February 27–March 2, 2019
Minneapolis, MN, USA

Association for Computing Machinery

Advancing Computing as a Science & Profession

SIGCSE'19

Proceedings of the 50th ACM Technical Symposium on Computer Science Education

Sponsored by:

ACM SIGCSE

Symposium Co-Chairs:

Elizabeth K. Hawthorne & Manuel A. Pérez-Quiñones

Program Co-Chairs:

Sarah Heckman & Jian Zhang

Association for
Computing Machinery

Advancing Computing as a Science & Profession

The Association for Computing Machinery
1601 Broadway, 10th Floor
New York, NY 10019-7434

ISBN: 978-1-4503-5890-3 (Digital)

ISBN: 978-1-4503-6741-7 (Print)

Additional copies may be ordered prepaid from:

ACM Order Department
PO Box 30777
New York, NY 10087-0777, USA

Phone: 1-800-342-6626 (USA and Canada)
+1-212-626-0500 (Global)
Fax: +1-212-944-1318
E-mail: acmhelp@acm.org
Hours of Operation: 8:30 am – 4:30 pm ET

Welcome from the SIGCSE Chair

Welcome to the 50th SIGCSE Technical Symposium on Computer Science Education (the 2019 Symposium), the premiere technical conference for computer science educators. The 2019 Symposium is sponsored by the Association for Computing Machinery (ACM) Special Interest Group on Computer Science Education (SIGCSE).

SIGCSE has the third largest membership of any of ACM's Special Interest Groups (SIG), and is among the oldest SIGs. Only ten SIGs were founded prior to 1968 when SIGCSE was formed, and two other SIGs shared their 50th anniversary in 2018 with SIGCSE. The SIGCSE Board and many other SIGCSE volunteers celebrated the 50th anniversary last year, but I would like to give a special thanks to two people. Briana Morrison, who is on the SIGCSE Board, created a series of weekly postings about SIGCSE's anniversary. These postings were shared on the listserv and published on SIGCSE's web site, and I know that many of you, myself included, enjoyed them. I would also like to thank Jane Prey, who is a long-time SIGCSE volunteer and previous SIGCSE award winner, for her work as the guest editor of a special issue of ACM Inroads celebrating SIGCSE's anniversary.

However, the celebration for the SIG is far from over. This year marks the 50th Technical Symposium, an achievement that even fewer SIGs share, as only six ACM SIGs have conferences that have been held 50 or more times. Further, the SIGCSE Symposium is thriving. The past several years have seen large increases in attendance at the conference, and this year will be even better thanks in part to the 50th anniversary committee. Adrienne Decker, who is a SIGCSE Board member and chairing the committee, Carl Alphonce, and Kurt Eiselt have worked for more than a year to put together a series of special events at the 50th Symposium. There will be a track focused on anniversary content that includes peer-reviewed papers and panels and invited discussants. Previous conference co-chairs have been invited to attend the conference and will be recognized for their work. The Travel Grant program has been expanded to 50 people for the anniversary, which should bring a new group of educators to our community. There will be special ribbons, stickers, and mementos for all attendees, and there will be a 50th anniversary booth and signage throughout the conference providing information about the conference history. Finally, the committee has worked with a historian, the Charles Babbage Institute, and Computing Educator's Oral History Project to bring content to attendees and have attendees contribute to the organizations' initiatives. On behalf of the SIGCSE Board I would like to thank the 50th anniversary committee for all of their hard work.

Of course, none of the activities at the 2019 Symposium would have been possible without the dedicated effort of conference co-chairs Manuel Pérez-Quiñones and Beth Hawthorne. They have spent countless hours ensuring that the 50th Technical Symposium will an event to remember. They and their committee of nearly 100 people have put together an engaging and innovative program, created opportunities for networking, and handled all the issues big and small that come with a conference of this size. On behalf of the SIGCSE organization and Board, I thank Manuel and Beth for their hard work, innovative ideas, excellent communication, and sense of humor.

Along with everything else you can expect to see this year, the conference provides us with a chance to honor two people for their contributions to computer science education and the SIGCSE community. The annual SIGCSE award for Outstanding Contribution to Computer Science Education will be given to Mark Guzdial at the University of Michigan. Mark has worked to transform wide-scale teaching practice through contextualized computing education, most notably with the Media Computation curriculum, advocated and supported policy changes supporting computing for all in many states in the U.S., published core research in computing education over decades, and helped to foster the next generation of computing educators through his mentorship. It is difficult to find someone in the SIGCSE community who has not read something written by Mark, including the thousands of regular readers of his long-standing blog on computing education. He has also contributed significantly as an organizer of two SIGCSE conferences and served on the SIGCSE Board. Mark has touched the computing education community and SIGCSE in many ways throughout the years, and our community is better for it. The annual SIGCSE award for Lifetime Service will be given to Gloria Childress Townsend at DePauw University. Gloria has worked tirelessly on behalf of diversity and inclusion in computing. She was a co-founder and co-facilitator of the SIGCSE Committee on Expanding the Women-in-Computing Community, a committee that has led birds-of-a-feather sessions at the Technical Symposium annually since 2005. Gloria worked for decades with ACM-W serving on the Executive Board and as ACM-W chair. She conceived of the idea of small regional celebrations of women in computing and worked as a guide and leader for these celebrations as they spread from the United States across the globe. Her extensive service to the computing education community has helped it to reach people who might not have joined without her hard work. Please join me and the rest of the SIGCSE Board in congratulating both of them on their well-deserved awards.

The 50th SIGCSE Technical Symposium will be an amazing event. I hope that you enjoy the celebrations, learn something new about computing education, meet new colleagues and friends, and stay warm in chilly Minneapolis. Enjoy the conference!

Amber Settle
SIGCSE Chair, 2016-2019

SIGCSE 2019 Chairs Welcome

Welcome to the 50th ACM Technical Symposium on Computer Science Education! Our theme this year is Celebrating the 50 Technical Symposia that has taken us from a small gathering of Computing Education enthusiasts in Texas in 1970 to the largest computing education conference in the world. The first SIGCSE Technical Symposium had over 40 papers submitted, 18 of them were accepted. For the 50th symposium, we received 526 paper submissions and accepted 169. In addition, the program has grown to include the ACM Student Research Competition, posters, demos, birds-of-a-feather, panels, special sessions, pre-symposium events, and workshops. Including all tracks, we received 994 submissions, from over 50 countries, with a total of 2668 unique authors representing over 800 organizations. And the participating organizations cover the gamut of K-12, community colleges, public and private universities and colleges, non-profits, corporate entities, government offices, and national laboratories. The growth of this conference parallels the growth of interest in the understanding and study of computing. We have plenty of reasons to celebrate the 50th gathering of our community.

With the growth of the computing education community, so has grown attendance at SIGCSE. In 1972 attendance was around 300 participants. Last year attendance surpassed 1500, and it was the third year in a row with record attendance. What is often missed is that conferences like SIGCSE are run by volunteers. All reviewers, associate program chairs, committee members, symposium and program chairs, and students are volunteers. All are giving their time to help participate in the dissemination of the greatest ideas and research results having to do with computing education.

The 2019 program continues to grow. This year we have a number of presentations exploring our history - in a special 50th celebration track, alongside of the now traditional coverage of topics in computing education, including active learning, AP exams, CS1, computational thinking, issues of diversity, tools, assessment, curriculum issues, etc. As is customary, we have other events that share our passion for computing education and are co-located with us. RESPECT 2019, the fourth international conference on Research on Equity and Sustained Participation in Engineering, Computing, and Technology will take place on Wednesday. We also have the SIGCSE sponsored New Chairs Roundtable as well as a number of pre-symposia, workshops, sponsored and affiliated events to complement our already robust offerings.

We are honored to have Dr. Freeman Habrowski, III, President of the University of Maryland, Baltimore County as our opening keynote. Among his many accomplishments, he chaired the committee that produced the National Academies' report, *Expanding Underrepresented Minority Participation: America's Science and Technology Talent at the Crossroads.* He will share a 50-year perspective on American society with a particular focus on technology, student success, and inclusion in computing.

We are also honored to have Dr. Blair Taylor of Towson University who consults with the NSA's College of Cyber, as a subject matter expert on long-term strategies to build the nation's cyber workforce. In the closing keynote, Dr. Taylor will share her experiences and perspectives on the future of integrating cybersecurity into computer science education.

The SIGCSE Symposium promotes high-quality scholarship and community engagement around computer science education. We continued the practice of reviewer discussions, an expanded associate program committee, and three paper submissions tracks, recognizing the differences in scope and review criteria between (1) CS education research, (2) experience reports and tools, and (3) curricula initiatives. In 2019, we changed the paper length up to a full 6 pages of content with a 7th page available for acknowledgments and references. These innovations have made our reviewing process more tailored and transparent. 797 volunteers provided each Paper with at least 5 reviews; and all other submissions with at least 3 reviews. Reviewers, along with 69 Associate Program Chairs and 14 Track Chairs, discussed submissions to come to a consensus. Program Chairs made final selections based on recommendations, importance, novelty, and timeliness. Table 1 table shows the number of submissions reviewed and accepted in each category.

Table 1: SIGCSE 2019 Submission and Acceptance Statistics

Track	# Submitted	# Accepted	Acceptance Rate
Papers (CS Education Research, Experience Reports and Tools, Curricula Initiatives)	526	169	32%
Panels	40	18	45%
Special Sessions	28	15	54%
Workshops	57	30	53%
ACM Student Research Competition	35	19	54%
Birds of a Feather	58	30	52%
Demos	24	11	46%
Lightning Talks	29	22	76%
Nifty Assignments	53	6	11%
Posters	144	90	63%

We are privileged to have exhibitors and supporters who champion CS education. This year's supporters include: Platinum: GitHub Education, Google, and Microsoft; Gold: Codio, Intel, Oracle Academy, Turing's Craft, and zyBooks; Silver: ABET, IBM, Gradescope by Turnitin, Mimir, and Vocareum; and Bronze: AnitaB.org.

This year the Program Chairs selected three best papers from each of the paper tracks for their accomplishment of high quality, novelty and broad appeal to reviewers. All best papers received at least one nomination from reviewers, high ratings, and excellent comments from reviewers. The top three papers in each track are shown below and highlighted throughout the printed program.

Best Papers for CS Education Research		
1	First Things First: Providing Metacognitive Scaffolding for Interpreting Problem Prompts James Prather *Abilene Christian University*, Raymond Pettit *Abilene Christian* University, Brett A. Becker *University College Dublin*, Paul Denny *The University of Auckland*, Dastyni Loksa *University of Washington*, Alani Peters *Abilene Christian University*, Zachary Albrecht *Abilene Christian University*, Krista Masci *Abilene Christian University*	Fri 11:10am Hyatt: Greenway J (2nd floor)
2	Assessing Incremental Testing Practices and Their Impact on Project Outcomes Ayaan M. Kazerouni *Virginia Tech*, Clifford A. Shaffer *Virginia Tech*, Stephen H. Edwards *Virginia Tech*, Francisco Servant *Virginia Tech*	Thu 3:45pm Hyatt: Greenway D/E (2nd floor)
3	Exploring the Value of Different Data Sources for Predicting Student Performance in Multiple CS Courses Soohyun Nam Liao *University of California, San Diego*, Daniel Zingaro *University of Toronto Mississauga*, Christine Alvarado *University of California, San Diego*, William G. Griswold *University of California, San Diego*, Leo Porter *University of California at San Diego*	Thu 11:10am Millennium: Grand South (1st floor)
Best Papers for Experience Reports and Tools		
1	Computer Science Principles for Teachers of Blind and Visually Impaired Students Andreas Stefik *University of Nevada, Las Vegas*, Richard E. Ladner *University of Washington*, William Allee *University of Nevada, Las Vegas*, Sean Mealin *North Carolina State University*	Fri 2:10pm Millennium: Grand South (1st floor)
2	Developing Soft and Technical Skills Through Multi-Semester, Remotely Mentored, Community-Service Projects Janet Davis *Whitman College*, Samuel A. Rebelsky *Grinnell College*	Thu 11:10am Hyatt: Greenway J (2nd floor)
3	Visualizing Classic Synchronization Problems: Dining Philosophers, Producers-Consumers, and Readers-Writers Joel C. Adams *Calvin College*, Elizabeth R. Koning *Calvin College*, Christiaan D. Hazlett *University of Illinois at Urbana-Champaign*	Fri 4:35pm Millennium: Grand South (1st floor)
Best Papers for Curricula Initiatives		
1	');DROP TABLE textbooks;--: An Argument for SQL Injection Coverage in Database Textbooks Cynthia Taylor *Oberlin College*, Saheel Sakharkar *University of Illinois at Chicago*	Thu 2:10pm Hyatt: Greenway A (2nd floor)
2	A Flexible Curriculum for Promoting Inclusion through Peer Mentorship Heather Pon-Barry *Mount Holyoke College*, Audrey St. John *Mount Holyoke College*, Becky Wai-Ling Packard *Mount Holyoke College*, Barbara Rotundo *Mount Holyoke College*	Sat 12:05pm Hyatt: Greenway J (2nd floor)
3	PythonSneks: An Open-Source, Instructionally-Designed Introductory Curriculum with Action-Design Research Austin Cory Bart *University of Delaware*, Allie Sarver *Virginia Tech*, Michael Friend *Virginia Tech*, Larry Cox *Virginia Tech*	Thu 1:45pm Millennium: Grand Central (1st floor)

This event owes many thanks to the SIGCSE Board for their guidance over the years. In addition, many organizations and their representatives had a hand in the success of this event. In no particular order: the planners at dLPLAN Meetings | Events: Dorothea Heck, Peggy Robins, Angelina Palmieri, and Betsy Fenwick; the Symposium Site Coordinators: Bob Beck and Paul Tymann; the ACM staff: April Mosqus and Donna Cappo; representatives from Sheridan: Lisa Tolles; Bill Guckert from WRG Design, Cindy Lathrop from the Hyatt Regency Minneapolis, and Melissa Jetson from Meet Minneapolis. We thank our home institutions for their generous support by allowing us to devote time to serve the SIGCSE community.

Finally, we are tremendously grateful for the engagement and support of the SIGCSE community and countless volunteers over the first 50 Symposia, and we look forward to the continued growth of this vibrant academic community. Let the celebration begin!

Elizabeth K. Hawthorne
Symposium Co-Chair
Union County College

Manuel A. Pérez-Quiñones
Symposium Co-Chair
University of North Carolina at Charlotte

Sarah Heckman
Program Co-Chair
North Carolina State University

Jian Zhang
Program Co-Chair
Texas Woman's University

Table of Contents

Paper Session: Tools 1

Session Chair: Charles Dierbach *(Towson University)*

Paper Session: Practice & Problems

Session Chair: Paul Denny *(The University of Auckland)*

Paper Session: Process & Performance

Session Chair: Razvan Alexandru Mezei *(Saint Martin's University)*

Paper Session: Autograders

Session Chair: Karen Jin *(University of New Hampshire)*

Paper Session: Capstones & Projects

Session Chair: Michelle Friend *(University of Nebraska Omaha)*

Special Session: SIGCSE Reads 2019: Discussion and Q & A

Session: SIGCSE@50 - CS1

Session Chair: James Caristi *(Valparaiso University)*

Paper Session: Camps

Session Chair: William H. Bares *(College of Charleston)*

Paper Session: Story & Video

Session Chair: Caroline Budwell *(Virginia Commonwealth University)*

Paper Session: Games & Gamification

Session Chair: Kalpathi Subramanian *(University of North Carolina at Charlotte)*

Paper Session: Testing 1

Session Chair: Mohsen Dorodchi *(University of North Carolina at Charlotte)*

Panel: The Reality of Inclusion:

Special Session: ACM Task Force on Data Science Education

Panel: CS Principles Higher Education Pathways

Session: SIGCSE@50 - Computing Education Research

Session: Morning Keynote & 2019 SIGCSE Award for Outstanding Contribution to Computer Science Education

Session Chairs: Elizabeth K. Hawthorne *(Union County College)*;
Manuel A. Pérez-Quiñones *(University of North Carolina at Charlotte)*

Paper Session: Online

Session Chair: Bernd Bruegge *(Technical University Munich)*

Paper Session: Mistakes and Errors

Session Chair: Ben Stephenson *(University of Calgary)*

Paper Session: Instruments 1

Session Chair: Steven Bogaerts *(DePauw University)*

Paper Session: Testing 2

Session Chair: Clifford A. Shaffer *(Virginia Tech)*

Paper Session: Teaching Practice 2

Session Chair: Matthew Hertz *(University at Buffalo)*

Paper Session: Assessment 2

Session Chair: Eileen T. Kraemer *(Clemson University)*

Special Session: Leading Conversations about Microaggressions, Bias, and Other Difficult Topics

Panel: Wrestling with Retention in the CS Major: Report from the ACM Retention Committee

Panel: Why and How to Spend a Sabbatical in Industry

Session: SIGCSE@50 - CS0

Session Chair: Leigh Ann Delyser *(CSforALL)*

Paper Session: Physical Computing

Session Chair: Barbara Anthony *(Southwestern University)*

Paper Session: Professional Skills

Session Chair: Victoria Hong *(St. Joseph's College)*

Paper Session: Attitudinal

Session Chair: Bob Edmison *(Virginia Tech)*

Special Session: Microteaching

Panel: Community College Transfer Pathways

Special Session: Curious about Student Participation in Humanitarian Open Source Software?

Session: SIGCSE@50 - Broadening Participation

Session Chair: Alison Derbenwick Miller *(Oracle)*

Session: Keynote

Session Chair: Elizabeth K. Hawthorne *(Union County College)*

Paper Session: Professional Development 1

Session Chair: Diana Cukierman *(Simon Fraser University)*

Paper Session: REU

Session Chair: Aarathi Prasad *(Skidmore College)*

Paper Session: Expectations

Session Chair: Brian Harrington *(University of Toronto Scarborough)*

Paper Session: Outreach

Session Chair: Alison Clear *(Eastern Institute of Technology)*

Paper Session: Theory & Mat

Session Chair: Shanon Reckinger *(University of Illinois Chicago)*

Paper Session: Pair Programming

Session Chair: Albert Chan *(Fayetteville State University)*

Paper Session: Access

Session Chair: Jennifer Parham-Mocello *(Oregon State University)*

Paper Session: Culture & Language

Session Chair: Andrew J. Ko *(University of Washington)*

Paper Session: Inclusion

Session Chair: Brandon Myers *(University of Iowa)*

Paper Session: Blocks

Session Chair: Denise Case *(Northwest Missouri State University)*

Friday Workshops

Saturday Workshops

Birds of a Feather Flock #1

Session Chair: Mary Anne Egan *(Siena College)*, Mark Sherriff *(University of Virginia)*

Birds of a Feather Flock #2

Session Chairs: Mary Anne Egan *(Siena College)*, Mark Sherriff *(University of Virginia)*

Poster Session #1

Session Chairs: Laurence D. Merkle *(Air Force Institute of Technology)*,
S. Monisha Pulimood *(The College of New Jersey)*

Poster Session #3

Session Chairs: Laurence D. Merkle *(Air Force Institute of Technology)*, S. Monisha Pulimood *(The College of New Jersey)*

Lightning Talks #1

Session Chairs: Lina Battestilli *(NC State University)*, Peter-Michael Osera *(Grinnell College)*

Lightning Talks #2

Session Chairs: Lina Battestilli *(NC State University)*, Peter-Michael Osera *(Grinnell College))*

Demonstrations

Session Chairs: Lina Battestilli *(NC State University)*, Peter-Michael Osera *(Grinnell College)*

ACM SRC: ACM Student Research Competition

Session Chairs: Jessica Schmidt *(NC State University)*, Stephen Hughes *(Coe College)*

Recipients of the SIGCSE Award for Outstanding Contribution to Computer Science Education

1981 **William F. Atchison**, *University of Maryland*
1982 **Alan Perlis**, *Yale University*
1983 **Karl V . Karlstrom**, *Prentice-Hall*
1985 **Elliot I. Organick**, *University of Utah*
1986 **Donald Knuth**, *Stanford University*
1987 **Niklaus Wirth**, *ETH, Zurich*
1988 **Grace Murray Hopper**, *Rear Admiral, USN, Digital Equipment Corp.*
1989 **Edsger W. Dijkstra**, *The University of Texas at Austin*
1990 **Curriculum '68 Committee**:
William F. Atchison, Samuel D. Conte, John Hamblen, Thomas E. Hull, Thomas A. Keenan, William B. Kehl, Edward J. McClusey, Silvio O. Navarro, Werner Rheinboldt, Earl J. Schweppe, William Viavant, David M. Young, Jr.
1991 **David Gries**, *Cornell University*
1992 **Daniel D. McCracken**, *City College, City University of New York*
1993 **Alan C. Kay**, *Apple Computer*
1994 **Norman E. Gibbs**, *Software Engineering Institute*
1995 **Robert M. Aiken**, *Temple University*
1996 **Nell B. Dale**, *The University of Texas at Austin*
1997 **Andrew Tannenbaum**, *Vrije University*
1998 **William A. Wulf**, *University of Virginia and National Academy of Engineering*
1999 **Peter J. Denning**, *George Mason University*
2000 **Andries Van Dam**, *Brown University*
2001 **Allen B. Tucker**, *Bowdoin College*
2002 **Elliot Soloway**, *University of Michigan*
2003 **Eric Roberts**, *Stanford University*
2004 **Mordechai Ben-Ari**, *Weizmann Institute of Science*
2005 **Kim Bruce**, *Williams College*
2006 **Richard Pattis**, *Carnegie Mellon University*
2007 **Judith Gal-Ezer,** *Open University of Israel* and **John Hughes**, *University of Technology, Sydney*
2008 **Randy Pausch,** *Carnegie Mellon University*
2009 **Elliot B. Koffman**, *Temple University*
2010 **Sally Fincher,** *University of Kent, Canterbury*
2011 **Matthias Felleisen,** *Northeastern University*
2012 **Harold (Hal) Abelson,** *Massachusetts Institute of Technology*
2013 **Michael Kölling**, *University of Kent, Canterbury*
2014 **Robert M. Panoff,** *The Shodor Education Foundation, Inc.*
2015 **Mark Allen Weiss,** *Florida International University*
2016 **Jan Cuny,** *National Science Foundation*
2017 **Gail Chapman,** *Exploring Computer Science*
2018 **Tim Bell**, *University of Canterbury, New Zealand*
2019 **Mark Guzdial**, *University of Michigan*

Recipients of the SIGCSE Lifetime Service Award

1997 **Richard Austing**, *University of Maryland*
1998 **Della Bonnette**, *University of Southwestern Louisiana*
1999 **Robert Aiken**, *Temple University*
2000 **James E. Miller**, *University of Southern Mississippi*
2001 **Lillian N. (Boots) Cassel**, *Villanova University*
2002 **Joe Turner**, *Clemson University and Zayed University*
2003 **Harriet Taylor**, *National Science Foundation and Louisiana State University*
2004 **Bruce Klein**, *Grand V alley State University*
2005 **Andrew McGettrick**, *University of Strathclyde*
2006 **Joyce Currie Little**, *Towson State University*
2007 **John Impagliazzo**, *Hofstra University*
2008 **Dennis Frailey**, *Raytheon Corporation*
2009 **Michael J. Clancy**, *University of California, Berkeley*
2010 **Peter Denning**, *Naval Postgraduate School*
2011 **Gordon Davies**, *Open University*
2012 **Jane Prey**, *Microsoft Research*
2013 **Henry Walker**, *Grinnell College*
2014 **Andrea Lawrence**, *Spelman College*
2015 **Frank H. Young**, *Rose-Hulman Institute of Technology*
2016 **Barbara Boucher Owens**, *Southwestern University*
2017 **Mats Daniels**, *Uppsala University*
2018 **Eric Roberts**, *Stanford University*
2019 **Gloria Childress Townsend**, *DePauw University*

SIGCSE 2019 Technical Symposium Organization

Symposium Co-Chairs: Elizabeth K. Hawthorne *(Union County College, USA)*
Manuel A. Pérez-Quiñones *(University of North Carolina at Charlotte, USA)*

Program Co-Chairs: Sarah Heckman *(North Carolina State University, USA)*
Jian Zhang *(Texas Woman's University, USA)*

Program Committee

Special Sessions and Panels Co-Chairs: Christina Gardner-McCune (*University of Florida, USA)*
Alvaro Monge *(California State University, Long Beach, USA)*

Workshop Co-Chairs: Brett Becker *(University College Dublin, Ireland)*
Pam Cutter *(Kalamazoo College, USA)*

Poster Co-Chairs: Laurence D. Merkle *(Air Force Institute of Technology, USA)*
S. Monisha Pulimood *(The College of New Jersey, USA)*

Birds of a Feather Co-Chairs: Mary Anne Egan *(Siena College, USA)*
Mark Sherriff *(University of Virginia, USA)*

Demos and Lightning Talks Co-Chairs: Lina Battestilli *(North Carolina State University, USA)*
Peter-Michael Osera *(Grinnell College, USA)*

Student Research Competition Co-Chairs: Jessica Schmidt *(North Carolina State University, USA)*
Stephen Hughes *(Coe College, USA)*

Nifty Assignments Co-Chairs: Nick Parlante *(Stanford University, USA)*
Julie Zelenski *(Stanford University, USA)*

Organizing Committee

Accessibility Chair Stacy Branham *(University of California, Irvine, USA)*

Pre-Symposium & Affiliated Events: John Dougherty *(Haverford College, USA)*
Diana Cukierman *(Simon Fraser University, Canada)*

Registration: Lynn Degler *(Rose-Hulman Institute of Technology, USA)*
Cary Laxer *(Rose-Hulman Institute of Technology, USA)*
Laurence D. Merkle *(Air Force Institute of Technology, USA)*

Publications: Ruth Anderson (*University of Washington, USA*)

Database Administrator: Leen-Kiat Soh (*University of Nebraska, Lincoln, USA*)
Mark Sherriff (*University of Virginia, USA*)

Webmaster: Josh Hug (*University of California, Berkeley, USA*)
Matt Jadud *(Bates College, USA)*

Treasurer: Paul Tymann *(Rochester Institute of Technology, USA)*

Evaluations: Phil East *(University of Northern Iowa, USA)*

Supporter/Exhibitor Liaison: Dave Musicant *(Carleton College, USA)*
Jodi Tims *(Baldwin Wallace University, USA)*

Student Volunteers & Activities: Sara Melnick *(Independent)*
Darakhshan Mir *(Bucknell University, USA)*
Samuel A. Rebelsky *(Grinnell College, USA)*

K-12 Liaison: Leigh Ann Sudol-DeLyser *(CSforALL, USA)*
Ria Galanos *(Thomas Jefferson High School for Science and Technology, USA)*

Community College Liaison: Cara Tang *(Portland Community College, USA)*

International Liaison: Jennifer Campbell *(University of Toronto, Canada)*

Kids' Camp: Dale-Marie Wilson *(University of North Carolina at Charlotte, USA)*
Meghan Allen *(University of British Columbia, Canada)*

Puzzles, Social, & Board Games: Steven Wolfman *(University of British Columbia, Canada)*
Zach Butler *(Rochester Institute of Technology, USA)*

Publicity and Social Media: Adam Blank *(University of Washington, USA)*
John Lewis *(Virginia Tech, USA)*

Local Arrangements: Jigang Liu *(Metropolitan State University, USA)*

50th Celebration Planning Committee: Adrienne Decker *(University at Buffalo, USA)*
Kurt Eiselt *(University of California, Davis, USA)*
Carl Alphonce *(University at Buffalo, USA)*

International Committee Members: Meghan Allen *(The University of British Columbia, Canada)*
Miles Berry *(University of Roehampton, United Kingdom)*
Karen Bradshaw *(Rhodes University, South Africa)*
Ernesto Cuadros-Vargas *(UTEC, Peru)*
Paul Denny *(University of Auckland, New Zealand)*
Rita Garcia *(Adelaide, Australia)*
Orit Hazzan *(Technion, Israel)*
Arto Hellas *(University of Helsinki, Finland)*
Carsten Kleiner *(Hochschule Hannover, Germany)*
Wendy Powley *(Queen's University, Canada)*
Marco Silva *(Federal University of Technology, Brazil)*
Abhijat Vichare *(Persistent, India)*
Hironori Washizaki *(Waseda University, Japan)*
Gary Wong *(University of Hong Kong, Hong Kong)*
Ming Zhang *(Peking University, China)*

Associate Program Chairs: Eric Aaron *(Colby College, USA)*
Joel C. Adams *(Calvin College, USA)*
Rajeev Agrawal *(US Army Engineer Research and Development Center, USA)*
Meghan Allen *(The University of British Columbia, Canada)*
Carl Alphonce *(University at Buffalo, USA)*
Christine Alvarado *(University of California San Diego, USA)*
Ruth Anderson *(University of Washington, USA)*
Barbara Anthony *(Southwestern University, USA)*
Julio César Bahamón *(University of North Carolina at Charlotte, USA)*
Mark Bailey *(Hamilton College, USA)*
Tiffany Barnes *(North Carolina State University, USA)*
Brett A. Becker *(University College Dublin, Ireland)*
Marie Bienkowski *(SRI International, USA)*
Kevin Buffardi *(California State University - Chico, USA)*
Alistair Campbell *(Hamilton College, USA)*
Paul Cao *(University of California San Diego, USA)*
Albert Chan *(Fayetteville State University, USA)*
Peter J. Clarke *(Florida International University, USA)*
Steve Cooper *(University of Nebraska-Lincoln, USA)*
Ernesto Cuadros-Vargas *(San Pablo Catholic University, Peru)*
Adrienne Decker *(University at Buffalo, USA)*
Leigh Ann DeLyser *(CSforALL, USA)*
Mohsen Dorodchi *(University of North Carolina at Charlotte, USA)*
John P. Dougherty *(Haverford College, USA)*
Maureen Doyle *(Northern Kentucky University, USA)*
Joshua Eckroth *(Stetson University, USA)*
Stephen Edwards *(Virginia Tech, USA)*
Matthew Forshaw *(Newcastle University, United Kingdom)*
Allan Fowler *(Kennesaw State University, USA)*
Michelle Friend *(University of Nebraska Omaha, USA)*
Chris Gregg *(Stanford University, USA)*
Cecily Heiner *(Southern Utah University, USA)*
Sharon Hsiao *(Arizona State University, USA)*
Helen Hu *(Westminster College, USA)*
Mark J. Johnson *(Central College, USA)*
Maria Jump *(Northeastern University -- Charlotte, USA)*
Carsten Kleiner *(University of Applied Science and Arts Hannover, Germany)*
Andrew J. Ko *(University of Washington, USA)*
Stephan Krusche *(Technical University of Munich, Germany)*
David Levine *(Saint Bonaventure University, USA)*
Andrew Luxton-Reilly *(The University of Auckland, New Zealand)*

Associate Program Chairs (continued):

Bruce R. Maxim *(University of Michigan, USA)*
Lester I. McCann *(University of Arizona, USA)*
Susan Mengel *(Texas Tech University, USA)*
Laurence D. Merkle *(Air Force Institute of Technology, USA)*
Craig Miller *(DePaul University, USA)*
Robert Noonan *(William and Mary, USA)*
Jody Paul *(Metropolitan State University of Denver, USA)*
Leo Porter *(University of California San Diego, USA)*
Wendy Powley *(Queen's University, Canada)*
Samuel A. Rebelsky *(Grinnell College, USA)*
Suzanne Rivoire *(Sonoma State University, USA)*
Susan Rodger *(Duke University, USA)*
Ingrid Russell *(University of Hartford, USA)*
Mark Sherriff *(University of Virginia, USA)*
Swapneel Sheth *(University of Pennsylvania, USA)*
Simon *(University of Newcastle, Australia)*
Melissa Stange *(Lord Fairfax Community College, USA)*
Ben Stephenson *(University of Calgary, Canada)*
Jim Teresco *(Siena College, USA)*
Luther Tychonievich *(University of Virginia, USA)*
Paul Tymann *(Rochester Institute of Technology, USA)*
Frank Vahid *(University of California, Riverside, USA)*
Jan Vahrenhold *(Westfälische Wilhelms-Universität Münster, Germany)*
Abhijat Vichare *(Abhijat Research and Software, India)*
Ellen Walker *(Hiram College, USA)*
Henry Walker *(Grinnell College, USA)*
Charles Wallace *(Michigan Technological University, USA)*
Ursula Wolz *(Bennington College, USA)*

ACM Student Research Competition (SRC) Reviewers

Mohammad Q. Azhar (BMCC, The City University Of New York)
Doug Baldwin (SUNY Geneseo)
Judith Bayard Cushing (The Evergreen State College)
David Bunde (Knox College)
Michael Cotterell (University of Georgia)
Barb Cutler (Rensselaer Polytechnic Institute)
Mohsen Dorodchi (University of North Carolina at Charlotte)
Maureen Doyle (Northern Kentucky University)
Hillary Fleenor (Columbus State University)
Eric Fouh (Lehigh University)
S. Jane Fritz (St. Joseph's College)
J Paul Gibson (Mines Telecom)
Carlos Guerrero (Universitat de les Illes Balears)
Geoffrey Herman (University of Illinois at Urbana-Champaign)
Roberto Hoyle (Oberlin College)
Dugald Hutchings (Elon University)
Wei Jin (Georgia Gwinnett College)
Lisa Lacher (University of Houston - Clear Lake)
David Levine (Saint Bonaventure University)
Zilu Liang (Tokyo Institute of Technology)
Sa Liu (Harrisburg University of Science and Technology)
James McGuffee (Christian Brothers University)
Chao Mei (University of Texas at San Antonio)
Xenia Mountrouidou (College of Charleston)
Dave Musicant (Carleton College)
Arnold Pears (KTH Royal Institute of Technology)
Yang Song (University of North Carolina Wilmington)
Izak Van Zyl (Cape Peninsula University of Technology)
Ellen Walker (Hiram College)
Nikhil Yadav (St. John's University)
Jeong Yang (Texas A&M University-San Antonio)
Lan Yang (California State Polytechnic University, Pomona)

BOF Reviewers

Shakil Akhtar (Clayton State University)
Mark Allison (University of Michigan-Flint)
Nada Basit (University of Virginia)
Michael Bauer (Leeward Community College)
Leland Beck (San Diego State University)
Marjahan Begum (Copenhagen Business School)
Christopher Bohn (University of Nebraska-Lincoln)
Dennis Bouvier (Southern Illinois University Edwardsville)
Kevin Buell (Arizona State University)
Deanne Cranford-Wesley (Forsyth Technical Community College)
Rosiane de Freitas (IComp/UFAM)
Toby Donaldson (Simon Fraser University)
Huseyin Ergin (Ball State University)
Razieh Fathi (University at Buffalo)
Yujian Fu (Alabama A&M University)
Anna Förster (University of Bremen)
Charles Garrod (Carnegie Mellon University)
Chris Gregg (Stanford University)
Caroline Hardin (University of Wisconsin-Madison)
Cinda Heeren (UBC)
Michael Hilton (Carnegie Mellon University)
Thomas Horton (Univ. of Virginia, Dept. of Computer Science)
Justin Hsia (University of Washington)
Jim Huggins (Kettering University)
Colin Johnson (University of Kent)
Deborah Kariuki (CSForAll)
Richard Kick (Newbury Park High School)
Joan Krone (Denison University)
David Largent (Ball State University)
Melinda Mcdaniel (Georgia Institute of Technology)
Charlie Mcdowell (UC Santa Cruz)
Alvaro Monge (California State University Long Beach)
Krish Narayanan (Eastern Michigan University)
Keith O'Hara (Bard College)
Swati Padhee (Wright State University)
James Paterson (Glasgow Caledonian University)
Fabio Petrillo (Universite du Quebec a Chicoutimi)
Donna Reese (Mississippi State University)
Matt Roberts (Macquarie University)
Jason Schultz (Bemidji State University)
Amber Solomon (Georgia Institute of Technology)
Lei Tang (Rice University)
Fatma Tarlaci (Stanford University)
George Thomas (University of Wisconsin Oshkosh)
Kim Tracy (Rose-Hulman Institute of Technology)
Anthony Varghese (University of Wisconsin-River Falls)

Demonstration Reviewers

Michal Aibin (British Columbia Institute of Technology)
David Arnow (Brooklyn College (CUNY))

Ajay Bandi (Northwest Missouri State University)
James Chegwidden (Tarrant County College)
Josh Dehlinger (Towson University)
Kathleen Ericson (University of Tennessee at Martin)
Paul Fodor (Stony Brook University)
Adam Gaweda (North Carolina State University)
Olga Glebova (Georgia State University)
Javier Gonzalez-Sanchez (Arizona State University)
Marco Aurélio Graciotto Silva (Federal University of Technology - Paraná)
James Heliotis (Rochester Institute of Technology)
Kimberly Hermans (University of California, Irvine)
David Hovemeyer (York College of Pennsylvania)
Hasan Jamil (University of Idaho)
Amir Kamil (University of California, Berkeley)
Young Lee (none)
Idongesit Mkpong-Ruffin (Faulkner University)
Jared O'Leary (BootUp)
Lawrence Osborne (Lamar University Faculty)
Christian Roberson (Florida Southern College)
Raja Sooriamurthi (Carnegie Mellon University)
William Thacker (Winthrop University)

Lightning Talk Reviewers

Reem Ali (University of Minnesota)
Meghan Allen (The University of British Columbia)
Beverly Bachmayer (Intel)
Matthew Barr (University of Glasgow)
Lillian Cassel (Villanova University)
Albert Chan (Fayetteville State University)
Edward Chapin (University of Maryand Eastern Shore)
Jonathan Corley (University of West Georgia)
Diana Cukierman (Simon Fraser University)
Venu Dasigi (Bowling Green State University)
Alex Edgcomb (Sr. Software Engineer at zyBooks. Research Specialist at UC Riverside.)
Heidi Ellis (Western New England University)
Theodore Hays (Clemson University Undergraduate Research Team)
Cruz Izu (The University of Adelaide)
James Kolasa (Bluegrass Community and Technical College)
Violetta Lonati (University of Milan)
Manuel Martins Barata (ISEL - Instituto Superior de Engenharia de Lisboa)
Razvan Alexandru Mezei (Saint Martin's University)
Diba Mirza (University of California Santa Barbara)
Christopher Moretti (Princeton University)
Briana Morrison (University of Nebraska at Omaha)
Anurag Nagar (The University of Texas at Dallas)
Peter Ohmann (College of St. Benedict / St. John's University)
Andrew Rasmussen (Chicago Public Schools)
Tim Sisson (Cleveland State University)
Nadine von Frankenberg Und Ludwigsdorff (Technical University of Munich)
Kendra Walther (University of Southern California)
Arthur Yanushka (Christian Brothers University)

Nifty Assignment Reviewers

Joseph Ahor Abandoh-Sam (Valley View University)
Owen Astrachan (Duke University)
Arvind Bhusnurmath (University of Pennsylvania)
James H. Davenport (University of Bath)
Giuseppe De Ruvo (The University of Auckland)
Zhijiang Dong (Middle Tennessee State University)
Colin S. Gordon (Drexel University)
Jean Goulet (Universite de Sherbrooke)
Michael Guerzhoy (Princeton University)
Fahmida Hamid (University of North Texas)
Nadeem Hamid (Berry College)
Matthew Hertz (University at Buffalo)
Sarah J Huibregtse (Rochester Institute of Technology)
Janet Jenkins (University of North Alabama)
Osvaldo Jimenez (University of the Pacific)
Pankaj Kamthan (Concordia University)
Amanpreet Kapoor (University of Florida)
Bo Kim (Southern New Hampshire University)
Ana Paula Ludtke Ferreira (Universidade Federal do Pampa)
Suzanne Matthews (United States Military Academy)
Afsaneh Minaie (Utah Valley University)
Benjamin Mitchell (Villanova University)
Linda Null (The Pennsylvania State University)
Joe Politz (University of California San Diego)
Aarathi Prasad (Skidmore College)

John Rager (Amherst College)
Saquib Razak (Carnegie Mellon University)
David Reed (Creighton University)
Mike Scott (University of Texas at Austin - Computer Science Departmnet)
Nigamanth Sridhar (Cleveland State University)
Ben Stephenson (University of Calgary)
Amber Stubbs (Simmons College)
Deborah Trytten (University of Oklahoma)
Giovanni Vincenti (University of Baltimore)
Alan Whitehurst (Southern Virginia University)
Victor Winter (University of Nebraska at Omaha)

Panel Session Reviewers

Andrew Allen (Georgia Southern University)
Alice Armstrong (Shippensburg University)
Cathy Bareiss (Olivet Nazarene University)
Arvind Bhusnurmath (University of Pennsylvania)
Carlos Cabrera (Florida International University)
Cengiz Gunay (Georgia Gwinnett College)
Hoda Hosny (AUC Egypt)
Justin Hsia (University of Washington)
Joseph Isaac (University of Florida)
Yerika Jimenez (University of Florida)
Colin Johnson (University of Kent)
Amanpreet Kapoor (University of Florida)
Joe Kmoch (JK Consulting)
Joaquim Madeira (University of Aveiro)
Robyn Moncrief (National Louis University)
Dave Musicant (Carleton College)
Keith O'Hara (Bard College)
Peter-Michael Osera (Grinnell College)
Imani Palmer (University of Illinois at Urbana-Champaign)
Rosario Robinson (FocusGears)
Jerry Roth (Vanderbilt University)
Anya Tafliovich (University of Toronto)
Terry Tang (Rice University)
S. Rebecca Thomas (Bard College)
Hakan Tuzun (Hacettepe University)
Linda Werner (University of CA, Santa Cruz)
Howard Whitston (University of South Alabama)
Adrienne Decker (University at Buffalo)

Paper Reviewers

Joseph A. Abandoh-Sam (Valley View University)
Ahmed Abukmail (University of Houston-Clear Lake)
Donald Acton (The University of British Columbia)
Joshua Adams (Saint Leo University)
Paul Addison (Ivy Tech Community College)
Ashish Aggarwal (University of Florida)
Irfan Ahmed (Virginia Commonwealth University)
Michal Aibin (British Columbia Institute of Technology)
Efthimia Aivaloglou (Open Universiteit)
Mete Akcaoglu (Michigan State University)
Bita Akram (North Carolina State University)
Saeed Al-Haj (Ohio Northern University)
Hisham Al-Mubaid (University of Houston-clear lake)
Jennifer Albert (The Citadel)
Ibrahim Albluwi (Princeton University)
Farha Ali (Lander University)
Mark Allison (University of Michigan-Flint)
Cecilia Ovesdotter Alm (Rochester Institute of Technology)
Roberto Almeida Bittencourt (UEFS - State University of Feira de Santana)
Asm Iftekhar Anam (University of Wisconsin - Green Bay)
Maurício Aniche (Delft University of Technology)
Craig Anslow (Victoria University of Wellington)
Gabriella Anton (Northwestern University)
Vaibhav Anu (Montclair State University)
John Anvik (Department of Mathematics and Computer Science, University of Lethbridge)
Ajayi Anwansedo (Southern University and A & M)
Saira Anwar (Purdue University)
Eduardo Aranha (UFRN)
Luis Gustavo J. Araujo (State University of Feira de Santana)
António Araújo (University of Porto)
Alex Aravind (University of Northern British Columbia)
David Arnow (Brooklyn College (CUNY))
Muhammad Rizwan Asghar (The University of Auckland)
Thomas Babbitt (USMA)
Monica Babes-Vroman (Rutgers University)
Donald Bagert (Benedictine College)
Connor Bain (Northwestern Universtiy)
Doug Baldwin (SUNY Geneseo)
Robert Ball (Weber State University)
Michael Ball (University of California, Berkeley)
Ajay Bandi (Northwest Missouri State University)
Shankar M. Banik (The Citadel)
William Bares (College of Charleston)
Lecia Barker (University of Colorado Boulder)

Ian Barland (Radford University)
David Barnes (University of Kent)
Matthew Barr (University of Glasgow)
Phillip Barry (University of Minnesota)
Lina Battestilli (North Carolina State University)
Daniel Bauer (Columbia University)
Michael Bauer (Leeward Community College)
Judith Bayard Cushing (The Evergreen State College)
Marjahan Begum (Copenhagen Business School)
Fabiane Benitti (UFSC)
Angela Berardinelli (Mercyhurst University)
Mario Luca Bernardi (Giustino Fortunato University)
Andrew Berns (University of Northern Iowa)
Gianmario Besana (DePaul University)
Bradley Beth (The University of Texas at Austin)
Arnab Bhattacharya (Indian Institute of Technology, Kanpur)
Debasis Bhattacharya (University of Hawaii Maui College)
Saúl Blanco (Indiana University Bloomington)
Michael Bloodgood (The College of New Jersey)
Richard Blumenthal (Regis University)
Ryan Bockmon (Univeristy of Nebraska - Lincoln)
Elizabeth Boese (University of Colorado - Boulder)
Steven Bogaerts (DePauw University)
Christopher Bohn (University of Nebraska-Lincoln)
Bill Booth (Baylor University)
Otto Borchert (Missouri Southern State University)
João Marcelo Borovina Josko (Federal Universty of ABC - Sao Paulo - Brazil)
Durell Bouchard (Roanoke College)
Eric Bouwers (Squla)
Jeremy Bradbury (University of Ontario Institute of Technology)
Andrej Brodnik (University of Ljubljana)
Neil Brown (King's College London)
Glenn Bruns (California State University Monterey Bay)
Dennis Brylow (Marquette University)
Karan K. Budhraja (University of Maryland, Baltimore County)
Philip Buffum (North Carolina State University)
David Burlinson (University of North Carolina at Charlotte)
Jeffrey Bush (University of Colorado Boulder)
Zack Butler (Rochester Institute of Technology)
Candido Cabo (City University of New York)
Ricardo Caceffo (University of Campinas (Unicamp), Brazil)
Yu Cai (Michigan Technological University)
Andre P. Calitz (none)
Jennifer Campbell (University of Toronto)
Soraya Cardenas (Cascadia College)
Lori Carter (Point Loma Nazarene University)
Leandro Carvalho (Institute of Computing - Universidade Federal do Amazonas)
Lillian Cassel (Villanova University)
Francisco Enrique Vicente Castro (Worcester Polytechnic Institute)
Veronica Catete (North Carolina State University)
Veronica Catete (North Carolina State University)
Sharath Chandrashekhara (University at Buffalo)
Bruce Char (Drexel University Department of Computer Science)
Ankur Chattopadhyay (University of Wisconsin - Green Bay)
James Chegwidden (Tarrant County College)
Robert Chen (Framingham State University (retired))
Juan Chen (College of Computer, National University of Defense Technology, China)
Wai Chong Chia (Sunway University)
Sridhar Chimalakonda (Indian Institute of Technology - Tirupati)
Donald Chinn (University of Washington)
Vanea Chiprianov (University of Pau)
Radhouane Chouchane (Columbus State University)
Cheng Yu Chung (Arizona State University)
Christos Chytas (Carl von Ossietzky Universität Oldenburg)
John Cigas (Park University)
Dawn Cizmar (St. Edwards University)
Jaclyn Cohen (Open.Michigan Initiative)
Rachel Cole (Research Alliance for New York City Schools)
Randy Connolly (Mount Royal University)
Phillip Conrad (UC Santa Barbara)
Jonathan Corley (University of West Georgia)
Mary Courtney (Pace University)
Andrew Csizmadia (Newman University)
Kathryn Cunningham (Georgia Institute of Technology)
Edwin Curran (University of Ulster)
Mónica Isabel T. Da Costa (EST - IPCB)
Omar Darwish (Texas Woman's Univery)
Venu Dasigi (Bowling Green State University)

James H. Davenport (University of Bath)
Karen C. Davis (Miami University)
Don Davis (University of Texas at San Antonio)
Rosiane de Freitas (IComp/UFAM)
Giuseppe De Ruvo (The University of Auckland)
Debzani Deb (Winston-salem state university)
Nasrin Dehbozorgi (University of North Carolina at Charlotte)
Josh Dehlinger (Towson University)
Fabian Deitelhoff (FH Dortmund)
Rafael Del Vado Vírseda (Universidad Complutense de Madrid. Departamento de Sistemas Informáticos y Computación)
Marie-Anne Demuynck (Texas Woman's University)
Yuli Deng (Arizona State University)
Kamyar Dezhgosha (University of Illinois at Springfield)
Christo Dichev (WSSU)
Darina Dicheva (Winston-Salem State University)
Suzanne W. Dietrich (Arizona State University)
Betsy DiSalvo (Georgia Institute of Technology)
Zachary Dodds (Harvey Mudd College)
Anca Doloc-Mihu (Georgia Gwinnett College)
Robert Domanski (City University of New York)
Toby Donaldson (Simon Fraser University)
Yihuan Dong (North Carolina State University)
Zhijiang Dong (Middle Tennessee State University)
John Dooley (Knox College)
Felicia Doswell (Norfolk State University)
John A. Doucette (New College of Florida)
Toby Dragon (Ithaca College)
J. Philip East (University of Northern Iowa)
Alex Edgcomb (Sr. Software Engineer at zyBooks. Research Specialist at UC Riverside.)
Bob Edmison (Virginia Tech)
John Edwards (Utah State University)
Roger Eggen (University of North Florida)
Jesse Eickholt (Central Michigan University)
Farjana Eishita (University of New Orleans)
Yasmine El-Glaly (Rochester Institute of Technology)
Daniel Ellsworth (Colorado College)
Richard Enbody (Michigan State University)
Kirankumar Eranki (Indian Institute of Technology Bombay)
Huseyin Ergin (Ball State University)
Barbara Ericson (University of Michigan)
Yadran Eterovic (Pontificia Universidad Catlica de Chile)
Cheri Fancsali (Research Alliance for NYC Schools)
Mohammed Farghally (Virginia Tech)
Mojtaba Sedigh Fazli (University of Georgia)
Yvon Feaster (Clemson University)
Alan Fekete (The University of Sydney)
Russell Feldhausen (Kansas State University)
Maria Lydia Fioravanti (University of São Paulo)
Hillary Fleenor (Columbus State University)
Paul Fodor (Stony Brook University)
Daniel Fokum (The University of the West Indies)
Samantha S. Foley (University of Wisconsin-La Crosse)
Anna Förster (University of Bremen)
Eric Fouh (Lehigh University)
Susan Eileen Fox (Macalester College)
Ellen Francine Barbosa (ICMC/USP)
Anna Frankfurt (University of Prince Edward Island)
Diana Franklin (UChicago STEM Education)
Gordon Fraser (University of Passau)
Frank Friedman (Temple University)
Ilenia Fronza (Free University of Bolzano / Bozen)
Yujian Fu (Alabama A&M University)
Muztaba Fuad (Winston-Salem State University)
Ramona Fuentes-Valdéz (Tecnológico de Monterrey)
Paulo Gabriel Gadelha Queiroz (ufersa)
Dilrukshi Gamage (University of Moratuwa)
Saturnino Garcia (University of San Diego)
Christina Gardner-McCune (University of Florida)
Charles Garrod (Carnegie Mellon University)
Megean Garvin (UMBC)
Alessio Gaspar (University of South Florida Polytechnic)
Isabela Gasparini (UDESC)
Adam Gaweda (North Carolina State University)
Edward F. Gehringer (North Carolina State University)
Alexandra Gendreau Chakarov (University of Colorado Boulder)
Paul Gestwicki (Ball State University)
Uttam Ghosh (Vanderbilt University)
Nasser Giacaman (The University of Auckland)
J Paul Gibson (Mines Telecom)
Niki Gitinabard (North Carolina State University)

Richard Glassey (Robert Gordon University)
Ira Goldstein (Siena College)
Mercedes Gómez-Albarrán (Universidad Complutense de Madrid)
Javier Gonzalez-Huerta (Blekinge Institue of Technology)
Javier Gonzalez-Sanchez (Arizona State University)
Ana I. González-Tablas (University Carlos III de Madrid)
Colin S. Gordon (Drexel University)
Jean Goulet (Universite de Sherbrooke)
Marco Aurélio Graciotto Silva (Federal University of Technology - Paraná)
Joanthan Gratch (Texas Woman's University)
Jean M. Griffin (Google)
Tor-Morten Grønli (Westerdals Oslo ACT)
Joshua Gross (Blackburn)
Carlos Guerrero (Universitat de les Illes Balears)
Francisco J. Gutierrez (Computer Science Department, University of Chile)
Mandlenkosi Gwetu (UKZN)
Steve Hadfield (US Air Force Academy)
Ayman Hajja (College Of Charleston)
Hossein Hakimzadeh (Indiana University Bloomington)
Margeret Hall (School of Interdisciplinary Informatics, University of Nebraska Omaha)
Ranette Halverson (Midwestern State University)
Tom Halverson (Dakota State University)
Alan Hamlett (WakaTime)
Sally Hamouda (Rhode IslandCollege)
Meng Han (Kennesaw State University)
Qiang Hao (Computer Science & SMATE, Western Washington University)
David Harvie (United States Military Academy)
J. Scott Hawker (Rochester Institute of Technology)
Elizabeth Hawthorne (Union County College)
Alan Hayes (University of Bath)
Orit Hazzan (Technion - Israel Institute of Technology)
Bastiaan Heeren (Open University, The Netherlands)
Fredrik Heintz (Linköping University)
David Heise (Lincoln University)
Arto Hellas (University of Helsinki)
Shelly Heller (George Washington University)
Austin Henley (University of Tennessee)
Julie Henry (PreCISE - UNamur)
Suvineetha Herath (Carl Sandburg College)
Geoffrey Herman (University of Illinois at Urbana-Champaign)
Kimberly Hermans (University of California, Irvine)
Arnon Hershkovitz (Tel Aviv University)
Matthew Hertz (University at Buffalo)
Michael Hewner (Rose Hulman Institute of Techonology)
Timothy Highley (La Salle University)
Curt Hill (Valley City State University)
Michael Hilton (Carnegie Mellon University)
Mark Holliday (Western Carolina University)
Charles G Hoot (NW Missouri State University)
Cay Horstmann (San Jose State University)
Thomas B. Horton (Univ. of Virginia, Dept. of Computer Science)
David Hovemeyer (York College of Pennsylvania)
Christopher Hovey (University of Colorado Boulder)
Brian Howard (DePauw University)
Iris Howley (Williams College)
Aleata Hubbard (WestEd)
Jim Huggins (Kettering University)
Janet Hughes (The Open University)
Sarah J Huibregtse (Rochester Institute of Technology)
Dugald Hutchings (Elon University)
Nicole Hutchins (Vanderbilt University)
Jorge Eduardo Ibarra-Esquer (Universidad Autónoma de Baja California)
Ahmed Ibrahim (University of Virginia)
Michelle Ichinco (University of Massachusetts Lowell)
Md Athar Imtiaz (The University of Auckland)
Cruz Izu (The University of Adelaide)
Jana Jackova (Matej Bel University)
Filip Jagodzinski (Western Washington University)
Eissa Jamil (Edge Technovations LLC)
Hasan Jamil (University of Idaho)
Gayithri Jayathirtha (University of Pennsylvania)
Johan Jeuring (Open Universiteit Nederland and Universiteit Utrecht)
Osvaldo Jimenez (University of the Pacific)
Yerika Jimenez (University of Florida)
Haojian Jin (Carnegie Mellon University)
Karen Jin (University of New Hampshire)
Wei Jin (Georgia Gwinnett College)
Mike Jipping (Hope College)
William Joel (Graphics Research Group / WCSU)
Jeremiah Johnson (University of New Hampshire)
Julie Johnson (Vanderbilt University)
Chris Johnson (University of Wisconsin, Eau Claire)

Naomi Johnson (University of Virginia)
Maria José Marcelino (University of Coimbra)
Swaroop Joshi (The Ohio State University)
Dennis Kafura (Virginia Tech)
Antti-Juhani Kaijanaho (University of Jyvaskyla, Faculty of Information Technology)
Tetsuro Kakeshita (Saga University)
Maria Kallia (King's College London)
Amanpreet Kapoor (University of Florida)
Amey Karkare (Indian Institute of Technology, Kanpur)
Ayaan Kazerouni (Virginia Tech)
William Kerney (Clovis Community College)
Fazel Keshtkar (ST John's University)
Daehee Kim (California State University - Stanislaus)
Meen Chul Kim (Drexel University)
Bo Kim (Southern New Hampshire University)
Jason King (North Carolina State University)
Jason King (North Carolina State University)
Styliani Kleanthous (University of Cyprus)
Devorah Kletenik (City University of New York)
John Kloosterman (University of Michigan)
Jane Kochanov (Penn State Harrisburg)
Kyu Han Koh (California State University, Stanislaus)
Tobias Kohn (University of Cambridge)
James Kolasa (Bluegrass Community and Technical College)
Meir Komar (JCT)
G. Ayorkor Korsah (Ashesi University)
Brittany Ann Kos (University of Colorado Boulder)
Joan Krone (Denison University)
Jw Kruger (Unisa SBL)
Shreya Kumar (University of Notre Dame)
Zachary Kurmas (Grand Valley State University)
Clif Kussmaul (Muhlenberg College)
Lisa Lacher (University of Houston - Clear Lake)
Richard Ladner (University of Washington)
Christopher I. G. Lanclos (Mississippi State University)
Dieter Landes (University of Applied Sciences and Arts)
Matthew Lang (Google)
Joan Langdon (Bowie State University)
Yedidyah Langsam (City University of New York)
D. Brian Larkins (Rhodes College)
John Lasseter (Hobart & William Smith Colleges)
Celine Latulipe (University of North Carolina at Charlotte)
Alina Lazar (Youngstown State University)
Akos Ledeczi (Vanderbilt University)
Annie En-Shiun Lee (University of Waterloo)
Gilliean Lee (Lander University)
Irene Lee (Massachusetts Institute of Technology)
Michael Lee (New Jersey Institute of Technology)
Tsee Lee (Brooklyn Technical High School)
Young Lee (none)
Zachary Lehman (University of California, Los Angeles)
Chi-Un Lei (The University of Hong Kong)
Juho Leinonen (University of Helsinki)
Pedro Leite (Donnelly College)
Matt Lepinski (New College of Florida)
Terry Letsche (Wartburg College)
Kees Leune (Adelphi University)
Grace Lew (Biola University)
Gary Lewandowski (Xavier University)
Peilong Li (University of Massachusetts Lowell)
Toby Jia-Jun Li (Human-Computer Interaction Institute, Carnegie Mellon University)
Zilu Liang (Tokyo Institute of Technology)
Chun Wai Liew (Lafayette College)
Mark Liffiton (Illinois Wesleyan University)
Seongtaek Lim (Cornell Tech)
Yu-Tzu Lin (National Taiwan Normal University)
Panos Linos (Butler University)
Joshua Littenberg-Tobias (MIT)
Hong Liu (Indiana University Kokomo)
Jiangjiang Liu (Lamar)
Qiang Liu (College of Computer, National University of Defense Technology)
Jigang Liu (Metropolitan State University)
Li Liu (California State University, Northridge)
Matija Lokar (University of Ljubljana)
Violetta Lonati (University of Milan)
Dobrila Lopez (Curtin University)
Leonardo Lucena (Instituto Federal do Rio Grande do Norte)
Marcia Lucena (UFRN)
Stephanie Ludi (University of North Texas)
Ana Paula Ludtke Ferreira (Universidade Federal do Pampa)
Roman Lysecky (University of Arizona)
Nicholas Lytle (North Carolina State University)
Reza M. Parizi (Kennesaw State University)
David Malan (Harvard University)
Samuel Mann (Otago Polytechnic)
Farshid Marbouti (San Jose State University)

Daniela Marghitu (Auburn University)
Thomas Marlowe (Seton Hall University)
Maíra Marques Samary (Universidad de Chile)
Manuel Martins Barata (ISEL - Instituto Superior de Engenharia de Lisboa)
Julian Mason (Toyota Research Institute)
Raina Mason (Southern Cross University)
William Mason (Georgia Institute of Technology)
Ecivaldo Matos (UFBA - Universidade Federal da Bahia)
Suzanne Matthews (United States Military Academy)
Bruce Maxwell (Colby College)
Keith Maycock (National College of Ireland)
Chris Mayfield (James Madison University)
Jean Mayo (Michigan Technological University)
Robert McCloskey (University of Scranton)
O. William Mcclung (Nebraska Wesleyan University)
Frank Mccown (Harding University)
Chris McDonald (The Univ. of Western Australia)
Charlie Mcdowell (UC Santa Cruz)
James McGuffee (Christian Brothers University)
John McManus (Randolph-Macon College)
Pedro Medeiros (Universidade Nova de Lisboa- Dep. Informática)
Chao Mei (KENNESAW STATE UNIVERSITY Search)
Alexandra Mendes (Teesside University)
Suzanne Menzel (Indiana University Bloomington)
Jose Carlos Metrolho (IPCB)
Razvan Alexandru Mezei (Saint Martin's University)
Afsaneh Minaie (Utah Valley University)
Mia Minnes (University of California San Diego)
Jose Miro-Julia (UIB)
Diba Mirza (University of California Santa Barbara)
Allison Mishkin (University of Oxford)
Amitabh Mishra (University of West Florida)
Sumita Mishra (Rochester Institute of Technology)
Benjamin R. Mitchell (Villanova University)
Idongesit Mkpong-Ruffin (Faulkner University)
Karina Mochetti (UFF)
Selvarajah Mohanarajah (UNC-Pembroke)
Gabriela Moise (Petroleum-Gas University of Ploiesti)
Mattia Monga (Università degli Studi di Milano - Dip. di Informatica)
Alvaro Monge (California State University Long Beach)
Christopher Moretti (Princeton University)
Michael Morgan (Monash University)
Mirella M. Moro (Univ. Federal de Minas Gerais - UFMG)
Niema Moshiri (University of California San Diego)
Frank Moss (Claremont Graduate University)
Sukanya Kannan Moudgalya (Michigan State University)
Xenia Mountrouidou (College of Charleston)
Michael G Murphy (retired)
Paolo Musmarra (Università degli Studi di Salerno)
Brandon Myers (University of Iowa)
Muhammad Nadeem (Mississippi State University)
Anurag Nagar (The University of Texas at Dallas)
Pedro Najera (Tecnologico de Monterrey, Campus Cuernavaca)
Fabiola Nakamura (Universidade Federal do Amazonas)
Mourya Reddy Narasareddygari (North Dakota State University)
Mamoun Nawahdah (Birzeit University)
Fariha Naz (Simon Fraser University)
Patrick Ndayizigamiye (University of KwaZulu-Natal)
Marion Neumann (Washington Universoty in St. Louis)
Ha Nguyen (University of California-Irvine)
Jaye Nias (Spelman College)
Delmer Nicholson (University of Cincinnati Clermont College)
Emma Norling (The University of Sheffield)
Cindy Norris (Appalachian State University)
Sarah M North (Kennesaw State University)
Theodore S. Norvell (Memorial University of Newfoundland)
Linda Null (The Pennsylvania State University)
Brian O'Neill (Western New England University)
Suhaib Obeidat (Bloomfield College)
Peter Ohmann (College of St. Benedict / St. John's University)
Edward Okie (Radford University)
Oluwakemi Ola (UBC)
John Oliver (Cal Poly)
Lawrence Osborne (Lamar University Faculty)
Radek Oslejsek (Masaryk University)
Joseph Osunde (The Open University, United Kingdom)

Vanessa Stangherlin Machado Paixão-Cortes (PUCRS / URI)
Yin Pan (none)
Greta Pangborn (Saint Michael's College)
Katarina Pantic (Utah State University)
Jennifer Parham-Mocello (Oregon State University)
Joonsuk Park (University of Richmond)
Younghee Park (San Jose State University)
Youngki Park (Chuncheon National University of Education)
Young Park (Bradley University)
Hyesung Park (Georgia Gwinnett College)
Rob Parke (University of Southern California)
Miranda Parker (Georgia Institute of Technology)
Rick Parker (University of Colorado Boulder)
Pablo Parra (University of Alcala)
Leo Natan Paschoal (University of São Paulo)
James Paterson (Glasgow Caledonian University)
Joslenne Pena (The Pennsylvania State University)
Bin Peng (Park University)
Markeya Peteranetz (University of Nebraska-Lincoln)
Teresa Peterman (GVSU)
Andrew Petersen (University of Toronto)
Peter Peterson (University of Minnesota)
Zachary Peterson (Cal Poly, San Luis Obispo)
Iasonas Petras (Princeton University)
Fabio Petrillo (Universite du Quebec a Chicoutimi)
Raymond Pettit (University of Virginia)
Matthew Peveler (Rensselaer Polytechnic Institute)
Phu H. Phung (University of Dayton)
Gustavo Pinto (UFPA)
Blagovesta Pirelli (Ecole Polytechnique Fédérale de Lausanne)
Lambros Piskopos (Wilbur Wright College)
Enrico Pontelli (New Mexico State University)
Jari Porras (LUT)
Lori Postner (Nassau Community College)
James Prather (Abilene Christian University)
Thomas W. Price (North Carolina State University)
Abena Primo (Huston-Tillotson University)
Christopher Proctor (Stanford University)
Lauren Provost (Simmons College)
Keith Quille (Institute of Technology Tallaght)
Beth Quinn (NCWIT)
John Rager (Amherst College)
Saty Raghavachary (University of Southern California)
Brian Railing (Carnegie Mellon University)
Sagar Raina (Mount Saint Mary College)
Rajendra Raj (Rochester Institute of Techinology)
Damith Chatura Rajapakse (National University of Singapore)
Raghuram Ramanujan (Davidson College)
Devina Ramduny-Ellis (Greenhead College)
Shikha Raturi (University of the South Pacific)
Saquib Razak (Carnegie Mellon University)
Elissa M. Redmiles (University of Maryland)
Michael Redmond (La Salle University, Philadelphia, PA, USA)
Donna Reese (Mississippi State University)
Christine Reilly (Skidmore College)
Yolanda Reimer (University of Montana)
Detlef Rick (University of Hamburg)
Charles Riedesel (University of Nebraska - Lincoln)
Kathryn E Ringland (Northwestern University)
Kelly Rivers (Carnegie Mellon University)
Christian Roberson (Florida Southern College)
Nicholas Rosasco (Valparaiso University)
Joel Ross (U Washington iSchool)
Guido Rößling ()
Anthony Ruocco (Roger Williams University)
Ryan Rybarczyk (Butler University)
Mehran Sahami (Stanford University)
Mariam Salloum (UC Riverside)
Ian Sanders (unisa)
Kari Sandouka (Dordt College)
Sreecharan Sankaranarayanan (Carnegie Mellon University)
Cassandra Scharber (University of Minnesota)
Jessica Young Schmidt (North Carolina State University)
Karl Schmitt (Valparaiso University)
Kaye Schroeder (National American University, The College of St. Scholastica)
Jason Schultz (Bemidji State University)
Stephanie Schwartz (Millersville University)
Michael James Scott (Falmouth University)
Bruno Sena (University of São Paulo)
Mazyar Seraj (University of Bremen)
Adolfo Gustavo Serra Seca Neto (UTFPR)

Christian Servin (El Paso Community College)
Michael Shah (Tufts University)
Bonita Sharif (University of Nebraska - Lincoln)
Mohamed Shehab (University of North Carolina at Charlotte)
Amit Shesh (Northeastern University)
Yasuto Shirai (Shizuoka University)
Angela Siegel (Dalhousie University)
Bill Siever (Washington University)
Scott Sigman (Drury University)
Jorge Silveyra (Muhlenberg College)
Maninder Singh (North Dakota State University)
Tim Sisson (Cleveland State University)
Harvey Siy (University of Nebraska at Omaha)
Thérèse Smith (Worcester Polytechnic Institute)
Takako Soma (Illinois College)
Raja Sooriamurthi (Carnegie Mellon University)
Shvetha Soundararajan (George Mason University)
Greg Speegle (Baylor University)
Ellen Spertus (Mills College)
Nathan Sprague (James Madison University)
Nigamanth Sridhar (Cleveland State University)
Bernhard Standl (Vienna University of Technology)
Andreas Steffens (RWTH Aachen University)
Kristin Stephens-Martinez (University of California, Berkeley)
Tom Stokke (University of North Dakota)
Jeffrey Stone (The Pennsylvania State University)
Kristina Striegnitz (Union College)
Kalpathi Subramanian (The University of N Carolina at Charlotte)
Valerie Summet (Rollins College)
Durga Suresh-Menon (Wentworth Institute of Technology)
Valdemar Švábenský (Masaryk University)
Alaaeddin Swidan (Delft University of Technology)
Claudia Szabo (The University of Adelaide)
Toni Taipalus (University of Jyväskylä)
Robert Tairas (Vanderbilt University)
Paul Talaga (University of Indianapolis)
Burcin Tamer (Computing Research Association)
Sheng Tan (Florida State University)
Fatma Tarlaci (Stanford University)
Micah Taylor (The University of North Carolina at Chapel Hill)
Cynthia Taylor (Oberlin College)
Rita Tesseroli (UFPR)
William Thacker (Winthrop University)
Anastasios Theodoropoulos (University of Peloponnese)
Charles Thevathayan (RMIT University)
George Thomas (University of Wisconsin Oshkosh)
Megan Thomas (California State University, Stanislaus)
Brian Thoms (California State University Channel Islands)
Armando Maciel Toda (University of São Paulo)
Kim Tracy (Rose-Hulman Institute of Technology)
Christian Trefftz (Grand Valley State University)
Deborah Trytten (University of Oklahoma)
Jennifer Tsan (North Carolina State University)
Liviana Tudor (Petroleum-Gas University of Ploiesti, Romania)
Claude Turner (Norfolk State University)
Martin Ukrop (Faculty of Informatics, Masaryk University, Czech Republic)
Ian Utting (University of Kent)
David Valentine (Grove City College)
Eliana Valenzuela-Andrade (University of Puerto Rico at Arecibo)
Robert Van Camp (Marietta College)
Sarah Van Wart (University of California, Berkeley)
Izak Van Zyl (Cape Peninsula University of Technology)
James Vanderhyde (Saint Xavier University)
Anthony Varghese (University of Wisconsin-River Falls)
Jorge Vasconcelos (National Autonomous University of Mexico (UNAM))
Nanette Veilleux (Simmons College)
J. Ángel Velázquez-Iturbide (Universidad Rey Juan Carlos)
Gabriela Vilanova (UNPA)
Giovanni Vincenti (University of Baltimore)
Rebecca Vivian (The University of Adelaide)
David Voorhees (Le Moyne College)
Jan Vykopal (Masaryk University)
Rosita Wachenchauzer (Universidad Nacional de Tres de Febrero)
Amber Wagner (Kennesaw State University)
Sally K Wahba (NetApp)
Mike Wallinga (Northwestern College)
Kendra Walther (University of Southern California)
Patrick Wang (Institut Supérieur d'Électronique de Paris)
Sujing Wang (Lamar University)
Yi Wang (Rochester Institute of Technology)
Stan Warford (Pepperdine University)
Jayce R. Warner (The University of Texas at Austin)
Kevin Waterman (EDC)
Andrew Watkins (Baldwin Wallace University)

Neftali Watkinson (University of California, Irvine)
Josh Weese (Kansas State University)
Bingyang Wei (Texas Christian University)
Dee Weikle (James Madison University)
Troy Weingart (United Stated Air Force Academy Dept of Computer Science)
David Weintrop (University of Maryland)
Richard Weiss (The Evergreen State College)
Kevin Wendt (University of Minnesota)
Xiaojing Weng (The Education University of Hong Kong)
Elizabeth White (George Mason University)
Alan Whitehurst (Southern Virginia University)
Michael Whitney (Winthrop University)
Eliane Wiese (University of Utah)
Jim Williams (University of Wisconsin-Madison)
Craig Wills (Worcester Polytechnic Institute)
Victor Winter (University of Nebraska at Omaha)
Zoe Wood (Cal Poly)
Heather Wright (Computing Research Association)
Jinyue Xia (University Of North Carolina Charlotte)
Benjamin Xie (University of Washington)
Mamta Yadav (Texas A&M University - Corpus Christi)
Nikhil Yadav (St. John's University)
Jeong Yang (Texas A&M University-San Antonio)
Lan Yang (California State Polytechnic University, Pomona)
Arthur Yanushka (Christian Brothers University)
Sejong Yoon (The College of New Jersey)
Timothy Yuen (University of Texas at San Antonio)
Zhen Zeng (Arizona State Univeristy)
Jinghua Zhang (Winston-Salem State University)
Yuanlin Zhang (Texas Tech University)
Ming Zhao (Arizona State University)
Rui Zhi (North Carolina State University)
Craig Zilles (University of Illinois at Urbana-Champaign)

Poster Reviewers

Seth Adjei (Northern Kentucky University)
Ashish Aggarwal (University of Florida)
Jennifer Albert (The Citadel)
Gabriella Anton (Northwestern University)
Saira Anwar (Purdue University)
Luis Gustavo J. Araujo (State University of Feira de Santana)
Monica Babes-Vroman (Rutgers University)
Donald Bagert (Benedictine College)
Michael Ball (University of California, Berkeley)
Mario Luca Bernardi (Giustino Fortunato University)
Bradley Beth (The University of Texas at Austin)
Manish Bhatt (University of New Orleans)
Esdras Bispo Jr. (Federal University of Goiás)
Jeremy Bradbury (University of Ontario Institute of Technology)
Andrej Brodnik (University of Ljubljana)
Ricardo Caceffo (University of Campinas (Unicamp), Brazil)
Ankur Chattopadhyay (University of Wisconsin - Green Bay)
Radhouane Chouchane (Columbus State University)
Vincent Cicirello (Stockton University)
Alison Clear (EIT)
Phillip Conrad (UC Santa Barbara)
Andrew Csizmadia (Newman University)
Fabian Deitelhoff (FH Dortmund)
Gabriella Dodero (ASLERD)
Mohsen Dorodchi (University of North Carolina at Charlotte)
Felicia Doswell (Norfolk State University)
Bob Edmison (Virginia Tech)
Kurt Eiselt (University of California, Davis)
Daniel Ellsworth (Colorado College)
Yadran Eterovic (Pontificia Universidad Catlica de Chile)
Mohammed Farghally (Virginia Tech)
Russell Feldhausen (Kansas State University)
Ronald Finkbine (Indiana University Southeast)
Susan Eileen Fox (Macalester College)
Kathleen Freeman (University of Oregon)
Ilenia Fronza (Free University of Bolzano / Bozen)
Alessio Gaspar (University of South Florida Polytechnic)
Richard Glassey (Robert Gordon University)
Mark Gondree (Sonoma State University)
Ana I. González-Tablas (University Carlos III de Madrid)
Isabela Hidalgo (University of South Florida)
Timothy Highley (La Salle University)
José Ramón Hilera (Universidad de Alcalá)
Brian Howard (DePauw University)
Jana Jackova (Matej Bel University)
Yerika Jimenez (University of Florida)
Kartik Palani Kartik Palani (University of Illinois at Urbana-Champaign)

Fazel Keshtkar (ST John's University)
Edward Kim (Villanova University)
Meen Chul Kim (Drexel University)
Carsten Kleiner (University of Applied Science and Arts Hannover)
Joe Kmoch (JK Consulting)
Kyu Han Koh (California State University, Stanislaus)
Joan Langdon (Bowie State University)
Bobby Law (Glasgow Caledonian University)
Alina Lazar (Youngstown State University)
Christopher League (LIU Brooklyn)
Chi-Un Lei (The University of Hong Kong)
Peilong Li (University of Massachusetts Lowell)
Yu-Tzu Lin (National Taiwan Normal University)
Qiang Liu (College of Computer, National University of Defense Technology)
Nicholas Lytle (North Carolina State University)
Mirella M. Moro (Univ. Federal de Minas Gerais - UFMG)
Joaquim Madeira (University of Aveiro)
Olaf Manuel Maennel (Tallinn University of Technology)
Maria Jose Marcelino (University of Coimbra)
Bruce Maxwell (Colby College)
Lester McCann (University of Arizona)
Ralph Eric McGregor (Bridgewater College)
Pedro Medeiros (Universidade Nova de Lisboa- Dep. Informática)
Alexandra Mendes (Teesside University)
Jose Carlos Metrolho (IPCB)
Gabriela Moise (Petroleum-Gas University of Ploiesti)
Niema Moshiri (University of California San Diego)
Shamsi Moussavi (MassBay Community College)
Srikanth Mudigonda (Saint Louis University)
Paolo Musmarra (Università degli Studi di Salerno)
Nilufer Onder (Michigan Technological University)
Daniel Paiva (Universidade Tecnológica Federal do Paraná)
Youngki Park (Chuncheon National University of Education)
Matthew Peveler (Rensselaer Polytechnic Institute)
Enrico Pontelli (New Mexico State University)
Sagar Raina (Mount Saint Mary College)
Ali Raza (University of Colorado Boulder)
Detlef Rick (University of Hamburg)
Charles Riedesel (University of Nebraska - Lincoln)
Marc Rigas (The Pennsylvania State University)
Suzanne Rivoire (Sonoma State University)
Kaye Schroeder (National American University, The College of St. Scholastica)
Ching-Kuang Shene (Michigan Technological University)
Yasuto Shirai (Shizuoka University)
Bill Siever (Washington University)
Maninder Singh (North Dakota State University)
Varsha Srikanth Koushik (University of Colorado Boulder)
Melissa Stange (Lord Fairfax Community College)
Andreas Steffens (RWTH Aachen University)
Paul Talaga (University of Indianapolis)
Rita Tesseroli (UFPR)
Brian Thoms (California State University Channel Islands)
Armando Toda (University of São Paulo)
Tammy Vandegrift (University of Portland)
Jorge Vasconcelos (National Autonomous University of Mexico (UNAM))
Rebecca Vivian (The University of Adelaide)
Amber Wagner (Kennesaw State University)
Patrick Wang (Institut Supérieur d'Électronique de Paris)
Howard Whitston (University of South Alabama)
Craig Wills (Worcester Polytechnic Institute)
Steven Wolfman (The University of British Columbia)
Fan Yang (Stanford University)
H. Kai Yang (Seattle College)
Yueming Yang (Baldwin Wallace University)
Jones Yu (Wentworth Institute of Technology)
Yuanlin Zhang (Texas Tech University)

Special Session Reviewers

Andrew Allen (Georgia Southern University)
Isabel Azevedo (ISEP)
Beverly Bachmayer (Intel)
Leland Beck (San Diego State University)
S. Jane Fritz (St. Joseph's College)
Olga Glebova (Georgia State University)
Mark Gondree (Sonoma State University)
Colin Johnson (University of Kent)
Michael Kirkpatrick (James Madison University)
Swathi Kurunji (Teradata)
Steven Mcgee (The Learning Partnership)

Louis Mchugh (Illinois Institute of Technology)
Sara More (Johns Hopkins Department of Computer Science)
Imani Palmer (University of Illinois at Urbana-Champaign)
Andy Rasmussen (Chicago Public Schools)
Matt Roberts (Macquarie University)
Tobias Rocha (UFRN)
Rehmat Ullah (Hongik University)
Tammy Vandegrift (University of Portland)
Ming Zhang (Peking University)
Sanja Zivanovic (Barry University)

Workshop Reviewers

Raman Adaikkalavan (Indiana University South Bend)
Mohammad Q. Azhar (BMCC, The City University Of New York)
Luciana Benotti (Universidad Nacional de Cordoba)
Marc Berges (Technische Universität München, TUM School of Education)
Erik Brunvand (University of Utah)
David Bunde (Knox College)
Richard Burns (West Chester University)
Michael Cotterell (University of Georgia)
Lawrence D'Antonio (Ramapo College)
Luigi De Russis (Politecnico di Torino)
Nate Derbinsky (Northeastern University)
Priscilla Dodds (Georgia State University)
Ali Ebnenasir (Michigan Technological University)
Kathleen Ericson (University of Tennessee at Martin)
Mark Floryan (University of Virginia)
Joshua T. Guerin (University of Tennessee at Martin)
Yasemin Gulbahar (Ankara University)
Brian Harrington (University of Toronto)
Cinda Heeren (UBC)
Wen-Jung Hsin (Park University)
Kartik Palani Kartik Palani (University of Illinois at Urbana-Champaign)
Anastasia Kurdia (Tulane University)
David Largent (Ball State University)
Cam Macdonell (MacEwan University)
Melinda Mcdaniel (Georgia Institute of Technology)
Srikanth Mudigonda (Saint Louis University)
Daniel Costa De Paiva (Universidade Tecnológica Federal do Paraná)
Shari Plantz-Masters (Regus University)
Joe Politz (University of California San Diego)
Traci Sarmiento (United States Air Force Academy)
Ching-Kuang Shene (Michigan Technological University)
Varsha Srikanth Koushik (University of Colorado Boulder)
Nadine von Frankenberg Und Ludwigsdorff (Technical University of Munich)
Steven Wolfman (The University of British Columbia)
Jidong Xiao (Boise State University)
Fan Yang (Stanford University)
Rina Zviel-Girshin (Ruppin Academic Center)

SIGCSE 2019 Sponsors & Supporters

Platinum Supporters:

Microsoft

GitHub Education

Google

Gold Supporters:

codio

intel

ORACLE Academy

zyBooks

turingscraft

Silver Supporters:

ABET

IBM

Mimir

gradescope by turnitin

vocareum

Bronze Supporters:

ANITA B.ORG

Pursuing the Dream: A 50-Year Perspective on American Society, Technology, and Inclusion in Computing

Freeman A. Hrabowski, III
President
University of Maryland, Baltimore County (UMBC)
Baltimore, MD, USA
hrabowski@umbc.edu

ABSTRACT

Rapid and dramatic demographic and technological changes require our nation's schools, colleges, and universities to work with agility in preparing students – particularly those from diverse backgrounds – for careers in science, technology, engineering, and math (STEM) fields, including computer science. Exploring the interplay of technology, education, and inclusion over the past 50 years, Dr. Hrabowski examines what this means for our future work in higher education. Computing education provides a critically important case. As the sector evolves rapidly, many well-paid jobs go unfilled and we must explore ways to draw on talent wherever it is found. Emphasizing themes from his TED talk on student success, Dr. Hrabowski focuses our attention on the importance of high expectations and hard work, building community among students, faculty engagement with students, and rigorous assessment of what works. He assesses the way innovative approaches – including course re-design, active and experiential learning, research, and partnerships with companies and agencies – promote student success, inclusive excellence, and achievement for all students both in STEM generally and computer science in particular.

KEYWORDS

Computer Science Education

ACM Reference format:

Freeman A. Hrabowski. 2019. Pursuing the Dream: A 50-Year Perspective on American Society, Technology, and Inclusion in Computing. In *SIGCSE'19: The 50th ACM Technical Symposium on Computer Science Education, Feb 27-Mar 2, 2019, Minneapolis, MN, USA.* ACM, New York, NY, USA, 1 pages. https://doi.org/10.1145/3287324.3290951

BIOGRAPHY

Dr. Freeman A. Hrabowski, President of University of Maryland, Baltimore County (UMBC) since 1992, is a consultant on science and math education to national agencies, universities, and school systems. He was named by President Obama to chair the President's Advisory Commission on Educational Excellence for African Americans. He also chaired the National Academies' committee that produced the report, Expanding Underrepresented Minority Participation: America's Science and Technology Talent at the Crossroads (2011). His 2013 TED talk highlights the "Four Pillars of College Success in Science."

Named one of the 100 Most Influential People in the World by TIME (2012) and one of America's Best Leaders by U.S. News & World Report (2008), he also received TIAA-CREF's Theodore M. Hesburgh Award for Leadership Excellence (2011), the Carnegie Corporation's Academic Leadership Award (2011), and the Heinz Award (2012) for contributions to improving the "Human Condition." UMBC has been recognized as a model for inclusive excellence by such publications as U.S. News, which the past eight years has recognized UMBC as a national leader in academic innovation and undergraduate teaching. Dr. Hrabowski's most recent book, Holding Fast to Dreams: Empowering Youth from the Civil Rights Crusade to STEM Achievement, describes the events and experiences that played a central role in his development as an educator and leader.

ACM ISBN 978-1-4503-5890-3/19/02.
https://doi.org/10.1145/3287324.3290951

A Module-based Approach to Teaching Big data and Cloud Computing Topics at CS Undergraduate Level

Debzani Deb
Department of Computer Science
Winston-Salem State University
Winston-Salem, NC, USA
debd@wssu.edu

Muztaba Fuad
Department of Computer Science
Winston-Salem State University
Winston-Salem, NC, USA
fuadmo@wssu.edu

Keith Irwin
Department of Computer Science
Winston-Salem State University
Winston-Salem, NC, USA
irwinke@wssu.edu

ABSTRACT

Big data and cloud computing collectively offer a paradigm shift in the way businesses are now acquiring, using and managing information technology. This creates the need for every CS student to be equipped with foundational knowledge in this collective paradigm and to possess some hands-on experience in deploying and managing big data applications in the cloud. We argue that, for substantial coverage of big data and cloud computing concepts and skills, the relevant topics need to be integrated into multiple core courses across the undergraduate CS curriculum rather than creating additional standalone core or elective courses and performing a major overhaul of the curriculum. Our approach to including these topics is to develop autonomous learning modules for specific core courses in which their coverage might find an appropriate context. In this paper, three such modules are discussed and our classroom experiences during these interventions are documented. So far, we have achieved reasonable success in attaining student learning outcomes, enhanced engagement, and interests. Our objective is to share our experience with the academics who aim at incorporating similar pedagogy and to receive feedback about our approach.

CCS CONCEPTS

Social and professional topics ~ Computer science education • Social and professional topics ~ Information technology education • Computer systems organization ~ Cloud computing

KEYWORDS

Big data; Cloud computing; Curriculum; Mapreduce; Apache Spark.

ACM Reference format:

Debzani Deb, Muztaba Fuad, Keith Irwin. 2019. A Module-based Approach to Teaching Big data and Cloud Computing Topics at CS Undergraduate Level. In *Proceedings of 50th ACM Technical Symposium on Computer Science Education (SIGCSE '19), February 27-March 2, 2019, Minneapolis, MN, USA.* ACM, NY, NY, USA, 7 pages. https://doi.org/10.1145/3287324.3287494

SIGCSE '19, February 27-March 2, 2019, Minneapolis, MN, USA

ACM ISBN 978-1-4503-5890-3/19/02...$15.00
https://doi.org/10.1145/3287324.3287494

1. Introduction

In today's world, the analysis of 'big data' becomes a high priority task for many fields of study and data-driven discovery and decision processes now guide many sectors of our business and economy. At the development level, analyzing big data requires proficiency in specialized algorithms and methodologies due to the fundamentally distributed and parallel nature of the workloads, while, at the infrastructure level, cloud computing skills are paramount to acquire a pool of virtual resources in a 'pay-as-you-go' fashion to deploy and manage these workloads. Big data and cloud computing collectively offer a paradigm shift in the way businesses are now acquiring, using and managing information technology. With the fast growth of this paradigm, businesses are struggling to find experienced people who not only have the deep analytical skills, but also have the data hosting, storage and management skills to effectively leverage this collective model. This observation is supported by the recent prediction, made by the International Data Corporation (IDC), that by 2020 big data staffing shortages will expand from analysts and data scientists to include architects and experts in data management. Increasing adoption of this collective paradigm in solving problems from a variety of domains is also making study and research on this paradigm crucial.

It is immensely important that every CS and IT undergraduate student be equipped with foundational knowledge in this collective paradigm and be provided with hands-on experience in deploying and managing big data applications in the cloud, to acquire skills that are necessary to meet current and future industry demands as well as to enable them to carry out applied research in this paradigm. However, the challenge is that many of the tools and techniques of the big data and cloud computing paradigm have emerged only in the last few years and have not yet transitioned into the most recent ACM/IEEE Joint Curriculum recommendations [1] or the ABET curriculum requirements [2]. Many 2-year and 4-year institutions develop their CS curriculum around these guidelines and requirements and as a result cannot afford to include these contemporary topics within a core course in their densely packed curricula.

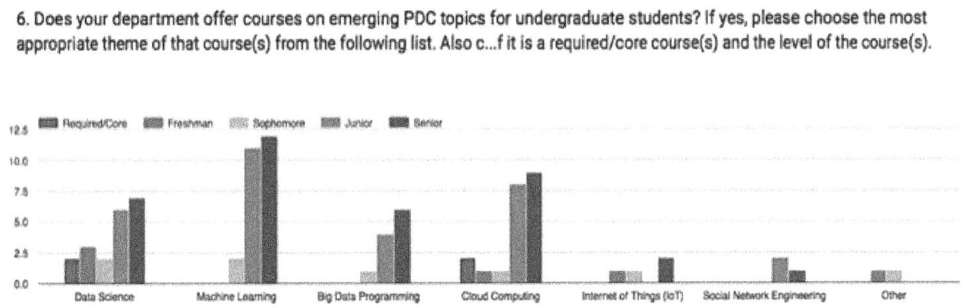

Figure 1: SIGCSE Listserv survey results

We argue that for substantial coverage of big data and cloud computing concepts and skills, students need to be intervened more often, gradually, and the topics should be integrated into multiple core courses of the curriculum. Our approach to including these topics is to develop a series of short, self-contained learning modules with specific learning goals, lessons plans, and assessment resources, and to suggest specific core courses in which their coverage might find an appropriate context. Each module covers topics of the collective paradigm in the context of a conventional core CS/IT course, thus enabling us to better expose students to the big data and cloud computing concepts without a major overhaul of the curriculum. Providing students with hands-on experience is vital and therefore the modules are designed with a rich set of tutorials, sample programs, descriptions of cloud-based resources and substantial hands-on projects. Reusability and adaptability are other major concerns, and as a result the modules are designed to be autonomous, made available for downloading [3], and detailed enough for easier adoption by other instructors with minimal experience. This paper details the deployment of the modules in specific courses at our institution, however, they could be adapted for deployment in some other courses with minimal effort.

In this paper, we report on our experiences in offering three such modules in respective courses. More specifically, we discuss the learning outcomes, module content, assessment instruments, and student assessment and survey results. Our objective is to share our experience with the instructors who aim at incorporating similar pedagogy that enhance student knowledge on this collective paradigm. The rest of the paper is organized as follows: Section 2 discusses the related initiatives for including big data and cloud computing topics into the curriculum, section 3 details the modules and their classroom deployments and section 4 concludes the paper.

2. Related Works

Limited by the fact that there are no standard guidelines provided by ACM or ABET to integrate the big data and cloud computing topics into the CS curriculum, the computer science education community has taken multiple approaches to address the need to produce a satisfactory number of well-trained professionals in these fields. Our extensive literature survey identifies three such approaches from Academia. Firstly, several institutions offer non-core specialized courses [4, 5, 6] to cover a variety of aspects of data science and big data analytics, where students are primarily taught data acquisition, cleaning, analytical and visualization skills. While these courses help students in developing skills related to transforming data into knowledge, they do not provide the students with concepts and experiences related to hosting, storing, and deploying application within the cloud environment and scaling up applications within performance and budgetary constraints. A second category of approaches integrates big data and/or cloud computing topics in existing CS/IT courses (mostly non-core) such as Parallel and Distributed Computing, High Performance Computing, Networking, Cybersecurity etc. These interventions are often sporadic, mostly ignited by the instructor's own interests and experiences and therefore are not capable of garnering a substantial student interest and knowledge on this collective paradigm. A few research-intensive universities offer specialized standalone courses [7, 8, 9, 10] such as "Cloud computing", "Big data management" etc., where the abovementioned collective paradigm is addressed to a greater extent. However, being an elective (non-core) course offered at a handful of universities, only a handful of students receive the benefit.

The abovementioned approaches are limited in intervening a substantial portion of the CS/IT undergraduate student population with necessary expertise of this collective paradigm as they are mostly undertaken via non-core and special topic courses. A survey was recently administered through SIGCSE listserv regarding the CDER curriculum initiative on parallel and distributed computing (PDC) [11] and one of the questions asked the participants about the emerging topic courses that their departments are offering and whether these courses are core (required) or not. Fig. 1 shows the summarized results based on 35 responses. It is important to note that although many different institutions are conducting many specialized courses that are related to big data and cloud computing at the junior or the senior level, very few of them are core courses and therefore a complete and massive adoption of these topics are yet not possible within this framework. There is a big gap between the advances in big data and cloud computing and their inclusion in college-level instructions and this paper aims to address this gap by proposing an alternative module-based approach that covers the related concepts through a set of autonomous modules dispersed over several core courses across the curriculum.

3. Details of the Modules

The proposed modules are designed to be short and autonomous for easier adoption and as a result, each of them spans two 75-minute class periods and includes specific learning goals, lecture notes, and assessment resources. The assessment resources contain quiz questions, tutorials, sample programs, cloud-based resources, hands-on projects etc. Detailed tutorials are developed for multiple platforms, enabling straightforward adoption at other institutions. The modules are expected to be taught in a lecture-lab setting, where the first class is typically used for discussing the new concepts and techniques, and the second class is used to introduce students to the hands-on project along with the necessary tools and resources they will require to complete the project. The take home project contains multiple tasks and usually has two weeks of deadline.

The first of the three modules is designed to expose students to the cloud computing fundamentals and to provide them with hands-on experience in using the public cloud environment. The module is adopted to the core "Computer Architecture" (CA) course at our institution. It is important to provide context for the module within the typical course materials where it is deployed so that the module is not perceived by the students as an isolated and disruptive topic. In the CA class, this context is established by asking students to execute CPU/IO benchmarking applications (typical CA topics) in the cloud setting. The second module is focused on MapReduce programming and popular cloud analytics engines (such as Hadoop and Spark) and is deployed in the "Analysis of Algorithm" (AA) class. The context is established by allowing students explore the cost vs. performance tradeoff for running analytics applications within the cloud environment. The third module is designed with the aim of illustrating the importance of SQL within various big database management systems (BDBMS) and is deployed within a "Database Management" (DB) course. The students could easily see the connection when they utilize Spark-SQL programs to load and query both structed and unstructured data sets. The following few sections discuss each module along with the student assessment results in the intervened semesters.

3.1 "Computer Architecture" (CA) Module

This module is integrated into the "Computer Architecture" class and is designed to expose students to virtualization and cloud computing fundamentals and to provide students with hands-on experiences in using AWS cloud. At our institution, this is a required course for both CS and IT majors and mostly junior and senior students attend the course. Specific learning outcomes are

1. Recognize the key properties, techniques, strengths and challenges of cloud computing (CA-LO1).
2. Develop hands-on experience with AWS web interface for virtual machine (VM) provisioning and management. (CA-LO2).

3.1.1 Lesson Plan. The first 75-minute class is lecture-based and includes discussion on important cloud computing characteristics such as scalability, on-demand access, measured services, and elasticity. The lecture then explains resource sharing and virtualization while pointing out its important aspects such as migration, timesharing, isolation etc. Finally, the lecture explores the benefits of utilizing cloud services within a business and the challenges associated with adoption, such as data confidentiality, performance unpredictability, etc. The second class mainly comprises a tutorial and a lab session that instructs students the basic provisioning and management of AWS EC2 instances.

3.1.2 Assessment Instruments. Student learning was assessed by utilizing an exam composed of factual questions and a hands-on project involving AWS EC2 services. The exam includes true/false, multiple choice and analytical questions and focuses on gauging the progress students have made retaining concepts related to virtualization and cloud computing fundamentals. As part of the hands-on project, students are asked to perform the following tasks

Task 1: Create two EC2 instances with different hardware and software configurations.

Task 2: Analyze instance performances by benchmarking them with CPU- and IO-bound applications and determine how performance scales with the different VM types.

Task 3: Represent results of the analysis graphically and report on them critically.

Students are asked to utilize Systester [12] as CPU-bound benchmark, which calculates the nth digit of π using the Gauss-Legendre algorithm, while experimenting with various values of n such as 128K, 256K, 512K, 1M, 2M, 8M, 16M. Additionally, the project requires the students to use the *iozone* benchmarking tool from the Phoronix [13] benchmarking suite to assess IO performances. Students set up experiments to benchmark both read and write performances by running *iozone* for different record sizes (4KB and 64KB) and file sizes (512 MB, 2GB, and 8GB). The experiments were repeated for both instances, the results were expressed graphically, and the students were further asked to critically evaluate their performance analysis results.

3.1.3 Assessment Results. This module was deployed in the Spring 2018 offering of the CA class with 29 students in it. Overall, students performed well (mean:13, median:13, standard deviation: 1.34) in answering the exam questions (out of 15). These statistics indicate students' knowledge acquisition on the concerned topics and therefore show the module's effectiveness in attaining the first learning outcome (CA-LO1). Students were able to accomplish the project with 40% of them achieving A grade, 20% of them achieving B grade, 15% of them securing C grade, and 25% of them attaining D/F grades. Even though, all students were comfortable with the AWS web interface for VM management (especially, after the detailed tutorial session) and accomplished Task 1 successfully (CA-LO2), some had trouble correctly executing the benchmarking applications on the VM instances (Task 2), and a group of students faced challenges while comparing and presenting their results and reporting on them critically (Task 3). It is clear that the student population being part of two different majors and backgrounds (CS and IT) was an important factor that contributed to the assessment results, and that the module would benefit more if it were offered to a particular major and tailored accordingly. However, we did not have the opportunity at our institution to accommodate that.

3.2 "Analysis of Algorithm" (AA) Module

This module is designed for the students of the Algorithm course with the goal of introducing the popular cloud analytics engines such as Hadoop and Spark. This module is targeted only for the CS majors, who have completed CS1, CS2, and a data structure course and are comfortable with and reasonably proficient using programming languages such as Java or Python. The learning outcomes of the module are

1. Recognize the key properties, techniques, strengths and challenges of MapReduce and Spark Framework (AA-LO1).
2. Build scalable applications based on MapReduce programming model using Hadoop and HDFS. (AA-LO2).
3. Develop basic experience with big data analysis on cloud platforms with performance and cost constraints using Spark/Hadoop platforms (AA-LO3).

3.2.1 Lesson Plan. The first 75-minute class is lecture-based and explores parallel computing at the beginning and introduces MapReduce as a framework that can quickly process large data sets by splitting them into individual chunks that are processed in parallel. The basics of MapReduce programming are then covered with example codes. Apache Hadoop, as an implementation of the MapReduce model, is then introduced along with its distributed file system HDFS. The concept of a Hadoop cluster along with the master-worker framework is briefly explored. Lastly, the problems with the classic MapReduce programming is discussed briefly and the need for an in-memory analytic engine such as Apache Spark is emphasized with a brief description of Spark's runtime environment.

The second class, on the other hand, is a lab-based class where the instructor provides some demonstrations and a tutorial for the students to follow. The tutorial provides instructions on running Hadoop through Cloudera's VM [14] on the local machine. It also provides students with step by step instruction of setting up HDFS, compiling and executing a MapReduce application, and retrieving output from HDFS. Lastly, the tutorial introduces students to Chameleon cloud [15] and shows them how to ssh to a particular Chameleon instance (all students are registered and added to our Chameleon project before the tutorial starts). We implemented a Spark on YARN cluster (with HDFS) on the Chameleon Cloud and the compiled Spark application that the students use for experimentation along with the datasets are pre-loaded to that instance. The concerned Spark application finds the trending topics given the Wikipedia page views information [16]. During the lab session, students are taught how to execute a Spark application in Yarn cluster by using the *spark-submit* command, and how to configure cluster resources for its execution by varying parameters such as *--num-executors*, *--executor-memory*, and *--executor-cores*. Students are also taught to verify the current resource allocation and to check the execution time and other performance metrics of a spark application by using Spark's web user interface (UI).

3.2.2 Assessment Instruments. This module is assessed by utilizing both hands-on project and exam questions. There are four multiple-choice questions and two design questions developed to assess students' comprehension of the Hadoop/Spark framework and the MapReduce programming model. In the design questions, students are asked to write pseudocode of map and reduce functions (or a series of them) for certain cases. The hands-on project, on the other hand, is built on top of the lab session and includes the following tasks:

Task 1: Modify existing MapReduce code to fulfill new requirements.

Task 2: Develop basic MapReduce program from scratch.

Task 3: Explore Spark application performance in the cloud environment through running them with various runtime configuration settings, and to gain some insight about the resource provisioning and the performance vs. cost tradeoff. Students are presented with two Wikipedia data sets (100GB and 200GB) and are provided with two Spark clusters (one-node cluster and two-node cluster, each compute node with 24 cores, 128 GB memory) in the Chameleon testbed. Students are asked to run the trending Wikipedia Spark application with the given two input datasets while trying various configuration setups for both clusters. Although use of Chameleon is free of charge, we introduce a basic cost model to the students (i.e. 1 service unit = 1 core with 1 GB memory) and ask them to compare different cluster configurations and gain some insight about performance vs. cost tradeoff. Students are further asked to write a report detailing their experimental results and their findings along with their supporting arguments.

3.2.3 Assessment Results. The module was deployed in the Spring 2017 offering of the AA course (N:13). All students were CS majors and were mostly juniors. On average, students attained 68% on the four multiple choice questions in the final exam. For the two design questions, students' average scores were 62% and 38%. The second design question (with average score 38%) involves writing a series of *map* and *reduce* tasks; and while many students provided a partially correct answer, only a few figured it out completely. These results indicate that the students were able to comprehend the concepts taught as part of the module and were able to answer both multiple choice and analytical questions successfully to a certain extent. After the rigorous lab session and many other individual troubleshooting sessions supported by the instructor and TAs, all students were able to perform Task 1 of the project, Task 2 was successfully completed by 85% of the students, and Task 3 was completed successfully by only 30% of the students. Overall, the student assessment results justify the module and show its effectiveness in achieving the proposed learning outcomes. Student assessment results of the multiple choice and analytical questions evidently supports students' in-depth understanding of the covered concepts (AA-LO1). The results of the first two project tasks show student competency in developing simple MapReduce applications (AA-LO2). The final task in the project exposed students to the cloud-enabled Spark environment and allowed them to understand runtime tradeoffs (AA-LO3); however, only a few students were able to complete this task.

3.3 "Database Management" (DB) Module

Currently, numerous application scenarios require processing very large datasets in a highly scalable and distributed fashion. Various types of big data systems have been designed to address this challenge and many of them have recognized the strengths of SQL as a query language. The proposed module for the introductory Database Management course is designed to expose students to the various types of big data systems and to integrate the study of SQL within these systems. This is a required course for both CS and IT majors at our institution and is typically attended by sophomore and junior students. The learning outcomes are

1. Recognize the key properties, strengths, and limitations of important big database management system (BDBMS) such as MapReduce, No-SQL, and New-SQL. (DB-LO1)
2. Develop hands-on experience in using SQL within Spark framework to load and query big datasets. (DB-LO2)

3.3.1 Lesson Plan. The first class (lecture) discusses limitations of relational database systems, and key properties, strengths, and limitations of various big data management systems such as MapReduce, No-SQL, and New-SQL. The second class starts with an introduction to the Spark distributed data processing framework, with Spark-SQL being a module within it for handling structed data processing. The lecture then introduces the students to the concept of DataFrames, emphasizing it can be created from a wide array of sources. The instructor then provides students with a tutorial and source code that instructs students the process of utilizing Jupyter notebook for developing and executing Spark-SQL applications. The tutorial provides instruction on creating DataFrames from JSON and CSV files, on manipulating them, and on running SQL queries programmatically within them.

3.3.2 Assessment Instruments A hands-on project and exam questions are utilized as assessment instruments. The exam contains four multiple choice questions that assess students' understanding of No-SQL and New-SQL systems and a detailed analytical question that assesses their comprehension of Spark-SQL programming. The hands-on project is a progression of the tutorial and involves developing a Spark application that loads historical Facebook stock prices [17] and uses Spark SQL to query the data. The dataset is downloaded as a CSV file, where each record contains the stock values of a single date and includes the following attributes*: date, open price, high price, low price, close price, volume*, and *adjClose* (close price adjusted for dividends and splits). Students are asked to develop a Spark-SQL application that loads the file, creates a DataFrame based on the content, registers the DataFrame as a SQL temporary view, and then includes queries that show the answers to the following questions

1. Show all records that have gained value during daily transaction in the year 2018 (close >= open).
2. Which day did Facebook stock gain maximum value?
3. Show the first 10 highest stock values.
4. Show the average sale volume for last 5 years.
5. Add two more questions and write queries to answer them.

Students were taught to infer schema based on JSON and CSV input during the tutorials and the project requires them to perform similar inference while querying the Facebook data set. However, the project also contains a challenging part where the students are required to load and query a text file where schema should be enforced programmatically. Students are not explicitly taught the schema enforcement but are provided with some resources that they might find useful.

3.3.3 Assessment Results Overall, students were able to complete the project (infer schema automatically) while 63% of them attained A grade, 25% of them attained B grade and 12% attained C grade. The challenging part (define schema programmatically), however was successfully completed by only 12% of the students. Overall the students' quiz performance validates their thorough understanding of the key properties of the various BDBMS systems (DB-LO1) and their project grades reflect their competency in developing a Spark-SQL application in analyzing and querying big datasets (DB-LO2).

3.4 Student Interest and Learning Experience

A three-question student survey was designed to asses students' perceptions of their learning experiences and their level of confidence and interests and is administered after each intervention. The students provide their opinions about the three statements using a Likert scale of five values such as Strongly Agree, Agree, Neutral, Disagree and Strongly Disagree. The questions are as follows, where X refers to the module specific topics in each survey

- Q1 - I found the topics X interesting.
- Q2 - If a friend asks me what X are, I will be able to explain for 2-3 minutes.
- Q3 – I would like to learn more about X and would like to explore more in my future courses.

Fig. 2 shows the student survey results for the Computer Architecture course. It is evident from the results that the students positively attested the enhancements due to the module. More specifically, 79% of the students found (strongly agreed or agreed) the conveyed topics interesting, 72% of them strongly agreed or agreed that they are well-versed on the topics, and 86% reported their desire to learn the topics more after the intervention. Fig. 3 shows the student survey results for the Algorithm course and all (100%) students found (strongly agreed or agreed) the conveyed topics interesting after the intervention. Similarly, 61% of the students strongly agreed or agreed that they are well-versed on the topics and 77% of the students expressed their eagerness to learn more. The survey results for the Database Management course is shown in Fig. 4 where 73% of the students attested (strongly agreed or agreed) the conveyed topics as interesting, 60% of the students strongly agreed or agreed that they are well-versed on the topics, and 87% of the students revealed their desire to learn the topics more. The relatively higher number of agreements with the self-reflection survey questions demonstrate that the students valued the experience, felt comfortable with the module content and grew further interest even though the duration of the intervention was very short.

4. Conclusions

The goal of this study is to explore the integration of big data and cloud computing modules into core undergraduate CS/IT courses and to evaluate its effectiveness. A substantial advantage of the modular approach is that a large number of CS/IT majors can be exposed to these contemporary topics and technologies via systematic and increasing integration throughout the computing curricula, and without the need of developing an additional core or elective course. This paper presents three such modules and our classroom experiences while deploying them. The student-generated evidence based on student performance and survey data supports our pedagogy, inspires us to continuously assess and update our interventions, and allows us to extend our interventions across multiple courses and semesters. The assessment results clearly show that the students were able to relate to the topics very well, found them to be interesting enough to explore and to retain, and developed significant interest and confidence after the interventions.

Development of this module content, lab and project-related artifacts such as tutorial, compiled programs, cloud instructions, input datasets, and assessment instruments required a large time investment. Instructors planning to reuse these modules must be well-prepared and organized in the classrooms to utilize their time in the best possible way. Our class size was rather small, and the instructors and their research assistants were able to support each student's needs in a timely manner. However, instructors who are planning to offer a similar module to a larger class must acquire enough TA resources for the duration of the module.

One limitation of the study is the lower number of students impacted by the modules and therefore, further repetitions of the interventions are paramount to make stronger conclusions about their effectiveness.

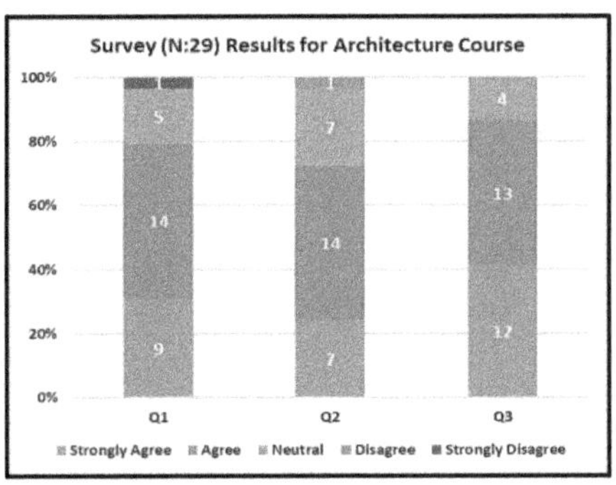

Figure 2: Students' Survey Results for CA Course.

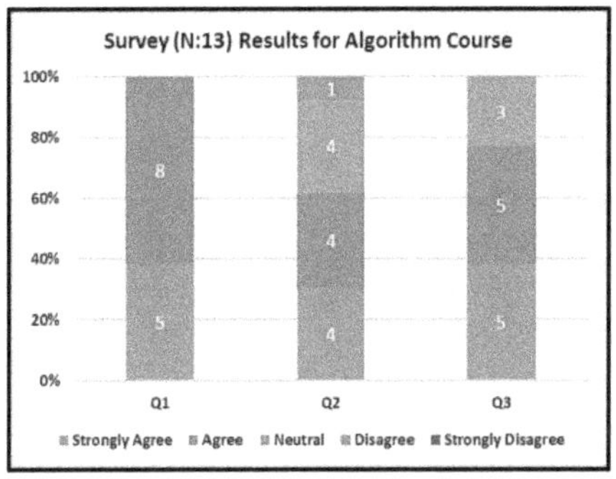

Figure 3: Students' Survey Results for AA Course.

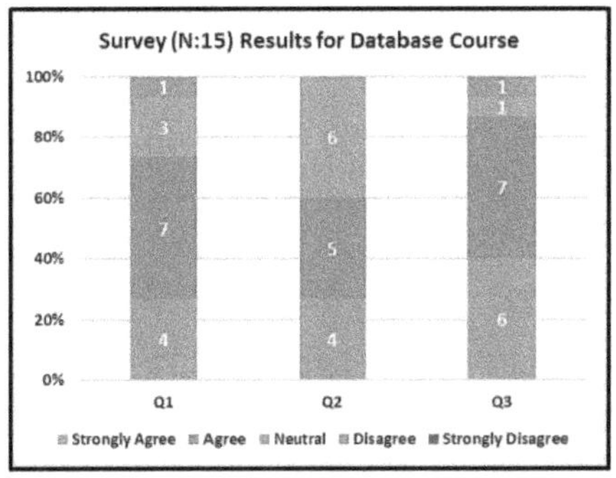

Figure 4: Students' Survey Results for DM Course.

In the future, we would like to perform research on more gradual and systematic integration of the developed modules across the curriculum, and research on assessing their collective effectiveness, rather than measuring the efficacy of a single module.

ACKNOWLEDGMENTS

This research was supported by National Science Foundation Award # 1600864.

REFERENCES

[1] Joint Task Force on Computing Curricula, Association for Computing Machinery (ACM) and IEEE Computer Society. 2013. Computer Science Curricula, 2013.

[2] Criteria for accrediting computing programs, 2017-2018 ccreditation cycle, http://www.abet.org/wp-content/uploads/2016/12/C001-17-18-CAC-Criteria-10-29-16-1.pdf

[3] http://ibigcloud.altl.org/resources.html, 2018.

[4] B. Ramamurthy, "A Practical and Sustainable Model for Learning and Teaching Data Science", Proceedings of the 47th ACM Technical Symposium on Computing Science Education (SIGCSE), March, 2016.

[5] S. J. Matthews, "Using Phoenix++ MapReduce to introduce undergraduate students to parallel computing", Journal of Computing Sciences in Colleges, vol. 32 Issue 6, June 2017.

[6] J. Eckroth, "Teaching Future Big Data Analysts: Curriculum and Experience Report", IEEE International Parallel and Distributed Processing Symposium Workshops (IPDPSW), May, 2017.

[7] A. S. Rabkin, C. Reiss, R. Katz, and D. Patterson. "Experiences teaching mapreduce in the cloud", In Proceedings of the 43rd ACM Technical Symposium on Computer Science Education (SIGCSE), 2012.

[8] M. S. Rehman, J. Boles, M. Hammoud, M. F. Sakr, "A Cloud Computing Course: From Systems to Services, Proceedings of the 46th ACM Technical Symposium on Computer Science Education (SIGCSE), 2015.

[9] CS5412: Cloud Computing, http://www.cs.cornell.edu/courses/cs5412/2018sp/

[10] CS309: Cloud Computing http://cs309a.stanford.edu/

[11] Center for Parallel and Distributed Computing Curriculum Development and Education resources (CDER), https://grid.cs.gsu.edu/~tcpp/curriculum/

[12] System Stability Tester, http://systester.sourceforge.net/

[13] Phoronix Test Suite, https://www.phoronix-test-suite.com/

[14] Cloudera, Cloudera QuickStart VM https://www.cloudera.com/downloads/quickstart_vms/5-12.html

[15] Chameleon cloud, https://www.chameleoncloud.org

[16] Wikipedia Page Views http://dumps.wikimedia.org/other/pagecounts-raw/

[17] Historial Facebook Stock Prices, https://finance.yahoo.com/quote/FB/history/

Embracing the Liberal Arts in an Interdisciplinary Data Analytics Program

Jessen Havill
Department of Mathematics & Computer Science
Data Analytics Program
Denison University
Granville, Ohio
havill@denison.edu

ABSTRACT

In 2016, we launched an interdisciplinary, undergraduate Data Analytics major that extends the definition of "interdisciplinary" beyond computer science, mathematics, and statistics to the natural and social sciences, humanities, and fine arts. Our program was conceived, and continues to be administered, as an independent academic unit by a Committee of faculty representing ten disciplines. Students majoring in Data Analytics complete four or more mathematics and computer science courses, four project-oriented Data Analytics courses, three to four courses in one of seven applied domains, and a required summer internship. Data Analytics courses are taught by both dedicated Data Analytics faculty and other faculty from the Committee. Partnerships with campus offices, alumni, businesses, and nonprofits have enhanced both coursework and internship opportunities. The major's popularity has exceeded our expectations, and has succeeded in attracting students with a variety of academic interests, many of whom would not have otherwise pursued a computational or quantitative major.

CCS CONCEPTS

• **Social and professional topics → Computing education**;

KEYWORDS

Data Science, Data Analytics, Curriculum, Liberal Arts

ACM Reference Format:
Jessen Havill. 2019. Embracing the Liberal Arts in an Interdisciplinary Data Analytics Program. In *Proceedings of the 50th ACM Technical Symposium on Computer Science Education (SIGCSE '19), February 27–March 2, 2019, Minneapolis, MN, USA.* ACM, New York, NY, USA, 6 pages. https://doi.org/10.1145/3287324.3287436

1 INTRODUCTION

With the growing availability of huge amounts of data and their increased application in a variety of sectors, undergraduate Data Science and Analytics programs (majors and minors) are on the rise. Anecdotally, it appears that most of these new programs, especially at smaller colleges, are growing out of Computer Science, Mathematics, Statistics, and/or Business departments as alternatives to their established majors [3, 4, 20].

At Denison University, we created an interdisciplinary Data Analytics program, administered as a standalone entity, that takes a more holistic approach to integrating this new discipline into an undergraduate curriculum. Now in its third year, enrollment in the major has grown well beyond our expectations. We believe that our program is unique in at least two ways. First, we recognize the value of Denison's liberal arts curriculum, and actively promote liberal arts values both through the structure of the major and in the content of unique, interdisciplinary core courses. Second, the major is designed to appeal to students with a broad array of interests and backgrounds. This is achieved by intentionally integrating disciplines beyond the quantitative sciences from the outset and establishing a low barrier to entry into the major.

In the following sections, we describe in detail the structure of the major, recount how the major originated and was developed, discuss our goals and the principles we followed in designing the program, and share our results and plans for the future.

ACM ISBN 978-1-4503-5890-3/19/02...$15.00
https://doi.org/10.1145/3287324.3287436

2 THE DATA ANALYTICS MAJOR

Denison University is a highly selective liberal arts college located about 30 miles east of Columbus, Ohio that enrolls approximately 2300 undergraduate students. Among peer institutions, our student body is fairly diverse: 20 percent are first-generation college students, 23 percent are domestic students of color, and 16 percent are international. The college offers 50 undergraduate majors and has no graduate programs.

Denison's Data Analytics (DA) major requires 11–12 courses, plus an internship. These requirements are divided into four components, color coded in Figure 1:

(1) computer science and mathematics foundation (yellow),
(2) project-oriented Data Analytics courses (blue),
(3) courses in an applied domain (green), and
(4) summer internship or research project (pink).

The first and third components, and to a lesser extent the fourth, are similar to other Data Science programs. The second component, however, and the way in which the program is administered and staffed, differentiates it from most, if not all, existing programs. In the remainder of this section, we will describe each component in more detail.

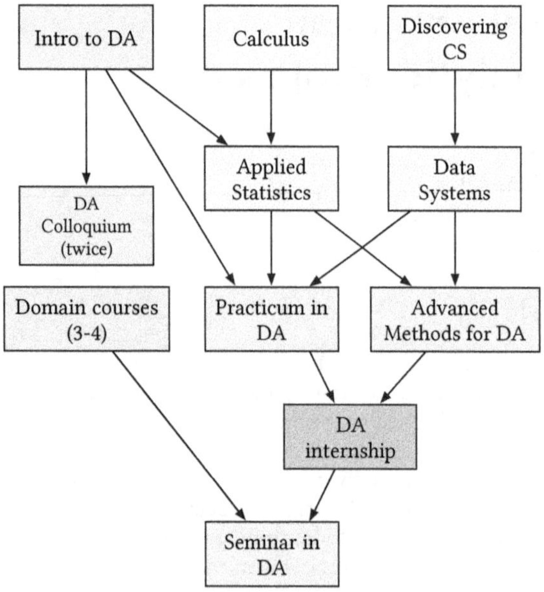

Figure 1: Components and course flow in the Data Analytics major. Computer science and mathematics foundation courses are shaded yellow, Data Analytics courses are shaded blue, domain courses are shaded green, and the internship is shaded pink.

2.1 Computer science and mathematics foundation

DA majors take a minimum of two computer science courses: *Discovering Computer Science* and *Data Systems. Discovering Computer Science* is a project-oriented course that teaches computational problem solving and the principles of computer science through simulations and data-oriented problems in the natural or social sciences [5, 12]. *Data Systems* is a novel new course that teaches introductory students, with only one previous CS course, how to work with tabular, relational and hierarchical data models, and interact with data sources via web APIs. Both courses are also required for our major in Computer Science, and utilize the Python programming language. *Data Systems* also introduces SQL.

DA majors also take at least two mathematics courses: *Calculus* (single variable or multivariable, depending on placement) and *Applied Statistics. Applied Statistics* covers calculus-based probability, experimental design, data collection, statistical inference, hypothesis testing, and regression analysis. Students are introduced to programming in the R language in both this course and *Introduction to Data Analytics* (below).

Students who wish to deepen their technical knowledge, or who are interested in pursuing data science in graduate school, are encouraged to take additional mathematics (e.g., linear algebra and differential equations, statistical modeling, operations research) and/or computer science (e.g., data structures, database design, artificial intelligence, high performance computing) courses. Some students choose to further pursue a major or minor in Computer Science or Mathematics.

2.2 Project-oriented Data Analytics courses

The core of the DA major consists of four interdisciplinary courses, plus a once-weekly colloquium, that are administered by the DA program. All of these courses engage students in active learning through work on applied, interdisciplinary projects and emphasize communication and teamwork in lab environments.

Introduction to Data Analytics has no prerequisites and is intended to give new students a broad introduction to the data analysis cycle and applications thereof. Through a sequence of projects, the course introduces students to different types of data, basic data collection, programming with data (in R), wrangling data into a tidy format, and elementary descriptive and predictive statistics. The projects are intentionally drawn from a diversity of application areas (e.g., political science, economics, sociology, biology, city planning, psychology, entertainment, sports). Crucially, the course also emphasizes how to effectively visualize and present, orally and in writing, the results of data analysis to a nontechnical audience. Throughout, students are challenged to confront ethical issues arising from the collection, interpretation, presentation, and application of data about human beings.

Practicum in Data Analytics is taken by DA majors in the fall semester of their junior year. In this course, students, in small groups, synthesize, hone, and translate their data analytics skills in the context of semester-long consulting projects with real clients. The clients so far have primarily been campus offices — the Registrar (room utilization), Sustainability (energy usage and carbon neutrality), the library (reference desk usage), Athletics (player metrics for men's basketball), and the Annual Fund — but we are also starting to work with businesses (e.g., a west coast insurance company) and local non-profits (e.g., a local affordable housing coalition). Each student group starts with a project prospectus and works with its client over the course of the semester to produce the desired product. Emphasis is placed on the iterative nature of the data analysis cycle, dealing with ambiguity, effectively working with clients, developing professional visualization and presentation skills, and ethical/social implications of policy recommendations on end users. Students are free to use whatever tools are best for the task at hand (e.g., Python, R, SQL, Tableau, Stata). Overall, the course provides students with a valuable "real world" experience in a safe environment that tolerates failures, and challenges students to learn from them. The course also acts as a prelude to students' summer internships (more below).

Advanced Methods for Data Analytics develops students' understanding of cutting-edge algorithms for data analytics, and how they can be used to answer questions about real-world problems. The emphasis is on modern machine learning methods (both supervised and unsupervised), but also covers topics such as missing data, optimization, dimensionality reduction, and network analysis. As with other DA courses, these techniques are learned through work on projects from a variety of domains (e.g., fraud detection, movie recommendations, online ad placement, a soup kitchen optimization, Egyptian hieroglyphic recognition).

Seminar in Data Analytics is the senior major capstone experience. Each student undertakes an independent consulting or research project over the course of the semester. The project is expected to synthesize each student's accumulated skillset, applied to a problem in their chosen domain (more below). Weekly seminar meetings provide opportunities to share updates, get critical feedback, and discuss other topics of interest. The course culminates in significant individual research papers and oral presentations.

Finally, starting next year, the *Data Analytics Colloquium* will be a 1-credit (full courses are normally 4 credits) once-weekly opportunity for DA majors to gather to hear from guest speakers and discuss data analytics topics of interest. The overarching theme of the colloquium will be "Data Analytics Across the Liberal Arts." The course must be taken twice by majors: once as a sophomore, and again as either a junior or senior. For sophomore students, the colloquium will provide an initial exposure to advanced methods, wicked problem solving, and possible career paths in the field. For upper-level students, the colloquium will build on their course and/or work experiences, and allow them to share these connections with less experienced students. Because sophomore and junior/senior students will be enrolled in the class together, and faculty from across campus will be invited to give presentations, this course will help to build community among students across levels and with faculty with diverse interests and expertise.

2.3 Courses in an applied domain

Because no data exists in a vacuum, each DA major must choose an applied domain in which to specialize. The goal of this specialization is to understand the types of questions that data are used to answer in that discipline, and how data are collected and interpreted in this context. There are currently seven available domains:

- Anthropology and Sociology,
- Biology,
- Economics,
- Philosophy,
- Physics,
- Political Science, and
- Psychology.

In each domain, students take 3–4 prescribed courses. (Some disciplines allow elective choices.) Included in each set of courses is an "analytics-intensive" course (often that discipline's research methods course). Alternatively, students are invited to design their own domain; these proposals are evaluated based on their coherence and whether they satisfy the goals laid out above.

Our embrace of the liberal arts is perhaps most exemplified by the newly added Philosophy option. Students choosing this domain take one course each in ethics, philosophy of science, and logic. These courses equip students with an appreciation of the history and complexity of moral issues and normative theories so they can investigate and address the ethical challenges that arise in solving analytical problems. They are also a natural way to deepen students' appreciation of what is distinctive about data analytics and to sharpen their critical assessment of its tools and applications. We anticipate that DA students focusing in Philosophy may also pursue questions being addressed in experimental philosophy [10].

2.4 Summer internship or research project

Finally, every DA major is required to undertake a DA-focused internship or research project during the summer between their junior and senior year. The internship experience places students in authentic situations in which to apply their skills and learn more about their particular interest areas. The summer internship (or research project) is intentionally situated between the practicum and the senior seminar; the former prepares students to effectively navigate the internship and be an effective contributor, while the latter gives students an opportunity to reflect on their experience and further investigate problems they encountered.

While students are ultimately responsible for securing their own internship, we have been able to facilitate a number of opportunities through relationships with alumni and local organizations, and a close partnership with our career exploration center.

3 ORIGIN AND DEVELOPMENT

The germination of the Data Analytics major officially began in late 2014, but seeds had been planted over the last decade. During this time, with the growing availability of large datasets, our Mathematics and Computer Science department began to increasingly lean toward data-oriented content in our introductory and elective courses. Across campus, some natural and social science departments were also moving in more data-oriented directions, both in faculty and student research and in their research methods courses. Taken as a whole, it was becoming increasingly clear that data analytics was developing into a new fundamental mode of inquiry that is not specific to any one discipline.

Echoing this sentiment, in response to a call for new academic programs in Fall 2014, two new data analytics/science majors were proposed. These proposals led to conversations among a group of like-minded faculty from seven disciplines in the social and natural sciences (Biology, Computer Science, Economics, Mathematics, Political Science, Psychology, and Sociology/Anthropology). This enlightening and fruitful dialogue stretched over all of 2015. At the time, we were aware of very few model undergraduate Data Analytics/Science programs [3, 4, 13], and none that were appropriate for our liberal arts curriculum. As we discuss in more detail below, we paid particular attention to designing a broad and inclusive program that would create synergy with our liberal arts mission and leverage strengths that were already present. We submitted our consensus proposal for the Data Analytics major in late 2015, and it was approved by the Faculty in Spring 2016. The program officially began in Fall 2016, with the first majors eligible to graduate in May 2019.

4 PRINCIPLES AND GOALS

Since the inception of our program, a handful of curricular guides for data science majors have been published [9, 14, 19].[1] The structure of our major is mostly consistent with these recommendations with two notable differences. First, our program more intentionally integrates the liberal arts and disciplinary perspectives outside of computer science and mathematics into its core. Second, our program has fewer mathematics and computer science requirements than other programs in data science. In what follows, we explain our rationale behind these decisions by highlighting two main principles upon which we designed the major: the centrality of the liberal arts and broadening participation in the program.

[1] Three Denison DA faculty contributed to the PCMI report [9].

4.1 Embracing the liberal arts

The Data Analytics program embraces, rather than competes with, Denison's liberal arts curriculum. In an oft-cited article, William Cronon describes ten qualities of a liberally educated person. He sums them up with this description of the tenth quality, that liberally educated people "Only connect...:"

> More than anything else, being an educated person means being able to see connections that allow one to make sense of the world and act within it in creative ways. Every one of the qualities I have described here—listening, reading, talking, writing, puzzle solving, truth seeking, seeing through other people's eyes, leading, working in a community—is finally about connecting. [8]

The value of these qualities to science education in general has long been recognized. In 1999, Nobel Laureate Thomas Cech wrote that,

> ...in history, literature, and the arts one is presented with diverse, often mutually contradictory "data"—different points of view due to incomplete knowledge or the different backgrounds of those doing the viewing. One learns to distill the critical elements from the irrelevant, synthesize seemingly discordant observations, and develop a strong argument. ... Scientists need the same skills as humanists to cut through misleading observations and arrive at a defensible interpretation, and intellectual cross-training in the humanities exercises the relevant portions of the brain. [6]

More recently, multiple authors [7, 11, 15, 17, 22] have expounded on the values that the liberal arts bring to Data Science education in particular. They warn of reducing data science to a set of techniques, ignoring the benefits that cultural knowledge and empathy can bring, skills that are best learned through the humanities and arts. For example, Andy Cotgreave, Senior Technical Evangelist at Tableau, writes, "Liberal arts skills are needed at every level of data science, from storytelling and communication of insights through to the training and interpreting of the most advanced machine learning applications in your business." [7] *Data ethnographers* [18, 21] with diverse cultural perspectives are needed to critically evaluate both the data that goes into an analysis and the policies it recommends. Insufficient attention to these issues has caused many well-documented machine learning failures in recent years [16]. Finally, DJ Patil, former Chief Data Scientist of the United States, recently remarked, "If you want to be great, make sure you have a good dose of liberal arts in your training. That is fundamental." [17]

Denison's Data Analytics program promotes the values of the liberal arts both in the structure of the major and within its courses. With regard to the former, each student's 3–4 course domain specialization gives them meaningful exposure to data methodology and concerns grounded in a particular discipline. Notably, we encourage students to approach this experience as a bidirectional exchange. Our emphasis is not simply on applying data analytics techniques to domain-specific data; rather, we recognize the oft-overlooked value that quantitative methodologists bring to our students' education. These domain connections are reinforced through the individual research projects that students complete in their senior seminar. In addition, to afford students the freedom to pursue a well-rounded education, the size of the major is consistent with the College's "rule of thirds" for students' typical 32-course degree: one third major, one third general education requirements, and one third electives. The general education requirements ensure that students acquire a broad education and their freedom with electives allows them to explore further, pursue a second major, or deepen their quantitative skills.

Within the Data Analytics courses described above, liberal arts values are emphasized in a variety of ways. First, the introductory and *Advanced Methods* courses are organized around a sequence of projects that are drawn from a diverse set of disciplines. Through these projects, students explore the rich diversity of the ways in which information is collected, understood, analyzed, and communicated. Effective communication and ethics are two themes common to all Data Analytics classes. They include instruction on, and repeated practice with, clear and concise communication of results—visual, oral, and written—to both technical and nontechnical audiences. And they force students to reflect on and address ethical and fairness concerns arising from the collection and handling of human (and other sensitive) data, and interpreting and reporting inferential conclusions based on them. In addition, in the *Practicum*, students grapple with real problems which force them to become more comfortable with ambiguity and uncertainty. In their communication with clients, students must learn to listen, question their assumptions, and see issues from other points of view. And, in this environment, gaps in students' domain and/or technical knowledge inevitably arise during the semester, pushing students to become independent learners and adopt a growth mindset.

4.2 Broadening student participation

In designing the Data Analytics major, we wanted to welcome a more diverse pool of students than is typically attracted to a quantitative major like computer science. Notably, we intentionally left the word "science" out of the name of the program, opting for "Data Analytics" over "Data Science," to signal that this course of study is not geared exclusively to science-oriented students. For the same reason, we proposed to administer Data Analytics as a standalone interdisciplinary program that is independent of (but collaborates with) the Mathematics and Computer Science department. To staff the program, we hired three new faculty – a quantitative ecologist, an applied mathematician, and a statistician – whose home department is Data Analytics. The program continues to be administered by a diverse Committee that includes the three DA faculty and faculty from several other departments. The directorship of the program will rotate among these departments moving forward. In addition, *Introduction to Data Analytics* has thus far been taught by faculty with primary expertise in mathematics, statistics, biology, psychology, and political science. These decisions serve to position Data Analytics as a discipline that spans a range of application areas and is not "siloed" in any one department or division of the College.

For the same reasons, we designed the curriculum to provide sufficient technical skills without over-emphasizing them relative to

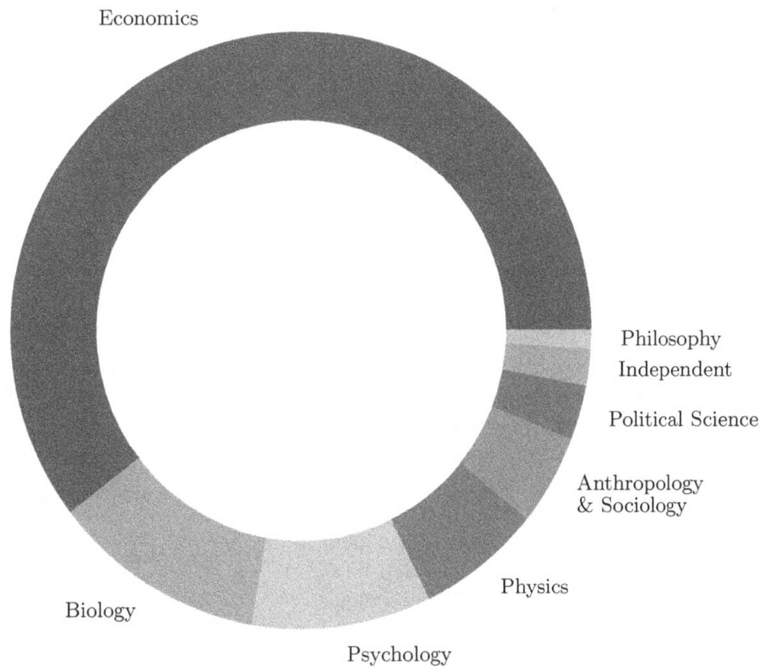

Figure 2: Distribution of Data Analytics majors' chosen domains.

other skills and points of view inherent in this interdisciplinary field. Only requiring four computer science and mathematics courses makes the major more welcoming to students who are apprehensive about quantitative subjects or who have less mathematical preparation. And none of these courses is a prerequisite for our *Introduction to Data Analytics* course, which gently orients students to the field. Additional technical skills are taught in the core DA courses, but in a more holistic way, integrating them with topics like project management, visualization, and communication. (As stated above, students who want to delve more deeply are encouraged to pursue additional courses or a minor/major in computer science or mathematics.) Simultaneously emphasizing the importance of expertise in another discipline (i.e., the domain) appeals to students' existing interests and gives them a "hook" into the major. In these ways, we want to provide a relatively low barrier to entry while meeting students where they are with respect to academic interest.

5 RESULTS

Our novel Data Analytics curriculum has been even more successful than we anticipated. Over the first four semesters of the program, we have offered 13 sections of Introduction to Data Analytics, enrolling approximately 240 students in total. At the end of the program's second academic year (2017–2018), there were already about 100 declared DA majors among the first year, sophomore, and junior classes. Overall, 37% of our majors are women, and this percentage has been rising with each class year.

At the end of the 2018–2019 academic year, our first year with graduating seniors, we anticipate that we will enroll approximately 130 total declared majors, and that we will graduate 27. This would make DA the fifth or sixth largest major at the College in only its third year. Although comparison data is hard to come by, the outdated data that is available [1–3] suggests that our enrollments may be higher than other undergraduate Data Science programs, even at much larger institutions.

We have DA majors with a variety of interests, and are finding that students are coming to DA from a variety of different directions. As illustrated in Figure 2, about half of the majors have chosen to focus in Economics (one of the largest majors at the College), and the remaining half are approximately evenly distributed among the remaining domains. 58% of our majors are currently double majors; 17% are double majoring in Mathematics or Computer Science.

One year into the program, in Fall 2017, we sought insight into introductory students' interest in Data Analytics by asking them, "What aspect of the Data Analytics major is the most appealing or exciting to you?" Their replies generally fell into three categories. About half wrote about integrating data analytics with other interests, for example:

> I love the idea of being able to use both my love for math/analytics and my love of humanities/social sciences in the same career.

> It is a very applicable skill in the workforce today and I can pair it with another interest of mine, psychology.

Another 40% wrote about the broad career opportunities, for example:

> The most appealing aspect is that Data Analytics can take you in many different directions, meaning there are a lot of fields you can go into with a DA major.

> I am interested in being fluent in computer languages such as R as a skill set and working with nonprofits and other humanitarian organizations.

And the final 15% cited their interest in statistics and/or computing, for example:

> I love being able to create graphs out of code, I find it absolutely fascinating!

> The statistics aspect, as well as finding patterns and deciphering what it means in the grand scheme of things.

During the summer of 2018, all 27 rising seniors were successful in securing a DA-oriented internship or research experience. Students worked in a wide variety of sectors, including health care, pharmaceuticals, logistics, criminology, animal care, nonprofits, consulting, dining, retail, insurance, finance, energy, e-commerce/billing, transportation, physics, and athletics. Most students secured these opportunities on their own, with the help of our career exploration center, but we were also able to facilitate some exclusive opportunities by actively pursuing relationships with alumni and local businesses and nonprofits. These relationships have also led to class visits and panels in which our students have the opportunity to learn from practitioners.

6 FUTURE PLANS

Based on student feedback, we are currently exploring additional domains in sports analytics, data journalism, and geosciences. In the future, we would also like to open up possibilities in linguistics, humanistic macroanalysis, and the arts. In the latter vein, we are looking forward to welcoming later this year an artist who creates data-inspired sculpture and a pianist who also works in AI.

We are also likely to propose in the immediate future a Bachelor of Science in Data Science program to better accommodate our students with deeper technical interests. As mentioned previously, these students are currently pursuing a double major or minor in Computer Science or Mathematics. This new option would streamline their requirements, providing for more room in their schedules for other electives.

ACKNOWLEDGEMENTS

I would be remiss in not acknowledging the good work of my colleagues in creating and maintaining the Data Analytics program: Anthony Bonifonte (Data Analytics), Laura Boyd (Economics), Michael Brady (Political Science), Thomas Bressoud (Computer Science), Paul Djupe (Political Science), Mine Dogucu (Data Analytics), Fareeda Griffith (Anthropology and Sociology), Erin Henshaw (Psychology), Ashwin Lall (Computer Science), Andy McCall (Biology), Matthew Neal (Mathematics), Sarah Supp (Data Analytics), and David White (Mathematics).

REFERENCES

[1] American Statistical Association. New Undergraduate Data Science Programs. Amstat News, July, 2015, http://magazine.amstat.org/blog/2015/07/01/new-undergraduate-data-science-programs/, accessed August 30, 2018.

[2] American Statistical Association. New Undergraduate Data Science Programs. Amstat News, August, 2015, http://magazine.amstat.org/blog/2015/08/01/new-undergraduate-data-science-programs-2/, accessed August 30, 2018.

[3] Paul Anderson, James Bowring, Renée McCauley, George Pothering and Christopher Starr. An Undergraduate Degree in Data Science: Curriculum and a Decade of Implementation Experience. In *Proceedings of the 45th ACM Technical Symposium on Computer Science Education*, pages 145–150, 2014.

[4] Paul Anderson, James McGuffee, and David Uminsky. Data Science As an Undergraduate Degree. In *Proceedings of the 45th ACM Technical Symposium on Computer Science Education*, pages 705–706, 2014.

[5] Douglas Baldwin, Valerie Barr, Amy Briggs, Jessen Havill, Bruce Maxwell, and Henry M. Walker. CS 1: Beyond Programming. In *Proceedings of the 48th ACM SIGCSE Technical Symposium on Computer Science Education*, pages 677–678, 2017.

[6] Thomas R. Cech. Science at Liberal Arts Colleges: A Better Education? Daedalus 128:1, pages 195–216, 1999.

[7] Andy Cotgreave. Your analytics team needs a liberal arts major. InfoWorld, April 4, 2018, http://www.infoworld.com/article/3267998/analytics/your-analytics-team-needs-a-liberal-arts-major.html, accessed August 30, 2018.

[8] William Cronon. "Only Connect...": The Goals of a Liberal Education. The American Scholar 67:4, 1998.

[9] Richard D. De Veaux, et al. Curriculum Guidelines for Undergraduate Programs in Data Science. Annual Review of Statistics and its Application 4:2.1–2.16, 2017.

[10] Experimental Philosophy. http://experimental-philosophy.yale.edu/ExperimentalPhilosophy.html, accessed August 30, 2018.

[11] Scott Hartley. The Fuzzy and the Techie: Why the Liberal Arts Will Rule the Digital World. Houghton Mifflin Harcourt, 2017.

[12] Jessen Havill. Discovering Computer Science: Interdisciplinary Problems, Principles, and Python Programming. *Chapman & Hall/CRC Press*, 2016.

[13] Aparna Mahadev and Karl R. Wurst. Developing Concentrations in Big Data Analytics and Software Development at a Small Liberal Arts University. Journal of Computing Sciences in Colleges 30:3, pages 92–98, 2015.

[14] National Academies of Sciences, Engineering, and Medicine. Data Science for Undergraduates: Opportunities and Options. The National Academies Press, doi.org/10.17226/25104, 2018.

[15] JM Olejarz Liberal Arts in the Data Age. Harvard Business Review, July–August, 2017, http://hbr.org/2017/07/liberal-arts-in-the-data-age, accessed August 30, 2018.

[16] Cathy O'Neil. Weapons of Math Destruction: How Big Data Increases Inequality and Threatens Democracy. Crown Publishing Group, 2016.

[17] DJ Patil. Big Data, and How It Can Solve the World's Most Pressing Problems. Lecture presented at The Ohio State University, September 19, 2018, https://livestream.com/WOSU/DJPatil/videos/180512174, accessed November 26, 2018.

[18] Sarah Pink, Deborah Lupton, Martin Berg, Paul Dourish, Adrian Dyer, Vaike Fors, Edgar Gómez Cruz, Heather Horst, Pilar Lacasa, John Postill, Shanti Sumartojo, and Emma Witkowski. DATA ETHNOGRAPHIES (1): personal data in an uncertain world. Data Ethnographies Lab, 2016, https://dataethnographies.com/paper-i-personal-data-in-an-uncertain-world/, accessed November 26, 2018.

[19] Renata Rawlings-Goss. Keeping Data Science Broad: Negotiating the Digital and Data Divide Among Higher Education Institutions. South Big Data Innovation Hub, 2018, https://southbigdatahub.org/programs/keeping-data-science-broad/, accessed August 30, 2018.

[20] Ryan Swanstrom. College and University Data Science Degrees. http://datascience.community/colleges, accessed August 30, 2018.

[21] Tricia Wang. Why Big Data Needs Thick Data. https://medium.com/ethnography-matters/why-big-data-needs-thick-data-b4b3e75e3d7, accessed November 26, 2018.

[22] Adam Weinberg. Data Analytics and the Liberal Arts. Huffington Post blog, April 19, 2016, http://www.huffingtonpost.com/adam-weinberg/data-analytics-and-the-li_b_9721312.html, accessed August 30, 2018.

A Novel Course in Data Systems with Minimal Prerequisites

Thomas C. Bressoud
Denison University
Granville, Ohio
bressoud@denison.edu

Gavin Thomas
Denison University
Granville, Ohio
thomas_g8@denison.edu

ABSTRACT

The need for understanding data systems, from the structure and constraints of data models to the client-server mechanisms for acquiring and curating data, includes not just computer science students, but extends to data science students and students in a wide range of interdisciplinary programs. In this paper we describe the design and implementation of a second course in computer science, whose data-centric focus emphasizes structural models of data and the skills involved in acquiring and transforming data into forms amenable for analysis. We argue that, from a user-not-designer perspective, these topics need not wait for an upper-level database course, but to achieve sufficient depth, an introductory computer science course is appropriate and sufficient as a prerequisite.

CCS CONCEPTS

• **Information systems** → *Relational database model; Hierarchical data models; Semi-structured data; RESTful web services;* • **Networks** → *Network design principles; Application layer protocols;* • **Computer systems organization** → *Client-server architectures;*

KEYWORDS

Computer science education; CS2; data science; curriculum; data models; client-server

ACM Reference Format:
Thomas C. Bressoud and Gavin Thomas. 2019. A Novel Course in Data Systems with Minimal Prerequisites. In *Proceedings of the 50th ACM Technical Symposium on Computer Science Education (SIGCSE '19), February 27-March 2, 2019, Minneapolis, MN, USA.* ACM, New York, NY, USA, 7 pages. https://doi.org/10.1145/3287324.3287425

1 INTRODUCTION

The sources and forms of data, along with the demand for acquiring, processing, and analyzing that data are increasing at a prodigious rate[1, 3, 6]. From a curricular perspective, majors, programs, and courses are being designed to enable interested students to understand these topics and prepare themselves for the practice of these associated data skills[2, 5, 8, 14]. As the sources and forms of data increase, with a commensurate increase in the data providers and interfaces for accessing data, so too must our interpretation of what constitutes a data system[4].

SIGCSE '19, February 27-March 2, 2019, Minneapolis, MN, USA

ACM ISBN 978-1-4503-5890-3/19/02.
https://doi.org/10.1145/3287324.3287425

The student audience for such curricular efforts is broadening as well. We identify three student constituencies:

- **Computer Science:** students recognizing the value of acquiring and transforming data, and the synergy of this activity with the systems and algorithmic problem-solving aspects of the computer science discipline.
- **Data Science/Data Analytics:** students pursuing these new and emerging undergraduate majors, who desire to build algorithmic and practical skills with an eye towards enabling data exploration, visualization, statistical analysis, and application of machine-learning techniques for use in coursework as well as in practicums and internships.
- **Multidisciplinary/domain-centric:** students whose focus is on practical aspects of acquiring and transforming data for use in their own disciplines. These include students in social sciences as well as natural sciences, and often these students want to learn this material as a prelude to a "methods" course specific to their discipline.

Others[8] have called the union of these audiences the "data-centric" audience, and we extend this idea to define the set of data-related topics and the desired level of understanding the *data-aptitude* for these students. We see two primary dimensions to data-aptitude, corresponding to the *sources* and *forms* of data. Data sources range from local files to relational databases to network-based data providers. Data forms, provided by data sources, range from comma-separated-value flat files to the tables within a relational database to XML and JSON to unstructured data and HTML. Data sources may be further distinguished by the protection and privacy associated with the data they provide. Some data is explicitly open and freely available, while other data may be limited to use by particular applications, and still other data may be comprised of protected resources of one or more authorized resource owners.

Many of the topics associated with data-aptitude have homes spread through the computer science curriculum. In the ACM curricular guidelines [9], the Information Management (IM) knowledge area includes relational databases and data models; the Network Computing (NC) and Systems Foundations (SF) include aspects of client-server computing and the protocols upon which the APIs for accessing provider data are built.

In curricular guidelines [13], and in many actual majors [9], parts of this material can be found in a *Database Systems* course. Such courses are strong on the relational data model, emphasize normalization and design of schema to enforce desirable properties and constraints, and often include mathematical underpinnings of the model and systems design aspects allowing for efficient realizations of database systems.

Database systems courses typically require prerequisites of a CS1 class, an Intro to Systems/Computer Organization class, a Data

Structures class, and a class and/or material in discrete mathematics supporting sets and relations, and so the database systems class is most often not taken until a student is in the late stages of their educational career. In smaller institutions, based on rotations of class offerings, a student may not be able to take a database systems class at all. Being able to actually use the database-relevant material in projects or other classes is not possible. And because of its focus on the relational model and the systems design aspects of efficient database system realizations, it is too narrow to satisfy the needs defined for data-aptitude.

At the other end of the spectrum, and recognizing the needs of data-aptitude and the growing audience of data-centric students, recent efforts have focused on incorporating data-aptitude as part of the CS1 experience. At St. Olaf, Hall-Holt and Sanft have incorporated aspects of data acquisition and analysis along with statistics in an introductory "statistics-infused" CS offering [8]. Anderson et al. use Data Programming in a CS1 class [2]. More broadly, Kaplan has written about teaching computation to undergraduates across the natural and social sciences [10] with a data focus and has a book that uses R and Data Computation for introductory computer science/data science[11]. Earlier work by Sullivan also uses a data centric introduction to computer science and targets the broader non-majors audience [14].

There are some clear advantages to such CS1+data approaches. Students are introduced early to data-aptitude topics alongside algorithmic problem solving. By learning some of this material in a first course, students can bring this newfound knowledge to bear in downstream courses and projects. And clearly it helps to address the need of the growing population of the data-centric student audience. Additionally, having introductory computer science and data-aptitude in a single course has significant appeal on already-crowded majors, including new data science majors as well as students with a data focus in majors in the other natural and social sciences.

Unfortunately, such an all-in-one solution can come at a price: too much content for a single course. Students can feel overwhelmed when data-aptitude content and goals are added to the existing content and goals of an introductory computer science course. Students have difficulty in differentiating the competing aspects of what they are learning, from algorithmic problem solving, programming language syntax, separation of internal/memory resident data structures from external files and formats, statistics, and data acquisition through various means, from files to URL s to more complex networking-based communication exchange. There is also the significant danger that, for the data topics, we try to simplify by "teaching to an interface", focusing on the calls and arguments for a supporting package, and de-emphasizing the underlying systems principles and implementations that are beneath the surface.

To simultaneously solve many of the disadvantages of a late-curriculum and narrow database systems course as well as the content overload and potential lack of data-aptitude depth of a CS1+data approach, we advocate for an early data systems course with a prerequisite of a CS1 class. We define data systems broadly, including relational database systems as well as those systems providing data across the Internet in a client-server manner in the form of web service APIs, like REST (REpresentational State Transfer)[7]. This course differentiates and focuses on the understanding and *using* of these data systems, rather than the *design* of such systems, allowing us to shed much of the material that would be contained in a database systems course. This course would not replace the database systems course; rather, with only a 20% content overlap, it would provide students a foundational understanding of the topics at an earlier stage in their education.

This course employs *data models* as a framework for learning about the various forms of data, from a simple tabular model with appropriate constraints to the relational data model to a hierarchical data model as needed by our definition of data-aptitude. In the data sources dimension, the course follows a progression of data sources, starting the students with local files, moving on to a MySQL database server as representative of relational databases, and then covering more advanced client-server interaction over HTTP using provider APIs, and also extracting data from HTML and addressing protected resources. In this way, we feel we can cover the topics of data-aptitude in sufficient depth beyond a single CS1+data course, while keeping material broad and applicable to the wide range of data-centric students.

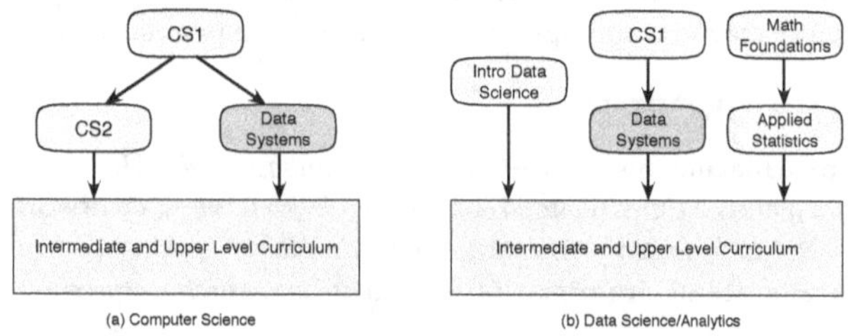

Figure 1: Curricular Context for Data Systems Course

In Figure 1, we show in (a) our proposed course in the context of the early part of a computer science major. Note that we are not replacing a program's CS2 course, but rather suggest a second course that could be taken concurrently with a traditional CS2. In summer of 2016, the Park City Math Institute held a three week program for Undergraduate Faculty on developing guidelines for a Data Science curriculum[5]; in (b), we show a permutation of that curriculum and show our proposed course within it. This fits well with the guidelines' desire for a second course in computer science centered around data acquisition and curation. One could also envision the two course sequence of CS1 followed by our proposed course as an excellent fit for the multi-disciplinary/non-major student constituency.

Our institution and department has designed and, in the 2017-2018 academic year, implemented such a course, supporting a broader systems experience for our computer science students and integral to our institution's emerging data analysis (DA) major. This new course is now required for both majors.

2 COURSE CONTENT

The Data Systems Architecture, as illustrated in Figure 2, enables us to see the elements of the course content. As introduced in Section 1, the two primary dimensions of course content involve the *sources* of data from data systems and the *forms* of that data. On the right side of the figure, we depict the primary data sources, that of local files, database systems, web servers, and providers exporting APIs by which their data may be accessed. Each of the

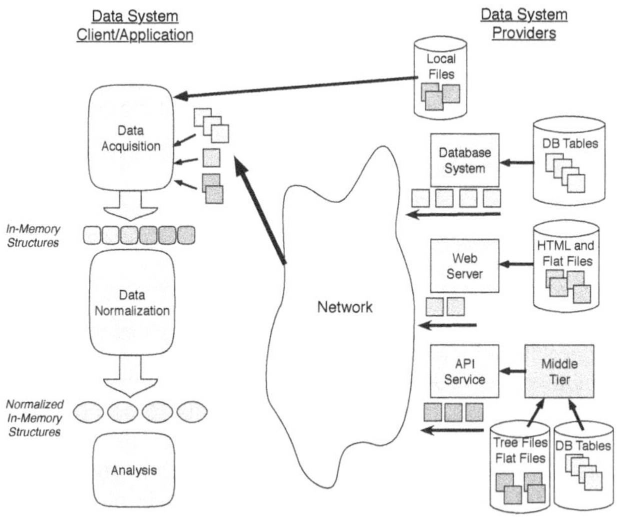

Figure 2: Data Systems Architecture

sources may deliver their data in one or more of the data forms covered in the course. The left side of the figure depicts the main phases of the data pipeline necessary for client applications that are on the consumer side of data systems. The process starts with data acquisition, which may come from local files, or over the network, and proceeds to data normalization, where the data is transformed to satisfy constraints and to put it into a form amenable for analysis.

2.1 Data Models

We use *data models* as the framework by which we cover the various forms and associated formats of data. A data model consists of:

- *structure*: typically one or more two-dimensional structures, or a tree structure,
- *operations*: given the structure, how do we extract, modify, and transform data in that structure, and
- *constraints*: within the structure, what are the legal data types, legal values for elements, and legal relationships between some elements and one or more other elements.

This course investigates three data models, starting with a simple tabular data model, progressing through the relational data model, and then covering the hierarchical data model.

Tabular Data Model. The tabular data model focuses on primarily single table datasets with row and column dimensions. In this model, we are interested in in-memory representations of tabular data with sufficient power in their operations to allow extracting and updating subsets of rows and columns, working with columns as vectors, and transforming from one tabular representation to another. In Python, we use the pandas module to provide such facility.

To enable effective analysis, which includes partitioning data, computing on partitions, and combining results[15], the data must conform to particular constraints, with variables representing columns, and rows defining appropriate functional dependencies between independent variables and dependent variables[1]. Data can be represented in tables in many different ways, but most do not conform to these constraints, and, in the tabular model, constraints are not enforced, but are merely a convention. So the course must teach recognition of violations of the model constraints, and how to transform into its normal form.

The course starts from CS1 topics of two-dimensional data structures using native Python data structures, like lists of lists and dictionaries of lists. We begin with basic line-by-line processing of flat delimited files as a way of building into the topic. This corresponds to the upper right part of Figure 2 with data acquisition from local files. Coverage of the model progresses through various techniques of transforming and normalizing the data[2], thus allowing for exploration/visualization and downstream analysis. Transformation and other complex operations are discussed algorithmically, to allow generalization to other languages and packages. At the end of this section, students are given a project with real-world datasets that they must understand and normalize to allow visualization and communication/interpretation of the underlying data.

Relational Data Model. One of the most important forms of data, and its associated data model, is the relational database system and model. Grounded in nearly 50 years of development and an important element of many larger systems, we cover this model from a primarily client/user perspective. This corresponds in Figure 2 to the second source on the right of the data system providers and, on the left, by using SQL as part of data acquisition and then transforming results into appropriate in-memory structures.

By using the tabular data model as a foundation, we start with projecting columns and selecting rows from single relations/tables, drawing parallels with the prior material, and seeing some of the differences of a declarative versus procedural style of operation. We then extend to multiple tables using join operations to see how the relational model uses constraints on foreign and primary keys to build one-many and many-many relationships.

Utilizing existing well-designed databases as examples, we cover, at an intuitive level, various aspects of sound database design. We use elements of the convention-based constraints of the tabular model to arrive at an intuitive understanding of third normal form. By using database schema, the students see the benefit of design preceding data population, and how a database system can enforce many of the desired constraints in this model, to avoid errors before-the-fact. Coverage of this section concludes with simple, but sound, database design, table creation, and row insertion for some existing datasets derived from the earlier section on the tabular data model.

The relational data model is reinforced and content synthesized in the student's second project, in which they have access to a few significantly large relational databases and conceive of and build queries of significant complexity, and interpret results.

Hierarchical Data Model. When we interact with data systems on the Internet, many providers structure and represent provided data in a flexible form based on a tree data model. Dominant specific examples include XML and JSON formats, but the tree inherent in an HTML document is another significant example. These correspond, in Figure 2, to the "Tree Files" and "HTML Files" in the lower two providers types on the right side of the figure. Data acquisition for tree formatted files can also be provided by local files.[3]

[1] Called *tidy data*[16] by the data science community.

[2] Variously called cleaning, wrangling, and munging by the data science community.

[3] We use the lxml module to support this data model.

Given a tree or subtree, the operations of this model include procedural tree traversal and the extraction of data (tags, text, and attributes) from the nodes of the tree. This model also gives us the opportunity, on the XML and HTML side, to look at declarative operations using XPath. We are also able to see how trees can represent both the notion of a single table, or a set of tables, all within a single file. Constraints in this model are either by convention, or can be explicit, using mechanisms such as Document Type Definition (DTD), or an XML Schema Definition (XSD).

Unstructured Data. Much of the time, data may not be structured in one of the covered forms, and a client, after data acquisition, must perform advanced pattern matching and extract fields of data out of one or more unstructured collections of data. To accommodate this reality, the course includes a unit on pattern matching and regular expressions. The focus is on recognizing the patterns that exist in unstructured data and understanding the tools by which the data can be extracted, regex capture groups, for instance. Using these tools, students build tabular data structures from unstructured data.

2.2 Data Sources

As described above in both the tabular data model and the hierarchical data model, we begin with local files to build our understanding of the model before we move into more complicated means of data acquisition. We progress from there, during coverage of the relational model, to an external database management system as the source of the data. We use a MySQL server available on the local network and shared by all the students in the class. Each student has their own login, within which they can CREATE and INSERT in tables, and each has SELECT access to numerous databases and tables used in the class. Students learn the various parts of the URL employed as a *connection string* to establish communication with the database and are introduced to basic networking ideas like a machine and its address, and a protocol by which a client makes requests that are processed and result in a response by the server. They also see, by example, the notion of data resources having an ownership (the user) and protection for these owned resources.

Our next source of data are web servers, corresponding to the middle provider type on the right side of Figure 2. Students learn the basics of the HyperText Transfer Protocol (HTTP) as a network client that must specify the machine and protocol for a connection over the network. They then must construct and issue requests (GET and POST) and be able to retrieve and understand the constituent parts of the meta-data and data of the response. This type of data source can provide delimited flat files, HTML files, or even XML/JSON files. Given this data source, and combining with the knowledge from the hierarchical data model, students combine these to understand web scraping as an application of these ideas.

With the foundation of HTTP, we then turn to API-based data providers[4], as represented by the bottom right of Figure 2. We extend our understanding of the resource path part of a URL in an HTTP GET or POST to give an *endpoint* of a provider, and the use of URL parameters and HTTP header key/value pairs to parameterize requests made of an endpoint. We can then extend our ideas about authentication and authorization to allow for client applications as an entity that can be authenticated and resources from a provider as being "owned" by a principal, who may not be the same as the writer of the application. We use OAuth with real-world providers to facilitate this material.

[4]We focus on RESTful APIs as appropriate for students in this class

2.3 Classroom Approach

Because of the importance of visualization in exploring acquired data, asking interesting initial questions about a dataset, and communicating such pre-analysis to an audience. We employ the use of Tableau, software available both online and in desktop version, as a powerful tool for generating such visualizations. Once data is in a normalized form from our tabular data model, it is relatively straightforward to build quality visualizations, and the students in this class employ Tabeau in all of their projects.

We use real-world datasets for all projects and most of the examples and practicums in the course. There is an abundance of data, and one of the goals of the course is to understand how to take "messy" real-world data and, in a clear and systematic way, normalize it into a usable form.

In addition to the projects associated with the tabular and relational data models, we use a synthesis final project. Students must employ most of the aspects learned in the class, from using multiple providers, and at least one of those providers must hold protected resources, and the students must engage OAuth to gain authorized access to these resources. Students must build a simple, sound database with data derived from their data acquisition and data normalization. Finally, students must visualize and ask interesting questions of their data.

The topics covered by week in the semester are give in Table 1:

Week	Topic Coverage
1	Python Foundations and Review
2	Tabular Model Structure and Operations using pandas Module
3	Tabular Constraints/Tidy Data Recognition and Transformation
4	Relational Database Access and Single Table SQL
5	Relational Database Multiple Table Joins, Grouping, and Aggregation
6	Programming in sqlalchemy and Sound Database Design
7	Regular Expressions; Networking Fundamentals
8	HTTP Definition and use with the requests module
9	Hierarchical Model - Structure, Operations, JSON Intro
10	XML and XPath using lxml
11	HTML and Web Scraping
12	Authentication, Authorization and OAuth2
13	Basic REST API Services
14	Authorized REST API Services

Table 1: Course Topics by Week

3 INAUGURAL YEAR STUDENT AUDIENCE

In the 2017-2018 academic year, we offered a total of four sections of data systems, each capped at 24 students – three sections in Fall 2017, and one in Spring 2018. All sections filled, and, after initial-semester attrition, we ended with a population of 64 students in Fall 2017 and 26 students in Spring 2018. From an initial class survey, we describe the basic demographics of the student audience in this section, along with their self-reported confidence/proficiency in some of the topics assumed from the CS1 prerequisite.

Over the four sections, 52% of the students were sophomores, 41% were juniors, and 7% were seniors. The number of juniors and seniors is expected to reduce as we move forward, with fewer upperclass students needing to satisfy this new requirement. The female/male ratio in this initial year was 20%/80%, but our data analytics offerings have been showing more diverse appeal, and so we hope our ratio of females taking this course will increase.

Because of the DA major introduction in the prior academic year, and the addition of this course as a required in the computer science major, there was a backlog of demand, including from students further along in their program. We expect, in subsequent offerings, for the class year distribution to shift toward predominantly sophomores, as opposed to the 52% sophomore and 41% juniors seen in this first year.

Majors, as a percentage of the class population, differed significantly between the two semesters, as can be seen in Figure 3. In the fall, nearly 60% of the students were computer science majors, and only 32% were data analytics majors. In the spring, these ratios swapped. In Section 1, we identified three student constituencies, the CS students, the data analytics students, and the multidisciplinary students. Our data-analytics program emphasizes interdisciplinary integration, and so the data analytics majors shown here are really a mix between the data analytics and multidisciplinary constituencies. We do hope that demand from students in other majors ("Other" in the graph) will increase as we move forward.

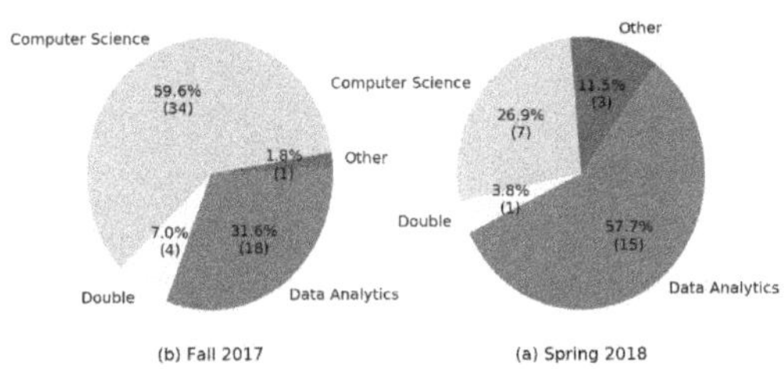

Figure 3: F17 and S18 Distribution by Major

We decided to use Python in a single language approach to this data systems class, because it is taught in our CS1 courses. This allows students to focus on the topics we present, rather than needing to also learn a new language. In the initial survey, designed to understand sufficiency in CS1 topics and to aid in some initial review, we asked students their self-assessed level of understanding in a number of the Python programming topics. In particular we asked students to assess their proficiency in the usage and methods of strings, lists, and dictionaries, the usage and construction of two-dimensional data structures, and creation of basic graphs through plotting packages. Figure 4 shows the results of these survey questions, where students ranked their proficiency on a 1 to 7 scale (bigger is better).

On the positive side, for all six topic areas, the significant majority of the distribution is at ratings of 5-7. Students clearly felt most proficient in lists and strings, followed by dictionaries and objects. The distribution of proficiency on graphics has greater spread, as does two-dimensional representations. Given coverage late in our CS1 offerings, this is not unexpected.

4 EVALUATION AND STUDENT FEEDBACK

We employed multiple surveys to gather student feedback on interest and efficacy of this course. Students were given an initial survey, to gather demographics and solicit feedback on proficiency

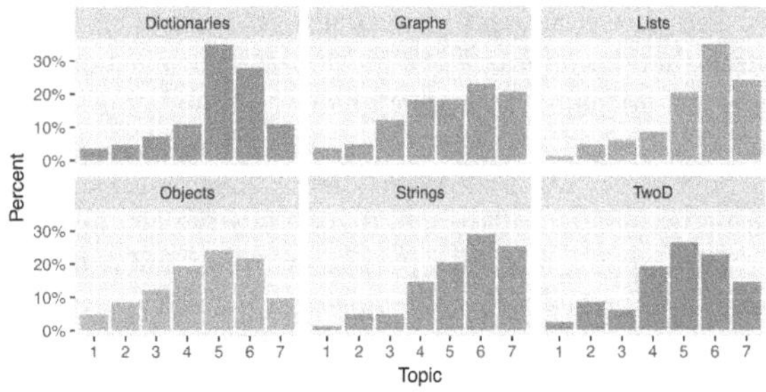

Figure 4: CS1 Topic Proficiency

in CS1 topics and opinions on the expected usefulness of the data systems topics. Students were also given surveys mid-semester and end-semester, asking about learning outcomes in each of the covered topics. Finally, we conducted a follow-up survey aligned near the end of students' summer experiences to help understand applications of the course materials to courses, internships, and projects after the class was over.[5] Out of 90 total students, 85 responded to the initial survey, 72 to the mid-semester survey, and 64 to the end-semester survey. The post-survey only went out to students who agreed to be contacted for follow-up, and we received 29 responses from 60 such students.[6]

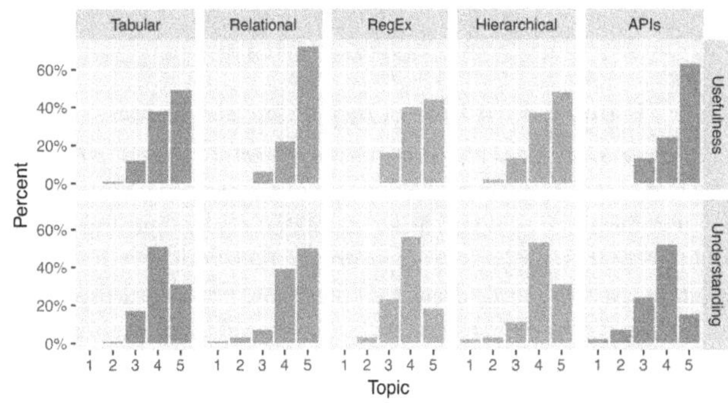

Figure 5: Usefulness and Understanding by Topic

Figure 5 shows percentages of respondents rating, on a 1-5 scale, for each of five central topic areas. In the top row of the figure, students rate their expectation on the usefulness of the topic, prior to coverage. In the bottom row, students self-assess their understanding of the topic material after coverage. The first, second, and fourth column correspond to the data models covered in the course. The column headed RegEx corresponds to coverage of regular expressions, addressed in the course for handling unstructured data. The final APIs column encompasses both simple web server access, as well as more complex authenticated and authorized REST APIs. Even before coverage, students' expectations were high for the usefulness of all of these topics, with Relational and APIs as the perceived "most useful". Further, their self-assessed level of understanding is quite good across all five topics. Using total percentage of 4 plus 5 ratings as a metric, Relational is at the top with 89% 4s and 5s, Hierarchical, Tabular, and RegEx are in the middle at 84%, 82%, and 74%, respectively, and understanding of APIs at 67% 4s

[5] All surveys were anonymous, were with informed consent, were completed without the instructor in the room, and students were reminded that they always had the choice to not take the survey.

[6] For a solicitation to students during their summer, we felt a nearly 50% response rate quite good.

and 5s. These are very positive outcomes of the course, and support our thesis that this approach of a broad-based introduction to data systems is sufficiently accessible given the foundation of a CS1 course.

The post-survey was undertaken after receiving unsolicited feedback from students describing how they had employed data systems course learning in internships, personal projects, and research experiences after the course was completed. To avoid anecdotal and biased reporting, we designed and sent the post survey out to the broader audience of students from all sections asking, in particular, whether students had employed what they had learned in the course, if so, in what kinds of post-course activity, and then, to rate the importance of the data systems class topics in the context of their post-course work. Of the 29 respondents, 27 (93%) indicated use of these topics in some post-course project or activity, and most applied their learning in multiple activities. Of these, 44% used their skills in projects for other courses, 60% in internship or REU experiences, and an amazing 78% in personal or outside projects.

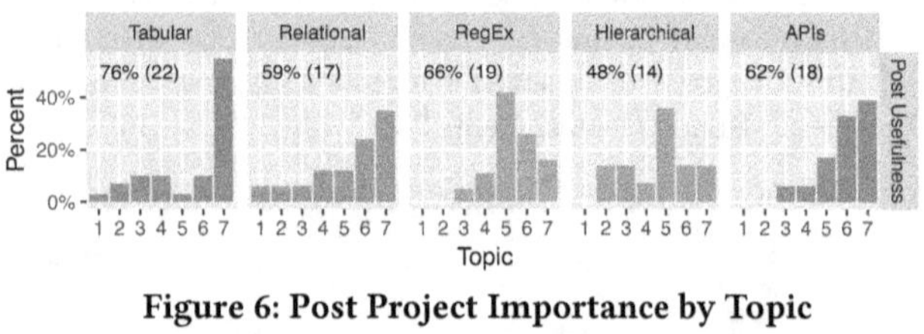

Figure 6: Post Project Importance by Topic

In Figure 6, we depict both the usage of each of the course topic areas and their importance in the post-course project. The usage is shown in each topic column as an annotated percentage and count (out of 29) that employed that topic area in their project. Given that a student used the topic area, we asked how important the topic was to their work. We can see that 76% of the students used Tabular (structure and cleaning/normalization) in their projects and that it was considered very important in the work. Regular expressions were used by a significant number of students, but their importance would appear to have been secondary. APIs, when used, were quite important. And the hierarchical model was used least at 48%, with more of a spread in importance. These numbers clearly support both the selection of content in our course design and, by the fact that so many students have integrated their learning so quickly into work following the class, both within and outside their academic endeavors, clearly argues for such a course being early in their curriculum.

Category	1	2	3	4	5		1	2	3	4	5
Effort	0	2%	4%	45%	49%		0	0	5%	25%	70%
Knowledge	0	2%	9%	32%	57%		0	0	0	20%	80%
Challenge	0	0	13%	40%	47%		0	0	10%	30%	60%
Overall	2%	4%	28%	42%	25%		0	0	5%	35%	60%

Table 2: Course Evaluation Results

Table 2 presents the results of the standard university course evaluations for the two offered semesters. Ratings are on a 1 to 5 scale and, for comparison, we use percentages of counts for each category. The number of evaluation respondents was 52 for the fall (on the left) and 20 for the spring (on the right). In both semesters, students were challenged by the material of the class, and significant effort was required. The knowledge and overall ratings differ between the two semesters, with both having greater spread, and a few students giving the fall instance of the course as low as a 1 or 2. The overall ratings and knowledge were remarkably good for the spring instance of the class. From the instructor's point of view, the course improved between the two semesters. Based on the fall feedback, some material was reduced and refined, and there were some changes to the ordering of topics as well.

In the post-survey, we asked students, with the benefit of hindsight after the course was complete, how they would compare their learning in this course to other courses at the university, and how they would rate the course overall. The course comparison question received 14 (48%) ratings of 6 and 12 (35%) ratings of 7, on a 7 point scale. The hindsight rating of the course overall received 13 (45%) ratings of 4 and 14 (48%) ratings of 5, on a 5 point scale.

When asked in the post-survey to describe their projects and how they had used what they learned, we received a rich set of answers. Some of these internship experiences include students working in physics, actuarial science, data science, banking, software engineering, academic research, and even for the government. Personal projects include stock market analysis, Chicago speed camera analysis, creating Twitter bots, personalizing Spotify, IMDb movies analysis, ESPN baseball analysis, and many more. The interesting and diverse responses, and the excitement conveyed by the students has been perhaps the most rewarding aspect of this undertaking.

5 CONCLUSIONS

The course, in design and in result, has been very successful, but it also has had its challenges. First and foremost involves the resources for students to use in the class. There is no single textbook that covers our desired topics. Books on database systems are too narrow and contain much material that we do not cover. Books on Python modules teach skills focused on a particular interface and lack the framework of the data models or the generality to see how a new interface or different language might accomplish the same goals. Instead, we relied on many online resources in combination with a significant number of Jupyter notebooks [12] written to both engage the students and to convey material. Some students, with good note-taking and skills at managing this disparate set of resources, adapted well, but for others it was a significant challenge. The second biggest challenge was trying to "do too much" in the fall version of the class. We reduced student workload somewhat, dropped a few secondary topics, and reordered slightly, to allow some of the more interesting *data sources* dimension of the class to occur earlier in the semester. These adjustments made a significant difference for the spring semester.

In summary, we have designed and developed a new data systems course that addresses the needs of our curriculum, introducing systems topics earlier and allowing downstream use of the knowledge gained. The course addresses the needs of the growing data-centric audience with a foundation of data-aptitude that can be implemented in institutions with data science programs or traditional computer science programs. We cover a significant range of topics in both the forms and the sources of data. Finally, we avoid content-overload and can attain greater depth by relying on a CS1 prerequisite.

REFERENCES

[1] 2017. *White paper: Top Ten Big Data Trends.* Technical Report 849188. Tableau Software.

[2] Ruth E. Anderson, Michael D. Ernst, Robert Ordóñez, Paul Pham, and Ben Tribelhorn. 2015. A Data Programming CS1 Course. In *Proceedings of the 46th ACM Technical Symposium on Computer Science Education (SIGCSE '15).* ACM, New York, NY, USA, 150–155. https://doi.org/10.1145/2676723.2677309

[3] Randy Bean. 2015. Making the Case for the 'Long Tail' of Big Data. *Wall Street Journal* (Aug 2015).

[4] Peter Cornillon. 2005. What Is a Data System, Anyway? *EDUCAUSE Review* 40, 2 (March/April 2005), 10–11.

[5] Richard D. De Veaux, Mahesh Agarwal, Maia Averett, Benjamin S. Baumer, Andrew Bray, Thomas C. Bressoud, Lance Bryant, Lei Z. Cheng, Amanda Francis, Robert Gould, Albert Y. Kim, Matt Kretchmar, Qin Lu, Ann Moskol, Deborah Nolan, Roberto Pelayo, Sean Raleigh, Ricky J. Sethi, Mutiara Sondjaja, Neelesh Tiruviluamala, Paul X. Uhlig, Talitha M. Washington, Curtis L. Wesley, David White, and Ping Ye. 2017. Curriculum Guidelines for Undergraduate Programs in Data Science. *Annual Review of Statistics and Its Application* 4, 1 (2017), 15–30. https://doi.org/10.1146/annurev-statistics-060116-053930 arXiv:https://doi.org/10.1146/annurev-statistics-060116-053930

[6] Peter ffoulkes. 2017. *White paper: InsideBIGDATA Guide to The Intelligent Use of Big Data on an Industrial Scale.* Technical Report. insideBigData. https://insidebigdata.com/2017/02/16/the-exponential-growth-of-data/

[7] Roy T. Fielding and Richard N. Taylor. 2000. Principled Design of the Modern Web Architecture. In *Proceedings of the 22nd International Conference on Software Engineering.* IEEE, 407–416.

[8] Olaf A. Hall-Holt and Kevin R. Sanft. 2015. Statistics-infused Introduction to Computer Science. In *Proceedings of the 46th ACM Technical Symposium on Computer Science Education (SIGCSE '15).* ACM, New York, NY, USA, 138–143. https://doi.org/10.1145/2676723.2677218

[9] Association for Computing Machinery (ACM) Joint Task Force on Computing Curricula and IEEE Computer Society. 2013. *Computer Science Curricula 2013: Curriculum Guidelines for Undergraduate Degree Programs in Computer Science.* ACM, New York, NY, USA. 999133.

[10] Daniel T. Kaplan. 2004. Teaching Computation to Undergraduate Scientists. In *Proceedings of the 35th SIGCSE Technical Symposium on Computer Science Education (SIGCSE '04).* ACM, New York, NY, USA, 358–362. https://doi.org/10.1145/971300.971424

[11] Daniel T. Kaplan. 2015. *Data Computing: An Introduction to Wrangling and Visualization with R.* Project MOSAIC.

[12] Thomas Kluyver, Benjamin Ragan-Kelley, Fernando Pérez, Brian Granger, Matthias Bussonnier, Jonathan Frederic, Kyle Kelley, Jessica Hamrick, Jason Grout, Sylvain Corlay, Paul Ivanov, Damián Avila, Safia Abdalla, and Carol Willing. 2016. Jupyter Notebooks – a publishing format for reproducible computational workflows. In *Positioning and Power in Academic Publishing: Players, Agents and Agendas*, F. Loizides and B. Schmidt (Eds.). IOS Press, 87 – 90.

[13] Task Group on Information Technology Curricula. 2017. *Information Technology Curricula 2017: Curriculum Guidelines for Baccalaureate Degree Programs in Information Technology.* ACM, New York, NY, USA.

[14] David G. Sullivan. 2013. A Data-centric Introduction to Computer Science for Non-majors. In *Proceeding of the 44th ACM Technical Symposium on Computer Science Education (SIGCSE '13).* ACM, New York, NY, USA, 71–76. https://doi.org/10.1145/2445196.2445222

[15] Hadley Wickham. 2011. The Split-Apply-Combine Strategy for Data Analysis. *Journal of Statistical Software, Articles* 40, 1 (2011). https://www.jstatsoft.org/v040/i01

[16] Hadley Wickham. 2014. Tidy Data. *Journal of Statistical Software, Articles* 59, 10 (2014), 1–23. https://doi.org/10.18637/jss.v059.i10

Investigating the Impact of Group Size on Non-Programming Exercises in CS Education Courses

Full Paper

L.D. Miller
Computer Science and Engineering
University of Nebraska - Lincoln
ldee.miller@gmail.com

Leen-Kiat Soh
Computer Science and Engineering
University of Nebraska - Lincoln
lksoh@cse.unl.edu

Markeya S. Peteranetz
Computer Science and Engineering
University of Nebraska - Lincoln
markeya.dubbs@huskers.unl.edu

ABSTRACT

Computer science (CS) courses are taught with increasing emphasis on group work and with non-programming exercises facilitating peer-based learning, computational thinking, and problem solving. However, relatively little work has been done to investigate the interaction of group work and non-programming exercises because collaborative, non-programming work is usually open-ended and requires analysis of unstructured, natural language responses. In this paper, we consider collaborative, non-programming work consisting of online wiki text from 236 groups in nine different CS1 and higher-level courses at a large Midwestern university. Our investigation uses analysis tools with natural language processing (NLP) and statistical analysis components. First, NLP uses IBM Watson Personality Insights to automatically convert students' collaborative wiki text into a Big Five model. This model is useful as a quality metric on group work since Big Five factors such as Openness and Conscientiousness are strongly related to both academic performance and learning. Then, statistical analysis generates regression models on group size and each Big Five trait that make up the factors. Our results show that increasing group size has a significant impact on collaborative, non-programming work in CS1 courses, but not for such work in higher-level courses. Furthermore, increasing group size can have either a positive or negative impact on the Big Five traits. These findings imply the feasibility of using such tools to automatically assess the quality of non-programming group exercises and offer evidence for effective group sizes.

CCS CONCEPTS

• **Social and professional topics** → Computational thinking; • **Applied computing** → Collaborative learning; E-learning;

KEYWORDS

CS Education, Non-Programming Exercises, Group Work, Natural Language Processing, Statistical Analysis

SIGCSE'19, February 27–March 2, 2019, Minneapolis, MN, USA

ACM ISBN 978-1-4503-5890-3/19/2...$15.00
https://doi.org/10.1145/3287324.3287400

ACM Reference Format:
L.D. Miller, Leen-Kiat Soh, and Markeya S. Peteranetz. 2019. Investigating the Impact of Group Size on Non-Programming Exercises in CS Education Courses: Full Paper. In *SIGCSE '19: 50th ACM Technical Symposium on Computer Science Education, February 27–March 2, 2019, Minneapolis, MN, USA.* ACM, New York, NY, USA, 7 pages. https://doi.org/10.1145/3287324.3287400

1 INTRODUCTION

Computer science (CS) courses are taught with increasing emphasis on group work. Group work helps prepare students for an industry where software is developed in teams [4, 21, 27] such as the popular Agile software development approach [18, 39]. Furthermore, group work helps students develop the "soft skills" necessary for the workplace such as problem solving, self-motivation, leadership, communication, and interpersonal skills. Employers understand the need for these "soft skills" and often value them as much or more than technical skills for employees [18, 27]. Finally, group work has academic benefits for students and instructors in CS with potentially higher retention rates [8] and grades [16] particularly for underrepresented students [12].

At the same time, CS courses are taught with increasing emphasis on moving away from traditional programming exercises. The idea is to provide instruction on the same computational thinking skills, but simplify or remove entirely components which can be frustrating or intimidating to students (especially first year students or those without programming background) such as code syntax [9]. These approaches range from Alice [9, 11] and Scratch [5] which use drag-and-drop programming in custom-made integrated development environments (IDEs) to full on CS Unplugged [2] which uses non-programming exercises where students discuss and write exercise responses entirely using natural language [20, 26, 36]. Both these approaches have been shown to provide significant improvements to student grades [11, 36].

Despite these separate benefits, relatively little work has been done on the interaction of group work and non-programming exercises. Programming IDEs, including Alice and Scratch, track actions important for group work such as when members uploaded revisions and also analyze whether those revisions ran correctly. On the other hand, actions in non-programming exercises are (1) harder to track since students can communicate through diverse means (e.g., social media) and (2) harder to analyze since exercise content is written in natural language. Without such research, finding an effective group size for non-programming exercises can be operationally difficult. Instead, instructors use ad hoc group sizes for these exercises which dampen the benefits of group work when there is too much work for the group or members can complete the exercises solo, or simply just use the same group size as that used in programming exercises. Ultimately, this can increase student dissatisfaction with group work and non-programming exercises even when those exercises are otherwise effective for instruction on computational thinking [24].

Therefore, we propose the use of alternative analysis tools to *help researchers and instructors evaluate group work, particularly for non-programming exercises.* These tools include two components: (1) advanced natural language processing (NLP) software and (2) statistical analysis dashboard. The NLP software provides quality metrics for the group work written by students, while the dashboard provides statistical analysis on the metrics such as an individual metric broken down by group size. Together, quality metrics and statistical analysis informs researchers on the interaction of group work and non-programming exercises and informs instructors on how group size impacts student activities and performance with those exercises. These tools could also be used to augment other approaches than non-programming exercises such as using NLP to evaluate group discussions in Alice, and to complement group work analysis on programming exercises such as using tracked keystrokes or versions of code check-in, to ultimately form a more comprehensive and meaningful assessment of student group work and learning.

In this paper, we evaluate an analytical process of using NLP and statistical tools on data collected from nine different CS courses at a large Midwestern university, including CS1 and higher-level CS courses. The data collected were from the collaborative text (i.e., online wikis) written by students working in groups to complete non-programming exercises known as the Computational Creativity Exercises [36]. These exercises use active learning, group work, and problem-based learning to teach students creative and computational thinking skills. Students experienced improved individual learning [37] consistent with that expected from collaborative writing [7]. During our analytical process, the NLP component analyzes the collaboratively written texts using IBM Watson Personality Insights [14]. This state-of-the-art NLP software models the collaboratively written texts using a full Big Five personality profile. This profile is useful as a quality metric on group work since Big Five variables such as Openness and Conscientiousness are strongly related to both academic performance and learning [10, 17, 25]. The statistical analysis dashboard provides separate analyses for both the CS1 and higher-level CS courses using R [33]. Both show how all the different Big Five factors are affected by changes in group size.

For this paper, stemming from our overall goal of investigating the impact of group size for non-programming exercises in CS courses, we focus on the following research questions:

- RQ #1: Does increasing group size have a significant impact on the quality of non-programming exercises-e.g., collaborative wiki essays-for CS1, measured using the Big Five factors?
- RQ #2: Does group size impact students' work quality differently in higher-level CS courses than in CS1?

The rest of this paper is organized as follows. Section 2 provides background on the non-programming exercises and group work in CS. Section 3 discusses the analytical tools in detail. Section 4 provides the results for the tools evaluated across nine different CS courses with nearly 250 groups. Finally, we conclude and discuss future work.

2 BACKGROUND AND RELATED WORK

2.1 Non-Traditional Exercises

As previously discussed, CS courses are moving away from using only traditional programming exercises in classrooms. Traditional programming exercises often contain syntax which is frustrating for new students [9] distracting them from developing computational thinking skills which require more than being able to program [40].

Non-traditional exercises range from enhanced programming environment approaches that support syntax-free, drag-and-drop programming such as Alice [9, 11] and Scratch [5] to full on CS Unplugged approaches that do away with programming completely. These latter approaches replace programming with natural language exercises [20, 26, 36]. Both enhanced programming environments and CS Unplugged approaches are effective and have been shown to improve student grades [11, 36].

Meanwhile, the original focus of CS Unplugged was non-programming exercises for K-12 students where instructors lacked the time, computers, or experience to use traditional programming exercises [2, 3, 26]. Nevertheless, interest in CS Unplugged has steadily increased at the college-level for several reasons: (a) non-programming exercises are easier to understand for non-majors and students with diverse backgrounds [6], (b) non-programming exercises are easier to deploy and grade in large sized courses and massive open online courses [20], and (c) non-programming exercises are effective at providing instruction on computational thinking skills important for college-level courses [36].

This paper focuses on non-programming exercises as grading these exercises in large classrooms is challenging and assessment based on this type of exercises has been less investigated. Having said that, our proposed analytical process could also be used for, say, enhanced programming environment exercises. As an example, the analytical tools could analyze group discussions in Alice to form a more meaningful assessment of student group work and learning. We will return to this discussion in Section 5 as future work.

2.2 Computational Creativity Exercises

For this paper, we used the data collected from students completing non-programming exercises called the computational creativity exercises (CCEs) [23]. In these exercises, group members used an online wiki which functions similarly to any collaborative writing assignment: each member could add to the wiki or edit work written by other group members. Collaborative writing has long been known to improve (individual) student learning [7]. Recent work has also reported the benefits of using collaborative writing in CS courses [1, 32].

CCEs expand on collaborative writing with exercises designed to *boost both creative and computational thinking skills* using a combination of problem solving, written analysis, and reflection. Students working in groups on these CCEs experienced improved individual learning in their CS courses [37]. Each CCE contains four standard components: (1) *Objectives* describing the computational thinking skills covered in that exercise (such as abstraction); (2) *Tasks* describing the individual tasks that each student in the group must complete; (3) *Light Bulbs* providing direct connections between exercise tasks and CS topics; and (4) *Questions* asking open-ended analysis and reflection questions for group members to discuss.

We evaluated six CCEs previously deployed to both CS1 and higher-level CS courses. The descriptions for those exercises are taken from [37]: (1) *Cipher*: Devise an encoding scheme to encode questions for other teams to compete to decode; (2) *Everyday Object*: Describe inputs, outputs, and functionalities for an existing object (e.g., nail clippers); (3) *Exploring*: Explore an existing location and document the senor stimuli observed there; (4) *Pathfinding*: Create a step-by-step set of instructions to create a quilt pattern; (5) *Storytelling*: Write story chapters independently and then work as a team to resolve conflicts and inconsistencies; and (6) *Thinking Inside the Box*: Test an alien machine without causing harm while attempting to reveal the functionalities of the machine.

2.3 Group Work

Group work has been studied for quite some time both (a) in K-12 and college level courses and (b) for CS and other fields. Results show that group work improves student achievement for K-12 and college [19]. Compared to working individually, group work in CS courses allow students to achieve higher retention rates [8] and grades [16] particularly for underrepresented students [12]. Furthermore, for CS, group work is important because modern soft-ware is developed in teams [4, 21, 27] such as the popular Agile soft-ware development approach [18, 39]. As previously mentioned, team development requires individuals with "soft skills" such as problem solving, self-motivation, leadership, communication, and interpersonal skills. Employers value these "soft skills" as much or more than technical skills for employees [18, 27].

Researchers have studied many different approaches for adding group work to CS courses [12]. For traditional programming exercises, pair programming has been studied extensively with groups of 2 students: one student acting as the driver controlling the keyboard and mouse while the other acts as the navigator [38]. Group work has also been previously tried for non-traditional exercises, but instructors tend to use ad hoc group sizes (such as simply allowing students to pick the groups) and have not extensively analyzed exercise content produced by these groups. Examples include group work designed for peer support with group sizes of 2-3 [15] and group work on software development projects with group sizes of 4-6 students [21] and 5 students [34].

Much less work has been done on investigating the impact of group sizes. Larger groups are recommended on semester-long projects involving students from multiple classes [27]. However, results on whether larger groups are better than smaller groups are often contradictory. For example, [30] found that students preferred working in discussion groups of size 2 over size 4 whereas [13] reported a significant positive relationship between (increasing) group size and higher level knowledge construction in groups.

3 ANALYSIS TOOLS

This section describes the (1) data collection, (2) advanced natural language processing (NLP), and (3) statistical analysis for our proposed analysis tools. As previously mentioned, the IBM Watson Personality Insights uses NLP to derive from collaboratively written text the set of Big Five personality profiles. Although Big Five profiles are designed to be intuitive (e.g., higher imagination is usually preferred), connecting the results to previous research on group work requires a working understanding of the Big Five. Therefore, we provide a detailed description of the Big Five traits used after describing Personality Insights.

3.1 Data Collection

The data collection is based on the deployment of the CCEs previously described (Section 2.2) to nine different CS courses at a large Midwestern university.

The nine different CS courses include six CS1 courses and three higher-level CS courses. The six CS1 courses include all the different versions available at that university including CS1 designed for (a) CS majors, (b) engineering majors, and (c) honors students in a CS/business crossover program. The three higher-level CS courses include intermediate (year 2-3) courses covering CS hardware and algorithm design.

Students were required to complete the CCEs with collaborative writing essays using an online wiki. The CCEs were graded and counted collectively as 5% of students' course grade. Students were allowed to form their own groups for the CCEs using the online wiki, but random assignment and group merging services were also available. In particular, group merging was used to keep the groups from dropping in size as students dropped from a course during the semester.

In total, we consider collaborative writing essays on the CCEs collected from 149 different groups in CS1 and 87 different groups in higher-level CS courses. The analysis tools preprocess the essay content automatically to remove HTML and other special characters. And the essays are stored with only group names as identifiers to protect the privacy of students.

3.2 Advanced Natural Language Processing

Here we provide a description on the IBM Watson Personality Insights and the Big Five traits used.

Personality Insights. IBM Watson Personality Insights is a natural language processing module of the well-known Watson AI system which defeated human experts on the *Jeopardy!* game show in 2011. Personality Insights uses state-of-the-art natural language processing (NLP) to derive from text the set of Big Five personality profiles [14]. First, Personality Insights uses a word-embedded technique called GloVe [28] to obtain a vector representation for the text. Then, this vector is fed into a machine learning algorithm trained on thousands of users which predicts Big Five traits for the text. Although details on the machine learning algorithm are proprietary, its validity was established by comparing the Big Five profiles predicted by the algorithm to Big Five profiles based on surveys [31, 35]. More specifically, the mean absolute error and correlation validate that Big Five profiles from Personality Insights are quite similar to those for survey-based Big Five profiles on the same users.

Personality Insights operates as part of the IBM cloud and provides a relatively simple abstract programming interface (API) for use. The machine learning algorithm is already trained and immutable. As such, the order and content of the text uploaded have no impact on the Big Five model predicted. In the results below, we uploaded each essay one at a time to the cloud using the API. After running the algorithm, Personality Insights returned a separate Big Five profile for each essay with different traits.

Big Five. The five-factor personality model is most commonly assessed using a complex questionnaire such as NEO Personality Inventory-Revised [22]. This questionnaire has a five-point Likert scale paired with 240 items that assess 30 different traits (sometimes called facets). Each set of six traits define one of the five factors important for this personality and behavior model: Openness, Conscientiousness, Extraversion, Agreeableness, and Emotional Range (also called Neuroticism).

For this initial work, we evaluate our analysis tools on three of the five main factors: *Openness, Conscientiousness, and Agreeableness.* As personality traits reflected in individuals, these three factors have been consistently connected to both academic performance and learning [10, 17, 25]. As such, these factors are probably the most immediately interesting for instructors and researchers. (Evaluation on the other two, more emotional, factors is discussed in the future work.) The 18 different traits corresponding to the three factors are described in detail in Table 1 with descriptions paraphrased from [14] and [22].

Finally, as previously discussed, IBM Watson Personality Insights uses a machine learning approach to predict the scores for the Big Five model [14]. These scores are given on a percentile range of 0-100 comparing the traits to those found in the thousands of writing samples used for training. As such, *an Imagination score of 90% in the results below means that the essay content is more imaginative than 90% of the baseline* (rather than 90% imaginative which would be nonsensical).

Table 1: Descriptions of traits for Openness, Conscientiousness, and Agreeableness-Big Five factors used in the results.

Openness	**Individuals who score high...**
Adventurousness	Are eager to try new activities and experience different things.
Artistic interests	Love beauty, both in art and in nature.
Emotionality	Have good awareness of their own feelings.
Imagination	View the real world as often too ordinary.
Intellect	Are intellectually curious and tend to think in symbols and abstractions.
Authority challenging	Have a readiness to challenge authority, convention, and traditional values.
Conscientiousness	**Individuals who score high...**
Achievement striving	Try hard to achieve excellence.
Cautiousness	Are disposed to think through possibilities carefully before acting.
Dutifulness	Have a strong sense of duty and obligation.
Orderliness	Are well-organized, tidy, and neat.
Self discipline	Have the self-discipline to persist at difficult or unpleasant tasks until they are completed.
Self efficacy	Confident in their ability to accomplish things.
Agreeableness	**Individuals who score high...**
Altruism	Find that helping others is genuinely rewarding.
Cooperation	Dislike confrontation. Willing to compromise.
Modesty	Are unassuming, self-effacing, and humble.
Uncompromising	See no need for pretense or manipulation when dealing with others.
Sympathy	Are tender-hearted and compassionate.
Trust	Assume that most people are fundamentally fair, honest, and have good intentions.

3.3 Statistical Analysis

The analysis tools automatically calculate statistics on the Big Five traits using the R programming language. R is a free and open-source language which includes a large range of statistical models and allows for data organization, statistical analysis, and graphical representation using the same software. The results below *use separate regression models to measure the impact of changing group size on each Big Five trait.* The model provides a slope for each trait along with statistical significance (with F-test).

4 RESULTS

Tables 2-3 shows the results of our analysis across nine different CS courses with 236 groups. Both tables provide results measuring the impact of group size on Big Five traits for the Openness, Conscientiousness, and Agreeableness factors. Table 2 provides those results for CS1, based on 149 groups, while Table 3 them for higher-level CS courses, based on 87 groups. Both tables are organized in the same way. First, the average, predicted score for each Big Five trait is given separately for groups sizes 1-5 (S1-S5). The largest value for a single trait has a blue background, while the smallest has a red background. Larger groups (size 6-7) are not included because there are fewer than five such groups and they are only found in one course. Second, the slope for the regression model with standardized coefficients and statistical significance using a F-test (Reg. and Sig.) are given for each Big Five trait. This model is run using all scores for groups sizes 1-5 (not just the average scores).

4.1 CS1 Results

Table 2 provides considerably interesting analysis tool results for the CS1 courses. First, overall, ***group size seems to have a significant impact on all three Big Five factors*** (Openness, Conscientiousness, and Agreeableness) with statistical significance on 4/6 of the traits for each factor. As previously mentioned, these factors are important for CS education because they have been consistently connected to academic performance and learning [10, 17, 25]. That being said, increasing group size impacts the Big Five factors in decidedly different ways.

Openness. At first, increasing group size seems to have a mixed impact on Openness traits. Imagination and Emotionality traits both go up significantly with increasing group size, while Adventurousness and Authority challenging both go down significantly. One possible interpretation is larger groups were more likely to revise and "soften" the bold aspects of language that are scored as Adventurous or Authority challenging. Larger groups result in written essays which are more empathetic and imaginative, but also remain more focused on the topic under discussion for the assignment. These results are particularly interesting since students work together on the CCEs remotely using an online wiki rather than directly in class. Larger groups could act a kind of remote peer pressure on students encouraging them to take the CCEs seriously and make insightful revisions to avoid upsetting a larger number of their peers. At this point, we conclude that increasing group size improves most Openness traits on the CCE non-programming exercises. Future work investigating the impact of group size on Openness for groups working together remotely vs. directly in the classroom should be considered.

Conscientiousness. Increasing group size reduces most Conscientiousness traits on the CCE non-programming exercises. Achievement striving, Orderliness, Self discipline, and Self efficacy all go down significantly with increasing group size. To an extent, these results should be expected since the written essays from larger groups are likely going to be less cohesive, less smooth, and less logically consistent than essays written by a single individual. The CCE non-programming exercises place emphasis on getting all students to contribute to the written essays. However, in larger groups, members might end up placing less emphasis making sure those essays are rigorously proofed and edited. Larger groups and lack of editing combine to lower Conscientiousness scores from Personality Insights which compares against the writing samples used for training. In a way, to improve Conscientiousness, this type of non-programming exercises should place emphasis on making sure or incentivizing that content is proofed and edited. Future work investigating the impact of group size on Conscientiousness should consider including a group leader who guides the essay writing including editing.

Agreeableness. Increasing group size has a mixed impact on Agreeableness traits for the CCEs. Altruism and Sympathy both go up significantly with increasing group size, while Cooperation and Uncompromising go down significantly. Altruism and Sympathy and Uncompromising are arguably more important for CCEs to help students describe, document, and create in the written essays because there are more viewpoints involved in the writing process when the group size is larger. We speculate that the reduction in Cooperation make sense as larger groups will have more voices which are less cohesive leading to a final product that appears to be more confrontational. As previously mentioned, the CCEs emphasize individual contribution and do not explicitly encourage electing a group leader guiding the essay writing. Meanwhile, we realized that the online wiki also has a separate discussion forum from the written essay. When we went back to look at the forum, we found that most students actually used social media for discussion (e.g., Facebook). Would including those discussions improve the scores on Cooperation and Uncompromising as group size increases? Future work investigating the impact of group size on Agreeableness' traits should include social media discussions.

Discussion. The results in Section 4.1 show that increasing group sizes have a significant impact on non-programming exercises for CS1 measured using the Big Five factors (RQ #1). Increasing group sizes (1) improves most Openness traits, (2) reduces most Conscientiousness traits, and (3) has a mixed impact on Agreeableness traits. These results have different takeaways for instructors and researchers.

Table 2: CS1 regression results measuring the impact of group size on Big Five traits. S1-S5 gives trait for group sizes with max (blue) and min (red), Reg. gives the slope for model, Sig. gives statistical significance ($^* \leq 0.1$, $^{**} \leq 0.05$, $^{***} \leq 0.01$)

Openness	S1	S2	S3	S4	S5	Reg.	Sig.
Adventurousness	0.42	0.36	0.31	0.27	0.22	-0.05	***
Artistic interests	0.55	0.60	0.56	0.64	0.65	0.02	
Emotionality	0.26	0.38	0.37	0.54	0.54	0.07	***
Imagination	0.67	0.73	0.78	0.84	0.85	0.05	***
Intellect	0.97	0.98	0.97	0.98	0.98	0.00	
Authority challenging	0.88	0.88	0.83	0.77	0.77	-0.03	***
Conscientiousness	**S1**	**S2**	**S3**	**S4**	**S5**	**Reg.**	**Sig.**
Achievement striving	0.43	0.42	0.36	0.25	0.24	-0.05	***
Cautiousness	0.76	0.80	0.73	0.76	0.76	0.00	
Dutifulness	0.44	0.42	0.42	0.48	0.44	0.00	
Orderliness	0.51	0.44	0.42	0.36	0.37	-0.03	***
Self discipline	0.32	0.24	0.22	0.09	0.10	-0.06	***
Self efficacy	0.51	0.45	0.38	0.25	0.27	-0.06	***
Agreeableness	**S1**	**S2**	**S3**	**S4**	**S5**	**Reg.**	**Sig.**
Altruism	0.41	0.48	0.47	0.58	0.56	0.04	***
Cooperation	0.55	0.55	0.49	0.50	0.44	-0.03	**
Modesty	0.51	0.54	0.57	0.56	0.54	0.01	
Uncompromising	0.51	0.52	0.43	0.40	0.41	-0.03	**
Sympathy	0.57	0.69	0.65	0.83	0.80	0.06	***
Trust	0.43	0.42	0.41	0.37	0.38	-0.01	

First, instructors can use these results as a guide for tradeoffs in group size on non-programming exercises. The instructor can decide which traits are most important on the exercises and set the group size accordingly. As an example, exercises which emphasize Imagination should use larger groups, while those which emphasize Orderliness should use smaller groups.

Second, researchers should use these results as a starting point to supplement or complement their designs. Although using our analysis tools to evaluate non-programming exercises content using Big Five factors seems promising, some results are influenced by design choices in the CCEs (e.g., no group leader). As such, additional work must be done to further evaluate (a) the impact of group size on the Big Five factors (as previously suggested) and (b) the analysis tools on other non-programming exercises with different design choices.

4.2 Higher-Level Results

Table 3 provides analysis tool results for the higher-level courses. Overall, group size does not have a significant impact on all three Big Five factors (Openness, Conscientiousness, and Agreeableness) with statistical significance on only 2/18 traits. We might be tempted to speculate that group work has nothing to do with these results:

Table 3: Higher-Level CS regression results measuring the impact of group size on Big Five traits. S1-S5 gives trait for group sizes with max (blue) and min (red), Reg. gives the slope for model, Sig. gives statistical significance (* ≤ 0.1, ** ≤ 0.05, * ≤ 0.01).**

Openness	S1	S2	S3	S4	Reg.	Sig.
Adventurousness	0.51	0.45	0.44	0.53	0.00	
Artistic interests	0.52	0.65	0.63	0.66	0.04	
Emotionality	0.19	0.17	0.17	0.13	-0.02	
Imagination	0.51	0.74	0.72	0.67	0.05	
Intellect	0.97	0.98	0.97	0.99	0.00	
Authority challenging	0.89	0.94	0.95	0.92	0.01	
Conscientiousness	**S1**	**S2**	**S3**	**S4**	**Reg.**	**Sig.**
Achievement striving	0.56	0.42	0.46	0.47	-0.02	
Cautiousness	0.87	0.77	0.80	0.84	-0.01	
Dutifulness	0.57	0.35	0.37	0.40	-0.05	*
Orderliness	0.65	0.52	0.56	0.61	-0.01	
Self discipline	0.50	0.29	0.33	0.36	-0.04	
Self efficacy	0.59	0.52	0.53	0.51	-0.02	
Agreeableness	**S1**	**S2**	**S3**	**S4**	**Reg.**	**Sig.**
Altruism	0.46	0.34	0.33	0.28	-0.06	***
Cooperation	0.73	0.52	0.55	0.59	-0.04	
Modesty	0.66	0.51	0.50	0.56	-0.04	
Uncompromising	0.66	0.44	0.47	0.53	-0.04	
Sympathy	0.56	0.57	0.49	0.50	-0.03	
Trust	0.43	0.45	0.43	0.40	-0.01	

the CCEs are simply too easy for higher-level CS students. However, recent work from others has shown that the CCEs helped with learning in higher-level students [29]. As such, the differences between Tables 2-3 point to a fundamental difference in group work between CS1 and higher-level CS students when using the non-programming exercises. Older students potentially have more experience with group work and are less affected by the size of the group they are working in.

Openness. Students in higher-level courses (1) have very high levels of Authority challenging and (2) Adventurousness and Authority challenging both increase with group size. Imagination does increase at S2, but then actually goes down as group size increases. As previously mentioned, increasing Adventurousness and Authority challenging can be undesirable for assignments. In general, where larger groups are beneficial for Openness in CS1 students, the opposite may be true for students in higher-level courses. One explanation is that these students, having gone through their first or second year of courses, are more independent and have better problem solving skills and more structured reasoning processes. Thus, working in a smaller or a larger group does not impact the quality of the collaborative wiki essay significantly.

Conscientiousness and Agreeableness. Students in higher-level courses have the highest values for traits at S1-S2 before an observable decline in all traits across both factors. These results provide additional evidence that increasing group size dose not impact the quality of these students' collaborative work, or if there is impact, it appears to be more negative than positive.

Discussion. The results in Section 4.2 show that group size does not impact higher-level CS courses as much as CS1 (RQ #2). The difference is probably in how students view group work since students in higher-level courses still benefit from using the exercises [29]. We speculate that students in higher-level courses are more adept at working independently and have stronger knowledge on the subject matter that they are capable of producing similar quality of work by themselves or as a team. Nevertheless, these results demonstrate how the analysis tools could provide important information to instructors allowing for redesigning of group assignments to invoke more meaningful teamwork.

5 CONCLUSIONS

CS courses are being taught with increasing emphasis on group work and non-programming exercises, but little work has been done investigating the impact of group size on these exercises. The reason is that student responses to non-programming exercises are often written in natural language making analysis difficult. We propose analysis tools which use natural language processing and statistical analysis to evaluate collaborative, non-programming work effectively. These tools use IBM Watson Personality Insights to convert the natural language into a Big Five profile and then generates statistical models on the group size and Big Five traits on factors important for learning (e.g., Openness). Our results show that increasing group size seems to have a significant impact on non-programming exercises for CS1. Also, increasing group size does not have as much of an impact on higher-level CS courses as it does in CS1. Instead, there appears to be a difference between students working in a group or not in a group.

We have only started evaluating group work on non-programming exercises. We have already mentioned future work on the impact of groups working remotely vs. directly, the presence of a group leader, and the inclusion of social media discussions. Also, while the CCEs provide general benefits for all students [36], we also intend to investigate whether presence in groups with high Big Five scores correlates with individual performance in the CS classroom in the same way that prior research has shown the traits in individuals are associated with learning outcomes.

Finally, the analysis tools using Personality Insights have a huge potential for use with other research areas. First, the tools could be used for the enhanced programming environments such as Alice and Scratch. In addition to monitoring student programming, these environments could obtain a more complete picture by analyzing the quality of group discussions. Second, massive open online courses could use these tools for the analysis of group discussions and exercise content which requires natural language responses.

6 ACKNOWLEDGMENTS

This work was partially supported by the National Science Foundation with grants no. 1122956 and 1431874. Further support was provided with a UNL Phase II Pathways to Interdisciplinary Research Centers grant.

REFERENCES

[1] Oluwabunmi Adewoyin, Kewen Wu, and Julita Vassileva. 2015. Exploiting the Use of Wikis to Support Collaborative Writing: A Case Study of an Undergraduate Computer Science Class. In *Proceedings of the International Conference on Collaboration and Technology (CRIWG 2015)*. 111–123.

[2] Tim Bell, Jason Alexander, Isaac Freeman, and Mick Grimley. 2009. Computer Science Unplugged: school students doing real computing without computers. *New Zealand Journal of Applied Computing & Information Technology* 13, 1 (2009), 20–29.

[3] Tim Bell, Paul Curzon, Quintin Cutts, Valentina Dagiene, and Bruria Haberman. 2011. Overcoming Obstacles to CS Education by Using Non-programming Outreach Programmes. In *Proceedings of International Conference on Informatics in Schools: Situation, Evolution, and Perspectives (ISSEP'11)*. 71–81.

[4] Jürgen Börstler and Thomas Hilburn. 2016. Team Projects in Computing Education. *ACM Transactions on Computing Education* 16, 2 (2016), 1–4.

[5] Karen Brennan and Mitchel Resnick. 2012. New frameworks for studying and assessing the development of computational thinking. In *Proceedings of American Educational Research Association meeting*. Vancouver, British Columbia, Canada, 1–25.

[6] Richard Brown and Elizabeth Shoop. 2011. Modules in Community: Injecting More Parallelism Into Computer Science Curricula. In *Proceedings of the 42rd ACM Technical Symposium on Computer Science Education (SIGCSE'11)*. Dallas, Texas, USA, 447–452.

[7] Rafael Calvo, Stephen T. O'Rourke, Janet Jones, Kalina Yacef, and Peter Reimann. 2011. Collaborative Writing Support Tools on the Cloud. *IEEE Transactions on Learning Technology* 4, 1 (2011), 81–97.

[8] Adam Carter, Christopher Hundhausen, and Olusola Adesope. 2017. Blending Measures of Programming and Social Behavior into Predictive Models of Student Achievement in Early Computing Courses. *ACM Transactions on Computing Education* 17, 3 (2017), 1–20.

[9] Stephen Cooper, Wanda Dann, and Randy Pausch. 2003. Teaching Objects-first In Introductory Computer Science. In *Proceedings of the 34th ACM Technical Symposium on Computer Science Education (SIGCSE'03)*. Reno, Nevada, USA, 1–5.

[10] Holger Danielsiek and Jan Vahrenhold. 2016. Stay on These Roads: Potential Factors Indicating Students' Performance in a CS2 Course. In *Proceedings of the 47th ACM Technical Symposium on Computer Science Education (SIGCSE'16)*. Memphis, Tennessee, USA, 12–17.

[11] Wanda Dann, Dennis Cosgrove, Don Slater, Dave Culyba, and Steve Cooper. 2012. Mediated transfer: Alice 3 to Java. In *Proceedings of the 43rd ACM Technical Symposium on Computer Science Education (SIGCSE'12)*. Raleigh, North Carolina, USA, 141–146.

[12] Scott Grissom, Renée McCauley, and Laurie Murphy. 2018. How Student Centered is the Computer Science Classroom? A Survey of College Faculty. *ACM Transactions on Computing Education* 18, 1 (2018), 1–27.

[13] Khe Foon Hew and Wing Sum Cheung. 2911. Higher-level knowledge construction in asynchronous online discussions: an analysis of group size, duration of online discussion, and student facilitation techniques. *Instructional Science* 39 (2911), 303–319.

[14] IBM Cloud Docs. 2017. *The science behind the service.* IBM. https://console.bluemix.net/docs/services/personality-insights/science.html#science

[15] Ville Isomöttönen and Ville Tirronen. 2017. Flipping and BlendingâĂŤAn Action Research Project on Improving a Functional Programming Course. *ACM Transactions on Computing Education* 17, 1 (2017), 1–35.

[16] Erkki Kaila, Einari Kurvinen, Erno Lokkila, and Mikko-Jussi Laakso. 2016. Redesigning an Object-Oriented Programming Course. *ACM Transactions on Computing Education* 16, 4 (2016), 1–21.

[17] Meera Komarraju, Steven Karau, Ronald Schmeck, and Alen Avdic. 2011. The Big Five personality traits, learning styles, and academic achievement. *Personality and Individual Differences* 51 (2011), 472–477.

[18] David Largent. 2016. Measuring and Understanding Team Development by Capturing Self-assessed Enthusiasm and Skill Levels. *ACM Transactions on Computing Education* 16, 2 (2016), 1–27.

[19] Yiping Lou, Philip Abrami, John Spence, Catherine Poulsen, Bette Chambers, and Sylvia Apollonia. 1996. Within-Class Grouping: A Meta-Analysis. *Review of Educational Research* 66, 4 (1996), 423–458.

[20] Mary Lou Maher, Celine Latulipe, Heather Lipford, and Audrey Rorrer. 2015. Flipped Classroom Strategies for CS Education. In *Proceedings of the 46th ACM Technical Symposium on Computer Science Education (SIGCSE'15)*. Kansas City, Missouri, USA, 218–223.

[21] Linda Marshall, Vreda Pieterse, Lisa Thompson, and Dina Venter. 2016. Exploration of Participation in Student Software Engineering Teams. *ACM Transactions on Computing Education* 16, 2 (2016), 1–38.

[22] Robert McCrae and Paul Costa. 2010. *NEO inventories professional manual.* Psychological Assessment Resources, Odessa, Florida, USA.

[23] L.D. Miller, Leen-Kiat Soh, Vlad Chiriacescu, Elizabeth Ingraham, Duane Shell, and Melissa Hazley. 2014. Integrating computational and creative thinking to improve learning and performance in CS1. In *Proceedings of the 45th ACM Technical Symposium on Computer Science Education (SIGCSE'18)*. Atlanta, Georgia, USA, 475–480.

[24] L.D. Miller, Leen-Kiat Soh, Vlad Chiriacescu, Elizabeth Ingraham, Duane Shell, Stephen Ramsey, and Melissa Hazley. 2013. Improving learning of computational thinking using creative competency exercises in college CS-1 computer science courses. In *Proceedings of 2013 IEEE Frontiers in Education Conference (FIE'13)*. 1426–1432.

[25] Erik Noftle and Richard Robins. 2007. Personality Predictors of Academic Outcomes: Big Five Correlates of GPA and SAT Scores. *Journal of Personality and Social Psychology,* 93, 1 (2007), 116–130.

[26] Youwen Ouyang, Katherine Hayden, and Julie Remold. 2018. Introducing Computational Thinking through Non-Programming Science Activities. In *Proceedings of the 49th ACM Technical Symposium on Computer Science Education (SIGCSE'18)*. Baltimore, Maryland, USA, 308–313.

[27] Robert Pastel, Marika Seigel, Wei Zhang, and Alex Mayer. 2015. Team Building in Multidisciplinary Client-Sponsored Project Courses. *ACM Transactions on Computing Education* 15, 4 (2015), 1–24.

[28] Jeffrey Pennington, Richard Socher, and Christopher Manning. 2014. GloVe: Global Vectors for Word Representation. In *Proceedings of the 2014 Conference on Empirical Methods in Natural Language Processing (EMNLP)*. 1532–1543.

[29] Markeya Peteranetz, Shiyuan Wang, Duane Shell, Abraham Flanigan, and Leen-Kiat Soh. 2018. Examining the Impact of Computational Creativity Exercises on College Computer Science Students' Learning, Achievement, Self-Efficacy, and Creativity. In *Proceedings of the 49th ACM Technical Symposium on Computer Science Education (SIGCSE'18)*. Baltimore, Maryland, USA, 155–160.

[30] Johanna Pirker, Maria Riffnaller-Schiefer, and Christian Gütl. 2014. Motivational Active Learning âĂŞ Engaging UniversityStudents in Computer Science Education. In *Proceedings of the 2014 conference on Innovation & technology in computer science education (ITiCSE'14)*. Uppsala, Sweden, 297–302.

[31] Barbara Plank and Dirk Hovy. 2015. Personality Traits on Twitter -or- How to Get 1,500 Personality Tests in a Week. In *Proceedings of the 6th Workshop on Computational Approaches to Subjectivity, Sentiment and Social Media Analysis (WASSA 2015)*. 92–98.

[32] Elvira Popescu, Mihai Dascalu, Alex Becheru, Scott Crossley, and Stefan Trausan-Matu. 2016. Predicting Student Performance and Differences in Learning Styles based on Textual Complexity Indices applied on Blog and Microblog Posts. In *Proceedings of IEEE 16th International Conference on Advanced Learning Technologies (ICALT 2016)*. 184–188.

[33] R Core Team. 2015. *R: A Language and Environment for Statistical Computing.* R Foundation for Statistical Computing, Vienna, Austria. https://www.R-project.org/

[34] Kurt Schneider, Olga Liskin, Hilko Paulsen, and Simone Kauffeld. 2015. Media, Mood, and Meetings: Related to Project Success? *ACM Transactions on Computing Education* 15, 4 (2015), 1–33.

[35] Andrew Schwartz, Johannes Eichstaedt, Margaret Kern, Lukasz Dziurzynski, Stephanie Ramones, Megha Agrawal, Achal Shah, Michal Kosinksi, and David Stillwell. 2013. Personality, Gender, and Age in the Language of Social Media: The Open-Vocabulary Approach. *PLoS One* 8, 9 (2013), 1–16.

[36] Duane Shell and Leen-Kiat Soh. 2013. Profiles of Motivated Self-Regulation in College Computer Science Courses: Differences in Major Versus Required Non-major Courses. *Journal of Science Education and Technology* 22 (2013), 899–913.

[37] Duane Shell, Leen-Kiat Soh, Abraham Flanigan, Markeya Peteranetz, and Elizabeth Ingraham. 2017. Improving Students' Learning and Achievement in CS Classrooms through Computational Creativity Exercises that Integrate Computational and Creative Thinking. In *Proceedings of the 48th ACM Technical Symposium on Computer Science Education (SIGCSE'17)*. Seattle, Washington, USA, 543–548.

[38] Karthikeyan Umapathy and Albert Ritzhaupt. 2017. A Meta-Analysis of Pair-Programming in Computer Programming Courses: Implications for Educational Practice. *ACM Transactions on Computing Education* 17, 4 (2017), 1–13.

[39] Rebecca Vivian, Katrina Falkner, Nickolas Falkner, and Hamid Tarmazdi. 2016. A Method to Analyze Computer Science Students' Teamwork in Online Collaborative Learning Environments. *ACM Transactions on Computing Education* 16, 2 (2016), 1–28.

[40] Jeannette Wing. 2006. Computational Thinking. *Commun. ACM* 49, 3 (2006), 33–35.

Developing Soft and Technical Skills Through Multi-Semester, Remotely Mentored, Community-Service Projects

Janet Davis
Whitman College
davisj@whitman.edu

Samuel A. Rebelsky
Grinnell College
rebelsky@grinnell.edu

ABSTRACT

For the past four years, we have taught a reimagined software design course with typical and atypical components. Projects form the core of the course: Students work in teams of 4-6 people to develop non-mission-critical software for local non-profits, building their engagement with the community and helping them understand the broader impact of their work. These projects require multiple semesters to complete. Since students typically enroll for the course for one semester, this model gives students the novel experience of legacy software. We also provide each team with an alumni mentor who helps them navigate not only technical problems but also the challenges of working with a real-world, non-technical client.

These aspects of the course also develop our students' soft skills. They learn to work with a team, to communicate with non-technical clients, to work with remote collaborators (or mentors), and to think ahead to those who will take on the project in the next semester. As we tell our students, these skills are often as crucial as their technical skills.

In this paper, we report on the design of the course and describe some of the challenges associated with this model (e.g., projects that inadvertently reveal information, clients who switch management or expectations, and projects that become obsolete) and provide suggestions for those who might want to adopt a similar approach.

CCS CONCEPTS

• **Social and professional topics** → **Computing education**; **Software engineering education**; • **Software and its engineering** → *Designing software*; *Programming teams*.

KEYWORDS

Software engineering, Software design, Soft skills, Community service, Ruby on Rails, Alumni engagement

ACM Reference Format:

Janet Davis and Samuel A. Rebelsky. 2019. Developing Soft and Technical Skills Through Multi-Semester, Remotely Mentored, Community-Service Projects. In *Proceedings of the 50th ACM Technical Symposium on Computer Science Education (SIGCSE '19), February 27-March 2, 2019, Minneapolis, MN, USA*. ACM, New York, NY, USA, 7 pages. https://doi.org/10.1145/3287324.3287508

SIGCSE '19, February 27-March 2, 2019, Minneapolis, MN, USA

ACM ISBN 978-1-4503-5890-3/19/02...$15.00
https://doi.org/10.1145/3287324.3287508

1 INTRODUCTION

Software design and software engineering form a core part of the undergraduate computer science curriculum. However, perspectives on the content and structure of software design courses vary significantly. Some focus on formal methods (e.g., [7, 14]). Some consider strategies such as design patterns, while others compare plan-and-document with agile methodologies [8]. Some excite students through the use of video games (e.g., [17–19]). Many are now adopting an emphasis on service to the community [2, 3, 11–13], such as the Posse group's work on humanitarian free and open-source software (HFOSS) [16].

The role of projects also varies significantly. Some curricula place a small project in the software design or software engineering course and then follow with a capstone project. For others, the project is the center of the software design course, with everything else done in support of it. In either model, it can be difficult to scope projects so that students can successfully complete them in one term or even one academic year.

In this paper, we reflect on the curriculum model that we have employed for the past four years. The model introduces a novel constellation of features, including (a) community non-profit organizations who serve as project clients; (b) multi-semester projects that students often join in the middle; (c) two separate half-courses, one that introduces the principles and practices necessary for the design of a medium-scale project and one that comprises the project itself; (d) an emphasis on Web-based software with a common platform; (e) the use of a MOOC/SPOC to ground learning; (f) alumni mentors who advise project teams; and (g) a partnership with our career development office; At the same time, the course relies on many traditional components, including a focus on agile methodologies and object-oriented design. Together, these many parts provide students with a strong background in software design and, as importantly, to build equally valuable soft skills.

In section 2, we describe the institutional and departmental context for the curriculum. In section 3, we explore the goals and design of the new software design course. In section 4, we report on selected "war stories" that have contributed to student learning and that others may find instructive. In section 5, we describe some outcomes. Finally, in section 6, we provide recommendations for others interested in adapting some or all of these practices.

2 CONTEXT

Grinnell College is a small (1700 students), rural, highly selective liberal arts college. While it is difficult to quantify student ability, standardized test scores are high: the 75th percentile scores are 33 (ACT) and 1540 (new SAT composite), and the 25th percentile scores are 30 and 1370. Like many institutions, we have seen our computer science program expand rapidly. During the time of this project, we have gone from graduating between twelve and fifteen CS majors per year to graduating nearly sixty CS majors each year.

As is often the case at liberal arts colleges, our institution considers the major a small part of the overall undergraduate experience. Policies dictate that major requirements may not consist of more than eight courses plus a few non-departmental requirements. Our current requirements include a three-course, multi-language, introductory sequence; systems (either architecture or operating systems); upper-level algorithm design and analysis; theory of computation; software design; and one departmental elective. CS majors must also take three semesters of mathematics and statistics, including calculus, discrete mathematics, and a third course of the student's choice.

Despite these limitations, we provide our students with a strong and comprehensive undergraduate education, enough so that our CS curriculum serves as one of the curricular exemplars in the recent ACM/IEEE Curricular Guidelines [1].

Nonetheless, the software design curriculum has been particularly problematic. As one colleague put it, "software design often feels like a bunch of disconnected topics with a large, ambiguous project tied on." Throughout the years, we have offered the course in multiple forms, with different languages, emphases, and textbooks. In most cases, students did not take what we hoped out of the course. The course also received low end-of-course ratings, no matter who taught it. Even when a model seemed successful for one semester, subsequent offerings showed less success.

3 COURSE DESIGN

In spring 2014, we undertook a complete redesign of the course. Beyond engaging students in a moderately large project and teaching software design principles and practices, we had a variety of other goals. We wanted to provide students with a more realistic design experience, one more akin to what they would encounter after college. We know students are more successful when they are invested in their projects, so we wanted projects whose benefit they understood. We wanted to help students build not only technical skills, but also soft skills.We also felt a strong commitment to including service learning within our curriculum. And, to be honest, we wanted a course that students rated more highly.

These goals led us to a variety of design decisions for the course.

Community non-profits as project partners. In determining the kinds of projects we would use, we decided to focus on local non-profit organizations. Student engagement with the community provides an important opportunity. One of us had recently worked with a student team to complete a moderate-scale project for a local organization, and it was clear that many other organizations in our community also had needs for custom software. We decided early on that we would focus on non-mission-critical software; we did not want schedule slippage or poor design to negatively impact these community partners.[1] Even with that more limited scope, there is still a significant need. As one partner put it, "There are a lot of programs that would make our work easier, but that we can't afford and that would still need customization. Knowing that we might eventually get some of that software is a huge benefit."

At the same time, these projects provide value to our students. While the use of external clients is common practice in software design courses, we see particular value in community service projects. As is the case in many other courses with such projects (e.g., [2–4, 11–13]), our students regularly note that it feels much more rewarding to know that they are making software that others will use and that will benefit our community, particularly when compared to projects in other classes, whose audience appears to be only the professor or classmates. These community service projects also support the college's broader mission to "graduate individuals ... who are prepared in life and work to use their knowledge and their abilities to serve the common good." [9] While contributing to open source projects also lets students serve the common good, as in the work of Liu [13] or the Humanitarian Free and Open-Source community [2], we find the focus on local community is particularly motivating to our students. The chance to meet face-to-face with those being served has an important impact, as does the sense of continuity, knowing that partners depend on the software continuing to work in the future.

In the four years of the course, we have partnered with a diverse group of non-profits, including an umbrella "back office" that serves many non-profits in our community, two different food banks, a local no-kill animal shelter, a retirement community, a pre-kindergarten program, a retirement home, a sexual assault support group, and a county-wide service organization. The diversity of organizational interests supports a broad spectrum of projects.

Multi-semester projects. Inspired by Engineering Projects in Community Service (EPICS) at Purdue University [4], we decided to adopt multi-semester projects. This not only allows projects to expand to their natural scope, but also gives students a more realistic and somewhat less stressful experience. Since students often join projects in the middle, they have a realistic experience of reading and extending legacy code. By eliminating the expectation that students finish the project by the end of the semester, we alleviate some of the stress and frustration students typically feel; this model includes neither the traditional end-of-semester "death march" nor the dissatisfaction students often feel when they must reduce the scope of the project to complete it by the end of the semester. Finally, by continuing projects over multiple semesters, we remove some of the burden of extension and maintenance from instructors.

Of course, not all projects get finished. And some that get finished still don't get adopted. In those cases, our partner in the career-development offices regularly reminds students that the partner non-profits still received benefit from the *process*; thinking carefully about requirements and workflows can sometimes be as important as the software itself. This acknowledgement of "alternate value" helps make the process rather than the product the focus, emphasizing the importance of soft skills in interactions with partners and of continuing relationships. This emphasis distinguishes our approach from other software design courses with a strong community service component, such as the work of Leidig et al. [11, 12], that focus primarily on the product.

Course structure. Previously, we offered software design as a single four-credit course that included both principles and practices

[1]We use the term "partner" to emphasize the importance of reciprocity in which both students and partner organizations gain from the relationship. Using this term rather than "client" also avoids confusion, because most of our partner organizations have their own clients.

and a project component. We decoupled the two halves. That is, we offered a two-credit course in principles and practices and a separate two-credit "practicum" in which the students apply those principles and practices to a project with community partners.

Our chief intention was to make it easier for students to repeat the practicum, either working on the same project for multiple semesters or joining different projects in different stages of completion. However, the increased flexibility also made it easier for some students to put together a course plan. The department also started to offer additional two-credit courses in other areas, making it possible for students to combine one of the software design half-courses with an elective.

Ruby on Rails. Supporting a wide variety of multi-semester projects suggested that we should use a single language and platform for all the projects. Although students in our program already knew a variety of languages, including Java, we decided to use Ruby on Rails as the primary platform. We saw many advantages to this platform. Rails embraces a model-view-controller framework that we consider it important to master. Moreover, Rails is an "opinionated" framework which pushes developers towards consistent coding practices and design decisions. When things go right, Rails provides an efficient and straightforward development environment. A large number of modules for common tasks (a.k.a. "gems") are available, which gives students not only a more efficient development pathway, but also a more realistic development process. Ruby provides a very different model of object-oriented programming than does Java, which helps students broaden their understanding of object-oriented design.[2] There are also many resources for helping students learn software design with Ruby, including many that are available for free or at low cost (e.g., [6, 10]).

However, the use of Ruby on Rails did not come without other costs. In particular, it meant that we had to devote a non-trivial amount of time during the semester teaching students both Ruby and Rails, time which delayed the start of their projects.

Agile project management. Like many others, we chose to have students manage their project using an agile approach. A few advantages particularly stood out for this course: User stories are an accessible way to communicate requirements for non-technical partners, as well as students. The product manager role provides a consistent point of contact for partners. Many students were already comfortable with pair programming from our introductory sequence, and embraced the practice of working together in the same room. Iteration demos hold students accountable on a regular basis. We also had students estimate story points, which allowed them to assess their own pace and progress by measuring velocity for each iteration. Iteration retrospectives provide a structured opportunity for students to reflect on their experiences and change their practices. Since several two-week iterations fit into a semester, there are several such opportunities for learning.

One particularly useful concept is time-boxing. As we all know, projects expand to fill more than available time. Particularly since the project course was designed as a two-credit half-course, we made it clear to students that we were not expecting a particular product by a particular date; our focus was instead on the thought and effort they expended on the project. We encouraged them to time-box their work: work for at least N hours per week, but no more than N+M hours. We also encouraged student to time-box tasks and user stories, and to reconsider their planning if not completed in the allocated time. "Stretch goals" let students make further progress if tasks were completed more quickly than expected.

An affiliated MOOC/SPOC. After making many of the design decisions described above, we were fortunate to discover that Fox and Patterson had released a relevant textbook [6] and affiliated MOOC (Massive, Open, Online Course) [5]. We were particularly excited to find a textbook providing an integrated approach to learning Ruby on Rails and agile software development, including processes for working with a team and with an external client. We were invited to participate through an affiliated SPOC (Small, Personalized, Online Course), which provided access to lecture videos, programming assignments, and quizzes, as well as a community of teachers using the same resources.

The SPOC model also gave students the opportunity to explore online learning, a model that they will likely need after college. Through assignments that asked them to compare their experience reading the textbook and watching the associated recorded lectures, we helped students think about mechanisms of learning that best serve them.[3]

Alumni mentors. Students engaging in these projects benefit from multiple kinds of mentoring. They need advice on design. They need help finding the libraries that will best serve their project. They need help navigating the complexities of working with a non-technical partner. They need ways to handle the ambiguities inherent in building new software, from forming appropriate requirements to recovering from surprising and inexplicable bugs.

While we have a successful peer mentoring program within the department, we decided that the students would be better served by alumni mentors who had significant experience working with Ruby on Rails. Ruby on Rails is a complex ecosystem and one that evolves frequently; practitioners who use it daily can draw on comprehsensive knowledge and understanding than ours. Alumni mentors can also give students a sense of how their work reflected actual industry practice; it's one thing to hear from a faculty member that a technique or approach is useful, it's another to hear it from someone who uses it in industry. The alumni mentors also provide an opportunity for students to consider what their life might be like after college. Many mentors have dealt with the complexity of non-technical clients and provide a resource for students struggling with those issues. By relying on remote alumni mentors, we would give students the experience of working with others who are not physically present. Finally, the cohort of alumni mentors can serve as a broader "panel of advisors" to all projects.

This program also builds deeper relationships between alumni and the college. Our Office of Alumni Relations reports that many alumni clamor for more opportunities to support students.

Partnering with the career development office. Because the software design course naturally connects to their post-college work and because working with a non-technical partner requires a

[2]We found it useful to support this understanding with a professional text on object-oriented design in Ruby.[15]

[3]Many also appreciated our instructions to watch the video lecture with no distractions and with a notebook in hand.

very different skill set, we partnered with the career development office to present in class at the beginning of the semester.

While we formed project teams primarily on the basis of student interest in project topics and partners, we emphasized the importance of diverse skills and perspectives within teams. For the first two years of the course, a member of the career development office joined the class to give students a personal inventory, such as Myers-Briggs or Strengths Finder, and to help help students explore the meanings of their results.[4] They also helped students understand how different characteristics affect their teams and the benefits of building teams with multiple talents.

More importantly, a member of the office helps the students understand the complexities and subtleties of working in our community. We are fortunate that our career development office has a community outreach coordinator who can speak not only to issues of professionalism, but also to broader issues of our community. The discussion touches on a broad variety of issues, including socio-economic status[5], network access[6], biases townspeople have about college students, and biases students have about the townspeople.

Most importantly, our coordinator helps tease out issues through interactive discussion, as the following examples illustrate.

You want to be professional in your conversations with your client. Should you contact your client via text messages? No, of course not. *You'll find that it depends on the particular partners. In fact, some of our partners prefer text messages. It lets them easily group the messages and reply on their own timeframe. The most important thing is that you understand your client's preferred mode of communication.*

What about clothes? Should men wear a button-down shirt and a tie to meetings? That seems professional. *Once again, it depends on who you are meeting with. If you to a meeting with farmers on their farm, and wear dress shoes and a button-down shirt, they may think that you are setting yourself above them, that you are not very sensible, or both. You should usually dress at about the same level as your client, so make sure to pay attention in your first meeting. I'm happy to advise you about what is appropriate for that first meeting.*

You need to meet with your client. How much lead time is necessary? It depends. *It's good to see that you've learned. Some clients have full schedules and may want as much as two-weeks of lead time before you meet. I'd recommend that you set up your meeting time for the semester in advance. You should also agree on mechanisms for contacting them when you have short followup questions that do not require an in-person meeting. Others clients unpredictable schedules and won't want to schedule more than a few days in advance. Just make sure that you learn what is best for your client.*

[4]We have discontinued the use of these instruments based on discussions with our colleagues in Psychology who expressed reservations about their validity. However, we have found some success in providing students with a list of characteristics and descriptions of those characteristics, asking them to pick those that best describe themselves, and then having them share with their project team. That approach provides three useful outcomes: It helps them understand the kinds of characteristics that are discussed in the workplace, it encourages them to self-reflect, and it provides a good starting point for team formation.

[5]For example, students are surprised to hear that while the unemployment rate in town is at about 3%, over one-third of students in our school district are eligible for free or reduced lunches.

[6]Students are surprised to hear that for many families, broadband is not a possibility and cell-phone data is their primary connection to the Internet.

4 WAR STORIES

Of course, not everything goes smoothly. In this section, we describe some problems we've encountered and suggest lessons from each.

Revealing an AWS key. We ask students to use Git to manage their projects. While many have prior experience with Git, most expand their understanding and usage, moving from a single branch to multiple branches, and from pushing to sending pull requests. Because many students had learned Git informally and because the Internet is full of mediocre advice, some students employ poor Git practices. For example, there is a group of students who frequently write "`git add .; git commit`.[7]" As one might expect, that can lead to inappropriate materials in public repositories.

We discovered one such case indirectly. The instructor received a call from Amazon.com asking, "Do you realize that $5,000 has been charged to your AWS account in the past two days?"[8] It appears that students joining a project in the second semester had ignored their predecessors' instructions and put the AWS key in a public repository. Since repositories are regularly scraped for such keys, it took little time for the now-public key to be found and used.[9]

That experience proved instructive not just for that semester's students but also for subsequent students. Students learned not only that there are consequences when they inappropriately reveal information, but also that such experiences are not uncommon. The more important lessons were about the technical and nontechnical issues involved in keeping some information private in a project that is primarily public. Students needed to figure out technical issues, such as how to update the `.gitignore` file to ensure that the key would not be included even by someone new to the project who follows poor Git practices, how to configure the system to read that key from an environment variable, and how to set environment variables in a platform like Heroku. But they also needed to decide on practices. For example, how do you share a private key among team members without accidentally revealing it to others? While there are some common practices, and any organization they joined would have standards, we saw value in letting students think through the issue and compare strategies.

Revealing personal information. Lazy Git practice has created other problems. One group, while developing an online directory for a local retirement community, accidentally included photographs of all the residents in their public GitHub repository. In addition to the obvious privacy issues, adding a large number of photographs significantly increases the download time for cloning the repository.

Fortunately, we caught this problem before any personal information was revealed.[10] Students had to learn how to "scrub" a GitHub repository: beyond removing the photographs from the repository, it was essential for them to remove the photographs from the repository's history.

This experience highlighted an issue that students regularly struggle with: The overall structure of the project should be public so that others can adapt or adopt it, but some portions need to be

[7]That is, add any new or changed files in or below the current directory and commit those files to the repository.

[8]During development, the instructor had allowed the students to set up an AWS account and to use his credit card.

[9]Fortunately, an Amazon employee noted that Amazon had also found the key in the repository, was sympathetic, and waived the charge.

[10]It helps that the photos were all in a single zip file.

customized for the client. How do you appropriately separate the two? Admittedly, this remains an issue that students struggle with. Too often, they consider the two aspects of the project together, rather than separately. We continue to draw on this example in helping them reflect on this design issue.

Uncooperative IT departments. We have had at least two instances in which students finished a project for a larger non-profit with its own IT department and then found the IT staff less cooperative than we expected. In one case, the software effectively disappeared after it was passed to the client's IT department. They thanked us, but did not seem to have the time or enthusiasm to install it. In the second case, the IT staff agreed to provide a server for the students to install software, but it took two months of conversation to open port 80 on that server. At that point, students students were left without enough time to complete a release.

In both cases, we were able to help students focus on positive outcomes. While the projects did not get released, they had some confidence that they would benefit others by releasing their software with an open source license. In both cases, it was clear that their regular client meetings had evolved partners' thinking about their projects and processes.

We continue to explore ways to handle this broader issue of transitioning the project to partner organizations. In most cases, it appears that using a common cloud platform, such as Heroku, serves both the students and the partner organizations well.

Changes in management. Through the years, management of our partner organizations has sometimes changed. Often, the new manager has a very different view of what the project should do. In one case, the initial project request was for a group text messaging system with a Web interface. We'd been surprised by the original project requirements since free software with similar functionality exists. However, the client felt that they had particular enough requirements that a custom solution was necessary. When management changed, the usage model also changed. Instead of a Web interface, the client now wanted what was essentially a text-message expander; they would text to one number and have that text broadcast to a variety of other numbers. Students met the change with good nature; they arranged for a phone number, identified and incorporated SMS receipt libraries, explored security issues, such as how to limit who could use the service, and designed a protocol to make it easy for the client to select the recipient list. Then management changed again. And the new manager decided that free software did a good enough job.

This situation was particularly challenging to help students through. Since the organization's personnel changed, we could not emphasize the broader benefits to organizational understanding. Because similar free software existed, students did not think that there would be a benefit to releasing their work as free-and-open-source software. In the end, we focused on what the students had learned from the project and on ways they could share that knowledge with future students who might need to incorporate SMS in future projects.

5 OUTCOMES

We have seen a variety of positive outcomes from the redesign. As already mentioned, the design provides clearer connections to their post-college careers and work experiences and students feel more committed to these projects because they understand the potential impact. More broadly, they understand that the work they can do as computer scientists can have real and meaningful value.

We see significant growth in student's soft skills, a particularly important learning outcome. Because students must regularly meet with a non-technical partner, understand the partner's needs, and describe their technical work to the partner, they greatly expand their communication skills. As is often the case with small teams, they develop better interpersonal skills. Because we ask them to reflect on and compare their individual strengths at the start of the semester, they think more broadly about those skills and the skills a successful project requires. Because we do not require that projects be finished in the semester and because we tell the students to time-box their work, they not only feel less stress, but are more willing to agree upon appropriate levels of ambition.

Ruby on Rails has proven both a strength and a weakness of the course. By the end of the semester, when they've started to develop a better understanding of the Rails model, many students now realize that they are able to put together a small, database-backed, Web application in about a week of full-time work, at least if everything goes as expected. That realization gives them a sense of self-efficacy and accomplishment. At the same time, most also understand that if things don't go right, and they often don't, there are additional challenges to face.

We hope that these kinds of challenges help them develop broader skills in learning how to learn. Most are used to situations in which the answers can be found in a textbook, from the instructor, or, too frequently, on Stack Overflow. Doing design and facing unexpected problems leads students to situations in which they can't immediately find an answer. What do you do when Stack Overflow doesn't answer your question? They must develop skills in debugging (and in test-driven design that helps them debug), in searching broadly and on sites like Stack Overflow to find relevant answers, in analyzing the applicability of advice that doesn't quite match their problem, in adapting other solutions to their situation, and finally, in asking mentors for help. Some clearly develop these skills.

We also hope that these projects help students develop more of a tolerance of ambiguity. Most are accustomed to assignments with clear requirements; some find themselves frustrated that these project are open ended and, in many cases, they must develop their own requirements or, more precisely, translate their clients' requirements.

Unfortunately, we have not seen as many positive effects on end-of-course evaluations as we had hoped. While some students describe the course as the center of their CS education, others seem to find it almost pointless. As one student puts it, "In this course, more than most, what you get out of this course depends directly on what you put into the course." We continue to explore ways to help students better understand and embrace these benefits.

6 CONCLUSION AND RECOMMENDATIONS

By using a variety of traditional (e.g., real-world projects, agile practices) and novel components (e.g., alumni mentors, multi-semester projects, collaboration with the career development office), this course gives students more realistic experiences in software design.

These experiences develop not only technical skills but the less quantifiable soft skills that are essential to their future success.

While we find the combination of course design components particularly successful, others may find it useful to adapt just a few. Recommendations associated with some of the more novel aspects of the course follow.

Identifying alumni mentors. We have found LinkedIn to be a particularly useful tool for identifying alumni mentors. A search for people who attended the institution and who had experience with Ruby on Rails produced a small, but sufficiently large, list. Discussions with other faculty in the department helped us choose who to prioritize. The response rate to invitations was high.

Other approaches are possible. One might search a departmental alumni database, if one is available. One might broadcast a message to a mailing list of departmental alumni, although that approach might have the disadvantage of some alumni feeling disheartened that they volunteered and were not selected. They might be invited to serve as readers of the projects or to provide backup advice.[11]

It is also worth considering what to do across semesters: Do mentors continue from semester to semester, do you recruit a new cohort each semester, or do you rotate a few in and out each semester? We chose to use the same cohort of alumni each semester. By preserving the cohort, we ensure that the alumni develop a deeper understanding of the course and what students are and are not capable of. Alumni mentors also provide some institutional memory for ongoing projects as students come and go; that can be particularly helpful if the course rotates between faculty members. Of course, there are also benefits in a rotating group of mentors, including providing a wider range of experiences and expanding the opportunities for student-alumni connections.

Partnering with career development. We have found it productive to partner with our career development office. The training they give students before meeting with community partners and the guidance that they give throughout the semester are invaluable. For those reasons, we highly recommend partnering with your corresponding office.

In the absence of such institutional support, it is still possible to run your own "preparing to meet with your community partner" session. As we suggest in the section on our work with career development, it is useful to help students get a broader sense of issues in the community, to help students unpack their own biases about the community the likely biases the community has about them, and to help them figure out the non-technical questions to discuss in the first meeting with the client. You will find it useful to brainstorm with the students to help them prepare appropriate questions for their first partner meetings.

Identifying community partners. Getting the right partners is important. The course requires not only projects of the right scope and scale, but also partners who will understand the issues associated with working with a student development team and who is willing to accept a slow development process. You learn many of these things in preliminary meetings with potential partners; we recommend having such meetings in the prior semester, if at all possible. Expect to interview many more potential partners than the number of projects you need.

We are fortunate to have an outreach coordinator who helps with these kinds of issues. Among other things, they are careful to make sure that neither side overcommits. Our coordinator is particularly good at saying "that seems like too much", particularly when we discuss the scale of the project or the time commitments on both sides. They have also been useful in helping the partner understand possible projects and accept the limitations of working with students.

If your institution has someone in this role, we encourage you to work with them. If not, it is worthwhile to recruit someone who can serve a similar role–someone who can provide context, who listens carefully, and who cautions both sides against over-committing.

Choosing a common technology. While the choice of Ruby on Rails in particular had both benefits and drawbacks, the choice of a common technology for all projects had clear benefits. It lets us devote time and resources to explicitly teaching the technology, as appropriate to a course sometimes taken by sophomores. It lets students learn from each other's mistakes and triumphs. It let us recruit mentors with relevant technical expertise before we knew exactly what the projects would be, and has allowed mentors to continue their involvements as projects have changed. Finally, it limited the range of appropriate projects, which helped us communicate more concretely with potential partners about what our students could do in the course.

Time-boxing. We highly recommend timeboxing, both of individual tasks and of students' total hours of work on the project each week. That said, time-boxing is strange to most students. They are used to assignments which demand a particular product meeting detailed requirements. You support them in embracing the time-box model by providing clear expectations about process and quality and by giving regular feedback, particularly early in the semester. We have found weekly individual and group reports to be particularly useful.

Contextualizing the course. As we have suggested, not every student embraces the course. It is therefore essential to provide appropriate context for the course at the beginning of the semester. Explain to students what you expect them to get out of the course. For example, we focus on the benefits of learning soft skills, of making a difference in the community, of encountering more realistic situations, of developing the ability to put together a real product, and of recovering from difficulties.

ACKNOWLEDGMENTS

We appreciate the support of our community partners in this endeavor. They've been helpful, cooperative, and understanding. Our alumni mentors have also made for much better projects; their willingness to support our students with no compensation is a testimony to their commitment to our institution, the department, and the discipline. Our partners in Careers, Life, and Service, particularly Susan Sanning, have been essential to the class; we particularly appreciate their permission to share simulated versions of their Q&A session with the students.

[11]For example, please monitor this Slack channel for general questions on Ruby, Rails, and object-oriented design.

REFERENCES

[1] Association for Computing Machinery (ACM) and IEEE Computer Society Joint Task Force on Computing Curricula. 2013. *Computer Science Curricula 2013: Curriculum Guidelines for Undergraduate Degree Programs in Computer Science.* ACM, New York, NY, USA. 999133.

[2] Grant Braught, John Maccormick, James Bowring, Quinn Burke, Barbara Cutler, David Goldschmidt, Mukkai Krishnamoorthy, Wesley Turner, Steven Huss-Lederman, Bonnie Mackellar, and Allen Tucker. 2018. A Multi-Institutional Perspective on H/FOSS Projects in the Computing Curriculum. *ACM Trans. Comput. Educ.* 18, 2, Article 7 (July 2018), 31 pages. https://doi.org/10.1145/3145476

[3] Michael Buckley, Helene Kershner, Kris Schindler, Carl Alphonce, and Jennifer Braswell. 2004. Benefits of Using Socially-relevant Projects in Computer Science and Engineering Education. In *Proceedings of the 35th SIGCSE Technical Symposium on Computer Science Education (SIGCSE '04).* ACM, New York, NY, USA, 482–486. https://doi.org/10.1145/971300.971463

[4] Edward J. Coyle, Leah H. Jamieson, and William C. Oakes. 2006. 2005 Bernard M. Gordon Prize Lecture: Integrating Engineering Education and Community Service: Themes for the Future of Engineering Education. *Journal of Engineering Education* 95, 1 (2006), 7–11. https://doi.org/10.1002/j.2168-9830.2006.tb00873.x arXiv:https://onlinelibrary.wiley.com/doi/pdf/10.1002/j.2168-9830.2006.tb00873.x

[5] Armando Fox. 2014. Using MOOCs to Reinvigorate Software Engineering Education (Keynote). In *Companion Proceedings of the 36th International Conference on Software Engineering (ICSE Companion 2014).* ACM, New York, NY, USA, 255–255. https://doi.org/10.1145/2591062.2600730

[6] Armando Fox and David Patterson. 2014. *Engineering Software as a Service: An Agile Approach Using Cloud Computing.* Strawberry Canyon LLC.

[7] I. A. Garcia and C. L. Pacheco. 2014. Using TSPi and PBL to Support Software Engineering Education in an Upper-level Undergraduate Course. *Comput. Appl. Eng. Educ.* 22, 4 (Dec. 2014), 736–749. https://doi.org/10.1002/cae.21566

[8] Paul Gestwicki. 2018. Design and Evaluation of an Undergraduate Course on Software Development Practices. In *Proceedings of the 49th ACM Technical Symposium on Computer Science Education (SIGCSE '18).* ACM, New York, NY, USA, 221–226. https://doi.org/10.1145/3159450.3159542

[9] Grinnell College. [n. d.]. Mission statement. Online document available at https://www.grinnell.edu/about/mission.

[10] Michael Hartl. 2016. *The Ruby on Rails Tutorial, 4th Edition.* Addison-Wesley.

[11] David K. Lange, Roger C. Ferguson, and Paul M. Leidig. 2011. An Update on the Use of Community-based Non-profit Organizations in Capstone Projects. In *Proceedings of the 16th Annual Joint Conference on Innovation and Technology in Computer Science Education (ITiCSE '11).* ACM, New York, NY, USA, 372–372. https://doi.org/10.1145/1999747.1999885

[12] Paul M. Leidig, Roger Ferguson, and Jonathan Leidig. 2006. The Use of Community-based Non-profit Organizations in Information Systems Capstone Projects. In *Proceedings of the 11th Annual SIGCSE Conference on Innovation and Technology in Computer Science Education (ITICSE '06).* ACM, New York, NY, USA, 148–152. https://doi.org/10.1145/1140124.1140165

[13] Chang Liu. 2005. Enriching Software Engineering Courses with Service-learning Projects and the Open-source Approach. In *Proceedings of the 27th International Conference on Software Engineering (ICSE '05).* ACM, New York, NY, USA, 613–614. https://doi.org/10.1145/1062455.1062566

[14] Shaoying Liu, Kazuhiro Takahashi, Toshinori Hayashi, and Toshihiro Nakayama. 2009. Teaching Formal Methods in the Context of Software Engineering. *SIGCSE Bull.* 41, 2 (June 2009), 17–23. https://doi.org/10.1145/1595453.1595457

[15] Sandi Metz. 2012. *Pratical Object-Oriented Design in Ruby: An Agile Primer.* Addison-Wesley.

[16] Lori Postner, Heidi J.C. Ellis, and Gregory W. Hislop. 2018. A Survey of Instructors' Experiences Supporting Student Learning Using HFOSS Projects. In *Proceedings of the 49th ACM Technical Symposium on Computer Science Education (SIGCSE '18).* ACM, New York, NY, USA, 203–208. https://doi.org/10.1145/3159450.3159524

[17] Elizabeth Sweedyk. 2011. How Middle School Teachers Solved Our SE Project Problems. In *Proceedings of the 2011 24th IEEE-CS Conference on Software Engineering Education and Training (CSEET '11).* IEEE Computer Society, Washington, DC, USA, 449–453. https://doi.org/10.1109/CSEET.2011.5876123

[18] Elizabeth Sweedyk and Robert M. Keller. 2005. Fun and Games: A New Software Engineering Course. In *Proceedings of the 10th Annual SIGCSE Conference on Innovation and Technology in Computer Science Education (ITiCSE '05).* ACM, New York, NY, USA, 138–142. https://doi.org/10.1145/1067445.1067485

[19] Ursula Wolz and Sarah Monisha Pulimood. 2007. An Integrated Approach to Project Management Through Classic CS III and Video Game Development. In *Proceedings of the 38th SIGCSE Technical Symposium on Computer Science Education (SIGCSE '07).* ACM, New York, NY, USA, 322–326. https://doi.org/10.1145/1227310.1227422

Does Social Sensitivity Impact Virtual Teams?

Lisa L. Lacher†
College of Science and Engineering
University of Houston – Clear Lake
Houston, Texas USA
Lacher@uhcl.edu

Cydnee Biehl
College of Science and Engineering
University of Houston – Clear Lake
Houston, Texas USA
BiehlC1770@uhcl.edu

ABSTRACT

Working effectively as part of a team is an incredibly important skill to learn. Most jobs require interacting and working with others and the outcome of a team project relies on the processes of the group members. Naturally, a positive team experience yields better results than a negative experience. The biggest indicators of a positive team experience are communication and collaboration, which are both soft skills associated with the social sensitivity of the group members. Previous research has found that social sensitivity influences the amount of communication and the ultimate performance of traditional face-to-face teams. However, virtual teamwork is becoming more common. Does social sensitivity have a similar influence in virtual teams? Virtual teams have different interactions than face-to-face teams because they use communication technologies, which can hinder certain human cognitive processes. Our current research focuses on the influence of social sensitivity on the amount of communication and the performance of students who work as a virtual team using text-based communication in Discord. We find that teams with higher average levels of social sensitivity communicate more and perform better, even if they work in a virtual environment using only text messaging.

CCS CONCEPTS

• Information Systems • Collaborative and social computing systems and tools

KEYWORDS: Collaboration, Communication, Social Sensitivity, Soft Skills, Teams, Teamwork, Virtual Teamwork

ACM Reference format:

Lisa L. Lacher & Cydnee Biehl. 2019. Does Social Sensitivity Impact Virtual Teams?. In *Proceedings of 50th ACM Technical Symposium on Computer Science Education (SIGCSE '19), February 27-March 2, 2019, Minneapolis, MN, USA.* ACM, New York, NY, USA, 7 pages.
https://doi.org/10.1145/3287324.3287409

ACM ISBN 978-1-4503-5890-3/19/02...$15.00
https://doi.org/10.1145/3287324.3287409

1 INTRODUCTION

The recent growth of teamwork in education and industry is due to the growing need for large, complex projects that require the skill set of many people to accomplish [1]. The success of a team's ability to function effectively relies on certain soft skills, such as collaboration and effective communication. Past studies indicate that using these soft skills to influence interpersonal interactions is imperative to team health, success, and a positive team experience [2]. In academia, team projects are used to help students gain build collaboration skills. Group projects and team assignments give students more opportunities to develop their soft skills however, students tend to have more negative experiences rather than positive when working in a team. This is partly due to troubles collaborating and working together [3]. Most prominently, students find 'social loafing' to be incredibly challenging – this is a behavior seen by team members where individuals do not do a fair share of project work [4,5]. While this is an issue in traditional face-to-face (F2F) teams, virtual teams are more susceptible to this challenge.

Wooley et al. [6] first established a correlation between social sensitivity (SS) and effective teamwork. They found that team performance was not driven by the intelligence of team individuals, but rather by how well teams conversed and contributed equally (measured by each individual's amount of speaking). In particular, groups with higher SS levels were more collectively intelligent. Other research [7] has found that teams with higher levels of SS perform better than teams with lower SS. This research involved traditional F2F teams; however, we were uncertain if this applies to virtual teams. Just as with F2F teams, teammates of virtual teams need to be aware of their interpersonal interactions with group members. SS is the ability to accurately understand the emotions of other people and react accordingly; it is reliably measurable and key to mediating teamwork satisfaction [1]. SS impacts a person's comprehension of others emotions by *looking* at their eyes. Our university is non-residential, thus students live off-campus. Plus, a majority of our course's students work more than twenty-hours per week. Consequently, it was essential for them to function like virtual teams. Our course also had deaf students who could not use verbal communication tools, thus we decided on using a tool that used a text-based environment. However, in a text-based virtual environment, it is impossible to look in teammates' eyes. Thus, our research goal is to examine the correlation between student virtual team participation and performance and the SS of the teammates.

The remainder of this paper is structured as follows. Section 2 provides background information on virtual teams, social sensitivity, instant messaging, and Discord. Section 3 describes the design of the empirical study conducted to investigate the effects of social sensitivity on virtual team performance. Section 4 describes the data analysis and results. Section 5 discusses the threats to validity. Section 6 provides a discussion of the results based on the analysis performed in Section 4. Section 7 concludes the paper and provides a summary of future research.

2 BACKGROUND AND RELATED WORK

The ability to work effectively in teams is a needed soft skill in all team environments. This is especially true in virtual teams as they are unique in terms of geographically dispersed members with limited physical contact [8]. Virtual teams usually refer to people who work from different locations and rely on communication technologies to collaborate. Because virtual teams lack physical presence with one another, they heavily rely on online communication tools to collaborate. By using effective instant messaging (IM) applications, virtual team interactions can lead to a more positive team experience [9]. Lack of equal contribution in a virtual team environment is a struggle due to the complications caused by trying to get everyone to work at the same capacity – should this fail, rifts in team health could occur [8]. For teams that must perform virtually, the challenges that were most reported were social loafing and group members not willing to point out the lack of performance by other members [10].

Virtual teams, while efficient, face many more challenges than teams that can meet physically. Communication between teammates is far more difficult in virtual teams than traditional teams. Project Management Institute considers communication between virtual team members to be approximately four times more challenging than communicating F2F [11]. Because virtual team members have limited, if any, physical interaction, online interactions are harder to gauge for those with lower levels of SS [8]. Since SS is comprehendible by recognition of facial emotion on a nonverbal level [1], in an online environment, understanding emotions through only text could prove difficult. Teammates should be cognizant of their words when communicating in a virtual setting due to the large margin for misinterpretation and uncertainty by chatting via text. Spreading knowledge F2F is much faster and gives little room for error in understanding compared to doing this virtually [12].

2.1 Social Sensitivity

SS is the capability of an individual to observe and comprehend the emotions of others and react accordingly. A common test to measure SS levels is "Reading the Mind in the Eyes" created by Baron-Cohen, which tests the ability of individuals to judge feelings by looking only at a person's eyes [13]. Baron-Cohen states that individuals in the fields of math, engineering, physics, and computer science tend to have lower SS than those in art, humanities, and social sciences [13], thus students in computing-related fields are prone to experience difficulties in teams.

Though SS is a skill that is different for everyone, the average SS of a team can predict the overall performance of the team [1,6,7]. Prior research states that teams with higher SS are more likely to work together in the future [1]. The quality of interactions between group members is essential for a positive team experience and that quality relies on the social sensitivity of each group member [14]. The success of a team relies very heavily on SS which is a factor to consider when forming teams. Due to SS being based upon individuals accurately distinguishing the emotions of another person and behaving accordingly, it's essential for team members to possess excellent relational skills to contribute to a positive team experience. Considering the correlation between SS and team outcome, it has primarily been examined in traditional F2F teams [1, 7] but there has been little examination on this correlation in virtual teams.

2.2 Instant Messaging

Instant messaging (IM) is text-based communication that more users are preferring over email due to the nearly immediate send and response times [15]. Currently, some IM tools are utilizing voice and video functionality to make messaging feel closer to physical communication. In cases like ours and many others, personal responsibilities, commute times, and conflicting schedules interfere with physical collaboration. When this happens, IM is most beneficial to allow for collaboration outside of scheduled class and work hours [8]. For example, our study examines students with a need for virtual team communication as none of them live on campus due to it being non-residential and they all have varying commute time.

2.3 Discord

Discord is a chat tool originally created for use in online gaming. Because this tool is well-liked in the gaming industry, we hoped that it would provide a useful and enjoyable environment for student communication and collaboration on educational projects. Discord is a free to use tool with open-source capabilities to give users the freedom and creativity to write bots within the software that can have the ability to automate tasks and messages for themselves and other users. This feature opens many possibilities for effective utilization. Recent studies [15] have shown that using this form of instant messaging tool has positively assisted and enhanced student to student interactions. Because Discord's communication is primarily text-based, these chat logs can be exported and retained via Discord History Tracker (DHT). Written as a browser script, DHT gives users the ability to download their chat history into a text file to save for their records or use as they see fit. When active, the script will take a few moments (depending on the number of messages to save) to load the entire chat history from the very first to the very last messages to a log that can be saved or appended for future use. When inactive, a user can upload these logs within a web browser to the DHT website to view all logs even after being deleted from the Discord chat. This is especially helpful to prevent the loss of messages due to people deleting them individually. DHT is also incredibly useful to save chat history for personal records or to run analysis on. Discord is one of many other online communication tools with an ability to foster collaboration and communication by allowing users to contribute when convenient to mitigate issues that interfere with physical group meetings.

3 STUDY DESIGN

We designed a mixed methods study to analyze the relationship between student team SS, communication amounts between those teams, IT team project quality, and satisfaction levels with team members. We investigate whether student teams with higher average SS have a positive correlation with their actual project performance as measured by grades. In this study, we also analyze the relationship between SS and team satisfaction based on peer reviews as well as the perceived team leaders.

3.1 Study Goals and Hypotheses

We formulated the following hypotheses:

Hypothesis 1: Student teams with higher average SS scores perform significantly better on the project.

Hypothesis 2: Student teams with higher average SS scores will communicate significantly more.

Hypothesis 3: Peers perceive students with lower SS scores as contributing less to the project.

Hypothesis 4: Team leaders would have the highest level of SS on the team.

3.2 Independent and Dependent Variables

The experiment manipulated the following independent variable:

a) *Social Sensitivity Score*: Each student participant completed the "Reading the Mind in the Eyes" test [13] in order to determine their individual SS score.

We measured the following dependent variables:

b) *Team Performance*: This measure includes the average scores on the three project deliverables for each team.

c) *Discord Chat*: This measure includes the total amount of text communication, determined by the sum of the number of words posted in Discord by each team member during the semester.

d) *Non-contributor*: Researchers assigned a binary value representing student contribution to the projects by evaluating peer comments related to student contribution.

3.3 Participating Subjects

Thirty-three undergraduate IT and computer information systems students participated in this study. The participating subjects (6 females and 27 males) worked in teams on a project involving researching, analyzing, evaluating, reporting and presenting an IT emerging technology. The National Center for Education Statistics [16] defines nontraditional students anyone who meets one of the following conditions: delays post-secondary enrollment, attends part-time, works full-time, or has dependents. Based on this definition, 15 of the students were traditional students and 18 students were non-traditional.

3.4 Artifacts

During the semester, each student team completed three projects. Each project consisted of an Evaluation, Feasibility or Recommendation Report and a group presentation based on a topic of their choice related to the following categories: IT infrastructure, security or Internet of Things, and any emerging information technology not previously covered. Teams chose different topics (such as DRaaS, 5G networks, 3D printers, RFID, virtualization, solid-state drives, security as a service, smart homes, IoT security, medical robotics, penetration testing, augmented reality in network education, evaluation methods for autonomous cars) and met virtually using Discord to produce these deliverables.

3.5 Experimental Procedure

We performed all surveys using Blackboard. The study steps are as follows:

a) *Step 1 – Test Subjects for Social Sensitivity*: We administered the "Reading the Mind in the Eyes" test [13] online at the beginning of the semester to measure each subject's SS. We provided a glossary [13] that contained a definition and sample sentence for each of the selection choices used in the test to help ensure that participants had a clear understanding of their definitions. The students were encouraged to study the glossary prior to the test and to refer to it as needed during the test.

b) *Step 2 – Forming Student Teams*: A pre-study student survey was done to find information such as whether students preferred to work alone or in teams and if they had previous professional IT experience. Because of class time constraints, we formed six teams so that each team would have twenty minutes to present. Eleven students indicated that they were currently working as IT professionals. Because previous experience can have a great impact on performance, we randomly assigned experienced students to each of six groups as evenly as possible. Then we randomly assigned all other students to those groups, thus each group had between five to six group members. All teams had a relatively even mix of traditional and non-traditional students.

c) *Step 3 – Peer-Self Evaluations*: At the end of each project, the students completed an evaluation on their perception of the contribution of each team member as well as themselves. The evaluation included questions related to how much each team member contributed to researching, creating and designing project materials, quality of contribution, equally splitting workload, and level of cooperation to create an overall percentage of total project contribution. We averaged the percentages for each team member.

d) *Step 4 – Evaluating Team Projects*: Scores were determined for each deliverable using detailed rubrics to structure the grading for both the project report and presentation. We used this grade for the team performance measure. However, individual team member scores were determined by multiplying their peer evaluated contribution percentage by the team score. It was determined that at least one team member should earn 100 percent of the earned team score. If peer evaluations did not score at least one member as contributing 100 percent, we scaled all of the peer evaluation percentages so that the top evaluation was 100 percent.

e) *Step 5 – Evaluate Quantity of Communication*: Teams were encouraged to use Discord to collaborate on their projects. Although Discord allows verbal communication, we turned that feature off so that students could only text. We did this so it is easier to capture the quantity of text communication than verbal communication and because one of the students in the course is deaf and Discord does not currently have a speech to text interface that s/he could use, thus we required all students to use text.

We downloaded each team's chat history, captured by Discord History Tracker, immediately after the completion of each project so that no additional chat messages would be included. We then wrote a Python program to analyze the data collected and recorded the number of words each team member texted. Students used many emoji's, web links and images in their text conversations. In our calculations, each emoji, web link, and image counted as one word. We totaled all the words texted by a team's members in order to calculate the total amount of communication produced by a team.

f) *Step 6 – Post-Study Survey*: We administered an eighteen-question survey to the students at the end of the semester. The post-study survey collected general demographics data, as well as data regarding the self-perceived effectiveness of each team, and various questions related to how their teams used Discord as well as the self-perceived usefulness and value of using Discord to collaborate on team projects. We told students we would not view survey results until after we submitted course grades. We did this so students would feel comfortable providing honest answers and not feel that their answers would affect their course grade.

3.6 Data Collection and Evaluation Criterion

Figure 1 shows individual student SS test scores for each of the 33 participating subjects. The SS scores range from a minimum of 14 to a maximum of 31, with most subjects scoring in the range of 23 to 27. Interestingly, our mean sample score of 25.03 was lower than the general population sample score of 26.2 reported by Baron-Cohen et al [13]. This lower than average score is similar to previous results that found that computing students had lower than average SS scores [1]. Team average SS scores were also calculated. The average team SS scores range from a minimum of 23 to a maximum of 26.4.

We summed the student team performances on the three project deliverables into a final project score for use in the analysis of the impact of the team's average SS on the project team scores. We averaged peer ratings for each team member from each project to create a peer satisfaction rating for each student. We analyzed peer evaluations for comments from peers that explicitly stated that a majority of peers were frustrated with that team member's lack of contribution. We also examined survey results to determine which students emerged as team leaders.

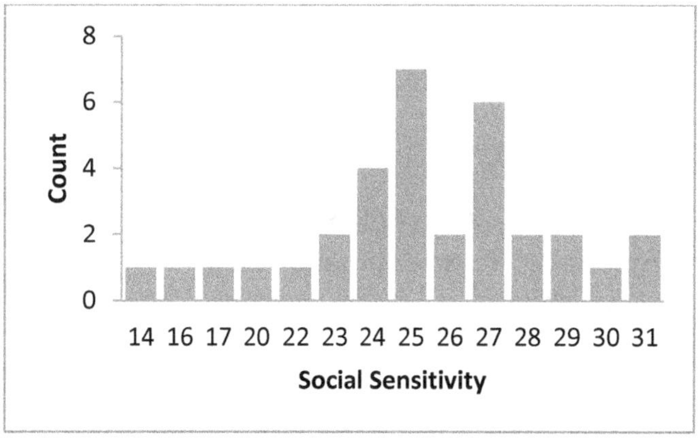

Figure 1. Individual Social Sensitivity Scores

4 DATA ANALYSIS AND RESULTS

This section is organized around the four hypotheses presented in Section 3.1 and provides analysis of the quantitative data that includes student's SS scores, their team's project performance, peer satisfaction, and team leader emergence. We used an alpha value of 0.05 for all statistical analysis and r2 value of 0.30 for correlations.

4.1 Analysis of the Effect of Social Sensitivity on Team's Project Performance

Earlier research [1,7] found that SS did have an effect on team performance for face-to-face teams. This section analyzes the connection between the student's SS and their performance on the team project that primarily took place within a virtual environment. Because each team consisted of five to six students, and the SS data from Step 1 was individual data, we combined the individual SS scores were into one team score. We calculated the SS score of each team by averaging the individual team member's SS scores. The performance of each team (i.e. project score) was the average of the raw team scores earned on each project.

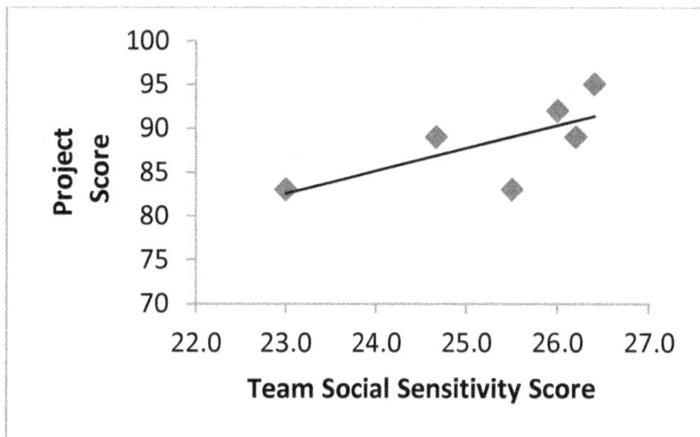

Figure 2. Effect of Social Sensitivity on Team Performance

Figure 2 plots each team's average SS score against their team total project score. To test hypothesis 1, we calculated a Pearson's product moment correlation coefficient to measure the relationship between team average SS and team performance. The results show that the team SS score had a significant positive correlation with the total team score with r(4) = 0.714. Based on these results, we show that teams with higher average SS performed significantly better on their project.

4.2 Analysis of the Effect of Social Sensitivity on Amount of Team Communication

We performed further analysis to investigate the connection between team SS and the amount of communication that occurs between virtual teams. Figure 3 plots each team's average SS score against their total project word count. To test hypothesis 2, we calculated a Pearson's product moment correlation coefficient to measure the relationship between team average SS and the quantity of team communication. The results show that the team SS score had a significant positive correlation with the total team communication with r(4) = 0.705. We also analyzed the relationship between individual SS scores (shown in Figure 1) and quantity of individual communication and with r(4)=0.255 we found no correlation. Based on these results, we show that teams with higher average SS communicate more on their projects.

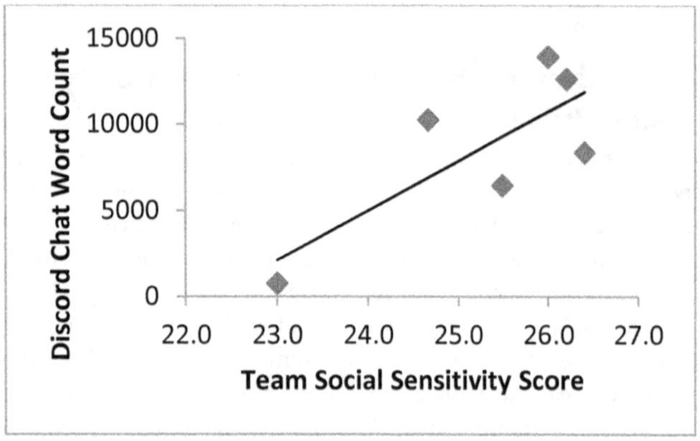

Figure 3. Effect of Social Sensitivity on Quantity of Team Communication

4.3 Analysis of the Effect of Social Sensitivity on Peer Perception of Team Member Contribution

One of our ultimate future goals for this project was to see if we could use Discord as a tool to improve teamwork and reduce conflict. One of the largest areas of conflict in student teams is social loafing [9]. We hypothesized that students who have a harder time understanding the emotions of their peers might be more susceptible of disengaging from the team and thus not contribute to the team's project. Originally, we had thought to average project peer evaluation ratings to determine average peer satisfaction. However, as we read through the comments we noticed that many students would be very frustrated with a team member who they felt did not contribute, but would still rate them fairly high because the team member was "part of the team" so we felt that an average peer rating would not be useful in determining this metric. Thus, we created a binary rating for each student within each project (1=contributed, 0=did not contribute) by analyzing the comments in the peer reviews. If the majority of team members specifically complained about a team member's lack of participation, then that team member received a contribution rating of 0 for that project. We then averaged those ratings to determine an overall course contribution rating. To test hypothesis 3, we calculated a Pearson's product moment correlation coefficient to measure the relationship between individual SS and contribution rating. The results show that individual SS score had a significant positive correlation with a lack of contribution with r(4) = 0.70 thus we conclude that appears that the lower the level of an individual's social sensitivity, the more at risk they are at not fully contributing to the project.

4.4 Analysis of the Effect of Social Sensitivity on Team Leader Characteristics

Empathy and good communication are a couple of the more important qualities of a good leader [18]. Salovey and Mayer [18] identify some of the characteristics of socially sensitive people to include the ability to admit mistakes, to accept others for who they are, to enhance other's moods, to be social problem solvers, to be flexible thinkers, and to have an interest in the world at large. This coupled with previous findings that teams with higher levels of SS communicate more led us to hypothesize that the team members that emerged as team leaders would have the highest levels of SS.

All teams expressed that they did not appoint leaders, but leaders emerged. Remarkably, every member on each team was consistent in who they identified as the leader of each team. However, with a r(4) = 0.324 we conclude that the person with the highest amount of SS is not necessarily going to be the natural leader of the team. It is interesting to note, but perhaps not surprising, that the leader identified by each team was a non-traditional student. However, when we ran an analysis on the average peer satisfaction levels (as determined by peer evaluations) of team leaders versus average peer satisfaction levels of all other team members, the results show that the group's positivity towards their leader was higher than the positivity with other team members by an amount that was statistically significant (p=0.001).

5 THREAT TO VALIDITY

Although the results of this study are encouraging, there are certain threats to validity that exists. One such threat is sample size. In the study, we see very strong correlations between SS, team project performance, amount of team communication, and lack of participation. The sample size is small, so further testing should be performed.

Another threat lies with the fact that some students may have had more familiarity with Discord than others. As mentioned earlier, Discord is a popular collaboration tool for gamers. One of the reasons for its popularity is its ease of use. In the pre-survey, we found that all students were familiar with texting and that many of the students (roughly one third) in our study did have previous exposure to Discord. To mitigate this threat, we randomly assigned team members, we provided training documents and held a training session in class to get students logged into their channels and initially communicating with their other team members.

Yet, another threat is that not all communication occurred in Discord. This class was not an online class and students did get to see their team members in class. This does help team members develop a certain amount of trust more quickly than if they had to work together completely online. Also, there is the availability of a wide variety of technological tools that virtual teams can use to collaborate and communicate (e.g. standard instant messaging, Slack, Google Hangouts, Skype, etc.) However, answers to questions on our post-survey allow us to conclude that other than the use of Google drive to assemble the written report and presentation slides, most teams primarily used Discord to communicate.

6 DISCUSSION OF RESULTS

One of our fundamental study findings is that SS appears to be a good predictor of team performance within teams that are required to work together virtually. Better team performance could be the result of the greater amount of communication that happens in teams with higher average levels of SS. This extends previous research [1, 7] that showed that SS had high impact on teams that were able to meet F2F. Students can definitely have difficulties with virtual teamwork. When having a F2F discussion with group members, there is an instantaneous response in communication and there can be response lags in a virtual environment - or no response at all. This can cause issues when needing to make important decisions or plans as a team and that can affect the success of the group. There also tends to be issues with understanding intent in text-based messages due to not being present to hear inflections in a person's voice. This is significant as misinterpreting messages can cause unnecessary rifts in team dynamic and can potentially damage the team's health as well as the accomplishments of the team. It appears that the higher levels of SS may help mitigate these issues.

Although we found correlations between team SS and team communication, we did not find any correlation between individual SS and individual levels of communication. This means that an individual's SS level does not have an impact on how much they personally communicate – they are not directly responsible for the higher quantity of communication by posting more chats. But instead, they appear to be indirectly responsible, perhaps by encouraging others to communicate more thus getting a greater diversity of ideas and input which, in turn, results in higher performance. We would need to do further analysis as we continue this study to gain a better understanding. We also did not find any correlation between the team leaders' SS and the amount that they communicated. However, when analyzing the post-survey we found that many of the identified leaders reported using open-ended questions and encouraging emoji's to foster more communication from others.

A very useful finding is that the lower the level of an individual's social sensitivity, the more at risk they are at for slacking on a project and not fully contributing. Although teams with higher levels of team SS tend to communicate more; we do not know how the quantity of communication for students with lower levels of SS would differ based on the higher or lower average level of the team social sensitivity. However, we hope that this finding can help signal educators that certain students might need more help and encouragement than others during these projects.

7 CONCLUSION AND FUTURE WORK

Our results indicate that the performance of virtual teams is positively correlated with the SS of its members. Our results also indicate that the amount of communication within a team also positively correlates with the SS its members. Our results also show that students with lower levels of SS may be at risk of not fully participating in team projects. Our study and results are novel in that we investigated the impact of SS in the virtual space. We believe these results are valuable. It has been shown that more communication between team members leads to higher quality work [1]. Of course, teams need members with the correct technical skill sets; however, with the growth of tele-work and virtual teams in industry, it may be valuable to consider using SS as an attribute to consider when forming teams. Using quantitative data related to work in virtual teams, our work demonstrates compelling preliminary results.

We will continue this research during subsequent offerings of this course to collect more data. We also plan on performing sentiment analysis on the Discord chat data to see if we can determine if SS has an impact, not only on the quantity of communication, but the quality of the communication as well. All teams go through the forming-storming-norming-performing stages of group development, but we would like to see if groups that have higher levels of SS get to the performing stages more quickly, and have a less turbulent journey through the other stages. We hope that by analyzing both the quantity and quality of communication will help us model when student groups are having troubles working together (beyond the typical difficulties of group development) so that we can create a bot for Discord that will automatically alert an instructor of the teamwork problem so an early intervention can help get the student team get back on track as soon as possible.

REFERENCES

[1] BENDER, L., WALIA, G., KAMBHAMPATY, K., NYGARD, K.E., AND NYGARD, T.E. 2012. Social sensitivity correlations with the effectiveness of team process performance. In *9th Annual International Conference on International Computing Education Research*, (Auckland, New Zealand), ICER'12. DOI: http://dx.doi.org/10.1145/2361276.2361285

[2] CHAN, C.L., JIANG, J.J., AND KLEIN, G. 2008. Team Task Skills as a Facilitator for Application and Development Skills. *IEEE Transactions on Engineering Management.* 55, 3 (Aug. 2008), 434-441.

[3] KAPP, E. 2009. Improving Student Teamwork in a Collaborative Project-Based Course. College Teaching 57, 3 (Summer 2009), 139–143. DOI: http://dx.doi.org/10.3200/ctch.57.3.139-143

[4] YANG, M. AND JIN, Y. 2008. An Examination of Team Effectiveness in Distributed and Co-Located Engineering Teams. *Int. J Engng. Ed., 24 (2)*, 400-408

[5] FONTENOT, M., CANALES, K., AND QUICKSALL, A. N. 2014. Taking care of the team in a first-year design experience course. In *2014 IEEE Frontiers in*

Education Conference Proceedings, (Madrid, Spain). DOI: http://dx.doi.org/10.1109/fie.2014.7044433
[6] WOOLLEY, A.W., CHABRIS, C.F., PENTLAND, A., HASHMI, N., AND MALONE, T.W. 2010. Evidence for a Collective Intelligence Factor in the Performance of Human Groups. *Science* 330, 6004, (686-688).
[7] BENDER, L., WALIA, G., KAMBHAMPATY, K., NYGARD, K.E., AND NYGARD, T.E., Social Sensitivity and Classroom Team Projects. In *Proceedings of the 43rd ACM Technical Symposium on Computer Science Education - SIGCSE 12,* (Raleigh, NC, USA).
[8] DULEBOHN, J.H. AND HOCH, J.E., Virtual Teams in Organizations, *Human Resource Management Review, Dec. 2017,* 569–574.
[9] PEÑARROJA, V., ORENGO, V., AND ZORNOZA, A., 2017. Reducing Perceived Social Loafing in Virtual Teams: The Effect of Team Feedback with Guided Reflexivity, *Journal of Applied Social Psychology,* 47, 8, 424–435.
[10] BORREGO, M., KARLIN, J., MCNAIR, L. D., AND BEDDOES, K. 2013. Team Effectiveness Theory from Industrial and Organizational Psychology Applied to Engineering Student Project Teams: A Research Review. *Journal of Engineering Education,* 102, 4, 472–512.
[11] RILEY, M. 2008. The Real Challenges of Leading Virtual Teams. In *PMI® Global Congress 2008,* (Denver, CO, USA), Project Management Institute.
[12] EDWARDS, A. AND WILSON, J. R. 2017. Implementing Virtual Teams: A Guide to Organizational and Human Factors. Routledge, London, UK.
[13] BARON-COHEN, S., WHEELWRIGHT, S., HILL, J., RASTE, Y., AND PLUMB, I. 2001. The 'Reading the Mind in the Eyes' Test Revised Version: A Study with Normal Adults, and Adults with Asperger Syndrome or High-functioning Autism. *Child Journal of Psychology and Psychiatry,* 42, 2, 241-251.
[14] CURŞEU, P. L., PLUUT, H., BOROŞ, S., AND MESLEC, N. 2014. The Magic of Collective Emotional Intelligence in Learning Groups: No Guys Needed for the Spell! *British Journal of Psychology,* 106, 2, 217–234.
[15] DRANGE, T. AND KARGAARD, J. 2017. Increasing Student/Student and Student/Lecturer Communication Through Available Tools to Create a Virtual Classroom Feeling in Online Education. In *The 13th International Scientific Conference eLearning and Software for Education,* (Bucharest, Romania).
[16] NCSE Definitions and Data. 2018. https://nces.ed.gov/pubs/web/97578e.asp
[17] CHU, J. 2016. The Impact of Ad hoc, Informal Communication on Virtual Team Effectiveness: A Study of IM Usage and Team Collaboration.
[18] SALOVEY, P. AND MAYER, J.D. 1990. Emotional Intelligence. *Imagination, Cognition, and Personality.* 9, 3, 185-211.

Student Performance in Computing Courses in the face of Growing Enrollments

Daniel T. Fokum
The University of the West Indies
Department of Computing
Mona, Jamaica
daniel.fokum@uwimona.edu.jm

Daniel N. Coore
The University of the West Indies
Department of Computing
Mona, Jamaica
daniel.coore@uwimona.edu.jm

Eyton Ferguson
The University of the West Indies
Department of Computing
Mona, Jamaica
eyton.ferguson@uwimona.edu.jm

Gunjan Mansingh
The University of the West Indies
Department of Computing
Mona, Jamaica
gunjuan.mansingh@uwimona.edu.jm

Carl Beckford
The University of the West Indies
Department of Computing
Mona, Jamaica
carl.beckford@uwimona.edu.jm

ABSTRACT

As computing enrollments have grown in the last decade there have been anecdotal claims from faculty that the discipline has attracted weaker students. To the best of our knowledge the only paper that has studied, and debunked, this claim has been based on data from an exclusive North American university. In this paper we examine data from six courses drawn taught over a 3 year period at a public university in a developing country. We find that in the case of the CS1 course, the distribution of student grades has fluctuated over this period. In addition, courses in object-oriented programming, networking, algorithms and discrete mathematics have also shown variation in student grades. We provide discussion as to why the grades in the courses show variation. We also explain why our findings differ from previous claims of stability in student grades.

CCS CONCEPTS

• **Social and professional topics** → *CS1*; *Student assessment*;

KEYWORDS

Enrollment growth; mixture modeling; student performance; introductory programming; algorithms

ACM Reference format:
Daniel T. Fokum, Daniel N. Coore, Eyton Ferguson, Gunjan Mansingh, and Carl Beckford. 2019. Student Performance in Computing Courses in the face of Growing Enrollments. In *Proceedings of the 50th ACM Technical Symposium on Computer Science Education, Minneapolis, MN, USA, February 27-March 2, 2019 (SIGCSE '19)*, 6 pages.
https://doi.org/10.1145/3287324.3287354

SIGCSE '19, February 27-March 2, 2019, Minneapolis, MN, USA

ACM ISBN 978-1-4503-5890-3/19/02...$15.00
https://doi.org/10.1145/3287324.3287354

1 INTRODUCTION

Computer Science (CS) enrollments have surged in the United States since 2006 [2]. Our institution, a public university in a developing country, has also experienced over 50% enrollment growth in its CS1 course. As CS enrollments have surged in the United States, there have been anecdotal claims that the discipline is attracting weaker students. However, using data from an eight year span at Stanford University, Sahami and Piech [7] showed that the distribution of student grades remained the same, and that there was no support for the claim that the CS discipline was attracting weaker student. The objectives of this paper are twofold:

(1) to determine if the observations of student performance at Stanford University–a private, selective institution–hold for a public university in a developing country.
(2) to evaluate the effectiveness of the methods of Sahami and Piech in the presence of data whose mixture models vary from one year to the next.

While the framing of the research questions above suggests that this is a replication study, it is not truly one because in our case the student assessments change from year to year. In Section 4 we discuss some additional reasons why this paper does not qualify as a true replication study, even though it seeks to answer the same questions as in [7].

The rest of this paper is laid out as follows: In Section 2 we discuss our data sources and how the data was analyzed. Section 3 presents our findings, while Section 4 interprets and discusses them and provides some closing remarks.

2 DATA AND METHODS

The data in this paper covers six computing courses and 17 grade distributions at our institution between 2014 and 2016. While our institution has experienced enrollment growth in our CS courses since 2011 as seen in Table 1, 2014 was chosen as the starting point for our study since our university changed the minimum pass mark in courses in 2014. The courses covered by this study are:

Table 1: Enrollment in various classes under consideration

Course	2011	2012	2013	2014	2015	2016
COMP1126	205	334	–	339	406	373
COMP1127	240	291	–	339	404	370
COMP1161	–	239	–	264	215	224
COMP2190	–	–	84	129	157	142
COMP2201	–	68	77	99	115	129
COMP2211	–	78	101	–	118	142

- COMP1126–*Introduction to Computing I* and COMP1127–*Introduction to Computing II.* Together, these courses constitute a CS1 sequence.
- COMP1161–*Object-oriented Programming.* A first year course, introducing students to object-oriented programming, using Java.
- COMP2190–*Net-Centric Computing.* A second year course that covers the basics of computer networking, web programming, and cryptography.
- COMP2201–*Discrete Mathematics for Computer Science.* A second year course that teaches students about counting, asymptotic analysis, recurrence relations, graphs, and finite automata.
- COMP2211–*Analysis of Algorithms.* A second year course that teaches students how to analyze computational complexity, and introduces the typical data structures and algorithms for dynamic data and graphs.

For each of the courses in our study, the course topics were stable over the period of the study. In order to reduce the influence of confounding factors in the delivery of each course, we only analyzed the years in which the course was offered in the same semester by the same instructor. In all, five distinct lecturers taught the six courses presented in this paper over the 2014–2016 time frame. COMP1126 and COMP1127 were taught by the same lecturer, while each of the other courses had a distinct lecturer. The primary change in each of the courses, from one year to the next, was the class size (see Table 1). For example, COMP1126 grew from about 200 students in Semester I 2011/12 to 373 students in Semester I 2016/17–a growth rate of over 90%. COMP1127 saw about 63% growth over that period, while COMP2190 and COMP2211 experienced 75% and 36% growth, respectively, between the 2013/14 and 2016/17 academic years. In 2016/17, three of the courses had a small drop in enrollment, however, enrollment in all the courses rebounded in the 2017/18 year.

In this paper we used the students' aggregate raw coursework scores in each of the courses listed above for our analysis. These coursework scores are composed of programming assignments and projects, written assignments, and a mid-semester test. For each course we started by considering the full set of grades collated at the end of the semester. From this set we excluded all records where the students had coursework grades of zero. Such cases arose when students registered for the course, and did not do any assignments, and failed to drop the course. For the first year courses (COMP1126, COMP1127, and COMP1161) the percentage of students who had missing coursework grades at the end of the semester ranged from 0% to a high of 11.3%. However, there was no qualitative relationship between course enrollment and the number of students with missing coursework grades. For the second year courses, the percentage of withdrawals ranged between 1.4% and 9.3%. As with the first year courses, there was no relationship between enrollment and the number of students with missing coursework grades. The data analysis in this paper used R [6] and open source packages to carry out modeling. The student grades for each course were read from LibreOffice data sheets, and all processing was done within R.

2.1 Methods

We began our analysis by plotting box plots to show the distribution of performance in each course over the years selected. We then performed $t-$ tests on the comparison of performance in each course's offering against a reference year's for that course. These $t-$ test results would indicate the extent to which one could assert that performance in the courses under study had changed over the years. We then built a mixture model for the data of each course's offering to examine what the analysis methods of Sahami and Piech [7] would yield for our data.

2.2 Mixture Modeling

A finite mixture model is a weighted sum of two or more component distributions [3]. Such a model is of the form:

$$g(X) = \sum_{j=1}^{m} \lambda_j \phi_j(X)$$

where λ_j represents the weight of the component distributions, and $\phi_j(X)$ represents the individual component distributions. In our case, we assumed that the grade distribution for the coursework grades in each of our classes was a sum of Gaussians. We used R [6] and the `mixtools` [1] package for R to carry out the mixture modeling. The `mixtools` package uses the Expectation Minimization (EM) algorithm to converge to values of the mean and standard deviation of the component Gaussians that are being fit, as well as weights of the component distributions in the mixture. Unlike [7], we did not assume that the grade distribution for each year was a sum of two Gaussians. Instead, we used a method within the `mixtools` package to sequentially test the number of components in the mixture models and make recommendations on the number of components in the fitted model. Sometimes, the tool recommended that the grades could be fit to just one, two, and occasionally 3 or 4 Gaussians, as shown in Table 7. It should be noted that while this paper modeled student performance as a sum of Gaussians, [5] has argued that CS grades are not in fact bimodal, and that more often than not they are either Gaussian or skewed.

3 RESULTS

3.1 Initial Comparison

Our analysis began by generating box plots showing the distribution of coursework grades for each of the six courses under consideration. Fig. 1 and 2 summarize the distribution of the coursework grades. The mean grade for each class is printed within each bar in the box plot. From Fig. 1 we can see some variation in the

Table 2: p-values of t-tests comparing to COMP1126 2014 class

Class	2015	2016
p-value	0.00	0.01
LL	-5.3	-2.1
UL	-3.4	-0.2

Table 3: p-values of t-tests comparing to COMP1127 2014 class

Class	2015	2016
p-value	0.00	0.00
LL	-3.9	-4.1
UL	-1.8	-2.1

mean coursework grades for the courses shown, thus, we need to determine if this variation is statistically significant.

Our next step in the analysis was to compare the mean coursework grade between one class and a reference group of that course. For all of the courses, except COMP2211, the reference group was the 2014 class because that was the year our institution changed the minimum pass grade. For COMP2211 the reference year was 2015, because the professor was on sabbatical in the 2014/15 year. In Tables 2–6, LL and UL refer to the lower and upper limits, respectively of the 95% confidence interval associated with the difference in the means. From Table 2 we see that for COMP1126, in both years, there was a statistically significant difference in means at the 95% confidence level, and that in both cases the later years outperformed the 2014 class. Table 3 shows the same general trend as for COMP1126, where the later years outperform the 2014 class. Tables 4 and 5 show that there is no statistically significant difference in means at the 95% confidence level for COMP1161 and COMP2190. For COMP2201, Table 6 shows that there is a statistically significant difference in performance between the 2015 and 2014 classes, with the former outperforming the 2014 class. However, for the later years, there is no statistically significant difference in mean coursework grades. Finally, a t-test shows that the 2016 class for COMP2211 underperformed the 2015 class ($t(235.7) = 5.46, p = 0.00$. The 95% confidence interval for the difference between the mean coursework grade for both populations is [4.2 : 8.9]). The lack of a statistically significant difference in means does not necessarily mean that the coursework grade distributions are similar for the courses. In Section 3.2 we fit the coursework grades for each course and class to a mixture of Gaussians to examine trends in the distribution of student grades.

3.2 Mixture Modeling Results

From Table 7 we can see that the first year courses (1126, 1127, and 1161) tend to require more distributions, while the advanced courses tend to require fewer distributions. This observation can be explained by the fact that the first year courses tend to attract a very broad set of students, while the advanced courses tend to only have students majoring or minoring in Computing disciplines. Our

Table 4: p-values of t-tests comparing to COMP1161 2014 class

Class	2015	2016
p-value	0.44	0.18
LL	-2.8	-0.7
UL	1.2	3.5

Table 5: p-values of t-tests comparing to COMP2190 2014 class

Class	2015	2016
p-value	0.39	0.47
LL	-3.3	-1.4
UL	1.3	3.1

Table 6: p-values of t-tests comparing to COMP2201 2014 class

Class	2015	2016	2017
p-value	0.00	0.77	0.41
LL	-5.0	-1.6	-2.7
UL	-1.1	2.2	1.1

Table 7: Number of distributions required to fit grades per course and year

	1126	1127	1161	2190	2201	2211
2016	3	3	2	1	2	2
2015	4	3	3	2	1	1
2014	2	4	3	2	1	-

observation on the number of distributions required to fit, especially for our CS1 sequence stands in contrast to [7], which found that two distributions were sufficient to fit CS1 grades at Stanford. When three distributions are required, it can be assumed that there are three distinct populations of weak, average, and high-performing students.

Fig. 3 summarizes the probability distribution fits for the 2016/17 academic year. We see from these plots that the fitted distributions provided reasonably good approximations of student coursework grades. It should be noted that the observation that either a single Gaussian or three Gaussians were required to fit student performance stands in contrast to [4], which found that two-component exponential distributions were enough to fit student performance in MOOCs.

3.3 Evolution of mixture components

Having established that we can fit the coursework grades to either one, two, or three component Gaussians, our next task was to investigate how these Gaussians evolved with time. In preparing this paper we tried different methods of labelling the components:

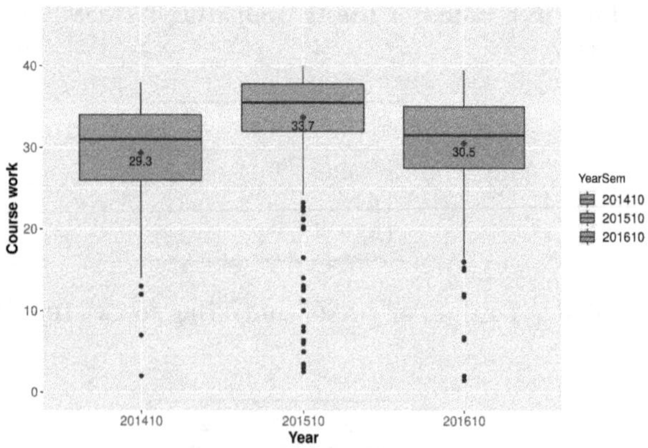

(a) COMP1126 (Intro. to Programming I)

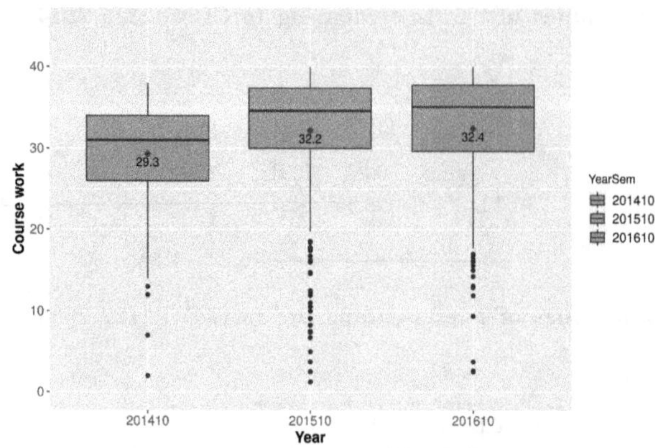

(b) COMP1127 (Intro. to Programming II)

Figure 1: Box plots summarizing course work grades in COMP1126 and COMP1127

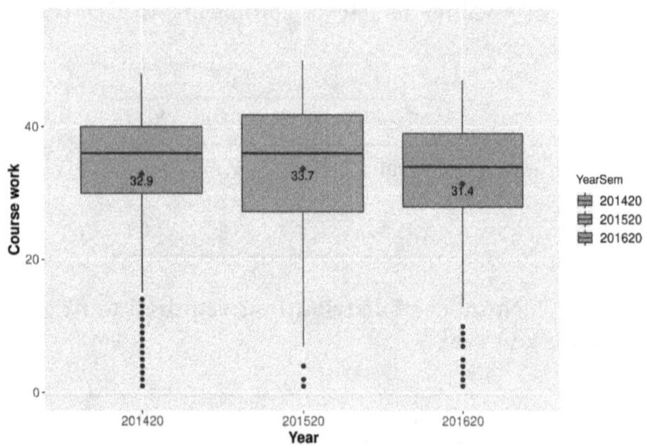

(a) COMP1161 (Object-oriented Programming)

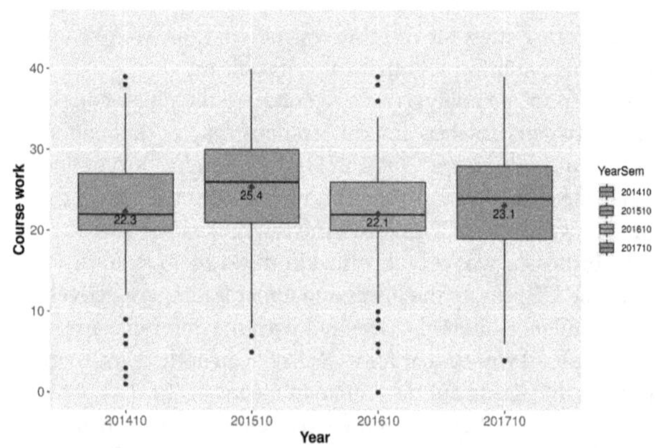

(b) COMP2201 (Discrete Mathematics)

Figure 2: Box plots summarizing course work grades in COMP1161 and COMP2201

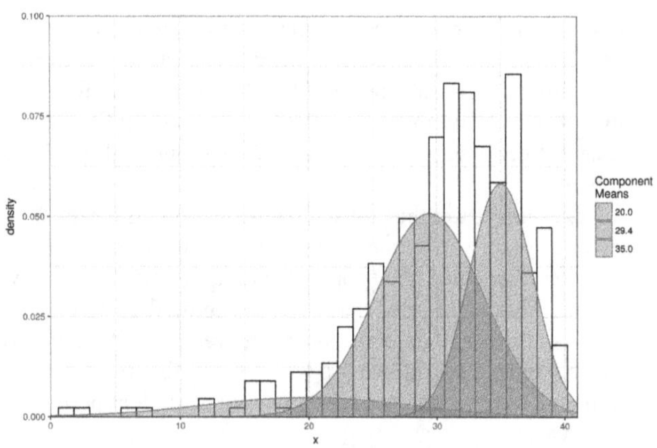

(a) Intro. to Computing I (COMP1126)

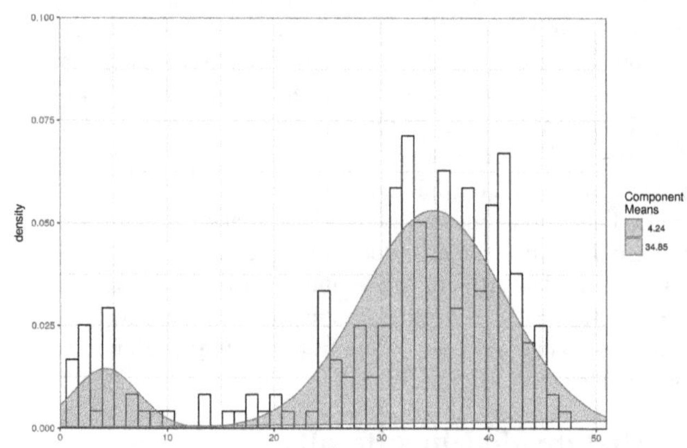

(b) Object-Oriented Programming (COMP1161)

Figure 3: Components of Gaussian mixtures for first year courses in 2016

by mean: the components were labeled in descending order of their mean values. That is, the component distribution with the highest mean was assigned to Component 1, the one with the next highest mean was assigned to Component 2, etc.

by weight: the components were labeled in descending order of their associated weights.

by variance: the components were labeled in descending order of their variance.

We eventually settled on labeling the components by variance. With this approach the first component had the highest variance. Since this component has the largest variance (and therefore standard deviation) in the mixture model, it accounts for the broadest range of performance of the students. From Fig. 4a we observed a lot of variation in the primary component of all of the courses. Over the 2014–2017 period, the component 1 means have gone up for COMP1127 (Into. to Computing I), COMP1161 (Object-Oriented Programming), and COMP2190 (Net Centric Computing), and have decreased for COMP2211. The rest of the courses have seen movement up and down. Fig. 4b shows that the component 2 means have increased over the 2014–2017 period for COMP1126 and COMP1127, and have decreased for COMP1161 and COMP2190. Two of the courses [COMP2201–Discrete Mathematics and COMP2211–Analysis of Algorithms] could be fitted with only one distribution in some of the years, and so we cannot identify any trends in the movement of the component 2 means. In the cases of COMP1126 and COMP1127, the component 2 mean always captures the average performing students. On the other hand the component 2 mean captures the failing students in COMP1161 in the 2015 and 2016 years.

From Fig. 4 we did not find sufficient evidence to report stability in student performance as was found in [7]. However, there is also no strong evidence that as enrollment has increased we are seeing poorer student performance.

Examining the means of each component, (regardless of how their labeling was defined) we found that the mean score for a component from one year to the next was not as consistent as Sahami and Piech found in their study at Stanford [7]. Sahami and Piech [7] reasoned that the group of students accounted for by the area under Component 1 where scores were below the mean for Component 1, could be regarded as the "weaker students". They used that definition to then compute the proportion of weaker students from one year to the next to argue that that proportion was not varying as the anecdotal perceptions seemed to imply. Given that we did not find the coherence of components across the years as they did, we modified the definition of "weaker student" to be those students who were accounted for by the overall model, whose mean score was less than the empirical mean of the class. Using that definition, we obtained the trend of proportions of weaker students shown in Fig. 5. With the exception of COMP1126 in Semester I 2012/13, our model shows that for COMP1126, in 2016 the probability of a student scoring less than the observed empirical mean for that year is about 42%. This is up from 29% in 2011/12. The outlier for COMP1126 is due to a handful of students getting very high passes in COMP1126 in Semester I 2012/13. This skews the empirical mean for the 2012/13 year, leading us to find a high probability for students scoring less than that mean. For COMP1127, the probability of a student scoring less than the empirical mean for 2016 is 37%. This is also up from 29% in 2011/12. A similar increase in the probability of students scoring less than the empirical mean for COMP2211 and COMP2190. In the case of COMP1161, there has been a slight decline in the probability of students scoring less than the empirical mean.

4 DISCUSSION AND CONCLUSION

Our results do not show the level of stability that was documented in [7]. There are several reasons for this: For one, thing our institution tends to attract more average students. A review of the average grade in the regional examination offered by our local examination body shows that students in our COMP1126 and COMP1127 classes had an entry grade of 3 (1 is the highest and best pass, while 5 is the lowest pass). Secondly, one of the authors of [7] stated that he had used the same set of assignments over a long period. On the other hand students at our institution are not bound by an honor code, and so instructors come up with new assignments every year. These new assignments, in spite of the instructors best efforts, can introduce some variation in the coursework grades. Another threat to the validity of our results comes from any changes to teaching methods or styles. For example, in 2015, the COMP2190 course moved away from using quizzes administered on a Learning Management System (LMS), to having short quizzes done in class every week. The quizzes still contributed the same proportion to the final grade, however, the students were being assessed differently. Finally, another threat to the results comes from differences in the tutors that were assigned to the courses from year to year. While the number of tutors assigned to courses has remained relatively constant in spite of enrollment growth, different tutors are assigned to the courses from year to year, and they would introduce minor differences in teaching methods.

In conclusion, in this paper we used mixture modeling to fit weighted sums of Gaussians to observed distributions of coursework grades from six computer science courses at our university. In order to limit confounding factors we constrained ourselves to courses that were taught by the same members of staff. Unlike Sahami and Piech [7], we found that our CS1 course required three component Gaussians, instead of solely two. For the advanced courses (Discrete Mathematics, Analysis of Algorithms and Net-Centric Computing) a two component Gaussian was sufficient to model performance. In fact, occasionally a single Gaussian was sufficient to model performance in advanced courses.

None of our courses exhibited the same level of consistency in performance over the years as the study at Stanford. While the variation in our findings could be interpreted to call into question the broad conclusion that [7] drew, we can also conclude that while it has been shown that the students at Stanford are not getting weaker, perhaps they are in other schools. This makes the case for having a a replication study for grades in a CS1 course done at another school, e.g., a publicly funded university in North America.

Given that we did not find the similar levels of consistency in performance as [7] we introduced a modified definition of a weaker student, wherein that individual scored less than the empirical mean. Using this definition we were able to show that the probability of a

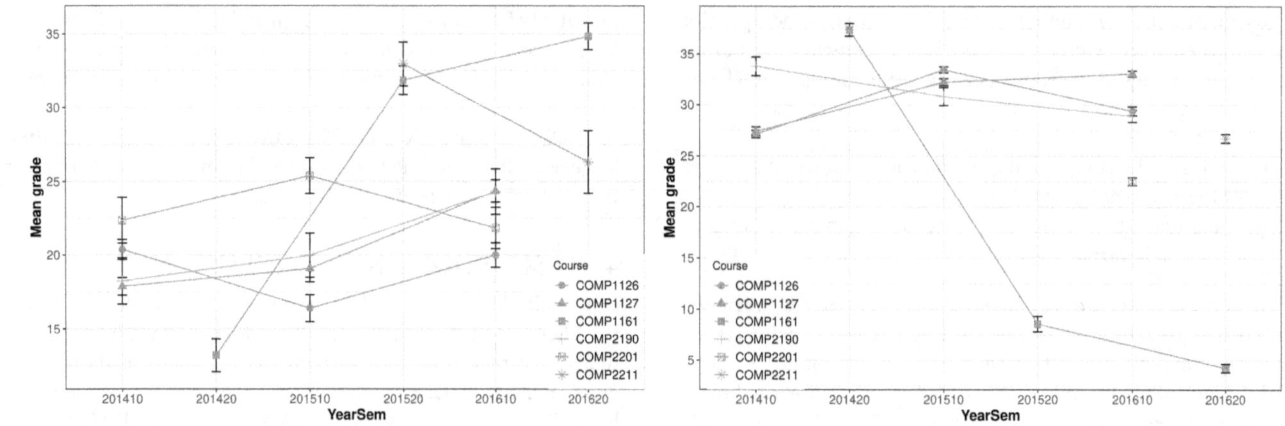

(a) Component 1 Means

(b) Component 2 Means

Figure 4: Variation in means of mixture components

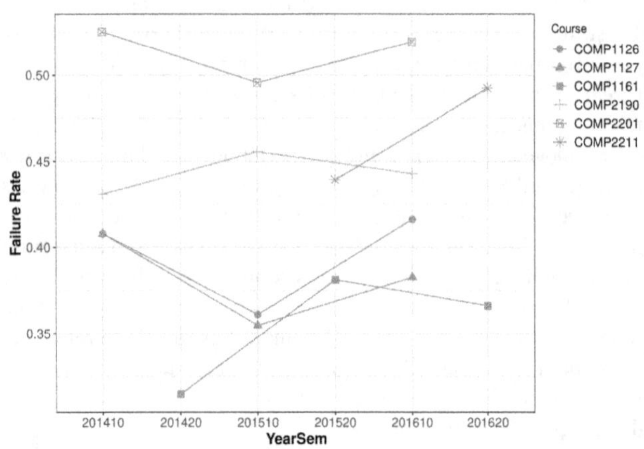

Figure 5: Percentage of weak students, i.e., those scoring less than the empirical mean

student scoring less than the empirical course mean had increased in most courses, except for COMP1161. It is quite curious that we did not see the same level of stability in student grades as [7]. We chalk up this difference to the fact that our institution is a public university that is not as selective as Stanford University. In addition, our institution does not have access to lots of resources, including graduate teaching assistants, that can allow it to scale up rapidly in response to increased enrollment, while keeping teaching quality the same.

REFERENCES

[1] T. Benaglia, D. Chauveau, D. Hunter, and D. Young. 2009. mixtools: An R Package for Analyzing Mixture Models. *Journal of Statistical Software, Articles* 32, 6 (2009), 1–29. https://doi.org/10.18637/jss.v032.i06

[2] Computing Research Association. 2017. *Generation CS: Computer Science Undergraduate Enrollments Surge Since 2006.* Technical Report. http://cra.org/data/Generation-CS/

[3] B. S. Everitt. 2006. Mixture Distributions-I. In *Encyclopedia of Statistical Sciences.* John Wiley & Sons, Inc., Hoboken, NJ, USA. https://doi.org/10.1002/0471667196.ess1655.pub2

[4] D. Koller, A. Ng, C. Do, and Z. Chen. 2013. Retention and Intention in Massive Open Online Courses. *EDUCAUSE Review* 48, 3 (2013), 62–63. https://doi.org/10.1145/2339055.2339064

[5] E. Patitsas, J. Berlin, M. Craig, and S. Easterbrook. 2016. Evidence That Computer Science Grades Are Not Bimodal. In *Proceedings of the 2016 ACM Conference on International Computing Education Research - ICER '16.* ACM Press, New York, New York, USA, 113–121. https://doi.org/10.1145/2960310.2960312

[6] R Core Team. 2014. R: A Language and Environment for Statistical Computing. (2014). http://www.R-project.org

[7] M. Sahami and C. Piech. 2016. As CS Enrollments Grow, Are We Attracting Weaker Students?. In *Proc. 47th ACM Technical Symposium on Computing Science Education (SIGCSE '16).* ACM, New York, NY, USA, 54–59. https://doi.org/10.1145/2839509.2844621

Understanding Who Enrolls in Introductory Computing Courses at Community Colleges

Beth A. Quinn†
NCWIT
University of Colorado
Boulder, CO, USA
beth.quinn@colorado.edu

Wendy M. DuBow
NCWIT
University of Colorado
Boulder, CO, USA
wendy.dubow@colorado.edu

David Sul
Sul & Associates
Petaluma, CA USA
dsul@sulandassociates.com

ABSTRACT

Effective teaching requires understanding where students are coming from. Retaining students who have been historically underrepresented in computing requires the same, especially in introductory courses. This paper draws from surveys of students in introductory computing courses at seven geographically dispersed community colleges. We use K-means cluster analysis to differentiate students based on their responses to questions measuring constructs related to student success in computing courses and persistence. The resulting five clusters were compared on outcome variables, including final grades, intent to persist in computing, and gender and race/ethnicity. We focus on community colleges because they are uniquely well-positioned to broaden participation in computing; however, the implications extend beyond the community college context. We conclude by discussing methodological and pedagogical implications, including how findings can challenge assumptions and stereotypes about introductory computing students.

KEYWORDS

introductory courses, cluster analysis, student demographics, broadening participation in computing

ACM Reference format:

Beth Quinn, Wendy DuBow and David Sul. 2018. Understanding Who Enrolls in Introductory Computing Courses at Community Colleges. In *Proceedings of 50th ACM Technical Symposium on Computer Science Education (SIGCSE '19), February 27-Mar. 2, 2019, Minneapolis, MN, USA.* ACM, NY, NY, USA, 7 pages. *7 pages.* https://doi.org/10.1145/1234567890

1 Introduction

In the first two years of college, students often take a variety of classes, as they figure out their interests, fulfill general education requirements, and learn how to navigate the post-secondary environment. As anyone who has taught introductory level courses knows, students end up in introductory classes for a variety of reasons and what they experience in that introductory class can change their academic path. Computer science (CS) education research suggests that a student's experience in the introductory CS classes can be critical points for sparking their interest in CS or turning them off [16,20,24,25]. As researchers interested in broadening participation in computing, our goal is to provide recommendations to faculty on how to do effective "in-reach" and to implement high-yield retention strategies. To do this, we need to understand the types of students who start in the introductory CS classes. This paper explores whether a clear typology of community college students in introductory CS courses can be determined and if demographic groups are distributed differently across these types.

In the last decade, increasing attention has been paid to the need to broaden participation in computing for reasons of equity and for the benefits that diversity of thought and background can bring to a field based on innovation. At the post-secondary level, some of these efforts have focused on changing introductory CS classes to be more inviting to different kinds of students [19,23,24]. Many of these efforts have been successful in attracting more students with diverse backgrounds to the major, particularly at elite colleges [7]. Still, some faculty may make unsupportable assumptions about their introductory students that can have implications for who is encouraged to continue in the field and who is not [9]. While it has been argued that making CS courses more welcoming to historically underrepresented populations makes them better for everyone, we need to know more about how that works.

In this paper, we outline a new approach to understanding differences and similarities among students enrolled in introductory computing courses. Rather than make a priori assumptions about demographic groups, we classify students based on constructs shown to influence success and persistence in computing, including prior programming experience [1,20], interest in computing [26], and assessment of skills and abilities related to success in computing [26]. We compare the resulting clusters of students on key outcome variables, including final grades and intent to persist in computing, and then on demographic classifications, such as gender and race/ethnicity.

This paper reports a preliminary application of this approach on students drawn from CS0 and CS1 courses from seven geographically dispersed community colleges in the United States. We focus on community colleges because of their mission to serve

ACM ISBN 978-1-4503-5890-3/19/02...$15.00
https://doi.org/10.1145/3287324.3287402

students in their local communities, whatever their background. Thus, they are uniquely well-positioned to broaden participation in computing. Because over 70% of the students in our sample intend to transfer to a 4-year institution, their educational trajectory has implications for 4-year departments. The others could complete their associate's degree or certificate and begin work in industry straight out of community college, so their trajectory affects the workforce more directly.

Data come from a National Science Foundation-funded project that piloted a new professional development program (PD) with community college faculty members from around the country. After faculty chose the course they deemed most pivotal in retaining students in their programs, we surveyed students in each of these "target courses" and interviewed a subset of their students.

2 Methods

The overall project included administration of a student survey at two points in time, and interviews with the participating faculty and a subset of students. For this paper, only data from surveys administered to, and interviews conducted with, students enrolled in the fall and spring terms AY 2017-2018 are reported.

Surveys were administered to students in the participating faculty members' target courses (CS0 or CS1) during a lab period early in the term. Students accessed the survey on lab computers via SurveyMonkey, and participation was voluntary. As incentive, students could opt in to a drawing for $100.

Within the survey, students could agree to be interviewed, and to date we have completed hour-long interviews with 25 students by videoconference or telephone. The semi-structured interview protocol contained questions about their motivations and expectations for attending a community college, their academic and career intentions, and their perceptions about computing. Interviews were recorded, transcribed, and coded using Dedoose (a qualitative analysis software program).

The survey [11] captures students' prior experience with computing, and in particular, with programming; their sense of belonging in computing; perceptions of the field of computing; and educational and career aspirations through a mix of open-ended questions, scale response grid questions (with a mix of 4- and 5-point scales), and single choice questions. Students were also asked to assess their anticipated self-efficacy in the course (e.g., keeping up with the work) and their skills and abilities related to success in computing (e.g., problem-solving). Multiple survey items were used to measure each construct. Most items were modified from existing surveys of computing students and of the general freshman population [3,4,5,19,21].

Survey participants were also asked for their gender identification (as an open-ended question), age, and race/ethnicity. They could select all racial/ethnic identities that applied out of a set modified from the HERI CIRP Freshman Survey [15]. For purposes of analysis, we define "minority" as those students reporting at least one non-White race or ethnicity (even if they also selected White). A related variable, "underrepresented minority in computing" (URMC) is based on the National Science Foundation's definition [22] and includes any student who selected Black, Hispanic, American Indian or Pacific Islander as one of their identities.

Key outcome measures are intention to major in a CS/IT field and intention to work in a computing field. We also collected final grades (with student permission) from each course instructor.

2.1 Scale Construction

For each group of items, we ran an exploratory factor analysis on the early course data from fall 2017, setting an eigenvalue ≥ 1 as the inclusion criteria for factors. All analyses were run using SPSS. Multifactor solutions were rotated using a VARIMAX technique. When two-factor solutions resulted, we ran separate factor analyses on the items that loaded together, if the groupings made conceptual sense, excluding items that failed to add explanatory value [10]. For example, programming-related items (e.g., "I enjoy the challenge of programming") loaded together on one factor and items measuring computing impact (e.g., "I would like to find technological solutions to world problems") loaded on a second factor.

We ran confirmatory factor analyses on data from students in spring 2018 courses. Subsequent analyses, reported here, are conducted on the combined fall and spring data, and include rerunning factor analyses to create factor scores.

The following constructs, measured as factor scores, are used in the subsequent analyses:

- Anticipatory course efficacy
- Self-assessment of CS-related skills and abilities
- Interest in programming
- Interest in other aspects of programming
- Perceptions about the field of computing
- Sense of belonging in computing
- Prior programming experience
- Prior experience in other aspects of computing

For a fuller description of these constructs, see [12].

2.2. Method of Classifying Students

To understand the types of students enrolling in introductory computing courses at community colleges, and in particular, to explore how introductory students cluster based on key constructs related to success and persistence in computing, we conducted a k-means cluster analysis on the resulting factor scores for all the relevant constructs [2,13]. By using this technique, we hope to challenge the tendency to essentialize differences between women and men (and likewise, among ethnic or racial groups). In our Conclusions, we explore the implications of this approach for pedagogy and the design of retention strategies.

As a clustering method, K-means partitions the data into k clusters based on minimal Euclidean distances from the assigned cluster's centroid (i.e., the mean distance of all cluster members). In SPSS, the algorithm begins by selecting the first k cases as starting centroids, assigning the remaining data to clusters based on their distance from each centroid. The centroid for each cluster is then recalculated and cases reassigned, as needed, to the nearest centroid. The algorithm terminates when no case is reassigned or when the predetermined number of iterations is reached.

Based on the number of constructs included in the analysis, we estimated that the likely number of groups would be between three and six. Because SPSS selects the first k cases as starting centroids, the solution is sensitive to order. Thus, we calculated solutions for 3<k<6, for five random sorts of the data [18]. All eight key constructs--measured as factor scores to standardize the variables--were used in the analysis. We then calculated Cramer's V for all possible solutions for each set of k solutions, resulting in five association matrices. High correlations among a particular set of solutions suggests that the solution is stable. Except for random sort 4, the three-centroid solution for all random sorts resulted in Cramer V correlations greater than .938, and the five-centroid solutions resulted in V correlations >.845. Lower correlations among the four-centroid solutions suggest that four categories are not as stable a solution. Since the five-centroid solution provided additional, meaningful differentiation among students over the three-centroid solution, we report on the five-centroid solution for random sort 2. See Figure 1 for the distribution of constructs across student clusters.

3 Results

3.1. Description of the Respondent Sample

Two hundred and ninety-two students completed at least part of the survey. Overall response rate is difficult to calculate since the survey was administered at slightly different weeks in each course and most faculty members did not have up-to-date enrollment rosters at the time. Figured conservatively, the response rate is within a range of 65-77%. There is, however, some variation on individual items, and thus on the scales.

Students from two colleges account for over 40% of the respondents (21.6% and 19.2%) since some faculty offered multiple sections both terms, and some faculty did not teach in spring. Almost 60% of respondents are CS/IT majors, 13% non-STEM majors and 11% engineering. CS0 accounted for 45% of respondents, while 55% were taking a more programming intensive CS1 course. The majority of students (+70%) intend to complete a bachelor's degree. Many (64%) were enrolled in the course because it was required, regardless of course level. CS0 students were slightly more likely than CS1 students to be taking the course because they felt it would be "interesting" (46% vs. 39%). (Students could choose more than one reason for taking the course.)

Men comprised 70% of the resulting sample, with women making up 25%; five percent declined to provide their gender. White men are the largest demographic group (33%) followed by men from minority groups historically underrepresented in computing ("URMC" which includes students identifying as Hispanic, African American, or Native/Pacific Islanders). Asian males make up 14% of the sample. White women and URMC women represent 10% each, followed by Asian women at 6%. A little over 7% of the sample declined to provide race/ethnicity data.

3.2 The Five Student Clusters

Eight scales were used in the cluster analyses. Because of missing data, the n for cluster membership is 275. Table 1 contains the mean factor scores and the range factor scores for each construct.

Factors	InAl	ExOn	InOn	ExAl	SemOp	Range
Anticipatory Self-efficacy	-0.33	0.36	0.29	-0.20	-0.35	-.2.4 to 7.3
Self-assessment	-0.55	0.60	0.36	-0.21	-0.20	-1.9 to 7.3
Programming Interest	-0.88	0.63	0.47	-0.42	0.17	--3.5 to 6.0
Other CS Interests	-0.72	0.43	0.48	-0.54	0.34	-2.2 to 5.4
Belonging	-0.63	0.53	0.44	-0.50	0.02	-2.3 to 6.4
Perceptions of Computing	-0.38	0.15	0.41	-0.54	0.00	-1.9 to 7.6
Prior Programming Exp.	-0.87	1.10	-0.19	1.06	-0.82	-.95 to 1.4
Other computing Exp.	-0.78	1.00	-0.71	0.11	0.74	-1.1 to 1.9

Table 1. Mean factor scores by cluster

Figure 1 is a graphic representation of Table 1, displaying the mean factor score for each cluster on the eight scales used in the factor analysis, arranged from left to right by the cluster with the most students (Inexperienced & Alienated) to the least (Semi-experienced & Open).

Figure 1. Mean factor scores by cluster

The "Inexperienced & Alienated" (InAl) students are the most common type (27%). These students report, on average, the lowest previous experience with and interest in programming and other computing activities, and the lowest sense of belonging in computing. They also report less positive beliefs about the field of computing and, perhaps not unsurprisingly, have the lowest average—but not the lowest—expectation of success in the course. We attribute InAl's lower scores to a lack of experience with and knowledge of the field of computing. They also report the lowest self-assessment on success-related skills and abilities, probably attributable to their lack of experience. It would be wrong, however, to assume that these students are uneducated or generally lacking in confidence.

Profile of an InAl: Victoria, an older student with two master's degrees and ambitions to start a business, comes to CS through an interest in data science. She talks with passion about having done "heavy lifting on market research" and "combing big data items" to inform decisions, and yet she remains unsure of her knowledge: "But then again, what do I know about data science and computers?" While InAls may be inexperienced with and unsure about computing, many have experience and interests in other domains that can be used to engage them in computing.

The "Experienced & Onboard" (ExOn) students are the next most common type, making up 21% of the sample. These students come into introductory courses with previous experience, confidence in their computing-related skills and abilities, and an expectation of success. They report the highest mean levels of experience with both programming and other computing activities (such as setting up a computer network), and the highest interest in programming and sense of belonging in computing. They score the second highest on socially-relevant computing interests and perceptions of the field.

Profile of an ExOn: Ryan, an 18-year old white man, aims to transfer as quickly as possible to get a bachelor's degree in CS. He took CS in high school, has coding and hardware experience, and loves it: "When I'm doing programming, I don't feel like it's school. . . I can spend like an entire day programming an assignment. That's probably why I did so well last semester." Ryan is intrinsically motivated: "They all weren't the most interesting assignments but they were still gratifying to finish. The coding is interesting." He says he's "pretty good" at math but doesn't "care for it." He has a growth mindset and understands both the difficulty and the time needed to learn CS: "I expected [it] to be difficult, I guess, and I think I did pretty well considering that."

The remainder of the sample is distributed fairly evenly across the other three types.

"The Inexperienced but Onboard" (InOn) (17%) report on average low levels of experience in programming and other computing activities, but high levels on all other constructs. For example, they score similarly to ExOns in self-assessments of their computing-related skills and abilities, and on expectations of success in the course. In addition, they score slightly higher than ExOns in their interest in computing areas that are more externally focused, such as finding technological solutions to world problems and helping people with computing problems.

Profile of an InOn: George, a 22-year-old Hispanic man, "grew up loving computers" but didn't have opportunities in high school to study CS. "I wish I had more experience ... and I wish I knew that I wanted to get into this earlier so... I could have just been practicing at home." He was enrolled at a 4-year institution as an undeclared major but had to drop out because of health, financial issues, and bad grades ("I kind of fell off"). His father, who works at a tech manufacturing company, got him a job working with robots. That experience changed him: "[I wrote] small scripts [to] see if [the device would] run 100 times without fail. If it does fail, find out why, so I could tell the engineer. I thought that was a lot of fun." He wants to get a BS in computing "because I know that once I get where I want to be... it's going to be somewhere where I can continue to shine."

The "Experienced but Alienated" (ExAl) students (18%) are almost the mirror image of the InOn Group. These students report mean levels of programming experience similar to the ExOns but differ significantly on almost every other construct. Compared to ExOns, they have lower levels of experience with non-programming related computing activities (but still score higher on this construct than the two other groups). However, on all other constructs they look more like the InAls. Because of their high levels of reported programming experience, their lower scores may be due to negative experiences rather than ignorance.

Profile of an ExAl: Olivia, a 20-year-old Latina woman, was a gamer in high school and had loved an app development class she took. She began at university with a CS major, dropped out for personal reasons, but then resumed the CS major at community college. After failing the math prerequisite, she decided to switch to art. She said, "At first it was pretty discouraging because I really wanted to be good at computer science." She worked hard but the inflexibility of programming meant she fell behind. She recalls, "I had really good grades in high school. I thought, 'Oh, this is going to be so easy,' like coding just looked so easy. But it's actually a lot of work." She believed that to be in CS, you needed to be an expert, and she had more expertise in art. To top it off, when she sought help for her CS class, she was ridiculed by the "rude" tutors.

The "Semi-Experienced & Open" (SemOp) (16%) report some experience with non-programming related computing activities but one of the lowest mean levels of experience with programming (similar to InAls). They score in the middle of the pack on interest in programming and other computing topics, and on sense of belonging and attitudes toward the field of computing. They tend, as a group, to report the lowest level of anticipated efficacy in the course and one of the lower self assessments of computing-related skills and abilities.

Profile of a SemOp: John is a 19-year-old white male who wants to transfer to get a BS. Currently, he is a Liberal Arts major but wants to pursue a Networking degree. He has no formal CS coursework, but he has taken a computer apart, has done some game modding, and has taught himself some programming. He is taking the introduction course because it is required, but also because he thinks it will be "useful" and "interesting." When asked what might "get in the way" of his success in computing, he said, "Just having to balance all of the other classes and getting past little mental blocks with my coding. Occasionally I have a problem with the conceptual ideas behind the code."

3.3 Cluster Comparisons: Academic Major and Outcomes

3.3.1. Distribution of majors across clusters. The majority of students (60%) in these courses are CS/IT majors and we find CS/IT majors in all clusters. There is, however, a modest but significant relationship between cluster membership and major (V=.218, p<.01). Unsurprisingly, CS/IT majors tend to be ExOns (27%) or InOns (22%). However, CS/IT majors are found in all clusters, including InAls (13%) and SemOps (19%). This aligns with previous research showing computing majors are less confident in their abilities than other STEM majors [24]. Not surprisingly, half of the undeclared students are "InAls." A similar pattern is true for Engineering and STEM majors enrolled in these introductory computing courses; 47% of these majors are InAls.

3.3.2. Sources of student previous experience in computing. The ExAls are most likely to have had a high school course (64% compared to 45% of the ExOns, the one group with higher levels of programming experience) (Cramer's V=.324, P<.01). There is also a significant relationship between cluster membership and the likelihood of being "self-taught" (Cramer's V=.453, p<.01). Only half (51%) of the ExAls are self-taught compared to almost 71% of ExOns and 60% of SemOps. Interestingly, 45% of the InOns, who report relatively lower levels of experience, report that they are self-taught and almost 28% had high school courses. (Students could select more than one source of their computing experience.)

3.3.3. Intent to transfer and reasons for taking the course. We find no significant relationship between intent to transfer and cluster membership. In this sample, most of the students (80%) are intending to complete a bachelor's degree. Students were also asked why they were taking the course (e.g., it's required, it's interesting, a friend recommended), selecting as many reasons as applicable. Across the sample, most students were taking an introductory computing course because it was required and/or because they found it "useful." We observed no significant relationship between reasons for taking the course and cluster membership, with one exception. InAls were less likely to be taking the course because it was required. Both InAl and InOn students were the most likely to say they were taking the course because it was "interesting" (48% and 47%, respectively).

3.3.4. Final course grades. While 85% of students completing the early survey (n=248) gave permission to share their final course grades, we have final course grade data for only 32% of the sample because some students dropped the course, some did not give permission for grade sharing, and some (6%) have missing data and cannot be assigned cluster memberships. Because of this, the grade analyses should be interpreted with caution. That said, while the ExOns had the highest mean course GPA and the SemOps (with low self-assessment and low anticipation of success) the lowest, we observed no significant relationship between cluster membership and the likelihood of passing the course (Cramer's V=.160, n.s.) or on final course GPA (F(4,186)=.925, p=.450).

3.3.5. Intent to work in computing. Students were asked if they "intend to work in a computing-related field." The majority of students (68%) declared that intention, but there was a significant relationship between cluster membership and intention (Cramer's V=.312, p<.01). Seventy-nine percent of ExOns said that was their intention and an additional 16% are already working in a computing field. The vast majority of InOn students (91%) also said they wanted to work in computing, but only one was already doing so. Interestingly, while they lack confidence in their academic skills, 84% of SemOps want to work in computing. InAls were the most likely to say they "didn't know" (43%), followed by ExAls (24%).

3.4 Cluster Comparisons: Demographics

As Figure 2 demonstrates, the clusters do not align neatly with gender and race/ethnicity categories, but there are some notable patterns. Women of all race/ethnicities predominate proportionally in the InAls, the most common student type in our sample. This group also contains a relatively larger proportion of Asian and URMC men, and the lowest proportion of white men.

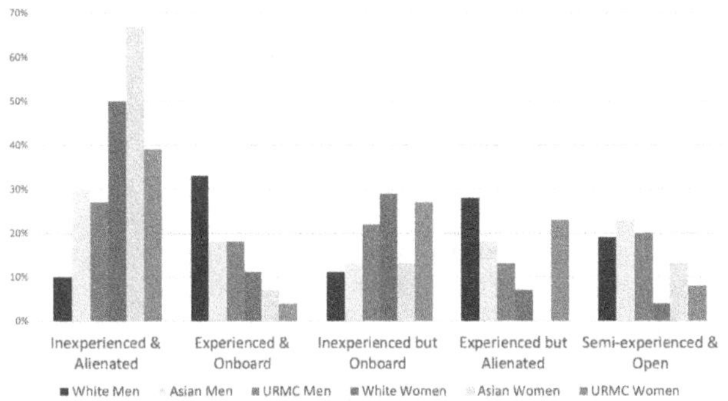

Figure 2. Clusters by intersectional identities

Men predominate proportionally in the ExOn and SemOp clusters, regardless of race/ethnicity. The SemOps have the second highest proportion of Asian men compared to other clusters. The InOn Group has a relatively high proportion of Asian and URMC men and women. The ExAls contain a low proportion of white women, and a higher proportion of the white and Asian men; no Asian women were in the ExAl cluster.

4 Conclusions

The K-Means cluster analysis allows us to explore how students can be grouped by key influencers other than race and gender. Rather than asking whether women and men differ on the construct and outcome measures, we developed "types" of students based on those measures. We examined whether women and men are distributed across the "types" of students. Along with helping us challenge essentialist assumptions, it also provides one way to statistically handle intersecting identities, where it matters not only that students are female or male, for instance, but also if they are a female or male of color.

The student clusters illustrate the challenges of teaching introductory computing courses, where student experiences, confidence, and impressions of the field can differ so dramatically [21]. The distribution of race and gender across clusters encourages us to deconstruct stereotypes we may have about who has the potential to be retained in computing. Importantly, the cluster analysis also has the potential to lead to insights into what instructors can do to actively retain students as they grapple with the content of a CS0 or CS1 class in their early years of post-secondary education. To this end, we offer some suggestions for ways to teach and retain the types that emerged from this sample.

The InAl Group: Because these students have the lowest interest and experience levels, and lower expectations for success, they may be most "susceptible" to being surprised by a positive experience in an introductory CS course. Remember: They were one of two groups most likely to say they were in the course because it was "interesting." Recognizing that a lack of experience with computing may lead to an expectation of failure, instructors can: (1) acknowledge the experience gap and scaffold instruction to bridge it, (2) provide explicit encouragement to individual students, and (3) connect computing content to student interests and their areas of existing expertise [14].

The ExOn Group: These students have both experience and interest, which brings a high expectation for succeeding in the class. ExOns are likely the easiest group to teach. However, the challenge is making sure they have good study and coding habits, and that in their confidence they don't overshadow, dominate, or intimidate other students.

The ExAl Group: While sharing similar experience levels with ExOns, ExAl students likely have had negative experiences with computing, whether before or during college. Thus, they need to be reinspired. Linking class activities and skills to real-world applications and fostering positive student community may help to retain these experienced students in the major.

The InOn Group: While they lack experience, InOn students are nearly as enthusiastic as ExOns, and in this sample, they are the most demographically diverse group. They need encouragement as they build the skills to match their interest. Instructors need to be cautious: Research suggests that computing interventions can sometimes dampen inexperienced students' interest in computing because they may not realize how hard computing can be, how exacting programming is, or how much time the class will take [17]. Thus, these students need scaffolding as well as a reason to stick it out. Even with confidence in their academic skills, the InOn group still may be vulnerable to intimidation by students with more experience.

The SemOp Group: These students have some general computing experiences (but not programming) and could skew positive or negative on their attitudes toward computing and toward their potential success in the course. As their name suggests ("Open"), they need direct encouragement to keep them motivated and to build their confidence. They scored low on self-assessment of computing abilities so will likely benefit from scaffolding.

In closing, we encourage faculty to bear in mind two student's perspectives on these introductory courses to remind ourselves how important the first courses are to recruitment and retention:

> If we're basing everything off this one class, we may see tech as this boring, mundane thing where we're just gonna sit at a desk typing up...programs, which is horribly dull.

> We need labs which are more relatable to students' everyday life...a little bit more fun for the students, to make them see, 'Oh! I actually like this! I don't know what I am doing but I like what the concept is!'

5 Limitations and Future Research

We want to note a few important limitations of our research as well as our plans for future research. First, the finding that the CS/IT major is distributed across clusters may be an artifact of the way students choose a major at community college and may not replicate at 4-year institutions. Second, it is notable that there wasn't a stronger association between cluster type and final grade, but students that dropped before final grades are not included in the sample, so their absence may well be suppressing an effect. However, while the sample size is relatively limited—both in terms of size and scope (all from community colleges)–the study is strengthened by the variety of institutions and backgrounds of students included in the dataset.

Because of the preliminary nature of these findings, the final version of the survey instrument and the cluster analytic technique are not ready for wide dissemination and use. In future work, we intend to validate the technique on a larger and differently constructed sample, including 4-year CS0 and CS1 students to account for structural differences between 4-year and 2-year institutions and potential differences between the kinds of students each institution type attracts. Once we have refined the statistical approaches and validated the student types, we will share our data collection and analytic techniques with the computing education community, where it could be helpful in two ways: (1) as a powerful theoretical frame for future research on pedagogical innovation informed by research-based constructs rather than a priori demographics, and (2) as support for CS0 and CS1 faculty by providing a helpful snapshot of the types of students they may encounter in their courses and insight into how to better teach and retain those students.

ACKNOWLEDGMENTS

We want to thank the participating faculty, who must remain unidentified, for their invaluable contributions to data collection and to our understanding of the community college context. We also thank our project Advisory Board—Cheryl Calhoun, Sarah Hug, Pat Morreale, Lisa Sandoval, Khallai Taylor, and Melanie Williamson—for their keen insights. Jamie Huber Ward contributed significantly to the professional development which is core to this project. Finally, we thank the students who participated in surveys and interviews. This research is supported by the National Science Foundation under Grant No. 1525652. Any opinions, findings, and conclusions expressed in this paper are those of the authors and do not necessarily reflect the views of the NSF.

REFERENCES

[1] Joanne M. Badagliacco, 1990. Gender and race differences in computing attitudes and experience. *Social Science Computer Review* 8, 1, (April 1990), 42–63. DOI: 10.1177/089443939000800105.

[2] Mark S. Aldenderfer and Roger K. Blashfield. 1984. *Cluster Analysis*. Sage, Beverly Hills, CA

[3] Center for Community College Student Engagement. 2015. *Community College Survey of Student Engagement (CCSSE)*. University of Texas, Austin, TX. Retrieved from http://www.ccsse.org/.

[4] Center for Community College Student Engagement. 2015. *Survey of Entering Student Engagement (SENSE)*. University of Texas, Austin, TX. Retrieved from http://www.ccsse.org/sense/.

[5] Center for Postsecondary Research. 2013. *National Survey of Student Engagement*. Indiana University School of Education, Bloomington, IN. Retrieved from http://nsse.indiana.edu/html/survey_instruments.cfm

[6] Computing Research Association. 2018. *The Data Buddies Project*. Retrieved from https://cra.org/cerp/data-buddies/

[7] Christianne Corbett and Catherine Hill. 2015. *Solving the Equation: The Variables for Women's Success in Engineering and Computing.* American Association of University Women, Washington, DC.

[8] Peter M. Crosta. 2014. Intensity and attachment: How the chaotic enrollment patterns of community college students relate to educational outcomes. *Community College Review* 42, 2 (February 2014), 118 - 142. https://doi.org/10.1177/0091552113518233

[9] Jill Denner, Linda Werner, Lisa O 'Connor, and Jill Glassman. 2014. Community college men and women: A test of three widely held beliefs about who pursues computer science. *Community College Review* 42, 4 (May 2014), 342–362.

[10] Christine Distefano, Min Zhu, and Diana Mîndrilă. 2009. Understanding and using factor scores: Considerations for the applied researcher. In *Practical Assessment, Research & Evaluation* 14, 20 (Oct. 2009), 1–11.

[11] Wendy M. DuBow and Beth A. Quinn. *EngageIT Early Course Survey.* Retrieved from https://tinyurl.com/Quinn-DubowStudentSurvey.

[12] Wendy M. DuBow and Beth A. Quinn. *EngageIT Early Course Survey Scales.* Retrieved from https://tinyurl.com/EngageIT-scales.

[13] John Fiedler and John J. McDonald. 1993. Market Figmentation: Clustering on factor scores versus individual variables. *AMA Adv. Res. Tech. Forum,* 1–14, 1993. Retrieved from https://tinyurl.com/Fielder-McDonald1993

[14] Andrea Forte and Mark Guzdial. 2005. Motivation and nonmajors in computer science: Identifying discrete audiences for introductory courses. *IEEE Transactions on Education* 48, 2 (May 2005), 248-253. DOI: 10.1109/TE.2004.842924

[15] Higher Education Research Institute. 2015. *CIRP Freshman Survey 2015.* Retrieved from https://heri.ucla.edu/cirp-freshman-survey.

[16] Catherine Hill, Christianne Corbett, and Andresse St Rose. 2010. *Why So Few? Women in Science, Technology, Engineering, and Mathematics.* American Association of University Women, Washington, DC. Retrieved from https://www.aauw.org/research/why-so-few.

[17] Yingdan Huang, Jane Meyers, Wendy M. DuBow, Zhen Wu and Michael Eisenberg. 2012. Programming plush toys as an introduction to computer science: The (fraught) question of motivation. In *Ubiquitous and Mobile Informal and Formal Learning in the Digital Age.* D.G. Sampson, P. Isaias, D. Ifenthaler, J.M. Spector (Eds.) New York, Springer. ISBN 978-1-4614-3328-6

[18] IBM, 2016. *K-Means Cluster (QUICK CLUSTER) Results Sensitive to Case Order.* Retrieved August 15, 2018 from http://www-01.ibm.com/support/docview.wss?uid=swg21476878.

[19] Kathleen J. Lehman, Linda J. Sax, and Hilary B. Zimmerman. 2017. Women planning to major in computer science: Who are they and what makes them unique? *Computer Science Education* 26, 4 (Jan 2017), 277-298.

[20] Jane Margolis and Allan Fisher. 2002. *Unlocking the Clubhouse: Women in Computing.* The MIT Press, Cambridge, MA.

[21] National Center for Women & Information Technology. 2015. *Survey-in-a-Box: Student Experience of the Major.* Retrieved from https://www.ncwit.org/resources/survey-box-student-experience-major-0.

[22] National Science Foundation. 2012. *CISE Strategic Plan for Broadening Participation.* National Science Foundation, Alexandria, VA. Retrieved from https://www.nsf.gov/cise/oad/cise_bp.jsp.

[23] Beth A. Quinn, Wendy M. DuBow, and Jamie Huber-Ward. 2018. Broadening participation in computing via professional development for community college CS/IT faculty. In *Proceedings of the 49th ACM Technical Symposium on Computer Science Education* (SIGCSE '18). ACM Press, New York, NY, 789–793. DOI: https://doi.org/10.1145/3159450.3159546

[24] Elaine Seymour and Nancy M. Hewitt. 1997. *Talking About Leaving: Why Undergraduates Leave the Sciences.* Westview Press, Boulder, CO.

[25] Henry M. Walker. 2017. Retention of students in introductory computing courses: Curricular Issues and Approaches. *ACM Inroads* 8, 4 (Oct. 2017), 12–12. DOI: 10.1145/3151936

[26] Susan Wiedenbeck. 2005. Factors affecting the success of non-majors in learning to program. In *Proceedings of the First International Workshop on Computing Education Research (ICER '05).* ACM, New York, NY, USA, 13-24. DOI: 10.1145/1089786.1089788.

Can Sending First and Second Year Computing Students to Technical Conferences Help Retention?

An Analysis of National Survey Data

Heather M. Wright
Center for Evaluating the Research Pipeline
Computing Research Association
Washington, DC, USA
heather@cra.org

N. Burçin Tamer
Center for Evaluating the Research Pipeline
Computing Research Association
Washington, DC, USA
burcin@cra.org

ABSTRACT

This research examines the relationship between undergraduate computing students' participation in technical conferences and psychological predictors of academic persistence. Studies have shown experiential educational activities, like conferences, encourage students' persistence in STEM; this is especially important for students underrepresented in the field, who are more likely than their well-represented peers to leave their degree programs. In recent years, academic literature has pointed to anecdotal evidence that conference participation for students early in their undergraduate education relates to students' persistence in STEM pathways. Using national survey data, we examine the relationship between conference participation and first and second year undergraduate students' persistence in computer science pathways. This paper presents results from a cross-sectional analysis and a two time-point analysis of national survey data collected from undergraduate students. Overall, we found that first and second year computing majors who attended a technical computing conference reported higher levels of belonging to their field and confidence to persist in their degree program than those who did not attend. We also found that conference participants' levels of belonging and self-confidence is higher than non-participants over time, even after controlling for initial levels at Time 1. Our analyses also showed that conference participation was associated with closing the gap in levels of belonging and self-confidence between students who are underrepresented in computing and those who are well-represented. Empirical results from this paper support anecdotal evidence that conference participation for students early in their undergraduate education may help retain students, and particularly underrepresented students, in computing majors in the long-term.

CCS CONCEPTS

• **Social and professional topics** → **Computing education**; *Race and ethnicity*; *Gender*.

SIGCSE '19, February 27-March 2, 2019, Minneapolis, MN, USA

ACM ISBN 978-1-4503-5890-3/19/02...$15.00
https://doi.org/10.1145/3287324.3287349

KEYWORDS

student retention; diversity; education research; belonging; self-confidence; technical conferences

ACM Reference Format:

Heather M. Wright and N. Burçin Tamer. 2019. Can Sending First and Second Year Computing Students to Technical Conferences Help Retention?: An Analysis of National Survey Data. In *Proceedings of the 50th ACM Technical Symposium on Computer Science Education (SIGCSE '19), February 27-March 2, 2019, Minneapolis, MN, USA.* ACM, New York, NY, USA, 7 pages. https://doi.org/10.1145/3287324.3287349

1 INTRODUCTION

It is widely known and understood that the field of computer science lacks diversity. Of Bachelor's degrees in computer science awarded in 2015, only 18% went to women and 20% went to students (both men and women) considered underrepresented racial/ethnic minorities (URM) in computing (e.g., Black/African American, Hispanic/Latino(a), and Alaska Natives/Pacific Islanders) [32]. At the graduate level, percentage of PhDs in computing awarded to women and URMs were 23% and 11%, respectively [32]. Although the proportion of women and URMs earning computer science degrees remains relatively low, the field of computing continues to grow each year [33, 46–48]. Further, a recent survey of Americans [15] found that 48% of respondents expect the number of STEM jobs to continually grow in the U.S. over the next decade, and 2 out of 5 believe worker shortages in STEM are at crisis levels. Despite this, less than half of parents in the survey sample encouraged their daughters to pursue STEM careers [15].

There have been several initiatives aimed at recruiting a diverse body of students in computing to help fill the growing needs of the country; most notably, the National Science Foundation (NSF) Directorate for Computer and Information Science and Engineering (CISE) released a Dear Colleague Letter in 2017 solidifying its commitment to broadening participation of underrepresented populations in computing fields [24]. This comes years after NSF's 2012 CISE Strategic Plan for Broadening Participation, which outlined CISE goals to take a leadership role in calling the community to action and raising awareness of issues related to underrepresented populations in STEM [18]. As the nation continues to place high importance on broadening participation of URMs and women, it is critical to understand the factors that relate to the success and retention of these students in the field.

2 EXPERIENTIAL LEARNING AND ENGAGEMENT

Researchers have long sought to understand why some students tend to leave their domain at higher rates than other groups of students; for example, literature has shown that women and URM students tend to leave, or seriously think about leaving [38] STEM fields at higher rates than men and racial majorities [14, 28, 37, 40].

Research shows that students who participate in extracurricular activities are less likely to drop out of school, especially if those activities help socially connect students with peers [30]. Further, experiential educational activities have been found to help students, and especially underrepresented students, persist in STEM fields [31, 35]. Engaging students in undergraduate research experiences has been shown to boost students' academic engagement and skill mastery, sense of belonging, and confidence to persist in academic degree programs [21, 25, 31]. Finally, experiential education can enhance the knowledge of, and engagement in, science among underrepresented minority youth [13].

While much is known about experiential education activities as they relate to formal research experiences and summer programs, less is known about the impact on conference engagement for undergraduate students in STEM fields; however, there is some evidence of the benefits of conference participation. For example, a 2009 study found that conference participation can improve communication skills and foster positive attitudes towards science careers [29]. Further, an exploratory analysis showed that computing majors who attended diversity focused conferences were more confident in their ability to complete their undergraduate degree in computing than those who had no experience attending these conferences [39]. Finally, a qualitative study examining the results of 90 in-depth interviews conducted over three years showed that engagement in conferences dedicated to undergraduate researchers helped develop skills like scientific communication and critical thinking, boost confidence, and give value to the importance of research engagement [42].

Recently, participation in academic conferences, especially for first and second year students, has been recommended as a mechanism for student engagement and retention. In 2006, faculty at Harvey Mudd College (HMC) began taking first-year women to the Grace Hopper Celebration of Women in Computing conference (GHC), which is an annual conference celebrating the achievements of women in computing. In combination with other efforts to recruit and retain women in computing, such as transforming the introductory computing course and expanding research opportunities to rising sophomores, HMC saw an increase in the percentage of women entering the major, as well as higher graduation rates among women in computing [1]. In addition, HMC learned from survey data that students who attended GHC were more likely to take computing courses and major in computing, which held true for both students who intended to major in computing, and those who did not, prior to entering college [2]. Finally, an ACM Inroads article published in 2017 was dedicated to supporting undergraduate students at conferences and how to encourage them to make the most of their experience [11].

Although recommendations around conference participation and student retention has encouraged faculty to enable first and second year students to attend conferences, an exploratory analysis showed that only a small portion of these students seem to be actually attending conferences; students in their third and fourth years of undergraduate study were more likely to have participated in technical conferences than first and second year students [44]. Even so, encouraging students early in their undergraduate education toward active learning activities may be an important step towards student retention [41].

2.1 Engaging First and Second Year Students

Engaging first and second year students may be particularly advantageous due to higher attrition rates among freshman undergraduate students. Data from the National Student Clearinghouse showed that for students who entered college in 2015, 26.6% of first year students dropped out of college completely; when analyzing those data by race and ethnicity, Black students had the lowest persistence rate (66.9%) followed by Hispanic students (72.5%) [9].

Researchers have posited psychological factors may be at play; studies investigating psychological outcome measures have examined the role that belonging takes in relation to students' academic persistence. Belonging, known as feeling welcomed and socially interconnected with others, has been argued as an inherit human need that can impact physical and emotional well-being, sense of identity and security, judgment, self-esteem, and academic engagement [6, 7, 10, 12, 26, 27, 34, 45].

In a longitudinal study examining sense of belonging among African American and White first year college students [20], researchers found that both groups of students equally reported a weaker sense of belonging over time; however, students who reported more academic integration showed stronger levels of belonging over time. They also found that both sense of belonging and institutional commitment were positively correlated with students' intentions to persist in their degree regardless of background.

Even so, studies have shown that URMs and women are particularly sensitive to the effects of belonging when it comes to their academic achievement and persistence [43]. Among Latino/a undergraduate students, researchers have found these students are more likely to think about leaving their degree when confronted with adversity and identity threat [23] and perceive a lack of social fit and support from peers and mentors [19].

When both belonging and self-efficacy (e.g., the belief and/or confidence in one's ability to perform tasks and achieve goals [3]) are low, researchers have found women are particularly likely to consider leaving their academic degree program across a range of STEM disciplines [28]. Just like belonging, self-efficacy has been theorized to play a major role in students' academic engagement, persistence, and future career choices [3–5, 36]. For example, a six-year longitudinal study of women in science and engineering (S&E) at the University of Washington [8] found that over time, women lose confidence (i.e., self-efficacy) in their academic abilities. While women intending to pursue an S&E major reported a strong initial level of confidence in their math and science abilities, their confidence levels dropped dramatically over the course of their first year of college; however, they also found that women who held high levels of confidence in their math and science abilities consistently over time were the ones more engaged in extracurricular and experiential learning activities, such as student societies, conferences, and internships.

Given that literature supports the idea that the first and second years of college are critical time periods, we theorize that incorporating experiential learning into the curriculum may act as a buffer from negative environmental and social factors that reduce belonging to the field and confidence to persist in computing. As a case in point, a study of Latino/a students showed that when students were socially and resourcefully supported in their first year of college, they showed positive academic and personal adjustment in the second year of college [22].

2.2 Research Questions and Hypotheses

To examine the relationship between conference participation and psychological predictors of students persistence in the field , we conducted two research studies. In our first study of a cross-sectional dataset, we asked how does conference participation *relate* to first and second year undergraduate students' persistence in computing pathways, and does that relationship differ for students who are considered underrepresented in computing?

In our second study, which uses a repeated measures design with two-time points, we asked how does conference participation *influence* first and second year undergraduate students' persistence in computing pathways, and does that relationship differ for students who are considered underrepresented in computing?

We hypothesized that students who participated in technical computing conferences would report a stronger sense of belonging and confidence to persist in computing (e.g., self-confidence) compared to those without conference participation. We also hypothesized that for underrepresented students, conference participation would have a greater impact on belonging and self-confidence than for well-represented students.

3 RESEARCH DESIGN

Each year, the Computing Research Association's Center for Evaluating the Research Pipeline (CERP) collects national survey data in an initiative called Data Buddies Survey (DBS). To do so, CERP researchers ask academic departments across the United States to distribute an anonymous survey link to students in their department. The online survey asks students who are affiliated with computing in some way (e.g., computing majors, minors, and those taking courses) about their degree program, psychosocial measures, and future career plans. At the end of the survey, students are given the option to complete future surveys, and students who agree to be tracked over time are contacted directly for the purpose of longitudinal data collection.

In Study 1, we examined DBS data collected from undergraduate students during the fall of 2016 [17]. In Study 2, we analyzed data collected at two points (2014 and 2015) from a panel of undergraduate students [16].

3.1 Participants

In our studies, survey respondents were drawn from DBS between 2014 and 2016. Undergraduate students in both studies were considered computing majors if they were in the following degree programs: computer science, computer information systems and/or informatics, bioinformatics, computing and business, information technology, computer engineering/software engineering, and any other degree related to computing (marked as "other computing-related degree"). Below, we describe participants specific to each study.

3.1.1 Study 1. In 2016, 11,753 undergraduate students responded to DBS. Among those, 2,662 first year and 2,366 second year students completed the survey. Students who were not computing majors and did not complete survey questions about their gender, racial/ethnic identity, or conference participation were excluded from the analysis. The final sample of first and second year students who were computing majors equaled 3,652. Of those, 18% had participated in a technical conference in computing and 42% were identified and coded as URMW [1].

3.1.2 Study 2. In 2014, 2,909 undergraduate students agreed to be contacted by CERP in the future, and 1,118 responded to the follow-up survey in 2015. Of these, 283 (26%) were first year and 328 (30%) were second year students. In order to examine the impact of conference participation early on in their career, we selected these first and second year students for our study. We further restricted our sample to only those students who had (a) not attended a conference during either of the data collection waves and (b) those who had attended a conference only during the 2014-2015 academic year. After dropping students who were not computing majors and those who had missing data in any of our independent and dependent variables, there were 347 students in the resulting dataset; 16% of these students attended a technical conference during the 2014-2015 academic year and 43% of the sample were coded as URMW.

3.2 Measures

This research focuses on the following subset of quantitative measures collected from DBS between 2014 and 2016.

3.2.1 Dependent Variables.

***Belonging*.** Survey respondents were asked on a Likert scale from *(1) Strongly disagree* to *(5) Strongly agree* to rate the degree to which they felt a sense of belonging in computing with the following three statements: "I feel like I belong in the computing community," "I feel like an outsider in the computing community," and "I feel welcomed in the computing community." Item "I feel like an outsider in the computing community" was reverse coded for analysis.

***Self-confidence*.** Survey respondents were asked on a Likert scale from *(1) Not at all* to *(5) Very* to rate the degree to which they felt confident to do the following: complete their undergraduate degree in computing, get admitted to a graduate computing program, find employment in their area of interest, and become a leader in the field of computing.

3.2.2 Independent Variables.

[1]Underrepresented minorities and women (URMW) included students who identified as a woman or as Black/African American, of Hispanic or Latino descent, Native Hawaiians/Pacific Islanders, or multiracial in which one of their multiracial identities included at least one of the earlier listed racial/ethnic groups.

Conference participation. Using a single binary item (Yes = 1 or No = 0), survey respondents were asked if they had participated in a technical conference related to computing over the past year.

URMW. To identify URMs and women, survey respondents were asked to provide their racial/ethnic identity and gender. Students who identified as a woman or as Black/African American, of Hispanic or Latino descent, Native Hawaiians/Pacific Islanders, or multiracial in which one of their multiracial identities included at least one of the earlier listed racial/ethnic groups were included as URMW (coded as 1). Students who identified as men and were also White/Caucasian or of Asian descent were categorized as majority men (e.g., not URMW; MM) and coded as 0.

3.3 Analysis

3.3.1 Study 1. Each item discussed above measuring sense of belonging and self-confidence were aggregated together to form two constructs. Each construct was tested for internal reliability. The reliability coefficient (Cronbach's alpha) for belonging was .75 and .74 for self-confidence. These values are considered to indicate satisfactory reliability.

To test our hypotheses, data were analyzed using separate two-way Analysis of Variance (ANOVA) models. Conference participation and URMW status were treated as two independent variables in each model. Belonging and self-confidence were treated as dependent variables separately. Statistical significance was determined using $p \leq .05$.

3.3.2 Study 2. The constructs used for sense of belonging and self-confidence were tested for reliability at both time 1 and time 2 by calculating Cronbach's alpha values. Sense of belonging measure had Cronbach's alpha values of .76 at time 1 and .84 at time 2. Self-confidence construct had Cronbach's alpha values of .74 at time 1 and .76 at time 2. Based on these alpha coefficients, these constructs have satisfactory reliability.

In order to test the changes in students' belonging and self-confidence, we used two-way repeated measures ANOVA models. In our models, belonging and self-confidence measures were the dependent variables while URMW and conference participation were independent variables. Note that belonging and self-confidence were modeled separately. Statistical significance was determined using $p \leq .05$.

4 RESULTS

In this section, we present our findings for each study by outcome measure.

4.1 Study 1

Belonging. In our analysis, we first looked at all first and second year students' sense of belonging as a function of their conference participation. Results indicated an effect of conference participation, $F(1, 3643) = 8.42, p \leq .01$; such that students who participated in a conference in the past year reported a stronger sense of belonging in computing than students who had no conference participation.

Next, we examined whether the effect of conference participation on first and second year students differed by their represented status (URMW vs MM). First, results revealed that MM students reported stronger confidence to persist in computing overall than URMW students ($F(1, 3643) = 155.14, p \leq .01$), regardless of conference participation. Second, we found that URMW first and second year students who participated in a conference reported a stronger sense of belonging than URWM students without conference participation, $F(1, 3643) = 9.31, p \leq .01$. Finally, results indicated no difference in belonging for MM as a function of their conference participation, $F(1, 3643) = .88, p = .35$. See Figure 1a for a visualization of these results, including 95% confidence intervals, based on mean values.

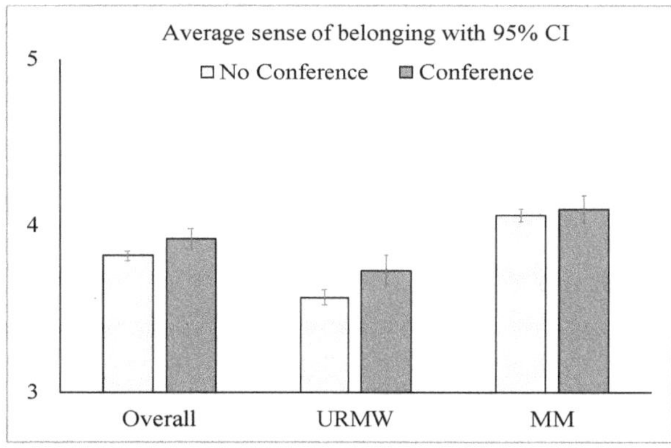

(a) Belonging

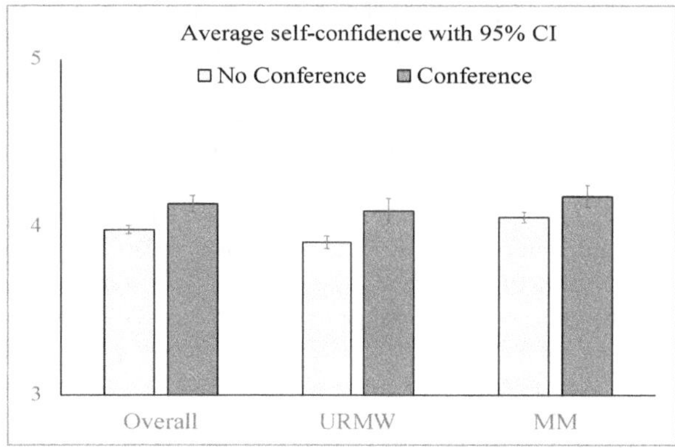

(b) Self-confidence

Figure 1: Study 1 Results-Sense of belonging and self-confidence by conference participation and group

Self-confidence. Next, we tested all first and second year students' confidence to persist in computing as a function of their conference participation. Results revealed that students with prior conference experience reported stronger confidence to persist in computing than non-participants, $F(1, 3645) = 31.24, p \leq .01$. When testing for differences in conference participation as a function of students representation status, results indicated both URMW ($F(1, 3643) = 20.01, p \leq .01$) and MM ($F(1, 3643) = 11.44, p \leq .01$) students reported stronger confidence if they had participated in a conference compared to URMW and MM students who had not participated in a conference.

Finally, while MM reported stronger self-confidence to persist in computing overall than URMW students ($F(1, 3645) = 18.16, p \leq .01$), the difference in confidence between MM and URMW students disappeared among conference participants, $F(1, 3645) = 3.09, p = .08$. See Figure 1b for a visualization of these results, including 95% confidence intervals, based on mean values.

4.2 Study 2

Belonging. We began by looking at time 2 pairwise comparisons in order to see if they aligned with our findings in Study 1. We found that conference participants at time 2 had a stronger sense of belonging than non-participants overall ($F(1, 343) = 4.96, p \leq .05$). When we look at this comparison for URMW and MM separately, we found that this difference was statistically significant only for the URMW students ($F(1, 343) = 6.98, p \leq .05$) and not for MM ($F(1, 343) = .04, p = .83$). These comparisons on data from 2015 replicated the results of Study 1.

Next, we examined the changes in students' sense of belonging over time. For the full sample, students who did not participate in a conference showed a statistically significant decrease in their sense of belonging over time ($F(1, 343) = 4.59, p \leq .05$). On the other hand, conference participants did not have a statistically significant change in their levels of belonging ($F(1, 343) = .22, p = .64$). When we looked at the change over time for URMW and MM separately, we found that while URMW students who did not participate in a conference showed a statistically significant decrease in their sense of belonging ($F(1, 343) = 4.73, p \leq .05$), URMW conference participants did not show a statistically significant change ($F(1, 343) = .22, p = .64$). MM did not have a statistically significant change in their belonging regardless of their conference participation (non-participants: $F(1, 343) = .52, p = .46$, participants: $F(1, 343) = .07, p = .79$). Figure 2a shows the results for the analysis of change in belonging over time, including 95% confidence intervals.

Self-confidence. We examined the pairwise comparisons at time 2 to understand if results aligned with our findings in Study 1. The overall comparison of conference participants and non-participants showed that students who participated in a conference had higher levels of confidence to persist in computing ($F(1, 343) = 6.51, p \leq .05$). Both URMW and MM conference participants had higher confidence to persist in computing; however, this comparison was not statistically significant for MM (URMW: $F(1, 343) = 4.07, p \leq .05$, MM: $F(1, 343) = 2.60, p = .11$) . While the overall difference of conference participants and non-participants aligned with that of Study 1, analyses in Study 2 did not show a statistically significant difference for MM.

When we looked at the effects of conference participation over time, we found that without conference participation, students' self-confidence decreased over time ($F(1, 343) = 7.95, p \leq .05$). On the other hand, conference participants did not experience a statistically significant change in their confidence to persist ($F(1, 343) = 2.68, p = .10$).

When we looked at this change for URMW and MM separately, our results showed that URMW non-participants showed a statistically significant decrease in their sense of belonging ($F(1, 343) = 5.49, p \leq .05$); MM non-participants did not have a statistically significant change in their self-confidence ($F(1, 343) = 2.53, p = .11$). For students who participated in a conference, neither URMW nor MM showed a statistically significant change in their confidence to persist in computing (URMW: $F(1, 343) = .36, p = .55$, MM: $F(1, 343) = 2.71, p = .10$). Figure 2b shows the results for the analysis of change in confidence to persist in computing over time, including 95% confidence intervals.

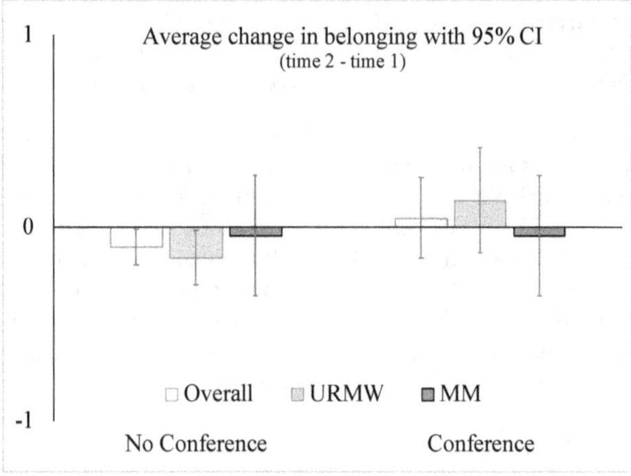

(a) Belonging

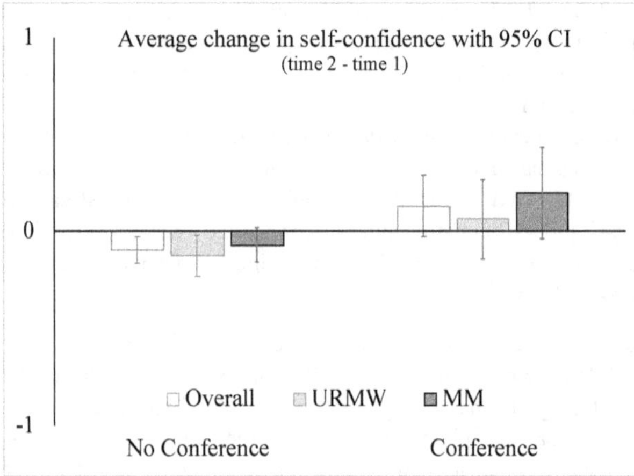

(b) Self-confidence

Figure 2: Study 2 Results- Sense of belonging and self-confidence by conference participation and group

5 DISCUSSION

We aimed to examine any relationship between conference participation and non-cognitive psychological factors related to students' persistence in computing. Specifically, we focused on first and second year undergraduate students, as intervening early on in these critical years may help retain students in the long term [20]. Studies have found that, especially in the case of women and racial/ethnic minorities, students experience a decline in their belonging and self-confidence after they enter into their degree programs [8, 20, 22].

We argue that, based on the evidence supporting the positive impact of experiential learning activities on students' sense of belonging and self-confidence [21, 29–31, 35, 39, 42], participating in conferences may help attenuate the conditions that result in attrition.

Our goal in the current research was to test our hypothesis that conference participation, an experiential learning opportunity, would have a positive impact on student retention in computing as measured in students' self-reported sense of belonging and confidence to persist in their field. We further hypothesized that this impact would be especially significant for URMW students, who tend to not only have comparatively lower levels of belonging and confidence to persist [28, 43], but also leave their degree programs at higher rates [14, 19, 23, 28, 37, 38, 40].

Taken together, results from our studies indicate that conference participants report higher levels of belonging and confidence in their ability to persist in computing. These findings were replicated in cross-sectional data from two separate years: 2015 in Study 2 and 2016 in Study 1. Our analysis also indicated that not only does conference participation benefit all students, URMW students seem to reap the most benefits from conference participation.

In Study 1, URMW students who participated in a conference had a stronger sense of belonging than non-participant URMW students, while MM's sense of belonging did not differ based on their conference participation. Overall, both URMW and MM conference participants were more confident in their ability to persist in computing compared to their non-participant counterparts. Even though URMW students as a whole had lower confidence levels than MM, this gap in confidence levels between URMW and MM students held only for those who did not participate in a conference and was not present for conference participants.

Study 2 showed that conference participation helped eliminate the decrease that is observed in non-participant URMW students' sense of belonging and confidence to persist over time. Overall, URMW students showed a decrease in their belonging and confidence levels over time while MM did not experience a significant change in either of these measures. However, URMW students who participated in a conference did not experience this decrease. MM's levels of belonging and confidence over time did not change regardless of their conference participation.

It is also important to note that while we observed statistically significant benefits of conference participation on students' sense of belonging and confidence to persist in computing, we also observed that URMW students reported both weaker belonging and confidence on average than MM students. This finding is consistent with existing research and theory that posits that students in underrepresented groups are more likely than their majority peers to feel like they do not belong and think about leaving their field, as discussed above; however, given that results from our study indicate conference participation may eliminate these differences, our research findings support recommendations to provide experiential learning opportunities to help retain students in the field.

5.1 Limitations and Future Work

More work is necessary to understand the extent to which conferences make an impact on student retention in the long-term. For example, while Study 2 examines two time points of data from a panel of students, additional time points can examine whether participation in conferences has a sustained impact on the students' belonging and confidence to persist. Additional time points of data would also allow for the examination of actual persistence; the current work only examines students' *confidence* to persist.

Furthermore, additional work is needed to examine causal mechanisms linking conference participation to higher belonging and confidence levels, which can help illuminate the way in which conferences (and other experiential learning interventions) influence students' persistence in the field. This would provide practitioners with more insight on what aspects of these activities are especially important for students and help inform decision-making related to broadening participation in computing. Additional work should also help identify other interventions that have similar positive impacts on students' belonging, self-confidence, and ultimately, their persistence. Because this study only examines one form of intervention, conference participation, additional research examining other forms of interventions will be an important consideration for future work.

Finally, as discussed earlier, a larger portion of undergraduates who attended conferences are more likely to be students who are further along in their degree programs [44], understandably, as these students have already engaged more deeply in their computing major. However, this research does not explore any impacts of conference participation on third and fourth year students. This research also does not explore impacts of conference participation on students in individual computing majors, nor does it examine group differences by students' individual racial/ethnic and gender identities. Future work should compare the differential impact of conference attendance on third and fourth year undergraduates versus first and second year students' psychological and environmental factors that are related to persistence, in addition to exploring differences in the impact of conference attendance on differing computing majors and group identities. Even so, this work is a first-step in understanding, empirically, whether it is worth the time and financial resources to send undergraduate students early in their education to conferences in computing; at present, research results suggest that it might be a worthwhile investment.

ACKNOWLEDGMENTS

This research was sponsored by NSF grants CNS-1246649 and DUE-1431112. We wish to thank Dr. Jane Stout for her intellectual contributions during the development stage of this research. We also wish to thank Data Buddies Survey departments for contributing to the data source for this paper (participating departments can be found here: https://cra.org/cerp/data-buddies/).

REFERENCES

[1] Christine Alvarado, Zachary Dodds, and Ran Libeskind-Hadas. 2012. Increasing Women's Participation in Computing at Harvey Mudd College. *ACM Inroads* 3, 4 (2012), 55–64. https://doi.org/10.1145/2381083.2381100

[2] Christine Alvarado and Eugene Judson. 2014. Using Targeted Conferences to Recruit Women into Computer Science. *Commun. ACM* 57, 3 (2014), 70–77. https://doi.org/10.1145/2500883

[3] Albert Bandura. 1977. Self-efficacy: Toward a unifying theory of behavioral change. *Psychological Review* (1977), 191–215.

[4] Albert Bandura. 1986. *Social foundations of thought and action: A social cognitive theory.* Prentice-Hall, Englewood Cliffs, NJ.

[5] Albert Bandura. 1997. *Self-Efficacy: The exercise of control.* W. H. Freeman, New York, NY.

[6] Roy F. Baumeister, C. Nathan DeWall, Natalie J Ciarocco, and Jean M. Twenge. 2005. Social exclusion impairs self-regulation. *Journal of Personality and Social Psychology* 88, 4 (2005), 589–604. https://doi.org/10.1037/0022-3514.88.4.589

[7] Roy F. Baumeister and Mark R. Leary. 1995. The need to belong: desire for interpersonal attachments as a fundamental human motivation. *Psychological Bulletin* 117, 3 (1995), 497–529. https://doi.org/10.1037/0033-2909.117.3.497

[8] Suzanne G. Brainard and Linda Carlin. 1998. A Six-Year Longitudinal Study of Undergraduate Women in Engineering and Science. 87, 4 (1998), 369–375. https://doi.org/10.1002/j.2168-9830.1998.tb00367.x

[9] National Student Clearinghouse Research Center. 2017. *Snapshot Report: First-year Persistence and Retention.* Technical Report. Herndon, VA. https://nscresearchcenter.org/wp-content/uploads/SnapshotReport28a.pdf

[10] Geoffrey L. Cohen and Julio Garcia. 2008. Identity, Belonging, and Achievement: A Model, Interventions, Implications. *Current Directions in Psychological Science* 17, 6 (2008), 365–369. https://doi.org/10.1111/j.1467-8721.2008.00607.x

[11] Janet Davis and Christine Alvarado. 2017. Supporting Undergraduates to Make the Most of Conferences. *ACM Inroads* 8, 3 (2017), 32–35. https://doi.org/10.1145/3123661

[12] Edward L. Deci and Richard M. Ryan. 2000. The "What" and "Why" of Goal Pursuits: Human Needs and the Self-Determination of Behavior. *Psychological Inquiry* 11, 4 (2000), 227–268. 10.1207/S15327965PLI1104_01.

[13] Cara M. Djonko-Moore, Jacqueline Leonard, Quintaniay Holifield, Elsa B. Bailey, and Sultan M. Almughyirah. 2018. Using Culturally Relevant Experiential Education to Enhance Urban Children's Knowledge and Engagement in Science. *Journal of Experiential Education* 41, 2 (2018), 137–153. https://doi.org/10.1177/1053825917742164

[14] Rogers Elliott, A. Christopher Strenta, Russell Adair, Michael Matier, and Jannah Scott. 1996. The role of ethnicity in choosing and leaving science in highly selective institutions. *Research in Higher Education* 37, 6 (1996), 681–709. https://doi.org/10.1007/BF01792952

[15] Emerson. 2018. Emerson Survey: 2 in 5 Americans Believe the STEM Worker Shortage is at Crisis Levels. (2018). https://www.emerson.com/en-us/news/corporate/2018-stem-survey

[16] Computing Research Association, Center for Evaluating the Research Pipeline. 2015. Data Buddies Survey Longitudinal Undergraduate Student Dataset (2014-1015). (2015). https://cra.org/cerp/data-buddies/

[17] Computing Research Association, Center for Evaluating the Research Pipeline. 2016. Data Buddies Survey Undergraduate Student Dataset. (2016). https://cra.org/cerp/data-buddies/

[18] National Science Foundation. 2012. CISE Strategic Plan for Broadening Participation. (2012). https://www.nsf.gov/cise/oad/cise_bp.jsp.

[19] Alberta M. Gloria, Jeanett Castellanos, Ambrocia G. Lopez, and Rocio Rosales. 2005. An Examination of Academic Nonpersistence Decisions of Latino Undergraduates. *Hispanic Journal of Behavioral Sciences* 27, 2 (2005), 202–223. https://doi.org/10.1177/0739986305275098

[20] Leslie R. M. Hausmann, Janet W. Schofield, and Rochelle L. Woods. 2007. Sense of Belonging as a Predictor of Intentions to Persist Among African American and White First-Year College Students. *Research in Higher Education* 48, 7 (2007), 803–839. https://doi.org/10.1007/s11162-007-9052-9

[21] Anne-Barrie Hunter, Sandra L. Laursen, and Elaine Seymour. 2007. Becoming a scientist: The role of undergraduate research in students' cognitive, personal, and professional development. *Science Education* 91, 1 (2007), 36–74. https://doi.org/10.1002/sce.20173

[22] Sylvia Hurtado, Deborah Faye Carter, and Albert Spuler. 1996. *Latino Student Transition to College: Assessing Difficulties and Factors in Successful College Adjustment.* Technical Report 2. 135–157 pages. https://doi.org/10.1007/BF01730113

[23] Dagoberto Heredia Jr., Brandy Piña Watson, Linda Castillo, Lizette Ojeda, and Miguel Ángel Cano. 2018. Academic Nonpersistence Among Latina/o College Students: Examining Cultural and Social Factors. *Journal of Diversity in Higher Education* 11, 2 (2018), 192–200. https://doi.org/10.1037/dhe0000041

[24] Jim Kurose. 2017. NSF 17-110 Dear colleague letter: Pursuing meaningful actions in support of broadening participation in computing (BPC). (2017). https://www.nsf.gov/pubs/2017/nsf17110/nsf17110.jsp

[25] David Lapatto. 2007. Undergraduate Research Experiences Support Science Career Decisions and Active Learning. *CBE Life Sciences Education* 6, 4 (2007), 297–306. https://doi.org/10.1187/cbe.07-06-0039

[26] Richard M. Lee, Matthew Draper, and Sujin Lee. 2001. Social Connectedness, Dysfunctional Interpersonal Behaviors, and Psychological Distress: Testing a Mediator Model. *Journal of Counseling Psychology* 48, 3 (2001), 310–318. https://doi.org/10.1037/2F0022-0167.48.3.310

[27] Richard M. Lee and Steven B. Robbins. 1998. The Relationship between Social Connectedness and Anxiety, Self-Esteem, and Social Identity. *Journal of Counseling Psychology* 45, 3 (1998), 338–345. https://doi.org/10.1037//0022-0167.45.3.338

[28] Karyn L. Lewis, Jane G. Stout, Noah D. Finkelstein, Steven J. Pollock, Akira Miyake, Geoff L. Cohen, and Tiffany A. Ito. 2017. Fitting in to Move Forward: Belonging, Gender, and Persistence in the Physical Sciences, Technology, Engineering, and Mathematics (pSTEM). *Psychology of Women Quarterly* 41, 4 (2017), 420–436. https://doi.org/10.1177/0361684317720186

[29] Patricia Ann Mabrouk. 2009. Survey Study Investigating the Significance of Conference Participation to Undergraduate Research Students. *Journal of Chemical Education* 86, 11 (2009), 1335–1340. https://doi.org/10.1021/ed086p1335

[30] Joseph L. Mahoney and Robert B. Cairns. 1997. Do Extracurricular Activities Protect Against Early School Dropout? *Developmental Psychology* 33, 2 (1997), 241–253. https://doi.org/10.1037/0012-1649.33.2.241

[31] Ama Nyame-Mensah. 2015. Strengthening the computing research pipeline through minority participation: The case for undergraduate research experiences. *2015 Research in Equity and Sustained Participation in Engineering, Computing, and Technology (RESPECT)* (2015), 1–7. https://doi.org/10.1109/RESPECT.2015.7296499

[32] U.S. Department of Education, Institute of Education Sciences, National Center for Education Statistics. 2015. Integrated Postsecondary Education Data System (IPEDS): Completions Survey. (2015). https://nces.ed.gov/ipeds/use-the-data

[33] Bureau of Labor Statistics, U.S. Department of Labor, Occupational Outlook Handbook. 2018. Computer and Information Technology Occupations. (2018). https://www.bls.gov/ooh/computer-and-information-technology/home.htm

[34] Laura D. Pittman and Adeya Richmond. 2007. Academic and Psychological Functioning in Late Adolescence: The Importance of School Belonging. *Journal of Experimental Education* 75, 4 (2007), 270–290. https://doi.org/10.3200/JEXE.75.4.270-292

[35] Susan H. Russell, Mary P. Hancock, and James McCullough. 2007. Benefits of Undergraduate Research Experiences. *Science* 316, 5824 (2007), 548–549. https://doi.org/10.1126/science.1140384

[36] Dale H. Schunk. 1991. Self-Efficacy and Academic Motivation. *Educational Psychologist* 26, 3-4 (1991), 207–231. https://doi.org/10.1080/00461520.1991.9653133

[37] A. Christopher Strenta, Rogers Elliott, Russell Adair, Michael Matier, and Jannah Scott. 1994. Choosing and leaving science in highly selective institutions. *Research in Higher Education* 35, 5 (1994), 513–547. https://doi.org/10.1007/BF02497086

[38] N. Burçin Tamer. 2018. About 1 in 3 Underrepresented Minority Students and Students with Disabilities (URMD) Reported Thinking About Leaving Their Graduate Program. *Computing Research News* 30, 5 (2018), 52. https://cra.org/crn/2018/05/about-1-in-3-underrepresented-minority-students-and-students-with-disabilities-urmd-reported-thinking-about-leaving-their-graduate-program/

[39] N. Burçin Tamer. 2018. Students who participated in diversity conferences are more confidence in their ability to complete their undergraduate degree in computing. *Computing Research News* 30, 7 (2018), 10–11. https://cra.org/crn/2018/08/diversity-conferences/

[40] N. Burçin Tamer and Jane G. Stout. 2016. *Recruitment and retention of undergraduate students in computing: Patterns by gender and race/ethnicity.* Technical Report. Washington, DC. https://cra.org/cerp/wp-content/uploads/sites/4/2017/05/CSRecruitmentRetention.pdf

[41] Vincent Tinto. 1999. Taking Retention Seriously: Rethinking the First Year of College. *NACADA Journal* 19, 2 (1999), 5–9. https://doi.org/10.12930/0271-9517-19.2.5

[42] Helen Walkington, Jennifer Hill, and Pauline E. Kneale. 2017. Reciprocal elucidation: A student-led pedagogy in multidisciplinary undergraduate research conferences. *Higher Education Research & Development* 36, 2 (2017), 416 – 429. https://doi.org/10.1080/07294360.2016.1208155

[43] Gregory M. Walton and Geoffrey L. Cohen. 2007. A Question of Belonging: Race, Social Fit, and Achievement. *Journal of Personality and Social Psychology* 92, 1 (2007), 82–96. https://doi.org/10.1037/0022-3514.92.1.82

[44] Heather M. Wright. 2017. Which students are attended technical conferences in computing? *Computing Research News* 29, 9 (2017), 13. http://cra.org/crn/2017/10/students-attending-technical-conferences-computing/

[45] Sharon Zumbrunn, Courtney McKim, Eric Buhs, and Leslie R. Hawley. 2014. Support, belonging, motivation, and engagement in the college classroom: A mixed method study. *Instructional Science* 42, 5 (2014), 661–684. https://doi.org/10.1007/s11251-014-9310-0

[46] Stewart Zweben and Betsy Bizot. 2016. 2015 Taulbee Survey: Continued booming undergraduate CS enrollment: Doctoral degree production dips slightly. *Computing Research News* 28, 5 (2016), 2–60.

[47] Stewart Zweben and Betsy Bizot. 2017. 2016 Taulbee Survey: Generation CS continues to produce record undergrad enrollment; Graduate degree production rises at both master's and doctoral levels. *Computing Research News* 29, 5 (2017), 3–51.

[48] Stewart Zweben and Betsy Bizot. 2018. 2017 CRA Taulbee Survey: Another year of record undergrad enrollment: Doctoral degree production steady while master's production rises again. *Computing Research News* 30, 5 (2018), 2–48.

Stride in BlueJ – Computing for All in an Educational IDE

Michael Kölling
King's College London
London, UK
michael.kolling@kcl.ac.uk

Neil C. C. Brown
King's College London
London, UK
neil.c.c.brown@kcl.ac.uk

Hamza Hamza
King's College London
London, UK
hamza.hamza@kcl.ac.uk

Davin McCall
King's College London
London, UK
davin.mccall@kcl.ac.uk

ABSTRACT

Block-based programming languages and environments have several benefits for introductory programming courses, compared to more traditional text-based languages. In particular, blocks remove the burden of learning language syntax and dealing with syntax-related errors. Many blocks-based environments are tightly focused on developing graphical games, stories and simulations, while the more general programming environments are typically text-based. In this tool paper, we describe the incorporation of a Stride editor within the BlueJ programming environment. Stride is a frame-based programming language, intended to combine the best of blocks and text programming, usable both as a stepping stone towards text-based languages and as a comprehensive language in its own right. The incorporation of Stride into BlueJ brings some aspects of block programming into a general purpose educational environment.

CCS CONCEPTS

• **Social and professional topics → Computing education**; • **General and reference →** *Design*;

KEYWORDS

BlueJ; Stride; Frame-based Editing

ACM Reference Format:

Michael Kölling, Neil C. C. Brown, Hamza Hamza, and Davin McCall. 2019. Stride in BlueJ – Computing for All in an Educational IDE. In *Proceedings of the 50th ACM Technical Symposium on Computer Science Education (SIGCSE '19), February 27-March 2, 2019, Minneapolis, MN, USA.* ACM, New York, NY, USA, 7 pages. https://doi.org/10.1145/3287324.3287462

1 INTRODUCTION

The teaching of programming, as part of computer science education, was long seen as a specialist skill relevant only to those who were considering a career in a computing-related discipline, or those with a special interest in the subject. As a result, programming was taught in specialist courses, either in higher education or in advanced, usually elective subjects in school.

In the last decade or so, computing has been increasingly viewed as a subject relevant to all learners, as part of a general education. Computer science – and with it, programming – is now often taught early in a school curriculum (in lower secondary school, or in primary school) [11]. This development represents perhaps the single most significant change in the teaching of programming in this century so far, and it has significant ramifications for the methods and tools that should be employed.

The trend towards teaching computing as a discipline for all, as part of a general education, brings with it an expectation that the content learned in this subject cover material that is generally useful in many domains. Consequently, arcane details that are only relevant to professional software developers working with specific systems, which may have been acceptable as part of a specialist programming course, are much harder to justify.

A common challenge in curriculum and tool design is, therefore, the separation of fundamental concepts from accidental complexities. While the former should be exposed as clearly as possible, the latter should be avoided as much as is practical.

In this paper, we discuss the design of a new version of a widely used introductory program development environment, BlueJ, to take account of this development. BlueJ was initially designed to allow development in the Java programming language. The use of Java, a language designed for professional software engineers, is defensible in specialist computer science courses, but much less so in a generalist educational setting with younger learners. Its sometimes arcane and error-prone syntax introduces a significant amount of accidental complexity, mastery of which is hard to justify if the goal is an understanding of fundamental and generic computing concepts.

As a result, we added support for a new, more suitable language to BlueJ: a language called *Stride* [7]. Stride differs from traditional text-based languages mostly in its program manipulation support, provided by its *frame-based editor.* In this paper, we describe and discuss the features of Stride, its integration into BlueJ, and the benefits that result for general early programming education from this design. A link to the full, downloadable system is provided at the end of this paper.

2 A SHORT HISTORY OF BLUEJ

BlueJ was initially designed for use at introductory university level. It is, however, also widely used at schools, usually in elective computer sciences courses in the last years of a school curriculum.

BlueJ differs from mainstream Java development environments in its interface and functionality. The interface emphasises program structure, classes and objects. In its main window, BlueJ shows a simplified UML diagram and a visualisation of objects, which can be interactively created (Figure 1). BlueJ has functionality specifically designed to aid the learning of object-oriented programming, such as the ability to interactively invoke individual methods of arbitrary objects, supply parameters, observe return values, and inspect object state.

SIGCSE '19, February 27-March 2, 2019, Minneapolis, MN, USA

ACM ISBN 978-1-4503-5890-3/19/02...$15.00
https://doi.org/10.1145/3287324.3287462

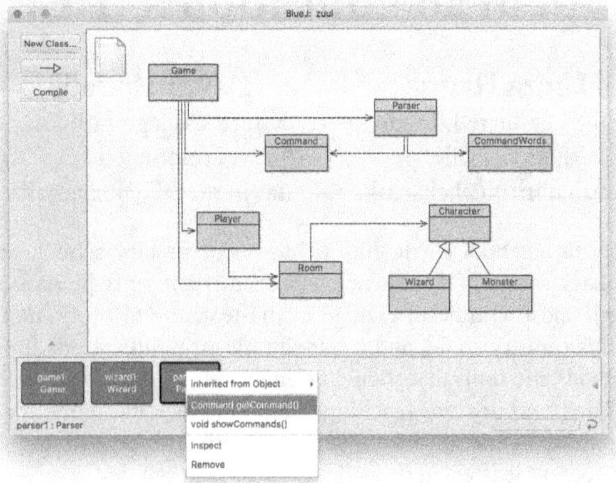

Figure 1: The main window of BlueJ, showing the class diagram and three objects on the object bench. Individual method can be invoked on objects via a context menu.

Figure 2: The BlueJ Java editor with scope highlighting, providing dynamic background colouring.

The main interface of the environment is significantly simpler and easier to learn to master than that of professional IDEs. BlueJ is, however, not a subset or cut-down version of a standard IDE: its aim is not to offer fewer features but to offer different features. Many of the educationally important interaction features are not available in other IDEs.

While BlueJ's original functionality provided significant innovation in IDE design and interaction, the programming language supported was standard Java. In the early versions of BlueJ, the editor for program entry and manipulation was a standard text editor, not significantly different from many other editors in use in programming systems.

BlueJ 3.0, released in 2010, introduced a new editor that supported scope highlighting (Figure 2). This functionality addressed one of the most common programming problems for beginners: the management of nested scopes. Beginning programmers often did not maintain consistent indentation and struggled with balancing the scope-defining brackets. Missing or surplus brackets were common and hard to diagnose. Auto-indentation and scope highlighting made these kinds of errors more obvious: The editor provides dynamic, real-time background colouring which makes spotting unbalanced brackets easier. It also aids in general readability of the code. The program manipulation, however, is character-based, and scope highlighting does little to prevent errors being made in the first place.

The overall abstractions provided via the main BlueJ interface worked well to illustrate important concepts, even for generalist programming courses with younger learners. The Java language, however, and particularly the text-based editor, introduced a significant amount of unnecessary complexity that resulted in frequent problems, usually with small-scale syntax issues. Spending time fixing such errors has little benefit for the understanding of fundamental programming principles.

3 THE RISE OF BLOCKS

When programming teaching was considered for younger audiences, including children under ten years old, text-based systems were not feasible. Instead, block-based languages, such as Scratch [8] became popular, which can be used at that age group.

Block-based languages introduced a number of important innovations that provide significant benefits for younger learners: Syntax errors were largely impossible to make, program statements were more readable due to labelling that is closer to natural language, and statements were discoverable by being presented on a block palette for experimentation and discovery.

Most importantly for our discussion: block-based languages removed much of the accidental complexity of dealing with character-based syntax and allowed learners and teachers to concentrate on the underlying computational concepts.

4 FROM BLOCKS TO TEXT

While block-based languages reduce or remove many potential syntax-related stumbling blocks that might obstruct the initial progress of a novice programmer, and are well-suited to younger programmers, they have some drawbacks in relation to the viscosity of the editing process: small code fragments which may be simple in appearance and function require a non-trivial amount of user action to create and place correctly, as each block must be dragged in from the palette. This quickly becomes a restrictive factor in the ability of the learner to create larger programs.

An additional limitation is inherent in learners' perception of the system: students may perceive a block-based language as a "toy" language [9], not suitable for real-world programming. This may affect their motivation and impact their desire to learn.

To alleviate the eventual frustration with block-based programming, a curriculum must at some point transition to a more traditional language and environment. In schools with a full computer science curriculum, such as those in England, this transition from blocks to a text-based environment typically occurs between school years 7 and 9 (age 12 to 14). However, this transition is not without its difficulties, as students encounter a raft of potential errors and pitfalls that were not possible in a purely block-based environment. Previous work [6] has identified a number of significant challenges that students face:

(1) Reduced readability due to terser and more punctuation-heavy syntax.
(2) The necessity of memorising commands rather than selecting them from a palette, and of memorising syntactical structure.
(3) The increased need for typing and spelling skills.
(4) An increased number of available commands.
(5) The need to match method call syntax with method definitions residing elsewhere in the code.
(6) Understanding how syntactical elements are used to group compound statements and determine lexical scope.
(7) More complex type systems.
(8) More complex and more technical error messages.
(9) Managing manual layout, in particular indentation.
(10) A potentially different programming paradigm.

The significant set of issues illustrates the challenge of transitioning from a block-based to a text-based programming language. This leads us to pose two questions:

(1) How can we better support learners in the transition from block-based to text-based programming?
(2) Can we apply any aspects of the block-based approach to improve editors for more comprehensive, general programming languages? Although the editing viscosity can make block-based programming unattractive for larger projects, it does also provide some clear advantages. Some of these advantages might also be provided by a hybrid approach that lies somewhere between fully block-based and text-based programming.

In the following section, we introduce *Stride*, a programming language and corresponding editor designed around frame-based editing, a new editing paradigm which incorporates aspects of both block- and text-based programming. Stride both provides an intermediate transitional path for learners, and serves as an example to show that a comprehensive programming language which is suitable for larger and more complex projects can benefit from the ideas of block-based programming editors.

5 STRIDE

Stride is a Java-like programming language manipulated in a *frame-based programming editor*. Statements and other structural elements in the Stride language are represented in its editor as *frames*, coloured nested boxes that can be directly manipulated by the user (Figure 3). Frames are first-class interface elements: they can be inserted and deleted with a single keypress, or dragged and dropped into different location with the mouse. A context menu for common operations is available for all frames.

Frames are always present in their entirety: They are inserted and deleted in atomic operations, either with a single-key keyboard command, or by selection with the mouse from a palette (see below). Structurally incomplete statements, such as if-statements with a

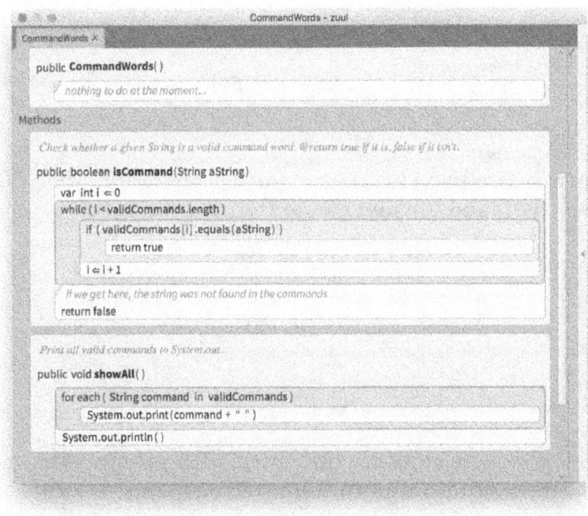

Figure 3: The Stride editor. Statements are represented by frames with a different background colour.

Figure 4: A frame for an if-statement with two empty slots: a text-slot for the condition, and a frame-slot for the body.

missing closing bracket, cannot exist, thus avoiding a large class of common syntax errors.

Frames, when inserted, may contain *slots* – holes to be filled to complete the statement. Slots are presented with white background, indicating an incomplete frame (Figure 4). Two types of slots exist: *text slots* for the insertion of expressions, and *frame slots* which hold nested frames.

Stride can be written and manipulated entirely with the keyboard. In contrast to block-based systems, the frame editor always displays a cursor to mark the editing locus. When the cursor is in a frame slot, a frame cursor is displayed that allows the entry of further frames. Focusing a text slot displays a text cursor that allows semi-structured text entry (Figure 5). Thus, editing, while exhibiting some properties similar to block-based systems, is quicker and more efficient than block-based systems which rely entirely on mouse interaction for manipulation.

While frames at the statement level automatically avoid many structural syntax errors, expressions and identifiers are not represented by frames. Here, text entry provides input significantly faster and more flexible than in block systems. Some structure is enforced in these text slots: Entry of parentheses, for example, is always in pairs. Entering or deleting one parenthesis will automatically enter

Figure 5: The two cursors for editing operation: the frame cursor (left) and the text cursor (right).

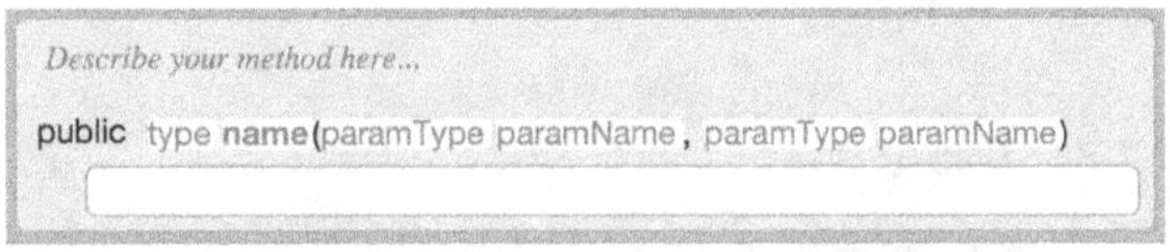

Figure 6: Frame slots are presented with prompts that provide information about the required elements.

or delete its matching counterpart. No unbalanced brackets can ever exist.

Semi-structured text entry represents a compromise between flexibility and error avoidance: It allows some syntax errors to be made in return for more flexible and faster program manipulation. Thus, Stride's syntax error characteristics sit between those of block-based and text-based systems: It avoids some common syntax errors, leading to fewer errors than in text systems, but allows others which are not possible in block-based systems.

Semantically, Stride is very similar to Java, with only minor differences in language constructs and an identical object model and type system. Most importantly, it is interoperable with Java, allowing full use of the standard Java libraries. Thus, the full functionality of the Java ecosystem is available. In fact, Stride and Java classes can be used side-by-side in the same BlueJ project.

A more detailed description of the features of Stride and its frame based editor is presented elsewhere [7].

6 REDUCING COMPLEXITY

Stride's frame editor provides several features that reduce cognitive load for novice programmers, avoid the need to memorise unnecessary detail and aid the transition from block-based programming systems.

6.1 Code structure

The editor provides an overall template for the class definition, with clearly labelled areas for fields, constructors and methods. These program elements, as well as statements, can only be inserted where they are syntactically valid.

Frames, when they are dragged, can only be dropped at syntactically valid places in the source code. Thus, structurally valid code is maintained at all times. The atomic insertion and manipulation of frames also ensures that detailed statement syntax, such as the punctuation required for a for-loop, does not need to be memorised or typed by the novice learner. Both the requirement of memorisation of syntax and the requirement of accurate typing typically present barriers for young learners in text-based systems.

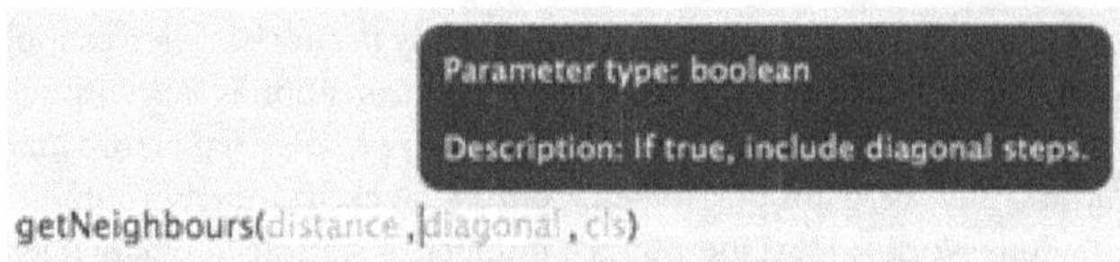

Figure 7: Parameter slots show formal parameter names; additional information is displayed on demand.

Figure 8: Frame slots are presented with prompts that provide information about the required elements.

6.2 Prompts and help

When compound frames are created, prompt texts in empty slots provide information about the program element expected (Figure 6). These prompts provide valuable help to beginners who may not remember the syntactical structure of a given statement.

Other prompt texts remain useful even after statement structures have become familiar. In method-call frames, for example, entering a valid method name automatically creates slots for each expected parameter with prompt texts displaying the parameter name. Hovering over the parameter slots with the mouse displays additional information in a popup, including the expected parameter type and a help text (Figure 7). These mechanisms make the available information much more visible at the point of insertion and reduce cognitive load for the learner.

6.3 Restricted entry

Some type of slots only allow a small number of possible values; in these cases entry is as a selection from a valid value set (Figure 8). Values in these selection slots can be typed, with completions of the typed prefix displayed and offered for selection. Beginners can inspect the full set of available choices.

6.4 Improved error display

Errors in Stride are displayed as red underlines in the program code. Focusing on the error location with the mouse or text cursor displays the error message, and may offer possible fixes (Figure 9). If a fix is offered, it can be selected from the popup to be enacted automatically.

Because of the enforced statement structure of the program text, error messages are generally more accurate than in freeform text editors. The error location can always be correctly attributed to a specific slot. Situations typical in text-based systems, where an error is reported far from its actual cause, cannot arise in Stride.

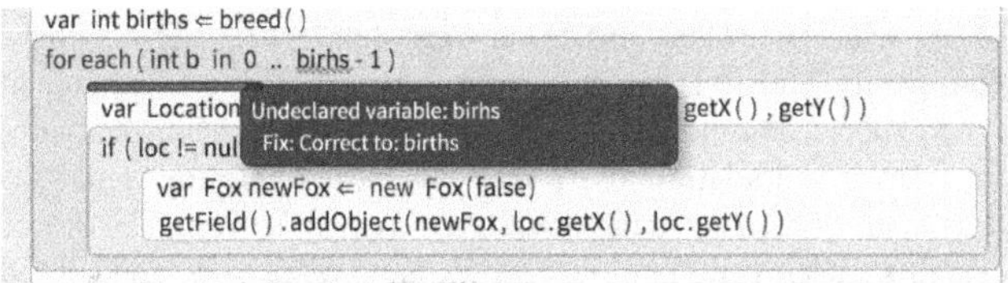

Figure 9: Errors may be followed by suggested fixes, which can be selected to enact the fix.

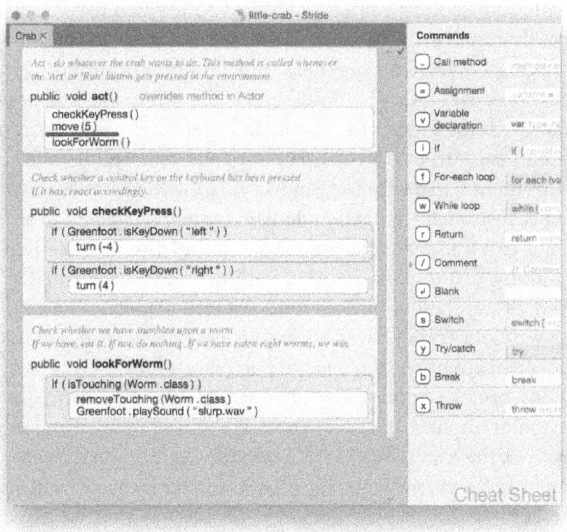

Figure 10: The right-hand side cheat sheet shows the available frames that can be inserted at the current frame cursor position.

6.5 The 'Cheat Sheet'

To aid in the memorisation of available statements and their key commands, a selection palette – named the "Cheat Sheet" – can optionally be displayed at the right-hand side of the editor (Figure 10). This cheat sheet always displays the complete set of available frame options, together with their keyboard shortcuts. A mouse click on a command in the cheat sheet inserts the corresponding frame in the code (as does, of course, activation of its command key). The cheat sheet is context sensitive: it displays only language elements that are syntactically valid at the current cursor position.

The cheat sheet provides an aid for recognition over recall, as the typical block palettes do in block-based systems. In contrast to block systems, not all method calls are listed individually (but rather, "Call method" is listed as a single frame type). As a result, the number of choices at any time is limited, and all available frames can easily be displayed. (The example shown in Figure 10 indeed shows all available program statement types.)

Investigation and choice of individual methods is provided via method call auto-completion functionality.

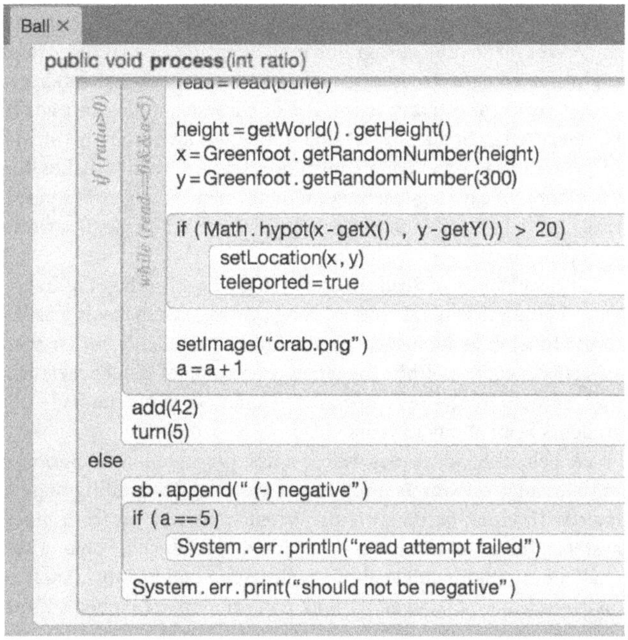

Figure 11: When code scrolls out of view, method headers are pinned to the top of the editor window. Header text of scopes that are not fully visible is displayed in the side bar of the scope frame.

6.6 Visual aids

The move away from characters as the basic unit of representation of program text opens the door for many options of visual program presentation that adds additional useful information for programmers. Figure 11 shows two examples of this: When longer methods scroll partially out of view, it is generally useful to still be able to tell which method is currently displayed. Consequently, the Stride editor pins the method header to the top of the window and scrolls the method body underneath.

In similar fashion, when the header of long scope frames scrolls out of view, the header text is displayed in the left indent area of the frame.

Both these examples demonstrate how the move away from plain text editors opens opportunities for better program display that increases readability.

7 STRIDE IN BLUEJ

Stride was originally implemented in the Greenfoot IDE [5], which – like many block-based systems – is a development environment with a restricted application domain: It is designed exclusively for the development of two-dimensional graphical applications, typically simple games or simulations. With the release of BlueJ 4.0, Stride is now available in BlueJ, a general-purpose IDE with a generic, non-restricted application domain – alongside the pre-existing Java editor.

The availability of Stride in BlueJ brings frame-based editing to a more general application domain that was previously covered only by Java, and not typically addressed by block-based environments.

Typical BlueJ-based teaching examples include GUI programs using Swing or JavaFX, programs implementing or making use of sophisticated data structures, applications connecting to databases or networks, and many more. All of these examples can easily be rewritten in Stride. In fact, BlueJ includes an automatic Stride-to-Java and Java-to-Stride conversion feature, which makes the translation of existing teaching examples easy. The translation feature also helps students in the progression from Stride to writing Java programs.

The availability of Stride in BlueJ brings the advantages of frame-based editing to general programming courses, and makes it feasible to use BlueJ in generalist courses aimed at all students, rather than specialist electives. While the target user group of BlueJ previously was learners from age 16 upwards, we now recommend use with students from about 13 years old.

We believe Stride serves well as a first programming experience at that age group, or as a follow-on system after gaining experience with block-based systems. When transitioning from block systems, the problems listed in section 4 are reduced. Some of the challenges remain and lead to new learning and insights (such as an extended command set, a more powerful object model, a more generic type system), while many of the incidental, purely syntactic complications are avoided [6].

When Stride is used in general programming courses for all students, its use serves two different purposes for two distinct user groups. For learners who do not want to progress further in software development, Stride can be the endpoint of programming education. All meaningful programming concepts can be illustrated with Stride, and the subsequent learning of specific text-based syntax or professional development tools serves little purpose for a generalist education.

For programmers who want to progress to more powerful systems, on the other hand, Stride serves as a well-working stepping stone into fully text-based Java. The concepts learned in Stride translate directly into traditional languages and environments, and a Java-preview feature in the Stride editor helps in investigating syntactic differences that remain.

This combination ensures that interested students can progress to other systems smoothly, while those wanting to get an insight into the concepts of programming in general are not distracted by unnecessary syntactic problems.

8 EVALUATION

Prior to the addition of Stride, BlueJ already contained support for the Blackbox project [1], which tracks the programming activity of opted-in BlueJ users. Blackbox has support for global data collection, and for supporting local studies by tagging users of interest, with access available to interested researchers. Support for tracking Stride users has been added to Blackbox, which can thus be used as an evaluation platform.

Currently, Stride use is low in BlueJ due to it being a recent addition. We can examine whether users are using the keyboard controls – a distinctive feature of Stride – or whether they are using the mouse as they would in other blocks editors. Looking at the data up to 2018-08-06 (all numbers to nearest 100), we find that 13,500 frame insertions were performed by clicking on the cheat sheet, whereas 30,300 insertions were done using the keyboard commands. Thus it seems that most users are taking advantage of the keyboard commands to insert frames. Looking at the statistics for frame manipulation, there were 800 paste operations and 1300 drag operations, suggesting that the ability to drag frames by mouse remains a useful and popular way to manipulate code, and is used more than the clipboard.

9 RELATED WORK

There are many existing purely text-based and purely block-based programming languages, that we will not list here, as we are interested in hybrid approaches like Stride – in which there has been increasing interest. Currently the closest system to Stride is GP, a block-based system for general purpose programming [10]. GP shares some aspects with Stride, such as the ability to edit block-like syntax with the keyboard. The main difference is that GP retains Scratch's pattern of having a different customised block for each environment capability (e.g. move, turn), which limits its use to strongly restricted application domains, whereas Stride has a single method-call frame which can be used to call any Java method.

Looking to the past, structure editors, such as Boxer [2] and Barista [4], and older editors like GNOME [3], share various features with our frame-based editor. Structure editors failed to gain widespread adoption. We believe one reason for this was the poor usability of older editors. For example, navigating a structured expression often used abstract syntax tree-based navigation, so that to move in the expression "1 + 2" from the 1 to the plus, the user had to press the up cursor key. This is logical in terms of internal syntax trees, but to a novice programmer, it is counter-intuitive. (In Stride, this is achieved by pressing the right cursor key). Another issue is that many structure editors became structure editor generators, as many programmers realised that it was possible to generate an editor automatically from language grammar descriptions. Our experience with Stride suggests that many design decisions in editors need to consider carefully the language grammar, rather than being language-agnostic. Finally, previous structure editors enforced fixed structure all the way down, as Scratch does. We believe that this is too cumbersome for large program manipulation; our approach of having structure at high-levels and free-form text at lower levels is a more promising practical compromise. A fuller discussion of prior related work is presented elsewhere [7].

10 CONCLUSIONS

A programming environment for beginners should minimise accidental complexity. The main interface of BlueJ and the design of its interaction facilities for easy compilation, execution and testing of code have followed this principle for a long time.

BlueJ's reliance on standard text-based Java programming, however, still introduced a notable hurdle for beginners, especially younger beginners. The text editor presented complexity for little educational gain. With the addition of Stride, BlueJ removes another layer of complexity that enables novices to make fewer errors, progress more smoothly and better concentrate on fundamental programming concepts.

Download: BlueJ 4.*x* can be downloaded at www.bluej.org. BlueJ is free, open source and supports both Java and Stride.

REFERENCES

[1] Neil C. C. Brown, Michael Kölling, Davin McCall, and Ian Utting. 2014. Blackbox: A Large Scale Repository of Novice Programmers' Activity. In *Proceedings of the 45th ACM Technical Symposium on Computer Science Education (SIGCSE '14)*. ACM, New York, NY, USA, 223–228. https://doi.org/10.1145/2538862.2538924

[2] Andrea A diSessa. 1997. Twenty reasons why you should use Boxer (instead of Logo). In *Learning & Exploring with Logo: Proceedings of the Sixth European Logo Conference*. 7–27.

[3] David B. Garlan and Philip L. Miller. 1984. GNOME: An Introductory Programming Environment Based on a Family of Structure Editors. In *Proceedings of the First ACM SIGSOFT/SIGPLAN Software Engineering Symposium on Practical Software Development Environments (SDE 1)*. ACM, New York, NY, USA, 65–72. https://doi.org/10.1145/800020.808250

[4] Andrew J. Ko and Brad A. Myers. 2006. Barista: An Implementation Framework for Enabling New Tools, Interaction Techniques and Views in Code Editors. In *Proceedings of the SIGCHI Conference on Human Factors in Computing Systems (CHI '06)*. ACM, New York, NY, USA, 387–396. https://doi.org/10.1145/1124772.1124831

[5] Michael Kölling. 2010. The Greenfoot Programming Environment. *Trans. Comput. Educ.* 10, 4, Article 14 (Nov. 2010), 21 pages. https://doi.org/10.1145/1868358.1868361

[6] Michael Kölling, Neil C. C. Brown, and Amjad Altadmri. 2015. Frame-Based Editing: Easing the Transition from Blocks to Text-Based Programming. In *Proceedings of the Workshop in Primary and Secondary Computing Education (WiPSCE '15)*. ACM, New York, NY, USA, 29–38. https://doi.org/10.1145/2818314.2818331

[7] Michael Kölling, Neil C. C. Brown, and Amjad Altadmri. 2017. Frame-Based Editing. *Visual Languages and Sentient Systems* 3 (2017), 40–67.

[8] John Maloney, Mitchel Resnick, Natalie Rusk, Brian Silverman, and Evelyn Eastmond. 2010. The Scratch Programming Language and Environment. *Trans. Comput. Educ.* 10, 4, Article 16 (Nov. 2010), 15 pages. https://doi.org/10.1145/1868358.1868363

[9] José Alfredo Martínez-Valdés, J. Ángel Velázquez-Iturbide, and Raquel Hijón-Neira. 2017. A (Relatively) Unsatisfactory Experience of Use of Scratch in CS1. In *Proceedings of the 5th International Conference on Technological Ecosystems for Enhancing Multiculturality (TEEM 2017)*. ACM, New York, NY, USA, Article 8, 7 pages. https://doi.org/10.1145/3144826.3145356

[10] Jens Mönig, Yoshiki Ohshima, and John Maloney. 2015. Blocks at Your Fingertips: Blurring the Line Between Blocks and Text in GP. In *Proceedings of the 2015 IEEE Blocks and Beyond Workshop (Blocks and Beyond) (BLOCKS AND BEYOND '15)*. IEEE Computer Society, Washington, DC, USA, 51–53. https://doi.org/10.1109/BLOCKS.2015.7369001

[11] Informatics Europe & ACM Europe Working Group on Informatics Education. 2013. *Informatics education: Europe cannot afford to miss the boat.* Technical Report. ACM Europe.

uAssign: Scalable Interactive Activities for Teaching the Unix Terminal

Jacob Bailey
University of Illinois at Urbana-Champaign
Urbana, Illinois
jbbaile2@illinois.edu

Craig Zilles
University of Illinois at Urbana-Champaign
Urbana, Illinois
zilles@illinois.edu

ABSTRACT

We describe uAssign, an assignment system for teaching and assessing command line terminal skills. uAssign allows instructors to create auto-graded terminal assignments that require students to perform a high-level action that can be completed in many ways. Assignments can be randomized so that students can't re-use old solutions. uAssign is implemented via an in-browser terminal emulator that uses WebSockets to connect to a Docker container. Performance testing and its use in a large-enrollment lecture course show that it is efficient enough to handle a large number of concurrent users. A survey of students shows significant improvement in terminal skill confidence after using uAssign and that students have a high level of satisfaction with uAssign assignments.

CCS CONCEPTS

• **Applied computing** → **Education**; **Computer-assisted instruction**; *E-learning*;

KEYWORDS

assessment, Unix, terminal, command-line, auto-grading, scalable

ACM Reference Format:

Jacob Bailey and Craig Zilles. 2019. uAssign: Scalable Interactive Activities for Teaching the Unix Terminal. In *Proceedings of the 50th ACM Technical Symposium on Computer Science Education (SIGCSE '19), February 27-March 2, 2019, Minneapolis, MN, USA.* ACM, New York, NY, USA, 7 pages. https://doi.org/10.1145/3287324.3287458

1 INTRODUCTION

The continued increase in enrollment in computer science programs has created demand for scalable assessment technology for homework and exams. Technology for code auto-grading and plagiarism detection are widely used, and recent research has explored scalable techniques for giving personalized feedback on style and design [10, 13]. This technology, however, has largely focused on programming assignments, which is but only one part of being a successful computing professional.

One of the areas that has not been given a lot of focus is *terminal skills*. The terminal, or command-line, generally refers to the text-based interface that exists on nearly all computers. At a terminal, you have access to common utilities to perform actions on the system (file management, program execution) without using a graphical interface. A user can perform simple tasks, but also construct more complicated commands to do things that would be inefficient to do by hand. These sorts of skills are an important tool in the toolbox of computing practitioners but are often relegated to course Wiki pages and informal help from lab instructors, with assessment either non-existent or only through basic testing with multiple-choice quizzes.

In this paper, we describe **uAssign** (available as open source [5]), a scalable approach to teaching and assessing Unix terminal skills. In designing uAssign, we had four main goals:

(1) The assignments should provide an authentic terminal experience where students can explore the current state of the machine and complete the assignments using many possible strategies (i.e., not merely checking that the student typed in a specific command).
(2) The platform should be flexible enough to support a wide range of terminal assignments and, also, support randomization so that unique problem instances can be given to each student to prevent sharing solutions.
(3) The platform should have high availability and scale gracefully, preventing abuse and resource exhaustion independent of user actions.
(4) Terminal assignments should be accessible to students in a convenient, platform-independent manner, ideally available through the the same interface that students are using for their other online homework.

uAssign achieves these goals through the composition of a collection of existing technologies, including Docker containers, WebSockets, and an in-browser terminal emulator. Using uAssign, a student will be able to open their browser and be presented with a real, working terminal attached to a live system in which they can complete their assignment, as shown in Figure 1.

Specifically, this paper makes the following contributions:

(1) We describe the design of the uAssign server, including its management of container life cycles and its integration into a representative web homework interface in Section 2, with special attention to how to quickly provision containers in Section 2.1 and security in Section 2.2.
(2) We present the results of a survey including information on students' prior terminal experience and the efficacy of uAssign in teaching terminal skills.
(3) We present performance results demonstrating that uAssign scales sufficiently for large enrollment classes.

SIGCSE '19, February 27-March 2, 2019, Minneapolis, MN, USA

ACM ISBN 978-1-4503-5890-3/19/02.
https://doi.org/10.1145/3287324.3287458

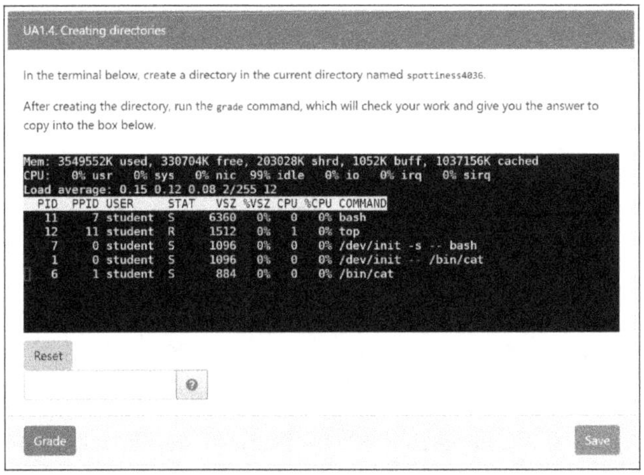

Figure 1: An example uAssign session for an introductory question demonstrating that the terminal has standard capabilities like `top`**.**

Additional implementation details and survey results can be found in Bailey's Master's thesis [6].

2 DESIGN AND IMPLEMENTATION

The key idea for making terminal assignments that provide an authentic terminal experience is to provide students access to an actual terminal that they can interact with. The uAssign system does this through running a Docker[1] container (a light weight "virtual machine") for each student assignment on a server and providing access to these containers through an in-browser terminal emulator. This requires students to be on the Internet when they complete the assignment, but provides low latency interaction with a terminal in a secure, platform independent way.

In principle, uAssign's software architecture could be paired with any learning management system (LMS); the implementation of uAssign that we describe below is for an embedding in the PrairieLearn [18] LMS that is used for other assignments in the course in which it was deployed.

The uAssign terminal assignment system is composed of three independent parts, illustrated in Figure 2:

(1) The uAssign server (shown on the right), responsible for managing the lifetimes of assignment instances and their associated Docker containers on the server,
(2) A PrairieLearn server-side component (bottom left), responsible for providing assignment specifications (randomly parameterized to prevent cheating) and recording completion in the grade book, and
(3) A PrairieLearn client-side terminal interface (top left) that mediates the interaction between the user and their container.

The standard flow through the system begins with a request for a new problem, causing the server-side PrairieLearn component to

[1]Docker is a popular container platform which makes use of a kernel's isolation features [1]. Core to Docker is its daemon (`dockerd`), which manages containers and exposes a REST API, allowing a client to build images, create and manage containers, as well as other container-related tasks. This library-like interface enables Docker to be used as part of a system that wants to work with containers programmatically.

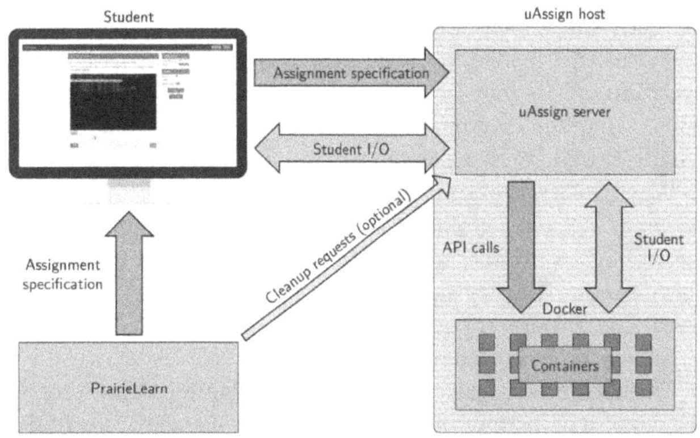

Figure 2: uAssign comprises three actors: (1) the LMS (PrairieLearn) provides assignment specifications, (2) the student's web browser displays the terminal, and (3) the uAssign server manages the Docker containers and mediates communication between the student and their container.

construct an assignment specification. This specification consists of a description of how the uAssign server should initialize the Docker container, including what files and directories should be created and any commands to be issued on the machine before control is transferred over to the user. To make assignments unique between users, we vary the names and contents of files and the names and hierarchy of directories. Our implementation encodes the specification as a JSON document with a UUID as a unique identifier and provides the specification to the student's web browser along with the client-side code.

The browser forwards this assignment specification to the uAssign server. Upon receipt, uAssign uses the provided UUID to see if this assignment is already in progress, and, if not, creates the container using the specification (discussed in detail in Section 2.1) and an *instance* record to track the relationship between this assignment specification and the container. If the instance record already exists, perhaps because the student is returning from having navigated away from the assignment, they are re-connected to their container.

The terminal session is then displayed in the student's browser using a series of components. On the client side, we use the `hterm` [2] terminal emulator written in JavaScript and a WebSocket to communicate to the uAssign server. Since `hterm` only provides functions to write data to the terminal and hooks to capture input text and key combinations, as well as the terminal's dimensions, we had to write client side code to proxy data from `hterm` over the WebSocket. The protocol we use to communicate between the client and the server is one derived from the protocol used by terminado [9], an application for proxying a terminal to a Python Tornado server. The uAssign server then proxies the I/O to the container, using the instance records to identify the correct container.

Currently, grading is accomplished through the use of "secrets". This is a design decision resulting from a desire to loosely couple the uAssign server from the LMS that is hosting the assignments. In some cases, the secret is discovered by doing the assignment (e.g., a `grep` assignment asks students to provide the name of the file containing a given string). In other assignments, a `grade` executable is placed in the container, which students can run to validate that a task (e.g., the appropriate set of files were deleted) was done correctly and dispense the secret. The secrets are unique for each student and provided to the container as part of the assignment specification. Students cut and paste the secrets from the terminal window into the encompassing PrairieLearn window and press the "Grade" button, then presented with their score.

When an assignment is graded, PrairieLearn sends the uAssign server a "cleanup request", which instructs the uAssign server to cleanup any resources associated with that specific assignment specification. These cleanup requests are provided on a best-effort basis. The uAssign server will also deallocate resources for an assignment if it has been idle for a few hours.

The user interface also includes a "reset" button. When pressed, the client will instruct the uAssign it to force an early cleanup of the active instance. Once the instance has been removed, the client will repeat sending its assignment specification. Since the instance was removed, the student will be presented with another instance of the same specification, effectively resetting the assignment.

2.1 Building containers faster than Dockerfiles

uAssign does not use Docker's standard method of configuring containers (`Dockerfiles`) because they are much too slow for our purpose. Our use of Docker is very different from what its authors intended. Docker was designed with the expectation of simultaneously running a large number of containers, but generally initializing those containers using a relatively small number of "images". As such, Docker does not optimize generating new images for speed, but, rather, for minimizing storage and network bandwidth. Docker images are internally organized into layers, where each layer represents the difference between the current image and the last, permitting significant sharing between similar images.

In uAssign, however, we want every container to have a unique image, so that we can give slightly different versions of the assignment to each student. In early versions, uAssign generated images with templatized Dockerfiles, providing the specification as the template's context. But, Docker's excessive I/O from generating the layers – each directive in a Dockerfile adds a layer – created problems both from a latency standpoint and caused I/O to become a scalability bottleneck. Also, Dockerfiles' use of syntax-significant whitespace made templating fragile.

Instead, uAssign skips this build process altogether and uses a custom JavaScript routine to perform actions directly on the target container as directed by the assignment specification. In this way, build time is reduced significantly. Our specifications even support identifying which actions can be performed in parallel, whereas Dockerfiles can only be executed one directive at a time.

We find that uAssign's implementation results in a 2 to 3 times speed up relative to a traditional Docker build. Figure 3 compares the container build time (averaged across 50 runs), as measured on the uAssign server, between our custom script (`index.js`) and the straightforward Dockerfile implementation. Across a collection of representative assignments, we find that uAssign's implementation is able to keep wait times in a tolerable range [15].

2.2 Security concerns and misuse protection

uAssign was designed to be as secure as possible while still providing students with an accurate environment to complete their

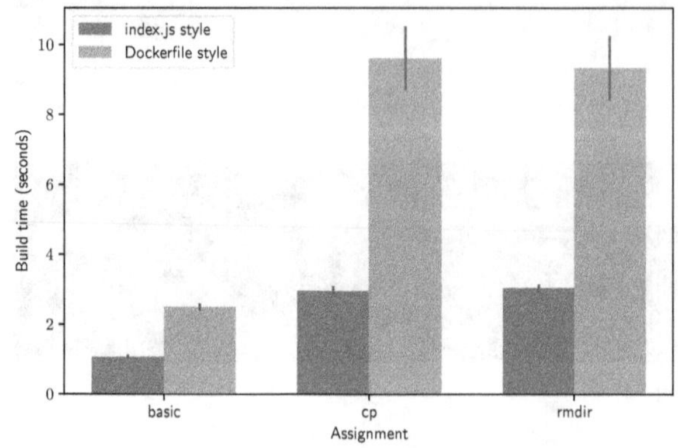

Figure 3: A comparison of build times using uAssign's actions (`index.js`) and Docker's own build system. The "basic" assignment asks students to read a file and answer with its contents. The "cp" assignment asks students to copy a file from one location to another. The "rmdir" assignment asks students to remove a directory. The "cp" and "rmdir" assignments have longer build times because they involve building a Go binary for grading.

assignments. Since uAssign gives a user access to a real container on a real machine, special care must be taken to ensure that privilege is not abused. uAssign, much like every other service which operates on the open Internet, needs to protect against general third-party attacks. As such, it implements standard security measures, including HTTPS (with built-in LetsEncrypt support for free certificate issuance), Secure WebSockets, and a CORS policy.

But, in addition to those third-party attacks, uAssign also needs to be able to protect against potential attacks by its users on the assignments themselves, as well as the resources that the assignments use. There are two main concerns: (1) students attempting to get credit without completing the assignment, and (2) users using the containers for something other than their intended purpose.

The most obvious point of attack for bypassing the assignment is the assignment specification, which contains all of the information needed to solve the problem, including the secret itself. Perhaps surprisingly, our implementation of uAssign actually passes the specification through the client browser in its effort to decouple the uAssign server from PrairieLearn. To prevent the user from accessing the contents of the specification, it is encrypted using shared-key encryption via AES with HMAC-SHA-256 verification.

Additionally, during the development of the course material for uAssign, we found that some students were able to extract strings from our grading binaries (written in Go), giving them a very easy way to obtain secrets. In order to mitigate this sort of attack, the secrets are compiled in an obfuscated form (gzip'ed, then XORed with a mask, and then base64 encoded), which the grading binary can decode when it runs. While this method is not foolproof, it would require more effort to bypass than to just do the assignment.

Because uAssign provides command line access to the containers it hosts, we must make efforts to prevent the containers themselves from being abused (e.g., to run Bitcoin miners or DDOS attacks). Our container security has three main elements: (1) Docker-imposed resource limits, (2) disconnecting the container from the network, and (3) preventing simultaneous connections to a container.

Docker natively provides the following resource limiting features [3]:

- Memory usage limits, by specifying a hard maximum in bytes.
- CPU quotas, by specifying what percentage of the system a container is allowed to use before being unscheduled.
- Process limits (similar to `ulimit`), specifying the maximum number of processes a container can spawn.

The main resource that isn't well limited is disk storage. Docker *has* the ability to limit storage usage, but only via a global setting. For example, setting the limit to 500 MB means that a container which reaches 500 MB of data will no longer be able to write to its filesystem. This cannot be customized per container, so the limit must be set to the largest size they expect *any* container to use.

Docker also manages networking for its containers, creating networks and virtual network adapters. In the case of uAssign, networking is available to a container while it is being configured, but is disabled before a student has access.

Finally, instances are only allowed to be connected to a single terminal emulator at a time. If another client attempts to connect to the same instance, the first connection is terminated, and the second takes its place. This prevents uAssign from being used for unintended purposes that involve multiple connections to the same container, such as a make-shift chat room.

3 EXPERIMENTAL RESULTS

During the Fall 2017 and Spring 2018 semesters, uAssign was used in a second programming class for CS majors. In was used by 127 and 264 students, respectively, in the Fall and Spring semesters. The students were given five weekly homework assignments containing 35 exercises that included directory navigation, listing, and removing, file copying, moving, renaming, and deleting, hidden files, file modification times, globbing, grep, tar and zip files, find, pipes, and C compilation. Students on average take about 3 minutes to do each exercise.

We conducted a survey during the Spring semester covering student preferences of operating system, their confidence in terminal skills, and uAssign's usability, which is described in Section 3.1. In Section 3.2, we describe an in-class stress test that we performed to identify scalability bottlenecks.

3.1 Student Survey Results

With IRB approval, the survey was performed online and students were incentivized to participate in the survey via a raffle of gift cards. In total, 57 students participated out of an enrollment of 264, constituting a respondent rate of 22%.

We asked students to self-rate their proficiency in the terminal on a scale from 1 to 5 (from "no experience" to "very experienced"), both before and after completing uAssign's terminal assignments, as shown in Figure 4. Over all respondents, we saw the mean increase from 2.40 to 3.42 – an increase of 1.02 on a five point scale – from completing the assignments. Breaking down the data by operating system preference (Table 1), Windows users self-report benefiting the most from the terminal assignments, followed by MacOS users.

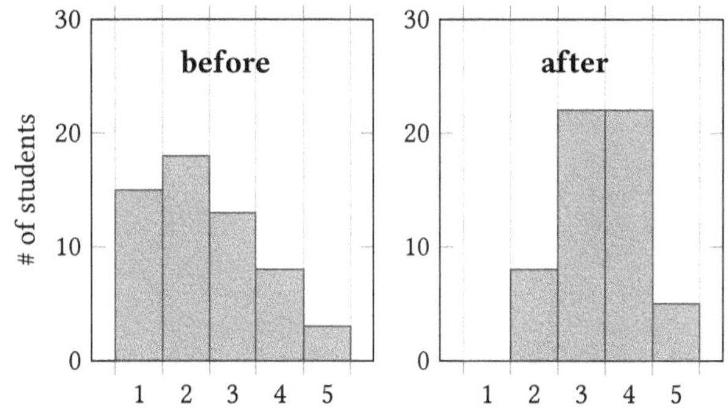

Figure 4: Student responses to "Rate your proficiency with the command line" before and after the terminal assignments.

Users who used Linux as their primary operating system reported no improvement, likely because they were already proficient.

We also see positive results with respect to the affective dimension. Students have very high perceptions of the utility of terminal skills (mean: 4.67, std dev: .58), as shown in Figure 5. Students were likewise satisfied with uAssign's user interface (mean: 4.37, std dev: .67, Figure 6 Perceptions of whether the assignments were good use of their time were also positive, but not as strong (mean: 3.63, std dev: .99, Figure 7).

Our survey suggests, however, that our assignments have likely not yet given students enough practice with the terminal. Only 60% of the participants stated that they felt confident they could use common terminal utilities, 40% still either disagree or are unsure (mean: 3.75, std dev: 1.11, Figure 8). When asked about their confidence with reading `--help` and `man` pages, 35% of participants aren't confident (mean: 3.86, std dev: .97, Figure 9). Also, participants still tend to prefer GUI tools to the command line for filesystem tasks (mean: 3.46, std dev: 1.18, Figure 10).

3.2 Performance stress testing

The only heavyweight activity on the uAssign server is spinning up new containers; once the container exists, it takes minimal network bandwidth and CPU to handle the terminal interactions. Spinning up containers became a significant bottleneck in our original Dockerfile-based implementation in Fall 2017, with students having to wait multiple minutes for their terminal to appear when the server was loaded.

With the revised container-building implementation described in Section 2.1, we stopped receiving performance complaints from students in Spring 2018. While this was a clear improvement, we weren't confident that we had removed the bottleneck, since students typically complete assignments on their own schedule over the course of many days.

To observe the server's behavior under controlled load, we performed a pair of stress tests in Spring 2018, where students were asked to access their terminal assignments simultaneously in lecture. Each lecture section involved roughly 80 concurrent users completing assignments with the uAssign server running on an AWS `t2.medium` instance. In both tests, mean and median container construction latency increased to around 15 seconds, which

Table 1: Self-reported improvement in terminal skill confidence, by operating system.

Primary		Primary + Secondary	
OS (% of participants)	Avg. Improvement	Secondary OS	Avg. Improvement
Windows (54.39%)	+1.323	Linux (15.79%)	+1.889
		N/A (36.84%)	+1.095
		MacOS (1.75%)	+1.0
MacOS (40.35%)	+0.739	N/A (28.07%)	+0.875
		Windows (3.51%)	+0.5
		Linux (8.77%)	+0.4
Linux (5.26%)	+0.0	Windows (5.26%)	+0.0

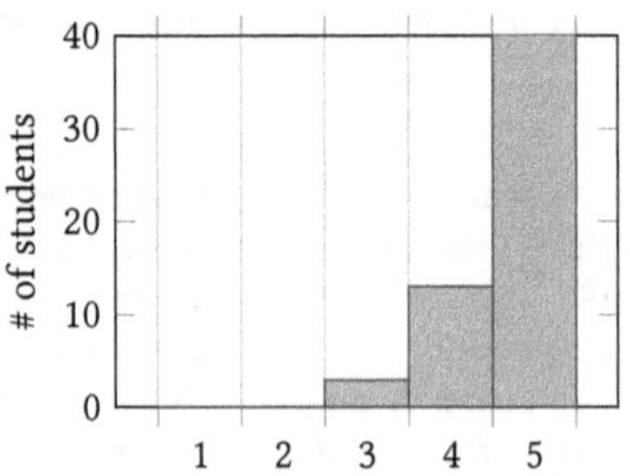

Figure 5: "I believe terminal skills are useful."

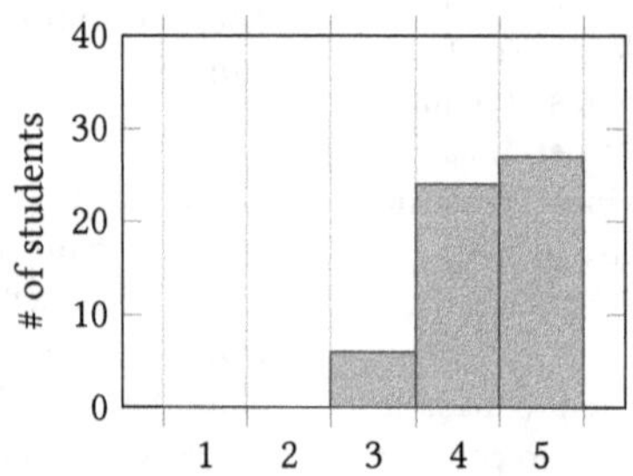

Figure 6: "The terminal assignment system provided a friendly user interface."

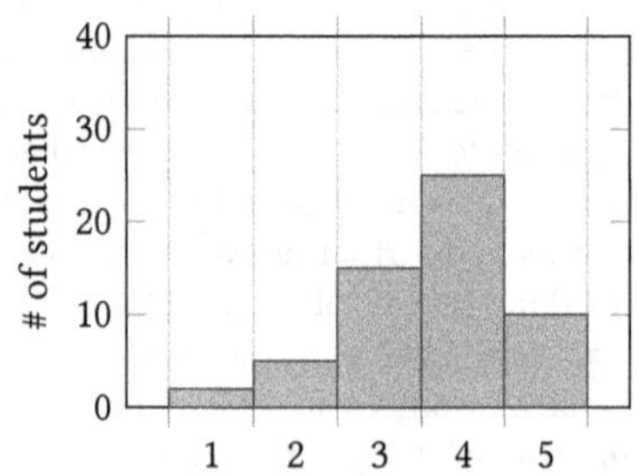

Figure 7: "My time was well-spent completing terminal assignments."

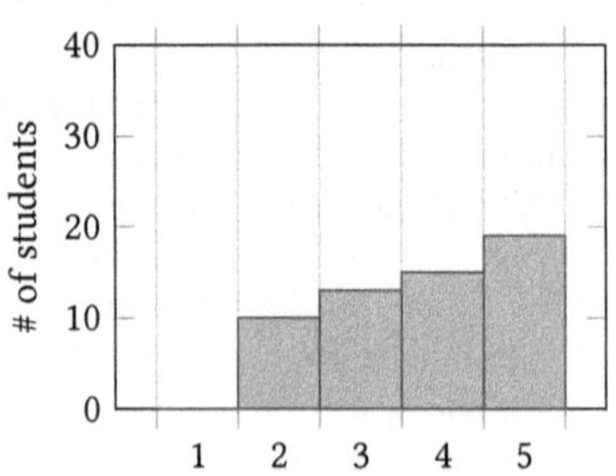

Figure 8: "I am confident that I can use common terminal utilities."

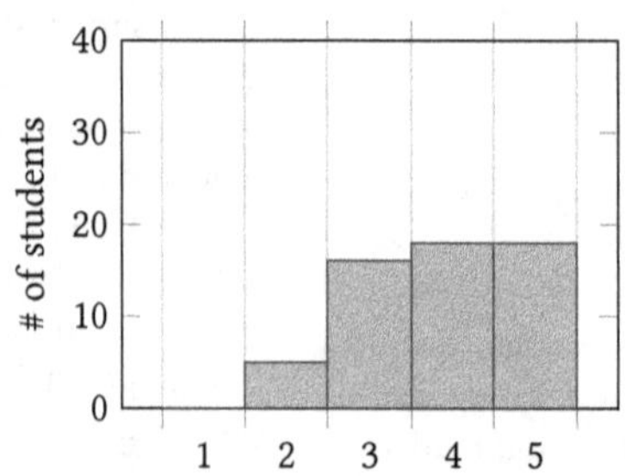

Figure 9: "I am confident that I can read terminal utility 'help' documentation (`-h`, `--help`) and man pages."

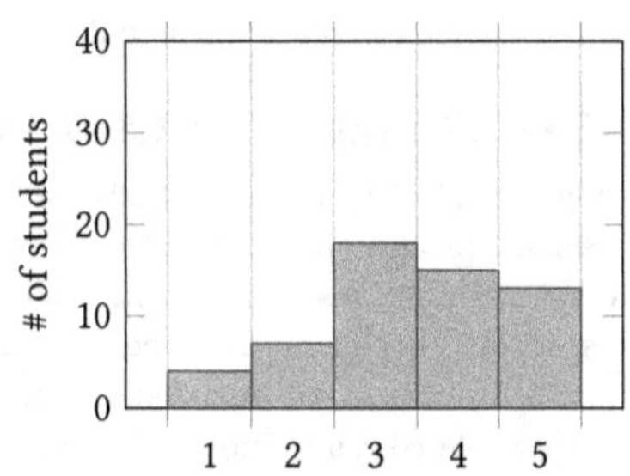

Figure 10: "I prefer performing common filesystem tasks in a GUI, rather than in the terminal."

is tolerable, and the terminals had no noticeable latency once their containers had been created.

These results make us comfortable running assignments with uAssign for class sizes up to 500 students on `t2.medium` instance, because the rate that students will construct containers is practically limited by the rate at which they can complete the assignments, even if all of the students were to wait to complete the assignments until the deadline. We believe that a slightly larger AWS instance with additional CPU and I/O bandwidth would be sufficient for even the largest computing classes at our university. Data collected on the uAssign host using `collectl` [17] shows that only CPU utilization was significantly affected by the stress test as shown in Figure 11; memory usage increased only a few hundred megabytes, and network usage was negligible. Additionally, scalability could be increased through the use of a filesystem with native Docker storage support like `btrfs`, where no extra work is needed to create a container's storage space.

4 RELATED WORK

Previous efforts to support the teaching and assessment of terminal skills can be categorized into four main types: (1) self-guided instruction tools, (2) traditional lessons with pencil/paper quizzes, (3) the use of virtual machines to teach system administration, and (4) web-based systems that present tasks for students with a means for validating that the assignment was completed.

Included with UNIX v7, *learn* [12] created an interactive environment to teach terminal usage by interpreting "CAI" (computer aided instruction) scripts. Lessons varied from basic command usage and filesystem navigation to the C programming language. Intended for self-guided instruction only, this software lacked any sort of assessment outside of completion of a given lesson.

Terminal skills have also been taught using traditional in-class lessons and hand-graded quizzes [11, 16]. Using quizzes (be they paper or online) may not fully assess skills, relying on a student to answer a question by statement, rather than perform some task.

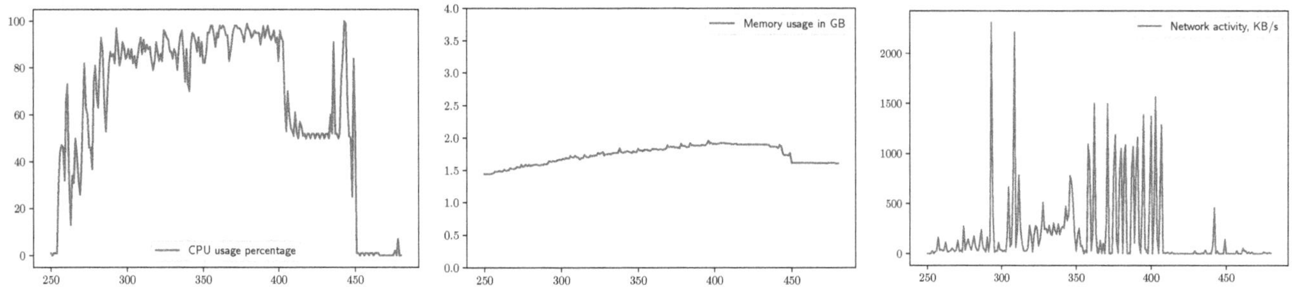

Figure 11: CPU, memory, and network bandwidth usage during our first stress test. The X-axis indicates time in seconds, with the stress test starting approximately 250 seconds after `collectl` was started.

Virtual machines are often used to teach system administration, so that learners don't break actual systems. "User Mode Linux" (U-ML) [8] allows students to connect to a custom Linux derivative running as a VM, over emulated serial lines provided by the VM host, where students can perform administration tasks such as simulated system updates and service management. "Virtual Lab" uses a web interface to provide access to its virtualized environment [7]. The client browser uses AJAX requests to send a user's command to the server. The server then uses SSH to run the command and captures and returns the full output back to the user as an HTTP response. This interface is not a "true" terminal, as it is not interactive (i.e., you cannot run editors, live-updating programs like `top`, or cancel execution). Neither system appears to integrate instant feedback/auto-grading.

The final category of related work are the peers of uAssign, web-based terminal assessment tools that permit randomization of assignments and support for auto-grading. "Unix-training" presents its lessons as a treasure hunt, where each step (e.g., compiling code, creating shell pipelines, accessing remote systems over SSH) gives you information to help you solve the next step [14]. Each student's path is unique to them, generated psuedorandomly (using some hashing of user information), and interactions with a web app tracks a student's progress. Unlike uAssign, this system relies on students having their own *NIX machines for course work.

The closest related work to uAssign is the concurrently developed TuxLab project [4]. Both uAssign and TuxLab work off of the same core principle – exposing customized Docker containers to students to complete terminal assignments. Both use instructor-written JavaScript code to efficiently configure containers by directly performing tasks on the container before the student connects. Both set resource limitations on the containers for performance isolation and to prevent abuse; both set CPU/memory limits, but uAssign's current deployment also limits disk usage.

The main difference is that TuxLab is designed as a stand-alone learning web app, where uAssign is designed to be integrated into an existing LMS. This design choice gives TuxLab an extra level of control and a more integrated user interface (a terminal on the right, reference on the left) and allows the web app to grade the container directly. uAssign design means that students don't have to learn an new interface (something they value according to the survey), but necessitates the use of a grading binary installed in the container for our current implementation.

In addition, TuxLab gives students access to its containers differently than uAssign. TuxLab's Docker containers run in Docker Swarm. Students connect to containers via SSH (with an in-browser SSH client) to an SSH proxy on the TuxLab server, which then connects to the container. This is required due to the way Swarm operates, abstracting containers to "services", where the only interaction with a container's I/O is through Docker-collected logs or though the Internet to a server running in that service, at an IP address in the Swarm network that is essentially randomized. A consequence of this design is that in the current implementation, TuxLab containers continue to have Internet access even after setup, which opens up assignment instances to unwanted capabilities such as package downloads (usurping any instructor-defined setup), communication with outside help, or even malicious servers. Also, since uAssign controls container lifetimes (instead of Swarm), students can navigate away from a problem and return to their container with all of their work still saved.

5 CONCLUSION AND FUTURE WORK

uAssign's implementation demonstrates that authentic assessments for terminal skills can be built in a scalable and secure manner. uAssign gives instructors the opportunity to add terminal-based content to their courses and computer-based exams [19, 20], without sacrificing flexibility in implementation. Through surveys, it's clear that there is a benefit for students, especially those who have not been exposed to the command line and that the current workflow is positive and worth continuing.

There is, however, work to still be done a few dimensions. First, we'd like to extend the range and depth of assignments that have been developed for uAssign. While our students reported significant growth in terminal skills, most students still didn't feel fully comfortable with the terminal. We believe that additional and more varied practice will help them develop that comfort.

Second, we plan to proliferate these terminal assignments to other programming courses. First we will deploy them in other introductory programming courses at our university that serve other populations. Beyond that, we feel there is an opportunity to develop a service that could be used at other universities.

Third, uAssign could be used to study how students learn terminal skills and identify misconceptions. Because uAssign proxies all input and output from its containers to students, we could log the student actions and perform educational pattern mining and qualitative analysis of these traces.

REFERENCES

[1] [n. d.]. Docker. https://www.docker.com/. Accessed: 2018-04-02.

[2] [n. d.]. hterm. https://chromium.googlesource.com/apps/libapps/+/master/hterm. Accessed: 2018-04-01.

[3] [n. d.]. Limit a container's resources | Docker Documentation. https://docs.docker.com/config/containers/resource_constraints/. Accessed: 2018-04-02.

[4] [n. d.]. TuxLab. http://tuxlab.org. Accessed: 2018-03-18.

[5] [n. d.]. uAssign Github repository. https://github.com/jakebailey/ua.

[6] Jacob Bailey. 2018. *uAssign: Scalable and flexible interactive activities for teaching the UNIX terminal.* Master's thesis. University of Illinois at Urbana-Champaign, http://hdl.handle.net/2142/101068.

[7] K. C. Bandi, A. K. Nori, V. Choppella, and S. Kode. 2011. A Virtual Laboratory for Teaching Linux on the Web. In *2011 IEEE International Conference on Technology for Education.* 212–215. https://doi.org/10.1109/T4E.2011.41

[8] Renzo Davoli. 2004. Teaching Operating Systems Administration with User Mode Linux. In *Proceedings of the 9th Annual SIGCSE Conference on Innovation and Technology in Computer Science Education (ITiCSE '04).* ACM, New York, NY, USA, 112–116. https://doi.org/10.1145/1007996.1008027

[9] Jupyter development team and Ramalingam Saravanan. [n. d.]. terminado. https://github.com/jupyter/terminado. Accessed: 2018-04-01.

[10] Andrew Head, Elena Glassman, Gustavo Soares, Ryo Suzuki, Lucas Figueredo, Loris D'Antoni, and Björn Hartmann. 2017. Writing Reusable Code Feedback at Scale with Mixed-Initiative Program Synthesis. In *Proceedings of the Fourth (2017) ACM Conference on Learning @ Scale (L@S '17).* ACM, New York, NY, USA, 89–98. https://doi.org/10.1145/3051457.3051467

[11] Tyson Kendon and Ben Stephenson. 2016. Unix Literacy for First-Year Computer Science Students. In *Proceedings of the 21st Western Canadian Conference on Computing Education (WCCCE '16).* ACM, New York, NY, USA, Article 14, 4 pages. https://doi.org/10.1145/2910925.2910930

[12] Brian W. Kernighan and Michael E. Lesk. 1979. LEARN – Computer-Aided Instruction on UNIX. In *UNIX Programmer's Manual.* Vol. 2. https://s3.amazonaws.com/plan9-bell-labs/7thEdMan/v7vol2a.pdf

[13] Joseph Bahman Moghadam, Rohan Roy Choudhury, HeZheng Yin, and Armando Fox. 2015. AutoStyle: Toward Coding Style Feedback at Scale. In *Proceedings of the Second (2015) ACM Conference on Learning@ Scale.* ACM, 261–266. https://doi.org/10.1145/2724660.2728672

[14] Matthieu Moy. 2011. Efficient and Playful Tools to Teach Unix to New Students. In *Proceedings of the 16th Annual Joint Conference on Innovation and Technology in Computer Science Education (ITiCSE '11).* ACM, New York, NY, USA, 93–97. https://doi.org/10.1145/1999747.1999776 Source code/wiki at http://matthieu-moy.fr/spip/?Unix-training-a-set-of-tools-to.

[15] Fiona Fui-Hoon Nah. 2004. A study on tolerable waiting time: how long are Web users willing to wait? *Behaviour & Information Technology* 23, 3 (2004), 153–163. https://doi.org/10.1080/01449290410001669914 arXiv:https://doi.org/10.1080/01449290410001669914

[16] Lawrence Osborne. 1992. Teaching C with UNIX for College Credit to Professional Programmers. *SIGCSE Bull.* 24, 4 (Dec. 1992), 43–48. https://doi.org/10.1145/141837.141852

[17] Mark Seger. [n. d.]. collectl. http://collectl.sourceforge.net/. Accessed: 2018-04-02.

[18] Matthew West, Geoffrey L. Herman, and Craig Zilles. 2015. PrairieLearn: Mastery-based online problem solving with adaptive scoring and recommendations driven by machine learning. In *2015 ASEE Annual Conference & Exposition.* ASEE Conferences, Seattle, Washington. https://peer.asee.org/24575.

[19] Craig Zilles, Robert Timothy Deloatch, Jacob Bailey, Bhuwan B. Khattar, Wade Fagen, Cinda Heeren, David Mussulman, and Matthew West. 2015. Computerized Testing: A Vision and Initial Experiences. In *2015 ASEE Annual Conference & Exposition.* ASEE Conferences, Seattle, Washington. https://peer.asee.org/23726.

[20] C. Zilles, M. West, D. Mussulman, and T. Bretl. 2018. Making Testing Less Trying: Lessons Learned from Operating a Computer-Based Testing Facility. In *Frontiers in Education.* http://zilles.cs.illinois.edu/papers/zilles_cbtf_fie_2018.pdf

MYR: A Web-Based Platform for Teaching Coding Using VR

Christopher Berns*
University of Massachusetts Lowell
Lowell, Massachusetts
christopher_berns@student.uml.edu

Grace Chin†
University of Massachusetts Lowell
Lowell, Massachusetts
grace_chin@student.uml.edu

Joel Savitz‡
University of Massachusetts Lowell
Lowell, Massachusetts
joel_savitz@student.uml.edu

Jason Kiesling§
University of Massachusetts Lowell
Lowell, Massachusetts
jason_kiesling@student.uml.edu

Fred Martin¶
University of Massachusetts Lowell
Lowell, Massachusetts
fred_martin@uml.edu

ABSTRACT

MYR is a browser-based, educational platform built to spark student interest in computer science by allowing users to write code that generates three-dimensional, animated scenes in virtual reality. The interface consists of two primary components: (1) an integrated editor, which leverages the MYR API and the A-Frame entity-component-system, and (2) a real-time renderer that displays the corresponding scene. The scenes, which vary in complexity, are viewable using virtual reality headsets, smartphones, and any device that supports a web browser.

By providing access to the specific domain of virtual reality to students, the system aims to make computer science concepts tangible for novice programmers. The MYR development team conducted pilot tests with middle school students in order to collect feedback from this audience. The larger goal of the project is to develop MYR as a research tool to gain insight into computing students' success, motivation, and confidence in learning computing.

The technical implementation, the results of the pilot tests, and the larger vision for future work are discussed in this paper.

CCS CONCEPTS

• **Applied computing → Interactive learning environments**;

KEYWORDS

WebVR, virtual reality, educational tools, research tools, web-based tools, classroom, software

*Undergraduate student research assistant at the Engaging Computing Lab.
†Undergraduate student research assistant at the Engaging Computing Lab.
‡Undergraduate student research assistant at the Engaging Computing Lab.
§Undergraduate student research assistant at the Engaging Computing Lab.
¶Professor and director of the Engaging Computing Group.

SIGCSE'19, February 27–March 2, 2019, Minneapolis, MN, USA

ACM ISBN 978-1-4503-5890-3/19/2...$15.00
https://doi.org/10.1145/3287324.3287482

ACM Reference Format:
Christopher Berns, Grace Chin, Joel Savitz, Jason Kiesling, and Fred Martin. 2019. MYR: A Web-Based Platform for Teaching Coding Using VR. In *SIGCSE '19: 50th ACM Technical Symposium on Computer Science Education, February 27–March 2, 2019, Minneapolis, MN, USA.* ACM, New York, NY, USA, 7 pages. https://doi.org/10.1145/3287324.3287482

1 INTRODUCTION

MYR (short for "My Reality") is a beginner-friendly integrated development environment (IDE) for creating web-based virtual reality scenes and experiences. It is built to deliver an engaging experience that can be used by students, educators, and computer artists alike.

We anticipate that providing a means for students to create virtual reality scenes programmatically will foster increased interest in CS for students from a wide range of backgrounds. We believe this can be achieved by providing code libraries, curricular materials developed in collaboration with teachers—such as lessons, activities, and assessments—and technology for CS education in the context of VR programming.

Early on we saw potential in A-Frame[1], a popular JavaScript library for creating virtual reality scenes in the browser, and decided to extend its capabilities with three clear goals in mind:

(1) to create an engaging environment structured around learning text-based programming fundamentals,
(2) to make it available to as many people as possible within a reasonable budget, and
(3) to provide a tool that is capable of aiding research in the field of CS Ed.

Since the MYR editor supports all JavaScript language features, it allows students to engage with common CS concepts, including sequences, loops, functions, events, conditionals, operators, and data. This provides users a platform to create inspiring, creative 3D scenes while simultaneously learning functional, declarative programming.

MYR supports a variety of different virtual reality headsets, including the higher-end HTC Vive and Oculus Rift and the more affordable Google Cardboard. This is important to the educational setting, as it allows institutions to be flexible within their budgets. It also provides an opportunity for interdisciplinary contexts and scenarios in CS Ed that lead to inclusion of many different groups of people in computing.

MYR includes a cloud-based data collection system with which the scenes that have been rendered are captured and stored. This information can then be used to analyze qualitative and engagement-related data, to measure users' learning progress and retention rates, and to research users' problem solving approaches and difficulties. All of this will aid in the development of relevant software features and inform decisions leading to engaging students from many backgrounds.

2 BACKGROUND

Research by Mannila et al. (2006) has shown that programming languages of a lesser syntactic complexity are correlated with fewer syntax and logic errors and thus lead to higher student success rates overall. By choosing a simple language, educators can effectively introduce fundamental programming concepts and skills to potential CS professionals and prepare the foundation that allows for a smooth transition to more complex languages [11].

There are many tools that try to achieve an appropriate level of support for empowering novice programmers. In particular, educational programming languages and environments are engaging to students when they enable them to build their own interactive media—that is, mobile applications, games, experiences, and art [10]. When students use tools such as Logo, Processing, and Scratch to design and implement interactive media, they exercise *computational thinking*, which Cuny, Snyder, and Wing define as "the thought processes involved in formulating problems and their solutions so that the solutions are represented in a form that can be effectively carried out by an information-processing agent" [7]. The recreational aspect enhances the reward level, opening the door to an exciting world of computer graphics at an early point in a student's CS career [12].

We wanted to build upon this prior work by exploring programming in a reinvigorated medium for creating immersive and highly interactive experiences: web-based virtual reality. Virtual reality enhances the learning experience by providing a world which students can explore—from ideas with which they are familiar to out-of-world ideas which they cannot experience in real life [9]. Previously, utilizing virtual reality technology had certain barriers: accessibility, cost, and technical skill. Now the implementation and adoption of WebVR has made creating and sharing virtual reality experiences highly accessible without set-up requirements, since it can be done through the ubiquitous web browser. Low-cost virtual reality headset technology has made it possible for more people to enjoy the immersive experience virtual reality offers.

There are several existing examples of 3D WebVR digital environments influencing K-12 students' digital literacy development and interdisciplinary lifelong learning [8]. Though these tools are impactful, there is a shortage of tools that balance ease-of-use and sophistication while providing an experience that effectively teaches computational thinking. On one hand, A-Frame by itself provides an inspector environment that makes it easy to create complex three-dimensional scenes, but lacks an intuitive platform to teach CS concepts. On the other hand, an industry-standard game engine like Unity[5] allows a user to program highly sophisticated scenes, but the level of competence necessary to use the program effectively renders it inaccessible to novice programmers. MYR aims to bridge this divide, balancing ease-of-use with education efficacy.

3 OVERVIEW OF MYR

In this section, we describe the design of MYR.

3.1 Entity-component-system

MYR uses the entity-component-system (ECS) of A-Frame [1], a framework developed for creating virtual experiences in the browser using WebVR [6], WebGL [2], and three.js [4]. A-Frame components are reusable and modular chunks of data that users can plug into an entity in order to add appearance, behavior, or functionality. This design pattern has seen recent attention in the field of game development. As described by Unity, "With ECS, we are moving from the object-oriented to a data-oriented design, which means it's easier to reuse code and easier for others to grasp and contribute to it" [5]. An ECS does this by favoring composition over inheritance. This is done by defining every entity simply as a composition of one or more single purpose components. These types of systems are easier to understand as they avoid deep inheritance hierarchies and provide a clear abstraction at both the entity and component level. This is a central reason why the MYR team believes it is likely to be a great experience for the beginner programmer.

In order to make the ECS viable for MYR, it had to be as fault-tolerant as possible. This was accomplished by supplying all of the needed components for a variety of primitive entities with minimal effort. The function call `box()` creates an entity with six different components: a geometry component, a position component, a scale component, a rotation component, a material component, and an ID component, as shown in Table 1.

Table 1: Components in entity created by the `box()` function call.

ID	`box1`
geometry	`{primitive: box}`
material	`{color: 'red'}`
position	`{x: 0, y: 0, z: 0}`
scale	`{x: 1, y: 1, z: 1}`
rotation	`{x: 0, y: 0, z: 0}`

These details are initially abstracted away from the user, but each component can be explored individually. MYR helps make this exploration feel natural and focused on one or two components at a time because they only pertain to a single set of details about the entity. Once users understand how to make a red box, for example, they have a number of different components to explore next. One student may choose to explore the material component, playing with different color combinations and patterns; another may choose to add animations and work on making an animated scene. There are countless ways to explore each entity and expand upon it, another powerful idea behind the decision to build on the ECS of A-Frame.

3.2 Cursor

Fundamentally, a *cursor* is something that preserves state in order to produce subsequent artifacts. In most cases, this leaves some sort of mark on the scene. The process of producing more complicated structures comes from mutations to the cursor rather than the elements themselves.

The idea of a cursor originally manifested in a physical robot turtle which was controlled with a simple API using Logo [12, 13]. The physical turtle became an on-screen turtle in later Logo implementations. This idea of a drawing cursor was later adopted in the Processing language.

When children thought about how to draw with the Logo turtle, they would imagine how their own bodies would move. Papert termed this "body syntonic" thinking, which we can now see as a form of computational thinking [14].

Following the example of these other educational tools, MYR adopts the idea of a cursor for drawing and augments it slightly by using the cursor as a component factory to create the subsequent entities for the ECS.

In order for the cursor to produce a variety of different components, it must have certain properties at all times. By default, MYR supplies all of the parameters to produce all of the components needed by each of the primitive entities it supports. At creation of the entity, the cursor uses its current parameters and creates the appropriate components. The function call `setColor('blue')` will update the MYR cursor with new parameters. The next entity that requires a material component will have blue as its color property.

3.3 An Example

Figure 1 shows a simple MYR program and the resulting image it creates—an ice cream cone. This is done using a global state, or cursor, which will be discussed further.

The following code creates the ice cream cone by:

(1) setting the cursor's color to #A05526 or sienna,
(2) setting the cursor's X, Y and Z position to 0, 1, and -2.5, respectively,
(3) setting the cursor's X, Y and Z scale to 0.5, 1, and 0.5 respectively,
(4) setting the cursor's X-axis rotation to 180 degrees,
(5) drawing a cone shape using the current parameters of the cursor,
(6) setting the cursor's color to lightblue,
(7) setting the cursor's X, Y and Z position to 0, 1.6, and -2.5 respectively,
(8) setting the cursor's X, Y and Z scale to 0.5, 0.4, and 0.5 respectively, and
(9) drawing a sphere shape using the current parameters of the cursor.

3.4 The MYR API

The development of the API was a primary focus of the MYR development team. The choice to adopt the notion of a cursor helped significantly. The entire MYR API only ever interacts with this cursor, making it easy to understand. This single point of interaction coupled with the expressiveness of an ECS provides MYR with an API that is both beginner-friendly and expressive.

```
setColor('#A0522D');       // sienna
setPosition(0, 1, -2.5);
setScale(0.5, 1, 0.5);
setRotation(180, 0, 0);
cone();
setColor('lightblue');
setPosition(0, 1.6, -2.5);
setScale(0.5, 0.4, 0.5);
sphere();
```

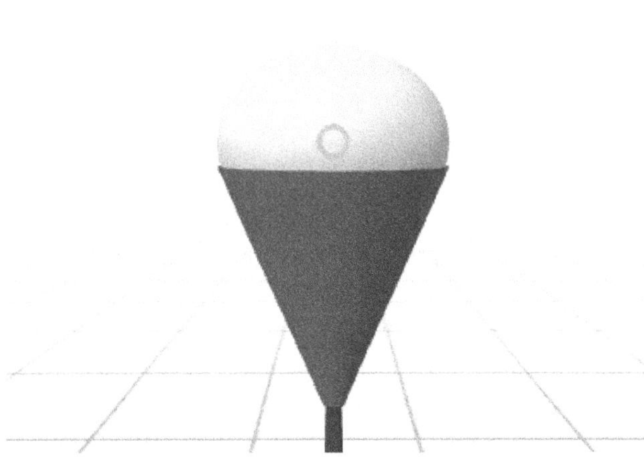

Figure 1: MYR code and resulting image of an ice cream cone

The MYR API also handles some of the more difficult parts of managing the components of each entity. In most cases, components do not interfere with each other, because they are single-purpose, but in certain situations access to the previously defined components is necessary. The expression `fadeIn( box() )` takes the `box` entity as its first parameter and then adds the fadeIn animation component. The fadeIn animation component handles the shift from an invisible entity to one that can be observed in the scene. In this case, however, the cursor must also access the previously defined material component and add the transparency property to it. This forces the cursor to retain a copy of its previous work in order to access the entities it has previously defined. While this does break the typical notion of a cursor, it is an important change necessary to support the ECS.

Ultimately, it is the control over the interaction with the cursor that helps MYR offer a rich, unified API that is within reach of beginners. It supports many geometric entities and simple animations to be explored, and when coupled with simple constructs, like functions and loops, the user can quickly create building blocks for more advanced entities in subsequent work.

3.5 Groups

In order to make MYR more engaging for advanced users, the team developed *groups*, a powerful feature of the MYR API. Like normal entities, group entities have scale, position, and rotation components. However, in lieu of material and geometry components, they have a component that is comprised of other entities. Groups give the user the ability to create nested entities–black boxes, so to speak, that can contain other entities or even other groups. Once entities are placed inside of a black box, the user can manipulate the black box as a whole without altering the appearance and relative positioning of the entities contained.

Groups were originally implemented to provide an entity that could be used to simultaneously manipulate multiple entities, e.g. for animations. Subsequently, the team was working to model molecular geometries in MYR, that is, to illustrate the positioning of atoms in molecules. Without the use of groups, the desired models could still be achieved, but altering their scale and position was tedious and and calculation-intensive. By using groups to define the molecules, rescaling and repositioning became easy, because not only did we only have to change the group's scale and position components, but we were also able to use whole numbers for these values.

Convinced that groups could be used in more elaborate ways, we began experimenting with the use of groups inside of functions that returned the group itself. This made the groups dynamic and reusable. By using groups in this way, as well as a simple loop, a crystal structure of molecules can be modeled in MYR. This is demonstrated in Figure 2.

This simple idea of grouping has had a profound effect on the capabilities of MYR. We believe that this will make MYR more enjoyable for anyone who wants to make more elaborate and robust scenes.

```
for (let i = 0; i < 21; i += 7) {
   for (let j = 0; j < 21; j += 7) {
      for (let k = 0; k < 21; k += 7) {
         my_molecule({x: i, y: j, z: k});
      }
   }
}
```

Figure 2: By calling a function that takes a position as an argument and returns a group within a nested for loop, one can model a crystal structure of molecules in MYR.

4 APPLICATION FEATURES

Figure 3 shows the MYR environment in action. The environment runs as a web application inside a modern web browser. The left side is the code-editing area, and the right side is the renderer.

The top row contains the following buttons (from left to right):

- menu to load examples,
- "play" to render a scene,
- "stop" to stop the render of scene,
- "plus" to create a new scene,
- "save" to preserve the scene,
- "folders" to open up previous work and examples,
- "help" to bring up the MYR reference,
- "cog" which offers different view options, and
- login for logging in using a Google account.

In the lower-right corner of the image is the "goggles" button, which converts the display to a full-screen virtual reality render.

4.1 IDE

The MYR application, at its core, is a tool for writing code. Providing a fully integrated development environment is critical to MYR's success. The IDE includes two key components: the editor and the renderer. The editor supports some of the most common features in modern text editors. This includes:

(1) common word processing features, such as keyboard shortcuts, drag-and-drop text, and cut, copy, and paste functionality,
(2) development features such as live syntax checking, code folding, comment toggling, and syntax highlighting, and
(3) a custom-built autocomplete engine to display the MYR API.

MYR's set of features is intended to get users working quickly with tools, and also offer more development-oriented features as well. Exposure helps introduce them to common IDE features and helps them be more productive. Offering a rich feature set helps ensure that the tools are continually able to support the users' best work as they become more proficient.

The IDE also includes a perspective representation of the scene. On a desktop or laptop computer, the scene can be explored with a keyboard and mouse. On a mobile device or virtual reality viewer, the scene can be explored using the device's orientation and screen presses. The user also has the option to leave the editor behind and jump straight into the virtual reality scene itself. Going from the code to the viewer is seamless with just a click of a button.

As with any new tool, there is an initial learning curve. To help ease the learning process, MYR's IDE provides a color-coded reference for its entire API. Learning the API is also facilitated with the autocomplete feature. These features give users an experience that is intuitive and modern.

4.2 Real-time sync

One of the challenges of using virtual reality is the amount of time spent compiling and transferring the scene for viewing. In many cases, this can detract from the enjoyability of the experience.

In practical use, MYR developers edit their code on a desktop or laptop computer, and open the same project on a viewer (e.g. a mobile phone with Google Cardboard). Code changes on the development computer are then immediately viewable on the virtual reality device. The ability to go from code to scene supports an iterative approach, allowing users to frequently test their code.

MYR also provides the ability to publish a scene to multiple clients for viewing. When working in MYR, the user only needs to save the scene to distribute it to all clients. This feature was

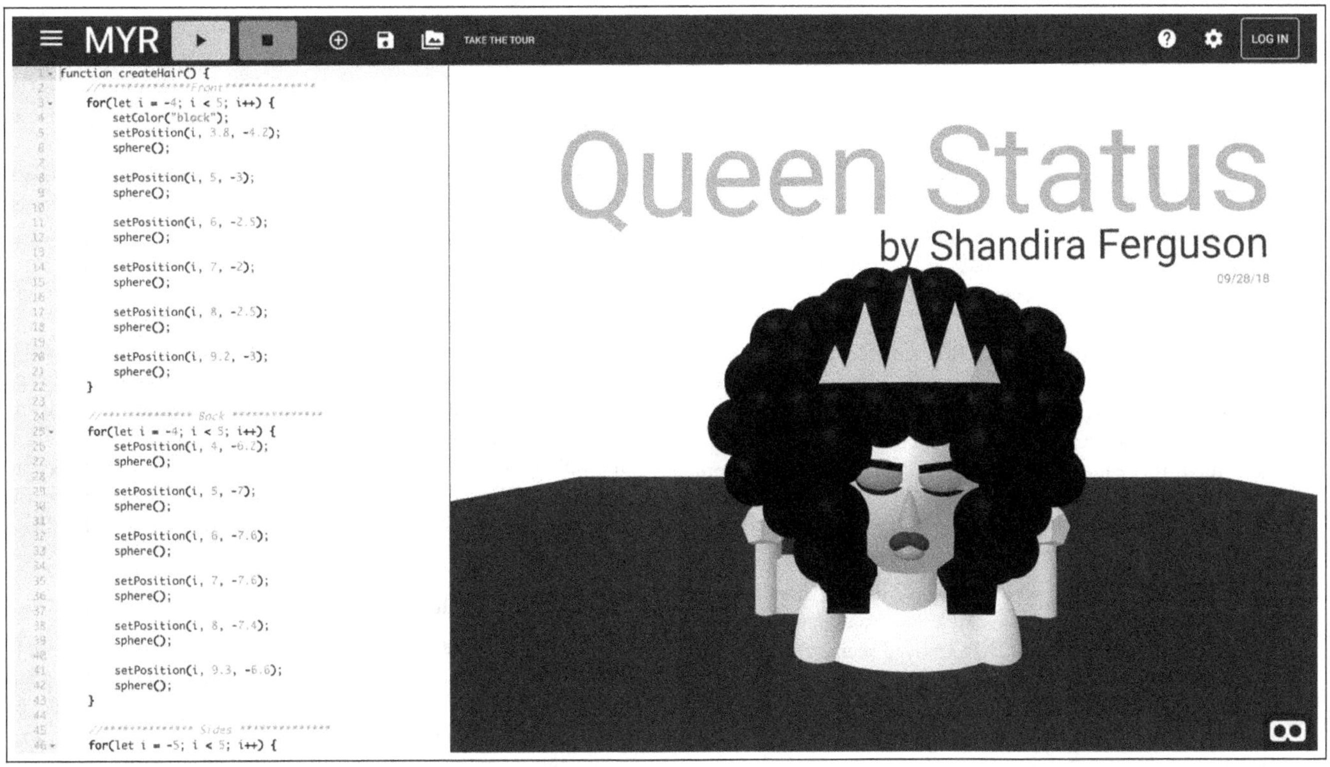

Figure 3: The MYR IDE features the code editor (left) and the resulting scene (right).

developed using Google's Firebase, a serverless architecture service. It provides an easy way for multiple clients to listen for changes in a shared database with minimal effort by the development team.

4.3 Sharing

Learning from example is a staple in many learning environments. The MYR team spent a significant amount of time providing illustrative examples of scenes in MYR. All of these examples are available through a gallery in the IDE. To encourage extension of these examples, the user is able to quickly access, modify, and then save them as their own. This allows the examples to be easily used by an instructor to deliver starter code to students, who can then extend it to meet a certain set of challenges in a curriculum.

The ability to share, however, goes far beyond just delivering samples and starter code. Presently, every project is public and can be shared easily via simple web link. Sharing one's work with others has the potential to keep authors engaged and give them a sense of accomplishment. This approach is intended to build a community of developers and allow them to share their work freely with one another.

4.4 Snapshot capture

While MYR can support imaginative work, it can also be used to conduct research. MYR uses the popular web library Redux for its application state management. By accessing this store, MYR is able to capture the entire state of the application and upload it via HTTPS to its back-end in Firebase.

Snapshots capture the entire state of the application, including the code the user wrote, which user wrote it, and the timestamp at which it was written. The MYR team is then able to produce a timeline from each render to the next. When processing this timeline, certain meta properties arise independent of the code itself.

Perhaps the most significant pieces of data that MYR generates are the rate at which the render system produces errors and the average amount of time between render attempts. These are aspects of particular concern for our current research efforts. The code itself is also useful for gaining insight into different problem solving approaches and even into metrics such as color choice.

5 PILOT TESTING

In July 2018, we ran pilot tests with 13 middle school students as part of a computing camp taught in an urban-rim city in the Northeastern USA. We observed how the students interacted with MYR and gathered feedback about the students' overall experience.

We performed our pilot tests on students who had little, if any, prior experience with either text-based programming or virtual reality. We worked with each student for 20 minutes, presenting them with three scenes and giving them different tasks for them to attempt to complete by modifying the provided starter code. We gave them minimal assistance when it came to task completion.

In the first scene, students were asked complete tasks involving setting colors and using coordinates to place a block between two existing ones. In the second scene, students were presented with two blocks and challenged to add a third one by using a function. In the third scene, students added a scoop of ice cream to the cone example previously discussed.

5.1 Student performance

Some of the tasks were easily accomplished by students, while others proved to be more challenging.

From the first scene, 11 of 13 students were able to find the correct line number of the code that set the color of a box entity, and 10 of 13 were able to create a third block (8 of them in the correct position).

From the second scene, about function modification, only 5 of 13 succeeded. We realized that functions were a new concept to our test group; none of the students used functions in the third scene task, where such use would have been applicable.

From the third scene, 11 of the 13 were able to add the second "scoop" of ice cream.

5.2 Student feedback

When students were asked what they liked about using a educational virtual reality tool, they stated that the visual aspect improves the overall learning experience. They enjoyed seeing the output of their code, the fascination of creating a new world, the simplicity of using it on a smartphone, the creative control they got over what was displayed in the scene, and simply "everything."

The survey asked students if they were interested in exploring MYR more, ten students responded "yes" and three students responded "maybe." None of our students responded "no." Regarding programming approach, six students preferred text-based programming, five students preferred block-based programming, and two students did not have a preference.

On a scale from one to five, with five being the highest, students were asked to rate how much virtual reality enhanced their experience. Three students rated it a five, seven students rated it a four, and three students rated it a three.

5.3 Takeaways

The results of our preliminary trial were positive. We saw high engagement among all participants. But what was even more surprising was that the enthusiasm persisted, even when they encountered challenging situations. Perhaps our expectations for the students were too high relative to their age group, but despite the difficulty they had completing the assigned tasks, everyone was eager to come back and give it another try.

6 FUTURE WORK

Based on the feedback we received during the pilot testing and from conversations with CS educators, we are developing new features that make using MYR in the classroom easier for early adopters. The following section describes our plans for future work.

6.1 Integrated curricula

One of the biggest challenges the team faced when conducting its pilot tests was delivering the instructions to the user. It was difficult to give consistent guidance from one user to the next. A script could not cover every scenario, and the instructions naturally improved as we learned what works and what does not. The need to provide a consistent interaction from user to user is critical to conducting proper research. Therefore, we plan to develop an integrated curriculum system in MYR, to complement its existing examples library.

As an educational tool, having an integrated curriculum has been demonstrated to be effective (e.g., Codecademy [3] and many other guided programming systems).

The MYR team also recognizes the challenges of creating lesson plans. We are planning a system for the development of different curricula to be integrated into the coding environment itself.

It is further important to draw on the experience of other CS educators. This is why we hope to make this feature available and easy to use, for anyone willing to put together a curriculum using MYR. The MYR team believes that a wide range of curricula is not only beneficial to the user but also to understand how best to teach MYR. With permission of the authors, MYR will provide this curriculum for other instructors in the hope that they will offer a variety of different lessons to suit many tastes.

7 CONCLUSIONS

MYR seeks to deliver the best experience for beginners who want to explore programming and virtual reality. One of our primary goals going forward is to deliver a scalable system that can be deployed in classrooms and also enjoyed at home. We aim to make this tool available to any CS educator, allowing them to supplement their curriculum with an educational adventure into virtual reality.

Inspired by all of the previous work in educational computing, MYR can encourage new programmers by seizing on the recent excitement about virtual reality. MYR was developed specifically to overcome obstacles in virtual reality programming. Features like its real-time sync can be used to alleviate the hardware challenges associated with virtual reality, and by targeting a wide range of headsets, like the Google Cardboard, MYR helps make virtual reality economical for school budgets.

In an effort to investigate the role virtual reality can have in teaching CS, we developed a powerful tool that we hope is adopted by educators. We believe that offering this immersive environment can have a profound effect on overall attitudes towards learning programming. Our initial research looks promising. Students remained engaged and excited about the material. Our results are encouraging as students persisted and maintained positive attitudes despite challenges. Since virtual reality offers an effective platform for immersive, educational experiences, we have the opportunity to bring virtual reality to the classroom.

MYR can be accessed at `learnmyr.org`.

8 ACKNOWLEDGMENTS

We would like to thank Chike Abuah for his significant initial contributions to the MYR project. We would like to thank Vrinda Punj and Elena Izotova for their contributions to the MYR system. We would like to thank Sasha Wilkinson, who reviewed our paper draft. We would like to thank Akira Kamiya for supporting our work with students in the summer camps. This material is based upon work supported by the National Science Foundation under Grant No. 1433592.

REFERENCES

[1] [n. d.]. A-Frame – Make WebVR. https://aframe.io/

[2] [n. d.]. https://get.webgl.org. https://get.webgl.org/

[3] [n. d.]. Learn to Code - for Free | Codecademy. https://www.codecademy.com/

[4] [n. d.]. three.js - Javascript 3D library. https://threejs.org/

[5] [n. d.]. Unity. https://unity3d.com

[6] [n. d.]. WebVR - Bringing Virtual Reality to the Web. https://webvr.info/

[7] Karen Brennan. 2018. New frameworks for studying and assessing the development of computational thinking. (08 2018).

[8] Jorge Ferreira Franco and Roseli de Deus Lopes. 2009. Three-dimensional Digital Enviroments and Computer Graphics Influencing K-12 Individuals' Digital Literacy Development and Interdisciplinary Lifelong Learning. In *ACM SIGGRAPH ASIA 2009 Educators Program (SIGGRAPH ASIA '09)*. ACM, New York, NY, USA, Article 15, 8 pages. https://doi.org/10.1145/1666611.1666626

[9] Soomin Kim, Wookjae Maeng, Cindy Oh, Joonmin Lee, Seo-young Lee, Jeewon Choi, Gil Whan Hwang, Guhyun Hwang, Hyunsung Kim, Joonseok Kim, and Joonhwan Lee. 2017. Immersive VR for Numerical Engagement. In *Proceedings of the 23rd ACM Symposium on Virtual Reality Software and Technology (VRST '17)*. ACM, New York, NY, USA, Article 64, 2 pages. https://doi.org/10.1145/3139131.3141207

[10] Colleen M. Lewis. 2010. How Programming Environment Shapes Perception, Learning and Goals: Logo vs. Scratch. In *Proceedings of the 41st ACM Technical Symposium on Computer Science Education (SIGCSE '10)*. ACM, New York, NY, USA, 346–350. https://doi.org/10.1145/1734263.1734383

[11] Linda Mannila, Mia Peltomäki, and Tapio Salakoski. 2006. What about a simple language? Analyzing the difficulties in learning to program. *Computer Science Education* 16, 3 (2006), 211–227. https://doi.org/10.1080/08993400600912384 arXiv:https://doi.org/10.1080/08993400600912384

[12] Tanya Markow, Eugene Ressler, and Jean Blair. 2006. Catch That Speeding Turtle: Latching Onto Fun Graphics in CS1. *Ada Lett.* XXVI, 3 (Nov. 2006), 29–34. https://doi.org/10.1145/1185875.1185648

[13] Seymour Papert. 1972. On Making a Theorem for a Child. In *Proceedings of the ACM Annual Conference - Volume 1 (ACM '72)*. ACM, New York, NY, USA, 345–349. https://doi.org/10.1145/800193.569942

[14] Seymour Papert. 1980. *Mindstorms: Children, computers, and powerful ideas.* Basic Books, Inc.

Exploring the Applicability of Simple Syntax Writing Practice for Learning Programming

Antti Leinonen
University of Helsinki
Helsinki, Finland
antti.leinonen@helsinki.fi

Henrik Nygren
University of Helsinki
Helsinki, Finland
henrik.nygren@helsinki.fi

Nea Pirttinen
University of Helsinki
Helsinki, Finland
nea.pirttinen@cs.helsinki.fi

Arto Hellas
University of Helsinki
Helsinki, Finland
arto.hellas@cs.helsinki.fi

Juho Leinonen
University of Helsinki
Helsinki, Finland
juho.leinonen@helsinki.fi

ABSTRACT

When learning programming, students learn the syntax of a programming language, the semantics underlying the syntax, and practice applying the language in solving programming problems. Research has suggested that simply the syntax may be hard to learn. In this article, we study difficulty of learning the syntax of a programming language. We have constructed a tool that provides students code that they write character-by-character. When writing, the tool automatically highlights each character in code that is incorrectly typed, and through the highlight-based feedback directs students into writing correct syntax. We conducted a randomized controlled trial in an introductory programming course organized in Java. One half of the population had the tool in the course material immediately before programming exercises where the practiced syntax was used, while the other half of the course population did not have the tool, thus approaching the exercises in a traditional way. Our results imply that isolated syntax writing practice may not be a meaningful addition to the arsenal used for teaching programming, at least when the programming course utilizes a large set of small programming exercises. We encourage researchers to replicate our work in contexts where syntax seems to be an issue.

CCS CONCEPTS

• **Social and professional topics → Computing education**; • **Applied computing → Interactive learning environments**;

KEYWORDS

syntax practice, writing code, embedded tool

ACM Reference Format:
Antti Leinonen, Henrik Nygren, Nea Pirttinen, Arto Hellas, and Juho Leinonen. 2019. Exploring the Applicability of Simple Syntax Writing Practice for Learning Programming. In *Proceedings of the 50th ACM Technical Symposium on Computer Science Education (SIGCSE '19), February 27-March 2, 2019, Minneapolis, MN, USA.* ACM, New York, NY, USA, 7 pages. https://doi.org/10.1145/3287324.3287378

ACM ISBN 978-1-4503-5890-3/19/02...$15.00
https://doi.org/10.1145/3287324.3287378

1 INTRODUCTION

When learning to program, students work in an interlocked domain where challenges in one area contribute to challenges in other areas. For example, du Boulay [9] proposes five overlapping domains: understanding what programs are; forming an understanding of how computers execute programs; learning the notation and syntax of a language; learning structures that are used for solving programming problems; and learning the pragmatic skills needed for example in testing and debugging programs. When interviewing students, Lahtinen et al. [12] observed that difficulties with syntax are intertwined with other difficulties such as understanding program structures, understanding how to design programs, and dividing functionality of a program into smaller components.

Being able to write syntactically correct programs is a fundamental part of being able to program. Ng and Bereiter [16] suggest that learning to program starts with learning the syntax, which is followed by learning the structure and style. Here, making errors such as adding a semicolon after a conditional or a loop by mistake can take plenty of time to identify and fix [1]. Syntax errors are not problematic for only the struggling students as noted by Denny et al [8]: "*all students spent a similar amount of time solving the most common errors no matter what quartile they were in*".

Intuitively, if students practice writing syntax through mimicking small code samples, and the writing practice is designed so that the students receive character-by-character feedback on whether what they wrote is correct, students should be able to learn to avoid the major pitfalls related to typing the practiced syntactic constructs. Previously, the importance of training syntax has been highlighted in SyntaxTrain [15], which is a tool that shows students a syntax diagram – effectively a flow diagram – and information on possible errors on a line.

In order to study whether simple syntax writing practice reduces syntax errors and improves students' performance in related programming problems, we have constructed a tool that is used for practicing code writing. For each character that the student types in the tool, the tool shows whether the character corresponds to the expected input and consequently highlights errors in syntax.

Our tool differs from SyntaxTrain in three ways. First, there are no flow diagrams as the students have not yet learned how to interpret them, second, the feedback is given on a character-by-character level, and third, our tool is directly embedded within the material.

We have conducted a randomized controlled trial where a part of the course population was presented with the tool before programming exercises where the practiced syntax was first used, and the other part of the course population worked on the programming exercises without separate syntax practice. We study whether there are differences in the populations in terms of effort – when measured through programming exercise -specific events such as keystrokes within the programming environment – and time used for the programming exercises.

This article is organized as follows. The next section outlines existing research on errors that students encounter when writing programs and considers the meaningfulness of isolated practice. Then, in Section 3, we outline our methodology, which includes the research questions, the context of the study, and the tool. The results of the study are presented in Section 4, and the implications of the results are discussed in Section 5, which also includes limitations of our study. Finally, Section 6 concludes the article and outlines possible future work.

2 BACKGROUND

When learning to program, a big part of the issues that novice programmers face is related to syntax. Robins et al. studied problem distributions in a CS1 course [19]. They studied the different types of issues for which students seek help during their programming laboratory sessions. The majority of the issues that students faced were categorized as "trivial mechanics", which were defined as "trivial problems with little mechanical details". These included issues with braces, brackets, semicolons, typos and spelling, Java and file naming conventions, forgotten import statements, formatting output, tidiness, indenting, and comments. All of the trivial mechanics issues are syntax related.

Jadud [11] studied novice programmers' "compilation behavior", i.e. the way how novices behave when encountering a syntax error. Jadud observed that the efforts related to fixing syntax errors were related to course outcomes and that the capability of handling syntax errors – *Error Quotient* – could be used to predict exercise and exam grades. This signifies the importance of teaching students to tackle syntactic issues or avoiding them altogether by separating syntax practice from concept practice. His article reports also an interesting vignette that followed a student's behavior during a part of a compilation session: it might take over an hour to fix a simple misplacement of a beginning brace due to the student not being able to understand the error messages provided by the compiler.

The environment in which Jadud's work was conducted in, BlueJ [20], was later augmented with data collection facilities by Brown et al. [5]. In an analysis of 37 million compilation events from BlueJ, Altamdri et al. [1] identified a set of frequently observed syntax errors. These included:

(1) Unbalanced parentheses, brackets, braces or quotation marks, or trying to enclose one with another.
(2) Confusing an assignment operator with a comparison operator.
(3) Including parameter types in method calls.

When comparing the results of Altamdri et al. with other studies on compilation errors, there are discrepancies which may be related to the potpourri of backgrounds and teaching approaches. For example, in the work of Denny et al. [8], the most frequent syntax errors were "Cannot resolve identifier", type mismatch, and missing semicolon – none of which are highlighted as very frequent in the study by Altamdri et al.

Even seemingly very simple things like writing the print command in Java can cause problems to students. The way how students write their first programs was studied by Vihavainen et al. [25] who identified four distinct mistake categories related to writing the print command. These were as follows:

(1) mixing up upper- and lowercase letters, for example writing *System* in *System.out.println* with a lowercase *s*,
(2) using other characters instead of periods to separate words, for example writing *System-out-println*,
(3) various mistakes with string literals, such as forgetting quotation marks or the word *out* when trying to print something, and
(4) general typing mistakes without clear misconceptions.

One of the suggestions that Vihavainen et al. propose is that the root of many problems seems to lie within the syntax of programming languages, which is usually very different from natural languages. They also noted that modern programming environments provide students with plenty of support as they are writing their programs. They noticed that many of the students used copy and paste in the exercises during the first week, but most of them utilized the "sout" shortcut instead during the second week of the course. In addition, in their context, only a very small portion of the students submitted code with syntax errors. In the case of an error, students fixed it locally before submitting to the server.

As syntax seems to be an issue in programming, as evidenced by the preceding research, one could suggest practicing it. Many support dividing learned content into smaller pieces that are first practiced separately and then integrated together [14, 21–23, 26]. Such practice can be done, for example, under the guidance of a tutor or a peer who provides the learner with more challenging tasks as they are progressing, within a tutoring system, or within an e-book that interleaves theory and practice. Isolated practice can be beneficial for the learner as it can be used to reduce the cognitive load that is associated with the actual task [3].

As being able to write correct syntax is a cornerstone in writing programs, doing small syntax practice before programming tasks could be beneficial. For example, Ng and Bereiter [16] have suggested that learning the style and structure of programs are preceded by learning the syntax. Once students have internalized syntax, they should be able to ignore the details of the syntax during program design and construction, allowing them to direct attention to more relevant parts of the program [18].

3 RESEARCH DESIGN

Here, we first describe the context of the study and the syntax practice tool in more detail and then outline our research questions and methodology.

3.1 Context

The data for this study comes from a seven-week introductory programming course organized at the University of Helsinki during the fall of 2017. The programming course is the first course that freshmen who major in computer science take. Approximately one third of the course participants study computer science as their major, while the rest come from various backgrounds ranging from pedagogy to medicine.

The course follows an online textbook with theory, quiz, and programming exercise parts. The quizzes are done within the course material, while the programming exercises are completed in a separate programming environment that collects snapshots of students' programming process. The course also includes weekly lectures. The lectures are in the beginning of the week and the exercise deadlines at the end of the week. In this study, we focus on the first two weeks of the course, which cover the principles of procedural programming with Java. The topics include input/output, variables, conditionals, loops, and lists.

The course material has been written to follow the principles of the Extreme Apprenticeship method [26], which emphasizes that most of the students' time in the course should be spent on solving programming exercises. The majority of the exercises are small, and sequential programming exercises form larger programs as they are completed. The first two weeks under study have almost sixty programming exercises altogether.

3.2 Tool description

The tool consists of two main elements. The first element is used to show the code that the student has to write, and the second element is used to provide the input field into which the students are expected to write the code. The input field has three functionalities: first, the input field highlights wrongly written syntax, second, the input field blocks copying and pasting – that is, students must write the code –, and third, the input field records whatever the user writes for future analysis, given the online learning material provides a server for the tool where the data should be stored.

The syntax to highlight is generated from a template, which is also used to generate the code that the student must write. The code that the students are expected to write can be restricted, for example, to only a single statement. For example, in the example illustrated in Figure 1, the students do not need to write the class and method body. They are only expected to write the for-statement, i.e. the following:

```
for (int i = 0; i < 10; i++) {
    System.out.println(i * i);
}
```

Figure 1 also highlights what happens if the syntax is written incorrectly. In the example, the user has mistakenly added a semicolon after the `for`-loop statement. In the Figure, the highlight has been emphasized with an arrow for readability purposes. Once the code is correctly written, the red cross in the lower right corner of the input field changes into a green check mark.

The tool was embedded in the online learning material on the first and second week of the course. It was placed so that students would use it to practice the same syntactic keywords that were present in the following exercises. For example, the first iteration of

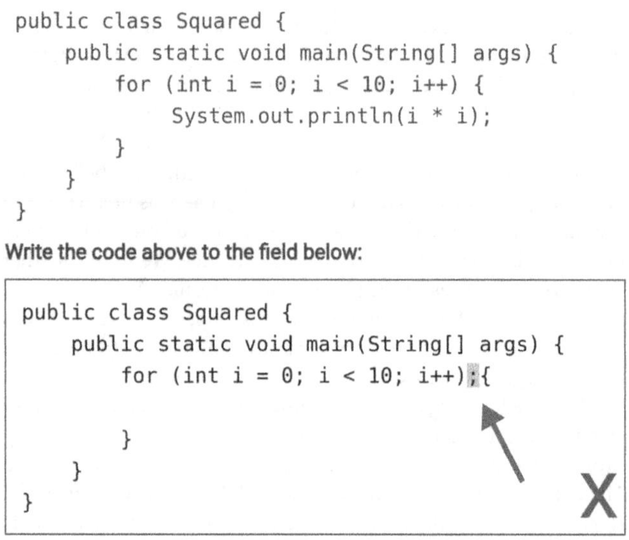

Figure 1: Illustration of the code that the student is expected to write and the input prompt of the tool. In the figure, the student has mistakenly added a semicolon after the for-statement, which is highlighted and must be fixed.

the tool practiced Java's print statement, and it was placed right before the first programming exercises such as writing the traditional program that outputs "Hello World!".

3.3 Data collection

Students encountered the tool in the material in the first two weeks for a total of five times. The tool was included when key syntax was introduced. The syntax in our study were the print statement (exercise 1), reading input (exercise 2), if-clause (exercise 3), while-clause (exercise 4), and method body (exercise 5), later referred to as Ex. 1 to 5. We examined data from the five instances where the tool was embedded in the material and each programming exercise that was given immediately after each syntax practice.

In order to determine the amount of time and the number of events required to complete the exercises, we used a NetBeans [4] programming environment plugin called Test My Code (TMC) [17], which collects students' keystrokes and events within the programming environment. The data also includes timestamps, which we used to study how much time students spent on the exercises.

For this study, we focused on character insertion and deletion events in order to analyze code written by the students themselves (and not for example copy-pasted). Similar insertion and deletion keystroke data with timestamps was collected from the tool.

3.4 Research questions

Our research questions for this study are as follows:

- RQ1. Do students who see the syntax practice tool have fewer events for the exercises when compared to those who did not see the tool?

- RQ2. Do students who see the syntax practice tool use less time for programming exercises when compared to those who did not see the tool?
- RQ3. Do students who see the syntax practice tool use less time in total for the syntax practice and programming exercises when compared to those who did not see the tool?

The study was conducted as a randomized controlled trial. The participants of the course were divided randomly into two groups A and B: group A (control) did not see the syntax practice tool in the material, while group B (treatment) did. In randomly assigned groups external factors such as initial skill levels should be approximately equal between the groups.

3.5 Group formation

As our study is an A/B-study, where group A consists of students who did not see the tool, and B of students who saw the tool, we compare these two groups in our analysis. Since the tool is voluntary to use and students in our study did not receive course points or other incentives for using the tool, some of the students in group B chose not to use the tool.

Thus, in addition to the A/B study, we further study group B (students who saw the tool) separately based on whether students in the group actually used the tool or not. In the analysis, the students from group B who did not use the tool were assigned into group C, while the students who used the tool were assigned into group D. Here, using the tool means that the student completed a syntax writing task in the tool correctly.

The division to groups C and D was done per exercise, depending on whether the student had completed the tool previous to the analyzed exercise. Exercise specific division was done so that the exercise data would better reflect the effects of the tool on the students' coding process for the said exercise as the completion of the tool later on in the material would not have helped on the earlier exercises. All participants had the same programming exercises.

3.6 Analysis

The purpose of the study was to analyze whether the syntax practice tool influences students' behavior in programming exercises. We study this both through the amount of individual events that students produce within the syntax practice tool for each particular syntax construct and within the programming environment in the programming exercises immediately following the syntax practices. In addition to the events, we also study the time that students used in the syntax practice tool and within the programming environment.

To answer the first research question, *Do students who see the syntax practice tool have fewer events for the exercises when compared to those who did not see the tool?*, we studied whether the students in group B had fewer keystroke events in the exercise data than the students in group A on average. We only included inserting and removing code as the number of times the students ran, tested or submitted their progress is irrelevant to the purpose of the tool.

To answer the second research question, *Do students who see the syntax practice tool use less time for programming exercises when compared to those who did not see the tool?*, we analyzed the time used for the exercise. We calculated the time between the first and last keystroke. We removed gaps in the snapshot timestamps that were over five minutes long as we did not want to include any pauses that students took. For this, we again compared the performance of group B against group A.

To answer the third research question, *Do students who see the syntax practice tool use less time in total for the syntax practice and programming exercises when compared to those who did not see the tool?*, we included the time spent on the tool for the students in group B when comparing time usage for the following exercise. This was done as it could be argued that even if students may complete exercises faster after using the tool, the tool is only useful if the total time in both the exercise and the tool is smaller for those students who saw the tool.

For all three comparisons, we used the Kolmogorov-Smirnov test [13] for examining whether the groups' differences were statistically significantly different, and corrected the results for multiple tests using the Holm-Sidak correction method [10].

4 RESULTS

4.1 Descriptive Statistics

A total of 249 students in the course consented for their data to be used in this research. From these 249 students, 17 had to be excluded as they did not provide the needed snapshot data. From the remaining 232 students, 125 students were in group A, meaning that they did not see the tool in the course material. Group B consisted of 107 students, which was split into groups C and D, that is, the students who saw the tool but ignored it (group C) and students who completed the tool (group D). The division to groups C and D was done per exercise, where group D consisted of the students who completed the tool previous to the analyzed exercise. Table 1a shows the number of students in groups A, B, C, and D per exercise.

4.2 Events and tool usage

Our first research question asks if the students who saw the tool had fewer typing events in the exercises after the tool than those who did not see the tool. Our hypothesis was that the students who saw the tool would have fewer events as they would make fewer typos while writing the syntax. However, it would seem that the tool did not help, that is, the students who saw the tool did not make fewer typos. Table 1b shows the median of the number of typing events between the groups. The differences between the number of typing events of the students who did not see the tool (group A) and those who saw it (group B) are not statistically significant based on the Kolmogorov-Smirnov test [13] in any of the exercises.

4.3 Time and tool usage

Our second research question focuses on whether the students who saw the tool used less time answering the programming exercises than those who did not see the tool. We studied the amount of time the students used on answering the programming exercises by calculating the time between their first and last keystrokes. We removed over five minute breaks between keystrokes to reduce the effect of taking breaks on the results. Table 1c shows the medians of the amount of time the group used per exercise. The differences in the time usage between groups are not statistically significant based on the Kolmogorov-Smirnov test.

	Ex. 1	Ex. 2	Ex. 3	Ex. 4	Ex. 5
No tool (A)	125	125	125	125	125
Tool (B)	107	107	107	107	107
Ignored tool (C)	50	36	50	47	59
Used tool (D)	57	71	57	60	48

(a) Number of students per group.

	Ex. 1	Ex. 2	Ex. 3	Ex. 4	Ex. 5
No tool (A)	52.68	141.56	146.96	164.69	60.74
Tool (B)	55.30	172.77	158.93	179.13	51.62
Ignored tool (C)	57.56	127.68	156.76	162.67	45.69
Used tool (D)	53.49	191.80	160.49	189.00	59.47

(b) Event counts (median) for completing the exercise following the syntax practice tool.

	Ex. 1	Ex. 2	Ex. 3	Ex. 4	Ex. 5
No tool (A)	1.90	3.80	2.91	3.99	0.84
Tool (B)	1.81	5.54	2.98	4.35	0.88
Ignored tool (C)	1.66	3.19	2.87	3.53	0.86
Used tool (D)	1.92	6.53	3.05	4.84	0.90

(c) Time in minutes (median) for completing the exercise following syntax practice tool.

	Ex. 1	Ex. 2	Ex. 3	Ex. 4	Ex. 5
No tool (A)	1.90	3.80	2.91	3.99	0.84
Tool (B)	2.19	6.22	4.65	5.07	1.51
Ignored tool (C)	1.73	3.68	3.55	3.76	1.11
Used tool (D)	2.56	7.29	5.43	5.86	2.05

(d) Time in minutes (median) when syntax practice and exercise time has been combined.

Table 1: Descriptive statistics of groups. Group A refers to students who did not have the tool in the material and B to students who did have the tool in the material. Group B is also split into two subgroups: Group C refers to those who saw the tool but did not use it and D to those who saw the tool and used it at least once. None of the differences between A and B are statistically significant based on the Kolmogorov-Smirnov test.

Our third research question is near identical to our second research question with the exception that we include the time used on the tool for the students who saw it. When comparing the time usages between the students who saw the tool (group B) and those who did not (group A), the results were not statistically significant based on the Kolmogorov-Smirnov test. The medians of time usage for groups A, B, C and D can be seen in table 1d.

Finally, we also compared the total time spent on exercises and the tools from groups C and D who both saw the tool. The comparison result from the Kolmogorov-Smirnov test was initially statistically significant showing difference between the groups, but after correcting our analysis for multiple comparisons using the Holm-Sidak correction method [10] the differences were not statistically significant.

5 DISCUSSION

5.1 Revisiting the research questions

In this study, we conducted a randomized controlled trial in order to determine whether light syntax practice would reduce the effort needed to complete related programming exercises in an introductory programming course. The effort that students invest into the exercises was studied from three perspectives: (1) the number of edit events in the exercises, (2) the amount of time that students spend on the exercise, and (3) the combined time in the practice system and the programming exercises.

The results, as outlined in the previous section, suggest that simple syntax practice does not improve students' performance in the subsequent programming exercises. No statistically significant differences were observed between the control group who did not have the syntax practice tool embedded to their learning material, and the treatment group who had the syntax practice tool immediately before the programming exercises where the syntax was used.

The results we observed suggest that the tool is not helpful, at least as it is. All of the results were statistically insignificant, which means that the people who saw the tool did not perform considerably better than those who did not see the tool. Next, we explore some of the possible explanations for our findings.

5.2 Separate syntax practice

The way how exercises are integrated into the learning environment plays a role in students' learning. If the exercises are placed in different locations or systems, it is possible that students must split their attention which increases extraneous cognitive load [6]. In our context, the syntax practice was conducted within the online learning material into which the syntax practice tool was embedded. The decision to embed the component into the learning material was partially driven by making a system that would be easy to share with others. In hindsight, however, it is possible that this decision also decreased the efficiency of the practice system.

From the perspective of reducing unnecessary cognitive load, supporting systems should be integrated into the environments in which students work [24]. For example, when programming exercises are worked on within a programming environment, having programming-related feedback such as syntax practice integrated into the environment would likely be a meaningful choice. On the other hand, if programming exercises are embedded to the online learning materials using tools such as Python Classroom Response System [28], it is possible that syntax practice within the online learning materials would be more beneficial as well.

Another way to address the issue, i.e. split-attention effect, was recently proposed by Altadmri et al [2]. They have developed a frame-based editing approach where syntactic commands, such as "if", once finished, are "glued" into place similar to block-based programming languages. While the system does not specifically focus on syntax practice, the approach shows promise in reducing problems with syntax.

In addition to the location of the syntax practice tool, another factor in its effectiveness could be its frequency in the course material. As the tool appeared only once per practiced syntactic keyword, simply having more syntax practice could have been beneficial.

5.3 Course organization

Course organization and management can influence students' learning. In the studied context, the course pedagogy focuses heavily on students working with small programming exercises that together combine into larger programs. The smallest exercises can effectively be seen as typing practice within the programming environment as the material provides examples that are very similar to the smallest exercises. It is possible that the use of small exercises within the course influences the need for syntax practice. There is some evidence that the use of such exercises can lead to students starting their work earlier, and thus also performing better [7].

We determined, in a post hoc fashion, whether some of the errors highlighted in related studies such as [1] were an issue in the studied context. We analyzed the keystroke data to identify conditionals and loops with functionality disabled with a semicolon, that is:

```
if (condition); {
    // code
}
while (condition); {
    // code
}
```

From the population of 232 students, none had encountered the above issues within the studied data set, which consisted of two weeks of an introductory programming course. While this is anecdotal and by no means representative of all syntax errors, it is possible that the course pedagogy and the way how the course is organized influences the errors that students encounter. Consequently, it could be meaningful to attempt to use our tool in contexts where students are more prone to struggle with syntax errors.

Furthermore, similar to the study reported in [25], many of the students used shortcuts when completing the course exercises. For example, some copied and pasted statements from the material and only changed the content, while others used shortcuts and autocomplete features. It is possible that the course format plays a role here too: the course has a two-hour weekly lecture where the teacher primarily focuses on live coding and worked examples. However, attendance is not mandatory and not all students attended the lecture. While we have no exact data on attendance, the responsible lecturer stated that approximately half of the students in the course attended the first two lectures relevant to this study.

5.4 Exercise complexity and syntax errors

Continuing with the above observation, that is, none of the students in the studied context had particular syntax errors, it is possible that the complexity of the studied programming exercises was too low. Due to the way the course is organized, the exercises that students are given after a new topic are initially small and then grow into larger problems. As syntax practice was conducted when a new topic was introduced, the exercises may have simply been too trivial for the students.

The complexity of problems and syntax errors have been linked in research. For example, as noted by Winslow [27],"*Given a new, unfamiliar language, the syntax is not the problem, learning how to use and combine the statements to achieve the desired effect is difficult*". The influence of the program complexity on syntax errors should be studied further in the future.

6 CONCLUSIONS

In this article, we reported a randomized controlled trial that evaluated the applicability of isolated syntax practice for learning programming. The isolated syntax practice was implemented as a component that was embedded in the learning materials immediately before the programming exercises where the students were expected to use the practiced syntax. The study was motivated through the research that points out that some struggle with syntax [1], and that the struggles with syntax errors are not only limited to the students who perform more poorly in courses [8].

Our results show that isolated syntax practice does not help student performance in subsequent programming exercises when measured in terms of total events or time needed to complete the exercises. Similarly, when comparing the total time used for the programming exercise combined with the typing practice, there was no statistically significant difference between the populations in the randomized controlled trial. At the same time, our experimental setup made it possible to not use the tool even if students were placed in the typing practice group.

In the discussion, we explored possibilities for why the result turned out as it did. A few of the possibilities include the pedagogy of the studied course: the participants in the course practice programming with tens of weekly exercises, some of which are used to highlight syntactic constructs that students are expected to learn. It is possible that the first exercises where syntax is practiced are sufficient and no separate practice is needed. It is also possible that the context in which the syntax practice was performed (that is, the online learning material) is too different from the programming environment where the programming exercises were worked on.

Currently, we are looking for other variables that could influence the outcomes such as previous programming background and other factors. Given, for example, information on previous programming background, we could look into whether the tool could be beneficial for students who have not previously programmed. We are also looking for researchers and educators whose students work with large programming exercises or whose students complete their programming exercises within online learning materials. Having someone replicate our study, with possibly contradictory results, would provide further insight into why syntax may be hard for some students.

REFERENCES

[1] Amjad Altadmri and Neil CC Brown. 2015. 37 million compilations: Investigating novice programming mistakes in large-scale student data. In *Proceedings of the 46th ACM Technical Symposium on Computer Science Education*. ACM, 522–527.

[2] Amjad Altadmri, Michael Kolling, and Neil CC Brown. 2016. The cost of syntax and how to avoid it: Text versus frame-based editing. In *2016 IEEE 40th Annual Computer Software and Applications Conference (COMPSAC)*. IEEE, 748–753.

[3] Paul Ayres. 2013. Can the isolated-elements strategy be improved by targeting points of high cognitive load for additional practice? *Learning and Instruction* 23 (2013), 115–124.

[4] Tim Boudreau, Jesse Glick, Simeon Greene, Vaughn Spurlin, and Jack J Woehr. 2002. *NetBeans: the definitive guide: developing, debugging, and deploying Java code.* " O'Reilly Media, Inc.".

[5] Neil Christopher Charles Brown, Michael Kölling, Davin McCall, and Ian Utting. 2014. Blackbox: a large scale repository of novice programmers' activity. In *Proceedings of the 45th ACM technical symposium on Computer science education.* ACM, 223–228.

[6] Paul Chandler and John Sweller. 1992. The split-attention effect as a factor in the design of instruction. *British Journal of Educational Psychology* 62, 2 (1992), 233–246.

[7] Paul Denny, Andrew Luxton-Reilly, Michelle Craig, and Andrew Petersen. 2018. Improving Complex Task Performance Using a Sequence of Simple Practice Tasks. In *Proceedings of the 23rd Annual ACM Conference on Innovation and Technology in Computer Science Education (ITiCSE 2018).* ACM, New York, NY, USA, 4–9. https://doi.org/10.1145/3197091.3197141

[8] Paul Denny, Andrew Luxton-Reilly, and Ewan Tempero. 2012. All Syntax Errors Are Not Equal. In *Proceedings of the 17th ACM Annual Conference on Innovation and Technology in Computer Science Education (ITiCSE '12).* ACM, New York, NY, USA, 75–80. https://doi.org/10.1145/2325296.2325318

[9] Benedict Du Boulay. 1986. Some difficulties of learning to program. *Journal of Educational Computing Research* 2, 1 (1986), 57–73.

[10] Sture Holm. 1979. A simple sequentially rejective multiple test procedure. *Scandinavian journal of statistics* (1979), 65–70.

[11] Matthew C Jadud. 2006. Methods and tools for exploring novice compilation behaviour. In *Proceedings of the second international workshop on Computing education research.* ACM, 73–84.

[12] Essi Lahtinen, Kirsti Ala-Mutka, and Hannu-Matti Järvinen. 2005. A Study of the Difficulties of Novice Programmers. In *Proceedings of the 10th Annual SIGCSE Conference on Innovation and Technology in Computer Science Education (ITiCSE '05).* ACM, New York, NY, USA, 14–18. https://doi.org/10.1145/1067445.1067453

[13] Raul HC Lopes. 2011. Kolmogorov-smirnov test. In *International encyclopedia of statistical science.* Springer, 718–720.

[14] Andrew Luxton-Reilly, Brett A. Becker, Yingjun Cao, Roger McDermott, Claudio Mirolo, Andreas Mühling, Andrew Petersen, Kate Sanders, Simon, and Jacqueline Whalley. 2017. Developing Assessments to Determine Mastery of Programming Fundamentals. In *Proceedings of the 2017 ACM Conference on Innovation and Technology in Computer Science Education (ITiCSE '17).* ACM, New York, NY, USA, 388–388. https://doi.org/10.1145/3059009.3081327

[15] Andreas Leon Aagaard Moth, Joergen Villadsen, and Mordechai Ben-Ari. 2011. SyntaxTrain: relieving the pain of learning syntax. In *Proceedings of the 16th annual joint conference on Innovation and technology in computer science education.* ACM, 387–387.

[16] Evelyn Ng and Carl Bereiter. 1991. Three levels of goal orientation in learning. *Journal of the Learning Sciences* 1, 3-4 (1991), 243–271.

[17] Martin Pärtel, Matti Luukkainen, Arto Vihavainen, and Thomas Vikberg. 2013. Test my code. *International Journal of Technology Enhanced Learning 2* 5, 3-4 (2013), 271–283.

[18] Robert S Rist. 1989. Schema creation in programming. *Cognitive Science* 13, 3 (1989), 389–414.

[19] Anthony Robins, Patricia Haden, and Sandy Garner. 2006. Problem distributions in a CS1 course. In *Proceedings of the 8th Australasian Conference on Computing Education-Volume 52.* Australian Computer Society, Inc., 165–173.

[20] Dean Sanders, Phillip Heeler, and Carol Spradling. 2001. Introduction to BlueJ: a Java development environment. In *Journal of Computing Sciences in Colleges*, Vol. 16. Consortium for Computing Sciences in Colleges, 257–258.

[21] R Keith Sawyer. 2005. *The Cambridge handbook of the learning sciences.* Cambridge University Press.

[22] Juha Sorva and Otto Seppälä. 2014. Research-based Design of the First Weeks of CS1. In *Proceedings of the 14th Koli Calling International Conference on Computing Education Research (Koli Calling '14).* ACM, New York, NY, USA, 71–80. https://doi.org/10.1145/2674683.2674690

[23] Jeroen JG Van Merriënboer, Richard E Clark, and Marcel BM De Croock. 2002. Blueprints for complex learning: The 4C/ID-model. *Educational technology research and development* 50, 2 (2002), 39–61.

[24] Jeroen JG Van Merriënboer, Paul A Kirschner, and Liesbeth Kester. 2003. Taking the load off a learner's mind: Instructional design for complex learning. *Educational psychologist* 38, 1 (2003), 5–13.

[25] Arto Vihavainen, Juha Helminen, and Petri Ihantola. 2014. How Novices Tackle Their First Lines of Code in an IDE: Analysis of Programming Session Traces. In *Proceedings of the 14th Koli Calling International Conference on Computing Education Research (Koli Calling '14).* ACM, New York, NY, USA, 109–116. https://doi.org/10.1145/2674683.2674692

[26] Arto Vihavainen, Matti Paksula, and Matti Luukkainen. 2011. Extreme Apprenticeship Method in Teaching Programming for Beginners. In *Proceedings of the 42Nd ACM Technical Symposium on Computer Science Education (SIGCSE '11).* ACM, New York, NY, USA, 93–98. https://doi.org/10.1145/1953163.1953196

[27] Leon E. Winslow. 1996. Programming Pedagogy&Mdash;a Psychological Overview. *SIGCSE Bull.* 28, 3 (Sept. 1996), 17–22. https://doi.org/10.1145/234867.234872

[28] Daniel Zingaro, Yuliya Cherenkova, Olessia Karpova, and Andrew Petersen. 2013. Facilitating code-writing in PI classes. In *Proceeding of the 44th ACM technical symposium on Computer science education.* ACM, 585–590.

Stochastic Tree-Based Generation of Program-Tracing Practice Questions

Anderson Thomas
The George Washington University
Washington, DC
athomas1@gwmail.gwu.edu

Troy Stopera
The George Washington University
Washington, DC
troystopera@gwmail.gwu.edu

Pablo Frank-Bolton
The George Washington University
Washington, DC
pfrank@gwmail.gwu.edu

Rahul Simha
The George Washington University
Washington, DC
simha@gwmail.gwu.edu

ABSTRACT

Recent work [6, 23] has shown that mental program-execution exercises, in the form of Parson's puzzles or program-tracing, are effective in improving student performance in intro CS courses. This form of practice is promising because its low cost of creation and short duration (for the student) can promote the significant practice needed for learning. The goal of this paper is to enable wider use of such exercises through large-scale automated generation of short, multiple-choice mental execution questions. The challenge in automation is to algorithmically generate effective *distractors* (plausible, but incorrect choices), and to generate questions of varying levels of difficulty and whose difficulty level can be set by the instructor. In this paper, we propose a language-generalizable approach for automatically generating a practically unlimited number of such exercises, each constructed to a designated level of difficulty and incorporating the core programming-in-the-small themes: assignment, conditionals, loops, and arrays. The stochastic tree-based generation algorithm and a subsequent simulation of execution also enable generating effective distractors since all possible execution paths are readily available in the tree at the time of generation, and the distractors, therefore, correspond to reasonable (but ultimately incorrect) paths of execution. Furthermore, the approach is easily transferable to other languages with little effort. The generated questions are delivered through a mobile app that can be customized by the instructor to vary the questions generated and to introduce interleaving to take advantage of the spacing effect. Preliminary student feedback on the experience has been positive.

KEYWORDS

Intro CS, Question Generation, Practice Tools

ACM ISBN 978-1-4503-5890-3/19/02...$15.00
https://doi.org/10.1145/3287324.3287492

ACM Reference Format:
Anderson Thomas, Troy Stopera, Pablo Frank-Bolton, and Rahul Simha. 2019. Stochastic Tree-Based Generation of Program-Tracing Practice Questions. In *Proceedings of the 50th ACM Technical Symposium on Computer Science Education (SIGCSE '19), February 27-March 2, 2019, Minneapolis, MN, USA.* ACM, New York, NY, USA, 7 pages. https://doi.org/10.1145/3287324.3287492

1 INTRODUCTION

The past decade has seen a surge of interest in enhancing student learning in introductory programming courses with activities that go beyond the traditional lecture followed by programming assignment [9, 10, 19]. One such enhancement, the use of program-tracing exercises, has been correlated to an improvement in the quality of programming skill in students [6, 18, 19, 23]. Systematically offering students many small exercises, in various gradations of difficulty and repeatedly, also aligns well with research from the science of learning, for example, *deliberate practice* [7], in which exercises are customized to the individual learner's level, provide immediate feedback, and are in the learner's *zone of proximal development* – just slightly harder than what the learner is capable of. An ideal support system for deliberate practice in programming, in addition to regular programming assignments, should also allow the instructor to set some broad parameters (numbers of questions, mix of difficulty levels), should be efficient in generation to enable scaling with numbers of students, and should reach students where they are (on their smartphones) to encourage repeated practice. These requirements pose a problem for hand-crafting custom questions, already a significant time sink for instructors, who might opt-out of these approaches to avoid the additional overhead.

One way to generate lots of questions is to use *question templates* that let an instructor specify which parts of a question can be randomly generated or selected, which then enables automated grading [3, 4, 8, 10, 11, 14, 17, 23]. The human effort involved in template-generated questions is both its advantage and disadvantage. Instructors thoughtfully generate and identify opportunities for learning through careful crafting of templates, expertly judge the level of difficulty, and are even able to include appropriate hints if the generated question is incorrectly answered. At the same time, the writing of templates takes time, as does vetting the generated questions, and ensuring that at least some distractors in each question are meaningful.

The goal of this paper is to ask whether a more automated approach – ours is called GenCODE – can be effective. In particular, can an algorithm judge the difficulty level during generation, provide sufficient variety, and most importantly, create meaningful distractors? We propose a stochastic tree-based approach that works in two phases, first to generate the code for a tracing exercise, and second, to generate the distractors for multiple-choice questions. (The latter is less important in variations where students must fill code.) The first phase mirrors a recursive-descent parser in that a tree similar to a parse-tree is constructed by randomly expanding nodes representing statements into assignments, loops, conditionals – some of which have statement-blocks that are then recursively expanded. The second phase simulates the execution of the generated tree to explore a variety of execution paths with the intent of identifying incorrect distractors which might appear plausible to students.

The GenCODE system itself consists of an instructor interface that gives the instructor the ability to set broad parameters. The generated questions are then available to the instructor for further editing or vetting, if the instructor so chooses. The questions are then delivered to a smartphone app, where they are gamified into various levels to encourage students to win points. As each student starts to answer questions and "level up" in the game, they are given harder questions. Furthermore, when a student incorrectly answers a question, the system will ensure that the question is presented back to the student *at a later time*, to exploit the learning that arises from the *spacing effect* [2].

GenCODE was piloted in a brief two-week trial in an introductory semester-long programming course (in Java) at our university during the Fall of 2017 and Spring 2018. Our main findings in this experience-report are the following. First, when human experts evaluate the difficulty level of generated questions, the human rating of difficulty has reasonably close correlation to the algorithm's rating of difficulty, suggesting that the approach has the potential for producing questions in the the desired student's zone of proximal development. Second, students were found to often get questions wrong and get the same questions wrong multiple times, which suggests that the algorithmically produced distractors are reasonable.

Third, students surveyed about their experience responded positively, appreciating the opportunity for low-stakes practice. Finally, using a Turing test, we attempted to discern whether experts (seniors, grads) could distinguish between the algorithm's generated questions and similar hand-crafted questions from other experts. Here, we discovered that our approach needs refinement: human experts were able to intuit some inexplicable signature from the algorithm-generated questions. Accordingly, some surface features of the tree-generated code may need modification; however, the questions are nonetheless useful for practice.

In the following sections we describe the related work on question generation and the implementation details of our system, followed by a discussion of the types of questions involved and the response to the system.

2 RELATED WORK

Computer Science educational research has investigated a variety of approaches to support the learning of programming that go beyond the typical weekly programming exercises, including for example, pair-programming, live coding and gamification. Program-tracing, the focus of this paper, is one such approach that researchers have found effective [16, 18, 19]. For example, Kumar et al [16], used a controlled study to show that code-tracing can improve code-writing abilities of students. A concomitant growth in delivery platforms has accompanied the interest in types of exercises: many researchers have elected to build systems designed to work on mobile devices [5, 12, 20]. This has allowed researchers to create program-assembly questions based on predefined code snippets. These findings have led to the integration of programming questions into new mediums, as seen in the work of Oyalere et al [20], where gamification is applied to Parsons Puzzles. Deb et al.[5] extend these tracing tasks with the inclusion of per-question feedback. More recently, Ericson et al. [6] found that program-question generation with automated feedback provides a system for reducing the time-cost of practicing programming through tracing activities, while yielding the equivalent results to activities that focus on writing code. Particular focus has surrounded Parson's Programming Puzzles[21], which are puzzle-like questions where students complete programs by correctly ordering code snippets.

In related work, the description of a program's execution as a method of explaining the correct answer has been shown to yield improved program writing skills in students [4, 8]. Focusing on the specific domain of *counter-controlled loops*, Kumar [4] presents a template-based system for generating C++ code snippets and questions. In [22], Prados et al. obtain some reuse of their system by changing the programming language of the generated code snippets.

Brusilovsky et al. focused on the development of tools for out-of-classroom self-assessment [3]. In their study, students answered sets of template-generated questions, resulting in the detection of a significant improvement of student understanding of program semantics. Variability in the generated material was obtained through the use of randomized parameters within highly structured code snippets [3]. With respect to the domain of *variable scope*, Fernandes et al. [8] found improved learning when studying the coupling of a question generator and a feedback system. In the work of Kumar at al. [14] on question generation, and specifically on domain-tree models capable of describing scope, the authors describe a system notable for being capable of providing feedback at various conceptual levels. In addition, the authors found improved learning when studying the coupling of a question generator and a feedback system. The work of Hsiao et al [10] describes in detail QuizJET, a templating system for object-oriented programming. QuizJET was designed to focus on a narrow subset of programming concepts and required on the order of 100 handcrafted templates for generating questions. These studies showcase the ability of templating systems to cover and provide materials for new topic domains but simultaneously illustrate the difficulty of extending them to new topics. With a different approach, Zavala et al. [23] move away from the strict templating systems and use ontological elements to provide randomized questions. Through the use of linked open data, Zavala et al. were able to add relevance to questions from real data sources. This approach, as well as the one we describe in this paper, lends itself to a more scalable paradigm for question generation. Related to this, we note that others have focused on providing feedback or tutoring specialized topics [1, 3, 8, 11–13, 15].

In contrast, our work is primarily aimed at simplifying and automating the *generation* of program-tracing questions by exploring whether structural (tree-based) algorithms have the potential of generating useful questions.

3 THE GENCODE ALGORITHM AND SYSTEM

In the following sections, we describe the stochastic tree-based approach to the generation of multiple-choice program-tracing questions, and the methods used to obtain variability in structure and difficulty. GenCODE is itself written in Java and currently generates Java questions, although the approach is easily applied to other languages.

3.1 Generating Program Structure

We start by describing the first step in generating a question: the generation of the code on which the tracing question is based. At the current time, GenCODE is capable of generating programs on topics such as *assignments*, *for-loops*, *conditionals*, and *for-arrays*. These, in turn may be combined (sequentially or through nesting) to create problems of increased complexity. The instructor indicates the topics of interest, with a broad difficulty category (easy, medium, hard) for each topic, which GenCODE then uses to generate questions.

As mentioned earlier, the general principle used is to generate recursively a tree that resembles a parse-tree by starting with a root node (a code block), which then has randomly generated child nodes (statements), each of which can be recursively expanded at random. However, solely using a language grammar to randomly generate terminal strings (programs, in this case) can result in strange-looking and unrealistic code, or sometimes, code that does not execute, and thereafter creating the burden of vetting on the part of the instructor. To constrain this process and generate valid code useful for tracing questions, we use three strategies with the goal of creating program-tracing questions that are restricted by parameters selected by the instructor, guaranteed to execute, and useful in bringing out common student misconceptions.

The first strategy is to present the instructor with an interface to specify topic combinations. These options are interpreted from the topics indicated by the instructor to the form of *patterns*. A pattern is the desired outline of the target program, along with a limited nesting depth. Currently, GenCODE has implemented seven patterns encompassing the following basic intro-CS topics: *for-loops*, *conditionals*, and *for-arrays*. The patterns are:

- Nested Patterns: These combine building blocks (NestedLoop, NestedConditional, and NetstedLoopConditional)
- Non-Nested Patterns: These provide a non-nested block (SingleLoop, SingleConditional, and ComboLoopConditional)
- Manipulation patterns: These manipulate some part of the code to create *distractor* answers: (ArrayWalk and LoopSkipManip)

The hope is that, through a quick glance at the name, an instructor can intuit the type of code that will be generated. At this time, any of these may be freely combined, except for *conditionals* and *for-arrays* (which remains a work in progress).

Note that patterns differ from templates in the amount and type of information that is predefined. While templates usually fix structure and alter coefficients and constants, our patterns are simple outlines of topic combinations that can be recursively expanded. The actual tree depth of any generated code can vary because the elements of the tree are randomly generated.

The second strategy is to limit the depth because, if a generated program is too long and unwieldy, program tracing becomes too difficult for intro-CS students.

The third strategy is to build the tree not out of traditional grammar elements but out of larger units called *blocks* that better align with the goals of identifying opportunities for learning. For example, an *evaluation block* can be a boolean expression (that itself may contain arithmetic expression) built out of variables declared prior to the block. Such a block can be used in a conditional or in a for-loop. What makes this higher-level structure useful is that the handling of an alternative execution pathway from an evaluation block is similar regardless of where it is used. In this manner, we also define other blocks such as *statement blocks*, and *component blocks*. A statement-block is equivalent to a leaf node in the tree, consisting of simple variable declaration or assignment, while a *component block* can be instantiated, for example, as a for-loop (which itself has a component block and evaluation block). Lastly, because tracing questions most often involve program output, a component block may include a print statement.

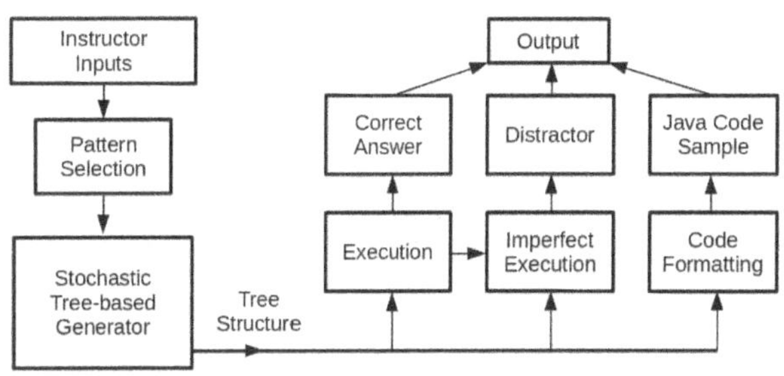

Figure 1: GenCODE structure

Figure 1 shows a high-level overview of the components in the system. The instructor specifies generation parameters (patterns and difficulty levels), and the tree-based algorithm generates a code snippet in the form of a tree. The tree is then explored for execution pathways, as explained below, to generate the correct answer and distractors that are clearly different yet plausible.

Two example code snippets are shown below. Both were generated by GenCODE when given the input topics "for-loops and for-arrays", and difficulty setting of 0.1 (easy), and 0.9 (hard), respectively.

```
public int easy_example(){
  int[] a = {18, 11, 37, 33, 27, 21};
  int b = 99;
  int c = 97;

  for (int c=0; c<a.length; c = c+1){
    a[c] = c;
    b = b*c;
  }
  return a[5];
}
```

```
public int hard_example(){
  int[] a = {46, 21, 62, 75, 96, 89, 84, 92, 51, 85};
  int b = 47;
  int c = 97;
  int[] d = {33, 46, 72, 2, 81, 84, 18, 89, 66};
  int e = 96;

  for (int f=0; f<d.length; f = f+1){
    for (int g=0; g<10; g = g+2){
      for (int h=5; h>=2; h = h-2){
        d[f] = g;
        e = e*h;
      }
    }
  }
  return d[5];
}
```

For the *easy* case, the correct choice is *5*, with distractors of: *8*, *6*, and *3*. For the *hard* case, the correct choice is *8*, with distractors of: *9*, *6*, and *11*. It is a simple matter to modify the difficulty settings inside GenCODE to narrow or widen the difference between extreme difficulty settings. For the pilot where the system was tested, the settings were adjusted to a more "narrow" spread so that even the "hard" problems are solvable by novice programmers.

3.2 Virtual Execution of Generated Code

Rather than generating code that is then compiled for actual execution, we simulate the execution within the tree itself. This is useful because the tree is a convenient structure that embodies all possible execution paths, some of which serve as candidates for producing distractors, and it is a convenient code data-structure for tracking variables and making adjustments.

The execution simulation tracks variables and the values in them, because ultimately, the values of some variables are printed (or returned) and are therefore ideal for generating "What does this method print (or return)?" questions. The simulation engine is independent of the generation, and can simulate any combination of topics and depth when given a tree.

Distractors, in a multiple-choice setting, are possible answers that vary in their similarity to the correct option. Good distractors are plausible answers that cause the student to pause and think carefully. Generally, the more plausible the distractors, the harder the question. During the simulation, the algorithm can change the path of execution at will, sometimes stopping for a partial answer (the current state of the variable to be printed), or following an alternative (but ultimately wrong) path of execution. For example, one distractor could offer an answer choice that results from having stopped a loop before its completion. Another might obtain a faulty final state by skipping an iteration step. The resulting final value of the incomplete or modified execution can be used as a distractor answer.

One important aspect of this procedure is that the choosing of each type of erroneous option (incomplete execution, skipped iterations, inverse logic, etc) points to specific conceptual errors that the student might be consistently falling prey to. This might give an insight into conceptual gaps that the student may have and help craft corrective actions (by designing specific sets of questions) that precisely target them.

3.3 Question Difficulty

One of the key principles of *deliberate practice*, the well-studied theory of how practice needs to be structured [7], is that practice exercises need to be in the learner's zone of proximal development: just slightly harder than what their current ability can tackle. For automated generation, this translates into the problem of generating questions with a target level of difficulty so that, as students gain in performance, the system presents with increasingly harder questions. This goal is challenging both because question hardness is subjective and we know little about the connection between program structure and the difficulty of resulting questions about tracing the program.

Our approach for this aspect of the system is to start with something heuristic, and to test the results with actual users assessing the level of difficulty. In this way, if there is reasonable correlation, the heuristic approach can be used to generate questions with a desired level of difficulty in order to support optimal practice. For the heuristic, we loosely use a combination of the program elements and its length as a measure, and successively build a piece of code that meets the target level of complexity, which we use as a proxy for the level of question difficulty. The instructor chooses a difficulty level between 0 (easiest) and 1 (hardest). Then, to generate a question with the requisite difficulty, the algorithm first randomly chooses a pattern and then uses the recursive generation approach to extend the complexity of the code to achieve the target difficulty level. The actual assessment of individual component difficulty is heuristic, and initially devised through some trial and error. In the next section, we describe the results of some user testing that supports our general approach although further refinement is needed for higher accuracy in difficulty-level generation.

3.4 Preliminary Trial and Lessons Learned

Our generated questions have focused on program tracing in a multiple-choice format. Both the correct answer and distractor answers are determined by virtually executing the generated code in the way explained in Section 3.2. As mentioned earlier, generated questions are delivered to students on an app downloaded to their smartphones. This app is part of the mobile platform developed by this research group for delivering practice questions for any course (a similar experiment with Biology questions is underway). The platform tracks the performance of every individual on every question, and recycles questions (after a gap in time) that a learner got wrong, while also providing an instructor with a dashboard of student activity.

Our pilot was performed at the end of the Fall 2017 and Spring 2018 semesters at our university. The course in both cases was the standard CS-1 course (in Java) offered to majors and non-majors alike. The questions were generated and given to student volunteers in the course ($N = 79$) about two weeks before the final exam, as practice for the final exam. Exercises focused on *for-loops*, *conditionals*, *for-loops* with *conditionals*, and *for-loops* with *for-arrays*. The initial question generation process resulted in a set of 200 questions. Some of the original questions (complex conditionals) were discarded due to their length, which did not fit the course objectives. In future iterations, maximum problem length may be added as an input parameter.

3.5 Types of generated questions

3.5.1 Conditionals . The evaluation of expressions, as used in conditionals, to their final Boolean values prepares students to learn more complex programming blocks such as *for-loops*. In these challenges, students must correctly follow the path of a variable through a series of manipulations. While nesting conditional statements is one way to increase the difficulty level, an excessive use of nesting results in spaghetti-looking code. Therefore, the generation also combines conditionals with loops.

3.5.2 For-Loops . Understanding simple and nested for-loops, especially those that manipulate variables across scope, encourages students to build upon their knowledge of execution order and conditionals. Eventually, the hope is that students come closer to viewing simple *for-loops* as an operation, instead of having to unroll each loop during execution.

3.5.3 For-Loops and Conditionals . Combining a *for-loop* with *conditionals* is a staple of programming, and therefore useful as a practice exercise. The conditionals can exist both outside and inside the loop, and can be nested. The resulting problems usually have distractors that students find challenging, especially if the iteration variable is used in generating the distractor.

3.5.4 For-Loops and For-Arrays . Since arrays are important and are often the first type of data structure seen by students, GenCODE generates questions that combine loops and arrays. These questions are particularly useful when the array itself is modified inside the loop, and when the loop iteration variable is featured in the array references.

4 RESULTS

In the following parts, we discuss the results of the approach used to set difficulty, and the responses from the students that participated.

4.1 Difficulty and Executable Blocks

We use the term *executable-block* to approximate what is sometimes called a *basic block* in compiler terminology: a piece of code that executes linearly without branching. Thus, a compiled program is a collection of basic blocks connected through jump instructions. Since we are using a tree representation for a generated program, we use the term executable-block because it also captures smaller elements such as declaration and expressions. For example, a *for-loop* has at least four executable blocks that make up its declaration, comparison, and stepping logic. Figure 2 shows the relation between the target difficulty (entered by the instructor) difficulty and the total number of executable blocks, organized by topic (In the Figure, *ARRAY* represents the *for-array* topic).

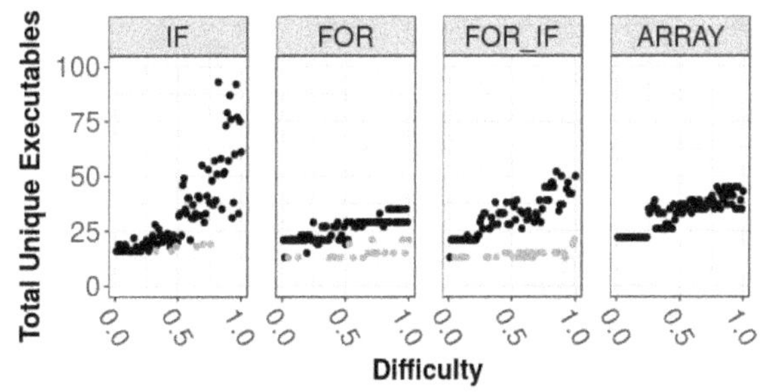

Figure 2: Difficulty Input Vs Number of Executables for each topic. Light points can be identified and discarded for being too easy.

As one would expect, the size and complexity of the programs increase as the input difficulty parameter increases. This, in addition to the patterns, allows the system to generate sets of problems that vary in difficulty and topic and that can be easily adjusted to fit a desired challenge level. Given the probabilistic nature of the question generation, some questions do not include programming blocks that provide added complexity and therefore remain "easy". These can be seen as the sets of points with few executable blocks, despite the increasing target difficulty. These cases are easily identifiable and future versions of GenCODE will adjust for this issue by eliminating them.

4.2 Number of Useful questions

Even without discarding the trivial cases shown as lighter points in Figure 2, the ratio of useful questions was high. The ratios for each question type are shown in Table 1. This means that for the *conditionals* and for the *for-loops*, the instructor will have to discard half of the generated questions, while for the *for-loops* with *conditionals*, and for *for-arrays*, the instructor must discard about one in twenty.

Table 1: Ratio of Useful questions

IF	53.6%
FOR	54.1%
FOR_IF	96.6%
FOR_ARRAY	93.3%

4.3 Generated vs. Perceived Difficulty

In order to determine the degree to which input (or generated) difficulty adhered to perceived difficulty, we conducted a small survey where 12 experienced programmers where asked to label 36 questions as being "easy", "medium", or "hard". We compared the actual difficulty and the assigned label. Two instances were left unlabeled for a total of 430 labeled difficulties. As can be seen in Table 2 and Figure 3, the distribution of difficulty labels is reasonably aligned with the desired difficulties in the sense that the peak of each of the label categories lies on the actual difficulty.

Table 2: Difficulty Assignment Table

		Labeled		
		Easy	Medium	Hard
Created	Easy	112	16	2
	Medium	66	75	15
	Hard	31	70	43

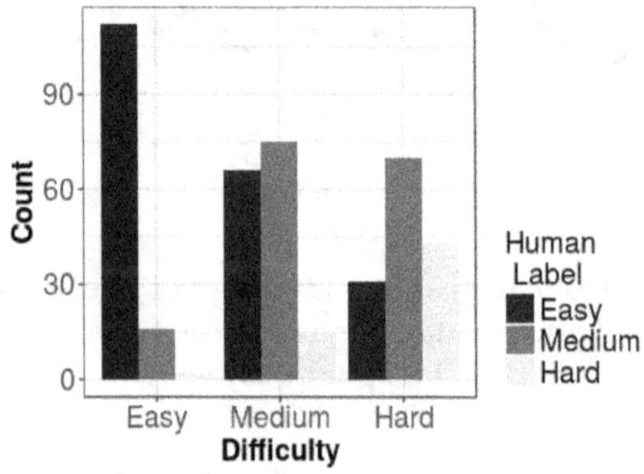

Figure 3: Difficulty VS Human Labeling

4.4 Student Response

A survey of student experience was collected at the end of the semester. Figure 4 shows the distribution of responses when students where asked "To what extent did the practice exercises help you prepare for the exam?" (in Figure 4a); and when they were asked "To what extent did the practice exercises help uncover some gap in your understanding (that perhaps led you to review some concept)?" (in Figure 4b).

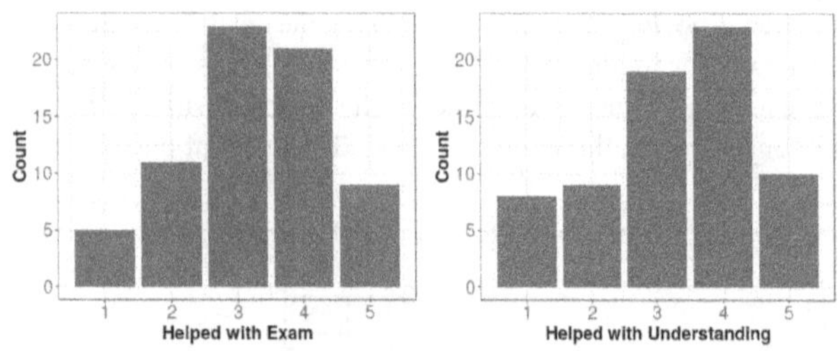

(a) (b)

Figure 4: Perceived effect of using the system on the final exam 4a and for conceptual understanding 4b.

As can be seen in Figure 4, while there was a generally positive effect of the use of GenCODE to help prepare students for the final exam, the main effect was on helping students identify erroneous concepts. This suggests the possibility of implementing such as system from the start of a semester, rather as a simple practice and review tool. These conclusions are supported by the responses from students where 75% preferred to have the tool introduced early in the course; 3% preferred somewhere in the middle; and 22% prefer it as a practice tool for the final exam.

5 DISCUSSION

The stochastic tree-based generation algorithm is a compromise between using a database of templates and pure generation from the target language's grammar. The latter produces too many unrealistic and unwieldy code snippets, while the former incurs instructor overhead. The stochasticity in generation enables scaling and repeated practice of the same level of difficulty.

The higher-level tree-based approach allows topic combinations as well as a reasonable way to achieve target difficulty levels, a necessary condition for reliably generating questions in a gradation of difficulty. In terms of difficulty variation, GenCODE uses the pattern tiers and probabilistic nesting and concatenation of programming blocks. This procedural generation system resulted in a reasonably close correlation between the generated and human-labeled difficulties. Combining the analysis of the results obtained with the adjustable method of increasing difficulty can allow the instructor to develop questions in the student's zone of proximal development.

Another benefit of the stochastic tree approach is the fact that it can be easily extended to other languages. The blocks represent programming concepts that are combined to produce the tree, which is used, in turn, to obtain the correct answer and the appropriate distractors. The only element that needs to be adjusted is the module that generates the sample code to produce the actual question, and small changes to the execution engine.

Our analysis of the trial showed that students get questions wrong on all difficulty tiers with similar frequencies, which points to the effectiveness of the distractor generation.

An additional aspect of interest is the possibility of using the tree of a programming question to infer difficulty. While the initial results linking the number of executable blocks and input difficulty point towards a correlation between the two, there still remains the question of whether or not the reverse is true: if the parsing of an existing problem into its constituent unique executable blocks lend itself to an extraction of difficulty.

While the original intention was to use the system as a practice tool for the final exam, a significant amount of students found it extremely useful in helping them detect, and then correct, conceptual errors. Most of the user comments focused on the utility of "walking through" problems, especially for the topic of *loops* and *nested loops*. Other sample comments:

- "The whole structure of the problems was useful to be able to mentally walk through a program instead of just clicking 'run' "
- "Help finding the output of a complex method"
- "I discovered how much improvement I needed in interpreting other's code"
- "When helping me to find where I need to put the most studying in"
- "It helped me practice reading code instead of just writing it"

In the course of the study, we discovered that the produced output still needs some work to be indistinguishable from handcrafted problems. Details in the produced questions seem to suggest to the user that a question has been artificially generated. One example given was: "A few questions had expressions like "if a >

a", which seemed like something a human would be unlikely to include". While the tool was found to be beneficial for practice and for concept clarification, by presenting more realistic instances of programming questions, the usefulness of the tool would increase.

Note that this project has not conducted a learning effectiveness study, for which we rely on the works of [6, 23]. Nonetheless, further study is warranted to compare the effectiveness of particular types of questions.

6 CONCLUSIONS AND FUTURE WORK

This paper explored the potential of automated generation of multiple-choice program-tracing questions using a stochastic tree-based approach. The approach offers the advantage of high scalability, correlation with desired difficulty levels, and easy portability to other languages. A preliminary trial resulted in supporting these goals, along with positive feedback from students.

In the future, we intend to quantitatively evaluate the learning effectiveness of the tool when used as support for conceptual clarification when introduced at the beginning of a course and not just as an exam practice resource. In addition, we plan on refining the procedural question generation to detect and discard those questions that present syntax that is clearly artificial.

ACKNOWLEDGEMENTS

The authors would like to acknowledge the efforts of Michael Goddard, a GW undergraduate who developed an exploratory prototype for his senior project, and Jennifer Hill, who developed much of the server/app combination that was used to distribute the generated questions. Part of this effort was supported through NSF award 1347516.

REFERENCES

[1] Stina Bridgeman, Michael T. Goodrich, Stephen G. Kobourov, and Roberto Tamassia. 2000. PILOT: an interactive tool for learning and grading. ACM Press, 139–143. https://doi.org/10.1145/330908.331843

[2] Peter C Brown, Henry L Roediger III, and Mark A McDaniel. 2014. *Make it stick.* Harvard University Press.

[3] Peter Brusilovsky and Sergey Sosnovsky. 2005. Individualized exercises for self-assessment of programming knowledge: An evaluation of QuizPACK. *Journal on Educational Resources in Computing* 5, 3 (Sept. 2005), 6–es. https://doi.org/10.1145/1163405.1163411

[4] G. Dancik and A. Kumar. 2003. A tutor for counter-controlled loop concepts and its evaluation, Vol. 1. IEEE, T3C_7–T3C_12. https://doi.org/10.1109/FIE.2003.1263331

[5] Debzani Deb, Mohammad Muztaba Fuad, and Mallek Kanan. 2017. Creating engaging exercises with mobile response system (MRS). In *Proceedings of the 2017 ACM SIGCSE Technical Symposium on Computer Science Education.* ACM, 147–152.

[6] Barbara J Ericson, Lauren E Margulieux, and Jochen Rick. 2017. Solving parsons problems versus fixing and writing code. In *Proceedings of the 17th Koli Calling Conference on Computing Education Research.* ACM, 20–29.

[7] K Anders Ericsson, Robert R Hoffman, Aaron Kozbelt, and A Mark Williams. 2018. *The Cambridge handbook of expertise and expert performance.* Cambridge University Press.

[8] Eric Fernandes and Amruth N. Kumar. 2004. A tutor on scope for the programming languages course. *ACM SIGCSE Bulletin* 36, 1 (March 2004), 90. https://doi.org/10.1145/1028174.971332

[9] Michail N Giannakos. 2013. Enjoy and learn with educational games: Examining factors affecting learning performance. *Computers & Education* 68 (2013), 429–439.

[10] I-Han Hsiao, Peter Brusilovsky, and Sergey Sosnovsky. 2008. Web-based parameterized questions for object-oriented programming. Association for the Advancement of Computing in Education (AACE), 3728–3735.

[11] I.-H. Hsiao, S. Sosnovsky, and P. Brusilovsky. 2010. Guiding students to the right questions: adaptive navigation support in an E-Learning system for Java programming: Adaptive navigation support in E-Learning. *Journal of Computer Assisted Learning* 26, 4 (July 2010), 270–283. https://doi.org/10.1111/j.1365-2729.2010.00365.x

[12] Petri Ihantola, Juha Helminen, and Ville Karavirta. 2013. How to study programming on mobile touch devices: interactive Python code exercises. ACM Press, 51–58. https://doi.org/10.1145/2526968.2526974

[13] Ville Karavirta, Juha Helminen, and Petri Ihantola. 2012. A mobile learning application for parsons problems with automatic feedback. ACM Press, 11–18. https://doi.org/10.1145/2401796.2401798

[14] Amruth N. Kumar. 2005. Generation of problems, answers, grade, and feedback—case study of a fully automated tutor. *Journal on Educational Resources in Computing* 5, 3 (Sept. 2005), 3–es. https://doi.org/10.1145/1163405.1163408

[15] Amruth N. Kumar. 2005. Results from the evaluation of the effectiveness of an online tutor on expression evaluation. *ACM SIGCSE Bulletin* 37, 1 (Feb. 2005), 216. https://doi.org/10.1145/1047124.1047422

[16] Amruth N Kumar. 2015. Solving code-tracing problems and its effect on code-writing skills pertaining to program semantics. In *Proceedings of the 2015 ACM Conference on Innovation and Technology in Computer Science Education.* ACM, 314–319.

[17] Amruth N. Kumar. 2018. Epplets: A Tool for Solving Parsons Puzzles. ACM Press, 527–532. https://doi.org/10.1145/3159450.3159576

[18] Raymond Lister, Colin Fidge, and Donna Teague. 2009. Further evidence of a relationship between explaining, tracing and writing skills in introductory programming. ACM Press, 161. https://doi.org/10.1145/1562877.1562930

[19] Mike Lopez, Jacqueline Whalley, Phil Robbins, and Raymond Lister. 2008. Relationships between reading, tracing and writing skills in introductory programming. ACM Press, 101–112. https://doi.org/10.1145/1404520.1404531

[20] Solomon Sunday Oyelere, Jarkko Suhonen, and Teemu H. Laine. 2017. Integrating parson's programming puzzles into a game-based mobile learning application. ACM Press, 158–162. https://doi.org/10.1145/3141880.3141882

[21] Dale Parsons and Patricia Haden. [n. d.]. Parson's Programming Puzzles: A Fun and Effective Learning Tool for First Programming Courses, Vol. Vol. 52. Australian Computer Society, Inc., Australia, 157–163.

[22] Ferran Prados, Imma Boada, Josep Soler, and Jordi Poch. 2005. Automatic generation and correction of technical exercises. In *International conference on engineering and computer education: Icece*, Vol. 5.

[23] Laura Zavala and Benito Mendoza. 2018. On the Use of Semantic-Based AIG to Automatically Generate Programming Exercises. In *Proceedings of the 49th ACM Technical Symposium on Computer Science Education.* ACM, 14–19.

Exploring the Impact of Worked Examples in a Novice Programming Environment

Rui Zhi, Thomas W. Price, Samiha Marwan, Alexandra Milliken, Tiffany Barnes, Min Chi
North Carolina State University
Raleigh, NC
rzhi,twprice,samarwan,aamillik,tmbarnes,mchi@ncsu.edu

ABSTRACT

Research in a variety of domains has shown that viewing worked examples (WEs) can be a more efficient way to learn than solving equivalent problems. We designed a Peer Code Helper system to display WEs, along with scaffolded self-explanation prompts, in a block-based, novice programming environment called Snap*!*. We evaluated our system during a high school summer camp with 22 students. Participants completed three programming problems with access to WEs on either the first or second problem. We found that WEs did not significantly impact students' learning, but may have impacted students' intrinsic cognitive load, suggesting that our WEs with scaffolded prompts may be an inherently different learning task. Our results show that WEs saved students time on initial tasks compared to writing code, but some of the time saved was lost in subsequent programming tasks. Overall, students with WEs completed more tasks within a fixed time period, but not significantly more. WEs may improve students' learning efficiency when programming, but these effects are nuanced and merit further study.

ACM Reference Format:

Rui Zhi, Thomas W. Price, Samiha Marwan, Alexandra Milliken, Tiffany Barnes, Min Chi. 2019. Exploring the Impact of Worked Examples in a Novice Programming Environment. In *Proceedings of the 50th ACM Technical Symposium on Computer Science Education (SIGCSE '19), February 27-March 2, 2019, Minneapolis, MN, USA.* ACM, New York, NY, USA, 7 pages. https://doi.org/10.1145/3287324.3287385

1 INTRODUCTION AND BACKGROUND

In computing classrooms, students are often expected to learn by solving programming problems independently. An alternative approach is to show students worked examples (WEs), that guide the student through solving the problem, step by step. WEs have been studied in a variety of domains [9, 10, 20], and the results consistently show that replacing some or all practice problems with WEs results in higher learning efficiency, where students take less time to learn the same amount of content. One way WEs may increase learning efficiency is by reducing students' cognitive load, or mental effort when learning [18]. Though a number of studies have explored the impact of WEs in the domain of programming [2, 3, 12, 14, 22–24], few of these studies have specifically compared WEs to traditional problem solving [22], especially in novice programming environments [23].

In this work, we present the "Peer Code Helper" (PCH), which integrates WEs into the Snap*!* programming environment [4]. We evaluated the PCH and the impact of programming WEs during a high school summer camp with 22 students. We found that access to WEs did not significantly impact students' learning, though they may have impacted students' intrinsic cognitive load. Students with WEs on a problem completed more objectives on that problem, but this difference was not significant. Our results suggest that WEs allowed students to work more efficiently on the first few problem objectives, but they took longer to complete subsequent objectives that were not supported with WEs. The difference in the time taken on each subsequent objective between students with and without WEs closed over time, and difference in problem solving speed was still much less than the time saved by the WEs on the first few objectives. Our findings show that WEs may help students solve more objectives in the same amount of time, but further study is needed to confirm this result.

1.1 Cognitive Load Theory

Our work is based on Cognitive Load Theory (CLT), which describes the relationship between mental effort and learning [21]. CLT believes that all learning activities impose a *cognitive load* on working memory, and this cognitive load comes in three categories: intrinsic, extraneous, and germane. Intrinsic load comes from the inherent difficulty or effort required to accomplish the learning task. Extraneous load comes from the way information or tasks are presented. Germane load refers to the work or effort needed to create new, permanent knowledge. CLT posits that humans have limited working memory, and it suggests that students' learning can be impaired if instructional materials require students to hold excessive amounts of information in working memory. Since the intrinsic load and extraneous load are additive [19], extraneous load should be minimized to maximize germane load and thus learning. Motivated by CLT, we integrated WEs into Snap*!* with the goal of reducing students' extraneous cognitive load while working on open-ended programming problems.

1.2 Worked Examples

A worked example (WE) teaches students how to solve a problem by directly presenting a solution for the problem. It is an effective instructional strategy to help novices learn complex tasks and has been studied for decades [18]. Prior studies have explored the

SIGCSE '19, February 27-March 2, 2019, Minneapolis, MN, USA

ACM ISBN 978-1-4503-5890-3/19/02...$15.00
https://doi.org/10.1145/3287324.3287385

effect of WEs in different disciplines, including algebra [20], propositional logic proofs [9], and stoichiometry [10]. Empirical studies have shown that WEs are more beneficial to novice learners compared with traditional problem solving in learning algebra [20]. Sweller and Cooper found that students who were presented with WE problems solved similar problems quicker and with fewer errors than students who solved the same problems themselves [20]. McLaren et al. compared four different instructional designs in a stoichiometry tutor. They found that students in the WE condition performed similarly in the post-test but were more efficient in finishing intervention problems and with less cognitive load, compared to students in other conditions including problem solving, erroneous worked examples, and tutored problem solving [10]. In an intelligent tutoring system for teaching and practicing propositional logic problems in discrete math, Liu et al.'s [9] work shows that WEs are beneficial to undergraduate students in the first few problems they solve but less beneficial for later problems in the students' homework set.

Worked examples have also been studied in the domain of programming. Some studies suggest using WEs in programming for teaching novices. Pirolli and Anderson investigated how three novices learned recursive functions and found that they relied heavily on examples while writing new programs [14]. Informed by the results from cognitive science and educational psychology, Caspersen and Bennedsen proposed a model which treats WEs as one of the fundamental principles of programming education [2]. Vihavainen et al. extended Caspersen and Bennedsen's work and proposed a model, which also suggests using WEs in study materials and lectures [24].

Others have investigated the impact of WEs experimentally. Trafton and Reiser's study suggests interleaving WEs with similar practice problems to maximize students learning gains, compared to blocking WEs with problems, or solving equivalent problems by writing LISP programs [22]. Recently, Ericson et al. found that interleaving WEs with Parsons problems can improve programming learning efficiency compared to WEs paired with writing code or fixing code [3]. Patitsas et al. investigated the effect of comparing and contrasting multiple solutions, by presenting the different solutions (WEs) side by side. They found that students in the comparing and contrasting condition showed greater learning gains for procedural knowledge and flexibility than students in the WE condition [13]. However, to our knowledge, only Trafton and Reiser directly evaluate the effectiveness of WEs by comparing them to equivalent problem solving tasks, but their results may not apply to novice programming environment.

In novice programming environment, Ichinco et al. showed that novices struggle to use WEs to solve block-based programming problems [6]. For example, they found that novices have difficulty in understanding the examples and finding relevant blocks to finish the programming task. To limit the impact of this difficult transfer task, we hand-selected WEs and presented them in small steps with scaffolded self-explanation prompts in PCH. Merriënboer and Croock found that *incomplete* WEs, in which students are given part of a WE and asked to complete the rest, improved novice's programming performance and post-test scores, compared with those who only had the WEs as a reference[23]. Inspired by this, our PCH provides students the WEs as starter code for their own solutions once students have completed their self-explanation prompts. Motivated by results from these studies, we combined the incomplete WEs with WE steps and investigated the impact of *incomplete* WEs on novice programming. Our prior work with WEs in a novice programming game showed that when students are given only WEs, they may skip through them quickly without learning [26].

1.3 Self Explanation

Self-explanation is an instructional strategy which requires the learner to reflect and generate explanations about the learning material. It has been shown that combining self-explanation with WEs can be especially beneficial to students' learning [1]. A review of self-explanation shows that along with WEs, self-explanation prompts help students foster greater understanding [16] and improves students' problem solving performance [12]. Morrison et al. showed that students who self-explained subgoal labels perform better than those who were not given subgoal labels [12]. Self-explanation has different forms, including open-ended, menu-based, focused, scaffolded, and resource-based self-explanations [16]. Berthold found that scaffolded self-explanation prompts following WEs were more beneficial to students in terms of conceptual and procedural understanding than open-ended self-explanation prompts in multimedia environments [1]. Therefore, our PCH system provides scaffolded self-explanation prompts, that guide students to reflect on WE code.

2 METHOD

To investigate the impact of incomplete worked examples (WEs) on novice programmers' learning outcomes, we designed a "Peer Code Helper" (PCH) feature in Snap*!* to demonstrate the first few steps of a programming problem as structured WEs. We evaluated the impact of these PCH WEs as compared with traditional problem solving during a high school coding camp for girls in summer 2018. Specifically, we investigated the following research questions. How does having access to WEs during a programming problem impact: **RQ1**: Students' learning during the problem? **RQ2**: Students' perceived difficulty and cognitive load with respect to the problem? **RQ3**: Students' programming efficiency?

2.1 The Peer Code Helper

We designed and developed the Peer Code Helper (PCH) [1] interface to present interactive WEs in a block-based programming environment called Snap*!*, which is used extensively in the Beauty and Joy of Computing (BJC) AP Computer Science Principles curriculum [4]. Our design is based on the implementation of WEs [23] and self-explanation prompts in other domains [1] as described in the related work. PCH shows students the first few steps for solving the given problem. A step was designed to be a meaningful chunk of code to finish an objective of a problem (e.g. draw a square/circle), though the exact example code may not end up in the final solution. For each step, we first show some starting code ("before code"), without the step completed, and ask the student to run it and answer questions related to the function of the code via scaffolded self explanations, as shown in Figure 1. Then we show what the code looks like after the step has been completed ("after code") and

[1]Contact the first author to request a copy of the system.

ask them to run the new code and consider why each new piece of code was added. Students can compare the "before" and "after" code and reflect on the changes between the two examples. When showing the next example step, the previous "after" code becomes the new "before" code.

We use the Stencil technique [8] to direct students' attention to the example code by enclosing it within a transparent stencil and hiding other components. The example code is runnable but not editable. When asking questions about the code, we used a *scaffolded* self-explanation prompt to help the student reflect on the code because prior work suggests that scaffolded prompts are more effective than open-ended prompts [1]. Students must fill in the blanks to explain what the "before code" does and then how the new parts improve the "after code". Students can run the example code and view its visual output. Then students can reflect on the example code and its output, complete the self-explanation prompt, and click the "Submit" button to go to the next step. After finishing all the WE steps, each piece of example code, commented with its explanation, is provided to the student within the Snap*!* scripting window. Students can then edit the code to build their solution.

2.2 Participants & Procedure

We studied the effects of WEs in Snap*!* on the first 2 days of a 5-day computing summer camp with 22 female high school students, grades 8-9 (ages 13-15). Five students were excluded from the study, leaving 17 students with 6 who identified as African-American, 4 as White, 1 Hispanic, and 6 as multiple ethnicities. About half (9/17) self-identified as having some programming experience and the rest (8/17) as having none or very little.

We adapted 3 drawing-themed programming problems with increasing difficulty from the BJC curriculum [4]. The first problem, Daisy Design, is to write a program to draw a pattern of circles. Its common solution has ~7 lines of code using procedures and loops. The second problem, Spiral Polygon, is to draw a polygon in a spiral shape. Its common solution is 7 ~10 lines of code and uses procedures, loops, and variables. The third problem, Brick Wall, uses ~25 lines of code with procedures, loops, variables, and conditionals. Each problem has a set of goal objectives and several stretch objectives in case some students finished early.

The study used a matched pairs, switching replication design as shown in Table 1 to investigate the impact of WEs on problem 1, and whether or not it matters which problem receives WE support. In Step 0, the instructor led an introduction to programming in Snap*!*, including loops, variables, conditionals, and procedures. In Step 1, students took the pre-test and the pre-survey, and were randomly assigned to groups (E1 receiving WEs on problem 1, E2 with WEs on problem 2), with matched pairs according to pre-test scores. The pre-test, and isomorphic post-test1 and post-test2, were adapted from the block-based version of the Commutative Assessments [25], with 16 multiple-choice questions on variables, loops, procedures, and conditionals. Each topic has four types of questions: code tracing, code comprehension, code completion, and WEs (designed to exactly match PCH WEs). Next, the instructor demonstrated PCH (Step 2) and all the students started problem 1 (Step 3). Camp instructors followed a tutoring protocol to ensure that each student received the same quality and quantity of help, using an audio recorder to capture the dialogue of these help episodes, and record who they helped, the help duration (time), and the type of help (e.g. high-level planning, programming, debugging, interface related). Then students completed the post-test1 and the cognitive load instrument to measure their perceived cognitive load (Step 4). We used the CS Cognitive Load Component Survey (CS CLCS) [11] as our cognitive load instrument. On day 2, students repeated the process for problem 2 (Step 5 ~7). Additionally, they completed problem 3 as a performance post-test, without WEs (Step 8) and filled in post-surveys (Step 9).

During the study, we collected data including participants' interaction with the system (e.g. clicking a button, altering or running their program) and regular snapshots of the students' code with timestamps when they are modified. During the study, students were also able to ask for help from instructors and volunteers, and we also recorded the frequency and duration of the help requests that students made. After the study, we graded students' code to measure the code quality and students' programming performance.

Table 1: Study Outline

Step	Group E1	Group E2	Time
0	Snap*!* Introduction (taught by camp instructor)		90 minutes
1	Experience pre-survey + Knowledge pre-test		35 minutes
2	Introduce the Peer Code Helper		10 minutes
3	E1: Problem 1 (WEs)	E2: Problem 1 (no WEs)	45 minutes
4	Post-test1 + Cognitive load survey		25 minutes
Second Day			
5	Re-introduce the Peer Code Helper		5 minutes
6	E1: Problem 2 (no WEs)	E2: Problem 2 (WEs)	45 minutes
7	Post-test2 + Cognitive load survey		25 minutes
8	Problem 3 (Brick Wall, no WEs)		45 minutes
9	Demographics (post-survey) + Cognitive load survey		15 minutes

3 RESULTS

Our original data included 22 students, 10 in group E1 (receiving WEs on problem 1), and 12 in group E2 (receiving WEs on problem 2). However, five students were excluded from survey and assessment analysis because they were not present for the whole study (2) or encountered errors in Snap*!* that caused them to lose significant programming progress (3) . After excluding these students, there are 9 students in Group E1 and 8 students in Group E2.

3.1 RQ1: Assessments Analysis

For our analysis of pre- and post-tests, we exclude one additional student from Group E1 who did not fill in post-test1, leaving 8 students in each group. Test results for students' pre-test, post-test1 and post-test2 are shown in Table 2. We compared the pre-test scores between groups and found no significant difference ($t(13.96) = -0.4$, $p = .64$, $d = .24$). We then ran a 2x3 mixed ANOVA on students' test scores, with group (E1 v. E2) as a between-subjects factor and test time (pre-test, post-test1, and post-test2) as within-subjects factor. There was a main effect of test time ($F_{2,28} = 5.26$, $p < .05$, partial $\eta^2 = .27$), indicating students' test scores changed significantly from pre-test to the two post-tests as shown in table 2.

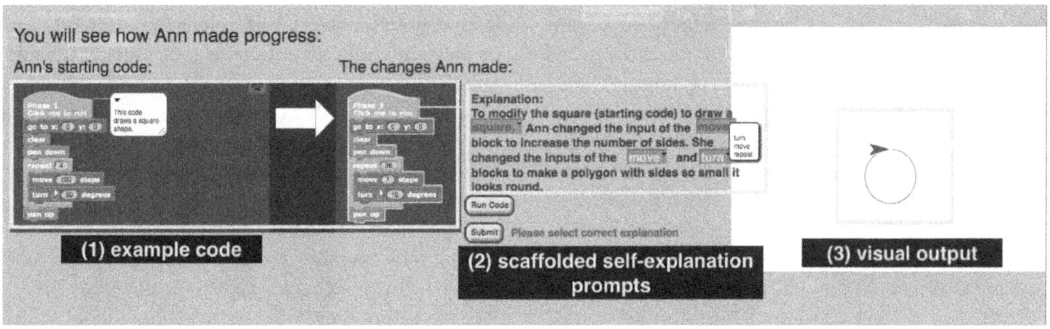

Figure 1: Peer Code Helper Interface. Students can run the example code (1), reflect on the output (3), and explain the code (2). Examples are shown side by side. Fill-in-blanks answer choices are marked correct in green or incorrect in red.

We found statistically significant improvements for all students from both pre-test to post-test2 ($t(15) = 3.05, p < .01, d = .30$) and post-test1 to post-test2 ($t(15) = 2.49, p < .05, d = .24$), but not from pre-test to post-test1 ($t(15) = -0.86, p = .40, d = .08$). This suggests that most of students' learning occurred during the second problem.

Table 2: Mean (SD) pre-test, post-test1, and post-test2 scores

	Pre-test	Post-test1	Post-test2
Group E1 (N=8)	8.13 (4.22)	8.38 (3.62)	9.13 (3.83)
Group E2 (N=8)	7.13 (4.02)	7.50 (3.21)	8.50 (4.21)

There was no main effect of group, indicating that there was not a statistically significant difference in mean test score between the two groups ($F_{1,14} = 0.20, p = .66$, partial $\eta^2 = .014$). Additionally, there was no statistically significant interaction between group and test time ($F_{2,28} = 0.13, p = .88$, partial $\eta^2 = .009$), indicating that students in both groups had similar learning across the study.

We also analyzed the test score for each type of problem (code tracing, code comprehension, code completion, and WE) but found no statistically significant difference on any of the measurements above. To understand the impact of WEs on help requests, we ran an 2x3 mixed ANOVA on the number of help requests, with group as a between-subjects factor and problem as a within-subject factor. We found no significant main or interaction effects ($F_{2,28} = 2.15$, $p = .14$, partial $\eta^2 = .13$), indicating that WEs likely did not impact the number of help requests students made, and nor did the problem, despite increasing levels of problem difficulty.

3.2 RQ2: Cognitive Load Analysis

We used the CS CLCS [11] to measure students' cognitive load. We excluded data from one additional student from Group E1 for this analysis because that student did not answer the survey after finishing problem 3, leaving 8 students in each group. The average factor scores of cognitive load in each category are shown in Table 3.

We ran a 2x3 mixed ANOVA on each type of the cognitive load (CL) scores, with group as a between-subject factor and problem as within-subjects factor. We did not find any significant result for extraneous load or germane load. For the intrinsic load, there was not a significant main effect of group ($F_{1,14} = 0.10, p = .76$, partial

Table 3: Mean (SD) factor score of cognitive load (IL - Intrinsic Load, EL - Extraneous Load, GL - Germane Load)

	Problem 1			Problem 2			Problem 3		
	IL	EL	GL	IL	EL	GL	IL	EL	GL
Group E1	4.3	3.5	6.6	**6.4**	3.3	6.7	5.3	3.4	7.9
N = 8	(2.4)	(3.7)	(3.2)	**(2.4)**	(2.8)	(2.4)	(3.3)	(2.5)	(2.6)
Group E2	4.9	3.4	8.6	**3.8**	2.7	8.0	6.3	4.9	7.6
N = 8	(2.6)	(2.6)	(1.6)	**(1.9)**	(1.7)	(2.1)	(2.8)	(3.5)	(2.3)

$\eta^2 = .007$) or problem ($F_{2,28} = 1.78, p = .19$, partial $\eta^2 = .11$) factors, but there was a statistically significant interaction *between* group and problem on the intrinsic load scores ($F_{2,28} = 4.65, p < .05$, partial $\eta^2 = .25$). This indicates that the two groups experienced different levels of intrinsic CL on different problems, which may be due to the WEs. We investigated this further with post hoc t-tests and found that E1 students' intrinsic load on problem 1 was significantly lower than on problem 2 ($t(7) = -3.51, p < .01, d = 0.83$), but no such results were found for E2. Similarly, we found E2 students' intrinsic load on problem 2 was significantly lower than that on problem 3 ($t(7) = -4.52, p < .01, d = 1.04$), but no such results were found for E1. This suggests that both groups experienced lower intrinsic CL on problems *with WEs* than on the following, more difficult problem *without WEs*. Comparing the two groups, we find that the difference in intrinsic load between E1 and E2 is not statistically significant for problem 1 ($t(13.91) = 0.40, p = .69$, $d = 0.20$). However, it is significant for problem 2, with a large effect size ($t(13.19) = -2.33, p < .05, d = -1.16$). One interpretation of these results is that students experienced reduced intrinsic CL when using WEs. This would be consistent with results from work by Gerjets et al., who evaluated "modular worked examples," which, like our WEs, emphasized breaking a problem down into steps [5]. However, another interpretation is that students experienced *higher* intrinsic CL on problem solving that *followed* a WE, which made it seem harder by contrast.

3.3 RQ3: Programming Efficiency

Previous research in other domains has shown that replacing problem solving exercises with worked examples (WEs) can increase learning efficiency by decreasing the *time* that students take to complete the exercises without affecting how much they learn. Similarly, RQ3 investigates the impact of WEs on the time taken to complete programming practice problems, or programming efficiency. However, because most students did not complete the *whole* problem within the allotted 45 minutes, we analyze completion time for smaller objectives within each problem.

To investigate students' programming efficiency, two researchers graded all students' submitted code by marking each problem's objectives as either complete or incomplete. For complete objectives, the researchers also marked the time when the student first completed the objective. The three problems (Daisy Design, Spiral Polygon and Brick Wall) had 9, 5 and 5 objectives, respectively. The two researchers reached an inter-rater reliability between 0.744 and 0.979 for first 15 student submissions (5 in each problem). Then the researchers discussed and resolved all the conflicts and graded the rest of student code separately. On the first problem, 2 out of 9 objectives were covered in the WEs (22%) and on the second problem, 1 out of 5 was (20%); we refer to these as "WE objectives." On each problem we removed some students from our analysis who lost their work due to errors in Snap*!*, leaving 9, 10, and 10 students in E1 and 10, 9, and 10 students in E2 on the three problems, respectively.

Figure 2 shows the average number of objectives completed for each group, over time. On both Daisy Design and Spiral Polygon, the group with WEs (E1 and E2, respectively), had more objectives completed at all times throughout the 45 minute work period, while on Brick Wall (with no WEs) there is little difference. These differences between groups is most apparent at the beginning of the curves, when students are completing the WE objectives, though the same trends holds, even if we do not include the WE objectives. On Daisy Design, it took the WE group (E1) a median 3.5 minutes to complete the WE portion of the problem. It took the non-WE group (E2) a median 22.5 minutes to accomplish the same WE objectives by writing code, with 20% of students never finishing the WE objectives in the 45 minutes given. A Mann-Whitney U Test shows that, even ignoring students who did not finish the objectives, this difference in time is significant ($W = 2$; $p = 0.001$). Similarly, on Spiral Polygon, the WE group (E2) took a median 2.5 minutes on the WE portion of the problem, and the non-WE group (E1) took 30.4 minutes, with 40% of students failing to achieve the objectives on 45 minutes. This difference in time is also significant ($W = 54$; $p < 0.001$). It is not surprising that the WE group, who only had to read code and answer questions, finished this content much faster (6-12 times faster), but the magnitude of the difference is worth noting. Based on these results, we can say the WEs saved students lots of time (19-24 minutes on a 45 minute problem), and allowed all students to finish the WE objectives (compared to only 80% and 60% for non-WE students).

However, looking past the WE objectives in Figure 2, we see that the differences between the two groups closes over time. On Daisy Design, the WE group (E1) end with a median 6 objectives complete (67%), compared to 5 objectives (56%) for the non-WE group (E2), and the difference is not significant ($W = 56.0$; $p = 0.382$). On Spiral Polygon, the WE group (E2) ends with a median 2 objectives complete (40%), compared to 1 objective (20%) for the non-WE group (E1), and the difference is not significant ($W = 31.5$; $p = 0.270$). This suggests that WEs may have impacted students' overall performance, but the difference was not significant. One possible explanation for the lack of a significant difference in programming is that while WEs save students time initially, it takes those students additional time to process the WE code they are given, and they work less efficiently at writing code after receiving a WE.

We investigated how the programming efficiency of students who just received WE code compares to those who just wrote equivalent code on their own. Starting from the time each student completed the WE objectives, we calculated how much additional time it took them to complete the next 1, 2 and 3 objectives. Some students finished the WE objectives slowly, or not at all, and ran out of time before they could complete additional objectives. However, for most objectives, enough students finished that we can still calculate the median time for each group (the time at which 50% of students finished and objective) or the first-quartile (Q1) time (when 25% of students finished). To do this, we make the simplifying assumption that the students who completed the WE objectives the slowest would have completed additional objectives *no quicker than* the other students in their group.

Table 4: The first-quartile (Q1) and median (Med) time (in minutes) taken by the WE and non-WE groups to complete 1, 2 and 3 additional objectives after the WE objectives, as well as the proportion that Comp. each objective

		WE Group			Non-WE Group		
	Addt'l Objs	Q1 time	Med time	Comp.	Q1 time	Med time	Comp.
Daisy	WE+1	7.5	9.5	100%	0.0	0.0	80%
	WE+2	14.2	24.8	78%	4.7	11.0	60%
	WE+3	23.3		44%	13.4		30%
Polygon	WE+1	12.0		44%	2.6		50%
	WE+2	13.0		44%	10.4		50%
	WE+3	29.4		44%	>39.6		20%

The results of this analysis are given in Table 4. For Daisy Design, we see that the median student in the WE-group (E1) took 9.5 minutes to complete their next objective, while the median student in the non-WE group (E2) took 0 minutes (they accomplished the next objective at the same time as the WE objectives). This occurred because the next objective was to move code into a procedure, and many students in the non-WE group simply wrote their code in a procedure from the beginning. The next two objectives also take the WE group longer. For Spiral Polygon, no additional objectives were completed by more than half of students, so we can only compute the Q1 time. Similarly, it takes the WE group much longer to accomplish one additional objective (Q1 = 12.0m) compared to the non-WE group (Q1 = 2.6m), but this gap quickly reduces for the second objective, and even reverses by the third (where not even 25% of non-WE of students had completed the third objective by 39 minutes). From this, we conclude that, after completing the WE-supported objectives, students with WEs initially worked less efficiently, especially since non-WE students could accomplish additional objectives *while* completing the WE objectives (e.g. putting code into a procedure). However, it also seems that this difference decreases over time. In addition, the difference never exceeded 15 minutes on Daisy Design, and 10 minutes on Spiral Polygon, which is still far less time than the WEs saved the median student on each

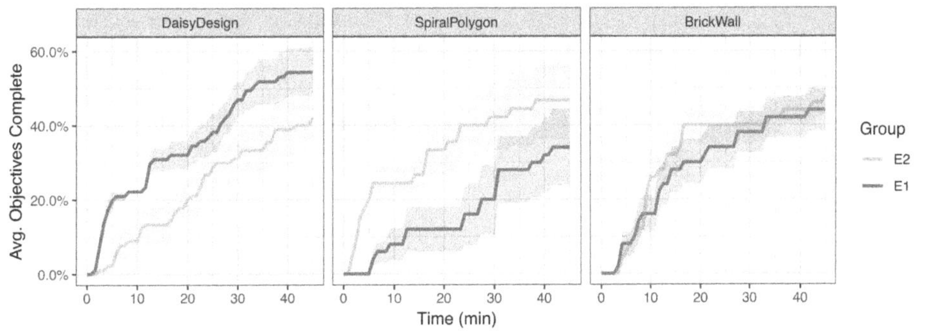

Figure 2: The average number of objectives completed by each group over time, with shading indicating ± 1 standard error.

problem (19 and 24 minutes, respectively). This helps to explain why the WE group accomplished more objectives on both problems, but the difference was not significant.

3.4 Post-survey Feedback

We asked students for feedback on the Peer Code Helper (PCH) at the end of the study. When asked if they would like to use the PCH on a future problem, 35% of students said yes and 12% said no, with the rest uncertain. We found that the 2 students said "no" had very high pre-test scores (over 75%), indicating that some more advanced students may not appreciate WEs, as found in previous work [7]. The participants who were uncertain about the PCH indicated that they preferred the challenge of working independently, saying, "it's good to have a challenge, but it's also nice... to make it a little bit easier.", and "I liked the ... feeling of success from figuring it out for myself, but sometimes the instructions are really helpful when I get stuck." Students' desire for independence is a common reason that they avoid help when programming, and overcoming this barrier can be very challenging [15]. However, many students wrote about how they appreciated the PCH, emphasizing how it helped them to "see how to go from one step to the next" and "know what to do... and... figure it out faster," and that the PCH "gave me somewhere to start coding from." When asked about their favorite parts of the PCH, students specifically mentioned how it gave "comments beforehand to help us understand how to begin the code." Paired with the other results presented here, this indicates that the PCH is an overall improvement to Snap*!*, which students generally prefer over purely independent programming.

4 DISCUSSION & CONCLUSION

We did not find significant differences in learning based on post-test scores. However, results suggest that most of students' learning occurred during problem 2. This may be because students solve problem 2 on second day of the study, after having more time to reflect and digest the concepts learned in problem 1. There was no difference in learning between groups on the WE problems. This is consistent with previous WE studies [10, 17], where students learned more efficiently with WEs, but they did not learn more, since both groups were exposed to the same learning content. The problems in our study contained core objectives (e.g. draw the daisy design), followed by more open-ended objectives (make the design colorful) which do not include new programming concepts. Since most students in both groups completed the core objectives, it is not surprising that there was no significant difference in their learning.

We found significant differences between the groups' intrinsic cognitive load for problem 2 but not for problem 1. It is interesting that we observed differences in *intrinsic* load, which is assumed to be inherent in the learning task, rather than *extraneous* load, which is assumed to be the result of our instructional design. This may be because WEs represent an inherently different learning task than problem solving. We also found both groups experienced higher intrinsic load on problems *without WEs* that followed problems *with WEs*. This may indicate that our design of WEs increased students' perceived difficulty of problem solving immediate following WEs.

Our analysis of programming efficiency suggests that initially, WEs save students considerable time in completing programming objectives (up to half of the time allotted), but that students take longer to complete later objectives. We hypothesize this is because students require time to process the WE code and begin to write their own code. However, the time saved is longer than the time students need to complete additional objectives, which allowed students who received WEs to complete more objectives overall on both problems 1 and 2, although this difference was not significant due to the low sample size.

Threats to Validity: This is an exploratory study with a small sample size, which makes it difficult to rule out possible differences between groups. All of the programming problems involved drawing patterns, and our design of WEs may not generalize to problems that lack visual output. The self-selected summer campers and may be more motivated to learn, but may have taken the assessments less seriously than other student populations. Participants' learning gains may also have come from repeated exposure to tests.

In conclusion, this study evaluates the impact of incomplete WEs, along with scaffolded self-explanation prompts, on learning, cognitive load, and efficiency in block-based programming activities in a high school summer camp. We found that WEs may have an effect on students' intrinsic cognitive load, but further research is needed how and why they have this effect. Our results also suggest that programming WEs may improve students' programming efficiency in the short term, but that students do require additional time to process WEs before they can construct their own code.

Acknowledgements: This material is based upon work supported by the National Science Foundation under grant 1623470.

REFERENCES

[1] Kirsten Berthold, Tessa HS Eysink, and Alexander Renkl. 2009. Assisting self-explanation prompts are more effective than open prompts when learning with multiple representations. *Instructional Science* 37, 4 (2009), 345–363.

[2] Michael E Caspersen and Jens Bennedsen. 2007. Instructional design of a programming course: a learning theoretic approach. In *Proceedings of the third international workshop on Computing education research*. ACM, 111–122.

[3] Barbara J Ericson, Lauren E Margulieux, and Jochen Rick. 2017. Solving parsons problems versus fixing and writing code. In *Proceedings of the 17th Koli Calling Conference on Computing Education Research*. ACM, 20–29.

[4] Dan Garcia, Brian Harvey, and Tiffany Barnes. 2015. The beauty and joy of computing. *ACM Inroads* 6, 4 (2015), 71–79.

[5] Peter Gerjets, Katharina Scheiter, and Richard Catrambone. 2006. Can learning from molar and modular worked examples be enhanced by providing instructional explanations and prompting self-explanations? *Learning and Instruction* 16, 2 (2006), 104–121.

[6] Michelle Ichinco, Kyle J Harms, and Caitlin Kelleher. 2017. Towards Understanding Successful Novice Example User in Blocks-Based Programming. *Journal of Visual Languages and Sentient Systems* 3 (2017), 101–118.

[7] Slava Kalyuga, Paul Ayres, Paul Chandler, and John Sweller. 2003. The Expertise Reversal Effect. *Educational Psychologist* 38, 1 (2003), 23–31.

[8] Caitlin Kelleher and Randy Pausch. 2005. Stencils-based tutorials: design and evaluation. In *Proceedings of the SIGCHI conference on Human factors in computing systems*. ACM, 541–550.

[9] Zhongxiu Liu, Behrooz Mostafavi, and Tiffany Barnes. 2016. Combining Worked Examples and Problem Solving in a Data-Driven Logic Tutor. In *International Conference on Intelligent Tutoring Systems*. Springer, 347–353.

[10] Bruce M McLaren, Tamara van Gog, Craig Ganoe, David Yaron, and Michael Karabinos. 2014. Exploring the assistance dilemma: Comparing instructional support in examples and problems. In *International Conference on Intelligent Tutoring Systems*. Springer, 354–361.

[11] Briana B Morrison, Brian Dorn, and Mark Guzdial. 2014. Measuring cognitive load in introductory CS: adaptation of an instrument. In *Proceedings of the tenth annual conference on International computing education research*. ACM, 131–138.

[12] Briana B Morrison, Lauren E Margulieux, and Mark Guzdial. 2015. Subgoals, context, and worked examples in learning computing problem solving. In *Proceedings of the eleventh annual international conference on international computing education research*. ACM, 21–29.

[13] Elizabeth Patitsas, Michelle Craig, and Steve Easterbrook. 2013. Comparing and contrasting different algorithms leads to increased student learning. In *Proceedings of the ninth annual international ACM conference on International computing education research*. ACM, 145–152.

[14] Peter L Pirolli and John R Anderson. 1985. The role of learning from examples in the acquisition of recursive programming skills. *Canadian Journal of Psychology/Revue canadienne de psychologie* 39, 2 (1985), 240.

[15] Thomas W Price, Zhongxiu Liu, Veronica Cateté, and Tiffany Barnes. 2017. Factors Influencing Students' Help-Seeking Behavior while Programming with Human and Computer Tutors. In *Proceedings of the 2017 ACM Conference on International Computing Education Research*. ACM, 127–135.

[16] Marguerite Roy and Michelene TH Chi. 2005. The self-explanation principle in multimedia learning. *The Cambridge handbook of multimedia learning* (2005), 271–286.

[17] Ron JCM Salden, Kenneth R Koedinger, Alexander Renkl, Vincent Aleven, and Bruce M McLaren. 2010. Accounting for beneficial effects of worked examples in tutored problem solving. *Educational Psychology Review* 22, 4 (2010), 379–392.

[18] John Sweller. 2006. The worked example effect and human cognition. *Learning and instruction* 16, 2 (2006), 165–169.

[19] John Sweller. 2010. Element interactivity and intrinsic, extraneous, and germane cognitive load. *Educational psychology review* 22, 2 (2010), 123–138.

[20] John Sweller and Graham A Cooper. 1985. The use of worked examples as a substitute for problem solving in learning algebra. *Cognition and instruction* (1985).

[21] John Sweller, Jeroen JG Van Merrienboer, and Fred GWC Paas. 1998. Cognitive architecture and instructional design. *Educational psychology review* 10, 3 (1998).

[22] J Gregory Trafton and Brian J Reiser. 1993. Studying examples and solving problems: Contributions to skill acquisition. In *Proceedings of the 15th conference of the Cognitive Science Society*. Citeseer, 1017–1022.

[23] Jeroen JG Van Merriënboer and Marcel BM De Croock. 1992. Strategies for computer-based programming instruction: Program completion vs. program generation. *Journal of Educational Computing Research* 8, 3 (1992), 365–394.

[24] Arto Vihavainen, Matti Paksula, and Matti Luukkainen. 2011. Extreme apprenticeship method in teaching programming for beginners. In *Proceedings of the 42nd ACM technical symposium on Computer science education*. ACM, 93–98.

[25] David Weintrop and Uri Wilensky. 2015. Using Commutative Assessments to Compare Conceptual Understanding in Blocks-based and Text-based Programs.. In *ICER*, Vol. 15. 101–110.

[26] Rui Zhi. 2018. Exploring Data-driven Worked Examples for Block-based Programming. In *Proceedings of the 2018 ACM Conference on International Computing Education Research*. ACM, 294–295.

Coding Demonstration Videos for CS1

Ben Stephenson
University of Calgary
Calgary, Alberta, Canada
ben.stephenson@ucalgary.ca

ABSTRACT

This experience report describes a faculty member's effort to create educational videos that support students' learning in a programming intensive CS1 class, along with an evaluation of their use by students. The videos that were created were supplementary in nature, providing students with an optional opportunity to go back and re-watch live coding demonstrations performed in class. The production process used to create the videos is described, along with several lessons learned during this undertaking. Student usage data is reported, along with survey results collected from 164 students. Survey results show that a strong majority of students who watched the videos believed that the videos helped them learn the material in the course. Several risks that should be considered before creating custom programming video content for a course are also discussed.

ACM Reference Format:
Ben Stephenson. 2019. Coding Demonstration Videos for CS1. In *Proceedings of the 50th ACM Technical Symposium on Computer Science Education (SIGCSE '19), February 27-March 2, 2019, Minneapolis, MN, USA.* ACM, New York, NY, USA, 7 pages. https://doi.org/10.1145/3287324.3287445

1 INTRODUCTION

In recent years, we have taught almost two dozen sections of large enrollment programming intensive CS1 courses. Our teaching in these courses frequently includes live Python coding demonstrations where a problem statement is presented to the students, the steps needed to solve the problem are identified, the code to implement the solution is written during class with input from the students, and the resulting program is run. Several prior studies have shown that live coding is an effective teaching strategy [5, 14, 15] because it captures the programming process, not just the end result.

While we strongly believe that live coding is a valuable part of our teaching, some students have expressed that it can be difficult to take notes during the demonstrations because it is much easier for the instructor to edit a line (or insert several new lines) in the editor than it is for students to make similar changes in their notes. Students who miss a class, for whatever reason, are also unable to benefit from the live coding demonstration because it is a one-time performance. While the program is posted on the course website, it only captures the result of the demonstration. It fails to capture the process followed to reach that point, and as such, is not nearly as valuable as seeing the demonstration.

SIGCSE '19, February 27-March 2, 2019, Minneapolis, MN, USA

ACM ISBN 978-1-4503-5890-3/19/02...$15.00
https://doi.org/10.1145/3287324.3287445

Introductory:
- Convert from one unit of pressure to another
- Compute the payment amount for a car loan

Decision Making:
- Identify the state of matter given its temperature
- Convert from a letter grade to a number of grade points
- Compute the amount of federal income tax payable

Iteration:
- Compute the average of a collection of numbers
- Fill a graphics window with a smooth color gradient

Functions:
- Draw different types of music notes on the screen

Data Structures:
- Compute the median of a list of numbers
- Compute the mode of a list using a dictionary

File I/O:
- Count the lines, words and characters in a file

Table 1: Examples for which Videos were Created

Our goal was to take live coding to the next level by allowing students to re-watch many of our live coding demonstrations at times and places of their choice. We accomplished this goal by producing quality videos of 11 of the examples that we have used consistently over the past several offerings of our CS1 courses. A brief summary of the examples that we selected can be found in Table 1. The videos were created without financial cost or assistance from support staff.

Each video captures an explanation of the problem, an outline of the steps needed to solve it, the development of the code, and at least one trace of the program. The videos range in length from 3 minutes 50 seconds to 10 minutes 34 seconds, with an average duration of 6 minutes 30 seconds, and only one video exceeding the previously published recommendation that screencasts / podcasts should be limited to 10 minutes [2, 8]. The visual component of the video consists of slides and screen recordings while the audio consists of narration that describes each task as it is performed. The process used to create these videos, along with several lessons learned during the process are described in the sections that follow.

2 CREATING VIDEOS FOR CS1

2.1 Goals and Uses

Our goal was to produce high quality videos (within the limits of what we could do on our own) that students could use to review in-class demonstrations that were difficult to capture in their notes. In particular, we wanted to ensure that the material was taught effectively in the videos and that their quality did not deter students

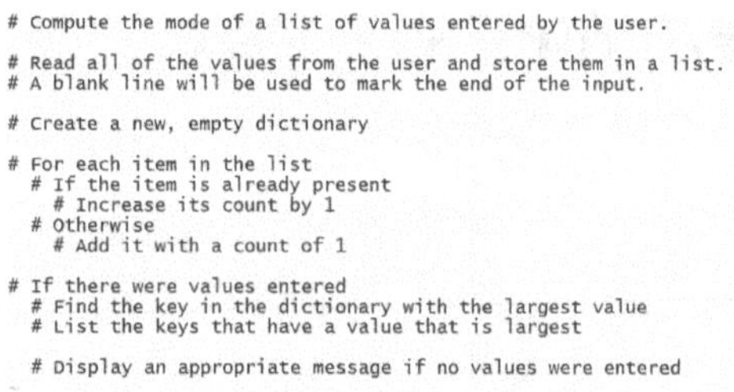

(a) Problem Solving

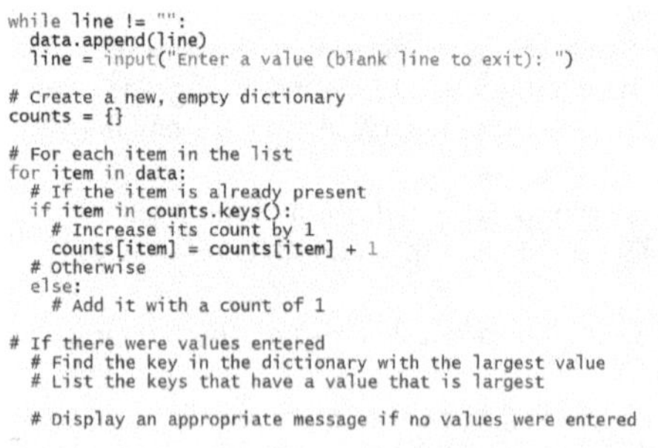

(b) Coding

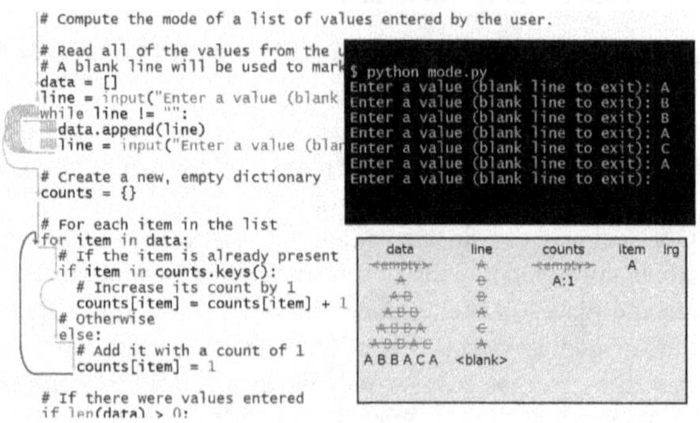

(c) Running

Figure 1: Segments in a Programming Demonstration Video

from using them. While simply recording our class demonstrations might have produced results that were, in some sense, more realistic, we do not believe that they would have been as helpful to students. The awkward pauses, unintended missteps, and fumbling for the right word that occurs during a live demonstration would have wasted time in the videos and, we believe, their unpolished nature would have made them less desirable to watch. Recording the demonstrations separately ensured that the solution progressed in a pedagogically sound manner, that the audio and video elements were clear and well synchronized with each other, and that all of the time in the video was used in a beneficial manner.

Use of the videos was entirely optional. Making them available allowed interested students to go back and see something again that was missed during class, and to a lesser extent, provided a mechanism for students that missed a class to catch up on some of the material. Since the videos only repeated the live coding portion of our lectures they were not a substitute for regular attendance.

All of our videos include the following segments:

- Introduction: The problem is described, and any background information needed to solve it is presented.
- Problem Solving: The steps needed to solve the problem are identified and entered into the source file as comments.
- Coding: Python code is written to implement each step in the solution.
- Running: The program is run and its execution is visualized using lines, arrows, and a trace table.
- Conclusion: The narrator brings the video to a close and the complete source code is shown again.

Representative screen shots of some of these segments can be found in Figure 1.

2.2 Video Creation Process

We used the following steps to create each of our videos.

Identifying an Example: We always selected examples that we have used in previous years. We did not create videos for new examples because we did not want to invest time and effort into creating a video for an example that might not resonate with students when used in the classroom. The examples that we selected varied in length from 12 to 38 lines of code and span the full gamut of programming topics taught in the course.

Script Writing: We wrote a complete script for each video. The scripts received multiple editing passes to ensure that they were clear, concise and sounded natural when spoken.

Audio Recording: Once the script was written the audio was recorded. Audio recording was performed separately from the screen capture recording so that the audio would be clear and properly paced without the awkward pauses that are inevitable when typing and speaking at the same time. During recording, we continued to make minor adjustments to the script to make the narration more natural. The audio was recorded using a Samsung Meteor Mic and Audacity audio software. We were able to borrow the microphone from another unit on campus (purchasing one would have been less than $100). Audacity is available from http://audacityteam.org/ at no cost.

Problem Solving and Coding Screen Capture: During this phase, we recorded ourselves typing the program into our editor. We began each demonstration by writing comments that described the steps that were going to be used to solve the problem. Then we wrote the Python code needed to implement each step. Both the comments and Python code were not necessarily created from top to bottom. At times we completed the steps non-sequentially because there was a pedagogical benefit to doing so. We used CamStudio (http://camstudio.org/) for screen recording because it was available without cost and used lossless compression.

Tracing the Program: The program was executed after it was created. Screen recording software was used to capture the command prompt / terminal window that showed the program being started, the input values being entered, and the results being displayed. Arrows were drawn in sequence to show the flow of control through the program, and a trace table was constructed so that students could see the values of the variables change as the trace progressed.

Introduction and Overlays: Each video began with a title slide that briefly described the problem and supplied needed information like definitions, formulas or numeric constants. A small number of the videos also included overlays that temporarily appeared on top of the code to provide additional information or highlighted specific programming language features.

Assembly and Post-Production: Once all of the audio and graphical content was created, it was assembled into a video using Adobe Premier Pro (http://www.adobe.com/). During this process, we removed errors from the audio (such as stumbling and having to restart a sentence), removed significant typos, and adjusted the timing, as needed, to keep the audio and graphical content synchronized. Video effects, such as cropping and overlaying two video segments were used to allow the terminal window and the program code to be displayed simultaneously and smooth scrolling effects were added to longer examples that would not fit comfortably on one screen. Finally, cross-fade transitions were added between video segments to avoid jarring cuts from the introductory slides to the editor, and from the editor to the running program.

Export, Upload and Captioning: The video was exported from Adobe Premiere Pro and uploaded to YouTube. Captions were initially added using YouTube's automatic captioning feature. Then those captions were edited to correct errors and improve the capitalization and punctuation. Hosting our videos on YouTube made it easy for our students to view them on nearly any operating system and device. Using YouTube also made it easy to make the videos publicly available so that students and educators outside of our institution could also benefit from them.

3 LESSONS LEARNED

There are many papers, books and websites that include advice on how to create effective videos, some examples of which include [1, 2, 7, 9, 10, 12, 16, 18]. While this information certainly helped us, it failed to prepare us for some surprises (pleasant and otherwise) that were specific to the creation of coding demonstration videos. The remainder of this section reports several lessons learned which are specific to this type of video, and supplements the general advice that others have reported previously.

Lesson #1: It Takes Time to Create Coding Videos

Based on previous work [2, 16], we knew that it was going to take time to create quality videos, but we didn't appreciate just how much time would be needed. Our first video was under 4 minutes in length and took more than 20 hours to produce. This was partly because we were learning the process and the tools, but it was also because it took a surprisingly large amount of time to construct program traces and closely synchronize the narration with the video of the program being created. One of the last videos that we produced was just over 7 minutes and 'only' took 10 hours 6 minutes to create. The amount of time spent on each task during its production is summarized in Table 2. With a little bit more practice we expect to reduce the creation time to approximately 1 hour per minute of video.

Task		**Time (minutes)**
Identifying an Example:		1
Script Writing:		90
Audio Recording:		30
Coding and Running Screen Capture:		20
Tracing the Program:		60
Introduction and Overlays:		5
Assembly and Post Production:		
Assembly of the coding:	90	
Assembly of the tracing:	195*	
Minor audio adjustments:	35	
Assembly and Post Production Total:		320
Export, Upload and Captioning:		
Export the video from Adobe Premiere:	15	
Upload to YouTube:	5	
Watch the 'final' version of the video:	10	
Changes needed after 'final' viewing:	15	
Export the video (again):	15	
Upload to YouTube (again):	5	
Captioning:	15	
Export, Upload and Captioning Total:		80
Total:		**606**

Table 2: Time Spent Producing a Video

Lesson #2: Recording the Coding was Easy

We expected that recording the creation of the program would be a tedious and difficult task. How would we ever create a program that was a couple dozen lines long without making any typos? While this was initially a significant source of stress for us, it turned out that it was not a problem. We found that the number of typos could be minimized by printing out the completed program and copying it instead of actually programming it. We also found that small typos simply did not matter. A mistyped character that was quickly deleted was only on the screen for a fraction of a second, and then it was gone and forgotten. Larger typos that required a significant amount of backspacing were removed because we didn't think that students were interested in watching us attempt to type the line correctly multiple times. These kinds of errors were easily removed in post-production as long as the final version of the line that was entered was correct.

Lesson #3: Easy Iteration is Valuable

Every video that we created included at least one trace of the completed program. In our early videos we created the traces by drawing the arrows and the trace table in PowerPoint. While this worked well enough for short traces, it was difficult to revise the trace if we decided to change something after it was initially created because several frames needed to be modified. As our traces grew longer, more and more frames needed to be modified to make a change, and this became a barrier to improving the traces. We overcame this problem by generating the arrows and trace table with a Python program. The traces were easy to revise because all of the images containing arrows and the trace table could be regenerated with one command. Making improvements to the traces

*The amount of time spent assembling the audio and video for the tracing portion of this video was atypically large because multiple attempts were needed to create a visually appealing spatial layout of the material.

in an iterative manner resulted in better animations that matched the narration exactly.

Lesson #4: Time Recoding is Very Helpful

We found the ability to stretch or compress time (time recoding) incredibly helpful when synchronizing the audio and visual content. The video could be sped up when several lines of code needed to be entered that required little verbal explanation. Similarly, the video could be slowed down, or even completely stopped, to allow a longer explanation to be completed before the next lines of code were displayed.

4 STUDENT USAGE AND IMPRESSIONS

During the Winter 2017 academic term, we used our newly created videos in a large CS1 course for non-majors. The course focused on imperative programming in Python. Its assessments consisted of 7 small exercises, 4 larger assignments, a midterm exam, and a final exam.

Students were given the option to complete an on-line survey about the videos for a small amount of extra credit (approximately 0.5% of their final grade). A total of 166 responses were received (that included consent to use the data for research purposes) from the 295 students enrolled in the course. While the survey was not anonymous students were still able to provide their honest opinions without fear of reprisal because the student responses were anonymized by a third party before they were provided to the course instructor and the data was not made available to the course instructor until the deadline for grade appeals had passed. Two responses were discarded because they were both submitted by the same student and the answers provided were contradictory. This left a total of 164 valid survey responses, which was a valid response rate of 55.6 percent. Of those 164 valid responses, 132 students indicated that they watched at least one of the videos.

4.1 Utility of the Videos

Our survey included questions that asked students whether or not the videos were helpful when completing various assessments in the course. Students responded using a 5-point Likert scale with values strongly agree, agree, neutral, disagree and strongly disagree. Students that didn't watch the videos selected a separate "I didn't watch the videos" response item.

Of students that watched the videos, the majority agreed or strongly agreed that the videos helped them with each assessment type. Students found the videos most helpful when completing the small exercises, with 68.5 percent of students that watched the videos agreeing or strongly agreeing that they were helpful for this assessment type. A smaller number of students found the videos helpful for other assessment types, with 54.4 percent agreeing or strongly agreeing that the videos were helpful when completing the four larger assignments, and 53.1 percent reporting that the videos were helpful when preparing for the midterm and/or final exam.

Students were also asked whether or not the videos were helpful for learning the course material in general, rather than focusing on a specific type of assessment. Approximately 78.3 percent of students that watched the videos agreed or strongly agreed with the statement "I believe that watching the videos helped me learn the material for this course". Only 4.9 percent disagreed with this statement, and no students strongly disagreed with it. In addition, 87.1 percent of students that watched the videos agreed or strongly agreed with the statement "I would recommend that other students taking this course watch the videos".

Finally, approximately 62.8 percent of students that watched the videos agreed or strongly agreed that "Watching the videos helped me answer a question that I would have otherwise needed to ask a TA or the course instructor". At our institution class sizes are increasing while the amount of TA support being provided is decreasing. As a result, we found this outcome particularly encouraging because it suggests that the videos reduced the amount of student email we had to respond to, in addition to being valued by the students.

4.2 Quality of the Videos

Students were also asked several questions about the quality of the videos. In each case, they indicated whether the aspect under consideration was poor, fair, good or excellent. Students that didn't watch the videos selected a separate "I didn't watch the videos" response item.

The audio and visual aspects of the videos were rated similarly by students, with 91.6 percent of students that watched the videos reporting that the audio was either good (55.0 percent) or excellent (36.6 percent) and 93.9 percent reporting that the visual aspects of the video were either good (52.7 percent) or excellent (41.2 percent). No students rated either the audio or visual aspects of the videos as poor.

When students were asked about the way that the material was taught in the videos, 89.3 percent reported that it was either good (51.1 percent) or excellent (38.2 percent). Approximately 97.7 percent of students that watched the videos responded with either good (61.5 percent) or excellent (36.2 percent) to the statement "All things considered, the overall quality of the video was ...". No students indicated that the material was taught poorly or that the overall quality of the videos was poor.

Overall, these results show that good, though not necessarily excellent, results can be achieved when a faculty member produces their own videos without assistance from support staff or substantial financial cost.

4.3 Usage Patterns

We analyzed the usage data provided by YouTube to determine when students viewed our videos[†]. The first video was posted on January 18, 2017, after the fifth one-hour class of the semester. The 10 remaining videos were posted throughout the semester after each example was presented in class. Usage data was collected until the final exam was completed. A total of 1,280 views occurred during this time.

Figure 2 shows the number of video views by date. The dates that the videos were released to the students are shaded. Light-weight solid lines are used to mark the due dates for the small exercises

[†]The videos were unlisted during this study. As a result, the usage data only includes views by our students. The videos have since been made public so that students and teachers outside of our institution can benefit from them.

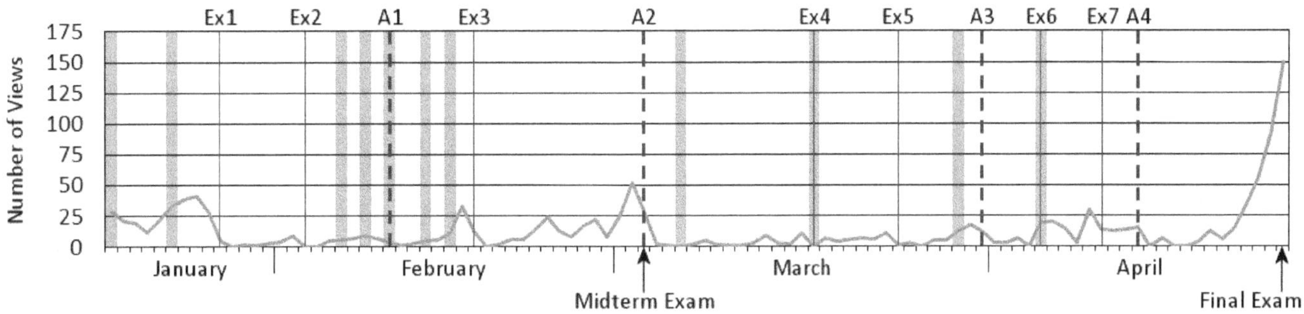

Figure 2: Number of Videos Viewed by Date

(labeled Ex1 through Ex7), while the heavier dashed lines denote the due dates for the larger assignments (labeled A1 through A4). There is a gap in the video release dates at the end of January due to approximately four classes spent on data representation, and there is a gap in late February due to Reading Week.

As Figure 2 shows, the number of views was largest in the days immediately ahead of the final exam, with the peak occurring on the day of the exam‡. The second largest peak occurred immediately ahead of the midterm exam. Due to unfortunate scheduling, the out-of-class midterm exam was on the same day that Assignment 2 was due. As a result, we can't determine whether that peak was due to the exam, the assignment, or a combination of the two. Most of the remaining peaks were on either the day that an assignment or exercise was due, or the immediately preceding day.

These results show that students were using the videos most heavily when preparing for the final exam. We suspect that this was, at least in part, due to the final exam occurring late in the final exam timetable (there was a 13 day gap between the last day of classes and the exam). More generally, many of the views are correlated with the due dates for assessments in the course. While we might have preferred to see our students use the videos more evenly throughout the semester, we were not particularly surprised by this pattern which suggests that students were using the videos to learn the material immediately before assessments.

4.4 Qualitative Responses

Our survey included three open-ended questions that asked students what they liked most about the videos, what they would suggest changing about them, and what, if anything, discouraged or prevented them from watching. An open-coding approach was used to identify and group common themes within the responses to each question.

4.4.1 What Did You Like Most? The most common response to this question, reported by 27 students, indicated that students liked that the videos captured the process used to create the programs, not just the final results. Other common responses included that the length of the videos was appropriate (17 students) and that the videos could be accessed any time (14 students). That the videos could be paused, rewound or viewed at a student's own pace was highlighted by 13 students.

There was also one relatively uncommon answer that we found noteworthy. Five students specifically stated that they liked that the videos were available even though they didn't watch any of them. These students seemed comforted by the fact that this resource was available if needed even though they never actually made use of it.

4.4.2 What Would You Change? The most common response to this question indicated that more videos should be created (27 students). This was closely followed by responses that explicitly stated that nothing should be changed about the videos (26 students). Other common answers included that the videos should be longer (16 students), which was indicated by either explicitly stating such, or by providing suggestions that would require the length of the videos to increase, such as speaking more slowly. Finally, nine students suggested improving the audio, with several of these students describing the narration as wooden or robotic. Overall, these responses suggest that there are few, if any, major problems with the videos. We will attempt to address the audio concerns raised by a small number of students by further emphasizing enthusiasm in the videos that we expect to create in the future.

4.4.3 What Discouraged You from Watching? Students most commonly reported that nothing discouraged or prevent them from watching the videos, with 33 responses explicitly stating such. This was closely followed by responses that indicated that it wasn't necessary to watch the videos because the student was already familiar with the material (30 students). These responses often specifically mentioned that the student was familiar with the material because he or she had seen the example when it was presented in class. Less frequent responses to this question included lacking time to watch the videos (8 students), not realizing that the videos were available (6 students), lacking motivation or procrastination (4 students) and technical difficulties (3 students).

5 RISKS

We plan to use the videos that we have created for many years to come, but there are several risks that could prevent us from doing so. Similar risks exist at many other institutions. We hope that discussing the risks will allow others to mitigate them before investing a significant amount of time and effort into the creation of their own materials.

In our department, the languages used in CS1 and CS2 are set by a committee rather than by individual instructors. Our videos will be much less useful when this committee decides to change

‡The exam was at 7:00pm, giving students ample time to study on the day of the exam.

the language used in CS1 at some point in the future. While we will have some influence on that decision, ultimately, we do not have control over the language of instruction used in the courses, and as a result, it could change despite our objection.

Python 3 is not compatible with Python 2. From this we can infer that it is possible, and perhaps even likely, that Python 4 will not be compatible with Python 3. While we will not have to move to Python 4 as soon as it is released, the pressure to move will increase over time as Python 3 resources go out of print and students express their desire to learn the current version of the language.

Our department generally strives for consistency in teaching assignments from year to year, but an unexpected resignation, retirement or maternity / parental leave can cause sudden changes, as can a pleasant surprise like hiring a new colleague. While another instructor might continue to use the videos we have created, they might choose other resources instead. Even if the videos continue to be used by another instructor, the benefit will not accrue to the person who invested the time needed to create them.

Finally, examples that include time-sensitive data or cultural references will become dated. While there are some very good examples that include such references, we would recommend creating videos for them sparingly because they may not resonate with students in subsequent years, and as such, videos that include them will typically have a shorter useful lifespan than videos that do not.

We will only be able to fully assess the value of this project once we know how many times we were able to use the videos. While we certainly hope to use them for several years to come, there is some risk that this will not occur, and the effort expended to create them will substantially overshadow the benefits. By being aware of these risks, we can work to mitigate them and maximize the likelihood that the videos will be used long enough to (more than) justify the time and effort needed to create them.

6 RELATED WORK

Numerous courses make use of video, either as the primary mode of instruction or to supplement face-to-face instruction. Examples that specifically address programming include work that compared video tutorials and in-person tutorials at the Open University of Israel [19] and work at Drake University that compared video lectures to in-person lectures when teaching the programming unit in a CS0 course [13]. Other examples include a study examining a variety of technological interventions, including video, in courses that included instruction on C++, SQL and COBOL [20], and an examination of the impact of video lectures on a multi-media programming course [11].

We are aware of four previous studies that specifically focus on screencast videos or animations that demonstrate programming examples [3, 4, 6, 17]. Two of these studies each report usage data for a small number of students (55 in [4] and 20 in [6]), and a small amount of data about students' impressions of the videos was reported by Bennedsen and Casperson in [4]. More recently, Sharrock and Aycock have each described browser-based tools for demonstrating programming, but no data from students is reported in Sharrock's study [17] while Aycock's work only includes a few student comments that were collected from the end-of-course evaluations [3]. Our work builds on these previous studies by reporting usage data for 295 students, as well as survey data collected from 164 respondents. We have also identified and articulated several risks that content creators should consider that have not previously been reported.

7 FUTURE WORK

The videos that we created demonstrate the incremental nature of problem solving and programming, but, in most cases, do not include the kinds of errors that new programmers commonly make. For example, none of the videos demonstrate how to respond to an error message such as "SyntaxError: EOL while scanning string literal". When programming in front of the class we show that such errors are a normal part of the programming process and we teach students how to respond to them effectively. In the future we anticipate creating additional videos that focus on debugging with the hope that such videos will further help students build the skills that they need to be effective programmers.

Another area that could be explored in the future is the costs and benefits associated with creating polished videos. Does time spent on editing increase the likelihood that students will watch the videos? What impact, if any, does the presence or absence of stumbles, missteps and errors have on student learning? A subsequent study could collect the data that would be needed to answer these questions.

8 CONCLUSION

This paper has reported on our experience building supplementary videos that allowed our students to re-watch the live coding demonstrations that we completed in class. Our contributions include identifying several lessons learned that are specific to the production of coding demonstration videos, survey data from a large CS1 class that shows that, overall, students found the videos helpful, and the identification of several risks that instructors considering similar projects should work to mitigate.

Based on our experience, would we recommend that others produce coding demonstration videos to supplement live coding demonstrations in their courses? Our answer is a qualified "yes". Quality results can be achieved for minimal, if any, financial cost, and the data that we collected shows that benefits were achieved. More than half of students that watched the videos reported that they were helpful when completing assessments, 62.8 percent reported that the videos helped answer a question that they would have otherwise needed to ask the instructor or a TA, and 87.1 percent reported that they would recommend that other students taking the course watch the videos.

But we also want other instructors to go into the process with their eyes open. It takes a significant amount of time and effort, both to learn the tools and to use them to achieve polished results, and there are some risks to long-term use that must be considered. When these risks can be mitigated it is likely that the videos will be used enough times to justify the effort needed to create them. However, when these risks cannot be mitigated, for whatever reason, we recommend proceeding with significant, even extreme, caution as the time needed to create the videos simply isn't worthwhile if they cannot be used several times. Instead, we believe that instructors in such circumstances would be better off employing other techniques to assist students.

REFERENCES

[1] Creating course videos, n.d. Retrieved July 27, 2017 from https://www.rit.edu/-academicaffairs/tls/course-development/creating-videos/.

[2] Screencasts, n.d. Retrieved July 27, 2017 from https://uwaterloo.ca/centre-for-teaching-excellence/teaching-resources/teaching-tips/educational-technologies/all/screencasts/.

[3] J. Aycock. Stick to the script: Lightweight recording and playback of live coding. In *Proceedings of the 23rd Annual ACM Conference on Innovation and Technology in Computer Science Education*, ITiCSE 2018, pages 350–351, New York, NY, USA, 2018. ACM.

[4] J. Bennedsen and M. E. Caspersen. Revealing the programming process. In *Proceedings of the 36th SIGCSE Technical Symposium on Computer Science Education*, SIGCSE '05, pages 186–190, New York, NY, USA, 2005. ACM.

[5] J. Bennedsen and M. E. Caspersen. *Exposing the Programming Process*, pages 6–16. Springer Berlin Heidelberg, Berlin, Heidelberg, 2008.

[6] C. Boisvert. Web animation to communicate iterative development. In *Proceedings of the 11th Annual SIGCSE Conference on Innovation and Technology in Computer Science Education*, ITiCSE '06, pages 173–177, New York, NY, USA, 2006. ACM.

[7] C. Brame. Effective educational videos, 2015. Retrieved July 27, 2017 from https://cft.vanderbilt.edu/guides-sub-pages/effective-educational-videos/.

[8] P. Edirisingha, G. Salmon, and M. Nie. Developing pedagogical podcasts. In G. Salmon and P. Edirisingha, editors, *Podcasting for Learning in Universities*, chapter 15, pages 153–168. McGraw-Hill Education, 2008.

[9] D. Garcia, M. Ball, and A. Parikh. L@S 2014 demo: Best practices for MOOC video. In *Proceedings of the First ACM Conference on Learning @ Scale*, L@S '14, pages 217–218, New York, NY, USA, 2014. ACM.

[10] M. Gilbert. *edX E-Learning Course Development.* Community experience distilled. Packt Publishing, 2015.

[11] A. Karakostas, S. Demetriadis, V. Ragazou, and M. Amarlariotou. e-lectures to support blended instruction in multimedia programming course. In *Proceedings of the Fifteenth Annual Conference on Innovation and Technology in Computer Science Education*, ITiCSE '10, pages 189–193, New York, NY, USA, 2010. ACM.

[12] J. Kim, P. J. Guo, D. T. Seaton, P. Mitros, K. Z. Gajos, and R. C. Miller. Understanding in-video dropouts and interaction peaks in online lecture videos. In *Proceedings of the First ACM Conference on Learning @ Scale*, L@S '14, pages 31–40, New York, NY, USA, 2014. ACM.

[13] E. D. Manley and T. M. Urness. Video-based instruction for introductory computer programming. *J. Comput. Sci. Coll.*, 29(5):221–227, May 2014.

[14] J. Paxton. Live programming as a lecture technique. *J. Comput. Sci. Coll.*, 18(2):51–56, Dec. 2002.

[15] M. J. Rubin. The effectiveness of live-coding to teach introductory programming. In *Proceeding of the 44th ACM Technical Symposium on Computer Science Education*, SIGCSE '13, pages 651–656, New York, NY, USA, 2013. ACM.

[16] D. C. Schmidt and Z. McCormick. Producing and delivering a Coursera MOOC on pattern-oriented software architecture for concurrent and networked software. In *Proceedings of the 2013 Companion Publication for Conference on Systems, Programming, & Applications: Software for Humanity*, SPLASH '13, pages 167–176, New York, NY, USA, 2013. ACM.

[17] R. Sharrock, E. Hamonic, M. Hiron, and S. Carlier. Codecast: An innovative technology to facilitate teaching and learning computer programming in a C language online course. In *Proceedings of the Fourth ACM Conference on Learning @ Scale*, L@S '17, pages 147–148, New York, NY, USA, 2017. ACM.

[18] S. Thornton, C. Riley, and M. E. Wiltrout. Criteria for video engagement in a biology MOOC. In *Proceedings of the Fourth ACM Conference on Learning @ Scale*, L@S '17, pages 291–294, New York, NY, USA, 2017. ACM.

[19] T. Vilner, E. Zur, and R. Sagi. Integrating video components in CS1. In *Proceedings of the 43rd ACM Technical Symposium on Computer Science Education*, SIGCSE '12, pages 123–128, New York, NY, USA, 2012. ACM.

[20] R. Vinaja. The use of lecture videos, ebooks, and clickers in computer courses. *J. Comput. Sci. Coll.*, 30(2):23–32, Dec. 2014.

Exploring the Value of Different Data Sources for Predicting Student Performance in Multiple CS Courses

Soohyun Nam Liao
University of California, San Diego

Daniel Zingaro
University of Toronto Mississauga

Christine Alvarado
University of California, San Diego

William G. Griswold
University of California, San Diego

Leo Porter
University of California, San Diego

ABSTRACT

A number of recent studies in computer science education have explored the value of various data sources for early prediction of students' overall course performance. These data sources include responses to clicker questions, prerequisite knowledge, instrumented student IDEs, quizzes, and assignments. However, these data sources are often examined in isolation or in a single course. Which data sources are most valuable, and does course context matter? To answer these questions, this study collected student grades on prerequisite courses, Peer Instruction clicker responses, online quizzes, and assignments, from five courses (over 1000 students) across the CS curriculum at two institutions. A trend emerges suggesting that for upper-division courses, prerequisite grades are most predictive; for introductory programming courses, where no prerequisite grades were available, clicker responses were the most predictive. In concert, prerequisites and clicker responses generally provide highly accurate predictions early in the term, with assignments and online quizzes sometimes providing incremental improvements. Implications of these results for both researchers and practitioners are discussed.

CCS CONCEPTS

• **Social and professional topics → Computing education; Computer science education; CS1;**

KEYWORDS

machine learning, prediction, student outcomes, low-performing students, CS1, CS2, Data Structures, Architecture

ACM Reference Format:

Soohyun Nam Liao, Daniel Zingaro, Christine Alvarado, William G. Griswold, and Leo Porter. 2019. Exploring the Value of Different Data Sources for Predicting Student Performance in Multiple CS Courses. In *Proceedings of the 50th ACM Technical Symposium on Computer Science Education (SIGCSE '19), February 27-March 2, 2019, Minneapolis, MN, USA.* ACM, New York, NY, USA, 7 pages. https://doi.org/10.1145/3287324.3287407

SIGCSE '19, February 27-March 2, 2019, Minneapolis, MN, USA

ACM ISBN 978-1-4503-5890-3/19/02...$15.00
https://doi.org/10.1145/3287324.3287407

1 INTRODUCTION

Failure rates in computer science courses can be high, both in introductory computing [24] and in follow on courses [15]. This problem is exacerbated by current high enrollments [6] because growing class sizes make it increasingly difficult for instructors to identify who among their students is in trouble. As a result, the computing education research community has been studying automated means of identifying at-risk students early in the term so that instructors might be able to intervene. Some prior studies focused on introductory courses, looking at relationships between student outcomes and pre-class experiences or characteristics (SAT score, gender, prior programming experience, achievement goals etc.) [12, 14, 19, 22, 26, 29]. Other work has leveraged educational technology to collect student data, such as programming behavior, types of questions asked on online forums, and clicker data from Peer Instruction [17, 21, 23]. Much of this work has focused on understanding characteristics of low- or high-performing students based on data from a single term, though a few recent studies have predicted overall course performance across terms by using machine learning models built with clicker data [11] and assignments [3, 5].

One limitation of previous prediction studies is that they largely focus on introductory programming courses, leaving a gap in our understanding of the factors that might be predictive for later courses. In addition, many of those studies focus on single data sources, rather than the ways in which multiple sources might work in concert.

In this study, we collect grades in prerequisite computer science courses (when applicable), assignments, online quizzes, and clicker data from five different CS courses (both lower- and upper-division) across two separate institutions. In each case, we examine the value of each of these data sources in building a predictive model, where the model is trained on data from one term and then applied to students in a subsequent term. We find, as one might expect, that for upper-division courses, grades in prerequisite courses are particularly strong predictors. Adding clicker data improves the model in general for all five courses, including two introductory programming courses where prerequisite CS grades are not available. By contrast, assignments and online quizzes improve the model only marginally, compared to prerequisite courses and clicker data. In concert, prerequisite grades and clicker data provide particularly accurate predictions. As such, instructors wishing to identify low-performing students early in the term may wish to prioritize the collection of these data sources.

Table 1: Dataset Details

ID	Course Name	Inst†	Size‡	Course Topics	Prerequisites
CS1P	CS1 in Python	A	192 / 142	variables, datatypes, functions, conditionals, loops, and sorting algorithms	None
CS1J	CS1 in Java	B	373 / 374	variables, methods, conditionals, loops, and objects	None
CS2J	CS2 in Java	B	169 / 176	arrays, lists, stacks, queues, sorting algorithms, and runtime analysis	CS1
DataStr	Advanced Data Structures	B	197 / 191	trees, balanced search trees, hashtables, tries, Huffman coding, and graph search	CS2, Programming Tools Lab, Discrete Mathematics, Computer Organization
Arch	Introductory Computer Architecture	B	339 / 266	ISA, performance, single/multi-cycle processors, pipelining, and caches	Computer Organization, Digital Logic, Digital Logic Lab

† Institution ‡ Size of Training Set / Test Set

Table 2: Data Sources Used in the Present Study

ID	Description	Preprocessing Method	CS1P	CS1J	CS2J	DataStr	Arch
p	Final grades from prerequisite courses	Numerical grade			✓	✓	✓
c	In-class clicker correctness	Average correctness	✓	✓	✓	✓	✓
a	Take-home assignment grades	Average score		✓	✓	✓	✓
q	Online quiz grades	Average score	✓	✓	✓	✓	✓

2 BACKGROUND

Accurately predicting student performance in CS courses is a longstanding goal of CS education researchers [20]. Given the elevated failure rates often reported in CS courses [24], the hope is to be able to identify at-risk students in a timely manner, so that there is opportunity to alert students or help them make progress.

Much of the relevant work relies on static factors that can be measured at the start of a course but that cannot be easily changed. Such factors include gender, prior experience, achievement goals, and self-efficacy [19, 26, 29]. While some success has been met using such approaches [18], correlations between these factors and course outcomes tend to be low or do not consistently replicate [25].

Fortunately, we can also avail ourselves of data generated by modern educational technology. In contrast to static data, this dynamic data is generated as the course unfolds, and provides a more nuanced understanding of how students progress through and interact with course material. One strand of this research leverages Peer Instruction (PI) clicker data, using student in-class responses from early in the term to predict course outcomes [11, 17]. Another strand uses instrumented software to capture student process and behavioral data, such as total keypresses when programming [3], time and changes between compilations [25], and time spent with particular elements in online modules [10].

We note two related gaps in the body of literature summarized above. First, the extant research push is largely focused on making predictions in CS1 courses, with very little action in other courses [8]. Second, students taking CS1 courses are very likely in their first year of study, so such research cannot include student grades in prerequisite courses. Some work suggests that grades in prerequisite courses are useful for predicting student progression through a CS degree program [4], but that work does not consider dynamic predictors of performance. In summary, while in CS1 the efficacy of static predictors tends to pale in comparison to that of dynamic predictors, it is not known to what extent prerequisite grades and dynamic predictors may work together to predict outcomes in more advanced courses. The present paper addresses these research gaps: we study a variety of courses in the undergraduate CS curriculum, and (for more advanced courses) make predictions using both static and dynamic predictors.

3 METHOD

Our work was guided by two central research questions:

- **RQ1:** What is the value of each of our data sources for predicting student performance in computing?
- **RQ2:** How do prediction accuracies improve as we use multiple data sources?

Given these research questions, we provide background information on our datasets and how we create models to predict student performance and evaluate those predictions.

3.1 Our Datasets

We obtained our data from five courses across the CS curriculum at two North American research-focused institutions with institutional approval to study human subjects. Table 1 provides course details, including course topics and numbers of students in each dataset. Note that for each course we have two terms' worth of data, one used for training and the other for testing. This cross-term modeling approach captures authentic variation in natural teaching environments, including changes in courses and exams [3, 11]. Our data includes two CS1 courses, one from each institution; these courses were taught completely separately and not coordinated across institutions.

Table 2 describes the modeling features used for the present study. We selected relatively common course components within these five courses to predict student performance: course prerequisites, clicker responses, assignments, and online quizzes. Course prerequisites (see the Prerequisites column in Table 1) are not available for CS1, as it is the first CS course taken by students at these institutions. Clicker data was available for all five courses, as all instructors used Peer Instruction [7] in class. Peer Instruction involves the use of conceptually-rich multiple-choice questions to which students respond individually and then in groups. The questions are designed to target student difficulties and misconceptions, and are informed by teaching experience, research literature, and available question banks. Assignment grades were incorporated into four of the models; no assignment data was available for CS1P, because the first assignment in that course was due later in the term. Arch students completed individual assignments. In the other courses, pair programming was required (CS1J) or encouraged (CS1P, CS2J, DataStr). Online quiz data was available in all courses through pre-class reading quizzes; CS2J also had review quizzes assessing what students learned in the past week.

3.2 Model Generation

Our model generation process can be divided into four major steps: defining early prediction, defining low-performing students, pre-processing the data, and training a model. We used the glm R function [2] to generate and evaluate prediction models.

Defining early prediction. Similar to prior studies, we produce predictions using only data collected during the first 3 weeks of each term [11, 17]. By making predictions this early in the term, the belief is that potential interventions may be possible even before the first midterm exam.

Defining low-performing students. We defined low-performing students to be those who are ranked in the bottom 40% on the final exam. This is based on prior literature [11] where instructors selected the bottom 40% to be the group of students likely in need of assistance.

Preprocessing. We preprocessed each data source as indicated in the Preprocessing Method column of Table 2. Each data source was distilled into a single value per student, except for prerequisites where we used one value per prerequisite course grade. We collected final letter grades from the prerequisite courses, and then converted these letter grades into numerical grades on a 0-4.33 scale, so A+ became 4.33, A became 4.0, A- became 3.67, and so on. For clicker data, we used records of student responses to each clicker question, following prior work [17] stating that student clicker correctness is correlated with final exam performance. Specifically, we assigned -1, 0, and 1 for incorrect, no response, and correct, respectively, and calculated the average of all clicker questions for each student. Similarly, for assignments and quizzes, we calculated average grades, after scaling the maximum possible score of each assessment item to be 1.0 to correct for different maximum possible scores. As a final step, we normalized each data feature to have a normal distribution.

Training. We trained a Logistic regression model [27] to perform binary classification (low-performing vs. high-performing) for each course. We selected logistic regression after exploring a number of different models for accuracy, simplicity, and ability to work well with a small number of input features. The model was trained on data from an earlier term with the data sources as features and with the binary outcome labels of low-performing or high-performing based on final exam score.

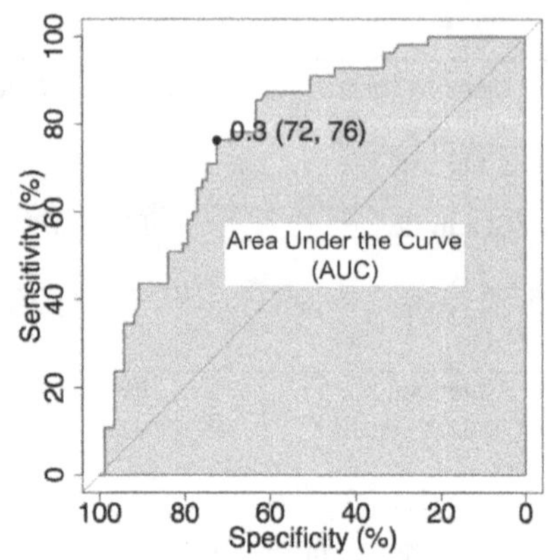

Figure 1: An Example ROC Curve

3.3 Model Analysis

Given the model created using the previous term of data (training set), we make predictions on the subsequent term (test set) and evaluate those predictions using a common graph in machine learning called a Receiver Operating Characteristic (ROC) curve, which plots the performance of a model as its parameters are varied. An example ROC curve is provided in Figure 1. The x-axis plots how accurately a model identifies high-performing students (specificity) and the y-axis plots how accurately a model identifies low-performing students (sensitivity). The output of the logistic regression model is a number between 0 and 1 representing the probability that a particular student is low-performing. We can trade off the specificity and sensitivity of our model by varying the probability threshold we use to decide whether a student is classified as high- or low-performing. This trade-off is what is shown in the ROC curve; each point on the curve corresponds to a different selected value for the probability threshold. For example, the point corresponding to a probability threshold of 0.3 is shown in Figure 1. This example point, for this model at this threshold, produces a specificity of 72% and a sensitivity of 76%.

When evaluating the overall modeling performance, the Area Under the Curve (AUC) on an ROC curve is commonly used as it captures, in effect, how close to an ideal curve is provided by the model. Figure 1 visualizes the AUC in blue. Overall, a high AUC (closer to 1.0) implies a better model as it is better capable of capturing sensitivity and specificity.

3.4 Analysis of Multiple Sources

Ultimately, we use a combination of multiple data sources to train and test the model using the AUC described above. We would like to know whether adding a data source leads to improvement in the model. However, one cannot directly determine whether a model is statistically better than another based on resultant AUC curves. As such, we begin by determining whether adding a specific data source is statistically significant, and to do so, we run a likelihood ratio test [13] (using the lrtest R package [1]). This test compares two models, before and after adding a specific data source, and

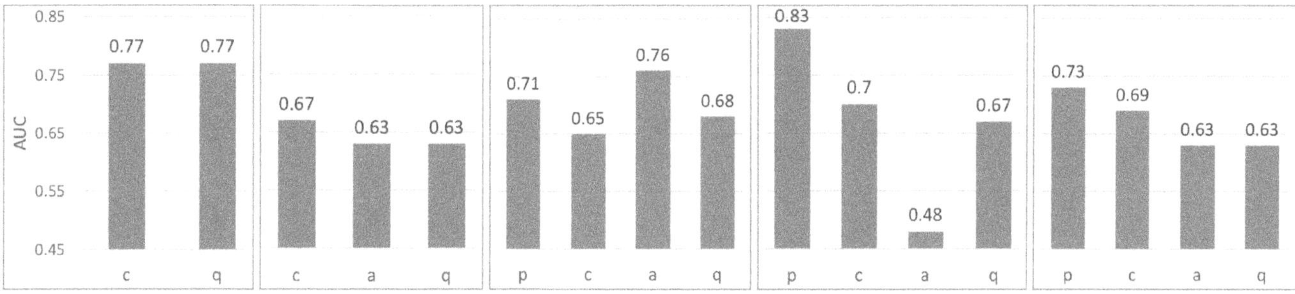

(a) CS1P (b) CS1J (c) CS2J (d) DataStr (e) Arch

Figure 2: AUC When Modeling with Individual Data Sources

returns a p-value to show whether adding that data source statistically changes the generated model. We define statistical significance at the $p < 0.05$ level. There is an important distinction between this analysis and the model analysis from Section 3.3 in that likelihood ratio tests are performed on the training set data only, whereas evaluation with an AUC occurs on a test set. This has the important consequence for our evaluation that a statistically significant improvement in the model's accuracy for the training set, evidenced by the likelihood ratio, may not necessarily translate to an improved result for the AUC on the test set (due to potential overfitting, changes across terms, etc.).

4 RESULTS

We first examine the value of different data sources (RQ1) and then explore how model accuracy improves as we use multiple data sources (RQ2).

4.1 RQ1: Value of Different Data Sources

To determine which data sources are most valuable, first we examine the resultant AUC of each data source when used in isolation and then we determine whether adding each source statistically significantly improves the model using likelihood ratio analysis.

4.1.1 Value of Data Sources in Isolation. Figure 2 provides the resultant AUC for the test set when using each data source individually, collected from the five courses. Recall that CS1 courses do not have any course prerequisites at our institutions, so they do not include results from prerequisite data. Moreover, CS1P did not have any assignments due within the first three weeks of the term, so Figure 2a does not have results on assignments.

On average, prerequisite data (p in Figure 2) returns the best AUC (0.76) out of all data sources. This implies that for courses beyond CS1 (even as early as CS2), prerequisite grades are a powerful predictor of student outcomes. The next highest average AUC (0.70) is provided by clicker data (c), confirming prior work that this data source as a valuable predictor of student outcomes [11, 17]. Online quizzes and assignments provide similar AUC for CS1J and Arch; assignments are better for CS2J; and quizzes are better for DataStr. Although the Average AUC is 0.68 and 0.63 for online quizzes and assignments, respectively, the inconsistencies between courses means no clear trend between online quizzes and assignments has emerged. Overall, the trend is that prerequisites are more valuable than clickers and clickers are more valuable than assignments or quizzes. In DataStr, we see that assignments have effectively no predictive power, as the associated AUC is worse than random guessing (i.e., AUC < 0.5). This is further discussed in Section 5.

Table 3: Statistical Significance of Adding Data Sources

	CS1P	CS1J	CS2J	DataStr	Arch
'p' only	N/A	N/A	***	***	***
Add 'c' to 'p'	***	***	*		***
Add 'a' to 'pc'	N/A		*	*	***
Add 'q' to 'pca'		***			***

$^{*}p < 0.05$, $^{**}p < 0.01$, $^{***}p < 0.001$

4.1.2 Value of Data Sources Relative to Each Other. Next, we determine which data sources add statistical significance to the model accuracy. For example, although online quizzes in isolation have some predictive power, perhaps the variance explained by that data source is already better explained by the clicker data.

To perform this evaluation, we test how well the generated model performs as we add one additional data source at a time. Specifically, the initial model with one data source is compared against a null model with only the intercept term to determine the statistical significance of the initial model. We then determine whether adding an additional data source improves the model for the training set.

Likelihood ratio analysis depends heavily on the order that one adds the data sources. For example, if one adds data sources ordered from least predictive to most predictive, then the least predictive are more apt to be deemed significant. As such, we used the common approach in likelihood ratio analysis of adding data sources from most to least predictive (based on our results from Section 4.1.1). We therefore start with prerequisite data, then sequentially add clicker, assignment, and online quiz data. (We additionally experimented with a variety of different orders, and the overall conclusions remained the same.)

Table 3 shows whether adding each data source makes any statistically significant changes in the generated model. The initial model based only on either prerequisite data (CS2J, DataStr, Arch) or clicker data (CS1P, CS1J) is always meaningful compared to the null model. Clicker data is statistically significant overall, not only when compared to the null model (CS1P, CS1J), but also when added to the model with prerequisite data only (CS2J, DataStr, Arch). Also, adding assignment data is statistically significant in all courses but CS1J. Lastly, adding online quiz data on top of prerequisite, clicker,

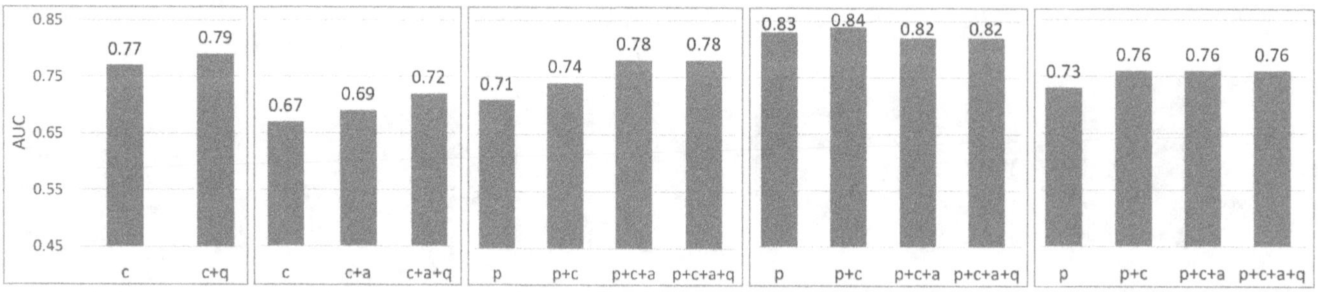

(a) CS1P (b) CS1J (c) CS2J (d) DataStr (e) Arch

Figure 3: AUC When Modeling with Combination of Data Sources

and assignment data statistically significantly improves only the model for two courses (CS1J, Arch).

Overall, this statistical analysis confirms findings from Section 4.1.1 that the value of our data sources, from most to least, is as follows: prerequisites, clickers, assignments, and online quizzes.

4.2 RQ2: Combining Different Data Sources

Similar to Section 4.1.2, we examine how the model improves as we add additional data sources. Rather than focusing on the statistical significance of the model for the training set, however, here we look at the resultant AUC for the test set when building a model with a combination of data sources. Because the statistical analysis in Section 4.1.2 was on the training set only, and the analysis here is for the training and test sets combined, we again note that data sources found "significant" in Section 4.1.2 may not translate to improved accuracy here.

Figure 3 shows how AUC changes as we add more data to the model. Overall, AUC improves as we add more data, except in DataStr and Arch. In those two cases, the model with both prerequisites and clickers performs quite well, but the additional data does not improve (and sometimes hurts) the model accuracy. The fact that prerequisites and clickers are more meaningful than the other sources for DataStr and Arch was also noticeable when we evaluated each data source individually (see Figure 2d and Figure 2e). One might suppose that there is a ceiling to the possible prediction accuracy in our courses, given different student demographics, different topic orderings, and different exams each term. It is unclear whether such a ceiling effect is limiting further prediction accuracy for DataStr.

For CS1P, CS1J, and CS2J, the model generally improves as more data sources are added (with the exception of online quizzes for CS2J). This finding may suggest that the multiple data sources collectively improves accuracy; but one might also argue that accuracy is generally quite high already with just two data sources, and that the additional sources only provide marginal improvements.

5 DISCUSSION

This section discusses implications of our results and provides suggestions for instructors wishing to use various data sources to identify low-performing students. We also explain why we selected these data sources and possible threats to validity of our results.

5.1 Implications

Our work adds to our understanding of how to predict student outcomes by examining the value of different data sources. To our knowledge, this is the first work that uses various data sources, collected in multiple courses across the CS curriculum, from multiple institutions, to perform cross-term predictions.

Prerequisite Grades. Of the four data sources, prerequisite course data is the most predictive. This predictive power relates to the number of prerequisite courses for each course. For instance, CS2J had only one prerequisite (CS1), while Arch and DataStr had two and three, respectively; in turn, the AUC of the prerequisite-only model of CS2J is the lowest, followed by Arch, then by DataStr.

The predictive power of prerequisite grades is unsurprising when one considers that a final grade in a course represents a student's overall academic performance throughout the term. Specifically, the final grade includes direct observations of a student's class performance, often including attendance, assignment grades, midterm exam grades, final exam grades, and so on. Moreover, it likely also captures some underlying factors that lead to student success on these assessments (motivation, study strategies, background knowledge, etc.). Lastly, a single term of data represents a full 10-12 weeks (at our institutions) of student performance. Recall that our other data sources were collected over a comparably brief three-week period. Given these differences in duration, it is somewhat astonishing that our other sources are as powerful as they are.

One important benefit of prerequisites being so predictive for upper-division courses is that this data is available at the beginning of a term, before collecting any data from the course itself. This suggests the possibility of offering support before the course officially begins. For example, refresher sessions could be offered, and students could be emailed to encourage participation.

Clicker Responses. Clicker data is the second best predictor of student performance, supporting prior findings that use clicker data for prediction [11, 17]. Peer Instruction questions may be particularly predictive as they are designed to address core concepts and highlight common misconceptions. In addition, these questions in our courses are graded on participation rather than correctness [16]. This gives students the freedom to represent their understanding accurately, as there is no grade incentive to solicit assistance. For those who have adopted Peer Instruction in their courses, clicker data is automatically available. Scoring clicker questions presents a small overhead, but is likely performed as part of teaching the course. Those not using Peer Instruction, by contrast, could use multiple-choice questions as part of online quizzes instead [11].

Assignments and Online Quizzes. Our AUC results imply that the additional value of assignments or online quizzes beyond prerequisite and clicker data is relatively small. Two exceptions are the addition of assignment and quiz data to CS1J, and the addition of assignment data to CS2J. In each of these courses, neither the clicker-only model (for CS1J) nor the prerequisite-only model (for CS2J) was as predictive as for the other courses, so this may have allowed more room for improvement from additional data sources. Why prerequisite data and clicker data were less predictive for these two classes is enigmatic, and could stem from a variety of factors (key differences in exams across terms, multiple CS1 courses feeding a single CS2 course, quality of clicker questions, etc.). We leave this as a topic for future inquiry. In addition to the AUC results, the likelihood ratio test results showed that online quiz data does not statistically significantly improve the generated model for most courses. Thus, if an instructor already has prerequisite course grades and clicker data, it may not be worth the additional effort to add assignments and online quizzes to a prediction model.

The poor performance of assignments as a predictor of success in DataStr was initially surprising. However, upon reflection, we observed that there were only two DataStr assignments given in the first three weeks of the term: one was a pre-class survey and the other was a programming assignment that is easier than other assignments given later in the course. The relative low difficulty of the programming assignment (and subsequently high grades on average) may explain the lackluster performance of assignments as a predictor of overall course performance.

Combining Data Sources. Overall, our results demonstrate that prediction accuracy often improves when adding additional data sources. When choosing to collect data, instructors may wish to prioritize the more predictive data sources of prerequisites and clicker responses. Instructors may consider augmenting the model with other data sources, with the proviso that accuracy gains may be limited.

5.2 Ease of Collecting Data Sources

We selected the data sources used in this study as they are generally easy to obtain. Three of the sources (clickers, assignments, and quizzes) are often already part of course assessments. The remaining source (prerequisites) is already available in the school database (although we recognize that access to this data may be limited depending on institution). One might be able to obtain grades in prerequisites through a start-of-term survey of students, though there may be concerns about reminding students of previously poor performance at the outset of a new course. These sources differ from some of those used in prior studies, where data was gathered using an extra instrument, such as a survey, pre- or post-test, or programming IDE [3, 29]. In contrast, we anticipate no significant burden for instructors to use the data sources in our study other than retrieving the required data and, in the case of clicker questions, marking the correct answer if not marked.

Prior work has demonstrated a relationship between prior programming knowledge and success in CS1 [9, 28]. We considered using a measure of prior knowledge as an alternative to prerequisite grades but did not do so because the data is a burden for instructors to collect, and because collecting accurate data requires asking students to solve programming-related questions that might be intimidating to those lacking prior knowledge. An alternative to explore in the future may be APCS grades or high school math grades, but in our experience instructors rarely have access to such data.

5.3 Threats to Validity

Although we included multiple courses, both lower- and upper-division, the data from the upper-division courses (DataStr and Arch) were collected only at a single institution. That said, these upper-division courses were taught by different instructors, so our results are not biased to a single instructor. In addition, we used logistic regression as it provided strong prediction accuracy for a binary outcome given only a few features per student. To arrive at that modeling technique, we tried a variety of models commonly used in machine learning (e.g., SVM and random forest) and selected logistic regression based on its consistently strong results. As our findings are based on using logistic regression, our results may be biased by our choice of modeling technique.

6 CONCLUSION

Our work analyzes the predictability of different data sources and how prediction performance improves when combining multiple data sources. We collected students' prerequisite course grades, clicker correctness, assignment grades, and online quiz grades, and applied logistic regression to produce cross-term predictions (as one might do to authentically predict in practice). Overall, our results demonstrate that prerequisite course grades (when available) predict student performance most strongly, followed by clicker data, assignments, and online quizzes. Combining prerequisite and clicker data often improves the model's prediction accuracy; however, adding assignments and quizzes to that already accurate model often does not increase the accuracy further.

This work adds to our knowledge of predicting outcomes in computing by comparing different data sources collected from the same population to determine which are most meaningful. The data sources selected for the work are those generally available to instructors, reducing the barrier for instructors to adopt these techniques. We note also that prerequisite and clicker data are available early: prerequisite data before the start of class, and clicker data from the first lecture (though several weeks of clicker data are likely required for accurate modeling [11]). The findings are generally consistent across five different computing courses (including both lower- and upper-division courses) and are collected from two institutions. Overall, our findings suggest that instructors wishing to identify low-performing students should leverage prerequisite course grades and clicker questions to make that determination.

7 ACKNOWLEDGEMENTS

We greatly appreciate the reviewers for their helpful feedback. This work was supported in part by NSF award 1712508.

REFERENCES

[1] https://www.rdocumentation.org/packages/lmtest/versions/0.9-36/topics/lrtest.

[2] https://www.rdocumentation.org/packages/stats/versions/3.5.1/topics/glm.

[3] A. Ahadi, R. Lister, H. Haapala, and A. Vihavainen. Exploring machine learning methods to automatically identify students in need of assistance. In *Proceedings of the 11th Conference on International Computing Education Research*, pages 121–130, 2015.

[4] A. Anthony and M. Raney. Bayesian network analysis of computer science grade distributions. In *Proceedings of the 43rd Technical Symposium on Computer Science Education*, pages 649–654, 2012.

[5] K. Castro-Wunsch, A. Ahadi, and A. Petersen. Evaluating neural networks as a method for identifying students in need of assistance. In *Proceedings of the 48th Technical Symposium on Computer Science Education*, pages 111–116, 2017.

[6] CRA Enrollment Committee Institution Subgroup. Generation CS: Computer science undergraduate enrollments surge since 2006. Computing Research Association, 2017.

[7] C. H. Crouch and E. Mazur. Peer instruction: Ten years of experience and results. *American Journal of Physics*, 69, 2001.

[8] H. Danielsiek and J. Vahrenhold. Stay on these roads: Potential factors indicating students' performance in a CS2 course. In *Proceedings of the 47th Technical Symposium on Computer Science Education*, pages 12–17, 2016.

[9] D. Hagan and S. Markham. Does it help to have some programming experience before beginning a computing degree program? In *ACM SIGCSE Bulletin*, volume 32, pages 25–28, 2000.

[10] L. Leppänen, J. Leinonen, P. Ihantola, and A. Hellas. Predicting academic success based on learning material usage. In *Proceedings of the 18th Conference on Information Technology Education*, pages 13–18, 2017.

[11] S. N. Liao, D. Zingaro, M. A. Laurenzano, W. G. Griswold, and L. Porter. Lightweight, early identification of at-risk CS1 students. In *Proceedings of the 12th Conference on International Computing Education Research*, pages 123–131, 2016.

[12] A. Lishinski, A. Yadav, J. Good, and R. Enbody. Learning to program: Gender differences and interactive effects of students' motivation, goals, and self-efficacy on performance. In *Proceedings of the 12th Conference on International Computing Education Research*, pages 211–220, 2016.

[13] M. Natrella. NIST/SEMATECH e-handbook of statistical methods. http://www.itl.nist.gov/div898/handbook, 2010.

[14] C. G. Petersen and T. G. Howe. Predicting Academic Success in Introduction to Computers. *Association for Educational Data Systems*, 12(4):182–191, 1979.

[15] L. Porter, C. Bailey Lee, and B. Simon. Halving fail rates using peer instruction: a study of four computer science courses. In *Proceedings of the 44th technical symposium on Computer science education*, pages 177–182, 2013.

[16] L. Porter, D. Bouvier, Q. Cutts, S. Grissom, C. Lee, R. McCartney, D. Zingaro, and B. Simon. A multi-institutional study of peer instruction in introductory computing. In *Proceedings of the 47th Technical Symposium on Computer Science Education*, pages 358–363, 2016.

[17] L. Porter, D. Zingaro, and R. Lister. Predicting student success using fine grain clicker data. In *Proceedings of the 10th Conference on International Computing Education Research*, pages 51–58, 2014.

[18] K. Quille and S. Bergin. Programming: Predicting student success early in CS1. a re-validation and replication study. In *Proceedings of the 23rd Conference on Innovation and Technology in Computer Science Education*, pages 15–20, 2018.

[19] V. Ramalingam, D. LaBelle, and S. Wiedenbeck. Self-efficacy and mental models in learning to program. *SIGCSE Bulletin*, 36:171–175, 2004.

[20] A. Robins. Learning edge momentum: A new account of outcomes. *Computer Science Education*, 20(1):37–71, 2010.

[21] M. M. T. Rodrigo, R. S. Baker, M. C. Jadud, A. C. M. Amarra, T. Dy, M. B. V. Espejo-Lahoz, S. A. L. Lim, S. A. Pascua, J. O. Sugay, and E. S. Tabanao. Affective and behavioral predictors of novice programmer achievement. In *Proceedings of the 14th Conference on Innovation and Technology in Computer Science Education*, pages 156–160, 2009.

[22] V. L. Sauter. Predicting computer programming skill. *Computers & Education*, 10(2):299–302, 1986.

[23] M. Vellukunnel, P. Buffum, K. E. Boyer, J. Forbes, S. Heckman, and K. Mayer-Patel. Deconstructing the discussion forum: Student questions and computer science learning. In *Proceedings of the 48th Technical Symposium on Computer Science Education*, pages 603–608, 2017.

[24] C. Watson and F. W. Li. Failure rates in introductory programming revisited. In *Proceedings of the 19th Conference on Innovation and Technology in Computer Science Education*, pages 39–44, 2014.

[25] C. Watson, F. W. Li, and J. L. Godwin. No tests required: Comparing traditional and dynamic predictors of programming success. In *Proceedings of the 45th Technical Symposium on Computer Science Education*, pages 469–474, 2014.

[26] B. C. Wilson and S. Shrock. Contributing to success in an introductory computer science course: a study of twelve factors. *SIGCSE Bulletin*, 33:184–188, 2001.

[27] J. R. Wilson and K. A. Lorenz. Short history of the logistic regression model. In *Modeling Binary Correlated Responses using SAS, SPSS and R*, pages 17–23, 2015.

[28] D. Zingaro. Peer instruction contributes to self-efficacy in CS1. In *Proceedings of the 45th technical symposium on Computer science education*, pages 373–378, 2014.

[29] D. Zingaro, M. Craig, L. Porter, B. A. Becker, Y. Cao, P. Conrad, D. Cukierman, A. Hellas, D. Loksa, and N. Thota. Achievement goals in CS1: Replication and extension. In *Proceedings of the 49th Technical Symposium on Computer Science Education*, pages 687–692, 2018.

The PyramidSnapshot Challenge: Understanding student process from visual output of programs

Lisa Yan
Stanford University
yanlisa@stanford.edu

Nick McKeown
Stanford University
nickm@stanford.edu

Chris Piech
Stanford University
piech@cs.stanford.edu

ABSTRACT

In the ideal CS1 classroom, we should understand programming process—how student code evolves over time. However, for graphics-based programming assignments, the task of understanding and grading final solutions, let alone thousands of intermediate steps, is incredibly labor-intensive. In this work, we present a challenge, a dataset, and a promising first solution to autonomously use image output to identify functional, intermediate stages of a student solution. By using computer vision techniques to associate visual output of intermediate student code with functional progress, we supplement a lot of the teacher labor associated with understanding graphics-based, open-ended assignments. We hope our publication of the dataset used in our case study sparks discussion in the community on how to analyze programs with visual program output.

CCS CONCEPTS

• Social and professional topics → Computing education; • Computing methodologies → Computer vision;

KEYWORDS

Programming courses; student process; teaching at scale; undergraduate courses; computer vision

ACM Reference Format:

Lisa Yan, Nick McKeown, and Chris Piech. 2019. The PyramidSnapshot Challenge: Understanding student process from visual output of programs. In *Proceedings of 50th ACM Technical Symposium on Computer Science Education, Minneapolis, MN, USA, February 27–March 2, 2019 (SIGCSE'19),* 7 pages. https://doi.org/10.1145/3287324.3287386

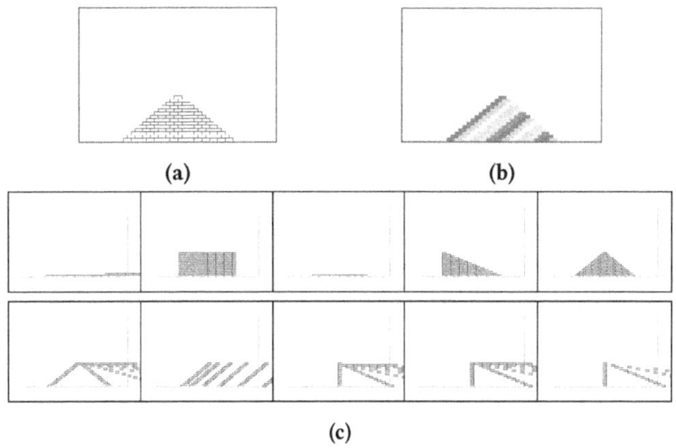

Figure 1: The Pyramid assignment. (a) A full-credit and (b) an extra credit final submission. (c) A series of image outputs of a typical student (top) and a student either tinkering or taking an incorrect path (bottom).

1 INTRODUCTION

First-time CS students learn by programming—they must design an approach, debug their code, and iteratively improve towards a final solution. For a teacher, however, a single timestamped submission per student at the end of this process is insufficient to capture all the intermediate steps a student has taken towards a solution. Even when such progress data is available, it is often intractable to analyze this data in a meaningful way that maps student code to *milestones*, or incremental attempts towards the assignment goal. If teachers could characterize individual and aggregate progress through an assignment, they could better understand how their students think about course concepts.

However, student process is highly variable. Unit testing and other automated assessment tools are often only designed to test functionality of the final submission, and teachers would have to design and engineer additional tests for identifying intermediate milestones. Existing tools are also difficult to tailor to *graphics-based* programming assignments, which have recently gained popularity in many CS1 courses. Due to their open-ended nature—enabling programmers of all levels to get quick, visual feedback in an exploratory environment—the large solution spaces often render unit-testing development or syntax-based code analysis insufficient for final submissions, much less intermediate code snapshots.

Despite the up-front complexity of autonomously analyzing functionality of graphics-based coding tasks, advances in computer vision in other fields have matched [14] and, more recently, surpassed [36] human ability to detect objects from pixel input. In spite of their effectiveness, contemporary vision classification techniques have rarely been applied to student code, as many state-of-the-art techniques are *supervised*—requiring well-labeled, plentiful data, which student assignment data often lacks.

In this work, we marry the two fields of understanding students and improving computer vision by presenting the community with a computer vision challenge rooted in CS education: autonomously characterize student progress on a graphics-based programming task by looking at intermediate image output. The PyramidSnapshot dataset[1] is a large, annotated set of images, each tagged with one

SIGCSE'19, February 27–March 2, 2019, Minneapolis, MN, USA

ACM ISBN 978-1-4503-5890-3/19/02...$15.00
https://doi.org/10.1145/3287324.3287386

[1]Dataset available at http://stanford.edu/~cpiech/pyramidsnapshot/challenge.html.

of 16 milestone labels mapping to functional progress towards the assignment goals of Pyramid, a canonical CS1 graphics-based task (Figure 1). The dataset contains timestamped, program image output of 2633 students over 26 CS1 offerings from the same university, corresponding to 101,636 images of intermediate work, of which 84,127 are annotated with milestones.

Our work is a first step towards a deeper understanding of how students work through graphics-based assignments. We hope that our publication of the PyramidSnapshot dataset is a useful case study on how to prepare graphics-based student data for quantitative functional analysis, as well as how to glean pedagogical insights from such fine-grained data. In this work we describe our approach to labeling a complex dataset by hand, and we show that a neural network-based classifier can extend human labeling effort reasonably well. Finally, we share our insights into how to visualize student process to identify different student work patterns.

2 RELATED WORK

There is a growing body of work on automated assessment tools, which are designed to understand and give feedback to students. Many courses also employ test-driven learning, where students use a provided set of unit tests or write their own using a system like Web-CAT [8, 13]. However, unit tests in general are often brittle, time-consuming to develop, and hard to apply to graphics assignments, which allow for variation among correct solutions. Thus, most contemporary work aims to understand student programs based on abstract syntax tree (AST) structure [10, 19, 21, 29, 32]. While these approaches work for short programs with low complexity, Huang et al. found that implementing AST-based feedback in general is as hard a task as autonomously understanding natural language [11].

To make CS courses more accessible for a diverse set of learners, classrooms should promote multiple paths for learning [31]. Some programming languages inherently encourage exploration, such as Scratch [27] and Alice [7]. For text-based programming languages, on the other hand, creativity is pushed to the assignments, which are often open-ended tasks that support visual output [15, 22, 28, 30]. Flexible assignments support not only *planners*, who strategically plan their route to the answer, but also *tinkerers*, who make incremental, exploratory steps towards the solution [3]. Assignment work patterns are often strong indicators of student performance in the course, from debugging behavior [17] and subgoal planning [20] to likelihood for plagiarism [35] and amount of tinkering [5].

It is difficult to autonomously understand the final solution that a student submits. It is even harder to derive insights from the process of how a student solution evolves over time. Existing work that characterizes student work patterns often use low-level indicators of student progress, such as code diffs, completion times, or errors [1, 2, 5, 6, 12]. While there have been studies on functional progress of student solutions in variable-constrained or block-based environments [24, 25, 33], our work is the first to identify program functionality over the course of an open-ended graphics assignment. We circumvent the difficulty of AST-based functionality analysis by using *pixel-based* visual program output.

In 2013, a team of researchers from DeepMind demonstrated that a convolutional neural network based algorithm could learn to play Atari games as well as humans using only pixel output [18]. Because the Atari games used in the DeepMind paper are very similar in complexity to the outputs of assignments typical in CS1 and CS2 classes—and some of the Atari games are in fact classic homework assignments [22]—we have reason to believe that modern computer vision algorithms should be able to understand the output of our student's graphical programs from the pixel level. Despite this potential, to the best of our knowledge, the capacity for understanding graphics prior to this paper has been used mostly to play and rarely to educate. Open datasets have been integral to the early evolution of computer vision techniques [9, 14, 16]; we hope that our dataset will help the CS education community evolve.

3 DATA

The Pyramid assignment is a sub-problem in the second week of a 10-week CS1 course at Stanford. The assignment is scoped as the students' first exposure to variables, object manipulation, and for-loop indexing. As part of their individual, take-home assignment, students use Java's ACM graphics library to draw bricks on the screen and construct a pyramid shape (Figure 1a), and they are awarded extra credit points if they can extend the correct pyramid (Figure 1b). The solution requires nested loops and the computation of several intermediate variables:

```
public void run()            // draw a pyramid
  for(int i = 0; i < BRICKS_IN_BASE; i++)
    // calculate row variables
    int nBricks = BRICKS_IN_BASE - i;
    int rowWidth = nBricks * BRICK_WIDTH;
    double rowY = HEIGHT-(i+1)*BRICK_HEIGHT;
    double rowX = (WIDTH - rowWidth)/2.0;
    // draw a single row
    for(int j = 0; j < nBricks; j++)
      // add a single brick
      double x = rowX + j * BRICK_WIDTH;
      rect(x, rowY, BRICK_WIDTH, BRICK_HEIGHT);
```

To collect intermediate student data, we modified the Eclipse Integrated Development Environment (IDE) to support *snapshotting* of student code as they work through the assignment. [25]. The IDE manages a git repository that stores a snapshot of student code whenever a student compiles and runs the assignment, meaning that snapshot frequency could be on the order of minutes when a student is actively working. Then, when the student submits their final program for grading, the IDE automatically packages up the repository and stores it on the course server.

In the CS1 course studied, the Pyramid assignment has been used for many years, with little variation in assignment scope and grading rubric. We analyzed 2,633 student submissions from as far back as 2007 (where the bulk of data was collected between 2012 and 2014) by compiling and running all Pyramid code files in git repositories to generate timestamped images. Figure 3 shows the distributions of the number of snapshots ($\mu = 52, \sigma = 59$) and hours spent ($\mu = 1.7, \sigma = 1.5$) for each pyramid submission. Of the 138,531 snapshots in our dataset, we successfully generated 101,636 images; 36,895 snapshots had runtime or compile errors.

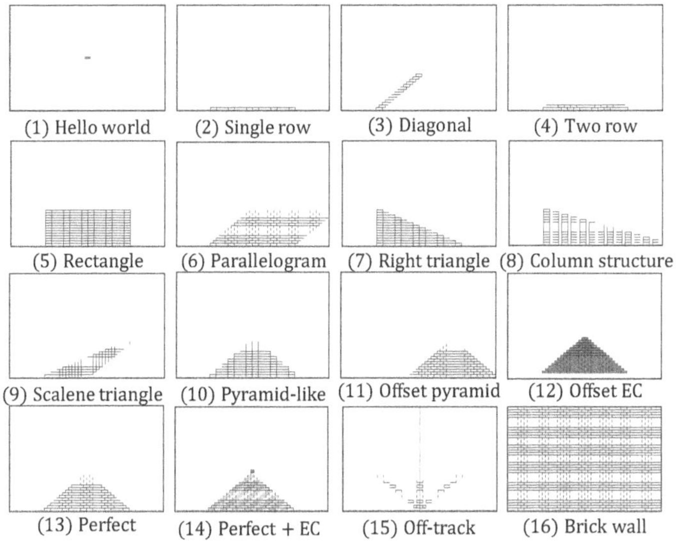

(a)

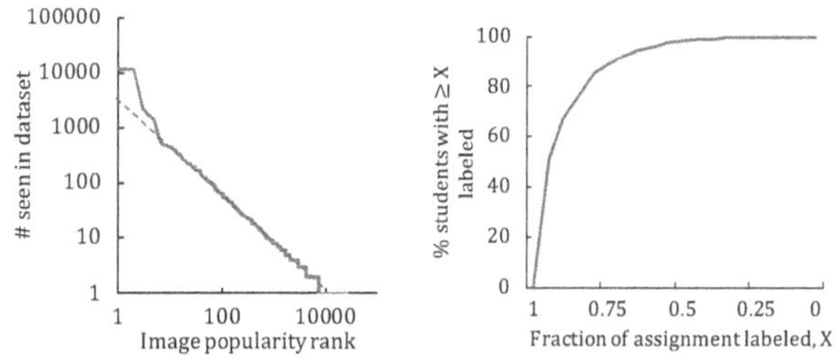

(b) (c)

	# Snapshots	Unique images	Effort score
Total	138531	27220	5.1
Labeled	84127	12077	7.0
Unlabeled	17509	15143	1.2
Error	36895	–	–

(d)

Figure 2: (a) Examples from the 16 milestone category labels in the PyramidSnapshot dataset; EC stands for Extra Credit. (b) Zipf distribution of the dataset images. (c) CDF of the fraction of a repository labeled with the effort strategy in Section 3.2. (d) Label coverage of the PyramidSnapshot dataset.

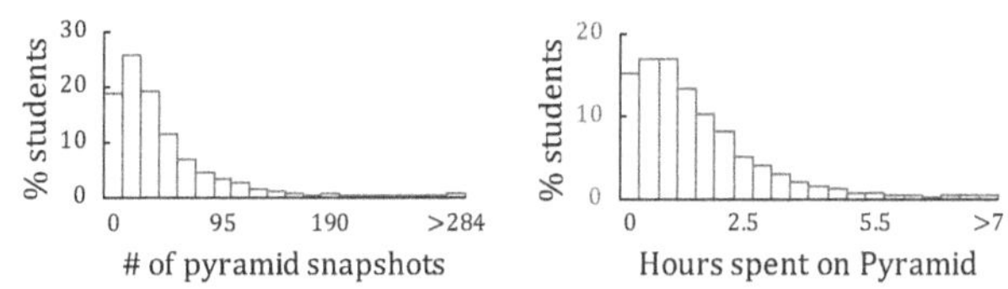

(a) (b)

Figure 3: Pyramid work time analysis: (a) number of snapshots per student; (b) hours spent on the assignment.

3.1 Dataset complexity

For a graphics-based assignment like Pyramid, we claim that using image output to represent the functionality of student work is less complex—and therefore easier to work with—than using a text-based representation like Abstract Syntax Trees (ASTs). Like many other coding assignment datasets that have been analyzed in the past, the frequency distributions of both the Pyramid assignment code Abstract Syntax Trees (ASTs) and the image output files follow Zipf's law, the same distribution as natural language. One of the implications of this insight is that the exponent s of the Zipf fit can be used as a measure of the complexity of a programming dataset, where a higher exponent means that a dataset has a higher probability of observing the same solution more than once and is thus less complex [23]. The frequency distribution of Pyramid ASTs fits to a Zipf exponent $s = 0.57$, which is notably more complex when compared to logistic regression implementations ($s = 1.82$) and CS1 first week homeworks ($s = 2.67$) [26]. On the other hand, the Pyramid *image outputs* have Zipf distribution with exponent $s = 0.78$ (Figure 2b), suggesting that modern tools for understanding images may be more effective than an AST-based approach for understanding functionality of intermediate solutions.

3.2 Labeling milestones efficiently

The PyramidSnapshot dataset comes with *milestone labels*; that is, each image is categorized into one of our 16 visual categories of intermediate work. Figure 2a shows an example image for each of these milestones. Our milestone labels are mutually exclusive by design: an image must be either a scalene triangle or a pyramid-like image object, for example. We understand that there could be potential overlap in these milestones, but we chose exclusive labels because separable labels enable easier, clearer analysis. It is worth keeping in mind that there is a huge variation of images within each category; for example, Milestone 15 (Off-track) was marked for any image that was unable to be categorized by the other labels.

It would be an insurmountable task by a team of three researchers to label over 101,000 images in our PyramidSnapshot dataset. However, we observe from the Zipf distribution of the data (Figure 2b that only 27,220 (27%) of these are unique. Furthermore, the perfect pyramid (Milestone 13) in our dataset is the most frequent and occurs over 11,000 times across all student work, and the ten most popular images cover 20,219 images (20%) in our 101,636 image dataset. Using the Zipf distribution, one can label unique images to milestones in order of popularity in the dataset; a single researcher labeled 12,077 unique images with corresponding milestones in 20 hours over three days, covering 84,127 images (83%) of the actual dataset (Figure 2d). The *effort score* in Figure 2d characterizes the gain of labeling a unique image as the frequency of that image appearing in the overall dataset; the average effort score of unique images labeled was about 7 repeated images. On the other hand, each remaining unlabeled unique image appeared on average 1.2 times in the dataset, meaning that we would not have gained much with this labeling strategy had we continued into the tail of the distribution. Figure 2c shows that about 90% of students have at least 75% of their repositories labeled after using this strategy of labeling more popular images first.

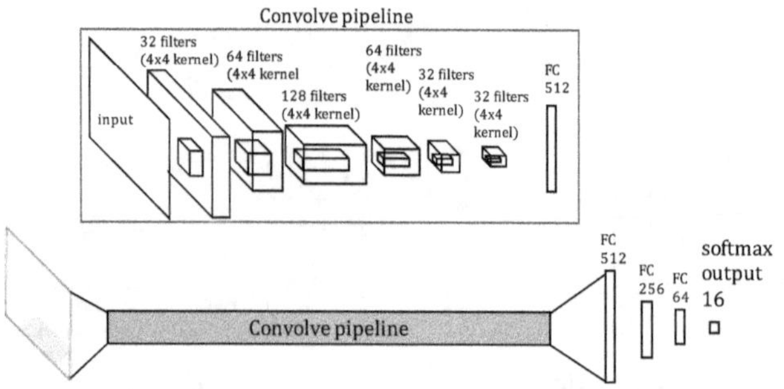

Figure 4: The neural network for milestone classification.

4 METHOD

We realize that assigning intermediate images to milestones presents a scalability issue for other assignments, even if we use image frequency to reduce labeling effort. We therefore explore how the accuracy of a classification model works as we vary N, the number of most popular images that we label, defined as our *training set* size. In this section, we define potential models for classifying intermediate snapshots by milestone, and we also outline an approach to answering a secondary question—whether classifying image output is sufficient for grading final submissions.

4.1 Classifying milestones

Given a training set of the N most popular images, we consider three models for classifying our images with milestones. Our first approach is based on the premise of unit testing: select one representative image for each milestone, and for each test image, predict a milestone only if the test image pixels exactly match that of the reference; otherwise it predicts nothing. We keep $N = 15$ unit testing images; we do not save a representative image for the Off-track milestone (Milestone 15). The second approach, K-nearest neighbors (KNN), is a common baseline used for computer vision [14]; for each test image, define the K nearest neighbors as the K images from the reference training set that have minimum sum-squared-difference (pixel-wise), and predict the most common milestone out of the nearest neighbors. Our third approach is a deep learning approach: train a convolutional neural network (Figure 4) to return the most likely milestone label based on processing a grayscaled, downsampled image of dimension $346 \times 477 \times 1$ with a 1.2-million parameter model. The model parameters are trained by optimizing a softmax cross-entropy loss over the N most popular images.

4.2 Extending classification to final solutions

In parallel with our goal to capture functionality of intermediate work, we also want to study whether an image-based, deep-learning approach is effective for autograding final submissions. From anecdotal experience, graphics assignments tend to be more difficult and time-consuming to grade than their command-line counterparts, mainly because the set of possible correct graphical outputs is often not well-defined. To grade our Pyramid assignment, a grader runs student final submission code with five predetermined sets of parameters which vary the brick size and Pyramid dimensions, then evaluates the student on a rubric set of 9 items, where for each item the grader marks a binary pass/fail by looking at both the student's code and five test results. We compare two approaches; the first is a unit-test-based model, where we have one counterexample image per rubric and we compare pixel-wise for exact match of output images. The second is a convolutional neural network approach with a similar structure to the milestone predictor in Figure 4; we train one pipeline for each of the five test output images and replace the classification layer with a sigmoid binary predictor per rubric; our model has 5.1 million parameters. We use a slightly different (non-public) dataset of 4383 Pyramid final code submissions with grades between 2009 and 2017.

5 RESULTS

To evaluate our three approaches to classifying milestones from graphical image input, we trained each classifier with a varying size of N on our training set of the most popular images, and we evaluated its overall accuracy on two datasets: the *validation set*, composed of the top 11,000 popular images (corresponding to 70% of our image dataset), and the *tail set*, composed of the remaining 1,077 labeled images. We use the validation set to decide which classifiers work for common snapshots; the tail set accuracy is an indicator for whether our classifiers work on rarely seen snapshots.

We first discuss accuracy results on the validation set. The results for each classifier with the best choice of training set size N is reported as overall accuracy in classifying all 16 milestones in Figure 5a; we can immediately see that our neural network outperforms the other two unit-test and KNN ($K = 100$) models. We also report a higher-level statistic of overall accuracy over *knowledge stages*, which reduces our 16-dimension milestone space into five meaningful stages of knowledge, organized based on whether students are working on a single loop (Stage 1), a nested loop (Stage 2), adjusting brick offset within the nested loop (Stage 3), or completed with the assignment and going beyond what is expected (Stage 4). The remaining four stages are grouped as "Other/Off-track." We note that higher-level abstracted knowledge stages are more meaningful for a human grader as such stages will not differentiate between two milestones associated with the same level of student cognitive understanding. In Figure 5b we report our neural network accuracy for predicting a milestone that is in the same knowledge stage as the correct milestone label; the model reports at least 70% accuracy for Stages 1, 2, and 3, which are the most formative ones in terms of determining student progress towards the assignment goal, and therefore the low accuracy in identifying Stage 4 is acceptable. However, we realize that there is room for accuracy improvement across all knowledge stages for future work.

To understand how the model connects image to label, we use the t-SNE algorithm to compress the model's internal image representation into a 2-D, clustered visualization. Figure 5c shows that our image embeddings roughly cluster by their milestone; however, there are some perfect pyramid images (Milestone 13, red) hidden among the Hello world milestones (Milestone 1, blue). Upon checking these incorrectly classified images, we found that some of them depicted a very small pyramid, which could easily be misclassified as a single block, but others were simply incorrectly placed in the embedding space. Our hypothesis is that since unique images of single bricks dominate our dataset, our model has a tendency to predict Milestone 1 in the absence of any other strong indicators.

Overall accuracy	Unit test (N = 15)	KNN (K = 100, N = 11000)	Neural network (N = 11000)
By milestone (16 milestones)	.275	.037	.562
By knowledge stage (5 stages)	.275	.552	.649

(a)

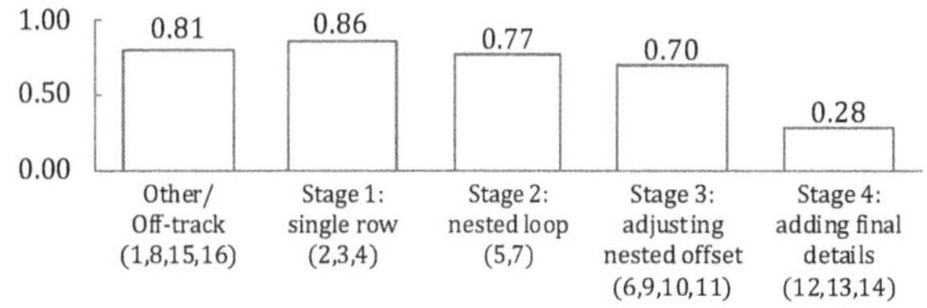

(b)

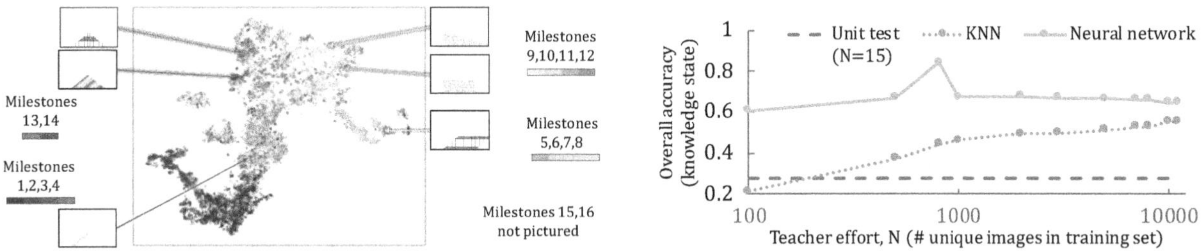

(c) (d)

Figure 5: Milestone classification results. (a) Accuracy of each model (with training set size N) by milestone and by knowledge stage on the 11,000 most popular images. A closer analysis of the neural network model (N = 11000) shown by (b) Accuracy breakdown by knowledge stage, and (c) t-SNE plot of model embeddings, color-coded by milestone. (d) Overall accuracy (by knowledge stage) of KNN and neural network models with varying training set sizes N.

	Unit test image		Neural network	
	F1	Acc	F1	Acc
Train	0.15	0.95	0.65	0.97
Test	0.15	0.95	0.50	0.96

Figure 6: Average accuracy and F1 scores when predicting rubrics on final submissions.

We realize that it may seem intractable to extend our approach to other graphics-based assignments due to the sheer *effort* required to label the intermediate images for training data. We use the labeling scheme from Section 3.2 to create a training set consisting of the N most popular images; we then evaluate the performance of the KNN and neural network models with different training set sizes N, and we evaluate their performance on the top 11,000 most popular images (Figure 5d). Naturally, the KNN model performs best with a huge dataset, but what is surprising is that the neural network already outperforms the other two models even with only $N = 100$ items in the training set. There is a small peak at $N = 800$ for the neural network model; this artifact is because the model correctly predicted the milestones of some high-rank images, therefore weighting the accuracy upwards; this trend goes away when we compare accuracy across unique images only. In general, the takeaway that we can get just over 60% accuracy with just $N = 100$ labeled data points is very promising.

We also evaluated our images solely on the tail images in the distribution, the 1,077 least popular (labeled) images in the tail set. All three models performed poorly: Unit test reported 0% accuracy (due to its pixel-based exact match strategy), and both KNN and our neural network model performed with less than 1% accuracy for almost all choices of our training set. This is a huge area in which future models can improve; the more reliable we are in predicting the tail of our model, the more confident we can be in imputing milestone labels on unlabeled images in our dataset.

Final submissions evaluation. We report in Figure 6 our results of running our two final submission grading models. The average F1 scores and accuracies are evaluated on a validation set of 438 submissions; the neural network was trained on a set of 3945 submissions, and the unit-test model had 7 exact match reference images. Both models have very high average accuracies; however, this is because very few students get marked off for any of the 9 items in the rubric (the average frequency of incorrect rubric items was 10%). We therefore prioritize the F1 score metric, which is a harmonic mean of the precision and recall scores (measuring false positive and false negatives). We notice that the F1 scores for our neural network model are low for two reasons: first, several rubric items were code-based student misconceptions (e.g., incorrectly indexing either the inner or outer loop of a two-level nested loop, leading to indistinguishable final image outputs). Second, the rubrics marked for two different students with the same set of five unit-test images could vary widely. For example, for the 1485 student solutions that had the correct image output for all five brick configurations, there were at least 20 different rubric assignments, some with at most three rubric items marked off. Our image output-based approaches are not reliable enough to grade CS1 graphics assignments, but they are useful for labeling intermediate milestone work.

6 DISCUSSION

By splitting our milestone classification task into two phases—human labeling and deep-learning-facilitated labeling, we are able to achieve modest success on predicting the correct milestone label for any image. We use our milestone information to gauge how much time a student spends on average in each of our knowledge stages to decide which content to emphasize in classroom teaching.

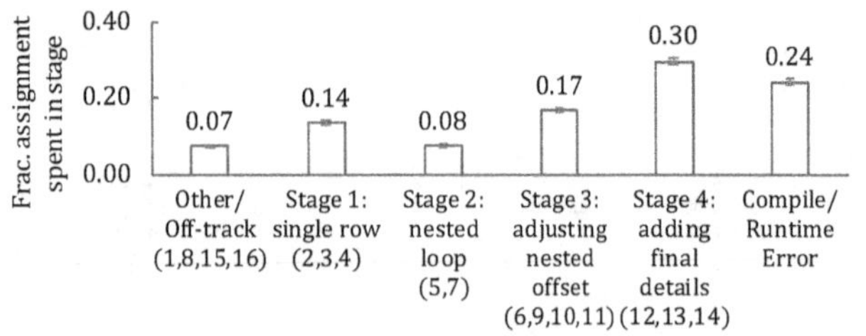

Figure 7: Average amount of assignment (by number of commits) that students spent in different knowledge stages.

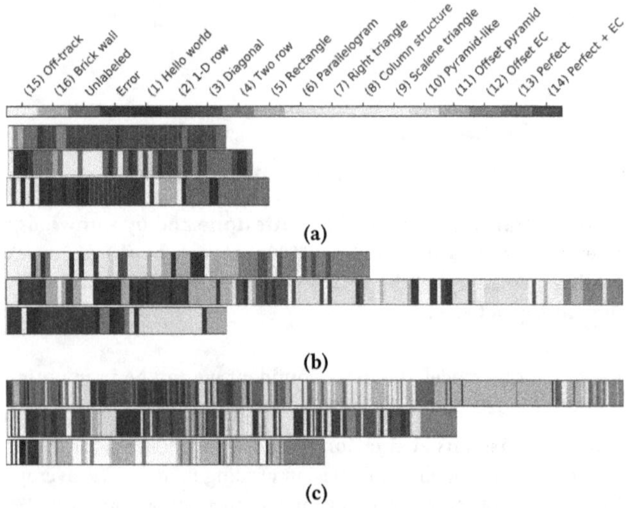

Figure 8: Student work patterns during the Pyramid assignment; a student's work is displayed as a horizontal strip over time, where each vertical slice is one snapshot. Three students respectively scoring in the (a) 99th percentile, and (b) 3rd percentile or lower on the midterm exam; (c) three students with long trajectories of work. Best viewed in color.

Figure 7 graphs the mean (±1 SE) fraction of commits spent in each of the knowledge stages, where we use our neural network predictor to *impute* the knowledge stages of the remaining 12% of the dataset, and the number of commits student spends each stage before moving on. We observe that on average, students spend 17% of their time in Stage 3, where they must manipulate the loop index to correctly offset blocks in different rows of the Pyramid. Understandably, students spend most of their time (30%) adding final details and finishing up (Stage 4). Knowing this time distribution can inform which concepts students struggle with; after this analysis, instructors devoted more time in class to discussing loop index manipulation skills needed for Stage 3.

We can also use milestone information to get a holistic view of students' functional progress over the Pyramid assignment; we show this via a case study of students based on their milestone traversal behavior. In Figure 8, we impute labels and visualize student work over time as a heatmap that indicates when students are in Stage 1 or 2 (blue colors), Stage 3 (yellow and green), or Stage 4 (red). After imputing the milestones on the remaining unlabeled snapshots, we found some very telling examples of how different students work on the assignment over time. When we compare high-performing students (Figure 8a) with low-performing (Figure 8b), we observe that these groups of students tend to concentrate their work in different stages. All three high-performing students have few snapshots in Stages 2 and 3, instead spending a significant portion of their time working on the perfect pyramid (Milestone 13). In contrast, the low-performing students spend a large fraction of time in Stage 3's early milestones that emphasize brick offset adjustments. One student also fails to reach the correct solution, ending instead in the offset pyramid milestone (Milestone 11).

From our data, we can also visually discern between certain students who were struggling to get anything working and those who were tinkering [5, 31]—where a student spends a long time at a particular knowledge stage not because they are stuck, but because they are exploring the solution space. Figure 8c shows three students that have used over 100 snapshots for the Pyramid assignment. The first two students spend a large portion of their time working in Stage 1. In contrast, the last student spends most of their time in a late Stage 3 milestone, the offset pyramid (Milestone 11), suggesting some sort of tinkering and adjustment. When we connect these work patterns with their performance on the midterm, the first two students score in the 19th and 21st percentile, respectively, while the third student scores in the 73rd percentile.

7 FUTURE WORK AND CONCLUSION

Our anecdotal analysis of this dataset suggests there is merit to observing snapshot histories with respect to milestone evolution. Having functional labels for snapshotted student data can be used in conjunction with existing indicators of progress, like error messages and code length [4, 5, 12], to predict student performance. As future work, we can cluster students and identify in aggregate which work patterns are correlated with stronger student performance. Future classrooms may evaluate student process in addition to final submission correctness; the color-coded heat map characterizing functionality over time provides a quick reference for instructors to detect which snapshots are pivotal for student learning. Towards this end, we have deployed the image label predictor as part of an in-classroom tool that allows teachers to interact with students and discuss the meta-process of how they program [34]. In this work, we have only scratched the surface of pedagogical insights that can be gleaned from more detailed analyses of student progress; by publishing our dataset, we hope that other researchers can improve upon our work to better understand how students code.

We realize that labeling intermediate snapshots is a human effort that is time-intensive for teachers and researchers. To see whether our approach was tractable for other assignments, we analyzed the tradeoffs between human labeling the most popular images and subsequent neural network-based labeling of remaining images. In our study, a simple neural network model trained on the 100 most popular images performs relatively well, suggesting that labeling for functionality is not as daunting as it may seem. Yet our biggest contribution is publishing the labeled PyramidSnapshot dataset used in this work as a new, annotated benchmark with two benefits to the community: to evaluate autonomous prediction for functionality of intermediate student program output, and to analyze student work patterns with greater detail than before.

REFERENCES

[1] Alireza Ahadi, Raymond Lister, Heikki Haapala, and Arto Vihavainen. 2015. Exploring Machine Learning Methods to Automatically Identify Students in Need of Assistance. In *Proceedings of the Eleventh Annual International Conference on International Computing Education Research (ICER '15)*. ACM, New York, NY, USA, 121–130. https://doi.org/10.1145/2787622.2787717

[2] Brett A. Becker. 2016. A New Metric to Quantify Repeated Compiler Errors for Novice Programmers. In *Proceedings of the 2016 ACM Conference on Innovation and Technology in Computer Science Education (ITiCSE '16)*. ACM, New York, NY, USA, 296–301. https://doi.org/10.1145/2899415.2899463

[3] Matthew Berland, Taylor Martin, Tom Benton, Carmen Petrick Smith, and Don Davis. 2013. Using Learning Analytics to Understand the Learning Pathways of Novice Programmers. *Journal of the Learning Sciences* 22, 4 (2013), 564–599. https://doi.org/10.1080/10508406.2013.836655

[4] Paulo Blikstein. 2011. Using Learning Analytics to Assess Students' Behavior in Open-ended Programming Tasks. In *Proceedings of the 1st International Conference on Learning Analytics and Knowledge (LAK '11)*. ACM, New York, NY, USA, 110–116. https://doi.org/10.1145/2090116.2090132

[5] Paulo Blikstein, Marcelo Worsley, Chris Piech, Mehran Sahami, Steven Cooper, and Daphne Koller. 2014. Programming pluralism: Using learning analytics to detect patterns in the learning of computer programming. *Journal of the Learning Sciences* 23, 4 (2014), 561–599.

[6] Adam S. Carter, Christopher D. Hundhausen, and Olusola Adesope. 2015. The Normalized Programming State Model: Predicting Student Performance in Computing Courses Based on Programming Behavior. In *Proceedings of the Eleventh Annual International Conference on International Computing Education Research (ICER '15)*. ACM, New York, NY, USA, 141–150. https://doi.org/10.1145/2787622.2787710

[7] Wanda P. Dann, Stephen Cooper, and Randy Pausch. 2008. *Learning To Program with Alice* (2 ed.). Prentice Hall Press, Upper Saddle River, NJ, USA.

[8] Stephen H. Edwards and Manuel A. Perez-Quinones. 2008. Web-CAT: Automatically Grading Programming Assignments. In *Proceedings of the 13th Annual Conference on Innovation and Technology in Computer Science Education (ITiCSE '08)*. ACM, New York, NY, USA, 328–328. https://doi.org/10.1145/1384271.1384371

[9] Mark Everingham, Luc Gool, Christopher K. Williams, John Winn, and Andrew Zisserman. 2010. The Pascal Visual Object Classes (VOC) Challenge. *Int. J. Comput. Vision* 88, 2 (June 2010), 303–338. https://doi.org/10.1007/s11263-009-0275-4

[10] David Hovemeyer, Arto Hellas, Andrew Petersen, and Jaime Spacco. 2016. Control-flow-only abstract syntax trees for analyzing students' programming progress. In *Proceedings of the 2016 ACM Conference on International Computing Education Research*. ACM, 63–72.

[11] Jonathan Huang, Chris Piech, Andy Nguyen, and Leonidas Guibas. 2013. Syntactic and functional variability of a million code submissions in a machine learning mooc. In *AIED 2013 Workshops Proceedings Volume*. 25.

[12] Matthew C. Jadud. 2006. Methods and Tools for Exploring Novice Compilation Behaviour. In *Proceedings of the Second International Workshop on Computing Education Research (ICER '06)*. ACM, New York, NY, USA, 73–84. https://doi.org/10.1145/1151588.1151600

[13] David S Janzen and Hossein Saiedian. 2006. Test-driven learning: intrinsic integration of testing into the CS/SE curriculum. In *ACM SIGCSE Bulletin*, Vol. 38. ACM, 254–258.

[14] Alex Krizhevsky, Ilya Sutskever, and Geoffrey E Hinton. 2012. ImageNet classification with deep convolutional neural networks. In *Advances in neural information processing systems*. 1097–1105.

[15] Lucas Layman, Laurie Williams, and Kelli Slaten. 2007. Note to Self: Make Assignments Meaningful. In *Proceedings of the 38th SIGCSE Technical Symposium on Computer Science Education (SIGCSE '07)*. ACM, New York, NY, USA, 459–463. https://doi.org/10.1145/1227310.1227466

[16] Yann LeCun and Corinna Cortes. 2010. MNIST handwritten digit database. (2010). http://yann.lecun.com/exdb/mnist/

[17] Colleen M. Lewis. 2012. The Importance of Students' Attention to Program State: A Case Study of Debugging Behavior. In *Proceedings of the Ninth Annual International Conference on International Computing Education Research (ICER '12)*. ACM, New York, NY, USA, 127–134. https://doi.org/10.1145/2361276.2361301

[18] Volodymyr Mnih, Koray Kavukcuoglu, David Silver, Alex Graves, Ioannis Antonoglou, Daan Wierstra, and Martin Riedmiller. 2013. Playing Atari with Deep Reinforcement Learning. *arXiv preprint arXiv:1312.5602* (2013).

[19] Bassam Mokbel, Sebastian Gross, Benjamin Paassen, Niels Pinkwart, and Barbara Hammer. 2013. Domain-independent proximity measures in intelligent tutoring systems. In *Educational Data Mining 2013*.

[20] Briana B. Morrison, Lauren E. Margulieux, and Mark Guzdial. 2015. Subgoals, Context, and Worked Examples in Learning Computing Problem Solving. In *Proceedings of the Eleventh Annual International Conference on International Computing Education Research (ICER '15)*. ACM, New York, NY, USA, 21–29. https://doi.org/10.1145/2787622.2787733

[21] Lili Mou, Ge Li, Lu Zhang, Tao Wang, and Zhi Jin. 2016. Convolutional Neural Networks over Tree Structures for Programming Language Processing. In *AAAI*, Vol. 2. 4.

[22] Nick Parlante, Steven A Wolfman, Lester I McCann, Eric Roberts, Chris Nevison, John Motil, Jerry Cain, and Stuart Reges. 2006. Nifty assignments. In *ACM SIGCSE Bulletin*, Vol. 38. ACM, 562–563.

[23] Steven T. Piantadosi. 2014. Zipf's word frequency law in natural language: A critical review and future directions. *Psychonomic Bulletin & Review* 21, 5 (2014), 1112–1130. https://doi.org/10.3758/s13423-014-0585-6

[24] Chris Piech, Jonathan Huang, Andy Nguyen, Mike Phulsuksombati, Mehran Sahami, and Leonidas Guibas. 2015. Learning Program Embeddings to Propagate Feedback on Student Code. In *Proceedings of the 32nd International Conference on Machine Learning (Proceedings of Machine Learning Research)*, Francis Bach and David Blei (Eds.), Vol. 37. PMLR, Lille, France, 1093–1102.

[25] Chris Piech, Mehran Sahami, Daphne Koller, Steve Cooper, and Paulo Blikstein. 2012. Modeling how students learn to program. In *Proceedings of the 43rd ACM technical symposium on Computer Science Education*. ACM, 153–160.

[26] Chris J. Piech. 2016. *Uncovering Patterns in Student Work: Machine Learning to Understand Human Learning*. Ph.D. Dissertation. Stanford University.

[27] Mitchel Resnick, John Maloney, Andrés Monroy-Hernández, Natalie Rusk, Evelyn Eastmond, Karen Brennan, Amon Millner, Eric Rosenbaum, Jay Silver, Brian Silverman, and Yasmin Kafai. 2009. Scratch: Programming for All. *Commun. ACM* 52, 11 (Nov. 2009), 60–67. https://doi.org/10.1145/1592761.1592779

[28] Eric Roberts. 2000. Strategies for Encouraging Individual Achievement in Introductory Computer Science Courses. In *Proceedings of the Thirty-first SIGCSE Technical Symposium on Computer Science Education (SIGCSE '00)*. ACM, New York, NY, USA, 295–299. https://doi.org/10.1145/330908.331873

[29] Stephanie Rogers, Dan Garcia, John F. Canny, Steven Tang, and Daniel Kang. 2014. *ACES: Automatic Evaluation of Coding Style*. Master's thesis. EECS Department, University of California, Berkeley. http://www2.eecs.berkeley.edu/Pubs/TechRpts/2014/EECS-2014-77.html

[30] Elizabeth Sweedyk, Marianne deLaet, Michael C. Slattery, and James Kuffner. 2005. Computer Games and CS Education: Why and How. In *Proceedings of the 36th SIGCSE Technical Symposium on Computer Science Education (SIGCSE '05)*. ACM, New York, NY, USA, 256–257. https://doi.org/10.1145/1047344.1047433

[31] Sherry Turkle and Seymour Papert. 1990. Epistemological Pluralism: Styles and Voices within the Computer Culture. *Signs: Journal of Women in Culture and Society* 16, 1 (1990), 128–157. https://doi.org/10.1086/494648

[32] Ke Wang, Rishabh Singh, and Zhendong Su. 2018. Dynamic Neural Program Embedding for Program Repair. *International Conference on Learning Representations* (2018).

[33] Lisa Wang, Angela Sy, Larry Liu, and Chris Piech. 2017. Deep Knowledge Tracing On Programming Exercises. In *Proceedings of the Fourth (2017) ACM Conference on Learning @ Scale (L@S '17)*. ACM, New York, NY, USA, 201–204. https://doi.org/10.1145/3051457.3053985

[34] Lisa Yan, Annie Hu, and Chris Piech. 2019. Pensieve: Feedback on Coding Process for Novices. In *Proceedings of the 50th ACM Technical Symposium on Computer Science Education (SIGCSE '19)*. ACM, New York, NY, USA. https://doi.org/10.1145/3287324.3287483

[35] Lisa Yan, Nick McKeown, Mehran Sahami, and Chris Piech. 2018. TMOSS: Using Intermediate Assignment Work to Understand Excessive Collaboration in Large Classes. In *Proceedings of the 49th ACM Technical Symposium on Computer Science Education (SIGCSE '18)*. ACM, New York, NY, USA, 110–115. https://doi.org/10.1145/3159450.3159490

[36] Barret Zoph, Vijay Vasudevan, Jonathon Shlens, and Quoc V Le. 2017. Learning transferable architectures for scalable image recognition. *arXiv preprint arXiv:1707.07012* (2017).

Approaches for Coordinating eTextbooks, Online Programming Practice, Automated Grading, and More into One Course

Margaret Ellis, Clifford A. Shaffer, and Stephen H. Edwards
Virginia Tech
Blacksburg, VA
maellis1|shaffer|s.edwards@vt.edu

ABSTRACT

We share approaches for coordinating the use of many online educational tools within a CS2 course, including an eTextbook, automated grading system, programming practice website, diagramming tool, and debugger. These work with other commonly used tools such as a response system, forum, version control system, and our learning management system. We describe a number of approaches to deal with the potential negative effects of adopting so many tools. To improve student success we scaffold tool use by staging the addition of tools and by introducing individual tools in phases, we test tool assignments before student use, and we adapt tool use based on student feedback and performance. We streamline course management by consulting mentors who have used the tools before, starting small with room to grow, and choosing tools that simplify student account and grade management across multiple tools.

CCS CONCEPTS

• **Social and professional topics → Computing education**;

KEYWORDS

tool use, CS2, instruction, course management

ACM Reference Format:

Margaret Ellis, Clifford A. Shaffer, and Stephen H. Edwards. 2019. Approaches for Coordinating eTextbooks, Online Programming Practice, Automated Grading, and More into One Course. In *Proceedings of the 50th ACM Technical Symposium on Computer Science Education (SIGCSE '19), February 27-March 2, 2019, Minneapolis, MN, USA.* ACM, New York, NY, USA, 7 pages. https://doi.org/10.1145/3287324.3287487

1 INTRODUCTION

With continuing advances in CS Education Research, there is an ever-growing collection of high-quality online educational tools available to instructors for use in their courses. In this experience report we share our experience integrating several such tools into a CS2 course, and describe approaches that others can use to manage the process of adopting many such tools in an education setting. We describe the context of our course and our experiences with using WebCat [1], OpenDSA[2], CodeWorkout[3], and Lucid Chart [4], all in conjunction with more typical educational tools such as Canvas (our LMS), Eclipse and iClickers. We want students to take advantage of available tools that allow them to explore, practice, tinker, and build professional skills. Yet we do not want to overwhelm either the students or the instructional team. The overarching approaches we used can be grouped into two main categories: 1) improving instruction and student learning, and 2) streamlining course management for the instructor. To improve instruction and student learning we use scaffolding to phase in the use of multiple tools and for learning individual tools incrementally. We test tool-based assignments before student use to verify clarity and correctness, gauge difficulty, and assess the amount of time necessary to complete the assignment. We also modify our use of individual tools based on student experiences and feedback.

Our approaches to streamline course management for instructors help save time and reduce the risk of error. When integrating multiple tools into this course we have benefited from consulting mentors who have used a given tool before. We also start small with room to grow in the use of more complex tools, and we prefer to choose tools that simplify student account and grade management across multiple tools. We will report on our specific experiences and within that we describe some guiding principles that can be applied generally in various instructional settings.

2 BACKGROUND

Student success has been linked to student self-efficacy, and targeting instruction to improve student confidence with a specific task can improve student persistence [10]. A key objective of our CS2 course design is to improve student self-efficacy, so our approach to integrating and using tools is done with this in mind. Four key areas of influence impact self-efficacy: vicarious experiences, mastery experiences, social persuasion, and physiological response [2]. Tools that provide accessible practice to students can help improve their confidence in the practice area with mastery experiences, particularly when the lessons are sequenced from simple to more complex and students are able to monitor their understanding. Tools that provide accurate non-negative feedback can maintain students' confidence by social persuasion. If students' frustration with challenging concepts can be minimized while they have a satisfying experience then the physiological response positively influences self-efficacy [3]. In a study of CS majors, students reported that they gained confidence by tinkering outside of class, and a personal

ACM ISBN 978-1-4503-5890-3/19/02...$15.00
https://doi.org/10.1145/3287324.3287487

[1] web-cat.org
[2] opendsa.org
[3] codeworkout.cs.vt.edu
[4] www.lucidchart.com

factor that predicts interest in Computer Science is the willingness to engage in constant practice [1].

Practice with a tool can help build student self-efficacy with that tool and improve student success in a course. Furthermore, building student confidence at learning new tools could have a broad impact by increasing students' initiative and willingness to tinker with and explore tools throughout their career.

Some tools are specifically designed to enhance learning or automate course management (e.g., CodeWorkout, OpenDSA, Web-CAT, iClicker, Piazza), and others are designed to complete a task that is expected of computing professionals (diagramming tools, IDEs). Previous research and reports discuss the use of online coding tools, visualization tools, eTextbooks, auto grading tools, student response tools, and online forums. Many instructors believe that online coding tools reduce the dropout rates in introductory programming classes [20], and these tools have been shown to be useful in helping students master syntax of programming languages [13]. There are claims that coding tools increase the self-confidence of students in Computer Science [4, 15], while visualization is useful for novices and programmers in general [11, 14]. It is widely accepted in Computer Science education research that automating processes, such as grading, can save resources and also seems to overall positively impact academic performance [7, 21]. If used thoughtfully, it is also commonly accepted that response systems such as iClickers and online forums such as piazza also improve student learning [6, 12].

Despite the benefits of using the aforementioned educational tools, some instructors still do not take advantage of tools in their courses for a variety of reasons. Educators need to feel a sense of control for successful adoption of a tool. Training and tutorials that recognize operational and pedagogical difficulties that can arise help reduce educators' anxiety [16, 17]. It can be difficult for educators to find guidance regarding effective use of educational tools such as algorithm visualization, but experiences and lessons learned from others can save time and allow educators to make better choices [19]. Educators are less willing to adopt a system unless its usefulness has been demonstrated. But even though the usefulness of online coding tools has received attention from researchers, use of such tools is still not widespread by educators [5]. Researchers recognize time as the major impediment to instructors' adoption of visualization tools which is further exacerbated by course integration issues [18]. The next wave of challenges for instructors who are already using tools is determining how many and what tools to use, and how to effectively integrate them. We share our approaches to help other instructors expand and coordinate their tool use with a greater sense of control and confidence so they can improve student learning and reduce administrative work.

3 COURSE DESCRIPTION

Our CS2 course covers an introduction to data structures, efficiency, and Object Oriented design with Java as the programming language. There are typically two lecture sections of 100-300 students who have a variety of backgrounds. Students have obtained credit for a prerequisite introductory programming course, either in our CS software engineering sequence, at a community college or another 4-year institution, or by obtaining AP Computer Science A credit.

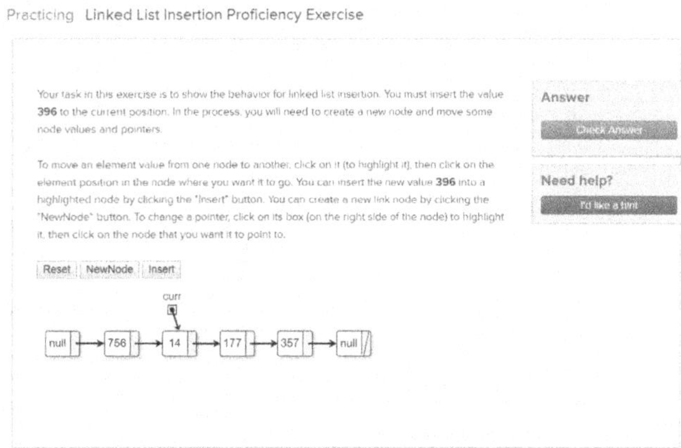

Figure 1: Example of an OpenDSA interactive exercise.

Students who took the prerequisite programming course at our institution come to our course familiar with unit testing and our style and documentation standards. They will have already used two of the tools discussed here: Web-CAT (for managing submissions of programming projects and auto-grading via unit testing) and CodeWorkout (which auto-grades small programming exercises). However, a significant fraction of the students in the course have not used these tools, are not familiar with our style and documentation standards, and have never written unit tests or used an auto-grader system. Our CS2 course is taught using Java, and there are typically a few students whose only prior programming course used a different programming language.

Students attend two traditional lecture sections and a two-hour lab each week. Labs and programming projects are submitted to Web-CAT for feedback and grading. Our current institutional Learning Management System (LMS) is Canvas. In addition to lab and projects, students have programming practice assignments in CodeWorkout and OpenDSA. CodeWorkout is used on tests for coding questions. OpenDSA is an interactive eTextbook which is customizable but already has significant content available for data structures. Students are assigned OpenDSA reading and problems throughout the semester, and they find the visualizations and practice useful. An example exercise is shown in Figure 1. Students also have design assignments for which they use a diagramming tool of their choosing. We use Piazza heavily as the course forum, and we use iClickers for in-lecture active learning.

In 2015 we restructured the course content in order to synchronize lab activities, lecture material and progressively more involved projects. We incorporated scaffolding throughout the course. Students are given pre-reading assignments and quizzes in preparation for lecture, and the labs are broken into pre-labs, labs and post-labs. We include iClicker questions in the lecture material. When we redesigned the course we continued to use Web-CAT but wrote new tests and hints for reference tests focusing on expected behavior instead of specific methods, with a goal of keeping the messages constructive and positive.

Table 1: Tools used in CS2

Tool Name	Purpose	Introduced	Integrates with
Canvas	Learning Management System(LMS)	week 1	
Web-CAT	auto-grading and feedback system	week 1	Canvas
iClicker	active learning response system	week 2	Canvas and spreadsheets
OpenDSA	eTextBook with algorithm and data structure visualization	week 5	Separate Canvas Course
Lucidchart	optional online collaborative diagramming tool	week 5	Google Docs, pdf
Eclipse Debugger	Debugger	week 5	Web-CAT
CodeWorkout	online coding practice and assessment	week 6	Canvas

4 LESSONS LEARNED

4.1 Approaches for Student Success

Students start with varying backgrounds, so the initial weeks can be intimidating and there can be a steeper learning curve for some students than for others. Scaffolding tool use helps alleviate the initial challenges. We scaffold tool use by starting with small introductory activities, including demonstrations in lecture and with videos, and eventually expect students to use tools in context. Pro-actively testing tools and corresponding instructions with consideration for difficulty and approximate time required improves student success and minimizes unanticipated frustrations. Assessing student feedback and performance allows us to make adaptations to tool use, activity directions, and overall course instruction.

4.1.1 Scaffold tool use. Our approach to integrating multiple tools is to phase them in throughout the semester, and to provide instruction for each when introduced. At the beginning of the course students are trying to learn the course routines, CS concepts, and new tools. To keep them from feeling intimidated and overwhelmed we phase in tools over time. We make the learning curve for individual tools more gradual by exposing students to tools at increasing levels of detail and difficulty over time. We attempt to lessen the cognitive load on students so that they are not simultaneously trying to master a new concept and a new tool. By scaffolding the introduction of tools and the learning of specific tools we give students the opportunity for mastery experiences that are sequenced from simple to more complex to build their confidence.

4.1.2 Add tools to the course in stages. In Table 1 we list tools used in the course and when they are introduced in order to ease students into the semester. In the first week of the course students start the routines of going to lab and submitting to Web-CAT. They also begin weekly pre-reading assignments with quizzes on Canvas. In the second week we expect students to use their iClickers in class, and the forum becomes more active. After a few weeks, students are comfortable with the overall course management and tools. Many of them need this time to adjust to programming expectations reinforced by Web-CAT, which includes style and unit test coverage. This gives them the opportunity to practice and gain confidence in this software development setting.

After several weeks, when students are accustomed to the course, we demonstrate the debugger. Students also have their first assignments using a diagramming tool and their eTextbook. In the following week they have on-line programming practice to help prepare them for the upcoming testing experience.

4.1.3 Introduce specific tools with increasing levels of difficulty. To lessen the cognitive load on students, we scaffold the assignments that use the tools. This eases the students into using the tool. We use a variety of techniques such as having a small assignment with the specific objective of familiarizing students with the tool, modeling use of the tool in class, and having assignments with increasingly involved use of the tool. The first day that we introduce using iClickers is a practice day, and we do not count the points so as to ease into use and make sure the logistics are correct. These smaller experiences set the students up for success and allow them to get positive feedback as they build skills.

In the week when students use the Web-CAT project autograder for the first time, we provide detailed lab instructions for doing Web-CAT submissions. The corresponding post-lab activity is an exploration of the Web-CAT results in order to further familiarize students with the tool. This eases students into using Web-CAT. Subsequent Web-CAT lab and project instructions are less detailed.

The first semester that we used the OpenDSA eTextbook, we did not initially demonstrate it in lecture. From forum and office hours interactions, we realized that students were getting stuck on those questions that require problem solving, particularly about algorithm analysis and recursion. Students actually needed help with course skills and concepts more than tool use. When we demonstrated OpenDSA problems in lecture, we found that students were more comfortable after they watched us solve just a couple problems. Providing this vicarious experience for them builds their confidence in solving these types of problem. As a result they start the homework assignments sooner and ask fewer questions. Similarly for CodeWorkout, students can use the tool and understand the feedback but might need help with some of the Computer Science context. Most CodeWorkout questions require students to write member methods for a class. This is disorienting for some students until they see a solved example. After that, they are more comfortable and successful solving future questions.

Many students do not begin the semester debugging their code with a source-line debugger. We notice that students are intimidated by the eclipse debugger until they have one-to-one coaching in office hours, at which point they value it and become proficient with it. In the first semester that we used the debugger, we did introduce it in lecture and lab, but then we realized we needed a lab dedicated solely to that topic. We have since also added more early exposure to the debugger. By week 5 we have demonstrated using the debugger in lecture to see the contents of a linked structure. In the post-lab the following week, students further explore the lab code using the debugger and are given a corresponding quiz. This increases self-efficacy with the debugger around the time that their programming projects are becoming larger. In Week 9 we have a lab dedicated to debugging. The students find this frustrating, but more of them begin using the debugger, which we observe helps them in the projects.

The final project requires students to work in a group to iteratively design and implement a program. For each of the four programming projects that precede the final group project, the students are given design guidelines. In preparation for creating their own design with a UML diagram, students are initially asked to create a simple UML diagram of existing code containing only two Java classes. This experience helps familiarize them with using the diagramming tool when the diagram difficulty is low. We also provide our own brief video tutorials, and we vet and link to existing tutorials. Lab and project instructions provide UML diagrams as examples, and the tool is not phased in until Week 4, with the complexity of its use increasing over the semester. This is an example of phasing in a tool over time, so students are comfortable with it by the time that they use it for their more high-stakes final project.

4.1.4 Test tool assignments with consideration for clarity, difficulty and timing. Working through assignment instructions well before they are assigned is valuable because it improves the instructions and overall assignment. Actually completing an assignment allows instructors to verify that students are set up for success with clear directions, pages with working links and images, the necessary pre-requisite skills, and the appropriate time-frame to complete the assignment. Pro-actively testing instructions reduces student questions and increases their comfort, and saves time in the long run for the instructional staff. Having other instructors or teaching assistants test the assignment is ideal, but minimally the author themself can work back through the instructions with fresh eyes well after it was drafted.

As part of our lab restructuring, we broke each into pre-lab, lab, and post-lab. In the first semester we had the TAs work through the labs in advance using a rubric such as the one shown in Figure 2. As detailed in the checklist, we test the instructions on Canvas, the down-loadable code skeleton, and the Web-CAT configuration. We reduce confusion in lab when the Canvas instructions are clear and complete. Assignment testing also uncovers potential issues with our Web-CAT reference tests and feedback messages. Our expectations about student performance and the amount of time required to complete the lab is improved by having someone time themselves to complete the assignment. With assignment testing the resulting instructions are clearer, and adjusted expectations are more reasonable. This reduces student anxiety and frustration while still challenging them.

Each semester we have different assistants solve our CodeWorkout questions, and we verify that the timing, difficulty and instructions are appropriate. Even after multiple iterations, we still discover ways that we can improve instructions or how we write our unit tests. Here are examples of feedback that we gained from testing our instructions:

"The only problem I encountered is for union, the instructions didn't say you can't edit the original bags, but CodeWorkout won't let you pass if you modify the original bags."

Checklist for Lab Review

1. Review Pre-lab and solutions, check if well connected to lab
2. Read lab instructions
    a. **verify all links work**
    b. **verify images work**
    c. **take a careful look at code blocks and check formatting**
3. Make sure skeleton formatting is reasonable
4. Verify skeleton downloads correctly
5. Solve the lab yourself
6. Review Solution against yours (we can reuse former solution or your new one)
7. Submit Solution(s) to WebCAT
    a. check for reasonable error feedback on WebCAT
    b. check deadline times for each lab
8. Review Lab Notes from last year regarding the lab and make it usable for team
9. Review Post-lab and solutions
    a. check if well connected to lab
    b. check deadline times
10. Send feedback to me and communicate/work back and forth
11. Report out to the team (by Sunday)
12. Make sure google drive directories have latest skeleton and solution, rename any former one with _prev. Both the Skeletons and Solutions directory

Figure 2: Example checklist for testing lab instructions

"I was of the opinion that when the second bag is null, the bag returned should be a new bag with all the elements in the current bag, rather than just returning a reference to the current bag, but if that's not a requirement then it shouldn't create any confusion for students since both approaches work."

Testing CodeWorkout questions helps us anticipate multiple solution approaches and how we might need to improve our unit tests. We have also found that we need to be mindful of what methods the students need to know in order to solve the problem (e.g. `String substring(int, int)`, `double pow(double, double)`, `int parseInt(String)`). Testing helps us to flesh this out and decide what additional information students might need.

We have found that integrating tools requires additional time spent by the instructional staff on configuring tools and testing the assignments up front in order for students to have a smooth experience. Fortunately, the tools that we use have also successfully reduced the time spent grading by our TAs and instructors, so there is more time available for configuring and testing. Even with the additional time spent in preparation, the end result is more time available for student contact.

4.1.5 Consider student input and experience. Watching and talking to students about using tools enlightens us and debunks preconceived notions about their experience with, and perception of, the tools. This allows us to make adjustments that improve student learning.

By watching students and looking at their submission history, we could see that many students were submitting to Web-CAT heavily to receive feedback while not thinking through their submissions thoroughly on their own. These students were using Web-CAT feedback to make guesses until they had full code coverage for their own tests, and likewise making small changes until they pass all of our tests, seemingly without regard for the bigger picture of the assignment or overall test cases for the problem. One of the goals of an auto-grading system that requires student tests and provides feedback is to promote reflection-in-action, however student patterns of over-submitting are well documented [9] [8]. An adjustment that we made was to configure the use of "submission energy", which is a mechanism to limit the frequency with which students can submit to Web-CAT. This causes students to think through the problem more thoroughly and learn more from the assignment.

When we began updating this course we knew we wanted to increase student engagement. Some of our faculty had formerly experienced frustration with response systems, and others did not want to require students to make additional purchases. By talking with students, we discovered that because most of them also take Physics, they already have iClickers. So our use of iClickers was adapted to mirror how our colleagues in Physics use them. This simplified our ramp up, and was convenient for students because it was already a familiar tool. Paying attention to students and talking to them allowed us to come up with this solution.

4.2 Approaches for Instructor Success

Instructor time is valuable. If instructors can spend less time on administrative work then they have more time to spend with students and improving curriculum. We try to streamline the use of multiple tools in one course in order to save time and reduce errors. We consult mentors to head off difficulties, and we start small to ease into teaching with a new tool. We pick tools that integrate well with each other, particularly for managing grades.

4.2.1 Consult a mentor who has used the tool before. Finding a mentor who has used a given tool is valuable for avoiding pitfalls and quickly resolving logistical issues. Having a mentor is especially helpful for guidance on how to handle absences, late work, and how to accommodate students with special services needs.

When we changed the lab structure and set up all new projects for the course, it was advantageous to have a mentor for using Web-CAT. It made us more efficient in setting up configurations for assignments and in writing tests. Experienced users could provide guidance not just on syntax for test messages, but various approaches on how and when to give students feedback on failed tests. Seeing examples of a mentor's previous configurations helped to accommodate late submissions with automatic point deductions. For a tool as complicated as Web-CAT, it is ideal to build community and corporate knowledge from semester to semester in the form of experienced TAs training new TAs, and having the experienced TAs write training manuals for new TAs who will have to pick up being tool administrators.

Having a mentor for CodeWorkout was useful for realizing what previous content was already available. It was also important for logistical nuisances such as knowing to use the same name for the assignment in Canvas and CodeWorkout, and being sure to synchronize settings and time constraints across course sections. A mentor was also useful for demonstrating how to provide alternate test times and extended time. The begin and end dates can be adjusted and so can the time alloted. Having a mentor saved time and allowed us to anticipate and resolve logistical issues.

When we decided to use iClickers, we consulted with our colleagues in Physics. We had a meeting to discuss their approaches and steps for setting up iClickers across our institution. They showed us how they installed and configured the software and also explained their grading scheme and course guidelines. When they described some of their management efforts with grading and especially dealing with absences, we chose to take a simpler overall approach. We followed their advice to require students to only use the iClickers to respond and not their phones. Their guidance helped us head off logistical issues and made getting started with iClickers run smoothly.

4.2.2 Start small with room to grow. We avoid investing significant time and effort on a tool or corresponding assignments until we are confident it will yield positive learning experiences for our students. We will not really know this until we try the tool, so we start with a small number of assignments and keep the grading value of the assignments low. It is easier to start with a tool that provides some ready-made content, this allows you to initially spend your efforts on integrating the tool versus creating content. If the tool is also customizable then we improve and enhance our approaches either throughout the semester or from semester to semester. As discussed above, it is useful to test any ready-made content before assigning it to students.

The first semester that we used CodeWorkout, we began with pre-existing questions about arrays. CodeWorkout was familiar to some students who had used it in our CS1 course the previous semester. CodeWorkout was not familar to all the students, and it had not been used before in the CS2 course, so we eased into it. We created a couple of practice assignments with new data structure content that the students did for low point homework, and then used it in an exam. The following semester we added working an assignment during lecture. In the future we plan to create more CS2 content to use for active learning during lectures.

We do not make tool activities worth many points and we do not over-promise how we will use or grade activities with the tool. For example, there are many OpenDSA questions, but they are worth only 2% of the students' overall grade. However, they have great value to the students as practice. One semester our server running OpenDSA restarted overnight, and students who completed the assignment before the server crashed lost their grades, while students who did the assignment after the crash were graded normally. So we follow a two-level approach here. In the long term, we want to fix the underlying problem before the next semester (or work with the tool developers if appropriate). In the meantime, we can take the simple route and give everyone credit for that set of questions. This is why it is a good idea to keep the percentage of the grade and the level of instructor effort at a minimal level until you have confidence in the tool.

Integrating multiple tools is more manageable because we start small and then gradually increased tool usage, which mitigates risk and allows us to adapt and enhance how we incorporate the tools over time.

4.2.3 Choose tools that simplify management of student accounts and grades. As much as possible, we use tools that simplify course administration. This reduces errors and frees up instructor time to focus on students and instruction. We manually manage student accounts and porting grades as needed, but in most cases our tools are set up to communicate automatically.

Web-CAT now allows us to port grades directly to Canvas. In the past we would download a gradesheet from Canvas to ensure the proper column title for the grades that we were uploading. We learned to be sure to delete spreadsheet columns for other assignments so as to not unintentionally overwrite them when we upload. Keeping this spreadsheet open in Excel simultaneously with a tools' spreadsheet allows one sheet to reference the other using the Excel VLOOKUP command as needed to manually port grades.

Having the grades port directly from Web-CAT to Canvas takes significantly less time than any manual process and greatly reduces error in the transfer. We had formerly made errors such as porting grades over to the wrong assignment in the LMS or having all the student grades shifted down a row. Another key administrative benefit to grades automatically porting is that late grades are handled seamlessly. When we ported the grades manually, there would be added administrative work and more errors for the scenario where we ported grades for an assignment from Web-CAT to Canvas and then one student's grade was later changed in Web-CAT but this was not reflected in Canvas.

OpenDSA is now fully integrated with Canvas, so students do not need a separate account, and grades are automatically ported. Before OpenDSA automatically ported the grades over to Canvas, the student accounts were not necessarily the same. It is important that the roll from your LMS and the roll from your tool share some attribute that uniquely identifies each student. This is typically the student ID number or the institutional email. We formerly had grade errors because, despite instructions, some students would use a personal email to self-enroll in OpenDSA and then there was no shared unique key with the Canvas roll. Furthermore, some students would enroll in OpenDSA multiple times with various emails, so grades could be scattered across OpenDSA accounts, and various subsets might or might not get ported to Canvas. Having synchronized student accounts eliminates these issues and saves instructor time.

CodeWorkout can now be launched via Canvas, and grades are automatically ported over. However, we experienced similar issues with CodeWorkout as we formerly did with OpenDSA if we allowed students to self-enroll in CodeWorkout. Issues arose when students created multiple accounts and used different emails for their accounts, and additionally we had complications when students enrolled in the wrong or multiple sections of the course, which then affects their assignment settings. Using student accounts directly from Canvas in CodeWorkout, and not allowing students to self-enroll, saves time and reduces errors.

4.3 Potential Pitfalls

Integrating multiple tools into a course can positively impact student learning and instructor routines, but there are increased opportunities for complications. Our approaches have helped us proactively avoid many frustrations but there remain situations that can easily be mis-managed, especially when configuring a variety of tools independently.

One interesting example of a configuration issue and potential pitfall is whether students can rework the problems to study for a test. Some questions we ask ourselves are: Do the students have access to previously worked problems? If they rework them will they get regraded? If they rework them will they count as late? Currently we handle this in OpenDSA by closing assignments when they are due and then downloading grades before reopening questions the week before a test so students can use them for more practice.

Another interesting example of a configuration issue and potential pitfall is whether to record the grade for the last or best attempt from a student. This is the kind of option that may go unnoticed at first without a mentor. We find that on CodeWorkout we should take the best attempt since they might run out of time, but on Web-CAT we should take the last attempt since they are under less time pressure to make thoughtful decision about their submissions.

Hurdles such as these support the case that it is advisable to test your process with colleagues, teaching assistants, or by setting up multiple accounts of your own to enable testing. Versions, installation processes, interfaces, and security issues can change between semesters, so it is best to re-test to avoid unexpected student frustration. New issues can arise, but also, former issues might be resolved with updates.

5 CONCLUSIONS AND FUTURE WORK

By maintaining focus on student success and trying to streamline the process for instructors we have been able to integrate many tools into one course. We improve student success by scaffolding tool use, testing tool assignments before student use, and conscientiously paying attention to student feedback and behavior. We improve the experience for instructors by consulting mentors, starting small, and choosing tools that simplify course management. These approaches can be applied across educational settings. We reported on our experience with a large, in-person lecture. But many of these strategies can be applied to smaller classes, labs, and on-line courses. Our checklist in Figure 2 can be found at http://people.cs.vt.edu/~maellis1/teaching_resources/ and adapted to various circumstances.

Our future work includes integrating more active learning during lecture by expanding our use of CodeWorkout. We hope to improve student comprehension by using new content form OpenDSA with interactive questions for linked structures. We will also be adopting a version of Web-CAT with enhanced student feedback. While students benefit from scaffolding the use of the debugger, we plan to reduce the cognitive load for the debugger lab by making it about a programming concept that students have previously mastered. We are currently applying these approaches for integrating multiple tools into an updated version of our Problem Solving in CS course.

ACKNOWLEDGMENTS

We gratefully acknowledge the support of the National Science Foundation under Grant DLR-1740765. We thank our colleagues Jack Lesko and Manuel Pérez-Quiñones for their constructive discussions during the course of the work described here.

REFERENCES

[1] C.T. Amelink, K. Davis, B.G. Ryder, and M.O. Ellis. 2018. Exploring Factors Influencing the Continued Interest in a Computer Science Major. In *2018 ASEE Annual Conference & Exposition*.

[2] A. Bandura. 1977. Self-efficacy: Toward a unifying theory of behavioral change. *Psychological Review* 84 (1977), 191–215.

[3] M. Beier, J. Lesko, and C. Amelink. 2018. Engineering Self-Efficacy: What it is, Why it Matters, and How to Encourage it! https://www.wepan.org/page/SelfEfficacy.

[4] Luciana Benotti, Federico Aloi, Franco Bulgarelli, and Marcos J. Gomez. 2018. The Effect of a Web-based Coding Tool with Automatic Feedback on Students' Performance and Perceptions. In *Proceedings of the 49th ACM Technical Symposium on Computer Science Education (SIGCSE '18)*. 2–7.

[5] P. Brusilovsky, S.H. Edwards, A. Kumar, L. Malmi, L. Benotti, D. Buck, P. Ihantola, R. Prince, T. Sirkiä, S. Sosnovsky, J. Urquiza, A. Vihavainen, and M. Wollowski. 2014. Increasing Adoption of Smart Learning Content for Computer Science Education. In *Proceedings of the Working Group Reports of the 2014 on Innovation & Technology in Computer Science Education Conference (ITiCSE-WGR '14)*. 31–57.

[6] A.T. Chamillard. 2011. Using a Student Response System in CS1 and CS2. In *Proceedings of the 42nd ACM Technical Symposium on Computer Science Education (SIGCSE '11)*. 299–304.

[7] B. Cheanga, A. Kurniaa, A. Limb, and W.C. Oonc. 2002. On automated grading of programming assignments in an academic institution. *Computers & Education*, 121–131. Issue 41.

[8] S.H. Edwards. 2004. Using software testing to move students from trial-and-error to reflection-in-action. In *Proceedings of the 35th SIGCSE Technical Symposium on Computer Science Education (SIGCSE '04)*. 26–30.

[9] S.H. Edwards, J. Snyder, M.A. Pérez-Quiñones, A. Allevato, K. Dongkwan, and B. Tretola. 2009. Comparing Effective and Ineffective Behaviors of Student Programmers. In *Proceedings of the Fifth International Workshop on Computing Education and Research (ICER '09)*. 3–14.

[10] J.V. Ernst, B.D. Bowen, and T.O. Williams. 2016. Freshman Engineering Students At-Risk Of Non-Matriculation: Self-Efficacy For Academic Learning. *American Journal of Engineering Education* 7 (June 2016), 9–18.

[11] E. Fouh, M. Akbar, and C.A. Shaffer. 2012. The Role of Visualization in Computer Science Education. *Computers in the Schools* 29 (2012), 95–117. Issue 1-2.

[12] D.D. Garcia, L. Aaronson, S. Kenner, C. Lewis, and S. Rodger. 2016. Technology We Can't Live Without!, Revisited. In *Proceedings of the 47th ACM Technical Symposium on Computing Science Education (SIGCSE '16)*. 236–237.

[13] P. Ihantola, A. Vihavainen, A. Ahadi, M. Butler, J. Börstler, S.H. Edwards, E. Isohanni, A. Korhonen, A. Petersen, K. Rivers, M.Á. Rubio, J. Sheard, B. Skupas, J. Spacco, C. Szabo, and D. Toll. 2015. Educational Data Mining and Learning Analytics in Programming: Literature Review and Case Studies. In *Proceedings of the 2015 ITiCSE on Working Group Reports (ITICSE-WGR '15)*. 41–63.

[14] R. Ishizue, K. Sakamoto, H. Washizaki, and Y. Fukazawa. 2018. PVC: Visualizing C Programs on Web Browsers for Novices. In *Proceedings of the 49th ACM Technical Symposium on Computer Science Education (SIGCSE '18)*. 245–250.

[15] A.N. Kumar. 2008. The Effect of Using Problem-solving Software Tutors on the Self-confidence of Female Students. *SIGCSE Bull.* 40, 1 (March 2008), 523–527.

[16] R.B. Levy and M. Ben-Ari. 2007. We Work So Hard and They Don'T Use It: Acceptance of Software Tools by Teachers. In *Proceedings of the 12th Annual SIGCSE Conference on Innovation and Technology in Computer Science Education (ITiCSE '07)*. ACM, New York, NY, USA, 246–250. https://doi.org/10.1145/1268784.1268856

[17] R.B. Levy and M. Ben-Ari. 2008. Perceived behavior control and its influence on the adoption of software tools. In *Proceedings of the 13th annual conference on Innovation and technology in computer science education (ITiCSE '08)*. ACM, 169–173. https://doi.org/10.1145/1384271.1384318

[18] T. Naps, S. Cooper, B. Koldehofe, C. Leska, G. Rößling, W. Dann, A. Korhonen, L. Malmi, J. Rantakokko, R.J. Ross, J. Anderson, R. Fleischer, M. Kuittinen, and M. McNally. 2003. Evaluation the educational impact of visualization. In *Working Group Reports from the Symposium on Innovation and Technology in Computer Science Education (ITiCSE-WGR '03)*. 124–136.

[19] C.A. Shaffer, M.L. Cooper, A.J.D. Alon, M. Akbar, M. Stewart, S. Ponce, and S.H. Edwards. 2010. Algorithm Visualization: The State of the Field. *ACM Transactions on Computing Education* 10 (August 2010), 1–22.

[20] C. Watson and F.W.B. Li. 2014. Failure Rates in Introductory Programming Revisited. In *Proceedings of the 2014 Conference on Innovation & Technology in Computer Science Education (ITiCSE '14)*. 39–44.

[21] C. Wilcox. 2015. The Role of Automation in Undergraduate Computer Science Education. In *Proceedings of the 46th ACM Technical Symposium on Computer Science Education (SIGCSE '15)*. 90–95.

Autograding Distributed Algorithms in Networked Containers

Evan Maicus
Rensselaer Polytechnic Institute
maicue@rpi.edu

Matthew Peveler
Rensselaer Polytechnic Institute
pevelm@rpi.edu

Stacy Patterson
Rensselaer Polytechnic Institute
sep@cs.rpi.edu

Barbara Cutler
Rensselaer Polytechnic Institute
cutler@cs.rpi.edu

ABSTRACT

We present a container-based system to automatically run and evaluate networked applications that implement distributed algorithms. Our implementation of this design leverages lightweight, networked Docker containers to provide students with fast, accurate, and helpful feedback about the correctness of their submitted code. We provide a simple, easy-to-use interface for instructors to specify networks, deploy and run instances of student and instructor code, and to log and collect statistics concerning node connection types and message content. Instructors further have the ability to control network features such as message delay, drop, and reorder. Running student programs can be interfaced with via stream-controlled standard input or through additional containers running custom instructor software. Student program behavior can be automatically evaluated by analyzing console or file output and instructor-specified rules regarding network communications. Program behavior, including logs of all messages passed within the system, can optionally be displayed to the student to aid in development and debugging. We evaluate the utility of this design and implementation for managing the submission and robust and secure testing of programming projects in a large enrollment theory of distributed systems course. This research has been implemented as an extension to Submitty, an open source, language-agnostic course management platform with automated testing and automated grading of student programming assignments. Submitty supports all levels of courses, from introductory to advanced special topics, and includes features for manual grading by TAs, version control, team submission, discussion forums, and plagiarism detection.

CCS CONCEPTS

• **Computing Education** → Computing Education Programs; Computer Science Education;

KEYWORDS

Distributed Systems, Testing, Autograding, Container

SIGCSE '19, February 27-March 2, 2019, Minneapolis, MN, USA

ACM ISBN 978-1-4503-5890-3/19/02...$15.00
https://doi.org/10.1145/3287324.3287505

ACM Reference Format:
Evan Maicus, Matthew Peveler, Stacy Patterson, and Barbara Cutler. 2019. Autograding Distributed Algorithms in Networked Containers. In *Proceedings of the 50th ACM Technical Symposium on Computer Science Education (SIGCSE '19), February 27-March 2, 2019, Minneapolis, MN, USA.* ACM, New York, NY, USA, 6 pages. https://doi.org/10.1145/3287324.3287505

1 INTRODUCTION

Testing and grading networked programming assignments is a complex endeavor. As a first step, the tester must distribute student code to many nodes — running either locally or remotely — each of which must be configured to properly execute the student application. These nodes must be configured to communicate with one another, often utilizing manually-specified ip addresses and ports. It is possible to run all instances of student code from a single host; however, the algorithm will be less likely to encounter the realities of networked communication over the Internet, including delays, packet loss, and packet corruption or duplication. Once the student assignment is installed, running, and networked on all nodes, the grader must interface with it. Manual testing is often conducted via multiple ssh terminals to provide a sequence of input to the different nodes. It can be difficult to satisfactorily test resilience to simultaneous inputs across many hosts.

1.1 Manual Testing & Grading

Manual grading of distributed applications is typically done by issuing a command, waiting for the system to react and stabilize, and then checking the resulting state of the system. Student code is usually viewed by the instructor as a black box, as even a correct implementation could result in different outputs on subsequent runs due to issues of concurrency and network delay. Take, as an example, manually grading a distributed calendar application, in which no two events may be scheduled at the same time for the same user, but in which any user many enroll another in an activity. First, a command from the instructor might prompt a node in the system to enter an event into the calendar. The instructor, then, must wait while the nodes of the network determine whether the newly entered event is non-conflicting. When the system has stabilized, the instructor can check each node to see whether they agree on the state of the calendar. If all nodes agree on a valid calendar, the student receives credit for this rubric item. If the student's results are invalid, or, worse, one or more of the student nodes crash, the instructor must adapt, restart the grading system, or award the student zero credit on subsequent tests.

1.2 Grading by Live Demonstration

As a result of these difficulties, instructors may opt to schedule in-person code demonstration sessions during which students bring their completed assignments and run them through a series of live testcases. Because the student is presumably well acquainted with their own implementation and interface, they can more rapidly configure and manipulate the system to demonstrate adherence to assignment specifications. The student arrives with the code already configured and running on multiple hosts, allowing the demonstration time to focus on providing test inputs to the system and discussing the output and implementation details. However, even live demos have hiccups with unexpected bugs and the instructor often must think on their feet, as it is not often possible to restart testing altogether. As a result, if live testcase 1 is a failure, the expected output from live testcase 2 must be adjusted. Sometimes, however, failures are so catastrophic that testcase 2 becomes impossible.

1.3 Contributions

Our contributions are as follows:

- We present the design and implementation of a system for automatically running and grading networked, distributed applications within Submitty, an open source course management and autograding system [12].
- The design allows instructors to manipulate network features such as message delay and loss on a per-connection basis, to enforce restrictions regarding which nodes are allowed to communicate, to require that student code uses a particular protocol (e.g., TCP or UDP) to pass messages, and to connect and disconnect nodes from a network.
- Our system allows instructors to interface with and provide input to running student distributed applications in a scripted way, facilitating automated testing of student code.
- The system logs information about all messages and message content passed between the networked nodes. This log can be leveraged to automatically evaluate the efficiency of an implementation and may also be provided to students as a learning aid and debugging tool.
- The module for the generation of container networks and deployment of student code can also be as a standalone tool. This tool may be utilized by students during development and by instructors to facilitate live student demonstrations.

2 RELATED WORK

As enrollment sizes have increased in Computer Science programs, professors have turned to autograding solutions, both commercial [4], and homegrown [15]. The use of such automated grading platforms has been claimed to be an economic [16] and logistical [15] necessity for the professors and institutions that are able to employ them. However, not all programming assignments are a good fit for the traditional autograding scheme of running a single instance of student code, piping it inputs, and then difference checking its output against a known solution. In particular, autograding assignments that require networked instances of student code are not feasible in the majority of autograding solutions.

This apparent lack of support is due at least in part to the difficulties of automatically testing the correctness of distributed applications. Issues of concurrency and sub-optimal network conditions yield outputs that are difficult to debug, as "happens before" relationships can be impossible to establish without a reliable global clock [3]. This issue is exacerbated by the problem of distributed state, which makes log and output analysis a challenging task. To combat issues of concurrency and nondeterministic message orderings, some systems decompose tests into a set of abstract pre- and post- conditions, rather than defining a single, fixed valid output [8]. In such a testcase, a precondition might be that the state of a distributed calendar is inconsistent because a conflicting event has been entered. The postcondition, then, would be that a valid calendar is decided upon by the nodes in the network. Other systems, meanwhile, attempt to sidestep the problem of concurrency entirely by testing distributed applications component by component [14]. In such systems, rather than passively assessing a distributed system as it runs, unit tests are performed by "separating system components from the environment." In contrast, other testing frameworks aim to allow developers to subject their applications to the full wrath of a stressful network. This can be done by integrating a transparent "degrader", which sits between the nodes of a system and intercepts all messages. The degrader acts as a relay, and can modify message content, delay, and drop rates. [7]. Alternatively, a less intrusive approach can be taken to inject delays via a network emulator directly on connections between network nodes without the need for interception [1, 13]. This process, known as "fuzzing," is necessary to tease out unknown errors from a system. Packet loss rates of about 0.1% are expected in realistic conditions — a packet loss rate of 1% is considered problematic and 5% is a "severe failure" [10].

3 SYSTEM REQUIREMENTS

Our system was designed to support RPI's Distributed Systems and Algorithms course, an elective of the Computer Science major taken by juniors, seniors, and graduate students. To fairly, robustly, and efficiently test and evaluate student work, the autograder must:

- **Automatically create a reasonably sized student network.** Manual testing during live demos of typical projects for this course requires as many as eight student nodes. The hardware for the server should therefore be able to run a minimum of eight simultaneous containers.
- **Keep network specification simple but powerful.** Network configuration should have reasonable default values so that instructors can quickly build autograders for simple examples, while remaining customizable to facilitate and control complex test cases.
- **Facilitate scripted interaction via standard input and capture of all program output.** Automated validation and scoring can be performed on captured program output.
- **Support common message passing protocols and a variety of programming languages.** We have implemented and tested support for both TCP and UDP protocols, and students have chosen from Java or Python for their implementations. The Submitty platform supports a comprehensive set of programming languages.

- **Be highly reusable.** The automated creation of networks and deployment of student code is a useful tool independent of the autograding pipeline. This module should be self contained, so that it can be leveraged by students during development and by instructors for additional, unscripted testing and grading.
- **Provide an interface for professors to subject student programs to stressful network conditions.** Subjecting distributed applications to stressful but realistic conditions can be useful in revealing hidden implementation issues [7, 10]. To this end, our system should include tools with which instructors can subject student assignments to network conditions including packet loss, corruption, duplication, and delay.
- **Provide students with meaningful feedback for debugging purposes.** Automated grading is not only about assigning students a numeric grade, it is also an opportunity to help them understand why they did not receive full credit and (if allowed by the course syllabus) to revise and resubmit their projects. Like other autograding platforms, Submitty supports multiple submissions [15] and access to files, standard output, and message logs produced during testing to facilitate debugging of distributed applications [3].

4 IMPLEMENTATION

4.1 Isolating Docker Communications

For the implementation of our system, we focus on leveraging Docker containers [5] — lightweight, secure environments that are virtualized at the operating system level and used to execute applications. Docker containers can effectively and securely execute and autograde student code within many different types of runtime environments [9, 11]. We considered multiple network emulation schemes before settling on this decision, including the use of physical host PCs, virtual machines, emulation schemes involving multiprocessing, and the use of cloud services such as Amazon EC2 instances — virtual servers provided through Amazon's cloud services [2]. The decision to use Docker containers was made based on the following factors:

- **Cost** Many Docker containers can run on a single physical host server, making it far more cost effective than using multiple networked physical PCs. Docker is open-source, and free to use on your own hardware. In contrast, cloud-based container/virtual machine services have a fee per unit of time.
- **Ease of Configuration** Docker containers and networks are simple to configure [6]. In Submitty, we allow instructors to provide DockerFiles so they can easily specify course, assignment, or testcase specific packages.
- **Network Emulation** Docker provides native support for networks with arbitrary topology among containers. We leverage these networks to log all messages passed by the student application.
- **Security and Isolation** Docker containers isolate student code from the host operating system. Docker networking solutions prevent one student's code from communicating with that of another student's being graded in parallel. This represents a real advantage over multiprocessing solutions or physical machines with known hostnames or IP addresses.
- **Ease of Interface** Because all Docker instances are run on a single host server, a wrapper script may maintain handles on all running instances. This makes it simple to attach and pipe standard input to running Docker instances in an immediate fashion without maintaining multiple ssh connections.
- **Performant** Docker containers are quick to spin up - it is possible to create and start a new batch of containers for a given testcase in only a few seconds. Furthermore, Docker containers are more efficient than virtual machines and have a small impact on their host machine's resources. In stress-tests with single threaded, non-networked programs with and without Docker containers, we found that overall CPU and memory usage increased by less than 1% each [9].
- **Scalable** While it falls outside of the scope of our current work, Docker networks are scalable and may be distributed across multiple physical host servers, making it possible to deploy and test swarm applications [17].

4.2 Router: Intercept and Log All Messages

Our goal is to allow instructors to subject student programs to stressful network conditions and to change these conditions over time. Similar to the "degrader" presented in [7], we introduce an additional, invisible node to the network that we call the *router*. The router intercepts and logs all messages, applying rules regarding message delay, loss, and reorder that may be unique for each host-port pair. While the injection of such a node into the student network is more intrusive than other solutions [1, 13], it facilitates other desired features such as allowing students to study, learn, and debug with access to a detailed message log; limiting network communication to specified protocols; and evaluating student code based on volume and patterns of communication. Furthermore, specification of custom network rules is simple within such a model; within our system, the router is implemented in Python and can be customized or replaced by an instructor to delay, drop, reorder, or otherwise directly manipulate student messages. To accommodate assignments that require a less intrusive model, testcases can be run in "routerless" mode, without message logging or manipulation.

Our router node is invisible to the student application — no modifications are necessary to the student code — yet all network communications pass through this router, allowing it to manipulate traffic in any way necessary. If we have two nodes, A and B, and A sends a message A $\rightarrow$ B, the message, in actuality, follows the path A $\rightarrow$ router $\rightarrow$ B. However, neither A nor B are aware that the message passed through the router rather than directly from A to B. To accomplish this we leverage the power of Docker network aliasing:

- Each container in a Docker network may have a unique alias and may be contacted by this alias by any other node in the network.
- While Docker aliases must be unique among the aliases on a network, they need not be unique across all networks.
- A Docker container may simultaneously be connected to multiple networks.

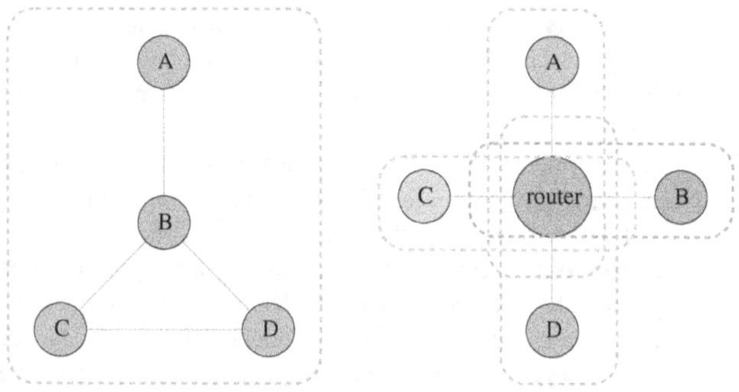

Figure 1: On the left, we illustrate a conceptual network for a student program with four nodes. On the right, we illustrate the actual connectivity using multiple Docker networks and our router.

Thus, we create two Docker networks (A, router), and (B, router). However, on the network (A, router), we give the router the alias "B" and A the alias "A_Actual" On the (B, router) network, we give the router the alias "A" and B the alias "B_Actual." Therefore, in the eyes A, the router is B, and in the eyes of B, the router is A. The router, meanwhile, can retrieve the true identities of A and B using the "_Actual" aliases. This use of one network for each node in the system carries with it the added benefit of making it impossible for a student process to interface with containers other than the router. This network architecture is illustrated in Figure 1.

The router can intercept and forward all messages as they move through the system. To facilitate this, the necessary network information is provided to a student process via an automatically generated `knownhosts.txt` file which contains the addresses of hosts on the system and the ports on which they will be listening. The student program must parse this file and use this information to establish the necessary connections. Our design requires that we add the constraint that port assignments are unique across the entirety of the system. This constraint does not represent a significant limitation on the program.

By default, the router will listen for both UDP and TCP connections, and provide students with both UDP and TCP versions of the `knownhosts.txt` file. Upon initialization, our router creates a "switchboard" dictionary, that maps a port to a sender, recipient, and connection type (UDP or TCP). Leveraging this switchboard, it is simple for instructors to modify the router to add rules regarding network stress by recipient, sender, or port.

4.3 Network Configuration

Ease-of-configuration is of prime importance when developing autograding tools for instructors. Simple test cases should leverage default system configurations and require only short, intuitive, and human-readable autograding configuration files. To this end, our system pares network specification down to five simple but powerful parameters (Figure 2). The first of these, "use_router," determines whether or not the router node will be injected into the student network. The instructor may either specify a custom router or the default logging router will be inserted. The "container_name" field allows the instructor to give a container an

```
{
  "use_router" : true,
  "containers" : [
    {
      "container_name" : "container0",
      "container_image" : "python:3.6",
      "outgoing_connections" : ["container1"],
      "commands" : ["python3 server.py"]
    },
    {
      "container_name" : "container1",
      "container_image" : "python:3.6",
      "outgoing_connections" : ["container0"],
      "commands" : ["python3 client.py"]
    }
  ]
}
```

Figure 2: Specification of a Docker network for a testcase.

application-meaningful designation. If unspecified the container names default to "container0", "container1", etc. The container name is used when defining network connections and as the name of the directory where student output is archived. The "container_image" field specifies the Docker container image. If unspecified at the container level within the test case, the system will check for a "container_image" at the global level for this autograding configuration. If unspecified, the system will default to a custom Ubuntu image appropriate for typical introductory Python/C++/Java programming assignments. The "outgoing_connections" field allows the instructor to specify one way channels of communication between containers in the network. If unspecified, this field defaults to all other containers created for this testcase. The combination of the outgoing_connections across all containers for a testcase is used to generate the `knownhosts.txt` file. Finally, the "commands" array is an array of one or more of unix commands to be executed sequentially within the container.

Network configuration JSON objects (Figure 2) are presented to our system embedded in a JSON array. For each testcase, new Docker containers and networks are created. As a result, each new testcase can test different types of containers, network sizes, and network conditions. For each testcase, the output of the run is stored in an individual folder, which is then fed directly into our existing Submitty autograder validation pipeline.

4.4 Methods of Evaluation and Autograding

We provide many methods for instructors to interface with student distributed applications. In some cases, it is enough to merely initialize a student node with some known state, either via command line arguments or through the use of an initialization file. In such cases, the nodes of the student application must be capable of achieving the goal of a testcase without additional instructor intervention. For example, in the distributed calendar assignment, an initial testcase may determine whether the nodes of the student application can reach consensus on startup from initially inconsistent or incomplete state — a task that may be performed without additional instructor prompts or instructions.

In cases where interaction is needed, instructors may provide and deploy their own code within an additional container on a testcase's network. For assignments in which students are asked

```
{
  "dispatcher_actions" :
  [
    {
      "action" : "stdin",
      "containers" : ["container0"],
      "string" : "This will be piped to container0\n"
    },
    {
      "action" : "delay",
      "seconds" : 2
    },
    {
      "action" : "stdin",
      "containers" : ["container1"],
      "string" : "This is piped to container1 2 sec later\n"
    }
  ]
}
```

Figure 3: The specification of a list of dispatcher actions.

to implement only certain portions of a distributed algorithm, this instructor node may represent one or more modules of the whole system. For example, the instructor may write a server node while the student writes a client node (or vice versa). The student's code must then interface with the instructor-written module(s), and then (typically) the standard output of the instructor module can be directly used for validation/autograding of the student code. This type of "object instantiation" [16] can provide students with invaluable experience with complicated systems without asking them to implement every module themselves.

The student may also be asked to implement an entire distributed system – for example a distributed calendar – while the instructor deploys one or more "client" nodes within the network. These instructor written clients perform an automated batch of actions (with appropriate time delays), connecting to different student containers and sending them messages. In the case of the distributed calendar assignment, the client might attempt to schedule an event while connected to one node, then access the event while connected to another. In a more complicated testcase, the instructor may create a client in which two threads of execution connect to student nodes and issue multiple sets of commands concurrently.

Some assignments lend themselves to an even more direct and simple method of communication. To this end, we allow instructors to "dispatch" strings to the standard input of running Docker containers. A sample of the syntax for specifying these actions is shown in Figure 3. Dispatched actions take four forms: delay, standard input, stop, and start actions. Actions are performed sequentially, with no default delay between them. Standard input actions may target one or more containers, allowing professors to quickly and easily broadcast the same message to many student processes. Start and stop actions may be used to connect or disconnect nodes in the student network – a feature which is helpful for testing program resilience to system faults. This method of delivering input to student code is especially useful when testing peer-to-peer applications. For example, in the calendar assignment, each node in the system may be used to represent a user. To specify a testcase on such a network, an instructor may dispatch standard input to multiple nodes, creating or canceling calendar events. If, at the end of these actions, all nodes agree on a valid calendar, the student would receive full credit for the testcase. To test an assignment for fault tolerance, an instructor might choose to stop a student node mid-testcase execution. After more standard input actions are processed, the node can be restarted into a system that has changed since it was last active. After the system has stabilized, the instructor may query the nodes of the network to see if they have reached an acceptable consensus.

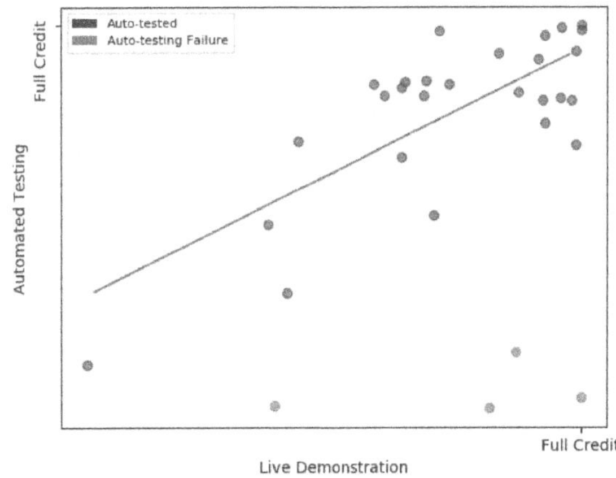

Figure 4: A scatterplot correlating live demonstration scores to automated testing of a Distributed Systems and Algorithms midterm project. 5% noise has been added to all values for anonymity.

5 RESULTS: CASE STUDY

A core component of RPI's Distributed Systems and Algorithms course has been the twice yearly live demonstration of student projects. These demonstrations consist of a one on one, 20 minute code presentation, during which the instructor guides the student through a suite of testcases. This term, limited automated testing with Submitty was used as a prerequisite for participation. Students received the benefit of multiple submissions with testing feedback, and the demonstrations went more smoothly, as the student implementations had undergone preliminary testing.

After the live demonstrations for this term's distributed calendar midterm project, we adapted the set of demonstration testcases to a more complete set of automated tests. The live testcase script included seven tests. These ranged in difficulty from entering an event into the calendar to testing resilience to node failure. The tests were designed by the instructor to provide good coverage of the problem specification.

Testcases for the live demonstration were developed to build upon one another, with the ending state of a testcase presumed to carry into the next. In order to capture this feature, each of our testcases began with the state-changing actions from those prior. This term, projects were submitted by 31 teams of students. Our system successfully tested 27 of these projects automatically. The four remaining submissions had automated testing failures that will require further investigation to debug and prevent (either by making the system more robust, or by providing appropriate feedback to the instructor and/or student about misunderstandings in the system or assignment specification). Had a complete test suite been available earlier in the project period, allowing early submission and resubmission, we are confident that the students would have successfully adapted their implementations to meet the requirements of automated testing.

The results of all submissions are depicted in Figure 4. All datapoints have been perturbed with 5% noise on each axis to help preserve student anonymity. The (unperturbed) results of these testcases display a Pearson Correlation Coefficient of 0.78, and show that our system is capable of successfully evaluating the challenging testcases from RPI's Distributed Systems and Algorithms course. The four assignments with auto-testing failures shown in red were omitted from the Pearson calculation. Autotesting was performed in parallel, and the complete test suite took fewer than 2 minutes for each student team submission. Much of this time was used for initialization, as student nodes were given five seconds to fully initialize per testcase. This startup time helps to ensure that student code is not given inputs before it is fully operational.

6 DISCUSSION & LIMITATIONS

We have detailed a new framework for automatically running and grading networked, distributed applications within Submitty, an open-source course management and autograding platform. We have presented a simple yet powerful means by which instructors may specify automatically-generated networks of nodes and deploy student code to those nodes. We have introduced the design and implementation of a "router," for logging and manipulating all messages sent through a student network. We have evaluated and implemented a number of methods for interacting with student distributed applications including the use of "object instantiation", an instructor-written client, and directly via standard input. This implementation has been successful in grading RPI's Distributed Systems and Algorithms course.

The open source Submitty course management and autograding system has served CS courses of all levels at RPI since 2014. It has become indispensable as the size of all of our courses has grown in recent years. The success of this extension for autograding projects in the Distributed Systems and Algorithms course has piqued interest among instructors, and our solution will be deployed in our Operating Systems and Network Programming courses in future semesters.

7 FUTURE WORK

Our current router implementation is limited in that it expects every network connection to use a unique port. This means that if a node is expecting connections from two others, it must open two sockets. Investigation is ongoing to create a new version of the default router which will allow many to one communication.

We would like to streamline the process of developing autograding configuration files. Our current syntax is flexible, powerful, and customizable; however, a suite of testcases for an assignment can have duplication between tests that use similar container networks, dispatched commands, and autograding validation. We plan to explore methods of reducing redundancy and to develop a web GUI for autograding configuration.

REFERENCES

[1] K. Alnawasreh, P. Pelliccione, Z. Hao, M. RÃĕnge, and A. Bertolino. 2017. Online Robustness Testing of Distributed Embedded Systems: An Industrial Approach. In *2017 IEEE/ACM 39th International Conference on Software Engineering: Software Engineering in Practice Track (ICSE-SEIP)*. 133–142. https://doi.org/10.1109/ICSE-SEIP.2017.17

[2] Amazon. 2006-2018. Amazon EC2. https://aws.amazon.com/ec2/

[3] Ivan Beschastnikh, Patty Wang, Yuriy Brun, and Michael D Ernst. 2016. Debugging Distributed Systems. *Queue* 14, 2, Article 50 (March 2016), 20 pages. https://doi.org/10.1145/2927299.2940294

[4] John DeNero, Sumukh Sridhara, Manuel Pérez-Quiñones, Aatish Nayak, and Ben Leong. 2017. Beyond Autograding: Advances in Student Feedback Platforms. In *Proceedings of the 2017 ACM SIGCSE Technical Symposium on Computer Science Education (SIGCSE '17)*. ACM, New York, NY, USA, 651–652. https://doi.org/10.1145/3017680.3017686

[5] Docker. 2013-2018. https://www.docker.com/

[6] Federico Kereki. 2015. Concerning Containers' Connections: On Docker Networking. *Linux J.* 2015, 254, Article 2 (June 2015). http://dl.acm.org/citation.cfm?id=2807678.2807680

[7] R. LÃijbke, D. Schuster, and A. Schill. 2013. Reproducing Network Conditions for Tests of Large-Scale Distributed Systems. In *2013 13th IEEE/ACM International Symposium on Cluster, Cloud, and Grid Computing*. 74–77. https://doi.org/10.1109/CCGrid.2013.70

[8] A. Marroquin, D. Gonzalez, and S. Maag. 2015. Testing distributed systems with test cases dependencies architecture. In *2015 7th IEEE Latin-American Conference on Communications (LATINCOM)*. 1–6. https://doi.org/10.1109/LATINCOM.2015.7430116

[9] Matthew Peveler, Evan Maicus, and Barbara Cutler. 2019. Comparing Jailed Sandboxes vs Containers within an Autograding System. In *Proceedings of the 2019 ACM SIGCSE Technical Symposium on Computer Science Education (SIGCSE '19)*. ACM, New York, NY, USA.

[10] A. Rusan and R. Vasiu. 2015. Emulation of backhaul packet loss on the LTE S1-U interface and impact on end user throughput. In *2015 IEEE International Conference on Intelligent Computer Communication and Processing (ICCP)*. 529–536. https://doi.org/10.1109/ICCP.2015.7312715

[11] František Špaček, Radomír Sohlich, and Tomáš Dulík. 2015. Docker as Platform for Assignments Evaluation. *Procedia Engineering* 100 (2015), 1665–1671.

[12] Submitty. 2014-2018. http://www.submitty.org/

[13] TERRA NULLIS. 2018. Pumba - Chaos Testing for Docker. https://alexei-led.github.io/post/pumba_docker_chaos_testing/

[14] C. Torens and L. Ebrecht. 2010. RemoteTest: A Framework for Testing Distributed Systems. In *2010 Fifth International Conference on Software Engineering Advances*. 441–446. https://doi.org/10.1109/ICSEA.2010.75

[15] Chris Wilcox. 2015. The Role of Automation in Undergraduate Computer Science Education. In *Proceedings of the 46th ACM Technical Symposium on Computer Science Education (SIGCSE '15)*. ACM, New York, NY, USA, 90–95. https://doi.org/10.1145/2676723.2677226

[16] Chris Wilcox. 2016. Testing Strategies for the Automated Grading of Student Programs. In *Proceedings of the 47th ACM Technical Symposium on Computing Science Education (SIGCSE '16)*. ACM, New York, NY, USA, 437–442. https://doi.org/10.1145/2839509.2844616

[17] H. Zeng, B. Wang, W. Deng, and W. Zhang. 2017. Measurement and Evaluation for Docker Container Networking. In *2017 International Conference on Cyber-Enabled Distributed Computing and Knowledge Discovery (CyberC)*. 105–108. https://doi.org/10.1109/CyberC.2017.78

Comparing Jailed Sandboxes vs Containers Within an Autograding System

Matthew Peveler
Rensselaer Polytechnic Institute
pevelm@rpi.edu

Evan Maicus
Rensselaer Polytechnic Institute
maicue@rpi.edu

Barbara Cutler
Rensselaer Polytechnic Institute
cutler@cs.rpi.edu

ABSTRACT

With the continued growth of enrollment within computer science courses, it has become an increasing necessity to utilize autograding systems. These systems have historically graded assignments through either a *jailed sandbox* environment or within a *virtual machine* (VM). For a VM, each submission is given its own instantiation of a guest operating system and virtual hardware that runs atop the host system, preventing anything that runs within the VM communicating with any other VM or the host. However, using these VMs are costly in terms of system resources, making it less than ideal for running student submissions given reasonable, limited resources. Jailed sandboxes, on the other hand, run on the host itself, thus taking up minimal resources, and utilize a security model that restricts the process to specified directories on the system. However, due to running on the host machine, the approach suffers as new courses utilize autograding and bring their own set of potentially conflicting requirements for programming languages and system packages. Over the past several years, *containers* have seen growing popularity in usage within the software engineering industry as well as within autograding systems. Containers provide similar benefits of isolation as a VM while maintaining similar resource cost to running within a jailed sandbox environment. We present the implementation of both a jailed sandbox and container-based autograder, compare the running time and memory usage of the two implementations, and discuss the overall resource usage.

CCS CONCEPTS

• **Social and professional topics** → *Computer science education*; *Software engineering education*; • **Applied computing** → *Interactive learning environments*; *Learning management systems*;

KEYWORDS

Containers, Jailed Sandbox, Autograding, Docker

ACM Reference Format:
Matthew Peveler, Evan Maicus, and Barbara Cutler. 2019. Comparing Jailed Sandboxes vs Containers Within an Autograding System. In *Proceedings of the 50th ACM Technical Symposium on Computer Science Education (SIGCSE '19), February 27-March 2, 2019, Minneapolis, MN, USA.* ACM, New York, NY, USA, Article 4, 7 pages. https://doi.org/10.1145/3287324.3287507

SIGCSE '19, February 27-March 2, 2019, Minneapolis, MN, USA

ACM ISBN 978-1-4503-5890-3/19/02...$15.00
https://doi.org/10.1145/3287324.3287507

1 INTRODUCTION

The demand for computing professionals across industries continues to grow. In conjunction, universities are seeing a growth in enrollment in CS courses and are having to teach and grade larger classes [3]. To handle this surge, many are turning to autograding systems, whether they be commercial or homegrown, to provide automated feedback to students on their assignments [4]. Increasingly, these systems are being seen as an absolute necessity for instructors as it no longer feasible to provide adequate manual feedback on each homework submission from a student [23]. In addition to this, instructors may wish to use a variety of programming languages and system resources to teach their courses. A study of CS1 courses in the UK found that 13 different programming languages were used [17]. Additionally, given that many of the languages identified on that list release new versions at least annually (or in the case of Javascript, a major revision biannually), ensuring the instructors have a specific version within an autograding system requires a flexible design, especially as instructors within the same department may disagree about the specific version of a language they wish to use for their courses.

We consider the following requirements necessary for a robust and flexible autograding system. These aspects are independent of the details of any assignment or grading evaluation criteria.

- A student should be able to submit an assignment multiple times, and should receive prompt automated testing feedback for each attempt.
- A student should not be able to view the submission files or autograding results of any other student on the server.
- A student's submission should be subjected to some limitations on allowed runtime, memory usage, size of generated artifacts, etc. to prevent runaway processes.
- A student may not affect the host system.
- A student may not utilize resources not explicitly granted to them as part of the autograding process (such as accessing the Internet).

Autograding systems have historically been implemented using either a jailed sandbox, which is fast and light on resources, but hard to isolate specific versions of dependencies per assignment, or a virtual machine/external server, which is slower, but allows for a full separation of dependencies per assignment per VM, assuming a unique VM per assignment configuration. Relatively recently, containers have seen a surge in popularity within the computing industry as a middle ground between jailed sandboxes and virtual machines, drawing upon each environments' strengths while avoiding their weaknesses. These traits, therefore, suggest that containers are potentially ideal for autograding. Within this paper, we examine and draw comparisons between the jailed sandbox environment versus utilization of containers. For the latter, we utilize the Docker [5] platform, which has greatly popularized usage of containers in both industry as well as for autograding. Through the course of the paper, we use Docker interchangeablely with containers, but recognize that containers predates Docker, and that there are alternatives, such as Core OS rkt[19], for creating and managing containers. Virtual Machines and external servers (such as the Amazon EC2 platform [2]) are omitted from consideration. Utilization of VMs for proper isolation proves far too heavy in terms of used system resources as well as boot times, which often takes over a minute. While we could leave a VM booted continuously to avoid the boot time, we would then have to load the required dependencies for multiple courses/assignments such that it would then have the same issues as the jailed sandbox. Additionally, a booted VM generally requires upwards of 512MB of RAM which it will consume so long as it lives so that it can perform tasks that make sense within a desktop/server environment, but not necessarily for autograding. External servers are rejected due to the high associated cost of running them throughout the semester and/or explicit fees per submission per unit of autograding time. Furthermore, external servers face many of the same problems as VMs in addition to connection delays between the submission server and the external testing server.

In this paper, we provide a comparison of a jailed sandbox environment versus using containers for autograding. In Section 3, we introduce Submitty [21], our open-source course management platform for collecting, automated testing, and automated grading of programming assignments. In Section 4, we describe our jailed sandbox autograding implementation and the pros and cons of this approach. In Section 5, we discuss our implementation of autograding via Docker and its strengths and weaknesses. In Section 6, we measure the performance of these two approaches, covering resources used on the machine as well as time spent grading an assignment. In Section 7, we conclude our paper and discuss promising future lines of research for this work.

2 RELATED WORK

Many different autograding platforms have been created focusing on different aspects of the process. The first comprehensive surveys were done of such systems and their history in 2005 [1, 6]. Ihantola et al. point out in their survey of autograders that even though many of the developed prototypes are not open sourced or released [11]. However, the systems do have common functionalities. Additionally, prior work has been done to document many of the potential attack vectors a student may use in their submission [7] that a robust autograding environment must be able to handle.

Furthermore, while prior work discusses autograders, what they should do, and how they should operate [24], they largely gloss over the exact specifics of the environment within which they operate and provide little context for why they decided on a given environment. Additionally, beyond work done by Špaček et al. on how one might structure an autograder to utilize Docker [20], there is very little literature on using Docker for autograding, or the considerations one must take in using it. To our knowledge, there does not exist a work that provides a comparison of resource usage and throughput of a jailed sandbox vs. Docker for an autograding environment.

3 OUR AUTOGRADER IMPLEMENTATION

Within our university, we have implemented our own open source autograding system, Submitty [21]. Submitty has been in use in the Computer Science Department at Rensselaer Polytechnic Institute since 2014, and during the last year, was used by a dozen courses per semester with more than 2000 enrolled students combined. For our deployed server installation we use Ubuntu 18.04 and the packages that come with it, but Submitty also supports for Ubuntu 16.04 and Debian 7. Within this system, we have support for about 8 programming languages (e.g. Python, C++, Java, C, Scheme) used in our courses, as well as an equal number of instrumentation packages to performance static analysis, monitor memory usage, run test suites, etc.

To create a new assignment, an instructor writes a JSON specification file that describes any necessary compilation steps for the assignment, the testcases to be run, and how to validate the output from the code, most commonly using some variation of Myer's Diff [18] (e.g. doing a strict diff, allowing for lines to appear in any order, ignoring whitespace differences) or through usage of an automated test suite, like JUnit [12]. Students can re-submit the assignment multiple times before the submission deadline, each time receiving feedback on the success or failure of the *non-hidden* automated tests. Note: We suggest that instructors include additional *hidden* test cases to ensure that students do not simple hard-code solutions to the published test suite. Once the submission deadline is passed, student work may be further assessed manually by an instructor or TAs via an web interface that shows a rubric, as well as the output of each individual testcase, as well as the student's submitted code.

The instructor specifies how they wish students to submit to the server, either utilizing a drag-and-drop interface, or by using Git [9] version control wherein the server will clone the student's repository. The autograding pipeline is modular and allows for selection and customization of alternative grading methods (e.g., jailed sandbox vs. Docker) from within the JSON configuration. The Submitty system configuration allows specification of the overall number of concurrent autograders (based on server hardware specifications). We utilize this system and its associated autograding pipeline to analyze these two environments to compare and contrast the performance of the two implementations.

4 AUTOGRADING VIA JAILED SANDBOXES

A popular approach to handling autograding is to utilize a jailed sandbox environment, which is conceptually straightforward. In a jailed sandbox, the autograding process is run directly on the host machine utilizing whatever services/packages have been installed there. To achieve the secured sandbox so as to achieve our previously stated requirements, we have sufficient *untrusted* users. These users only have access to files within a specific workspace directory with access restricted to a single untrusted user. The autograding process for a student submission is then roughly as follows:

(1) Copy a student's submission into the untrusted user workspace
(2) Compile the student's submission as that untrusted user

(3) Run the testcases for the student's submission as that untrusted user
(4) Validate the results from the testcases
(5) Move the final results out of the untrusted user workspace

To perform this process, a user with a higher permission level does the first action of copying in the required files. The higher level user then executes the compilation, testing, and validation script as the reduced-privilege untrusted user. To further enhance security we could also use `chroot` to more robustly restrict the workspace to the working directory and to ensure that the untrusted user cannot access any files on the system with mistakenly set permissions and removing any environment settings for the system so as to prevent the untrusted user from accessing them. To restrict the actions and resources available to the student code, the untrusted user is limited to a whitelist of allowed system calls using the Linux `seccomp` library [22].

To protect the host system from programs that may unintentionally, accidentally, or maliciously hog CPU or RAM, open excessively-many files, attempt to write infinite length files, or "fork-bomb" the system with too many threads or processes, RLimits are put in place on the executing process. Anytime a process attempts to violate one of these limits, a related signal is sent to the process (such as SIGXCPU for using too much of the CPU), which is then translated internally to a SIGKILL on execution of the student's code.

While the jailed sandbox is in some ways straightforward and efficient, it also has significant drawbacks, principally in what resources remain available to the student code. Because student code is being run directly on the host machine, any program or package that's installed on the machine could potentially be run by the student. Students may have access to programs that an instructor did not want a student to use and did not even realize is installed on the host. While an instructor can use a `seccomp` to prevent a student from running additional processes from their code, if that filter is not used, then a student would potentially `exec` any program installed on the machine. However, while it is possible to handle this via a more complex virtualization of the filesystem, this adds additional complication for setting up an assignment for an instructor and for a system administrator to ensure correctness. Furthermore, many programming languages, such as Python, make use of modules. These modules are often times installed globally on the system such that any user may use them, which may complicate things when one class expressly wants students to use a module that another class directly forbids. Some of these languages feature methods of creating "virtual environments" that only have access to specific modules installed into the environment, utilization of them is language specific and complicated to fold into a jailed sandbox, while still maintaining an ease of use to instructors.

5 AUTOGRADING VIA DOCKER

An alternative to autograding via a jailed sandbox is to use containers. While much of the underlying technology of containers (such as cgroups and namespaces) have been around for over a decade, they have received a lot of recent attention due to Docker, which has allowed a lower barrier of entry to using containers. Containers provide a lightweight alternative to virtual machines, while still providing isolation of running processes from the host machine. This is accomplished by providing virtualization at the operating system level, which allows use of resources of the host system and its kernel. Containers share the base components of their runtime with the host as well as other containers which leads to a smaller footprint in running the containers. This is in contrast to VMs which perform their virtualization at the hardware level and prevent sharing of resources with other VMs. To make use of containers, much like for a VM, one needs to create an *image* that is used to create independent, isolated containers. We can easily create specialized container images targeting a specific language or specific packages without impacting other courses or existing assignments. This allows instructors to create unique environments for their courses, with whatever languages or packages they might want without affecting the host system or the containers prepared for other courses or assignments. Additionally, through the use of containers, it becomes possible to automatically test and grade networked or distributed programs that utilize isolated networks wherein the containers communicate to each other [13, 16].

The autograding process for Docker adds some additional steps over the jailed sandbox environment:

(1) Copy a student's submission into untrusted user workspace
(2) Create a container, mounting the untrusted user workspace to that container
(3) Execute the compilation step for an assignment
(4) Execute each testcase for the assignment
(5) Execute validation over the test cases results
(6) Destroy the container
(7) Move the results from the untrusted user workspace

We still utilize our implementation of a jailed sandbox inside of the container for added security and per testcase resource restrictions. Docker can be configured to similarly limit the CPU and memory a container uses. While this does effectively cover a similar effect as some of the RLimits from before, we still require RLimits to limit the size of files created by runaway processes.

5.1 Security Considerations

By default, utilization of a container provides isolation of automated testing of a student's submission from other students as well as the host machine. Additionally, by default, a container is not allowed to communicate with the outside Internet. In addition to these container-specific details, we also utilize parts of the security model built around the sandbox environment. This means that within our container, we utilize seccomp to specify what system calls are allowed to be made in execution of their programs. However, it should be noted here that given that one could run any OS within a container, not just one matching the host, a common pitfall of seccomp is to not consider how a different OS may require different filter flags to achieve the same result within seccomp [8].

However, unlike in the sandbox environment, the default user that runs a process within a Docker container is root. Additionally, the folder that was mounted into the container in step (2) above has the same owner/group as the host system. This means that it's not enough to simply not run as root, but rather we must run as the same untrusted user inside the container that owns that workspace. While it's possible to exec a command on container creation to create the necessary user, Docker also allows one to pass in a specific group ID (GID) and user ID (UID) to execute all commands within a container under. These IDs need not exist on the container, and so long as you do not attempt to get the name of the user/group (such as via whoami), this works seamlessly, and removes the risk of running programs within the container as root.

5.2 Docker Images

A necessary step of autograding via Docker containers is the creation of Docker images. For VM images, a user generally installs an OS, installs some packages, and then creates an archive out of the resulting image or uses provisioning software (e.g. Chef, Salt, Puppet) with its own format to create an image. These steps are either manually labor-intensive in the case of the former or require knowledge of the specialized format in the latter. In contrast, Docker images are specified by creating a *Dockerfile*. This file begins with a base image (major linux distros such as Ubuntu and Debian are available as base images) is specified to build from and then a series of *RUN* commands to be executed on that base image using the default shell of that distro (e.g. bash). Docker then handles getting the base image and running each command, returning a built image, without requiring the user to manually type the commands inside the VM. However, to produces the smallest possible Docker images, one must condense run commands as much as possible and not add unnecessary packages. Listing 1 presents a sample Dockerfile built from the Debian base image.

```
FROM debian:stretch-slim

RUN apt-get update \
    && apt-get -y --no-install-recommends install \
        grep \
        libseccomp-dev \
        libseccomp2 \
    && rm -rf /var/lib/apt/lists/*

CMD ["/bin/bash"]
```

Listing 1: Example Dockerfile

To keep the size of Debian and Ubuntu images small, we use the *no-install-recommends* flag, we remove the cache of available packages created by the *apt-get update* command, and we execute these commands in a single RUN line. The choice of base image is significant as well. Table 1 presents the base size of four popular Docker images.

Image	Size
alpine:3.8	4.41MB
ubuntu:18.04	84.1MB
debian:stretch-slim	55.3MB
debian:stretch	101MB

Table 1: Popular Docker images and their sizes

While it would seem that one would want to always use Alpine [15] thanks to its very small footprint, it can be more difficult to add the necessary programs and packages. For example, Alpine does not come with the `glibc` and it is not easy to build packages like Clang6 without prior Alpine experience. Thus, we selected the *debian:stretch-slim* image thanks to its more familiar interface, general ease in building any package, relatively small size, and similarity to our host OS Ubuntu (to avoid problems with seccomp).

Submitty allow instructors to specify their own complete Dockerfile, or use our simple command-line interface to mix and match Dockerfile components (such as Python 3.6, Clang 6, Java8, etc.) and specify additional system packages and language modules.Instructors specify the appropriate Docker image within the assignment configuration JSON. Additionally, these images can be distributed to students for use during offline development and testing.

6 PERFORMANCE ANALYSIS

While containers are billed as being lightweight compared to virtual machines, they are not as lightweight as a jailed sandbox, due to the additional OS virtualization layer. To analyze these costs, we identified several busy periods of student submissions from a prior term. Even the busiest time periods did not overwhelm the CPU or memory resources of our server hardware (which is ensured by our conservative limit of the machine to grading at most ten assignments in parallel). We selected the busiest four hour period during the Fall 2017 that semester – a time period with ~540 unique submissions in our CS1 and CS2 courses. The period selected occurred the night of their common assignment deadline and happened on the 9th week of the semester when both classes are tackling more compute-intensive assignments. The submissions gave us a mix of perfect full-credit submissions, submissions earning partial credit, submissions that failed to compile or run at all, and submissions that entered into infinite loops. We then took this time period and replayed it (and repeated the time period) with different time speedups over an hour to artificially stress the hardware and test the scalability. We also increased the number of allowed concurrent autograding processes. We repeated each simulation twice, running it first under the jailed sandbox setup, and then running it using Docker containers. Fo the Docker test, we prepared a single "master" image with both Python and C++, and additional utilities used by CS2, such as Valgrind, as well as some extraneous packages, with a total image size of 2.1 GB. The system hardware we utilized for these tests was a Dell Poweredge R520 with an Intel Xeon ES-2470 (20 Cores, 40 Threads) CPU and 32 GB of RAM.

During the execution of the time period we measured the following statistics:

- Number of active graders every 0.1 seconds
- CPU utilization percentage every 0.1 seconds
- Memory usage every 0.1 seconds
- Time taken for a submission to be executed and graded
- Time spent by a submission waiting in the queue for grading to begin
- Time spent creating a container (for Docker)
- Time spent destroying a container (for Docker)

These measures were then averaged over every minute within the one hour. For time spent, for any minute that did not have any processes either finish grading or finish waiting, we took the average of its nearest neighbors that did have those values. We then plotted the system performance metrics against each other in terms of percentage used versus the overall amount available and then

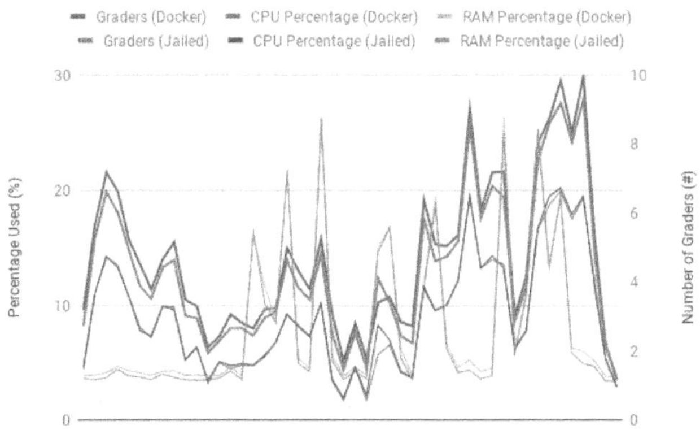

Figure 1: Resource usage for 4X simulation

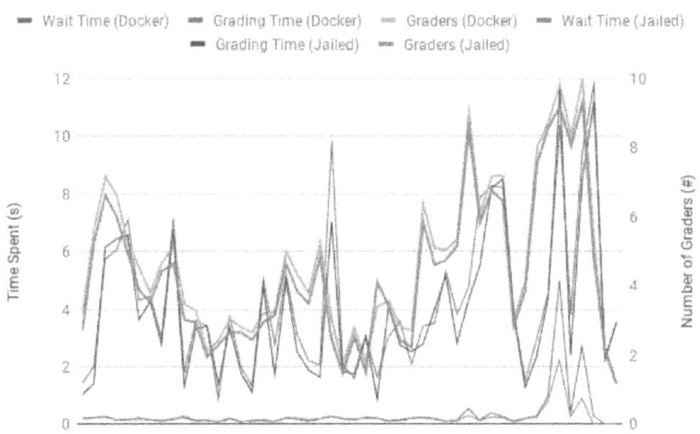

Figure 2: Average time spent for 4X simulation

created a plot of the average time spent grading and average time spent waiting.

6.1 Results

For our first considered simulation, we took the four hour block and replayed it once within an hour block (4X the recorded load). Within that block, we allowed for 10 concurrent graders to operate. The results of this simulation are shown in Figures 1 and 2. The CPU used for Docker versus the jailed system are roughly equivalent. The RAM, while higher for Docker, had on average less than a percent difference. The time used for grading is also roughly comparable, with an average of 0.6 seconds more spent for Docker versus the jailed sandbox and then an almost equal time spent waiting for each submission throughout. However, we see Docker has two periods where the wait time deviates from the jailed sandbox wait time (the first around 3 seconds and the second around 2 seconds). Just before the assignment deadline (at the end of the 4 hour window) the machine has reached our conservative limit of concurrent autograding processes. This happens because for each container, we spent around ~1.4 seconds for creating the container, and about ~1 second for destroying the container, making each grader last an extra ~2.4 seconds with Docker versus the jailed sandbox. While the production server could handle this load without an increase in wait time, the slight overhead of Docker did result in a small wait time for the equivalent simulation replay.

For our second presented simulation, we took the same four hour block and condensed it to 15 minutes, and then replayed that 4x to make up the hour (effectively a 16X of realtime recorded load). We also bumped up the number of allowed concurrent graders to be 28 to partially handle the simulated increase in submissions per hour. Note that the number of concurrent graders is still less than the number of threaded cores on the machine (40), which should not unduly stress the machine for the single-threaded student assignments in our CS1 and CS2 courses. The results of this simulation are shown in Figures 3 and 4. Here, we see that Docker ends up utilizing all of the concurrent graders for a large fraction of the simulation hour. This ends up causing Docker to start utilizing more RAM (with a peak difference of about 15%) and CPU (with a peak difference of about 5%). The jailed sandbox environment on the other hand never needed to use all of the graders at one time. More importantly, we see a far more drastic change in the amount of time taken to grade an assignment and the wait time per submission. Docker, once maxed out, with the additional time cost of creating and destroying containers, cascades through the system to subsequent submissions, giving larger fluctuations in the amount of time spent waiting for an assignment to start grading, which at the worst of times added almost an additional 25 seconds of waiting, and on average was above 10 additional seconds. By contrast, the jailed sandbox ran more efficiently, maintaining a wait time that was close to zero seconds spent waiting per submission. While under the full load of the concurrent graders, we saw that the time taken on average to create a container to be 7.4 seconds and destroying a container to be 3.3 seconds.

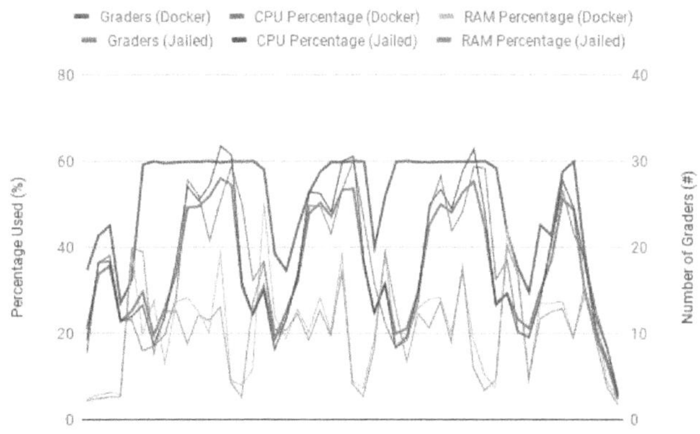

Figure 3: Resource usage for 16X simulation

6.2 Discussion

From these results, we can conclude that while containers do have a cost related to them in terms of resources, the primary cost is paid in terms of time taken with container creation and destruction. Even when not all graders were being utilized on a machine, each student on average experienced an additional 2 seconds slowdown

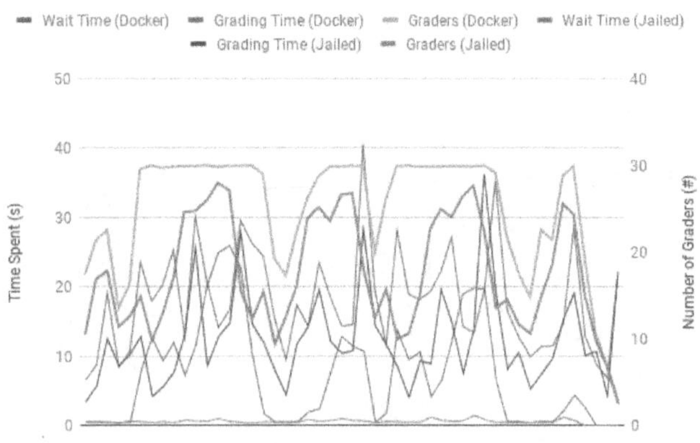

Figure 4: Average time spent for 16X simulation

per submission. However, once the server was under a full load, that time rose to an average of almost 11 seconds per submission. While not a drastic change in time taken, any time increase to a student is disliked, especially during that the busiest and most stressful period before the assignment deadline.

The spikes in the grading time in the data largely corresponded to students who had submitted programs that had infinite loops that would therefore run for several minutes until finally being killed off by the system via the RLimit. While this affected the average grading time for an assignment in the time slice where it occurred, more importantly, it meant that a grader was taken out of circulation for an abnormally long time which ended up causing a cascade effect on other graders that were potentially similarly hogged and which ended up causing more severe fluctuations in wait time and grade time for submissions.

Finally, the image that we was used for these test was not specialized per class or per assignment, rather bringing in all packages that might be needed for multiple courses, resulting in a relative large image size. By creating more specialized images per course and per assignment, we may see that the amount of time taken in creation and destruction of a container decreases as well, while secondarily also not requiring as much space on the host environment's hard drive to store the container.

We did attempt to test Docker underneath additional concurrent graders (up to 40) for the 16X simulated test case; however, the system was not stable. Grading processes would crash when container creation failed showing a definite limitation of using Docker for autograding. When we equivalently bumped up the number of concurrent graders for the jailed sandbox environment beyond the number of threads on the machine, the system and grading processes ran slower, but remained stable and operational. More development will be needed to tune the system and robustly handle near-capacity autograding load in containers.

7 CONCLUSION

Given the results of our performance testing, switching from the jailed sandbox to Docker containers for autograding is quite promising. In this work, we discussed the configuration, strengths, and weaknesses of both implementations. We analyzed the CPU and RAM utilization and timing statistics over the lifetime of the autograding processes for submitted assignments. Through this, we found relatively negligible differences in performance between the two environments, except when the machine was under a significant load at which point containers started to perform much worse in terms of time taken for container creation and destruction. Overall, we believe that the strengths of containers far outweigh the weaknesses, with the caution that care should be taken to tune the system configuration for large loads and further investigate issues impacting of system robustness.

In this work, we utilize a simplistic view of the container life cycle as it is applied to autograding. As shown in Section 5, within a single autograder process, a container is created, the student's code is run and evaluated, and then the container is destroyed. However, as shown in Section 6, most of the time cost of using a container is in the construction and destruction portions of that life cycle. Looking forward, we would like to investigate ways to mitigate these costs so that to a student, the time cost of using a container vs a jailed sandbox is relatively equal. We first consider the startup cost.

To improve this, we take inspiration from other sources (e.g. web servers, databases) and how they handle fluctuations in load. With these services, it is common to define a "pool" of available workers for a given process, oftentimes defining a minimum number of workers in the pool as well as the maximum size that it can grow to. Similarly, for the containers, we can work to maintain a container pool such that for a new submission, it can take a container from the pool instead of having to create the containers on-demand for all submissions. However, unlike the aforementioned examples, to maintain the flexibility that container usage affords us, we must further investigate algorithms to handle which container images we need to fill our pool with. As a first step in this direction, we can maintain a count of images used within some time frame, and then fill our pool with the most used images within that frame, with the expectation that the next submission will draw from the same distribution. Further work around this would be to investigate and utilize forms of machine learning and analysis to allow us to tune this pool on demand.

Opposite the start up time of containers, to improve the destruction time, we can offset this process to be done outside of the core process of autograding of a submission. To do this, we can create a container garbage collector that cleans up containers asynchronously at some fixed interval. Implementations of these strategies, while allowing for a better throughput has to be balanced out with the potential increase in number of containers that may exist at one time, especially in regards to a GC for recycling old containers. As stated, in Section 6, we found that once we had too many running containers at once, Docker would start to error out in attempting to create more.

REFERENCES

[1] Kirsti M Ala-Mutka. 2005. A Survey of Automated Assessment Approaches for Programming Assignments. *Computer Science Education* 15, 2 (2005), 83–102. https://doi.org/10.1080/08993400500150747 arXiv:https://doi.org/10.1080/08993400500150747
[2] Amazon. 2006-2018. Amazon EC2. https://aws.amazon.com/ec2/
[3] Computing Research Association. 2017. *Generation CS: CS Undergraduate Enrollments Surge Since 2006.* Technical Report.

[4] John DeNero, Sumukh Sridhara, Manuel Pérez-Quiñones, Aatish Nayak, and Ben Leong. 2017. Beyond Autograding: Advances in Student Feedback Platforms. In *Proceedings of the 2017 ACM SIGCSE Technical Symposium on Computer Science Education (SIGCSE '17)*. ACM, New York, NY, USA, 651–652. https://doi.org/10.1145/3017680.3017686

[5] Docker. 2013-2018. https://www.docker.com/

[6] Christopher Douce, David Livingstone, and James Orwell. 2005. Automatic Test-based Assessment of Programming: A Review. *J. Educ. Resour. Comput.* 5, 3, Article 4 (Sept. 2005). https://doi.org/10.1145/1163405.1163409

[7] Michal Forisek. 2007. Security of Programming Contest Systems.

[8] Tal Garfinkel. 2003. Traps and Pitfalls: Practical Problems in System Call Interposition Based Security Tools. In *Proceedings of the Network and Distributed System Security Symposium (NDSS)*.

[9] Git. 2005-2018. https://git-scm.com/

[10] Georgiana Haldeman, Andrew Tjang, Monica Babeş-Vroman, Stephen Bartos, Jay Shah, Danielle Yucht, and Thu D. Nguyen. 2018. Providing Meaningful Feedback for Autograding of Programming Assignments. In *Proceedings of the 49th ACM Technical Symposium on Computer Science Education (SIGCSE '18)*. ACM, New York, NY, USA, 278–283. https://doi.org/10.1145/3159450.3159502

[11] Petri Ihantola, Tuukka Ahoniemi, Ville Karavirta, and Otto Seppälä. 2010. Review of Recent Systems for Automatic Assessment of Programming Assignments. In *Proceedings of the 10th Koli Calling International Conference on Computing Education Research (Koli Calling '10)*. ACM, New York, NY, USA, 86–93. https://doi.org/10.1145/1930464.1930480

[12] JUnit. 2018. https://junit.org/junit5/

[13] Federico Kereki. 2015. Concerning Containers' Connections: On Docker Networking. *Linux J.* 2015, 254, Article 2 (June 2015). http://dl.acm.org/citation.cfm?id=2807678.2807680

[14] Stephan Krusche and Andreas Seitz. 2018. ArTEMiS: An Automatic Assessment Management System for Interactive Learning. In *Proceedings of the 49th ACM Technical Symposium on Computer Science Education (SIGCSE '18)*. ACM, New York, NY, USA, 284–289. https://doi.org/10.1145/3159450.3159602

[15] Alpine Linux. 2018. https://alpinelinux.org/

[16] Evan Maicus, Matthew Peveler, Stacy Patterson, and Barbara Cutler. 2019. Autograding Distributed Algorithms in Networked Containers. In *Proceedings of the 2019 ACM SIGCSE Technical Symposium on Computer Science Education (SIGCSE '19)*. ACM, New York, NY, USA.

[17] Ellen Murphy, Tom Crick, and James H. Davenport. 2017. An Analysis of Introductory Programming Courses at UK Universities. *Programming Journal* 1 (2017), 18.

[18] Eugene W. Myers. 1986. An O(ND) difference algorithm and its variations. *Algorithmica* 1, 1 (01 Nov 1986), 251–266. https://doi.org/10.1007/BF01840446

[19] Core OS. 2014-2018. rkt. https://coreos.com/rkt/

[20] František Špaček, Radomír Sohlich, and Tomáš Dulík. 2015. Docker as Platform for Assignments Evaluation. *Procedia Engineering* 100 (2015), 1665–1671.

[21] Submitty. 2014-2018. http://www.submitty.org/

[22] Wikipedia. 2018. Seccomp. https://en.wikipedia.org/w/index.php?title=Seccomp&oldid=853577449 [Online; accessed 27-August-2018].

[23] Chris Wilcox. 2015. The Role of Automation in Undergraduate Computer Science Education. In *Proceedings of the 46th ACM Technical Symposium on Computer Science Education (SIGCSE '15)*. ACM, New York, NY, USA, 90–95. https://doi.org/10.1145/2676723.2677226

[24] Chris Wilcox. 2016. Testing Strategies for the Automated Grading of Student Programs. In *Proceedings of the 47th ACM Technical Symposium on Computing Science Education (SIGCSE '16)*. ACM, New York, NY, USA, 437–442. https://doi.org/10.1145/2839509.2844616

Trial by Flyer: Building Quadcopters From Scratch in a Ten-Week Capstone Course

Steven Swanson
University of Califonia, San Diego
San Diego, California
swanson@cs.ucsd.edu

ABSTRACT

We describe our experience teaching an intensive capstone course in which pairs of students build the hardware and software for a remote-controller quad-rotor aircraft (i.e., a quadcopter or "drone") from scratch in one 10-week quarter. The course covers printed circuit board (PCB) design and assembly, basic control theory and sensor fusion, and embedded systems programming. To reduce the workload on course staff and provide higher-quality feedback on student designs, we have implemented an automated PCB design checking tool/autograder. We describe the course content in detail, identify the challenges it presents to students and course staff, and propose changes to further increase student success and improve the scalability of the course.

CCS CONCEPTS

• **Social and professional topics → Model curricula**; • **Hardware → PCB design and layout**; • **Computer systems organization →** Robotic control; Embedded software.

KEYWORDS

Quadcopters, Capstone, Robotics

ACM Reference Format:

Steven Swanson. 2019. Trial by Flyer: Building Quadcopters From Scratch in a Ten-Week Capstone Course. In *Proceedings of the 50th ACM Technical Symposium on Computer Science Education (SIGCSE '19), February 27-March 2, 2019, Minneapolis, MN, USA.* ACM, New York, NY, USA, 7 pages. https://doi.org/10.1145/3287324.3287451

1 INTRODUCTION

Compute-capable devices and robots are permeating every aspect of our students' lives, and many of the "killer apps" of the future will lie at the intersection of the computing and the physical world – robotics, the internet of things, personal electronics, etc. Students prepared to create those applications must understand how to design, build, and debug systems that include both code and physical components. Likewise, programming has become an integral part of every engineering discipline, so many engineering students can benefit from hands-on experience building a programming complex systems. Educators have devised a wide range of capstone courses to provide students with experience at the boundary of hardware and software [20, 22–25], but providing this experience in the face of growing enrollments is a significant challenge.

To provide students with project-based, hands-on experience we have developed a 10-week (one academic quarter) capstone, interdisciplinary course in which students design and build all of the hardware and software components of a remote-controlled quadrotor aircraft (or "quadcopter"). The course content includes embedded system/microcontroller programming, debugging software-controlled mechanical systems, working on interdisciplinary teams, PCB design, basic sensing and control theory, and practical skills in PCB assembly, soldering, and debugging electro-mechanical systems. The class targets senior undergraduate (or graduate) computer science, computer engineering, and other engineering students. We have taught the class annually for the last four years in the computer science and engineering department at the University of California, San Diego. The class has been growing in size and most recently had 24 students working in twelve groups.

A particularly challenging aspect of teaching the course is providing detailed, thorough, and reliable design reviews for student designs. Even a small error in the PCB design can lead to failure, and most teams require multiple reviews before their design is ready to manufacture. The workload can be crushing for the instructors.

To remedy this problem, we developed an automatic design checker call *QuadLint* that can verify many aspects of student designs. The tool drastically reduces the number of human design reviews required and lets those reviews focus on less tedious aspects of the design review process. It is thorough enough to fully automate grading for some of the preliminary labs in the course. We believe QuadLint is the first autograder to handle PCB designs.

apluThe emphasis on building hardware is unusual for a computer science course, but understanding how to build computer systems is critical for students hoping to craft next-generation devices that rely on the careful blending of hardware and software[1].

The course materials are all freely available online[2]. The only exceptions are a complete "solution" to the project and the source code for our automatic design checker. We are happy to share these with educators.

Based on surveys, course evaluations, and anecdotal reports, students find the class to be very challenging, but also exciting, engaging, educational, and fun. The course staff reports that it is great fun to teach as well.

This paper describes the course content, the challenges that arise in teaching the class, our design checking tool, and student reflections on the course. Most of the descriptions reflect the most recent instance of the class (Spring 2018). We also detail our plans for the next version which will address many of these challenges and should allow the class to grow further in size.

2 PROJECT OVERVIEW

The class is an intensive, capstone-style course. It moves very quickly and students need to stay engaged and work hard to succeed. With just a very few exceptions over the last four years, students rise to the course's challenge with aplomb.

SIGCSE '19, February 27-March 2, 2019, Minneapolis, MN, USA

ACM ISBN 978-1-4503-5890-3/19/02.
https://doi.org/10.1145/3287324.3287451

[1] Also, as Turing Award winner Alan Kay famously said "People who are really serious about software should make their own hardware"

[2] https://sites.google.com/a/eng.ucsd.edu/quadcopterclass/
https://github.com/NVSL?q=QuadClass

Figure 1: Photos from the Class – (From left to right) Two student quadcopters (top and bottom), the old test stand (top) and the new (bottom), and the current, expensive remote control (top) and the cost-optimized version (bottom).

H1: Eagle Intro	Complete an Eagle tutorial on building libraries, schematic assembly, layout, design checks, and CAM file generation.
H2: PCB Libraries	Build several Eagle library parts (of varying complexity) from scratch by reading and interpreting data sheets.
H3: Schematic creation	Create the schematic for their quadcopter based on a combination of reference designs, written specifications, and datasheets. Design an LED-based lighting element.
H4: PCB Layout	Design the shape of their PCB and layout the components to meet mechanical, electrical, and aesthetic constraints.
H5: PCB Assembly	Assemble their PCB using solder paste, tweezers, and a reflow oven.
S1: Software Intro	Setup the Arduino IDE and program their remote control and PID test stand to allow remote control of the motor speed. Assemble a PID test stand.
S2: Sensing	Implement sensor filtering and fusion using software and the IMU's internal filters to provide clean, low-noise measurements of the quadcopter's orientation.
S3: PID	Implement a one-channel PID controller to stabilize the PID test stand. Control the pitch of the test stand using their remote control.
S4: Flight Control	Implement flight operation functions such as "arming" the quadcopter and calibrating of the gimbals and IMU.
H6: Flight!	Combine the above elements to make their quadcopter fly.

Table 1: Lab Descriptions – The course comprises ten labs broken into three groups. Many of the hardware and software labs run concurrently to fit them all into ten weeks.

The quadcopters that students design use a PCB to host their electronics and to serve as its airframe (Figure 1-left). They measure less than 10 cm on a side and are suitable for flight indoors over short distances. The motors are moderately powerful, "brushed" electric motors powered by a small lithium-polymer (LiPo) battery, and we use small, plastic propellers. The quadcopters are easy to operate safely, and a blow from the propeller at full speed is painful but not particularly dangerous. Students wear eye protection around their flying quadcopters.

The quadcopters use an Arduino-compatible, 16 MHz Atmega128RFA microcontroller [19] that includes an IEEE 802.15.4 [16] radio. To measure the quadcopter's orientation, we use an inertial measurement unit (IMU) [28] that contains a 3-axis accelerometer and a 3-axis gyroscope. The purpose-built remote control (Figure 1-right) uses the same microcontroller, providing a uniform programming environment for the course.

We teach the class in a "Makerspace" run by our engineering school to support hands-on engineering courses. It provides an array of useful equipment, including high-quality soldering equipment, a professional reflow soldering oven, a laser cutter, and an array of hand tools.

3 COURSE CONTENT

The course breaks building a quadcopter into four high-level tasks: designing the PCB, implementing the flight control software, assembling the PCB, and getting the quadcopter flying. Below we describe each of these tasks, key challenges they present for the students and the course staff, and how we approach them in the class. Table 1 briefly describes the course's ten labs.

3.1 Designing and Manufacturing PCBs

The first task introduces students to the key concepts of PCBs design, the tools and processes used to design and manufacture them, and best practices for PCB design.

They complete labs Lab H1 and Lab H2 on their own. For the remaining labs, they work in pairs. We manufacture the student PCBs through JLPCB [12]. The boards usually arrive with 5-7 days of ordering. We build four-layer PCBs.

Key Topics This task addresses the following concepts and skills.

(1) **PCB principles:** What PCBs are, how they work, and how they are manufactured.

(2) **PCB Design Tools:** The abstractions and concepts that PCB design tools provide to describe PCB designs – schematics, part libraries, layers, design rules, etc.
(3) **Design From Example:** How to adapt reference designs to a particular application.
(4) **Design From Datasheet:** How to interpret device datasheets to integrate a device into a design.
(5) **Part Selection:** How to select appropriate components for a design from among many, many options.
(6) **Design Requirements:** How to describe, interpret and satisfy electrical, mechanical, and application requirements for a PCB.
(7) **PCB Design Best Practices:** How to design schematics and PCBs that functional, manufacturable, and comprehensible to other engineers.
(8) **PCB Manufacturing Process:** How to prepare a design for manufacturing and interpret the design requirements of a particular manufacturer.
(9) **The Cost of PCB Errors:** The importance of detailed design review and attention to detail in PCB design.

The last point represents a significant departure from most other areas of computer science, where the compile-test-debug cycle is extremely short and fixing many errors is nearly free. In the class, an error in a student design can delay their project by at least two weeks – an eternity in a ten-week class. In the real world, PCB design errors can take months to address.

Student Challenges Students face two types of challenge in this part of the class.

The first is using the tools. We use the "standard" version of Autodesk's Eagle PCB design package. It is free for students and relatively simple to use, but its interface has some rough edges.

Second, some students struggle with the "correct by inspection" requirement that comes with designing PCBs. For some, this requirement is stressful. Others struggle to pay enough attention to detail while reviewing their design.

Staff Challenges The main challenge for the course staff is performing design checks to help ensure the student's PCBs will work. The typical quadcopter schematic has ~190 electrical connections and an error in any of them can cause the board to fail. In addition, there are numerous constraints that the PCB layout must meet in order to work properly. Checking these is tedious, time-consuming, and the staff can easily overlook subtle problems. The workload compounds because the students must keep revising their designs until they are correct.

We address this challenge in three ways. First, we require the students to "pay" for design reviews (see below). Second, students perform a peer design review for the schematic and another for the PCB layout. Third, the staff only performs careful design checks on the final schematic and layout. The earlier labs rely mostly on automated design checks (See Section 5).

Teaching The PCB portion of the course moves very quickly and starts the first day of class. In quick succession, students learn the basics of Eagle (Lab H1 – 2 days), how to build high-quality PCB libraries (Lab H2 – 1 week), and then design (Lab H3 – 1.5 weeks) and layout (Lab H4 – 1.5 weeks) their PCB.

We introduce each topic with a lecture and then describe the lab and demonstrate the key features of Eagle they will use. We also describe the electrical components they will use and discuss how to interpret and use datasheets and reference designs.

We use an unusual method for grading the hardware labs that reflects the fact that, in the real world, PCB design errors are expensive. Students "pay" for design reviews (by course staff or QuadLint) with points deducted from their lab grade. This incentivizes them to find and fix problems themselves by inspection rather than relying on QuadLint or the staff.

The labs are worth 10 points. We give them 12 points to start and subtract 0.5 points for each design review they request. Completing a lab requires passing both a QuadLint review and a human review, so they can score up to 11 out of 10. We do not deduct points for anything else on the PCB design labs – the lab must be completed correctly for them to move on. This may seem harsh, but the alternative is manufacturing a PCB with known flaws, which is pointless.

3.2 Implementing Flight Control Software

The flight control software task provides students with first-hand experience implementing a software system that controls a real-world device, comprises two communicating components (the remote and the quadcopter), and presents challenging debugging problems. The two central challenges are 1) combining the inputs from the gyroscope and the accelerometer to provide accurate, responsive measurement of the quadcopter's orientation and 2) implementing and tuning a proportional, integral, derivative (PID) [14] controller to control that orientation.

We provide some pre-built equipment for this portion of the course: a PID test stand (Figure 1 top-middle). The test stand supports a mockup that closely matches components of the quadcopter they will build. It has a microprocessor break-out board (red) [26, 27][3], an IMU breakout board (blue) [17, 18], and a laser-cut plywood frame. It has a pivot that allows the mockup to tip back and forth, simulating a quadcopter that moves on one axis.

We leverage the open-source library support for the IMU [5, 7, 8] and microcontroller [9, 26] provided by SparkFun [1] and Adafruit [2].

Key Topics This task addresses the following concepts and skills:
(1) **Attitude sensing:** How to measure orientation by combining gyroscope and accelerometer measurements.
(2) **Sensor Filtering:** How to use the IMU's built-in filtering facilities to reduce the burden on software.
(3) **Complementary Filtering:** How to use a complementary filter to combine sensor inputs to provide more stable, lower-noise measurements.
(4) **Basic PID control:** How PID controllers work and how to implement and tune them in software.
(5) **Debugging physical systems:** How to debug and tune software that controls a physical system.

Items two through four are the subjects of entire courses (which most student have not taken). We cover the basics and provide intuition for the underlying theory.

Student Challenges Students struggle with several aspects of this task. The first is that the notion of "correctness" for both the filtering and PID code is qualitative rather than quantitative. We provide guidance about the how algorithms should behave, but there is not a crisply-defined "correct" answer.

Second, poor performance can stem from many sources: Conceptual misunderstanding, algorithm implementation errors, arithmetic problems (e.g., overflow), misconfiguration of the IMU, and poor parameter settings. Finding the root cause of a problem can be hard.

Staff Challenges The main staff challenge is to help the students in debugging their code efficiently. The algorithms are not very

[3]Unfortunately, Sparkfun has discontinued this breakout board. We have a good number of them, but we are migrating away from it (see Section 7).

complex, but there are many ways to implement them and getting oriented in each team's code base is impractical.

Instead, when they face a problem, we have students verify that individual components of the system are working properly starting with the simplest. For instance, for trouble with a PID controller, we ask them to verify the correctness of their raw sensor readings, then their filtering code, etc. to identify where, exactly, the problem lies.

Teaching We divide this task into three labs, each with an associated lecture. The first (Lab S1 – 1 week) covers the basic hardware components on the remote and the quadcopter. They assemble code from example programs to demonstrate that they can read sensor data from the IMU and control the speed of motors on their test stand using the remote control.

Lab S2 (1.5 weeks) and the associated lecture covers sensor filtering. The students use a complementary filter [15] combined with the IMU's built-in high- and low-pass filters to generate accurate, low-noise orientation measurements.

In Lab S3 (1.5 weeks) they implement a PID controller to stabilize and control the pitch of the test stand. They must implement PID correctly, tune its parameters, and translate the controller's output to motor power levels.

3.3 PCB Assembly

This task teaches how to assemble a moderately complex PCB. It is a delicate and potentially frustrating process.

Key Topics We teach the following skills:

(1) **Reflow soldering:** How reflow soldering works and how to achieve good results, including how to applying solder paste to the board.
(2) **Placing parts:** How to place parts precisely with tweezers and how to ensure the correct orientation of polarized parts.
(3) **PCB rework techniques:** How to fix common problems in hand-assembled PCBs.
(4) **Hand soldering:** How to solder through-hole components by hand.
(5) **Flashing the bootloader:** How to install the low-level firmware on their microcontroller.
(6) **Testing and bring up:** How to systematically check that each component of their quadcopter is functioning properly.

Student Challenges Assembling boards is hard for several reasons. First, many students have no experience soldering. Common problems include a lack of patience, applying too much solder paste, and applying it imprecisely.

Soldering the IMU is especially challenging. In the latest iteration of the class, the failure rate was 75%, and several teams resorted to "hot wiring" the IMU breakout board onto their quadcopter. This is a clear area where we need to provide a better method[4]

Staff Challenges This has emerged as the most labor-intensive section of the class for the staff, especially since QuadLint has taken on many of the design reviews. The boards come back from the manufacturer in batches, so many groups need intensive, one-on-one guidance about part placement, etc. at the same time. This leads to extremely busy staff, extended lab hours, and a lot of student waiting.

Teaching We provide a brief lecture about reflow soldering and a small group tutorial about applying solder paste and placing parts.

[4]Interestingly, in previous years the success rate has much higher. Several things have changed since then, but the most likely culprit seems to be low-quality solder paste.

3.4 Flight

In the final stage (Lab H6) of the course, students combine their PID controller software with their PCB to create working, flying quadcopter. This includes extending the flight control software from one-axis (pitch) to three (pitch, roll, and yaw), loading it onto their PCB, tuning it to achieve stable flight. Stable hovering counts as success.

Key Topics The key skills covered include the following:

(1) **Integration and testing:** How to generalize their PID controller to work in a more challenging environment.
(2) **Flying a quadcopter:** How to maneuver a quadcopter safely.

Student Challenges Student success during for stage varies widely. Some students get it working quickly, but others struggle, and many do not succeed. In some cases, failure has a clear cause (e.g., their PID from Lab S2 did not work well). In other cases, the cause is less clear. It would be useful to perform interviews with teams to understand what went wrong.

Staff Challenges The challenges here are similar to those for the flight controller portion of the class. The staff mostly provide debugging and moral support to frustrated students.

Teaching There is no additional material to present for this portion of the class. Students start this lab when they have finished Lab H5 and Lab S4 and work on it until the end of the quarter. In the best case, they have three weeks. Some have just a few days.

4 LOGISTICS

Running the course successfully has required us to carefully manage class size and the course schedule. We have also worked to craft a grading scheme to reward student effort and account for the challenging nature of the course.

Please see the appendix of [30] for a more detailed discussion of course logistics.

4.1 Admissions

Students must apply to take the course. We advertise to graduate and undergraduates across the school of engineering, drawing students mostly from computer science, electrical engineering, mechanical and aerospace engineering, and math.

We accept students based on some demonstration of success in projects-based coursework and GPA. We also prioritize students graduating before the next iteration of the class. The last time we taught the class (Spring 2018), we had 119 applicants, accepted 41, and 24 ended up attending the class: Twelve computer science, computer engineering, or robotics students, nine mechanical or aerospace engineering, and three math.

4.2 Schedule

The course schedule is very tight, since our university runs on 10-week quarters. We meet twice a week with a 1.5-hour lecture section followed immediately by 1.5 hours of lab time. The boundary between the lecture and lab is blurry.

We run the hardware and software labs in parallel. We lecture about and then start a new lab roughly every day for the first three weeks of the quarter. From that point on, groups progress at different rates.

Figure 2 illustrates the nominal schedule (down the center of the figure) and the slippage that invariably occurs (the outer edges). The largest delays are in finalizing the PCB layout, assembly, and completing the PID controller and flight software.

In earlier versions of the course, we noticed that students (especially computer science majors) would devote too much time to

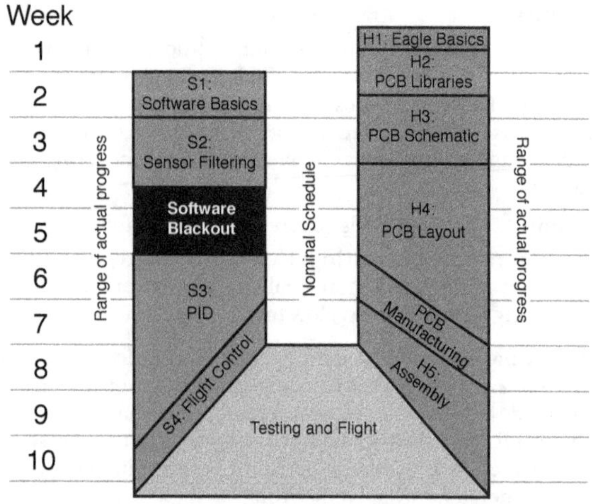

Figure 2: Course Schedule – The schedule for the class moves quickly but accommodates delays. The nominal schedule (down the center) leaves over three weeks for students to get their quadcopters flying. In practice, the timeline varies widely between groups (the edges).

Lab S2 rather than finalizing their PCB layouts. To prevent this, we added a "software blackout" when they must focus only on their PCB layouts and the course staff refuses to answer questions about the software labs.

We do not enforce deadlines on any of the labs after Lab H3.

4.3 Grading

Aside from the "pay-for-review" grading mechanism described above, grading in the course is a combination of participation (showing and doing work), and "checking off" the completion of the labs. Our experience is that students, almost without exception, have worked hard and learned a great deal, even if their quadcopter does not fly in the end. Generally speaking, working hard in the class will earn a "B", and any semblance of flight earns an "A". Stable flight rates an "A+".

4.4 Staffing

The course staffs usually consists of the instructor and one TA. When we have taught the class, the instructor has been deeply involved in designing and running the labs. The staff needs to be familiar with all of the course content and have practical experience with designing, assembling, and debugging PCBs. Experience with PID control is also very useful, although that (and the other software components) are easier to pick up "on the fly," if the staff has general experience with Arduino programming, since errors are less costly and debugging is easier.

The best preparation for teaching the class is doing the project start-to-finish.

4.5 Equipment

The course requires hand-soldering, reflow soldering, and the facilities to build a test stand.

A good soldering iron is necessary, but not terribly expensive. We use soldering irons similar to the Hakko FX-888D ($110).

For reflow, we use a high-end reflow oven, but this is not necessary. The first three iterations of the course used a "heat gun" (i.e., paint stripper) instead of the reflow oven and the results were very good. There is also a rich DIY reflow soldering community online.

We use the laser cutter to build the test stands, but in earlier iterations we 3D-printed the test stands or let the students devise their own testing rig. They showed remarkable ingenuity with materials including rubber bands, cardboard, and popsicle sticks.

5 AUTOMATED DESIGN CHECKS

Checking PCB schematics and layouts is a time consuming, error-prone, and critical to maximizing student success in the class. In the earlier versions of the course, the course staff would quickly become overwhelmed with design reviews. This led to uncaught errors and exhaustion. The effort required effectively limited the number of students we could accommodate in the class.

To reduce this burden, we developed a custom, web-based course management tool called QuadLint that performs automated checks on student PCB schematics and layouts and some other useful classroom functions (e.g., tracking student progress and submitting labs).

QuadLint is, we believe, the first autograder that checks specific design requirements for PCB designs. All PCB design tools provide a suite of design rule checks (DRC) and some PCB manufacturing houses provide automated tests for manufacturability [13], but QuadLint provides an extensible, programmable mechanism for checking the higher-level correctness of designs.

5.1 Checking Designs

QuadLint has two modes. The *quick check* mode generates warnings that flag common violations of good PCB/schematic design style, similar to the checks `lint` performs on source code. These style checks could be applied to any PCB design. Failure to fix a warning will not, in itself, negatively impact the function of the PCB. Students can run quick checks as frequently as they want.

QuadLint's *full check* mode identifies errors that are likely to cause their PCB to not work correctly. Most of these checks only apply to quadcopters designed in this class: They are extremely specific to the reference designs, datasheets, and specifications we provided. The students "pay" for each full check with 0.5 points off their score for the current lab. This prevents them from relying on QuadLint – if they ever design a PCB on their own, they will not have the benefit of QuadLint's detailed checks to catch their errors.

QuadLint lets students explain why they feel a particular error or warning is unjustified. Once they have fixed or explained all their errors and warnings, they submit the design for human review (which costs another 0.5 points). The course staff looks at their explanations and can approve or reject them and provide written feedback. If errors remain, the students fix them and resubmit. If there are no errors, they move on to the next lab.

QuadLint can perform a nearly complete check of student schematics (i.e., QuadLint passes, it will work). Checking PCB layouts is more difficult because many of the requirements are geometric or spatial.

5.2 Implementation

QuadLint runs in the cloud on Google's AppEngine [21]. It is written in Python and relies heavily on the Swoop library [29] for reading and manipulating Eagle PCB design files. We are happy to share the source code with educators.

6 STUDENT FEEDBACK

Based on anonymous course evaluations administered at the end of the class, students enjoy the class and find it valuable. Among 12 respondents from the most recent class of 24 students, 100% of students rated their enjoyment of the class a 4 ("some") or 5 ("a lot") out of 5. 93% of the students answered "yes" or "probably" (4 or 5 out of 5) to whether they could build a PCB on their own, all of them felt more confident soldering, and 91% felt more confident in debugging electronics. 70% of students thought the pace of the course was "just right" or "could have been a bit faster", and the remainder felt it "could have been a bit slower."

7 FUTURE IMPROVEMENTS

Planning is already underway for the next iteration of the course, and we are making some significant changes and smaller adjustments to improve the student success rates and reduce (or least more evenly distribute) work for the staff. Below we detail the planned changes for each of course's four main task.

7.1 Designing and Manufacturing PCBs

We are continuing to refine QuadLint to catch more common (and uncommon) errors in student designs and we are also adding features that will make it easier for less expert course staff to perform design reviews. We are working on ways to make the peer-design reviews more useful and effective.

7.2 Implementing Flight Control Software

The breakout board-based PID testing setup leads to several problems: Building it takes time and the electrical connections can be unreliable which leads to problems in the software labs.

We are addressing all of these problems by replacing the breakout-board based design with a newly-designed PCB that integrates all the components of their final design. This will attach to laser-cut arms to hold motors. The result will essentially be a quadcopter that fits on a newly-designed, larger test stand (Figure 1-bottom-middle) that will also accommodate their final quadcopters. The new board will use the same components and circuits as their final designs, so the work they do in the software labs should transfer better to their quadcopters.

7.3 PCB Assembly

The biggest problems we face in PCB assembly are the low success rate for soldering IMUs, the huge spike in staff workload that occurs during the assembly process, and the amount of time it takes students to assemble their quadcopters. We plan several changes that will address these challenges.

The first is that we have been experimenting with better soldering techniques for the IMU and considering different IMUs that come in easier-to-solder packages [6].

The second is that we will have students assemble the PCB for their remote control. The remote control assembly lab will run early in the course, and we will divide the class into 2-3 cohorts that will do the lab at staggered times, to make teaching and supporting them more manageable. We will provide "loaner" remotes to ensure that groups can make progress on other labs if assembly goes poorly.

Finally, we will use stencils to apply solder paste to the PCBs instead of plastic syringes. It is faster, more precise, yields better-looking PCBs, and is how "real" PCBs are assembled.

7.4 Flight

No significant changes are planned, but the changes outlined above should leave students with more time at the end of the class to get their quadcopters flying.

7.5 Cost

A frequent complaint about the course is that the students cannot continue working on their quadcopters after the course ends since they cannot keep the remote controls. The reason for this is that

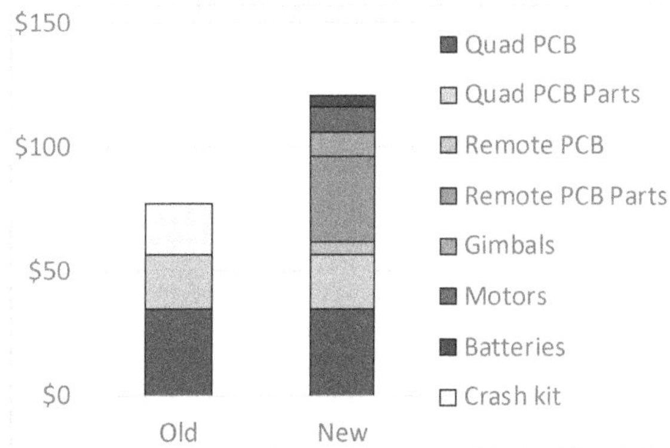

Figure 3: Per-student Costs – The per-student cost for the most recent iteration (left) did not include the remote. Our planned changes will raise costs, but students will have everything they need to program their quadcopter after the class.

the remote controls (Figure 1-top-right) we have been using are expensive – ~$150. The quadcopter costs about ~$35 per board plus $40 in for the components (including a "crash kit" [10] that provides batteries, motors, etc. as spare parts for a small, commercial quadcopter), so charging a lab fee large enough to provide a full set of hardware for each student to keep is not feasible.

We have set a goal of reducing costs enough to let each student keep a remote, a quadcopter, and all the other necessary equipment for ~$120. Figure 3 shows the breakdown in per-student cost for the last iteration of the class and the projections for the new version. Note that the per-student cost goes up, but in the new version, they can keep the remote.

The new remote (Figure 1-bottom-right) dispenses with useful-but-expensive on-board LCD for displaying status information ($25). We also added an integrated LiPo battery charger, so they can charge their own batteries. The remote uses the same kind of battery as the quadcopter. Further savings come from buying electrical components [11], motors [3], and batteries [4] in larger quantities (i.e., enough for 2-3 years of the course). Ordering in small quantities costs $10-$20 per student.

8 CONCLUSION

Many of the "killer apps" of the near future will lie at the intersection hardware, software, sensing, robotics, and/or wireless communications. Building a quadcopter gives students hands-on training in all of these aspects of system design simultaneously.

Building a quadcopter from scratch is 10 weeks is challenging, and fitting all of the necessary material into a single academic quarter has required careful planning and refinement over several iterations of the course. Students almost universally enjoy the class and report they learn many useful skills over the course of the quarter.

There is still much room for improvement. We are planning changes that should increase student success rate and allow us to scale the class to meet the growing demand for project-based courses from students.

ACKNOWLEDGMENTS

We would like to thank the reviewers for their constructive comments and Leo Porter for his comments and guidance. We would also like to thank Jorge Garza for TAing the course several times and debugging many, many problems.

REFERENCES

[1] http://sparkfun.com.
[2] http://adafruit.com.
[3] 4pcs 8520 motor 16000kv 1.0mm shaft jst1.25 connector. https://www.alibaba.com/product-detail/4pcs-8520-motor-16000kv-1-0mm_60753394316.html.
[4] 5pcs tenergy 3.7v 380mah lipo battery. https://www.amazon.com/gp/product/-B00HS5Y6G4.
[5] Adafruit lsm9ds1 library. https://github.com/adafruit/Adafruit_LSM9DS1.
[6] Adafruit precision nxp 9-dof breakout board - fxos8700 + fxas21002. https://www.adafruit.com/product/3463.
[7] Adafruit unified sensor driver. https://github.com/adafruit/Adafruit_Sensor.
[8] Ahrs (attitude and heading reference system) for adafruit's 9dof and 10dof breakouts. https://github.com/adafruit/Adafruit_AHRS.
[9] Atmega128rfa1 development board. https://github.com/sparkfun/-ATmega128RFA1_Dev.
[10] Avawo for hubsan x4 h107c parts crash pack 8-in-1 quadcopter red/white spare. https://www.amazon.com/gp/product/B00RROB6Q4.
[11] Digikey. http://digikey.com.
[12] Jlcpcb. https://jlcpcb.com/.
[13] Pcb file checker. https://www.4pcb.com/pcb-preorder.html.
[14] Pid controller. https://en.wikipedia.org/wiki/PID_controller.
[15] Reading a imu without kalman: The complementary filter. http://www.pieter-jan.com/node/11.
[16] Eee 802.15 wpan™ task group 4 (tg4). http://www.ieee802.org/15/pub/TG4.html.
[17] Adafruit 9-dof accel/mag/gyro+temp breakout board - lsm9ds1. https://www.adafruit.com/product/3387.
[18] Adafruit lsm9ds1 accelerometer + gyro + magnetometer 9-dof breakout. https://learn.adafruit.com/adafruit-lsm9ds1-accelerometer-plus-gyro-plus-magnetometer-9-dof-breakout.
[19] 8-bit avr microcontroller with low power 2.4ghz transceiver for zigbee and ieee 802.15.4. https://www.microchip.com/wwwproducts/en/ATmega128rfa1.
[20] R. W. Beard. Robot soccer: an ideal senior design experience. In *Proceedings of the 2000 American Control Conference. ACC (IEEE Cat. No.00CH36334)*, volume 6, pages 3975–3979 vol.6, June 2000.
[21] Google app engine. https://cloud.google.com/appengine/.
[22] D. J. Jackson and K. G. Ricks. Fpga-based autonomous vehicle competitions in a capstone design course. In *2005 IEEE International Conference on Microelectronic Systems Education (MSE'05)*, pages 9–10, June 2005.
[23] J. C. Jensen, E. A. Lee, and S. A. Seshia. An introductory capstone design course on embedded systems. In *2011 IEEE International Symposium of Circuits and Systems (ISCAS)*, pages 1199–1202, May 2011.
[24] A. Saad. Mobile robotics as the platform for undergraduate capstone electrical and computer engineering design projects. In *34th Annual Frontiers in Education, 2004. FIE 2004.*, pages S2G–7, Oct 2004.
[25] A. Saad. Senior capstone design experiences for abet accredited undergraduate electrical and computer engineering education. In *Proceedings 2007 IEEE SoutheastCon*, pages 294–299, March 2007.
[26] Atmega128rfa1 dev board hookup guide. https://learn.sparkfun.com/tutorials/-atmega128rfa1-dev-board-hookup-guide.
[27] Atmega128rfa1 development board. https://www.sparkfun.com/products/retired/-11197.
[28] inemo inertial module: 3d accelerometer, 3d gyroscope, 3d magnetometer. https://www.st.com/en/mems-and-sensors/lsm9ds1.html.
[29] Swoop. https://pypi.org/project/Swoop/.
[30] Steven Swanson. Trial by flyer: Building quadcopters from scratch in a ten-week capstone course, 2018. https://arxiv.org/abs/1810.07646.

Redesigning a Software Development Course as a Preparation for a Capstone: An Experience Report

Yekaterina Kharitonova*
UC Santa Barbara
Santa Barbara, CA
ykk@cs.ucsb.edu

Yi Luo
Harvey Mudd College
Claremont, CA
yluo@hmc.edu

Jeho Park
Claremont McKenna College
Claremont, CA
jeho.park@cmc.edu

ABSTRACT

Students need a wide variety of skills before they can successfully engage in real-world projects with paying customers. Some of these skills, such as the "soft skills" of communicating with a non-technical customer and working in a larger team to collaboratively develop a project, are generally not present in Computer Science courses. In this paper, we discuss our experience teaching these skills and explain the structure of our redesigned Software Development course and how it aligns with the Capstone experience. We believe that the concepts we introduced during our redesign can be useful to any educator wanting to include collaborative project-based work in their courses. To enable faculty to apply and enhance these concepts, the resources that we used in this course, which include activities, templates, guidelines, rubrics, and questionnaires, are available as an open source project at https://team-repo.github.io/.

ACM Reference Format:
Yekaterina Kharitonova, Yi Luo, and Jeho Park. 2019. Redesigning a Software Development Course as a Preparation for a Capstone: An Experience Report. In *Proceedings of the 50th ACM Technical Symposium on Computer Science Education (SIGCSE '19), February 27-March 2, 2019, Minneapolis, MN, USA.* ACM, New York, NY, USA, 7 pages. https://doi.org/10.1145/3287324.3287498

1 INTRODUCTION

Numerous instructors reported that teaching group-based software development projects is challenging [2, 4, 11]. Olarte et al. [26] carried out a survey study and identified a gap between students and their instructor's perceptions of key aspects of capstone projects, e.g., project characteristics, student competency, advisor involvement, and perceived learning (technology, methodology, project management). In our experience teaching such courses, it is usually students' first time working in a team of three or more members. It is also potentially their first exposure to designing an open-ended project, defending their design decisions, managing their time, and actively coordinating with other team members, to name a few. Naturally, many of students' complaints about the course are attributed to their inexperience and an expected discomfort of needing to step outside of their comfort zone. While that notion is true in many ways, we saw them as an indication for potential improvements in how we teach these skills, the activities students engage during class, and how these improvements could be tied to students' preparation for their capstone experience.

This report emerged from the discussions that began within a three-person Critical Friends circle [24]. The circle's participants – the two instructors in Ireland, who are part of the Adult and Community Education cohort at Maynooth University, and this paper's lead author – did not share the same academic discipline, yet each implemented team-based work and reflective exercises. As we reflected on our courses and compared our students' experiences, we noted similarities in our beliefs in the benefits of group work and reflective practices but started to question if our students held similar beliefs. By sharing our teaching materials, we could begin to compare the effect of certain practices and activities, and how they are perceived by the students across diverse disciplines, institutions, and cultures.

We based the redesign of our Software Development course on the software engineering concept of a "code smell" [16], which is a characteristic of the code that is indicative of a bigger problem. We treated students' dissatisfactions with the course as "course smells" and looked for ways to address underlying problems. This report is intended to outline the potential issues, considerations, attempted solutions, and recommendations to aid those who are contemplating pursuing a similar path with their courses. Similar insights are provided by Herbert [18] in her reflections on 17 years of capstone project coordination.

In this paper, we describe some of the most common "course smells" and students' attitudes behind them in Section 4.1. We then list the implementations of our course redesign in Section 4.3, where each part of the redesign helps address at least one of the skills necessary for students to have a positive capstone experience (outlined in Section 3). We close by discussing possible future work considerations.

*Dr. Kharitonova was a visiting professor at Harvey Mudd College, where she mentored students in both the Software Development and Capstone courses.

SIGCSE '19, February 27-March 2, 2019, Minneapolis, MN, USA

ACM ISBN 978-1-4503-5890-3/19/02...$15.00
https://doi.org/10.1145/3287324.3287498

2 RELATED WORK

This experience report is based on the existing work on project-based learning in computer science capstone courses and means of equipping computer science students with soft skills to succeed in collaborative projects. Project-based learning (PBL) is a well-known approach to teaching computer science courses [15, 25, 28] and is necessary to prepare software engineering students for a creative and collaborative career [10]. Capstone projects/courses are one of the common ways in which PBL is used in computer science programs [1, 13]. Dugan Jr [9] studied about 200 research papers about computer science capstone courses and reported that a common capstone course model is a semester-long course which required students to complete a large software engineering project. However, a variant course model teaches the process of software engineering in one semester and allows students to focus on applying that process to a project in the second semester. In our case, our two-semester capstone and the software development course are more in line with this variant model. More recently, Greenberg Davis and Zilora [17] compared two very different capstone course schedules and structures. Our course redesign included elements from both courses, such as self-selected teams and instructor-selected projects, and shared many course schedule elements, such as presentation and poster sessions, project plan, and use case analysis. In their paper, Fedoruk et al. [14] presented their model of student-initiated capstone projects [14]. We model their approach to fostering student interest and motivation through such projects by giving students a chance to build a project of their choice while they are familiarizing themselves with the new software framework. Given that our students are not familiar with the framework/language, the resulting depth and breadth of the projects that they are able to complete in just a few weeks of such exploration varies significantly, affecting their perceptions of the course.

While our course redesign improved students' experience in the course, the rigorous evaluation of the results is not the focus of this report. There are, however, previous studies that touched upon the assessment of course redesigns. Faust et al. [12] redesigned their three-quarter long capstone program in Electrical and Computer Engineering. This program included a one-quarter lecture course and a two-quarter capstone project. They introduced more project management and communication topics, and added a term-long practicum project in the lecture course, which mimicked an industry-sponsored project. The redesign was validated through multiple data resources such as focus groups and surveys. Deepamala and Shobha [7] redesigned a computer science engineering capstone course based on observations of previous academic years. Team structure and project management were included in the rubrics, and their study discovered improved program outcomes, which they calculated by mapping rubrics to the course outcomes. Dong and Guo [8] investigated the course redesign strategies of integrating collaborative project-based learning in senior computer courses in a three-year longitudinal study. Surveys, classroom observations, and focus groups indicated the scalable and open-structured project design match the learning needs of senior students, and confirmed the effectiveness of an active learning environment which is more collaborative and has adequate scaffolding.

3 CAPSTONE COURSE: STRUCTURE AND GOALS

The Computer Science (CS) capstone project at Harvey Mudd College (HMC) is a year-long course in which teams of three to five students in their senior year tackle a problem proposed by the client sponsoring the project. This is a required three-credit-hour course, where *all* teams meet together for a 50-minute weekly meeting over a 15-week semester (typically those meetings are devoted to teams' presentations about their work). Each team has at least one faculty advisor who helps facilitate team activities and a sponsor-appointed liaison who provides the domain expertise; both schedule separate weekly check-ins with the team. Students work on the project during several additional meetings that each team schedules throughout the week.

Most sponsors are not based locally, so the weekly status updates happen via the telecommunication channels. Typically, students meet with the liaison(s) at a reception at the beginning of the academic year, which, in addition to the informal introductions, serves as an initial project-clarification meeting. Almost every team will also go on a 'site visit' to meet the liaison(s) at the sponsor's office. This meeting is usually meant for students to gather detailed requirements, learn more about the problem they are working on, and meet more people from the sponsoring organization.

Each team produces various deliverables throughout the year, which range from presentations and written reports to prototypes and demos. The sponsor owns all project results. Project work culminates in a campus-wide poster session and formal presentations at the end of the year.

The main goal of the capstone course is to provide students an opportunity to solve real-world problems in CS while providing value to the sponsor in return for funding the project(s). As such, in addition to the technical skills and foundational CS knowledge, students need to be comfortable with the following set of skills, regardless of their project:

- oral and written communication (e.g., explaining the project, clarifying the tradeoffs of the proposed solution, describing the progress and results)
- team organization and management (e.g., addressing personality, skill, or attitude differences, promoting collaboration and healthy interactions, scheduling and task distribution)
- project planning (e.g., researching and scoping the project, collecting user requirements)
- time management (e.g., regularly completing work on schedule)
- software/code maintenance (e.g., version control, setting up and learning about new software, libraries, legacy code)

In this paper, we are presenting our redesign of only the Software Development course: the capstone course was not changed.

4 SOFTWARE DEVELOPMENT COURSE REDESIGN

Since the Software Development course is a prerequisite for taking the capstone, we redesigned it to allow students to practice the above-listed skills in a collaborative environment to better prepare them for the capstone experience. While we focus on the relationship to the capstone experience, we would like to emphasize that this work could more broadly be applied to any future practical experience.

4.1 Course Structure, History, and Challenges

The Software Development course is a three-credit-hour course required for all CS majors, and is typically taken by students in their junior year. The course meets three times a week for two 75-minute lectures and one 50-minute lab over a 15-week semester. The course is offered either as a single expanded section or as two or more sections with about 20 students in each section. The labs, which are intended as hands-on work sessions, usually combine students from all sections. In addition to the instructor, course staff includes a group of tutors and graders who help with course administration. These student assistants are typically chosen from the students who have taken the course.

This course has undergone many changes at HMC. Sometimes, the course focused on providing students with an overview of the field and the software engineering tools and practices, other times, the focus was on the specific software tool that students learned during the course. In all iterations of the course, however, students always engaged in some type a group project.

Historically, the course has been a challenge to teach, specifically because of how it was perceived by the students. Students' dissatisfaction with the course stems from some of the following reasons ("course smells"):

Culture: Course reputation skews students' attitudes before they even take the course.

- "Soft skills" needed for the course were seen as inferior to the technical skills required by the other courses.
- Open-ended nature of the projects and the lack of explicit, step-by-step guidelines made students perceive the course as being "unorganized".
- Emphasis of the course was unclear, especially with the frequently changing instructors bringing varied styles of instruction.
- Quality and success of projects varied, causing the spread of "urban legends".
- Variability of student experiences during the capstone course made some students question the usefulness of this course.

Tediousness: Assignments in the course (especially with the focus on planning, reporting, and documentation) are seen as busywork that takes away from the development.

- Students wanted more emphasis on software and tools.
- Administrative overhead of planning and managing a project was frustrating.
- Writing component was strongly disliked, often due to the previous lack of practice with technical reports.

Lack of engagement: Lecture material is seen as not relevant to projects.

- Best practices are considered "common sense" that can be shared on a handout.
- Learning about the evolution of the field is not seen as useful to their immediate work.
- Large number of students had summer internships and are familiar with some of the presented concepts.
- Previous experience makes students believe it is more representative of the "real world" and should remove the need for this class since they know the material already.

Structure and speed of feedback: Course schedule could be better and feedback turnaround can always be faster.

As the reader could probably tell, these discouraging attitudes are ongoing challenges that are not unique to our course. We hope that by discussing our course elements and considerations of the redesign, instructors can use some of our experiences, insights, and developed materials in their courses.

4.2 Redesign Considerations

In redesigning the course in order to better prepare students for their capstone work, we no longer had to question whether to focus on the *software* development or on the software *development*. The former would have required specific tools and exercises to get students to practice using various technologies, many of which might not be relevant for the capstone projects. Given the wide variety of software tools that teams use depending on their capstone sponsor, we decided to focus the course on the *process* of development, i.e., *how* students develop a project, rather than on providing the knowledge of a specific language or a software tool. This is not to say that we did not use or provide information about specific technologies: for example, we introduced version control using the currently popular `git` and its distributed version hosted by GitHub. However, our focus was mainly on how to use this (or a similar) tool in developing, managing, and maintaining a project in a collaborative environment.

The main questions for the course redesign revolved around the following themes:

Teamwork

- How many students should be on a team?
- How is the project manager (PM) chosen?

Projects

- How soon to introduce students to their projects? When should they start working on them?
- What type of projects to include? Should there be external clients? Should students propose their own projects? Should teams work on the same project?
- Should all teams use the same software framework?

Activities

- Which activities to include to help students develop and practice skills needed for the capstone experience?

4.3 Redesign implementation

The course redesign took place over the course of four semesters: in the first semester of the redesign, the course was co-taught by the first author and the instructor who previously taught this course for several semesters, while in the other three semesters, the course was taught solely by the first author.

4.3.1 ***Team size.*** Teamwork considerations (see Section 4.2) stayed the same as they were before the redesign. Students usually self-organize into the teams of four (with some teams of three or five, depending on the class size). If there are three or fewer students on a team, then it gets harder to motivate the need for collaborative project management tools: students tend to think of them as an annoying overhead, since it can be easier to coordinate tasks without them. If there are five or more students, it can become challenging to coordinate work and to ensure that everyone on the team can make a substantial contribution. Additionally, managing team dynamics and scheduling can become trickier as the group gets larger. Four students per team seems to work well for us, especially, since that is the usual number of students on a capstone team.

4.3.2 ***Project Manager (PM)***. The selection of a PM for the team is rather unique in our course: the PM rotated after each phase of the project, giving *every* student a chance to try out this role. Sometimes, if the class size does not evenly divide into teams of four, students in a team of five can decide in which phase they want to have two PMs. The order in which students assume this role is decided within each team with rough guidelines from the instructor. As a result, each team member will serve as a PM for their team for one phase (approximately two weeks) and be a software engineer for the other three phases. This practice is especially beneficial for the minority students and those whose personality or circumstances do not usually place them in a leadership position. Additionally, it is valuable for everyone on the team to learn from each other: by being exposed to various styles of leadership, students experience how well they interact with and respond to them.

Students in the course tend to like that they get to be a PM; they might not necessarily like the experience with their team/project but they seem to value that they got to have this experience, making them more aware whether they want to take on this role during the capstone. As one of the students put it in their final reflection: "*I originally thought I wanted to be a PM, but after being one for two weeks I realized that I most definitely prefer to be a developer (this was evidenced by my inability to stay out of each of the developer's hair!). However, I understand that project management is an important aspect of a developer's work as well, and gained insight into the best practices for me...*"

This information is especially useful for students, since during the capstone, the team has the same PM for the entire project, but the PM can also switch for the second semester. Similar rotational leadership was implemented by Danielewicz-Betz and Kawaguchi [5] who assigned computer science students to collaborative teams to work on projects for real customers. Focus was placed on project management skills, overall understanding of organizational issues, and activating students' multi-directional communication with teachers, fellow students, coaches, and customers. Usually the most motivated students ended up leading a team.

4.3.3 ***PM Presentations***. Before the redesign, PMs selected a software engineering design pattern and then presented it to the class. The presentations were generally around ten minutes, followed by a couple of minutes of Q&A. Because the content of those presentations was not necessarily directly relevant to the majority of the projects, students often complained that the presentations felt like a waste of their time, even though they got to practice their oral communication skills and received feedback from their peers (everyone in the class submits a form with their feedback, which is then anonymously shared with the presenter).

As the first step of the redesign, we instead asked the PMs for each phase to present their team's progress. Liu [22] investigated how students perceived different types of project presentations and this survey study concluded that short and frequent presentations help student make constant progress in term-long projects. Our redesign of PM presentations is in accordance with this finding. The new focus of the presentations also aligned well with the types of presentations that occur during the capstone course. The peer review, which sometimes included suggestions for the current state of the project, became more relevant to the teams and allowed them to practice giving and receiving written feedback. As a result of this change, the number of complaints about the PM presentations reduced to zero. In the following semesters, we started recording the presentations and asked students to submit a short reflection on their talk without seeing the video first (but having read peer feedback). At the end of the course, they had to watch the video and submit a written reflection on it. There were still no complaints about the presentations, the video, or the reflection, and students now had the benefit of having reflected on ways in which they can potentially improve their future presentations. Here is a sample from a student's reflection: "*In my first presentation reflection, I wrote about the effectiveness of my eye contact, gestures and movements. Watching the video, I noticed how often I looked at the slides on the computer in front of me; it was quite distracting, and I now understand the comments left by my peers when they said that I needed to look more at the audience. I also remember feeling very nervous during the presentation, and my nervousness was very evident to the viewer watching my presentation. However, I agreed with the comments of my peers when they said that I was very energetic and enthusiastic. Practicing for my presentation, I was worried it would be too boring or dry and was pleasantly surprised and happy to see that it was not.*" The video also provided students with an objective way to evaluate their assumptions, which is evident from reflections such as this one: "*From the video, I can actually see that I was saying a lot of filler words which is weird when I was so certain I wasn't. I also thought I was speaking very loudly but I can barely hear myself in the video.*"

A similar process was described by Dascalu et al. [6] where they implemented a computer science capstone course to also focus on team collaboration and communication in the streamlined software engineering process. Students worked in teams of three or four members and each team presented three times in a semester on the specification, design, and the final product. Similar to our course redesign, those presentations were recorded for students to review their performance.

4.3.4 ***Course Schedule***. The second semester of the redesign saw the most drastic changes to the course. In order to create a new reputation for the course, we had to make it unrecognizably different without changing the course number. To do so, we first changed the course schedule.

Before the redesign, students formed teams and began working on their projects starting the second week of the semester. There were four phases (also known as Agile *sprints*), each three weeks long. The new format included two main stages: the first stage (the first six weeks of the course) was devoted to learning and practicing concepts, e.g., the Agile process and version control, while the second stage was dedicated to the team project. The project work was still carried out in four sprints, except they were now two weeks long, which is closer to the industry standard of an Agile sprint. The tighter iterations helped students stay on track better, which was similar to the conclusion that Liu described in their survey study [22]. Murphy et al. [25] also used four two-week iterations in their two-course sequence of projects for real customers.

The two stages allowed us to use the lectures in the first stage to introduce students to the concepts that would be useful to them in the second stage. We provided them with the hands-on exercises and gave them some time to explore and practice those concepts without the pressure of also needing to make progress on the project. Such setup is also in line with Kolb's Experiential Learning Cycle [23] in which a person progresses through four stages: 1) their concrete experience is followed by 2) observing and reflecting on that experience, leading to 3) their creation of abstract concepts (analysis) and generalizations (conclusions) 4) used to test hypotheses in the future situations, looping back to the first stage.

4.3.5 ***Software Framework***. The other big change in the course was the switch to a new development environment (Ruby on Rails), which everyone in the class had to use. In previous semesters, students were developing on three different platforms (iOS, Android, web), which provided more flexibility in the types of projects that students could work on, but it also meant that the course staff could not effectively help everyone (or even most of them). Additionally, due to the vast variability in their development environments, some lecture materials and assignment instructions were not directly applicable to some teams, which was one of the main contributors to students' dissatisfaction with the course.

The Rails framework was new to almost everyone, including the course staff, which is why one of the early assignments in the course was to follow a video tutorial to build an app from scratch: this way, we could get the issues sorted out on a toy app, before students dove into their project. It gave everyone a chance to get the development environment set up on their computers and get oriented in it. Even the students who had lots of previous technical experience could still learn something new for them, while the less experienced students felt a bit less intimidated, since nobody was "an expert". Wilson [30] emphasized the importance of creating an atmosphere of "we are all in here to learn together," which was one of several recommendations that was based on the survey results of over 850 students taking college computer courses. Similar framing was discussed by Barker et al. [3] for creating supportive classroom climates. Lewis [21] also pointed out that it is important for the instructor to embrace questions they cannot answer, since it allows them to model a "growth mindset" and create a classroom culture that supports all students in computing.

Rails provides a beginner-friendly framework that allows one to have something up and running in less than an hour. It allowed students to create web apps, which they do not get to do in other courses. Having a standardized platform allowed the staff to share more focused resources, write clearer assignments, simplify debugging, and allow students to ask each other for troubleshooting tips. Students were given a chance to work on a toy project of their choosing by following and potentially combining various tutorials that they discovered. While most students enjoyed this exploration and valued an early exposure of learning to scale down their ambitions by first implementing a minimum viable product (MVP), several students still struggled and ended up disliking both, using Rails and the open-ended nature of this assignment. Given that Rails enforces a particular structure, it is necessary to learn how to implement things "the Rails way", which students were not explicitly taught, and few took the time to figure out.

When selecting a framework for the course, it is useful to keep in mind the frequency with which it updates, as well as the date of the latest major version. At the time we selected Rails 5.0 as our framework, it was less than a year old. The new update brought an ability to easily create chats and notifications [27], which allowed for more interactive and engaging apps. However, it also meant that there were fewer tutorials that showcased the new features, and the existing tutorials demonstrated features that were no longer supported, which greatly confused the students. We recommend giving students a starting structure for how to begin learning a new framework. Creating such (open-source) tutorials and guidelines could be a useful class exercise/assignment.

4.3.6 ***External Clients and Projects***. The clients for the projects are typically community partners (usually faculty or staff) who were either recruited by the instructor or who approached the instructor with a problem that they hoped students could solve. As part of the redesign, we allowed the clients to be other students who were not taking the course, and who were leading a project on campus, e.g., for a student organization.

Once the second stage of the class started, the lab session every other week was dedicated to the in-class client-team meetings. If a client was unable to meet during the lab, the team was responsible for coordinating an alternative meeting time.

Unlike the sponsors for the capstone project, the clients for this course did not have to pay for students to work on their project. Clients usually provided a short summary outlining the motivation for their project and a list of desired features. The instructor met with the clients before the course had started to discuss any details and to ensure that the client understands that students might not complete the project or deliver a functional product. Sometimes, the client continued collaborating with the course for several semesters, and, the new teams got to inherit previous teams' work. Sometimes, depending on the quality of the legacy code, teams ended up extending the prototype's functionality, and sometimes, they had to go with a complete re-write. Even in the cases of the complete overhaul of the code base, students benefited from having an existing proof-of-concept, which also helped them during the requirements-gathering phase.

Usually, it is best when a client has a strong vision for the final product or has a prototype. Exposing students to non-technical clients can be very useful in improving students' communication abilities, yet, it can pose challenges with calibrating expectations. If a client is unaware of what is possible and/or really happy with whatever students deliver, it seems to take away the team's motivation to strive to improve (because it does not seem to matter how well they do) and can lead to students' dissatisfaction with the project.

Additionally, we strongly discourage the instructor from being a project client; students end up feeling more on-guard: not knowing when they were being evaluated, they feel less comfortable asking the instructor for help or clarifications, which they otherwise would do with the client.

4.3.7 ***Status Reports***. In our course, students are responsible for maintaining a work log and for submitting weekly status updates. Writing these reports helps students practice documenting and communicating their progress in sufficient detail to the course staff. Additionally, the number of hours that a student works is factored into the grade for each of their weekly status reports. To discourage students from doing all their work at the last minute [19], students are supposed to work eight hours each week and receive additional credit only for two extra hours (regardless of how many hours over the eight-hour limit they actually worked). This requirement generates a lot of students' pushback due to various reasons. For some students, eight hours is not enough time, since they end up working more (either because they are making a lot of progress or they are naturally slower than the assumed pace); for others, it is too much time, and they do not know what to fill it with every week. For most students, writing these reports is the first time they need to formally plan and keep track of their progress, and they dislike how much it challenges the way they tend to work. Most of them, instead of planning their week in advance and keeping track of their efforts as they work, end up writing their log at the end of the week, trying to remember what they have done. Others, having developed their own successful workflow, find the provided system cumbersome and not needed.

The motivation behind the redesign of status reports was twofold: 1) streamline the project reporting and add a reflective summary component to reduce students' perception that the reports are busywork; 2) speed up and simplify the grading process to provide better feedback. Before the redesign, students had to submit their status reports in response to weekly quizzes on Canvas (http://canvas.instructure.com), where each section of the report, e.g., "Accomplishments" and "Next Week's Plans", was submitted as a short answer. Each quiz question was graded based on the rubric, with the feedback included in the "Additional comments" section of each question. Students either composed their answers on the day the quiz was due or, if they kept track of their work and plans elsewhere, they had to copy-paste it into the quiz, resulting in unnecessary work. For students who did not track their progress consistently and, thus, did not plan their work well, their "Next Week's Plans" did not necessarily match their "Accomplishments" from the corresponding week. However, it was difficult for the staff to spot these inconsistencies, because it required looking through previous quizzes, adding inconvenient work.

The redesign of the status report introduced a new format: a continuous document that students were supposed to add to over course of the semester. At the beginning of the semester, we shared a Google Doc template with the status report prompts. We asked students to list their reports in reverse chronological order to the same document to facilitate continuity and coherence between plans and progress from week to week. Students were continually encouraged to periodically review what they learned and planned in previous weeks to make more informed plans. At the end of the semester, when students assembled their portfolio and had to look through all of their status reports, majority of final reflections included an acknowledgement (sometimes, with an element of surprise) of how much they actually did and/or learned in the course. The following comment from a student's final portfolio reflection summarizes well most students' general attitude: "*Although I didn't enjoy doing status reports, in retrospect, they were helpful in outlining what I have done every week and how I've progressed.*"

Grading status reports that were written as a continuous log made it easy to see students' progress and compare it with previous weeks. Additionally, we recommend that when a student is a PM, they submit a modified version of the weekly report, which focuses on the status of the entire project and summarizes each teammate's contributions. These reports provide an easy way for staff to keep track of the project progress: the ambiguity or the lack of sufficient detail are typically early warnings that a team is beginning to flounder. Students should be informed of this sign, and encouraged to communicate within the team to resolve the blocks and/or reach out to staff for help.

4.3.8 ***Portfolio.*** As part of the redesign, we introduced a new assignment, which, in addition to simplifying students' final grade assessment for the instructor, provided students with an opportunity to think back on their work in the course. At the end of the semester, students had to submit a portfolio with their individual deliverables to help them reflect on their experience, efficiency, and effectiveness. Each student submitted a single PDF document, which included their status reports, a PM presentation reflection and a postmortem reflection, extra credit submissions (if they had any, e.g., a reflection about the guest speaker's talk), and a final overall portfolio reflection. This assignment was mainly aimed at the "tediousness" component of students' complaints. It was evident that students gained additional insights about their experience and performance in the course, and shows how important reflection can be in helping students assess how much they learned: "*After compiling my portfolio and seeing the semester's work all in one place, I can safely say I learned a lot more in this class than I originally thought! Although I don't think my portfolio is an accurate depiction of the amount of technical work that my group and I did this semester, I think it gives a good sense of what our project was about and the progress we made on it.*" Students' comments such as the following are the best illustration of how valuable reflective exercises can be and how well they relate to Kolb's Experiential Learning Cycle: "*After gathering and reading through this documentation from throughout the semester, I am thankful for all the opportunities to reflect on my work ...The [reflections] all presented opportunities to acknowledge both my strengths and weaknesses during this semester, and grow from that acknowledgement. One of the main lessons this class has instilled in me is that to be a skilled software developer is not all about technical ability; it is also about teamwork, collaboration, communication, self-critique, and personal growth.*"

5 FUTURE WORK

Much work still needs to be done in determining the variables and metrics to use in the evaluation of the course's effectiveness in preparing students for the capstone experience. Perhaps, adopting the assessment model introduced by Vasilevskaya et al. [29] or Lape et al. [20], and augmenting it with our proposed redesign elements, would capture students' changing attitudes as they progress through the course and help evaluate their learning. It would be informative to collect, analyze, and share qualitative and quantitative data about each course aspect. It would also be useful to run a longitudinal study with pre-/post-surveys, e.g., for students who experienced the rotating PM role, to measure their confidence in and preparedness for being a PM during the Software Development course and then during the capstone.

We also hope that faculty (and potentially industry partners) will get engaged in our open source project at https://team-repo.github.io and help with creating effective materials for teaching project-based courses that incorporate teamwork and reflection.

ACKNOWLEDGMENTS

The authors would like to thank the anonymous reviewers and Critical Friends – Lisa Parce and Michael Russell – for their insightful comments. A special thanks to the Software Development instructors whose experience and materials informed and enabled the redesign. We would also like to thank the friends and family without whose understanding and support this report would not exist.

REFERENCES

[1] Robert Adams and Carsten Kleiner. 2016. Collaboration Support in an International Computer Science Capstone Course. In *International Conference on Social Computing and Social Media.* Springer, 313–323.

[2] Craig Anslow and Frank Maurer. 2015. An experience report at teaching a group based agile software development project course. In *Proceedings of the 46th ACM Technical Symposium on Computer Science Education.* ACM, 500–505.

[3] Lecia J. Barker, Melissa O'Neill, and Nida Kazim. 2014. Framing Classroom Climate for Student Learning and Retention in Computer Science. In *Proceedings of the 45th ACM Technical Symposium on Computer Science Education (SIGCSE '14).* ACM, New York, NY, USA, 319–324. https://doi.org/10.1145/2538862.2538959

[4] Michelle Craig, Phill Conrad, Dylan Lynch, Natasha Lee, and Laura Anthony. 2018. Listening to early career software developers. *Journal of Computing Sciences in Colleges* 33, 4 (2018), 138–149.

[5] Anna Danielewicz-Betz and Tatsuki Kawaguchi. 2014. Gaining hands-on experience via collaborative learning: Interactive computer science courses. In *Interactive Collaborative Learning (ICL), 2014 International Conference on.* IEEE, 403–409.

[6] Sergiu M Dascalu, Yaakov L Varol, Frederick C Harris, and Brian T Westphal. 2005. Computer science capstone course senior projects: from project idea to prototype implementation. In *Frontiers in Education, 2005. FIE'05. Proceedings 35th Annual Conference.* IEEE, S3J–1.

[7] N Deepamala and G Shobha. 2018. Effective approach in making Capstone project a holistic learning experience to students of undergraduate computer science engineering program. *JOTSE* 8, 4 (2018), 420–438.

[8] Jianyu Dong and Huiping Guo. 2014. Effective Course Redesign Strategies to Integrate Collaborative PBL in Senior Computer Engineering/Computer Science Courses. In *2014 ASEE Annual Conference & Exposition.* ASEE Conferences, Indianapolis, Indiana. https://peer.asee.org/20345.

[9] Robert F Dugan Jr. 2011. A survey of computer science capstone course literature. *Computer Science Education* 21, 3 (2011), 201–267.

[10] Dora Dzvonyar, Lukas Alperowitz, Dominic Henze, and Bernd Bruegge. 2018. Team Composition in Software Engineering Project Courses. *SEEMâĂŽ18* (2018).

[11] Heidi J. C. Ellis, Gregory W. Hislop, Stoney Jackson, and Lori Postner. 2015. Team Project Experiences in Humanitarian Free and Open Source Software (HFOSS). *Trans. Comput. Educ.* 15, 4, Article 18 (Dec. 2015), 23 pages. https://doi.org/10.1145/2684812

[12] Mark Faust, Andrew Greenberg, and Branimir Pejcinovic. 2012. Redesign of senior capstone program in electrical and computer engineering and its assessment. In *2012 Frontiers in Education Conference Proceedings.* IEEE, 1–6.

[13] Alan Fedoruk, Mingwei Gong, and Michael McCarthy. 2014. Student initiated capstone projects. In *Proceedings of the 15th Annual Conference on Information technology education.* ACM, 65–70.

[14] Alan Fedoruk, Mingwei Gong, and Michael McCarthy. 2014. Student Initiated Capstone Projects. In *Proceedings of the 15th Annual Conference on Information Technology Education (SIGITE '14).* ACM, New York, NY, USA, 65–70. https://doi.org/10.1145/2656450.2656475

[15] Maria Lydia Fioravanti, Bruno Sena, Leo Natan Paschoal, Laíza R Silva, Ana P Allian, Elisa Y Nakagawa, Simone RS Souza, Seiji Isotani, and Ellen F Barbosa. 2018. Integrating Project Based Learning and Project Management for Software Engineering Teaching: An Experience Report. In *Proceedings of the 49th ACM Technical Symposium on Computer Science Education.* ACM, 806–811.

[16] Martin Fowler. 1999. *Refactoring. Improving the Design of Existing Code.* Addison-Wesley.

[17] Hollis Greenberg Davis and Stephen J. Zilora. 2016. A Tale of Two Capstones. In *Proceedings of the 17th Annual Conference on Information Technology Education (SIGITE '16).* ACM, New York, NY, USA, 130–135. https://doi.org/10.1145/2978192.2978234

[18] Nicole Herbert. 2018. Reflections on 17 Years of ICT Capstone Project Coordination: Effective Strategies for Managing Clients, Teams and Assessment. In *Proceedings of the 49th ACM Technical Symposium on Computer Science Education (SIGCSE '18).* ACM, New York, NY, USA, 215–220. https://doi.org/10.1145/3159450.3159584

[19] Nicole Herbert and Zhong Wang. 2007. Student Timesheets Can Aid in Curriculum Coordination. In *Proceedings of the Ninth Australasian Conference on Computing Education - Volume 66 (ACE '07).* Australian Computer Society, Inc., Darlinghurst, Australia, Australia, 73–80. http://dl.acm.org/citation.cfm?id=1273672.1273681

[20] Nancy K. Lape, Lori Bassman, Christopher Clark, Albert Dato, Angela M. Lee, Matthew Spencer, Erik Spjut, and Laura Palucki Blake. 2017. Integrating Theory and Hands-On Practice using Underwater Robotics in a Multidisciplinary Introductory Engineering Course. In *2017 ASEE Annual Conference & Exposition.* ASEE Conferences, Columbus, Ohio. https://peer.asee.org/28561.

[21] Colleen M. Lewis. 2017. ACM RETENTION COMMITTEE: Twelve Tips for Creating a Culture That Supports All Students in Computing. *ACM Inroads* 8, 4 (Oct. 2017), 17–20. https://doi.org/10.1145/3148524

[22] Chang Liu. 2006. Software project demonstrations as not only an assessment tool but also a learning tool. In *ACM SIGCSE Bulletin*, Vol. 38. ACM, 423–427.

[23] McLeod, S. A. 2017. Kolb - learning styles. Retrieved Aug 24, 2018 from www.simplypsychology.org/learning-kolb.html

[24] Jean McNiff and Jack Whitehead. 2011. *All you need to know about action research.* Sage Publications.

[25] Christian Murphy, Swapneel Sheth, and Sydney Morton. 2017. A Two-Course Sequence of Real Projects for Real Customers. In *Proceedings of the 2017 ACM SIGCSE Technical Symposium on Computer Science Education.* ACM, 417–422.

[26] Juan José Olarte, César Domı, Arturo Jaime, Francisco José Garcı, et al. 2016. Student and Staff Perceptions of Key Aspects of Computer Science Engineering Capstone Projects. *IEEE Transactions on Education* 59, 1 (2016), 45–51.

[27] RailsHistory 2016. Ruby on Rails Version History by Daniel Kehoe. Retrieved Aug 27, 2018 from https://railsapps.github.io/rails-release-history.html

[28] Swapneel Sheth, Christian Murphy, Kenneth A Ross, and Dennis Shasha. 2016. A course on programming and problem solving. In *Proceedings of the 47th ACM Technical Symposium on Computing Science Education.* ACM, 323–328.

[29] Maria Vasilevskaya, David Broman, and Kristian Sandahl. 2014. An assessment model for large project courses. In *Proceedings of the 45th ACM technical symposium on Computer science education.* ACM, 253–258.

[30] Brenda Cantwell Wilson. 2004. A Study of Learning Environments Associated with Computer Courses: Can We Teach Them Better? *J. Comput. Sci. Coll.* 20, 2 (Dec. 2004), 267–273. http://dl.acm.org/citation.cfm?id=1040151.1040185

Experiential Learning of Software Project Management and Software Development via Course Collaboration

Stefan C. Christov
Quinnipiac University
Hamden, CT
stefan.christov@quinnipiac.edu

Mark E. Hoffman
Quinnipiac University
Hamden, CT
mark.hoffman@quinnipiac.edu

ABSTRACT

The skills to effectively manage software development teams and to productively interact with a project manager are important in the computing professions. Teaching these skills in a traditional academic setting, however, is challenging. To support the experiential learning of these skills, we established a collaboration between two computing courses, a sophomore-level one and a senior-level one, where the seniors serve as managers of teams of sophomores on a semester-long project. This paper describes the collaboration and evaluates it in terms of student learning and experience based on three iterations of that collaboration. The associated course materials and evaluation instruments are made publicly available.

CCS CONCEPTS

• **Social and professional topics → Computing education**;

KEYWORDS

Software project management, collaborative teaching, experiential learning, software development

ACM Reference Format:

Stefan C. Christov and Mark E. Hoffman. 2019. Experiential Learning of Software Project Management and Software Development via Course Collaboration. In *Proc. of the 50th ACM Technical Symposium on Computer Science Education (SIGCSE '19), February 27-March 2, 2019, Minneapolis, MN, USA.* ACM, New York, NY, USA, 7 pages. https://doi.org/10.1145/3287324.3287457

1 INTRODUCTION

Software project management (SPM) is recognized as an important skill in software engineering and in project management in general. Software engineering management, including subareas such as project initiation and scope definition, project planning and estimation, and project measurement and control, is one of the knowledge areas in the Software Engineering Body of Knowledge [11]. Also, recently, the Software Extension to the Project Management Body of Knowledge [12] was approved by both the Project Management Institute [2] and the IEEE Computer Society [1].

Teaching SPM skills in a traditional academic setting, however, is challenging primarily due to the difficulty of providing students with opportunities to apply the SPM theory they learn. To truly practice SPM skills, a student needs to manage a relatively long-term, non-trivial software project executed by a team of software developers. Running such a project, finding such teams, and empowering students to be in a managerial position is logistically difficult. Thus, SPM is often taught via imaginary or non-concurrent software projects where the course instructor provides project materials, such as requirements or design documents, and asks students to apply SPM knowledge to generate another set of documents, such as effort/size estimates or a project plan. Such projects allow students to practice some aspects of SPM, but they preclude the opportunity to exercise other important aspects. These other aspects include the enactment of a project plan, and especially the typically iterative, incremental nature of planning and estimation based on what is learned during an ongoing project, as well as the human aspect of SPM, including intensive communication with developers and potentially dealing with intricate personality issues.

To address the above challenges, we established a collaboration between a sophomore-level Introduction to Software Development (ISD) course and a senior-level SPM course in which the seniors serve as managers of teams of sophomores on a semester-long project. This collaboration allows the seniors to exercise the variety of SPM skills discussed above and the sophomores to experience interacting with a manager. We also found that the collaboration supports other non-SPM related skills in the ISD course.

The main contributions of our work are: a pedagogical framework for conducting an undergraduate SPM-related course collaboration; an evaluation methodology for assessing and continuously improving such collaboration; and results on student learning and experience based on a three-year study as well as lessons learned. We also make publicly available all course materials associated with the collaboration and all evaluation instruments.

The next section of this paper discusses related work. Section 3 describes our approach to supporting experiential learning of SPM and Section 4 presents how we evaluated that approach. Evaluation results are discussed in Section 5 and Section 6 concludes the paper.

2 RELATED WORK

The importance of providing students with opportunities to apply the theoretical knowledge obtained in computer science (CS) and software engineering (SE) courses has been widely recognized (e.g., [9, 16]). A survey of the SE education literature in the period 1982-2013 indicates that the most widely used approach to providing practical experiences in SE education is "learn by doing" [20].

To support "learn by doing" in the context of SPM, course collaborations have been previously used, although surprisingly few are reported in the literature. Bavota et al. [4] as well as Maqsood and

SIGCSE '19, February 27-March 2, 2019, Minneapolis, MN, USA

ACM ISBN 978-1-4503-5890-3/19/02...$15.00
https://doi.org/10.1145/3287324.3287457

Javed [19] report collaborations between graduate SPM courses and other undergraduate courses where graduate students manage undergraduate students. The effectiveness of these collaborations is indirectly evaluated—in [4], by inferring learning success in terms of size and quality of the software systems produced and in [19] by comparing the structure of the graduate course to a capability maturity model [7]. In [4], a survey was also administered several years after the course completion and a positive general experience is reported. Detail about specific skills or knowledge that the course collaborations promoted is not provided.

Johns-Boast and Flint [13–15] describe a course collaboration at the undergraduate level where students in the senior part of a software development capstone course manage student teams in the junior part of that course. Based on feedback from different stakeholders (e.g., students and industrial partners), general benefits of this collaboration are noted. Few specifics are provided on SPM skills and knowledge obtained by students.

Besides through course collaborations, educators have supported practical SPM experience within a single course. For example, Bollin et al. use a simulation tool to teach SPM [5]. Malachowsky reports on observations related to introducing a project manager role in projects for an undergraduate Process and Project Management course [18]. Kuhrmann and Münch describe a teaching unit to support learning of group dynamics issues and strategies [17].

Other course collaborations not particularly focusing on SPM have been reported. These include studies of the feasibility of distributing large SE projects across the academic curriculum [8]; students from different courses collaborating by taking different roles in a simulated software factory [21]; teaching large scale teamwork in a small college environment by using multi-semester, multi-course projects [23]; collaboration between a graduate Education course and an undergraduate SE course [3]; and a collaboration between two graduate Distributed Software Development courses at two different universities [22].

Unlike [4] and [19], the work described in the current paper evaluates the collaboration between two undergraduate courses. Compared to [4], [13–15], and [19], we evaluate the collaboration in terms of specific skills and knowledge that the collaboration promotes for students in both courses. We also make publicly available all course material supporting the collaboration as well as the instruments used for evaluation and continuous course improvement. While all the single-course approaches described in [5, 17, 18] are useful for teaching certain SPM skills, we believe that the course collaboration approach presented in the current paper allows students to practice a richer set of SPM skills over a longer period of time. Our work is similar to the work described in [3, 8, 21–23] in terms of identifying general course collaboration issues and strategies to address them, but our work adds lessons learned specific to issues with and strategies for supporting learning of SPM.

3 APPROACH

This section describes the two courses that facilitate the reported collaboration, the structure of the most recent collaboration, and our continuous improvement process.

3.1 The ISD and SPM Courses

Introduction to Software Development (ISD) is a first semester, sophomore-level course required of CS and SE majors, and CS minors. Prior to taking the ISD course, CS and SE majors take an introductory programming course (CS1), a data structures course (CS2), and an object-oriented programming course (OOP). CS minors are not required to take the OOP course. Students work in teams of 4 or 5 on a semester-long software maintenance project that serves as a platform to exercise various software development practices.

Software Project Management (SPM) is a required course for SE majors, typically taken first semester of senior year. The course acquaints students with various aspects of SPM. Students are familiar with the ISD course having already taken it.

The topics covered and the deliverables produced each week in both courses are listed in Table 1. Detailed description of the ISD and SPM courses can be found in [10] and [6], respectively. Course materials are available online at https://tinyurl.com/y7kwdhzw.

3.2 ISD and SPM Course Collaboration

Beginning in 2015 (the first time the SPM course was offered), students in the SPM course were assigned to manage ISD student teams. The collaboration has evolved through a continuous improvement process described in Section 3.3. This section describes the most recent collaboration (2017).

Each SPM student (manager) is assigned to manage one ISD student team. Managers meet with their team weekly during one of the scheduled ISD class periods. At these meetings, managers perform a number of management tasks coordinated with the assignments in the ISD and SPM courses. The fourth column in Table 1 details the interaction between the ISD teams and their managers.

Managers work with their team to create a work plan at the beginning of each Scrum sprint, finalize all work unit assignments, and submit the work plan to the ISD instructor. Managers run the weekly team meetings by providing an agenda and submit minutes to the SPM instructor. Managers receive periodic individual team member status reports that they use to create individual and team performance evaluations. The managers' evaluations are factored in grades of the ISD students. Managers facilitate individual and team postmortems at the end of each Scrum sprint.

Managers also provide leadership and guidance to their teams. Managers sometimes need to motivate underperforming teams, provide moral support, and facilitate intra-team conflict. Managers do not code for their team, but are allowed to suggest strategies to facilitate coding tasks. Managers are free to share their experience as ISD students to facilitate their teams' success.

3.3 Continuous Improvement Process

Over the three years of this collaboration, we have used a continuous improvement process to identify issues and propose course changes to address them. During the fall, while the courses are in session, we gather data using the methods described in Section 4.2. After the courses end, during the winter and spring, we analyze the data to determine to what degree the course collaboration supports the courses' learning outcomes. Based on the analysis results, we propose changes for the collaboration and modify course materials based on these changes during the summer, prior to the next offering of the courses. The continues improvement process repeats, starting with the next offering of the courses.

Week	Topics in ISD Course	Deliverables in ISD Course	Interaction between ISD and SPM Courses	Topics in SPM Course	Deliverables in SPM Course
1	* Evaluation of an existing software system	* Software system evaluation report	* In-class weekly meeting between manager and team: introductions and ice breaking activity; installation and evaluation of software system to be maintained during the semester	* Intro to SPM * Human Aspects of SPM I: Teamwork	* Meeting minutes * Reading response assignments on characteristics of successful teams (NY Times article, NPR Podcast)
2	* Elicinting customer requirements	* Requirements report	* In-class weekly meeting: manager discusses with team strategies for teamwork success and consults team on requirements elicitation and specification * Out-of-class: manager is available to review requirements report	* Human Aspects of SPM II * Software Project Foundations	* Meeting minutes
3	* Specifying customer requirements	* Vision document * Backlog with bugs/enhancements	* In-class weekly meeting: manager consults team on bug/enhancement prioritization and vision statement * Out-of-class: manager is available to review vision dovument and backlog	* Software Project Estimation	* Meeting minutes * Initial estimation of size and effort for top 3 bugs/enhancements
4	* Process and configuration management tools	* Report on evaluation and selection of process and configuration management tools	* In-class weekly meeting: manager consults team on process and configuration management tools * Out-of-class: manager is available to review report on process and configuration management tools	* Project plans	* Meeting minutes * IEEE Standard 1058 project plan template tailored to team's project
5	* Test planning	* Test plan * Team charter	* In-class weekly meeting: manager consults team on test plan development and assists with team charter creation * Out-of-class: manager is available to review test plan and team charter	* Project planning techniques	* Meeting minutes * Work breakdown structure and work packages that describe work that team needs to perform to develop and present a test plan
6, 8, 10, 12	* Scrum Sprint week 1	* Individual status reports * Scrum meeting progress report	* In-class weekly meeting: manager assists team in selecting backlog items and creating a work plan. Manager has final word on work unit assignments and deadlines * Out-of-class: Manager monitors progress of team by providing written feedback on individual status reports; manager is available for guidance and advice	* Week 6: Project planning tools * Week 8: Measuring and controlling work products * Week 10: performance evaluation * Week 12: Managing risk	* First week of each Scrum sprint: meeting minutes, work plan, written feedback on individual status reports from team members * Week 6: project planning tools presentation * Week 8: Report on measuring different aspects of team's software system * Week 10: Performance evaluations of individual team members * Week 12: Report assessing risks for Scrum sprint IV
7, 9, 11, 13	* Scrum Sprint week 2	* Individual status reports * Scrum meeting progress report * Code * End-of-sprint demo * Updated backlog * Individual and team postmortems	* In-class weekly meeting: Manager and team discuss progress, issues that have arisen, and potential ways to deal with these issues * Out-of-class: Manager monitors progress of team by providing written feedback on individual status reports; manager is available for guidance and advice; manager participates in team's post-mortem meeting * Last class of Scrum sprint: manager attends team demo/presentation	* Week 7: Software Project Estimation II * Week 9: Midterm exam * Week 11: Managing and controlling work processes * Week 13: Ethics in SPM	* Second week of each Scrum sprint: meeting minutes, written feedback on individual status reports from team members, report on individual team member work unit completion, teamwork evaluation rubric * Week 7: COCOMO II estimation of effort and time for team's top 3 bugs/enhancements * Week 9: Midterm exam * Week 11: Report on effort analysis; earned value analysis problem set * Week 13: Report on ethical analysis of SPM issues in the "Case of the Killer Robot"
14	* Packaging and documenting software system	* Course project reflection paper * Final demo and presentation	* In-class weekly meeting: reflection on last Scrum sprint and the semester-long interaction between the team and the manager * Out-of-class: manager is available to provide advice/feedback on team's final demo and presentation	* Organizational issues in SPM	* Meeting minutes * Performance evaluations of team members * Course reflection paper
Exam Period	* Final Project Report		Final exam		

Table 1: The structure of the course collaboration.

4 EVALUATION METHODOLOGY

4.1 Participants

Participants for this study consisted of students enrolled in a sophomore-level ISD course and students enrolled in a senior-level SPM course (Table 2). In addition to CS and SE, several students pursued double majors while others minored in CS. The ISD course had two sections each year and students were randomly assigned to teams of 4 or 5 students within the same section. SPM students were randomly assigned to manage teams. The first year of the study, 2 SPM students managed 2 teams each; four teams did not have a manager. In 2016, 9 SPM students managed 7 teams; two teams had 2 managers. In 2017, 7 SPM students managed 7 of the 8 teams; one team did not have a manager.

		2015	2016	2017
ISD Course	Enrollment	34	29	38
	Major Distribution			
	CS	16	19	16
	SE	10	7	17
	Other	13	7	12
	Number of Teams	8	7	8
	Number of Managed Teams	4	7	7
SPM Course	Enrollment (all SE majors)	2	9	7
	Number of Managers	2	9	7

Table 2: ISD and SPM Participant Demographics.

4.2 Data Collection

Data for this study was collected using methods developed for the 2015 collaboration [6]. The methods include end-of-semester surveys, course reflections, and instructor observations throughout each semester. Based on the continuous improvement process described in Section 3.3, methods were revised in 2016 and 2017. Each method is described in detail below and the supporting data collection instruments are available online at https://tinyurl.com/y7kwdhzw. To reduce bias during data analysis, collected data were independently analyzed by two reviewers and discrepancies were resolved by reaching consensus.

End-of-Semester Student Surveys. At the end of each collaboration iteration, ISD students who had a manager and all SPM students participate in a survey that gathers data on student learning and experience and the effect of having or being a manager, respectively. Students assess how the collaboration contributed to their achievement of the course learning outcomes (CLOs) on a 5-point Likert scale (Strongly Disagree to Strongly Agree). The CLOs for both courses are listed in the bottom half of the two panels in Figure 1. An open-ended follow-up question invites students to describe any additional skills or knowledge acquired. Three open-ended questions ask students to assess what worked best, what needs improvement, and what should be changed, if given the opportunity.

The survey for the ISD students also asks them to assess their engagement with their manager by regularly attending meetings and communicating outside of meetings. The 2016 survey adds a question where students assess the amount of manager authority. The 2017 survey adds a question where students assess their manager's involvement with the team, keeping in mind that managers are not supposed to write code.

The survey for the SPM students also includes open-ended questions that ask students to assess their most important contribution to the team they managed and what the ISD and SPM instructors can do to make the learning experience useful and productive. The 2016 survey adds questions where SPM students assess their amount of authority, whether their responsibilities were clearly defined, the success of teamwork lessons added at the beginning of the course, the synchronization of SPM assignments with the ISD team workflow, and the workload for the course. The 2017 survey adds questions where SPM students assess their involvement as a manager with their team, keeping in mind that managers are not supposed to write code, and whether their team accurately understood their role as a manager.

End-of-Semester Student Course Reflections. Prior to this study, ISD students completed a graded end-of-semester course reflection. Questions guiding students' reflection were not altered for this study. These questions asked students to reflect on topics such as the most important thing learned in the course and the most important contribution the student made to the project. Each question required a detailed explanation supported by evidence from students' coursework. Student responses were reviewed for references to managers in any of the questions.

SPM students submitted a course reflection assignment in 2016 and 2017. In 2015, the course reflection was an interview conducted by the ISD and SPM instructors given that there were only 2 SPM students. This interview was guided by the same questions as on the written course reflection assignment. These questions asked students to reflect on topics such as what did or did not go well in the interaction with their team and what they would do differently if they could start the interaction from scratch.

Instructor Observations. The ISD and SPM instructors maintained a shared document each semester to record observations from meetings, conversations, and other experiences related to the collaboration. The format of the document was not particularly formal; however, it allowed observations to be recorded as they occurred. A major source of information were the ISD instructor's weekly half-hour visits to the SPM course where the current week's issues that arose in the collaboration were discussed with the managers.

5 RESULTS AND DISCUSSION

5.1 Educational benefits of the collaboration

Figure 1 shows the self-assessed achievement of the CLOs of the ISD and SPM courses reported in the end-of-semester surveys. Based on these results, the course collaboration is contributing to students' achievement of most of the CLOs. For the SPM course, the achievement of most CLOs was rated around 4.5 on average, which means that students agreed or strongly agreed that the collaboration contributed to their achievement of these CLOs. For the ISD course, most of the CLOs were rated around 4, the "Agree" level. It is not surprising that the collaboration has a slightly stronger contribution to the achievement of CLOs in the SPM course than in the ISD course because serving as a manager of a real team exercises a large set of project management skills. Working under a manager allows ISD students to exercise important software development skills, such as working on a team and evaluating and maintaining a software product, but other skills in the ISD course, such as explaining social and ethical implications of software development were addressed by other components of the ISD course.

The self-assessed level of achievement of CLOs increased from the first course collaboration in 2015 to the third course collaboration in 2017. We believe this is a result of the continuous improvement process described in Section 3.3. Note that some of the CLOs received a lower score in 2016 compared to 2015 (all CLOs received higher score in 2017 compared to 2015 and 2016). The dip in 2016 is most likely due to making significant modifications to the course collaboration in 2016 based on limited experience (the collaboration in 2015 that involved only two managers). There were also numerous scheduling conflicts in 2016, making the interaction between managers and their teams difficult. The issues encountered in 2016 were carefully analyzed and addressed in the 2017 collaboration (see discussion in Section 5.2).

The end-of-semester surveys and reflections from the SPM course indicated that the course collaboration contributed to the SPM students' learning and practicing of soft skills in SPM, such as leading a meeting, handling difficult team members, and conducting performance evaluations. This is a strong advantage of an SPM course that allows students to manage a software development team compared to traditional SPM courses that lack such a component.

The ISD students reported multiple benefits of having a manager. For example, the managers provided useful advice during the course project, coordinated and organized their teams, set expectations and reviewed project artifacts. Some managers also provided moral support and even taught their teams some software development technologies, such as Git. It is interesting to note that the number of unsolicited comments about the benefit of having a manager in the ISD end-of-semester reflections substantially increased in 2017. The manager-related comments in 2017 were also more specific compared to similar comments from previous years. We believe this is an indication of the ISD students' increased involvement with their manager and better understanding of the manager's role.

5.2 Structuring the collaboration

Establishing the collaboration between the ISD and SPM courses posed several challenges. One of the most important challenges was providing sufficient time for interaction between teams and

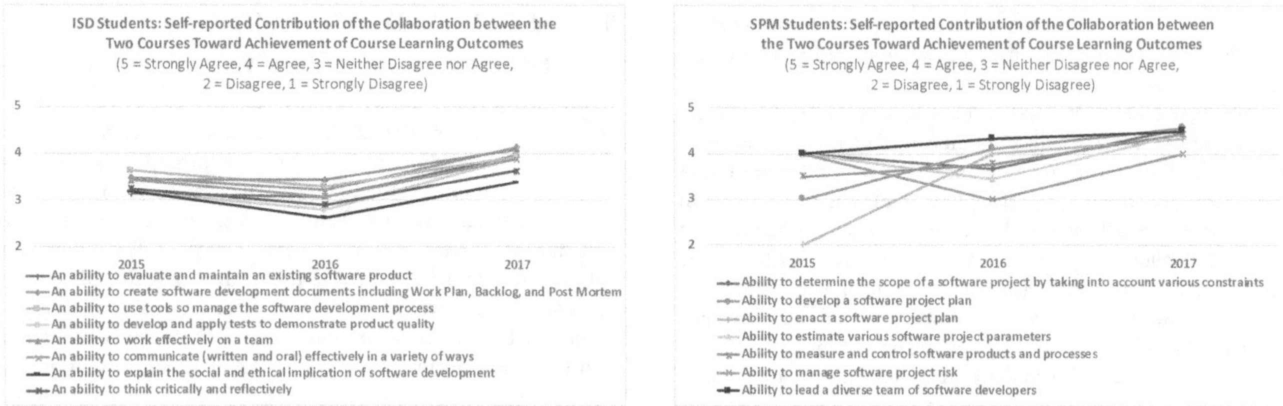

Figure 1: Self-assessed achievement of CLOs.

their managers. In 2015 and 2016, we asked the managers and their teams to find a time period outside of class for a weekly meeting. This proved to be difficult due to scheduling conflicts and due to some students' time management problems. To address this issue, in 2017 we added a lab to the SPM course that consisted of the SPM students attending one class period of the ISD course per week to meet with their teams. This lab does not increase the credit hours of the SPM course as it is considered part of the out-of-class time students need to spend working on the course. In 2017, multiple students commented in the end-of-semester surveys and reflections that these meetings significantly facilitated the course collaboration. Students also indicated that using a group chat service to communicate outside of in-person meetings was useful.

Determining the right amount of authority for the managers is an important challenge. The managers' authority during the first course collaboration in 2015 primarily consisted of requiring the ISD teams to consult their managers regarding various project issues at least once a week and to submit some project artifacts to the manager prior to submitting them to the course instructor. There was no mechanism for a manager to affect the grade of the managed students as we were reluctant to have students influence the grade of other students, especially with no prior experience on this collaboration. The amount of manager authority in 2015, however, was determined to be insufficient by both ISD and SPM students as the SPM students acted more as consultants than as managers. As a result, we gradually increased the manager's authority in 2016 and 2017 to the level described in Section 3.2.

This gradual increase of manager authority seems to have had a positive effect. In 2017, the majority of the ISD and SPM students considered the amount of manager authority "just about right" (Figure 2). The course instructors also observed that teams tended to follow their manager's guidance and complete tasks assigned by the managers by the deadlines set by the managers. Figure 2 suggests that with the gradual increase of manager authority from 2016 to 2017, a larger percentage of the ISD students (about 64%) considered the amount of manager authority appropriate rather than low in 2017 compared to 2016 (about 48%), with still about a third of the ISD students in 2017 desiring more manager authority. This result is consistent with the instructors' observation that ISD students tend to appreciate higher manager authority which seems to correlate with more support from the manager in various aspects of the software development project, including resolving team conflicts and dealing with less engaged/underperforming team members. On the other hand, Figure 2 suggests that the gradual increase of manager authority from 2016 to 2017 was associated with smaller, but still substantial, percentage of SPM students considering the amount of manager authority appropriate in 2017 (about 57%) than in 2016 (about 89%). Interestingly, however, the SPM students who did not consider the amount of manager authority appropriate in 2017, fall on both sides of "Just about right"—namely "High" and "Low". This might be due to varying personal managing styles (e.g., hands-off vs. hands-on) and/or not clearly communicating the same expectations to ISD and SPM students.

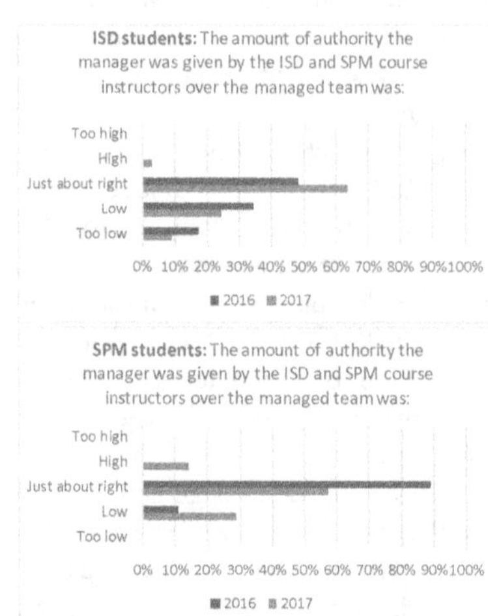

Figure 2: Amount of manager authority.

Besides providing managers with appropriate amount of authority, setting up the course collaboration such that the manager is appropriately involved with his/her team is challenging. Manager involvement was incrementally increased over the three course offerings. The activities not directly related to manager authority, but promoting manager involvement are the weekly meetings with the managed team, attending the team presentation at the end of each Scrum sprint, and participating in team postmortems. An appropriate amount of manager involvement seems to have been achieved in Fall 2017 based on the survey results—79% of the ISD students and 100% of the SPM students rated the amount of manager involvement as "Just about right."

Achieving appropriate amount of manager authority and involvement might have come at the expense of reaching or slightly exceeding an appropriate workload limit in the SPM course. Whereas in 2016, 100% of the respondents of the SPM end-of-semester survey indicated that the workload was "just about right", only about "57%" gave this answer in 2017 and 43% considered the workload high or too high. Based on our analysis of the 2017 data, we believe we could reduce the workload of SPM students without hurting the collaboration. One possibility is to reduce the amount of paperwork, such as status reports ISD students submit to SPM students to review. Student feedback suggests that these reports duplicate the weekly meetings between managers and teams.

Overall, the structure of the course collaboration has stabilized. Our analysis of the 2017 data suggests fewer potential changes compared to previous course offerings. In the end-of-semester reflections, the focus of student writing has shifted from complaints and suggestions for course changes to reporting of learning diverse skills and discussing the benefits of the course collaboration.

An open issue that remains to be addressed is dealing with "underperforming managers." As in most courses, the SPM course can have a range of students in terms of academic strength and commitment. Thus, there are sometimes students who end up being underperforming managers. This could be particularly problematic in the context of the course collaboration as not only the grade of that underperforming SPM student is affected, but also the learning experience and potentially the grade of the ISD students in this manager's team. Some of the strategies we are considering to deal with this issue include compiling a collection of supporting material for underperforming managers (such as tips and best practices based on our experience so far) and soliciting manager evaluations from the managed teams to identify early signs of underperformance that would allow instructors to intervene early in the semester. We are also careful in designing the grading scheme in the ISD course in a way that the ISD students' grade is minimally affected by underperforming managers.

5.3 Workload of course instructors

The course collaboration did not substantially increase the workload of the instructors of the ISD and SPM courses during the semester and no teaching assistants (TAs) were used. In addition to the regular duties associated with the ISD course, the ISD instructor attended the SPM class for 30 minutes each week to discuss with the managers the weekly progress of the teams and any issues that might have arisen. The total time commitment was about 7 hours. The SPM instructor attended the first and the last class of each of the two sections of the ISD course to introduce the course collaboration and to provide feedback on final presentations, respectively. The total time commitment was about 3.5 hours. In addition, the ISD and SPM instructors met with each other for about 45 minutes two times during the semester to coordinate the course collaboration.

Most of the instructor time on the course collaboration was spent between semesters (in the summer) to analyze data from the previous course offering and continuously improve the collaboration as discussed in Section 3.3. The instructors met in person 3-4 times on average for approximately 1.5 hours each summer. In addition, each instructor individually analyzed data and made course modifications for about 10-15 hours total.

We believe that the educational benefits associated with the course collaboration described in Section 5.1 substantially outweigh the instructor workload associated with supporting this collaboration. The additional workload during the semester is minimal and amortized over 16 weeks; the workload for course improvements between semesters is both essential for careful evidence-based course development and has been decreasing as the course collaboration has stabilized.

5.4 Limitations

The course collaboration was implemented and evaluated in a teaching-focused institution with small class sizes (at most 24 students) and no TAs. Scaling such a collaboration to a different setting, e.g., an institution with large class sizes and heavy reliance on TAs, will most likely be associated with different obstacles, such as coordinating a large number of teams and TAs, and might lead to different results. The detailed coordination structure outlined in Table 1, the complete set of supporting course material we provide, and the continuous improvement methodology should significantly facilitate the replication of our experience.

We have a curriculum structure (the ISD course, the SPM course, and the weekly lab in the SPM course) that affords the opportunity to implement this type of collaboration. Other institutions might not have such a structure. Most computing programs, however, offer a course on software engineering/development and such a course could be combined with a concurrent SPM-related elective or a graduate course to implement a similar collaboration. In addition to establishing a curriculum structure, we are working on additional mechanisms (e.g., further synchronizing assignments and course materials) to institutionalize the course collaboration, so that it can continue when other instructors teach these courses.

We evaluated the course collaboration on a relatively small number of course offerings, three, but the course structure and the educational observations seem to be stabilizing, which supports the validity of the presented results. Much of the data we analyzed is self-reported by students. This data is consistent, however, with the observations instructors made over the three course offerings. We are also considering approaches for performing further quantitative evaluation, such as using the grades of course assignments and mapping these assignments to learning outcomes.

6 CONCLUSION AND FUTURE WORK

The skills to effectively manage software development teams and to productively interact with a project manager are important in the computing professions, but providing opportunities to exercise these skills in an academic setting is challenging. To support the experiential learning of these skills, we established a collaboration between two computing courses. Our results indicate that this collaboration has been successful in terms of supporting course learning outcomes and practicing soft-skill aspects of SPM, which are difficult to practice in SPM courses that do not involve managing a team. The course collaboration is also feasible in terms of course instructors' workload. Important issues for establishing such a collaboration and strategies to address them have been identified. To further facilitate the implementation of such collaboration by others, all course materials and evaluation instruments to support continuous improvement are made publicly available. In the future, we plan to explore approaches for handling underperforming managers and quantitatively evaluating the collaboration.

REFERENCES

[1] 2018. IEEE Computer Society. www.computer.org.
[2] 2018. Project Management Institute. www.pmi.org.
[3] H. U. Asuncion, R. L. Angotti, and K. Sung. 2012. Work in progress: Sustainable projects for software engineering courses: Collaborating with technology courses. In *2012 Frontiers in Education Conference Proceedings*. 1–6. https://doi.org/10.1109/FIE.2012.6462274
[4] Gabriele Bavota, Andrea De Lucia, Fausto Fasano, Rocco Oliveto, and Carlo Zottoli. 2012. Teaching Software Engineering and Software Project Management: An Integrated and Practical Approach. In *Proceedings of the 34th International Conference on Software Engineering (ICSE '12)*. IEEE Press, Piscataway, NJ, USA, 1155–1164. http://dl.acm.org/citation.cfm?id=2337223.2337375
[5] A. Bollin, E. Hochmüller, and R. T. Mittermeir. 2011. Teaching software project management using simulations. In *2011 24th IEEE-CS Conference on Software Engineering Education and Training (CSEE T)*. 81–90. https://doi.org/10.1109/CSEET.2011.5876160
[6] Stefan C. Christov and Mark E. Hoffman. 2016. Evaluating the Collaboration between a Software Project Management Course and a Software Development Course in Terms of Student Learning and Experience. In *American Society for Engineering Education (ASEE) 123rd Annual Conference and Exposition*. ASEE Conferences, New Orleans, Louisiana.
[7] CMMI Product Team. 2006. *CMMI for Development, Version 1.2.* Technical Report CMU/SEI-2006-TR-008. Software Engineering Institute, Carnegie Mellon University, Pittsburgh, PA. http://resources.sei.cmu.edu/library/asset-view.cfm?AssetID=8091
[8] James B. Fenwick, Jr. and Barry L. Kurtz. 2005. Intra-curriculum Software Engineering Education. In *Proceedings of the 36th SIGCSE Technical Symposium on Computer Science Education (SIGCSE '05)*. ACM, New York, NY, USA, 540–544. https://doi.org/10.1145/1047344.1047513
[9] Sally Fincher, Marian Petre, and Martyn Clark (Eds.). 2001. *Computer Science Project Work: Principles and Pragmatics.* Springer-Verlag, London, UK, UK.
[10] Mark E. Hoffman and Stefan C. Christov. 2017. Guiding Principles and Pedagogical Tools for an Introductory Software Development Course. In *American Society for Engineering Education (ASEE) Annual Conference and Exposition.*
[11] IEEE Computer Society, Pierre Bourque, and Richard E. Fairley. 2014. *Guide to the Software Engineering Body of Knowledge (SWEBOK®): Version 3.0* (3rd ed.). IEEE Computer Society Press, Los Alamitos, CA, USA.
[12] Project Management Institute. 2013. *Software Extension to PMBOK™Guide–Fifth Edition.* Project Management Institute.
[13] Lynette Johns-Boast. 2010. Group Work and Individual Assessment. In *21st Annual Conference of the Australasian Association of Engineering Education.* 46–51.
[14] Lynette Johns-Boast and Shayne Flint. 2009. Providing students with 'real-world' experience through university group projects. In *20th Annual Conference of the Australasian Association for Engineering Education.* 299–304.
[15] L. Johns-Boast and S. Flint. 2013. Simulating industry: An innovative software engineering capstone design course. In *2013 IEEE Frontiers in Education Conference (FIE)*. 1782–1788. https://doi.org/10.1109/FIE.2013.6685145
[16] Joint Task Force on Computing Curricula, ACM and IEEE Computer Society. 2013. *Computer Science Curricula 2013: Curriculum Guidelines for Undergraduate Degree Programs in Computer Science.* ACM, New York, NY, USA.
[17] Marco Kuhrmann and Jürgen Münch. 2016. When Teams Go Crazy: An Environment to Experience Group Dynamics in Software Project Management Courses. In *Proceedings of the 38th International Conference on Software Engineering Companion (ICSE '16)*. ACM, New York, NY, USA, 412–421. https://doi.org/10.1145/2889160.2889194
[18] Samuel A. Malachowsky. 2015. Implementing Project Managers in the Software Engineering Classroom. In *2015 ASEE Annual Conference and Exposition.* ASEE Conferences, Seattle, Washington. https://peer.asee.org/24249.
[19] Manzile Maqsood and Talha Javed. 2007. Practicum in Software Project Management: An Endeavor to Effective and Pragmatic Software Project Management Education. In *Proceedings of the the 6th Joint Meeting of the European Software Engineering Conference and the ACM SIGSOFT Symposium on The Foundations of Software Engineering (ESEC-FSE '07)*. ACM, New York, NY, USA, 471–480. https://doi.org/10.1145/1287624.1287691
[20] M. R. Marques, A. Quispe, and S. F. Ochoa. 2014. A systematic mapping study on practical approaches to teaching software engineering. In *2014 IEEE Frontiers in Education Conference (FIE)*. 1–8. https://doi.org/10.1109/FIE.2014.7044277
[21] J.D. Tvedt, R. Tesoriero, and K.A. Gary. 2001. The Software Factory: combining undergraduate computer science and software engineering education. In *ICSE 2001. Proceedings of the 23rd International Conference on Software Engineering.* 633–642. https://doi.org/10.1109/ICSE.2001.919137
[22] Igor Čavrak, Marin Orlić, and Ivica Crnković. 2012. Collaboration Patterns in Distributed Software Development Projects. In *Proceedings of the 34th International Conference on Software Engineering (ICSE '12)*. IEEE Press, Piscataway, NJ, USA, 1235–1244. http://dl.acm.org/citation.cfm?id=2337223.2337386
[23] Ellen L. Walker and Oberta A. Slotterbeck. 2002. Incorporating Realistic Teamwork into a Small College Software Engineering Curriculum. *J. Comput. Sci. Coll.* 17, 6 (May 2002), 115–123. http://dl.acm.org/citation.cfm?id=775742.775765

Propagating Educational Innovations

Heather Bort
Marquette University
Milwaukee, WI, USA
heather.bort@marquette.edu

David P. Bunde
Knox College
Galesburg, IL, USA
dbunde@knox.edu

Zack Butler
Rochester Inst. of Tech.
Rochester, NY, USA
zjb@cs.rit.edu

Christopher Lynnly Hovey
University of Colorado Boulder
Boulder, CO, USA
hoveyc@colorado.edu

Cynthia Taylor
Oberlin College
Oberlin, OH, USA
cynthia.taylor@oberlin.edu

ABSTRACT

Many great teaching techniques are presented every year at SIGCSE and other CS education conferences. Unfortunately, most of them achieve very limited adoption, with few instructors incorporating these ideas into their classrooms. There is significant literature on how to encourage instructors to adopt educational innovations in other STEM fields, but the CS education community has made only limited strides in this area. This session will feature an interactive discussion of some of the barriers that prevent the adoption of good ideas, what solutions are available, and a brief presentation of the results of an ITiCSE working group on this topic. Attendees will leave the session better equipped to promote the adoption of educational innovations, either their own or ones that they have decided to champion.

ACM Reference Format:
Heather Bort, David P. Bunde, Zack Butler, Christopher Lynnly Hovey, and Cynthia Taylor. 2019. Propagating Educational Innovations. In *Proceedings of the 50th ACM Technical Symposium on Computer Science Education (SIGCSE '19), February 27-March 2, 2019, Minneapolis, MN, USA.* ACM, New York, NY, USA, 2 pages. https://doi.org/10.1145/3287324.3287526

1 SUMMARY

To have significant impact in the community, an educational innovation (e.g. a tool, curriculum change, or pedagogical technique) must be adopted by many other instructors beyond its creator(s). Despite this, many people attempting to develop educational innovations, even those seeking external grant support, fail to adequately plan for recruiting and supporting adopters [2]. It is not enough to try to disseminate the innovation by publishing papers on its effectiveness; instead a significant effort must be devoted to its *propagation*, the process of actually increasing the number of instructors using it in their classrooms.

There is a substantial collection of literature on propagating educational innovations in STEM—particularly in physics eduction—but relatively little in CS specifically, and the CS education research community seems to have limited awareness of it. This led us (with others) to participate in an ITiCSE working group that summarized existing literature on propagation in general, and its relation to CS higher education. We are proposing this special session to share our work in an interactive way and to initiate a community-level conversation on propagating educational innovations. We believe that this session will lay important groundwork for propagating the innovations presented each year in this conference, which will benefit the SIGCSE community and the computing higher education community in general.

SIGCSE '19, February 27-March 2, 2019, Minneapolis, MN, USA

ACM ISBN 978-1-4503-5890-3/19/02.
https://doi.org/10.1145/3287324.3287526

2 OBJECTIVE

Our overall goal is to promote the idea that propagation requires specific planning. While we do not view this idea as controversial, our sense is that the community is generally unaware of the literature on promoting propagation, and that most of its members do not undertake such planning. Our goal is to change this situation.

After our session, attendees will be able to do the following:

- Identify individual, social, and institutional barriers that can prevent others from adopting educational innovations.
- Explain some strategies for overcoming those barriers.
- Find appropriate high-level resources from which to get more information, including our working group report and a short book on planning for propagation [1].

Given the limited time, we do not expect attendees to become propagation experts during the session. Rather, we see this time as the beginning of their exposure— they confront the fact that propagation is not automatic, talk about some of the issues, learn some of the high-level results, and gain resources for their own further study of the topic. To this end, we will provide them with a handout including best practices and pointers to further literature.

In addition to our goals for attendees, we plan to learn from members of the community about their perception of barriers to innovation and what would help them adopt. This is a check on the existing literature, most of which is from other STEM fields rather than CS specifically. In addition, the organizers plan to continue raising awareness of propagation planning after SIGCSE, so we are seeking feedback on the helpfulness of the work we have done so far and we hope to solicit ideas for future activities.

3 EXPECTATIONS

Our target audience is anyone with a current or future interest in promoting an educational innovation, either their own or one they have previously adopted. This includes everyone at SIGCSE.

The session will cover what we consider to be the most important conclusions of our working group report. We are using an interactive style that asks attendees to explore the material based on their own experiences. This style fits our goals both by helping attendees learn the material and by implicitly pointing out possible differences between propagating educational innovations in CS and in other STEM fields, where most prior research was done. Incidentally, we will also be incorporating and modeling evidence-based teaching practices in leading the session, which will maximize participants' engagement and learning through our session.

4 SESSION OUTLINE

4.1 Introduction (8 minutes)

After introducing ourselves, we will give examples of innovations and define propagation. To motivate the session, we will present the highlights of a paper reporting that most NSF CCLI[1] proposals had no propagation plan and few had visible results [2]. We will also provide participants with an overview of the session.

4.2 Breakout sessions (57 minutes)

The bulk of the special session will be a series of scaffolded discussions in small groups, followed by "report outs," large-group discussion, and a brief presentation by the organizers of the related literature. During the breakout time, session organizers will circulate around the room to encourage discussion. Session segments will be as follows:

- **Group formation (7 min).** Attendees organize into groups of 4–5 people and introduce themselves for 1–2 minutes each. In particular, we will have them mention educational innovations that they have tried to propagate, that they have adopted themselves, or that they considered but decided not to adopt. The rest of the conversation will be grounded in these experiences.
- **Motivating potential adopters (19 min).** Discussion of why attendees decided to try an innovation. What were their goals and how did they pick a particular innovation? (Where did they hear about it and what convinced them to try it?) Discussion within their group, followed by report out, whole-group discussion, and presentation on reasons given in surveys and the role of instructor identity. The goal is to show that instructors are not just rational evaluators of possible options and that some kinds of appeals are likely to be more effective than others.
- **Listing of challenges/obstacles to adoption (12 min).** Generation of a list of what prevents people from adopting. We will specifically prompt both for individual barriers (e.g. it uses a different programming language) and institutional barriers (e.g. needing to convince colleagues to change a course that is also taught by others or which is a prerequisite). Groups will come up with their own lists and then these are reported out so that all attendees can see them and use them for the next breakout.
- **Addressing challenges/obstacles (19 min).** Next, groups will talk about strategies for addressing the challenges. These will be reported out, followed by a whole-group discussion of commonalities and themes. Then, the organizers will summarize relevant literature.

4.3 Summary (10 minutes)

The organizers will reiterate the need for specific planning for successful propagation, as well as presenting an overview of other topics from our working group report that were not covered in the session. We will make a specific point to introduce other materials in the literature, including giving out a handout with best practices for adoption and pointers to the literature. Any remaining time will be for general discussion.

5 PRESENTERS

All the presenters were members of a working group on propagating educational innovations at ITiCSE 2018. **Heather Bort** is a doctoral candidate at Marquette University and a member of the PUMP-CS project. Her work focuses on incorporating CS concepts within Humanities contexts for non-major courses. **David Bunde** is an Associate Professor at Knox College. He works to propagate techniques for parallel programming education and peer instruction, an active learning pedagogy. **Zack Butler** is a Professor at the Rochester Institute of Technology. He has studied the use of puzzles as a gender- and experience-neutral context for introductory CS courses. **Chris Hovey** is a social scientist in the Department of Information Science at the University of Colorado Boulder. His research focuses on what influences CS faculty to try out and routinely use innovative teaching practices, especially those that promote gender diversity and student retention, in undergraduate and graduate education. His most recent project surveyed over 800 instructors and professors across the U.S. about their adoption of innovative teaching in introductory CS courses. **Cynthia Taylor** is an Assistant Professor at Oberlin College who does research on active learning and assessment of student learning. She works to propagate peer instruction and concept inventories.

6 SUITABILITY FOR A SPECIAL SESSION

We believe a special session is the right way to present this material. It is not new research, but an important community conversation and a topic that CS education needs to learn from other fields. A panel would also be suitable except that potential panelists are not people who would typically attend SIGCSE, since they are outside CS education. A special session also allows the interactive style we propose here, which is particularly suited to our goals and which we hope will contribute to other conversations between SIGCSE attendees.

REFERENCES

[1] C. Henderson, R. Cole, J. Froyd, D. Friedrichsen, R. Khatri, and C. Stanford. 2015. *Designing Educational Innovations for Sustained Adoption: A How-To Guide for Education Developers Who Want to Increase the Impact of Their Work.* Increase the Impact, Kalamazoo, MI.

[2] C. Stanford, R. Cole, J. Froyd, C. Henderson, D. Friedrichsen, and R. Khatri. 2017. Analysis of propagation plans in NSF-funded education development projects. *J. Sci. Educ. Technol.* 28 (2017), 418–437.

[1]CCLI was an NSF program for educational innovation; it is a predecessor to the current IUSE program.

Rethinking Debugging as Productive Failure for CS Education

Yasmin B. Kafai[†]
Graduate School of Education
University of Pennsylvania
Philadelphia PA USA
kafai@upenn.edu

David DeLiema
School of Education
University of California, Berkeley
Berkeley CA USA
deliema@berkeley.edu

Deborah A. Fields
College of Education
Utah State University
Logan UT USA
deborah.fields@usu.edu

Gary Lewandowski
College of Arts and Sciences
Xavier University
Cincinnati OH USA
lewandow@xavier.edu

Colleen Lewis
Computer Science Department
Harvey Mudd College
Claremont CA USA
lewis@cs.hmc.edu

ABSTRACT

Computational thinking has become the calling card for re-introducing coding into schools. While much attention has focused on how students engage in designing systems, applications, and other computational artifacts as a measure of success for computational thinking, far fewer efforts have focused on what goes into remediating problems in designing systems and interactions because learners invariably make mistakes that need fixing—or debugging. In this panel, we examine the often overlooked practice of debugging that presents significant learning challenges (and opportunities) to students in completing assignments and instructional challenges to teachers in helping students to succeed in their classrooms. The panel participants will review what we know and don't know about debugging, discuss ways to conceptualize and study debugging, and present instructional approaches for helping teachers and students to engage productively in debugging situations.

CCS CONCEPTS: • Computing Education

KEYWORDS

Computing education, computational thinking, debugging

ACM Reference:

Yasmin B. Kafai, David DeLiema, Deborah Fields, Gary Lewandowski, & Colleen Lewis. 2019. Rethinking Debugging as Productive Failure for CS Education. In *Proceedings of the 50th ACM Technical Symposium on Computer Science Education (SIGCSE'19). Feb. 27-Mar.2, 2019, Minneapolis, MN, USA.* ACM, New York, NY, 2 pages. https://doi.org/10.1145/3287324.3287333

1 Introduction

Debugging has always been an essential part of programming. As Papert [9] noted, "when you learn to program a computer you almost never get it right the first time" (p. 23). Thus, computation involves the practice of continually diagnosing and fixing problems. Looking at research on debugging from the early days of educational computing, we know a lot about novice programmers' bug types, and their processes and problems with identifying bugs [8]. Beyond mere syntax issues, novices' bugs are also semantic in nature, dealing with more thorny issues of errors in run-time or logic, thereby reflecting their underlying understanding of computation itself. More recent pedagogical approaches offer new ways by reframing debugging as opportunities for "productive failure," or the counterintuitive notion that failure precedes later success in learning [3]. Current research on productive failure highlights the role of multiple representations and solutions, activation of prior knowledge, and nature of peer support, in order to identify which dimensions are most productive for different students and conditions [4, 5]. This panel will present different perspectives on debugging, starting with an overview of what we know about student challenges and instructional approaches (Lewandowski), followed by research on students and teachers approaches to debugging (DeLiema), and instructional approaches at the high school (Fields) and college (Lewis) levels.

[†]Moderator

SIGCSE '19, February 27-March 2, 2019, Minneapolis, MN, USA

ACM ISBN 978-1-4503-5890-3/19/02. https://doi.org/10.1145/3287324.3287333

1.1 Gary Lewandowski

We are fortunate to have literature on debugging that dates back to the 70s and continues to have relevance for understanding the challenges students face and ideas for approaching instruction. Generally speaking, we understand that bugs occur most typically when students experience a cognitive breakdown in skills, rules, or knowledge. The most prevalent kinds of bugs are missing or malformed plan executions, sometimes due to fragile language skills, and other times what Knuth describes as "algorithm awry." A particular challenge in debugging is the ability to think about the overall system that they are building, which makes it more difficult to locate their bugs. Thus, some of the suggested instructional approaches are guides to help students pursue either forward or backward reasoning about the bugs. The good news is that there is evidence that when taught a debugging technique, students will use it! Productive failure is likely to fit into the existing literature as a guiding principle that bugs are a part of the programming process that can lead us to insight on the problem being solved and better (correct) solutions.

Gary Lewandowski is a Professor of Computer Science at Xavier University where he experiences the joys of failure and debugging on a daily basis while teaching CS and human-centered making, and while serving as Associate Dean. His research interests include debugging processes of students as part of a larger interest in the assets students bring to their study of CS.

1.2 David DeLiema

When teachers, researchers, and parents talk about children handling failure in the learning process in *productive* ways, what might they mean? Blending prior theoretical and empirical research on failure and debugging [3,10], learning conjectures from a multi-year design-research project [1], and micro-longitudinal analyses of a 6th grader's approach to debugging computer code over two weeks, I propose five characteristics of how students handle failure that each mark a unique facet of productivity: whether (1) problems get fixed, (2) students learn to avoid specific (recurring) problems, (3) students know and learn strategies for debugging novel problems, (4) students drive the process of debugging problems, and (5) students calibrate confidence to the tractability of a problem. Drawing on data that triangulates student participation, reflection, and artifacts, I argue that newcomers should foreground and background these facets in different configurations at different points for focused practice. This study sets a foundation for research on particular characteristics of the social and material contexts that shape how newcomers to a discipline approach failure.

David DeLiema is a Postdoctoral Researcher in the Graduate School of Education at UC Berkeley where he studies failure, embodied learning, and epistemic cognition.

1.3 Deborah Fields

I argue for a broad view of debugging since it can involve important thinking processes. I am particularly aware of these thinking processes in the context of physically embodied projects such as electronic textiles. E-textiles involve making fabric-based projects by sewing sensors and microcontrollers using conductive thread to make computational circuits. Intersections of crafting, circuitry, and computation make tracing root causes tricky, demanding strategic debugging and revisions productive for learning [7]. In working with hundreds of students creating e-textiles over the past decade we have noted beyond identifying syntax errors, debugging can involve problem-solving, iterative testing, isolating problems, hypothesis testing, and even working with an intended audience for one's project [2]. In addition to arguing for an expansive consideration of debugging, I also argue that we should help students become aware of the thinking skills they use in debugging projects. We have explored using reflective portfolios for this purpose, inviting students to share things that went wrong and how they resolved those problems. Meta-reflection on debugging has strong potential for helping students develop conscious strategies for debugging.

Deborah Fields is an Associate Research Professor at Utah State University, where she investigates student learning through making creative computational artifacts, studying relationships between design, personal relevance, and learning.

1.4 Colleen Lewis

As a CS education researcher, I hypothesize that debugging is particularly challenging to teach because students over classify bugs as "silly mistakes" and thus disregard the importance of their debugging practice [6]. If a student has enough expertise to *find* the bug, this expertise is likely sufficient to *fix*. That is, once you *find* a bug, it is often trivial to *fix* it. If a bug appears to be trivial, the process of finding the bug may also be dismissed as trivial. I try to support my students in developing their debugging skills by giving students assignments that require debugging and by embedding debugging advice where they will come across it when they need it (i.e., as a comment within provided test cases and on a poster in the computer labs csteachingtips.org/tips-for-tutors).

Colleen Lewis is the McGregor-Girand Associate Professor of CS at Harvey Mudd College. At UC Berkeley, Lewis completed a PhD in education and an MS in CS. Her research seeks to identify effective teaching practices for creating equitable learning spaces. Lewis curates CSTeachingTips.org, a NSF-sponsored project for disseminating effective CS teaching practices.

REFERENCES

[1] David DeLiema. 2017. Co-constructed failure narratives in mathematics tutoring. *Instructional Science, 45*, 6 (Dec. 2017), 709-735.

[2] Gayithri Jayathirtha, Deborah A. Fields, and Yasmin B. Kafai. 2018. Computational concepts, practices, and collaboration in high school students' debugging electronic textile projects. In *Proceedings of International Conference on Computational Thinking Education* (CTE '18), The Education University of Hong Kong, Hong Kong, China.

[3] Manu Kapur. 2016. Examining productive failure, productive success, unproductive failure, and unproductive success in learning. *Educational Psychologist, 51*, 2 (April 2016), 289–299.

[4] Manu Kapur and Katherine Bielaczyc. 2012. Designing for productive failure. *Journal of the Learning Sciences, 21*, 1 (June 2011), 45-83.

[5] Manu Kapur and Nikol. Rummel. 2012. Productive failure in learning from generation and invention activities. *Instructional Science, 40*(4), (July 2012) 645-650.

[6] Colleen M. Lewis. 2012. The Importance of Students' Attention to Program State: A Case Study of Debugging Behavior. In *Proceedings of the International Computer Science Education Research Workshop (ICER '12)*. ACM, Auckland, NZ, 127-134.

[7] Breanne K. Litts, Yasmin B. Kafai, Kristin A. Searle, and Emily Dieckmeyer. 2016. Perceptions of productive failure in design projects: High school students' challenges in making electronic textiles. In Proceedings of the International Conference of the Learning Sciences (ICLS '16). International Society of the Learning Sciences, Singapore, 498-505.

[8] Renee McCauley, Sue Fitzgerald, Gary Lewandowski, Laurie Murphy, Beth Simon, Lynda Thomas, and Carol Zander. 2008. Debugging: A review of the literature from an educational perspective. *Computer Science Education, 18*, 2, (June 2008) 67-92.

[9] Seymour Papert. 1980. *Mindstorms: Children, computers, and powerful ideas*. Basic Books, Inc., New York, NY.

[10] Andreas Zeller. 2009. *Why programs fail: a guide to systematic debugging*. Elsevier, Burlington, MA.

Special Session: Process Skills in Computer Science

Helen H. Hu
Westminster College
Salt Lake City, UT, USA
hhu@westminstercollege.edu

Chris Mayfield
James Madison University
Harrisonburg, VA, USA
mayfiecs@jmu.edu

Clif Kussmaul
Muhlenberg College
Allentown, PA, USA
clif@kussmaul.org

ABSTRACT

Process skills (also known as professional skills, lifelong learning skills, workplace skills, transferable skills, or soft skills) are an important aspect of computer science education. Learning objectives for computer science courses often include the development of process skills like critical thinking, problem solving, and teamwork, but many instructors struggle with how to encourage and measure the development of these skills. This special session will introduce detailed rubrics for assessing process skills in a manner that will model POGIL (Process Oriented Guided Inquiry Learning) facilitation techniques. Presenters will demonstrate how to use one set of these rubrics in an active learning classroom (*i.e.*, POGIL) to provide students with feedback. The other set of rubrics assess process skills on student work and can be used with any classroom. Attendees will leave the session with a better understanding of key process skills in computer science, how to assess student interactions and student work for these skills, and how a POGIL classroom facilitates the development of critical thinking, information processing, and teamwork. This special session will appeal to any K-12 teacher or college instructor interested in developing students' process skills in a computer science class.

CCS CONCEPTS

• **Social and professional topics → Computer science education;**

KEYWORDS

Process Skills, Active Learning, Critical Thinking, Teamwork, POGIL

ACM Reference Format:
Helen H. Hu, Chris Mayfield, and Clif Kussmaul. 2019. Special Session: Process Skills in Computer Science. In *Proceedings of the 50th ACM Technical Symposium on Computer Science Education (SIGCSE '19), February 27-March 2, 2019, Minneapolis, MN, USA.* ACM, New York, NY, USA, 2 pages. https://doi.org/10.1145/3287324.3287520

1 OVERALL OBJECTIVE

Process skills are key to student success in school as well as their future career trajectories. This special session will disseminate state-of-the-art resources from multiple NSF-funded projects that focus on process skills development. It will be organized as a tutorial in which participants discuss how to teach process skills and practice assessing student work in their courses. Participants will experience using the rubrics in an active learning classroom (POGIL).

The ELIPSS project (http://elipss.com/) has developed two sets of detailed rubrics for assessing process skills and providing feedback to students [1]. One set of rubrics is intended for assessing process skills on student *products* (e.g., programs and other student written work), and the other set is designed for student *interactions* observed during group work in the classroom. Instructors can further the development of their students' process skills by providing feedback that identifies strengths, weaknesses, and areas that need work. While the rubrics can be used in any classroom, they work especially well in active learning environments, such as POGIL.

The IntroCS-POGIL project (http://introcspogil.org/) has created a new professional development program for faculty wishing to adopt POGIL in introductory computer science courses. POGIL (Process Oriented Guided Inquiry Learning) engages students by grouping them in teams to work collaboratively through activities and construct their own understanding of computer science content. POGIL activities are carefully designed to foster student development of process skills like information processing, critical thinking, and teamwork. Each POGIL activity typically includes 2–3 computer science content learning objectives and 1–2 process skill goals. After completing the POGIL activities, students are often expected to reflect and report on their process skills used during the activity.

Both projects use the *Operationalized Process Skill Definitions* developed by the POGIL Project (see https://pogil.org/educators/additional-resources). The following table gives examples of these process skills applied to computer science courses:

Process Skill	CS Examples
Information Processing	Predicting effects of code execution Converting pseudocode to code
Critical Thinking	Identifying common syntax errors Writing test cases
Problem Solving	Developing pseudocode Debugging code
Oral & Written Communication	Presenting algorithms Writing documentation
Teamwork	Collaborative development Designing an API

2 OUTLINE OF SESSION

This special session will begin by clarifying how students might demonstrate process skills in a computer science class. Process skills rubrics will be introduced in a manner that will model POGIL facilitation techniques and provide an interactive venue for learning about POGIL and asking questions about developing process

SIGCSE '19, February 27-March 2, 2019, Minneapolis, MN, USA

ACM ISBN 978-1-4503-5890-3/19/02.
https://doi.org/10.1145/3287324.3287520

skills. Guidance on how to use these rubrics with students will be provided. The presenters will end the session with links on how to access the process skills rubrics (at http://elipss.com) and POGIL activities (at http://cspogil.org), and will provide information about the support available to computing faculty adopting POGIL for computing classes.

15 minutes	*Process Skills Discussion* Explore definitions and examples
25 minutes	*Introduction to ELIPSS Rubrics* Rubric exploration activity Practice applying the rubrics
20 minutes	*Interactive Classroom Activity* Experience POGIL as students would Discuss how to give students feedback
10 minutes	*Opportunities to Learn More* IntroCS-POGIL and ELIPSS Projects CS-POGIL activity collections
20 minutes	*Q&A Discussion* Likely to happen throughout the session

2.1 Helen H. Hu

In my introductory computer science classes, my students discuss the importance of process skills, and I use this discussion to motivate the group work and POGIL learning teams. I have found that the POGIL classroom structure has improved the collaboration and teamwork in my classes. During the first weeks of the semester, my students are expected to complete a reflective report on which process skills are strengths and which ones could be improved. I then introduce the ELIPSS rubrics to help students understand how to improve in each area. Since adopting POGIL, I have seen increases in student engagement levels as well as in my female students' pass rates [2]. My POGIL activities include instructor guides with tips on how an instructor should facilitate the activity and support the development of process skills.

2.2 Chris Mayfield

I teach with POGIL primarily in my introductory courses, and I find it rewarding to help students develop their process skills. It's important to make process skills an explicit part of your objectives and assessments; they won't just happen automatically. For the past several years, I have been writing new POGIL activity collections for CS1 in both Java and Python (available upon request). Each activity has a specific process skill goal that students make progress toward as they work through the questions in teams. Focusing on process skills enhances learning because it affects the way students demonstrate their mastery of the content. As a member of the ELIPSS collaboration team, I have facilitated multiple workshops on assessing process skills and providing feedback. This special session will be a unique combination of ELIPSS materials and IntroCS-POGIL resources, tailored for a CS audience.

2.3 Clif Kussmaul

I use POGIL activities across the curriculum, from CS1, through Computer Organization and Software Engineering, to Artificial Intelligence. I have also led POGIL workshops for faculty across the US and in other countries. In both classes and workshops, I observe that to play a sport or a musical instrument, people need to practice and develop specific skills, ideally with a coach, and often with other players. A good coach provides constructive feedback, but also assigns drills and other activities to help players practice skills before using them in more realistic settings. Computer science and other academic subjects should use the same ideas to help students practice and develop process skills both within and across disciplines.

3 EXPECTATIONS

This special session should appeal to K-12 teachers and university instructors interested in process skills development, especially but not limited to active learning classrooms. Attendees will experience how students discover computer science concepts for themselves and develop problem solving, critical thinking, and communication skills while working through POGIL activities. They will learn how POGIL and these rubrics have been used in CS classrooms, how to access rubrics and POGIL materials, and how to learn more through POGIL workshops and regional meetings hosted by the National POGIL Office (https://pogil.org/events).

4 SUITABILITY

The flexibility of the special session will allow for participants to engage in exploring the rubrics in a POGIL classroom environment. It is easy to briefly describe POGIL, but actually experiencing POGIL helps many teachers to really understand the key principles and practices. Similarly, POGIL is implemented in different ways depending on students, courses, and other factors, so providing multiple perspectives helps teachers understand the range of options. Thus, a special session enables us to help instructors better understand both the rubrics and the POGIL approach to support process skills development in any course.

ACKNOWLEDGMENTS

The authors thank the National Science Foundation for support under awards NSF DUE-1044679, DUE-1524399, DUE-1524936, DUE-1524965, and DUE-1626765. All opinions reflected in this paper are those of the authors and not necessarily those of the National Science Foundation.

REFERENCES

[1] Renee Cole. 2018. Enhancing Learning by Assessing Professional Skills in Student Group Interactions and Written Work. In *125th American Society for Engineering Education Conference.*

[2] Helen H. Hu and Tricia D. Shepherd. 2014. Teaching CS 1 with POGIL Activities and Roles. In *Proceedings of the 45th ACM Technical Symposium on Computer Science Education (SIGCSE '14).* ACM, New York, NY, USA, 127–132. https://doi.org/10.1145/2538862.2538954

Cybersecurity Program Accreditation: Benefits and Challenges

Rajendra K. Raj
Rochester Institute of Technology
Rochester, New York, USA
rkr@cs.rit.edu

Vijay Anand
Southeast Missouri State University
Cape Girardeau, Missouri, USA
vanand@semo.edu

David Gibson
United States Air Force Academy
Colorado Springs, Colorado, USA
david.gibson@usafa.edu

Siddharth Kaza
Towson University
Towson, Maryland, USA
SKaza@towson.edu

Andrew Phillips
United States Naval Academy
Annapolis, Maryland, USA
aphillips@usna.edu

ABSTRACT

The Curricular Guidelines for Post-Secondary Degree Programs in Cybersecurity (CSEC 2017) released by the Joint Task Force of the ACM, IEEE Computer Society, AIS and IFIP have begun to define the academic field of cybersecurity. Increasing numbers of institutions are now offering full-fledged undergraduate cybersecurity degree programs. However, as the CSEC 2017 guidelines do not define what constitutes a standalone undergraduate cybersecurity degree, the computing community needs to agree on parameters of what such a degree ought to be. To this end, ABET has created flexible accreditation criteria for cybersecurity programs guided extensively by CSEC 2017 and community input. These criteria were used to conduct pilot accreditation visits of four distinct cybersecurity programs in 2017-18.

This panel discusses benefits, challenges, and costs of cybersecurity program accreditation. The panelists, who represent the first four ABET-accredited cybersecurity programs, will discuss major curricular features of their programs, their motivation for participating in the pilot accreditation, the effort in preparing for accreditation, and the benefits anticipated both for their programs and the larger computing community due to program accreditation.

CCS CONCEPTS

• **Social and professional topics → Accreditation; Model curricula; Computing education programs;**

KEYWORDS

Program accreditation, cybersecurity education, computer security education, information assurance education.

ACM Reference Format:
Rajendra K. Raj, Vijay Anand, David Gibson, Siddharth Kaza, and Andrew Phillips. 2019. Cybersecurity Program Accreditation: Benefits and Challenges. In *Proceedings of the 50th ACM Technical Symposium on Computer Science Education (SIGCSE '19), February 27-March 2, 2019, Minneapolis, MN, USA.* ACM, New York, NY, USA, 2 pages. https://doi.org/10.1145/3287324.3287325

SIGCSE '19, February 27-March 2, 2019, Minneapolis, MN, USA

ACM ISBN 978-1-4503-5890-3/19/02.
https://doi.org/10.1145/3287324.3287325

1 SUMMARY

The worldwide demand for cybersecurity professionals has been addressed by various training programs and specialized certificates for current practitioners. Designation as a National Center of Academic Excellence (CAE) in Cyber Defense or Cyber Operations [4] have helped US institutions get started in this space. With many institutions beginning to develop undergraduate cybersecurity programs, there is a need to establish cybersecurity as a formal academic discipline. Shared expectations of the core knowledge, skills, and abilities of cybersecurity program graduates will help institutions developing curricula and employers hiring graduates [3].

The CSEC 2017 [2] curricular guidelines from the Joint Task Force of the ACM, IEEE Computer Society, AIS, and IFIP describe different aspects of cybersecurity education, but do not define what constitutes an undergraduate cybersecurity program. To establish what constitutes an accreditable 4-year undergraduate cybersecurity degree program, the Computing Accreditation Commission (CAC) of ABET has developed accreditation criteria for cybersecurity degree programs based largely on the CSEC 2017 guidelines and community input [1]. ABET's approach provides flexibility for a variety of cybersecurity programs to meet the criteria, while supporting outcomes, quality, and continuous improvement.

For the first time, four cybersecurity programs were accredited by ABET in 2017-18. The panelists, who represent these first four ABET-accredited programs, will discuss unique aspects of their programs, their motivations for seeking accreditation, and challenges faced in creating accreditable programs. The panel continues the dialog of what constitutes a proper academic undergraduate cybersecurity program.

Table 1 outlines the panel structure. The moderator will introduce the panelists and briefly discuss the background cybersecurity education. The panelists' position statements are shown in the next section. Ample time is reserved for audience participation.

Table 1: Panel Structure

	Description	Duration
1	Introductions and Background	8 minutes
2	Panelists' Presentations	32 minutes
3	Audience Q & A	30 minutes
4	Summary	5 minutes

2 POSITION STATEMENTS

2.1 Rajendra K. Raj

Rajendra K. Raj, a professor of computer science at Rochester Institute of Technology, heads the department's security cluster. He co-chaired ABET's CAC criteria committee that created the new cybersecurity program criteria that will become official in 2019-20.

Raj will moderate the panel, introduce the panelists, and briefly outline the background in cybersecurity education leading to the ABET accreditation criteria for cybersecurity. He will also facilitate the audience Q & A and discussion, and summarize the session.

2.2 Vijay Anand

Vijay Anand is associate professor of computer science at Southeast Missouri State University and a member of the Missouri Governor's Cybersecurity Task Force. Moving from industry to academia, he established Southeast's Cybersecurity program in 2011. Anand's research interests include real-time adaptability of Trusted Platform Modules to evolving threats, process institutionalization and improvements of security frameworks, intrusion detection, secure data transfer, usable security and privacy concerns.

Anand will discuss distinct features of Southeast's cybersecurity degree program that emphasizes industry needs of cybersecurity. He will discuss the the highly-technical, hands-on and comprehensive cybersecurity that is constantly evolving based on industry feedback. Anand will present the comprehensiveness of the curriculum, which covers technical (software, hardware, communication, and infrastructure), business processes, compliance and operational aspects, along with the infrastructure needed to support hands-on learning. He will also address the validation of Southeast's cybersecurity program through ABET accreditation.

2.3 David Gibson

David Gibson is Professor Emeritus of Computer Science at the United States Air Force Academy (USAFA). He led USAFA's Computer Science department for 14 years, and the development and operation of USAFA's cyber education, training, and research programs including establishment of the Cyber Science degree. Gibson has held positions at the National Security Agency and Cyber Command. An ABET volunteer for 18 years, he served on the Cyber Education Project and the CSEC 2017 Joint Task Force.

Gibson will discuss the evolution of USAFA's cyber program from its roots in computer science to the recent establishment of a distinct Cyber Science degree that is a technically-rigorous program that prepares graduates to serve as military officers conducting both offensive and defensive cyber operations and leading others in the same. Gibson will discuss the USAFA's Computer Science and Cyber Science programs, and compare the benefits and costs of program accreditation by ABET and designation by NSA as a National Center of Academic Excellence in Cyber Operations.

2.4 Siddharth Kaza

Sidd Kaza is Chairperson of Computer and Information Sciences at Towson University, Maryland. His interests lie in cybersecurity education, learning sciences, and application development. His projects under the Cyber4All umbrella (towson.edu/cyber4all) have been funded by the National Science Foundation, Department of Defense, Maryland Higher Education Commission, and others. Kaza served on the CSEC 2017 Joint Task Force and serves on the advisory board of the CSEC2Y curricular guidelines.

Kaza will discuss distinct features of Towson's cybersecurity program that is strongly rooted in computer science. The program, also designated as a National Center of Excellence in Cyber Operations, is focused on technical rigor in network security, application software, reverse engineering, and cyber operations. The program has been the tip-of-the-spear at Towson and helps create an institutional environment that holds four other programs in cybersecurity. Kaza will highlight challenges in maintaining cutting-edge programs and retaining faculty, while adhering to accreditation and designation requirements.

2.5 Andrew Phillips

Andrew Phillips is Academic Dean and Provost at the United States Naval Academy (USNA). Responsible for leadership of all facets of the Naval Academy academic program, Phillips led the development of the Center for Cyber Security Studies and the majors in Cyber Operations. Phillips is a past President of the Computer Science Accreditation Board (CSAB) and a CSAB Fellow, and a Team Chair/Program Evaluator for both ABET and the Middle States Commission on Higher Education.

Phillips will discuss the distinct features of USNA's Cyber Operations program that was designed to acknowledge the growing demand for cyber expertise in the Navy and Marine Corps. In that warfare centric context, fusing both offensive and defensive disciplines together is essential to understanding cyberspace operations. Because of the focus on adversaries, on maintaining operations in the presences of risk and threats, and on offensive techniques, the newly created Cyber Science Department was given the latitude to create a truly interdisciplinary blend of both technical and non-technical course material. Each of the Cyber Science Department courses specifically focus on offensive capabilities and/or defensive strategies, with a holistic view of what can be done from a technical or capabilities perspective as well as the legal/ethical perspective and the social engineering/human factors aspect of the adversary.

ACKNOWLEDGEMENTS

Anand acknowledges the immense support provided to Southeast's cybersecurity program by both the current and former presidents of Southeast Missouri State University, Dr. Carlos Vargas and Dr. Kenneth Dobbins. Raj acknowledges support provided by the US National Science Foundation under Award No. DGE-1433736.

REFERENCES

[1] ABET, Inc. 2018. Criteria for Accrediting Computing Programs. Effective for Review During the 2018-19 Accreditation Cycle. (2018). http://www.abet.org/wp-content/uploads/2018/02/C001-18-19-CAC-Criteria-Version-2.0-updated-02-12-18.pdf Accessed: November 6, 2018.

[2] Joint Task Force on Cybersecurity Education. 2017. *Cybersecurity Curricula 2017.* Technical Report. ACM, IEEE-CS, AIS SIGSEC, and IFIP WG 11.8. DOI: http://dx.doi.org/10.1145/3184594

[3] R. K. Raj and A. Parrish. 2018. Toward Standards in Undergraduate Cybersecurity Education in 2018. *Computer* 51, 2 (February 2018), 72–75. DOI: http://dx.doi.org/10.1109/MC.2018.1451658

[4] US National Security Agency and the Department of Homeland Security. 2018. Centers of Academic Excellence in Cybersecurity. (2018). https://www.nsa.gov/resources/educators/centers-academic-excellence Accessed: November 6, 2018.

What Have We Talked About?

An Analysis of the SIGCSE-Members Listserv

Austin Cory Bart
University of Delaware
Newark, DE
acbart@udel.edu

Clifford A. Shaffer
Virginia Tech
Blacksburg, VA
shaffer@vt.edu

ABSTRACT

The SIGCSE-Members listserv has been archiving posts by the Computer Science Education community for the past 22 years. This paper characterizes the post collection, in order to better understand the nature of the community from a quantitative perspective. We apply a number of email mining techniques, including a topical analysis through N-grams. Threads, posters, and posts are characterized in terms of duration and temporally. We also demonstrate how emails from the listserv can be successfully classified using machine learning algorithms, and report on an unsuccessful attempt to predict thread popularity. All of the scripts we used to collect, process, and analyze the data are freely available in the hopes that other researchers will replicate, refine, and extend our results.

CCS CONCEPTS

• **Social and professional topics → Computing education**; *Computing organizations*; • **Applied computing** → Document management and text processing;

KEYWORDS

Email; Listserv; Computing Educators; SIGCSE; SIGCSE-members

ACM Reference format:
Austin Cory Bart and Clifford A. Shaffer. 2019. What Have We Talked About?. In *Proceedings of Proceedings of the 50th ACM Technical Symposium on Computer Science Education, Minneapolis, MN, USA, February 27-March 2, 2019 (SIGCSE '19)*, 6 pages.
https://doi.org/10.1145/3287324.3287441

1 INTRODUCTION

The SIGCSE-Members listserv archives posts made by its members dating back to October 1996. This paper characterizes the collection of posts, in order to better understand the SIGCSE community. To our knowledge, this is the first attempt at a formal, quantitative analysis of the SIGCSE-Members mailing list. Previously, Kim Bruce published a summary of a particularly fervent conversation from the mailing list in an ITiCSE working group [4], which was followed up by a phenomenographical analysis [2]. Otherwise, there has been little reference to the mailing list in formal CS Ed research.

General analyses of email lists and on-line communities has been a wide area of study for decades, and the techniques used can vary substantially. [1] gives a useful overview of various problems and methods by reviewing a plethora of relevant papers in this area. As a subfield of text categorization, typical subproblems include N-gram analysis, temporal information analysis, and thread clustering. We tackle a number of these problems. For this paper, we ignore the most typical form of email classification (spam analysis), due to the highly-curated nature of the SIGCSE-members listserv.

1.1 Audience and Contributions

The primary audience of this paper are members of the Computing Education community who are interested in better understanding this professional community of practice. This paper could also be of broader interest to researchers in more general education who want to observe an exemplar sub-community, or to social interaction researchers interested in a professional education community. Educators that are new to the SIGCSE-Members listserv, and are interested in getting involved in the mailing list, should also find the analysis a useful introduction.

This paper makes the following contributions in service of these audiences:

- A time-oriented review of popular post topics through N-gram analysis of expected and common keywords,
- Visualizations of post characteristics based on analysis of thread length, thread duration, and post size,
- Visualizations of temporal posting trends by analyzing posts' submission date and time,
- A description of the frequency of job and conference ads using a supervised classification algorithm,
- A description of poster behavior based on analysis of the number of submissions from each poster,
- An attempt at predicting thread popularity from quantitative factors, and
- The release of the email processing scripts into a public repository.

2 DATA COLLECTION

The SIGCSE-Members listserv is restricted to posting by confirmed SIGCSE members; before receiving access, users must confirm their ACM membership ID with the listserv administrators via email [8]. The site maintains a public archive of all posts [1]. This public archive was scraped, processed, and analyzed using custom-made Python

[1] https://listserv.acm.org/SCRIPTS/WA-ACMLPX.CGI?A0=SIGCSE-MEMBERS

SIGCSE '19, February 27-March 2, 2019, Minneapolis, MN, USA

ACM ISBN 978-1-4503-5890-3/19/02...$15.00
https://doi.org/10.1145/3287324.3287441

scripts. To encourage replication and extension of our analyses, we make these scripts publicly available through a GitHub repository [2]. The following data were collected from the archive about every email posted from October 1996 to April 2017:

- The body of the email (either as unicode text or HTML).
- The subject line of the email.
- Any attachments to the email, including the MIME filetype.
- The name of the sender (but not their email, as described below).
- The timestamp of the email, with second-level resolution.
- The conversation thread that the email belongs to (and its position within the thread).

Email address normalization is a challenging problem in email mining, because of how names and addresses can be inconsistently aliased between accounts and mail management systems [3]. The SIGCSE archive does not reveal posters' emails addresses unless the viewer logs in as a confirmed member. For simplicity, we only collected data that was publicly viewable without logging in. This means that, although we collected user-friendly names of users, we did not collect the exact email address that sent each email. Therefore, the following methodology was used to normalize posters:

(1) Names were converted to lower case.
(2) Unnecessary titles were stripped out (e.g., "dr" or "doctor").
(3) Each full name was split into a set of names and sorted (e.g., the name "charles babbage" would be converted to the list "babbage, charles") in order to avoid common reorderings of names.

Once the email bodies and subjects were downloaded, the posts were processed by applying the following transformations:

- Special unicode characters were converted to similar ascii characters, in order to simplify textual analysis. This may have effects on the analysis with regards to international participants in the listserv, suggesting a direction for follow-up studies.
- HTML files were converted to a plain-text representation using the Python Html2Text library [3].
- Quoted text that was repeated in replies were removed.
- Signatures and authorship lines were removed.

Overall, 17795 emails were downloaded and processed using the above methodology. The remainder of this paper is dedicated to describing our own preliminary analyses of the archive.

3 TOPICAL ANALYSIS

Figure 1 shows the top 41 longest threads and the number of posts in that thread (all of which had at least 20 posts), organized by the year that the thread was made. This list demonstrates the range of topics covered on the Listserv, including debates about best practices ("Value of Unit Testing"), programming language arguments ("Java vs. C"), pedagogical conversations ("Students who get help from online forums"), community and professional conversations ("Faculty who are poor teachers - why do we tolerate them"), and even some humor ("Fun - how do you know if you are an old CS prof").

[2]https://github.com/acbart/sigcse-mail
[3]https://github.com/aaronsw/html2text

Year	#	Subject
1996	27	More on CSAB
1999	22	Story on Computer education in today's Chronicle Online
	25	Grad School
2000	38	Simplified Java IO for CS1
2004	36	ACM Java Task Force announcement
	24	Java vs C
2005	24	Decline in CS enrollment - was Re: Two replies to Duben and to Shaffer
	22	Elimination of Computer Science Courses from the High Schools List of NCAA-Approved Core Courses
	55	Differential Equations
2006	24	Intro to programming course without reference to any languages
	25	What price publications
	21	Java Programming IDE
	23	Coder Jobs Painfully Stable
	48	I Object
2007	27	Carrots Sticks and women
2008	22	CS - science or engineering - was calculus?
	29	Are CSI and CSII language independent?
2009	24	Need for a CS version of the Order of the Engineer
	41	Is Obtaining ABET Accreditation for a Doctoral Granting Institutions Undergraduate Program Worth the Effort?
	21	Looking for information on how Java-first schools handle the topic of pointers
2010	22	Outrage: Albion College board axes CS ignoring shared governance
	39	CSI functions first
	22	Article in today's Chronicle
2011	21	SIGCSE Robot Hoedown attracts Senators attention
	31	Designing a CS classroom
2012	35	Python better than Java for CS1
	29	Students who get help from online forums
	26	Recursion Question
	33	Resell your books
	21	computer science majors study less on average than elementary education majors
2013	36	Handwriting code on exams
2014	22	Summer reading
	36	Getting college credit from MOOCs
	23	systems that detect plagiarism in programming assignments
	29	Computer Engineering Barbie
2016	94	Fun - how do you know if you are an old CS prof
	31	Faculty who are poor teachers - why do we tolerate them?
2017	25	Value of Unit Testing
	22	workflow for easilly adding feedback to code while grading
	23	Can we talk about documenting our code?
2018	22	Functional programming in intro CS course

Figure 1: The 41 Longest Threads, Ordered by Time

Figure 2 shows the results of targeted unigram and bigram analysis of common phrases over each year. Each plot represents a different grouping of phrases and words. The number of occurrences of the word or phrase were divided by the total number of words from that year in order to provide a time-adjusted proportion.

Figure 2a shows the word usage rate over years across various programming languages. Java has almost always been the top language discussed. C and C++ are also frequent topics, although somewhat less so. Python has grown dramatically in popularity since the early 2000s. In general, however, the discussion of all of these languages seems to have decreased in the past decade. There was surprisingly little conversation about Scheme, Racket, or JavaScript, to the point where they could not be reasonably included in the visualization.

Figure 2b shows the trends in the use of gendered language over years. Two kinds of words were counted as gendered: "Male" and "Female". Male words include "men", "boys", "gentlemen", "his", "he"; female words include "women", "girls", "ladies", "her", and "she". In the first decade of the mailing list, most years had more male words used than female. However, that trend changed around 2007. Since about 2012, there has been more female gendered words used than male. We suggest that this trend reflects the increased emphasis within the SIGCSE community on the gender balance problem.

Figure 2c shows use of the terms "CS0", "CS1", "CS2", and "CS3" over time. These terms describe introductory courses at various levels [5]. CS1 was easily the most popular term, followed by CS2.

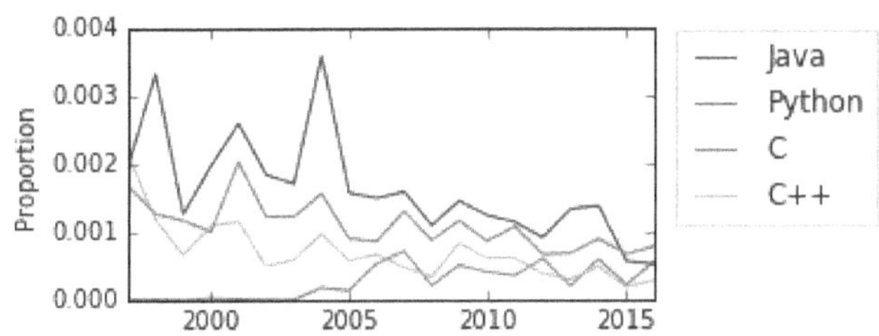

(a) Programming Languages

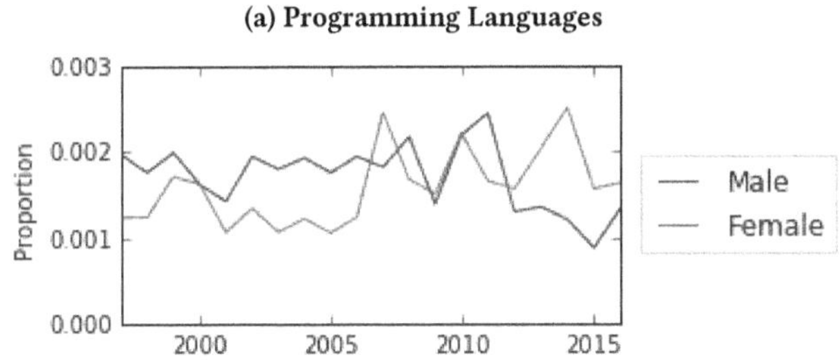

(b) Gendered Words

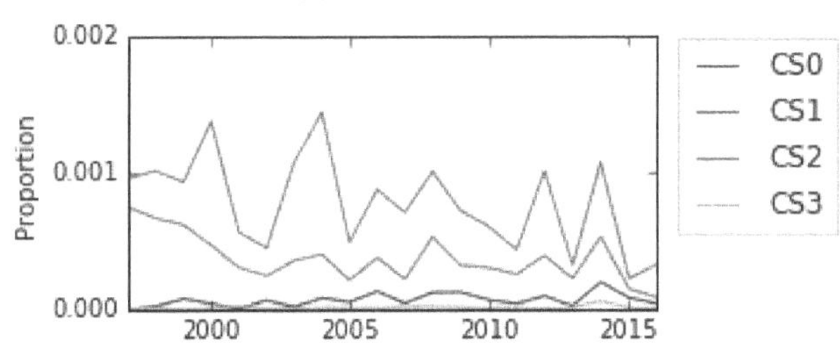

(c) CS Levels

Figure 2: N-gram Analysis over Years

CS0 was consistently ranked third, while CS3 was barely ever used (a grand total of 22 times over the two decades). Note that this analysis targeted these literal terms, and not common synonyms (e.g., "Data Structures and Algorithms" for CS3).

A few additional observations follow. The term "undergraduate" consistently appeared twice as frequently as "graduate". The terms "teaching" and "research" appeared equally often. The terms "K-12", "Middle School", and "High School" were almost unused until 2007, when they began skyrocketing in popularity.

4 POST AND THREAD CHARACTERISTICS

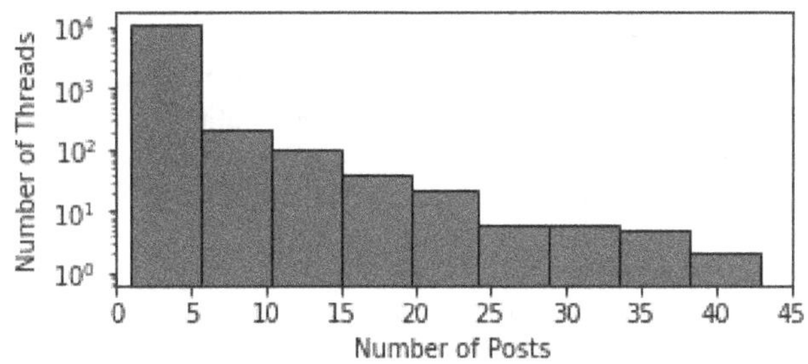

Figure 3: Distribution of Thread Sizes

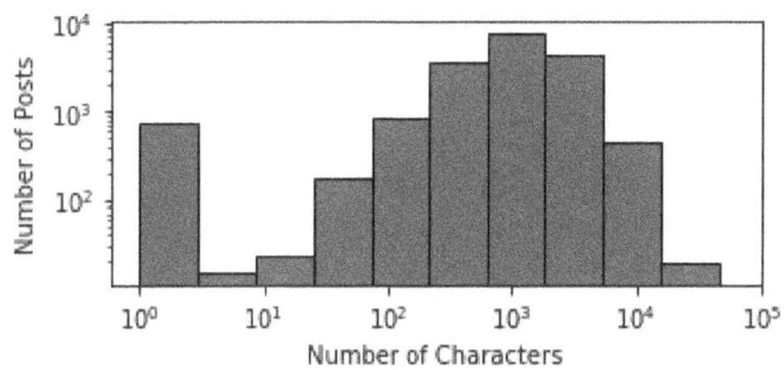

Figure 4: Distribution of Post Lengths

Figure 3 and 4 shows the distribution of email thread sizes and individual email length, respectively. The first graph is logarithmic on the y-axis, while the second is logarithmic on both axes. Most threads tend to be small, lasting only one or two posts (57.5%). Only one thread was longer than 60 posts, totaling 91 posts ("fun -> how do you know if you are an old CS prof?"), in addition to 4 separate follow-up threads. Similar to thread length, most posts tended to be short, with less than 5000 characters. (Note that SIGCSE-Members listserv moderators traditionally monitor and heavily discourage including large amounts of text from earlier posts in any reply, which will affect post lengths.) The overall distribution of post lengths is log-normal, centered roughly around 1500 characters (about half a page of text). Only one post was more than 40,000 characters, a particularly long notification about the 1997 IEEE Conference on Software Engineering Education and Training. A large number of posts were less than 10 characters, which could be caused by inadequacies in the processing methodology used, trivial posts made in reply to another post, or posts that were just an attachment.

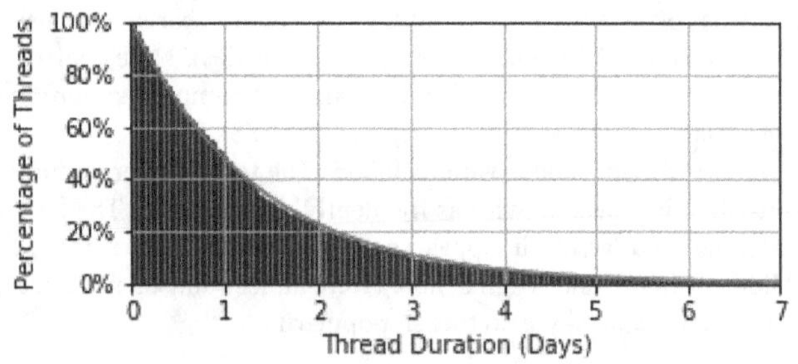

Figure 5: Non-trivial Thread Duration

Figure 5 is a bar chart of the duration of non-trivial threads; each bar represents the percentage of threads that last at least that number of hours (with 24 bars between each unit on the x-axis). In this case, non-trivial threads were any thread that had at least one reply [6]. These durations follow a power law, as shown by the red regression line with the following formula:

$$\%\, of\ Threads\ Ended = \frac{1}{2.1^{days}}$$

The Mean Squared Error of this regression rounds to 0 (approximately 0.00003). The implication is fairly straightforward: almost half (47.6%) of all non-trivial threads end after a day, roughly a quarter (22.7%) end after two days, a tenth (10.8%) after three days, and so on. Previous studies of forum and email thread lengths suggest that long-tail, power-law distributions are fairly common in online communications [3].

5 TEMPORAL ANALYSIS

Figure 6 shows trends over time in user posting behavior. Each of the four graphs show a different granularity of time: over the entire time period, grouped by month, grouped by day of the week, and grouped by the time of day. These posting habits reveal behavior within the SIGCSE-members listserv. Although not particularly surprising, participants tend to avoid posting during non-work hours, on weekends, and during holiday seasons. These patterns should be considered when waiting on responses or when trying to decide when to post messages.

The Yearly trend shows a chaotic growth over the past two decades. The variation over time is considerably higher than in other graphs. However, linear regression reveals a significant ($p <$ .01) but tiny ($slope = .13$) positive trend. This suggests that the rate of posting has relatively increased over the years, but with strong fluctuation – most likely due to the cyclical boom/bust cycles seen in computer science programs. The most sustained activity seems to have occurred during the 2009-2010 time period, while the lowest was during the 2001-2003 time period.

The Monthly distribution reveals that users are disengaged during the summer months and during the winter holidays. Although January quickly peaks with new posts, the rest of the spring is a slow downward trend until posts fall off sharply in June. When most US Fall semesters begin in September, posts also pick up and eventually peak in October, before falling back down in November. It is unclear exactly why posts peak so heavily in January, but two hypotheses are: 1) anticipation of the SIGCSE conference, or 2) to make up for lost time during December. Of course, there is high variation within most months, so these conclusions are tenuous.

The day-of-the-week graph shows the frequency of emails sent during days of the week. This graph indicates that for any given day of the week, there are typically no posts. When posts do occur, they tend to happen considerably more often on weekdays than on weekends. This suggests that most posters disengage during the weekend. There appears to be a generally negative trend during the week, at least in terms of the heavily active days. If accurate, then this implies that posters steadily disengage over the course of the week.

The final graph shows the frequency of posts over hours of the day. Similar to the day of week graph, most hours have no emails posted. However, the graph does seem to show three distinct periods: busy in the morning, moderately busy in the evening, and quiet during the night. One conclusion is that SIGCSE posters tend to catch up on their correspondence early in the day and trail off over time, mostly disengaging after work. Timezone data was not always available for each post. When it was available, all times were adjusted to Greenwich Mean Time in order to meaningfully compare post times from a common vantage point.

6 JOBS AND CONFERENCES

When reviewing the posts in the archive, a large number of job and conference ads were noted. Machine Learning was used to classify each post based on the type of post, a common technique in email classification [9]. For training data, 303 posts were manually tagged as either "Normal Conversation" (200), "Job Ad" (52), or "Conference Discussion" (51). These posts were then analyzed in a Support-Vector Machine with stochastic gradient descent (SGD) learning, using the body of the post as a Bag-of-Words, via the Scikit-Learn Python package [7]. The performance of the classifier was impressive, with perfect precision, recall, and F1-scores based on the test data.

The classifier suggests that 2322 job ads and 2368 conference-related posts have been made on the listserv. The percentage of job ads and conference posts were surprisingly similar (14.3% and 14.0% respectively) over the entire dataset. However, the yearly rate shown in Figure 7 reveals that neither rate has been constant; conference posts have slowly but steadily increased, while job ads faced a period of decline during the mid-2000s before resuming growth in the past half-decade. This closely matches the boom/bust cycles previously seen in computing education. Figure 8 shows the monthly trend in job posts. Job ads appear to be seasonal: most posts come out during the fall, and few posts come during the summer (a significant difference, according to a one-way ANOVA with $p < 0.05$). This matches the authors' intuitions about hiring schedules.

7 POSTER BEHAVIOR

Our next form of analysis attempts to determine the behavioral patterns of the typical posters to the listserv. Previously, we described how poster names were normalized to more accurately group posts by repeated users. After this process was applied, 2205 estimated unique posters were found. The distribution of posts per poster is given in Figure 9 . The median number of messages per poster

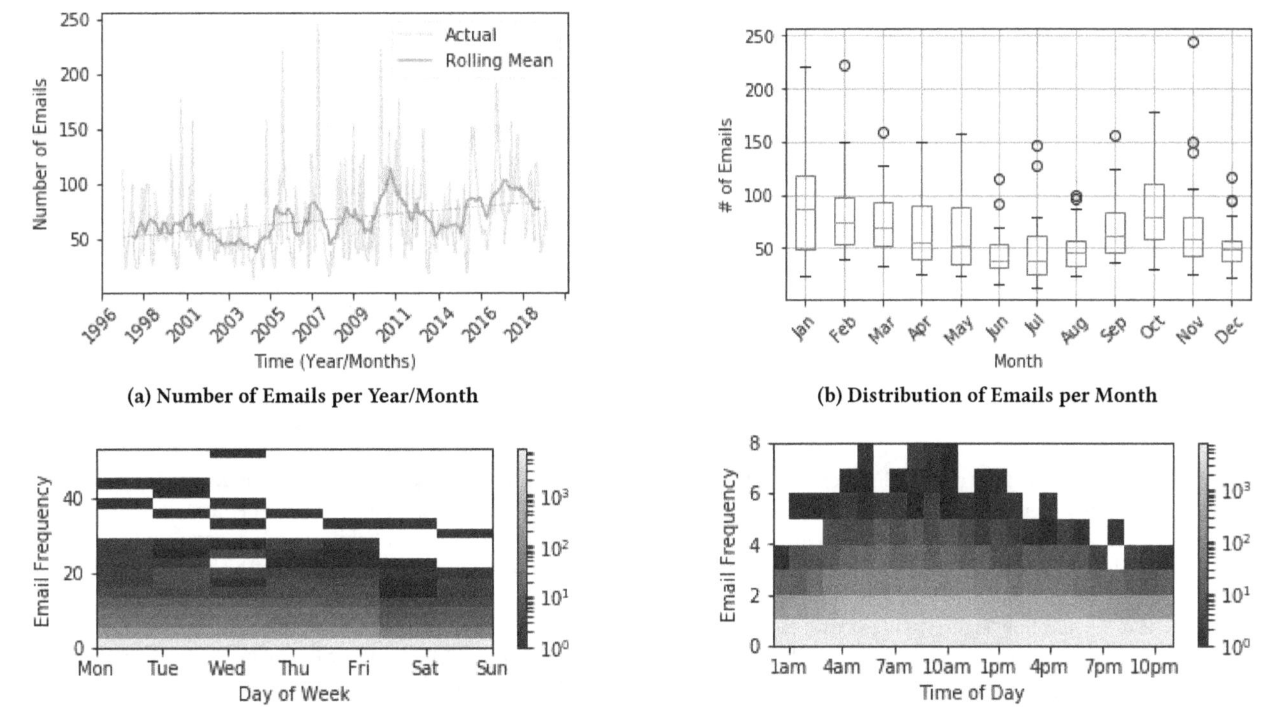

(a) Number of Emails per Year/Month

(b) Distribution of Emails per Month

(c) Frequency Distribution of Emails by Hour

(d) Frequency Distribution of Emails by Day of Week

Figure 6: Posts over Time

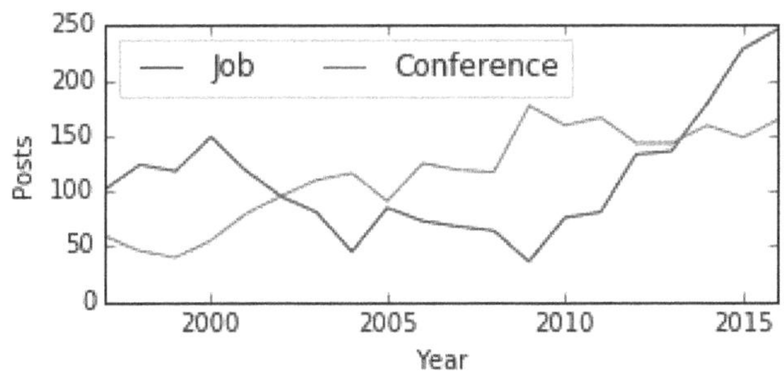

Figure 7: Post Types by year

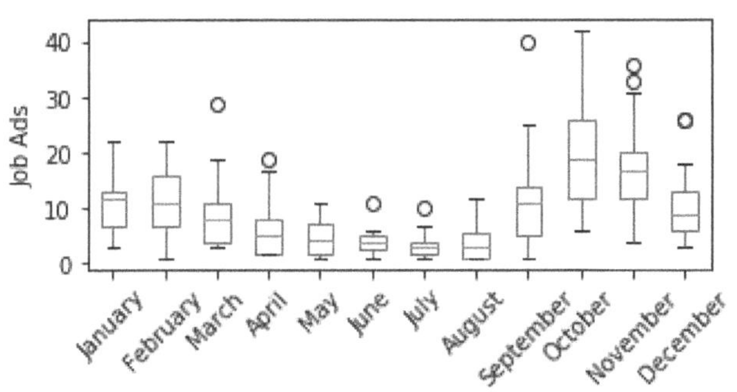

Figure 8: Distribution of Job Ads per Month

is 2, with 51.3% of all posters having 2 or fewer posts associated with their normalized name. Table 1 breaks down the frequency and

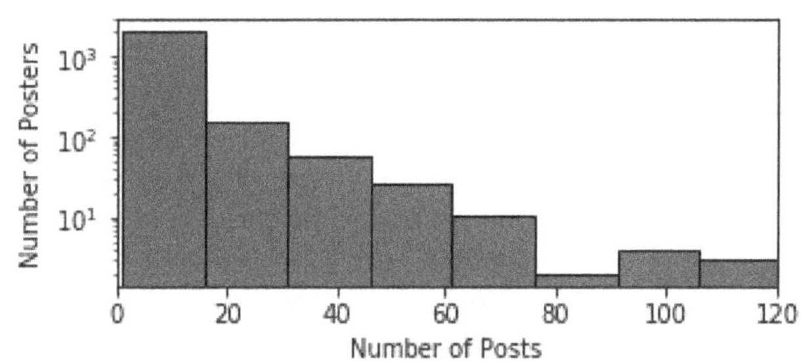

Figure 9: Distribution of Posts per User

percentages of four different kinds of posters: Quiet (1-2 posts), Typical posters (3-20 posts), Active (21-50 posts), and Super-active (>50 posts). From this, it can be seen that the bulk of the posts are made by regular posters, but that active and super-active posters both contribute large numbers of posts, despite making up a relatively small percentage of the total number of posters.

Poster Type	Threshold	Posters	Posts
Quiet	1-2 posts	1184 (50.9%)	1491 (8.4%)
Regular	3-20 posts	944 (40.6%)	6864 (38.6%)
Active	21-50 posts	154 (6.6%)	4849 (27.2%)
Super	>50 posts	43 (1.8%)	4590 (25.8%)
Total	Any posts	2325	17794

Table 1: Poster Type Frequencies

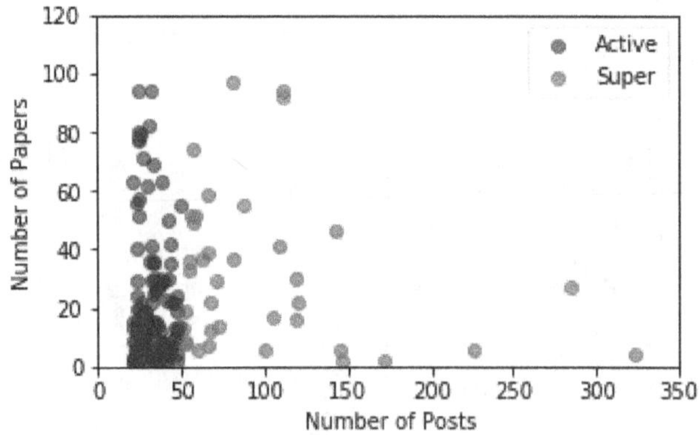

Figure 10: Productivity vs. Activity of Active Users

All of the active members of the mailing list were identified and manually researched in order to correlate their mailing list activity with their research productivity, as defined by their publication count within the SIGCSE Collection of the ACM Digital Library [4]. Note that this collection includes several publications, including SIGCSE, ICER, ITiCSE, and Koli. Figure 10 is a scatter plot showing the relationship between the users' posts and their SIGCSE publications for active and super-active users. Surprisingly, there was no significant correlation between activity and productivity. There were a number of users who published frequently without posting to the mailing list, and many active users with few publications within the SIGCSE publication archives.

8 THREAD POPULARITY REGRESSION

For our final analysis, an attempt was made to statistically predict what makes for a popular thread. We hypothesized that some subset of the posts' temporal information (i.e. month, hour of day, day of week), post length (characters), and the presence of questions (approximated by the number of question marks), would allow us to predict the size of a thread (which would serve as the thread's popularity). First, we attempted to stepwise fit a linear regression model for each possible subset of the factors. Second, we classified each continuous variable into finite categories (e.g., hour could be classified as "morning", "evening", etc.) and used in a logistic regression model. However, in both cases, no models could be found to reasonably fit the data. In fact, the R^2 was $< .01$ in all such models that we attempted. This suggests that, despite clear patterns in user behavior, there are no predictable ways to increase user response using these simple statistical models generated from these factors.

9 CONCLUSIONS AND FUTURE WORK

We have characterized the SIGCSE Members mailing list in a number of ways. We performed some basic topical analyses to describe trends in discussion themes. Posts and posters were analyzed to derive email and thread characteristics, including from a temporal perspective. We report a successful application of machine learning to classify posts as job ads and conference discussion, and an unsuccessful attempt to predict thread popularity using statistical models. We hope that this reveals some deeper insight about the SIGCSE community, and gives the society an opportunity to reflect on where it has been over the past 20 years.

At this point, we have run a number of exploratory analyses on the collected archive of posts. However, we believe that there are still many more possible research questions to be explored using this dataset. As previously mentioned, we have open-sourced our collection and processing scripts in the hopes that interested readers will replicate, refine, and extend our investigations. As we review our work, we find some obvious areas for improvement. First, as described in our methodology, exact email addresses were not easily available in the public archive, which hampered our ability to conduct fine-grained analysis of users. A further analysis of this archive would benefit from using the associated email data to more precisely identify users. Techniques described by Bird et al [3] could be used in support of this approach. Second, this paper presents a largely quantitative analysis of the SIGCSE Mailing Archive, which illuminates certain aspects of the community. However, a qualitative analysis could shed insight on other aspects. Deeper analysis of posters' word usage, habits, and language could reveal potentially interesting information about the SIGCSE community. Proper qualitative and phenomenological analysis, such as that conducted by Anders et al [2], would be even more illuminating. Finally, there was little attempt to compare behavior by the SIGCSE-Members community against behavior on listservs supporting other types of communities.

[4]http://dl.acm.org/sig.cfm?id=SP927

REFERENCES

[1] Izzat Alsmadi and Ikdam Alhami. 2015. Clustering and classification of email contents. *Journal of King Saud University-Computer and Information Sciences* 27, 1 (2015), 46–57.

[2] Anders Berglund and Raymond Lister. Debating the OO Debate: Where is the Problem?. In *Proceedings of the Seventh Baltic Sea Conference on Computing Education Research - Volume 88 (Koli Calling '07)*. 171–174.

[3] Christian Bird, Alex Gourley, Prem Devanbu, Michael Gertz, and Anand Swaminathan. Mining email social networks. In *Proceedings of the 2006 international workshop on Mining software repositories*. 137–143.

[4] Kim B Bruce. 2004. Controversy on how to teach CS 1: a discussion on the SIGCSE-members mailing list. In *ACM SIGCSE Bulletin*, Vol. 36. 29–34.

[5] Curtis R. Cook. CS0: Computer Science Orientation Course *(SIGCSE '97)*. 87–91.

[6] Bryan Klimt and Yiming Yang. 2004. The enron corpus: A new dataset for email classification research. *Machine learning: ECML 2004* (2004), 217–226.

[7] F. Pedregosa, G. Varoquaux, A. Gramfort, V. Michel, B. Thirion, O. Grisel, M. Blondel, P. Prettenhofer, R. Weiss, V. Dubourg, J. Vanderplas, A. Passos, D. Cournapeau, M. Brucher, M. Perrot, and E. Duchesnay. 2011. Scikit-learn: Machine Learning in Python. *Journal of Machine Learning Research* 12 (2011), 2825–2830.

[8] Samuel Rebelsky and William J. Turner. 2017. Mailing Lists. http://sigcse.org/sigcse/membership/mailing-lists. (2017). Accessed: 2017-08-18.

[9] Seongwook Youn and Dennis McLeod. 2007. A comparative study for email classification. *Advances and innovations in systems, computing sciences and software engineering* (2007), 387–391.

CS Education Then and Now: Recollections and Reflections

Melinda McDaniel
(moderator)
Georgia Tech
College of Computing
Atlanta, GA USA
mcdaniel@cc.gatech.edu

John Cigas
Park University
Computer Science Dept.
Parkville, MO USA
cigas@acm.org

Briana B. Morrison
Univ. of Nebraska Omaha
College of IS&T
Omaha, NE USA
bbmorrison@unomaha.edu

Henry Walker
Grinnell College
Dept. of Computer Science
Grinnell, IA USA
walker@cs.grinnell.edu

ABSTRACT

How has CS education changed since SIGCSE first began in 1968? This panel of presenters, with 135 years of teaching instruction between them, will remind some attendees of what used to be and educate newer members on what life was like pre-internet. Topics to be discussed include changes in content, presentation medium, equipment and environment, students and audience, and pedagogy. Audience members will be engaged through peer instruction questions during and between topic discussions and may use their cellphones or laptops to respond to questions. This panel will allow our community to acknowledge the diversity and experience in our organization and celebrate our heritage. We believe old-timers who wish to reminisce and young, new instructors who are interested in a historical aspect will be interested in the session.

Keywords: Computer Science Education; K-12 Education; Interdisciplinary; Pedagogy; Outreach; Diversity

ACM Reference format:

Melinda McDaniel, John Cigas, Briana Morrison, and Henry Walker. 1997. CS Education Then and Now: Recollections and Reflections. In *Proceedings of the 50th ACM Technical Symposium on Computer Science Education (SIGCSE '19)*, Feb. 27-March 2, 2019, Minneapolis, MN, USA. ACM, NY, NY, USA, 2 pages. https://doi.org/10.1145/3287324.3287328

1. SUMMARY

How has CS education changed since SIGCSE first began in 1968? This panel of presenters, with 135 years of teaching instruction between them, will remind some attendees of what used to be and educate newer members on what life was like pre-internet. By remembering our roots and instruction in previous decades of computing education, we can begin to understand how far we have progressed, especially for our nascent field.

The panelists intend to address computing education topics familiar with all SIGCSE attendees and those that have experienced the most significant changes since the formation of the SIGCSE organization. The panelists will discuss changes to the content of computing discipline such as security concerns, Artificial Intelligence, and programming languages. We will discuss the presentation medium going from transparencies and projectors to online education and MOOCs. We will discuss the change in both equipment (mainframes and laptops) and environment (shared lab space to WIFI collaborations). We will discuss the change in the students we teach: from math majors to digital natives to CS For All. We will also discuss the change in pedagogy as we continue to research best practices for teaching and learning computing. Finally, we will have predictions for the future.

We will engage the audience with peer instruction questions allowing the audience to share anecdotes from their own personal history while celebrating our organization and heritage. We believe old-timers who wish to reminisce and young, new instructors who are interested in a historical aspect will be interested in the session.

2. PANEL STRUCTURE

After brief introductions, each panelist will have 10 minutes to focus on a specific topic as outlined in their position statements, including personal anecdotes. The panel as a whole will then discuss possible future directions of the field and what big changes we may see in the next 5 - 10 years. The remaining time will be spent answering questions from the audience, inviting others to share their experiences or predictions for the future.

The panel will utilize peer instruction technology during and between topic discussions to engage the audience. Attendees will be asked questions concerning their teaching experience, what programming languages they have taught, etc. and may use their cellphones or laptops to respond to questions. Answers will be shown immediately which will allow us to recognize the attendee who has taught the longest, the year of the earliest computer course taken, person who has taught the most programming languages, etc.

3. AUDIENCE (McDaniel)

While the structure of computer science education has changed tremendously in the last fifty years, the students themselves are also vastly different than they were in 1968. We are very aware of the transition between punch cards and the use of complex IDEs, but we must not lose sight of the changes in the students we teach that have also occurred. The student population is more diverse, more experienced with computers, and more confident. Although recent reports bemoan the lack of availability of computer science education courses prior to college [4], the number available is far greater than what was available in 1968. Furthermore, the students currently attending college have grown up with computers and, even if not able to learn computer programming, have been using

SIGCSE '19, February 27-March 2, 2019, Minneapolis, MN, USA

ACM ISBN 978-1-4503-5890-3/19/02.
https://doi.org/10.1145/3287324.3287328

computer applications since childhood. When SIGCSE began, the ability to use a mainframe computer required attending a separate building and came with it an awe that is not experienced by today's students. In this segment of the panel, I will discuss how the changes in the classroom environment as well as in the audience we are teaching affect student outcomes and how we, as instructors, can reach this ever changing audience.

Melinda began her Computer Science teaching career at Georgia Tech in 1984 while working on her master's degree. After graduating and completing 20 years of teaching CS in high school (including AP Computer science from Pascal to Java), she decided to return to school for a PhD. Now she teaches at her Alma Mater and especially enjoys inspiring non-majors to see the value and joy of learning to code.

4. CONTENT (Morrison)

All one has to do is look at the evolution of ACM curriculum standards over the years to see the progression and growth of the computing discipline. What began as an offshoot of math has grown and splintered into areas such as information technology, software engineering, information assurance, information sciences, and data science just to name a few. Originally teaching students FORTRAN and COBOL to become employed by the Department of Defense or large businesses, we now educate students for practically all career areas in any number of languages. We now struggle with how to fit all the needed topics into the limited number of credit hours available in a degree program. My talk will review the growth of the topics within the discipline and our continuous need to adapt to new discoveries within the field.

Briana earned a Computer Engineering bachelor's degree in 1987 from Tulane University. She worked for IBM as a software developer for 8 years before transitioning to academia. After earning her Master's in CS at Southern Polytechnic State University she began teaching there, first as an adjunct and then as an instructor. During her 20 years at SPSU she served as the coordinator of the undergraduate CS program and helped to establish the Computer Game Design and Development program. After earning her PhD at Georgia Tech in 2016 she is now at University of Nebraska Omaha.

5. ENVIRONMENT (Cigas)

Marshall McLuhan's phrase 'the medium is the message' aptly applies to the equipment and technology applicable to computer science education. I started programming with punch cards and a compiler turnaround time often measured in hours. The strategies I learned to work in that environment are not the same as those used by today's students, who can collaboratively program with me from across the country using a shared IDE. Here I will review some of these changes in technology over the years and the effects they had on my students and my own behaviors.

John has been teaching at the university level since the early 80's. Most of his experience is at liberal arts schools, where he's had the opportunity to teach a variety of courses through the years. Currently he's trying to figure out how best to use technology to deliver programming classes online.

6. PEDAGOGY (Walker)

In 1968, lecture was used almost exclusively for computing and mathematics courses. Although biology, chemistry, and physics regularly utilized separate, supervised labs, closed labs in computing and math were quite rare. In the 1980s through the mid 1990s, much discussion focused on the role, if any, of labs within a computing curriculum. In the early 1990s, the role, substance, and significance of lab sessions evolved, and educators also identified the nature of the facilities to support these labs [2, Abstract]. By 1996, curricular recommendations from the Liberal Arts Computer Science Consortium required formal labs for CS1 and CS2, including the statement that formal labs, "should not be limited to skills acquisition labs (e.g., learning to use a debugger or editor), but should be based on the principles of the scientific method, including experimentation, observation, data collection, data analysis, and hypothesis confirmation or rejection" [3, p. 89].

Also in the early 1990s, R. R. Hake conducted a landmark study of 6542 physics students in 62 introductory courses between 1992 and 1996. Hake concluded, "48 courses ... which made substantial use of IE [interactive engagement or active learning] methods achieved an average gain ... almost two standard deviations ... above that of the traditional courses" [1, p. 64]. Since that time, numerous experiments, studies, and experiences within computing have evolved to promote active student learning, while also seeking to meet recent challenges due to increasing enrollments. Many other studies, in numerous disciplines including computing, reached the same conclusion that pedagogy promoting active student engagement can have a strong impact on student learning.

Henry's first computer science teaching job involved giving some non-credit lectures (on FORTRAN coding) about 1968. He started academic teaching as a mathematics instructor at M.I.T. in 1973, the year he received his PhD.. Over the years, he has engaged in numerous discussions of computing education in general and pedagogy in particular---most recently in his book, "Teaching Computing: A Practitioner's Perspective," Taylor and Francis, 2018. He has taught CS for more than 50 years.

7. ACKNOWLEDGEMENTS

This panel of presenters would like to thank Dr. Olga Glebova for serving as our master of ceremonies. Dr. Glebova is a Lecturer for Georgia State University where she has taught Algorithms, Introduction to Programming, and Discrete Mathematics for three years.

8. REFERENCES

[1] Hake, R.R. 1998. A six-thousand-student survey of mechanics test data for introductory physics courses. In *American Journal of Physics.* 66(1) (January 1998). 133–137.

[2] Parker, J., Cupper, R., Molnar, D., and Scragg, G. 1990. Laboratories in the Computer Science Curriculum. In *Journal of Computer Science Education* (1990). 205-221.

[3] Walker, H.M. and Schneider, G.M. 1996. A revised model curriculum for a liberal arts degree in computer science. In *Communications of the ACM* 39(12) (December 1996). 85–95.

[4] Webb, M. et al. Computer science in K-12 school curricula of the 2lst century: Why, what and when? In *Education and Information Technologies* 22.2 (2017). 445-468.

A Top-Ten List for 50-50

Gloria Childress Townsend
Professor of Computer Science
DePauw University
Greencastle IN, USA
gct@depauw.edu

ABSTRACT

SIGCSE addresses gender issues in computing year after year. At DePauw University, we learned from SIGCSE's lessons – and those taught by ACM's Council on Women in Computing – and recently awarded 47% of our computer science undergraduate degrees to women. This talk provides a rapid-fire countdown of ten of our most effective strategies that created our 47% class.

KEYWORDS

Computer Science Education, Gender

ACM Reference format:

Gloria Childress Townsend. 2019. A Top-Ten List for 50-50. In *SIGCSE'19: The 50th ACM Technical Symposium on Computer Science Education, Feb 27-Mar 2, 2019, Minneapolis, MN, USA.* ACM, New York, NY, USA, 1 pages. https://doi.org/10.1145/3287324.3290952

BIOGRAPHY

Gloria Childress Townsend, Professor of Computer Science, has taught at DePauw University for thirty-nine years and chaired her department for seven years. She founded ACM Celebrations and chaired the ACM-W Chapters project, during her seventeen-year tenure with ACM's Council on Women in Computing. Her research interests include evolutionary computation and gender issues in computing.

SIGCSE '19, February 27-March 2, 2019, Minneapolis, MN, USA

ACM ISBN 978-1-4503-5890-3/19/02.
https://doi.org/10.1145/3287324.3290952

A Learning Platform for SQL Injection

Nada Basit
University of Virginia
basit@virginia.edu

Abdeltawab Hendawi
University of Virginia
hendawi@virginia.edu

Joseph Chen
University of Virginia
jmc2fz@virginia.edu

Alexander Sun
University of Virginia
ahs9vt@virginia.edu

ABSTRACT

We present a web application system where users can learn about and practice SQL injection attacks. Our system is designed for students in a university level database or computer security class, and is aimed towards students familiar with SQL but with little experience in web security. Our platform currently contains 12 levels, each of which demonstrates a SQL vulnerability that the user must exploit. For each level, we explain the goal of the challenge, and also provide detailed solutions. Our system provides advantages over other methods of teaching SQL injection because it is hands-on, the challenges provide a greater scope of vulnerability coverage, and is easily extensible, allowing instructors to add their own SQL injection problems for their students.

CCS CONCEPTS

• **Security and privacy → Database and storage security**; • **Applied computing → Interactive learning environments**;

KEYWORDS

SQL injection; database security; learning tool; education

ACM Reference Format:
Nada Basit, Abdeltawab Hendawi, Joseph Chen, and Alexander Sun. 2019. A Learning Platform for SQL Injection. In *SIGCSE '19: 50th ACM Technical Symposium on Computer Science Education, February 27–March 2, 2019, Minneapolis, MN, USA.* ACM, New York, NY, USA, 7 pages. https://doi.org/10.1145/3287324.3287490

1 INTRODUCTION

In today's technology-driven society, website applications have a predominant role in everyday life. People use websites for online shopping, banking, communicating with friends, and much more. Many websites use databases in their backend to store user information. Because valuable information such as passwords, credit card numbers, or social security numbers are stored in those databases, they become common targets for malicious hackers.

SIGCSE'19, February 27–March 2, 2019, Minneapolis, MN, USA

ACM ISBN 978-1-4503-5890-3/19/2...$15.00
https://doi.org/10.1145/3287324.3287490

One common attack against SQL databases is known as SQL injection. SQL injection is a web vulnerability where malicious users input carefully crafted SQL statements into a website form. In order to execute the SQL query, websites often concatenate untrusted user input with code to be executed. Successful SQL injections have the potential to read sensitive data from a database or execute administrator actions [14]. According to the Open Web Application Security Project (OWASP), SQL injection is the most critical web vulnerability [11]. Similarly, according to MITRE's Common Weakness Enumeration, the most dangerous programming error is SQL injection [6]. SQL injection attacks have been used in real world websites on numerous occasions. In as early as 2002, over 200,000 credit card numbers were leaked from Guess.com using a SQL injection attack [1][10]. The year after, over 500,000 credit card numbers were leaked from PetCo.com using another SQL injection attack [7]. In 2013, the hacker group "RedHack" found a SQL injection vulnerability in the Istanbul Administration Site. They were able to erase people's debts to water, gas, electricity, and Internet companies [12]. They also tweeted the injection so that others could also exploit the vulnerability. Therefore, it is important that web developers understand the risk that SQL injection poses.

We believe there are two main reasons why SQL injection remains a problem today. One is that some web developers are either unaware or unconcerned about SQL injection, which causes the websites they create to be vulnerable. The second is that even if security is considered, hackers are constantly looking for new attacks to leverage. Even though there have been many countermeasures [2][3][4][8], each method begets another method of attack, and new vulnerabilities are continually being found. Although some of these vulnerabilities are reported, others go unreported and the public has no knowledge they exist. These factors make it difficult to keep our websites secure.

In this paper, we address the problem of SQL injection by describing a SQL injection learning platform we created. The platform is a web application that is designed to be used in a classroom setting. It demonstrates the vulnerabilities related to SQL present in web applications by allowing users to craft their own injections to hack into intentionally vulnerable databases. Our goal is that users will understand the importance and consequences of SQL injection through attempting injections themselves. The platform aims to address the lack of awareness of SQL injection by teaching and providing examples of SQL injection, and attempts to address newer vulnerabilities by being easily extensible. The platform is centered around a series of levels, which get progressively more difficult and build off the previous ones. Each level presents a different scenario, along with a vulnerable website form. The user must understand the scenario and then craft an appropriate SQL injection query which will exploit the vulnerability. Users create their own exploits because we believe a hands-on approach is more beneficial when conveying the importance of computer security.

Among the work that have tried to teach SQL injection, our platform differs in that it is user-friendly towards people who are new to SQL injection and provides extensibility to educators who want to add new levels. Some sites aim to be a practice tool with harder challenges without much guidance towards beginners. In contrast, our site aims to be a simple and effective teaching tool that starts users with basic challenges and progresses through harder problems.

We review related work in the area of teaching SQL injection in Section II. We then discuss an overview of our system, including the contents and architecture of our system, in Section III. In Section IV, we explain the extensibility of our system and show how a professor would add a new challenge to the site. In Section V, we explore each level, explaining the challenge, goal, and solution for each one. Finally, we present reflections on our tool in Section VI.

2 RELATED WORK

Uskov's paper [15] gives an overview of "Software and Web Applications Security" courses that are based on hands-on teaching of security topics, one of which is SQL injection. The course framework first gives an overview of SQL injection, explaining the vulnerability and under what circumstances it occurs. Next, a demonstration of the attack is shown, along with an example of a tautology SQL injection. The framework then shows how SQL injection can be prevented and defended against. Finally, the author provides some hands-on SQL injection assignments for students to try.

The authors in [9] present a survey of SQL injection attacks along with methods of prevention. They also discuss online practice tools that aid security professionals in testing their skills. These tools are similar to the platform that we have developed in that they are websites intentionally vulnerable to SQL injection and have the user practice exploiting them. These tools include DVMA (Damn Vulnerable Web App), Web Security Dojo, and OWASP. The authors go into the details of the pros and cons of these tools, for example, they mention that DVMA leaves out hints and explanations of exercises, how OWASP is completely Java-oriented, ignoring PHP, and how Web Security Dojo is not user-friendly for beginners to SQL injection. We took these considerations into account when designing our platform.

The authors in [13] created a way to teach database security through mobile labs. Their goal was to broaden mobile security education, and they built a mobile application for Android that consisted of several labs on computer security. The modules not only taught SQL injection but also focused on ethical issues and explained how to fix the vulnerability.

Chen and Tao [5] developed a teaching tool called SWEET, which uses virtualization so students can learn and practice web security in a safe environment. They illustrate most web security threats through the use of an external application called OWASP WebGoat. WebGoat contains a series of web challenges that tries to simulate real life situations such as stealing credit card numbers and logging into websites as admin. It includes SQL injection challenges that are friendly to new learners and can be adopted separately for different courses.

Besides the aforementioned related work, much of the work that has been done in developing database security curriculums are based on lectures, and not hands-on activities. However, besides published papers and pedagogical material, there exist several sites that offer SQL injection challenges. We reviewed a number of these sites, including SQLZoo, Overthewire, pentesterlab, the SEED project, the NICE challenge, and Hackme. Overall, we believe our platform offers two main improvements. First, we designed the site with extensibility in mind from the beginning. We attempted to make the process of adding new levels as simple as possible so that instructors can include their own problems for their students. The second is that our site is more user-friendly towards students who are new to SQL injection. Some websites are behind a paywall, or require users to first set up a virtual environment. In contrast, our challenges are free to access and are hosted online. Many of the existing sites are aimed at people who are already familiar with SQL injection and want to practice, consequently, their challenges can be unclear or even discouraging to beginners with little experience in security. Our platform starts with basic injection challenges, eventually building up to the more advanced ones. Along the way, we provide step-by-step explanations. Overall, the difference is that our platform aims to be a teaching tool rather than a practice tool.

3 SYSTEM OVERVIEW

Our system is a web application running on a LAMP (Linux, Apache, MariaDB, PHP) architecture. The application introduces the user to SQL injection and challenges users to write their own injections to solve increasingly difficult SQL injection problems. In addition to the SQL injection challenges, there is a wiki that guides the users as they progress through the challenges. The wiki focuses on conveying the important ideas and methods in SQL injection attacks, such as intuition for analyzing the situation and how to utilize SQL commands and syntax to craft exploits to retrieve the desired information.

Our platform has 12 challenges, each of which introduces a different type of SQL injection or vulnerability. Each of the challenges is associated with a different database, which contain the tables necessary to run the challenge. For each level, the website will execute a provided query that has been combined with the user input, which is an injection. When running the query, the SQL engine will fetch data from the corresponding database. The 12 databases are isolated from each other and are each associated with a MariaDB user that only has `SELECT` permissions for the corresponding database.

The process of submitting an injection is displayed in Figure 1. We describe the steps in more detail.

User Input For 11 of the levels, users are presented with a website that has a form with an empty query box. Users put their injection in the box and submit the form. One level does not have an input box, but rather asks the user to perform a SQL injection through a GET request. Each level has a provided query, which is what the user input will be inserted into. The provided query is given for the first few levels but is removed later to provide a

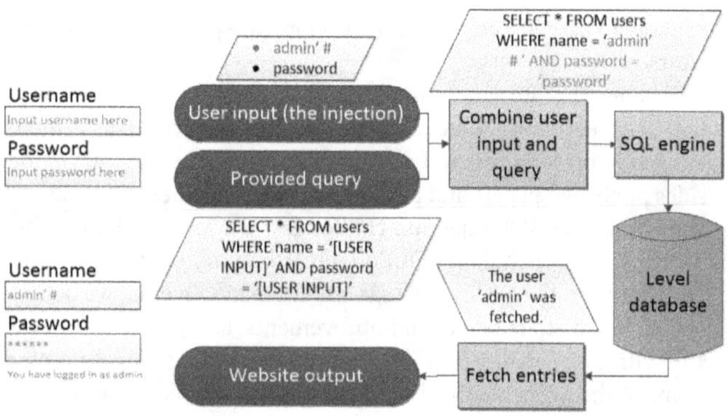

Figure 1: Process of submitting an injection, from user input to website output, with a username and password interface.

challenge. In Figure 1, the website has a login functionality where the provided query is

```
SELECT * FROM users WHERE name = [USER INPUT] AND
              password = [USER INPUT]
```

For the user input, the user should input an injection that allows them to log in as a specific user, in this example, the injection `admin'#` allows the user to log in as admin.

Combine user input and query All inputs through the input box are inserted into the SQL statement, just as in an actual web application, and then are processed and executed. The specifics of the combiner vary per level, but most work by concatenating sections of the provided query and user input together to get the entire injection. All levels that involve SQL injection do not sanitize queries, nor do they use prepared statements. The levels are designed to mimic insecure web pages that might not have any sanitization or protection.

SQL engine, Database The SQL statement, containing the user's injection, is executed. The engine goes to the database and searches through the rows of the `users` table.

Fetch entries The system goes through the rows of the table and retrieves the entries that matched the SQL query. In this example, the row of the table with username "admin" will be fetched.

Website Output The requested data is displayed on the website. The output format varies depending on the level. In some levels, a table of all the fetched data is displayed on the page, in other cases, only one row can be displayed at once. In more advanced levels, a restricted amount of information is returned to the user, such as "Your query has executed" without displaying the retrieved data. In the example above, the website will display "You have logged in as admin".

4 EXTENSIBILITY

A key feature of our system is that it was designed with extensibility in mind. SQL injection attacks are constantly evolving, and we would like our application to be able to adapt. In the future, when new vulnerabilities have been discovered, it will not be enough to just know how to solve the 12 challenges available on the current platform. In this section, we explain the process of adding another level to our site. Instructors that want to create a challenge that demonstrates a new vulnerability can do so by following these steps.

(1) First obtain the source code for the platform and get a copy of the site running for their own personal or classroom use. The platform should work on most UNIX based systems. We envision that every professor who uses our platform and wishes to extend the challenges will eventually have their own version of the site, with the 12 provided challenges and then followed by their own.
(2) Create a database called "level13", with tables, columns, and entries as necessary. Also, create a user called "level13" which has `SELECT` privileges for the level13 database. No other privileges should be granted unless they are needed for the challenge.
(3) There is a "levels/" folder where the necessary files for each level are stored. A new folder called "level13" should be created. In this folder needs to be a PHP file that contains the code to run the challenge.
(4) Finally, after the setup for the new level is done, a few minor changes must be made so that students can navigate to that challenge. On the webpage for each level, there is a button that links to the next, so a link should be created from level 12 to level 13. A level 13 button should also be added on the main page.

5 LEVEL OVERVIEW

In this section, we explain the objective of each challenge and the type of attack each level introduces. Each level follows the same overall format and is displayed in the screenshots below. In the white box, a description and goal of the level is provided. Next, there is an input box where users should input their injection. Some levels display the provided query concatenated with the user input to help students with their injections. After submitting the form, the results are displayed back to the user.

(1) **Display all rows of a table**

In the first level, users are given a form with an input box asking for a username. After submitting a username, all rows in the table `users_level1` that matched the given username will be retrieved and displayed. The challenge of this level is to use SQL injection to display all rows of this table, even though the user does not know all the usernames. The provided query is

```
SELECT username FROM users_level1 WHERE username =
              '[USER INPUT]'
```

The provided query contains a `WHERE` clause that checks whether the username in the table matched the inputted username. If the user inputs "Bob", all rows in the table with username "Bob" will be returned. To fetch every row in the table, we need to make the `WHERE` clause always true no matter the username. A well-known method is to use `' OR ''='`. The query with the injection is

```
SELECT username FROM users_level1 WHERE username = ''
              OR ''=''
```

where the text in red is the user input. The `WHERE` clause now checks if the username is the empty string, or if the empty string is equal to the empty string. As the second comparison will always be true, all rows of the tables will be fetched. Figure 2 displays the challenge, showing the general layout of each website and also the output from inputting the injection.

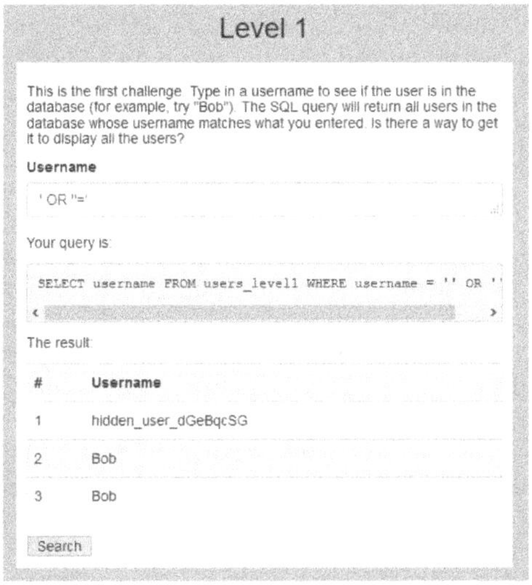

Figure 2: Level 1 page with injection query and output of usernames.

(2) **Display other tables in the database**

Level 2 asks the user to fetch the names of other tables in the database. The provided query is

```
SELECT username FROM users_level2 WHERE username =
'[USER INPUT]'
```

Students can fetch data from the TABLE_NAME column of the TABLES table of the INFORMATION_SCHEMA database using a query such as

```
SELECT TABLE_NAME FROM INFORMATION_SCHEMA.TABLES
```

To solve the challenge, the quotation mark should be closed and a query that selects table names should be appended using the UNION operator. Finally, the # symbol can be used to comment out the rest of the query to ignore the closing ' character. The injection is shown in the SQL statement below in red.

```
SELECT username FROM users_level2 WHERE username = ''
UNION SELECT TABLE_NAME FROM
INFORMATION_SCHEMA.TABLES #'
```

(3) **Find the column names of a table**

Level 3 asks for the column names of a hidden table in the database. This requires users to first list the tables, using the level 2 technique and then finding the columns in the other table. The provided query for visualization is given as:

```
SELECT username FROM users_level3 WHERE username =
'[USER INPUT]'
```

The first step is to use the injection from level 2 to list the table names in the database. After finding a suspicious table, students can find the column names of the table from the COLUMNS table in INFORMATION_SCHEMA. The injection is shown in the SQL statement below in red.

```
SELECT username FROM users_level3 WHERE username = ''
UNION SELECT COLUMN_NAME FROM
INFORMATION_SCHEMA.COLUMNS WHERE
TABLE_NAME='hidden_table_NSXOkukMOh'; #
```

(4) **Retrieve information about the database**

All SQL databases have a database name, DBMS version, and current user associated with it. The name of the database or current user can help with creating an injection and knowing the DBMS version helps with identifying known vulnerabilities. The query:

```
SELECT username FROM users_level4 WHERE username =
'[USER INPUT]'
```

The database name, username, and DBMS version can be retrieved using the DATABASE(), CURRENT_USER(), and VERSION() functions, respectively. Users can find these functions either through online search or the SQL manual. The query below shows the injection to accomplish this.

```
SELECT username FROM users_level4 WHERE username = ''
UNION SELECT DATABASE() UNION SELECT CURRENT_USER()
UNION SELECT VERSION() #'
```

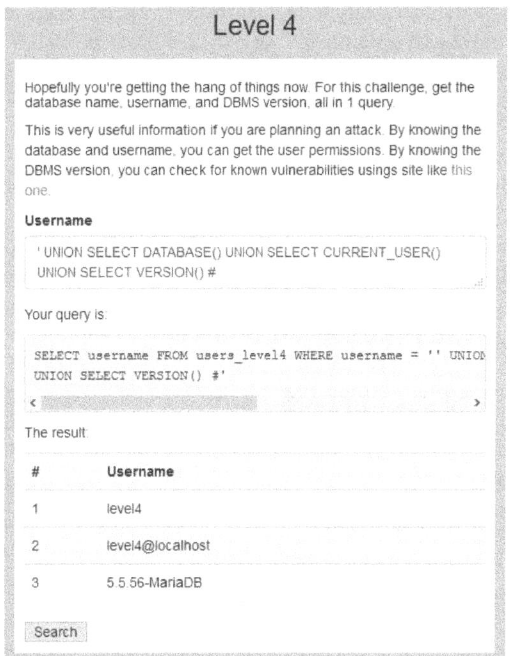

Figure 3: Level 4 page with injection query and output.

(5) **SQL injection through a GET request**

The form for this level does not have an input box. Rather, the user should input their injection through the GET request in the URL. The provided query is the same as in Level 1, so the level 1 SQL injection query can be reused. The current URL ends with

?username=Bob

which means that the website will send a GET request with the username equal to Bob. Students should replace Bob with the injection and must also learn about URL encoding.

(6) **Log in as admin**

This level challenges a student to log in as admin through a login form with username and password fields. The provided query is

```
SELECT username FROM users_level6 WHERE username =
    '[USER INPUT]' AND password = '[USER INPUT] '
```

This level is slightly different from the previous ones in that there are two inputs, one for the username and the other for the password. The query compares the given username and password to the entries in the table, and if they match, then the user will be logged in. The username is given as "admin", but the password is unknown. However, using SQL injection, the username check can be closed with a quote and the password check can be bypassed using #. The query is

```
SELECT username FROM users_level6 WHERE username =
    'admin' # ' AND password = '[USER INPUT] '
```

The result is that everything after the # is ignored and the SQL executor will only compare the usernames. This bypasses the need to know the password.

(7) **Retrieve admin's password**

Another vulnerability in login forms is that a malicious attacker can retrieve user passwords. The provided query is

```
SELECT username FROM users_level7 WHERE username =
    '[USER INPUT]' AND password = '[USER INPUT] '
```

The form will display whatever is selected from the query onto the website. Currently, the query selects usernames from the `users_level7` table. The solution to getting the password is making the form return the password instead of the username. From the provided query, students can deduce that there is a column named password that exists in the same table. Therefore, the username selection query can be closed and a new query that selects the admin's password can be appended.

(8) **Read a file on the server**

Hackers can use SQL injection to read files located on an improperly configured server and obtain sensitive information. This level demonstrates how file read is done through SQL. The query is:

```
SELECT username FROM users_level8 WHERE username =
                    '[USER INPUT] '
```

SQL has the built-in function `load_file()`, which will return the contents of a file. The query with the injection is

```
SELECT username FROM users_level8 WHERE username = ''
                    UNION SELECT
load_file('/var/lib/mysql-files/hidden_file.txt')#'
```

The filepath was given in the level description. For security reasons, the server was set up so that only files in that folder could be read from.

(9) **SQL Truncation attack**

Although not a injection, this challenge introduces a SQL vulnerability related to how MariaDB truncates entries in a table. When a user inputs a value into a database, sometimes MariaDB will truncate the input if it is larger than the maximum column width. To simulate this, a table was created where the maximum length of a username is 20 characters.

The site allows two actions, to register and to log in. The goal of the challenge is to log in as the admin user. The PHP source code was given for this level. When registering a user, the inputted username is first checked against the existing entries in the database, and this line of code is executed.

```
$username = trim(substr($_POST["username"], 0, 20))
```

Given a username input, the code takes the substring of the first 20 characters and then removes the whitespace from the substring. This means a 21 character input such as "admin   a" will be truncated to "admin   ", and then trimmed to just "admin". The check if the username is already in the database occurs before the trim, therefore, an account can be registered with that username and a new password, which will not be caught because "admin   a" is not equal to "admin". After this user is inserted into the database, students can log in with "admin" and the password they used.

(10) **Boolean SQL injection**

This level again challenges the student to fetch the admin password. However, in level 7 the website displayed the result of the query, which allowed us to directly print the password out on the page. However, this level only shows if the login was successful, without printing any information from the database onto the page.

One strategy is to brute force the admin password one letter at a time using the LIKE operator. For example, using this SQL injection:

```
admin' AND password LIKE 'a%'#
```

can determine if the password begins with the letter a. If the website displays that the login was successful, then the password starts with a. Otherwise, we try the next letter, b. Once the first character is found, which happens to be q, a second letter can be tested and so on until the full password is found. This type of attack is known as boolean SQL injection.

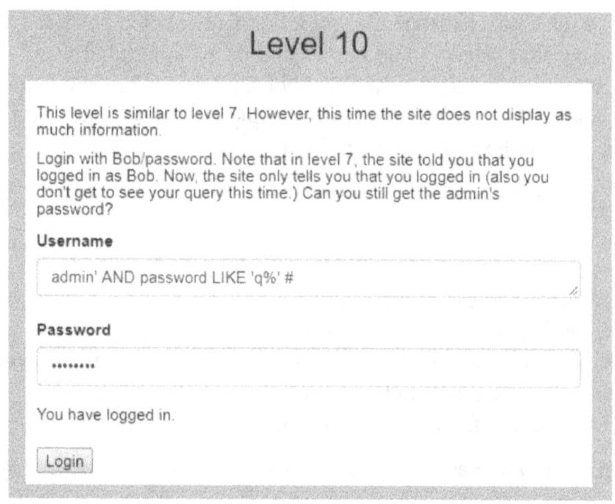

Figure 4: Level 10 page with the injection that shows the passwords starts with the letter q.

(11) **Retrieve table name and then admin password**

Level 11 is an extension of two previous levels, challenging the user to first find the table name and then the admin password. An additional challenge is that each query can only return one row of a table. Students need to use additional SQL commands to solve this challenge.

For this level, users first need to know the table name, which can be found using the injection from level 2. An additional challenge in this level is that only one row can be returned from the table at once. Students need to use additional SQL commands to solve this, such as the `OFFSET` operator or `GROUP_CONCAT`. After finding the table name, students can use the Level 7 query to finish the challenge.

(12) **Retrieve the admin password using a timing attack**

Level 12 is an important level which introduces side-channel attacks, namely a timing attack. Level 12 challenges the student to try to get the admin password when the form only displays that the query has finished executing. Because it only displays that the query has executed, previous attacks do not tell enough information to retrieve the password. The level 7 approach cannot be used because the admin's password is not displayed. The level 10 approach cannot be used because the server does not display if the query was successful, only that it has finished.

The solution for this level is the same as the solution for level 10, but with the addition of a timing attack. The query will delay the output by 5 seconds if the injection matched a row in the table, and immediately return the output otherwise. Using the MariaDB function `CASE`, a query can be built.

For example, a query can be built to check the letter `a`. The query will first check if the admin's password starts with `a`, just like in level 10. If it does, it will pause for 5 seconds, if the password does not start with `a`, it will not pause. From the user's perspective, if there is a 5 second pause, then a character of the password was found. This process is continued by checking `b`, then `c`, etc, just like in Level 10.

We have provided descriptions and explanations of the 12 levels we implemented for our SQL injection practice tool. We hope that they provide an idea of the type of injection and attack strategies we are aiming to teach. Future administrators can extend the website to include challenges that should build off the existing 12.

6 REFLECTIONS

The system was used during a Spring 2018 database systems course which had 117 students. The students were all 3rd or 4th year computer science majors. Students formed small groups of two or three and worked through the challenges on the platform together. They were asked to solve and review at least 4 of the challenges during class and finish for homework if necessary.

After the students completed the activity, they were asked to respond to a short survey as groups. Students were asked about which challenges they found most and least interesting or useful. They were also asked about their overall opinion of the site and for any other comments. Subjectively, the feedback was overall positive, with many students saying they enjoyed the platform and the challenges. Students liked the hands-on aspect of the tool and stated that certain aspects of our platform, such as the ability to see the injection within the query, were helpful to learn SQL injection. Collectively, they said that our platform was a nice way to learn about SQL injection. After reading through the student feedback, we believe our platform offers a practical way to teach SQL injection to students.

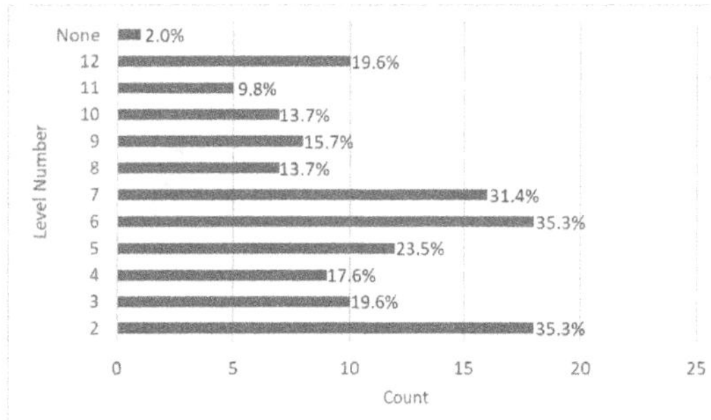

Figure 5: Levels students found most useful.

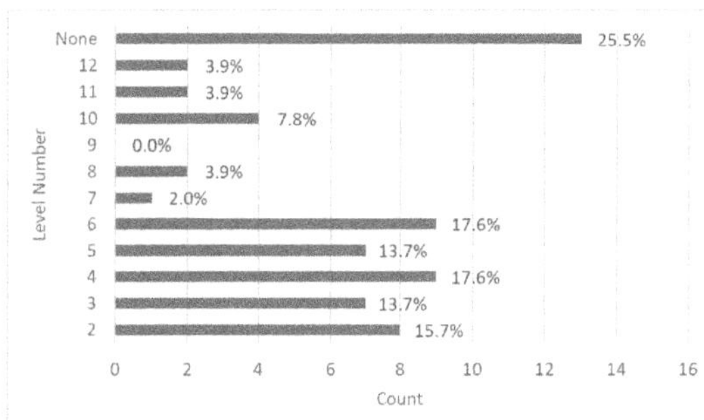

Figure 6: Levels students found least interesting.

Figures 5 and 6 show the student responses as to which levels they found most and least interesting or useful. Level 1 was not included in this survey because the professor demonstrated that challenge for the class. According to the survey, the most useful levels were levels 2 and 6, with 35.3% of the groups finding them useful. The least interesting were levels 4 and 6, with 17.6% of the groups finding them the least interesting.

We also read through the student comments and noted their reasons for not liking a level. The most common reason was that the level was too simple, and therefore not interesting. Some other faults were that it was unclear what to do, or too similar to a previous level. We noticed that most of the responses for the least interesting level were the first six levels. This is reasonable because we intended the introductory challenges to be simple.

In the future, we would like to integrate our platform into the course rather than having it be a separate activity. We will also take student feedback into consideration and improve the levels that students found unhelpful or unclear. Problems can be changed to have a different direction to make the challenge unique, and more context will be added so students find the challenges to be clear. More difficult SQL injection challenges can be included for advanced students. Finally, we would like our platform to be publicly available to other institutions so that instructors can add their own problems.

REFERENCES

[1] Aarafat Aldhaqm, Shukor Razak, Siti Othman, Abdulalem Aldolah, and Md Ngadi. 2016. Conceptual Investigation Process Model for Managing Database Forensic Investigation Knowledge. 12 (02 2016), 386–394.

[2] Sruthi Bandhakavi, Prithvi Bisht, P. Madhusudan, and V. N. Venkatakrishnan. 2007. CANDID: Preventing Sql Injection Attacks Using Dynamic Candidate Evaluations. In *Proceedings of the 14th ACM Conference on Computer and Communications Security (CCS '07)*. ACM, New York, NY, USA, 12–24. https://doi.org/10.1145/1315245.1315249

[3] Martin Bravenboer, Eelco Dolstra, and Eelco Visser. 2007. Preventing Injection Attacks with Syntax Embeddings. In *Proceedings of the 6th International Conference on Generative Programming and Component Engineering (GPCE '07)*. ACM, New York, NY, USA, 3–12. https://doi.org/10.1145/1289971.1289975

[4] Gregory Buehrer, Bruce W. Weide, and Paolo A. G. Sivilotti. 2005. Using Parse Tree Validation to Prevent SQL Injection Attacks. In *Proceedings of the 5th International Workshop on Software Engineering and Middleware (SEM '05)*. ACM, New York, NY, USA, 106–113. https://doi.org/10.1145/1108473.1108496

[5] L. Chen and L. Tao. 2011. Teaching Web Security Using Portable Virtual Labs. In *2011 IEEE 11th International Conference on Advanced Learning Technologies*. 491–495. https://doi.org/10.1109/ICALT.2011.153

[6] Steve Christey. [n. d.]. CWE -2011 CWE/SANS Top 25 Most Dangerous Software Errors. http://cwe.mitre.org/top25/.

[7] J Clarke. 2009. *SQL Injection Attacks and Defense*. 1–473 pages.

[8] William G. J. Halfond and Alessandro Orso. 2006. Preventing SQL Injection Attacks Using AMNESIA. In *Proceedings of the 28th International Conference on Software Engineering (ICSE '06)*. ACM, New York, NY, USA, 795–798. https://doi.org/10.1145/1134285.1134416

[9] Diallo Abdoulaye Kindy and Al-Sakib Khan Pathan. 2013. A Detailed Survey on Various Aspects of SQL Injection: Vulnerabilities, Innovative Attacks, and Remedies. *IJCNIS* 5 (2013).

[10] Odunayo Esther Oduntan and Temitope Sunday Aluko. 2014. Securing Web Application from Structured Query Language Injection Attacks : A Four-Tier Approach.

[11] OWASP. [n. d.]. OWASP Top 10 - 2017: The Ten Most Critical Web Application Security Risks.

[12] Burak Polat, Cemile Tokgöz Bakıroğlu, and Mira Elif Demirhan Sayın. 2013. Hactivism in Turkey: The Case of Redhack. 4 (10 2013). https://doi.org/10.5901/mjss.2013.v4n9p628

[13] Kai Qian, Dan Chia-Tien Lo, Hossain Shahriar, Lei Li, Fan Wu, and Prabir Bhattacharya. 2017. Learning database security with hands-on mobile labs. In *2017 IEEE Frontiers in Education Conference, FIE 2017, Indianapolis, IN, USA, October 18-21, 2017*. IEEE Computer Society, 1–6. https://doi.org/10.1109/FIE.2017.8190716

[14] A. K. Sood and R. J. Enbody. 2013. Targeted Cyberattacks: A Superset of Advanced Persistent Threats. *IEEE Security Privacy* 11, 1 (Jan 2013), 54–61. https://doi.org/10.1109/MSP.2012.90

[15] A. V. Uskov. 2013. Hands-On Teaching of Software and Web Applications Security. In *2013 3rd Interdisciplinary Engineering Design Education Conference*. 71–78. https://doi.org/10.1109/IEDEC.2013.6526763

');DROP TABLE textbooks;--

An Argument for SQL Injection Coverage in Database Textbooks

Cynthia Taylor
Oberlin College
ctaylor@oberlin.edu

Saheel Sakharkar
University of Illinois at Chicago
ssakha2@uic.edu

ABSTRACT

In this position paper, we look at the representation of SQL injection within undergraduate database textbooks, and argue that both discussion of security issues and security of example code must be improved. SQL injection is a common database exploit which takes advantage of programs that incorrectly incorporate user input into SQL statements. Teaching students how to write parameterized SQL statements is key to preventing this wide-spread attack. We look at the current editions of seven textbooks used at the top 50 US CS programs, and analyze their coverage of SQL injection, use of parameterized queries, and correctness of examples. We find a wide variety in the amount of coverage given to the topic, from none at all to in-depth coverage of defenses. Additionally, we find cases of SQL injectable code given as examples of how to correctly write queries in two of seven textbooks.

KEYWORDS

SQL injection, database textbooks, database security

ACM Reference Format:

Cynthia Taylor and Saheel Sakharkar. 2019. ');DROP TABLE textbooks;--: An Argument for SQL Injection Coverage in Database Textbooks. In *Proceedings of the 50th ACM Technical Symposium on Computer Science Education (SIGCSE '19), February 27-March 2, 2019, Minneapolis, MN, USA.* ACM, New York, NY, USA, 7 pages. https://doi.org/10.1145/3287324.3287429

1 INTRODUCTION

It has frequently been argued that if we want all students to be exposed to computer security and secure coding practices, these topics must be integrated into many CS courses, not isolated in computer security classes [17, 19–21, 33, 35]. However, even though including relevant security topics in courses has been promoted since the nineties [17, 33], many courses still do not cover them.

Education research has shown that textbooks frequently guide the topics covered in a course [11, 14]. Because textbooks help define what is covered, their inclusion of security topics can determine whether or not students are exposed to security guidelines and best practices. When assessing the current state of security coverage in courses, textbooks can give us important information about how likely a topic is to be included in most classes. Furthermore, adding security concepts into textbooks could be key to getting them widely discussed.

With that in mind, we look at a single security issue that we think all undergraduates should be exposed to, SQL injection, and analyze how it is covered in the most recent editions of database textbooks used in the top fifty Computer Science departments in the United States. SQL (Structured Query Language) is a family of languages used to run queries on databases. SQL injections take advantage of SQL queries which do not safeguard against improperly formatted user input, and as a result allow malevolent users to effectively run their own SQL statements against a database, allowing them to exfiltrate user information, log in as arbitrary users, and destroy data. SQL injection attacks have stolen credit card data, hacked the websites of election boards, and revealed cheating spouses [13, 32, 38]. SQL injection vulnerabilities are among the most common database vulnerabilities and have consistently appeared at the top of vulnerability lists [23, 39], despite the vulnerability being over fifteen years old [7]. These attacks have become even more common over time, as automated tools to detect and exploit them have become readily available [7].

This common attack can easily be prevented with proper coding techniques, namely using parameterized queries. The fact that vulnerable coding techniques are still commonly used has been blamed by some industry managers on a lack of education about this attack, with a recent article quoting one manager as saying "Any serious programmer should know about SQLi [SQL injection], but there's a massive shortage of programmers, so companies hire anyone even if they don't have the right training" [7]. The same article describes another manager who blames bad educational resources, saying "he lamented about the large number of tutorials available to web developers online that, instead of providing decent advice, detail how to make systems that are vulnerable to SQLi" [7].

Given that SQL injection can be prevented with a properly educated workforce, it is important that database textbooks demonstrate how to correctly parameterize queries to protect against it, and include in-depth discussion of the vulnerability and the importance of preventing it. In this work, we look at how commonly used database textbooks address the issue. We analyzed each textbook with regard to the following questions:

(1) Is SQL injection discussed in the textbook?
(2) Are there examples demonstrating how to incorporate user input while protecting against SQL injection?
(3) Are there SQL examples that would be vulnerable to SQL injection?

We find that there is a wide variety in how different texts discuss the issue, ranging from having code examples which are vulnerable to SQL injection, having no examples which take user input, or not

SIGCSE '19, February 27-March 2, 2019, Minneapolis, MN, USA

ACM ISBN 978-1-4503-5890-3/19/02...$15.00
https://doi.org/10.1145/3287324.3287429

Table 1: Text name, author, publication date, and number of universities using the text. All editions are the most recent for the text.

Text	Author	Pub. Date	Using Text
Database Management Systems, 3rd ed. [24]	Ramakrishnan	2002	16
Database System Concepts, 6th ed. [28]	Silberschatz	2010	10
Database Systems: The Complete Book, 2nd ed. [12]	Garcia-Molina	2008	10
Fundamentals of Database Systems, 7th ed. [9]	Elmasri	2015	4
Database Systems: A Practical Approach to Design, Implementation, and Management, 6th ed. [6]	Connolly	2014	2
Data Modeling Essentials, 3rd ed. [29]	Simsion	2004	1
Learning SQL, 2nd ed. [1]	Beaulieu	2009	1

discussing SQL injection at all within the text, to discussing the issue and dangers in depth and demonstrating the correct way to use variables within a SQL query. Across seven textbooks, we look at 745 SQL examples, of which only 59 incorporate user input. Of these 59, four examples include user input in ways that make them vulnerable to SQL injection. While this is only 6.8% of examples that include user input, any of these examples have the potential to make student code vulnerable to attack if the techniques are followed in deployed code. Given that SQL injection attempts against internet-deployed programs are inevitable in modern environments, this has the potential to cause real harm to users of these programs.

Even more troubling is that we find the majority of these textbooks (five out of seven) do not discuss SQL injection at all. This means that even if the book itself does not contain vulnerable examples, students who later find such examples on the internet tutorials and help sites (e.g., Stack Overflow) will be unlikely to recognize the code as dangerous.

In this position paper, we first analyze the most recent editions of popular database textbooks to quantify their coverage of SQL injection and defenses against it. Following this, we make recommendations for how instructors, textbooks authors, and the security community. We end with an argument on the importance of presenting secure code in textbooks.

2 SQL INJECTIONS AND HOW TO PREVENT THEM

There are a number of variants of SQL attacks, and a vast array of advice on how to prevent them [16, 27]. In a classic SQL injection, a malevolent actor takes advantage of improperly sanitized data input in order to run their own query against the database. The key to a successful SQL injection attack is the ability to have the database interpret user input as SQL code, rather than as data.

Consider the following dynamically constructed query, where the variables `user` and `pass` are input by the user and concatenated with the rest of the string to form a SQL query:

```
'SELECT * FROM usertable WHERE username="'
+ user + '" AND password="' + pass + '";'
```

A cooperative user will enter their username and password (say, "alice" and "rabbit"), to result in the string

```
SELECT * FROM usertable WHERE
username="alice" AND password="rabbit";
```

which will return all information on the user alice with password rabbit.

A malevolent user could enter `x" OR "1"="1` as the password. When the string is concatenated together, this will result in the following query:

```
SELECT * FROM usertable WHERE
username="alice" AND password="x" OR "1"="1";
```

By using a quote in their input string, the user causes the database to interpret OR as part of the SQL code rather than as part of the password, indicating that they should select information on the user either if the password is equal to x, or if the second part of the clause is true. The phrase `"1"="1"` will always evaluate to true, allowing a bad actor to pull details for any user. Using a similar phrase for the username will allow them to view the entire table without having to know specific usernames. Additionally, adding `;--` to the end of the input will end the SQL statement and comment out everything following on the same line. New SQL statements can be added between ending the previous statement and commenting out the rest of the line, allowing hackers to run arbitrary code against the database. While the details of this attack may vary depending on the SQL variant being used, the basic attack works across all SQL varietals.

The most effective measure for preventing SQL injection is always using parameterized queries to incorporate user input, rather than dynamically creating SQL statements via string concatenation. In the example above, a parameterized version of the query would look something like:

```
SELECT * FROM usertable WHERE username=@user
AND password=@pass;
```

At runtime, the values of @user and @pass will be programatically set to values input by the user. Using parameters allows the rest of the SQL statement to be compiled ahead of time, with only the parameters changing at run time. As a result, user input will always be treated as data and never be compiled into SQL, voiding the ability of user input to be interpreted semantically as part of SQL queries.

Using some sort of input filtering is additionally recommended to prevent obvious bad input, although the impossibility of being able to filter for every possible bad input means that input filtering alone is not enough. Additionally, there are many tools designed to

Table 2: Analysis of database texts and their SQL examples. Inputless queries refer to SQL statements that do not contain variables or user input. Parameter Queries refer to SQL statements that demonstrate using parameters for user input. Unsafe Queries refer to SQL statements which are vulnerable to SQL injection. SQLi mentions refer to in text discussions of SQL injection, and parameter mentions refere to in text discussion of how and why to use parameterized. The last two rows indicate whether or not the text contains content related to SQL injections, namely if it contains a chapter focusing on interfacing with SQL via applications or the web, and whether it contains a chapter on security.

	Ramakrishnan	Silberschatz	Garcia-Molina	Elmasri	Connolly	Simsion	Beaulieu
Inputless Queries	53	172	60	80	51	8	262
Parameter Queries	15	10	17	11	2	0	0
Unsafe Queries	0	0	2	2	0	0	0
SQLi Mentions	0	2	0	4	0	0	0
Parameter Mentions	0	1	0	4	0	0	0
Web/App Chapter	Yes	Yes	Yes	Yes	Yes	No	No
Security Chapter	Yes	Yes	Yes	Yes	Yes	No	No

detect or prevent SQL injection [16, 27]. We treat the coverage of these tools as out of the scope of this project (and did not see them mentioned in any of the textbooks we analyzed).

3 METHODOLOGY

To determine which textbooks to analyze, we began by compiling a list of database textbooks used by the top fifty Computer Science departments in the United States [31]. We looked at the syllabus of the most recently taught undergraduate database courses at each university. We used the most recent available edition of each textbook. The textbooks are listed by popularity in Table 1.

For each text, we looked at queries regarding creating and dropping tables; insert, update, and delete statements; join queries; views and cursors; and granting and revoking privileges. We did not count queries regarding constraints, triggers, and transactions. We only looked at examples within chapters, i.e. we skipped SQL examples/statements that were presented in end-of-chapter exercises and review questions.

Our categorization of the SQL examples separated them into three categories: examples with no input, parameterized examples, and unsafe examples. Queries with no input do not require any user information, and thus are protected from SQL injection by default. Parameterized queries demonstrate incorporating user input in a way that protects from SQL injection. Unsafe queries are susceptible to SQL injection and demonstrate bad practices when incorporating user input. We did not count examples as unsafe if they were included as part of of a discussion of SQL injection, i.e. if they were illustrating what not to do. We followed the OWASP guidelines [22] when deciding if an example was vulnerable to SQL injection, namely checking if the query was formed using string concatenation to add user inputs.

We also looked at mentions of SQL injection within the text, and counted the number of times the issue was discussed, as well as the number of discussions of using parametrized queries to prevent SQL injections. These counts looked for discussion within the text, rather than query examples. Lastly, we looked at whether the textbook had chapters discussing interfacing SQL with applications or the web or chapters discussing security as a proxy for whether SQL injection was within the scope of topics covered by the text.

4 RESULTS

The results of our categorization of the SQL examples and discussion in these database texts is presented in Table 2.

We found that database texts vary widely in all aspects of SQL injection coverage, ranging from not mentioning it at all or containing unsafe SQL query examples, to having explicit discussions of SQL injection and multiple examples demonstrating the correct way to handle user input. As shown in Table 2, most of the textbooks we looked at include examples of incorporating parameters to generate safe, non-injectable SQL queries. However, most do not explicitly discuss SQL injection. We also found two database texts, Molina [12] and Elmasri [9], which include unsafe examples that are easily SQL injectable, even though Elmasri [9] discusses parameterizing SQL queries to prevent SQL injection at other locations in the text.

4.1 Discussion of SQL Injection

Five of the seven textbooks we looked at do not mention SQL injection at all. Five of these seven textbooks had chapters on both using other programming languages to access SQL databases, and on database security, making SQL injection highly relevant to their content. However, only two of these textbooks explicitly discuss it.

Silberschatz [28] mentions SQL injection where relevant, both in the section on interfacing SQL with other programming languages and in a section on application security. It advises students to use parameterized statements. However, it implies that using parameters is equivalent to using a function to add escape characters around user input. This is incorrect, as using parameters allows SQL statements to be pre-compiled, and prevents any user input from being interpreted as code, while escaping user input is not recommended as a sole defense since imperfect escape functions can easily be subverted.

Elmasri [9] mentions SQL injection in the text next to an example of a properly parameterized query, and devotes a section of the security chapter to it. The advice in their security chapter generally follows best practices, recommending students use parameterized statements, and recommending filtering input while also pointing out its limitations (namely, the impossibility of filtering out all possible dangerous characters).

Listing 1: Figure 9.31 transcribed from Molina [12]

```
$result = $myCon->query("INSERT INTO
Starsln VALUES($_POST['title'],
$_POST['year'], $_POST['starName'])");
```

Listing 2: Figure 10.13 transcribed from Elmasri [9]

```
0) import java.io.* ;
1) import java.sql.*
 ...
2) class printDepartmentEmps {
3)  public static void main (String args [])
        throws SQLException, IOException{
4)  try { Class.forName("oracle.jbdc.driver.
        OracleDriver")
5)  } catch (ClassNotFoundException x){
6)      System.out.println ("Driver could not
            be loaded") ;
7)  }
8)  String dbacct, passwrd, lname ;
9)  Double salary ;
10) Integer dno ;
11) dbacct = readentry("Enter database
    account:");
12) passwrd = readentry("Enter password:") ;
13) Connection conn = DriverManager.
        getConnection
14)   ("jdbc:oracle:oci8:" + dbacct + "/"
            + passwrd) ;
15) dno = readentry("Enter a Department
        Number: ");
16) String q = "select Lname, Salary from
    EMPLOYEE where Dno = " + dno.tostring() ;
17) Statement s = conn.createStatement() ;
18) ResultSet r = s.executeQuery(q) ;
19) while (r.next()) {
20)     lname = r.getString(1) ;
21)     salary = r.getDoublde(2) ;
22)     system.out.printline(lname + salary) ;
23)  } }
24) }
```

Listing 3: Figure transcribed from Section 6.1.3 of Ramakrishnan [24]

```
char c_sqlstring[] = {"DELETE FROM Sailors
WHERE rating>5"};
EXEC SQL PREPARE readytogo FROM :csqlstring;
EXEC SQL EXECUTE readytogo;
```

Listing 4: Figure 9.10 transcribed from Molina [12]. An almost identical example exists as Figure 10.4 in Elmasri [9].

```
1) void readQuery() {
2)      EXEC SQL BEGIN DECLARE SECTION;
3)          char *query;
4)      EXEC SQL END DECLARE SECTION;

5)      /*prompt user for a query, allocate
        space (e.g., use malloc) and make
        shared variable :query point
        to the first character of the query */
6)      EXEC SQL PREPARE SQLquery from :query;
7)      EXEC SQL EXECUTE SQLquery;
    }
```

Listing 5: Figure 11.6 transcribed from Elmasri [9]

```
0)  require 'DB.php';
1)  $d = DB::connect('oci8://act:pass12@
                www.host.com/db1');
2)  if (DB::isError($d))
    { die("cannot connect - " .
      $d->getMessage()); }
...
3)  $q = $d->query("CREATE TABLE EMPLOYEE
4)              (Emp_id INT,
5)              Name VARCHAR(15),
6)              Job VARCHAR(10),
7)              Dno INT);" );
8)  if (DB::isError($q))
    { die("table creation not successful
          - " . $q->getMessage()); }
...
9)  $d->setErrorHandling(PEAR_ERROR_DIE);
...
10) $eid = $d->nextID('EMPLOYEE');
11) $q = $d->query("INSERT INTO EMPLOYEE
                VALUES
12)             ($eid,
                 $_POST['emp_name'],
                 $_POST['emp_job'],
                 $_POST['emp_dno'])" );
...
13) $eid = $d->nextID('EMPLOYEE');
14) $q = $d->query('INSERT INTO EMPLOYEE
                VALUES (?, ?, ?, ?)',
15) array($eid,
        $_POST['emp_name'],
        $_POST['emp_job'],
        $_POST['emp_dno']) );
```

How SQL injectable examples are framed and described is important. Listing 5 from Elmasri [9] demonstrates both the correct (lines 14-15) and incorrect (lines 11-12) way to incorporate form data into a SQL query using PHP. However, the fact that the first example should not be used is not discussed until two pages after the example in the text, and is not mentioned at all in the caption or on the page where the figure appears. This means a student who is skimming the text looking for an example to modify for their own code could simply copy the code that first appears in the example, without being aware that this is in fact an example of what they shouldn't do.

4.2 Demonstration of Parameterized Queries

Textbooks did much better with demonstrating parameterized queries, with five of the seven textbooks we looked at including examples of parameterized queries. This included every text that discussed interfacing with SQL from another programming language. This is very promising, as it shows that students are being shown the correct way to write queries.

The texts that did not cover them may consider parameterized queries to be out of the scope of what is covered in the text. For example, Simsion [29] focused on data modeling and only contained 8 SQL queries in total. Likewise, Beaulieu [1], while covering SQL queries in great detail with 262 query examples, did not discuss any techniques for using user input in queries, or writing queries to interface with the web or other programming languages. However, both these texts were being used in a database course at the same institution, where they were the only required textbooks, which means that students in that course had no text reference for parameterized queries.

4.3 SQL injectable examples

We found SQL injectable examples in two of the textbooks we looked at, as well as examples which introduced SQL injectable coding techniques while not being exploitable themselves.

The example shown in Listing 1 uses the PHP $_POST variable, which obtains user input from form elements. This means that any user input will be directly concatenated with the SQL statement, with no alteration. This example is clearly vulnerable to SQL injection, yet is presented in the text as the correct way to incorporate user input into SQL queries within a website. Students who follow this example in their code will be creating websites which are trivially hackable, and actively dangerous to their users.

Some of the examples, such as Listing 2, were not strictly SQL injectable but demonstrated a coding style that was. Listing 2 is not itself SQL injectable because `dno`, the value it reads in line 15 and concatenates into a SQL query in line 16, is read as a integer. However, this example introduces the student to the idea of creating SQL statements via string concatenation, and includes concatenating strings taken directly from the user in line 14. The idea that this might be dangerous is not mentioned anywhere in the text surrounding the example, although SQL injection is mentioned elsewhere in the text. Ramakrishnan [24] also discusses constructing dynamic SQL statements and while the example it gives, shown in Listing 3, is not SQL injectable (in fact, it does not involve any variables), it demonstrates a technique which enables SQL injection without any caution to the student about why one might want to be careful when using it.

Listing 4 is an example which appears in Molina [12], although an almost identical example appears within Elmasri [9]. This example is trivially SQL injectable, but at least makes clear to the student that the user will be able to run arbitrary code against the database (although the surrounding text does not explain why this might be a bad idea).

5 DISCUSSION

In this section, we discuss the ramifications of this work and offer recommendations for both instructors, textbook authors, and the security community.

5.1 Recommendations for Instructors

As SQL injection is one of the most exploited and most common software vulnerabilities, we urge instructors make it a priority in textbook selection, and to select textbooks carefully. Textbooks should always show parameterized statements in examples incorporating user input, and should explicitly discuss the danger and popularity of SQL injection attacks.

Our finding vulnerable code examples in multiple textbooks means that instructors must use caution when selecting a databases textbook. Choosing a textbook with these examples may do real harm in leading students to write vulnerable code. While instructors can cover the correct way to do this in class, separate from the textbook, students may continue to use the text as a reference after the course is over (and after their recollection of covered topics has faded). In this case, a textbook which demonstrates vulnerable SQL queries may actually be dangerous, as students copying such examples can introduce vulnerabilities in their own code. If an instructor must use one of these texts for some reason, we recommend they specifically point out the unsafe examples to students, and encourage the students to correct or cross them out within the text.

While this work considers currently popular database texts, new books and new editions will be released. When selecting a textbook, we recommend instructors carefully read chapters that cover interfacing with SQL through other languages or via the web, as this was where we found vulnerable examples, and where SQL injection should be mentioned. We also caution instructors against assuming that this problem will be solved in new textbook editions, as the most recent textbook we looked at ([9]) contained multiple SQL injectible code examples.

Lastly, regardless of the text used, we urge instructors to spend significant class time educating students on the very real danger of SQL injection attacks, and how they can defend their code against it.

5.2 Recommendations for Authors

Although we looked only at database texts, and only at one specific vulnerability, we suspect that textbooks in other subjects demonstrate insecure examples as well. (For example, a colleague recently shared an example from an introductory C text which was vulnerable to buffer overflows.) While in most cases making a mistake or not including information in a textbook may be merely regrettable, in the case of security this can be actively dangerous. For many security vulnerabilities, the best defense we have is educating programmers. The ramifications of not educating them in these cases is real harm to the users of their applications, in the form of stolen credit cards and identifiers, personal information being revealed, and more.

In the case where textbook authors are not security experts, collaboration with security researchers when writing textbooks could be beneficial. A "security editor" could check code examples, and recommend key security concerns to cover in the text, and where they should be covered.

In order to design secure applications, we must incorporate the idea of security from the very beginning of the design process, rather than attempting to add it on at the end. Likewise, if we want students to go on to write secure code, we must center the idea of security within their education, rather than isolating it to a separate chapter at the end of a textbook, or expecting it to be covered in a separate security course. It is unfortunate that we must expect that any application that is made public will be attacked. However, if we want users to be safe, we must emphasize that expectation within our topic coverage.

5.3 Implications for the Security Community

Since textbooks shape what is covered in class [11, 14], getting security topics into textbooks could have a dramatic impact on getting security integrated into courses. Our survey showed that three textbooks were used in 81% of the courses we looked at. Getting more security coverage in these textbooks would positively impact a huge number of students. Security educators should consider collaborating with textbook authors to ensure both secure code examples and integrated coverage of security topics. SQL injection is just one of many attacks where the solution is programmer education, and all signs indicate that we have a great deal of work to do within education before these problems are actually solved.

6 RELATED WORK

Prior work has looked at analyzing examples presented in computer science textbooks; our approach followed a model similar to Börstler et al. [2], where examples from commonly used introductory programming textbooks were reviewed for their quality. Within the context of databases, both Said et al. [25] and Conklin and Heinrich [5] compare the topics covered in various database textbooks, Said [25] being more focused on database security topics whereas Conklin [5] is more focused on database topics in general. However, neither focused specifically on SQL injection, as we do in this work.

Previous work has looked at how to incorporate security into database courses, frequently citing a current lack of coverage on the subject. Yang [34], Li et al. [18], Guimaraes et al. [15], and Stalvey et al. [30] all offer guidelines, coursework and labs on database security, which include SQL injection among other topics. A great deal of work has been done creating hands-on labs which teach SQL injection, to be used either in database or security courses. Yuan et al. [37] evaluates several different lab frameworks for teaching students about SQL injection, including [3, 4, 8, 36]. Other lab frameworks which include SQL injection are presented in [10, 18, 26]. Given the wide variety of lab work covering this topic, SQL injection is clearly considered an important topic by the security community.

7 CONCLUSION

The majority of textbooks we looked at did not discuss one of the most widespread and dangerous security problems today, SQL injection, an attack for which the most effective defense is programmer education. Additionally, multiple textbooks included code examples that would make programs vulnerable to this attack. Given the pervasiveness of SQL injection on the modern web, not educating students about it is irresponsible and dangerous, and supplying vulnerable code is actively harmful.

To stop SQL injection vulnerabilities in the wild, we need to educate students on how to defend against them. We need database textbooks not only to demonstrate parameterized queries, but to explain to students why it is important to use them. If we wish to secure the web in the future, both instructors and textbook authors need to emphasize the importance of protecting against this attack.

Given how easy and widely known the SQL injection attack is, it is at this point a fact of life that any code put on the internet will have SQL injection attempts against it. Students need to know that this is not an academic or abstract possibility, but something that will happen to their code. Most of the texts we looked at showed secure examples, but did not mention SQL injection or explain why using parameters was important. Without this knowledge, students who later see vulnerable code examples will not know that they show a coding style that will introduce dangerous vulnerabilities into their code.

It may be very tempting to view things like web programming or SQL injection as tangential to the core concepts of databases, and perhaps out of scope for textbooks. However, is very likely that in any databases course, some students will go on to write internet-facing code. Given the lack of dedicated web programming courses, this may be the only place students are exposed to creating SQL queries before they write applications that are widely used and publicly available via the web. Students who are not taught how to protect their queries from SQL injection in their databases course may end up learning about it only after their applications are hacked.

In our investigation, we saw that the same two textbooks are used by over half of the top fifty computer science programs in the US. A single textbook may be read by tens of thousands of students who eventually work in the tech industry. How that textbook deals with security issues may have a profound effect on the future of application security.

8 ACKNOWLEDGEMENTS

Thanks to Stephen Checkoway for many useful conversations, and to the anonymous reviewers for their helpful comments.

REFERENCES

[1] Beaulieu, A. *Learning SQL: Master SQL Fundamentals, 2nd Edition.* O'Reilly Media, 2009.

[2] Börstler, J., Nordström, M., and Paterson, J. H. On the quality of examples in introductory Java textbooks. *ACM Transactions on Computing Education (TOCE) 11*, 1 (2011), 3.

[3] Chen, L., Tao, L., Li, X., and Lin, C. A tool for teaching web application security. In *Proceedings of the 14th Colloquium for Information Systems Security Education* (2010), pp. 17–24.

[4] Chu, B., Stranathan, W., Cody, J., Peterson, J., Wenner, A., and Yu, H. Teaching secure software development with vulnerability assessment. In *Proceedings of the 13 Colloquium for Information Systems Security Education (CISSE 2009). Seattle, Washington* (2009).

[5] Conklin, M., and Heinrichs, L. In search of the right database text. *Journal of Computing Sciences in Colleges 21*, 2 (2005), 305–312.

[6] Connolly, T., and Begg, C. *Database Systems: A Practical Approach to Design, Implementation, and Management, 6th Edition.* Pearson, 2014.

[7] Cox, J. *The History of SQL Injection, the Hack That Will Never Go Away*, 2015. https://motherboard.vice.com/en_us/article/aekzez/the-history-of-sql-injection-the-hack-that-will-never-go-away, Accessed on 07/14/2017.

[8] Du, W., and Wang, R. Seed: A suite of instructional laboratories for computer security education. *Journal on Educational Resources in Computing (JERIC) 8*, 1 (2008), 3.

[9] Elmasri, R., and Navathe, S. B. *Fundamentals of Database Systems, 7th Edition.* Pearson, 2015.

[10] Ernits, M., Tammekänd, J., and Maennel, O. i-tee: A fully automated cyber defense competition for students. In *ACM SIGCOMM Computer Communication Review* (2015), vol. 45, ACM, pp. 113–114.

[11] Freeman, D. J., and Porter, A. C. Do textbooks dictate the content of mathematics instruction in elementary schools? *American educational research journal 26*, 3 (1989), 403–421.

[12] Garcia-Molina, H., Ullman, J. D., and Widom, J. *Database Systems: The Complete Book, 2nd Edition.* Pearson, 2008.

[13] Greenberg, A. *Hack Brief: As FBI Warns Election Sites Got Hacked, All Eyes Are on Russia*, 2016. https://www.wired.com/2016/08/hack-brief-fbi-warns-election-sites-got-hacked-eyes-russia//, Accessed on 08/10/2017.

[14] Grossman, P., and Thompson, C. Learning from curriculum materials: Scaffolds for new teachers? *Teaching and teacher education 24*, 8 (2008), 2014–2026.

[15] Guimaraes, M., Murray, M., and Austin, R. Incorporating database security courseware into a database security class. In *Proceedings of the 4th annual conference on Information security curriculum development* (2007), ACM, p. 5.

[16] Halfond, W. G., Viegas, J., and Orso, A. A classification of SQL-injection attacks and countermeasures. In *Proceedings of the IEEE International Symposium on Secure Software Engineering* (2006), vol. 1, IEEE, pp. 13–15.

[17] Irvine, C. E., Chin, S.-K., and Frincke, D. Integrating security into the curriculum. *IEEE Computer 31*, 12 (Dec. 1998), 25–30. Online at http://cisr.nps.edu/downloads/papers/98paper_integrate.pdf.

[18] Li, L., Qian, K., Chen, Q., Hasan, R., and Shao, G. Developing hands-on labware for emerging database security. In *Proceedings of the 17th Annual Conference on Information Technology Education* (2016), ACM, pp. 60–64.

[19] Meghanathan, N., Kim, H., and Moore, L. A. Incorporation of aspects of systems security and software security in senior capstone projects. In *Proceedings of ITNG 2012* (Apr. 2012), S. Latifi, Ed., IEEE Computer Society, pp. 319–324. Online at http://ieeexplore.ieee.org/xpl/articleDetails.jsp?arnumber=6209193.

[20] Mullins, P., Wolfe, J., Fry, M., Wynters, E., Calhoun, W., Montante, R., and Oblitey, W. Panel on integrating security concepts into existing computer courses. In *Proceedings of SIGCSE 2002* (Feb. 2002), S. Grissom and D. Knox, Eds., ACM Press, pp. 365–66. Online at http://dl.acm.org/citation.cfm?id=563480.

[21] Null, L. Integrating security across the computer science curriculum. *Journal of Computing Sciences in Colleges 19*, 5 (May 2004), 170–178. Online at http://dl.acm.org/citation.cfm?id=1060104.

[22] OWASP. *Reviewing Code for SQL Injection*, 2010. https://www.owasp.org/index.php/Reviewing_Code_for_SQL_Injection, Accessed on 11/17/2016.

[23] OWASP. *OWASP Top Ten Project*, 2017. https://www.owasp.org/index.php/Category:OWASP_Top_Ten_Project#tab=OWASP_Top_10_for_2017_Release_Candidate, Accessed on 7/14/2017.

[24] Ramakrishnan, R., and Gehrke, J. *Database Management Systems, 3rd Edition.* McGraw-Hill, 2002.

[25] Said, H. E., Guimaraes, M. A., Maamar, Z., and Jololian, L. Database and database application security. In *ACM SIGCSE Bulletin* (2009), vol. 41, ACM, pp. 90–93.

[26] Schweitzer, D., and Boleng, J. Designing web labs for teaching security concepts. *Journal of Computing Sciences in Colleges 25*, 2 (2009), 39–45.

[27] Shegokar, A. M., and Manjaramkar, A. K. A survey on SQL injection attack, detection and prevention techniques. *Int. J. Comput. Sci. Inf. Technol 5*, 2 (2014), 2553–2555.

[28] Silberschatz, A., Korth, H., and Sudarshan, S. *Database System Concepts, 6th Edition.* McGraw-Hill, 2010.

[29] Simsion, G., and Witt, G. *Data Modeling Essentials, 3rd Edition.* Morgan Kaufmann, 2004.

[30] Stalvey, R. H., Farkas, C., and Eastman, C. First use: introducing information security in high school oracle academy courses. In *Information Reuse and Integration (IRI), 2012 IEEE 13th International Conference on* (2012), IEEE, pp. 653–658.

[31] Stanger, M., and Martin, E. *The 50 Best Computer-Science and Engineering Schools in America*, 2015. http://www.businessinsider.com/best-computer-science-engineering-schools-in-america-2015-7, Accessed on 10/05/2016.

[32] Trainer, K. *Between 35,000 and 40,000 credit cards exposed to hackers after coding errors led to SQL Injection*, 2016. https://www.foregenix.com/blog/credit-cards-exposed-to-hackers-poor-coding-sql-injection.

[33] White, G., and Nordstrom, G. Security across the curriculum: Using computer security to teach computer science principles. In *Proceeding of NISSC 1996* (Oct. 1996), pp. 483–88. Online at http://csrc.nist.gov/nissc/1996/papers/NISSC96/paper003/sec_cur.pdf.

[34] Yang, L. Teaching database security and auditing. In *ACM SIGCSE Bulletin* (2009), vol. 41, ACM, pp. 241–245.

[35] Yang, T. A. Computer security and impact on computer science education. *Journal of Computing Sciences in Colleges 16*, 4 (2001), 233–246. Online at http://dl.acm.org/citation.cfm?id=378722.

[36] Yuan, X., Hernandez, J., Waddell, I., Chu, B., and Yu, H. Hands-on laboratory exercises for teaching software security. In *Proceedings of the 16th Colloquium for Information Systems Security Education* (2012).

[37] Yuan, X., Williams, I., Kim, T. H., Xu, J., Yu, H., and Kim, J. H. Evaluating hands-on labs for teaching sql injection: a comparative study. *Journal of Computing Sciences in Colleges 32*, 4 (2017), 33–39.

[38] Zetter, K. *Answers to Your Burning Questions on the Ashley Madison Hack*, 2015. https://www.wired.com/2015/08/ashley-madison-hack-everything-you-need-to-know-your-questions-explained/, Accessed on 08/10/2017.

[39] Zetter, K. *Hacker Lexicon: SQL Injections, an Everyday Hacker's Favorite Attack*, 2016. https://www.wired.com/2016/05/hacker-lexicon-sql-injections-everyday-hackers-favorite-attack/, Accessed on 01/17/2017.

What to Expect and What to Focus on in SQL Query Teaching

Toni Taipalus
University of Jyvaskyla
Jyvaskyla, Finland
toni.taipalus@jyu.fi

Piia Perälä
University of Jyvaskyla
Jyvaskyla, Finland
piia.m.h.perala@jyu.fi

ABSTRACT

In the process of learning a new computer language, writing erroneous statements is part of the learning experience. However, some errors persist throughout the query writing process and are never corrected. Structured Query Language (SQL) consists of a number of different concepts such as expressions, joins, grouping and ordering, all of which by nature invite different possible errors in the query writing process. Furthermore, some of these errors are relatively easy for a student to fix when compared to others. Using a data set from three student cohorts with the total of 744 students, we set out to explore which types of errors are persistent, i.e., more likely to be left uncorrected by the students. Additionally, based on the results, we contemplate which types of errors different query concepts seem to invite. The results show that syntax and semantic errors are less likely to persist than logical errors and complications. We expect that the results will help us understand which kind of errors students struggle with, and e.g., help teachers generate or choose more appropriate data for students to use when learning SQL.

CCS CONCEPTS

• **Social and professional topics → Computing education**; *Computational thinking*; *Student assessment*;

KEYWORDS

SQL, error, query language, database education, relational database

ACM Reference Format:
Toni Taipalus and Piia Perälä. 2019. What to Expect and What to Focus on in SQL Query Teaching. In *Proceedings of the 50th ACM Technical Symposium on Computer Science Education (SIGCSE '19), February 27-March 2, 2019, Minneapolis, MN, USA.* ACM, New York, NY, USA, 6 pages. https://doi.org/10.1145/3287324.3287359

1 INTRODUCTION

SQL has been taught at university level courses for decades, yet compared to programming languages, SQL has received relatively little attention in educational research. A number of new teaching methods have been presented to facilitate learning [5, 7–9], but scientific evidence on which parts of SQL students struggle with leaves room for interpretation.

This study is an attempt to address the issue of difficult, i.e., persistent errors in SQL. We consider an error persistent if it is present in a student's final answer to an exercise, i.e., the student did not fix the error during the query writing process. The aim of our study is to find out which errors are persistent, and then consider which query concepts invite which persistent errors. To that end, we analyzed the final answers of three student cohorts with the total of 744 students and over 8,700 SQL queries.

In Section 2, we discuss previous studies on SQL error categorization, and briefly explain the frameworks we chose for this study. In Section 3, we describe how we collected and analyzed the data, and in Section 4 we report our findings. In Section 5 we compare our findings to previous studies, and consider the practical implications and limitations of our research, as well as further research opportunities. Finally, in Section 6, we present conclusions.

2 BACKGROUND

2.1 Related Work

Previous SQL research in educational contexts mainly focuses on one of two perspectives. First, on the development and analysis of a particular tool for facilitating SQL learning, and second, on the study of student errors in SQL. The former class of SQL research is out of the scope of our study, but the latter class presents a number of error categorizations, which are needed to quantifiably measure and analyze student errors.

Brass and Goldberg [4] presented an extensive list of semantic errors to be used in database management system (DBMS) compilers, and a set of studies [1–3], which inspired us to this research, explored the frequencies of syntax and semantic errors students made when learning SQL. Ahadi et al. [1] used PostgreSQL to categorize syntax errors from over 160,000 SQL queries. Ahadi et al. [2] studied student errors in exercises with seven different query concepts, and, as the authors point out, theirs is the first published quantitative study of the relative student difficulties in regard to different SQL query concepts. Additionally, Ahadi et al. [3] closely investigated 551 queries that contained a semantic error which students were unable to correct.

Taipalus et al. [11] composed an unified error categorization and a framework of query concepts using earlier research [1, 2, 4, 10, 12]. These findings were validated and complemented by an analysis of over 33,000 SQL queries, and the categorization was based on the SQL standard, and is DBMS independent. The categorization mapped 105 errors and complications into four classes; 1) complications, which do not affect the result table; 2) logical errors, which affect the result table, and for which there exists a valid data demand (i.e., a natural language representation of what the query

SIGCSE '19, February 27-March 2, 2019, Minneapolis, MN, USA

ACM ISBN 978-1-4503-5890-3/19/02...$15.00
https://doi.org/10.1145/3287324.3287359

needs to return from the database); 3) semantic errors, which affect the result table, and for which there exists no valid data demand; and 4) syntax errors, which result in an error message instead of a result table.

2.2 Errors and Complications

We use the error categorization, and the query concept framework composed by Taipalus et al. [11], because both of them are wider than any of those presented in the previous studies. According to the categorization, there are three classes of errors in addition to complications. The 38 syntax errors are categorized into six categories; ambiguous database object (SYN-1), undefined database object (SYN-2), data type mismatch (SYN-3), illegal aggregate function placement (SYN-4), illegal or insufficient grouping (SYN-5), and common syntax error (SYN-6).

The 13 semantic errors are categorized into five categories; inconsistent expression (SEM-1), inconsistent join (SEM-2), missing join (SEM-3), duplicate rows (SEM-4), and redundant column output (SEM-5).

The 30 logical errors are categorized into six categories; operator error (LOG-1), join error (LOG-2), nesting error (LOG-3), expression error (LOG-4), projection error (LOG-5), and function error (LOG-6). The categorization points out that, while a semantic error is evident just by reading the query without knowing the data demand, a logical error can be identified only if the data demand is known.

Finally, in addition to errors, the framework contains 24 complications, which are, e.g., unnecessary joins and other structural problems which could be formulated in a simpler fashion. For brevity, we refer to all of these four classes simply as *errors*, when it is not necessary to differentiate errors from complications.

2.3 Query Concepts

As the base for our exercises, we use the the framework [11] which lists 18 query concepts, all of which are present at least once in the 15 exercises. Notably, all of the exercises test skill with more than one query concept, and, what's more, some query concepts invite others by design. All the query concepts per exercise are presented in Table 1.

While some of the concepts are basic, e.g., single-table queries, expressions, aggregate functions, and ordering, others, e.g., multiple source tables (i.e., data in the result table is projected or calculated from more than one source table), and parameter distinct (i.e., DISTINCT is required as an aggregate function parameter) are relatively difficult for an introductory database course. See to Taipalus et al. [11] for more detailed information about the query concepts, exercises, and error categories, as well as example data demands and queries for each of the 15 exercises.

3 METHOD

For this study, we had over 123,000 SQL queries which we collected from three student cohorts in a mandatory database course. The course consisted of lectures, voluntary exercises, exercise discussion sessions, and an exam. The students majored in computer science or information systems with no prior knowledge on using SQL. Each cohort answered to 15 SQL retrieval exercises. We designed the exercises using the query concept framework presented by Taipalus et al. [11], with the same query concepts, as well as the number of source and subject tables. In order to mitigate the polarization effect of the database business domain on the number of errors, we designed different database structures and business domains for each cohort.

Table 1: Query Concepts per Exercise [11]

Exercise	Concepts
A1	single-table; expressions
A2	single-table; expressions; ordering
A3	single-table; wildcard; expressions with nesting
B4	multi-table; expressions; facing foreign keys
B5	multi-table; expressions with nesting; ordering
B6	multi-table; expressions; does not exist
B7	multi-table; expressions; does not exist
B8	multi-table; expressions; does not exist; equal subqueries
B9	single-table; expressions; aggregate functions
B10	multi-table; expressions; multiple source tables
B11	multi-table; expressions; self-join; aggregate function evaluated against a column value; correlated subquery
B12	multi-table; expressions; aggregate function evaluated against a constant; uncorrelated subquery; parameter distinct
B13	multi-table; expressions; self-join
C14	multi-table; multiple source tables; aggregate functions; grouping
C15	multi-table; multiple source tables; aggregate functions; grouping; grouping restrictions; ordering

We also replicated the learning environment as presented by Taipalus et al. [11]. The students answered the 15 exercises during the course. The exercises were divided into three sets (A, B, and C in Table 1). For each set, the students had approximately one week to complete the exercises in the given set, in whatever order, and with unlimited tries. The learning environment was minimally controlled, and the students could use whatever material or forms of communication at their disposal, which more accurately mimics their future work environments, as argued for by Taipalus et al. [11]. The exercise discussion sessions were held after the weekly deadline had passed, and the sessions had no impact on the previous week's queries. The learning environment was effectively an interactive SQL prompt (SQLite) embedded into a web page. The correct result table was visible during the whole query writing process, which, in turn, constitutes as making the environment unnatural when compared to work environments.

In order to pinpoint persistent errors, we analyzed only final answers from each student, which left us with over 8,700 queries for further analysis. Out of these final queries, 2,765 were incorrect. We manually marked these errors according to the error categorization by Taipalus et al. [11]. Based on this, we approached error persistence from two perspectives; relative frequencies for each error category per exercise, and estimated means for each error class per exercise.

Table 2: Relative Error Frequencies by Error Category in Incorrect Final Answers, and Complications in All Final Answers

	A1	A2	A3	B4	B5	B6	B7	B8	B9	B10	B11	B12	B13	C14	C15
Correct	0.67	0.77	0.60	0.79	0.77	0.78	0.76	0.82	0.91	0.63	0.41	0.43	0.62	0.75	0.56
SYN-1 ambiguous database object	0.00	0.00	0.04	0.02	0.09	0.01	0.03	0.01	0.00	0.01	0.00	0.00	0.00	0.00	0.00
SYN-2 undefined database object	0.00	0.05	0.00	0.05	0.01	0.03	0.01	0.00	0.00	0.07	0.03	0.03	0.05	0.02	0.02
SYN-3 data type mismatch	0.07	0.00	0.32	0.09	0.23	0.11	0.03	0.03	0.00	0.02	0.01	0.01	0.09	0.06	0.00
SYN-4 ill. aggr. function placement	0.00	0.00	0.00	0.00	0.00	0.00	0.00	0.00	0.00	0.00	0.01	0.02	0.01	0.00	0.02
SYN-5 ill. or insufficient grouping	0.03	0.00	0.00	0.01	0.00	0.04	0.00	0.03	0.02	0.06	0.38	0.43	0.06	0.37	0.67
SYN-6 common syntax error	0.11	0.27	0.09	0.25	0.15	0.09	0.16	0.22	0.05	0.14	0.04	0.09	0.10	0.11	0.06
SEM-1 inconsistent expression	0.08	0.00	0.04	0.00	0.01	0.01	0.01	0.14	0.05	0.02	0.01	0.13	0.15	0.04	0.03
SEM-2 inconsistent join	0.00	0.00	0.00	0.04	0.00	0.01	0.00	0.01	0.00	0.00	0.00	0.01	0.02	0.01	0.00
SEM-3 missing join	0.00	0.00	0.00	0.01	0.05	0.06	0.05	0.04	0.00	0.34	0.09	0.03	0.08	0.13	0.03
SEM-4 duplicate rows	0.00	0.00	0.00	0.00	0.00	0.00	0.00	0.03	0.00	0.20	0.05	0.00	0.00	0.00	0.00
SEM-5 redundant column output	0.00	0.01	0.00	0.01	0.00	0.00	0.01	0.00	0.00	0.00	0.00	0.00	0.00	0.00	0.00
LOG-1 operator error	0.00	0.06	0.12	0.03	0.44	0.11	0.65	0.47	0.22	0.05	0.04	0.06	0.07	0.00	0.02
LOG-2 join error	0.00	0.00	0.00	0.34	0.15	0.23	0.19	0.35	0.00	0.40	0.07	0.20	0.39	0.06	0.02
LOG-3 nesting error	0.00	0.00	0.47	0.00	0.01	0.01	0.00	0.09	0.00	0.00	0.00	0.00	0.08	0.00	0.00
LOG-4 expression error	0.13	0.27	0.11	0.47	0.09	0.14	0.20	0.13	0.09	0.25	0.47	0.36	0.63	0.06	0.14
LOG-5 projection error	0.75	0.46	0.11	0.10	0.25	0.62	0.07	0.05	0.20	0.45	0.14	0.08	0.12	0.59	0.30
LOG-6 function error	0.00	0.00	0.00	0.00	0.00	0.00	0.00	0.00	0.75	0.00	0.01	0.60	0.00	0.25	0.25
Complication	0.05	0.07	0.14	0.37	0.08	0.33	0.37	0.12	0.06	0.46	0.41	0.21	0.40	0.31	0.17

We calculated the relative frequencies of different errors among incorrect final answers (N=2,765) in the 15 exercises, as we wanted to identify which query concepts invite which classes of errors. An answer was considered incorrect if it contained at least one syntax, semantic or logical error. Importantly, a complication by itself did not constitute in making an answer incorrect. In addition to errors, we calculated relative frequencies of complications among all final answers (N=8,773).

In order to identify persistent errors among exercises, we analyzed the data by counting the number of different classes of errors for each exercise. The homogeneity of variance was tested before analysis, and it was found that the data was overdispersed. Therefore, we modeled the data with negative binomial regression that is also common method for count data. Because our interest was in comparing the error rates under the different exercises, we added fixed effects of task to the model. The non-independence of the observations due to the fact that each student completed multiple exercises was modeled by including random effect of student in the model. We estimated the model using the SPSS (version 24) Mixed command, and interpreted the results by calculating the predicted number of errors and their confidence intervals (CI) for each exercise. We estimated the statistical significance using an overlap rule of 95% for the CI bars, as proposed by Cumming et al. [6].

4 RESULTS

4.1 Error Persistence for Error Categories

We collected success rates, relative error frequencies by error category in incorrect final answers, and complications in all final answers to Table 2. We ignored non-attempts, as not all students attempted to solve all exercises. Some errors were absent in some exercises altogether. Again, we observed high numbers of relative frequencies among logical errors when compared to other categories. In fact, for each of the logical error categories, at least one exercise yielded a relative frequency of at least 0.40. By contrast, e.g., illegal aggregate function placement (SYN-4), inconsistent join (SEM-2), and redundant column output (SEM-5) error categories had a relatively low highest relative frequency of at most 0.02. Complications were present in all exercises.

4.2 Error Persistence for Error Classes

We collected estimated means and CIs of syntax, semantic, and logical errors as well as complications in final answers per exercise to Table 3. Collectively, logical errors were more prominent than other error classes in all exercises. The results show that on average, students are more likely to commit persistent syntax errors in exercise C15 (estimate 0.828 with 95% CI [0.721, 0.951), whereas persistent semantic errors were most prominent in exercise B10 (estimate 0.855 with 95% CI [0.735, 0.995]).

Investigation concerning the class of logical errors showed that students committed fewer persistent logical errors in exercises A1, A2, A3, B11 and C15 when compared to exercises B6, B7, B9, B10, B12, and B13. The overall trend showed that, with a few exceptions, the means of logical errors increase over time, but in the final exercises C14 and C15, the means decreased.

Inspection of complications showed that students wrote more complications in exercises B10, B13, and C14 when compared to exercises A1, A3 and B5. Additionally, exercise B9 showed the widest CIs among all error classes.

Table 3: Estimated Means and CIs for Each Errors Class per Exercise

Exercise	Syntax errors			Semantic errors			Logical errors			Complications		
	Mean	95% CI LL	95% CI UL	Mean	95% CI LL	95% CI UL	Mean	95% CI LL	95% CI UL	Mean	95% CI LL	95% CI UL
A1	0.556	0.464	0.666	0.402	0.325	0.498	0.939	0.817	1.079	0.422	0.343	0.519
A2	0.533	0.426	0.666	0.370	0.283	0.485	0.845	0.708	1.009	0.491	0.390	0.620
A3	0.578	0.491	0.682	0.385	0.314	0.471	0.885	0.775	1.011	0.431	0.356	0.521
B4	0.566	0.455	0.704	0.392	0.301	0.510	1.098	0.939	1.285	0.539	0.431	0.675
B5	0.637	0.521	0.777	0.390	0.302	0.505	1.026	0.877	1.202	0.396	0.307	0.510
B6	0.555	0.444	0.693	0.395	0.303	0.515	1.266	1.092	1.467	0.532	0.424	0.667
B7	0.522	0.419	0.651	0.442	0.348	0.563	1.213	1.049	1.402	0.547	0.441	0.679
B8	0.505	0.386	0.660	0.602	0.470	0.770	1.171	0.982	1.397	0.555	0.430	0.716
B9	0.396	0.260	0.602	0.389	0.254	0.595	1.282	1.015	1.619	0.382	0.249	0.585
B10	0.639	0.537	0.759	0.855	0.735	0.995	1.325	1.175	1.494	0.652	0.550	0.774
B11	0.585	0.514	0.667	0.372	0.315	0.438	0.819	0.734	0.915	0.528	0.460	0.606
B12	0.687	0.598	0.791	0.467	0.394	0.554	1.409	1.278	1.553	0.540	0.461	0.632
B13	0.571	0.464	0.703	0.526	0.423	0.655	1.420	1.244	1.621	0.625	0.512	0.763
C14	0.692	0.569	0.841	0.440	0.344	0.562	1.062	0.907	1.243	0.630	0.514	0.773
C15	0.828	0.721	0.951	0.425	0.351	0.516	0.949	0.834	1.080	0.482	0.402	0.578

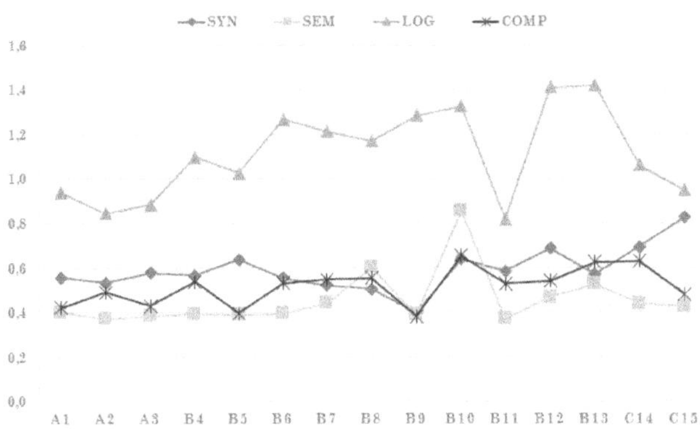

Figure 1: Estimated Means for Each Error Class

5 DISCUSSION

5.1 Persistent Errors in Previous Studies

Although Ahadi et al. [2] used slightly different query concepts, and did not quantitatively study which types of errors occur, we can compare the success rates of our results to theirs to gain understanding on which concepts students struggle with. Their study listed seven query concepts, five of which map to the framework [11] we used. *Simple, one table* [2] corresponds to *single-table* (exercises A1, A2 and A3). Their study reports success rate of 90%, while our rates vary from 60% to 77%. The success rate of a query with *group by* [2], which corresponds to *grouping* (exercise C14), is 75%, which is the same as in our results.

Their query for *group by with having* [2], which corresponds to our *grouping restrictions* (exercise C15), has a success rate of 61%, while ours is 56%. *Self-join* [2] corresponds to *self-join* (exercises B11 and B13), but the success rate of their study (24%) differs from ours (41% and 62%). Finally, *correlated subquery* [2] corresponds to *correlated subquery* (exercise B11), and the success rates are fairly similar with their 46% and our 41%. It is worth noting that most of our exercises tested more than one concept instead of just one. What differs between these two studies, is that the most difficult query concept in their results was self-join, but in our results the most difficult concepts were correlated and uncorrelated subqueries, with success rates of 41% and 43%, respectively.

An earlier study on syntax errors in the whole query writing process [1] (as opposed to our study, in which we only analyzed final answers) used PostgreSQL to categorize syntax errors, which makes the results uncomparable to ours. However, some similarities can be found, as the study points out *syntax error* (corresponds to SYN-6 common syntax error), *undefined column* and *undefined table* (SYN-2), and *grouping error* (SYN-5 illegal or insufficient grouping) among the most frequent syntax errors. Additionally, by examining the final incorrect answers, they discovered that 51% of students abandoned the exercise when they were not able to fix a syntactic error. Ahadi et al. [3] explored persistent semantic errors related to query concepts. The study lists several common errors, most of which correspond to the error categorization we used; *missing/wrong condition* (corresponds to LOG-4, also possibly SEM-1), *self-join not used* (SEM-3 missing join, also possibly SEM-2 inconsistent join), *missing group by or having clause* (SYN-5 illegal or insufficient grouping, and LOG-4 expression error), *use of wrong column* (SYN-5 illegal or insufficient grouping, and LOG-4 expression error), *missing order by clause* (LOG-5 projection error), *incorrect/incomplete column* (LOG-5 projection error), and *missing/extra column in select* (LOG-5 projection error). When compared to our findings in Table 2, these error categories are among the most prominent ones, and our findings seem to support theirs. Additionally, based on our results, data type mismatch (SYN-3), common syntax (SYN-6), operator (LOG-1), join (LOG-2), nesting (LOG-3) and function errors (LOG-6) were relatively frequent in the exercises.

In summary, the available evidence seems to suggest that students struggle with similar query concepts, and some errors are more persistent than others. The consensus view among our results and the results by Ahadi et al. [3] seems to be that the most persistent errors are illegal or insufficient grouping (SYN-5), common syntax error (SYN-6), inconsistent expression (SEM-1), inconsistent join (SEM-2), missing join (SEM-3), expression error (LOG-4), and projection error (LOG-5). Additionally, the results by Ahadi et al. [1] and Taipalus et al. [11] seem to agree that, among all queries, the most frequent syntax errors are common syntax errors (SYN-6), undefined database object errors (SYN-2), and, in queries involving aggregate functions, illegal or insufficient grouping errors (SYN-5).

5.2 Persistent Errors versus All Errors

Taipalus et al. [11] counted relative error frequencies in not just final answers, but during the whole query writing process, i.e., in all queries submitted to the DBMS. By comparing their results to those presented in Table 2, we can acquire some insight on which errors are common, but usually corrected by the students. First, rough comparison reveals that ambiguous database object (SYN-1) and illegal aggregate function placement errors (SYN-4) were uncommon in all and in final answers, while undefined database object errors (SYN-2) were common in all answers, but uncommon in final answers, i.e., usually corrected. The occurrence of data type mismatch (SYN-3) and illegal or insufficient grouping (SYN-5) appears to be closely related to the query concepts, as these errors were frequent in all and in final answers, but only in certain exercises. Common syntax errors (SYN-6) were common in all and in final answers.

The most frequent semantic errors among all and final answers were inconsistent expressions (SEM-1), and missing joins (SEM-3). In general, semantic errors were less frequent in both all and final answers than syntax errors, and the least frequent among all four error classes.

In general, logical errors were most frequent in all and in final answers. Interestingly, in 9 of the 15 exercises, operator errors (LOG-1) were more frequent in the final answers than in all answers. This suggests that operator errors are both common, and they have a high tendency to stay uncorrected. Join errors (LOG-2) were common in almost all multi-table queries, both all and final. Nesting errors (LOG-3) were common in queries which required nesting expressions (A3), or designing the subqueries by using previously uncommon nesting (B8). These errors, however, were closely related to the query concepts, and most of the exercises invited no such errors. Expression (LOG-4) and projection (LOG-5) errors were most common in all and in final answers. These types of errors seem relatively common in the query writing process, and are relatively difficult for students to fix. Smelcer [10] studied SQL query writing process in regard to short term memory, and the occurrence of these types of errors might be related to the thought process of a student translating the natural language data demand into SQL. Intuitively, function errors (LOG-6) occurred only in exercises involving aggregate functions (B9, B11, B12, C14, C15). With the exception of exercise B11, function errors were more common in final than in all answers. This suggests that function errors are difficult for students to fix.

Finally, while complications were relatively common in both all and in final answers, the number of final answers with complications was usually considerably lower than the number of all answers with complications. This suggests that, even though complications are still common, many of them are corrected during the query writing process.

In summary, different query concepts invite different errors by design, e.g., a query with aggregate functions invites the possibility of function errors. By examining the maximum error frequencies for each error category in all answers, we can determine the commonness of each error category, and, consequently, by examining the maximum error frequencies for each error category in all answers, we can determine the persistence of each error category. These things considered, it seems reasonable to assume that we as teachers and researchers should focus on errors which are both common and persistent. Our data indicates the same results as Taipalus et al. [11], i.e., such error categories with a maximum (and arbitrary) relative frequency of at least 0.40 are logical (LOG-1 through LOG-6), and illegal or insufficient grouping errors (SYN-5), as well as complications.

5.3 Persistent Errors and Query Concepts

Among syntax errors, the most persistent were data type mismatch (SYN-3), illegal or insufficient grouping (SYN-5), and common syntax errors (SYN-6). Common syntax errors were relatively frequent in all exercises. With the exception of exercise B13, data type mismatch errors seemed to decrease while the students completed more and more exercises, which might suggest that students learned to formulate queries in which the expressions were Boolean type. Illegal or insufficient grouping errors were common, but only in exercises involving aggregate functions (B11, B12, C14, C15), with the exception of exercise B9, which might be explained by the fact that B9 is the only single-table query with aggregate functions, and thus easier to solve. In terms of persistent syntax errors, answers to exercise C15 showed the most syntax errors. This might be explained by the query requiring the use of all six SQL clauses, as the second highest mean among syntax errors is in exercise C14, which, in turn, required the use of five SQL clauses, while all other exercises required the use of three to four clauses.

As seen in Fig. 1, the trend was that semantic errors were the least persistent among the four error classes. Among semantic errors, the most persistent were inconsistent expressions (SEM-1), inconsistent joins (SEM-2), and missing joins (SEM-3). Inconsistent expressions were relatively prominent compared to other semantic errors in almost all exercises. This is rather unsurprising, because expressions are required in almost all exercises (A1 through B13). Also, intuitively, missing and inconsistent joins were relatively common in all multi-table exercises (B4 through B8, and B10 through C15). Persistent semantic errors were most prominent in exercise B10. One explanation might be that this exercise is the first in which the result table must contain data from multiple tables, which in turn invites joins without subqueries. This might be the first time a student needs to use this approach, but it might not be evident that this approach is preferred.

Finally, and most importantly, logical errors were most persistent among the four error classes. Expression (LOG-4) and projection

Table 4: Which Persistent Errors to Expect

Concept	Expect
multi-table	SEM-2 inconsistent join, SEM-3 missing join, LOG-2 join error
equal subqueries	LOG-2 join error
self-join	LOG-2 join error
multiple source tables	SEM-3 missing join
aggregate functions	SYN-5 illegal or insufficient grouping, LOG-6 function error
(all)	SYN-6 common syntax error, LOG-4 expression error, LOG-5 projection error, complication

errors (LOG-5) were common across all exercises, and operator (LOG-1) and join errors (LOG-2) across almost all exercises. Among logical errors, nesting errors (LOG-3) were relatively uncommon, and the persistence of function errors (LOG-6) was closely related to query concepts involving the use of aggregate functions. Based on our results, we collected the different errors that some of the concepts invite to Table 4. For most of the concepts, however, the data showed no distinguishable patterns.

In conclusion, our results provide needed insight on which SQL errors students struggle with, and which aspects we as teachers and researchers should focus on when utilizing SQL. Although Taipalus et al. [11] proposed an operational model for designing SQL exercises and exercise database data, taking into account their framework's 105 different errors for each exercise is arguably an onerous task. We propose that teachers should start the exercise design by focusing on the most expected persistent errors first, and then work down to less common errors depending on their personal time and resource constraints. What's more, our study propounds the view that students are able to correct some types of errors by themselves, and therefore teaching should focus on errors which students struggle with.

5.4 Limitations and Further Research

We compared our results with certain previous studies [1–3], which did not use the same query concepts or error categorization. With this in mind, there is a chance of misinterpretation of the listed concepts and error categories. Furthermore, these concepts and categories might include or exclude aspects of the framework [11] we used. Finally, the framework lists multiple query concepts per exercise, while Ahadi et al. [2, 3] only list one. In some cases, this might be the result of different levels of specificity between the concept listings, but nonetheless makes the cause and effect analysis in our results more difficult, as it not clear whether frequent errors in any one exercise are caused by a particular query concept, or by a combination of two specific query concepts.

For further research, we propose a tool for automatically categorizing errors in student answers according to the error categorization by Taipalus et al. [11]. The categorization is extensive, and complications, semantic errors, and syntax errors must be analyzed by hand. This is further emphasized by the fact that the categorization is DBMS independent, which makes reliable syntax error discovery by a single DBMS unreliable. By automation, the categorization is open to larger datasets, and by making the automation of error categorization real-time, learning environments may provide students feedback as the query is being written.

6 CONCLUSION

In this study, we set out to investigate which errors are persistent, i.e., more difficult for students to fix, and which types of persistent errors different query concepts, such as joins or aggregate functions invite. The results show that logical errors and complications are more persistent than syntax or semantic errors. While function errors were common in exercises with certain query concepts, expression and projection errors were persistent in all exercises, regardless of the query concepts. We propose that while designing SQL exercises, teachers and researchers design the exercise data to take account most persistent errors, starting from the most common ones.

ACKNOWLEDGMENTS

The authors would like to thank Dr. Mikko Rönkkö for his invaluable advice and support regarding the methodology, and the anonymous reviewers for their comments and suggestions.

REFERENCES

[1] Alireza Ahadi, Vahid Behbood, Arto Vihavainen, Julia Prior, and Raymond Lister. 2016. Students' Syntactic Mistakes in Writing Seven Different Types of SQL Queries and its Application to Predicting Students' Success. In *Proceedings of the 47th ACM Technical Symposium on Computing Science Education (SIGCSE '16)*. ACM Press, New York, New York, USA, 401–406. https://doi.org/10.1145/2839509.2844640

[2] Alireza Ahadi, Julia Prior, Vahid Behbood, and Raymond Lister. 2015. A Quantitative Study of the Relative Difficulty for Novices of Writing Seven Different Types of SQL Queries. In *Proceedings of the 2015 ACM Conference on Innovation and Technology in Computer Science Education (ITiCSE '15)*. ACM Press, New York, New York, USA, 201–206. https://doi.org/10.1145/2729094.2742620

[3] Alireza Ahadi, Julia Prior, Vahid Behbood, and Raymond Lister. 2016. Students' Semantic Mistakes in Writing Seven Different Types of SQL Queries. In *Proceedings of the 2016 ACM Conference on Innovation and Technology in Computer Science Education (SIGCSE '16)*. 272–277. https://doi.org/10.1145/2899415.2899464

[4] Stefan Brass and Christian Goldberg. 2005. Semantic errors in SQL queries: A quite complete list. *Journal of Systems and Software* 79, 5 (2005), 630–644. https://doi.org/10.1016/j.jss.2005.06.028

[5] Luca Cagliero, Luigi De Russis, Laura Farinetti, and Teodoro Montanaro. 2018. Improving the Effectiveness of SQL Learning Practice: A Data-Driven Approach. In *2018 IEEE 42nd Annual Computer Software and Applications Conference (COMPSAC)*, Vol. 01. 980–989. https://doi.org/10.1109/COMPSAC.2018.00174

[6] Geoff Cumming, Fiona Fidler, and David L. Vaux. 2007. Error bars in experimental biology. *The Journal of Cell Biology* 177, 1 (2007), 7–11. https://doi.org/10.1083/jcb.200611141 arXiv:http://jcb.rupress.org/content/177/1/7.full.pdf

[7] Mohammad Dadashzadeh. 2003. A Simpler Approach to Set Comparison Queries in SQL. *Journal of Information Systems Education* 14, 4 (2003), 345–348.

[8] Victor M. Matos and Rebecca Grasser. 2002. Teaching Tip A Simpler (and Better) SQL Approach to Relational Division. *Journal of Information Systems Education* 13, 2 (2002), 85–88. http://jise.org/Volume13/Pdf/085.pdf

[9] Gang Qian. 2018. Teaching SQL: A Divide-and-conquer Method for Writing Queries. *Journal of Computing Sciences in Colleges* 33, 4 (April 2018), 37–44. http://dl.acm.org/citation.cfm?id=3199572.3199577

[10] John B Smelcer. 1995. User errors in database query composition. *International Journal of Human-Computer Studies* 42, 4 (Apr 1995), 353–381. https://doi.org/10.1006/ijhc.1995.1017

[11] Toni Taipalus, Mikko Siponen, and Tero Vartiainen. 2018. Errors and Complications in SQL Query Formulation. *ACM Transactions on Computing Education* 18, 3, Article 15 (Aug. 2018), 29 pages. https://doi.org/10.1145/3231712

[12] Charles Welty. 1985. Correcting user errors in SQL. *International Journal of Man-Machine Studies* 22, 4 (1985), 463–477. https://doi.org/10.1016/S0020-7373(85)80051-1

Perceived Benefits and Challenges of Learning Startup Methodologies for Software Engineering Students

Jorge Melegati
Free University of Bozen-Bolzano
Bolzano, Italy
jmelegatigoncalves@unibz.it

Rafael Chanin
PUCRS, School of Technology
Porto Alegre, Brazil
rafael.chanin@pucrs.br

Xiaofeng Wang
Free University of Bozen-Bolzano
Bolzano, Italy
xiaofeng.wang@unibz.it

Afonso Sales
PUCRS, School of Technology
Porto Alegre, Brazil
afonso.sales@pucrs.br

Rafael Prikladnicki
PUCRS, School of Technology
Porto Alegre, Brazil
rafaelp@pucrs.br

ABSTRACT

The need of skills other than technical from software developers is becoming evident. The DevOps movement is an example of that applied to operational tasks. Startup development methodologies focus on business activities in innovative organizations. Several universities offer courses based on these methodologies to software engineering students, mainly to improve their creativity, problem solving, and business skills. This paper investigates how software engineering students learned startup development methodologies and discusses what are the challenges and benefits in their learning process. We conducted a multi-method study in three different universities. The data was collected in two phases and analyzed using thematic analysis. Our study reveals that students realized the importance of collaboration with other courses and the importance of user involvement in development. However, students tend to over-simplify concepts, trying to adapt them to what they are familiar with. The results indicate the necessity of business education for technical students and directions for improvements.

CCS CONCEPTS

• **Social and professional topics → Software engineering education.**

KEYWORDS

Software Engineering Education; Lean Startup; Empirical Study

ACM Reference Format:
Jorge Melegati, Rafael Chanin, Xiaofeng Wang, Afonso Sales, and Rafael Prikladnicki. 2019. Perceived Benefits and Challenges of Learning Startup Methodologies for Software Engineering Students. In *Proceedings of the 50th ACM Technical Symposium on Computer Science Education (SIGCSE '19), February 27-March 2, 2019, Minneapolis, MN, USA.* ACM, New York, NY, USA, 7 pages. https://doi.org/10.1145/3287324.3287382

SIGCSE '19, February 27-March 2, 2019, Minneapolis, MN, USA

ACM ISBN 978-1-4503-5890-3/19/02...$15.00
https://doi.org/10.1145/3287324.3287382

1 INTRODUCTION

Nowadays, business education is becoming so relevant that some universities across the world have already recognized the importance of providing entrepreneurial skills to engineering students [27]. The fact is that being technically competent is not enough. Understanding customers' needs and knowing how to deliver real value to people is a must in this new economy. Even though some initiatives can be perceived in the academic world, the lack of business education to software engineering students has been a noted issue for a long time. Back in 2000, Shaw [32] already observed that software engineering students rarely faced nontechnical issues. In 2009, a survey of 119 Spanish students reported that they were not receiving enough training in innovation and entrepreneurship [14]. Several courses have focused on entrepreneurship for software engineering students in the last years [13, 19] and other studies focused on the importance of business concepts for technical students [20].

Some entrepreneurship courses teach emerging methodologies for startup development like Lean Startup [19, 24, 35] and Customer Development [9]. Fitzgerald and Stol [15] argue that these methodologies are consequence of the need of a closer integration between business needs and development. However, despite of consisting interesting concepts and ideas, these methodologies can be difficult to comprehend and to apply in practice [6], which may hinder software engineering students to grasp business skills by following the courses. To the best of our knowledge, this is a problem that has not been investigated in the literature. Therefore, this study focuses on the following research question:

What are the benefits and challenges of software engineering students learning the Lean Startup approach?

To answer the research question presented, we performed a multi-method study composed of two parts. Firstly, we studied two different teams of computer science students learning by applying the Lean Startup methodology to develop a new product or service. A set of benefits and challenges in the learning process perceived by the students were identified. Secondly, we conducted a survey to a group of students from a mobile application development course that also taught Lean Startup and Customer Development concepts to further examine some specific challenges discovered in the case study. We analyzed data in both parts using thematic analysis, a technique for identifying, analyzing and reporting patterns (themes) in qualitative data [33]. The results indicate that students understand the importance of collaboration with other courses, such as business development and marketing, and the importance of user involvement in development. However, they tend to simplify concepts, trying to adapt them to what they are familiar with, sometimes losing the main concepts behind the principles.

The remaining part of the paper is organized as follow: Section 2 presents the background on fundamental concepts. Section 3 reviews related work. Section 4 describes the research design, Section 5 presents the results, which are further interpreted and discussed in Section 6. Finally, Section 7 depicts our conclusion and final thoughts.

2 BACKGROUND

In this section, we discuss the definition of a startup and present two methodologies startup companies use: Lean Startup and Customer Development.

2.1 Startup definition

According to Blank and Dorf [4] a startup is a temporary organization that is searching for a sustainable and repeatable business model. Eric Ries [28] defines a startup as "*a human institution designed to create a new product or service under conditions of extreme uncertainty*". All startups share similar characteristics [34]: suffer from internal and external pressure; have limited resources; are young and immature; address dynamic technologies and markets; and present high market risk.

Regarding software development processes for startups, several strategies and approaches have been tested, but no significant results have been achieved [11, 34]. Since the most important goal of a startup is to find a sustainable business model before running out of resources, methods such as Customer Development [4] and Lean Startup [28] were proposed in order to address this objective. The following subsections present these methodologies' main concepts.

2.2 Customer Development

Steve Blank [3] created the Customer Development process based on the premise that most startups fail from a lack of customers rather than product development issues. He argues that there are several processes to manage product development, but there is no formal process to manage customer development.

The Customer Development process is divided into four phases:

- *Customer Discovery*: state and validate both the problem and the customer hypotheses. A startup should only move to the next phase once there are evidences that a group of customers are willing to pay to solve a given problem;
- *Customer Validation*: develop and test a sales process. If the startup is not able to validate the business model, it has to go back to the discovery phase. This move is called *pivot*;
- *Customer Creation*: once the business model is validated, it is time to grow the customer base in order to validate the business feasibility;
- *Company Building*: put formal management into place and create growth strategies to scale the business.

If a startup is not able to validate its business model before running out of resources, it will not succeed. Hence, it is very important to perform an effective customer discovery process [2]. This can be done by interviewing potential customers, using marketing strategies, such as developing landing pages or online advertisements to validate a given value proposition, or even by manually delivering the product/service to the customer (the concierge approach).

2.3 Lean Startup

Inspired by the Customer Development and Lean Manufacturing, Eric Ries proposed the Lean Startup. The method has the premise that every startup is a set of experiments to test hypotheses the startup makes about a given business idea. In order to do so, startups build minimum viable products (MVPs) [23].

An MVP is used to collect feedback from potential customers in order to identify and to model the next experiment [18]. One of the common issues with this approach is to understand what "minimal" and "viable" means [21]. The development of an MVP should focus on the smallest effort in order to test a given assumption of the business model and to obtain maximum validated learning.

Despite of the Lean Startup popularity, it is an approach proposed in a non-scientific book based on anecdotal evidences. Nevertheless, according to Frederiksen and Brem [16], there is substantial evidence in scientific literature to support the Lean Startup efficacy.

3 RELATED WORK

Chanin et al. [10] performed a systematic mapping study on software startup education and derived several interesting insights on how the Lean Startup principles are perceived by students. For instance, one of the reviewed studies (Rioja Del Rio et al. [29]) suggested the use of Business Model Canvas (BMC) [26] when working on software startup projects. The idea is that it allows students to analyze the big picture (all aspects of a business model). Otherwise they would just focus on technical issues. BMC entails the value proposition of the business, the customer segment, the channels to reach the customers, the relationships between them, key resources, key activities, key partners, revenue streams and cost structure.

Barbe [1] proposed a model that connects all aspects of a startup development: from the basic technical knowledge to the business acceleration and funding. The motivation for this model was businesses created by technical founders. If these founders lack business and/or soft skills, they will most likely fail or will need to find people with these skills. Hence, students not only learn the technical foundations for developing a software startup, but they are also exposed to the whole startup development process.

Zaina and Álvaro [38] proposed a methodology that combined user-centered design [30] and Lean Startup in order to foster innovation and entrepreneurial behavior in a software engineering course. The authors argued that computer related courses usually focused only on technical issues, and they did not instigate students to be creative and innovative. They conducted two case studies to verify the method effectiveness. The results indicate that students not only learned important business concepts, but also perceived the importance of understanding customers' needs.

Finally, Buffardi et al. [8] argued that it was very hard to emulate real world projects in an academic environment. When students work with "toy" projects, they end up learning technical content, but they do not experience real customer pressure, competition, and other "real life" situations. This study also brought in light (from

Nurkkala and Brandle [25]) the gaps between software engineering students' and industrial software engineers' experiences. They are sixfold: real product versus a project; long duration versus short duration; low turnover versus high turnover; high complexity versus low complexity; needs maintenance versus no maintenance; and real customers versus no customers. Hence, a methodology was proposed in order to minimize these gaps. The idea was to promote collaboration between software engineering and entrepreneurship students, who would act as customers. Even though software engineering students reported that the experience was relevant to them, the whole process just mimics a real project context. It is not ideal, but it gave students a good perception about what it took to develop a real startup. In this kind of situations, instructors need to evaluate the trade-offs. Depending on the characteristics of a course, it may be too difficult to address real projects.

In regards to challenges students face as well as benefits from courses on Lean Startup concepts, as far as the authors are concerned, there are no academic studies being undertaken.

4 RESEARCH DESIGN

In order to answer our research question, we followed a multi-method study design composed of two parts: (1) a multiple case study conducted in two sites, and (2) a survey applied to software engineering students in a third site.

4.1 Data collection

The first part consisted of a multiple case study [37] based on two cases within different educational configurations:

Case A. Two students in the end of a Computer Science course in a Brazilian university employed Lean Startup and agile methodologies in their bachelor thesis project. The group initially consisted of three students but after a few months one student dropped out and the first author acted as a mentor. The project consisted of building a website to inform students, professors and employees about events occurring in the university campus. It took approximately nine months from March to November 2016. Nonetheless, the effort was not equally distributed along the period.

Case B. Four students, one from a Master and three from a Bachelor program in Computer Science from an Italian university participated in the optional Lean Entrepreneurship course taught by the third author. The setup of the course was project-based, following a learning-by-doing style (the course was described in a previous paper [35]). They developed a project based on the business idea of their own: build a platform to connect car owners keen to rent their cars to possible renters when they were not using them. The course lasted four months, from October 2017 to January 2018.

We collected data mainly in the end of each project. For Case A, students developed a monograph (thesis) to be presented for evaluation that described all the tools used as well as the project history. The monograph had 65 pages written in Portuguese. Only the second half (starting from page 25) were valuable to this study: the remaining consisted of techniques and tools description used in the software development. The team described the product development in three iterations. Each iteration description has the following sections: building, diffusion, metrics and learning. We also included the emails exchanged between the mentor and the team. An initial set consisted of 150 emails had a team member as the sender or receiver. A subject analysis revealed that 10 of them were not related to the project. Most of them were about deadlines and meetings arrangements. We analyzed those related to the difficulties encountered by team members.

For Case B, the course ended with a retrospective session conducted by the teacher (the third author) in which the group depicted the project history. The first author also participated in this session as an observer. During the retrospective, students were asked to draw the journey during the course on an A0 paper sheet, using whatever format or notion that they deemed appropriate. Then they were asked to explain the drawn diagram. The retrospective session took more than one hour, and in the first nine minutes the team discussed internally what to drew. We recorded, and later transcribed, all conversations and discussions during the retrospective session.

The second part of this study consisted of a survey undertaken in a 2-year iOS application development course in Brazil. The class was composed of 40 students with strong software engineering background and 10 design students specialized in user experience for mobile applications.

During the course, students conducted various software development projects, classified as small tasks, nano and mini-challenges. At the end of the course, students worked on a final software development project (a big-challenge activity) which had a six-month duration. They always worked in groups (between three and six students) composed of developers and at least one designer.

The survey was performed following the guidelines proposed by Wohlin et al. [36]. Since this study focuses on software engineering students, we did not apply the survey on the design students. Therefore, the survey was sent to 40 individuals.

All students that participated in this survey have already received lessons on Lean Startup and Customer Development and have practiced and applied these concepts in various activities. The survey was intended to further explore the challenges identified in our multiple case study. In order to do so, we decided to present a small scenario that asked students how they could contribute to a project. The scenario is described as follows:

> *"An entrepreneur friend of yours comes to you with a project idea that he had not yet implemented. He wants to create an app/system that connects elderly people with technology teachers. His idea is to help people to get into the digital world (learn how to use an email, Facebook, Instagram, etc). At first, the business model would be to charge the elderly for the class and keep a commission (between 5% and 10%) and pass the remaining to the teacher. You like the idea and join the project. Before leaving, you received a task: describe, in your opinion, what and how you can help. The idea is to present the next steps and (given your expertise) how you are going to help this project."*

The idea behind this approach was to leave the floor open to students to develop their thoughts freely; we believe that if we had mentioned explicitly that we were working on a survey about Lean Startup/Customer Development, students would have been induced to answer accordingly. Students were asked to write down their answers in a text editor and send them to one of the authors.

4.2 Data analysis

The data analysis conducted in both parts employed mainly thematic analysis, following the scheme proposed by Braun and Clarke [7]. Although suggested to psychological studies, this approach has been commonly used in Software Engineering research [12].

In the first part, we labeled relevant pieces of data and initial themes emerged. The labeled excerpts were then grouped together. Through a comparison between them, we made some improvements. In addition, we conducted a cross-case analysis to compare the two cases related to their setup and results according to the themes identified in each individual case. In the second part, we analyzed the survey responses under the themes identified in the case studies.

5 RESULTS

This section presents our results. Section 5.1 presents findings from the multiple case study: a detailed description of each case and a cross-case analysis. Section 5.2 displays the survey results.

5.1 Multiple-case study

Case A. In this case, students never mentioned a business model for their project. Although Lean Startup can be useful to non-profit organizations, there was no concerns about how to support the project financially. One possibility that students mentioned in emails were that the project could substitute the pre-existent university events page. In this sense, also in the emails, there was a concern from the mentor about why users should switch to the new product. Regarding design and user experience, in the thesis, the text mentioned that suggestions made during first iteration focused on design aspects and still in the third iteration: *"most of the critics [...] were related to the experience provided by the site and that it was not attractive enough"*. Finally, for marketing and distribution, the difficulties were users acquisition and engagement. The first was present in each interaction description and they also wrote: *"with acquired learning, it was clear the importance of time spent in marketing"*. The latter was present in an email from one of team members: *"engagement: one of the challenges is to make the user to come back and give her interaction ways that make her want to come back every week to see all the events"*.

In the thesis, students made a conceptual error: they used the word "hypothesis" to describe a list of features to "create an interface". They confused hypothesis testing with building incrementally. A possible explanation is that the Build-Measure-Learn cycle first step is to formulate hypothesis, so they felt obligated to write a hypothesis while reporting this interaction. Nevertheless, they followed a cyclical process as described in their thesis (Figure 1).

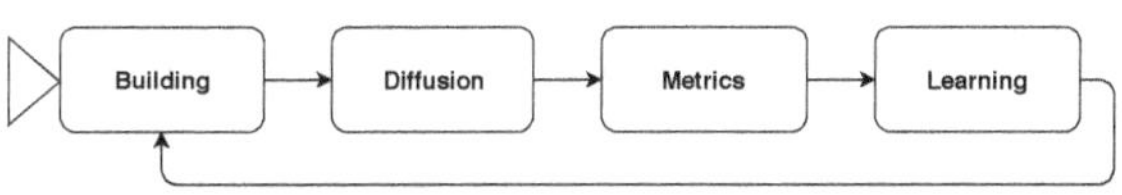

Figure 1: A schematic view of Group A's thesis.

It is interesting to show pieces of data where students highlight their learning: *"that demonstrated the importance of keeping development always in touch with the final user"* or *"the importance that the client represents in the process"*. Additionally, in their conclusions, they stated that: *"not always the concept about a project or a product idea by developers point of view is, in fact, a need to the target users"*.

Case B. From a business perspective, the second group mentioned that the mentor drew attention to the need of a specific insurance to make the product viable. Although such insurance was fundamental to the product viability, the group had already started developing software architecture. Regarding design and UX, they said that they still needed help to understand *"what the consumer wants"*. They also mentioned that they were not able to create an interesting logo that could enhance product adoption.

The tendency to follow a straight path is clear in the picture the second group drew (Figure 2). Although classes in the course advocated the Build-Measure-Learn cycle from the Lean Startup methodology [28], the depicted flow still recalls the waterfall process. The group also mentioned in the retrospective while discussing the insurance: *"we started the implementation of the website after the form. We didn't think about it"*. During the retrospective, the team also made a conceptual error: when asked what an MVP was, they replied: *"MVP is just the minimum set of features we should put in our platform"*. Instead, according to Lean Startup, MVP is the minimum set of features one should implement to test a hypothesis that may not even be in the final product.

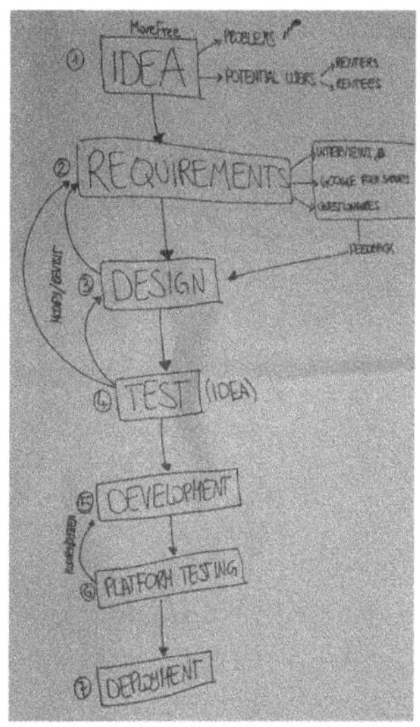

Figure 2: Flow draw by the second group.

As takeaways from the course, this group mentioned: *"what the consumer wants is more important than you implementing"* and *"if it does not put value to the market, there's no sense to making it"*.

Cross-case analysis. Although students had similar team sizes and backgrounds, they followed really different processes. The first group performed a cyclical process trying to formulate hypothesis and to validate them, that is, following a Build-Measure-Learn cycle. They also focused on customer feedback that comprehends a good part of the methodology [17]. Meanwhile, the second group basically followed a straight plan (having the idea, gathering requirements, designing and testing the idea, development, platform testing and deployment), even after participating in classes about the Lean Startup methodology. In software startups, Giardino et al. [18] already saw this plan driven approach as waste and a reason for startups' failure. Meanwhile, Bosch et al. [6] argue that agile and lean practices are better for early stage software startups.

A possible explanation is that first group students was more engaged in learning the methodology or really developing a viable product. Another possibility would be that they are better students than the second group. Even if these hypotheses are correct, an element should have been more important to guide a group: the mentor. For the second group, the mentor had an important act telling them about the insurance issue. However, students did not mention anything else about her performance. For the first group, the first author acted as a mentor highlighting the importance of customer feedback and hypothesis testing, guiding the students to focus on them. The second group mentioned another interesting point: *"it's different from the other courses: you're given [a task] and deliver [it]; that is, there's no market connection"*.

There were, though, some similarities between the two cases. First, neither teams worried about business issues: Case A students did not come up with a clear business model and Case B students ignored concerns about insurance and continued developing the technical solution. Of course, the academic environment may be the reason of such insouciance about business. Second, both teams recognized the importance of validation and customer feedback.

Thematic analysis identified 11 themes categorized in the two categories: *Benefits* and *Challenges*, as described in Table 1.

Table 1: Themes found in first phase.

Category	Theme
Benefits	Business learning Design learning Feedback importance Marketing learning Success based on metrics Team building learning User experience learning
Challenges	Business perspective ignored Conceptual errors

The benefits include students learning regarding different areas:

- **Design:** for instance, all suggestions in the first iteration of Case A concerned design issues;
- **Team building:** like a student in Case B mentioned: *"people from different backgrounds can give different opinions"*;
- **Marketing and distribution:** as Case A thesis states: *"with the acquired knowledge it is clear the importance of time dedicated to distribution"*;
- **Business:** Case A thesis states: *"not always the idea of determined project or idea from the perspective of developers is, in fact, a necessity of targeted users"*.

Besides that, several excerpts show the importance of user feedback during projects development. For instance, in Case A's students wrote: *"Although the alerts page visits had a peak after launching, the feature was abandoned by users, generating almost no visits. This shows that possibly it wouldn't be interest to invest in its development."*

The challenges comprises the avoidance to tackle business issues as mentioned earlier, the tendency to follow a straight plan focusing on technical challenges and difficulty to understand some concepts, like MVP. In this regard, in Case A, students used hypothesis as a synonym of prototype. Besides that, team members from Case B defined MVP as *"just the minimum set of features we should put in our platform"* instead of the correct concept of validation.

5.2 Survey results

From the 40 students surveyed, 37 answered (92,5% response rate). In the large majority (28 times), students focused on the *validation* of the idea, highlighting the **business learning** the course enabled. In their answers, students generally described how they would perform validation. The most common technique was *interview*, mentioned 11 times. In a student words: *"To interview the target audience and to understand what is its real needs and difficulties."*. Other tools mentioned were prototype (6), concierge (2) and talking to close people, like relatives (2). However, several students (6) did not detail how they would perform the validation they proposed. In summary, there is no learning cycle, in Lean Startup terms, in this process. Even though some learning happens during validation, this approach resembles a traditional software/business requirement process. These answers also illustrate **conceptual errors** students make. Figure 3 summarizes this idea: students understand validation as a step to get to the implementation, and not as a learning process.

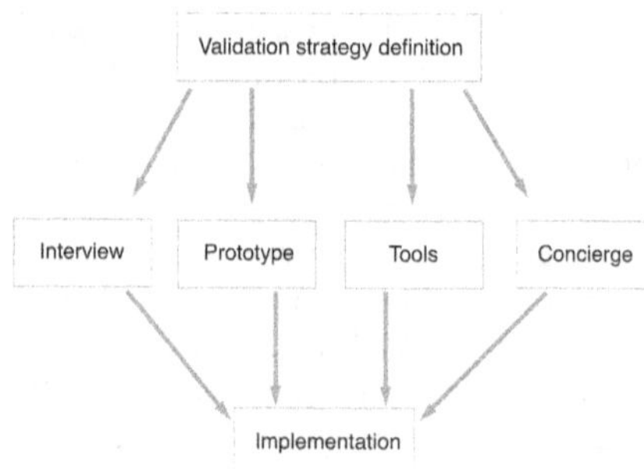

Figure 3: Students' perceptions on validation.

As another example of **conceptual errors**, five respondents criticized the idea without proposing to validate it. One student said that he would not participate in the project: *"I think the idea will not work, because doing an app to connect people that do not know how to use technology will not be effective to reach them, because they will never succeed to use this app without previous knowledge. The app will not reach its target audience. I suggest to pivot the idea."*. It is understandable to have personal opinions about an idea, but, the Lean Startup process makes it clear that one should look for facts, and not opinions. This outcome showed us how personal opinions and beliefs have a significant influence on startup projects.

Five times students focused on promote themselves to the fictional job and three of them would not even test the idea. For instance, *"I could contribute by developing the project, helping with brainstorm dynamics, prototypes ideas, etc. I could also help to put the platform website up, the meeting schedule service and an iOS app, organizing and managing the team if necessary."*.

Three students highlighted the importance of **listening to user feedback**. One student mentioned that *"it is highly important, as soon as we develop some features, to test with the audience in order to receive feedback so possible changes could be made"*.

Marketing and distribution concerns were mentioned 3 times. For instance, one student said: *"Besides that, I would do ads in games that elderly people use to play [some mobile games] and advertise the platform there".*

Students mentioned concerns about **user experience** 6 times. One student described: *"To facilitate the app user flow and to avoid that the user loses herself, I would leave the minimum of options available in the screens. Besides that, I would put some gamification elements to make the user experience more pleasant".*

6 DISCUSSION

Our results suggest that a Lean Startup or Customer Development course indeed makes software engineering students aware of business related concerns of a software product like marketing. In our case studies, both groups tried to validate their business assumptions about users, although to different levels of success. Moreover, Case A also faced several issues about user interface and distribution. One reason that Team B have not have confronted them may be the shorter period spent in the project. Students' statements about learning also corroborate this observation.

Nevertheless, students face difficulties to avoid a straight plan focusing on technical challenges. They had already absorbed the plan-driven idea of "getting things done". From the first phase, two facts support this finding: from Case A, the observation from the first author as a mentor that the group tended to focus on developing the solution and, from Case B, the flow students drew. In the second phase, such an issue happens when students described technical plans on what to be done next ignoring a validation stage. Even when they suggested a validation stage, they do not think it in a cyclical manner: adding a validation as an initial stage to be performed before implementation.

In addition, students still struggle to understand concepts such as MVP and validation, generally using them as synonyms of simpler and already known concepts: MVPs as prototypes and validations as interviews. For example, students in Case B defined incorrectly an MVP as a product with a small set of features, ignoring the concept of business hypothesis, the practice core. In Case A, students wrongly used the term "hypothesis" to designate a prototype. For validation, Case B students and many survey respondents described the employment of interviews without further details.

Based on our findings, we suggest that software engineering students to be immersed in the concept of software business and customer relationships earlier in their formation process. More practical courses with real users or customers could be a solution. Such courses would be in line with the move from product to services seen in software products where "companies must transition from working with planned releases with detailed requirement specifications to continuously experimenting with customers" [5]. Since Case A's results were slightly better in than Case B (students performed a cyclical process focused on customer feedback), some indications could be gathered from Case A which suggest how to improve students' business capabilities. In this case, the mentor encouraged students to work in cycles and real users interacted with the platform. The problems they had with imprecise concepts and the lack of concern about the project's business sustainability should be the focus for improvement in the future courses.

6.1 Threats to validity

Runeson and Höst [31] describe a common scheme to assess threats to validity when reporting a case study composed by four aspects: construct validity, internal validity, external validity and reliability.

Construct validity reflects "to what extent the operational measures that are studied really represent what the researcher have in mind" [31]. The use of multiple information sources for both case studies reduces this issue as suggested by Yin [37].

Internal validity is related to causal relationships and represents the possibility of other factors not taken into account also explain a consequence. Although this study is exploratory, we used pieces of data to support each claim in data analysis and explored alternative explanations like students drivers. Triangulation of data from different sources within each case study also improved internal validity [22]. Another threat was that the first author was the first group mentor and it could have biased the data analysis. A detailed procedure and the results presentation to the other coauthors who were not involved in the cases mitigated this issue.

The use of three student groups in three different scenarios in two countries improved **external validity**.

The use of thematic analysis improved the **reliability** which goal is "to minimize errors and biases in the study", that is, if another researcher performs the same study in the future, she reaches the same results [37]. Besides that, the paper describes all steps performed in data collection and analysis.

7 CONCLUSIONS

This study focused on the challenges and benefits of startup methodologies courses for software engineering students. We performed a multiple-case study and a survey with students in three different contexts from two countries. Our results indicate that students understood the importance of business concepts and developed several soft skills, but still struggle to understand key aspects of the Lean Startup methodology, usually over-simplifying them, and experience a tendency to follow a straight path focused on technical success.

Based on the difficulties found, we proposed some insights that could be used to create or improve business and innovation related courses taught to computer science and similar areas. Lecturers should be concerned with important concepts, like MVP and validation, and perform a deeper inspection to check students' understanding of these concepts. They should also organize their practical courses to encourage students to follow a cyclical path avoiding the tendency to pursue a straight path.

Our results stimulate further studies on introducing business and innovation education into computer science and software engineering courses. For instance, it would be interesting to verify whether introducing these concepts in the beginning of the course, when students are less biased, could bring better learning results.

ACKNOWLEDGMENT

This work is partially funded by FAPERGS (17/2551-0001/205-4). The authors would like to thank the students who participated in this study.

REFERENCES

[1] D.F. Barbe. 2010. A Model of Cross Disciplinary Education, Technology Transfer and Teaching Non-Technical Skills for Engineers. In *Transforming Engineering Education: Creating Interdisciplinary Skills for Complex Global Environments*. IEEE Computer Society, Dublin, Ireland, 1–32.

[2] T. Batova, D. Clark, and D. Card. 2016. Challenges of lean customer discovery as invention. In *2016 IEEE International Professional Communication Conference (IPCC)*. 1–5.

[3] S. Blank. 2013. *The Four Steps to the Epiphany: Successful Strategies for Products That Win*. K&S Ranch, Incorporated.

[4] S. Blank and B. Dorf. 2012. *The Startup Owner's Manual: The Step-by-step Guide for Building a Great Company*. K&S Ranch, Incorporated.

[5] J. Bosch. 2016. Speed, Data, and Ecosystems: The Future of Software Engineering. *IEEE Software* 33, 1 (jan 2016), 82–88.

[6] J. Bosch, H.H. Olsson, J. Björk, and J. Ljungblad. 2013. The Early Stage Software Startup Development Model: A Framework for Operationalizing Lean Principles in Software Startups. *Lean Enterprise Software and Systems* (2013), 1–15.

[7] V. Braun and V. Clarke. 2006. Using thematic analysis in psychology. *Qualitative Research in Psychology* 3, 2 (jan 2006), 77–101.

[8] K. Buffardi, C. Robb, and D. Rahn. 2017. Tech startups: realistic software engineering projects with interdisciplinary collaboration. *Journal of Computing Sciences in Colleges* 32, 4 (2017), 93–98.

[9] R. Chanin, L. Pompermaier, K. Fraga, A. Sales, and R. Prikladnicki. 2017. Applying Customer Development for Software Requirements in a Startup Development Program. In *Proceedings - 2017 IEEE/ACM 1st International Workshop on Software Engineering for Startups, SoftStart 2017*. 2–5.

[10] R. Chanin, A. Sales, L. Pompermaier, and R. Prikladnicki. 2018. A Systematic Mapping Study On Software Startups Education. In *2018 Evaluation and Assessment in Software Engineering, EASE 2018*. 163–168.

[11] G. Coleman and R. O'Connor. 2008. An investigation into software development process formation in software startups. *Journal of Enterprise Information Management* 21, 6 (2008), 633–648.

[12] D. S. Cruzes and T. Dyba. 2011. Recommended Steps for Thematic Synthesis in Software Engineering. *2011 International Symposium on Empirical Software Engineering and Measurement* 7491 (2011), 275–284.

[13] E.F.Z. da Cruz and A. Alvaro. 2013. Introduction of entrepreneurship and innovation subjects in a computer science course in Brazil. In *2013 IEEE Frontiers in Education Conference (FIE)*. 1881–1887.

[14] M. Edwards, L. M. Sánchez-Ruiz, E. Tovar-Caro, and E. Ballester-Sarrias. 2009. Engineering students' perceptions of innovation and entrepreneurship competences. *Proceedings - Frontiers in Education Conference, FIE* (2009).

[15] B. Fitzgerald and K.J. Stol. 2017. Continuous software engineering: A roadmap and agenda. *Journal of Systems and Software* 123 (2017), 176–189.

[16] D.L. Frederiksen and A. Brem. 2017. How do entrepreneurs think they create value? A scientific reflection of Eric Ries' Lean Startup approach. *International Entrepreneurship and Management Journal* 13, 1 (2017), 169–189.

[17] A. Ghezzi, A. Cavallaro, A. Rangone, and R. Balocco. 2015. A Comparative Study on the Impact of Business Model Design & Lean Startup Approach versus Traditional Business Plan on Mobile Startups Performance. *Proceedings of the 17th International Conference on Enterprise Information Systems* (2015), 196–203.

[18] C. Giardino, X. Wang, and P. Abrahamsson. 2014. Why early-stage software startups fail: A behavioral framework. *Lecture Notes in Business Information Processing* 182 LNBIP (2014), 27–41.

[19] R. Harms. 2015. Self-regulated learning, team learning and project performance in entrepreneurship education: Learning in a lean startup environment. *Technological Forecasting and Social Change* 100 (2015), 21–28.

[20] J. Kontio, M. Ahokas, P. Poyry, J. Warsta, M.M. Makela, and P. Tyrvainen. 2006. Software Business Education for Software Engineers: Towards an Integrated Curriculum. *19th Conference on Software Engineering Education and Training Workshops (CSEETW'06)* (2006), 4–7.

[21] V. Lenarduzzi and D. Taibi. 2016. MVP Explained: A Systematic Mapping Study on the Definitions of Minimal Viable Product. In *2016 42th Euromicro Conference on Software Engineering and Advanced Applications (SEAA)*. 112–119.

[22] T.C. Lethbridge, S.E. Sim, and J. Singer. 2005. Studying software engineers: Data collection techniques for software field studies. *Empirical Software Engineering* 10, 3 (2005), 311–341.

[23] S.-C. Li. 2007. The Role of Value Proposition and Value Co-Production in New Internet Startups: How New Venture e-Businesses Achieve Competitive Advantage. In *Portland Int. Center for Management of Engineering and Technology (PICMET)*. 1126–1132.

[24] C. Nobel. 2011. Teaching a 'Lean Startup' Strategy. *Harvard Business School* (2011), 1–2.

[25] T. Nurkkala and S. Brandle. 2011. Software studio: teaching professional software engineering. In *Proceedings of the 42nd ACM Technical Symposium on Computer Science Education*. Dallas, TX, USA, 153–158.

[26] A. Osterwalder and Y. Pigneur. 2010. *Business model generation: a handbook for visionaries, game changers, and challengers*. John Wiley & Sons.

[27] J. Porter, J. Morgan, R. Lester, A. Steele, J. Vanegas, and R. Hill. 2015. A course in innovative product design: A collaboration between architecture, business, and engineering. In *Proceedings of 2015 IEEE Frontiers in Education Conference (FIE)*. IEEE Computer Society, El Paso, TX, USA, 1–5.

[28] E. Ries. 2011. *The Lean Startup: How Today's Entrepreneurs Use Continuous Innovation to Create Radically Successful Businesses*. Crown Business.

[29] C. Rioja Del Rio, A. Morgado-Estevez, and J.J. Dominguez-Jimenez. 2014. Entrepreneurship and lean manufacturing for software engineering. In *SEFI Annual Conference 2014*. Birmingham, UK.

[30] J. Rubin and D. Chisnell. 2008. *Handbook of usability testing: how to plan, design and conduct effective tests*. John Wiley & Sons.

[31] P. Runeson and M. Höst. 2009. Guidelines for conducting and reporting case study research in software engineering. *Empirical Software Engineering* 14, 2 (2009), 131–164.

[32] M. Shaw. 2000. Software engineering education. In *Proceedings of the conference on The future of Software engineering - ICSE '00*. ACM Press, New York, New York, USA, 371–380.

[33] A. Strauss, J.M. Corbin, and J. Corbin. 1998. *Basics of Qualitative Research: Techniques and Procedures for Developing Grounded Theory*. SAGE Publications.

[34] S. M. Sutton. 2000. The role of process in software start-up. *IEEE Software* 17, 4 (Jul 2000), 33–39.

[35] X. Wang, D. Khanna, and P. Abrahamsson. 2016. Teaching Lean Startup at University: An Experience Report. In *International Workshop on Software Startups (IWSS) co-located with 22nd ICE/IEEE International Technology Management Conference*.

[36] C. Wohlin, P. Runeson, M. Höst, M.C. Ohlsson, B. Regnell, and A. Wesslén. 2012. *Experimentation in software engineering*. Springer Science & Business Media.

[37] R.K. Yin. 2003. *Case Study Research: Design and Methods*. SAGE Publications.

[38] L.A.M. Zaina and A. Alvaro. 2015. A Design Methodology for User-centered Innovation in the Software Development Area. *Journal of Systems and Software* 110, C (2015), 155–177.

Motivating Students Beyond Course Requirements with a Serious Game

Stacey Watson
Nazareth College
Pittsford, NY
swatson0@naz.edu

Heather Richter Lipford
University of North Carolina at Charlotte
Charlotte, NC
Heather.Lipford@uncc.edu

ABSTRACT

Educators are challenged to provide computer science students enough skills-based practice within the confines of a course. Yet it is also difficult to motivate students to spend additional time for further practice outside of course requirements. We are investigating games and gamification as methods for motivating students to engage in additional practice. In this paper, we report on the study of a fantasy-themed serious game to teach Ruby programming skills. We examine how well it motivated students to complete additional levels of the game than was assigned for course credit in an undergraduate Software Engineering course. Of the 185 student participants, 42.78% completed one or more optional game levels. These students spent more than twice as much time playing than their counterparts who only completed the mandatory game levels.

CCS CONCEPTS

• **Applied computing → Computer-assisted instruction**;

KEYWORDS

co-curricular, motivation, gamification, serious games

ACM Reference Format:
Stacey Watson and Heather Richter Lipford. 2019. Motivating Students Beyond Course Requirements with a Serious Game. In *Proceedings of the 50th ACM Technical Symposium on Computer Science Education (SIGCSE '19), February 27-March 2, 2019, Minneapolis, MN, USA.* ACM, New York, NY, USA, 7 pages. https://doi.org/10.1145/3287324.3287364

1 INTRODUCTION

Researchers have noted that video games motivate users to engage with unparalleled levels of intensity for long periods of time [4]. This is largely attributed to the idea that games elicit powerful human emotions such as joy, frustration and curiosity [14]. Educators, seeking to tap into the powerful motivating effect of games, have found that using games and game elements in educational contexts can motivate students to put forth more effort [3], which can improve learning outcomes[2] as a result.

The main focus of educational games, however, should not be on the game itself, but rather should be about "incentivizing the right behavior that is aligned with the educational goals" [8]. In computer science, educational goals can include skills that require repeated practice to achieve mastery. Yet there may not be enough time in a typical course to cover the depth and frequency of skills practice necessary to gain fluency in the discipline. Therefore, we believe that practice outside of class is an important component of computer science education. However, as students have many demands on their time, it is challenging to motivate them to go beyond course requirements in order to further improve their skills.

In this paper, we explore whether a game and gamification will motivate students to engage in co-curricular activities designed to encourage them to explore content and to practice skills even when they are not required for course credit. More specifically, we utilize a fantasy-themed serious game along with a leaderboard to teach Ruby programming skills within a Software Engineering course. Our results are promising, as a large number of students did spend additional time completing game levels beyond what was assigned and did spend more time on task.

2 RELATED WORK

Serious games educate individuals within particular contexts using game thinking and game mechanics [7][4]. In other words, serious games are games that are meant to do more than entertain.

Educational researchers have found that such games motivate their target audience and can lead to increased learning outcomes. In Buckley et al.'s [2] study, for example, student learning outcomes were shown to increase as a result of a game where 156 online students bought and traded fictitious contracts and earned virtual money based on the accuracy of their forecasts.

Serious games have also been used in computer science education contexts, such as Robocode [18] in which players use Java programming skills to develop a robot tank to compete against tanks programmed by other players, and CoLoBoT [5], in which players use C, C++ or Java programming skills to colonize a planet. Muratet et al. [16] [17] developed and evaluated a real-time strategy game, Prog&Play, to teach their students programming skills. The serious game group performed better on the mid-term and final exams than the control group without the game, and students responded that they enjoyed the game campaigns. There are a number of other games mentioned in the literature for teaching programming or other CS skills, but these lack in-depth evaluation of their use and effectiveness [20][12][10] and/or have primarily been used within course requirements.

We believe that learning to program, as well as learning other computing skills, requires students to spend time on their own honing those skills. Thus, we believe more work needs to be done to determine if serious games would motivate students to go beyond

SIGCSE '19, February 27-March 2, 2019, Minneapolis, MN, USA

ACM ISBN 978-1-4503-5890-3/19/02...$15.00
https://doi.org/10.1145/3287324.3287364

the course requirements toward mastering the skills rather than only completing the minimum course requirements.

There are co-curricular serious games for computer science students in the form of hack-a-thons, robotics competitions, and capture the flag (CTF) competitions. Typically, these competitive events are offered as a co-curricular experience rather than being incorporated into a particular course and require students to have prepared in advance for the competitions. The challenge is that most of these competitive academic events require many weeks of preparation and take place over several days. This serves to limit the number of competitions that take place each year which, in turn, limits participation to those institutions with available travel funding and who have faculty with the time to train students outside of class time and to accompany student teams to the competitions.

One exception to examining co-curricular learning is the work of Ibanez et al.[6], who utilized a gamified learning platform called Q-Learning-G in a C programming course. They found that many students continued working on tasks even after earning the maximum possible score, with surveys indicating that many students were motivated by earning all of the badges. However, Ibanez et al.'s was a small case study, where the game aimed to teach core course content. We seek to expand upon this work with a larger study, where the learning goals of the game support but are not the primary course goals.

To summarize, research into games and gamification at the college level has been shown to motivate students to engage more fully in their coursework. However, very little of this research explores whether games and gamification would motivate students to go beyond course requirements. In general, co-curricular activities in computer science are limited to heavy-weight events as hack-a-thons and capture-the-flag competitions, which limit participation. Thus we seek to contribute more research on ways to motivate students to go beyond the basic requirements and to spend more time honing their skills without cutting into class time.

3 RESEARCH QUESTIONS

Our primary research goal is to provide a better understanding of how games and gamification, specifically a serious game, impact student motivation to engage in additional game levels beyond what is required for course credit.

This paper concentrates on two main questions in addressing the primary research goal:

R1. Will a serious game motivate students to go beyond the requirements for course credit to develop programming skills?
R2. Will a leaderboard motivate students to go beyond the requirements for course credit to develop programming skills?

We examined these questions over two semesters in one section of an undergraduate Software Engineering course at the University of North Carolina at Charlotte, a large public university (where the primary author was also the instructor). We added a serious game, described below, with a certain level of completion required and remaining levels optional. We also added a leaderboard to the Learning Management System with the top ten scorers as the game itself did not include competition with peers and studies have shown that competition is a motivational mechanism for some individuals [19]. We examined and compared completion data for both semesters, completion times for the second semester, as well as student survey responses about the game and the leaderboard, to examine how well this serious game engaged students to go beyond the required levels.

4 METHOD

4.1 Study Design

At the University of North Carolina at Charlotte, students in the Software Engineering course (ITSC 3155) learn Ruby and the Rails framework as the tools for applying software engineering principles.

The Ruby programming language is new to the students, and is significantly different from the Java students learn in their Freshman and Sophomore computing courses. However, as software engineering principles and not the programming language or framework are the primary learning objectives, it is important for students to practice on their own. In past semesters, the course instructor assigned some online tutorials on the topic, but it was clear that students needed something that would motivate them to engage in additional practice outside of class time.

As such, we decided to use Ruby Warrior [1], an interactive game designed by Ryan Bates to teach the Ruby programming language as well as some artificial intelligence concepts, to make this topic more engaging for students. This serious game not only includes points and levels, but also includes key game elements such as competition and challenges in the form of foes to defeat and captives to rescue.

In this game, which is installed via a Ruby gem (library), students write Ruby code that will enable their warrior to climb a tower to reach a precious Ruby at the top. On each floor of the tower, they must write code that will instruct their warrior to reach the stairs to the next floor, battling enemies and rescuing captives along the way. The level instructions, provided in a README file that updates each time they clear a level, gives players a sense for what each floor contains, but it is up to the students to program enough artificial intelligence into their warrior to find their own way. See Figure 1.

Once a player writes code that they believe will provide the artificial intelligence for their warrior to clear the level, they run the Ruby Warrior command and can watch as their warrior attempts to make its way to the stairs for that level. Once a level is cleared, the cumulative score and level is displayed. See Figure 2.

There are ten floors of the tower to clear to reach the top and two levels of difficulty: beginner and intermediate. The beginner level 1 requires only the use of a single line of code with the warrior.walk! method, whereas level 10 requires the use of loops, conditionals and other programming logic along with strategic use of game objects and methods. There is also an epic mode for both the beginner and intermediate levels where students try to write code that will work for all ten levels.

RubyWarrior has been mentioned in a number of academic papers that review games designed to help improve programming or computing competency [20][12][10]. However, none of these papers study the game itself.

```
README
Level 2

It is too dark to see anything, but you smell sludge nearby.

Tip: Use warrior.feel.empty? to see if there is anything in front of you,
and warrior.attack! to fight it. Remember, you can only do one action
(ending in !) per turn.

 --------
|@  s  >|
 --------

  > = Stairs
  @ = Warrior1 (20 HP)
  s = Sludge (12 HP)


Warrior Abilities:

  warrior.feel
    Returns a Space for the given direction (forward by default).

  warrior.attack!
    Attacks a unit in given direction (forward by default).

  warrior.walk!
    Move in the given direction (forward by default).


When you're done editing player.rb, run the rubywarrior command again.
```

Figure 1: Ruby Warrior README

```
Warrior1 attacks forward and hits Sludge
Sludge takes 5 damage, -3 health power left
Sludge dies
Warrior1 earns 12 points
- turn 7 -
 --------
|  @    >|
 --------
Warrior1 walks forward
- turn 8 -
 --------
|   @   >|
 --------
Warrior1 walks forward
- turn 9 -
 --------
|    @ >|
 --------
Warrior1 walks forward
- turn 10 -
 --------
|     @>|
 --------
Warrior1 walks forward
Success! You have found the stairs.
Level Score: 12
Time Bonus: 10
Clear Bonus: 4
Total Score: 10 + 26 = 36
```

Figure 2: Clearing a Level in Ruby Warrior

4.2 Study Procedure

Students were introduced to the Ruby Warrior exercise during class where they were encouraged to work within light-weight teams [11] to defeat the levels in the game. We estimated that it would take students 50 minutes to complete the first three beginner levels, which would fit into the time allotted during class for the exercise.

In an assignment posted in the Learning Management System (LMS), students were provided installation and grading instructions with a deadline set for the end of the week. Students were required to complete the first three beginner levels for full course credit but were told that a leaderboard would be posted with the top ten student scores so as to motivate students who enjoy competition.

In the Fall 2017 semester of the study, students submitted screenshots with their earned final score for each level. In the Spring 2018 semester of the study, the students submitted time-stamped logs of all in-game interactions.

Students were encouraged to continue to play for four more weeks as a way to prepare for the first course test and for a chance to improve their standing on the leaderboard. They submitted game progress to the LMS in these subsequent weeks, but did not receive course credit for additional levels and/or higher scores achieved. A leaderboard was posted on the LMS course home page and was highlighted in class to encourage students to continue to play.

Survey comments in the Fall 2017 semester of the study revealed an unexpected consequence of the leaderboard: some students continued to play but did not submit their scores as they knew they had not yet achieved a high enough score to earn a place on the leaderboard. As a result, in the Spring 2018 semester of the study, 5 course points could be earned for submitting logs, regardless of whether or not students continued to play.

After the final week of the study, we sent a recruitment email for students to complete a brief online survey about the exercise. Students were required to consent to participate in the anonymous survey, which included some basic demographic questions as well as questions about computer, mobile and board game behaviors, level attained in the game, perceptions about the game and about how the game and the leaderboard impacted the students' motivation to continue playing.

As a study by Landers and Landers [9] has shown that the higher motivation generated by games and gamified approaches leads to increased time-on-task, which is a leading indicator for learning outcomes, we focused on completion levels and time spent for our study. Anonymous level completion data were collected from the LMS for both semesters and console log completion time data were collected from the second semester. Our study methods and data collection were approved by our institution's Institutional Review Board (IRB).

4.3 Participants

Study participants were students in two semesters of one section of an upper-division Software Engineering course (ITSC 3155) at the University of North Carolina at Charlotte.

The sample was comprised of 185 computer science majors (aged 19-38, μ = 22, σ = 3.22). Among the participants, 154 (83.2%) were male and 31 (16.8%) were female. The grade point average (GPA) of the participants ranged from 1.97 to 4.0 (μ = 3.2, σ = 0.53). Of the participants, 17 identified as African American, 8 as Any 2 or More Races, 1 as American Indian, 25 as Asian or Pacific Islander, 87 as Caucasian, 9 as Hispanic, 6 as International and 32 did not specific their race/ethnicity.

5 RESULTS

5.1 Game Performance

Our primary measures were the number of levels completed and the time spent on the game activity by the students.

5.1.1 Levels Completed. As illustrated in Table 1, which summarizes the completion rates of the mandatory versus optional game levels, 42.78% of the students completed one or more optional game levels. All but 2 students were able to complete the levels assigned for course credit and 56.11% of participants completed only the mandatory levels. Eleven students (6.11%) completed all ten of the beginner levels to earn the top spots on the leaderboard.

Levels	% Participants
Some Mandatory	1.11%
Only Mandatory	56.11%
One or More Optional	42.78%
All Optional *	6.11%

Table 1: Levels Completed

* The All Optional group is included in the One or More Optional group

5.1.2 Time Spent. The total time students spent in the game was gathered in this study through console logging in the second semester. As students worked on Ruby Warrior over several weeks, we set a maximum threshold of 30 minutes for any attempt at defeating a level. If students took longer than 30 minutes to run the next Ruby Warrior command, we assumed the student stepped away for hours or days. In this case, the time was replaced with an average attempt time for the class as a whole.

This calculated total time increased according to how many levels they completed. Students who completed only the mandatory levels spent a mean time of 45.74 minutes in the game, those who completed one or more optional levels spent a mean time of 110.53 minutes in the game and those who completed all optional levels spent a mean time of 162.43 minutes in the game. These results are depicted in Table 2.

Levels Completed	Mean
Only Mandatory	45.74
One or More Optional	110.53
All Optional *	162.43

Table 2: Minutes Spent Playing - Spring 2018

* The All Optional group is included in the One or More Optional group

This increased time is expected as it would take students longer to complete additional levels. However, when mean time per level was calculated, there was no significant difference (p-value 0.2) in the mean minutes per level. Students who completed all of the mandatory levels did so with a mean time of 15.25 minutes per level and students who completed one or more of the optional levels did so with a mean time of 18.02 minutes per level. See Table 3.

5.1.3 Level Attempts. An attempt in Ruby Warrior is defined as the player running their new code through the interpreter to see if their warrior has enough artificial intelligence to make it through the level to the stairs. There was no significant difference (p-value 0.9) in the mean attempts per level between students who completed only the mandatory levels and those who completed one or more of the optional levels. Students who completed all of the mandatory levels did so in an average of 6.33 attempts per level and students who completed one or more of the optional levels did so in an average of 6.04 attempts per level. The students who completed all optional levels did so in an average of 7.24 attempts per level. See Table 3.

Levels	Attempts per Level	Minutes per Level
Some Mandatory	6.33	15.25
One or More Optional	6.04	18.01
All Optional *	7.24	18.05

Table 3: Mean Attempts and Minutes per Level - Spring 2018

* The All Optional group is included in the One or More Optional group

5.1.4 Participation Over Time. In terms of participation over time, logs revealed that the majority of the students (78.95% in Fall 2017 and 70.19% in Spring 2018) stopped playing after the first week. However, as mentioned earlier, participation in later weeks in the Fall 2017 was under-reported due to an unexpected consequence of the leaderboard - surveys indicated that at least some students who did not earn a high enough score to make it into the leaderboard continued to play the game.

The total percent of students who played in each week for the Spring semester is depicted in Figure 3. It is important to note that there was a different subset of participants in each week of the semester. Some of the later participants skipped a week or more before participating again. The leaderboard standings shifted in each of the weeks of the study in both semesters.

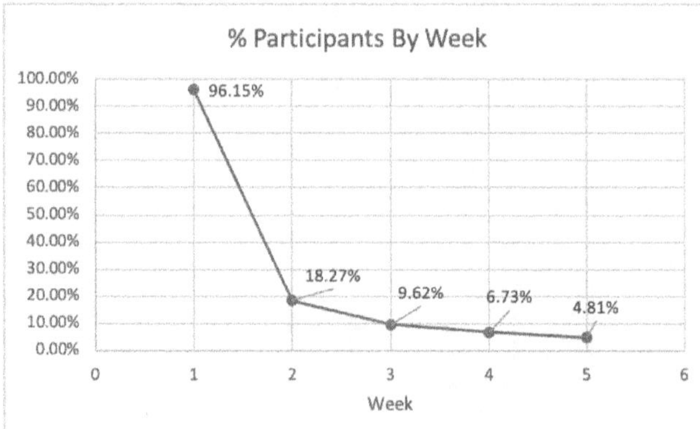

Figure 3: Participation over Time - Spring 2018

5.2 Student Perceptions

A survey regarding their perceptions of the Ruby Warrior game was completed by 57% (103) of students across both semesters of the study.

Students in each semesters were asked the extent to which they agreed with the following statements on a scale of 1 to 4 with 1 representing "strongly disagree" and 4 representing "strongly agree":

(1) *Ruby Warrior was a good addition to the course.*

(2) *I wished we could have played more games like Ruby Warrior in the course.*
(3) *Ruby Warrior increased my motivation to learn the topic(s).*
(4) *Ruby Warrior increased my motivation to complete more levels than what was required for course credit.*

The percent of the students who responded to each question and to each answer choice is depicted in Figure 4.

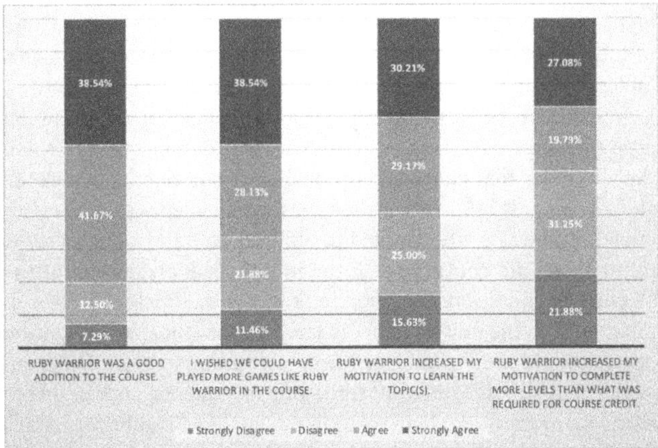

Figure 4: Quantitative Survey Results - Fall 2017/Spring 2018

Students in the second semester of the study were additionally asked the extent to which they agreed with the following statements on a scale of 1 to 4 with 1 representing "strongly disagree" and 4 representing "strongly agree". Three example comments from participants in the study are as follows:

(1) *Ruby Warrior increased my motivation to continue to play in subsequent weeks*
(2) *The leaderboard increased my motivation to complete more levels than was required for course credit.*
(3) *The leaderboard increased my motivation to continue to play Ruby Warrior in subsequent weeks.*

The percent of the students who responded to each question and to each answer choice is depicted in Figure 5.

We also asked several open ended questions. Over both semesters, 39.13% (27/69) of the responses to the question "What did you like about Ruby Warrior?" indicated that the game was "interesting" and included words such as "fun", "engaging", "interactive" "entertaining", "not boring" and so forth. For example, one such comment was that the game *"...was an interesting and entertaining way to apply my knowledge of Ruby, and assisted me in practicing coding in ruby."* (P3).

Of the responses, 17.4% (12/69) indicated that the game provided a challenge and helped students learn the material and included words and phrases such as "unlocking the next level", "challenge", "learn", "required you to think", or otherwise indicated that students felt the game left them feeling challenged and accomplished for having solved each level. For example, one such comment was as follows: *"I like games in general, figuring out the logic and finishing a level was rewarding"* (P33)

We also asked an open-ended question about what students did not like about the game. Across both semesters of the study, 45 students responded to this question. These responses primarily had to do with the lack of compelling graphics or student time constraints.

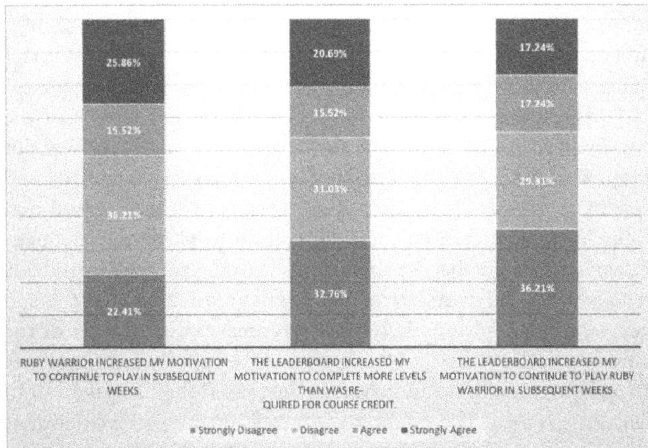

Figure 5: Quantitative Survey Results - Spring 2018

Of the responses, 20.0% (9/45) comments expressed that they did not like the simple text interface and wished that Ruby Warrior had graphics. An example comment from a participant in the study is as follows: *"I don't mind text-based games, but a graphical version would be better."* (P29).

Of the responses, 17.8% (8/45) of the comments mentioned that it was time-consuming and time constraints kept them from playing. An example comment from a participant in the study is as follows: *"I didn't like how we were expected to do Ruby Warrior outside of class for the most part. I have 4 other classes and I did not have the time to put into it in the subsequent weeks. Overall I think it will benefit a lot of students, but due to time constraints and not having many directions to go off of to help make it easier when you don't have the time I lost interest later on. It was very motivating at first and I tried to make the most of it."* (P23).

In the Spring 2018 semester, we added a question that asked why they stopped at the level that they did to see if we could uncover why some students were not motivated to continue playing. Again, time constraints were prominent in these comments. In fact, 70.3% (26/37) of students said that they stopped because they did not have the time to continue. One of these students wished they could go on and another planned to continue when time allowed. An example comments from participants in the study is as follows: *"I still plan to do epic mode on Spring break, and maybe intermediate some time later."* (P21).

Only 8.1% (3/37) of the responses explicitly indicated that they were simply not motivated or interested in playing. For example, one participant said they weren't *"motivated enough to continue"* (P11).

6 DISCUSSION

The study did successfully motivate 42.8% of the students to complete more than the required game levels, mainly in the first week of the study. Furthermore, the log data collected in the Spring 2018 semester of the study revealed that students who completed one or more optional levels spent an average of 64.79 additional minutes and an average of 40.31 additional attempts in the Ruby Warrior game than their peers who only completed the mandatory levels.

Furthermore, the survey results indicated that 43.69% of the survey participants agreed or strongly agreed that Ruby Warrior motivated them to complete more levels than were required and 46.55% of the survey participants agreed or strongly agreed that Ruby Warrior increased their motivation to play in subsequent weeks. As this number was consistent with the percent of students who actually did complete more than the required levels, the survey respondents were likely to be a representative sample of the students in the class. 55.34% of the survey participants agreed or strongly agreed that Ruby Warrior increased their motivation to learn the topics. The qualitative survey questions revealed that students were motivated to play and complete additional levels because the game was fun, interesting and/or challenging.

These results suggest that while some students may not have found a game to be motivating, there were students who expressed that a game will motivate them to engage in extra practice even if it is not required for course credit. Thus, our primary goal was accomplished. We were able to motivate a number of students to spend additional time practicing their Ruby programming skills than was required.

Additionally, on the quantitative survey question which asked students whether the leaderboard motivated them to complete more levels than were required, 36.21% of the students who completed this question responded that they agreed or strongly agreed with this statement. Therefore, the leaderboard, in that it allowed competitive students a way to measure their progress against the top scorers, was an additional motivating element for at least some students. Furthermore, some students mentioned the leaderboard in the responses to the qualitative question about what they liked about Ruby Warrior or what motivated them to continue past the required levels.

As such, the survey results indicate that the leaderboard did motivate at least some of the students to go beyond course credit requirements to develop technical skills (R2) in the Ruby programming language, which suggests that pairing a leaderboard with such exercises will motivate at least some students to practice programming skills beyond what is required for course credit.

7 LIMITATIONS

This study was wholly focused on student motivation and engagement as leading indicators of learning outcomes and did not attempt to measure gains in learning outcomes for those students who spent additional time in the game. Furthermore, the impact of the leaderboard was measured by survey results rather than a between-subjects comparison. Although the survey results indicate that the leaderboard had some impact on student motivation to complete more levels in Ruby Warrior, it may have had the opposite effect on students who are averse to competition. Also, as we inserted this one game into a semester-long course, we could not account for how much our results have to do with the novelty of a single gamified intervention. Finally, this study did not compare serious games with other methods of motivating students to engage in co-curricular activities.

8 CONCLUSIONS AND FUTURE WORK

With regard to our first research question, "will a serious game motivate students to go beyond the requirements for course credit to develop programming skills?" (R1), our results clearly show that in this instance, yes they did. Of the participants, 42.78% did go on to complete one or more of the optional levels and did spend additional time and attempts in the game. Furthermore, student survey results indicated that they were motivated to not only complete the optional levels, but also to learn the topic itself. These results are promising, but need further investigation to more deeply understand how and when such games can motivate students.

In terms of the participation over time, student engagement did drop off sharply after the first week, seeming to support the research that suggests that gamified approaches are more effective in the short-term [13] [15]. However, it was worth keeping the exercise open for students who wanted to dip back into the game as some participants did continue past the initial week even without the promise of course credit. Also, there were other factors to bear in mind, such as the finite number of levels or the students' perception of what more they could learn from continuing to play. Different games may provide different trade-offs to students, and be able to motivate more students to continue to engage in additional skills practice.

In future studies, it would be helpful to examine the impact of adding a small amount of course credit for completing at least one additional level in subsequent weeks. The addition of credit may be the hook needed to entice more students to re-engage in the game, and once they have done so, the challenge may well lead to an even higher percent of students who complete levels beyond what is required for course credit.

While we were only able to gather survey results on our research question "will a leaderboard motivate students to go beyond the requirements for course credit to develop programming skills?" (R2), we did discover that some survey respondents felt the leaderboard motivated them to go beyond the required levels and to a lesser extent, to learn the topic. In future studies it would be helpful to attempt to isolate the leaderboard effect, perhaps with a between subjects study design and to add a survey question to try to identify students who were competition-averse and, as such, less motivated to continue because of the leaderboard.

Nonetheless, these results do show that games have the potential to motivate computing students to spend more time on co-curricular learning activities, and we encourage other researchers to further pursue co-curricular games in computer science.

REFERENCES

[1] Ryan Bates. 2012. Ruby Warrior. https://github.com/ryanb/ruby-warrior. Accessed: 2017-09-03.

[2] Patrick Buckley and Elaine Doyle. 2016. Gamification and student motivation. *Interactive Learning Environments* 24, 6 (2016), 1162–1175. http://dblp.uni-trier.de/db/journals/ile/ile24.html#BuckleyD16

[3] Adrian Dabrowski, Markus Kammerstetter, Eduard Thamm, Edgar Weippl, and Wolfgang Kastner. 2015. Leveraging Competitive Gamification for Sustainable Fun and Profit in Security Education. In *2015 USENIX Summit on Gaming, Games, and Gamification in Security Education (3GSE 15)*. USENIX Association. http://blogs.usenix.org/conference/3gse15/summit-program/presentation/dabrowski

[4] Sebastian Deterding, Dan Dixon, Rilla Khaled, and Lennart Nacke. 2011. From Game Design Elements to Gamefulness: Defining "Gamification". In *Proceedings of the 15th International Academic MindTrek Conference: Envisioning Future Media Environments (MindTrek '11)*. ACM, 9–15. https://doi.org/10.1145/2181037.2181040

[5] Epsitec Games. 2017. CoLoBoT. http://www.ceebot.com/colobot/index-e.php. Accessed: 2017-10-03.

[6] M. B. Ibanez, A. Di-Serio, and C. Delgado-Kloos. 2014. Gamification for Engaging Computer Science Students in Learning Activities: A Case Study. *IEEE Transactions on Learning Technologies* 7, 3 (July 2014), 291–301. https://doi.org/10.1109/TLT.2014.2329293

[7] Karl M Kapp. 2012. *The gamification of learning and instruction: game-based methods and strategies for training and education.* John Wiley & Sons.

[8] Ferial Khaddage and Christoph Lattemann. 2015. Towards mobilizing mathematics via gamification and mobile applications. *Mobile Learning and STEM: Case Studies in Practice* (2015), 263.

[9] Richard N. Landers and Amy K. Landers. 2014. An Empirical Test of the Theory of Gamified Learning. *Simulation & Gaming* 45, 6 (2014), 769–785.

[10] Lieve Laporte and Bieke Zaman. 2016. Informing Content-driven Design of Computer Programming Games: a Problems Analysis and a Game Review. In *Proceedings of the 9th Nordic Conference on Human-Computer Interaction.* ACM, 61.

[11] Celine Latulipe, N Bruce Long, and Carlos E Seminario. 2015. Structuring flipped classes with lightweight teams and gamification. In *Proceedings of the 46th ACM Technical Symposium on Computer Science Education.* ACM, 392–397.

[12] Michael J Lee, Faezeh Bahmani, Irwin Kwan, Jilian LaFerte, Polina Charters, Amber Horvath, Fanny Luor, Jill Cao, Catherine Law, Michael Beswetherick, et al. 2014. Principles of a debugging-first puzzle game for computing education. In *Visual Languages and Human-Centric Computing (VL/HCC), 2014 IEEE Symposium on.* IEEE, 57–64.

[13] Jemma Looyestyn, Jocelyn Kernot, Kobie Boshoff, Jillian Ryan, Sarah Edney, and Carol Maher. 2017. Does gamification increase engagement with online programs? A systematic review. *PLOS ONE* 12, 3 (03 2017), 1–19. https://doi.org/10.1371/journal.pone.0173403

[14] Jane McGonigal. 2011. *Reality is Broken: Why Games Make Us Better and How They Can Change the World.* Jonathan Cape.

[15] Elisa D. Mekler, Florian BrÃijhlmann, Klaus Opwis, and Alexandre N. Tuch. 2013. Do points, levels and leaderboards harm intrinsic motivation?: an empirical analysis of common gamification elements.. In *Gamification*, Lennart E. Nacke, Kevin A. Harrigan, and Neil Randall (Eds.). ACM, 66–73. http://dblp.uni-trier.de/db/conf/gamification/gamification2013.html#MeklerBOT13

[16] Mathieu Muratet, Patrice Torguet, Jean-Pierre Jessel, and Fabienne Viallet. 2009. Towards a serious game to help students learn computer programming. *International Journal of Computer Games Technology* 2009 (2009), 3.

[17] Mathieu Muratet, Patrice Torguet, Fabienne Viallet, and Jean-Pierre Jessel. 2011. Experimental feedback on Prog&Play: a serious game for programming practice. In *Computer Graphics Forum*, Vol. 30. Wiley Online Library, 61–73.

[18] Robocode. 2017. Robocode. http://robocode.sourceforge.net. Accessed: 2017-10-03.

[19] John L Sherry, Kristen Lucas, Bradley S Greenberg, and Ken Lachlan. 2006. Video game uses and gratifications as predictors of use and game preference. *Playing video games: Motives, responses, and consequences* 24, 1 (2006), 213–224.

[20] Adilson Vahldick, António José Mendes, and Maria José Marcelino. 2014. A review of games designed to improve introductory computer programming competencies. In *Frontiers in Education Conference (FIE), 2014 IEEE.* IEEE, 1–7.

Active Learning with LEGO for Software Requirements

Stan Kurkovsky
Central Connecticut State University
New Britain, CT
kurkovsky@ccsu.edu

Stephanie Ludi
University of North Texas
Denton, TX
stephanie.ludi@unt.edu

Linda Clark
Central Connecticut State University
New Britain, CT
lclark@ccsu.edu

ABSTRACT

Case studies are one of the best active learning approaches for teaching software engineering in general and requirements engineering in particular. They offer an effective approach to understanding a system or a phenomenon that are too large or too difficult to represent in a lab setting. As a tangible manipulative, LEGO works well to support designing hands-on case studies that mix studying software engineering concepts with the elements of team building and playful creativity. In our project, we study the role that LEGO has in engaging students in software engineering through a set of activities that leverage the case study and play aspects. This paper presents our design approach for requirements engineering activities, as well as current results from classroom testing with a focus on student engagement with the subject matter.

CCS CONCEPTS

• **Social and professional topics** → **Software engineering education**; • **Software and its engineering** → *Requirements analysis*;

KEYWORDS

Software requirements, software engineering, active learning, LEGO

ACM Reference Format:
Stan Kurkovsky, Stephanie Ludi, and Linda Clark. 2019. Active Learning with LEGO for Software Requirements. In *Proceedings of the 50th ACM Technical Symposium on Computer Science Education (SIGCSE '19), February 27-March 2, 2019, Minneapolis, MN, USA.* ACM, New York, NY, USA, 7 pages. https://doi.org/10.1145/3287324.3287444

1 INTRODUCTION

Software engineering (SE) is often called a 'wicked problem' because the resulting software is full of complex interdependencies due to incomplete, contradictory, and volatile requirements [6]. Students often find it difficult to work on problems that do not have a single well-defined solution, where problem statements are ambiguous and vague, or when classroom examples have to be applied to different scenarios or domains [15]. For these reasons, it is sensible to rely less on lecture and focus more on active learning experiences mimicking what students may encounter in "real-world" SE.

As a discipline within SE, requirements engineering (RE) may be a particularly wicked problem [4, 15, 24, 27]. Wicked problems cannot be solved by applying a single standard approach or a single set of common procedures from a textbook. In order to learn how to solve RE problems, students need hands-on experience with practical scenarios, which could come from participating in actual software projects, simulations, role-playing, case studies, or other experiential learning activities [8, 13]. These activities provide a safe environment for students to learn from their own failures [28]. When it comes to learning activities in RE, it is especially important to focus on team-based exercises, which come closest to mimicking RE processes in real-word projects. Most importantly, building such experiences in a team setting creates an environment well-suited for open-ended problems offering a wide variety of possible scenarios and solutions informed by a diverse range of individual experiences, opinions, and emotions [24].

Case studies are one of the best active learning tools for teaching SE, offering an effective approach to understanding a system or a phenomenon too large or too difficult to represent in a lab setting. Whether case studies are text-based or hands-on, they help answer detailed *how* and *why* questions, which offers a deeper insight into chains of cause and effect concerning the system's behavior [25].

As a tangible manipulative, LEGO works well to support designing hands-on case studies that mix learning SE concepts with the elements of team building and playful creativity. While LEGO is associated with constructing concrete structures such as buildings, cars or even robots, the dynamic nature of LEGO also allows it to represent more abstract concepts [9]. For example, LEGO pieces in isolation or when assembled into small builds can represent lines of code, subsystems or parts of a software development process [14].

Play in a classroom environment offers many important features to aid in the learning process. Play provides a safe environment where failure is acceptable because "it's just a game." Play is voluntary and nobody is forced or coerced to participate. Play is fun and it is something that people want to do. Play is improvisational and provides an avenue to express creativity and imagination, which is especially important in design-centric computer science courses.

In our project, we study LEGO's role in engaging SE students through a set of activities that leverage the described case study and play aspects. Activity and resource development is part of this project[1], whereby faculty teaching SE or related courses can use the activities in isolation or as a set to engage students in the material. SE concepts represented include architectural design, change management, dependability, and object-oriented interfaces. This work describes our design approach for RE activities, as well as current results from classroom testing with a focus on student engagement with the subject matter.

ACM ISBN 978-1-4503-5890-3/19/02...$15.00
https://doi.org/10.1145/3287324.3287444

[1]http://web.ccsu.edu/lego-se/

2 REQUIREMENTS ENGINEERING IN THE CLASSROOM

The importance of RE in software engineering practice, research, and education has long been recognized [16, 19, 20]. However, according to a recent survey of software RE education literature covering 79 papers published prior to 2015 [20], most students are not only unaware of modern RE practices, but are also disinterested in studying them [5, 12, 26]. This could be due to the prevailing student interest towards technical aspects of SE, as opposed to its social dimension exemplified in the RE discipline. This trend is extremely worrisome because as a discipline, RE encompasses understanding the dependencies among the stakeholders, processes, and systems in order to gather, analyze, prioritize, document, review, and manage the requirements for a software system throughout its complete lifecycle [29].

RE is a highly creative process. Whether considering requirements for an existing, new, or a future system, RE process requires a significant degree of insight, experience, and creativity [17]. Creativity can be defined as "the interplay between ability and process by which an individual or group produces an outcome or product that is both novel and useful as defined within some social context".

Many SE novices, most students included, do not take RE seriously enough because it does not immediately result in program code [7, 12]. A traditional approach to computing education essentially encourages this kind of neglectful approach to software requirements. Computer science and SE students begin by acquiring a lot of technical knowledge, which almost always starts with learning how to program. Even in the assignments given in later courses, students are often rewarded mostly for the correctness of implementation. In fact, RE may seem entirely unnecessary because many assignments and projects given to students may already include all requirements spelled out for them. Consequently, many students perceive RE activities as not particularly important because they are almost always less technical than other SE activities such as design, implementation, and testing. Consequently, the importance of software requirements and the RE process may not start to emerge until students begin facing complex problems.

We believe that RE should be studied in a constructive setting that promotes practical application of theoretical knowledge. An active learning environment that prominently features group work with plenty of peer learning opportunities may be a suitable setting to achieve that goal. Ideally, we would like students to test the textbook ideas in a hands-on setting against the backdrop of their practical experiences accumulated thus far. In this approach, students will be able to build new mental models and develop new concepts and attitudes based on their previous knowledge and experience. This approach underscores the fact that although knowledge construction is personal in nature, knowledge sharing is inherently a collaborative and social endeavor, which is achieved through reflection on decisions and actions in order to internalize the newly acquired knowledge [3]. In-class group activities based on the preceding lecture material is a key mechanism to solidify the corresponding course material through peer learning. Ensuing discussions or role-playing can be helpful for students to apply new material in a dynamic way, to challenge themselves and peers, and provide constructive criticism to each other. Well-designed group exercises can allow all students to participate in a safe and non-intimidating way by relating the main topic of the exercise to a well-known or an easy to understand system or context.

Current research indicates that using games in education improves student engagement, helps reinforce conceptual elements through their practical application, leading to a better retention of the course material. Educational games help promote friendly competition, as well as student emotional engagement with the course content [29]. Emotions generated by playing an interesting game can help students create conceptual models providing internalized meaning to the new concepts [2]. Additionally, people tend to be engaged by the novelty of experiences, making them likely to retain information associated with a delivery method that breaks the monotony of a traditional lecture.

A number of reports on using games to teach SE indicate that successful strategies include using a variety of activities that combine practice of new concepts with recall of previous material. Game-based activities are especially well-suited for reinforcing knowledge learned earlier and when it is combined with other instructional approaches [28]. Team-based setting is optimal because it supports collaboration, encourages everyone's participation, reduces the risk of embarrassment, and provides plenty of opportunities for peer learning [2, 12, 28]. Any such activity must culminate in an instructor-led debrief, during which students are typically asked to comment on the ways that the activity reinforces the concept, reflect on their own experiences, and hear the others' thoughts [26, 28]. Open-ended questions help students strengthen the connections between the activity and the course material, ensuring a deeper understanding and better retention of the material [18].

According to several recent surveys describing various efforts to use games and other active learning exercises for SE education and training [21, 28], RE appears to be the most neglected area with the smallest number of documented experience reports. At the same time, it is clear that graduates entering the software industry must possess a strong set of both technical and soft skills, while RE exemplifies an intersection of these skill sets. Many researchers and practitioners argue that strengthening the skills of SE professionals in the area of RE is a key success factor in most SE projects [10, 20].

SE educators and practitioners must not forget that SE's social dimension is integral to the discipline, but is frequently overshadowed by technical aspects of practice [1, 4, 27]. Of all areas of knowledge and practice comprising SE, RE is perhaps one area that impacts this social dimension the most. Although interpersonal communication and teamwork are key enabling factors in all software process activities, they usually involve interactions on technical topics with like-minded technically-inclined individuals. RE, however, calls for an effective communication with a broad range of people who have different backgrounds and goals and who may not always have a clear idea about their wants and needs. RE addresses social dimension issues by emphasizing two aspects of communication: documenting and understanding. On the one hand, RE focuses on documenting the customer needs and desires, and expressing them in the form understandable by software engineers. This implies that customers know what they want, and that information can be expressed using some mutually acceptable formalisms. On the other hand, any documentation produced as a result of RE activities aims to support and improve software engineers' understanding of the customers' needs. Furthermore, RE activities should also aim to help customers crystallize their understanding of their own needs. The process that leads to developing this mutual understanding is one of the main reasons why social dimension of RE is so important. Modern software processes, such as agile methodology, de-emphasize documentation in favor of close involvement of and frequent interactions with the customer. This focus on understanding underscores the need for instilling social competencies into the modern software professionals' skill set.

3 REQUIREMENTS ENGINEERING AND LEGO

This paper focuses on RE, whose activities transcend the process model used (e.g. waterfall, agile), and include requirements elicitation, analysis, documentation, and validation. Conceptually, RE activities can be challenging for students as many introductory SE courses provide students with the project requirements. Thus, students can feel as if the activities are partially completed for them. The other issue that can arise is that activities involving interaction with users/customers makes some students uncomfortable as such interaction is so different from their typical project work.

This section discusses RE modules, as well as observations in conducting the corresponding LEGO-based activities in class. While this set of modules focuses on RE, each offers a different perspective, as well as focus on specific concepts within requirements. An instructor would not use them all at once, but instead weave them into appropriate parts of the course, especially if agile or incremental process models are used as part of the course.

Each module is outlined in a consistent manner and includes an overview, learning outcomes, materials & supplies, an outline for conducting the activity, as well as instructor notes/observations.

3.1 Module 1: Requirements Elicitation and System Refactoring in an Agile Environment

This module offers a concise experience on the importance of requirements elicitation via stakeholder interaction, while illustrating the role of reflection and refactoring in agile software process.[2] In this module, students work on small teams to build a system prototype, manifesting as a house. The stakeholder is the instructor, who has a set of requirements in mind that the house should possess. Students are instructed to devise effective questions for the stakeholder, whereby the responses are used to prototype the system based on the derived features. The activity can be conducted as 2 or 3 sprints. At the end of each sprint, each team presents their system to the class and the stakeholder offers feedback on requirements coverage. At the beginning of the second and third sprint, the stakeholder changes a requirement that would require refactoring of the prototype.

The learning objectives associated with Module 1 are:

- Devise a set of appropriate elicitation questions to gather requirements from a stakeholder;
- Generate a set of requirements based on stakeholder interaction;
- Describe the importance of reflecting on team effectiveness and the role of refactoring in an agile environment;
- Validate a set of requirements for completeness and accuracy.

The module is designed for a class size of 20 and upwards of 70, where the students work in teams of 5. Some flexibility in terms of duration also is designed into the module, where the minimum time is 50 minutes (2 sprints) to a maximum 70 minutes for 3 sprints.

Each team has its own LEGO kit, either based on the LEGO Serious Play kit or a compendium of classic LEGO bricks, windows, doors, trees/flowers, and some minifigures. The teams can work around their respective tables, where each team should have a LEGO baseplate to build their prototype. Additionally, sticky notes and pens or access to a whiteboard is useful for sharing the requirements that their prototype represents.

To help scope the prototype, the following initial requirements are provided to the instructor: house shall have 3 rooms, where each room has a window and a doorway; house shall be single story, with a single (front) door; doors and doorways shall be sized to fit a minifigure; a single outer wall shall be a solid color; the house shall have landscaping. Note: this is intentionally vague as these parts may not be consistent across kits.

The module is conducted in 2 sprints (50 minutes) or 3 sprints (70 minutes). The 2-sprint module is presented here, the 3rd sprint is a repetition of sprint 2 with additional reflection. The first sprint focuses on requirements elicitation and delivering an initial prototype. In the 30-minute sprint, students prototype a system (a house). Students, working in small teams, are instructed to devise effective questions for the stakeholder in the simulation of elicitation, where the responses are used to prototype the system based on the derived features. Each team must decide what 3-4 questions will be the most effective to gather requirements. Teams write their questions on post-its or on their whiteboard. The team raises their hands when they need to interact with the stakeholder. The stakeholder needs to respond to the question as it was written, i.e. if a team wrote a question as a yes/no question then the response needs to be yes/no.

The student teams then build their prototype based on the stakeholder responses. The teams document the requirements they elicited on sticky notes. At the end of the sprint, each team briefly explains their prototype in terms of what requirements it represents. Each team places their sticky notes on the board for everyone in the class to view. Next, the stakeholder shares the initial requirements that they wanted (setting aside these sticky notes or circling them to call them out), and asks teams to reflect on how effective their questions were at eliciting these requirements.

During Sprint 2, the teams focus on refactoring based on a new requirement given by the stakeholder. Suggested requirements are: a loft needs to be added to the house; the solid color wall needs to be striped with 2 alternating colors; the roof needs a skylight.

For the 20-minute sprint, the teams have time to refactor their system to meet the new requirement. They also need to meet any prior requirements that were missed. At the end of the sprint, each team briefly explains their prototype in terms of what feature it represents and how the prototype was refactored to meet the revised requirements. Also, how did the team work to refactor the prototype efficiently? What could have been done to be more efficient? The team and stakeholder do a final check of the requirements

[2] http://web.ccsu.edu/lego-se/modules/RequirementsValidation.html

for coverage and accuracy. Students discuss any ambiguities or accuracy issues.

If a third sprint is conducted, students are able to reflect further on how their refactoring strategies evolved, as well as any requirements coverage/accuracy issues. The design choice to designate an optional third sprint is to provide flexibility since some classes may meet for 50 minutes while others may meet for 80 minutes.

The instructor notes provide some tips for the instructor, based on initial module testing and general observations by the authors:

- In a large class, keeping track of who asked what questions or what the instructor responded is required. The instructor can do so via a notepad, their tablet, or some other mechanism.
- In a class that meets for 50-minutes, time management is particularly needed though having a mechanism such as a timer or clock will help with keeping track of the time regardless of the class meeting duration.

3.2 Module 2: Requirements Elicitation and Analysis

In this module, students work as a team to prototype a system competing against a well-known social media system (e.g. Facebook, Twitter, Instagram, SoundCloud) or a well-defined hardware system (e.g. Roomba vacuum, Nest learning thermostat, or Amazon Echo).[3] Students brainstorm and identify a set of features that will implement the core functionality and help the new system distinguish itself from the competition.

The learning objectives of this module include:

- Synthesize a core set of system requirements;
- Generalize a set of requirements by identifying related and overlapping requirements;
- Distinguish between functional, non-functional, and domain requirements;
- Validate requirements for completeness and consistency.

The prerequisites of this module include basic familiarity with software requirements, as well as prior exposure to the principles of LEGO Serious Play [11, 14]. This activity is about 60 minutes long and works well for a single team of up to 25 participants. It has been offered successfully with team sizes ranging from 5 to 25.

Materials and supplies necessary to run this activity include a LEGO set for each student, such as a LEGO Serious Play 'exploration bag' or any cheap ($5) LEGO Classic, LEGO City, LEGO Friends, or a similar set. Alternatively, all students can share one large LEGO set with a diverse combination of bricks. A set of minifigures with accessories may also be useful. Some sticky notes and markers will also be needed. Each student requires a separate small building space with one additional table to place all models.

The module consists of two parts: requirements elicitation (using LEGO Serious Play for ideation) and analysis (not using LEGO).

Requirements elicitation begins with explaining the problem to the students: we are building a competitor to a well-known social media system or a well-defined hardware system. We need to brainstorm and come up with some features that will implement the core functionality and help us distinguish ourselves from the competition. It is important to emphasize the word 'features,' not requirements or functionality. It is important to use a well-known system as a reference, so that students would have enough general knowledge about it while providing enough room for interpretation and extension. The instructor asks an open-ended question: what features would you envision in the system? In response to that, each student builds a LEGO model representing a single feature of the system. Then, following the principles of LEGO Serious Play, students take turns to briefly explain the ideas behind the LEGO models they built and the system features they represent. Everyone takes turns to speak keeping the stories related to their LEGO models. The learning point is that many students may come up with similar ideas, but everyone has a different perspective. It is important to consider everyone's input to obtain a holistic unbiased picture. In requirements elicitation, all stakeholders have an opportunity to contribute their input to the list of requirements. Right after presenting their features of the system, each student writes down a few words on a sticky note describing their main idea. All sticky notes are collected and placed on the board where everyone can see them. This allows the students to make their ideas more concrete and formulate them in a concise form. This ideation process may be repeated, because a single round may not be sufficient to generate all important ideas. Only after seeing the results of one round on the board, students may start to come up with really interesting features.

Once the ideas for the proposed system features are in place, the elicited requirements can be analyzed. The instructor can ask the class to suggest some logical groupings of the requirements. It is possible that some requirements may be similar or overlapping, while clusters of requirements could help us identify and focus on the core functionality of the system. We should also reject those requirements that don't make sense. A learning point here is that it takes a collective effort to see the 'big picture' in order to identify what is important/relevant and what is not. At this point, the requirements can be divided into three categories: functional, non-functional, and domain requirements. Following that, the requirements can be checked for completeness. The instructor could prompt students with these questions: what are the most important requirements, did we miss anything important, are there any assumptions that must be identified as separate requirements? The resulting set of requirements should also be checked for consistency: are there any ambiguities or contradictions?

Running the activities of this module with a group of students, it is important to keep in mind a few practical points:

- It's OK to propose similar requirements during the first phase. In fact, it is very helpful to have such similar/duplicating requirements to make the learning points stronger.
- It is very important to keep a close eye on the clock during the second part of the exercise to ensure that there's enough time for every part of this activity. As with all such activities, the key to achieving the learning points is in the discussions, all of which are concentrated in the second part.

3.3 Discussion

Two of the three co-authors work at two different institutions. One of the authors is at Central Connecticut State University, a medium-sized public university with classes consisting of 25-30 students.

[3] http://web.ccsu.edu/lego-se/modules/RequirementsElicitation.html

Another co-author works at University of North Texas, a large public university with class sizes ranging between 45-70 students.

Although both learning modules described here are conducted in a team setting, the purpose is to engage each student with the material and to reflect on the concepts/process. As such, the stopping points where teams are asked to reflect are critical. However, it is important to note that each student on the team must contribute to the activity, reflect of what was learned, and share with the class as a whole. Without this, some students may not be engaged and feel that the activity is a diversion. To mitigate this risk, the use of the appropriate terms as they are being introduced/used in class helps solidify that connection.

These modules can be scaled up/down to fit various class sizes. For one of the authors, SE class sizes are typically between 45 and 67 students. As such, conducting modules in teams is helpful in managing resources and time. Even so, piloting module 1 has provided the author with some observations to help in devising tips for replication elsewhere with similar class sizes, as well as feedback for future development. For example, module 1 has been run successfully with larger class sizes, though the challenge is having enough time to facilitate discussion with large numbers of teams (8 or more). Module 2 has been successfully run in various configurations: one large team of up to 20 students, or two or more smaller teams of 8-10 students working in parallel. For larger classes, a TA can serve as an additional. Teams of 4-5 students works well for large classes as it allows each person to participate, while balancing the time needed by the instructor to interact with the teams.

4 EVALUATION

This study took place at a regional master's public institution located in the Northeastern US. During the Fall 2017 semester, participating students enrolled in a senior SE course required for all undergraduate computer science students. All 21 of the students enrolled in the course consented to participate in the study.

4.1 Materials

The Motivated Strategies for Learning Questionnaire (MSLQ) [22] is a 44-items questionnaire with a 5-point Likert scale response ranging from "strongly disagree" to "strongly agree." The MSLQ measures student motivational orientation, cognitive engagement, and self-regulation in the classroom. The cognitive variables and self-regulation are hallmarks of students who choose to be more cognitively engaged [22]. The MSLQ has five subscales: test anxiety, self-regulation, self-efficacy, cognitive strategy use, and intrinsic value. The MSLQ lends itself to subscale comparisons or global composite scores. Empirical validation of the subscales includes significant relationships with prior academic performance [22] and later academic performance [23]. Open-ended questions listed in the Appendix included constructs relevant to the process of building the model, abstract thinking, and the use of LEGO models as representations of abstract ideas.

4.2 Procedures

During the second week of class, the course instructor invited the researcher to meet with the students during a class period. Students were informed of the study and consent to participate was obtained.

Table 1: Descriptive Statistics for the Pre-Module Continuous Variables

	Control M (SD)	LEGO M (SD)	Total M (SD)
Self-Efficacy	3.66 (.72)	3.65 (.62)	3.66 (.65)
Intrinsic Value	4.36 (.37)	4.27 (.40)	4.31 (.38)
Cognitive Strategy Use	3.55 (.27)	3.53 (.43)	3.54 (.35)
Self-Regulation	3.37 (.32)	3.34 (.37)	3.36 (.34)
Test Anxiety	2.77 (1.05)	2.73 (1.08)	2.75 (1.04)
GPA	3.13 (.38)	3.13 (.42)	3.13 (.39)

Table 2: Descriptive Statistics for Post-Module MSLQ Scores

	Control M (SD)	LEGO M (SD)	Total M (SD)
Self-Efficacy	3.47 (.60)	3.80 (.61)	3.64 (.61)
Intrinsic Value	3.84 (.43)	4.22 (.42)	4.04 (.46)
Cognitive Strategy Use	3.56 (.36)	3.60 (.47)	3.58 (.41)
Self-Regulation	3.31 (.68)	3.42 (.42)	3.37 (.55)
Test Anxiety	3.23 (.85)	2.82 (1.11)	3.02 (.99)
Total Score	3.52 (.34)	3.66 (.33)	3.62 (.34)

During this class, a paper and pencil version of the MSLQ was administered.

Students were matched on the MSLQ subscale scores, MSLQ overall score, and cumulative grade point averages. One student from each pair was randomly assigned to one of two groups, LEGO or control. With uneven numbers, the remaining student was assigned to the LEGO group. During the module, the two groups met in two separate rooms. One room included the LEGO group and the primary course instructor; the control group met in a separate room with a second instructor. Each instructor followed identical module scripts, with the exception of working with LEGO versus working through the example on the whiteboard.

The following class meeting, the LEGO group met with the researcher and responded to a series of open ended questions in a focus group format. At the same time, the control group had a debrief with the control group instructor.

Four weeks following the module, a paper and pencil mid-term exam was administered to the entire class. Two items embedded in the exam measured the ability of students to identify system requirements, resolve ambiguities, and express them in the form of user stories. The mid-term items were blindly graded by the course instructor using a scale of 0 to 10, with 10 being a perfect score.

At the end of the semester, a second paper and pencil administration of the MSLQ was given to both groups by the researcher.

4.3 Results

4.3.1 Quantitative Data. Of the 21 students, 3 were female and 18 were male. The control group of 10 students included one female, and the LEGO group 2 females. Because the groups were matched on the MSLQ and GPA values, the two groups did not differ significantly on any of these measures, as shown in Table 1.

Both groups share the same trend among the MSLQ subscales on the initial administration, for all subscales. Overall intrinsic value is the highest construct (M=4.31, SD=.38), followed by self-efficacy (M=3.66, SD=.65). Cognitive strategy use (M=3.54, SD=.35) and self-regulation (M=3.36, SD=.34) were rated lower, however means for both subscales fell into the "agree" Likert category. The lowest subscale was test-anxiety (M=2.75, SD=1.04), both groups tending not to rate themselves as anxious.

These similarities were maintained after the intervention, yielding non-significant differences both between the pre- and post intervention, as well as between the two groups using bootstrapped confidence intervals and a significance level of .05 (Table 2). Specifically, intrinsic value for the LEGO group (M=4.22, SD=42) and control group (M=3.84, SD=.43) were again the highest values. The non-significant differences for LEGO group members for self-efficacy (M=3.80, SD=.61), cognitive strategy use (M=3.60, SD=.47), and self-regulation (M=3.42, SD=.42) were similar to control group means (M=3.47, SD=.60), (M=3.56, SD=.36), and (M=3.31, SD=.68) respectively. While overall test anxiety rose slightly after the intervention (M=3.02, SD=.99), LEGO group mean scores of (M=2.82, SD=1.11) were similar to control scores of M=3.23, SD=.85.

As a measure of academic performance, the two mid-term items reflected the module content. Both groups of students exhibited similar non-statistically significant strong performances on these items, with means above 9.0 for both groups on both items, no student receiving less than a score of 7 on either item.

4.3.2 *Qualitative Data.* Of more interest were the open-ended comments from participants in the LEGO group. Overall, the students expressed positive comments about the activity. Students liked the interpersonal interaction, *"discussing in small group, learn from each other, better than working individually."* While this the activity was challenging, it was also rewarding, *"trying to represent that idea with LEGO was initially confusing but doing so helped me visualize and further develop that idea."* Several reported the impact that working with LEGO had the problem-solving process. *"LEGO did help to an extent to see the software development process from another perspective besides UML modeling or staring at a terminal."* One student went so far to describe the thought process used while engaging in the activity: *"By thinking about how to build the model to properly show my feature, I thought of which features of the model would contradict my feature and cause issues with the model, and then I was able to abstractly consider why a model would fail from those features in order to apply it to the context of the social media site, which helped me to explain what I meant."*

Finally, the students reported that using LEGO moved their thinking beyond concrete conceptualizations to abstract. This higher-order thinking is a pedagogical challenge for most faculty, but from the student comments, LEGO may be tapping into this cognitive function *"by having LEGO to describe my example I had to go abstract and think about what is the fundamental idea behind the design pattern rather than thinking about just the example."*

Overall themes from the qualitative remarks touch on important pedagogical constructs in engaging post-secondary students in STEM education, active learning, problem solving, and abstract thinking. Within the student development process, moving students to interactive classroom activities can be met with resistance. The use of LEGO created an environment in which students interacted with peers and the instructor. The students reported an increased ability to problem solve, a key component particularly within STEM applied skills. These results are consistent with creating a learner-centered environment to maximize instruction of undergraduate STEM majors.

4.3.3 *Threats to Validity.* While the administration of the module is a pilot, a one-time experience with LEGO may not be sufficient to elicit changes in cognitive motivation as measured by the MSLQ. Additionally, the student comments along with the literature related to play suggest that abstract thinking as opposed to motivation may be a more appropriate measure of the impact of LEGO on cognitive function. A final consideration for the validity of the results reflects the study design. Because the two groups were from the same class, the students may have discussed the experience between groups, hence diluting the uniqueness of the groups. These factors likely contributed to the lack of significant findings within the quantitative results. It may be possible that working with LEGO does not impact motivation, but instead, the ability to engage in abstract thinking. Hence, along with the limitations of the study design, the construct of interest may have been incorrectly identified.

5 SUMMARY

This paper outlined our ongoing work to develop active learning modules that reinforce a broad range of SE concepts. RE is an integral component of the SE discipline, which, unfortunately, often gets overlooked by many students, educators, and practitioners. Here, we detailed two active learning modules focusing on RE. Both of these modules have been tested a number of times with different groups of students and at different institutions. Our evaluation of the impact on student learning shows that students are enthusiastic about using LEGO-based learning modules in the classroom, while their feedback indicates a number of tangible benefits helping students achieve their learning goals.

We aim to expand the assessment to both institutions in order to study the effectiveness of the activities on different groups of students, including diverse student samples in large classroom settings (60+ students per section). At the University of North Texas, the SE course will soon become a 3rd-year course; the impact on student learning under the new course constraints will also be of interest. Our goal is to provide activities that can be used in different instructional contexts, so the evaluation will provide evidence to support the aim.

As assessment of these modules continues, the researchers are currently investigating the impact of the LEGO modules on abstract thinking. In order to ensure validity of the intervention, the LEGO activates will occur in two separate classes and include three modules over the course of an academic semester. It is anticipated these adjustments in the assessment methods will enhance the validity of the interventions and result in gaining more knowledge about the cognitive changes brought about by the LEGO play.

ACKNOWLEDGMENTS

This work is supported in part by the National Science Foundation IUSE program awards 1611905 and 1709244.

REFERENCES

[1] B. Al-Ani and N. Yusop. 2004. Role-playing, group work and other ambitious teaching methods in a large requirements engineering course. In *Proceedings. 11th IEEE International Conference and Workshop on the Engineering of Computer-Based Systems, 2004.* 299–306.
[2] J. Beatty and M. Alexander. 2008. Games-Based Requirements Engineering Training: An Initial Experience Report. In *2008 16th IEEE International Requirements Engineering Conference.* 211–216.
[3] Mordechai Ben-Ari. 1998. Constructivism in Computer Science Education. *SIGCSE Bull.* 30, 1 (March 1998), 257–261.
[4] J. A. Bubenko. 1995. Challenges in requirements engineering. In *Requirements Engineering, 1995., Proceedings of the Second IEEE International Symposium on.* 160–162.
[5] David Callele and Dwight Makaroff. 2006. Teaching Requirements Engineering to an Unsuspecting Audience. *SIGCSE Bull.* 38, 1 (March 2006), 433–437.
[6] Peter DeGrace and Leslie Hulet Stahl. 1990. *Wicked Problems, Righteous Solutions.* Yourdon Press, Upper Saddle River, NJ, USA.
[7] J. M. Fernandes, R. J. Machado, and S. B. Seidman. 2009. A Requirements Engineering and Management Training Course for Software Development Professionals. In *2009 22nd Conference on Software Engineering Education and Training.* 20–25.
[8] K. Garg and V. Varma. 2007. A Study of the Effectiveness of Case Study Approach in Software Engineering Education. In *20th Conference on Software Engineering Education Training (CSEET'07).* 309–316.
[9] David Gauntlett. 2014. The LEGO System as a tool for thinking, creativity, and changing the world. In *LEGO Studies: Examining the Building Blocks of a Transmedial Phenomenon*, Mark Wolf (Ed.). Routledge, New York.
[10] Hubert F. Hofmann and Franz Lehner. 2001. Requirements Engineering As a Success Factor in Software Projects. *IEEE Softw.* 18, 4 (July 2001), 58–66.
[11] Alison James. 2013. Lego Serious Play: a three-dimensional approach to learning development. *Journal of Learning Development in Higher Education* 9, 6 (2013).
[12] E. Knauss, K. Schneider, and K. Stapel. 2008. A Game for Taking Requirements Engineering More Seriously. In *2008 Third International Workshop on Multimedia and Enjoyable Requirements Engineering - Beyond Mere Descriptions and with More Fun and Games.* 22–26.
[13] D.A. Kolb. 1984. *Experiential Learning: Experience as the Source of Learning and Development.* Prentice-Hall.
[14] Stan Kurkovsky. 2015. Teaching Software Engineering with LEGO Serious Play. In *Proceedings of the 2015 ACM Conference on Innovation and Technology in Computer Science Education (ITiCSE '15).* ACM, New York, NY, USA, 213–218.
[15] Connolly Thomas M., Stansfield Mark, and Hainey Thomas. 2007. An application of games-based learning within software engineering. *British Journal of Educational Technology* 38, 3 (2007), 416–428.
[16] C. J. Neill and P. A. Laplante. 2003. Requirements engineering: the state of the practice. *IEEE Software* 20, 6 (Nov 2003), 40–45.
[17] Lemai Nguyen and Graeme Shanks. 2009. A Framework for Understanding Creativity in Requirements Engineering. *Inf. Softw. Technol.* 51, 3 (March 2009), 655–662.
[18] Scott Nicholson. 2015. *A RECIPE for Meaningful Gamification.* Springer International Publishing, Cham, 1–20.
[19] Bashar Nuseibeh and Steve Easterbrook. 2000. Requirements Engineering: A Roadmap. In *Proceedings of the Conference on The Future of Software Engineering (ICSE '00).* ACM, New York, NY, USA, 35–46.
[20] Sofia Ouhbi, Ali Idri, José Luis Fernández-Alemán, and Ambrosio Toval. 2015. Requirements Engineering Education: A Systematic Mapping Study. *Requir. Eng.* 20, 2 (June 2015), 119–138.
[21] Oscar Pedreira, FÃllix GarcÃŋa, Nieves Brisaboa, and Mario Piattini. 2015. Gamification in software engineering âĂŞ A systematic mapping. *Information and Software Technology* 57 (2015), 157 – 168.
[22] Paul R. Pintrich and Elisabeth V. De Groot. 1990. Motivational and self-regulated learning components of classroom academic performance. *Journal of Educational Psychology* (1990), 33–40.
[23] Paul R. Pintrich, David A. F. Smith, Teresa Garcia, and Wilbert J. Mckeachie. 1993. Reliability and Predictive Validity of the Motivated Strategies for Learning Questionnaire (Mslq). *Educational and Psychological Measurement* 53, 3 (1993), 801–813.
[24] Gil Regev, Donald C. Gause, and Alain Wegmann. 2009. Experiential learning approach for requirements engineering education. *Requirements Engineering* 14, 4 (20 Jun 2009), 269.
[25] Per Runeson, Martin Host, Austen Rainer, and Bjorn Regnell. 2012. *Case Study Research in Software Engineering: Guidelines and Examples* (1st ed.). Wiley Publishing.
[26] R. Smith and O. Gotel. 2008. Gameplay to Introduce and Reinforce Requirements Engineering Practices. In *2008 16th IEEE International Requirements Engineering Conference.* 95–104.
[27] Hans van Vliet. 2006. Reflections on Software Engineering Education. In *Software Engineering Education in the Modern Age*, Paola Inverardi and Mehdi Jazayeri (Eds.). Springer Berlin Heidelberg, Berlin, Heidelberg, 1–10.
[28] C. G. von Wangenheim and F. Shull. 2009. To Game or Not to Game? *IEEE Software* 26, 2 (March 2009), 92–94.
[29] D. Zowghi and S. Paryani. 2003. Teaching requirements engineering through role playing: lessons learnt. In *Proceedings. 11th IEEE International Requirements Engineering Conference, 2003.* 233–241.

A APPENDIX: OPEN-ENDED QUESTIONS

Question 1: Comment about your thoughts when you were actually building your LEGO model. For example, were you thinking about how to represent the actual feature, the fit of the feature into the system, the function of the feature?

Question 2: You had to build a LEGO model representing a software feature you'd like to propose. Did LEGO help you crystallize your idea? If so, how? If not, why do you think it didn't help?

Question 3: Before you heard what your classmates said about their LEGO models, what were some of your impressions when you saw your classmates' LEGO models?

Effects of a Pathfinding Program Visualization on Algorithm Development

Nicholas Lytle
North Carolina State University
Raleigh, NC
nalytle@ncsu.edu

Mark Floryan
University of Virginia
Charlottesville, VA
mrf8t@virginia.edu

Tiffany Barnes
North Carolina State University
Raleigh, NC
tmbarnes@ncsu.edu

ABSTRACT

Program Visualizations (PVs) have been used as educational tools to allow students to visually inspect the runtime behavior of their code. However, many of these systems act as low-level visual debuggers not high-level abstractions of program behavior. Additionally, evaluations of these systems tend to focus more on student engagement or opinion in using the system and not on artifacts produced using the system. This paper discusses the effectiveness of a PV developed to aide students in an undergraduate Artificial Intelligence class on a pathfinding homework assignment. Students in 4 semesters of the course were tasked to develop pathfinding algorithms for an agent to navigate worlds in cases of both certain and uncertain world information. Students in 2 semesters of the course were given access to a PV that allowed them to see a visual representation of their agent navigating the world in either information condition. The final agents developed by these students were compared with those developed by students who never received the PV. Comparisons were made on the performance of these agents in both cases of uncertain and certain world information on several test worlds. Student written reports for the Experimental condition were also analyzed. The results showed significant differences in the performance of the algorithms developed in both certain and uncertain world information. Student reflections on using the PV within the written reports provide insight into how the PV informed the design and development of their submission.

CCS CONCEPTS

• **Human-centered computing → Visualization.**

KEYWORDS

pathfinding, constructivism, visualization

ACM Reference Format:

Nicholas Lytle, Mark Floryan, and Tiffany Barnes. 2019. Effects of a Pathfinding Program Visualization on Algorithm Development. In *Proceedings of the 50th ACM Technical Symposium on Computer Science Education (SIGCSE '19), February 27-March 2, 2019, Minneapolis, MN, USA.* ACM, New York, NY, USA, 7 pages. https://doi.org/10.1145/3287324.3287391

SIGCSE '19, February 27-March 2, 2019, Minneapolis, MN, USA

ACM ISBN 978-1-4503-5890-3/19/02...$15.00
https://doi.org/10.1145/3287324.3287391

1 INTRODUCTION

Program and Algorithm Visualizations (PVs and AVs) have been long studied within Computer Science[6]. While their efficacy is varied[11], it is generally accepted that visualizations that engage students in an active learning process fair better than those that don't[9]. These findings have been supported by the learning theory of constructivism [5] as PVs and AVs allow students to create their own models of understanding through actively engaging with a visualization. This insight has lead to the development of successful interactive AVs and PVs as well as frameworks to allow students and instructors to build their own visualizations [10].

While much has been done to characterize and categorize visualizations, evaluations have remained fairly the same, primarily focusing on either usability of the system or post-test score differences between those who were given the system and those that weren't [21]. Further, most visualization tools primarily focus on *understanding* classic algorithms such as Djisktra's[18] or A* [1] and not using visualizations for algorithm *development*. In order to fully investigate the potential of visualizations, domains should be chosen and visualizations should be built that allow for more potential for individual knowledge construction through algorithm design and development for ill-defined problems. Further, evaluation methods should be chosen that focus more on the artifacts constructed through using a PV rather than transfer of knowledge. Finally, investigative methods should be taken to corroborate previous intuitions about how students engage with visualizations during development.

We present an assignment for an Artificial Intelligence class that tasks students to build pathfinding algorithms for an agent under two scenarios: one in which the agent has complete knowledge of the world state and one in which the agent has uncertain knowledge. After two semester of the assignment, a visualization (GUI) was developed that allowed students to see how their pathfinding agent was performing on given test inputs and make informed changes as necessary. To investigate the impact of this GUI, we look at the final produced pathfinding algorithms for both certain and uncertain cases. We also analyze student written reports to see whether or not arguments can be made that the students participated in an active learning and development process while using the visualization. Through this, we attempt to answer these research questions:

- **RQ1** How does the GUI affect algorithm performance in certain information cases?
- **RQ2** How does the GUI affect algorithm performance in uncertain information cases?
- **RQ3** How do students report using the GUI in the development of their algorithms?

Previous work and educational theory that motivates this system are discussed in Section 2. The methodology is detailed in Section 3 beginning with an overview of the assignment, the visualization tool that was developed, and the method of data analysis that was conducted on the resulting submissions. Section 4 outlines the results and Section 5 discusses them trying to connect findings into the context of previous research. Finally, Section 6 concludes the work with future directions and overall recommendations.

2 RELATED WORK

Software Visualization (SV) has a long history within the field of Computer Science [6]. Hundreds of systems have been developed [19] to aide in all course levels from Introductory Computer Science [21] to Data Structures and Algorithms courses [8]. As the literature is expansive, a full review of systems is out of the scope of this paper but good starting resources are Hundhausen's Meta-Analysis [9], Shaffer et al. [20] and Urquiza-Fuentes et al. [23].

As many systems exist, taxonomies have developed to categorize these SVs. Two broad subcategories of SVs that are widely accepted are Algorithm Visualizations(AVs), systems that provide higher-level visual abstractions of an algorithm, and Program Visualizations (PVs), systems that show low-level behavior of programs in a visual environment [15]. These systems have also been categorized on other metrics including levels of engagement the user has with the system (e.g. viewing a visualization passively vs. constructing one's own visualization [12]) as well as method of implementation and use (e.g. script-based, compiler-based, etc. [23]).

A meta-analysis by Hundhausen of AVs showed that it is not the visual displayed, but the level of student engagement with the system that predicts an AV's success [9]. This lead to further investigations of AVs and PVs by engagement level which have corroborated these findings [7, 23]. Hundhausen argued the original results can be explained by the learning theory of constructivism[5] as a visualization tool that students actively engage with provides an experiential learning context that is conducive for knowledge construction. Concepts from constructivism have been strongly motivated to be incorporated into computer science education [2] and the pedagogical theories that have taken inspiration from constructivism (namely constructionism [14]) have been the basis for numerous successful computer science educational projects (e.g. Scratch [17], LOGO[13],etc.).

While some AVs and PVs have shown pedagogical success, most systems have demonstrated this through similar evaluation methods. Most often, systems are only evaluated once and are only evaluated through usability studies (Sorva et al. reported that 50% of the successful studies they reviewed were solely focused on usability[21]). Even in cases where controlled experiments exist, evaluations mainly focus on transfer through post-test questions (reading and writing tasks) to measure algorithm understanding[21]. While transfer and application are important to investigate, examining the success of developed artifacts created through using a visualization can provide additional insight into its effectiveness. In addition, it is also important to take measures to investigate past claims about how students engage with the visualization and examine their development process.

To accomplish this, it is important to choose a domain where these evaluations can take place and provide meaningful insight. One candidate is in developing pathfinding algorithms. Many visualizations already exist for graph algorithms [1, 18, 22]. These systems, like most visualizations, primarily focus on teaching or helping students develop classic algorithms such as Djikstra's or A*. However, pathfinding problem domains can be constructed in which elements of the environment can make these classic algorithms unsuitable as solutions. Presenting students with an ill-defined problem such as this can potentially encourage problem-solving behavior, lead to a breadth of solutions, and encourage active engagement with a visualization created to aid the design and development process.

3 METHODOLOGY

3.1 Assignment

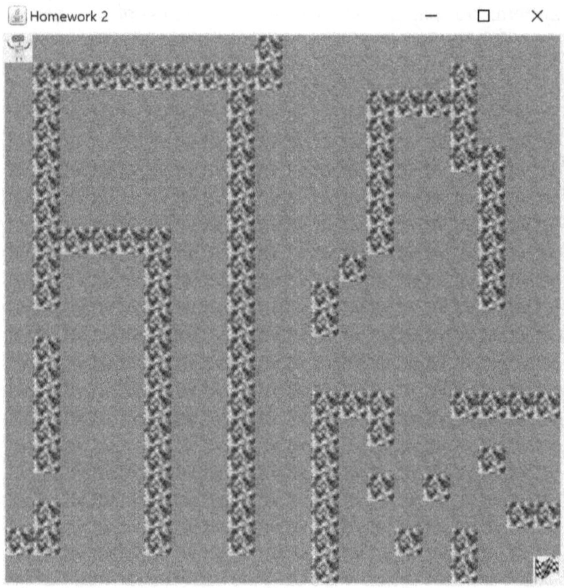

Figure 1: The GUI displaying World 4 with open (Green) and closed (Red) tiles. The agent starts at Top Left and must navigate to Goal (bottom right).

The assignment, a programming task written in Java, asked students to develop pathfinding algorithms and write a report on their development process. Through a basic API, students had to extend a *Robot* class that acted as the agent for pathfinding. This robot would be placed at a starting location in a grid-based *World* loaded from a text file, where each space in the World is either *open* (passable) or *closed* (impassible). A Robot is able to move through a method, moveRobot(), to any neighboring location (defined as the Moore neighborhood with r=1 [24]) so long as the position is open. The students must write a method, TravelToDestination(), that for any given World, will navigate the Robot from the starting location to the goal location. For every call of moveRobot() (regardless of whether or not the move was successful), a counter increases and students must develop their TravelToDestination() method to reach the goal state in the fewest number of moves. If their algorithm reached the goal state, the number of moves the robot took was printed out to the console.

Students had to develop algorithms to account for two cases: one where the robot could have *certain* information about the layout of the World and one in which the robot had *uncertain* information. In both cases, a Robot had a method, PingMap(), which took in a location and returned whether the position was open or closed. For the certainty case, this method call always returned the true value of the position which allowed students to get a complete read of the map. Because of this, students were encouraged to implement A* with an admissible heuristic (such as the Manhattan distance [3]) in order to create an optimal pathfinding algorithm for the certain case.

The other case was when the robot got uncertain information through pings about the state of a given location (i.e whether it was closed or open). The robot could again "ping" the status of a given location, but the accuracy of the returned answer was a function of how close the robot was to the given location. For example, a ping on a location that was right next to the robot would much more often return the true state, but pinging a location on the opposite end of the map would more closely return results resembling a coin-flip (i.e. returning open half the time and closed half the time). This presented students a problem in which a preset algorithm was unknown and tasked them to reason about the problem domain to come up with a solution.

Student submissions comprised of algorithms to account for both cases. Some submitted this as two conditions for the same Robot class while others submitted multiple classes. Students were also asked to complete a write-up in which they discussed the design of their algorithm, how they evaluated their performance, and how their code differs between the certain and uncertain cases. Students were graded through testing their algorithms on a set of 4 test worlds given to the students ahead of time. Students were graded in the certainty case by whether or not their algorithm took the same number of steps as the optimal path. Students were also graded by the average path length over multiple runs for a given world in the case where they were operating under uncertainty. Finally, student write ups were graded subjectively by the teaching staff in terms of thoughtfulness of reflection, their process for testing, and their algorithm design process.

The purpose of the assignment was to present students with a pathfinding problem that had both a well-defined and a more ill-defined component. The well-defined component, implementing A*, was used to determine whether or not students could successfully program an algorithm discussed within the class. The more ill-defined component was designing an effective algorithm given the constraints of the robot operating in the uncertain condition. Ill-defined problems have been shown to be effective in teaching problem-solving behavior in Computer Science classes [16], and presenting students with a problem in which no set solution was known allowed for students to engage thoughtfully in the development of their pathfinding algorithm.

3.2 Visualization

A simple program visualization was developed to allow students to watch their robot navigate through a given test world. The visualization acted as a separate callable line inside of the API which students could use at their discretion. When called, it produced a separate window that students could use to watch their robot navigate. Every call to moveRobot() in the students' code would change the robot's position on the screen (if it was a legal move) and the visualization would end and close if the robot reached the end state, reporting the number of moves taken as in the original assignment.

Like the programming assignment, the GUI ran in two modes: a mode displaying certain and uncertain information. In certain information, the entire world layout would be displayed. An example of this is shown in Figure 1 on Input 4. Here, the Robot Tile is the agent's current position, the flag tile is the goal, the green tiles represent open spaces while the red spaces represent impassable tiles.

The other mode, uncertain information, is shown in Figure 2. The visualization tool would show the open and closed tiles as described before *only* if the robot had previously traversed (or attempted to traverse) that tile. For every other position, the tile would show question marks denoting that that specific location's true value was unknown. Students were given one additional function, makeGuess(), to aid in this mode. Students could allow their algorithms to 'predict' the true nature of a tile as either open or closed and the image in the visualization would change accordingly (denoted as a mix between the question image and either the open or closed tile image).

The students had the ability to control many aspects of how the visualization ran. The entire animation displayed was controlled by the user as the visualization solely changed based off of their calls to moveRobot() or makeGuess(). Second, the students could change the speed in which the visualization would run (setting the size of the step of the visualization). Finally, the students had full access to the images for the visualization and could change them if desired. The visualization was completely voluntary and not necessary for testing or running their code. While simplistic, the visualization was meant to be used as a tool for actively engaging students in the development of their algorithms. By presenting students with a visual representation of their agent's actions based off of their algorithm at every stage of development, the hope was that students would be able to better diagnose their algorithm's behavior and make more informed decisions on how to better design their implementation.

3.3 Data and Testing

The data was collected from four semesters of an upper-level undergraduate Artificial Intelligence course at a public mid-atlantic research university. Two semesters had no access to the GUI and the algorithms developed from these semesters act as the Control Group. The Experimental Group comprises of the two semesters that had access to the GUI. Submissions often included multiple algorithms (often one for dealing with certain information and one for uncertain information) and so these had to be curated for testing. For the experimental group, 48 algorithms were submitted and

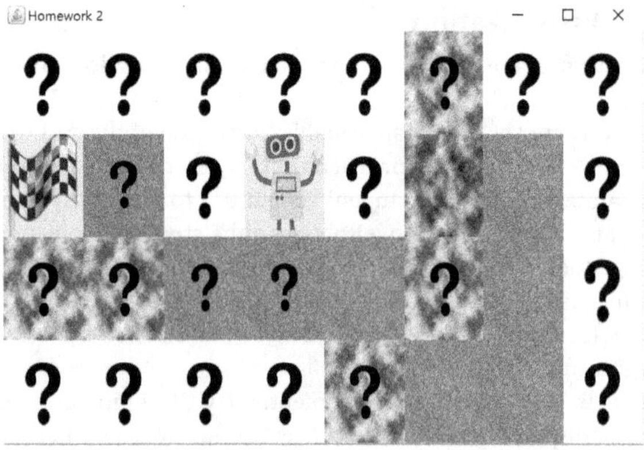

Figure 2: The GUI during an Uncertain World 2 Run. Currently unknown tiles are shown as '?s' with some locations resembling open or closed tiles to denote a guess.

tested for the certain case and 53 were submitted for the uncertain case while 100 and 126 algorithms were submitted and tested for the Control group's certain and uncertain cases respectively. Each set of algorithms were tested on the same 4 test worlds given to the students as test cases. For the certainty cases, the algorithms were run once and the number of steps taken was recorded. For the uncertain cases, the algorithms were run 8 times and the minimum path length, maximum path length, average path length, and standard deviation for the path lengths were recorded. Finally, to examine how the GUI influenced the development process, a question was added to the written report guideline asking students: "Was the GUI helpful to you? How did having the GUI influence how you tested and developed your AI (if at all)?". The 38 student responses that explicitly responded to this prompt within the Experimental group were qualitatively analyzed through open coding.

4 RESULTS

4.1 Certain Information

The results of comparing the certain information condition are show in Table 1. The proportions of students in both groups that got the optimal answer are reported. As the world complexity (and path length needed to get to the solution) increases, the success of the control group (N=100 algorithms) drops sharply from 73% of students getting the optimal answer for Input 1 to 45% for Input 4. In contrast, the Experimental group (N=48 algorithms), drops only from 79% on Input 1 to 65% on Input 4. A χ^2 test is calculated for each input and while the associated p-value decreases for each successive World, only the comparison between Input 4 results are significant at $p < .05$ ($\chi^2 = 4.98, p = .03$).

A similar comparison was done between the proportion of algorithms that executed (in this case, found a resulting path, regardless of whether or not the path was optimal) for both groups. The proportion of algorithms in the Experimental case that executed never dipped below 90% in any test case but the execution proportion was much more varied and lower for the Control condition. Once more, χ^2 tests are calculated and for Input 2 ($\chi^2 = 5.19, p = .02$), Input 3 ($\chi^2 = 6.26, p = .01$), and Input 4 ($\chi^2 = 5.19, p = .02$) the results are significant.

	Input 1	Input 2	Input 3	Input 4
Optimal Path Control	73%	65%	55%	45%
Optimal Path Experimental	79%	75%	67%	65%
χ^2 *Test*	p=.42	p=.22	p=.18	**p=.03***
Executed Control	82%	76%	74%	79%
Executed Experimental	94%	92%	92%	94%
χ^2 *Test*	p=.06	**p=.02***	**p=.01***	**p=.02***

Table 1: Percentage of algorithms in both the Experimental and Control Group that executed and found the optimal path on inputs in the certain condition.

4.2 Uncertain Information

The analysis for the case of uncertain world information is limited to World 3 and World 4. As in the case of the certain world knowledge, the proportion of algorithms in each condition that executed was inspected. While the proportion of algorithms that executed was higher in the experimental condition for both World 3 (43/53 vs. 82/126) and World 4 (42/53 vs. 82/126), Chi-Square tests show only a significant difference in World 3 executions ($\chi^2 = 4.56, p = .03$). As the algorithms were tested 8 times, an additional comparison was made between groups on whether or not they executed *every* time. Once more, the proportions for World 3 (42/53 vs. 73/126) and World 4 (36/53 vs. 73/126) favored the Experimental condition with again, only World 3 resulting in a significant difference ($\chi^2 = 7.37, p = .007$).

Comparisons were made between the minimum (or best case runs) of the algorithms 8 runs for both groups. The average best case run for each group was calculated for both World 3 (Experimental: 26.83, Control: 95.31) and World 4 (Experimental: 62.8, Control: 121.28). A Mann-Whitney Test was performed between the two sets of minimum runs for each group finding a significant difference in World 3 Best Case Runs (W = 1081, p < .001) but not for World 4 Best Case Runs (W = 1527.5, p =.3052). The proportion of algorithms whose best case was the optimal solution was also investigated for World 3 (12/43 vs. 7/82) and World 4 (8/42 vs 5/82). A Chi-Square Test reveals that there exists a significant difference in these proportions for both World 3 ($\chi^2 = 8.21, p = .004$) and World 4 ($\chi^2 = 4.96, p = .026$). Comparisons were also made for the maximum or worst case runs of each set of algorithms. For World 3, the average maximum run for the Experimental Condition was 81.1 against 373.03 for the control (A Mann-Whitney Test gives W = 992 p = < .001). For World 4, the average maximum path length run was 139.4 for the Experimental Condition vs 441.5 for the Control Group (W = 1200, p = .006).

As the algorithms were run multiple times, the average and standard deviations of the 8 runs were recorded. The average path length for the 8 runs was less for the Experimental Group in both World 3 (43.38 vs 194.71) and World 4 (95.91 vs. 202.75). A Mann-Whitney Test was performed and showed that these differences are significant in both World 3 (W = 874.5, p = < .001) and World 4 (W = 1245.5, p = .012). The standard deviations of the algorithms 8 runs were recorded with the Experimental Group having a smaller average SD in both cases (World 3: 18.7, World 4: 27.5) than the Control Group (World 3: 108.9, World 4:109.4). Through a Mann-Whitney Test on both groups, the difference is significant in both World 3 (W = 1188, p = 0.003) and World 4 (W = 1211, p = 0.007). To further investigate this, the proportion of algorithms whose standard deviation was 0 (meaning the algorithm returned the same path length every time) was also examined. For World 3, these proportions were (Experimental: 16/43, Control: 17/82) and for World 4, these proportions were (Experimental: 12/42, Control: 10/82). A Chi-Square Test shows that these differences are significant for both World 3 ($\chi^2 = 3.94, p = .047$) and World 4 ($\chi^2 = 5.10, p = .024$).

4.3 Development Process

38 reports addressed the question, "Was the GUI helpful to you? How did having the GUI influence how you tested and developed your AI (if at all)?" and 34 reported finding the GUI helpful. Responses went through a process of open coding performed by the lead author. In reviewing the codes and the responses, 5 major themes related to GUI use emerged. They are enumerated below.

GUI Presents a Fun, Easy Visual: Many students reported on how the visualization of the assignment made things not only easier, but more fun. While minimalistic, the GUI was positively received and as none of the images were locked, some students customized the look of the GUI ("I changed the images up to be more fun"). Students also reported how the GUI visual made things easier by allowing them to visually *see* the path and "see the robot as opposed to reading coordinates from the console".

GUI Helps Understand Agent Behavior: Students reported that the visual not only allowed them to see the world but gave "insight into how the algorithm is 'thinking'". The uncertain mode and the makeGuess() function were well received as allowing students to understand how uncertainty worked ("being able to see how he saw the environment is what helped me understand...").

GUI Helps with Design/Development: Many reported that specific design decisions for algorithms came from seeing how their robot operated within the GUI ("[it] helped us come up with the idea of storing the information the robot acquires as it goes", "it helped me come up with the idea to weighing the heuristic distance".)

GUI Helps with Debugging: Student discussed how the GUI was particularly helpful in debugging both in the certain case ("The GUI helped us realize that our A* algorithm was incorrect") and in the uncertain case ("I would not have seen that the robot was wasting many moves teetering between two sides of the map").

GUI Helps with Evaluation: Students reported using the GUI for evaluating their algorithm performance ("I used the GUI almost every time I tested the robot", "...we were able to understand the characteristics of a map better with the GUI and thus were able to understand the advantages and disadvantages of our algorithm").

5 DISCUSSION

5.1 Algorithm Evaluations

In addressing **RQ1**, "How does the GUI affect algorithm performance in certain information cases?", there was a noticeable difference between the two groups in pathfinding performance. The idea that a visualization *not* designed to show the steps of the algorithm (like a tradition AV) would still help algorithm performance was surprising. However, many students *specifically* mentioned getting tremendous help on the A* portion using the GUI mentioning how it "acted as a debugger for [their] implementation of the traditional A* algorithm". While the difference in proportion of students who got the optimal solution was only significant in World 4, as World 4 had the greatest complexity and longest number of steps in the optimal path (38 compared to 3,7, and 13 in Worlds 1, 2, and 3 respectively), it is possible that larger worlds could also yield similar results. The difference between the two groups on whether or not the algorithms actually executed was more pronounced with three of the test world differences being significant. This could suggest that the largest amount of aid that the GUI provided was actually getting students to create a functioning path. If the visualization does not show the robot moving towards the goal, it means that the student has to rework their algorithm in order to actually get the robot to move in the intended way. This clear visual representation of a failed scenario (one in which a path isn't found or the robot isn't moving) could be better for developing an understanding of what exactly is going wrong and thus be better for debugging. Students who have a better understanding of what is going wrong and are able to better debug their solutions most likely are more actively engaged in fixing their assignment code.

To answer **RQ2**, "How does the GUI affect algorithm performance in uncertain information cases?", several elements of algorithmic performance were measured, all favoring the Experimental group. The difference in program execution between groups was found in the uncertainty case for both the "at least once" and "every time" conditions. This could mean that students who were running their algorithm multiple times and saw hang ups were more likely to try to fix the hang up cases than those without the visualization. This could be because the visualization provided more information as to *how* the hang up was occurring (e.g. the student whose algorithm was 'teetering' between two sides of the map) than either no information or any command-line print-outs that a student might have added to debug. Algorithms in the Experimental condition also performed better in the best case scenarios with best cases more often being the optimal solution. This suggests that students in the Experimental condition were better at discovering the rules of the environment (or as students put it, understanding what the robot "knows") in order to come up with more optimal solutions. This also explains the difference in average case performance and worst case performance as the Experimental group was not as dramatically impacted by worst case outliers as the Control Group. This is most likely due to the fact that the algorithms in the Experimental condition also had considerably less variability between runs with a lower standard deviation between groups as well as more algorithms that ran consistently. This performance behavior would have been demonstrated to the user very differently between conditions. In the Control, only a number of steps would have been reported, while students in the GUI group might have chosen to watch their algorithm find a path which may have taken a considerably long time in the worst case scenarios. This difference in level of engagement could have actively discouraged students in the Experimental group from accepting these longer runs as valid behavior and encouraged them to fix and edit their code more so than the control group who might have been fine with just a number print out.

5.2 Development Process

To address **RQ3**, "How do students report using the GUI in the development of their algorithms?" the five themes discovered from the student responses were examined. It became clear that 4 of the 5 themes were related in the fact that they formed a process. These themes were that the GUI 1) Helps with Understanding Robot Behavior, 2) Informs Design/Development, 3) Helps with Debugging, and 4) Helps with Evaluation. Students descriptions of GUI use often reflected or mentioned these themes simultaneously or immediately after the other. Further, the four themes resembled well known cyclical design processes like a spiral software development process [4]. In this way, students use of the GUI can be explained by a cyclical development process of first understanding the current robot's behavior, coming up with a further design, refining and debugging the design, and then testing and evaluating the robot (This cycle is shown in Figure 3).

A case example from a student submission is chosen to highlight this development process. This student submitted 5 iterations of their robot class in various states of development. The student described five "generations of [their] robot design" in which they either add additional features such as a map "memory" (Iteration 3) or a "ping sensor trust limit" (Iteration 4) or instead refine and debug the previous design (Iterations 2 and 5). For each iteration, the student's *understanding* of the robot's current limitations, developed from *evaluating* the program's behavior, informs the next added *design* element or focuses their efforts on *debugging* the current performance. The average performance of each iteration of the algorithm is detailed in Table 2. Each iteration (except for two cases in World 4) improves on the performance of the last iteration showing a careful design and development process to ensure that progress is being made towards a better solution. The student expressed that the GUI was "predominantly helpful" in the development of their program and mentioned that they also used it to test their iterations.

From the case study and examination of student reports and connecting these results to the evaluations discussed previously, it is clear that there is indeed support for the constructivist insight proposed in previous studies. Students self-reported as well as demonstrated through their algorithm performance that they were able to construct better algorithms due to engaging with the GUI during development. While simplistic, the visualization provided an appropriate platform for knowledge construction about the rules of the assignment and presented appropriate feedback necessary to encourage informed algorithm design.

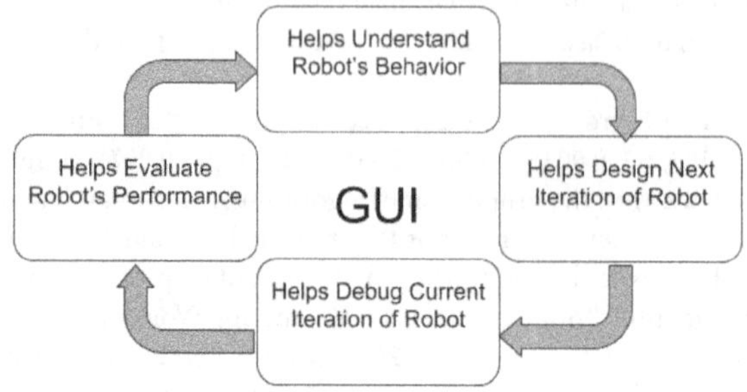

Figure 3: The cyclical process of GUI use with the 4 themes discovered from analyzing written reports.

Iteration	Input 1	Input 2	Input 3	Input 4
1: Base Bot	3.0	X	X	X
2: Modifies 1	3.0	11.0	50.6	106.4
3: Bot Has Memory	3.0	10.6	48.0	105.0
4: Limited Ping Trust	3.0	9.0	X	X
5: Refinement of 4	3.0	7.4	34.1	52.1

Table 2: Average number of steps for 5 iterations of an example student's algorithm development using the GUI (X denotes did not execute for the given test case).

6 CONCLUSION

With the results demonstrated, we show that even a simple PV can be enough to change student algorithm performance. In addition, results from analyzing the written reports provide support to previous studies that suggest students can engage in an active learning and development process when using a PV. Student suggestions inform a lot of future directions of this work. Suggestions given can be broadly categorized as either wanting more *control* over the runtime environment (e.g. wanting to be able to step through the program rather than have it auto-run) or wanting more *information* displayed during the runtime (e.g. having the row and column numbers labeled). Incorporating these changes and testing algorithm performance on groups with different added features can shed light into which have better effects on algorithm development.

Limitations of this work include the fact that the largest semester of data in the Control group is also the first implementation of this homework assignment, as there might have been effects from teaching staff in having to do this first iteration of the assignment. In addition, limiting analysis to only the 4 Worlds given as test input and only doing 8 runs for each algorithm in the uncertainty case was chosen to resemble the process done for grading, but it might not have been a large enough sampling or test pool to catch all the variability in an algorithm's performance.

We highly suggest that instructors develop their own simple PVs as even basic ones, as in the case of ours, can affect not only assignment engagement but also performance. In addition, instructors should consider incorporating more open-ended and ill-defined problems within their curricula to promote problem-solving behavior and design thinking.

REFERENCES

[1] G Michael Barnes. 2013. Using an instructor authored visual simulation framework in a CS3 course. *Journal of Computing Sciences in Colleges* 28, 4 (2013), 148–154.
[2] Mordechai Ben-Ari. 2001. Constructivism in computer science education. *Journal of Computers in Mathematics and Science Teaching* 20, 1 (2001), 45–73.
[3] Paul E Black. 2006. Manhattan distance. *Dictionary of Algorithms and Data Structures* 18 (2006), 2012.
[4] Barry W. Boehm. 1988. A spiral model of software development and enhancement. *Computer* 21, 5 (1988), 61–72.

[5] Thomas M Duffy and Donald J Cunningham. 1996. 7. Constructivism: Implications for the Design and Delivery of Instruction. (1996).

[6] Eric Fouh, Monika Akbar, and Clifford A Shaffer. 2012. The role of visualization in computer science education. *Computers in the Schools* 29, 1-2 (2012), 95–117.

[7] Scott Grissom, Myles F. McNally, and Tom Naps. 2003. Algorithm Visualization in CS Education: Comparing Levels of Student Engagement. In *Proceedings of the 2003 ACM Symposium on Software Visualization (SoftVis '03)*. ACM, New York, NY, USA, 87–94. https://doi.org/10.1145/774833.774846

[8] Christopher D Hundhausen. 2002. Integrating algorithm visualization technology into an undergraduate algorithms course: ethnographic studies of a social constructivist approach. *Computers & Education* 39, 3 (2002), 237–260.

[9] Christopher D Hundhausen, Sarah A Douglas, and John T Stasko. 2002. A meta-study of algorithm visualization effectiveness. *Journal of Visual Languages & Computing* 13, 3 (2002), 259–290.

[10] Ville Karavirta and Clifford A Shaffer. 2013. JSAV: the JavaScript algorithm visualization library. In *Proceedings of the 18th ACM conference on Innovation and technology in computer science education*. ACM, 159–164.

[11] Thomas Naps, Stephen Cooper, Boris Koldehofe, Charles Leska, Guido Rößling, Wanda Dann, Ari Korhonen, Lauri Malmi, Jarmo Rantakokko, Rockford J Ross, et al. 2003. Evaluating the educational impact of visualization. In *ACM Sigcse Bulletin*, Vol. 35. ACM, 124–136.

[12] Thomas L Naps, Guido Rößling, Vicki Almstrum, Wanda Dann, Rudolf Fleischer, Chris Hundhausen, Ari Korhonen, Lauri Malmi, Myles McNally, Susan Rodger, et al. 2002. Exploring the role of visualization and engagement in computer science education. In *ACM Sigcse Bulletin*, Vol. 35. ACM, 131–152.

[13] Seymour Papert. 1980. *Mindstorms: Children, computers, and powerful ideas*. Basic Books, Inc.

[14] Seymour Papert and Idit Harel. 1991. Situating constructionism. *Constructionism* 36, 2 (1991), 1–11.

[15] Blaine A. Price, Ronald Baecker, and Ian S. Small. [n. d.]. A principled taxonomy of software visualization. *J. Vis. Lang. Comput.* 4, 3 ([n. d.]), 211–266.

[16] David Reed. 2002. The use of ill-defined problems for developing problem-solving and empirical skills in CS1. *Journal of Computing Sciences in Colleges* 18, 1 (2002), 121–133.

[17] Mitchel Resnick, John Maloney, Andrés Monroy-Hernández, Natalie Rusk, Evelyn Eastmond, Karen Brennan, Amon Millner, Eric Rosenbaum, Jay Silver, Brian Silverman, et al. 2009. Scratch: programming for all. *Commun. ACM* 52, 11 (2009), 60–67.

[18] M Gloria Sánchez-Torrubia, Carmen Torres-Blanc, and Miguel A Lopez-Martinez. 2009. PathFinder: A visualization eMathTeacher for actively learning Dijkstra's algorithm. *Electronic Notes in Theoretical Computer Science* 224 (2009), 151–158.

[19] Clifford A. Shaffer, Matthew Cooper, and Stephen H. Edwards. 2007. Algorithm Visualization: A Report on the State of the Field. *SIGCSE Bull.* 39, 1 (March 2007), 150–154. https://doi.org/10.1145/1227504.1227366

[20] Clifford A Shaffer, Matthew L Cooper, Alexander Joel D Alon, Monika Akbar, Michael Stewart, Sean Ponce, and Stephen H Edwards. 2010. Algorithm visualization: The state of the field. *ACM Transactions on Computing Education (TOCE)* 10, 3 (2010), 9.

[21] Juha Sorva, Ville Karavirta, and Lauri Malmi. 2013. A review of generic program visualization systems for introductory programming education. *ACM Transactions on Computing Education (TOCE)* 13, 4 (2013), 15.

[22] Matthias F Stallmann. 2017. Algorithm Animation with Galant. *IEEE computer graphics and applications* 1 (2017), 8–14.

[23] Jaime Urquiza-Fuentes and J Ángel Velázquez-Iturbide. 2009. A survey of successful evaluations of program visualization and algorithm animation systems. *ACM Transactions on Computing Education (TOCE)* 9, 2 (2009), 9.

[24] Eric W Weisstein. 2005. Moore neighborhood. *From MathWorld–A Wolfram Web Resource. http://mathworld. wolfram. com/MooreNeighborhood. html* (2005).

Teaching Android Mobile Security

Jean-François Lalande
Valérie Viet Triem Tong
Pierre Graux
Guillaume Hiet
jean-francois.lalande@inria.fr
CentraleSupélec, Inria, Univ Rennes, CNRS, IRISA
Rennes, France

Wojciech Mazurczyk
Institute of Telecommunications
Warsaw University of Technology
Warsaw, Poland
wmazurczyk@tele.pw.edu.pl

Habiba Chaoui
National School of Applied Sciences, Ibn Tofail University
Kenitra, Morocco
habiba.chaoui@uit.ac.ma

Pascal Berthomé
INSA Centre Val de Loire, LIFO
Bourges, France
pascal.berthome@insa-cvl.fr

ABSTRACT

At present, computer science studies generally offer courses addressing mobile development and they use mobile technologies for illustrating theoretical concepts such as operating system, design patterns, and compilation because Android and iOS use a large variety of technologies for developing applications. Teaching courses on security is also becoming an important concern for academics, and the use of mobile platforms (such as Android) as supporting material is becoming a reasonable option. In this paper, we intend to bridge a gap in the literature by reversing this paradigm: Android is not only an opportunity to learn security concepts but requires strong pedagogical efforts for covering all the aspects of mobile security. Thus, we propose teaching Android mobile security through a two-dimensional approach. The first dimension addresses the cognitive process of the Bloom taxonomy, and the second dimension addresses the technical layers of the architecture of the Android operating system. We describe a set of comprehensive security laboratory courses covering various concepts, ranging from the application development perspective to a deep investigation of the Android Open Source Project and its interaction with the Linux kernel. We evaluated this approach, and our results verify that the designed security labs impart the required knowledge to the students.

CCS CONCEPTS

• **Applied computing → Education**; • **Security and privacy → Mobile platform security**; *Software security engineering*; **Software reverse engineering**.

This work has received a French government support granted to the COMIN Labs excellence laboratory and managed by the National Research Agency in the "Investing for the Future" program under reference ANR-10-LABX-07-01.

SIGCSE '19, February 27-March 2, 2019, Minneapolis, MN, USA

ACM ISBN 978-1-4503-5890-3/19/02...$15.00
https://doi.org/10.1145/3287324.3287406

KEYWORDS

teaching, mobile, security

ACM Reference Format:
Jean-François Lalande, Valérie Viet Triem Tong, Pierre Graux, Guillaume Hiet, Wojciech Mazurczyk, Habiba Chaoui, and Pascal Berthomé. 2019. Teaching Android Mobile Security. In *Proceedings of the 50th ACM Technical Symposium on Computer Science Education (SIGCSE '19), February 27-March 2, 2019, Minneapolis, MN, USA.* ACM, New York, NY, USA, 7 pages. https://doi.org/10.1145/3287324.3287406

1 INTRODUCTION

At present, Android programming is an integral part of most undergraduate studies in computer science. It was introduced as a complete knowledge area in 2013 (platform-based development) in the Curriculum Guidelines for Undergraduate Degree Programs in Computer Science [4]. The same year, security aspects were also introduced as a new knowledge area named "Information Assurance and Security." The Android platform can be used for a variety of learning purposes concerning operating system, wireless communications, advanced design pattern, etc. Skills in mobile programming are of significance as even web services generally develop a companion application that the user can install on a smartphone.

When addressing the security aspects of mobile computing, it is challenging to discuss concepts without referring to their implementation. Security concepts such as access control, authentication, or cryptography can still be presented as an independent course. However, the manner in which attackers attempt to bypass the implemented security countermeasures of modern smartphones should be presented with complete knowledge of the Android's internal aspects.

In this paper, we propose a set of labs intended to teach about threats and the security internals of Android applications and operating system. The approach is original in that it follows a progression based on the Bloom taxonomy [12] and works on the security aspects of the complete software stack of Android. We propose a variety of activities that enhance students' skills from those for developing simple applications to those for more complex activities such as analyzing vulnerable applications under attack or reversing packers. Additionally, the labs cover the different internal components of Android, which aids students to gain knowledge of the internal classes of the Android runtime, the execution and compilation of Android applications, and the link with the operating system. These two dimensions—the student cognitive process and the coverage of the different levels of the Android software stack—aid students to better analyze mobile security problems.

The paper is organized as follows: Section 2 summarizes the state of the art in the learning of Android development and security. Section 3 presents our approach, and Section 4 provides the technical details of each lab. Section 5 summarizes the feedback we have collected. Section 6 concludes the paper.

2 RELATED WORK

Application Development and Operating Systems with Android. It is apparent that a pre-requisite for teaching mobile security is fluency in the underlying programming language and the main concepts of application development. For example, Tigrek et al. [21] propose a minimal course for first year engineering students to discover Android programming. Among the presented principles, "How Without Why" (program based on tutorials) combined with "Just Enough Java" (learn the essential Java patterns) are effective for learning to develop an application, although is not sufficient for understanding the security impact of a selected implementation [1]. In Bloom's revised taxonomy of educational objectives [12], these two pieces of procedural knowledge are used to distinguish between "knowledge of subject-specific skills" and "knowledge of criteria for determining when to use appropriate procedures". Additionally, we consider that in the structure of the cognitive process (remember, understand, apply, analyze, evaluate, and create) the three last cognitive processes require a deep understanding of the internal aspects of mobile application and the underlying operating system.

The Android framework can also be used as supporting material to teach more general software engineering [5, 20] or operating system [2] concepts. Notwithstanding whether these works are effective for a better understanding of the concepts, most of the presented material does not describe the Android system with adequate details to aid the investigation of the security aspects of mobile devices.

Mobile Security. A few studies use Android as a platform for experimenting with general security notions, e.g., filtering traffic in firewalls [23] or countering Denial of Service attacks [22]. However, they do not address the specificities of mobile systems and applications.

A few previous works [10, 15, 25] have described the particularities of teaching security aspects of mobile applications and platforms. Nevertheless, in most cases, only foundational aspects that are relevant for Android developers are covered.

The approach of Guo *et al.* [10] is one of the works closest to our proposal. They have designed a labware of seven modules, which illustrates the concepts of mobile security and privacy. The learning approach is based on two main concepts. First, the course uses an attack/defense lab, where the students are required to implement attacks prior to implementing the corresponding protection mechanisms. Such an approach aids the students to better comprehend the security issue and to implement more effective protections. Secondly, the provided material (slide, tutorials) and the content of the labs can be used directly on real smartphones, enhancing the confidence of the students in their skills. Each lab intends to develop skills of protection against one type of threat. The fundamentals of Android security are introduced in different labs, such as those on the use of permissions or cryptographic API. Advanced threats and prevention mechanisms, such as buffer overflows or obfuscation, are discussed in a lab entitled "Secure Mobile App Development," which was under development at the time of the article writing.

In our opinion, these works lack progression in the Bloom taxonomy and do not cover the different levels of the Android software stack. The next section develops this concept before the description of the labs in Section 4.

Table 1: Attacks targeting different Android components

Components	Examples of attack	CVE
Applications	Android ransomware, spyware, adware	
AOSP classes	OpenSSLX509Certificate vulnerability [17]	2015-3825
DVM & ART	DoS via an unspecified Dalvik function	2009-3698
AOSP services	Janus: Hiding Payload & Bypass signatures	2017-13156
Kernel	Towelroot: Futex Requeue Kernel Exploit	2014-3153

3 LEARNING MOBILE SECURITY

A deeper understanding of all the security components of Android requires comprehension of the whole stack of technologies that is used by the Android Open Source Project (AOSP) [6, 9]. Describing security APIs from the developer's perspective can be a starting point for discovering features such as account management, permissions, and cryptographic primitives. Nevertheless, most of the security features are provided by the operating system, and explaining them requires sufficient knowledge of operating systems, runtime environments, and networks. Examples of such features are the installation process of applications, storage of credentials, role of SELinux, and update process of the operating system.

Additionally, students should comprehend the heterogeneous nature of the attacks likely to target Android devices. We have presented a few examples of vulnerabilities in Table 1 that illustrate the diversity of the likely threats. The kernel is the most challenging component to attack, and a representative vulnerability is the Futex vulnerability[1], which enables, under certain conditions, the execution of arbitrary code in the kernel mode and to root the phone. On top of the kernel, the Android services can be exploited, *e.g.*, the process that installs or updates applications. An example of such a threat is the Janus exploit that abuses a vulnerable signature verification implementation. Similar attacks target the direct environment of the malicious application, *i.e.*, the Dalvik virtual machine or the ART library that implements security verifications for the running application. Moreover, the attacker can attempt to abuse the SDK itself by identifying vulnerable classes [17] with controllable side-effects. Finally, and this constitutes a significant part of the attacks, the attacker does not exploit any vulnerability but performs malicious activities using the requested permissions. Examples of such applications are ransomware, cryptominers, and remote administration tools.

Taking these remarks into consideration, we describe the structure of the proposed labs and detail their content, in the next section.

[1] https://tinyhack.com/2014/07/07/exploiting-the-futex-bug-and-uncovering-towelroot

Table 2: Proposed security activities in Bloom taxonomy of cognitive process structure [12]

Soft. components \ Cognitive process	Remember	Understand	Apply	Analyze	Eval.	Create
Applications	DEV app development	MAL malware reverse				PROJ
AOSP classes		BANK banking app reverse	COV covert channels	CLASS vulnerable class loader		
DVM & ART				PACK reverse packers		
AOSP internals	INST compile, flash		MEM memory forensic	KERN ROP programming		
Kernel						

Table 3: Knowledge chapters for the DEV lab

Chapter 1
Application's architecture [13, 26] Designing graphical interfaces Messaging components
Chapter 2
Concurrency and synchronization Connectivity and sensors
Chapter 3
Security [6, 9] Wear OS [8] Firebase Cloud Messaging

4 ANDROID SECURITY LABS

4.1 Security Labs Design

We have developed several labs[2] which cover different Android components involved in the understanding of mobile security. We present these labs in Table 2, following Bloom's revised taxonomy of educational objectives [12]. Students should follow these labs from left to right in the table, eventually completing the sequence with a security project (PROJ) that corresponds to the deepest cognitive process of the taxonomy (Create).

The number of hours depends of the level of knowledge teachers intend to obtain. We distinguish three levels: level 1 (~2h) provides fundamental knowledge or focuses on a particular aspect; level 2 (~5h-8h) enables the student to cover more notions and practice with real devices; level 3 (~20h) aids the student to cover a large variety of notions or to work on a particular one with important software development. Most of the labs use level 1 or 2 (e.g., INST and MAL); however, a few of them (e.g., DEV and COV) can use level 3 or can be adapted as a security project (PROJ).

The first two labs (Remember process) train the students to develop Android applications (DEV) and to flash a custom Android image on a smartphone (INST). Such labs are typically observed in other available approaches [2, 20, 21]. Then, two labs enhance the students in the understanding of benign (BANK) and malicious applications (MAL) by reversing their bytecode. This aids the studying of attacks at the application level and their associated countermeasures (debugger detection, obfuscation, etc.) that can be used both by malicious and legitimate applications.

The subsequent labs correspond to the "Apply" step in the taxonomy. Students are encouraged to implement attacks and countermeasures with their previously acquired knowledge. For this purpose, we propose two use cases. The first one (COV) is proposed to defeat the Android access control system by implementing a covert channel between two applications that do not have permission to interact with each other. The second one (MEM) is proposed to exploit a dump of the volatile memory to recover certain confidential information. The likely benefit of these labs is to compel the students to obtain deeper knowledge of the low-level components of Android, *i.e.*, the leakage induced by the operating system and its primitives (COV) and the Dalvik (or Art) data structures used to represent the Java classes of the applications in volatile memory (MEM).

[2] https://gitlab.inria.fr/jlalande/teaching-android-mobile-security

Contrary to the previous labs, wherein students are completely guided while they practice, the three subsequent labs require the performance of security analysis (Analyze process). We provide the symptoms of certain issues to the students, and we expect an investigation and eventually certain remediation. In the first lab (CLASS), students are required to analyze an application that uses a vulnerable class loader. The second lab (PACK) proposes to analyze a malicious application obfuscated with packing techniques. The third lab (KERN) focuses on low level vulnerabilities by performing ROP attacks using gadgets of the kernel.

Note that no lab is classified in the "Evaluate" cognitive process as the distinction between "Analyze" and "Evaluate" is marginal. In particular, in [4], only three levels of mastery is proposed (familiarity, usage, assessment). Thus, we use only four levels of the Bloom taxonomy for classifying our labs; additionally, we propose various security projects (PROJ). They are designed to explore a specific subject with a large number of hours (level 3 or higher) for a group of students and may be linked to research activities.

4.2 DEV Lab: Android Development

The DEV lab provides the pre-requisite for understanding the fundamentals of Android development. We classify this lab in Bloom's taxonomy in the "Remember" process as we do not intend to train software developers and rather intend to teach the fundamentals for discussing security aspects. The topics covered depend on the amount of time allocated, and we distinguish three chapters of knowledge, as presented in Table 3.

Learning outcomes. At the end of the lab, we expect the students to comprehend the architecture and deployment of an Android application. The students should be capable of developing an application that communicates with a remote server, using REST API.

4.3 INST Lab - Compiling, Modifying, Flashing

Numerous other laboratories presented in this paper are required to be able to setup a clean image of the smartphone. As indicated by Guo et al. [10], students appreciate having a real device to experiment with while performing development or hacking activities. Moreover, it is occasionally more difficult to work with an emulator, for example to play with the different sensors, or to pair an emulated smartphone with an emulated Wear watch, which may require the installation of the Google APIs with an active Google account.

The INST lab (level 1) includes the compilation of a complete AOSP distribution for a Google Nexus 5 or 5X or Sony Xperia X smartphone and then the flashing of the compiled images. Additionally, the Nexus models offer the capability to debug the kernel output using serial headphone jack. For that purpose, we constructed a small serial debugger that aids students involved in advanced labs, where the kernel is modified and is likely to crash during runtime.

Learning outcomes. Students are able to customize the source of an operating system and install it on a device.

4.4 MAL Lab - Malware Reverse Engineering

The MAL lab consists in reversing several types of malware using different open source tools. The pedagogical goal of the lab is to demonstrate that each type of malware requires a custom reverse process. The lab consists of multiple exercises. Thus, the required number of hours can be adapted from level 1 to 3. In Bloom's taxonomy, we place this lab in the "Understand" process because we provide the students with the entire set of instructions for reversing the malware. We present the two most representative ones.

Programming an antidote for a ransomware. The students install a ransomware on a provided smartphone. They observe that the image files are encrypted by the malware. Then, the students explore the code using BytecodeViewer[3] or Jadx[4] in order to identify the service that encrypts the images. The code analysis reveals that the AES ciphering key used by the ransomware is a constant. Thus, after locating the deciphering code, the students modify the malicious application using to a bytecode editor so that it calls the deciphering code. Finally, they use this modified application to recover the images on the smartphone.

Observing spyware. The students are first required to reverse the spyware and locate the code that extracts personal data (accounts, phone number, IMEI) and the code that transmits the data to a remote server, whose domain name is identified. for the sake of simplicity. We also propose the observation of the leaked data in network traces as part of the lab in order to confirm the static analysis. To achieve this goal, the students setup a local web server, use the ngrok website[5] to create a public URL of the form x.ngrok.io, and link this URL to the local web server. Then, using a provided tool based on Soot[6], the students substitute the domain name used by the malware with this URL. Executing this new version of the malware enables one to capture the first requests that are responsible for leaking user's data.

Learning outcomes. Students comprehend the different types of threat that security analysts confront. They discover the process of reverse engineering with three approaches. This emphasizes the fact that security analysts have to adapt their methodology to the nature of the threat. At this stage, the investigation process is specified; however, students understand that a custom process should be designed for each malware.

[3]https://bytecodeviewer.com
[4]https://github.com/skylot/jadx
[5]Ngrog is a tunneling service from a public URL to a local server: https://ngrok.com
[6]http://sable.github.io/soot/

4.5 BANK Lab - Banking Application Reverse

This lab consists in reversing the authentication activity of a real banking application. This lab is completely guided, which places it in the "Understand" process of the taxonomy and aids to fit its duration to level 2.

The students are required to comprehend the protocol that is used by the application to authenticate the user to a remote server. The banking application receives a challenge from the server, which is used to generate a virtual keyboard. This permits the application to obfuscate the entered password.

First, students unpack the application and uncompile the bytecode into Java source code using Jadx. This phase aids them to identify the activities and classes involved in password encoding. Second, students observe the evolution of the application state. Using AndBug[7], students can put breakpoints on specific bytecode instructions. In particular, it aids them to identify the code that transmits the encoded password to the server. They also install a counterfeit certificate in the smartphone to bypass the verification of the remote server's authenticity. This permits them to monitor the network traffic using the Burp Suite proxy[8]. Finally, the students precisely identify the Java objects that encode the password and that are transmitted to the server when the user attempts to authenticate. By capturing both the challenge received from the server and the encoded password transmitted by the application, the students can recover the password.

Learning outcomes. Students comprehend the countermeasures used by applications for critical parts such as the authentication phase. They train themselves to bypass these countermeasures as a real attacker would. Working on attack design aids the understanding of the limits of current security implementations.

4.6 COV Lab - Developing Covert Channels

The COV lab (level 2 or 3) consists in developing a covert channel between two Android applications [14] in order to bypass the enforced security policy.

We provide two applications App1 and App2 to the students. App1 collects certain sensitive data of a user but does not have the permissions to use the network. App2 cannot access confidential data but has the necessary permissions to use the network. Those applications cooperate to leak the data. To achieve this, App1 establishes a local covert channel with App2 which is based on the remaining free space in the flash memory. This can encode the secret data bits if the sender (App1) creates and deletes large files. Snippets of code are provided to the students to aid them to develop the covert channel inside an asynchronous task. Moreover, countermeasures against such threats are discussed and analyzed. If time permits, certain countermeasures can be implemented using papers of the literature [14, 24].

Learning outcomes. By completing this lab, the students become aware of the threat posed by covert channels and the means by which an enforced security policy can be bypassed. Students can also discover advanced detection techniques.

[7]https://github.com/swdunlop/AndBug
[8]https://portswigger.net/burp

4.7 MEM Lab - Memory Dump Forensic

This lab (level 2) has been inspired by studies on recovering credentials from volatile memory [3, 19]. It is highly challenging for Java applications to clean their memory after allocating certain objects even after rebooting the device [16]. Thus, we have designed a lab wherein students inspect a dump of the memory obtained with Lime[9]. This dump is achieved after displaying a simple application with two `EditText` objects, which simulates an authentication activity. The goal of the lab is to capture the content of the two `EditText` objects from the dump.

Then, students should inspect the memory dump using the Volatility framework[10]. After identifying the Linux process corresponding to the Dalvik VM, we provide extensions for inspecting the heap of the virtual machine based on the work of Hilgers et al. [11]. Using Python scripts, students can manipulate classes and objects and their implementation at the C programming language level. Students are invited to write the script that enumerates all the classes and to identify the ones that extends `EditText`. This aids them to retrieve the credential from the memory dump.

Learning outcomes. Students comprehend the likely leaks induced by the memory management of Java-like virtual machines, Dalvik and Art. They are capable of conducting a simple forensic of a memory dump, which is of interest to digital investigators.

4.8 CLASS Lab - Vulnerable Class Loader

The CLASS lab (level 2) places the students in a situation wherein an attacker has compromised the remote server used by the application. We ask students to analyze and solve the situation following Bloom's taxonomy. This learning approach has already been investigated for learning web development in a secure manner [18]. In our lab, the vulnerable application loads a few classes from the remote server that is supposed to have been compromised by the attacker. The students have access to the source code of the first activity although not to the sources of the remote classes. They are required to investigate different attacks and if feasible, implement countermeasures.

The vulnerable application is composed of a regular activity that dynamically loads other activities from the remote server. The vulnerabilities are twofold. First, the application uses a custom class loader that is ineffectively implemented because it systematically loads classes from the remote resources rather than first asking the hierarchy of class loaders. Thus, the classes from the Android runtime such as `Checkbox` or `LinearLayout` can be overwritten by the downloaded activities. This can be used by the attacker to take control of the main activity. Secondly, the first activity stores certain confidential data in a static field. The attacker can access it later from the loaded activity, which is an unintentional leak of information. To disable those attacks, the students are required to patch the class loader and use an instance field rather than the static field.

Learning outcomes. Students should be capable of conducting a complete investigation of an application connected to a compromised server. Tthey should understand that an implementation can contain vulnerabilities if the developer does not comprehend the mechanisms induced by the used language or the operating system.

4.9 PACK Lab - Packers

The PACK lab (level 2) consists in reversing the MAL lab ransomware that are now obfuscated with different packing techniques. The packer uses native code to unpack the payload at runtime. The obfuscated methods are decoded immediately before being called and are re-encoded when they return. This lab requires a deep analysis to determine how the obfuscated code can be retrieved.

First, the students execute the applications in order to observe that they behave as those of the MAL lab. Then, they use Bytecode-Viewer or Jadx to inspect a specified malware sample and determine that the code of certain methods is empty. Using IDA Pro[11], the students are required to discover how the native code obfuscates the Java methods. At this stage of the lab, it is feasible to retrieve the original code of the malware sample.

However, additional ransomware samples using different packing algorithms are provided to the students. Consequently, new static analysis of each packing algorithm would be required, and therefore, we propose to switch to a dynamic approach. The students are guided to modify the code of AOSP: The Android VM is modified to dump the code of each method before executing them. We provide the most challenging parts of the modifications to the students to aid them to complete the lab. Based on the INST lab, the students flash the Sony Xperia X smartphone with the modified Android system. This permits them to automatically reverse all the samples.

Learning outcomes. Students comprehend and analyze the work achieved by a packer using ciphering algorithms. They also comprehend the benefit of a solution based on a combination of a static analysis and a dump that is performed during execution.

4.10 KERN Lab - Kernel ROP Attacks

The KERN lab (level 2 or 3) goes deeper into the security aspects related to Android's kernel. In this lab, we provide an emulator with a kernel containing a vulnerable driver. This driver can be exploited with a buffer overflow vulnerability that enables the execution of an arbitrary short payload. Because the kernel implements a `W xor X` policy, students are required to perform a ROP attack with gadgets available in the kernel. For achieving this step, students use ROPgadget[12] to search for gadgets in the `vmlinuz` file. The "Hello World" example consists in printing a message in the kernel logs. Students should learn to call the `printk` kernel function using several gadgets. If time permits, more complex attacks can be achieved to spy the memory of a targeted process.

Learning outcomes. This lab illustrates the importance of the security of all Android components. It trains students to perform attacks using multiple vectors including attacking the system itself.

The material associated to these labs can be found online at https://gitlab.inria.fr/jlalande/teaching-android-mobile-security

[9] https://github.com/504ensicsLabs/LiME
[10] https://www.volatilityfoundation.org/
[11] https://www.hex-rays.com/products/ida/
[12] https://github.com/JonathanSalwan/ROPgadget

Table 4: Evaluation of progress (δ) and average mark after labs (m) for each type of lab

	Attended lab:	DEV		INST		MAL		MEM		COV		CLASS	
	Nb of students:	$n = 27$		$n = 7$		$n = 28$		$n = 3$		$n = 11$		$n = 11$	
Questions	Scoring	δ	m	δ	m	δ	m	δ	mark	δ	m	δ	m
Are you able to develop an Android application that interacts with an HTTP server?	DEV	**+1.74**	**3.67**	+0.14	2.14	+0.75	2.64	+0.00	1.67	+0.18	2.36	+1.36	2.73
Are you able to compile and/or flash an Android distribution (e.g. AOSP)?	INST	+0.93	2.59	**+2.57**	**4.14**	+0.82	2.71	+0.00	1.00	+0.18	2.09	+0.55	1.91
Are you able to reverse Android malware?	MAL	+0.56	1.74	+1.29	2.29	**+1.46**	**2.96**	+0.00	1.00	+0.18	1.82	+0.55	1.73
Are you able to perform a forensic analysis of a dump of volatile Android memory?	MEM	+0.56	1.78	+0.86	1.86	+0.86	2.11	**+2.00**	**3.00**	+0.00	1.55	+0.18	1.27
Are you able to develop a covert channel to hide communication between two Android applications?	COV	+0.52	1.74	+0.00	1.00	+1.00	2.14	+0.00	1.00	**+2.45**	**3.82**	+0.36	1.55
Are you able to comprehend how a vulnerable class loader can be exploited and propose some patch?	CLASS	+0.44	1.59	+0.29	1.43	+0.96	2.21	+0.33	1.33	+0.09	1.64	**+0.91**	**2.27**

1 = Unknown – 2 = Discovering – 3 = Intermediate – 4 = Good knowledge – 5 = Advanced

5 EVALUATION

5.1 Audience

The presented labs have been used in several undergraduate programs in eight universities and engineering schools of three countries. We did not have the opportunity to play all the labs for the same pool of students. Nevertheless, multiple combinations of two or three labs have been tested. We have also used these labs for research summer schools and tutorials at international conferences for illustrating technical aspects of mobile security. Nevertheless, at the time of writing, the goal of this work is also to introduce the whole sequence of labs in the master degree curriculum, where security aspects have an important position.

5.2 Evaluation Design

We designed a survey for asking students to evaluate their capabilities with regard to the labs they attended. The concept was to ask the students to evaluate themselves regarding only one lab in order to measure the correlation between the lab they followed and the skill evaluated. If they followed two labs, we asked them to evaluate themselves with respect to the lab with the highest number of hours. The survey was sent in spring 2018 to the students we had taught between 2014 and 2018. From among the approximately 200 students, we obtained responses from 87.61% followed the lab a few months ago, 19% a year ago, 14% two years ago, and the remaining 6% over two years ago.

Table 4 presents the obtained results. The left column recalls the asked questions which correspond to the pedagogical goal of a lab. On the right, student evaluations have been reported in the column corresponding to the name of the lab they followed. With such a presentation of the results, the correlation should occur on the diagonal of the table. For evaluating each question, we used the following marking system inspired by the work of Campbell et al. [5]: 1) Unknown (No trace in my memory); 2) Discovering (I recall some of the content); 3) Intermediate (I understood most of the content); 4) Good knowledge (I am able to do the lab again, without a supervisor and with the help of documents); 5) Advanced (I can reuse my knowledge in another use case).

For each question, a student is asked to rate himself/herself "before" and "after" the lab, which enables the computation of a differential score corresponding to the difference in the mark before and after the lab. This provides more information than the raw mark does with regard to whether the students have previously followed courses on related topics. It enables the evaluation of the progress of the students irrespective of their starting point. In Table 4, m corresponds to the average of the marks "after the lab" (from one to five) and δ corresponds to the average of the differential marks.

5.3 Evaluation Results

The correlation between the labs and the evaluated skills is evident: for each lab, the highest scores correspond to the pedagogical goal of the lab. The improvement in student's skills on the diagonal is an average of +1.85, which is encouraging as it is approximately equivalent to shifting from "Discovering" to "Good knowledge." Only the CLASS lab achieves an improvement of +0.91. This can be explained by the level of difficulty of the lab, which corresponds to the Analyze phase of the taxonomy and requires substantial effort of investigation by the students. The CLASS lab also achieves a progression of +1.36 for the DEV lab. This can be explained by the fact that the CLASS lab involves HTTP requests.

The self-evaluation of skills by the students yielded an average mark of 3.31 on the diagonal. The marks of the MAL and MEM labs are approximately equal to 3, which is a reasonable result considering the technical challenge associated with them. The COV labs achieved the highest mark (3.82). We conjecture this to be a result of the high number of allocated hours for this lab. More simple activities achieve higher results (DEV, INST) as students feel comfortable when performing the labs.

The results confirm that the labs are aligned with their pedagogical goal. The marks reveal that students tend to evaluate their skills between intermediate and reasonable knowledge levels. Indeed, only years of practice can provide further knowledge.

6 CONCLUSION

This paper explores several technical aspects with regard to the learning of Android security. Based on Bloom's taxonomy, we designed various labs that aid students to learn more deeply about the internal aspects of Android. By programming attacks and studying malware or vulnerable applications, students are trained to analyze complex security problems. This pedagogical design aids them to improve their skills in mobile security by providing a deeper understanding of the complexity of the software components used by Google to design its operating system.

REFERENCES

[1] Yasemin Acar, Michael Backes, Sascha Fahl, Doowon Kim, Michelle L Mazurek, and Christian Stransky. 2016. You Get Where You're Looking for: The Impact of Information Sources on Code Security. In *IEEE Symposium on Security and Privacy*. IEEE Computer Society, 289–305. https://doi.org/10.1109/SP.2016.25

[2] Jeremy Andrus and Jason Nieh. 2012. Teaching operating systems using android. In *43rd ACM technical symposium on Computer Science Education*. ACM Press, Raleigh, North Carolina, USA, 613–618. https://doi.org/10.1145/2157136.2157312

[3] Dimitris Apostolopoulos and Giannis Marinakis. 2013. Discovering authentication credentials in volatile memory of Android mobile devices. In *12th IFIP Conference on e-Business, e-Services, e-Society*. Athens, Greece, 178–185. https://doi.org/10.1007/978-3-642-37437-1_15

[4] Muhammad Rizwan Asghar and Andrew Luxton-Reilly. 2018. Teaching Cyber Security Using Competitive Software Obfuscation and Reverse Engineering Activities. In *49th ACM Technical Symposium on Computer Science Education - SIGCSE '18*. ACM Press, Baltimore, MD, USA, 179–184. https://doi.org/10.1145/3159450.3159489

[5] Jennifer Campbell and Anya Tafliovich. 2015. An Experience Report: Using Mobile Development To Teach Software Design. In *46th ACM Technical Symposium on Computer Science Education - SIGCSE '15*. ACM Press, Kansas City, MO, USA, 506–511. https://doi.org/10.1145/2676723.2677307

[6] Nikolay Elenkov. 2014. *Android Security Internals: An In-Depth Guide to Android's Security Architecture*. No Starch Press.

[7] William Enck, Peter Gilbert, Byung-Gon Chun, Landon P. Cox, Jaeyeon Jung, Patrick McDaniel, and Anmol N. Sheth. 2010. TaintDroid: an information-flow tracking system for realtime privacy monitoring on smartphones. In *9th USENIX Symposium on Operating Systems Design and Implementation*. USENIX Association, Vancouver, BC, Canada, 393–407.

[8] Andrey Esakia, Shuo Niu, and D. Scott McCrickard. 2015. Augmenting Undergraduate Computer Science Education With Programmable Smartwatches. In *46th ACM Technical Symposium on Computer Science Education - SIGCSE '15*. ACM Press, Kansas City, MO, USA, 66–71. https://doi.org/10.1145/2676723.2677285

[9] Sheran Gunasekera. 2012. *Android Apps Security*. Apress.

[10] Minzhe Guo, Prabir Bhattacharya, Ming Yang, Kai Qian, and Li Yang. 2013. Learning mobile security with android security labware. In *44th ACM technical symposium on Computer science education - SIGCSE '15*. ACM Press, Kansas City, MO, USA, 675–680. https://doi.org/10.1145/2445196.2445394

[11] Christian Hilgers, Holger Macht, Tilo Muller, and Michael Spreitzenbarth. 2014. Post-Mortem Memory Analysis of Cold-Booted Android Devices. In *2014 Eighth International Conference on IT Security Incident Management & IT Forensics*. IEEE Computer Society, Munster, Germany, 62–75. https://doi.org/10.1109/IMF.2014.8

[12] David R Krathwohl. 2002. A Revision of Bloom's Taxonomy: An Overview. *Theory Into Practice* 41, 4 (2002), 212–218. https://doi.org/10.1207/s15430421tip4104_2

[13] Jonathan Levin. 2015. *Android Internals: A Confectioner's Cookbook*.

[14] Claudio Marforio, Hubert Ritzdorf, Aurélien Francillon, and Srdjan Capkun. 2012. Analysis of the communication between colluding applications on modern smartphones. In *28th Annual Computer Security Applications Conference*. ACM Press, Orlando, Florida, USA, 51–60. https://doi.org/10.1145/2420950.2420958

[15] Matthew Neis, Vincent Cefalu, and Ankur Chattopadhyay. 2018. Developing a Unique Android App-driven Nifty Middle-School Educational Module on Mobile Security for Driving Basic Information Security Awareness and Generating Interests in Cybersecurity. In *49th ACM Technical Symposium on Computer Science Education - SIGCSE '18*. ACM Press, Baltimore, MD, USA, 1081–1081. https://doi.org/10.1145/3159450.3162243

[16] Christoforos Ntantogian, Dimitris Apostolopoulos, Giannis Marinakis, and Christos Xenakis. 2014. Evaluating the privacy of Android mobile applications under forensic analysis. *Computers & Security* 42 (may 2014), 66–76. https://doi.org/10.1016/j.cose.2014.01.004

[17] Or Peles and Roee Hay. 2015. One Class to Rule Them All: 0-Day Deserialization Vulnerabilities in Android. In *9th USENIX Workshop on Offensive Technologies*. Washington, WA, USA, 1–12.

[18] Michael Sonntag. 2013. Learning security through insecurity. In *2nd International Conference on E-Learning and E-Technologies in Education*. Lodz, Poland, 143–148. https://doi.org/10.1109/ICeLeTE.2013.6644363

[19] Pasquale Stirparo, Igor Nai Fovino, and Ioannis Kounelis. 2013. Data-in-use leakages from Android memory - Test and analysis. In *9th IEEE International Conference on Wireless and Mobile Computing, Networking and Communications*. 718–725. https://doi.org/10.1109/WiMOB.2013.6673433

[20] Kelvin Sung and Arjmand Samuel. 2014. Mobile application development classes for the mobile era. In *2014 conference on Innovation & technology in computer science education*. ACM Press, Uppsala, Sweden, 141–146. https://doi.org/10.1145/2591708.2591710

[21] Seyitriza Tigrek and Mohammad Obadat. 2012. Teaching smartphones programming using (Android Java): Pedagogy and innovation. In *2012 International Conference on Information Technology Based Higher Education and Training*. IEEE Computer Society, 1–7. https://doi.org/10.1109/ITHET.2012.6246039

[22] Zouheir Trabelsi, Mohammed Al Matrooshi, and Saeed Al Bairaq. 2016. A Smartphone App for Enhancing Students' Hands-on Learning on Network and DoS Attacks Traffic Generation. In *17th Annual Conference on Information Technology Education*. ACM Press, Boston, MS, USA, 48–53. https://doi.org/10.1145/2978192.2978229

[23] Zouheir Trabelsi, Mohammed Al Matrooshi, Saeed Al Bairaq, Walid Ibrahim, and Mohammad M. Masud. 2017. Android based mobile apps for information security hands-on education. *Education and Information Technologies* 22, 1 (jan 2017), 125–144. https://doi.org/10.1007/s10639-015-9439-8

[24] Marcin Urbanski, Wojciech Mazurczyk, Jean-Francois Lalande, and Luca Caviglione. 2017. Detecting Local Covert Channels Using Process Activity Correlation on Android Smartphones. *International Journal of Computer Systems Science and Engineering* 32, 2 (March 2017).

[25] Xiaohong Yuan, Kenneth Williams, Scott McCrickard, Charles Hardnett, Litany H. Lineberry, Kelvin Bryant, Jinsheng Xu, Albert Esterline, Anyi Liu, Selvarajah Mohanarajah, and Rachel Rutledge. 2016. Teaching mobile computing and mobile security. In *IEEE Frontiers in Education Conference*. IEEE Computer Society, Erie, PA, USA, 1–6. https://doi.org/10.1109/FIE.2016.7757365

[26] Karim Yaghmour. [n. d.]. *Embedded Android: Porting, Extending, and Customizing*. O'Reilly Media, Inc.

Allowing and Fully Supporting Multiple Programming Languages in a Computer Graphics Course: An Experience

Amit Shesh
Northeastern University, Boston MA, USA
ashesh@ccs.neu.edu

ABSTRACT

This paper reports an experience of offering an introductory computer graphics course in two languages, Java and C++, in the same section. This was done to target a more diverse audience of students coming from different majors and concentrations. Students chose between these languages and could switch at any time during the course. All materials related to lectures, code examples and assignments were provided in both languages. Technical support was provided for both languages throughout the course. In order to streamline this effort programming environments and supporting tools were chosen and standardized for both languages. Student experience was monitored throughout the semester using survey instruments. The experience involved significant planning, overhead and expected and unexpected issues throughout the semester. Although this experience deals with a computer graphics course, we believe other courses, especially higher-level electives, can be made multi-lingual to cater to students with different backgrounds.

CCS CONCEPTS

• **Social and professional topics → Comp. Sci. education.**

KEYWORDS

Multilingual CS course; computer graphics; experience report

ACM Reference Format:
Amit Shesh. 2019. Allowing and Fully Supporting Multiple Programming Languages in a Computer Graphics Course: An Experience. In *Proceedings of the 50th ACM Technical Symposium on Computer Science Education (SIGCSE '19), February 27-March 2, 2019, Minneapolis, MN, USA.* ACM, New York, NY, USA, 7 pages. https://doi.org/10.1145/3287324.3287464

1 INTRODUCTION

Today's computing programs expose students to many programming languages and supporting tools. In addition students can choose from an increasing number of concentrations and minors related to computer science, each with its own set of requirements. As a result a computer science instructor faces a unique pedagogical challenge: choosing appropriate technology (e.g. programming language and supporting tools) for a course to not only satisfy its outcomes but also suit technical backgrounds, programming proficiency and expectations of students. This problem is often addressed more closely in the design and close alignment of lower-level "core" courses. However higher-level elective courses (such as computer graphics, HCI, etc.) typically enjoy more curricular freedom, and therefore are more prone to such challenges.

For example computer graphics is traditionally taught using OpenGL in many programs. C/C++ are the natural languages of choice with OpenGL, although many other languages now support OpenGL. However C/C++ has long fallen out of favor in introductory programming courses [18], and is often used only in systems courses. This means that many students enter a computer graphics course with a limited knowledge of C/C++, either from self-learning or other courses where they learned it on-the-fly.

One way to address this situation is to allow many programming languages and environments in a course and giving a choice to the students. A multilingual course may be a good option in many situations. Some courses naturally attract students of different (programming) backgrounds (e.g. CS and engineering students in a graphics course). Languages more appropriate for teaching may conflict those relevant and demanded by industry [15]. Some courses may have content that is language-agnostic (e.g. capstone courses that apply previously learned skills, algorithms courses with programming components). Some courses may be programming-intensive but expect students to learn relevant languages *on-the-side* (e.g. HCI). Courses that expose students to *new content* in multiple languages are relatively uncommon. Letting students choose languages in the structured setting of a course is good practice for when they would face this choice in the real world.

However implementing a multilingual course well has several *practical* challenges. The content of the course should work "equally well" with multiple languages for the choices to be equitable. If supporting tools are not chosen well, students may spend precious time and effort on logistics (e.g. the observed influence of programming environments on learning for novices [17] can occur in higher-level courses too). The overarching challenge is to *commit* to supporting the course in multiple languages: using all of them in lectures, code examples and assignments and providing technical support for them. This takes time and effort [19]. Our experience underscores the importance of this commitment: students may need significant help with issues that may be secondary to the course outcomes, but adversely affect their ability to learn and score well.

1.1 Reader Take-Away and Claims

This paper describes a computer graphics course. However we strive to generalize our experience and recommendations in a way that they are relevant to other (typically high-level elective) courses.

SIGCSE '19, February 27-March 2, 2019, Minneapolis, MN, USA

ACM ISBN 978-1-4503-5890-3/19/02...$15.00
https://doi.org/10.1145/3287324.3287464

Program	Spring 2016	Fall 2016	Fall 2017
CS	7	10	7
Minor in CS	1	1	0
CS + Math	8	8	8
CS + Game Design	13	1	0
CS + Interactive Media	8	2	1
CS + Digital Art	0	2	2
Engineering	1	2	1
CS (grad)	0	1	9
Other	0	1	1

Table 1: Student population in the course. The course was offered in two languages from the 2nd semester.

This paper focuses on the motivations, planning, logistics and pedagogical experience of such an endeavor. It does not claim that our approach results in greater student success or increase in student performance, although there is some evidence that it helps to attract students from different degree paths. We hope our experience will be useful to new and experienced instructors from planning, implementation and assessment perspectives.

2 FEASIBILITY AND BACKGROUND

What may be good *pedagogical* justification for offering a course in multiple languages? Some questions/criteria that we considered and are applicable to any course:

C1: Is there student demand? If there is a demographic that is typical in or targeted by the course that could benefit from using another language, this may be worthwhile. Examples include students from different majors, prior course work or work experience.

C2: Is there curricular demand? If the course satisfies requirements for a particular concentration, offering the course in a specific language may better match the goals of that concentration.

C3: Do all languages fit well with content? If a language makes implementation harder and/or time-consuming it may not be chosen by enough students. Or worse, students who choose it may face hardships and regret it.

C4: Are there support resources? Supporting additional languages requires relevant expertise in the course staff. A language that is allowed in the syllabus but not supported enough in office hours will likely not result in a positive student experience.

C5a: Is it appropriate to let students choose? Can students make make an informed choice of language? Have they had prior experience in self-learning a language to gauge their own ability?

C5b: How committed should students be to their choice? Will they be able to change their choice, and if so, how easily?

2.1 Background of our course

Our computer graphics course is an upper-level elective for undergraduates and is the first course on the subject in our program. The course content is a mix of conceptual knowledge and practical graphics programming. It uses OpenGL [7] and shader-based programming. We require support for OpenGL 3.3 or higher (most computers bought in the last 5 years would support this).

In addition to a traditional computer science major, we offer more than 20 *combined* majors with other colleges in art, science, engineering and humanities. Although there is a required "core" of programming courses, other supporting requirements and hence prior course work of students differ. Our course typically attracts about 6 – 7 of these combinations, along with some other majors (see Table 1). Often this course is cross-listed as a graduate-level course, attracting students with even more varying programming backgrounds that are not cultivated by our core courses. The undergraduate pre-requisite for this course is to have 1 semester of Java programming, although typically most students in this course have more than that. Graduate students are required to have "prior programming experience in a high-level language".

Computer graphics courses are typically offered in C++ (as evident from most common textbooks and OpenGL documentation using C/C++) and the language is still preferred in many graphics-related industries. However as most students in the course are typically from our CS programs, we were strongly advised to offer the course in Java in Spring 2016. We did so, but surprisingly several students wished the course was offered in C++ as well. We found that most of these students were in game-design-related programs (as revealed by them), which required C++. Engineering majors, although small in number, did not have any prior experience in Java. In later semesters we found a somewhat greater preference to C++ among graduate students as well. However a significant portion of other students still preferred Java. In an effort to make the course more inclusive to students from such different backgrounds, we decided to let each student choose between Java and C++. This would allow us to cater to not only our "traditional" CS students, but also combined and other majors and graduate students.

2.2 Course Outcomes

Our course outcomes remained the same before and after the language addition, with the exception of the italicized part. They are:

- Write simple as well as moderately complex graphics applications and shaders using OpenGL 3.3+ and GLSL *with Java and/or C++* that perform 2D and 3D interactive graphics.
- Explain the overall process of displaying static and dynamic graphical content on a screen
- Explain and implement several algorithms related to computer graphics
- Implement various processes and graphical operations such as modeling, viewing and rendering in 2D and 3D
- Use vector and matrix algebra, coordinate and solid geometry and physics to solve problems in computer graphics
- Implement a ray tracing application

2.3 Desired Pedagogical Outcomes

Retain original outcomes and course work: To maintain the quality of the course, we wanted to retain its outcomes and objectives of individual assignments in the 2-language version.

Provide all relevant material in both languages: We wanted to provide all examples (developed offline or as part of lectures) in both languages. A student should be able to download and run an example in the chosen IDE without any additional setup.

Retain original goals behind design of code: Many frameworks significantly scaffold over low-level details, which is not ideal when students are learning the basics. We build our own scaffolding with a *shallow* abstraction so that students may see low-level details. We wished to retain this aspect across both languages.

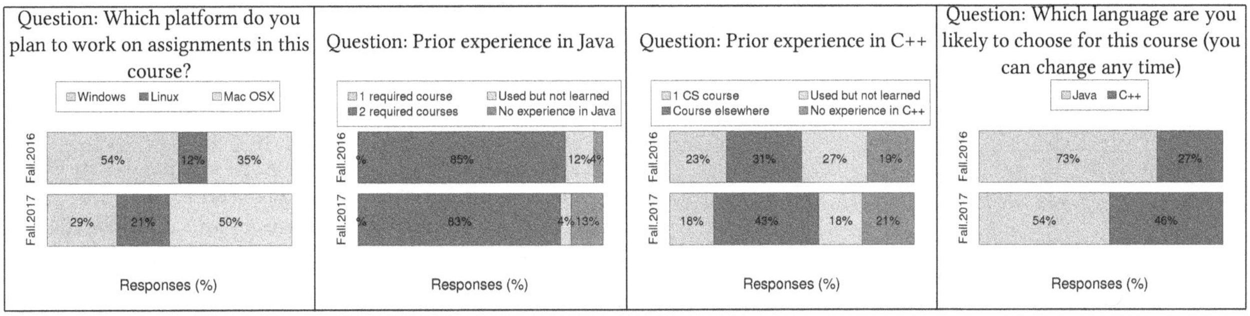

Figure 1: First-day survey responses in Fall 2016 (N=26) and Fall 2017 (N=29). Both semesters had 100% response rate.

No.	Question
Q1	My assessment of the level of difficulty of this assignment was: **(4-level Likert scale)**
Q2	The reason for my difficulty rating in the above question is:
Q3	Which language did you use to complete this assignment? **(C++, Java)**
Q4	For the language I chose for this assignment: I received adequate help from the course staff **(5-level Likert scale)**
Q5	In the language I chose for this assignment: I could find all the documentation that I was looking for (just language, not OpenGL) **(5-level Likert scale)**
Q6	In the language I chose for this assignment: I was satisfied with the level of documentation I found (for OpenGL, not the general language) **(5-level Likert scale)**
Q7	In the language I chose for this assignment: I had no problems related to syntax or debugging **(5-level Likert scale)**
Q8	I faced little to no platform-specific issues (i.e. related to your operating system) in this assignment **(5-level Likert scale)**
Q9	I am likely to continue using the same language that I used in this assignment, in the next assignment **(Yes/No)**
Q10	Was the language you used for this assignment different from earlier assignments? **(Yes/No)**
Q11	If you changed language, what was the reason you did? **(a)** I faced difficulty (syntax-wise) in my earlier choice **(b)** I had difficulty setting up the environment for my earlier choice **(c)** the partner I was worked with chose this language so I switched **(d)** Other reason **(e)** I did not change language

Table 2: Post-assignment survey. Students were required to fill out this survey after each of the first 4 assignments in Fall 2016.

Provide technical help in both languages and all platforms: We wanted to provide students with adequate technical help, across languages and platforms. Most students choose to work on their personal computers and create a healthy mix of language and platform (see Figure 2). Also most students do not understand enough the interplay between graphics programming, platform and GPU.
Difficulty independent of language choice: We wanted to make the coding examples equally understandable and documented in both languages. Secondly we wanted the expected effort on assignments to be equitable for both languages.
Freedom to make and change choice: We wanted students to choose between Java and C++, and also be able to switch languages between assignments if they wished. This is challenging because most assignments in this course build on each other. As stated above we did not want to abandon prior assignments.
Monitor student experience and seek feedback: In order to know and document student experience we wanted to get continuous feedback from them. This would make it easier for us to discover issues early on and take corrective action as necessary.

3 PLANNING THE COURSE

We started planning about one month before the Fall 2016 semester started (in retrospect, that was not enough). Incremental changes in the next semester did not take significant time. Subsequent subsections discuss specific planning items.

3.1 Instruments for Student Feedback

The first-day survey was optional for students, although they were told that taking it would help them choose their language. Figure 1 shows the questions for this survey and students' responses. It is interesting to note in students' responses that a higher percentage chose Java, although many had prior experience in C/C++. We think this may be because our CS2 and CS3 use Java and are required for all CS majors. In Fall 2017 the proportion of students choosing C++ increased, partly because of graduate students (they were 25% of the students in the course).

The post-assignment survey was administered at the end of an assignment to poll students' experience with the language of their choice. (Questions: Table 2, Responses: Figure 4). We made access to the next assignment contingent upon an attempt to complete the survey for the previous assignment, to ensure full participation.

As both instruments were designed to see if students had specific struggles, they were not anonymous. However they were not worth any grade, and students were assured that the responses were only to help them in case they were struggling[1].

[1]We subsequently have obtained IRB approval for using the data in this paper

Library	Opengl	UI Dev.	XML	Image I/O
JOGL [5] + Swing	✓	✓	✓	✓
freeglut [2] (C)	✓	Limited	X	X
SFML [10]	✓	Limited	X	✓
Qt [9] (C++)	✓	✓	✓	✓

Table 3: Survey of tools for Java and C++ (bold: our choices).

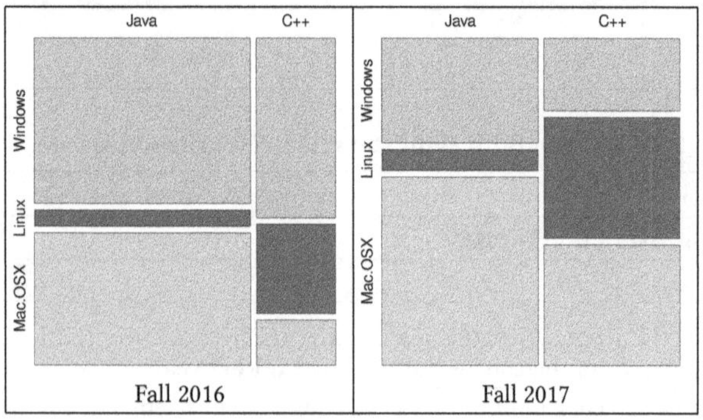

Figure 2: Language:Platform preferences of students according to the first-day survey responses. Please see Section 2.3.

3.2 Language tools

OpenGL is a rendering library originally written for the C language. Shader programs use a language called GLSL. OpenGL is implemented completely in the display driver of the computer. However OpenGL requires a "rendering context" (i.e. a window within which it may render). Therefore one must use a separate UI library that supports OpenGL. Also our coding examples required XML parsing, support for common image formats (to use images as textures) and some UI capability (mouse and key events).

We used the JOGL [5] library for Java as it is fairly mature and comprehensive. We used the IntelliJ [4] IDE as students were familiar with it from previous courses. There are several choices for C/C++. We surveyed several choices (summarized in Table 3). We chose Qt [9] because of its cross-platform support, completeness (one framework for all required capabilities) and *similarity to coding constructs* (a SAX parser and image I/O capabilities similar in design to Java). This last aspect helped us to homogenize the Java and C++ implementations. This facilitated a smooth transition from one language to another, in case a student wished to switch. We used the JOML library [6] in Java and the glm library [3] in C++ for matrix operations.

3.3 Design of code base

Figure 3 shows our common design that we implemented in both Java and C++. Creating and using one design upfront provided several advantages. The code base in both languages was similar as they emanated from the same design. This allowed students to compare and contrast implementations. Deploying examples was faster, as we would implement an example in one language and then quickly replicate it in the other. By further isolating library-dependent components in the design, changing libraries would be easier (e.g. one could change from Qt to another library in C++ and re-implement only classes shown in yellow in Figure 3).

Lang.	Fall 2016				Fall 2017				
	A1	A2	A3	A4	A1	A2	A3	A4	A5
Java	21	20	20	20	17	18	17	19	19
C++	5	6	6	6	12	11	12	10	10

Table 4: Use of languages for Assignments 1-4 in Fall 2016 and Assignments 1-5 in Fall 2017 (see Q3 in Table 2). A4 in Fall 2016 was roughly split into A4 and A5 in Fall 2017.

3.4 Implementation and Deployment of Code

We released implementations of the design in Figure 3 incrementally as the semester progressed. Examples provided to students were developed offline or interactively in class (see Section 4.1).

As noted by Angel *et al.* [14], there is a steep learning curve for shader-based OpenGL programming (drawing a simple triangle requires a preliminary understanding of the graphics pipeline, the program itself and two shader programs). We asked graded questions in the first two assignments of the course relevant to the provided implementation. Students were expected to read code, understand its design and answer questions based on them.

We had an unexpected issue in the code, that retrospectively was due to insufficient planning. We implemented interfaces as *pure virtual classes* in C++. About halfway through the semester we realized that there was no good way to implement *generic interfaces* in C++, as it does not allow *virtual template functions*. This caused a re-design of the C++ implementation, which although minor, was not backward compatible with the code released prior to the redesign. We provided 1 : 1 help to students using C++ who could not resolve these issues by themselves.

4 PRACTICAL EXPERIENCES

4.1 Student Experience

Lectures and logistics: In addition to spending some lecture time to explain setup issues, we provided video tutorials for both languages/environments for students. Throughout the course we showed and developed examples in lectures using both Java and C++, often using the first and highlighting the differences in the second. Occasionally there were class discussions about the difference in implementations between the two languages. The most substantive discussion was on the topic of memory layouts for shader programs. OpenGL and GLSL extensively use array operations (interleaving, fast indexing, etc.), and understanding this is instrumental to understanding buffer objects [14] which are the main data vehicles in shader-based graphics. While C/C++ implements this quite naturally with arrays, JOGL implements them using the Java Native Interface (JNI) and *FloatBuffer* and *IntBuffer* constructs that most students had never encountered before. When a program crashed due to incorrect buffer object allocation/usage students would get vague JVM crash messages that were difficult to debug without help (the corresponding messages in C++ were more helpful, or at least familiar because memory errors are more common).

Language change: Table 4 shows the distribution by language in Fall 2016 (N=26) and Fall 2017 (N=29). In Fall 2016 over 4 assignments we had a total of 8 instances of students changing languages, whereas there were 6 such instances in Fall 2017 over 5 assignments. Some stated reasons were: difficulty setting up environments for their initial choice on their machine (3 in 2016, 1 in

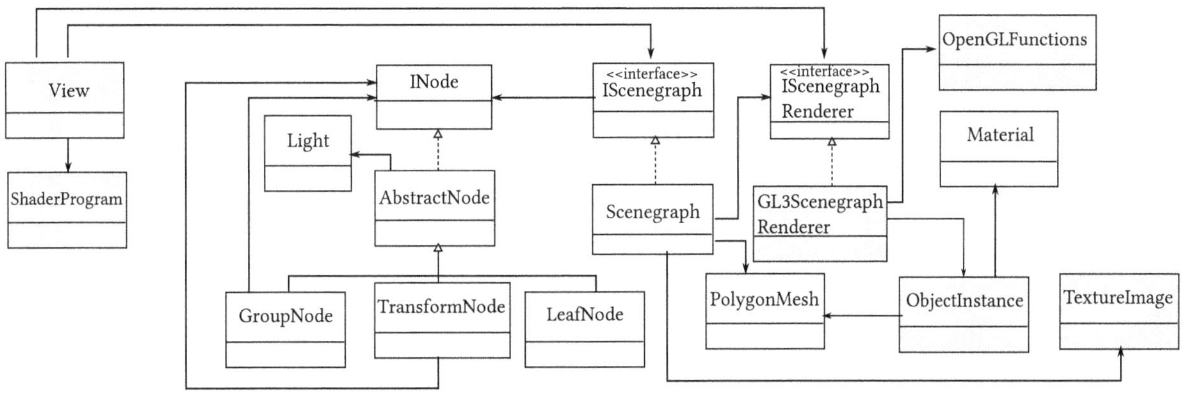

Figure 3: Design of our code base. Library-specific (JOGL/Qt) code was restricted to only some classes (in yellow). For example, if the C++ implementation shifted from Qt to a new library only the yellow classes would be re-implemented.

2017), syntax difficulties (1 in 2016, 2 in 2017), difficulty finding examples online (1 student in 2016), and switching because their partner used a different language (3 in 2016, 3 in 2017).

Student Feedback: Figure 4 shows the student responses to the post-assignment surveys shown in Table 2. In both semesters students seemed satisfied with the level of help they received (Q4). The satisfaction ratings for finding OpenGL documentation for their language were lower than expected (Row 2). Upon slicing the data by language (Rows 3,4) we find that the C++ responses seem to be somewhat higher. However the sample size for C++ is too low to make any conclusions. Students also did not report many issues related to platforms, other than those verbally communicated and addressed during office hours and in class.

4.2 Instructor Experience

Language and platform support: As Figure 2 shows the course had a mix of language:platform combinations. The decision to choose mature tools like Qt and JOGL helped to minimize compatibility issues. Nevertheless there were some idiosyncracies. Rendering of text using JOGL did not work on *some* Macs. This was eventually attributed to a bug in the JOGL library which was reported to developers. The design differences between Qt and JOGL APIs created some problems (Qt does not choose core shader profiles by default, JOGL does not allow specifying profiles explicitly). As a result the provided code examples not working for some students, in a somewhat unpredictable way. All such issues were eventually resolved.

In addition to language and platform, an unexpected third dimension emerged: graphics hardware. There were several instances where the same program would work differently (or not at all) for different vendors (e.g. Intel vs NVidia). Due to the age of their computers and graphics hardware there were issues with support for some GLSL versions. In at least two cases the culprit was the smart-switching technology (e.g. Nvidia Optimus [8]) that, unknown to them, caused their programs to run on the "less-capable" GPU. In some cases shader programs worked differently on different hardware even though they had the required OpenGL support. This is possibly because of vendor-dependent OpenGL drivers (we noticed many issues occurred on Macs).

Course staff: a continuing problem that we faced was the recruitment of students as competent graders/teaching assistants. There is no graphics research group of students which can be reliably be tapped to assist in teaching this course. We hope that eventually this course itself will create a pipeline of future graders but until then the instructors carry most of the load of helping students with their programming problems. The most compelling evidence of students needing support related to implementation rather than concepts was the time spent on off-line interaction, both scheduled (office hours, email, discussion forum) and unscheduled (help sessions after lecture, often measured in hours).

4.3 "Before and After" Comparison

Since we do not have survey data from Spring 2016 it is difficult to perform a "before-and-after" quantitative analysis. However some comparisons may be made. We retained the same course outcomes as described in Section 2.2, with the exception of adding the 2-language wording. We also retained the topics, lecture plans, course textbook and materials provided to the students, again with the exceptions of providing all code examples in two languages and language-specific setup tutorials. We also retained the objectives, basic themes and progression of all assignments. Finally we found no statistically significant differences between final grade distributions across these semesters (p=0.0912 in a 1-sided ANOVA test).

4.4 Lessons learned

Student use the flexibility: We were able to accommodate students from different backgrounds. Many students have a strong preference towards one language, but that language differs with background. Students saw examples in 2 languages, chose one and occasionally switched.

More robust testing and deployment is needed: A more robust testing plan for code examples is needed to streamline support and minimize "one-off" issues. We recommend picking students from class as *beta-testers* to periodically test code.

Language:Platform issues are more prevalent: We have experienced this (albeit on a smaller scale) even in monolingual courses. Students are often unaware of platform-specific issues, but it is an important experience for them to face and resolve them.

Taming language differences through design: We feel switching languages for students, and building code examples for instructors would have been tougher if the code design was not unified.

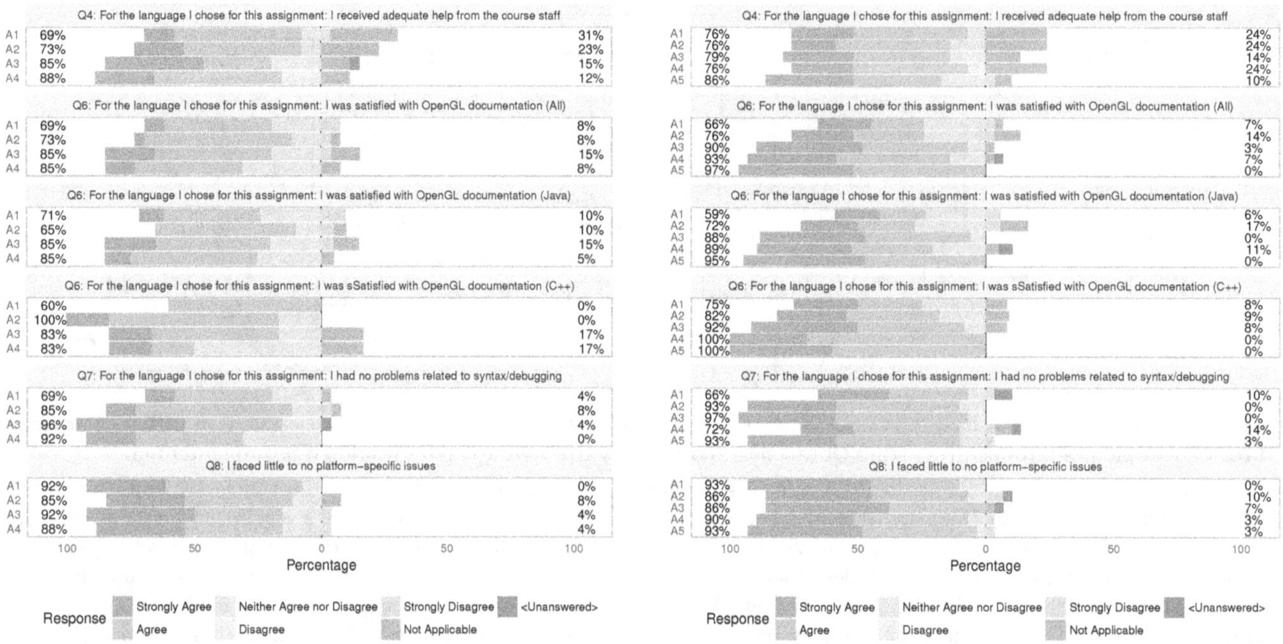

Figure 4: Student responses to questions 4, 6, 7 and 8 in the post-assignment surveys (see Table 2). Data was collected with surveys at the end of assignments A1-A4 for Fall 2016 and A1-A5 for Fall 2017.

5 CURRENT AND FUTURE INSIGHTS

Language choice: Java is not a popular language in computer graphics, and it was not our first choice of language. However being an introductory course, we have designed it to focus on concepts and theory, whereas efficiency and performance are somewhat secondary. Therefore choosing Java does not have a detrimental effect on the course objectives. We plan to explore WebGL with Javascript in the course in future. This may attract more students interested in applying graphics to web applications. However we expect challenges related to the unfamiliarity with Javascript.

Overhead: is it worth it? As discussed earlier, there is significant overhead to preparing course materials and their delivery in multiple languages. However much of this effort is one-time. Our experience shows that subsequent efforts to improve materials is incremental, especially after a basic design infrastructure is in place. Much of the software industry has moved away from working with a single-language ecosystem to using multiple languages as needs dictate. We think it is important to similarly convey to students how the concepts they learn apply (seamlessly, or with issues) across languages. This overall aim leads us to firmly believe that the associated overhead is well worth the learning benefits.

6 RELATED WORK

Computer graphics education has undergone a metamorphosis from the perspective of pedagogical style [13]. For reasons mentioned in Section 3.2 teaching computer graphics requires a significant usage of supporting tools and related platforms, ranging from desktop to mobile and web applications. Ackermann *et al.* [12] offer an exemplar experience of choosing between them as a significant component of the design of such a course. CGEMS [1] offers some evidence of the importance of programming materials in teaching graphics by its very existence and its growing repository of resources. Similar to computer graphics a case can be made for an equitable choice of programming languages and platforms in teaching other CS courses: mobile development [16] and operating systems [22] are two examples.

In general choosing a programming language for a course has been well-researched and debated. Language and tools are two of several factors in the teaching and success of introductory programming courses: see Pears *et al.* [21] for a survey. However the idea of making courses (especially higher level) multilingual does not seem well studied. This was somewhat surprising as we know from experience that many courses allow this to some degree. Leutenegger *et al.* [20] propose a sequence of introductory programming courses that switch languages between them, but each course uses one language. Tjaden *et al.* [23] make an argument similar to ours for a data structures courses. Although they emphasize a need to support code uniformly in all languages, their course content allows them to avoid specific programming examples in lectures.

7 CONCLUSION

Due to growing diversity in student backgrounds and prior experience it has become more important to offer courses with flexibility in the languages and tools used in them. Our experience shows how a computer graphics course can be offered with multiple languages that allows flexibility to students and enough technical support for them, without compromising on its outcomes and learning objectives. The same approach can be applied to other elective courses that may benefit from being multilingual.

ACKNOWLEDGMENTS

We thank the anonymous reviewers for their valuable feedback, suggestions for improvement of this paper and ideas for further investigation in this course.

REFERENCES

[1] 2017. CGEMS: Computer Graphics Educational Materials Source. https://education.siggraph.org/resources/cgems.
[2] 2017. FreeGLUT. http://freeglut.sourceforge.net/.
[3] 2017. GLM: OpenGL Mathematics. http://glm.g-truc.net/0.9.8/index.html.
[4] 2017. IntelliJ IDEA. https://www.jetbrains.com/idea/.
[5] 2017. The JOGL Project. http://jogamp.org/jogl/www/.
[6] 2017. JOML: Java OpenGL Math Library. https://github.com/JOML-CI.
[7] 2017. OpenGL. https://www.opengl.org/.
[8] 2017. Optimus Technology. http://www.nvidia.com/object/optimus_technology.html.
[9] 2017. Qt. https://www.qt.io/.
[10] 2017. SFML. https://www.sfml-dev.org/.
[11] 2018. QOpenGLFunctions: Qt encapsulation of OpenGL functions. http://doc.qt.io/qt-5/qopenglfunctions.html.
[12] Philipp Ackermann and Thomas Bach. 2015. Redesign of an Introductory Computer Graphics Course. In *EG 2015 - Education Papers*.
[13] Edward Angel, Steve Cunningham, Peter Shirley, and Kelvin Sung. 2006. Teaching Computer Graphics Without Raster-level Algorithms. In *Proc. SIGCSE*. 266–267.
[14] Edward Angel and Dave Shreiner. 2011. *Interactive Computer Graphics: A Top-Down Approach with Shader-Based OpenGL* (6th ed.). Addison-Wesley Publishing Company. 717–725 pages.
[15] Adair Dingle and Carol Zander. 2000. Assessing the Ripple Effect of CS1 Language Choice. *J. Comput. Sci. Coll.* 16, 2 (Oct. 2000), 85–93.
[16] Mark H. Goadrich and Michael P. Rogers. 2011. Smart Smartphone Development: IOS Versus Android. In *Proc. SIGCSE*. 607–612.
[17] Paul Gross and Kris Powers. 2005. Evaluating Assessments of Novice Programming Environments. In *Proc. ICER*. 99–110.
[18] Philip Guo. 2014. Python is now the most popular introductory teaching language at top us universities. *BLOG@ CACM, July* (2014), 47.
[19] PA Lee and Chris Phillips. 2003. *An assessment of c++ as an introductory teaching language*. Technical Report.
[20] Scott Leutenegger and Jeffrey Edgington. 2007. A Games First Approach to Teaching Introductory Programming. In *Proc. SIGCSE*. 115–118.
[21] Arnold Pears, Stephen Seidman, Lauri Malmi, Linda Mannila, Elizabeth Adams, Jens Bennedsen, Marie Devlin, and James Paterson. 2007. A Survey of Literature on the Teaching of Introductory Programming. In *Proc. ITiCSE-WGR*. 204–223.
[22] Robert J. Sheehan. 2007. Teaching Operating Systems with Ruby. In *Proc. ITiCSE*. 38–42.
[23] Brian Tjaden and Hannah Tang. 2003. Coding in Tongues: A Bilingual Programming Perspective to Data Structures. *J. Comput. Sci. Coll.* 18, 5 (2003), 151–158.

An Approach to Generate Virtual Tutors for Game Programming Classes

Alan de Oliveira Santana
Departamente of Informatics and Applied Mathematics
Federal University of Rio Grande do Norte
Natal Rio Grande do Norte Brazil
alandeoliveirasantana@gmail.com

Eduardo Aranha
Departamente of Informatics and Applied Mathematics
Federal University of Rio Grande do Norte
Natal Rio Grande do Norte Brazil
eduardoaranha@dimap.ufrn.br

ABSTRACT

Nowadays, researchers are looking for ways to adapt education to include technology and more engaging methods. For computer science courses, the use of problem-based learning, virtual tutors, learning style personalization and game programming are possible ways to achieve this goal. In this context, this work proposes and evaluates an approach to generate different kinds of virtual tutors (with various levels of interaction) for problem-based game programming classes. The system was evaluated in an experiment where two types of virtual tutors were proposed and generated considering two virtual game programming classes. Results showed that the use of virtual tutors promoted efficient learning and that the availability of different kinds of tutors can optimize individual engagement.

KEYWORDS

Virtual tutors; Education; Game programming classes

ACM Reference format:

Alan Santana & Eduardo Aranha. 2019. An Approach to Generate Virtual Tutors for Game Programming Class. In *Proceedings of 50th ACM Technical Symposium on Computer Science Education (SIGCSE '19), February 27-March 2, 2019, Minneapolis, MN, USA.* ACM, New York, NY, USA, 7 pages. https://doi.org/10.1145/3287324.3287414

1 Introduction

The clear majority of 21st century professions demand an understanding of Computer Science. Professionals of art and entertainment, communication, health, among others, need to have Computer Science as a science, in the search for solutions of problems of diverse areas, as well as in the construction of these solutions [1].

One engaging way to introduce students how to computer science is teaching how to program digital games [2]. Even though, programming can be a hard task to be learned and performed.

Among the new educational methodologies, there is the Project Based Learning (PBL), a scientific method that engage students in the investigation of authentic problems [3]. Hence, it qualifies students to learn and prepare themselves to solve different problems related to their professions [4]. In a PBL class, the teacher is responsible for presenting a challenge and guiding students along their learning path to find a solution, suggesting contents and research websites, and motivating the students to continue learning [5].

PBL's practical goal is to prepare students for professional challenges by developing skills (problem understanding, critical thinking, etc.) during the resolution process [6, 7]. This way, PBL is especially applicable to programming classes.

However, it is challenging to use PBL in large classes or long-distance education, due to the number of students to whom the teacher will need to offer support. In this context, the use of virtual tutors can reduce the demand for human teachers and also allow the use of different learning styles, possibly increasing student engagement and experience [8].

Hence, this work investigates and proposes an approach to generate virtual tutors that can support PBL programming classes. The research hypothesis of this work is that different kinds of virtual tutors can be generated for the same PBL game programming class, enabling more personalized and engaging learning. The proposed approach was implemented using two kinds of tutors and evaluated through a controlled experiment.

2 Background

In this section, the application of the PBL model in game programming classes and an overview of virtual tutors are presented.

2.1 PBL for Programming Classes

In the traditional education, teachers tell their student what to do, forcing them to memorize contents, but not necessarily to learn. In Project Based Learning (PBL), problems are presented to students, who should, in return, search for the knowledge required to develop a solution [7].

The PBL model is different from the traditional model because it exposes students to one or more problems, making them understand and identify these problems according to their previous knowledge. This enables students to find out what it

SIGCSE '19, February 27-March 2, 2019, Minneapolis, MN, USA

ACM ISBN 978-1-4503-5890-3/19/02...$15.00
https://doi.org/10.1145/3287324.3287414

takes to solve the presented problems. Finally, the student learns how to use the acquired knowledge to arrive at the solution [7].

The teaching process focuses on the student. Consequently, studies [7] indicate that the PBL model requires the teacher to be more participative, to do more planning, to carry out more participatory work in the educational institution and to make more decisions.

Therefore, the virtual tutors generated by the proposed tool intend to expose the problems to students and guide them through activities that exemplify how to solve the obstacle without delivering the answer directly. The goal is to engage students and make the learning process more fun and objective.

The approach that involves using virtual tutor based on PBL is well adaptable to gaming programming courses. Researches show that game programming courses are of interest to most students, which fits well into PBL's ultimate goal, that is, to help students become intrinsically motivated. This way, students are well motivated while learning programming, which makes the learning process far more productive [9].

The general approach of using PBL in programming classes seeks to train the student to learn how to learn by presenting poorly structured problems, thus keeping the tutor as a helper and guide throughout the learning process [9, 10].

2.2 Virtual Tutors

Virtual tutor systems are programs that simulate a human tutor on a particular task, such as indicating content, explaining or motivating students.

The vast number of different of possibilities allows virtual tutors to be used for a variety of purposes, such as a support system for adults who experience difficulties to learn second language [11] or evaluation and orientation systems in music courses [12].

One of the main advantages of using virtual tutors is that they are suitable for courses that do not have teachers available. This way, a virtual tutoring system makes it possible to reach students in a better way with lower costs with human tutors, apart from being able to use its methodology in more than one course at a time, thus becoming a multidisciplinary tool [13, 14].

For the most part, virtual tutoring systems are designed to be rich in features, but they often leave aside motivational characteristics. However, nowadays the literature already presents studies related to the development of charismatic tutors capable of engaging students [15, 16].

The actual architecture of the virtual tutoring systems is developed using the multi-agent model [17, 18] with the main efforts focused on the head and upper limbs [19]. Although the use of the whole body presents more possibilities, it is harder to be implanted [20].

Among the several types of tutors available, those who guide the student through an analysis of the way he or she uses the tool and their affective elements are one of the most widespread, since they allow the system to find ways to motivate the student [21, 22].

The most common form of virtual tutor interaction with the user is through gestures and text boxes. Some of the primary forms of nonverbal communication are facial expressions, head and eye movements [23], gestures [24] and trunk movements and posture [25 and 26].

Another form of interaction with users is the chat, which is based on the Alicebot project [27]. These works use the chat combined with the tutoring system intending to make classes more interactive and playful, resulting in more pleasant and productive learning [28, 29].

In this sense, the use of virtual tutors has a variety of ways to be produced and applied, which motivates the proposal to develop a system that generates different types of tutors for various student profiles.

3 Virtual Tutor Generation Approach

This paper proposes a generation approach for different kinds of virtual tutors and class contents. The approach is composed of three parts, the pedagogical behavior of the virtual tutor, the class content structure and the generation engine.

3.1 Pedagogical Behavior

The first part of this approach is related to the desired pedagogical tutor behavior. It defines a generic flow that different kinds of tutors can follow, in addition to their specific kinds of supported user interactions. A simplified sample flow is presented in Figure 1, showing the activities that virtual tutors should perform in a PBL game programming class.

In this flow, the virtual tutor welcomes the student and then presents a game (project) to be developed. Then, the student decides between seeing more details about the project or accessing the list of activities required to make the game. If complex, an activity is organized in a list of smaller activities. The tutor guides the student to access resources (videos, texts, online tutorial, etc.) to learn the knowledge and skills needed to develop each activity. After performing all required activities, the student can submit her project to reach the end of the class.

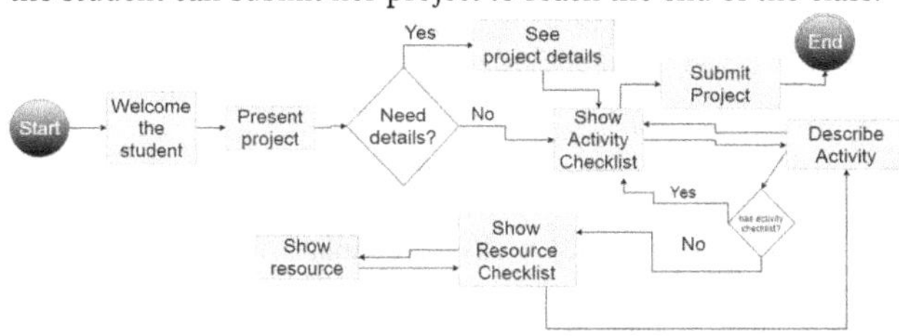

Figure 1: Sample of pedagogical behavior of the tutors.

3.2 Class Content Structure

The second part of the approach is the class content structure, which specifies the content of the class, including details about the project, activities to perform and resources that can be used to acquire the required knowledge. The class structure should be aligned with the pedagogical behavior model, to ensure that all required information about the class is being provided for the virtual tutor.

A possible class structure is presented in Figure 2, which is aligned with the pedagogical behavior presented in Figure 1. Based on that structure, the content of each class is specified as a project (game to develop) and a list of activities to develop the project. The project is detailed by instructional materials (video, texts, game URL, etc.). In addition, each project activity has a checklist, which can be related to sub-activities to perform or related instructional materials and learning evaluation instruments (questionnaires, code uploads, etc.).

3.3 Generation Engine

The third part of the proposed approach is the generation engine. This is a module that receives as input the pedagogical behavior model, the class content and the desired kind of virtual tutor. Based on that information, a virtual class is generated. It is important to notice that new pedagogical behavior or class content structure models may require adjusts in the generation engine implementation.

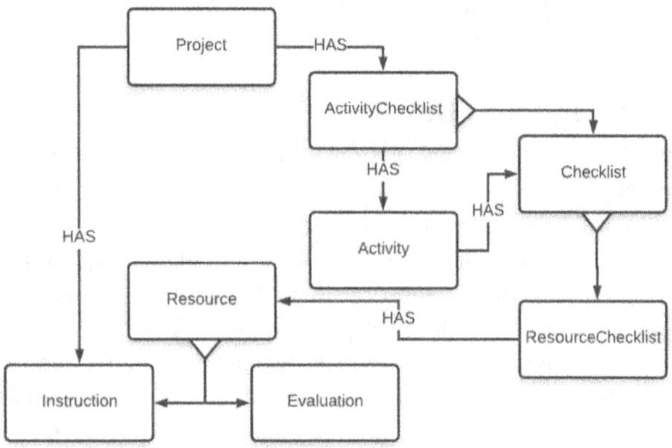

Figure 2: Class structure definition.

4 Approach in Action

The proposed approach was implemented considering the models presented in Figure 1 and 2. The implemented generation engine also considered two kinds of virtual tutors. The first format is called exhibitor tutor, while the second one is called chat tutor.

4.1 Exhibitor Tutor

The tutor exhibitor [30] seeks to simulate the presence of a teacher, listing the contents through screen transitions that seek to motivate the student to practice and follow a task order.

The format of the exhibiting tutor includes a set of pages that are categorized into models, the most important being the video model and the abstract model, responsible respectively for the presentation of the videos (which is the main source of knowledge of the tool) and the access options. These pages are loaded into a frame within a static home page, thereby reducing system load time.

In addition, the architecture of the exhibiting tutor is defined by an agent that acts in the environment changing the expressions of the tutor according to the actions of the user. In this way, their expressions focus on the presentation of content, simulating a teacher who guides the student to find the knowledge. Figure 3 shows the tutorial interface.

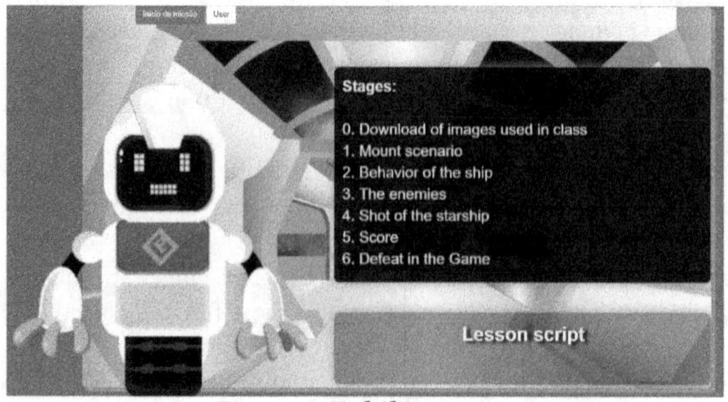

Figure 3: Exhibitor tutor.

4.2 Chat tutor

The chat tutor [31] seeks to simulate a real tutor using a chat room to interact with the student, motivating him or her to conduct the research. However, unlike the tutor exhibitor format, this tutor uses the interaction of the chat to deepen the contents.

The chat tutor format uses the intrinsic interaction of chats to motivate and engage students. This format allows the tutor to better present the content and objectives of the lesson. In this way, the tutor can give additional explanations about the content and maintain motivational dialogues.

The chat tutor format (see Figure 4) consists of an HTML5 page that interacts with an AIML-inspired JSON database.

This JSON database has specific tags for loading external content, such as videos, images and documents, which are interpreted by a pedagogical module responsible for maintaining the communication context between the student and the tutor.

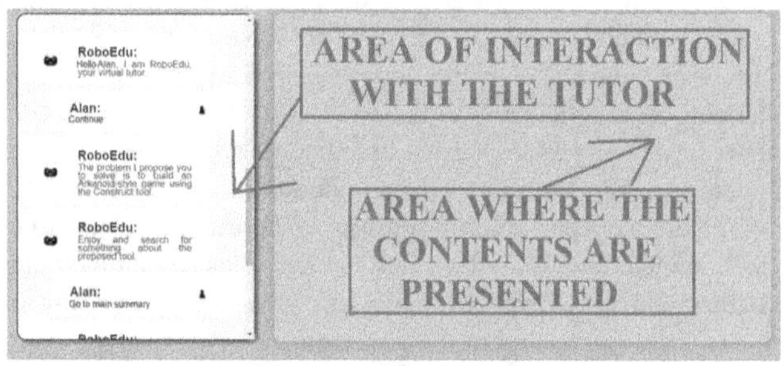

Figure 4: Chat tutor.

4.3 The generator and the tutors

Both tutors presented the same pedagogical behavior, being different only the content approach, differentiated by the form of access to knowledge base.

Thus, once the teacher generates a lesson through the generator, two distinct bases are generated, with their respective contexts necessary for the types of proposed tutors.

In this way, the main benefit that the generator causes in the development of data bases with different approaches, is the reduction of the time of creation of knowledge bases for the various tutors implemented, with average time gain of 1/X, where X is number of bases of data to be generated for tutors who presented the same content differently from one another.

5 Experimental Evaluation

To evaluate the proposed approach and its implementation, a controlled experiment was performed, as presented next. The goal is to verify if different kinds of generated virtual tutors can better attend the students' specific needs.

5.1 Research Questions

For this study, the following research questions were drawn to evaluate the proposal of the tutor generation system:

RQ1: Is there a common preference for the proposed virtual tutors formats?

RQ2: Did the students have fun during the classes with the virtual tutors?

RQ3: Were the participants able to develop the proposed games with the tutors?

RQ4: What format allows the class to be held in less time?

RQ5: In the students' opinion, what are the advantages and limitations of tutors?

RQ6: Is it possible to affirm that one of the virtual tutors contributed more than another to the students' engagement?

5.2 Experimental Design

For this experiment, the Latin Square design of experiment was selected. In a Latin Square design [32], the influence of two factors are controlled, which are in this experiment: the class (complexity, attractiveness, etc.); the participant (experience, engagement, etc.). Two PBL classes based on Arkanoid and a Starship game were developed and used as columns of the Latin Square (see Table 1). Then, 32 undergraduate students from different courses related to K-12 education were selected and organized as lines of 16 Latin Squares. For each Latin Square, a generated tutor was randomly selected (exhibitor or chat) to be used as treatment A or B of the Latin Square. In this way, every student attended both classes (Arkanoid or Starship) and used a different kind of generated virtual tutor in each class.

Table 1: Latin Square design of experiment.

	Arkanoid class	Starship class
Student n	A	B
Student n+1	B	A

The experiment was organized in 3-hour classes, once a week, for three weeks. In the first class, students were quickly introduced to the Construct2 game developing environment. Then, they were instructed on how to use the virtual tutors. The goal of the first class was to develop the Arkanoid-based game and each student used its randomly assigned virtual tutor for that.

The project of the second class was a Spaceship-based game and each student used a virtual tutor different from the one used in the first class. In the third class, students created their own game without support of a virtual tutor. The goal was to verify if the students learned how to create a game.

5.3 Data Collection Procedures

This experiment used three data sources to validate their results: system registration, questionnaires and observations. The system log consists of a simple text file that stores all user interactions with the tutors. This log has a writing protocol that allows the data to be analyzed in an organized way. The main actions that the log records are pause, plays and moves in the progress bars of the videos, as well as the options selected during each class. The other two sources of data for this experiment were questionnaires and observations.

The log analysis enabled the evaluation of how users manipulated the system, observing the duration of each individual class, resource accesses, interactions occurred, etc.. The questionnaire analysis summarizes the results obtained to allow a more accurate evaluation of the answers to the first four questions. For that, four questionnaires were developed, one for each class and format corresponding to the Latin square shown in Table 1. In addition, the observational analysis regards students' comments and behaviors made during the execution of the experiment.

5.4 Results

Next, the results of this experimental evaluation are discussed, according to each defined research question.

RQ1: Is there a common preference for the proposed virtual tutors formats? After the end of the second class, students were asked about what system they preferred to use and why. Results showed that 56.25% of the students chose the Tutor chat format compared to 43.75% who chose the tutor exhibitor.

Among the reasons for making that choice were responses such as that from a student who said that "chat is better because it allows the video to be more obvious." Another student adds, "I preferred the tutor chat because I felt like I was talking to a teacher." With regard to the tutor exhibitor, most of the students reported that they chose this format because the access to the videos is faster and more objective, without having to go through long conversations, as with tutor chat.

RQ2: Did the students have fun during the classes with the virtual tutors? The answer for this question were obtained from the questionnaire and observations in the classroom. The "Arkanoid Class" shows that 68.9% of students chose the "strongly agree" option for the affirmative of having fun in the class. Also, 18.8% chose "weakly agree" and 12.5% were "neutral" in Arkanoid class. Regarding the Spaceship class, 59.4% of the students scored "strongly agree", 18.8% chose "weakly agree", 15.6% were "neutral" and 6.3% chose to "weakly disagree". The observations in the classroom pointed that the inherent difficulty encountered in the development of the starship's game demonstrated that some students did not have much fun due to this difficulty.

One point that was observed during class was student`s smiles and laughs during videos and tutors interactions. There were also comments at the end of the class mentioning that "the class was cool". In this way, the class was considered to have fun during classes with both tutors.

RQ3: Were the participants able to develop the proposed games with the tutors? To answer these research questions it was analyzed whether students were able to develop the games for each tutor format. For that, we analyzed the success rates in completing the games for each format. The numbers obtained were:

Arkanoid class with Tutor chat: 13/16 (81.25%);
Arkanoid class with tutor exibidor: 12/16 (75.00%);
Starship class with Tutor chat: 12/16 (75.00%);
Starship class with Tutor exhibitor: 13/16 (81.25%).

These data showed that, on average, 78% of students completed the proposed games. This number was considered good according to the low level of previous experiences of the students. However, the data also suggest that the effectiveness of each tutor format can be influenced by the class (the virtual tutors have obtained different results in each class, although the results are very close).

RQ4: What format allows the class to be held in less time? Based on the log analysis, the first and last action in the system was observed. The Arkanoid class showed an average time of 144 minutes versus 138 minutes for the Starship class. One reason for this time reduction is that the second class (Starship) has similar contents to the first one (Arkanoid). However, the higher development complexity of the starship's game may have reduced this difference.

Also, in all classes, the Tutor chat format took about six minutes longer than the Tutor exhibitor. This possibly occurred mainly due to its textual interaction, which is based on typing.

RQ5: In the students' opinion, what are the advantages and limitations of the generated virtual tutors? These data were collected mainly from the questionnaire, which asked the students about the advantages and limitations of each tutor.

In general, students indicated that the tutors turned the classes more objective. One student quoted that "the main advantage is that you can understand most of the activity without the help of the teacher".

The tutors were also singled out as practical and facilitators of knowledge, through citations like "very practical, easy to handle." and "Video lessons are a great way to learn, demonstrating step by step the tools to the development of the game." Other students also reported that "it's a very intuitive way of doing things".

The interaction with the tutor was also pointed out as a facilitator, allowing the students to review the contents as needed, something that if done in a regular class with a real teacher, generates lost time, harming the whole class. Among the students' responses one replied that "we have the advantage of being able to pause or resume the video when doubts arise, in addition to being able to review it later." Another student pointed out that "the tutor helped me see where I went wrong and what to do".

However, some students also reported limitations on tutors. One of the limitations observed was the fact that the current version of the tutors does not have a system to manage doubts. Therefore, one student mentioned as a limitation that "he can not answer questions, but he is great as an instructor".

Another limitation pointed out was that of a student who preferred to use the Tutor exhibitor because he considered this more objective and because the Tutor chat indicated the content to be seen insistently. This student reported that "I think the chat often asks if the student wants to see a specific video, but besides that, it's great".

In general, according to the students, tutors presented more advantages than disadvantages. However, this data will be useful to improve what worked and make corrections to what did not please students so much. The main improvement would be to add artificial intelligence characteristics and adapt pedagogical behavior to respond to students' questions at run time.

RQ6: Is it possible to affirm that one of the virtual tutors contributed more than another to the students' engagement? The analysis of the questionnaires plus the observations made in the class, allowing to see the level of commitment of the students.

The first question of the questionnaire sought to know the level of motivation during the lesson. The data show that 59.9% of the students who passed the starship's game class reported that they strongly agree with the positive response to this research question, in addition to 31.2% who responded weakly agree. Responses about the Arkanoid game presented more positive data, with 75% of students reporting that they strongly agree with question 1.

The second question was about the motivation to learn with the proposed tutor. The Arkanoid class had 67.7% of the answers strongly agree and 25.8% agreed weakly. However, due to the difficulty of the ship's game, the tutor obtained more diversified results in the answers about this class. The data showed that 43.8% chose strongly agreed; 15.6% chose to weakly agree; 9.4% chose neutral; 21.9% weakly disagree; and 9.4% strongly disagree.

As can be seen in the responses of question 2 about the starship's game, most students reported that they were motivated, but the number of students thought was difficult was quite high, suggesting an improvement in the content of the game class of the ship.

The Question 3 sought to gather data on the ease of carrying out the proposed activities. As expected, the Arkanoid class presented satisfactory results, with 58.8% of the students saying that they strongly agreed and 32,4% agreed weakly on this issue.

Regarding the starship's game, 34.4% of the students agreed strongly, 43.8% agreed weakly and 12.5% presented neutral answers. These numbers were already expected due to the higher difficulty level of the starship's game class.

Question 4 was already discussed in this section and showed that, in general, students were able to perform classes with some ease, encountering occasional difficulties in the starship's game.

Finally, classroom observations revealed that students remained focused on the videos, even when they were struggling, performing the proposed tasks within the delimited deadlines, and did not stop working on the content to examine any other information not linked to the lesson, such as websites and mobile phones.

This was expected because the tutors keep the student busy and in constant interaction with the tool, resulting in a higher concentration.

Through the results of the questionnaires and the observations made in the classroom, it was possible to conclude that the students were committed and motivated to reach their objectives, allowing to affirm that the level of engagement that both tutors cause is practically the same, without a tutor who engage more the student than another.

5.5 Discussion about the results

Two types of classes were used, one that simulates a teacher and another that seeks to simulate a chat with a tutor.

The control group used compared the tutor exhibitor with the lesson only with the resources accessed sequentially and both using the format of missions.

The results showed that the use of the tutoring system left the classes productive due to the use of the tutor connected to the format of the lesson based on missions, because with short resources and objectives students can absorb information in a simpler and more objective way, besides the use tutoring and dynamics improve the level of confidence of students in developing the proposed games due also to the motivation and encouragement provided by the virtual tutor. Thus, it was concluded that using virtual tutors makes classes based on missions more productive, because in a same class there is a strong tendency to have more advanced or more capable students to absorb content more easily than others, who in turn need more encouragement and closeness with the teacher to ask questions or re-explain already existing content.

It was also observed that students after taking the first class and taking X time to complete the games, in the second class they tended to take a shorter time and to consult less the resources that they had previously studied.

This fact shows that the proposed dynamic format allowed the students who already mastered certain contents to skip the explanations about them, and the students with doubts quickly accessed the resources in the specific points that they needed.

Regarding the use of more than one type of tutorial approach, it was very beneficial for the class, which even without prior experience in programming or game development, managed to produce at rates of more than 85% the proposed games, in addition to having done so in a way playful and objective.

Given this validation, we tried to make the tutors generator easy and intuitive to use to allow teachers in general to use the tool that although implemented is still undergoing validation through a case study, where teachers should use the tool to create their classes and apply with their students, noting the impact on their use by teachers and students.

5.6 Threats to Validity

The controlled experiment has some threats to validity. One of them is the indirect analysis of the virtual tutor generation approach through the evaluation of two generated tutors. If the tutor formats selected to be generated are not good, the indirect evaluation of the generation approach would be not good too. However, we selected two tutor formats considered goods by previous works.

Also, the Starship class was harder than the Arknoid class. The Latin Square design of experiment controlled this threat and allowed a fair comparison between the two generated tutors. In this way, both tutors received a not so good evaluation in the Starship class.

Finally, this study only considered two tutor formats and two classes, as well as undergraduate students that are not from computer science (future teachers). Hence, results may vary in different scenarios.

6 Conclusion

This work proposes the development and evaluation of a virtual tutor generation system for different student profiles. For this, two formats of tutors were developed, one designed for more interactive classes and the other one for more objective classes.

Throughout the experiment, it was possible to see that for undergraduate students with little or no experience in system development, a virtual tutor generation system is feasible and indicated. This is mainly because, as the data obtained suggested, in class, there are students who need more information during the lessons, while others want to evolve fast without significant loss of time since they already know or can absorb content faster.

It was also found that the use of virtual tutors allowed the class to flow without pauses for explanations, content reinforcement or to answer doubts, which can result in time loss and break a class' line of reasoning.

Through these results, the tools will be improved by creating a system to answer questions. Also, artificial intelligence will be created, and new studies will be carried out to develop new types of tutors for other student profiles.

This study was financed in part by the Coordenação de Aperfeiçoamento de Pessoal de Nível Superior - Brasil (CAPES) - Finance Code 001.

This research was partially funded by INES 2.0, FACEPE grant APQ-0399-1.03/17, and CNPq grant 465614/2014-0

REFERENCES

[1] Voogt J. et al. 2017. The International Handbook of Information Technology in Primary and Secondary Education: Part 2. Society for Information Technology & Teacher Education International Conference (pp. 1082-1085). Association for the Advancement of Computing in Education (AACE).

[2] Thiago T. S. Reis. et al. 2016. Um relato de experiência da aplicação de videoaulas de programação de jogos digitais para alunos da educação básica. Anais do Workshop de Informática na Escola. p. 141.

[3] Blumenfeld P. C,, Soloway, E., Marx, R. W., Krajcik, J. S., Guzdial, M. and Palincsar A. 1991. Motivating project-based learning: Sustaining the doing, supporting the learning. Educational psychologist, 26(3-4), 369-398.

[4] Papert, S. and Harel, I. 1991. Situating constructionism. Constructionism, v. 36, n. 2, (pp. 1-11).

[5] Judy H. Helm and Lilian, G. Katz. 2016. Young Investigators: The Project Approach in the Early Years. 3. Ed, New York and London, Editora Teachers College Press.

[6] Grant M. 2002. Getting a grip on project-based learning: Theory, cases and recommendations. Meridian: A middle school computer technologies journal, 5(1), 83.

[7] Bell S. 2010. Project-based learning for the 21st century: Skills for the future. The Clearing House, 83(2), (pp. 39-43).
[8] Thiago T. S. Reis. et al. 2015. Investigando dois formatos de vídeo aulas de programação de jogos digitais para alunos do ensino médio. In Anais do Workshop de Informática na Escola. pp. 187.
[9] Soares A., Martin, N. L. and Fonseca, F. 2015. Teaching introductory programming with game design and problem-based learning. Issues in Information Systems, 16(3).
[10] Esteves M., Fonseca B., Morgado L. and Martins, P. 2009. Using Second Life for problem-based learning in computer science programming. Journal for Virtual Worlds Research, 2(1).
[11] Vogt P., Dunk S. and Poos P. 2017. Foreign Language Tutoring for Young Adults with Severe Learning Problems. In Proceedings of the Companion of the 2017 ACM/IEEE International Conference on Human-Robot Interaction (pp. 317-318).
[12] Nijholt A. Reidsma D. and Ebbers R. 2008. The Virtual Conductor: Learning and Teaching about Music, Performing, and Conducting. In: Eighth IEEE International Conference on Advanced Learning Technologies.
[13] Dang B. et al. 2011. The design and implementation of general tutor system for multi-disciplinary courses in virtual experiment. In e-Education, Entertainment and e-Management (ICEEE), 2011 International Conference on (pp. 178-181). IEEE.
[14] Amante B. and Campo D. Martínez, M. 2012. Multidisciplinary study of tutoring using virtual characters and Second Life. In Information Technology Based Higher Education and Training (ITHET), International Conference on (pp. 1-5).
[15] Mukherjee S. et al. 2013. Learner centered design approach for e-learning using 3D virtual tutors. In Technology for Education (T4E), 2013 IEEE Fifth International Conference on (pp. 133-134). IEEE.
[16] Park S. W. and Kim C. 2011. Designing a virtual tutee system to enhance college student motivation. In Advanced Learning Technologies (ICALT), 2011 11th IEEE International Conference on (pp. 199-201). IEEE.
[17] Tegos S. and Demetriadis S. 2017. Conversational Agents Improve Peer Learning through Building on Prior Knowledge. Journal of Educational Technology & Society, 20(1).
[18] Boudabous S., Kazar, O., and Laouar, M. R. 2017. Towards A Hospital Ubiquitous Learning System Based Agents. In Proceedings of the International Conference on Computing for Engineering and Sciences (pp. 56-62). ACM.
[19] Yan J. 2009. Modeling Life-like Behaviors of An Animated Virtual Tutor. In World Congress on Computer Science and Information Engineering.
[20] Glowinski D. 2011. Toward a Minimal Representation of Affective Gestures. In IEEE Transactions on Affective Computing, Vol. 2, No. 2, Apr.-Jun.
[21] Joseph F. 2014. Multimodal Analysis and Modeling of Nonverbal Behaviors during Tutoring. In ICMI 14, Proceedings of the 16th International Conference on Multimodal Interaction. (pp. 404-408). Istanbul, Turkey, Nov.
[22] Ren Y., Hasegawa-Johnson M. and Levinson, S. 2004. Semantic analysis for a speech user interface in an intelligent tutoring system. In IUI 04, Proceedings of the 9th international conference on Intelligent user interfaces, Madeira, Portugal, Jan.
[23] Bholsithi W. and Wongwaen N. 2014. 3D Avatar Developments in Real Time and Accuracy Assessments. In International Computer Science and Engineering Conference, pp.85-90.
[24] Ji-Hwan S. and Hyo-Sung A. 2012. Bio-insect and Artificial Robot Interaction using Cooperative Reinforcement Learning. In IEEE International Symposium on Intelligent Control, pp.1190-1194.
[25] Truschzinski M. et al. 2014. Deducing human emotions by robots: Computing basic non-verbal expressions of performed actions during a work task. In: IEEE International Symposium on Intelligent Control, pp.1342-1347.
[26] Plurkowski L., Chu, M. and Vinkhuyzen, E. 2011. The Implications of Interactional 'Repair' for Human-Robot Interaction Design. In: IEEE/WIC/ACM International Conference on Web Intelligence and Intelligent Agent Technology, pp.61-65.
[27] Wallace, R. 1995. ALICEBOT. The a.l.i.c.e a.i. foundation. In <http://www.alicebot.org> acess in 2017 jun 30.
[28] Jeffrey P. Bigjam et al. 2008. Inspiring blind high school students to pursue computer science with instant messaging chatbots. 39th SIGCSE technical symposium on Computer science education (pp. 449-453).
[29] Cooper S. 2012. Initial results of using an intelligent tutoring system with Alice. ITiCSE 12, Proceedings of the 17th ACM annual conference on Innovation and technology in computer science education, pp. 138-143.
[30] Alan O. Santana. Eduardo H. Aranha. 2018. Um Modelo de Chatbot para Aulas de Desenvolvimento de Jogos Digitais. COMPUTER ON THE BEACH, Florianópolis. Computer on the Beach, v.1. p.238 – 247.
[31] Alan O. Santana, Thiago T. S. Reis and Eduardo H. Aranha. 2017. Um Modelo de Tutor Virtual para Aulas Baseadas em Missões de Programação de Jogos Digitais. VI Congresso Brasileiro de Informática na Educação, Recife. v.1. p.1059 – 1068.
[32] John T. E. Richardson. 2018. Latin Square Design. Frey, Bruce B. ed. The SAGE Encyclopedia of Educational Research, Measurement, and Evaluation. SAGE Publications, p. 949.

Pensieve: Feedback on coding process for novices

Lisa Yan
Stanford University
yanlisa@stanford.edu

Annie Hu
Stanford University
anniehu@stanford.edu

Chris Piech
Stanford University
piech@cs.stanford.edu

ABSTRACT

In large undergraduate computer science classrooms, student learning on assignments is often gauged only by the work on their final solution, not by their programming process. As a consequence, teachers are unable to give detailed feedback on how students implement programming methodology, and novice students often lack a *metacognitive* understanding of how they learn. We introduce *Pensieve* as a drag-and-drop, open-source tool that organizes snapshots of student code as they progress through an assignment. The tool is designed to encourage sit-down conversations between student and teacher about the programming process. The easy visualization of code evolution over time facilitates the discussion of intermediate work and progress towards learning goals, both of which would otherwise be unapparent from a single final submission. This paper discusses the pedagogical foundations and technical details of *Pensieve* and describes results from a particular 207-student classroom deployment, suggesting that the tool has meaningful impacts on education for both the student and the teacher.

CCS CONCEPTS

• **Social and professional topics → CS1**; **Student assessment**;

KEYWORDS

Programming courses; assessment; pedagogy; formative feedback; metacognition

ACM Reference Format:

Lisa Yan, Annie Hu, and Chris Piech. 2019. Pensieve: Feedback on coding process for novices. In *Proceedings of 50th ACM Technical Symposium on Computer Science Education, Minneapolis, MN, USA, February 27–March 2, 2019 (SIGCSE'19)*, 7 pages. https://doi.org/10.1145/3287324.3287483

1 INTRODUCTION

Assignment feedback is a critical component of student learning [19, 34]. Given that one of the primary learning goals of CS1 is to teach students *how* to solve programming challenges, it would be immensely useful to provide formative feedback on *how* a student worked through solving an assignment. Yet for a variety of reasons, many contemporary classrooms only provide summative feedback on a student's final answer [23, 41]. The hours during which a student actively learns and interacts with the material are manifested in a single deliverable—a single snapshot into the student's thinking—from which an instructor must glean enough information to discuss student process. This misses the opportunity to give students feedback on their problem solving approaches and to help students develop metacognitive abilities [5, 9, 30, 34]. However, providing feedback on a final student submission is hard, and providing feedback on the hundreds of steps a student takes to get to their answer seems prohibitively difficult.

To enable feedback on student progress, we built *Pensieve*, a simple-to-use tool that provides an interactive visualization of student work history over the course of completing an assignment (Figure 1). *Pensieve* gives both students and teachers a means to see assignment progress—from the time a student first looked at assignment starter code to when they submit the final product—facilitating conversation around metacognition and student learning that is critical for introductory computer science learners. When teachers can observe a student's process, they are able to give timely feedback addressing student mistakes and to adjust and personalize their own teaching [6]. When students observe their own process—even in the absence of the instructor—they can internalize metacognitive observations [9]. Through our streamlined user interface, understanding progress becomes quick and feasible, even in a large classroom.

In this paper, we begin with an overview of the pedagogical motivations for the *Pensieve* tool (Sections 2 and 3). We then discuss the technical implementation details in Section 4. In Section 5, we share positive experiences by both teachers and students when *Pensieve* was deployed in a 10-week course. The tool was correlated with significantly better student performance, with a particularly large benefit for students with the least programming background. Furthermore, there was almost no additive effort for the teaching assistants to learn the tool, nor was it difficult to incorporate into the existing course pipeline. Finally, we close in Section 6 with best practices and discussion of how our tool can be used in many CS1 classrooms today. *Pensieve* is an open source tool which you can download and modify.[1]

2 PEDAGOGY AND MOTIVATION

Pensieve aims to "push back" somewhat against the trend of automated grading tools in classrooms by thoughtfully integrating a human grader into assignment feedback. We designed the tool with several objectives in mind:

(1) Foster metacognitive skills
(2) Identify methodology errors early
(3) Counteract plagiarism effects in a large classroom
(4) Gentle introduction of version control.

Our first objective is to develop metacognition in the way students learn computer science. A key finding of a landmark National

[1] https://github.com/chrispiech/pensieve

SIGCSE'19, February 27–March 2, 2019, Minneapolis, MN, USA

ACM ISBN 978-1-4503-5890-3/19/02...$15.00
https://doi.org/10.1145/3287324.3287483

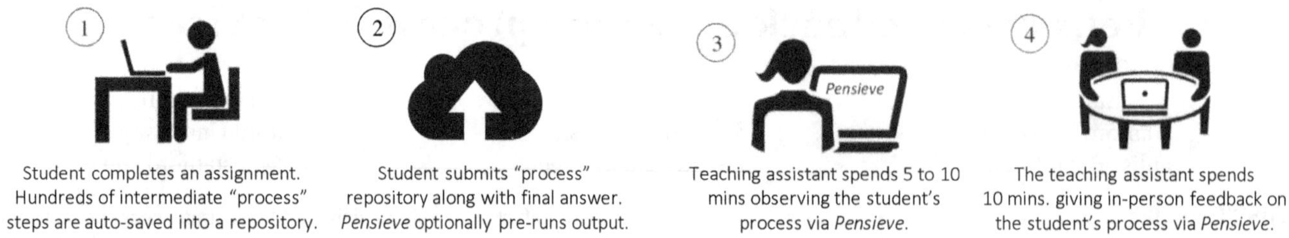

Figure 1: Pensieve allows teachers to visualize and give feedback on *how* a student progresses through an assignment.

Academy of Sciences study on learning science was the effectiveness of a metacognitive approach to instruction [7]. *Metacognition* is a learning theory for "thinking about thinking." To most effectively learn, students must not only understand the problem but also understand and reflect on where they are in the problem-solving process. Metacognitive practices directly correspond to increasing students' performance in evaluating concepts, one of the highest cognitive skill levels in Bloom's Revised Taxonomy for learning [2, 20, 39]. Research has also shown that students with stronger metacognitive awareness tend to perform better on programming tasks [4, 12, 18]. Importantly, metacognition directly supports the concept of a *growth mindset*, the theory that intelligence can be developed with experience [15]. Students who believe that ability is a fixed trait are at a significant disadvantage in STEM fields compared to their peers who believe in a growth mindset.

A related objective of our tool is to encourage early identification of methodology errors. Most assignments in large-scale computer science classes are assessed summatively: the teaching assistant sees and grades only the students' final submission. However, research has conclusively shown that nongraded *formative assessments*, or ongoing assessments designed to make students' thinking visible to both teachers and students, are key to improved learning [7, 22]. They allow teachers to identify which thought processes work for students and to provide useful, directed feedback so that each student can improve. As such, this goal is intertwined with our goal of fostering metacognition in computer science—through reflecting critically on their programming process, students will be able to both identify areas for improvement and understand how to achieve that improvement earlier.

Finally, by emphasizing the importance of the learning process, we hope that *Pensieve* can act as a preemptive deterrent to potential plagiarism. Students who plagiarize all or parts of their assignments stunt their metacognitive development in programming and reap fewer benefits from formative feedback. They may also become stuck in a cycle of plagiarism in which they are increasingly unable to complete work independently [40]. Many current approaches to combating plagiarism in large CS classrooms focus on detecting similar code in the final submission; however, this further reinforces the importance of the final grade received above the intrinsic value of learning how to learn, a way of thinking that underlies much student plagiarism [8]. We hope that by monitoring the development process [40], we can better support students who may otherwise feel overwhelmed and driven to plagiarize code.

3 RELATED WORK

In many large classrooms, the technology focus is on Automated Assessment Tools (AATs), which relegate a significant portion of the feedback pipeline to tools that support teacher- or student-written unit tests [1, 16, 21]. Larger classrooms like massive open online courses push towards full-automation by systems like intelligent tutoring systems to personalize the learning experience for online students [14]. In our study, we focus on large CS1 courses that have in-classroom human teacher support. While there is research on how to automate computer agents to personalize debugging hints per student [36], our work seeks solutions that allow humans to provide higher-level feedback on problem solving process.

Novice programmers benefit from metacognitive awareness. Loksa et al. found that students who are trained in problem solving procedures are more productive and have higher self-efficacy [28]. There are several metacognitive tools that have been studied in a CS context: Lee et al. found that personifying the programming process increases online engagement with a coding task [26]; Prather et al. discuss how metacognitive awareness ties into how students use AATs [32]; and Marceau et al. studied how novice programmers interact with error messages [29]. Outside of CS classrooms, Tanner et al. reported on generalizable teaching practices for promoting metacognition, such as instructor modeling of problem solving, tools to help students identify learning strategies, and guided reflection [38]. *Pensieve* incorporates all three of these strategies by engaging students—with the support of teaching assistants—with their own metacognitive understanding of computer science.

Formative feedback in the classroom can have a variety of impacts [3]. Van der Kleij et al. found that detailed feedback contributes more to student learning than feedback on correctness does [41]. Students also benefit more from an assignment when they have interactive, dialogue-based critiques with peers or instructors [9, 30]. We design our tool with the awareness that feedback is not a one-sided conversation; teachers should discuss with the students to promote student self-regulation of learning for the rest of the course [6].

Other classrooms have used version control systems to give formative feedback, as version control simplifies management of large courses [11] and makes it easier to identify problems in work habits and progress [24, 25, 35]. We take a slightly different approach, placing less emphasis on learning *how* to manage a version control system than on enabling self-evaluation from students and good feedback from teachers [27]. Our tool focuses on surfacing this information in a clear manner, providing a light introduction to the benefits of version control.

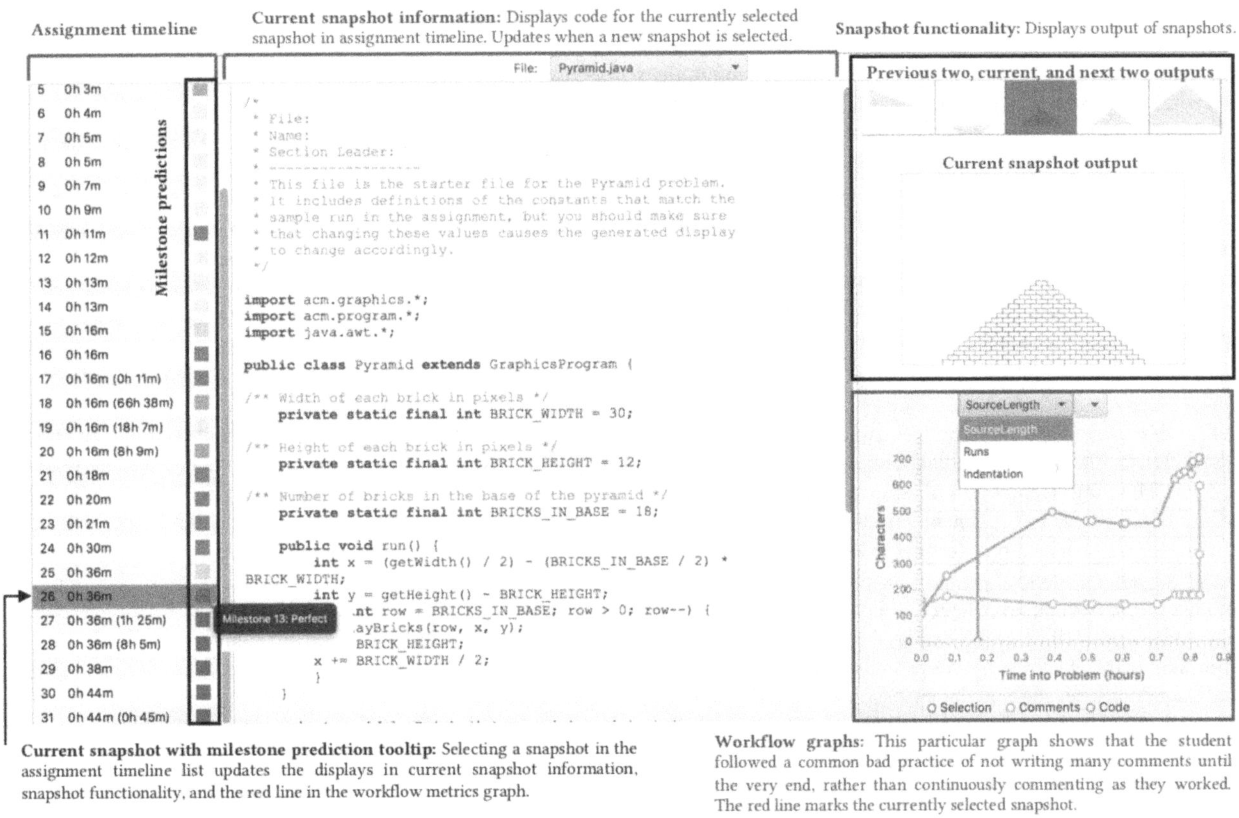

Figure 2: Diagram of *Pensieve* display, composed of four main components (discussed more in Section 4): Assignment timeline (left), Current snapshot information (center), Snapshot functionality (top right), and Workflow graphs (bottom right).

4 PENSIEVE DETAILS

Pensieve is primarily designed for educators to easily give feedback on student process. A pipeline of how it fits into a classroom is shown in Figure 1. As a student works on an assignment, their process is recorded as a local repository which is submitted along with their final answer. A screenshot of the *Pensieve* tool is shown in Figure 2. To use *Pensieve*, loaded with a student's process, the instructor interacts with the four main components of the tool: a timeline of snapshots for this program file (left panel), a selectable, highlightable text view of the snapshot code (center), the visual output corresponding to running the snapshot code (top-right), and metrics of this code file over time (bottom-right).

As part of our efforts to minimize instructor workload, *Pensieve* is designed to be a drag-and-drop, out-of-the-box tool for viewing student assignment progress. It is ported as a JAR file; an instructor can simply download the JAR into a student assignment folder, run it, and begin viewing student intermediate snapshot data.

4.1 Tool Implementation

The only required folder for *Pensieve* to work is a repository of *timestamped code* snapshots of a single student working on an assignment—data which is increasingly available to educators [33]. We currently represent timestamped code using the git abstraction: we customized the Eclipse IDE students use to automatically save student code at compile time (as described in [31]). However, *Pensieve* depends neither on the use of Eclipse nor Java in the classroom; it merely requires that student work be cached over time in a timestamped code folder. Our tool can work at a coarser granularity, such as on assignments that require students to commit periodically to an online storage platform like GitHub. The tool can also operate on setups like those on Code.org, which save snapshots whenever students run their code. We utilize the timestamped code repository to analyze both student code progress and timing information. In this section, we discuss interacting with the *Pensieve* tool for a single file in the timestamped code folder.

4.1.1 Assignment timeline. The leftmost panel of the tool (Figure 2) displays all captured snapshots for a given student file. Each entry in the timeline contains the snapshot index (in temporal order), the amount of time spent so far on this file, break time, and an optional color key indicating functional progress (discussed more in Section 4.1.4). Time spent on the assignment is calculated as an aggregate of relative timing information between this snapshot and the previous one. We mark break time in parentheses, where a break occurs when two consecutive snapshots' timestamps differ by more than 10 minutes. By browsing the timeline, an instructor can infer where students took substantial breaks to get a cursory glance of which snapshots would be worth closer attention.

4.1.2 Current snapshot information. Clicking on a snapshot entry in the Assignment timeline panel displays that snapshot's code in the center panel with appropriate syntax highlighting. Other than syntax and comment highlighting, the center panel is plaintext, allowing an instructor to select and copy code if additional verification is needed. The top-right panel is used to display this code's output when compiled and run; if the code has a compile or runtime error, nothing is shown. The example assignment shown in Figure 2 draws a pyramid-like object using Java's ACM library. It is important to note that Pensive is not running snapshot code live; the compiling and running of any student code is done in a preprocessing step. The details of designing such a preprocessor are discussed more in Section 4.1.4.

4.1.3 Workflow graphs. The bottom-right panel contains time series of various file metrics to visualize student progress and style over time. The SourceLength graph shown in Figure 2 displays code length (in green) and comment length (in yellow) in number of characters, as well as a red, vertical indicator of the currently selected snapshot's metrics. Another graph displays indentation errors over time—which are allowed in Java but are indicative of messy code—and a third graph displays custom metadata from the timestamped code directory; for example, our repositories also record the number of code runs per snapshot. Instructors can easily toggle between these time series, which are intended to highlight student work patterns, such as when they started thinking about good style and indentation, or whether the majority of their work and code changes were concentrated at the end of the timeline.

4.1.4 Snapshot functionality. The top-right panel visualizes the output of the currently selected code, if there were no compile or runtime errors. All outputs for all snapshots are run and saved prior to downloading and running *Pensieve* in a preprocessing step. In our implementation, this is performed on the course servers after students submit the assignment and before instructors begin grading. The preprocessor compiles and run each snapshot in each file; if there are no errors, then the output is saved into a separate folder. The *Pensieve* program then interfaces with the folder of outputs via a JSON metadata lookup, which associates the snapshot (represented by a (Unix Epoch timestamp, original filename) tuple) with the following features: a flag for compile error, a flag for runtime error, the output file path, and a milestone metric, of which the latter two are only valid if both error flags are off. Any additional metadata per snapshot can also be saved in this JSON lookup file.

In our example assignment, we mainly use graphics exercises based on the Java ACM library. As a result, output file paths point to saved output PNG files. However, one could easily run and save console program output as plain-text log-files, which can be displayed in the top-right panel of *Pensieve* with minor modifications. Milestone metrics are computed based on each snapshot's output; if there are unit tests for the assignment, this can simply be the number of passed unit tests. For our image files, we had an image classifier that determined a milestone number for each snapshot [42]. The milestone metric per snapshot is displayed as a small square color indicator in the left timeline panel; runtime and compile errors are assigned separate color indicators.

4.2 Classroom use

Pensieve is split into phases (Figure 1): first, a student works in their own environment (a lab computer, personal laptop, or in-browser app), which saves timestamped snapshots of their code progress. The student then submits their work to a database, where optional preprocessing occurs; for example, to generate and save snapshot output for later review. Then, the teacher downloads and reviews the student code submissions using *Pensieve*, and finally discusses the code with the student in a classroom.

In our classroom, eight students are assigned to a teaching assistant for the duration of the quarter; the teaching assistant's weekly responsibilities are to teach discussion sections and grade assignment work. The graders download the student code from the course database, typically a few days prior to the grading deadline, which is a week after the student submission deadline. At the time of grader download, *Pensieve* is already included as part of each student folder. Any preprocessing to generate visual program output or console output logs must be included in the student folders prior to download; this is done to ensure that the grader can run *Pensieve* as a lightweight tool on their own computers. The preprocessing step to generate and save graphical output on three separate code files for a 400-student class took about half a day. In the absence of a course database or preprocessor, a teacher can simply drop the *Pensieve* JAR into the assignment directory on the students' computer. Once the JAR is within the correct directory, teachers and students can navigate the timestamped code repository and discuss coding tips and misconceptions.

Teachers in our classroom provide assignment feedback to their students in two ways: the functional and style grades produced from a fixed rubric, and an *interactive grading* (IG) session [37], where the teacher and student sit down for a one-on-one, 15-minute session to discuss the student's code, any misconceptions, and tips to improve for future assignments. Teachers can use *Pensieve* during these IG sessions to identify, for example, places where students struggled with concepts or showed good style habits, and to gain a holistic view of how the student thought through the assignment. Grading is done independently from IG session outcomes; the purpose of the IG session is to maintain a conversation throughout the quarter so that students are actively reflecting on their coding progress.

In addition to the teacher-facing version of *Pensieve*, we provide a reduced version of the tool to the students so that they can look at their prior work and revert back to a previous version if needed *as they work on the assignment*; our tool at this point functions more as a welcoming, light version control software for students.

5 EXPERIENCE

At the time of writing this report, *Pensieve* has been used in two terms: Winter 2018 and Spring 2018. In the first term we refined the tool and teacher training procedures. In the second term (which we will refer to as the **Experience Term**), we evaluated the impact of the tool for the 207 students who took CS1.

We sought to evaluate the impact of our tool in three ways: (1) a formal qualitative analysis of how useful instructors found the tool, (2) an official university survey on how useful students found the tool, and (3) quantitative measures of performance on exams, time to complete assignments and honor code violations. All evaluations

Table 1: (a) Positive teacher feedback; (b) ways to improve.

(a)

% Agree	Item
90	Insights from *Pensieve* lead to "more actionable and specific assistance"
70	*Pensieve* "is helpful for showing instructors which students might need extra help"
–	Data on how long it takes students to complete assignments are "especially valuable"

(b)

% Agree	Item
80	Want an option "to show only major changes in code" to better prioritize information and feedback
75	Want more "student-facing features"
–	"All of the data *Pensieve* presents is helpful but can be overwhelming"

tell a consistent story of educational benefit that we expected to see given the improved pedagogical benefits.

5.1 Student and Teacher Perceptions

At the end of the Experience Term, we asked students to provide a Likert rating for the statement, "It was useful to see the process of how I learned using *Pensieve*," as part of their formal course evaluation. Students on average strongly agreed ($\mu = 4.6/5, \sigma = 0.6$). Furthermore, students gave a higher rating for the quality of course instruction and feedback ($\mu = 4.8, \sigma = 0.4$, where 5 = Excellent, and 4 = Good) than in previous terms ($\mu = 4.6, \sigma = 0.4$) for the Experience Term instructor. Response rate was 70%.

To measure how useful teaching assistants found our tool, we requested an external facilitator to conduct a small group instructional diagnosis (SGID) [10]. External evaluators met with 31 teaching assistants who used Pensieve in the Experience Term to discuss (1) whether using the tool improved the teachers' understanding of student learning process in CS, (2) if there were ways to improve the tool, and (3) if there were ways to improve how the tool was used in the classroom. The evaluators solicited feedback and consolidated major sentiments. To minimize bias, the instructor and researchers were not present during the SGID. The teaching assistants articulated that they found the tool to be useful, despite it requiring more work on their part (Table 1). The feedback session suggests that more teacher training or better highlighting within the tool would improve the teacher experience.

5.2 Learning Analysis

In addition to measuring the perception of students and teachers, we also place importance on quantifiable improvements in learning outcomes. Under our hypothesis that *Pensieve* had a substantial impact on student learning, we expected to see a notable change in student performance.

All measures are between the Experience Term ($N = 207$ students) where we deployed *Pensieve* and a Baseline Term with the same instructor, lectures and assignments, but without using the *Pensieve* tool ($N = 498$ students). The students in the Baseline Term had significantly **more** CS background than in the Experience Term. 37.4% of students in the Baseline Term reported > 10 hours of programming experience, vs 27.7% of students in the Experience Term. The Experience Term was 52% female vs 51% female in the baseline.

In the Experience Term, we provided our tool to the entire class (as opposed to running a randomized control trial), thus it is not possible to report on the causal impact of using *Pensieve*. While we could not observe causality, we can observe correlation. The co-occurrence of using the tool and notable learning improvement adds weight to our belief that the tool has a positive impact. To assess the co-occurrence of learning gains, we measured changes in (1) time spent on assignments after the *Pensieve*-assisted interactive grading assignment (2) exam performance and (3) plagiarism.

Assignment time: We used student assignment completion time as a pre-post measure of their ability to program. For each of Assignments 1, 2, and 3, we used students' intermediate progress records to calculate how long the assignment took (Note: students received the *Pensieve* "intervention" just before the due date for Assignment 2). The Experience Term saw a significant decrease in the number of hours spent on Assignment 3, the assignment due after the intervention (from an average completion time of 7.0 hours down to 6.3 hours, in Figure 3a). This decrease was particularly large given that in the Experience Term, students were slower on average to complete assignments *prior* to the Pensieve intervention. To account for this difference we calculate how long students in the Experience Term took to complete Assignment 3 (X_3) compared to their expected completion time had they been in the Baseline Term, given how long they spent on Assignment 1 ($\hat{X_3}|X_1$):

$$\begin{aligned}\text{Decrease in Assn 3 time} &= E[\hat{X_3}|X_1] - E[X_3]\\ &= 48 \text{ mins } (p < 0.0001)\end{aligned}$$

We observe an increase in Assignment 3 grades between the Baseline and Experience Term, but the change is not significant (δ = 3.2pp, $p = 0.07$). Most students in the Baseline Term already received high grades (μ = 98% in Baseline, μ = 101% in Experience).

Exam ability: On its own, the ability to complete an assignment faster does not indicate that students have learned more. Another measure is the difference in how well students performed on the class midterm (given just after the due date for Assignment 3). Since the exams were not identical we evaluated the difficulty (on a consistent scale) of each exam question and used Item Response Theory [17] to calculate a midterm "ability" score for each student, which would be comparable across quarters. We define a student's score for each question on the midterm exam as $S_{i,j} = n_j \cdot \sigma(a_i - d_j)$ where $S_{i,j}$ is the score of student i on question j, n_j is the number of points on the question, d_j is the difficulty of the question, and a_i is the ability of the student. We can then reverse calculate ability (a_i) given their observed score and problem difficulty. The difference in exam ability between terms is shown in Figure 3b. Student midterm abilities, measured on a scale from 0 to 10 increased from an average of 6.9 to an average of 7.6 ($p < 0.0001$).

Plagiarism: One of the theorized impacts of using Pensieve is that it would create a culture where plagiarism would be less prevalent: it is much harder to cheat if you are going to be presented with your process. For Assignment 3, trajectory-based plagiarism

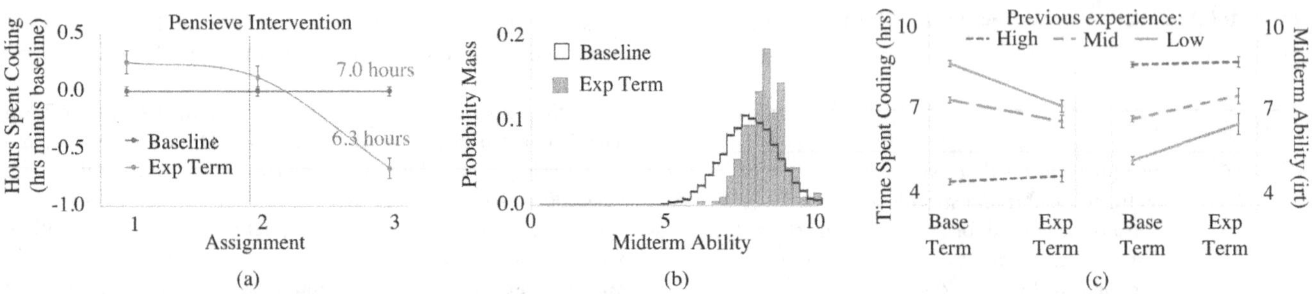

Figure 3: The difference in performance between the Baseline Term and the Experience (Exp) Term, where we deployed Pensieve. (a) Change in time to complete assignments. (b) Change in midterm ability. (c) Changes broken down for students with High, Mid and Low levels of initial CS background for: (left) time to complete assignment 3 and (right) midterm ability. All error bars are one standard error of the mean.

detection (TMOSS) shows a small decrease (from 4.3% of the class down to 3.9%) compared against previously published numbers from the same course [43].

Who benefits: Given that background knowledge outweighs many other factors for predicting student performance in CS1, we disaggregated our assignment time results and exam ability results based on the prior knowledge of students. We split students into three equal-sized terciles (Low, Mid, High) based on a background statistic, computed as a weighted sum of normalized: reported hours of experience (50%), Assignment 1 grade (30%) and Assignment 1 work time in hours (20%). Based on these splits we can see that the benefits of Pensieve were mainly experienced by the Low tercile (Figure 3c). The Mid tercile also had significant improvements; however the top tercile had negligible changes in midterm ability and assignment work time between the Baseline Term and the Experience Term.

Despite these promising results with *Pensieve*, there are many uncontrollable, confounding factors. In particular, teaching assistants are not required to use our tool, and it is highly likely that those who effectively use the tool are more effective teachers to begin with. Instead of taking our analysis as conclusive proof of the efficacy of *Pensieve*, it is better to see these results as a positive indication that such a tool improves the student learning experience.

6 BEST PRACTICES

In this section, we discuss best practices of *Pensieve* that were gleaned from our continued use of the tool and the conversations from the SGID sessions with teaching assistants.

When to use *Pensieve*: With the goal of developing student metacognition at an early stage, deploy *Pensieve* for the first few programming projects in a course. This enables teachers to identify process errors early on and recommend good programming practices, and develop a student's metacognition.

How to use *Pensieve*: *Pensieve* can be deployed in many ways. We believe that it is most valuable when teacher and student sit down together and use the tool to facilitate discussion. This type of conversation helps a teacher identify struggling students early on, so that they can be monitored and helped through the course. In our experience, keeping these short sessions ungraded helps to create an environment where students can ask questions about their own learning. Alternatively, the tool could be used for remote feedback, though we expect the missing human conversation will limit the impact on student learning.

Teacher training: Since our goal was to use *Pensieve* in student-teacher interactions, it is important to train teachers to use this tool effectively. Instruct teachers to foster conversations with students about problem solving techniques. We specifically focused on teaching teachers how to talk about top down "decomposition" and "iterative testing" [13]. We recommend teachers use the graphs to efficiently find the most "important" snapshots of progress—snapshots that illustrate conceptual changes.

Student messaging: *Pensieve* works best with fine-grained code snapshots of student process; naturally this brings up questions of student privacy. When presenting the tool to students, we made clear that our intentions were to help students learn as much as possible. Just like in other classes, the more a student shows their work the more helpful feedback a teacher can give. Similarly, when introducing *Pensieve* to students, it is an opportunity to explain that plagiarism is much more obvious when a teacher is looking at one's progress.

Currently, Pensieve is most valuable with a human teacher in the feedback process. There are many potential extensions to the tool that would add clearer information extraction and reduce teachers' burden, such as highlighting notable trends on the Workflow graphs or code diffs between snapshots. Still, it is an important first step in providing more formative, metacognitive feedback to students, and paves the way for better automated feedback in the future.

7 CONCLUSION

Perhaps one of the most important things *Pensieve* brings to the table is the ability to view progress in a tool that is useful for both the teacher *and* the student. This is a way to begin the conversation on metacognition—and a way to bring a human aspect back to programming despite the size of classrooms. Given how much time is needed to learn how to code, early feedback for beginning programmers is a highly efficient use of scarce resources, even for classrooms who do not have a low student-teacher ratio.

Students and teaching assistants had overwhelmingly positive feedback about using *Pensieve* in the classroom, and the courses where it was deployed had significant learning improvements. We invite you to use and improve on this novel, open-source way to give feedback on coding process.

REFERENCES

[1] Kirsti M. Ala-Mutka. 2005. A Survey of Automated Assessment Approaches for Programming Assignments. *Computer Science Education* 15, 2 (2005), 83–102. https://doi.org/10.1080/08993400500150747

[2] Lorin W. Anderson and David R. Krathwohl (Eds.). 2001. *A Taxonomy for Learning, Teaching, and Assessing. A Revision of Bloom's Taxonomy of Educational Objectives* (2 ed.). Allyn & Bacon, New York.

[3] Randy Elliot Bennett. 2011. Formative assessment: A critical review. *Assessment in Education: Principles, Policy & Practice* 18, 1 (2011), 5–25.

[4] Susan Bergin, Ronan Reilly, and Desmond Traynor. 2005. Examining the Role of Self-Regulated Learning on Introductory Programming Performance. In *Proceedings of the first international workshop on Computing education research (ICER '05)*. ACM, New York, NY, USA, 81–86. https://doi.org/10.1145/1089786.1089794

[5] Paul Black and Dylan Wiliam. 2009. Developing the theory of formative assessment. *Educational Assessment, Evaluation and Accountability(formerly: Journal of Personnel Evaluation in Education)* 21, 1 (23 Jan 2009), 5. https://doi.org/10.1007/s11092-008-9068-5

[6] David Boud and Elizabeth Molloy. 2013. Rethinking models of feedback for learning: the challenge of design. *Assessment & Evaluation in Higher Education* 38, 6 (2013), 698–712. https://doi.org/10.1080/02602938.2012.691462

[7] John D. Bransford, Ann L. Brown, and Rodney R. Cocking. 2000. *How People Learn*. National Academy Press.

[8] Tracey Bretag. 2013. Challenges in Addressing Plagiarism in Education. *PLoS Medicine* 10, 12 (2013).

[9] David Carless, Diane Salter, Min Yang, and Joy Lam. 2011. Developing sustainable feedback practices. *Studies in Higher Education* 36, 4 (2011), 395–407. https://doi.org/10.1080/03075071003642449

[10] D. Joseph Clark and Mark V. Redmond. 1982. Small group instructional diagnosis. ERIC.

[11] Curtis Clifton, Lisa C. Kaczmarczyk, and Michael Mrozek. 2007. Subverting the Fundamentals Sequence: Using Version Control to Enhance Course Management. In *Proceedings of the 38th SIGCSE technical symposium on Computer science education*. ACM, 86–90.

[12] Quintin Cutts, Emily Cutts, Stephen Draper, Patrick O'Donnell, and Peter Saffrey. 2010. Manipulating Mindset to Positively Influence Introductory Programming Performance. In *Proceedings of the 41st ACM Technical Symposium on Computer Science Education (SIGCSE '10)*. ACM, New York, NY, USA, 431–435. https://doi.org/10.1145/1734263.1734409

[13] Nell B. Dale. 2006. Most difficult topics in CS1: results of an online survey of educators. *ACM SIGCSE Bulletin* 38, 2 (2006), 49–53.

[14] Thanasis Daradoumis, Roxana Bassi, Fatos Xhafa, and Santi Caballé. 2013. A Review on Massive E-Learning (MOOC) Design, Delivery and Assessment. *2013 Eighth International Conference on P2P, Parallel, Grid, Cloud and Internet Computing* (2013), 208–213.

[15] Carol Dweck. 2008. *Mindsets and Math/Science Achievement*. New York: Carnegie Corporation of New York, Institute for Advanced Study, Commission on Mathematics and Science Education, New York, NY, USA.

[16] Stephen H. Edwards and Manuel A. Perez-Quinones. 2008. Web-CAT: Automatically Grading Programming Assignments. *SIGCSE Bull.* 40, 3 (June 2008), 328–328. https://doi.org/10.1145/1597849.1384371

[17] Susan E. Embretson and Steven P. Reise. 2013. *Item response theory*. Psychology Press.

[18] Anneli Eteläpelto. 1993. Metacognition and the Expertise of Computer Program Comprehension. *Scandinavian Journal of Educational Research* 37, 3 (1993), 243–254. https://doi.org/10.1080/0031383930370305

[19] Peter Ferguson. 2011. Student perceptions of quality feedback in teacher education. *Assessment & Evaluation in Higher Education* 36, 1 (2011), 51–62. https://doi.org/10.1080/02602930903197883

[20] Ursula Fuller, Colin G. Johnson, Tuukka Ahoniemi, Diana Cukierman, Isidoro Hernán-Losada, Jana Jackova, Essi Lahtinen, Tracy L. Lewis, Donna McGee Thompson, Charles Riedesel, and Errol Thompson. 2007. Developing a Computer Science-specific Learning Taxonomy. In *Working Group Reports on ITiCSE on Innovation and Technology in Computer Science Education (ITiCSE-WGR '07)*. ACM, New York, NY, USA, 152–170. https://doi.org/10.1145/1345443.1345438

[21] Petri Ihantola, Tuukka Ahoniemi, Ville Karavirta, and Otto Seppälä. 2010. Review of Recent Systems for Automatic Assessment of Programming Assignments. In *Proceedings of the 10th Koli Calling International Conference on Computing Education Research (Koli Calling '10)*. ACM, New York, NY, USA, 86–93. https://doi.org/10.1145/1930464.1930480

[22] Charles Juwah, Debra Macfarlane-Dick, Bob Matthew, David Nicol, David Ross, and Brenda Smith. 2004. Enhancing student learning through effective formative feedback. *The Higher Education Academy* 140 (2004).

[23] Hieke Keuning, Johan Jeuring, and Bastiaan Heeren. 2016. Towards a Systematic Review of Automated Feedback Generation for Programming Exercises. In *Proceedings of the 2016 ACM Conference on Innovation and Technology in Computer Science Education (ITiCSE '16)*. ACM, New York, NY, USA, 41–46. https://doi.org/10.1145/2899415.2899422

[24] Oren Laadan, Jason Nieh, and Nicolas Viennot. 2010. Teaching Operating Systems Using Virtual Appliances and Distributed Version Control. In *Proceedings of the 41st SIGCSE technical symposium on Computer science education*. ACM, 480–484.

[25] Joseph Lawrance, Seikyung Jung, and Charles Wiseman. 2013. Git on the cloud in the classroom. In *Proceedings of the 44th ACM technical symposium on Computer science education*. ACM, 639–644.

[26] Michael J. Lee and Andrew J. Ko. 2011. Personifying Programming Tool Feedback Improves Novice Programmers' Learning. In *Proceedings of the Seventh International Workshop on Computing Education Research (ICER '11)*. ACM, New York, NY, USA, 109–116. https://doi.org/10.1145/2016911.2016934

[27] Ying Liu, Eleni Stroulia, Kenny Wong, and Daniel German. 2004. CVS historical information to understand how students develop software. In *26th International Conference on Software Engineering*. International Workshop on Mining Software Repositories (MSR), 32–36.

[28] Dastyni Loksa, Andrew J. Ko, Will Jernigan, Alannah Oleson, Christopher J. Mendez, and Margaret M. Burnett. 2016. Programming, Problem Solving, and Self-Awareness: Effects of Explicit Guidance. In *Proceedings of the 2016 CHI Conference on Human Factors in Computing Systems (CHI '16)*. ACM, New York, NY, USA, 1449–1461. https://doi.org/10.1145/2858036.2858252

[29] Guillaume Marceau, Kathi Fisler, and Shriram Krishnamurthi. 2011. Mind Your Language: On Novices' Interactions with Error Messages. In *Proceedings of the 10th SIGPLAN Symposium on New Ideas, New Paradigms, and Reflections on Programming and Software (Onward! 2011)*. ACM, New York, NY, USA, 3–18. https://doi.org/10.1145/2048237.2048241

[30] David J. Nicol and Debra Macfarlan-Dick. 2006. Formative assessment and self-regulated learning: a model and seven principles of good feedback practice. *Studies in Higher Education* 31, 2 (2006), 199–218. https://doi.org/10.1080/03075070600572090

[31] Chris Piech, Mehran Sahami, Daphne Koller, Steve Cooper, and Paulo Blikstein. 2012. Modeling how students learn to program. In *Proceedings of the 43rd ACM technical symposium on Computer Science Education*. ACM, 153–160.

[32] James Prather, Raymond Pettit, Kayla McMurry, Alani Peters, John Homer, and Maxine Cohen. 2018. Metacognitive Difficulties Faced by Novice Programmers in Automated Assessment Tools. In *Proceedings of the 2018 ACM Conference on International Computing Education Research (ICER '18)*. ACM, New York, NY, USA, 41–50. https://doi.org/10.1145/3230977.3230981

[33] Thomas W. Price, Neil C.C. Brown, Chris Piech, and Kelly Rivers. 2017. Sharing and Using Programming Log Data (Abstract Only). In *Proceedings of the 2017 ACM SIGCSE Technical Symposium on Computer Science Education (SIGCSE '17)*. ACM, New York, NY, USA, 729–729. https://doi.org/10.1145/3017680.3022366

[34] Sarah Quinton and Teresa Smallbone. 2010. Feeding forward: using feedback to promote student reflection and learning–a teaching model. *Innovations in Education and Teaching International* 47, 1 (2010), 125–135. https://doi.org/10.1080/14703290903525911

[35] Karen L. Reid and Gregory V. Wilson. 2005. Learning by Doing: Introducing Version Control as a Way to Manage Student Assignments. In *Proceedings of the 36th SIGCSE technical symposium on Computer science education*. ACM, 272–276.

[36] Kelly Rivers and Kenneth R. Koedinger. 2017. Data-Driven Hint Generation in Vast Solution Spaces: a Self-Improving Python Programming Tutor. *International Journal of Artificial Intelligence in Education* 27, 1 (01 Mar 2017), 37–64. https://doi.org/10.1007/s40593-015-0070-z

[37] Eric Roberts, John Lilly, and Bryan Rollins. 1995. Using Undergraduates as Teaching Assistants in Introductory Programming Courses: An Update on the Stanford Experience. In *Proceedings of the twenty-sixth SIGCSE technical symposium on Computer science education*. ACM, 48–52.

[38] Kimberly Tanner. 2012. Promoting Student Metacognition. *CBE Life Sciences Education* 11, 2 (2012), 113–120.

[39] Errol Thompson, Andrew Luxton-Reilly, Jacqueline L. Whalley, Minjie Hu, and Phil Robbins. 2008. Bloom's Taxonomy for CS Assessment. In *Proceedings of the Tenth Conference on Australasian Computing Education - Volume 78 (ACE '08)*. Australian Computer Society, Inc., Darlinghurst, Australia, Australia, 155–161. http://dl.acm.org/citation.cfm?id=1379249.1379265

[40] Peter Vamplew and Julian Dermoudy. 2005. An Anti-Plagiarism Editor for Software Development Courses. In *Proceedings of the 7th Australasian Conference on Computing Education*. 83–90.

[41] Fabienne M. Van der Kleij, Remco C. W. Feskens, and Theo J. H. M. Eggen. 2015. Effects of Feedback in a Computer-Based Learning Environment on Students' Learning Outcomes: A Meta-Analysis. *Review of Educational Research* 85, 4 (2015), 475–511. https://doi.org/10.3102/0034654314564881

[42] Lisa Yan, Nick McKeown, and Chris Piech. 2019. The PyramidSnapshot Challenge: Understanding student process from visual output of programs. In *Proceedings of the 50th ACM Technical Symposium on Computer Science Education (SIGCSE '19)*. ACM, New York, NY, USA. https://doi.org/10.1145/3287324.3287386

[43] Lisa Yan, Nick McKeown, Mehran Sahami, and Chris Piech. 2018. TMOSS: Using Intermediate Assignment Work to Understand Excessive Collaboration in Large Classes. In *Proceedings of the 49th ACM Technical Symposium on Computer Science Education (SIGCSE '18)*. ACM, New York, NY, USA, 110–115. https://doi.org/10.1145/3159450.3159490

Experiences Using Heat Maps to Help Students Find Their Bugs: Problems and Solutions

Bob Edmison
Virginia Tech Department of Computer Science
Blacksburg, VA
bedmison@vt.edu

Stephen H. Edwards
Virginia Tech Department of Computer Science
Blacksburg, VA
edwards@cs.vt.edu

ABSTRACT

Automated grading systems provide feedback to students in a variety of ways, but usually focus on identifying incorrect program behaviors. Such systems provide notices of test case failures or runtime errors, but without debugging skills, students often become frustrated when they don't know where to start. They know their code has defects, but finding the problem may be beyond their experience, especially for beginners. An additional concern is balancing the need to provide enough direction to be useful, without giving the student so much direction that you effectively give them the answer. This paper presents our experience using heat maps to visually guide student attention to parts of their code that are most likely to contain problems. These visualizations are generated using existing tools that capture execution traces from instructor-written tests to identify which portions of the code are executed during tests that pass, and which portions are executed during tests that fail. Superimposing execution footprints allows statistical identification of locations in the student's code that are most likely to contain faults. This paper describes the results of using this feedback approach to help guide student attention with heat map visualizations over two semesters of CS1 involving over 700 students. Based on this experience, we analyze the utility of the heat maps, describe student perceptions of their helpfulness, and describe the unexpected challenges arising from students attempts to understand and apply this style of feedback. We conclude with concrete solutions proposed to improve how guiding feedback is presented to students.

CCS CONCEPTS

• **Human-centered computing → Heat maps**; • **Social and professional topics → Computer science education**; • **Applied computing → Computer-assisted instruction**; • **Software and its engineering → Software testing and debugging**;

KEYWORDS

debugging; testing; automatic fault localization; statistical fault localization; spectrum-based fault localization; SFL; automated grading; heat map; visualization; Web-CAT

SIGCSE'19, February 2019, Minneapolis, Minnesota USA

ACM ISBN 978-1-4503-5890-3/19/02...$15.00
https://doi.org/10.1145/3287324.3287474

ACM Reference Format:
Bob Edmison and Stephen H. Edwards. 2019. Experiences Using Heat Maps to Help Students Find Their Bugs: Problems and Solutions. In *Proceedings of ACM SIGCSE Conference (SIGCSE'19)*. ACM, New York, NY, USA, 7 pages. https://doi.org/10.1145/3287324.3287474

1 INTRODUCTION

Spectrum-based fault localization (SFL) is a technique used to shorten the cycle of testing code, diagnosing defects, repairing those defects, and then verifying the repair [14][1][5][6]. SFL creates what is referred to as a similarity coefficient that can be used to identify potentially defective or faulty code.

While SFL has applications in the professional world, like many software engineering techniques, it can also be applied in the classroom as students learn to design and implement software. Debugging is as much a skill as knowing when to employ the correct algorithm or control structure, but often students are not given any formal instruction in debugging techniques. We leave to the students to "figure it out". However, with CS programs struggling to address the growth in enrollment, and employers being less patient for new graduates to become productive, purposefully promoting debugging techniques is more important than ever.

In this paper, we report on a method that we have developed that uses spectrum-based fault location and data visualization to guide student debugging. Inspired by software engineering research, we automatically generate heat maps of student code highlighting where bugs are located, eliminating the need for instructor-written hints or tips and providing a more comprehensive and cohesive view of where students should focus their attention. Additionally, we report on our experience using this technique to provide feedback to our CS1 classes during the 2017/18 academic year, as well as techniques to address shortcomings in this approach we have identified.

2 BACKGROUND

2.1 Fault Location

The process of testing, debugging, and verification of software systems is a very expensive, resource intensive activity, mostly due to the labor-intensive nature of the debugging aspects of the process. A number of techniques have been proposed to automate the location of the defects that test cases identify. (see [18] for an excellent summary).

Spectrum-based fault localization (SFL) is a technique used to shorten the cycle of testing code, diagnosing defects, repairing those defects, and then verifying the repair [1]. SFL works by identifying the portions of a program that were activated when an error occurred [14]. The identification is accomplished by calculating a similarity coefficient, which ranks potential defect locations. Several methods.

One of the advantages of the SFL approach is that is does not require any foreknowledge of the program code or output. It can be applied at test-time using only a set of supplied test cases. The process then calculates a "suspiciousness" score, between zero and one, for each line of code based on the results of test cases applied during that testing run. If all of the tests pass, then the suspiciousness score for each line would be zero. If every test case failed on the same line, that line would be given a score of one.

Our approach here is implemented using the GZoltar library [4], which implements and extends the original Zoltar toolset [15]. Zoltar provides a method for identifying lines that cause multiple faults that is called BARINEL. This technique allows for a ranked list of possible debugging candidates to be returned, which is then translated to the locations within the program listing. In previous work [8], we validated this approach by using GZoltar to assess a set of student submissions, and then manually inspecting the results returned by GZoltar. We found that GZoltar scored the defective methods as the most suspicious 93% of the time.

Instructors don't typically have exercises to explicitly teach debugging strategies. It is a skill that is often learned by necessity and trial and error, with little in the way of focused feedback on the debugging task itself. Additionally, previous research [20] has questioned the efficacy of automated debugging in general. Our focus here is not to provide students with an automated debugging tool, but to provide a scaffold for them to learn how to approach debugging.

2.2 Heat Maps

Visualization of software statistics and faults is not a novel idea. Other systems [3][10] have been developed to visually display aspects of the metrics around software development. The Tarantula system [17] uses a system of pass/fail tests, and then visualizes the results within the context of the source code.

Existing feedback technology is limited in how it identifies and localizes software faults for many reasons, and currently relies almost entirely on instructor-provided names or messages. This places an extra burden on instructors and requires special skills to do well. Further, instructor-written feedback often does not reinforce a growth mindset and focuses on "what features are wrong". We have developed a new approach to providing feedback to assist students in debugging that leverages research from software engineering to generate fully automated "heat maps" of the statistically probable locations of bugs in student code. This visualization approach gives students both a big-picture view of where in their code they need to focus their attention, and also more actionable data about which specific location(s) they should investigate in detail. At the same time, it moves the feedback from value-based notions of "this feature is wrong" to more constructive concepts of "here is where you need to focus effort".

We recognize that later work [20] has questioned the efficacy of automated debugging in general, and on directing to defect locations specifically, that work focused on more advanced programmers. Our focus has been on providing a scaffold for novice developers to learn a process for debugging, by providing them automated, contextual guidance. In the future, we plan to investigate whether more advanced students benefit from this type of feedback, or if more feature-focused feedback provides a better experience for students.

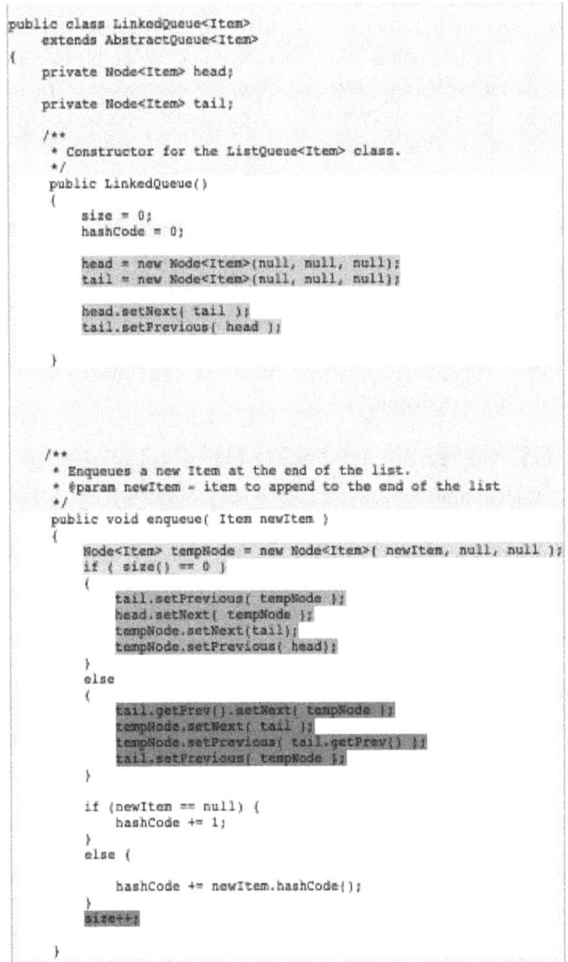

Figure 1: A sample source code heat map. Methods have a white background, and lines with a non-zero suspiciousness score are colored from yellow (0.01) to red (1.00).

3 GENERATING HEAT MAPS

Heat maps [25] are most commonly used in showing the concentration of occurrences at the intersection of two data points. Previous work has [11] has used heat maps to visualize the results of software testing over time as it relates to the changes in the source code. In our case, we created heat maps based on the suspiciousness scores generated from the results of SFL analysis of student code submissions.

For each student submission, the instructor's reference tests were applied to code using the GZoltar library [4], and the SFL results were recorded. We then created an HTML file that contains the source code for the student's submission. We then added styling to the file to visualize all of the lines of code that GZoltar identified as suspicious, based on the suspiciousness scored calculated (See Figure 1 as an example). This method of visualization shows the suggestions within the context of the source code for the submission. GZoltar reports a suspiciousness score of zero for lines that are executed in non-failing tests.

We used the HSV colorspace [16] to highlight lines that had a non-zero suspiciousness score, because it made it simple to convert the GZoltar scores into hue angles on the colorwheel. The color space we chose was between 0 (red) and $69.999\overline{9}$ (yellow) degrees, such that for a Gzoltar score:

$$colorScore = 70 - (GzoltarScore * 70)$$

Thus, the higher the Gzoltar suspiciousness score, the closer to red the source code line is displayed, the more suspicious the line is believed to be. Note also that we specifically ignore any line that has a suspiciousness score of zero. By doing this, we insure that only lines that GZoltar deems suspicious are colored. Thus, using heat maps, the student can quickly see the lines, and thus the methods, with the highest suspicion.

4 USING HEAT MAPS TO HELP STUDENTS

A significant amount of work, going back over 30 years, has been conducted looking at how novice programmers work and how they debug their code[7][21][22][2]. Additionally, much research, [12][13][23], has been conducted that studied the differences in debugging abilities and techniques employed by novice and expert programmers. Additionally, we know that situating the feedback within the context of the assignment is important to the learning process [24]. Finally, the feedback cycle of edit→submit→receive→revise can be critical for student performance [19]. This feedback cycle can create a problem for students when they encounter a bug in their code and the feedback they receive from the automated grader doesn't provide them the guidance they need to resolve the defect, or is provided out of context.

Students often believe, incorrectly, that an automated assessment system can figure out where the defects in their programs are, but that the instructor has configured the system not to reveal that information. In point of fact, while assessment systems can be quite effective in showing that bugs are present, simply knowing a problem exists is not the same as knowing its cause. Some instructors use different techniques to create reference test suites intended to aid in the task of locating bugs, but this work is time-consuming and the complexity of assignments can make this task challenging. Other instructors resort to giving the test data to students so students can examine the tests and run them themselves, but this relieves students of the obligation of self-checking their own work by writing their own tests, and still does not address the problem of finding bugs once they are revealed. Also, there is a balance that has to be struck between prompting the student as to where they might look to solve an issue versus telling them specifically "you're using an assignment instead of an equality operator in line 12".

The heat map visualization we have developed leverages automation to provide contextualized feedback to the students while encouraging them to debug on their own. There are many advantages to providing this form of visual feedback. First, it provides holistic feedback about the entire assignment, rather than textual feedback that is much more limited in scope. Rather than the instructor having the write feedback for every possible outcome, the heat map will automatically display all possible outcomes. Second, it provides location information within the student's solution, not a feature-oriented description. In effect, it is direct, location-based defect feedback instead of indirect information about what test case(s) failed. Novices don't have the domain knowledge that experts have [13], which makes a feature-based approached less appropriate for novice programmers. Third, by providing information about the entire assignment, students can choose which areas they wish to investigate. Fourth, by aggregating the statement-level data used to generate the visualization, it is also possible to rank entire methods in order of probability of containing bug(s). Fifth, it is fully automatic and requires no additional work on the part of instructors to write hints or feedback messages for students, or to consider how students might interpret (or misinterpret) the names of test cases.

Table 1: Heat map creation summary

Program	Students	Attempts	Displayed	Avg
Maze	259	1770	497	28.08%
Segregator	256	2287	983	42.98%
Battleship	254	1427	165	11.56%
AntsVsBees	256	2554	1386	54.27%
WxStation	174	1476	750	50.81%
	Total	**9514**	**3781**	**39.74%**

5 EXPERIENCE IN THE CLASSROOM

To test the efficacy of heat maps as a feedback strategy, we developed a plug-in for Web-CAT [9], the automated grading system that we use. When students submitted their assignments, the GZoltar library evaluated their code against the instructor's references tests. A heat map was then created and displayed back to the student within the context of the other feedback Web-CAT provided. We used this system during the 2017/18 academic year in our CS1 course. We evaluated five assignments in the Fall semester, and four in the Spring. In total, 893 students were enrolled, of which, 262 consented to participate in this study.

Heat maps were generated for each student submission, but not necessarily presented each time. We reserved heat map presentation until two conditions were satisfied:

- The student had at least 85% code coverage with their own test cases, **AND**
- The submission had to pass at least one reference test case.

The restrictions on presenting the heatmaps were meant to encourage students to continue to write their own tests, and not use the heat maps as a crutch or as an artificial view into the reference tests. The heat map is meant as a tool to provide a scaffold for them to approach debugging, not a substitute to writing their own tests, and imposing these restrictions before presenting the heat maps encourage that behavior.

5.1 Problems Identified in Use

At the end of each semester, we asked the students participating in the study to complete a survey about their experience with the heat map tool, and to provide their feedback. Based on observations on the behavior of the tool, and from reviewing the students' feedback, we have identified a number of issues associated with this approach.

One major shortcoming is the lack of visibility into the tests that failed. We are using the results of the instructor's reference tests when creating the heat maps, so the students don't have any access to the tests, which means they can't use the information encapsulated in the test case to localize the defect. Secondly, the nature of SFL means that the score for each line is based on the execution of the set of tests. We don't have a way of saying "The failure to test 1 contributed 23% and the failure of test 2 contributed 77% to the suspiciousness score of line 93".

Additionally, there is a misperception held by students that the auto-grader is "pointing to the bug", when, in fact, it is just evaluating the spectra of defects in the code, which may or may not include the actual location of the defect. Students believe that the heat maps should include the location of the defect, but that is not always true. If the student implemented the code, and it is defective, the defect will be present. However, if the error is a defect of omission, there is nothing to point to. The spectra will suggest an area to investigate, but it can't point to the location because the defect is code that doesn't exist.

5.2 Block-level Rather than Statement-level Localization

The nature of SFL means that suspiciousness scores for statements in a single block of code have the same score, because they are executed together. Unless the block has a single statement, the scores for a block will always be the same. In Figure 2, taken from a student submission, we see a constructor method has each line identified as suspicious. In fact, they are all considered equally suspicious.

Additionally, the way that SFL libraries typically behave is to create a *cumulative* suspiciousness score across all of the tests applied during the evaluation. In previous work [8], a manual evaluation of GZoltar results showed that because of this cumulative behavior, the suspiciousness was closer to the block-level than the statement-level.

From a student perspective, this can be confusing, because the heat map is presenting a block as being suspicious but isn't differentiating within the block where to look. That isn't terribly useful, and in fact could be less useful than looking at the error log, since the heat map will also reflect suspiciousness for locations along the call tree towards the defect. In the case of Figure 2, the error may be in `setActorChoices()`, and thus the call to the offending method is marked as suspicious.

5.3 Faults Due to Missing Code

In some cases, the defects are due to code that is missing, for example, unimplemented features, or a missing "else" conditional. In this case, the heat map can't highlight the problem (since the root cause doesn't actually exist), but it can highlight the code around the problem. Additionally, the heat map may highlight correct code

```
public Colony()
{
    super();

    QueensChamber queen = new QueensChamber();
    add(queen, 0, 3);
    Hive bees = new Hive();
    add(bees, 9, 3);

    setActorChoices(
        HarvesterAnt.class,
        ThrowerAnt.class,
        WallAnt.class,
        FireAnt.class,
        HungryAnt.class);

    food = 10;
}
```

Figure 2: A method showing multiple statements with the same suspiciousness.

that is executed at the wrong time because of the missing code. This mis-highlighting can cause students to mistrust heat maps or find them counter-productive, since they directly conflict with the model of the heat map helping point to the fault location.

Figure 3 demonstrates this behavior. In this case, the student has not implemented the `else` clause on the `if..else` statement, and the test case has attempted to test the scenario of `size == 0`. Notice that the SFL analysis has assigned a non-zero suspiciousness to the closing brace on the if clause. Since the else clause does not exist, this is the only place it makes sense for the suspiciousness score to be assigned for the missing else clause.

```
public String toString()
{
    String st = "";
    st += "<";
    if (size > 0)
    {
        Node temp = new Node(null);
        temp= front.getNext();
        while (temp != rear)
        {
            if (temp == rear.getPrevious())
            {
                st += temp.getElement() + ">";
                return st;
            }
            st += temp.getElement() + ", ";
            temp = temp.getNext();
        }
    }

    return st;
}
```

Figure 3: Heat map of method missing an `Else` condition.

5.4 Multiple Simultaneous Faults

In some cases, the heat map that is generated can have so many lines highlighted that it doesn't provide any meaningful insight to the student. Additionally, it can cause information overload for the student, making it difficult to know where to start. In Figure 4, a heat map of a student submission is shown where every non-comment line is highlighted. This isn't useful to the student, and in fact is frustrating, as the survey feedback showed.

Over-highlighting can happen when there aren't many simultaneous faults. It can happen when a key piece of code is defective, or one that is called may times throughout the execution of the application. In either scenario, the spectra generated for the execution will incorporate that code and all of the code that depends on it, resulting in spectra that indicate near universal code suspiciousness.

Figure 4: Heat map with all lines highlighted.

6 EVALUATION

We evaluated the heat maps in two ways. First, we surveyed students at the end of the semester and asked the students to indicate their agreement to a series of questions relating to the usefulness of the heat maps. The student responses (n=47) indicated that most found the heat maps hard to use, confusing, and that they did not improve the student's class performance. This was very discouraging, as we believed that this approach would be helpful to students, because it provides feedback for debugging that is within the context of their own source code, not just as a list of error statements in a separate display.

We also manually reviewed the heat maps that had been generated, created a summary analysis of the heat maps themselves, and we understood one reason why the heat maps were confusing. Figure 5 shows a graph of the percentage of heat map highlighted code as a percentage of non-comment lines of code (NCLOC) in the submission. In our initial deployment, we showed the results of all failed reference tests (indicated by the blue column).

Additionally, Figure 6 indicates the heat maps also have a broad highlighting of methods as well. Thus, the highlights are not concentrated in a small set of larger methods. They are spread out across the classes, touching code in many methods. This means that most students will be looking at a heat map with a significant portion of the source code identified as suspect in the heat map.

In attempt to address this issue, we reassessed the student submissions with a modified version of the heat map generator. Instead of showing the results for all of the failed tests, we generated heat maps based on the first failed test that was encountered by GZoltar. In order to insure that the suspiciousness for then entire set of spectra was consistent, we didn't stop testing, we merely noted the first failed test and displayed it by itself. The orange column in Figure 5 shows the results of the reassessment and suggests we were correct, but not to the extent that we expected. We would have hoped that the results would have shifted more to the left for the "first failed", indicating that fewer lines of code were being highlighted in more heat maps.

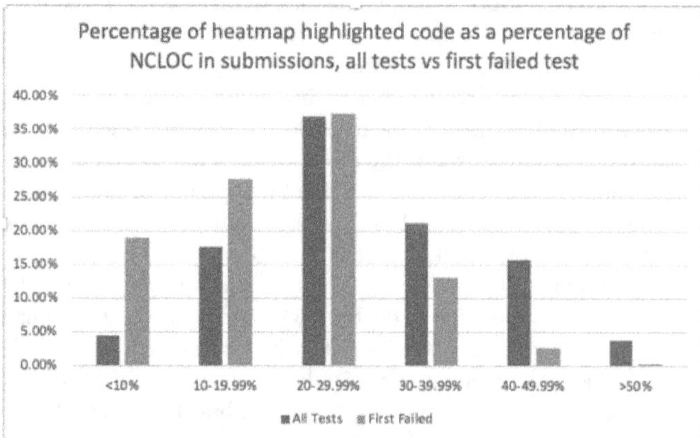

Figure 5: Heat map code highlighting as a percentage of NCLOC, all tests vs first failed test.

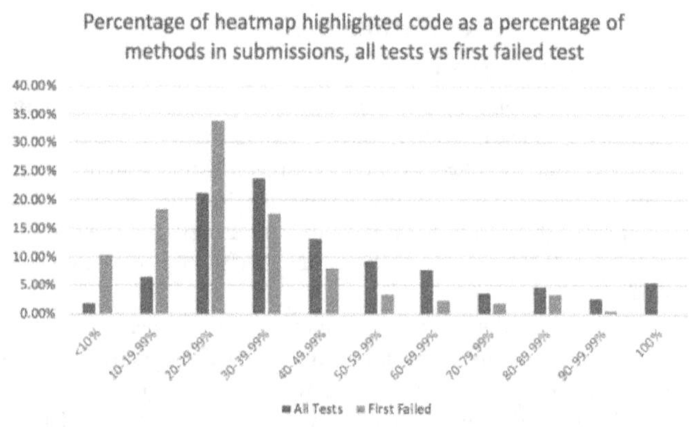

Figure 6: Heat map code highlighting as a percentage of methods, all tests vs first failed test.

Rather than focusing the student's efforts, the heat maps in their current configuration actually diffuse the focus. However, notice that like the lines of code, changing to a "first failed" reporting option does increase the percentage of the heat maps that have a lower percentage of methods highlighted in them, further reducing the noise to which students are subjected. Coupling this with the survey responses, it is clear that the current approach provides too much information in a way that is not directed enough for students, especially novice students, to gain much benefit.

7 LESSONS LEARNED

Based on our use of heat maps for two semesters, we have come away with some lessons learned about our experience.

First, it is not useful to generate heat maps when too many tests fail, or, more precisely, when too much of the program is highlighted by the spectra of failing tests. When the whole design is highlighted due to multiple simultaneous failures, the heat map is no longer helpful for localization. Above a certain point, the highlights become noise.

Second, instead of mapping all of the failed tests, instead, choice a model such as the first failing test to "mask" the heat map. This effectively focuses on displaying the slice of the heat map corresponding to one feature (and hopefully, one failure mode or fault). There is still the possibility that even in this model, a heat map could be drawn where all of the lines could be highlighted, such as a care where all test cases are failing regardless. This could be mitigated by adding additional checks in the auto-grader to limit the heat map display if the percentage of NCLOC from the project represented in the map is above a certain threshold.

As a step in this direction, we have developed a version of the heat map generator that allows the instructor to set a "failed test" depth, so that the map will only show the failed tests to this depth. Using the same submissions from the students in Fall 2017/Spring 2018 CS 1 courses, we re-created the heat maps, and then evaluated whether less code was being highlighted, as a percentage of NCLOC and methods in the student submissions. Figure 5 shows that the number of heat maps with a 20% or more of highlighted lines has decreased when we limit the heat map to reporting the results of the first failed test. Similarly, Figure 5 shows the percentage of code highlighted in heat maps also decreases when we limit the heat map to the first failed test, as shown by the orange column.

Third, label the heat map with the goal/feature being used as the filter. This can address the fact that students don't have access to the reference tests and don't know what is being tested. This helps balance the need to keep reference tests hidden, with the need of programmers to know what fault is being highlighted in the heat map. This will require additional effort on the part of the instructor, as this is effectively combining the functionality of a hinting system with the heat map. The hints or prompts will need to be meaningful, but not give too much away to the student.

Fourth, provide intentionally chosen labeling for heat maps to help students understand the correct interpretation and to preempt misconceptions about "the computer points out the bug". The heat maps as we have currently implemented them are displayed as simply the source code displayed in-line with the rest of the feedback provided by the auto-grader. We don't provide any prompts as to the interpretation of the heat map. Providing specific wording could help clarify the use of the heat map as well as address some of the issues associated with the limitations of the underlying SFL analysis. One possible explanation:

> Your submission has been analyzed using statistical fault location. In this heat map, colored lines indicate code executed during a failing test case, with more red lines indicating code that is less commonly (or never) executed in other passing test cases. A colored line is not necessarily defective itself, but it was definitely involved in the execution of a reference test case that failed. Note that a test may have failed because of missing code, as well as defective code.

8 CONCLUSIONS

Heat maps provide a way to visually display the results reference test outcomes within the context of student code assignments. However, their use has to be carefully planned and considered. As we have shown, it is easy to overload the student with more information than they are able to use or process, leading to frustration.

We have provided several alternative approaches for addressing these issues. Our plan is to first implement the "first failed" option in a class setting. We have shown here that this approach will lower the "noise" the students encounter, though perhaps not to the extent that we had expected. We now need to see if this change will improve student's perceptions of the utility of the heat map as a feedback mechanism.

Additionally, we plan to adjust the heat map interface itself. We plan to provide more guidance to the students about what the heat map can and, more importantly, can't do. Also, we are investigating integrating student tests into the heat map, using the heat map as a visualization of code coverage.

Finally, we plan to use the heat map in our data structures and algorithms course. We have a question about whether CS1 students may not be the best audience for this type of feedback system. It is possible that we are assuming a certain level of skill to use this tool that CS1 students don't possess yet when we present this feedback style to them. By offering the heat maps to more advanced students, we want to see if they are better equipped to benefit from them, or if they have similar issues as the CS1 students.

ACKNOWLEDGMENTS

This work is supported in part by the National Science Foundation under grant DUE-1625425. Any opinions, findings, conclusions, or recommendations expressed in this material are those of the authors and do not necessarily reflect the views of the National Science Foundation.

REFERENCES

[1] Rui Abreu, Peter Zoeteweij, Rob Golsteijn, and Arjan J C van Gemund. 2009. A practical evaluation of spectrum-based fault localization. *Journal of Systems and Software* 82, 11 (Nov. 2009), 1780–1792.

[2] Marzieh Ahmadzadeh, Dave Elliman, and Colin Higgins. 2005. An analysis of patterns of debugging among novice computer science students. In *ACM Innovation and Technology in Computer Science Education 2005*. ACM, New York, New York, USA, 84–88.

[3] Thomas Ball and Stephen G Eick. 1996. Software visualization in the large. *Computer* 29, 4 (April 1996), 33–43.

[4] José Campos, André Riboira, Alexandre Perez, and Rui Abreu. 2012. GZoltar: an eclipse plug-in for testing and debugging. In *Proceedings of the 27th IEEE/ACM International Conference on Automated Software Engineering*. ACM Request Permissions, Essen, Germany, 378–381.

[5] Mike Y Chen, Emre Kiciman, Eugene Fratkin, Armando Fox, and Eric Brewer. 2002. Pinpoint: problem determination in large, dynamic Internet services. In *International Conference on Dependable Systems and Networks*. IEEE, 595–604.

[6] Valentin Dallmeier, Christian Lindig, and Andreas Zeller. 2005. Lightweight Defect Localization for Java. In *European Conference on Object-Oriented Programming*, A P Black (Ed.). Springer Berlin Heidelberg, Berlin, Heidelberg, 528–550.

[7] B Du-Boulay. 1988. Some Difficulties of Learning to Program. *Studying the Novice Programmer* (1988), 286–300.

[8] Bob Edmison and Stephen H Edwards. 2015. Applying spectrum-based fault localization to generate debugging suggestions for student programmers. In *2015 IEEE International Symposium on Software Reliability Engineering Workshops (ISSREW)*. IEEE, 93–99.

[9] Stephen H Edwards and Manuel A Pérez-Quiñones. 2008. Web-CAT: automatically grading programming assignments. In *ACM annual conference on Innovation and Technology in Computer Science Education 2008*. ACM, 328.

[10] S C Eick, J L Steffen, and E E Sumner. 1992. Seesoft-a tool for visualizing line oriented software statistics. *IEEE Transactions on Software Engineering* 18, 11 (1992), 957–968.

[11] Alex Gerdes, Johan Jeuring, and Bastiaan Heeren. 2012. An interactive functional programming tutor. In *ACM Innovation and Technology in Computer Science Education 2005.* ACM, Haifa, Israel, 250–255.

[12] T Green and M Petre. 1996. Usability Analysis of Visual Programming Environments: A 'Cognitive Dimensions' Framework. *Journal of Visual Languages and Computing* 7, 2 (June 1996), 131–174.

[13] L Gugerty and G Olson. 1986. Debugging by skilled and novice programmers. In *ACM SIGCHI Bulletin Proceedings of the SIGCHI conference on Human factors in computing systems 1986.* ACM, New York, New York, USA, 171–174.

[14] Mary Jean Harrold, Gregg Rothermel, Kent Sayre, Rui Wu, and Liu Yi. 2000. An empirical investigation of the relationship between spectra differences and regression faults. *Journal of Software Testing, Verification and Reliability* 10, 3 (Sept. 2000), 171–194.

[15] Tom Janssen, Rui Abreu, and Arjan J C van Gemund. 2009. Zoltar: A Toolset for Automatic Fault Localization. In *2009 24th IEEE/ACM International Conference on Automated Software Engineering (ASE).* IEEE, 662–664.

[16] George H Joblove and Donald Greenberg. 1978. Color spaces for computer graphics. In *SIGGRAPH '78 Proceedings of the 5th annual conference on Computer graphics and interactive techniques.* ACM, ACM, New York, NY, 20–25.

[17] James A Jones and Mary Jean Harrold. 2005. Empirical evaluation of the tarantula automatic fault-localization technique. In *20th IEEE/ACM international Conference on Automated Software Engineering.* ACM, New York, NY, USA, 273–282.

[18] Xiaolin Ju, Shujuan Jiang, Xiang Chen, Xingya Wang, Yanmei Zhang, and Heling Cao. 2014. HSFal: Effective fault localization using hybrid spectrum of full slices and execution slices. *Journal of Systems and Software* 90 (April 2014), 3–17.

[19] Sudhir Mehta and Nem W Schlecht. 1998. Computerized assessment technique for large classes. *Journal of Engineering Education* 87 (April 1998), 167–172.

[20] Chris Parnin and Alessandro Orso. 2011. Are automated debugging techniques actually helping programmers?. In *International Symposium on Software Testing and Analysis 2011.* ACM, Toronto, ON, Canada, 199–209.

[21] Roy D Pea. 1986. Language-Independent Conceptual "Bugs" in Novice Programming:. *Journal of Educational Computing Research* 2, 1 (1986), 25–36.

[22] James G Spohrer and Elliot Soloway. 1986. Analyzing the high frequency bugs in novice programs. In *First Workshop on Empirical Studies of Programmers on Empirical Studies of Programmers.* Ablex Publishing Corp., Norwood, NJ, USA, 230–251.

[23] S Uchida, A Monden, H Iida, K Matsumoto, and H Kudo. [n. d.]. A multiple-view analysis model of debugging processes. In *2002 International Symposium on Empirical Software Engineering.* IEEE Comput. Soc, 139–147.

[24] S Wang and P Wu. 2008. The role of feedback and self-efficacy on web-based learning: The social cognitive perspective. *Computers & Education* 51, 4 (Dec. 2008), 1589–1598.

[25] Leland Wilkinson and Michael Friendly. 2009. The History of the Cluster Heat Map. *The American Statistician* 63, 2 (May 2009), 179–184.

On the Effects of Active Learning Environments in Computing Education

Tyler Greer
Computer Science
Western Washington University
greert2@wwu.edu

Qiang Hao
Computer Science & SMATE
Western Washington University
qiang.hao@wwu.edu

Mengguo Jing
Human Development and Family Studies
University of Wisconsin-Madison
mjing3@wisc.edu

Bradley Barnes
Computer Science
University of Georgia
bjb211@uga.edu

ABSTRACT

This replication study aims at both quantifying the effects of active learning classrooms in introductory programming courses (CS1) and overcoming some design and methodological limits of prior studies on this topic. 156 students enrolled in three different sections of the same CS1 participated in this study. The three sections differed from each other either in terms of learning pedagogies (conventional lecture vs. peer instruction) or physical learning environments (lecture hall vs. active learning classroom). This study did not replicate the findings of prior studies on this topic. Instead, this study found that when learning pedagogies were controlled, learning environments did not have significant influences on student performance. On the other hand, learning pedagogies were found to have significant influences on student performance. When peer instruction is conducted other than conventional lecturing, students tended to have significantly better performance. Such findings highlight the importance of active learning in computing education, and the feasibility of conducting active learning in CS1 despite of physical environment constraints. Additionally, such findings emphasize the necessity of replication studies on the topic of active learning environments, and invite debates on the investment decisions in active learning classrooms.

CCS CONCEPTS

• **Social and professional topics → Computer science education**; **Student assessment**; *Adult education*; • **Applied computing → Education**;

KEYWORDS

active learning environments, active learning classrooms, peer instruction, computing education

SIGCSE '19, February 27-March 2, 2019, Minneapolis, MN, USA

ACM ISBN 978-1-4503-5890-3/19/02...$15.00
https://doi.org/10.1145/3287324.3287345

ACM Reference Format:
Tyler Greer, Qiang Hao, Mengguo Jing, and Bradley Barnes. 2019. On the Effects of Active Learning Environments in Computing Education. In *Proceedings of the 50th ACM Technical Symposium on Computer Science Education (SIGCSE '19), February 27-March 2, 2019, Minneapolis, MN, USA.* ACM, New York, NY, USA, 6 pages. https://doi.org/10.1145/3287324.3287345

1 INTRODUCTION

Active learning classrooms were designed on the assumption that conventional lecture halls may not provide the best environment for active learning activities. Conventional lecture halls, featured by bolted seats in rows and centered teaching stages, can physically limit communications and interactions among students, especially in-class activities such as group discussion and collaborations in a large-scale class [1]. In contrast, active learning classrooms are designed to have movable chairs, round tables, and typically multimedia equipments to decentralize the role of instructors and encourage peer communications among students [2, 3]. Despite such physical advantages, active learning classrooms can accommodate fewer students, and take much more resources to build [4].

Abundant studies have confirmed the positive effects of active learning pedagogies in enhancing learning and teaching across different fields, but significantly fewer studies have investigated the effects of active learning classrooms. Most studied investigating the effects of active learning classrooms were conducted by same groups of researchers at three institutions in the United States, including North Carolina State University [5, 6], Massachusetts Institute of Technology [1], and University of Minnesota [7, 8], in the fields such as physics, chemistry, and biology. Surprisingly, few studies have explored the effects of active learning classrooms in computing education despite that different active learning approaches have been adopted and studied in many computer science courses across the world.

It is important to understand the effects of active learning classrooms on student learning for at least three reasons. First, it takes significantly more resources to build an active learning classroom or convert an existing lecture hall to an active learning classroom [4]. Second, given the same space, an active learning classroom can accommodate much fewer number of students. Most importantly, despite of the positive findings of prior studies on this topic, many of them may not be generalized due to both research design and methodological limits, such as continuous introduction of confounding factors, misuse of predictive models, and lack of control of false positive results [8–10].

Building on the prior studies and responding to the calls for more educational replication studies, this study aims at (1) quantifying the effects of active learning classrooms in Introductory Programming courses (CS1) by replicating the study of Hao et al. [9], and (2) overcoming the identified research design and methodological limits of prior studies. The results of this study contribute to the fine-grained understanding of the roles of physical environments and pedagogies in learning and teaching of programming, and the extent to which the prior findings can be generalized.

2 RELATED WORKS

2.1 Active Learning & Teaching in Computer Science: Peer Instruction

Many active learning approaches to improve student comprehension and performance have been explored and tested in computing education over the last three decades, such as team-based learning, paired-programming and peer instruction [11–14]. Among the many test pedagogical approaches, peer instruction was studied most extensively. Peer instruction is a student-centered approach that flips the traditional lecturing by moving information transfer out and moving information assimilation into the classroom [15]. When peer instruction is practiced, students are typically required to finish pre-class reading and pre-class practices. During the class time the reading and practices would be discussed and more related practices would follow.

Peer instruction has been consistently found effective in both upper and lower level courses of computing education. Specifically, peer instruction has been reported effective in improving student achievement, satisfaction and self-efficacy [11, 16–23]. In addition, peer instruction was also found effective in improving student retention rate in introductory programming courses [24, 25]. Recent research on the scalability of peer instruction studied class evaluations of computer science courses across a wide range of class sizes, ranging from around 50 to more than 300. Although a small decline in course evaluation was found as the class size increased, the efficacy of peer instruction was found robust [26].

Peer instruction works more effective than conventional lecturing because instructor explanation is replaced and augmented with carefully designed questions that students committed time to work on [24]. Students get a chance to fill up their understanding gaps through discussing with each other [23, 24]. Despite of the efficacy of peer instruction, it may still lose its "magic" if not well implemented. Porter et al. [20] suggested that it is essential for the instructors to make the adopted pedagogy clear to students and adjust the grading structure for a better balance between correctness and participation. In addition, the implementation takes more time and efforts to prepare than conventional lecturing, especially in a conventional lecture hall. It is understandable that instructors sometimes can not afford the time to implement peer instruction given limited preparation time and limited resources.

2.2 Physical Learning Environments: Active Learning Classrooms

Learning and teaching in school mainly happens in classrooms. Educational researchers hypothesized that the physical learning environment can either enhance or inhibit learning in 1970s [2]. Active learning classrooms are designed to better facilitate discussion and collaborations within small groups and across the whole class. Instead of having a teaching center and fixed forward-facing seats, active learning classrooms are featured by open spaces, movable chairs, writing surfaces, and a strong integration of learning technologies. It is important to note that an active learning classroom requires more resources during its construction, even if it is converted from an existing conventional classroom. Furthermore, an active learning classroom accommodates a significant smaller number of students than a conventional one [4]. As is reported by Park and Choi [4], the conversion from a conventional lecture hall to an active learning classroom with 30 seats cost about one hundred thousands dollars.

Two main projects, SCALE-UP and TEAL, pioneered the study of the active learning classrooms. The SCALE-UP project was conducted at North Carolina State University and TEAL project was conducted at Massachusetts Institute of Technology [1, 5, 10]. As pioneers of classroom design, both SCALE-UP; TEAL classrooms are featured with facilities and technologies that engage students in active learning, such as "abundant whiteboard space, round tables, chairs with wheels, laptop computers, projectors and monitors, an audio systems designed to allow the students to both hear the instructor and to respond" [27]. The ACL project at the University of Minnesota followed this efforts in both classroom design and studying the efficacy of such classrooms [3, 7, 8]. The efficacy of active learning classrooms have been mainly studied through the three projects in the academic fields such as physics, chemistry and biology [1, 3, 5, 7, 8]. Hao et al [9] was identified as the first study that investigated the effects of active learning classrooms in the context of computing education. The majority of these studies concluded that active learning classrooms had significantly positive effects on student achievement [3, 4, 8, 9]. However, the findings of many of such studies were limited by both research design and statistical analysis (see section titled "Motivation for Replication").

2.3 Motivation for Replication

This study aims at a conceptual replication of Hao et al [9] that overcomes the design and methodological limits of both Hao et al [9] and other prior studies on this topic. Two noticeable limits of such studies included the lack of control of confounding factors and the lack of control of false positives. Many prior studies on this topic failed to control the influences of learning pedagogies when reaching the conclusion that active learning environments contribute significantly to student performance [2, 7, 9]. Additionally, several studies involved comparison of multiple factors between two groups, which would increase the chances of random significant results. Significance levels were not properly corrected in such cases [3, 5, 28]. Therefore, this study aims at overcoming both limits and quantifying the effects of active learning environments in learning and teaching of programming.

3 METHODS

3.1 Research Design

A Three-Group design was used with the goal to separate two factors in focus: the learning environments and pedagogical approaches. By design, three different sections of an introductory computer science course were conducted in a large research university in the southeastern United States in spring 2017. The three sections each covered the same content and tested the students with the same examinations. Each section of the course differed in its combination of the physical learning environments and the implemented pedagogical approaches:

- Course One (Conventional): Conventional classroom + Conventional Lecturing
- Course Two (Active): Active learning classroom + Active Learning & Teaching
- Course Three (Hybrid): Conventional classroom + Active Learning & Teaching

It is worth noting that the limited number of active learning classrooms at the institution made their usage and scheduling extremely difficult. More importantly, statistically speaking, three-group design can sufficiently separate two factors in focus [29]. As the result, a combination of "active learning classroom" and "conventional lecturing" is not necessary. Furthermore, three other factors were controlled. Such factors including major, gender and age.

3.2 Experiment Contexts and Data Collection

Courses One and Three were taught in conventional lecture halls while Course Two was conducted in an active learning classroom. Course One was taught through conventional lectures, where students were recommended to read the textbook outside of class time but received the content in a series of conventional lectures. In contrast, peer instruction, one active learning approach, was practiced in the learning and teaching of Course Two and Three, where students were assigned daily reading as well as a small quiz based on the textbook and videos that the instructor created; both of these were to be completed before the start of class. In addition, in Course Two and Three, students worked in groups of three to solve problems from material that they were required to read. The instructor as well as teaching assistants were available during this time to answer questions on the material.

To fully control potential confounding factors, all sections of the course were taught by the same instructor. Additionaly, three control factors (major, gender and age) were collected from the institutional data warehouse. All the three course sections received 100-point two midterm and one final exam, which were treated as student course performance.

4 RESULTS

4.1 Descriptive Summary

The descriptive summary of the 156 students is presented in Table 1. To examine the group differences in terms of age, gender, and whether or not a student was majoring in computer science, one-way MANOVA was utilized. Because there were more than two comparisons over the same groups, Bonferroni Correction was applied to the significance levels in order to avoid false positive results. The adjusted significance levels were:

$$*p < 0.016; **p < 0.003; ***p < 0.0003 \quad (1)$$

The results did not show any significant group differences in terms of major [F(3, 123) = .225, p = .879] or age [F(36, 375) = 1.179, p = .227]. However, a significant difference in terms of gender [F(3, 123) = 6.385, p = .000] was found. Students in Course Three appeared to be older than their counterparts from Courses One and Two. Given that students did not have knowledge of the sections when registering the course, the difference is likely due to randomness. Although each section of the course was majority male (greater than 56% in all sections), it is worth noting that the percentage of female students is not significantly lower than male students.

Table 1: Descriptive Summary of Participants

	Course One (Conventional)	Course Two (Active)	Course Three (Hybrid)
Number of Students	69	42	45
Major			
CS Major	43.50%	33.30%	40%
Non-CS Major	56.50%	66.60%	60%
Gender			
Male	68.10%	61.90%	77.80%
Female	31.90%	38.10%	22.20%
Age (Mean Value)	19.452	19.976	21.022

4.2 Separating the Effects of Learning Environments and Pedagogical Approaches on Student Performance

MANCOVA was applied in order to examine the effects of pedagogical approaches and learning environments on the students' three exam performance (two midterm and one final exams). In this test of MANCOVA, the following control variables were used: age, gender, and whether or not students were majoring in computer science. All two-way and three-way interactions among the independent and control variables were taken into examination. Given that there were three exam performances to be compared across the three groups, Bonferroni Correction was applied to the significance levels in order to avoid false positive results. The adjusted significance levels were:

$$*p < 0.016; **p < 0.003; ***p < 0.0003 \quad (2)$$

Utilizing Pillai's trace, the pedagogical method factor was found to be significant (p < .016), and was the only factor or interaction that was found significant in the test. The results of the multivariate tests of all attributes on the exam results are presented in Table 2.

Table 2: Multivariate Tests

Attributes	Value	F	Significance Level
age	0.051	2.507	0.061
major	0.003	0.16	0.923
gender	0.05	2.481	0.064
ct	0.056	2.803	0.042
pm	0.085	4.382	0.006*
major * gender	0.008	0.399	0.754
major * ct	0.012	0.556	0.645
major * pm	0.025	1.215	0.307
gender * ct	0.009	0.418	0.74
gender * pm	0.024	1.154	0.33
major * gender * ct	0.035	1.686	0.173
major * gender * pm	0.055	2.722	0.047

major: whether majoring in computer science; ct: classroom type; pm: pedagogical methods
* p < .016; **p < .003; ***p < .0003

Discriminant Analysis was used to follow up the MANCOVA test to further confirm the findings from MANOVA. Two discriminant functions were revealed. The first explained 92.6% of the variance, canonical R2 = .10, whereas the second explained only 7.4%, canonical R2 = .008. In combination, these discriminant functions significantly differentiated Course Three from Course One and Course Two (λ = .894, $\chi 2$ = 17.1, p = .009**; see Figure 1 and 2), but removing the first function indicated that the second function did not significantly differentiate Course One from Course Two (λ = .991, $\chi 2$ = 1.317, p = .518; see Figure 1 and 2). In other words, a significant difference was found when the adopted pedagogical approaches were different, but no significant difference was observed when the learning environments were different.

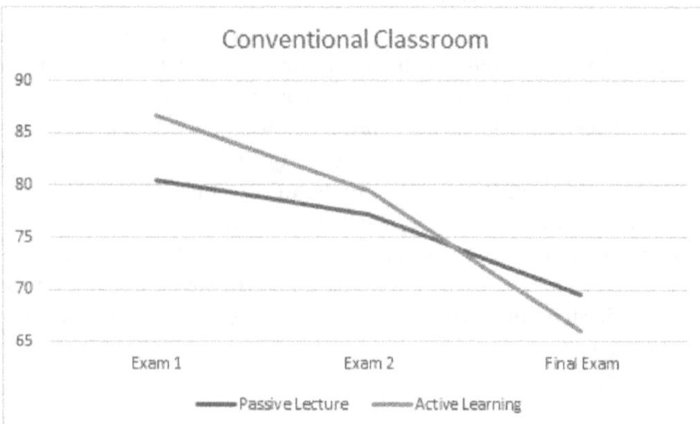

Figure 1: Student Performance Comparison between Course One and Three

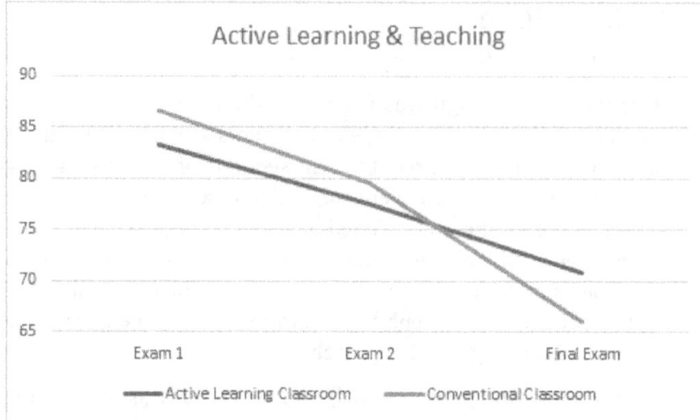

Figure 2: Student Performance Comparison between Course Two and Three

5 DISCUSSION

5.1 Efficacy of Active Learning: Does the Effect Come from the Environment or the Pedagogy?

Different from the finding of Hao et al [9] and many other prior studies [2, 7], this study found the effects of active learning environments on CS student performance to be insignificant. With a between-group design and strict control over significance levels, this study successfully separated the effects of learning environments from other potential confounding factors, among which the pedagogical approach is the most important one.

When controlling for other factors, significant differences were detected between different pedagogical approaches but not between learning environments. This finding reveals that the essence for effective learning and teaching lies more on the pedagogy than the physical space. Indeed, a well-design, technology-infused room with round tables allow students "face time" with peers and form groups naturally, while traditional lecture halls, especially those with chairs bolted in place, emphasize the instructor over the student and make group formation awkward and contrived. However, all these advantages are not guaranteed by the room per se, and effective learning are well facilitated with active learning and teaching pedagogies even in traditional classrooms.

In addition, our finding suggests to make better use of high-cost active learning classrooms with quality support from pedagogy and faculty rather than treat it as a one-time investment for ultimate solution. Overemphasis on the power of learning environment might be misleading as it weakens the roles of more essential factors. As a good example, the *Transform, Interact, Learn, Engage* classrooms at the University of Iowa are designed to support active learning, but faculties must undergo intensive training before they are allowed to teach their courses in such classrooms [27]. Unless faculty receive specific training about how to effectively use the tools to implement active learning and teaching pedagogies and how to design learning activities that are a good fit for the room, it is hard to say these rooms foster or constraints student learning.

5.2 Investment on Active Learning: Should We Invest in People or Classrooms?

Many large and well-funded institutions have initiated construction projects to bring active learning classrooms to their campuses. As such new classrooms full of technology become ready, instructors at such institutions have enthusiastically embraced them. However, not every institution has the capability of doing the same. As is reported by [4], upgrading a conventional classroom to an active one with 30 seats took more than one hundred thousand at their institution.

The findings of this study suggest that active learning and teaching can be conducted in conventional classrooms as effectively as in active learning classrooms. In other words, institutions with limited resources may not be able to build many active learning classrooms, but can still put resources into training their faculties on active learning practices. For instructors, at least CS faculties, having no access to active learning classrooms may not be a good reason for not practicing active learning. Although it can be less convenient to do so in a lecture hall, the benefits to students are still substantial. On the other hand, it is worth noting that having active learning classrooms should not be treated as the panacea by institutions. A recent study found that there was no significant increase in the use of active learning pedagogies in the collaborative classroom [30]. Without intentional training, faculties may choose the pedagogical approaches they are most familiar with despite of the physical spaces.

6 LIMITATIONS AND FUTURE STUDIES

The generalizability of the findings in this study could be limited for three reasons. First, all participants of this study came from the same course at the same institution. The course was solely taught by the same instructor during the experiment period. A different instructor or different sample of students might render the results different. Future studies may consider replications on a larger scale that involves multiple instructors from different institutions. Second, only one active learning approach, peer instruction, was practiced in the experiment. It is possible that peer instruction is least negatively affected by the learning environment compared with other learning and teaching approaches. Although peer instruction is well studied and highly applicable in computing education, it may not the same case for other fields such as chemistry or physics. If a different active learning approach is practiced in the experiment, the results might be different. Third, the pre-class activities, in-class activities, assignments, and exams given in the experimental course was designed and developed by the instructor. Future studies may consider using well-tested and publicly accessible activities and assignments (e.g., Nifty Assignments) and validated exams to strengthen the measurements.

7 CONCLUSIONS

This study intends to replicate the study of Hao et al [9] and overcome the identified research design and data analysis limits of Hao et al [9] and other prior studies on this topic. With a three-group design and strict significance-level corrections, this study did not replicate the findings of prior studies on the positive effects of active learning environments. Instead, we found that active learning pedagogies had significantly positive influences on computer science student performance, but active learning environments did not. Such findings highlighted the importance of active learning pedagogies in computing education, and the necessity to reflect on whether we should invest more in active learning classrooms. This study calls for more replication studies on the effects of active learning environments in computing education and other fields, and invites more debates on investment decisions on active learning classrooms.

REFERENCES

[1] Yehudit Judy Dori. Educational reform at mit: Advancing and evaluating technology-based projects on-and off-campus. *Journal of Science Education and Technology*, 16(4):279–281, 2007.

[2] Aimee Whiteside, D Christopher Brooks, and JD Walker. Making the case for space: Three years of empirical research on learning environments. *Educause Quarterly*, 33(3):11, 2010.

[3] D Christopher Brooks. Space matters: The impact of formal learning environments on student learning. *British Journal of Educational Technology*, 42(5): 719–726, 2011.

[4] Elisa L Park and Bo Keum Choi. Transformation of classroom spaces: Traditional versus active learning classroom in colleges. *Higher Education*, 68(5):749–771, 2014.

[5] Maria T Oliver-Hoyo, DeeDee Allen, William F Hunt, Joy Hutson, and Angela Pitts. Effects of an active learning environment: Teaching innovations at a research i institution. *Journal of Chemical Education*, 81(3):441, 2004.

[6] Robert Beichner. The scale-up project: a student-centered active learning environment for undergraduate programs. *An invited white paper for the National Academy of Sciences*, 2008.

[7] Paul Baepler, JD Walker, and Michelle Driessen. It's not about seat time: Blending, flipping, and efficiency in active learning classrooms. *Computers & Education*, 78: 227–236, 2014.

[8] Sehoya Cotner, Jessica Loper, JD Walker, and D Christopher Brooks. " it's not you, it's the room"âĂŤare the high-tech, active learning classrooms worth it? *Journal of College Science Teaching*, 42(6):82–88, 2013.

[9] Qiang Hao, Bradley Barnes, Ewan Wright, and Eunjung Kim. Effects of active learning environments and instructional methods in computer science education. In *Proceedings of the 49th ACM Technical Symposium on Computer Science Education*, pages 934–939. ACM, 2018.

[10] Yehudit Judy Dori and John Belcher. How does technology-enabled active learning affect undergraduate students' understanding of electromagnetism concepts? *The journal of the learning sciences*, 14(2):243–279, 2005.

[11] Beth Simon, Michael Kohanfars, Jeff Lee, Karen Tamayo, and Quintin Cutts. Experience report: peer instruction in introductory computing. In *Proceedings of the 41st ACM technical symposium on Computer science education*, pages 341–345. ACM, 2010.

[12] Brenda Timmerman and Robert Lingard. Assessment of active learning with upper division computer science students. In *Frontiers in Education, 2003. FIE 2003 33rd Annual*, volume 3, pages S1D–7. IEEE, 2003.

[13] Hossein Hakimzadeh, Raman Adaikkalavan, and Robert Batzinger. Successful implementation of an active learning laboratory in computer science. In *Proceedings of the 39th annual ACM SIGUCCS conference on User services*, pages 83–86. ACM, 2011.

[14] Jon DH Gaffney, Evan Richards, Mary Bridget Kustusch, Lin Ding, and Robert J Beichner. Scaling up education reform. *Journal of College Science Teaching*, 37(5): 48, 2008.

[15] Catherine H Crouch and Eric Mazur. Peer instruction: Ten years of experience and results. *American journal of physics*, 69(9):970–977, 2001.

[16] Deborah Allen and Kimberly Tanner. Infusing active learning into the large-enrollment biology class: seven strategies, from the simple to complex. *Cell biology education*, 4(4):262–268, 2005.

[17] Diane Ebert-May, Carol Brewer, and Sylvester Allred. Innovation in large lectures: Teaching for active learning. *Bioscience*, 47(9):601–607, 1997.

[18] David J Nicol and James T Boyle. Peer instruction versus class-wide discussion in large classes: A comparison of two interaction methods in the wired classroom. *Studies in higher education*, 28(4):457–473, 2003.

[19] I Michele and Ralph Preszler. Introductory biology course reform: A tale of two courses. *International Journal for the Scholarship of Teaching and Learning*, 8(2):5, 2014.

[20] Leo Porter, Dennis Bouvier, Quintin Cutts, Scott Grissom, Cynthia Lee, Robert McCartney, Daniel Zingaro, and Beth Simon. A multi-institutional study of peer instruction in introductory computing. In *Proceedings of the 47th ACM Technical Symposium on Computing Science Education*, pages 358–363. ACM, 2016.

[21] Leo Porter, Saturnino Garcia, John Glick, Andrew Matusiewicz, and Cynthia Taylor. Peer instruction in computer science at small liberal arts colleges. In *Proceedings of the 18th ACM conference on Innovation and technology in computer science education*, pages 129–134. ACM, 2013.

[22] Daniel Zingaro and Leo Porter. Peer instruction in computing: The value of instructor intervention. *Computers & Education*, 71:87–96, 2014.

[23] Cynthia Bailey Lee, Saturnino Garcia, and Leo Porter. Can peer instruction be effective in upper-division computer science courses? *ACM Transactions on Computing Education (TOCE)*, 13(3):12, 2013.

[24] Leo Porter, Cynthia Bailey Lee, and Beth Simon. Halving fail rates using peer instruction: a study of four computer science courses. In *Proceeding of the 44th ACM technical symposium on Computer science education*, pages 177–182. ACM, 2013.

[25] Qiang Hao. *Online Help Seeking in Computer Science Education*. PhD thesis, University of Georgia, 2017.

[26] Soohyun Nam Liao, William G Griswold, and Leo Porter. Impact of class size on student evaluations for traditional and peer instruction classrooms. In *Proceedings of the 2017 ACM SIGCSE Technical Symposium on Computer Science Education*, pages 375–380. ACM, 2017.

[27] Sam Van Horne, Cecilia Murniati, Jon DH Gaffney, and Maggie Jesse. Promoting active learning in technology-infused tile classrooms at the university of iowa. *Journal of Learning Spaces*, 1(2):n2, 2012.

[28] Leo Porter, Cynthia Bailey Lee, Beth Simon, and Daniel Zingaro. Peer instruction: do students really learn from peer discussion in computing? In *Proceedings of the seventh international workshop on Computing education research*, pages 45–52. ACM, 2011.

[29] Andy Field. *Discovering statistics using SPSS*. Sage publications, 2009.

[30] Theresa A Beery, Dustin Shell, Gordon Gillespie, and Eileen Werdman. The impact of learning space on teaching behaviors. *Nurse education in practice*, 13 (5):382–387, 2013.

Supporting Guided Inquiry with Cooperative Learning in Computer Organization

Yeajin Ham
Dept. of Educational Psychology & Learning Sciences
University of Iowa
Iowa City, Iowa, USA
yeajin-ham@uiowa.edu

Brandon Myers
Dept. of Computer Science
University of Iowa
Iowa City, Iowa, USA
brandon-d-myers@uiowa.edu

ABSTRACT

The computer organization course must help students acquire difficult conceptual knowledge and design skills, and improve their teamwork skills for subsequent project courses. Prior research supports that *cooperative learning*, in which students work together to achieve common goals, may address these challenges. We studied whether increasing the amount of guided inquiry activities and the cooperative support for it (teams and reflection) in an intermediate computer science course would improve achievement and engagement. The intervention group had lower scores on one of two achievement measures, lower engagement, and lower task value of collaborative activities. Qualitative analysis showed that students valued hands-on learning yet resisted guided inquiry, suggesting that sharing the purpose of each type of activity is important. Furthermore, the results showed that students valued learning with peers but were frustrated by group dysfunction, suggesting that instructors must address teamwork comprehensively to realize the benefits of cooperative learning.

KEYWORDS

guided inquiry; cooperative learning; collaborative learning; computer organization; computer architecture; POGIL

ACM Reference format:

Yeajin Ham and Brandon Myers. 2019. Supporting Guided Inquiry with Cooperative Learning in Computer Organization. In *Proceedings of the 50th ACM Technical Symposium on Computer Science Education (SIGCSE '19), Feb. 27 - Mar. 2, 2019, Minneapolis, MN, USA.* ACM, New York, NY, USA, 7 pages. https://doi.org/10.1145/3287324.3287355

SIGCSE'19, February 27-March 2, 2019, Minneapolis, MN, USA.

ACM ISBN 978-1-4503-5890-3/19/02...$15.00.
DOI: http://dx.doi.org/10.1145/3287324.3287355

1 INTRODUCTION

The computer organization course presents two instructional challenges. First, students struggle to acquire both conceptual knowledge [1], [2] and design skills. Second, at the University of Iowa, this prerequisite to upper-level coursework must prepare students for team projects.

A pedagogy called Peer Instruction [3] has shown promise for increasing achievement in computer science courses over traditional instruction [4]. These achievement gains rely on peer interaction [5][6], but students do not work in teams. One type of interaction that improves both achievement and teamwork skills is *cooperative learning* [7], in which students recognize the need to work together to achieve common goals.

We studied whether increased use and support of cooperative learning improved achievement, as well as constructs that mediate achievement, in two sections of a computer organization course. In the control section, students spent half the sessions on active learning lectures, lectures interspersed with interactive activities, and half in informal groups working on lab assignments and guided inquiry. In guided inquiry, students collaboratively work through scaffolded questioning to learn knowledge, reasoning skills, and practices in the discipline [8]. In the intervention section, we used additional supports for cooperative learning [9]. First, to support *positive interdependence*, that students share goals and recognize that they depend on each other to achieve them, students worked in stable teams. Second, to support *promotive interaction*, that the activities are worthy of group work, teams worked solely on lab assignments and guided inquiry. Finally, to support *group processing*, that students reflect on how to improve their team, teams completed reflections on teamwork and communication.

We measured achievement using scores on identical exam questions and a concept inventory. To explain achievement results, we measured task value, engagement, and perceptions of peer academic support. From open-ended post-test responses, we found themes for why students in each section found certain tasks helpful to their learning. Our contributions apply to intermediate level computer science courses taught with active learning:

- A quasi-experimental test of increased use of structures supporting cooperative learning

- Insights into why students view activities as helpful and unhelpful to their learning

The quantitative results of our study were null or negative. Students in the intervention showed lower achievement and engagement. However, the qualitative results of our study support that with comprehensive support for cooperative learning, this type of instruction could be effective.

2 BACKGROUND & RELATED WORK

2.1 Cooperative learning

There is evidence that active learning relies on peer interaction to produce learning gains [5][6][10]. A type of peer interaction called *cooperative learning* is often characterized by positive interdependence (students share goals and work together as a team to achieve them), individual accountability, promotive interaction (the work is worthy of a group discussion), the appropriate use of collaborative skills, and group processing (reflecting on interactions to improve them) [11][12]. Meta-analyses of cooperative learning in college courses found meaningful improvements in achievement [13]–[15]. Cooperative learning in CS1 was associated with lower rates of failure and withdrawal in CS2 [16] and increased achievement and programming self-efficacy if the instructor was trained in the pedagogy [17].

2.1.1 Supporting positive interdependence. An instructor can give multi-faceted problems, assigning different roles or expertise to group members, and giving bonuses for all individuals scoring well on an assessment [7]. This interdependence may be less present in Peer Instruction, where peers collaborate but are not accountable for each other. In our intervention group, we promoted positive interdependence by keeping students in teams for at least 4 weeks and assigning roles.

2.1.2 Supporting group processing. An instructor can have students reflect on the development of their teamwork and communication skills [18] and set and evaluate goals [7]. Our intervention supported group processing by having teams periodically answer prompts at the end of the session about how well the team is working.

2.1.3 Cooperative learning in computer organization. Titterton et al. [19] described a "lab-centric" computer organization course that included collaborative exercises, but it lacked positive interdependence. Experiments were limited to comparisons with traditional lecture-lab instruction [20]. Bruce described a VLSI course that included teams with designated roles working on circuit design problems [21] but did not have a baseline. Arbelaitz et al. [22] described a Computer Architecture course with cooperative learning to scaffold the teamwork of subsequent project based learning. For each of three intervention semesters, they found increased achievement over traditional instruction; however, they did not compare achievement between the active learning offerings. The cooperative learning instruction strategy that we adopted in our course was Process-Oriented Guided Inquiry Learning (POGIL).

2.3 POGIL

POGIL [23] is a classroom instruction strategy that combines cooperative learning and guided inquiry, in which students construct then apply new concepts in an experiential learning cycle [24]. In a POGIL learning cycle, students answer *exploration* questions about a model (e.g., data table, flowchart, code), which leads them to apply reasoning in *concept invention* (e.g., writing a definition, deriving a mathematical relationship). Finally, students answer *application* questions to apply the concept.

POGIL incorporates elements of cooperative learning. Constructing and applying new concepts in a guided inquiry activity requires students to discuss and challenge each other's assumptions and inferences, which is promotive interaction. Students work in groups of four and have roles to support positive interdependence. Furthermore, the activities develop students' *process skills*, including cognitive skills like critical thinking and social skills like communication and teamwork.

POGIL has been used in several disciplines including CS. Compared to traditional instruction, POGIL increased performance and engagement in college chemistry courses [25] and improved student achievement in CS1 [4]. The CS-POGIL project [26] has created and shared over 200 inquiry activities for CS, including some for computer organization. We used POGIL during both sections of our quasi-experiment, and the intervention group dedicated more than twice as many class sessions to it. We supported this increase with more emphasis on structures that make cooperative learning effective.

3 METHOD

The research questions for our work were:

RQ1: In computer organization, does replacing active learning lectures with additional guided inquiry and labs supported by teams and daily reflection improve student achievement?

RQ2: In computer organization, does replacing active learning lectures with additional guided inquiry and labs supported by teams and daily reflection improve engagement and factors that mediate engagement: peer academic support and task value?

To answer these questions, we conducted a quasi-experimental study over two semesters. Students in one semester experienced the control and students in the other experienced the intervention.

3.1 Context

We ran the study in the computer organization course during Fall 2017 and Spring 2018 semesters. The instructor taught the course both semesters in the same classroom, days, and time of day. Contact time was 50 minutes 3 days/week in a student-centered classroom with distributed laptops, screens, and whiteboards [27][28].

3.1.2 Preparation. Prior to the study semesters, the instructor taught the course twice using active learning lectures and once using the added approaches—labs and guided inquiry. That third offering was like the control semester. The instructor also had 30

Table 1. Participant demographics

	Control	Intervention
completed study	31 (of 68)	34 (of 51)
$4^{th}/3^{rd}/2^{nd}$ year	18/9/3	15/19/0
CS major	27	27

Table 2. Number of class sessions dedicated to each type of activity

	Control	Intervention
active learning lectures	19	1
lab assignments	8	12
guided inquiry	11	25
exam/review	3	3

hours of prior guidance on Backward Course Design [29] for this course.

3.2 Participants

Students had only one choice of section. During the second week of class, a researcher administered informed consent (IRB ID 201608778) and then sent the electronic pre-test to participants. The researcher not affiliated with the course administered consent to avoid bias by the instructor-researcher. The instructor did not have access to survey data or the list of participants until after final grades were approved. Table 1 lists the demographics of the participants. We also collected official university GPA to control for differences between the samples.

3.3 Control group

In the control semester, class sessions consisted of about half active learning lectures and half lab assignments and guided inquiry (see Table 2). The instructor and 1-2 teaching assistants facilitated the labs and guided inquiry.

3.3.1 Active learning lectures. These consist of a series of 10-minute mini-lectures followed by a brief design activity or Peer Instruction [3], in which students answer and discuss multiple choice questions on concepts.

3.3.2 Lab assignments. These comprise tutorials, experiments, and problem-solving using an assembly language simulator, C compiler, or digital logic simulator. The tutorial happened within a prelab that students had to complete before class. In experiments, students made predictions about what a program or circuit would do, shared those predictions on a class discussion board and tested the predictions using the tools. In problem solving, students built and tested small programs or circuits.

Labs were a hybrid of *open* and *closed* [30]. That is, the instructor gave time to complete most of the lab in class, but the lab was due a week after assigned.

3.3.3 Guided inquiry. We used POGIL for guided inquiry[1]. Students took on four common POGIL roles of Manager (keep on track), Recorder (write answers), Speaker (present answers), and Reflector (elicit balanced contributions, fill in exit slip during intervention).

[1] The activities follow the POGIL structure but have not yet been certified by The POGIL Project, so we call them *guided inquiry* in this paper.

Guided inquiry is a good match to the learning objectives of computer organization. Students invent concepts inductively by recognizing patterns (e.g., behavior of a program or circuit) or deductively by evaluating proposed solutions to a problem (e.g., various ways to implement procedure calls in assembly code). Concept invention is followed by application, where students write and debug programs and circuits. The inquiry activities used in the course can be found at CS-POGIL [31].

3.3.4 Collaboration in control group. For active learning lectures, the instructor encouraged students to work with others at their table to solve the problems after trying them independently. For lab assignments, students optionally collaborated with peers and were required to individually share hypotheses and definitions on the class online forum [19]. For guided inquiry, students formed groups at the beginning of each activity. Groups submitted a single copy of their answers for a participation grade.

3.4 Intervention group

During Spring 2018, the instructor used the intervention, where class sessions consisted entirely of lab assignments and guided inquiry. Table 2 lists the number of class sessions dedicated to each type of learning activity. The instructor replaced active learning lectures with guided inquiry and lab assignments. Students worked in teams (positive interdependence). In addition, for every class period, there was an exit slip that the Reflector responded to (group processing).

3.4.1 Collaboration in intervention group. Students worked on all in-class activities with their assigned team. To accommodate teams in the lab assignments, students shared predictions and outcomes with their team instead of on the class discussion board.

3.4.2 Team organization. Teams were together for four weeks and consisted of 3-4 students. In each week, the instructor rotated the student roles, which gives each student a chance to participate in different ways [7][18]. To form new teams at the end of a 4-week period, the instructor balanced the criteria of mixing prior pairings with student preference. The students picked teams for weeks 13-15 because they doubled as final project teams.

3.4.3 Exit slips. An exit slip consisted of *process questions* and *content questions.* The process questions promote group processing. They prompt the student to reflect on how their team is working together and what improvements they might make. The content questions assess the students on key learning objectives and prompt students to formulate questions so that the instructor may give tailored instruction next session. The instructor encouraged the Reflectors to ask teammates for input. Teams received grades for the guided inquiry activities by submitting their exit slips.

3.5 Measures of achievement

3.5.1 Final exams. The final exams had three identical multi-part questions and two different ones. There were two different questions because the control semester covered more content, specifically pipelining hazards and caches. We only used the three identical questions in our analysis. These questions covered: (1) concepts in architecture and digital logic, (2) design and analysis of microarchitecture and architecture, and (3) applications in digital logic.

The instructor shared the final exam with two colleagues to assess whether it assessed important learning objectives of computer organization. Both colleagues, one who had previously taught the course and the other who had taught a dependent course, approved of the exam.

3.5.2 *Concept inventory.* Concept inventories are multiple-choice assessments that measure conceptual understanding. The wrong choices are distractors that represent common misunderstandings that students hold. We used the Digital Logic Concept Inventory [32], which has been validated as a post-test of student understanding of concepts in digital logic [33]. The inventory was proctored during the last week of class, before final exams.

3.6 Questionnaire

The pre-test consisted of 15 items on intrinsic value and task value. The post-test consisted of 30 items on intrinsic value, task value, engagement, and peer academic support.

3.6.1 Engagement. Engagement is important to students' learning and achievement in higher education [34]. This construct is multi-faceted, so we included items that measured engagement in instructional activities and perceptions of social support and authenticity of tasks [35].

3.6.2 Intrinsic value. Intrinsic value refers to meaning given to learning tasks, which reflects whether students think what they learn is useful, important, or interesting [36]. To measure intrinsic value, we used items that were adapted from motivational beliefs scales [37].

3.6.3 Task value. Task value is the degree to which students perceive incentives for engaging in learning activities [38]. Students' task value has been supported as a predictor of choices related to achievement [39]. We asked how helpful each type of course activity was to their learning. The activities were: (abridged) "labs in class," "labs out of class," "readings", "lectures", "Peer Instruction", "guided inquiry", "homework", and "projects". To learn why students rated as they did, we also asked on the post-test two free response questions "Why did you rate [activities] as {helpful, unhelpful} to your learning?" We used open coding [40] to find themes and categorize responses. Two researchers independently formed codebooks, came to consensus on a codebook, independently coded, then came to consensus on codes. They assigned each response between one and four codes.

3.6.4 Peer academic support. Perceived support from teacher and peers may enhance students' engagement and motivation [41][42]. To measure peer academic support, we used a subscale of four items (e.g., "The students in this class like to help me learn") that has been associated with higher levels of cooperation [43].

4 RESULTS

4.1 Achievement

To see the effect of the intervention on achievement, we ran a multiple linear regression analysis that controlled for prior achievement using GPA. The model was *Achievement ~ Group + GPA.* The intervention group scored lower on the final exam than the control group (b= -1.560, t= -2.708, p=0.009) and this difference was statistically significant. We analyzed the three questions (listed in Section 3.5.1) separately. The results were (1) intervention group lower (b= -0.0125, t= -0.049, p=0.961) but not statistically significant, (2) intervention group lower (b= -2.560, t= -2.154, p=0.035) and statistically significant, and (3) intervention group lower (b= -1.615, t= -4.193, p<1e-4) and statistically significant. For DLCI score, the intervention group scored lower (b= -0.452, t= -1.156, p=0.253) but this difference was not statistically significant.

4.2 Engagement

We ran a multiple linear regression analysis to test the effect of the intervention on students' engagement while controlling for group differences. We specifically controlled for students' intrinsic value of the course, considering that intrinsic value is related to engagement and achievement [44]. The model was *Engagement ~ Group + Pre_Intrinsic_Value.* The intervention group had lower engagement than the control group (*b*= -2.934, t= -2.389, p=0.020) and this difference was statistically significant.

4.3 Peer academic support

We ran a multiple linear regression analysis to see the effect of the intervention on peer academic support. Since the task value of in-class collaborative activities at the beginning of the semester is related to orientation with regards to peers, we included it in the equation to control for group differences. The model was *Peer_Support ~ Group + Pre_collab_Task_Value.* The intervention group had higher peer support (*b*= 0.046, t= 0.056, p= 0.955) but this difference was not statistically significant.

4.4 Task value

4.4.1 Quantitative. We analyzed students' change in task value of course activities between the pre-test and post-test. We added the task value of labs-in-class, guided inquiry, and Peer Instruction into one construct called *collab3* (range 3 to 15). To test the difference between pre and post *collab3* (data not normally distributed) we ran a two-tailed Mann-Whitney (μ_{c2-c1}=0.43, μ_{i2-i1}= -1.0, p < 0.03). Since some students in the intervention may have pragmatically rated Peer Instruction lower because there was none of it in the intervention group, we excluded Peer Instruction from the construct *collab2* (range 2 to 10) and repeated the test (μ_{c2-c1}=0.23, μ_{i2-i1}= -0.70, p < 0.03). We also tested whether the decrease from pre-test to post-test of *collab3* and *collab2* in the intervention was significant using a two-tailed Wilcoxon signed-rank test (p < 0.03 and p < 0.04). The increases in the control were not statistically significant.

Table 3. Themes for the coded responses to post-test questions "Please explain why you rated the following activities as helpful/not helpful to your learning."

Why helpful?		Why not helpful?	
Theme	Example	Theme	Example
Application	"Working on the assignments and projects helped me to see how the concepts worked and how to use them."	Group process	"Attempting to take in information while attempting to focus on group interaction is far too distracting to perform either."
Learning with peers	"Working on actual code helps cement concepts, and explaining code helps to make you understand it better."	Unprepared for the work	"I would rather prefer lecture type model where the professor discusses all the concepts in class."
Feedback	"I usually find that an explanation of why I did something wrong makes it stick the most."	Help access	"...(labs outside of class) lacks the benefit of receiving help and feedback right away."
Coherence	"Having organized information relevant to the course material that can then be solidified by doing the homework..."	Difficulty	"The projects were very difficult, without time for trial and error, and often the bulk of the project was testing..."
Instructor help	"We had lots of time to work out what was correct and why, as well as having access to classmates and TAs for help..."	Type of activities	"Reading about coding doesn't help me learn very well, I tend to use the text more as a reference than required reading."

4.4.2 Qualitative. From responses to why activities were helpful or unhelpful, we identified 17 preliminary codes for helpful and 17 codes for unhelpful, and we grouped these codes into 5 categories for helpful and 5 categories for unhelpful (Table 3). Among the responses to the question asking why the activities were helpful, the category *Learning with peers* included the subcategory *Peer explanation* that refers to explanation by someone at the same level of understanding; for example, "sometime classmates' explanation about the knowledge is easier for me to understand than just listening to the professor." Students appreciated having access to help from peers, the instructor, and TAs (*instructor help). Application* included responses that expressed the value of "doing," "hands-on learning," and "applying concepts."

Regarding the reasons why activities were not helpful for learning, students mentioned being *unprepared for the work* in class. Of these, the subcategory *need to be taught before doing* includes comments such as "working on labs during class is not very helpful for me because most of us barely understand concept. We are not able to finish assigned work by our own without lecture." G*roup process* included comments about the challenges students encountered from group dysfunction, including preference for working alone, absent or unprepared group members, lack of social skills, and imbalance of work.

5 THREATS TO VALIDITY

5.1 External validity

External validity is the extent to which the conclusions of a study generalize to other contexts. We completed this study in a specific context: a specific computer organization course, set in an active learning classroom without a separate lab section, using guided inquiry, with one instructor, and students at one institution. While these control variables assisted the internal validity of the study, they limit generalizability. To support replications or similar studies, we have provided a replication package [45] containing the in-class activities and measurement instruments [46].

Our major curriculum presently has few prior in-class team experiences, so results may vary in departments that introduce cooperative learning experiences earlier [47].

The intervention changed multiple aspects of the course, making it difficult to tease apart the contributions of the independent variables (ratio of activities, presence of various cooperative learning structures). However, themes from our qualitative analysis helped us draw interesting conclusions.

The guided inquiry instruction may not have been representative of POGIL since the instructor had limited experience and had not yet certified the activities with expert POGIL reviewers. We partially mitigated this problem with the Summer 2017 pilot semester.

5.2 Internal validity

Internal validity is the extent to which the conclusions follow from the study. First, the fact that the instructor was on the research team may have biased the experiment. As discussed in 3.2, we took steps to reduce this bias.

Second, instructor graded the exams for each sample at different times, so they may have been graded differently. We mitigated accidental bias by keeping a rubric, notes for interpreting it, and referring to exemplars. Given those safeguards and the lack of an effect in the hypothesized direction, we decided not to regrade the exams as a mixed collection.

Third, the results could be explained by the instructor having more experience with Peer Instruction than guided inquiry (3 prior semesters versus 1). On the other hand, the instructor *improved* the quality of the inquiry activities between the control and intervention semesters.

Finally, the quasi-experiment was subject to selection bias and response bias due to our drawing of samples from different semesters and students opting into the study. In fact, Fall had a greater proportion of fourth years than Spring (Table 1). Other work evaluating POGIL in computer architecture courses found that the level of a student affected their response to the pedagogy [48]. We mitigated these biases in our analysis of achievement, engagement, and peer support by controlling for associated factors (Sections 4.1-4.3); however, we did not directly control for class year, so confounding factors may remain.

5.3 Construct validity

Construct validity is the extent to which a study measures what it claims to. Although we used a validated instrument for measuring peer academic support, we unintentionally used a four-point "Often" scale instead of its prescribed five-point "Agree" scale. Fortunately, Cronbach's alpha was > 0.8, which is in the acceptable range.

Our final exam may have not been a valid measure of achievement in computer organization. While we had other instructors review the exam (Section 3.5), it was not a formal process. We mitigated this weakness by having multiple measures of learning: the final exam and the externally validated DLCI.

The DLCI may not have been a reliable measure of student learning in our course. The reliability was <0.6, indicating students may have made errors due to reasons other than misunderstanding concepts, such as misreading or low incentive to try on an ungraded assessment.

6 DISCUSSION

Regarding RQ1, after controlling for prior achievement the intervention group had lower achievement on two of three final exam questions and no significant difference on the other final exam question and the concept inventory. We attribute the null and negative results partly to the decrease in engagement and task value of collaboration, the subject of RQ2.

Regarding RQ2, after controlling for preliminary intrinsic value, the intervention group had lower engagement. Also, students in the control increased their task value of collaborative activities, while students in the intervention decreased it. Although this result was initially discouraging, we think that there are interesting reasons for it.

First, while the intervention addressed positive interdependence and group processing in ways that the control did not, it may have insufficiently addressed factors of cooperative learning to support the increased amount of guided inquiry. Students in the intervention, which had much more guided inquiry, uniquely said that they *needed to be taught before doing*. This does not mean students did not like doing: the most common reason for helpfulness was *application*. Therefore, the instructor could better emphasize the value of the learning cycle of guided inquiry to see gains in task value.

Second, the increased amount of cooperation in the intervention may have lacked critical supports of cooperative learning. Students in the control mentioned being *unprepared* for in-class activities and students in both conditions mentioned various types of group dysfunction. Dysfunction may also have had a greater effect in the intervention when students had less ability to pick group members. Rotating roles once a week without revisiting them within the same team may have limited the effect of group processing. Finally, lack of individual accountability may be the most likely source of frustration for would-be engaged students. The *group process* subcategories on attendance, imbalance of work, and preparation in reasons for unhelpfulness suggest that we did not sufficiently address individual accountability. Some ways to increase individual accountability include using peer evaluations [49] and giving individual quizzes in class [11].

Preference for working alone came up seven times, which indicates that student opposition to cooperation, which some researchers feel is left out of cooperative learning models [50], needs to be considered. More favourably, *learning with peers* was mentioned in 18 why-helpful responses. These included subcategories that have been shown to promote learning: *peer explanation* [51], *help from peers* [52][53], and *exchange of ideas* [54]. This result indicates that plenty of students recognize the benefits of cooperative learning; therefore, we cautiously assert that engagement can be improved if cooperation is comprehensively supported.

7 CONCLUSION

In a quasi-experiment comparing two offerings of a computer organization course, we found that adding more guided inquiry supported by teams (*positive interdependence*) and teamwork skills reflections (*group processing*) lowered some measures of achievement and lowered engagement and task value of collaborative activities. To explain the results, we gathered themes from student explanations for why activities were helpful or unhelpful. The analysis showed that although students commonly valued hands-on learning, some in the intervention also felt they needed to be taught before doing. It also showed that although students commonly valued peer learning, some in both conditions also identified lack of preparation and group dysfunction as unhelpful. These results point to insufficient individual accountability to support the cooperative learning. Our study supports that Computer Organization students recognize some of the benefits of guided inquiry and cooperative learning but that the instructor needs to comprehensively support these strategies for them to succeed over other types of collaborative learning.

ACKNOWLEDGMENTS

An ACM SIGCSE Special Projects Award supported the creation of the POGIL activities used in the course. We also thank our anonymous reviewers for thoughtful feedback on improvements.

REFERENCES

[1] G. L. Herman, L. Kaczmarczyk, M. C. Loui, and C. Zilles, "Proof by Incomplete Enumeration and Other Logical Misconceptions," in *Proceedings of the Fourth international Workshop on Computing Education Research*, 2008, pp. 59–70.

[2] L. Porter, S. Garcia, H.-W. Tseng, and D. Zingaro, "Evaluating Student Understanding of Core Concepts in Computer Architecture," in *Proceedings of the 18th ACM conference on Innovation and technology in computer science education*, 2013, pp. 279–284.

[3] C. Bailey Lee, S. Garcia, and L. Porter, "Can peer instruction be effective in upper-division computer science courses?," *ACM Trans. Comput. Educ,*

vol. 13, 2013.

[4] H. H. Hu and T. D. Shepherd, "Teaching CS 1 with POGIL activities and roles," in *Proceedings of the 45th ACM technical symposium on Computer science education - SIGCSE '14*, 2014, pp. 127–132.

[5] D. L. Linton, J. K. Farmer, and E. Peterson, "Is Peer Interaction Necessary for Optimal Active Learning?," *CBE Life Sci. Educ.*, vol. 13, no. 2, pp. 243–52, 2014.

[6] L. Porter, C. B. Lee, B. Simon, and D. Zingaro, "Peer Instruction: Do Students Really Learn from Peer Discussion in Computing?," in *Proceedings of the seventh International Workshop on Computing Education Research, ACM*, 2011, pp. 45–52.

[7] R. M. Felder and R. Brent, "Cooperative Learning *," *Act. Learn. Model. from Anal. Sci. ACS Symp. Ser.*, vol. 970, pp. 34–53.

[8] C. E. Hmelo-Silver, R. G. Duncan, and C. A. Chinn, "Scaffolding and Achievement in Problem-Based and Inquiry Learning: A Response to Kirschner, Sweller, and Clark (2006)."

[9] D. W. Johnson and R. T. Johnson, "An Educational Psychology Success Story: Social Interdependence Theory and Cooperative Learning," *Educ. Res.*, 2009.

[10] M. K. Smith *et al.*, "Why peer discussion improves student performance on in-class concept questions.," *Science*, vol. 323, no. 5910, pp. 122–4, Jan. 2009.

[11] J. R. T. and S. K. A. Johnson D. W., "Active learning: Cooperation in the college classroom," *Annu. Rep. Educ. Psychol. Japan*, vol. 47, p. 140, 1991.

[12] D. W. Johnson and R. T. Johnson, "New Developments in Social Interdependence Theory," *Genet. Soc. Gen. Psychol. Monogr.*, no. 131:4, pp. 285–358, 2005.

[13] L. Springer, "Effects of Small-Group Learning on Undergraduates in Science, Mathematics, Engineering, and Technology: A Meta-Analysis," *Rev. Educ. Res.*, vol. 69, no. 1, pp. 21–51, 1999.

[14] D. W. Johnson, "Cooperative learning methods: A meta-analysis," 2000.

[15] C. W. Bowen, "A Quantitative Literature Review of Cooperative Learning Effects on High School and College Chemistry Achievement," *J. Chem. Educ.*, vol. 77, no. 1, p. 116, Jan. 2000.

[16] G. Gonzalez, "A systematic approach to active and cooperative learning in CS1 and its effects on CS2," *SIGCSE*, Mar. 2006.

[17] L. Beck and A. Chizhik, "Cooperative learning instructional methods for CS1: Design, implementation, and evaluation," *ACM Trans. Comput. Educ.*, vol. 13, no. 3, p. 10, 2013.

[18] D. Bunce *et al.*, "Instructors guide to POGIL."

[19] N. Titterton, C. M. Lewis, and M. J. Clancy, "Experiences with lab-centric instruction," *Com- Puter Sci. Educ.*, vol. 20, no. 2, pp. 79–102, 2010.

[20] C. M. Lewis, N. Titterton, and M. Clancy, "Developing Students' Self-Assessment Skills," *Consort. Comput. Sci. Coll.*, pp. 173–180, 2011.

[21] J. W. Bruce, "Active and Cooperative Learning in a VLSI Design Course: Lessons from the Trenches," in *ASEE Southeast Section Conference*, 2005.

[22] O. Arbelaitz, J. I. Martin, and J. Muguerza, "Analysis of Introducing Active Learning Methodologies in a Basic Computer Architecture Course," *IEEE Trans. Educ.*, vol. 58, no. 2, pp. 110–116, May 2015.

[23] R. S. Moog and J. N. Spencer, *Process Oriented Guided Inquiry Learning (POGIL)*, vol. 994. Washington, DC: American Chemical Society, 2008.

[24] D. A. Kolb, *Experiential learning: Experience as the source of learning and development.* FT press, 2014.

[25] "Effectiveness of POGIL," *pogil.org*, 2016. [Online]. Available: https://pogil.org/about/effectiveness. [Accessed: 20-Jul-2004].

[26] "CS-POGIL." [Online]. Available: http://cspogil.org. [Accessed: 19-Jun-2018].

[27] S. Ingram, B., Jesse, M., Fleagle, S., Florman, J., & Van Horne, "Transform, Interact, Learn, Engage (TILE): Creating Learning Spaces that Transform Undergraduate Education," in *Cases on Higher Education Spaces: Innovation, Collaboration, and Technology*, Hershey, PA: IGI Global, 2013, pp. 165–185.

[28] R. J. Beichner *et al.*, "The student-centered activities for large enrollment undergraduate programs (SCALE-UP) project," *Res. reform Univ. Phys.*, vol. 1, no. 1, pp. 2–39, 2007.

[29] L. D. Fink, *A Self-Directed Guide to Designing Courses for Significant Learning*. Jossey-Bass, 2003.

[30] M. Thweatt, Mack, Thweatt, and Mack, "CSI closed lab vs. open lab experiment," *ACM SIGCSE Bull.*, vol. 26, no. 1, pp. 80–82, Mar. 1994.

[31] "Architecture and Organization," *CS-POGIL*. [Online]. Available: http://cspogil.org/Architecture+and+Organization.

[32] G. L. Herman, M. C. Loui, and C. Zilles, "Creating the Digital Logic Concept Inventory," in *41st ACM Technical Symposium on Computer Science Education*, 2010, pp. 102–106.

[33] G. L. Herman, C. Zilles, and M. C. Loui, "A psychometric evaluation of the digital logic concept inventory," *Comput. Sci. Educ.*, vol. 24, no. 4, pp. 277–303, 2014.

[34] E. R. Kahu, "Framing student engagement in higher education," *Stud. High. Educ.*, vol. 38, no. 5, pp. 758–773, Jun. 2013.

[35] H. M. Marks, "Engagement in Instructional Activity: Patterns in the Elementary, Middle, and High School Years," *Am. Educ. Res. J.*, vol. 37, no. 1, pp. 153–184, 2000.

[36] A. Wigfield and J. S. Eccles, "Expectancy-Value Theory of Achievement Motivation," *Contemp. Educ. Psychol.*, vol. 25, pp. 68–81, 2000.

[37] P. R. Pintrich and E. V. de Groot, "Motivational and self-regulated learning components of classroom academic performance.," *J. Educ. Psychol.*, vol. 82, no. 1, pp. 33–40, 1990.

[38] M. Bong, "Role of Self-Efficacy and Task-Value in Predicting College Students' Course Performance and Future Enrollment Intentions," *Contemp. Educ. Psychol.*, vol. 26, no. 4, pp. 553–570, Oct. 2001.

[39] J. S. Eccles, "Subjective Task Value and the Eccles et al. Model of Achievement-Related Choices," in *Handbook of competence and motivation*, A. J. Elliot and C. S. Dweck, Eds. Guilford Publications, 2005, pp. 105–121.

[40] P. Burnard, "A method of analysing interview transcripts in qualitative research," *Nurse Educ. Today*, vol. 11, no. 6, pp. 461–466, Dec. 1991.

[41] E. A. Ruzek, C. A. Hafen, J. P. Allen, A. Gregory, A. Y. Mikami, and R. C. Pianta, "How teacher emotional support motivates students: The mediating roles of perceived peer relatedness, autonomy support, and competence," *Learn. Instr.*, vol. 42, pp. 95–103, Apr. 2016.

[42] G. Ghaith, "The relationship between cooperative learning, perception of social support, and academic achievement," *System*, vol. 30, pp. 263–273, 2002.

[43] D. W. Johnson, R. Johnson, and D. Anderson, "Social Interdependence and Classroom Climate," *J. Psychol.*, vol. 114, no. 1, pp. 135–142, May 1983.

[44] R. Pekrun, T. Goetz, W. Titz, and R. P. Perry, "Academic Emotions in Students' Self-Regulated Learning and Achievement: A Program of Qualitative and Quantitative Research," *Educ. Psychol.*, vol. 37, no. 2, pp. 91–105, Jun. 2002.

[45] F. Shull *et al.*, "Replicating software engineering experiments: addressing the tacit knowledge problem," in *Proceedings International Symposium on Empirical Software Engineering*, pp. 7–16.

[46] B. Myers, "Replication Package," 2018. [Online]. Available: https://bmyerz.github.io/sigcse2019-replication-package/.

[47] M. Phipps, C. Phipps, S. Kask, and S. Higgins, "University Students' Perceptions of Cooperative Learning: Implications for Administrators and Instructors," *J. Exp. Educ.*, vol. 24, no. 1, pp. 14–22, 2001.

[48] B. P. Railing, C. Taylor, and S. Garcia, "Using Active Learning Techniques in Mixed Undergraduate / Graduate Courses (Abstract Only)," in *Proceedings of the 46th ACM Technical Symposium on Computer Science Education - SIGCSE '15*, 2015, pp. 720–720.

[49] R. E. Stein, C. J. Colyer, and J. Manning, "Student Accountability in Team-based Learning Classes," *Teach. Sociol.*, 2016.

[50] K. J. Herrmann, "The impact of cooperative learning on student engagement: Results from an intervention," *Act. Learn. High. Educ.*, vol. 14, no. 3, pp. 175–187.

[51] J. A. Bargh and Y. Schul, "On the cognitive benefits of teaching.," *J. Educ. Psychol.*, vol. 72, no. 5, pp. 593–604, 1980.

[52] N. Webb, S. H. Farivar, and A. Mastergeorge, "Productive Helping in Cooperative Groups," *Theory Pract.*, vol. 41, pp. 13–20, 2002.

[53] N. Noddings, "Small groups as a setting for research on mathematical problem solving.," in *Teaching and learning mathematical problem*, E. A. Silver, Ed. Hillsdale, NJ: Lawrence Erlbaum Associates, 1985, pp. 345–359.

[54] J. Osborne, "Arguing to learn in science: the role of collaborative, critical discourse.," *Science*, vol. 328, no. 5977, pp. 463–6, Apr. 2010.

POGIL in Computer Science: Faculty Motivation and Challenges

Aman Yadav
Michigan State University
East Lansing, MI, USA
ayadav@msu.edu

Clif Kussmaul
Muhlenberg College
Allentown, PA, USA
clif@kussmaul.org

Chris Mayfield
James Madison University
Harrisonburg, VA, USA
mayfiecs@jmu.edu

Helen H. Hu
Westminster College
Salt Lake City, UT, USA
hhu@westminstercollege.edu

ABSTRACT

Introductory computer science courses face multiple challenges, including a broad range of content, diverse teaching methods, and the need to help students develop skills such as problem solving, critical thinking, and teamwork. One evidence-based approach to address these challenges is Process Oriented Guided Inquiry Learning (POGIL), in which student teams work on classroom activities specifically designed to help them construct understanding and develop key skills. While POGIL has been widely used and studied in Chemistry and other STEM fields, much less is known about how it is used in Computer Science.

In this study, we examined how faculty adopt POGIL for the first time in introductory CS classrooms. Using qualitative in-depth interviews, we investigated why faculty chose to adopt POGIL and their concerns about using it. Our results suggest that faculty motivations to use POGIL centered around improving student outcomes, including their learning and engagement. However, faculty also had concerns about using POGIL, which ranged from how POGIL impacts the curriculum to logistical and institutional barriers. We discuss the implications of these findings with respect to faculty development and active learning pedagogies.

CCS CONCEPTS

• **Social and professional topics → Computer science education**;

KEYWORDS

Active Learning, Faculty Development, Qualitative Interviews

ACM Reference Format:
Aman Yadav, Clif Kussmaul, Chris Mayfield, and Helen H. Hu. 2019. POGIL in Computer Science: Faculty Motivation and Challenges. In *Proceedings of the 50th ACM Technical Symposium on Computer Science Education (SIGCSE '19), February 27–March 2, 2019, Minneapolis, MN, USA.* ACM, New York, NY, USA, 6 pages. https://doi.org/10.1145/3287324.3287360

ACM ISBN 978-1-4503-5890-3/19/2...$15.00
https://doi.org/10.1145/3287324.3287360

1 INTRODUCTION

Introductory CS courses face a variety of challenges, whether in K-12 or in higher education. Many students have no prior exposure to the field, unlike nearly all students who take courses in mathematics and science. To succeed, CS students must develop a broad range of skills, such as teamwork, problem solving, and critical thinking, in addition to learning CS content. There are multiple approaches to teaching introductory CS (breadth-first, objects-first, etc.), and new languages, theories, tools, and practices are developed continually. CS faculty must spend time each year updating course content, reducing the time available to refine their pedagogical practices. Undergraduate CS faculty are usually trained as researchers, not educators, and are often unaware of effective teaching practices. The recent surge in CS enrollments exacerbates these challenges.

1.1 POGIL

A variety of evidence-based instructional practices have been developed and validated (e.g., [2], [15]). Many correspond to the ICAP model [1], which describes how learning increases as students shift from *passive*, to *active*, to *constructive* (creating their own understanding), to *interactive* (working with peers).

Process Oriented Guided Inquiry Learning (POGIL) is an evidence-based practice that is explicitly constructive and interactive. In a POGIL classroom, students work in teams of 3–4 on activities that are specifically designed to help guide student inquiry to construct their own understanding. At the same time, students develop process skills such as communication, teamwork, information processing, problem solving, and critical thinking. The instructor is not a lecturer or passive observer, but an active facilitator of student learning, who monitors progress, guides students to discuss insights and questions, and assists teams as needed. Prior work described POGIL in more detail, presented a sample activity (on stacks and queues) [12], and compared POGIL to other approaches (e.g., *Pair Programming*, *Peer Instruction*, and *Team-Based Learning*) [8]. A variety of POGIL activities for CS are listed at http://cspogil.org.

Numerous studies have examined the impact of POGIL (e.g., [3], [14],[16]). Most find that, compared to traditional approaches, attrition is lower, content mastery is greater, and students have more positive attitudes. After converting a CS1 course to POGIL, pass rates increased for female students but not males [9]. A POGIL CS Principles course increased student interest in taking additional CS courses [6]. In a software project course, POGIL helped students to understand the importance of communication in real projects [11].

1.2 Faculty Adoption

However, helping faculty to adopt evidence-based practices, including POGIL, can present significant challenges. A literature review on change in undergraduate STEM education [5] found that effective strategies for faculty professional development are aligned with or seek to change beliefs, involve long-term interventions (one semester or more), and approach education as a complex system. The review also identified two ineffective practices: top-down policy making, and simply making best practice materials available (e.g. on a website). In many cases, evidence-based strategies cannot be adopted directly, but must be adapted and customized for an institution, student population, and instructor.

For many faculty, it takes significant effort to shift from a familiar lecture-style to a POGIL-style classroom. Creating effective POGIL activities also requires significant effort, although other disciplines have found that activities, once written, can readily be adapted by other faculty. For example, a 2015 survey about faculty adoption of POGIL in CS identified several challenges, including lack of preparation time, availability of activities, and pressure to cover more content [7]. To help K-12 and college faculty adopt POGIL successfully, The POGIL Project (https://pogil.org) offers an extensive series of workshops on classroom facilitation, activity authoring, and related topics. However as suggested by the survey, literature review, and other research (e.g. [10]), many faculty who have adopted POGIL desire further training and mentoring beyond 1-day and 3-day workshops.

1.3 IntroCS POGIL Project

In response to these and other challenges, we have created a professional development program for CS faculty wishing to adopt POGIL in their introductory programming courses. Our *IntroCS POGIL* project seeks to improve faculty adoption and persistence with POGIL in three ways:

- *Materials:* Participants are given multiple collections of POGIL activities for CS1 in Java and Python with sample solutions and instructor guides.
- *Training:* A cohort of 10-15 participants attends a 3-day POGIL summer workshop, followed by a fourth day focused on CS pedagogy and individual course planning.
- *Support:* Participants are organized into teams of 2–4 faculty and each team has regular meetings with an experienced POGIL mentor to share questions, concerns, and insights.

In return, participants help the project to collect data, including student demographics, faculty and student interviews, surveys, learning assessments, and course outcomes.

This paper presents in-depth qualitative interview data from our first cohort of undergraduate faculty. The results complement and extend the literature on faculty motivation and challenges when adopting POGIL in computer science. In contrast to [7], which surveyed instructors who taught with POGIL for multiple years, our work focuses on faculty during their first year with POGIL. We study the impact of our professional development model (materials, training, and support) on faculty adoption and persistence. The specific examples that follow give further insight into how POGIL affects faculty teaching experiences and student outcomes in computer science.

2 METHODS

2.1 Participants

Twelve computer science faculty (seven female, five male) from the United States participated in the study. Based on Carnegie classification [4], ten faculty were from public institutions and two were from private institutions. One taught at a two year institution and the rest taught at four year institutions. Table 1 shows the demographic and university information for each participant.

All participating faculty were recruited via conference workshops and postings to the SIGCSE-members listserv to implement POGIL in introductory CS courses only (primarily CS1). As described in section 1.3, these faculty received collections of POGIL activities, attended summer workshops, and received mentoring on how to implement POGIL.

2.2 Data Collection and Analysis

Partway through their CS1 course, after faculty had implemented several POGIL activities, we invited them to participate in a qualitative interview. The purpose of the interview was to better understand their views about POGIL. Specifically, we wanted to get a picture of their motivation to use POGIL, how POGIL compared to the way they taught before, how their students responded to POGIL, and their concerns about using POGIL.

Each interview was conducted via phone or Google Hangouts and took an average of 22 minutes. The recorded interviews were transcribed, and the text files were imported into nVivo, a qualitative analysis software. The transcripts were read and analyzed by two researchers to see what themes and sub-themes emerged from the data. This bottom-up approach allowed us to maintain the primacy of the data rather than being influenced by our own preconceived notions of what it means to implement POGIL in CS1. In particular, we use an emergent coding method to identify the initial list of codes from the interview transcripts. The initial codes were combined and collapsed into conceptually-based themes, which represented faculty perspectives on implementing POGIL for the first time in their courses.

The analysis of the interviews revealed a number of themes related to faculty motivation to implement POGIL, challenges and issues they faced when implementing POGIL, and how their teaching practice changed as a result of using POGIL for the first time. Below we discuss these themes under two overarching categories: motivation for POGIL, and challenges/concerns when using POGIL.

3 MOTIVATION FOR POGIL

Faculty identified several reasons why they used POGIL that centered on improving student experience/outcomes, changing their teaching practices, and following other faculty recommendations.

3.1 Improving Student Experience/Outcomes

One sub-theme that emerged from the data was that faculty wanted to improve both the experience and learning of students in the CS1 course. One faculty, Christina, stated that:

> *I'm hoping it [POGIL] would be a better learning experience. They learn the concepts better and get better*

Table 1: Participant Demographics

Name*	Gender	Level	Status	Size and Setting
Rachel	Female	4-year	Public	Large, primarily nonresidential
Matthew	Male	4-year	Private	Small, highly residential
John	Male	4-year	Public	Large, primarily residential
Olivia	Female	4-year	Public	Medium, primarily nonresidential
Pavitra	Female	4-year	Public	Medium, primarily nonresidential
Emily	Female	4-year	Public	Medium, primarily nonresidential
David	Male	4-year	Public	Large, primarily residential
Kathryn	Female	2-year	Public	Very large
Christina	Female	4-year	Private	Medium, highly residential
Jen	Female	4-year	Public	Large, highly residential
Jack	Male	4-year	Public	Large, primarily residential
Ray	Male	4-year	Public	Large, primarily residential

* The names used are pseudonyms to protect their identity.

> *performance in the class; better experience. Most importantly, they are also learning the concepts. We can't have fun without learning. I'm hoping it will help them get better learning experience.*

Similarly, another faculty suggested that they wanted their students to get hands-on experience to help them have a good understanding, stating:

> *Mostly because I found especially the upper level computer science students don't get concepts as well, they are not conceptual thinkers; they are doers. Quite frankly, if it wasn't for computer science becoming a discipline, I probably wouldn't have got into academia because I tend to be more of active learner, too. I like hands-on; engineers are that way.*

Faculty also believed that POGIL would help students retain the concepts better as they moved to more advanced courses. For example, Kathryn said:

> *One area I'm especially interested is retention. When we measure how well the students are doing at the end of the term, that's one thing. How well are the students doing? Let's see one term later when they come back after summer break, you know, how well they are doing.*

3.2 Increasing Retention / Reducing Isolation

Christina also brought the idea of POGIL not only leading to better retention of material, but also better retention of students, stating:

> *Well, doing better and having better performance on the project. I'm hoping to see their better performance on the tasks. I'm hoping they have more retention in my class. They are really enjoying that. There's better retention from the CS1 to the next course. So those are the things. Better grades, perhaps—you know, fewer failing, fewer dropping.*

Similarly, Olivia suggested that POGIL will have positive effects on the weaker students. She said:

> *We have such a high DWF rate. I decided it was worth trying something new to see if we can help the struggling students. So I decided to give it a try.*

Faculty also hoped that, as a result of using POGIL, it would lead to more students coming to the class, as highlighted by Olivia:

> *One thing I am hoping to see it turn out a result in spring is that students start coming to class. Or when I say, 'Let's do the lab work,' and I'm hoping that this group activities are part of something that keeps them in the class and keeps them asking questions, and that improves their performances.*

In addition, another motivation for faculty was to better engage their students during class as highlighted by Matthew:

> *I want people [to be] more engaged. In my upper division courses, I do get a lot of give-and-take with the students, even when I lecture. But in the 100-level courses, they often just sit there and maybe they're there, maybe they're somewhere else, you know what I mean? I don't get a whole lot of interaction. I do, but it's just up to your student, and that bothers me. You know, I tried some strategies to get other people to engage in questions so that it starts out and stuff, but it's not often. I want to get them all engaged in it. POGIL looks like a way to do that.*

4 CHALLENGES/CONCERNS ABOUT POGIL

While faculty had various motivations to use POGIL, they also raised a number of concerns about implementing POGIL in their CS1 courses. These concerns were related to curricular issues, institutional challenges, student collaboration, and logistical problems. Below we discuss each of these sub-themes in detail.

4.1 Curricular Issues

Some themes emerged around faculty concerns related to how POGIL would support student learning in CS1. For example, faculty are concerned that active learning approaches like POGIL take more time that traditional lecture-based approaches. Matthew said:

> *The amount of time it takes to do POGIL is more than if you were just lecturing. So, there's always a concern about balancing active learning with actually covering the content.*

Rachel also discussed how POGIL was time intensive:

> *The one problem that I have with it: it just takes a long time to implement. It takes a long time to do a POGIL activity. It takes the bare minimum of an hour to do a POGIL activity, and I am actually behind in my content—two weeks behind. Because of the implementation of POGIL, I'm already two weeks behind and that just makes me very, very nervous... Like I said, the greatest concern that I have right now, that is always putting an extra beat in my heart, is not being able to cover all the content that I have to, especially in this intro-to-programming class. They have to come up with a basic level of knowledge so that when they move into that second class, they have seen stuff and they have learned stuff and experienced stuff. I can't miss content; I can't skip it. It's critically important that they know it and that they feel confident with it.*

The main concerns about lack of time to do POGIL was related to the pressure to cover content as highlighted by Pavitra:

> *I think the concern is usually time. I mean, we usually stress so much about being able to cover everything. You definitely have to get through everything. I think that is a major concern. I think it's just an additional set of activities that I'm doing. I mean, I've reduced the amount of time that I spend on slides. I usually now just show them the slides and tell them that it's there. But I think that's working on fine.*

Some faculty also discussed that the POGIL activities themselves were time consuming, as Christina stated:

> *Well, one concern is I'd like to know... my class is one hour and forty minutes. It's not short, I have time, I'm interested to see can they finish the activity during my class time. Yesterday they had it; they had fun, telling you this is great; they really liked it. We didn't finish the whole activity because I am doing other things. It was the first class in this semester, and there's a few administrative things I had to do, make sure that they can get on the system because some freshmen never had their account. And yesterday was rushed... I am basically saying, the length of the activity, as soon as it is going to be run, perhaps if it is too long, remove some of it. I thought the first activity I did was long.*

There were issues related to faculty themselves having the time needed to learn how to adapt their teaching to POGOL, as Christina stated:

> *But you know, it's time consuming. I'll spend more time on this. Because I need to learn what I am supposed to be doing, so I will try. I think time is the main thing. It is time learning some technology.*

When it came to how POGIL related to their own curricula, faculty were concerned that the activities did not always match their own materials and they were adapting the materials for their own need. Matthew stated:

> *The other challenges would just be the availability of materials, available materials. You know, one of my challenges is that I'm using a completely different set of tools and textbooks than the authors of materials. So, I have to be really strategic about where I can fit it in, and I'm doing things in a different order than they had, and things like that. In the repository, I mentioned earlier, there are second, third, elective types of courses with some materials that there's just not very many.*

4.2 Classroom Space Challenges

Multiple faculty also suggested that their typical classrooms were not well suited to the collaborative nature of POGIL. This is highlighted by Jack:

> *It's a challenge to get four students together comfortably where they can see each other. We've got tables that seat three students going across. And we line through them up side-by-side, so it's essentially rows of... the classroom I've got six students per row, to my left and to my right. The tables the way they are, they've got a board in front of them, so you just can't sit on the other side of the table comfortably. That's been the biggest issue. Just the logistics of getting people moved around.*

Similarly, Olivia suggested that her classroom is not set up to do POGIL, stating:

> *The biggest problem I have is that the classroom is not set up for it. The classroom is set up in traditional, all the seats and tables facing forward. And I'm having to rotate where each group meets, because quite honestly, some of the places I can't put them to work so much better. You know, in some cases, huddled with the computer between them, not really able to see each person well. So that's the biggest problem. We don't have any spare classroom we can move into temporarily, kind of thing.*

The faculty's lack of experience in teaching POGIL might also have contributed to seeing how POGIL would work in classroom space, as suggested by David, who said:

> *So far, like I said, the one thing, I mean, the room was a problem on my first day. Despite having visited the room in advance and looking at it, you know, I had planned to rearrange the furniture. But I just, with my lack of experience I guess, I couldn't foresee how very crowded the room would become and having to reset it quickly before the next class. I was worried about making a bad impression for the colleague who had followed me. That's a little bit of concern, but thankfully that has been sort of solved.*

4.3 Teamwork and Student Roles

Another issue faculty discussed was how to manage student roles given the collaborative nature of POGIL. In particular, faculty were concerned about the size of the group and how students would function within the group as highlighted by Emily, who said:

> *I'm struggling with how to manage your group, especially one group that has three or four people. So normally one out of three or four people always has free*

> *riders. You know, some people just do all the work for others to follow along, you know. It's kind of frustrating. If I focus on that, then the classroom moves very slow. Eventually, I don't know, I just did it one time, instead of three or four people, I went back to two people a group. You know, [my institution] has a small class. We have around 20 students per class. I thought 2 people per group with 10 teams I can manage pretty well. If I have three or four people a group, I have around 6 or 7 teams, you know? And it becomes difficult to manage. Especially four people is very difficult to manage.*

Given that students were working in teams, faculty also were concerned that not all students would contribute equally to the work. For example, Christina stated:

> *I also need to think about how to make sure that everybody is following their responsibility and roles. I am concerned about that one student actually taking lead and the others following. I want to make sure that doesn't happen. There's a tendency sometimes that someone with strong personality just takes lead and everyone say "yes, yes" and follows, without challenging them.*

Another challenge is how to manage groups when some finished sooner than others, as stated by Christina:

> *I want to make sure I know how to handle well the various completion rate of the students in this class. Some of them finished earlier than others, and I need to be ready to give them more things. I mean, I need to think about how to handle that. I talked about before, when I just gave them labs, now I have to be slightly different with how to do that, because we just stop at different stages.*

4.4 Institutional Challenges

Another theme that emerged was that faculty face institutional challenges when adopting new teaching approaches. This was mainly around how senior faculty were not open to changing what they have been doing. For example, Christina stated:

> *Well, you know, some faculty members are resistant to do something new. I don't know what exactly obstacle they think. They have to change the way things are accepted. Many of them are more senior faculty, they have a certain way of doing something. Or, maybe they believe in it, they believe what they are doing is successful, why try something new?*

Similarly, Kathryn stated that faculty who have been at the institutions for a number of years were reluctant to do something new, stating:

> *What I found in our college is the forerunners. Some faculty members have been there since 20+ years, and they have their way of teaching and they like the way of teaching. There's no interest to change it.*

One participant, David, also discussed that whether research or teaching was prioritized at the institution could be a barrier to faculty adopting POGIL. He stated:

> *[My University], at least the CS department here, you know, is not a research one school. Our incentives here are aligned with teaching. That makes POGIL sort of like a secure choice to be working on, for as far as my tenure-track position. If I were at a research position, like a tenure track professor at an R1 school, I am fairly certain that I will wait until after tenure to bother with POGIL, because my teaching would matter not at all and this takes, you know.*

5 DISCUSSION

The interviews and emergent themes provide a rich description of some of the challenges faced by faculty who adopt POGIL and other similar approaches to teaching. Some of these challenges can be addressed in faculty workshops and mentoring, and thus have given us insights to improve this ongoing project.

Faculty worry about the time required to implement POGIL (section 4.1). This is a common concern raised in nearly every POGIL workshop, despite evidence of POGIL's effectiveness (e.g.,[3], [14],[16]). When students truly understand key concepts and develop skills in teamwork, critical thinking, and problem solving, they become better learners, more able to learn new concepts and skills on their own.

Faculty also worry about the effort to adapt POGIL materials for their own courses. This highlights how materials created by faculty for their own classroom may require significant revision and refactoring to be readily adapted in other classrooms. The sets of POGIL materials provided in this project have instructor's guides that include learning objectives, sample answers, notes on pacing and discussion points, etc., but might benefit from more work to be more easily adapted by other faculty.

Faculty worry about interactions between POGIL and classroom layout (section 4.2). Faculty workshops on POGIL usually use teams of 4 sitting around a table; however, many faculty implement POGIL in classrooms or lecture halls with fixed seating. Thus, POGIL workshops should address how POGIL can be adapted to different classroom environments, and perhaps even model POGIL in other settings.

Faculty worry about teamwork and roles (section 4.3). This is an ongoing challenge, even for many experienced POGIL faculty, but it might also highlight how faculty are thinking more about what and how students learn, and less about "coverage".

Faculty worry about institutional challenges (section 4.4). This suggests that POGIL workshops and mentoring should do more to explore how often to use POGIL, how to present POGIL to students and colleagues, and how to present the effort and impact of POGIL in yearly evaluations and promotion packages.

6 CONCLUSIONS

Teaching with POGIL can be a significant paradigm shift for faculty, especially when adopting POGIL for the first time. But overall, the results are consistent with faculty perceptions of other active learning approaches (see e.g., [13]). Faculty are concerned about the amount of time needed to do POGIL well—both preparation time and classroom time. And they worry about "covering" less content during class time in order to facilitate the activities.

The concerns raised in the interviews illustrate the need for ongoing professional development and mentoring. Issues like the alignment of POGIL to a specific curriculum can be addressed through the creation of new materials. Others, such as class room space challenges and institutional barriers, require additional research and support.

In spite of their concerns, faculty continued to be motivated to use POGIL for reasons that ranged from:

- POGIL will help with retention
- POGIL will help weaker students and reduce isolation
- POGIL will improve student attendance and engagement
- POGIL will improve student performance

During the next phase of our research, we will examine the impact of POGIL adoption on student learning and outcomes. We are working with a wide range of faculty, from new assistant professors to full professors with decades of experience. We are particularly interested in how faculty perceptions change over time and how their teaching practices impact their students.

ACKNOWLEDGMENTS

The authors thank the National Science Foundation for support under award DUE-1626765. All opinions reflected in this paper are those of the authors and not necessarily those of the National Science Foundation.

REFERENCES

[1] Michelene T. H. Chi and Ruth Wylie. 2014. The ICAP framework: Linking cognitive engagement to active learning outcomes. *Educ. Psych.* 49 (2014), 219–243. Issue 4. https://doi.org/10.1080/00461520.2014.965823

[2] Thomas Eberlein, Jack Kampmeier, Vicki Minderhout, Richard S. Moog, Terry Platt, Pratibha Varma-Nelson, and Harry B. White. 2008. Pedagogies of engagement in science. *Biochemistry and Molecular Biology Education* 36 (2008), 262–273. Issue 4.

[3] John J. Farrell, Richard S. Moog, and James N. Spencer. 1999. A Guided-Inquiry General Chemistry course. *Journal of Chemical Education* 76, 4 (1999), 570–574.

[4] Indiana University Center for Postsecondary Research. 2015. The Carnegie classification of institutions of higher education.

[5] Charles Henderson, Andrea Beach, and Noah Finkelstein. 2011. Facilitating change in undergraduate STEM instructional practices: An analytic review of the literature. *Journal of Research in Science Teaching* 48, 8 (2011), 952–984. https://doi.org/10.1002/tea.20439

[6] H. H. Hu and P. B. Campbell. 2017. A Framework for Levels of Student Participation and Stages of Relevant Curriculum. *Computing in Science Engineering* 19, 3 (May 2017), 20–29. https://doi.org/10.1109/MCSE.2017.44

[7] Helen H. Hu, Clifton Kussmaul, Brian Knaeble, Chris Mayfield, and Aman Yadav. 2016. Results from a survey on faculty adoption of Process Oriented Guided Inquiry Learning (POGIL) in Computer Science. In *Proceedings of the Annual Conference on Innovation and Technology in Computer Science Education (ITiCSE).*

[8] Helen H. Hu and Tricia D. Shepherd. 2013. Using POGIL to help students learn to program. *Transactions on Computing Education* 13, 3 (2013), 13:1–13:23. https://doi.org/10.1145/2499947.2499950

[9] Helen H. Hu and Tricia D. Shepherd. 2014. Teaching CS 1 with POGIL activities and roles. In *Proceedings of the 45th ACM Tech. Sym. on CS Education.*

[10] Adrianna J. Kezar. 2011. What is the best way to achieve broader reach of improved practices in higher education? *Innovative Higher Education* 36, 3 (2011), 235–247. https://doi.org/10.1007/s10755-011-9174-z

[11] Shreya Kumar and Charles Wallace. 2014. Instruction in software project communication through guided inquiry and reflection. In *IEEE Frontiers in Edu. Conf.* Madrid, Spain.

[12] Clif Kussmaul. 2012. Process Oriented Guided Inquiry Learning (POGIL) for computer science.. In *Proceedings of the SIGCSE Technical Symposium on Computer Science Education.* Raleigh, NC, USA.

[13] Cynthia Bailey Lee, Saturnino Garcia, and Leo Porter. 2013. Can Peer Instruction be effective in upper-division Computer Science courses? *ACM Transactions on Computing Education* 13, 3 (2013), 12:1–12:22.

[14] Richard S Moog, Frank J Creegan, David M Hanson, James N Spencer, Andrei Straumanis, Diane M Bunce, and Troy Wolfskill. 2008. POGIL: Process Oriented Guided Inquiry Learning. In *Chemist's Guide to Effective Teaching: Vol II*, Norbert J. Pienta, Melanie M. Cooper, and Thomas J. Greenbowe (Eds.). Prentice Hall, 90–107.

[15] Michael Prince and Richard Felder. 2007. The many faces of inductive teaching and learning. *Journal of College Science Teaching* 5 (2007).

[16] Andrei Straumanis and Emily A Simons. 2008. A multi-institutional assessment of the use of POGIL in Organic Chemistry. In *Process Oriented Guided Inquiry Learning (POGIL)*, Vol. 994. American Chemical Society, 226–239.

Living-Learning Community for Women in Computer Science at Rutgers

Rebecca N. Wright
Rutgers University
rebecca.wright@rutgers.edu

Sally J. Nadler
Rutgers University
sjn6@echo.rutgers.edu

Thu D. Nguyen
Rutgers University
tdnguyen@cs.rutgers.edu

Cynthia N. Sanchez Gomez
Rutgers University
cysanche@echo.rutgers.edu

Heather M. Wright
Computing Research Association
heather@cra.org

ABSTRACT

We describe our experience developing and running a Computer Science Living-Learning Community (LLC) for first-year women at Rutgers University, now in its third year. Each year, around 20 first-year undergraduate women who intend to major in computer science (CS) apply and are selected to participate. LLC participants live in a common residence hall and are provided with an educational, mentoring, and community-building program that supports their progress as students and CS majors. Participants take a "house course," Great Ideas and Insights in Computer Science, as a group, and also take a course on Knowledge and Power: Issues in Women's Leadership. Program activities include study sessions and industry interactions, as well as opportunities to participate in K-12 outreach programs, hackathons, and computing research. To evaluate the program, participants and a similar comparison group are surveyed at the beginning and end of the academic year and a focus group is conducted with program participants. Program participants find the program valuable and would recommend it to others, but both program participants and the comparison group report some lack of confidence in their potential success as computer scientists.

CCS CONCEPTS

• **Social and professional topics → Computer science education; Women;**

KEYWORDS

living-learning communities; undergraduate education; gender and diversity

ACM Reference Format:
Rebecca N. Wright, Sally J. Nadler, Thu D. Nguyen, Cynthia N. Sanchez Gomez, and Heather M. Wright. 2019. Living-Learning Community for Women in Computer Science at Rutgers. In *Proceedings of the 50th ACM Technical Symposium on Computer Science Education (SIGCSE '19), February 27-March 2, 2019, Minneapolis, MN, USA.* ACM, New York, NY, USA, 7 pages. https://doi.org/10.1145/3287324.3287449

SIGCSE'19, February 27-March 2, 2019, Minneapolis, MN, USA

ACM ISBN 978-1-4503-5890-3/19/02.
https://doi.org/10.1145/3287324.3287449

1 INTRODUCTION

Undergraduate computer science enrollments have risen substantially in the last decade nationally, most years with double-digit percentage increases [2, 30]. But the percentage of women remains stubbornly low, at 19% of undergraduate computer science graduates in the United States and Canada in 2017, according to the Computing Research Association's Taulbee Survey [30]. In addition to the social justice issues associated with this disparity, the low participation of women in computer science (CS) negatively impacts the robustness of the computing workforce and the level of technical innovation possible in CS-based organizations. Increasing the participation of women in CS has been challenging because of a number of factors. For example, women feel out-of-place and unsupported in the current male-dominated environment [6, 17] and women report that they do not feel CS is connected to addressing real-world problems and helping people [18].

In order to help support undergraduate women to succeed as CS majors, Rutgers University, a large public R1 institution, has developed a living-learning community (LLC) for first-year undergraduate women in CS. Through an immersive educational and community-building experience, the program is designed to promote student engagement and success in CS. Specifically, the LLC incorporates mentoring, academic and professional development activities, a community of peers for friendship and academic support, and exposure to the issues and applications of CS. Our hope is that for first-year undergraduate women who are interested in majoring in CS, participation in the LLC will lead to participants declaring a CS major and persisting in the major.

Living-learning communities are programs based in college residence halls that link students' living environments with a particular academic theme or topic, supported by access to additional academic resources and support. LLCs have been shown to have a positive impact on undergraduate students in their first year and to provide students with a deeper and more integrated learning experience [9, 22, 24]. Living-learning communities for women in STEM have been shown to have positive impacts [14] and are considered a best practice by the Association of American Colleges and Universities, the National Science Foundation, the National Academies, and the American Association for University Women [1, 5, 8, 10]. Participation in living-learning programs has been shown to benefit undergraduates in both academic and social contexts including the transition to college, first-year retention, grade point average, civic engagement, critical thinking, and engaging in deep intellectual inquiry [3, 11, 15, 16, 20, 21, 25, 27]. Participating in an LLC is significantly and positively related to all significant types of student engagement, and increasing student engagement is in turn strongly related to educational gains [11, 12, 19, 20, 29]. There is also strong evidence that the primary benefits of LLCs are due to the indirect impact of the increased educational engagement that LLCs provide [13].

In computer science, revisiting the introductory sequence in computing to include a focus on big ideas and applications of value to society has been showing success in increasing and diversifying participation and excitement [4, 23]. There has also been research showing that women have better retention in the major if they have opportunities to work in small groups or pairs, and that pairs produce better results in any case [28]. Community-building, leadership, and outreach activities have also proven successful in promoting women's engagement in computing [7]. Our program incorporates these aspects.

In order to understand the impact of the program on women's engagement and persistence in computer science, a significant component of the project is the research and evaluation of the CS LLC and its impact on its participants. In this paper, we describe our living-learning community for women in computer science and our experiences with it after two cohorts of students (with the third currently participating as of this writing), in hopes that others might consider developing such programs at their own institutions.

2 LLC PROGRAM AND PLANNING

LLC participants live together in the same wing of one floor of a residence hall during their first year as undergraduates, and actively participate in required and optional program activities. The LLC program is supported by a staff program director, a faculty advisor, a graduate mentor, and a peer academic leader (PAL). The PAL is an upper-class student in a computing major that lives with the LLC participants. The PAL provides mentoring and academic support in the residence hall and serves as an immediate resource for LLC members. The graduate mentor is a graduate student in a computing major that assists with the operation of the LLC by helping students with their coursework and mentoring them on career development. Starting with cohort 2, we added a "big-little" mentoring program where earlier LLC students (LLC Bigs) could mentor first-year LLC students, and we arrange to hold special CS1 office hours for the LLC students. Our program draws on resources available in the CS department, the Douglass Residential College (formerly an undergraduate women's college within the university, now an intellectual community and residential program for undergraduate women within the university who chose to participate, henceforth referred to as DRC), and other parts of the university.

After their first year, LLC participants can remain connected to the program by participating as mentors in the "big-little" mentoring program, participating in selected program events, and through the social media group for all program cohorts. The social media group provides notice of various opportunities to participate in CS-related activities at Rutgers and elsewhere, including information about potential internships and research opportunities. Students also use it to communicate across cohorts.

Our program had 18 students in cohort 1 (academic year (AY) 2016–2017) and 20 students in cohort 2 (AY 2017-2018). Cohort 3, for AY 2018–2019, has 23 students. As we gain experience with the program and make improvements based on that experience, we envision growing the program size, perhaps up to as many as 40–50 students per year. Our expectation is that the program should be scalable to that size with only marginal increases in necessary resources. We describe our program as we have carried it out; we believe that an effective program could take place with somewhat fewer resources, such as having a single student take on the role of the PAL and the graduate mentor.

As a necessary component, running the program requires the ability to reach, and communicate with, students before they arrive on campus. It also requires communication with the housing office in order to reserve space in an appropriate residence hall and ensure the CS LLC student participants are placed there. Students in our LLC are recruited from a pool of women intending to major in CS, as indicated in their admission applications, who have been accepted into the university. Some participants have indicated that they were motivated to choose Rutgers because of the LLC. We advertise the program as part of the general admissions and recruitment process, which includes mailing and emailing marketing materials, phone calls, open houses/tours, and participation of LLC leadership in academic planning and advising days. Students must enroll at Rutgers before they can officially apply to the LLC, typically at the time that they make their on-campus housing requests. So far, we have followed the practice of accepting all eligible students who apply for the LLC until the available program slots have been filled. The program director also works with the enrollment management office to secure student scholarships for all women participating in the program as an additional benefit to LLC participants and as part of our institution's commitment to enhancing gender diversity in STEM, though this is not always possible and does not seem to be a necessary component of the program.

The program director and the faculty advisor recruit the graduate mentor, the PAL, and the LLC Bigs. For training them, we draw on the resources and experiences of DRC, which trains a larger group of graduate mentors, PALs, and Bigs. The director also works directly with other institutional offices to ensure an exceptional academic experience for the students. In collaboration with the academic advising office, students in the LLC are registered in the appropriate computer science and prerequisite or co-requisite math courses during their first semester at Rutgers. They are also given the opportunity to participate in an LLC-specific study group through our collaboration with the Rutgers Learning Center. All students have the same opportunity to participate in similar study groups for CS1 and CS2; our intervention here is to keep the LLC participants in the same study group.

The students in the LLC participate in a variety of academic, professional, and community building opportunities. Activities are a mix of events developed specifically for the LLC and those open to a broader audience (e.g., all DRC students), allowing the students to feel part of their own smaller community and the larger communities at, and beyond, our university. Professional development events range from general programs for women in STEM to CS-targeted networking opportunities and conferences. These are mostly organized by the director with assistance from the graduate mentor. Academic opportunities include the Bigs' office hours, study groups, study sessions for final exams, and the LLC's house course taught by the faculty advisor. Community-building opportunities are offered at multiple levels. The PAL organizes multiple activities within the residence hall while all LLC staff assist in the planning of larger community-building event, such as a welcome gathering and an end-of-year celebration.

In AY 2017–2018, there were 18 ongoing activities and events. In addition to those already mentioned, these include:

- **Study Smarter, Not Harder**: In collaboration with an on-campus learning center, students review a variety of study strategies that activate various types of learning used across multiple disciplines.
- **Douglass Project Open House**: This program introduces all DRC students in STEM to the Douglass Project for Women in STEM, including Douglass Project staff, programs, and resources available to the students.
- **DRC Career Conference**: This day-long conference is designed to educate DRC undergrads about career opportunities in particular industries and cross-cutting skills like networking and interviewing. The presenters are primarily Douglass alumnae, as well as other faculty and staff, and industry and nonprofit partners who work with DRC. Students hear from successful women (and some successful men) about their career paths.
- **CS Industry Leader Meet and Greet**: An opportunity for computer science students to meet a CS Industry leading figure. In Fall 2017, the speaker was a senior cybersecurity professional at the MITRE Corporation.
- **De-Stress Fest (Fall and Spring)**: The De-Stress Fest aims to foster community engagement before the end of the semester and provide a "stress-free" outlet for students to unwind.
- **C.A.V.E. Tour**: A private tour of the C.A.V.E. (Collaborative Academic Versatile Environment) offered to demonstrate the facilities and resources available to all CS students. The space is attached to the Computer Science department's instructional labs and is designed to provide a place for student informal tutoring, collaboration, and independent exploration of CS.
- **HackHERS**: HackHERS is the annual, woman-centric hackathon at our university, organized by the Women in Computer Science club and the Douglass Project for Women in STEM.
- **Networking Night**: The goal of this event is to provide an opportunity for DRC women to practice their networking skills and develop valuable connections with participating professionals.
- **Trip to Industry**: This one-day field trip provides the opportunity for students to meet professionals in the field of computing and technology and ask questions related to their respective career trajectories and work experience, while receiving a tour of their facilities.

In the fall of their first year, students enroll in the DRC class *Knowledge and Power* required for all DRC women. In the spring, they enroll in the "house course" for the LLC, *Great Ideas and Applications in Computer Science*, taught by their faculty advisor. This one-credit seminar course is designed to ensure that the LLC students have a shared class experience, to connect some of the topics students are learning in CS1 and CS2 to broader applications of CS, and to make thematic connections between various aspects of CS. The course includes high-level discussion of examples demonstrating how CS can have a positive impact on a wide variety of applications including everyday social problems; advanced science, engineering, and medical applications; journalism and politics; and commercial applications. The course also uses a few more detailed examples to highlight how underlying computational ideas such as abstraction, algorithms, and large-scale data processing play a role in these applications, as well as how programming is the enabler that turns these ideas into working systems. Students prepare brief presentations at the end of the semester on a CS-related project or topic of the students' choice, which can be a new project or something done in another course or as an extracurricular activity; students can work alone or in groups of two or three.

Students are connected to a variety of other CS-related opportunities and resources, including the Grace Hopper Celebration of Computing, a "Computing Corps" that provides CS outreach activities to middle school girls, opportunities for mentored research experiences, a variety of computing-related clubs, and CRA-W's Virtual Undergraduate Town Hall series.

3 OUR EXPERIENCE WITH TWO COHORTS

To understand the effectiveness of the LLC program and gain insight into the successes and potential improvements, we partnered with the Computing Research Association's Center for Evaluating the Research Pipeline (CERP), a research and evaluation center that collects and analyzes national survey data [26]. This paper is primarily about our experiences to date, including an overview in this section of our initial research findings. We hope to share more detailed research findings when they are more mature.

3.1 Evaluation Design

The LLC program was evaluated using a repeated measures quasi-experimental design that included both qualitative and quantitative methods to evaluate the efficacy of the program on participants' expected outcomes based on the goals of the program. LLC participants and a comparison group were surveyed at both the beginning (Time 1) and end (Time 2) of the AY. At the end of the AY, university staff held focus groups with LLC participants. CERP also carried out follow-up interviews with some members of cohort 1. Specifically, we describe the results of evaluation activities carried out according to the following schedule:

	Time 1 Survey	Time 2 Survey	Focus Group	Follow-up Interviews
Cohort 1	Oct/Nov'16	Apr'17	May'17	Jun'17
Cohort 2	Sep/Oct'17	Apr/May'18	Apr'18	N/A

LLC participants were recruited by LLC staff to complete CERP's survey. To recruit the comparison group of women each year, a flyer was shared with CS1 students inviting eligible students to participate in the study. Interested students emailed a CERP liaison and were screened for eligibility. Potential comparison group students were eligible for the survey if they were not part of the CS LLC and identified themselves as first-year students, women, and interested in majoring in CS.[1] Students who completed CERP's surveys were

[1] A possible limitation is that we did not include a requirement for living in an on-campus residential hall, which may make the comparison group less similar. We will require this for future comparison group eligibility.

given a $20 Amazon eGift card for each survey completed (Fall and Spring) as part of their participation in the study.

The CERP survey asked questions related to students' career goals and aspirations, sense of belonging and confidence in their abilities to succeed in computing, participation in various extra-curricular or co-curricular activities, and satisfaction with their departments. Interviews and focus groups with LLC participants collected further details more specific to the LLC program. We overview our initial research findings for cohorts 1 and 2 in Sections 3.2 and 3.3, respectively. Quantitative results were generated using one-way Anaysis of Variance (ANOVA) and repeated measures ANOVA.

3.2 Evaluation Results: Cohort 1

Cohort 1, beginning AY 2016–2017, initially comprised 18 students. One student went on medical leave early in the fall semester and did not participate in the evaluation activities. Accordingly, these results only include $n = 17$ LLC participants. The cohort 1 comparison group comprised $n = 34$ students. The self-reported demographics of both groups are as follows:

	Asian	Black	White	Multi Other	U.S. Citizen
Participants	53%	12%	29%	6%	71%
Comparison	79%	3%	15%	3%	79%

3.2.1 Cohort 1: Survey Results. Before measuring changes from Time 1 to Time 2, CERP examined Time 1 data to understand if the LLC group and the comparison group differed in any of the outcomes in this study. Time 1 data indicated that LLC participants and comparison students were statistically equivalent on most outcomes in this study, with the following exceptions:

- **The comparison group** was more interested in pursuing an interdisciplinary non-research career and more satisfied with the computing program at the university than LLC students.
- **LLC participants** reported more mentor support and were more involved in some computing-related activites than the comparison group.

Next, we measured whether students' responses at Time 2 differed from Time 1. Results indicated LLC and comparison groups reported statistically equivalent change over time on most outcomes in this study. Exceptions included the following:

- **LLC participants** reported stronger beliefs that computing ability is inborn; the comparison group showed no change.
- **LLC participants** reported less satisfaction with computing courses at the university and perceived a less supportive environment in the computing department over time; the comparison group showed no change.
- **LLC participants** participated in more conferences and attended more lectures during the school year than the comparison group.
- **LLC participants** show a significant decrease in computing self-efficacy over time. The comparison group also shows a decrease in computing self-efficacy over time, albeit to a lesser degree than LLC participants.

3.2.2 Cohort 1: Focus Group Results. A research faculty member held a focus group with four LLC participants before the end of the AY. Focus group participants spoke very positively about the LLC and its impact on their college experience. They also spoke highly of the faculty, staff, and mentors associated with the program; however, participants noted they did not know the graduate mentor well, which may be because she was not hired at the start of the program and she was not available on weekends.

Completing the sentence "*My year in the LLC has...*," participants said the following:

... *"enhanced my drive in continuing with CS because I have a group of people for support."*

... *"impacted me so much. As an international student, I can't imagine how my first year would be without the LLC. In such a big campus, making close friends is hard. With the LLC's impact, I am more confident about my academic goal."*

... *"been truly an amazing experience. I couldn't have asked for a better first year experience. ... "*

... *"[was] a year full of amazing support and new friendships that will last a lifetime."*

3.2.3 Cohort 1: Interview Results. CERP carried out interviews with five LLC participants via phone or Skype in June 2017. Questions were framed to gain insight into how the LLC might have contributed to participants' low satisfaction with the CS department, beliefs about the nature of computing ability, and low computing self-efficacy.

When asked for their opinions about the CS department, interviewees had both positive and negative things to say, including:

"I would recommend this department to a senior in high school. I like how welcoming some professors and organizations (USACS) could be. They are willing to help as long as you come prepared with questions."

"... [the department doesn't] like to encourage group work. Sometimes group work is the best way to succeed, like getting other people's opinions and ideas and working together."

Interviewees indicated they were not confident when they started college, even those with some CS pre-college background. Some also talked about how participating in the LLC helped boost their confidence:

"[When I started college, I was] scared! Everyone said CS was hard, and I barely knew anything. I took AP classes, but I didn't learn much from it. So I didn't take the exam or anything."

"I was definitely scared. After doing the LLC, I realized that pretty much everyone is the same. Pretty much everyone doesn't know anything. So I feel better. ... If I didn't join the LLC, I probably would have worked alone, so I probably would have stopped like halfway. ... I feel like I can handle it now with my peers. And if it's by myself, I would definitely give up."

Regarding beliefs about the nature of computing intelligence, some aspects of the responses showed a growth mindset, while others indicate a belief that computing skills come more naturally to some people than others:

"It's not like you're born with it. You practice it, you learn the skill. The more you practice, the more you will get used to it. . . . So I think it's a muscle training thing. . . . At the beginning of the year, I felt like some people [were] just good at it . . . But later on, I realized everyone is just the same. People start from the introduction classes, and [now I feel like] I can handle it."

"I initially thought computing skills is something you are born with, like everyone must be super good coders because they were born with this ability to think and process a certain way. But I think after taking my first intro classes, I've moved on from that. I am starting to see that it's not something people are born with, but it's something they have learned through thinking a specific way or through practicing the process."

Students talked at length about positive impacts of the LLC including the sense of community, access to information and resources, and mentorship:

"I would recommend this LLC for high school students. [Regarding] Douglass as a woman in this field, I felt kind of alone before I came in. Because everyone is saying CS is really hard for a woman. Even my mom still doesn't think it's a good idea. But after doing this LLC I feel really supported. Actually there are a lot of women like me doing the same thing, so I would recommend women do this."

"I've had girls who weren't in the LLC write me and say "you guys are so lucky, I wish I signed up for this, it's always nice to have a community..."

"The peer leader would always encourage us to take CS no matter what. She would always help us with any questions or concerns we had. I think it was helpful to have someone our age giving us advice."

"In the LLC we would also talk about if we weren't in the LLC we didn't think we would have continued with CS. . . . This community has helped me especially make it through to study CS. . . . I think it was the fact that I was able to work with a group of women going through the same struggles as me, understanding what I was feeling, was a really important thing to succeed. And I was able to find people who are not only good to work with in school, but good friends."

Participants also noted that they felt the LLC suffered due to some participants who didn't significantly engage with the group and weren't as interested in CS from the start:

"There was a group of us that I was in, like 10-12 people that connected very well. There were a few people who kind of stayed to themselves. . . . We tried to get everyone involved but it's hard. . . . We would do activities and a lot of them wouldn't show up."

"My roommate didn't know she was part of the LLC [upon arriving to campus in the fall]. Maybe it was because she was an international student, but I thought the person I was living with would be part of the LLC, and then I asked her and she said "I'm not even sure I want to do CS" I was like... Ok. It was a weird experience because I wasn't sure who was part of the LLC. Some people weren't sure what they signed up for."

Based on feedback from the cohort 1 participants as well as our direct experiences with the program, we made changes to ensure that the LLC participants understood that the program was directed to women wanting to major in computer science and that participants were intended to be an active part of the community. To this end, we began requiring LLC applicants to write a few sentences about why they want to study computer science and why they want to be in the LLC program.

3.3 Evaluation Results: Cohort 2

Cohort 2, beginning AY 2017–2018, initially comprised 20 students; however, one student went on leave in the fall semester and was not included in the analysis. Another student joined the program during the spring and was not included in survey distribution or the original cohort count. With changes in participants and non-response from two other students, the final sample for cohort 2 was $n = 17$ LLC students and $n = 32$ comparison group students. The self-reported demographics of both groups are as follows:

	Asian	Black	White	Multi Other	U.S. Citizen
Participants	65%	6%	0%	30%	75%
Comparison	77%	0%	20%	3%	77%

3.3.1 Cohort 2: Survey Results. Prior to examining any changes from Time 1 to Time 2 among cohort 2 students, we looked at differences between the comparison group and LLC participants at Time 1. Results were similar to findings for cohort 1. For most measures, both groups were statistically equivalent with the following exception:

- **LLC participants** reported stronger mentor support than the comparison group.

Next, we examined changes over time; results yielded both positive and concerning findings:

- **LLC participants** were more likely than the comparison group to indicate they intended to pursue their highest degree in a computing field at both Time 1 and Time 2.
- A higher proportion of **LLC participants** stayed in their CS major over time (88%) than the comparison group (53%).
- **LLC participants** reported stronger levels of mentorship overall than the comparison group.
- **LLC participants** reported more involvement in computing related activites (e.g., conferences, lectures by women, student groups).
- Both **LLC participants and comparison students** reported the following to the same degree over time:
  - weaker computing self-efficacy.
  - weaker belief that a career in computing could afford them opportunities to serve humanity and be in a position of influence in society.
  - stronger beliefs that computing ability is inborn.
  - stronger interest in non-computing careers.
  - less satisfaction with the computing program.
  - stronger feelings of threat.
  - weaker department support.
- While **LLC participants** reported overall stronger mentor support and peer support than the comparison group, an interaction effect revealed that LLC participants's perceived mentor support was weaker at Time 2 while the **comparison group's** perceived mentor support was stronger at Time 2.

3.3.2 Cohort 2: Focus Group Results. As with cohort 1, we held a focus group at the end of the spring semester with 14 LLC cohort 2 participants. Major findings from the focus group are as follows:

- Students shared positive evaluations of all staff associated with the LLC. Suggestions for improvement largely focus on programmatic and structural elements, such as more resources and clearer guidelines for how to use resources.
- The LLC is important for helping participants make connections with other students. This facet could be further strengthened, with student suggestions for improving the connectedness of students to one another and to computer science including: more hands-on activities, study groups, assignment to the same course sections, continued physical proximity after the first year, and additional events for the group.
- LLC participants were overwhelmingly positive about the role of their PAL peer mentor. They did not seem to benefit from peer mentoring relationships with the members of cohort 1.
- Students very much appreciated the trip to the tech firm in NYC and viewed it as a positive opportunity for both individual and cohort development.

Students were asked what aspects of the program worked well. The following quotes are examples from that discussion:

"*[The visit to the tech company] worked because we all came together, and we all saw where we can be in the future if we work hard ... it opened our eyes up to why we should continue.*"

"*[Living in the LLC] kept me more in touch with my major. Although there aren't a lot of resources, there are more than one would get if they were not a part of LLC.*"

One woman who described herself as shy said the LLC helped her make close friends and that—in a positive way—she is "*literally completely different*" than she was in high school. Asked to explain, she said participating in the LLC: "*made me realize that this is the person I am.*" An international student noted that when she came to the university, she knew no one, but that living in the LLC helped her make friends: "*I know people, I am making friends, I feel like, ok, I am not alone.*"

Suggestions for improvement from participants included the following:

- Clarify the role of the graduate mentor.
- More hands-on activities in the house course.
- Hold the house course during the fall semester.

4 LESSONS LEARNED AND FUTURE PLANS

Overall, evaluation findings between cohorts 1 and 2 suggest that while the program has not made dramatic impacts on students' outcomes over time, LLC participants describe the program as being important to them, and tend to report more mentor support than other women who are not in the LLC program. LLC participants also seem to have stronger intentions to persist in CS than the comparison group. However, both the LLC participants and the comparison group show concerning trends over time, which we will continue to address in coming years.

Since the psychological and aspirational outcomes decreased over time for both groups of women, we speculate that the reason for this decline is likely not due to women's participation in the LLC program. Instead, the research findings point to a potentially larger issue that affects first-year women in CS broadly at Rutgers (as well as possibly men and students at other institutions). These results also imply that the LLC program does not act as a "buffer" to environmental or cultural threats to the extent we might have expected. On the positive front, LLC women were more likely than the comparison group to report engagement in extracurricular activities related to women in computing. Engagement in these activities may help women's persistence in the long-term, because activities like conferences and groups for women expose students to real-world contexts, research innovations, and opportunities to broaden their professional networks. Nonetheless, simply continuing to increase engagement through an increased number of activities may not be a good approach because of the increased time commitment. We will work to understand these tradeoffs and relationships better in future assessments.

As a result of our cohort 1 evaluation findings, we modified our recruitment process to ensure that students understand that the program is intended for students who plan to major in CS (even if they have not yet had formal computing experience). Additionally, we are tracking the academic progression of students in the LLC to determine whether or not they persist through the CS intro sequence and ultimately declare a CS major. Students cannot declare a CS major at our institution until they have successfully completed this sequence, so we are only just now beginning to see some cohort 1 students declare a CS major.

We also made some changes regarding the graduate student mentor, as students from both cohorts felt they were unable to get to know the graduate mentor very well. During the second year, we ensured that the graduate mentor was hired by the start of the program, but evaluation findings show we still have room for improvement. We will continue to find more ways to foster interaction between LLC participants and the graduate mentor. Another lesson learned related to the need to be resilient to administrative delays outside of our control, as these caused disruption to our plans in multiple ways. Based on the excitement students reported in visiting local companies, and because the first cohort is now reaching the point in their studies where they interested in internships and thinking about post-college employment opportunities, we are working to have more interaction with industry. For example, we are looking to include additional student visits to industry sites, and we plan to hold panels and other activities on campus with tech industry participants.

The "big-little" mentoring of cohort 1 by cohort 2 was not as robust as we would like for this mentoring program. In the coming year, we are hoping to improve this aspect of the program through training sessions for the mentors from earlier cohorts and inviting them to participate in the welcome event and other selected LLC activities. Ideally, these modifications will enable the big-little mentoring program to serve two valuable purposes: providing additional mentoring for each new cohort and keeping earlier cohorts closely connected to the program.

Future work will continue to monitor the program and its participants in partnership with CERP. We will continue to make changes to the program based on evaluation results and seek a better understanding of the factors that may contribute to concerning results learned during the evaluation process. Because of the modest size of our program, the evaluation findings suffer from small sample sizes in each cohort. Combining samples over multiple years as the program progresses will yield larger sample sizes, allowing for a more reliable analysis than we can currently have. Larger sample sizes will also allow for the analysis of results based on demographic groups, which may also help explain some of the results to date.

We will continue to examine the impact of the LLC program with the third cohort. CERP has revisited the survey instrument to incorporate other measures that may point more directly to outcomes of the LLC program and ensure survey items are relevant to the respondents. If possible, CERP may also follow up with the first cohort of LLC and comparison students through surveys and/or interviews to understand if there are any long-term impacts of the LLC program undetected by the short-term results. Using CERP's Data Buddies Survey [26], we may also add a comparison group of men from our university to determine whether men demonstrate a similar downward trend from the start to the end of the academic year on psychological and aspirational outcomes, as well as compare our results with first-year students at other schools. With cohort 4, we plan to grow the program to 24-30 students.

As the early LLC cohorts reach the point of declaring majors, we will also track various kinds of retention and success: what proportion stay at Rutgers, declare and persist in a CS major or related major, how do they perform academically, what they go on to do after their undergraduate degree, and how do these compare to other students. Additionally, we will continue to seek more ways to keep the LLC participants engaged in the community as they progress through their time at Rutgers, as well as ways for current students to engage with graduated LLC participants (once we have them).

We hope that others may learn from our experience to develop similar programs at their institutions. Our program built heavily on the experience of DRC in running LLCs for women in other STEM areas, and we recommend that institutions draw on the specific resources at their institutions. In addition, we hope that knowledge from our program will smooth the pathway for programs even at institutions that do not have something like DRC to draw on. Ultimately, we hope this living-learning community—and others that might be developed like it—will help diversify the computing workforce by inspiring and motivating new generations of students to pursue degrees in CS and careers in technology broadly defined.

ACKNOWLEDGMENTS

This work was funded by the National Science Foundation under grant #1504775.

REFERENCES

[1] National Academies. 2007. *Beyond Bias and Barriers: Fulfilling the Potential of Women in Academic Science and Engineering.* The National Academies Press.

[2] National Academies. 2018. *Assessing and Responding to the Growth of Computer Science Undergraduate Enrollments.* The National Academies Press.

[3] C. Allen. 1999. Wiser women: Fostering undergraduate success in science and engineering with a residential academic program. *Journal of Women and Minorities in Science and Engineering* 5, 3 (1999), 265–277.

[4] Christine Alvarado, Zachary Dodds, and Ran Libeskind-Hadas. 2012. Increasing Women's Participation in Computing at Harvey Mudd College. *ACM Inroads* 3, 4 (2012), 55–64.

[5] Jayne E. Brownell and Lynne E. Swaner. 2010. *Five high-impact practices: Research on learning outcomes, completion and quality.* Association of American Colleges and Universities.

[6] S. Cheryan, V.C. Plaut, P.G. Davies, and C.M. Steele. 2009. Ambient belonging: How stereotypical cues impact gender participation in computer science. *Journal of Personality and Social Psychology* 97 (2009), 1045–1060.

[7] Teresa Dahlberg, Tiffany Barnes, Kim Buch, and Karen Bean. 2010. Applying service learning to computer science; attracting and engaging underrepresented students. *Computer Science Education* 20, 3 (2010), 169–180.

[8] National Science Foundation. 2003. *New Formulas for America's Workforce: Girls in Science and Engineering.* National Science Foundation.

[9] Faith Gabelnick, Jean MacGregor, Roberta S. Matthews, and Barbara Leigh Smith. 1990. Learning Community Models). *New directions for teaching and learning* 41 (1990), 19–37.

[10] Catherine Hill, Christianne Corbett, and Andresse St. Rose. 2010. *Why so Few? Women in Science, Technology, Engineering, and Mathematics.* American Association of University Women.

[11] K.K. Inkelas, Z.E. Daver, K.E. Vogt, and J.B. Leonard. 2007. Living-Learning programs and first-generation college students' academic and social transition to college. *Research in Higher Education* 48, 4 (2007), 403–434.

[12] Karen Kurotsuchi Inkelas. 2004. Does participation in ethnic cocurricular activities facilitate a sense of ethnic awareness and understanding? A study of Asian Pacific American undergraduates. *Journal of College Student Development* 45, 3 (2004), 285–302.

[13] Karen Kurotsuchi Inkelas. 2008. *National study of Living-Learning programs: 2007 report of findings.* Technical Report http://hdl.handle.net/1903/8392. University of Maryland.

[14] Karen Kurotsuchi Inkelas. 2011. Living-learning programs for women in STEM. *New Directions for Institutional Research* 152 (2011), 27–37.

[15] K. K. Inkelas, K.E. Vogt, S.D. Longerbeam, J. Owen, and D. Johnson. 2006. Measuring outcomes of living-learning programs: Examining college environments and student learning and development. *The Journal of General Education* 55, 1 (2006), 40–76.

[16] Karen Kurotsuch Inkelas and Jennifer L. Weisman. 2003. Different by design: An examination of student outcomes among participants in three types of Living-Learning programs. *Journal of College Student Development* 44, 3 (2003), 335–368.

[17] Karyn L. Lewis, Jane G. Stout, Noah D. Finkelstein, Steven J. Pollock, Akira Miyake, Geoff L. Cohen, and Tiffany A. Ito. 2017. Fitting in to Move Forward: Belonging, Gender, and Persistence in the Physical Sciences, Technology, Engineering, and Mathematics (pSTEM). *Psychology of Women Quarterly* 41, 4 (2017).

[18] Jane Margolis, Allan Fisher, and Faye Miller. 2000. The anatomy of interest. *Women's Studies Quarterly* 28, 1/2 (2000), 104–127.

[19] Gary Pike, George Kuh, and Alexander McCormick. 2011. An investigation of the contingent relationships between learning community participation and student engagement. *Research in Higher Education* 52, 3 (2011), 300–322.

[20] Gary R. Pike. 1999. The effects of residential learning communities and traditional residential living arrangements on educational gains during the first year of college. *Journal of College Student Development* 40, 3 (1999), 269–284.

[21] Louis Rocconi. 2011. The impact of learning communities on first year students' growth and development in college. *Research in Higher Education* 52, 2 (2011), 178–193.

[22] Nancy S. Shapiro and Jodi H. Levine. 1999. *Creating Learning Communities: A Practical Guide to Winning Support, Organizing for Change, and Implementing Programs.* Jossey-Bass.

[23] Lawrence Snyder, Tiffany Barnes, Dan Garcia, Jody Paul, and Beth Simon. 2012. The First Five Computer Science Principles Pilots: Summary and Comparisons. *ACM Inroads* 3, 2 (2012), 54–57.

[24] Matthew Soldner, Heather Rowan-Kenyon, Karen K.urotsuchi Inkelas, Jason Garvey, and Claire Robbins. 2012. Supporting students' intentions to persist in STEM disciplines: The role of living-learning programs among other social-cognitive factors. *The Journal of Higher Education* 83, 3 (2012), 311–336.

[25] Martha L. A. Stassen. 2003. Student outcomes: The impact of varying living-learning community models. *Research in Higher Education* 44, 5 (2003), 581–613.

[26] Jane Stout. 2013. Center for Evaluating the Research Pipeline (CERP): Providing a New Way to Evaluate Diversity Initiatives in Computing Research. *Computing Research News* 25, 7 (Aug. 2013). https://cra.org/crn/category/2013/vol-25no-7/

[27] Katalin Szelenyi and Karen Kurotsuchi Inkelas. 2011. The role of living-learning programs in women's plans to attend graduate school in STEM fields. *Research in Higher Education* 52, 4 (2011), 349–369.

[28] Linda Werner, Brian Hanks, and Charlie McDowell. 2004. Pair-Programming Helps Female Computer Science Students. *ACM Journal of Educational Resources in Computing* 4, 1 (2004).

[29] Chum-Mei Zhao and George Kuh. 2004. Adding value: Learning communities and student engagement. *Research in Higher Education* 45, 2 (2004), 115–138.

[30] Stuart Zweben and Betsy Bizot. 2018. 2017 CRA Taulbee Survey: Another Year of Record Undergrad Enrollment; Doctoral Degree Production Steady While Master's Production Rises Again. *Computing Research News* 30, 5 (May 2018). https://cra.org/crn/category/2018/vol-30-no-5/

Achieving Gender Balance through Creative Expression

William H. Bares, Bill Manaris, Renée McCauley, Christine Moore
Computer Science
College of Charleston
Charleston SC USA
{BaresWH | ManarisB | McCauleyR | MooreC}@cofc.edu

ABSTRACT

Increasing gender balance in computing is widely recognized by academic institutions, industry, and government agencies as an imperative. This paper describes how providing opportunities for creative expression early on and throughout the four years of an undergraduate computing degree achieves this goal. Prior studies have demonstrated that opportunity for creative expression has a positive effect on recruitment and retention of women, while conversely, lack of opportunity for creative expression has a negative effect. We describe our approach, integrated into a four-course sequence combining computing and the arts, so that other institutions may consider adopting it. Results of a six-year longitudinal study show that these courses attract, retain, and graduate 46% female students, while the corresponding number in our ABET-accredited Computer Science curriculum is approximately 20%. The paper concludes with general observations and suggests directions for future action in CS curricula design.

CCS CONCEPTS

• Computing Milieux • Computers and Education • Computer and Information Science Education

KEYWORDS

Creativity, art, contextualized computing, broadening participation, curriculum

ACM Reference format:

William Bares, Bill Manaris, Renée McCauley, and Christine Moore. 2019. Achieving Gender Balance through Creative Expression. In *Proceedings of ACM Special Interest Group on Computer Science Education (SIGCSE'19)* February 27-March 2, 2019, Minneapolis, MN, USA, *ACM, NY, NY, USA, 7 pages.* https://doi.org/10.1145/1234567890

1 Introduction

"Why, with so much sustained effort by so many individuals and organizations, is progress toward gender equity so slow?", Tims wonders in [32]. In particular, the national graduation rate of female students in computer science is close to 20% (i.e., 17.9% according to the Taulbee Survey [36] or 22.1% according to the ACM-NDC Survey [32]). This paper describes our experiences, over a six-year period, to achieve gender balance in computing.

The literature is full of articles offering perspectives and potential remedies to this gender balance problem. Some of these articles show that integrating creative expression with computer science results in courses that are often gender-balanced. For instance, Georgia Tech's bachelor's degree in Computational Media is reported to have 45.3% female enrollment, compared to 17.91% in the computer science degree [19]. Similarly, Barker reports that the Technology, Arts, & Media degree at the University of Colorado, Boulder has a 44.8% female enrollment [2, 3].

1.1 Our Experience – Computing in the Arts

At our institution, a six-year longitudinal study shows that our Computing in the Arts (CITA) degree attracts, retains, and graduates 46% female students, compared to approximately 20% in our ABET-accredited computer science (CSCI) degree. These figures were collected by analyzing anonymized course enrollment and graduation data supplied by our Office of Institutional Research. See [1] for further details of the study methodology and limitations. At the core of this CITA degree is a sequence of semester-long creative experiences that synthesize computing and one or more arts areas (music, visual art, theatre, or digital media). These synthesis courses are designed to ensure that students learn to use computational techniques, in general, and computer programming, in particular. Learning computer programming is central. It is used as a medium to create avant-garde artistic experiences, as well as to develop innovative computer applications informed / guided by artistic theory and practice.

More precisely, Table 1 shows enrollments by gender in CITA synthesis courses, over a six-year period, against comparable CSCI courses. These are comparable pairs of required courses, taken by respective majors (CITA and CSCI), during the freshman, sophomore, junior, and senior years. As can be seen, CITA courses consistently attract a higher percentage of female students than the corresponding CSCI courses. It should be noted that, while these CITA courses are required for CITA majors, the first- and second-year CITA courses are also frequently taken by non-majors. CITA majors also take CS1 and CS2, so they impact the higher percentages of female students in those courses as well. We also found that 44% of non-computing students who choose

SIGCSE '19, February 27-March 2, 2019, Minneapolis, MN, USA.

ACM ISBN 978-1-4503-5890-3/19/02...$15.00
https://doi.org/10.1145/1234567890

to enroll in a first-year CITA synthesis course are Arts or Business majors, while 49% of non-computing students attracted to CS1 are Lab Sciences and Math majors. Based on the first course alone, CITA appears to attract a different population from that of our Computer Science degree program [1].

Table 1. Enrollments in synthesis courses (2011-2017)

CITA Synthesis Courses				CSCI Courses			
Course	*F*	*M*	***F%***	*Course*	*F*	*M*	***F%***
Synth1	224	384	**36.8**	CS1	350	860	**28.9**
Synth2	50	107	**31.9**	CS2	217	650	**25.0**
Seminar	24	37	**39.4**	Soft Arch	56	241	**18.9**
Capstone	21	27	**43.8**	Practicum	45	199	**18.4**

This paper complements and completes the reporting in [1] by providing detailed information on the synthesis courses, so that other institutions may explore adopting this approach. This paper is organized as follows. Section 2 explores foundational, creative computing courses which influenced the design of the CITA synthesis courses. Section 3 describes the contents of the courses in detail for potential replication. Section 4 discusses how other institutions may apply similar approaches (and possibly degrees). Finally, Section 5 adds concluding remarks.

2 Foundations

2.1 Contextualized Computing

Contextualized computing focuses on applying computation in a particular domain of interest. Accordingly, contextualized computing pedagogy focuses on providing well-designed educational experiences that teach computing to develop applications in a particular context (e.g., Physics, or Media). Guzdial [17] describes the rationale for contextualized computing as follows:

> A context provides relevance and improves retention. Students are more likely to stick around if they understand the value of what they're learning. There is no evidence that they learn the material better, but they're more likely to be around in the second class, even if that's a normal decontextualized course. [p. 6]

Contextualized computing courses have been designed to overcome the perceptions among students that computer science is too abstract, emphasizes tedious details, and offers limited opportunities for creative expression. Cooper and Cunningham describe different efforts under the umbrella of contextualized computing, which aim to engage and retain students in learning computer science [10]. Uludag et al. [35] explore the combination of complementary technologies to increase appeal to broad audiences and attract both non-majors and majors. They incorporate visual programming with Scratch, App Inventor for mobile phones, and LEGO Mindstorms for robotics and engineering. La Marche [22] presents a contextualized-computing course centered on user-interface design. He discusses how contextual pedagogy may "lower failure rates, improve retention, increase student self-efficacy regarding programming, and increase positive views about computer science."

A major contribution in the area is by Guzdial [16], who along with various collaborators [14, 25, 28] introduced the concept of Media Computation [18]. This led to a Media Computation "movement" consisting of a large community of educators adopting Guzdial's pedagogical materials and introducing computer programming in the context of the arts. This resulted in our first contextualized-computing course offered in Fall 2006. Our course combined Python, fractals, L-Systems, and jMusic (a Java-based system for composing music with computers). Initially called "Media Computation", we soon renamed it "Computers, Music, and Art" (Fall 2007). Eventually, this became one of our required introductory courses in our computing in the arts degree (further discussed in section 3).

Overall, media computing courses have demonstrated lower failure rates compared to traditional computer science courses [12, 26, 29]. Media computation courses have induced greater interest in students to take additional media computation courses [13, 29, 30]. Guzdial reports results of a 10-year study of a media computation course showing a drop-rate of 12% (compared to 50% for conventional CS1). This course achieved a 40% enrollment of female students, with no notable differences in performance by gender. In a multi-year study, a combination of courses including media computation demonstrated an 18% improvement in retention one year later. This eventually led to development of the Georgia Tech Bachelor's degree in Computational Media, which in 2014 was reported to have 45.32% female enrollment as compared to only 17.91% female enrollment in the computer science major [19].

2.2 Creativity and Broadening Participation

Even though the number of female students attending college exceeds the number of male students, female students are less likely to choose science and technology careers [28]. The lack of women in the sciences has been likened to a "leaky pipeline" [7] from which female students leave at a greater rate than their male counterparts. CS enrollments are at an all-time high [9] at all types of institutions, (public and private, doctoral-granting and non-doctoral granting) with doctoral-granting reporting the largest increases. But women continue to be underrepresented, as the most recent Taulbee survey shows undergraduate CS enrollments by gender are 81.7% male to 18.35 female.

> ...the low number of women in CS hurts the ability of businesses to hire qualified employees. Another consideration is that the field loses an opportunity to harness women's perspectives and innovativeness. Important breakthroughs, creativity, and true innovation require outside-of-the-box thinking, which may be fostered by diversity [6].

Over the last few decades many have attempted to find reasons for this underrepresentation. Blickenstaff analyzes this issue and notes a range of possible causes identified in the literature, including differences in academic preparation for success in sciences, lack of female role models, and a negative perception of the sciences [7]. Others have identified issues related to lower levels of confidence [5], misperceptions of ability as compared to men [11], and self-efficacy [5, 11]. Others have noted that when women do start the degree, they drop out in greater numbers than their male counterparts [8, 9, 21].

Plucker et al. 2004 [24] define creativity as "the interaction among aptitude, process, and environment by which an individual or group produces a perceptible product that is both novel and useful as defined within a social context." Expressions of creativity are individualized "novel and personally meaningful interpretation of experiences, actions, and events." [4]. Research into the benefits of contextualized computing shows that creative expression is a significant factor for attracting and retaining students [13, 29, 30]. On the other hand, the lack of opportunity for creative expression is a significant factor as to why students, and especially women, leave Computer Science [10, 12]. Programming classes that afford students opportunities to be creative reported higher levels of motivation and interest [23]. Studies of software engineering practice have found that developers prefer to work on activities that they perceive as being creative [15]. Consequently, it seems advantageous to consider offering courses that integrate creative expression and computer science.

3 Synthesis Courses for Creative Expression

The synthesis courses, which contextualize art and computing, are vertically integrated throughout our CITA curriculum, and thus provide opportunities for creative expression throughout the undergraduate experience. However, the first- and second year courses are also taken by non-CITA majors, so even at institutions without dedicated degrees, courses integrating creative expression with computer science could bring more women to computing. Figure 1 illustrates the pathway through the CITA core curriculum.

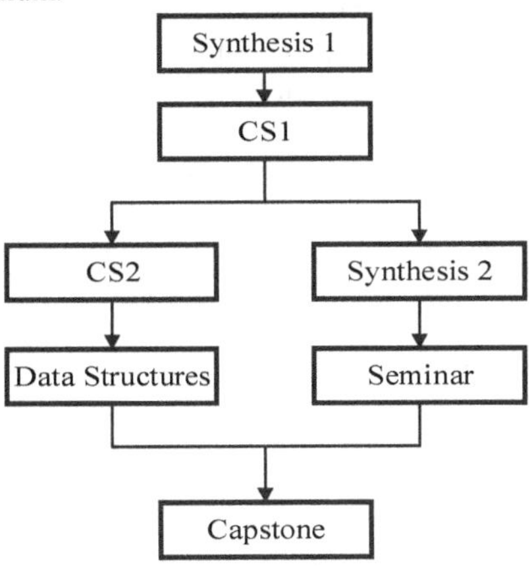

Figure 1: CITA curriculum pre-requisite course flow chart.

In addition to what is shown in Figure 1, CITA majors complete 9 credits in upper-division CSCI coursework, and 18 credits in their art concentration area. The first-year synthesis (Synthesis 1) courses seek to introduce basic programming concepts situated in an accessible and creative arts-themed context. The second-year synthesis course engages students in applying software development practices including iterative design, prototyping, peer evaluation of prototypes, and testing in the context of game programming. In the third-year synthesis course (Seminar), students develop a proposal for a capstone project, which synthesizes creativity in the arts with the tools and conceptual modeling systems of computing. The prerequisites for Seminar also include 3 courses in the student's chosen arts concentration (e.g., music, visual art, theatre, etc.).

3.1 Synthesis 1: Intro to Computing in the Arts

The first-year synthesis courses allow students to choose between creating animated short 3-D films, musical compositions and 2-D visualizations. These courses seek to introduce basic programming concepts situated in an accessible and creative arts-themed context. These courses do not expect students to have prior programming experience; they have no prerequisites and so are taken by students from various majors. However, these courses are required for CITA majors, and are recommended for Computer Science majors who have no programming experience, prior to enrolling in the first Computer Science course. These courses could be described as CS0.5 courses.

The first year-synthesis courses share the following computing learning outcomes:

- apply numeric and string data types to represent information,
- use variables in program development,
- understand arithmetic operators and use them to design expressions,
- understand for-loops and use them to design processes involving repetition,
- understand if statements and use them to design processes involving selection,
- understand functions and use them to design processes involving modularization,
- use predefined classes in program development (object-based programming),
- learn basic principles for group collaboration.

These computing learning outcomes span the AP Computer Science Principles Curriculum. This includes computational thinking practices (connecting computing, creating computational artifacts, abstracting, analyzing problems and artifacts, communicating, and collaborating), as well as the 7 Big Ideas: creativity, abstraction, data and information, algorithms, programming, the Internet, and global impact.

3.1.1 Animation and Virtual Worlds

The arts-related learning outcomes of this course highlight parallels between the software design and artistic design processes. Notably, both processes entail repeated cycles of design, construction, and evaluation, in which an artefact becomes gradually more refined. In the themed context of computer animation, students see the parallels between hand-drawn storyboards and algorithms written in pseudocode. All course assignments encourage creativity by defining a fixed set of requirements or demonstrable artistic or technical features leaving the students free to create their own characters, objects, scenes, or stories. The course currently uses Autodesk Maya with its built-in interactive Python code window, but could also use Blender 3-D. Example assignments include:

Modeling in 3-D: Create and texture paint an original 3-D character. First draw front and side profile sketches, which are imported into a 3-D modeling application to serve as guides. Apply polygon modeling tools to extrude, translate, rotate, scale, and subdivide to form desired the polygon mesh shape. Assign UV-texture coordinates to the model to create unwrapped 2-D outlines of patches of the model's skin. Use a 2-D paint program to color this unwrapped 2-D texture image. Submit the 3-D model, texture image, and rendered images showing the character from front and side views to compare the finished model to the initial design sketches. Students are free to model their work after an existing favorite character or original design.

Scripted scene layout: Create a 3-D scene composed of multiple instances of character models and objects. Students apply concepts of loops and selection statements to create instances (or copies) of their 3-D models, whose position and size are set by invoking the math library random number function. A selection statement inside the loop is used to randomly choose one of several 3-D models to be instanced. Students may use their 3-D character model created in the modeling assignment or borrow characters created by classmates to create a more complex scene. For example, students may create a space scene comprised of multiple different types of space craft and asteroids randomly scattered in space.

Scripted animated scene: Create a simulated particle system effect by applying concepts of loops, lists, and objects. Each particle is an object that has attributes of position and velocity. Students use a count-controlled loop to initialize the starting position and velocity of each particle. They next apply a count-controlled loop to simulate the animation for each particle. Nested inside the count-control loop is a conditional loop that animates the current particle until a stopping condition is reached, e.g. rain drop particle reaches the ground.

Final project: The course concludes with a two-person team project to create an original short animated story in which the team demonstrates creative contributions in story, characters, props, music, sound, or animation. Each student must individually demonstrate creative contribution in any two of these listed aspects plus original code to script scene layout or animation. Students practice their presentation skills by introducing their concept, presenting storyboards, blocking diagrams, and highlighting their respective contributions before screening their animated short film.

3.1.2 Computers, Music, and Art

This course's topics include computer programming and music through the study, transcription, and creation of musical works. Music topics may include notation, scales, key signatures, intervals, chord construction, sight-singing, ear training, and readings in music history and aesthetics. Computing topics include data types, variables, assignment, selection, iteration, lists, functions, classes, events, and graphical user interfaces. Students are introduced to the computer as a musical instrument and as a creative environment to develop fluency with musical practices such as algorithmic composition, developing simple computer instruments, and composing exercises based on models in electroacoustic music and minimalism. Students are required to produce various musical artifacts, ranging from the transcription of musical material (e.g., a favorite song or piece) to the development of solo and interactive group performances.

The course is taught in Python, using an approach blending programming and creative activities. It utilizes a special programming environment for creative programming in music and art, called JythonMusic [20]. JythonMusic provides libraries for music making, image manipulation, building graphical user interfaces (GUIs), and connecting computers to external MIDI and open sound control (OSC) devices, such as digital pianos, smartphones and tablets. Example assignments include:

Transcribe a favorite piece of music: Create a Python program that generates an interesting piece of music. This assignment focuses on creating interesting music with Python, MIDI melodies and harmony, and MIDI percussion. To prepare for this assignment, we study a program that creates a drum pattern consisting of kick, snare and hi-hat sounds, a program that creates a J.S. Bach canon, and a program that creates a minimalist piece ("Piano Phase" by Steve Reich). Students are presented with two options: either (a) find an interesting minimalist piece (e.g., by Philip Glass) and transcribe it, or (b) create your own song in JythonMusic. If a student chooses option (b), then the song needs to have both a melody and drums (all in MIDI).

Sonify an interesting image: Select an interesting image, and sonify (create music from it) using JythonMusic. Design the musical parameters (pitch, dynamics, timbre, panning, etc.) to use. You could use only part of the image, or different parts of the image for different part of the music. For example, convert a single ("rhythmically" interesting) row (or column) to a bass line. Or, create a recurring theme by sonifying a small (interesting) area of the image, and repeating it. Decide ahead of time if you will create continuous, chromatic, or diatonic music. Explore high-level structure of your music. Finally, you may add up to 20% of supporting (non-image generated) musical material, e.g., a low-pitched drone or an ambient background. Examples of student submissions may be found at http://bit.ly/visualSoundscapes2.

Final project: One way to conclude the course is with a laptop orchestra performance. Laptop orchestras became popular after the Princeton Laptop Orchestra (PLOrK) [33]. Such assignments make computing tasks more communal, which is appealing to students, especially women. Students program their computer in real time to perform musical tasks together with other members. For instance, in Fall 2010, we assigned Terry Reiley's "In C", in lieu of a comprehensive final exam [27]. Students pre-coded the 53 different patterns of the piece in one or more timbres (128 MIDI instruments). During the performance, students wrote necessary code to generate these different patterns in real time.

3.1.3 Digital Media Programming

Students learn the fundamentals of computer programming within the context of digital media and artistic expression. In addition to the computer science outcomes outlined above, the course also features design-related objectives. The application of foundational principles of design is the key to creating effective designs that have both visual and communicative success. The course requires students to apply the concept development process, which encompasses a sequence of steps that is common among problem-solving methodologies.

The course is taught primarily using Processing, a language for programming images, animation, sound, and games. Employing Java libraries as a base, Processing allows students to create compelling and beautiful designs while learning the fundamentals of computer programming. As illustrated in the example assignments discussed below, the course begins with creating static sketches in order to teach students how to code shapes, colors, and more complex composites on-screen. Then, as students increase their programming and design skills, programs become event-driven and interactive.

Let's Get Animated: Students create an aesthetically pleasing design using primitive geometric shapes. Then, they make it interactive. At this point in the course, students have learned how to code shapes, use built-in functions, such as random(), and create variables and control structures.

Create Visual Patterns: Students use some form of iteration to create a visually interesting, static pattern. Additionally, they use Boolean variables to overlay an additional pattern when the user interacts with the design.

Midterm Project: Halfway through the semester, students use functions or objects to create a more intricate animated design. They create at least three custom functions, and practice incremental development / testing to ensure that each function works correctly as a separate unit of code.

Final Project: Students design an interactive art composition or a game, while demonstrating a composite of knowledge and skills gained during the semester. At minimum, students are required to use classes and other programming constructs such as loops, conditionals, strings, and arrays. The project is judged on the effective implementation of design principles in the code. For example, create a three-level game in which a given number of oranges must be caught with the bucket before hitting the ground.

3.2 Synthesis 2: Game Programming

The second-year synthesis course engages students to create two-dimensional games from their favorite genres, such as arcade, role-playing, fantasy, sports, serious game, etc. This course teaches students to apply an iterative software design process involving repeated cycles of prototyping and evaluation to build interactive games. Students learn essential skills in Computer Science by developing and testing algorithms. The course spends comparable amount of time developing aesthetic and design skills.

The computing learning outcomes include creating, testing, and refining prototypes (paper, digital, and code), designing and applying test cases, applying classes to represent game objects, applying lists of objects to animate objects and check for collisions, applying two-dimensional lists to represent tile-based maps, and applying finite-state machines to control behavior of game objects, and maze navigation or wandering algorithms. For example, students apply finite-state machines to represent the chase and evade behaviors of ghosts in Pac-Man. Students also research and discuss profiles of diverse game designers and how serious games are used to communicate messages to audiences around the world.

The design outcomes are adapted from *Game Design Workshop* by Tracey Fullerton. Design outcomes include crafting aspects of a game to achieve desired player experience goals, creating engaging characters and stories, creating appealing interfaces that offer feedback, and developing balanced play mechanics that put the player in a state of "flow," where the level of challenge adapts to match a player's skill. Assignments define fixed artistic and technical requirements freeing students to define their own game objectives and artwork design. Typical assignments include:

Serious arcade game: Design a serious game based on the classic Activision Kaboom game mechanic, in which the player's character must move to catch falling objects. The game should raise awareness of a cause for social good. Develop your design through a paper prototype, feedback from testing your paper prototype with classmates, design test cases for collision interaction and application of game rules, code, and evaluate the resulting game using your test cases. Students take turns playtesting completed games in class and providing written feedback to the developer.

Final project: Design, implement, and test a maze-based game that demonstrates use of multiple classes to represent game objects and the tile maze. Apply finite-state machines to direct the behavior of non-player game objects. Apply collision detection to prevent the player and autonomous non-player objects from passing through barriers. Students are free to design game rules, art, and sounds to express their creativity. Develop design documentation that describes the objective, rules of play, maze, and game objects. Write a detailed testing plan and player-tester checklist that will be used to evaluate program correctness. Testing plan checklist items must be self-contained objective statements of expected correct behaviors. For example, the player-controlled object will re-appear on the opposite side of the screen when it goes beyond one of the four screen edges. Students give presentations of their game designs and take turns playtesting each other's games and completing playtest checklists.

This course could be taught using any number of development environments, but we have settled on Processing, since it bridges the Python and Java languages used in our CS1 and CS2 courses, both required for CITA majors. Again, CS1 is a prerequisite for this course. Processing also exposes students to a wide-variety of audio, visual, and media toolkits, which many students choose to use in the third-year and fourth-year synthesis projects.

3.3 Synthesis 3: Seminar

The third-year seminar and fourth year-capstone courses offer an even greater range of creative expression and exposure to software engineering. Students are encouraged to explore, design, and share their original concepts in a supportive, cooperative, and active-learning environment. The seminar and capstone experiences take place over a two-semester course sequence.

In the seminar students conduct literature searches to identify prior works that blend art and computing. They then brainstorm and refine their own artistic project ideas, through the same process of iterative prototyping practiced in the second-year synthesis course. In the most recent offering of the course, students must interact with faculty mentors in art and computing, who offer early feedback on artistic and computing aspects of the students' project ideas. These early contacts help students to (a) create projects that better synthesize art and computing, (b) identify and correct problems early on, and (c) help students to change directions when necessary.

By the end of the seminar, students must produce a working code prototype, possibly using and extending an existing code base for their chosen programming language / environment (e.g., Processing) and technology (e.g., Kinect sensors). Students independently explore and select development tools, such as Arduino, Processing, Java, and Unity Game Engine.

The seminar culminates with each student producing a detailed project proposal, which describes how the project integrates art and computing, illustrates its expected outputs and behaviors using mock displays or audio samples, details art and coding tasks, and estimates completion times for each task.

3.4 Synthesis 4: Capstone

During the fourth-year capstone practicum, students implement their projects according to the task descriptions and timeline milestones defined in their proposals. Course activities include:

- demonstrating progress towards timeline milestones;
- presenting work-in-progress demonstrations to the class;
- consulting with one art mentor and one computing mentor to solicit feedback on progress;
- blogging or journaling regularly to detail progress;
- offering constructive feedback to third-year synthesis students as they work through the process of identifying their projects;
- making a formal presentation of the completed project (as final exam); and
- submitting written report summarizing technical details of the solution and reflecting upon the completed work.

For example, one recent capstone student developed an interactive portfolio of autonomous virtual 3-D creature sculptures. The student modeled original 3-D creatures and brought them to life via C# programming in Unity Game Engine. The autonomous creatures respond to one another's presence, thus exhibiting variations in flocking, fleeing, and pursuit behaviors. This typical project exemplifies how creative expression is applied in both the arts and technology within the CITA degree. In addition, as the students graduate and seek employment or placement in graduate school, these projects become and invaluable part of their application portfolio.

4 Lessons to Apply

Similarly to us, independent CS education researchers report that synthesizing computer science with creative expression improves gender balance. Even if one cannot implement a whole curriculum, starting small – even at the level of a single course – has a positive impact. For instance, in our case, the courses "Computers, Music, and Arts" and "Game Programming" were offered before our CITA degree was designed (Fall 2006). We observed that these courses attracted many non-majors and women, encouraging us to create the CITA degree. Introducing opportunities for creative expression anywhere within a traditional Computer Science curriculum could help. For example, the concept of lists of objects may be taught in a typical CS2 or Data Structures course by implementing insert, search, and delete operations for student records. To offer greater opportunity for creative expression, lists of objects could be used to create an animated particle system effect. Other examples are described in [24]. Moreover, any computing (computer science, information systems, etc.) capstone sequence could involve development of art-inspired projects, offering creative experiences for students.

5 Conclusion

This paper presented our experiences with curriculum design that supports gender balance in computing. A six-year longitudinal study demonstrates that combining creative expression and the arts with core computer science courses (including computer programming, data structures and software engineering) results in graduating 46% female students (compared to the 20% nationwide statistic). This is a significant finding. Moreover, 72% of CITA graduates are placed in CITA-related jobs or graduate studies that involve computing or arts, with a majority of them in jobs that require their computing skills. This indicates that a CITA-like degree is a viable complement to a traditional Computer Science degree, as it prepares students for careers in computing, while at the same time equalizing the gender disparity found in traditional computing degrees.

In closing, by expanding our computing curricula to encompass the more creative aspects of human endeavor and interests, we may attract female students in approximately equal numbers to those of their male counterparts. This is a significant realization for designing future, gender-balanced computing curricula.

6 Acknowledgements

This work has been funded in part by NSF DUE (1323605 and 1044861).

REFERENCES

[1] Bares, W.H., Manaris, B. & McCauley, R. Gender Equity in Computer Science through Computing in the Arts – A Six-Year Longitudinal Study, Computer Science Education, 28, 3 (Sep. 2018), 191-210.

[2] Barker, L. J., Garvin-Doxas, K., & Roberts, E. What can computer science learn from a fine arts approach to teaching? In Proceeding of the 36th ACM Technical Symposium on Computer Science Education (St. Louis, MO, USA - February 23 - 27, 2005), ACM, NY, 421-425.

[3] F Barker, L. J. email communication, February 28, 2018.

[4] Beghetto, R. A. & Kaufman, J. C. Toward a broader conception of creativity: A case for mini-c creativity. Psychology of Aesthetics, Creativity, and the Arts, 1, 2 (May 2007), 73–79.

[5] Beyer, S. Gender differences in the accuracy of self-evaluations of performance, Journal of Personality and Social Psychology, 59, 5 (Nov. 1990), 960-970.

[6] Beyer, S. Why are women underrepresented in Computer Science? Gender differences in stereotypes, self-efficacy, values, and interests and predictors of future CS course-taking and grades, Computer Science Education, 24, 2-3 (Sep. 2014), 153-192.

[7] Blickenstaff, J.C. Women and science careers: leaky pipeline or gender filter?, Gender and Education, 17, 4 (Aug. 2006), 369—386.

[8] Brainard, S. and Carlin, L. 1998. A Six-Year Longitudinal Study of Undergraduate Women in Engineering and Science, Journal of Engineering Education, (87)4, pp. 369-375.

[9] Computing Research Association (2017). Generation CS: Computer Science Undergraduate Enrollments Surge Since 2006. http://cra.org/data/Generation-CS/

[10] Cooper, S. and Cunningham, S. 2010. Teaching computer science in context. ACM Inroads 1, 1 (March 2010), 5-8. DOI=http://dx.doi.org/10.1145/1721933.1721934

[11] Else-Quest, N., Mineo, C. and Higgins, A. 2013. Math and Science Attitudes and Achievement at the Intersection of Gender and Ethnicity, Psychology of Women Quarterly, (37)3, pp. 293-309.

[12] Forte, A. and Guzdial, M. Computers for Communication, Not Calculation: Media As a Motivation and Context for Learning, in Proceedings of the Proceedings of the 37th Annual Hawaii International Conference on System Sciences - Track 4 - Volume 4, (Big Island HI, USA – January 5-8, 2004) IEEE, Washington, DC, USA.

[13] Forte, A. and Guzdial, M. Motivation and nonmajors in computer science: identifying discrete audiences for introductory courses. IEEE Transactions on Education, 48, 2 (May 2005), 248-253.

[14] Garcia, D. and Barr, V. Guzdial, M. and Malan, D. 2013. Rediscovering the Passion, Beauty, Joy, and Awe: Making Computing Fun Again, Part 6, in Proceedings of the 44th ACM Technical Symposium on Computer Science Education (Denver, CO, USA – March 6-9, 2013) ACM, NY, USA, 379-380.

[15] Gu, M. and Tong, X. Towards Hypotheses on Creativity in Software Development. In 5th International Conference on Product Focused Software Process Improvement (PROFES), (Kausai Science City, Japan – June 13-15, 2005) Springer, NY, USA, 47–61.

[16] Guzdial, M. 2003. A Media Computation Course for Non-majors, SIGCSE Bulletin, 35, 3 (Sep. 2003), 104-108.

[17] Guzdial, Mark. Does Contextualized Computing Education Help?, ACM Inroads, 1,4 (Dec. 2010), 4-6.

[18] Guzdial, M. 2013. Exploring Hypotheses About Media Computation, in Proceedings of the 9th Annual International ACM Conference on International Computing Education Research, (La Jolla, CA, USA - August 12-14, 2013) ACM, NY, USA, 19-26.

[19] Guzdial, M. 2014. The most gender-balanced computing program in the USA: computational media at Georgia Tech, Computer Education Blog, September 2, 2014. https://computinged.wordpress.com/2014/09/02/the-most-gender-balanced-computing-program-in-the-usa/

[20] JythonMusic. http://jythonmusic.org

[21] Katz, S., Allbritton, D., Aronis, J., Wilson, C. and Soffa, M. Gender, Achievement, and Persistence in an Undergraduate Computer Science Program, SIGMIS Database, 37, 4 (Fall 2006), 42-57.

[22] La Marche, Jeffrey Steven. User Interface Computation As a Contextualized Approach for Introductory Computing Instruction, in Proceedings of the 9th Annual ACM International Computing Education Research Conference (La Holla, CA, USA – August 12-14, 2013) ACM, NY, USA, 179-180.

[23] Lewandowski, G., Johnson, E. and Goldweber, M. 2005. Fostering a creative interest in computer science. In Proceedings of the 36th SIGCSE technical symposium on Computer science education (St. Louis, MO, USA – February 23-27, 2005) ACM, NY, USA, 535-539.

[24] McCauley, R., Manaris, B., Heise, D., Sheller, C., Jolley, J., and Zaring, A. Computing in the Arts: Curricular Innovations and Results. In Proceedings of the 48th ACM Technical Symposium on Computer Science Education (Seattle, WA – March 8-11, 2017) ACM, NY, USA, 693-694.

[25] Plucker, J., Beghetto, R. A., & Dow, G. 2004. Why isn't creativity more important to educational psychologists? Potential, pitfalls, and future directions in creativity research. Educational Psychologist, 39, 2 (June 2004), 83–96.

[26] Porter, L. and Simon, B. 2013. Retaining Nearly One-third More Majors with a Trio of Instructional Best Practices in CS1, in Proceedings of the 44th ACM Technical Symposium on Computer Science Education (Denver, CO – March 6-9, 2013) ACM, NY, USA, 165-170.

[27] Rich, L., Perry, H. and Guzdial, M. 2004. A CS1 Course Designed to Address Interests of Women, in Proceedings of the 35th SIGCSE Technical Symposium on Computer Science Education (Norfolk, VA, USA – March 3-7, 2004) ACM, NY, USA, 190-194.

[28] Riley, T. 1989. In C, Score and Performing Directions, Celestial Harmonies.

[29] Simon, B. and Kinnunen, P., Porter, L. and Zazkis, D. Experience Report: CS1 for Majors with Media Computation, in Proceedings of the 15th Annual Conference on Innovation and Technology in Computer Science Education (Bilkent, Ankara, Turkey – June 26-30, 2010) ACM, NY, USA, 214-218.

[30] Sloan, R. and Troy, P. 2008. CS 0.5: A Better Approach to Introductory Computer Science for Majors, in Proceedings of the 39th SIGCSE Technical Symposium on Computer Science Education (Portland, OR, USA – March 12-15, 2008) ACM, NY, USA, 271-275.

[31] Tew, A., Fowler, C. and Guzdial, M. 2005. Tracking an Innovation in Introductory CS Education from a Research University to a Two-year College, in Proceedings of the 36th SIGCSE Technical Symposium on Computer Science Education (St. Louis, MO, USA – February 23-27, 2005) ACM, NY, USA, 416-420.

[32] Tims, J., Zweben, S., Timanovsky, Y. and Prey, J. ACM-NDC Study 2016–2017: Fifth Annual Study of Non-Doctoral-Granting Departments in Computing, ACM Inroads, 8(3), pp. 48-62, ACM, NY, USA.

[33] Tims, J. 2018. Achieving Gender Equity: ACM-W Can't Do It Alone. Communications of the ACM, February, 61(2), p. 5.

[34] Trueman, D., Cook, P., Smallwood, S. and Wang, G. 2006. 'PLOrk: The Princeton laptop orchestra, year 1', in Proceedings of the International Computer Music Conference (ICMC 2006), Michigan Publishing, 443–50.

[35] Uludag, S., Karakus, M. and Turner, S. Implementing IT0/CS0 with Scratch, App Inventor for Android, and Lego Mindstorms, in Proceedings of the 2011 Conference on Information Technology Education (West Point, NY - October 20—22, 2011) 183-190.

[36] Zweben, S. and Bizot, B. 2016 Taulbee Survey: Generation CS Continues to Produce Record Undergrad Enrollment; Graduate Degree Production Rises at both Master's and Doctoral Levels, Computing Research Association, https://cra.org/crn/wp-content/uploads/sites/7/2017/05/2016-Taulbee-Survey.pdf

Gender-balanced TAs from an Unbalanced Student Body

Amir Kamil
University of Michigan
akamil@umich.edu

James Juett
University of Michigan
jjuett@umich.edu

Andrew DeOrio
University of Michigan
awdeorio@umich.edu

ABSTRACT

Increasing participation of women and underrepresented minorities is a key challenge in the field of Computer Science Education. Balanced representation of these groups among teaching assistants in Computer Science courses influences recruitment and retention of underrepresented students. At the same time, the status-quo reduced participation of these students makes it more difficult to hire instructional staff from underrepresented groups.

In this paper, we describe our experience evaluating candidates with teaching-demonstration videos, followed by in-person interviews, to hire a gender-balanced set of undergraduate TAs for a large-scale CS2 course. Our research goal is to quantitatively assess gender balance throughout the hiring process.

Our initial applicant pool is just one-sixth women, but we found that women applicants perform better in our application process than men, resulting in a gender-balanced course staff without making hiring decisions based on the gender of applicants. We show that our approach results in a more gender-balanced teaching staff than hiring based on applicant GPA. We also use course-evaluation data to demonstrate that women perform as well as men as teaching assistants in CS2, and that the overall quality of our teaching assistants has remained high after the hiring-process change.

CCS CONCEPTS

• **Social and professional topics → Computing education**;

KEYWORDS

gender diversity, women in computer science, CS2, undergraduate TA, teaching staff, hiring practices, learning at scale

ACM Reference Format:

Amir Kamil, James Juett, and Andrew DeOrio. 2019. Gender-balanced TAs from an Unbalanced Student Body. In *Proceedings of the 50th ACM Technical Symposium on Computer Science Education (SIGCSE '19), February 27-March 2, 2019, Minneapolis, MN, USA.* ACM, New York, NY, USA, 7 pages. https://doi.org/10.1145/3287324.3287404

1 INTRODUCTION

Enrollment in undergraduate computer science programs and workplace demand for computer scientists are at an all-time high. Yet, women are underrepresented in computer science at all levels. Women account for only 23% of AP computer science test-takers, 18% of computer science degrees earned at major research universities, and 26% of professional computing occupations [7].

This work in particular is concerned with representation of women as undergraduate teaching assistants in CS courses. Undergraduate teaching assistants (TAs) are common in large-scale, modern computer science courses [8, 16, 17]. TAs form the front line of our courses, interacting with students in a variety of settings, including labs, discussions, office hours, in-class exercises, and online forums.

The underrepresentation of women in computer science programs presents a challenge for identifying and hiring a gender-balanced staff. At our university, the CS2 population is approximately 25% women. Furthermore, some of the same barriers to women's participation in CS generally may also discourage applying for TA positions. In our experience, the initial applicant pool for our CS2 course is approximately 16.5% women. As we describe in detail below, simple hiring schemes based on GPA or previous grade in the course result in a staff with the same gender-imbalance as the initial applicant pool.

In this paper, we describe an application and interview process we have used to consistently hire a gender-balanced staff over each of the past 5 semesters. Crucially, this has not required hiring less-qualified students to meet diversity goals. Rather, women who apply tend to perform better in teaching-demonstration videos and in-person interviews, which leads to a gender-balanced hiring ratio despite an imbalanced applicant pool.

The research questions we address in this work are:

- What gender balance is present at all phases of the application/interview process?
- Do men and women perform differently in evaluative measures used in the hiring process?

1.1 Background and Related Work

Evidence shows several factors contribute to underrepresentation of women in CS. At the college level, a lack of previous experience with CS is a key contributor; one large-scale study at Stanford University [15] found 42.4% of women entering college reported previous experience with CS, compared with 66.3% of men. Lack of previous experience with CS puts students at a disadvantage [1], and this imbalance can manifest in stronger positive attitudes toward computing among men entering college [2, 21]. Confidence also plays an important role in students' self-concept in their field, yet the Stanford study [15] found that among CS majors, women report much less confidence than men about their choice of major entering college. This is likely related to differing levels of exposure to CS before college.

At all levels, cultural norms and stereotypes about computer science can be a barrier to women's participation. Learning environments that match these stereotypes decrease women's interest in pursuing computer science [4, 14]. Many women in CS also face

ACM ISBN 978-1-4503-5890-3/19/02...$15.00
https://doi.org/10.1145/3287324.3287404

stereotype threat [4, 23], which occurs when an individual feels at risk of confirming negative stereotypes about a demographic or social group with which they identify. Empirical works show stereotype threat negatively impacts women's performance and feeling of belonging in STEM and CS fields [11, 20, 22].

These barriers are compounded by the existing underrepresentation of women in computer science. In a study of undergraduate students at Stanford University [15], 84% of women CS majors self-reported feeling like a gender minority, vs. 52% for women overall. Underrepresentation of women in teaching and leadership roles may reinforce this feeling and leads to fewer same-gender role models for women in computing courses. In CS courses, TAs often act as role models for students. Haller and Fossum [9] suggest students may have an easier time identifying with a successful TA who is just a few years ahead of them than with a professor or "famous" individual whose position seems out of reach. Roberts et al. [18] describe a "stepping-stone" model which stresses the importance of women at all levels of leadership in a course.

The presence of women as role models maintains the interest of women who already have exposure to computer science [6] and combats the shrinking pipeline of women in CS [3]. Contact with in-group experts is known to enhance women's self-concept and motivation in pursuing STEM fields, and can inoculate them against negative pressures of CS stereotypes [24], improving retention of women in CS programs. TA experience is an influential and motivating factor in encouraging women to pursue careers as CS teachers [19].

Several descriptions of TA hiring are in the literature. Decker et al. [5] describe a multi-phase hiring process in use at the University at Buffalo, which involves initial paper applications, in-person interviews, presentations on a course topic, and additional panel-style interviews with current TAs. Leyzberg et al. [13] discuss a formal interview process at Princeton in which faculty meet with students and evaluate them according to a common rubric, which the authors report has led to a fairer and more effective hiring process. We examine the impact of our TA hiring processes on the gender balance of our course staff.

2 METHODS

We proceed to describe the course that uses our interview process and its context in the curriculum. We then provide details about our interview process, as well as the statistical methods we used to analyze the data we collected through the process.

2.1 Description of the course

Our data set comes from a second-semester computer programming course at a the University of Michigan, a large, public, research institution. Students take an introductory CS1 course, followed by CS2, "Programming and Introductory Data Structures". While many students are aspiring computer science majors and minors, the course also has a diverse group of students from other majors who want a second computing course.

CS2 covers major computer science concepts including functional abstraction, data abstraction and dynamic resource management. Students are exposed to C++ features like arrays, structs, classes, pointers, inheritance, polymorphism, and recursion.

Each week, students attend two 80-minute lectures and a 2-hour lab. Labs are led by TAs and contain short assignments that reinforce the lecture material. There are two exams and 5 large programming assignments. A student's final grade is comprised by 40% projects, 5% labs, and 55% exams.

Programming assignments are substantial pieces of work and many student solutions reach 1,000 lines of code. A few examples include a machine-learning tool that predicts the subject of message-board posts, and a simple image-processing algorithm. Students work in optional partnerships on programming assignments. TAs hold regular office hours that primarily support questions about the projects and studying for exams.

2.2 TA Hiring Process

In this section, we describe the interview process we have used for the last five semesters, beginning in Fall 2016, based on the method used by Dr. Mary Lou Dorf's CS1 course. At a glance, our hiring process involves advertising our position, soliciting first-round applications (including a short teaching-demonstration video), reviewing first-round applications, and bringing in top candidates for a second-round of in-person interviews. During the interviews, each candidate participates in an interactive teaching demonstration and is evaluated based on a common rubric.

Prior to this TA hiring process, our method for hiring was more ad-hoc. There was little advertising, and interested students approached faculty to inquire about the position. We only interviewed a small subset of applicants, and the interview consisted of checking a student's knowledge of the material and their past experience with teaching or mentoring.

2.2.1 First-Round Applications. We advertise our TA positions widely and accept first-round applications from any interested students. A mass email soliciting applications is sent to all declared computer science majors and all students who have taken our CS2 course in the past year. We ask current TAs to advertise the position via word-of-mouth to their peers and to encourage current students to apply. A student group hosts a "What is it like to be an EECS TA" panel in which current TAs and instructors answer questions.

Our first-round application is available online. Information provided with the application describes the responsibilities of the position. Students are asked to provide their class standing, intended major, and current GPA. They also give free-response descriptions of why they would like to TA for our course and any previous teaching experience they have. Students are also allowed to submit a resume, but this is not required. The application is open for roughly one month. In the most recent semester, we received approximately 150 applications.

Students are also required to submit a 5-minute demonstration video with their initial application. Students are allowed to choose any topic related to course material and are free to style the video any way they like (e.g. a sample lesson plan, a mock office-hours session, exam review, etc.). We emphasize that the video need not be a polished, high-quality production, but should showcase their ability to convey ideas and their teaching style.

2.2.2 Selecting Finalists for In-Person Interviews. Students' initial applications are reviewed to select finalists for second-round, in-person interviews. The primary component of this process is evaluation of the teaching-demonstration videos. A single faculty member watches and evaluates each of the videos, assigning a score from 1-5. Videos that receive a score of 3.5 or higher (about 40-50% of applications) are split among remaining faculty to receive a second 1-5 score. Reviewing videos can be a significant time investment, but viewing at 2x speed works well and an accurate impression of quality can generally be formed within a few minutes. Overall, reviewing 100-150 videos requires 5-10 hours of faculty time.

The average score for each video is used as a primary component in determining who to invite for second-round interviews. While the top few candidates with near-perfect video scores (i.e. average 4.5 to 5) are almost always selected for interviews, there are inevitably several students essentially "tied" in the next echelon of video scores. We break the ties by considering the rest of the students' application materials, previous teaching experience, and personal experience faculty have with the students, if any.

The total number of finalists we interview depends on our anticipated staff needs. Roughly one-third to half of our in-person interviews yield candidates we would be happy to hire.

2.2.3 In-Person Interviews and Evaluation. Each finalist is invited to a 20-30 minute interview with two of our faculty. The first half of the interview consists of a few standard questions (e.g. "tell us about your motivation for teaching", "what works well about our course, and what would you change to improve it?", etc.) as well as free-form conversation intended to get to know the student and allow them to feel comfortable. We also ask each candidate a question about diversity and inclusion in our courses. The second half of the interview is a teaching demonstration on a fixed topic, which we tell the candidates in advance. The interviewers act as students, and the candidate is tasked with helping the mock students understand the topic at hand. Each interviewer ranks the candidate on a five-point scale on four categories: clarity, technical proficiency, use of whiteboard, and responsiveness to student questions and needs.

Once all the interviews are completed, the instructors rank candidates based on a combination of their numerical scores on the categories described above and their responses to the free-form questions. We do not consider the gender of applicants or TA diversity – the ranking is based solely on the candidates' performance in the in-person interview. The preference list is then passed on to the department, which hires staff from this list in order as positions become available. Overall, interviewing 20 students (yielding about 8 potential hires) takes 20 hours of faculty time.

2.3 Statistical methods

We analyzed three data sets: application-video scores, evaluations of in-person interviews, and student evaluations of course staff.

Scores for application videos were collected over five semesters, from Winter[1] 2016 through Winter 2018. We received a total of 459 applications from 397 unique candidates over that period. Our analysis considers only the first application from each candidate,

[1]The Winter term is January-April, and the Fall term is September-December.

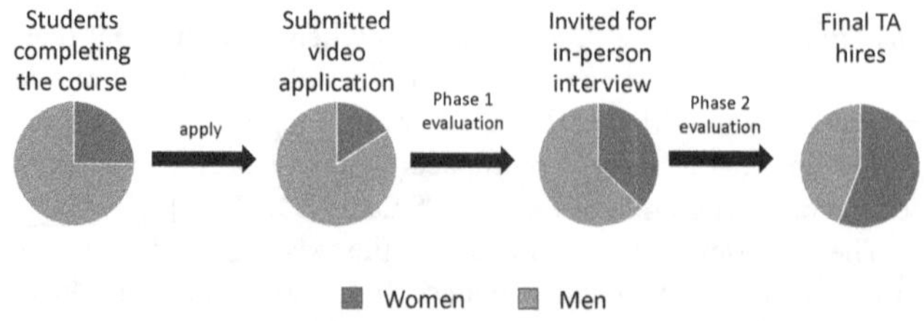

Figure 1: Hiring process overview, showing gender distribution at each step. Among students who complete the course, 25% are women. Of those, students who decide to apply for a TA position include 16.5% women. After the first interview phase which involves a teaching-demonstration video, the candidate pool contains 37% women. Finally, after an in-person interview, TA hires include 56% women.

using the average evaluation score from each reviewer of the candidate's video. We used the university's Learning Analytics Data Architecture (LARC) [12] system to determine applicants' genders, GPA at the time of application, and grade in our course. We applied a two-sided Student's t-test to determine if men and women candidates are distinguishable by video evaluation score, GPA, or grade in the course. Grades were converted to a numerical value (A+ = 4.3, A = 4.0, A- = 3.7, and so on) for analysis.

We collected scores for in-person interviews for the four categories of clarity, technical proficiency, use of whiteboard, and responsiveness to student questions and needs over the same five semesters. We applied a two-sided Student's t-test to the scores from each category, averaged over the reviewers for each candidate, to determine if men and women candidates perform differently.

Finally, we examined data from course evaluations conducted by the university over six semesters, from Fall 2015 through Winter 2018, to determine the overall effectiveness of each of our undergraduate teaching assistants. Effectiveness is on a five-point scale, and the evaluation system reports the interpolated median over the responses for each assistant. The group of evaluated assistants includes both TAs hired under a prior process, as well as those hired through the process described above. We applied two-sided Student's t-tests to determine if men and women received different ratings, as well as to compare the performance of TAs before our new process was in place to those hired under the new process.

3 RESULTS

Figure 1 shows a high-level overview of the application process and the resulting gender breakdown. The student population in the class is around 25% women, but our applicant pool has averaged 16.5% women over the course of this study. After our evaluation and interview process, 56% of the new course staff we hire are women.

In the rest of this section, we break down how women and men perform in each step of the application process. We also present data from course evaluations for staff we hire.

3.1 Impact of Initial Evaluation

Table 1 shows the results of evaluating applicants' video submissions. We only considered the first time an individual applied to our course, resulting in a data set with 18% women (though the

	Women	Men
Count	72	325
Score Mean	3.89	3.58
Score P-Value	0.000103	
GPA Mean	3.65	3.66
GPA P-Value	0.403	
Grade Mean	3.68	3.78
Grade P-Value	0.149	

Table 1: Data from initial application, which includes a teaching-demonstration video. The data include evaluation scores of the videos, overall GPA of applicants, and grade in the course.

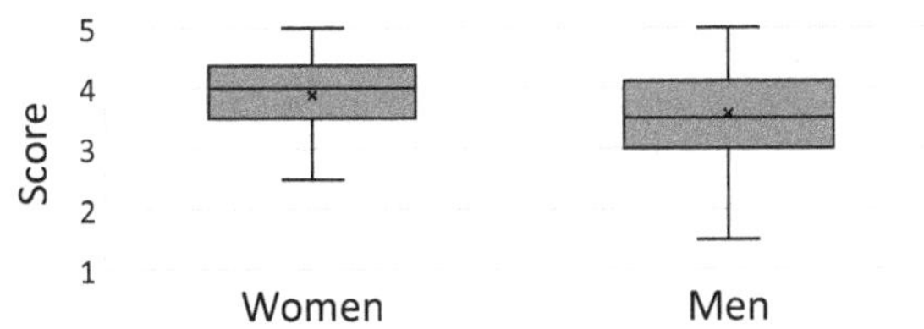

Figure 2: Initial evaluation scores of application, which includes a teaching-demonstration video. Boxes denote the quartiles, with an "X" indicating the mean.

applicant pool itself is 16.5% women). On average, women score about 9% higher than men, and the difference is statistically significant with a p-value of 0.000103. Figure 2 compares the distribution of women's scores with that of men.

We also examined how women and men applicants compare with respect to overall GPA and grade in the course. As the data in Table 1 shows, there is no statistically significant difference between the two applicant populations.

3.2 Impact of Interview

We interviewed a total of 95 candidates over five terms, with 37% women. Table 2 shows how women and men performed in the four categories of clarity, technical proficiency, use of whiteboard, and responsiveness to students. On average, women performed better than men in all four categories, and the difference was significant in every category except technical proficiency. Figure 3 illustrates the distribution of scores for all four categories.

3.3 Impact on Students

Table 3 presents data from course evaluations submitted by students for each staff member, and Figure 4 compares the distribution of scores by gender. Students are asked at the end of the term to evaluate each staff member on several metrics, including the all-encompassing "Overall, the instructor was effective." Our staff is rated as highly effective, averaging over 4.6 out of 5 possible with an overall student-response rate of 44%, and the data show no significant difference between women and men. This demonstrates that not only does our process result in hiring capable staff members,

	Women	Men
Count	35	60
Clarity Mean	4.01	3.52
Clarity P-Value	0.00293	
Technical Mean	3.93	3.65
Technical P-Value	0.0910	
Whiteboard Mean	4.07	3.51
Whiteboard P-Value	0.00258	
Responsiveness Mean	4.27	3.77
Responsiveness P-Value	0.0110	

Table 2: Interview scores in the categories of clarity, technical proficiency, use of whiteboard, and responsiveness to students.

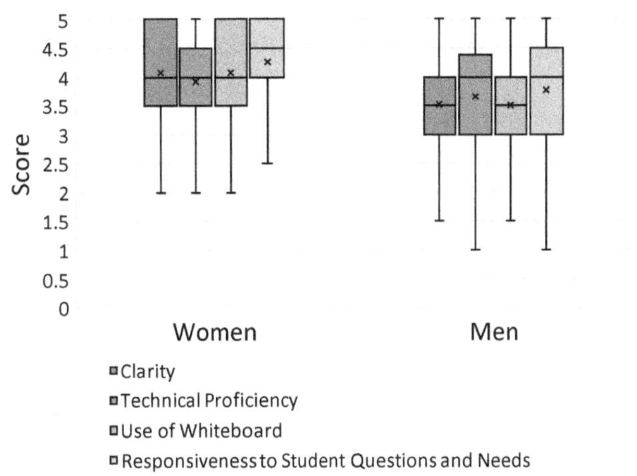

Figure 3: Interview evaluation score, by gender. An interview included a simulated office hours scenario, and interviewees were evaluated on clarity, technical competence, use of whiteboard, and responsiveness to (simulated) student questions. Boxes denote the quartiles, with an "X" indicating the mean.

	Women	Men	F15/W16	F17/W18
Count	52	47	22	41
Effective. Mean	4.65	4.62	4.56	4.63
Effective. P-Value	0.584		0.781	

Table 3: Data for student evaluations of TAs.

but that it results in both women and men staff who are highly effective.

We also compared course evaluations for staff hired before our process was in place to those hired afterwards. Table 3 compares scores in the Fall 2015 and Winter 2016 terms, which had no staff hired under the new process, to Fall 2017 and Winter 2018, where all but one staff member was hired using the process. The data show no significant difference between the two sets of staff members,

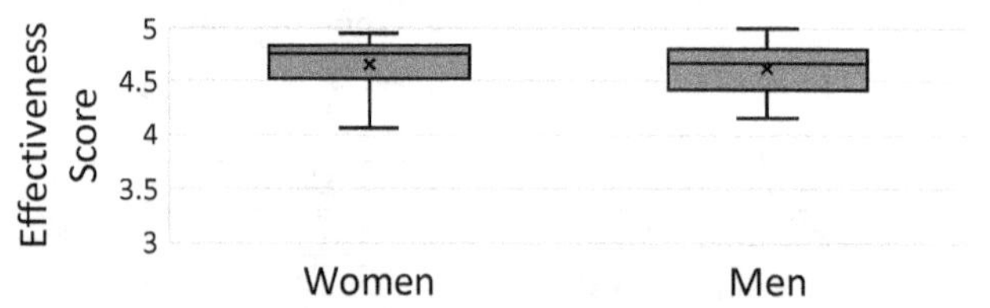

Figure 4: Student course evaluations of TAs, by TA gender. Students in each TA's lab section evaluated the TA in response to "Overall, the instructor was effective." Boxes denote the quartiles, with an "X" indicating the mean.

demonstrating that the diversity that resulted from the new process did not come at the cost of teaching effectiveness.

4 DISCUSSION

4.1 Qualitative Observations of Our Process

4.1.1 Initial Applications and Teaching-Demonstration Videos. By far, the most influential component in evaluating initial applications and deciding whom to interview is a candidate's teaching video. We have found that this provides invaluable insight into a candidate's ability to communicate clearly, appropriate use of aids such as a whiteboard or slide deck, and whether candidates explain at a pace and level that is appropriate for our students. The amount of work candidates put into their video is telling. It is surprising that some candidates that otherwise look good on paper submit a poorly-prepared, single-take video. The choice of format also informs our evaluation. For example, an interactive whiteboard session with real students is almost always more successful (and more appropriate for real teaching/learning) than a monologue. After experience with this process, judging candidates based only on paper applications would feel like being completely in the dark.

Application videos also allow our hiring process to scale to a large number of applicants. By dividing the work of evaluation between the faculty for the course, we have been able to evaluate almost 150 videos in just a few days, allowing us to identify the best candidates to bring in for in-depth, in-person interviews.

4.1.2 In-Person Interviews. The live teaching demonstration plays the largest role in determining which finalists we hire. A number of factors allow candidates to perform to their best ability and make objective evaluation across different students easier. We choose a fixed topic for all students and let them know in advance, so that they can prepare ahead of time. We let students know that the purpose of the demonstration is not to test their knowledge, but to see how they would teach and interact with real students. Along these lines, the faculty pretending to be students should be realistic; they should not ask overly tricky questions, act obstinately, or exaggerate confusions. A useful strategy is to borrow common misconceptions and/or questions we see in class.

4.2 Gender Balance/Imbalance Throughout Our Hiring Process

4.2.1 Initial Applications and Teaching-Demonstration Videos. Although women only account for 16.5% of our initial applicant pool, they make up 37% of the finalists selected for in-person interviews. That is, women who apply are three times more likely to be selected for an interview as men who apply.

A primary justification for this is that women tend to submit higher quality teaching-demonstration videos. A closer look at the distribution of video scores shows 75% of women score higher than 3.5, which is roughly our cutoff for acceptable videos that merit additional review by a second faculty member, whereas only 50% of men score above this threshold. That is, it appears a much higher percent of women who apply submit high-quality teaching demonstrations. It also appears that women perform better in our evaluation of additional criteria for students who score similarly on their teaching demos. The criteria include previous teaching experience, thoughtful responses to free-form questions, and whether any faculty personally recommend the candidate.

While we do not have evidence to explain why women tend to submit higher-quality teaching demonstrations, a possible factor is that self-selection processes by which students decide whether or not to apply may be different for men and women. For example, studies have found that among computer science students, women tend to have lower confidence in their computing abilities than men (e.g. [2, 10]). It may be this influences more severe self-selection of women than for men. Another possibility is that some of the challenges faced by women are formative in ways that strengthen their application. For example, women faced with lower confidence or stereotype threat may work especially hard to produce a high-quality teaching demo. Whatever the self-selection criteria may be, they do not appear to include GPA or grade in the course, as we have found that there is no statistically significant difference between the GPA or grades of men and women who apply.

4.2.2 In-Person Interviews. Though the pool of applicants selected for in-person interviews is just 37% women, women make up 56% of the staff we actually hire. Women we interview are twice as likely to be hired as men we interview. The primary reason for this is that they score higher than men in three of the four categories we use to evaluate their in-person teaching demonstrations. Anecdotally, women also seem to provide more thoughtful answers in the question/answer portion of the interview, but we do not have concrete data to evaluate the effects of this.

As with teaching-demonstration videos, we do not have evidence to explain why women do better in in-person interviews. It is striking that even after a first-step filtering process of evaluating videos, we find that women selected through that filter still do better than men who pass through the same filter. This suggests that both steps of the process are important in identifying the best candidates and achieving a gender-balanced yet effective staff.

4.2.3 Challenges. A significant challenge in our process is in getting women to apply in the first place. Despite the course being about 25% women, only an average of 16.5% of applicants in each term were women. Anecdotally, we have found that it requires more effort to convince promising women to apply than men. Furthermore, only 4% of women candidates applied more than once, while 16% of men candidates applied at least twice. This suggests that we should reach out to candidates who didn't quite make the cut to encourage them to apply again.

Cutoff	Count	% Women	% Men
GPA 4.0	29	24.1%	75.9%
GPA 3.9	102	17.6%	82.4%
GPA 3.8	146	17.1%	82.9%
GPA 3.7	199	16.6%	83.4%
GPA 3.6	247	17.0%	83.0%
CS2 Grade A+	62	17.7%	82.3%
CS2 Grade A	204	14.2%	85.8%
CS2 Grade A-	303	16.5%	83.5%
CS2 Grade B+	347	17.0%	83.0%

Table 4: Gender breakdown of applicants who meet various GPA or grade cutoff thresholds.

	GPA		CS2 Grade	
	Correl.	P-Value	Correl.	P-Value
Video	0.0620	0.218	0.0796	0.114
Clarity	0.0431	0.678	0.0747	0.472
Technical	0.107	0.303	0.129	0.214
Whiteboard	-0.0329	0.752	-0.00180	0.986
Responsiveness	-0.00439	0.966	0.0985	0.342
Course Evals	-0.0806	0.523	0.0566	0.654

Table 5: Correlation of GPA and grade in course to application-video score, scores for the four categories from in-person interviews, and course evaluations of TAs.

4.3 What-if? Hiring Based on GPA or Grade

We considered what our staff would look like if we hired solely based on overall GPA or grade in the course. Table 4 shows the gender breakdown of applicants under various cutoffs for GPA or grade. Regardless of the cutoff used, the ratio would not differ substantially from the 18% of first-time applicants who are women. In comparison, our interview process results in 2-3 times as many women as hiring based on GPA or grade would.

We also examined how GPA and grade correlate to scores for candidates' application videos. The "Video" row in Table 5 shows small positive correlations, but neither is statistically significant.

For the candidates we interviewed, we further compared how their GPA and grade in the course correlated with their scores for the four categories we evaluated during the interview. Table 5 shows all correlations are small and not statistically significant.

Finally, we considered the correlation between course evaluations for our staff and their GPA at time of hiring or grade in the course. Table 5 illustrates that neither correlation is statistically significant. This suggests that neither is a useful criterion for hiring staff in our course. We believe that a major reason for this is that most applicants have high enough GPA and grades to make both insignificant factors in the applicant's teaching effectiveness.

4.4 Limitations

A significant limitation to our study is that it only captures students who decide to go through the application process. The initial teaching-demonstration video is a barrier to entry, and we only evaluated candidates who put in the effort to submit a video.

It is not clear whether our application and interview process will translate to upper-level CS courses. While we have had success hiring excellent staff for CS2, it may be the criteria we use play a different role in upper-level courses. Additional criteria like further experience with specific subject matter may also be significant. Upper-level courses also tend to be smaller and faculty may know students personally, which gives additional information in evaluating candidates but may also make objectivity more difficult.

Another limitation is that our initial review of teaching videos and evaluation of in-person interviews could be influenced by implicit bias. We aim to counteract this by having multiple faculty review videos and each in-person interview, which gives multiple perspectives on each candidate's performance. We also use a multi-part rubric for our in-person interviews, which allows more objective evaluation of individual criteria. Finally, course-evaluation data show no significant difference in evaluation scores by gender, providing some evidence that our interview process is not biased.

5 CONCLUSIONS

In this study, we examined how an application process that incorporates teaching-demonstration videos and in-person interviews results in a gender-balanced course staff in a CS2 at a large, public institution. Despite the initial application pool being only 16.5% women, we ended up hiring a set of TAs that was 56% women, without making hiring decisions based on gender. Our analysis indicates women perform better in both the teaching videos they submit and in-person teaching demonstrations. We also showed that the resulting course staff was rated as highly effective by students, that there was no statistically significant difference in performance between the women and men on staff, and that the diversity produced by our hiring process did not come at the cost of reduced teaching effectiveness compared to previous terms.

We also observed that in our pool of applicants, GPA and grade in the course had no significant correlation with any of the evaluation metrics for application videos, in-person interviews, or course evaluations. Furthermore, there was no significant difference between women and men with respect to GPA or grade. This indicates that hiring solely based on GPA or grade would result in a gender ratio similar to that of the applicant pool without producing a more effective course staff.

Based on our analysis, we take several lessons that are likely to be applicable to similar courses at other institutions. The two-phase application process of teaching videos and in-person interviews scales to a large applicant pool while still producing an effective course staff. Evaluating applicants numerically on well-defined categories allows the evaluation effort to be split across multiple people and enables retrospective analysis such as this work. Combined with using two evaluators for each candidate, numerical scores may also reduce the likelihood of implicit bias. Finally, we believe that data collection is important to identify challenges in hiring a balanced staff, such as the underrepresentation of women in our applicant pool and the lower fraction of women than men who apply more than once.

REFERENCES

[1] Christine Alvarado, Gustavo Umbelino, and Mia Minnes. 2018. The persistent effect of pre-college computing experience on college CS course grades. In *Proceedings of the 49th ACM Technical Symposium on Computer Science Education*. ACM, 876–881.

[2] Sylvia Beyer, Kristina Rynes, Julie Perrault, Kelly Hay, and Susan Haller. 2003. Gender differences in computer science students. *ACM SIGCSE Bulletin* 35, 1 (2003), 49–53.

[3] Tracy Camp. 2002. The incredible shrinking pipeline. *ACM SIGCSE Bulletin* 34, 2 (2002), 129–134.

[4] Sapna Cheryan, Victoria C Plaut, Paul G Davies, and Claude M Steele. 2009. Ambient belonging: How stereotypical cues impact gender participation in computer science. *Journal of personality and social psychology* 97, 6 (2009), 1045.

[5] Adrienne Decker, Phil Ventura, and Christopher Egert. 2006. Through the looking glass: reflections on using undergraduate teaching assistants in CS1. *ACM SIGCSE Bulletin* 38, 1 (2006), 46–50.

[6] Benjamin J Drury, John Oliver Siy, and Sapna Cheryan. 2011. When do female role models benefit women? The importance of differentiating recruitment from retention in STEM. *Psychological Inquiry* 22, 4 (2011), 265–269.

[7] National Center for Women and Information Technology. 2018. By the Numbers. Retrieved August 8, 2018 from www.ncwit.org/bythenumbers

[8] Jeffrey Forbes, David J Malan, Heather Pon-Barry, Stuart Reges, and Mehran Sahami. 2017. Scaling introductory courses using undergraduate teaching assistants. In *Proceedings of the 2017 ACM SIGCSE Technical Symposium on Computer Science Education*. ACM, 657–658.

[9] Susan M Haller and Timothy V Fossum. 1998. Retaining women in CS with accessible role models. In *ACM SIGCSE Bulletin*, Vol. 30. ACM, 73–76.

[10] Sandra Katz, David Allbritton, John Aronis, Christine Wilson, and Mary Lou Soffa. 2006. Gender, achievement, and persistence in an undergraduate computer science program. *ACM SIGMIS Database: the DATABASE for Advances in Information Systems* 37, 4 (2006), 42–57.

[11] Amruth N Kumar. 2012. A study of stereotype threat in computer science. In *Proceedings of the 17th ACM annual conference on Innovation and technology in computer science education*. ACM, 273–278.

[12] LARC 2018. Learning Analytics Data Architecture, University of Michigan. https://enrollment.umich.edu/data-research/learning-analytics-data-architecture-larc

[13] Dan Leyzberg, Jérémie Lumbroso, and Christopher Moretti. 2017. Nailing the TA interview: Using a rubric to hire teaching assistants. In *Proceedings of the 2017 ACM Conference on Innovation and Technology in Computer Science Education*. ACM, 128–133.

[14] Allison Master, Sapna Cheryan, and Andrew N Meltzoff. 2016. Computing whether she belongs: Stereotypes undermine girls' interest and sense of belonging in computer science. *Journal of Educational Psychology* 108, 3 (2016), 424.

[15] Katie Redmond, Sarah Evans, and Mehran Sahami. 2013. A large-scale quantitative study of women in computer science at Stanford University. In *Proceeding of the 44th ACM technical symposium on Computer science education*. ACM, 439–444.

[16] Stuart Reges. 2003. Using undergraduates as teaching assistants at a state university. In *ACM SIGCSE Bulletin*, Vol. 35. ACM, 103–107.

[17] Eric Roberts, John Lilly, and Bryan Rollins. 1995. Using undergraduates as teaching assistants in introductory programming courses: An update on the Stanford experience. *ACM SIGCSE Bulletin* 27, 1 (1995), 48–52.

[18] Eric S Roberts, Marina Kassianidou, and Lilly Irani. 2002. Encouraging women in computer science. *ACM SIGCSE Bulletin* 34, 2 (2002), 84–88.

[19] Olgun Sadik. 2015. Encouraging women to become CS teachers. In *Proceedings of the Third Conference on GenderIT*. ACM, 57–61.

[20] Jenessa R Shapiro and Amy M Williams. 2012. The role of stereotype threats in undermining girls' and women's performance and interest in STEM fields. *Sex Roles* 66, 3-4 (2012), 175–183.

[21] Lily Shashaani. 1994. Gender-differences in computer experience and its influence on computer attitudes. *Journal of Educational Computing Research* 11, 4 (1994), 347–367.

[22] Steven J Spencer, Claude M Steele, and Diane M Quinn. 1999. Stereotype threat and women's math performance. *Journal of experimental social psychology* 35, 1 (1999), 4–28.

[23] Claude M Steele. 1997. A threat in the air: How stereotypes shape intellectual identity and performance. *American psychologist* 52, 6 (1997), 613.

[24] Jane G Stout, Nilanjana Dasgupta, Matthew Hunsinger, and Melissa A McManus. 2011. STEMing the tide: using ingroup experts to inoculate women's self-concept in science, technology, engineering, and mathematics (STEM). *Journal of personality and social psychology* 100, 2 (2011), 255.

PythonSneks: An Open-Source, Instructionally-Designed Introductory Curriculum with Action-Design Research

Austin Cory Bart
University of Delaware
Newark, DE
acbart@udel.edu

Allie Sarver
Virginia Tech
Blacksburg, VA
afsarver@vt.edu

Michael Friend
Virginia Tech
Blacksburg, VA
mrf7@vt.edu

Larry Cox II
Virginia Tech
Blacksburg, VA
lacox@vt.edu

ABSTRACT

Rising enrollments and limited instructor resources underscores the growing need for reusable, scalable curriculum. In this paper, we describe an open-source introductory Python course for non-Computer Science majors in STEM, designed following best practices of Instructional Design (a process similar to Software Engineering). The created resources include 234 learning objectives, 51 lesson videos, 45 lecture slides, 170 programming problems, 281 quiz questions, 6 unit tested projects, and 4 ethical prompts. A teaching field guide has also been produced as a result of this effort, documenting how to deploy this curriculum on a daily level. We describe our experiences deploying over two semesters. The course serviced over 500 students, with 100s in some sections. Along the way, two interventions were conducted in an Action Design Research style: one using Worked Examples, and another using Structured Small Groups. We report on the mixed results of these experiments, plus evaluations of the assignments from student surveys and statistical measures of item effectiveness. Finally, we describe lessons learned when following Instructional Design processes.

CCS CONCEPTS

• **Social and professional topics → Computing education; Model curricula; CS1;**

KEYWORDS

Python; Instructional Design; Open Curriculum

ACM Reference Format:
Austin Cory Bart, Allie Sarver, Michael Friend, and Larry Cox II. 2019. PythonSneks: An Open-Source, Instructionally-Designed Introductory Curriculum with Action-Design Research. In *Proceedings of Proceedings of the 50th ACM Technical Symposium on Computer Science Education (SIGCSE '19).* ACM, New York, NY, USA, 7 pages. https://doi.org/10.1145/3287324.3287428

ACM ISBN 978-1-4503-5890-3/19/02...$15.00
https://doi.org/10.1145/3287324.3287428

1 INTRODUCTION

Ever rising enrollments are bringing more students to computing courses, requiring more instructors and scalable curriculum. Frequently, these busy instructors are forced to reinvent much of their curriculum from scratch even as they gather materials from disparate external sources. The limited time and resources available leads to a lack of systematic processes in curriculum development, which can cause a wide range of issues: instructors focusing on lesson plans without reference to established assessments, course staff becoming out-of-sync on learning objectives, and untested assignments with errors and typos. The end result is overworked instructors struggling to make do with inadequate curriculum.

Curriculum Sharing is one mechanism that can reduce the burden on instructors. Open-sourced curriculum developed by other instructors can be adopted and improved. However, the authors have found few modern introductory computing curricula that follow best practices of *Instructional Design*: systematic construction of a curriculum, with parallels to Software Engineering. Most resources available are only parts of a full curriculum, not easily modified, and not tuned to a conventional undergraduate setting.

Working with an Instructional Designer, we created an introductory Python curriculum (PythonSneks) to fill this gap. Our vision is of an introductory curriculum that is easily adopted by instructors but inherently open and modifiable. The material is targeted at undergraduate non-computing majors with a range of prior experiences in a typical undergraduate setting, but suitable for other contexts. The course incorporates many modern pedagogical methods to reach large (100+) audiences: flipped-classroom lessons, peer instruction, active learning, and activities with immediate feedback. When deploying our course in the past year, the developers collected a large amount of data for course evaluation and answering research questions using an Action Research approach. We summarize the results of the above in the hopes that other adopters will use the materials to refine their own courses. Ultimately, this paper makes the following contributions:

- Description of the development, deployment, and evaluation of an open-source Python curriculum (available publicly at https://acbart.github.io/python-sneks/).
- Results from two experimental interventions on the courses' second offering, on Worked Examples and Structured Groups.
- Lessons for other curricula that seek to be open-source.

2 EXISTING CURRICULUM

As the most popular introductory language for university undergraduate courses [9], there are a large number of existing introductory Python curricula. Prior to developing our curriculum, we surveyed a number of courses from the literature and explicitly sought out more via a post on the SIGCSE-Members mailing list [2]. In this section, we review a subset of our findings, and discuss why we think our approach is a useful addition to the field. A complete listing of alternative curricula that we found is available at https://acbart.github.io/python-sneks/alternatives.

A recurring problem we found in reviewing courses is the limited accessibility of materials. For instance, [17] describes a curriculum, but provides no way to access materials. Although most instructors are willing to share when prompted, the social barrier of reaching out is often associated with unpackaged materials. Of course, there are projects that have published their materials. Chor & Hod describe a largely lecture-based curriculum (CS1001.py) focused on a wide range of Computer Science oriented topics (hashing, fibonacci, sorting, etc.) [6], representative of many similar approaches from the last few decades. Although suitable for students already interested in Computer Science, it is unclear how well such topics would appeal to broader, non-major audiences. Further, as we will describe, few such curricula follow principles of Instructional Design.

In response to the more abstract Computer Science courses, a number of courses have been created with a contextualized approach. Guzdial popularized a Python curriculum based on Media Computation in the early 2000s that saw wide-spread adoption [11]. This curriculum attempted to appeal to students' sense of interest in media and animation manipulation. Unfortunately, much of the curriculum's dependent technology seems to have stagnated [12]. Kafura et al describes an introductory Computational Thinking curriculum for non-majors based around Data Science [15], an arguably more authentic and useful context. However, because it was designed to be accessible for a wide audience, its learning objectives are targeted at a lowest common denominator of students and covers a limited set of topics.

Joyner's open MOOC-based curriculum is perhaps closest in our vision to an open introductory curriculum [14], and should be seen as a comparable project. Joyner's work is still being refined and disseminated, but preliminary reviews suggest there are many fine-grained differences in the approaches (e.g., different styles of material presentation, different content delivery platforms). For now, the course seems to be more biased towards its MOOC roots, without as much emphasis on the in-classroom perspective. Our hope is to design a curriculum that can be easily adaptable to instructors in traditional university settings. Another similarly high-quality open curriculum is the Exploring Computer Science program [8]. Although their materials are extremely well designed and articulated (including both assessments and learning objectives alongside their teaching field guide), the expected audience is primary and secondary schools. A number of companies and private entities have published free online curriculum for learning Python (e.g., CodeCademy, Coursera), but the materials are rarely open-source and are not tuned for university settings either. Evaluations of these curriculum are internal and not publicized.

There have been a number of papers that describe parts of curricula, projects, and assignments. There are even repositories (e.g., EngageCSEdu [19] and Ensemble [5]) of such materials. While many of these can become invaluable components of highly effective courses, it is critical to understand that, from an Instructional Design perspective, these are only *pieces* of a curriculum, whether they be interactive textbooks (e.g., [18]), lecture slides, or collections of auto-graded programming problems (e.g., CodingBat [22]). We argue that a curriculum is the sum of a large number of course artifacts that are designed to provide a series of learning experiences to learners, mediated into concrete course offerings by instructors. It is this sum of pieces that we seek to develop, disseminate, and evaluate in this publication, not individual components or ideas.

3 CONSTRUCTING A NEW CURRICULUM

After reviewing the above curricula, we chose to move forward with developing our own course. We do not claim that any particular element of our courses' design is ground-breaking. This is intentional – we seek to incorporate best practices and existing material. Instead, the major distinction of our curriculum from the prior work is the intersection of 3 principles:

(1) Materials should be documented and created in such a way that they can be shared externally in an editable way.
(2) Modern pedagogical techniques should be used to teach modern topics supported by modern technology.
(3) The course must scale to hundreds of students while still fitting within the conventional university course model.

3.1 Instructional Design

To satisfy our first principle, the lead course designer worked with an instructional designer and followed a formal Instructional Design model based on Dick & Carey [7]. Instructional Design is a systematic process akin to Software Engineering [3] that aligns learning outcomes, assessments, and instruction while simultaneously encouraging documentation and evaluation along the way.

We began with topics drawn from various sources, including syntactical features (e.g., how to write `for` loops), software engineering strategies (e.g., writing unit tests), computational theory (e.g., runtime complexity), and high-level critical thinking (e.g., solving open-ended problems). We oriented our topics around language features as an organizational aid: Figure 1 visualizes their order, divided into two strands of Data and Algorithms (branching off of Program Fundamentals). From the topics, 234 subordinate learning objectives were detailed and grouped, all descended from the following terminal learning objective: *"Create simple Python programs that solve problems."*

Parallel to the development of learning objectives, we conducted an analysis of the learners so we could establish appropriate criteria: student demographics and instructor interviews led to a determination of expected student prior skills and motivations. Informed by these analyses, we then transformed each subordinate learning objective into one or more assessment questions. Finally, instructional materials were prepared based directly on the objectives and assessments. These materials incorporated a mixture of presentation (asynchronous video lessons and synchronous lecture slides) and practice opportunities (programming problems, quiz and clicker

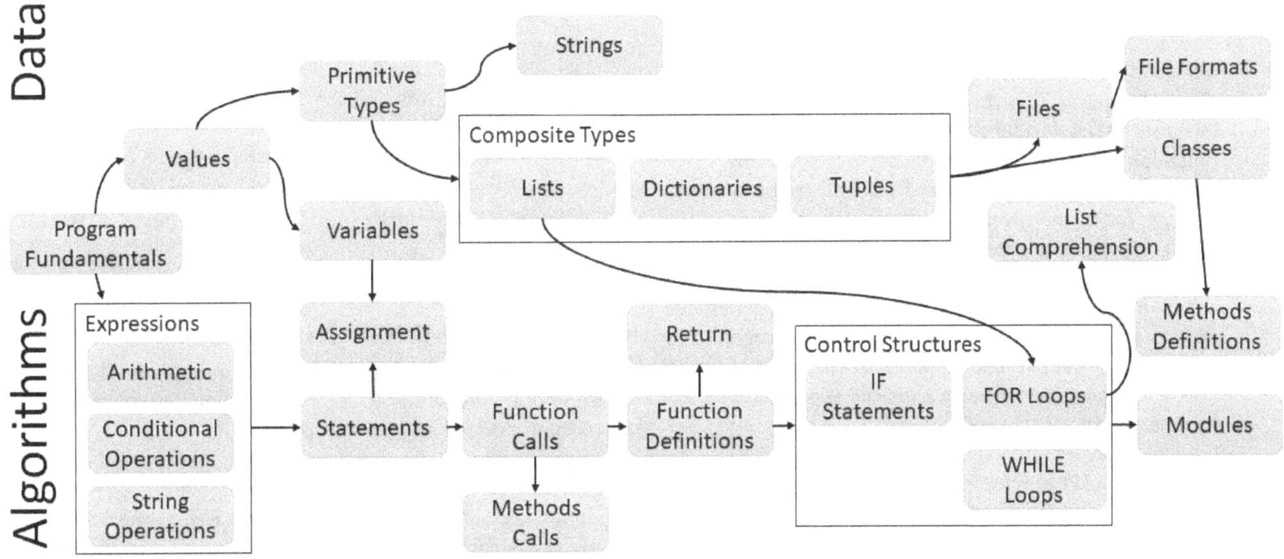

Figure 1: An Overview of the Sneks Curriculum, from a topics perspective

234	Learning objectives
281	Quiz Questions
170	Programming problems
51	Video lessons
45	Annotated Lecture Slides
6	Projects
4	Essay-based Ethics Assignments
2	Final Assessments
1	Teacher's Guidebook

Figure 2: Quantity of Curricular Resources

questions, essays, and projects). Along the way, we documented our instructional strategies into a Teacher's Guidebook (publicly available at https://acbart.github.io/python-sneks/). Figure 2 breaks down the complete set of created resources.

3.2 Pedagogy and Materials

In this section, we detail the pedagogy selected to deliver the course content. The Sneks curriculum is not meant to be revolutionary or experimental, it is meant to be well-engineered and clearly articulated. To that end, and in satisfaction of our second principle, most of the courses' pedagogy was selected based on best practices from the literature. Per our third principle, course materials were designed to fit into the framework of a typical undergraduate university course. For our purposes, this means a 14-week semester where students meet in-person for lecture and have access to a modern online learning management system (i.e., Canvas). However, we also wish to handle large classes of hundreds of students, so many decisions were motivated by scalability concerns.

To handle the large class sizes, a team of (largely undergraduate) teaching assistants supports the instructors by attending class, with a 30:1 student-to-staff ratio. The instructional staff met weekly to preview upcoming lessons, review previous assignments, coordinate grading, and receive pedagogical training. The training material was based off the curriculum by Tychonievich [27]; our strategies for deploying it are included in the Teacher's Guidebook.

The majority of the course content is delivered in a Flipped Classroom style [4, 13] via 51 asynchronous video lessons. Based on the guidelines of [10], each video was designed to be short (around 2-4 minutes) and concisely teach a small set of learning objectives. Each video has PDFs, narration, captions, and transcripts available. Lectures slides were also created, but are brief: the in-class lecture component lasts less than 20 minutes. Little didactic instruction is used during this time, instead focusing on Peer Instruction activities [23], live coding demos, and other active learning lecture strategies [24]. The majority of class time is instead dedicated to students completing assignments with help from the course staff.

Each video lesson is associated with a short quiz (averaging about 5 questions) of multiple choice, fill-in-the-blank, and other automatically graded conceptual questions. These quizzes are meant to be delivered in a mastery learning style, with students having repeated opportunities to complete them. Most lessons also have 3-4 programming problems associated with them. Like the quizzes, the programming assignments are automatically graded and paired with immediate feedback to scaffold the learners. These problems are small exercises, typically requiring less than 10 lines of code.

Lessons are organized into modules, and each module pair is capped with a project. Lessons align with the subordinate learning objectives, in the same way that the modules align with the major topics. The nature of the projects vary in topic, scope, and context. However, each attempts to incorporate opportunities for student agency and creativity, amusing stories, or other motivational elements.

(1) Turtle Art (Function calls): Use functions from the Turtle module to create a piece of art of their own design.
(2) Magical Banking (Function definitions and data passing): Integrate a black-box function and code a sequence of simple functions to make a banking application for wizards.
(3) Survey Statistics (For Loops and Lists): Develop a survey question for an alien overlord, gather responses, and analyze the data using simple iteration patterns.
(4) Text Adventure (While Loops and Dictionaries): Plan and create an interactive text-based adventure game with mutable, structured state based on a simple game framework.
(5) Data Science (Data Processing and Visualization): Analyze a self-selected dataset to generate visualizations and perform open-ended statistical explorations.
(6) Canvas Analyzer (Summative of all course topics): Use the Canvas LMS API to retrieve and analyze mock student data and the learner's actual course data.

Interweaved between the modules are 4 essays oriented around ethical dilemmas in computing. These essays are ordered to situate the students first as consumers of technology and then as producers of technology. Student responses are meant to be brief and are graded with an established rubric. For each prompt, students must 1) summarize a provided situation incorporating an ethical dilemma, 2) take a clear stance, 3) write a coherent argument supporting their stance, 4) reference a relevant ethical theory or guideline, and 5) write with understandable spelling, grammar, and punctuation.

The course is capped with a final exam based directly on the quizzes and programming questions. This exam is administered using the same platform as the other questions, and graded automatically. TA proctors are physically present to prevent cheating.

3.3 External Adoption

External adoption is a primary goal of the PythonSneks curriculum. The courses' components (and their source) are available through GitHub, while the course itself is available on the Canvas learning management system. Two audiences are in mind for these resources: power users who want a la carte access, and casual adopters who want to use the curriculum without modification. We encourage both cases, but request that adopters report their experiences (either informally or formally) using the GitHub Issue tracker and by filling out the Experience Report forms available in the repository.

Very little space in this paper is dedicated to the technology used in the course. Although our Teacher's Guide covers a number of options and our own reasoning for using various tools and platforms, our goal is to decouple the curriculum from the tools. The justification for this is that tools are transient: for example, the desktop programming environment used by students to complete projects (Spyder) is in the process of being retired – future semesters plan to use the educational Thonny environment, but there are a number of other viable options (PyCharm, Wing, etc.). To this end, many of the assignments and resources are being modified to be compliant with emerging standards developed for the CSSPlice project [1] to encourage adoption without respect to a particular tool.

[1]https://cssplice.github.io/

Project	Easy	Interest	Useful
Turtle Art	3	3	2
Magical Banking	2	3	3
Survey Statistics	2	3	3
Text Adventure	1	4	3
Data Science	3	3	4
Canvas Analyzer	1	3	3

Figure 3: Student Responses about Projects' Attributes

4 DEPLOYMENT AND EVALUATION

A critical element of the Sneks curriculum is pre-planned evaluation of the materials after its deployments. Evaluation is an important phase of any Instructional Design process, and critical to improvement. We present quantitative metrics of the quiz questions and programming problems, along with subjective student survey responses about the overall course components. In addition to the evaluation of the curriculum, we also conducted two quasi-experimental interventions. Issues with the course were identified in the fall as baseline data was collected. Several issues were particularly targeted in the Spring with interventions. In both cases, we attempted to apply emerging theories from the Computing Education literature that we hoped would overcome the issues. Each intervention was led by an undergraduate research assistant.

4.1 Evaluations

So far, the PythonSneks curriculum has been offered in Fall 2017 (281 students) and in Spring 2018 (240 students). Roughly 34% of students were female, and roughly 84% had some kind of prior programming experience (high school, another course at community college, etc.). The DFW (Ds, Fs, and Withdraws) rate was 7.1% in the fall and 7.3% in the spring. In this section, we offer some of the preliminary evaluations conducted of these offerings. The evaluations given here are not meant to be summative or definitive, but demonstrate the range of ways that the course can be measured.

Data was collected through both the LMS' grade systems, the coding platforms logging systems, and from surveys. These surveys were administered every other module to both students and teaching assistants. Student surveys asked questions about which learning resources were particularly helpful to their learning, their habits with regards to the video lessons, overall course motivation, and their suggestions for improvements to the modules they just completed. TA surveys asked questions about particular student misconceptions, useful teaching strategies, and suggestions for revising the most recent modules.

Figure 3 gives a summary of student responses to survey questions about the six course projects. For each project, students chose from 5-point likert style questions (e.g., "Very hard", "Somewhat hard", "Neither hard nor easy", "Somewhat easy", "Very easy" map to 0-4). The number shown is the median numeric response to each question, with the final column as a cumulative score for the project. Most projects were at least somewhat interesting to students, but they ranged in difficulty and usefulness. From a revision viewpoint, the final project's difficulty may be appropriate, but it would be

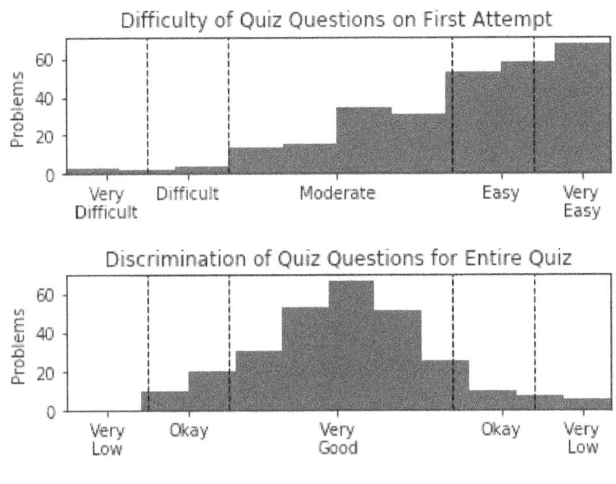

Figure 4: Summary of Quiz Questions

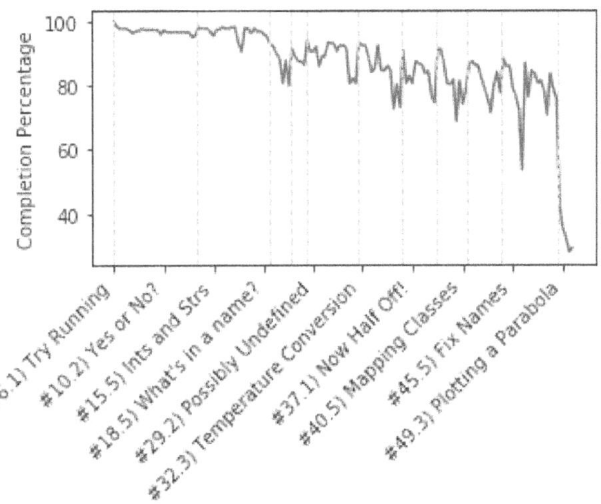

Figure 5: Completion of Programming Problems over Time

ideal if the project's interest or usefulness were higher to balance this out (as the Text Adventure accomplishes).

Figure 4 are histograms of the quiz questions' difficulty and discrimination. In this case, difficulty was measured as the proportion of students who gave a correct answer on their first attempt at a question; the X-axis has been labeled with an interpretation of these numbers. Discrimination is given as the Pearson correlation of each students' score with their overall quiz score, indicating how well this particular question predicts the quiz. Using these metrics, individual questions can be assessed for their fit. The distribution of question difficulty does suggest that most questions skew towards being easier, but that they tend to discriminate fairly well.

Figure 5 gives a time-oriented view of programming problem completion rate. The vertical lines indicate the start of a new module, while the blue line is the percentage of students who have completed a given problem. Although completion rates trend well over most of the course, they nosedive when the assignments overlap with the final project, possibly indicating a need to bifurcate the start of the project from the remainder of the assignments.

Upon finishing the second deployment of the Sneks curriculum, a total of 41 major redesign considerations were identified. These considerations have been divided into low (16), medium (21), and high (4) priority issues, and into categories such as organizational issues (*"TAs sometimes were unprepared: allocate time for TAs to try assignments as part of their job responsibilities"*), topical issues (*"String traversal is explained better in lecture than in the video lessons, so relevant content should be moved."*), and lingering student misconceptions (*" Students believe that variables passed into a function call must have the same name as the formal parameters"*).

4.2 Action Design Research

The next two sections describe interventions staged during the second offering of the course. Educational research is frequently confounded by the rapidly changing target space and variability between semesters, frustrating efforts to control populations for experimental validity. We share the beliefs suggested by Nelson and Ko [21], that the quest for unarguably valid experimental results is a detriment to progress in perfecting designs within computing education. The Sneks curriculum is ultimately a design artifact, and so frequently decisions were made that could affect the sanctity of our experiments. We allowed modifications in a systematic way that would contribute to the research space, while acknowledging the dynamic nature of educational settings. Therefore, we approach our modifications from a Action Design Research (ADR) perspective [26]. When ADR is used in an educational setting, the result is similar to Instructional Design: an iterative cycle of identifying problems in existing curricula, implementing changes, and observing the impact. Therefore, the interventions presented in this section should be taken with the caveat that the studies are static-group comparison designs, and understood for their limitations.

4.3 Worked Examples Intervention

Problem: Students struggle with difficult programming problems.

Theory: Worked Examples are examples of similar problems, consisting of a "problem formulation, solution steps, and the final answer itself" [25]. Prior work suggests providing Worked Examples with clear subgoal labels could help students deconstruct problems and improve performance [16, 20].

Hypothesis: Providing high quality Worked Examples could help students complete more problems faster and with less stress.

Research Questions:

(1) Do students take advantage of Worked Examples?
(2) Do Worked Examples improve performance?
(3) Do students find Worked Examples helpful?

Intervention: In the second course offering, 8 problems were selected as the hardest (based on the metric that it took students longer than average). Worked Examples were created for each problem and made available to students in the problem prompt.

Data Collection: Quantitative Data was collected via exercise completion rates and student interaction in the coding platform. Qualitative Data was collected via a survey on student opinion and usage of Worked Examples.

Results: Usage of the Worked Examples varied between problems, but roughly 42% of students took advantage of them. Surprisingly, students who took advantage of Worked Examples complete problems at roughly the same rate as those who did not. Students who used WEs actually took significantly more time to complete problems; focusing on students with no prior experience, we see those that used the WE actually took over twice the time as those who did not. However, almost 64% of students found the WEs to be helpful to their learning, with only 18% explicitly disagreeing.

Conclusion: The Worked Examples seemed to have minimal effect on the completion rate of problems, and possibly even negatively affected students by slowing them down, even though many students used them and found them helpful.

Limitations: First, all problems had high completion rates (80-90%) even before introducing Worked Examples. Second, the non-random assignment of students in the treatment could hide a more positive effect size. Third, it is possible that our WEs were more like tutorials than WEs.

4.4 Structured Groups Intervention

Problem: Students report that they do not feel prepared to begin a large-scale project

Theory: Micro-classes group students within a large lecture hall, previously shown to foster community [1].

Hypothesis: If students are given structure to form groups naturally, the enhanced community will contribute to their preparedness

Research Questions:

(1) Do groups increase students' sense of community?
(2) Is students' sense of community associated with their preparedness to begin a complex project?

Intervention: On the first class period after Project 2 began, the class was divided into 8 sections, each managed by a TA. Within each section, students were encouraged to organically form small groups. Students then worked together to answer questions about the upcoming project. Afterwards, students were prompted to begin working on the project together, with an emphasis on using student community to solve any problems they may come upon.

Data Collection: After two classes of project work, students took a Likert-style survey to assess their readiness to begin the project, their sense of classroom community, and if their sense of community was helpful in solving problems. This same survey was administered after the final project in the previous semester

Results: As shown in Figure 6, students reported a significantly (as evaluated by a Mann-Whitney U test) increased sense of community relative to the prior semester, but did not feel significantly more prepared to begin the project. There was a significant but moderate Spearman Rank Correlation of .41 between these metrics.

Conclusions: Although working with others did make a majority of students feel more prepared to start the project, the increased sense of community did not seem to help students feel more prepared to start their project.

Limitations: Data was never collected directly on whether students struggled to get started with each project, and the surveys were administered between different semesters for different projects. Finally, A possible limitation of student-selected peer groups is that novices working with novices may not feel that they have any new information, and will still need additional assistance.

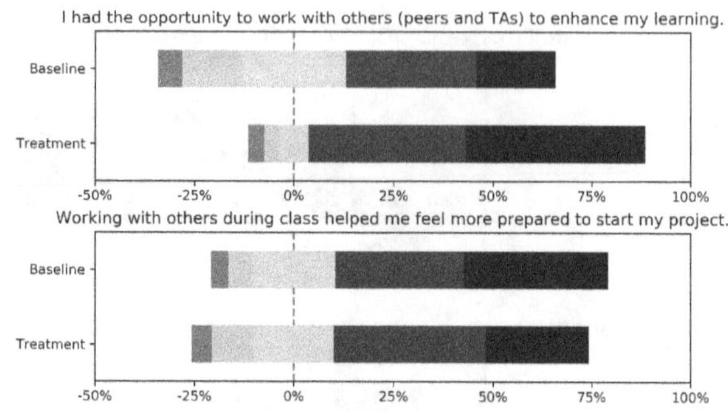

Figure 6: Students' Perceptions of Structured Groups

5 RECOMMENDATIONS

In this section, we describe lessons learned when developing.

1) Follow Instructional Design processes: Not only does ID provide a clear, systematic process to guide novice course developers, but it encourages high quality material that is well-aligned.

2) Design for privacy: As course resources are developed, consider how you will maintain question answer security and anonymize data for potential research publications and future course analysis. Once released, data can be difficult to remove from records.

3) Consider evaluations: How will you assess your questions for their quality? How will you know if students enjoyed your projects? Which resources were most helpful to students? Do not rely on anecdotal evidence, but collect concrete data.

4) Plan for a lengthy development process: As is frequently recognized, course development is a lengthy process. Course development began the summer before the course's first offering, and continued throughout despite full-time commitment from the primary developer. In the latter portions of the course, projects were frequently completed shortly before they were deployed.

6 CONCLUSIONS

In this paper, we describe an Instructional-Designed, open-source curriculum consisting of a large number of formal learning objectives, aligned assessments, and learning material. Although the Python Sneks curriculum has not been externally validated or summatively evaluated, it is not meant to represent a final version. In some sense, the curriculum is a straw-man, ready to be knocked down by more sophisticated curriculum with superior learning objectives and activities. We hope that our reporting on it will motivate not only external adoption, but also the creation and dissemination of other university-level open-source curricula that follow formal Instructional Design processes.

ACKNOWLEDGMENTS

The authors would like to thank the Virginia Tech Technology-enhanced Learning and Online Strategies (TLOS) group for their support in developing this course.

REFERENCES

[1] Christine Alvarado, Mia Minnes, and Leo Porter. 2017. Micro-Classes: A Structure for Improving Student Experience in Large Classes. In *Proceedings of the 2017 ACM SIGCSE Technical Symposium on Computer Science Education*. 21–26.

[2] Austin Cory Bart. 2017. What's Your Favorite "Introduction to Computing" with Python Curriculum? (2017). SIGCSE-Members Electronic Mailing List; posted on 27 Apr 2017.

[3] Austin Cory Bart and Clifford A Shaffer. 2016. Instructional Design is to Teaching as Software Engineering is to Programming. In *Proceedings of the 47th ACM Technical Symposium on Computing Science Education*. 240–241.

[4] Jennifer Campbell, Diane Horton, Michelle Craig, and Paul Gries. 2014. Evaluating an Inverted CS1. In *Proceedings of the 45th ACM Technical Symposium on Computer Science Education (SIGCSE '14)*.

[5] Lillian Boots Cassel, Ed Fox, Frank Shipman, Peter Brusilovsky, Weiguo Fax, Dan Garcia, Greg Hislop, Richard Furuta, Lois Delcambre, and Sridhara Potluri. 2010. Ensemble: enriching communities and collections to support education in computing: poster session. *Journal of Computing Sciences in Colleges* 25, 6 (2010), 224–226.

[6] Benny Chor and Rani Hod. 2012. CS1001.Py: A Topic-based Introduction to Computer Science. In *Proceedings of the 17th ACM Annual Conference on Innovation and Technology in Computer Science Education (ITiCSE '12)*. 215–220.

[7] Walter Dick, Lou Carey, and James O Carey. 2005. The systematic design of instruction. (2005).

[8] Joanna Goode, Gail Chapman, and Jane Margolis. 2012. Beyond curriculum: the exploring computer science program. *ACM Inroads* 3, 2 (2012).

[9] Philip Guo. 2014. Python is now the most popular introductory teaching language at top us universities. *BLOG@ CACM, July* (2014), 47.

[10] Philip J Guo, Juho Kim, and Rob Rubin. 2014. How video production affects student engagement: an empirical study of MOOC videos. In *Proceedings of the first ACM conference on Learning@ scale conference*.

[11] Mark Guzdial. 2003. A media computation course for non-majors. In *ACM SIGCSE Bulletin*, Vol. 35. 104–108.

[12] Mark Guzdial. 2016. Where are the Python 3 Libraries for Media Computation. (2016). https://computinged.wordpress.com/2016/08/19/where-are-the-python-3-libraries-for-media-computation/

[13] Diane Horton and Michelle Craig. 2015. Drop, Fail, Pass, Continue: Persistence in CS1 and Beyond in Traditional and Inverted Delivery. In *Proceedings of the 46th ACM Technical Symposium on Computer Science Education (SIGCSE '15)*.

[14] David A. Joyner. 2017. Congruency, Adaptivity, Modularity, and Personalization: Four Experiments in Teaching Introduction to Computing. In *Proceedings of the Fourth (2017) ACM Conference on Learning @ Scale (L@S '17)*. 307–310.

[15] Dennis Kafura, Austin Cory Bart, and Bushra Chowdhury. 2015. Design and Preliminary Results From a Computational Thinking Course. In *Proceedings of the 2015 ACM Conference on Innovation and Technology in Computer Science Education*. 63–68.

[16] Lauren E Margulieux and Richard Catrambone. 2014. Improving problem solving performance in computer-based learning environments through subgoal labels. In *Proceedings of the first ACM conference on Learning@ scale conference*.

[17] Cindy Marling and David Juedes. 2016. CS0 for Computer Science Majors at Ohio University *(SIGCSE '16)*. 138–143.

[18] B Miller, D Ranum, J Elkner, P Wentworth, AB Downey, C Meyers, and D Mitchell. 2012. How to think like a computer scientist. *Runestone Interactive Project (http://interactivepython. org/courselib/static/thinkcspy/index. html)* (2012).

[19] Alvaro E Monge, Cameron L Fadjo, Beth A Quinn, and Lecia J Barker. 2015. EngageCSEdu: engaging and retaining CS1 and CS2 students. *ACM Inroads* 6, 1 (2015), 6–11.

[20] Briana B Morrison, Lauren E Margulieux, and Mark Guzdial. 2015. Subgoals, context, and worked examples in learning computing problem solving. In *Proceedings of the eleventh annual international conference on international computing education research*.

[21] Greg L. Nelson and Andrew J. Ko. 2018. On Use of Theory in Computing Education Research. In *Proceedings of the 2018 ACM Conference on International Computing Education Research (ICER '18)*.

[22] Nick Parlante. 2015. CodingBat. *Com (Retrieved 1/08/2011 from http://codingbat. com, 2011)* (2015).

[23] Leo Porter, Dennis Bouvier, Quintin Cutts, Scott Grissom, Cynthia Lee, Robert McCartney, Daniel Zingaro, and Beth Simon. 2016. A Multi-institutional Study of Peer Instruction in Introductory Computing. In *Proceedings of the 47th ACM Technical Symposium on Computing Science Education (SIGCSE '16)*.

[24] Kate Sanders, Jonas Boustedt, Anna Eckerdal, Robert McCartney, and Carol Zander. 2017. Folk Pedagogy: Nobody Doesn'T Like Active Learning. In *Proceedings of the 2017 ACM Conference on International Computing Education Research (ICER '17)*.

[25] Ben Skudder and Andrew Luxton-Reilly. 2014. Worked examples in computer science. In *Proceedings of the Sixteenth Australasian Computing Education Conference-Volume 148*.

[26] Ernest T Stringer. 2008. *Action research in education*. Pearson Prentice Hall Upper Saddle River, NJ.

[27] Luther A. Tychonievich. 2017. Training Course for Teaching Assistants in Computing. (May 2017). https://www.cs.virginia.edu/luther/ta-training

Defining and Designing Computer Science Education in a K12 Public School District

Chris Proctor*
Stanford University
Stanford, CA
cproctor@stanford.edu

Maxwell Bigman†
Harvard University
Cambridge, MA
mbigman@gse.harvard.edu

Paulo Blikstein
Columbia University
New York, NY
paulob@tc.columbia.edu

ABSTRACT

Computer science is poised to become a core discipline in K12 education, however there are unresolved tensions between the definitions and purposes of computer science and public education. This study's goal is to explore how logistical and conceptual challenges emerge while designing a comprehensive K12 computer science program in a public school district. While the policy infrastructure for K12 computer science education is rapidly developing, few districts have yet implemented computer science as a core discipline in their K12 programs and very little research has explored the challenges involved in putting ideas into practice. This study reports on a committee designing a comprehensive K12 computer science education program at a small public school district in California. Through a grounded-theory qualitative interpretation of committee-member interviews and board meeting transcripts, we surfaced three themes which were the primary points of tension: how computer science is defined, how it ought to be taught, and what process ought to be used to answer these questions. Grounding these tensions in the academic discourse on K12 computer science education, this study offers recommendations to other districts designing comprehensive computer science education and suggests future directions of computer science education research that will be most useful to stakeholders of these processes.

CCS CONCEPTS

• **Social and professional topics → Computer science education; Computing literacy; K-12 education;** *Computational thinking*;

ACM Reference Format:
Chris Proctor, Maxwell Bigman, and Paulo Blikstein. 2019. Defining and Designing Computer Science Education in a K12 Public School District. In *Proceedings of the 50th ACM Technical Symposium on Computer Science Education (SIGCSE '19), February 27-March 2, 2019, Minneapolis, MN, USA.* ACM, New York, NY, USA, Article 4, 7 pages. https://doi.org/10.1145/3287324.3287440

*Equal first author
†Equal first author

SIGCSE '19, February 27-March 2, 2019, Minneapolis, MN, USA

ACM ISBN 978-1-4503-5890-3/19/02...$15.00
https://doi.org/10.1145/3287324.3287440

1 INTRODUCTION

Even though computers shape our political, economic, and social lives, K12 education in the United States does not include comprehensive computer science. When they are available at all, opportunities to learn computer science are marginal and piecemeal. AP CS enrolls mostly high-performing, college-bound students. Some students learn programming in extracurricular activities like robotics and maker spaces and clubs. Equity-focused interventions such as Exploring Computer Science [16] and Hour of Code have made progress in exposing more students to computer science. A thriving economy of educational technologies and out-of-school learning opportunities has emerged for those who can afford them. Computation rivals textual literacy in societal significance, but our schools do not systematically prepare children to participate as workers or citizens.

The computer science education community has made substantial progress on developing the infrastructure needed for comprehensive K12 CS education. Several CS curriculum standards have been published [13, 27]. The K-12 CS Framework [1] united the major stakeholders to produce a document intended as guidance to those developing standards and curricula. Various states have adopted existing computer science standards while others, including California and New York, are developing their own. At the same time, states are developing teacher credentialing standards [18] and teacher preparation programs to train computer science teachers.

As this infrastructure is still emerging in the United States, there are few examples of K12 CS program implementations, and very little research has been published on them. Several large urban school districts, including New York [29], San Francisco [28], and Los Angeles [19], are in the process of implementing K12 CS. The initial evaluation report on New York's CS4All initiative emphasizes the need for schools to develop local visions for computer science [29], and calls for case studies of school-based implementations (p. 55). We have been unable to find case studies documenting the process of designing and implementing K12 CS at smaller school districts. As other school districts consider making computer science a core K12 subject area, reports of prior experience will be valuable.

This case study of a small suburban school district's three-year process of designing a K12 CS program addresses this gap in research. Our analysis of interviews with committee members and presentations to the board of education surfaced three themes which were the focus of discussion and conflict in the committee and the broader community:

(1) What is the district's vision for computer science?
(2) How should the district's K12 CS program be implemented and taught?

(3) What process should be used to answer these questions (and who should participate)?

This study characterizes the development of each theme, grounds each in the broader discourse of computer science education, and offers recommendations for how other communities can engage productively with them. This study may be of interest to stakeholders of other school districts designing computer science programs, as well as academics studying teaching and learning in K12 CS. Stakeholders in other school districts–whether they are designing district-wide computer science programs or local implementations within large districts–may recognize the themes reported in this case study, and be able to avoid some of the conflict encountered in this district's process. The committee which is the focus of this study relied on existing research, but found it necessary to build their own shared understanding of what computer science is and how it should be taught. For researchers studying teaching and learning in computer science, the opportunity to see how academic discourse is taken up by practitioners may inform future research.

2 BACKGROUND

There is a substantial body of work considering teaching and learning in K12 CS. Although this study uses a grounded-theory approach [10] to surface the ways in which committee members came to understand computer science, this section summarizes the research which was the context for the committee's work and which frames the conversation to which this study contributes. Barr & Stephenson [3] argue for several ways the computer science education research community can contribute to the design and implementation of K12 programs. These include each of the major themes, listed above, which emerged from the interviews with committee members and board meeting transcripts.

Barr & Stephenson [3] emphasize the importance of uniting behind an "operational definition" (p. 49) of what is to be taught[1]. Each of the computer science standards documents has given a definition of computer science, and has acknowledged the difficulty of defining a young and dynamic field. Strategies for defining computer science fall into three broad groups. The first is identifying the fundamental ideas [8] or essential questions [30] at the heart of a field. This approach has been particularly attractive for computer science, which can be seen as a way of working directly with powerful ideas and thinking about thinking [22]. A second approach considers a field not as an abstract body of knowledge, but as a set of practices enacted within a community. To borrow a phrase from Roy Pea, computer science is what computer scientists do. An attractive feature of this framing is that it acknowledges cognition as situated [7] in the context of particular identities, cultures, tools, and spaces which can be important factors in equitable participation [4, 20, 21]. The K-12 CS Framework [1] and the revised CSTA standards [13] each define computer science in terms of concepts and practices. A third, more pragmatic, approach defines a field in terms of competencies. What exactly can experts do? Denning [12], for example, argues that computational thinking is a poorly-defined construct responsible for much confusion in K12 CS education, and that we would do better to focus on clearly-measurable outcomes aligned with the kinds of tasks computer scientists do in their daily work.

In considering how a computer science program ought to be implemented and taught, the computer science education community has sometimes emphasized interaction with computers over pedagogy. This is understandable, as thinking with computers is a core part of computer science [2], and many computer scientists have had profound personal experiences doing so. Computer science education pioneers such as Papert [22] valorized programming as a highly generative learning space, and software such as Scratch [24] has introduced millions of children to programming. Learning directly from computers remains an appealing option for scaling computer science education: Hour of Code is structured as student-guided tutorials with minimal peer or teacher interaction with no teacher expertise required [11]. However, research on supporting the development of interest and learners' identities in the face of negative stereotypes has shown the importance of supportive communities and personal relationships [4, 20, 21]. This research has spurred development of courses such as Exploring Computer Science [16], which revealed some of the challenges and opportunities involved with implementing computer science courses in a high school setting.

While the computer science education community has advocated for both top-down and bottom-up approaches, current K12 CS implementation work largely addresses policymakers and envisions centralized expert design being disseminated to schools and teachers for implementation via standards, teacher credentialing, and professional development. This may be driven by the ease with which digital resources can be distributed and by the corporate decision-making structures which have dominated education for much of the past century [9]. The alternative, distributed participatory design rooted in the values and identity of particular school communities, will become more feasible once there is a larger corps of K12 CS teachers to help lead the process. One of the findings of this study is the limits of scaling centralized decision-making: local stakeholders may need to construct shared understandings of fundamental questions about computer science.

3 METHODS

This study was conducted at a small wealthy suburban school district in California in which a committee composed of students, parents, teachers, and school leaders has spent the last three years designing a K12 CS program. The committee also generated implementation proposals, addressing questions such as how computer science should be integrated into elementary, middle, and high school, whether computer science should be a stand-alone course or integrated into other subject areas, whether there should be a computer science department, and whether a computer science course should be a graduation requirement. The district is unusual in its level of affluence and social capital. The high schools already offer numerous computer science courses, and several of the committee members have participated in K12 CS education leadership in various capacities.

[1]Barr & Stephenson address computer science but focus on computational thinking. As we understand the article, computational thinking is suggested as a candidate for an operational definition of K12 computer science.

Table 1: Frequency of qualitative codes in committee member interviews and board meeting transcripts

Code	Count
Theme 1: Definition	392
competencies	29
concepts	29
defining_education	46
framings	49
importance_of_defining_cs	8
practices	71
rationales	119
Theme 2: Curriculum and instruction	578
curriculum	394
implementation	45
pedagogy	139
Theme 3: Process	486
authorities	92
committee_participation	49
committee_roles	33
cs_inclusion	33
decision_making_structure	24
district_leadership	24
identity	199
politics	31

The texts analyzed in this study include semi-structured interviews with 9 core committee members and transcripts from presentations and public discussions at the district's Board of Education meetings in May 2017 and May 2018. The interviewees included parents, teachers, and school and district leaders. We used the committee's biweekly meeting minutes, written correspondence, and process documents to support our analysis.

We used a grounded theory approach, allowing themes to emerge from an iterative process of open coding. Because our goal was to understand how participants understood and framed the issues, our coding was primarily in vivo [25], noting how language is used in individual and social meaning-making, and in persuasive rhetoric. As we organized codes into thematic categories, we wrote analytical memos documenting our thinking and connecting the emergent themes to existing bodies of research [17]. The findings we present in the next section are supported by analysis of quotations and by patterns of codes in the transcripts. In subsequent work, we plan to deepen this analysis by discussing our findings with stakeholders and outside experts.

4 RESULTS

Table 1 shows the top two levels of the tree of qualitative codes which resulted from our iterative process of coding, analytical writing, and categorizing codes. The distribution of codes provides an overview of what committee member and participants in Board of Education meetings discussed, and is the basis of our analysis. The rest of this section analyzes each of the three top-level themes in turn.

4.1 What is computer science?

The first major theme was the committee's attempt to define computer science. The committee members unanimously agreed that computer science is important (though this was contested by some students and teachers at Board of Education meetings), but they invoked different rationales for why it is important. The most common rationales given were equity (52), early exposure for later interest development (21), economic opportunities (21), and a sense that computational literacy has become a skill necessary for everyday life or digital citizenship (17). Equity was stressed by the Board of Education and public commenters (37), and less frequently by the committee members (15). These rationales for the importance of computer science closely match those articulated by experts in the computer science education community[6].

The members had fundamental disagreements about what constitutes computer science and felt that their inability to agree on one definition blocked their effectiveness. One member, who has done graduate work in computer science, worked in the field, and participated in a nation-wide computer science standards committee, said, "everyone at some level was ignorant about what computer science is. So it's hard for us to define it. It's hard for us to know what it is. Only after being on the committee was I able to refine what I consider to be a pretty reasonable definition." When asked for individual definitions of computer science, committee members often referred to computing practices such as programming, computational thinking, and collaboration (100) and less frequently to core computing concepts such as abstraction, decomposition, and hardware (19). They also positioned computer science as part of broader concepts, defining it as part of what it means to be a well-educated adult today (30) and framing computer science metaphorically (47), for example as a language or as a way of using tools.

One particularly pronounced fault line was between committee members focused on bringing more students into computer science and those focused on developing students to their full potential. There need not be any intrinsic contradiction between inclusion and rigor, but differences in how each camp construed computer science made it difficult for them to understand and support each others' priorities. Those committee members who focused on inclusion overwhelmingly described computer science in terms of practices and developing the conditions under which beginners would be willing and able to participate. One teacher, describing a successful computer science lesson, reported, "every single child was not only super engaged, but it was the creative aspect, the problem solving and the teamwork that went with it and all of these other skills that I noticed. And that made learning more fun, of course. They were learning a lot." The committee members emphasizing rigor talked in terms of competencies such as programming and solving mathematical problems using the big ideas of computer science. A teacher taking this perspective argued that de-emphasizing programming (for example, through "unplugged" activities [5]) is a disservice to students: "If you're teaching origami in computer science class and some guy out in [a wealthy city] is teaching kids how to actually write programs, I've got very little doubt which kid is likely to be in better shape coming out of those two classes in terms of being able to function well at the next level. I think it's creating a chasm between the haves and the have-nots." This disagreement is rooted in different conceptions of what it means to do computer science.

This epistemological tension is paralleled in the academic debate over computational thinking [31], even though the term was used only 12 times in our corpus. Over the last decade, proponents of computational thinking have argued for a practice-focused vision of computer science, often including collaboration, creativity, and the construction of identities and communities where computational practices can emerge. Computational thinking has been useful to those arguing for teaching computer science at the elementary level, for interdisciplinary computer science, and as a lens on inclusion and equity. Others, likely in agreement with the teacher quoted in the previous paragraph, feel that computer science, and a useful definition of computational thinking, ought to be more narrowly defined, focusing on the application of core computational ideas through programming [12, 23]. Too heavy a reliance on computer science practices risks obscuring the powerful ideas that make the field transformative, empowering, and worth teaching.

The K12 CS framework takes an inclusive position, describing computer science in terms of concepts and practices. Four of the seven practices are identified as computational thinking, and they are privileged as "the heart of the computer science practices" (p. 67) While participants reported having read and discussed the standards documents cited above, they seldom referred to them while defining computer science. It might have benefitted the committee to consider the importance of practices and concepts in turn, as presented in the K12 framework. However, documents such as the K12 framework might also be more helpful if they voiced the epistemological tensions within the field, rather than attempting to resolve them in a unified front. Divergent definitions of computer science were an important source of tension of the committee, but they are not the only explanation for the divide described above. There were also interpersonal tensions rooted in how committee members construct identities as computer scientists and position themselves as experts. We return to issues of identity and power in the third major theme.

4.2 How should computer science be taught?

The second major theme that emerged from our research centered on the question of how computer science should be taught. The committee agreed that computational thinking should be an interdisciplinary strand woven into the curriculum in elementary and middle school, with specialists supporting classroom teachers. At the elementary level, the committee proposed incorporating unplugged activities [5] and robots into interdisciplinary lessons due to concerns about limiting students' screen time. At the middle school level, the committee proposed replacing discrete units in the math and science curriculum with computational approaches. The committee was overwhelmingly in favor of making one semester of computer science a graduation requirement, with 69% of the members supporting it, and only 15% against the idea (the other members abstained or tried to find a third way). One veteran computer science teacher cited how "every year we are losing more 700 students to computer science illiteracy and if we could just get a basic computer science class going for everyone...that hemorrhaging of knowledge in some sense could be evaded." Another computer science teacher said, "I'm definitely on the side of a requirement, if every student is forced into it, it may not have the effect it had on me, where you just throw your whole self into it and get excited about it, but at least it presents the opportunity." While there was broad support for a graduation requirement, there was substantial disagreement about what sort of course should be required. Mirroring the two different understandings of computer science, there was a group emphasizing rigor, and another group focused on exposure. The former group was interested in the AP Computer Science Principles course, citing "the number of people who have worked hard on that, including people from the university level," while the latter group was interested in emphasizing the broad applications of computer science in an inclusive manner. The committee ultimately did not reach an agreement on the nature of the required course, as they focused their efforts on first securing the graduation requirement.

The committee's proposal offered two potential paths to add the computer science requirement: by replacing another graduation requirement, or by adding a new requirement and thereby reducing the number of electives available to students. At the committee's presentation to the Board of Education in 2018, they received strong pushback from teachers from other departments, students, and some of the Board members. Two members of the History-Social Studies department presented at the Board meeting. They emphasized the importance of their courses, expressed frustration at not hearing about the committee's work earlier and questioned why every student needed computer science if they did not "desire to pursue technologies and system development." Given the nature of high school graduation requirements, adding any new requirements (computer science or otherwise) inherently is a zero-sum game. Goode & Margolis [16] came to a similar conclusion when trying to integrate their Exploring Computer science curriculum: "students' course schedules are so impacted by graduation and college-preparatory requirements that they are often not able to take any non college-preparatory electives." Debates about curricular requirements were often oriented toward the state's requirements and a possible future computer science requirement.

The students who spoke against the requirement cited the the overwhelming demands of the existing requirements, and the limited choice in their schedules. One student summed up a survey of his peers: "they're less against the idea of teaching computer science than they are with the idea of more requirements," instead suggesting that the district might "loosen up our curriculum and rethink that idea of what students must know, because right now we're all working under a system that's collapsing under its own weight." The second question of student autonomy and choice suggests a much bigger question in education: should students be able to choose their courses, or should districts determine what courses students need to take? On the other hand, one Board member argued for a requirement from an equity perspective: "if we believe that computer science is a critical skill for being a citizen in the modern world, then... we really can't accept a situation in which our female students and the underrepresented minority students are not participating in that at the same levels as other students. That really should be unacceptable to us, and I think a graduation requirement is a way of addressing that." Indeed, other implementation efforts have concluded that access is not enough to broaden participation

[15]. Furthermore, they suggest that an interdisciplnary approach to computer science education will not address the need to develop equitable practices. In combination with inclusive content and pedagogy which actively confronts negative stereotypes, widespread participation may ultimately depend on requiring students to take at least an introductory course [14, 15].

The debates about the nature of the graduation requirement suggests that it is important to include a wide variety of key stakeholders and incorporate their voices. Navigating the complexities of implementing computer science is inevitably situated in a political environment that goes beyond the discipline itself, and forces a district to consider major questions about requirements and goals. Behind these more immediate issues is the reality that the basic structure of secondary education has not changed in over a century in the US, and may be due for an overhaul. Our society's shift to computation as a medium of literacy would be well-suited as the basis of such a pivot, but waiting on such an overhaul before introducing computer science would not be an expedient strategy.

4.3 What process should be used to answer these questions?

The third major theme which emerged from our analysis was the question of how the design process ought to be conducted and who ought to participate. During interviews, committee members enthusiastically described how their identities as computer scientists developed. Their understandings of computer science were deeply grounded in these histories. The committee members who were most outspoken advocates for equitable participation had past experience with exclusionary stereotypes related to computer science and the factors which can support equitable participation. These included discussions of gender (31), race (7), social class (6), affect toward computer science (21), mentorship (4), and identities such as nerds (9). One teacher, who has decades of experience teaching math and computer science, described her initial interest in computer science: "It was just what you would expect. It was nerdy kids and nerdy me and very playful, very advanced math kind of kids and I kept wondering why we weren't getting more girls because I thought it was fun and I was a girl." She acknowledges the reality of disproportionately male participation and the stereotypes reinforcing this, while also offering herself as a counterexample to these stereotypes. From this teacher's perspective, the challenge is to let girls be nerdy too, or to let computer science be defined as playful, something other than just nerdy. No participants disagreed that culture and identity are important, but some did not describe their own development in these terms. Instead, their accounts emphasize the schools where they studied, the roles they occupied, and frequently hands-on opportunities with computers. Their equity-oriented work focused on outreach, trying to get underrepresented groups to enroll in the rigorous computer science courses, rather than redesigning the courses. To the extent that these teachers use their own histories as a guide, the link between their histories and the way they understand computer science is unsurprising.

When committee members positioned themselves as experts on computer science, they often referred to their professional or academic experience. However, these experiences did not automatically confer social capital. Some committee members presumed upon their expertise to make their claims authoritative. Others, despite years of professional experience and academic background, did not use their experience to make their voices more powerful. For example, one teacher and committee member said, "I worked for 15 years in the tech industry before I decided to teach elementary schools... My background is engineering but not computer science, though the work I was doing was programming. And so after fifteen years in the tech industry, I lost my job, I went back to school, I did my multiple subject credential, and I started teaching as an elementary school teacher." Throughout her interview, she supported her perspective on how computer science ought to be taught with detailed accounts of students' classroom experience, but avoided making general authoritative statements about what is best.

In some cases, the construction of expertise was explicitly about power and whose voice counts. One male teacher explicitly excluded the expertise of the women quoted in the previous paragraphs: "It's tough because, you know, I felt like [other male teacher] and I were the two subject matter experts in the room other than a couple of parents who were in the business. And I think both [other male teacher] and I at different times during the past couple years have, you know, threw our arms up." This teacher has strong views on what constitutes computer science and on how it should be taught, and frequently saw himself in the minority on the committee. These interactions portray computer science knowledge as situated in particular identities, contexts of use, and power relationships. This is a not a dominant perspective in computer science. Abstraction, one of the field's core ideas, relies on the objective representations of concepts[2]. As the computer science education community tackles the challenge of making computer science broadly accessible, we may also come to value a plurality of different manifestations of what it means to do computer science, each rooted in its own particular context of use.

In considering the question of process, the committee considered it a foregone conclusion that this needed to be inclusive, building a broadly-shared understanding of what computer science is, a consensus that it should be a core part of the curriculum, and agreement on how it should be implemented. The Board of Education charged the committee with including stakeholders including teachers, parents, students, and community members. At the two Board of Education presentations there was robust participation from members of all these constituencies, including committee members and those who did not participate. When, at the latest Board meeting, the committee encountered political opposition which stalled its progress, several committee members reflected on whether a different process might have been more effective. Some committee members felt that inclusion had come at the cost of efficiency (9), and felt that it would be better to move forward with a smaller, more united committee which could push for a single vision. Others argued for the opposite, that the committee should focus on community education (18) so that more teachers, parents, and students could come to an understanding of what computer science is and why it ought to be a district priority. One participant emphasized the political importance of community support: "In order to

[2]That said, some subfields, such as human-computer interaction and natural language processing, are fundamentally concerned with representing a plurality of interpretive processes.

sell this, we're going to need to have a district-wide community committee so that the community knows more about it and we get them on board." Several committee members pointed out the recursive challenge of sufficiently educating the school community about computer science so that the community would be able to meaningfully participate in designing a computer science education program.

5 DISCUSSION

Shortly before this study's publication, the district's Board of Education decided to delay enacting the committee's recommendations for a comprehensive K12 CS program with a one-semester graduation requirement. Instead, the board will convene a smaller, more focused task force for another year of study. While this committee's years of committed work undoubtedly advanced the cause of comprehensive K12 CS for every student in the district, their goal has not yet been met.

How might this experience contribute to the larger discourse of K12 CS education? The financial, cultural, and social capital which enabled this district to contemplate adopting K12 CS also set it apart from the vast majority of other districts in the United States and may limit the applicability of lessons learned here to other contexts. Would the process be less contentious in school districts which have less existing computer science expertise and fewer established programs? Would the debate be obviated in a large school district or statewide initiative, where policy can be unified and implementation guidance can be provided to individual schools? Is this a case of a district that went out too far ahead, before supporting research and policy infrastructure was in place?

We believe not. Interventions at scale, particularly those which are distributed online, may succeed in introducing students to computer science without requiring school communities to engage in the hard work of defining and designing local instantiations of computer science education. But lasting teaching and learning, which builds identities and expertise, takes place within communities of practice, populated by people acting from their own situated understandings and identities. In such an environment the issues identified in this study are likely to emerge. Participants are likely to act from their own definitions of computer science, which may be differently grounded in concepts, practices, or competencies. They are likely to be divided by competition for the scarce resources of curricular requirements, and by different opinions on whether computer science should be a standalone course or be integrated across disciplines. And all of these are likely to be shaped by participants' life histories with computer science, and the identities they have developed.

For stakeholders of schools designing comprehensive computer science programs, this study offers several lessons. It is important to realize that there are substantial, unresolved disagreements about what constitutes computer science, and that any implementation will need to take a stance on what matters most. Peoples' understanding of computer science will be situated in their own experience, and the process of developing a broadly-shared operative definition of computer science should include time to discuss these different backgrounds. In order to include participants without existing computer science experience, it may be necessary to invest in community education efforts. Despite these efforts, some people will be skeptical that computer science ought to be a priority; if they are not also included in the process they may solidify into an oppositional faction. The question of whether to require a separate computer science course may be a crux point, essential for equitable participation but also in competition with other priorities for the limited number of courses that can be required. The same factors which have historically excluded students from participating in computer science are likely to affect potential participants in the process of designing a computer science program.

For computer science education researchers, this study offers an example of how ideas from research were understood and used by one set of practitioners, and also surfaces some ways in which K12 CS education research will differ from research in the university setting. First, the divisions within academic computer science are not just an internal family affair. There may be value in further exploring the tension between different epistemological stances (concepts, practices, competencies), and in characterizing these tensions rather than trying to resolve them. It would be valuable to develop constructs which view computer science knowledge and expertise as situated in particular identities and cultures, and as part of broader educational goals. Pedagogical content knowledge [26], knowing not just the content, but also the many ways in which it can be effectively learned, is particularly important in K12 education, a setting in which success is demanded for every student and learning is more deeply intertwined with developmental processes. Such research will likely require participatory relationships between teachers and researchers. Ubiquitous issues of power and positionality between K12 teachers and academic researchers are likely to be particularly exacerbated in computer science, a field where experts (or even novices) have economic opportunities which substantially outstrip a teacher's salary.

6 CONCLUSION

Making computer science a core part of K12 education presents fundamental challenges to both fields, but we see them as productive tensions that may push each to grow and improve. Computer science developed as an unconventional, idiosyncratic field distinguished by a characteristic way of thinking, and by identities (geek, nerd, hacker) which have historically nurtured some marginalized people while excluding many others. However K-12 education is charged with designing learning experiences which work for all students, working within a system shaped by ongoing power struggles including race, gender, and social class. To meet the demands of K12 education, computer science must adapt to pluralistic ways of thinking and meet the needs of a more diverse set of practitioners. On the other hand, many have observed that our K12 public schools still fundamentally operate according to a model developed in the nineteenth century. Computer science may bring new technologies, pedagogies, ways of working, and levers for change such as transparency and analysis. This study offers an early sketch of how these tensions and possibilities may unfold.

REFERENCES

[1] 2016. K-12 Comptuer Science Framework.
[2] A. V. Aho. 2012. Computation and Computational Thinking. 55, 7 (2012), 832–835. https://doi.org/10.1093/comjnl/bxs074

[3] Valerie Barr and Chris Stephenson. 2011. Bringing computational thinking to K-12: what is Involved and what is the role of the computer science education community? 2, 1 (2011), 48–54.
[4] Brigid Barron. 2004. Learning ecologies for technological fluency: Gender and experience differences. 31, 1 (2004), 1–36.
[5] T Bell, I Witten, and M Felllows. [n. d.]. Computer Science Unplugged. www.csunplugged.org
[6] Paulo Blikstein. 2018. Pre-College Computer Science Education: A Survey of the Field.
[7] John Seely Brown, Allan Collins, and Paul Duguid. 1989. Situated Cognition and the Culture of Learning. 18, 1 (1989), 32. https://doi.org/10.2307/1176008
[8] Jerome S Bruner. 1960. *The process of education.* Harvard University Press.
[9] Raymond E Callahan. 1964. *Education and the cult of efficiency.* University of Chicago Press.
[10] Kathy Charmaz. 1996. Grounded Theory. In *Rethinking methods in psychology*, Jonathan A. Smith, Rom HarrÃľ, and Luk Van Langenhove (Eds.). Sage.
[11] code.org. 2018. How to teach one Hour of Code with your class. https://hourofcode.com/ac/how-to
[12] Peter J. Denning. 2017. Remaining trouble spots with computational thinking. 60, 6 (2017), 33–39. https://doi.org/10.1145/2998438
[13] CSTA Standards Task Force. 2017. Computer science standards.
[14] Joanna Goode. 2008. Increasing Diversity in K-12 computer science: Strategies from the field. In *ACM SIGCSE Bulletin*, Vol. 40. ACM, 362–366.
[15] Joanna Goode, Gail Chapman, and Jane Margolis. 2012. Beyond curriculum: the exploring computer science program. *ACM Inroads* 3, 2 (2012), 47–53.
[16] Joanna Goode and Jane Margolis. 2011. Exploring Computer Science: A Case Study of School Reform. 11, 2 (2011), 1–16. https://doi.org/10.1145/1993069.1993076
[17] Egon G Guba. 1981. Criteria for assessing the trustworthiness of naturalistic inquiries. *Ectj* 29, 2 (1981), 75.
[18] ISTE. [n. d.]. ISTE Standards for Computer Science Educators. http://www.iste.org/docs/pdfs/20-14_ISTE_Standards-CSE_PDF.pdf
[19] LAUSD. 2014. L.A. Unified Announces Larger Focus on Computer Science for K-12. (2014).
[20] Jane Margolis. 2010. *Stuck in the shallow end: Education, race, and computing.* MIT Press.
[21] Jane Margolis and Allan Fisher. 2003. *Unlocking the clubhouse: Women in computing.* MIT press.
[22] Seymour Papert. 1980. *Mindstorms: Children, computers, and powerful ideas.* Basic Books, Inc.
[23] Chris Proctor and Paulo Blikstein. 2018. How Broad is Computational Thinking? A Longitudinal Study of Practices Shaping Learning in Computer Science. (2018), 8.
[24] Mitchel Resnick, John Maloney, AndrÃľs Monroy-HernÃąndez, Natalie Rusk, Evelyn Eastmond, Karen Brennan, Amon Millner, Eric Rosenbaum, Jay Silver, Brian Silverman, and others. 2009. Scratch: programming for all. 52, 11 (2009), 60–67.
[25] Johnny Saldaña. 2015. *The coding manual for qualitative researchers.* Sage.
[26] Lee S Shulman. 1986. Those Who Understand: Knowledge Growth in Teaching. (1986), 11.
[27] Allen Tucker, Fadi Deek, Jill Jones, Dennis McCowan, Chris Stephenson, and Anita Verno. 2003. A Model Curriculum for K-12 Computer Science. (2003), 60.
[28] Bryan Twarek and Jim Ryan. 2015. The Need for Computer Science Education for All Students from PreâĂŘKindergarten to 12th Grade. https://drive.google.com/file/d/0B0TlX1G3mywqRGJKNkN2RXlZTWs/view?usp=embed_facebook
[29] Adriana Villavicencio, Cheri Fancsali, Wendy Martin, June Mark, and Rachel Cole. 2018. An Early Look at Teacher Training Opportunities and the Landscape of CS Implementation in Schools. (2018).
[30] Grant Wiggins and Jay McTighe. 2005. *Understanding by design.* Ascd.
[31] Jeannette M Wing. 2006. Computational thinking. *Commun. ACM* 49, 3 (2006), 33–35.

Developing Implementation Measures for K-12 Computer Science Curriculum Materials

Daisy Rutstein, Yuning Xu, Kevin McElhaney, Marie Bienkowski
SRI Education, SRI International
Menlo Park, CA, USA
daisy.rutstein@sri.com, yuning.xu@sri.com, kevin.mcelhaney@sri.com, marie.bienkowski@sri.com

ABSTRACT

As K-12 computer science (CS) education initiatives scale throughout the U.S., researchers seek to understand the context-specific relationships between CS instruction and student learning. Evaluation of instruction requires valid measures of curriculum implementation. We have developed measures for identifying conditions for successful implementation of an introductory high school computer science curriculum along two-dimensions: teaching quality and curriculum enactment. Additionally, we have defined three types of instructional strategies for teaching quality. Quantitative and qualitative data were collected from 53 teachers through surveys and interviews. Data were aggregated and integrated to derive scaled measures for the instructional strategies and curriculum adaptation, and implementation measures were correlated with student end-of-unit assessment data. We found potential factors that can enhance or impede the successful implementation of CS curriculum materials, and we have identified several broad issues associated with scaling up CS curricular implementation.

CCS CONCEPTS

Social and professional topics~K-12 education, Social and professional topics~Student assessment

KEYWORDS: Computational Thinking, Curriculum Implementation, Measurement

ACM Reference format:

Daisy Rustein, Yuning Xu, Kevin McElhaney, & Marie Bienkowski. 2018. Developing Implementation Measures for K-12 Computer Science Curriculum Materials. In *Proceedings of 50th ACM Technical Symposium on Computer Science Education (SIGCSE '19), February 27-March 2, 2019, Minneapolis, MN, USA.* ACM, New York, NY, USA, 7 pages. https://doi.org/10.1145/3287324.3287424

1 Introduction

The scope of K-12 CS curriculum development and adoption have greatly expanded in the U.S. over the last decade.

ACM ISBN 978-1-4503-5890-3/19/02...$15.00
https://doi.org/10.1145/3287324.3287494

Researchers and advocacy groups have been successful on several fronts, such as: creating the K-12 CS Framework [14] to inform the articulation of standards; promoting the inclusion of semester-long or full-year standalone CS courses in high school course offerings; integrating CS concepts and practices into K-12 mathematics and science classes [21]; and launching a successful Advanced Placement course that demonstrates potential to diversify the STEM workforce pipeline [2, 3]. At the same time, many K-12 CS courses are taught by teachers in departments such as math, science, and business [7] due to teacher shortages in STEM subjects, the newness of CS as a K-12 discipline, and schools' and districts' efforts to make CS courses available to their students [23]. These challenges highlight the need for researchers to examine (1) what constitutes high quality CS teaching and successful curriculum enactment and (2) the extent to which high teaching quality and successful curriculum enactment result in positive CS learning outcomes.

K-12 CS teaching may exhibit wide variation due to the diverse backgrounds and levels of experience teachers possess. Moreover, there is also variation in how schools, districts, and states include CS as part of their curricular programs. Characterizing how CS curricula are taught and enacted by different teachers and in different education contexts is centrally important to designing CS curriculum materials and teacher professional development (PD) opportunities [1]. Designers of curriculum materials such as Exploring Computer Science (ECS) [10] provide guidance and supporting resources for teachers to help them successfully enact CS lessons. The CS education research community needs ways to determine whether teachers' teaching strategies and enactment decisions are consistent with the underlying principles of the curriculum materials.

Prior work has addressed the development and validation of measures of computer science learning outcomes, such as students' proficiency with computational thinking concepts and practices [22]. In this paper, we extend that work to the measurement of curriculum implementation, focusing on ECS. We have defined a set of constructs underlying curriculum implementation, used them to develop measures of implementation, and conducted a study to characterize the relationships between aspects of curriculum implementation and student learning outcomes. To examine these relationships, we performed an analysis integrating attributes of teachers and their associated learning contexts, teachers' teaching strategies, and the fidelity of the curriculum enactment [e.g., 17, 20].

2 Background

ECS is a comprehensive school reform effort for computing education consisting of three elements: curriculum materials, teacher PD, and policy efforts [10]. It was developed with the goal to broaden the participation of traditionally underrepresented students in precollege computer science. The curriculum is made up of different units, each focusing on different aspects of computing. For example, the first unit focuses on human and computer interaction, while the second unit focuses on problem solving. The design of ECS is guided by the underlying principles of inquiry, equity, and collaboration. Inquiry-based learning constitutes an appropriate guiding principle for the design of ECS activities, as it emphasizes core concepts learned through engagement with disciplinary practices, student-centered teaching approaches, and open-ended, continuous, and formative assessment. [12].

Second, ECS is based on an *equitable* learning model. The curriculum activities reflect the notion that success in CS is attainable by and needed for all students regardless of their cultural, linguistic, or economic backgrounds. To achieve this aim, ECS strives to provide students with instructional experiences that are culturally relevant and meaningful to them and emphasize the impacts of computer science on contemporary society. This approach draws from the "funds of knowledge" perspective [15] and the national Algebra project [16], which include connections to community-based topics and address students' beliefs about their ability to learn mathematics.

Finally, collaborative work, peer-communication, and group discussion underpin many ECS activities. Having students work together provides the benefits of engaging with peers for learning and engagement. Activities are designed to encourage students to work in a variety of collaborative settings including elbow partners, pair-programming, and group research projects. This collaboration encourages conversations around computing topics.

In support of an initiative to engage K-12 teachers in rigorous secondary computer science teaching, the National Science Foundation and industry supporters funded the preparation and administration of several surveys of secondary CS teachers and teacher PD providers to characterize the CS education landscape [7]. The study found that more than half of teachers surveyed were not full-time CS teachers, and that they most often taught mathematics, technology skills, or science. Some teachers surveyed were drawn from business, information technology, and library science, and many of those surveyed were new to computer science. More than half were the sole CS teacher in their school, and 87% reported having an advocacy role for CS in their schools. The diversity of teacher backgrounds and ways that CS was incorporated into school and district educational infrastructure presents challenges to consistently implementing CS curriculum materials. Goode and Margolis [10] also reported the difficulties teachers face in implementing new curriculum based on their beliefs about (1) how and what students can learn, (2) the utility of inquiry approaches to teaching, (3) nature of science, and (4) the importance of students' prior knowledge. Further work [12] demonstrated that second-year teachers are less concerned with learning CS content, express increased readiness to implement pedagogical changes, and benefit from reflection on their teaching practice. These findings suggest context factors that affect the implementation of ECS.

Based on these studies, we identify five important factors that influence teachers' teaching practices and customizations to curriculum sequences and activities:

1. *Teacher background in CS*: knowledge of CS concepts and familiarity with CS pedagogy;
2. *State secondary school policies*: Graduation requirements, information technology literacy requirements, career technical education contexts;
3. *Regional workforce concerns*: Input from local industry;
4. *District/school CS context*: Initiatives that align with teaching; reform initiatives that could help or hinder (including those linked to accountability); afterschool programs in related topics such as robotics or technology; availability of technology for the classes and availability of AP CS at the school.
5. *Student background and prior achievement*: Socioeconomic status, gender, prior exposure to computing, access to technology, rigor of their academic program, grade in Algebra 1.

We frame these factors in terms of the human, social, and technical capital that teachers have at their disposal [19, 4]:

1. Human capital: A teacher might believe that they have taught themselves to program and studied the computational thinking practices, or they may view CS as aligning with STEM teaching initiatives at their school. Teachers will have different experiences with ECS PD and subsequent in-school support.

2. Social capital: This element includes the expertise that individuals can access to accomplish goals. For example, a teacher may belong to the local CSTA chapter or an online community.

3. Technical/resource capital: For CS, access to computers and the Internet with adequate performance can be important. Although ECS uses "unplugged" activities for teaching, many of the activities require the Internet and a programming environment. Another important resource is time: it would be unusual for a secondary CS teacher to be teaching only CS, so ECS teachers will have competing demands on their time.

These factors can shape the adoption of a new course like ECS and can influence the pedagogical approach teachers take once it is in place. Our study looked for evidence of important factors of ECS in enactment: inquiry, equity, and collaboration. Our specific research questions are:

1. What factors predict implementation of the inquiry-, equity-, and collaboration-based instructional strategies supported in the ECS program?
2. What factors predict the extent to which teachers adapt the ECS curriculum materials?
3. What factors enhance or impede the successful implementation of ECS?
4. How does curriculum implementation relate to student outcomes?

3 Methods

3.1 Modeling Curriculum Enactment and Teaching Quality

Researching the multiplicity of factors that can influence how a curriculum is implemented over a semester or a year and identifying the characteristics of the teaching of computer science is a complex endeavor. As researchers, we look for a way to make sense of the extensive set of factors and their influence relationships.

As mentioned above, we defined two high-level factors we believed would relate to student outcomes: teaching quality (which we defined as teachers' use of inquiry-, equity-, and collaborative-based teaching strategies) and curriculum enactment (which we defined as related to lessons modified, skipped, and added). We also hypothesized that there are many factors that could influence the degree of teaching quality and curriculum enactment. These factors include the attributes of the learning context (e.g., district, school and classroom characteristics) and teacher attributes (including the teacher's beliefs about the curriculum, the typical strategies the teacher uses in their classrooms, and the teacher's background characteristics.) Figure 1 shows our model for relating teacher and learning context attributes, aspects of implementation, and student outcomes.

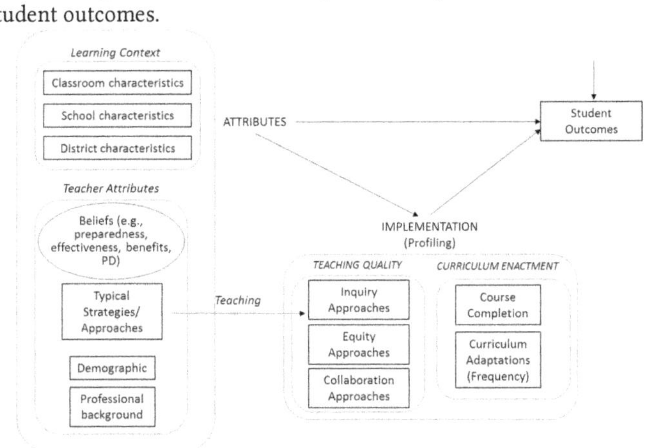

Figure 1: **Overall Model for Factors that Could Influence Student Outcomes**

Importantly, here we highlight the distinction between *teacher* quality and *teaching* quality [9]. This distinction aims to convey that how teachers employ teaching practices and teaching moves are open to change, improvement, and innovation over time [8, 13], and that teaching decisions are not static attributes of teachers. Our teaching quality measures target the teachers' teaching decisions, rather than characteristics of teachers themselves.

We further specified each of the constructs included in the model according to a set of variables, each of which we hypothesized would have either a positive or negative relationship to student learning outcomes. Measures were developed to capture these variables. Further information about how this model was operationalized is given below.

3.2 Operationalizing the Model

We developed a set of six surveys: one background survey (administered at the start of the year), one teacher PD survey (administered soon after the teacher PD workshop), and one unit survey for each of the first four ECS units (administered after each unit was taught). We focused on the first 4 units as those are considered the fundamental units (Unit 1 is about human/computer interaction, Unit 2 is about problem solving, Unit 3 focuses on web-design, and Unit 4 on programming). We also developed a student survey that asked questions around the students' demographic background and background with computer science concepts. The questions on the surveys were designed to measure the constructs specified in our model.

Fifty-three teachers completed at least one of the surveys and 34 teachers completed the background survey and at least one unit survey. Table 2 below presents the sample sizes for the teacher surveys and student assessments.

Table 2: Sample Sizes for Teacher Background Survey, PD Survey, End-Unit Surveys, and Student Assessments.

Data Collection Activity	Teacher N	Student N
Background Survey	36	-
Professional Development Survey	11	-
Pre-assessment	-	1133
ECS Unit 1	38	981
ECS Unit 2	37	892
ECS Unit 3	27	811
ECS Unit 4	28	586
Cumulative Assessment	-	780

Once the survey data were collected and coded, we re-examined the results of the survey to create a set of variables that could be included for each of the constructs in the model. These variables were generated using both a top-down approach (using our initial theoretical model as a guide) and a bottom-up approach (using statistical analysis and review of question responses to determine which questions had sufficient variability in responses to be included in the model). The final variables used for analysis can be either a composite variable that combines a set of survey questions or a variable based on a single survey question. Table 1 includes examples of survey questions related to the instructional strategies.

In addition to the set of selection answers on the surveys, there was a set of open-ended responses. These questions asked teachers to elaborate on aspects of their teaching, in particular to describe modifications they made to the curricular materials, or additional activities they used in the courses. These responses were then coded as to whether they indicated the teacher was engaging in one of the three types of teaching practices (inquiry, equity, or collaboration practices) or that they modified the curriculum.

The background survey for the teacher covered a variety of topics, including demographic information, prior CS experience, support for CS at the school level, beliefs about CS and ECS, and their typical teaching strategies. The PD survey included questions relating to the teacher's preparedness for teaching, and beliefs about the ECS curriculum.

So as not to overburden teachers with daily or weekly instructional logs, we administered a unit survey at the end of each unit, when teachers administering the end-of-unit assessment to their students. The end-of-unit surveys asked about their teaching assignment (unit 1 only), ECS classes, experience teaching the unit, modifying/skipping of topics, sense of preparedness to teach the unit, instructional activities taught, unit successes and challenges, availability of technology, and their overall ECS experience (units 3 and 4 only).

Table 1: Example survey questions for teaching quality factors

Inquiry-Based Practices
When teaching the unit, how often did you engage students in the following practice? • Students develop their own solutions to problems
Equity-Based Practices
Which of the following instructional successes did you encounter? • Opportunities for students to connect computational thinking to cultural backgrounds
Collaboration-Based Practices
When teaching the unit, how often did you engage students in the following practice? • Students collaborate or work in teams • Students present or communicate their ideas to peers

In the next phase we defined the theoretical model. Here we articulated hypotheses about the relationships between the variables to create a model that addresses the research questions. For example, Figure 2 illustrates our hypothesis that the likelihood that the teacher will implement inquiry-based teaching approaches will exhibit a positive relationship (indicated with a +) with a teacher's prior experience with inquiry and a negative relationship (indicated with a - sign) with number of non-inquiry-based (didactic) teaching approaches they use [5].

For research question 3, we defined successful implementation of the ECS curriculum as having higher instances of the approaches that are associated with teaching quality. We then categorized the types of modifications teachers reported according to whether they align with the pedagogy of the curriculum (e.g. adding activities that relate to the cultural background of the classrooms) or do not align (e.g. skipping activities). We then hypothesized whether these modifications relate positively or negatively to these variables. Here we included aspects that are often outside of the teachers control, such as the availability of technology (see Figure 3).

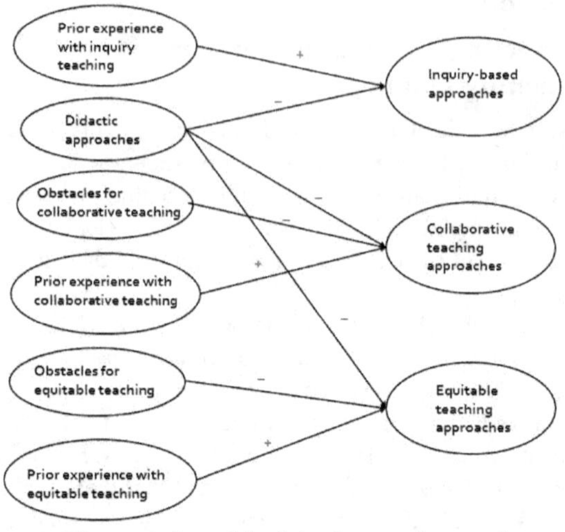

Figure 2: Theoretical model of the factors that predict teachers' implementation strategies

Figure 3: What factors enhance or impede the successful implementation of ECS?

Once we specified these models, we then tested them with the data. We started by determining if any of these variables had statistically significant correlations. We also examined the predictive capabilities of the variables in our theoretical model.

After we determined which factors might be predictors of the teaching quality and curricular enactment we examined the relationships among these variables and the student outcomes. The student outcomes were measured by four end-of-unit assessments, each given to the student at the end of instruction in the corresponding unit. We examined the relationships separately for each of the four unit assessments.

4. Results

4.1 Teaching Quality

4.1.1 Inquiry-based instructional strategy (IBIS)

We define the measure for IBIS based on both teachers' level on inquiry practices and their evaluations on successful classroom promotion regarding inquiry. Frequency of practices is prioritized over successful promotions in evaluating the implementation of IBIS. Table 4 presents the five levels for IBIS from low to high and the distributions of teachers on these levels by unit.

Table 4: Teacher Distributions on the Defined Measure for Inquiry-Based Instructional Strategy.

Levels of Inquiry-Based Instructional Strategy	Number of Teachers			
	Unit 1	Unit 2	Unit 3	Unit 4
L1: No practice regardless of success	0	0	0	0
L2: Low frequencies of practice + few success	3	2	0	0
L3: Low frequencies of practice + more success	5	4	1	1
L4: High frequencies of practice + few success	12	7	8	5
L5: High frequencies of practice + more success	17	22	18	22
Total N	37	35	27	28

The results showed high IBIS levels across all ECS units, with units 3 and 4 having the highest levels. The differences across units indicate the transition from lower to higher levels for some teachers as they progressed from unit 1 to unit 4. Such changes are likely due to the different nature of the different unit topics and activities.

4.1.2 Collaboration-based instructional strategy (CBIS)

As with IBIS, the measure for CBIS is also defined using the frequency of practices and the successful promotion of collaborative teaching. Table 5 presents teacher distributions on CBIS for the different units.

Table 5: Teacher Distributions on the Defined Measure for Collaboration-Based Instructional Strategy.

Levels of Collaboration-Based Instructional Strategy	Number of Teachers			
	Unit 1	Unit 2	Unit 3	Unit 4
L1: No practice regardless of success	0	0	0	0
L2: Low frequencies of practice + few success	4	4	4	5
L3: Low frequencies of practice + more success	1	3	5	4
L4: High frequencies of practice + few success	7	5	5	3
L5: High frequencies of practice + more success	25	23	13	16
Total N	37	35	27	28

High CBIS levels were found across all ECS units, but less so than IBIS. ECS units 1 and 2 had the highest CBIS levels. In contrast to IBIS, some teachers transitioned from higher to lower levels of CBIS as they progressed from unit 1 to unit 4. This trend might be due to the nature of units 3 and 4 where the focuses were on specific activities such as design and programming.

4.1.3 Equity-based instructional strategy (EBIS)

In the unit surveys, one of the close-ended questions targeted equitable teaching strategies. This question asks if teachers were successful in promoting computational thinking in their ECS classroom by providing opportunities for students to connect computational thinking to personal interests, cultural backgrounds, community problems, or social issues. The table below summarizes the percent of teachers who indicated successful promotion in each of the units. In all units, over half of the surveyed teachers indicated successful promotions. Unit 3 had a higher percent than the other units.

Table 6: Teacher Distributions on the Defined Measure for Equity-Based Instructional Strategy.

	Total Number of Teachers	% Teacher Indicated Successful Promotion
Unit 1	38	63.16%
Unit 2	37	64.86%
Unit 3	27	74.07%
Unit 4	28	64.29%

4.1.4 Factors enhancing or impeding IBIS, CBIS, and EBIS

For each of the instructional strategies, we correlated the measure for the strategy and the variables for teacher attributes and learning context. The results are presented in Table 7 below.

Teachers' prior experience with inquiry were found to moderately correlate with their ECS IBIS level for the first unit they taught. The levels of implementing EBIS were positively related to teachers' beliefs regarding culture relevance but were negatively related to the number of years of teaching CS and ECS for specific units.

Table 7: Correlations Between Measures for Instructional Strategies and Variables for Teacher Attribute and Learning Context.

		IBIS	CBIS	EBIS
Teacher Attributes	Prior inquiry experience	.49*** (Unit 1)		
	Belief: ECS benefits some or all	.36 (Unit 2)		
	Belief: Culture relevance did not decrease rigor			.38* (Unit 1) .47* (Unit 2)
	Belief: Culture relevance improves outcomes			.51* (Unit 3)
	Number of years teaching CS			-.59* (Unit 2)
	Number of years teaching ECS			-.49* (Unit 2)
	Industry experience			.56 (Unit 3)
Learning Context	Total instruction time	-.31 (Unit 1)		
	% of students with disability	-.39* (Unit 4)		

Note. Correlations smaller than .30 are not presented. $^{*}p<.05$, $^{***}p<.001$.

4.2 Curriculum Enactment

We operationalize curriculum enactment by examining the number of topics teachers modified, skipped, and added during each unit. Table 8 below shows the summary statistics for these three measures. On average, teachers made more modifications in units 1 and 3, and skipped more topics for units 3 and 4. More than a third of the teachers added their own topics in all units.

Table 8: Summary Statistics for Measures for Curriculum Adaptation

	Total Number of Topics	Average Number of Topics Modified	Average Number of Topics Skipped	Percent of Teachers Adding Any Topic
Unit 1 (N=37)	8	3.57	.19	45.16%
Unit 2 (N=34)	9	3.35	.32	46.67%
Unit 3 (N=27)	11	7.11	.81	34.62%
Unit 4 (N=28)	18	6.54	1.21	42.11%

Relationship between the levels of the instructional strategies and curriculum enactment were examined by correlating the corresponding measures. Teachers with prior experience with focal ECS instructional strategies (e.g. IBIS, CBIS) appear to be more inclined to modify units, perhaps because those strategies often require teachers to customize materials, so they are comfortable doing so. If there is some kind of well-established CS program at the school as evidenced by CS teaching experience or other CS classes, teachers are more likely to implement lessons "as-is". Additional evidence is needed to help understand the underlying causes.

On the other hand, access to technology matters for how lessons are implemented. If teachers lack technology or experience software issues, they tend to skip or replace certain lessons. If teachers have access to technology, they tend to use the curriculum more "as-is".

4.3 Teacher Implementation and Student Outcomes

We built hierarchical linear models (HLMs) to explore the impact of teacher implementation levels as well as the teacher and learning context attributes on student learning outcomes. At the end of each unit, students received a summative assessment that has been validated through a two-year pilot study. We used student scores on the end-unit assessment as an outcome measure, and measures developed for teacher implementation, teacher attributes, and learning context as classroom-level predictors for the HLM models. Student score on the pre-assessment was included as a student-level predictor in the model as well to account for variation at the student level. For each unit, we started with the student level predictors as defined by the theoretical model, then included the classroom level predictors and determined if there were interaction effects. This model was used to examine if the predictors were significant.

The results found students whose teachers reported higher unit IBIS or CBIS performed significantly better on the assessments for specific units. Higher level of CBIS was related to better performance on unit 1 (human-computer interaction) after accounting for the student- and classroom level covariates. Higher level IBIS was related to significantly better performance on unit 3 (web design).

In addition to the implementation levels, teacher attributes such as experience and the learning context such as CS presence appeared to have an impact on student learning. Specifically, students whose teachers reported more experience teaching CS courses performed significantly worse on the assessments across all units; whereas students whose teachers reported more experience teaching ECS courses performed better on unit 2 assessment (problem solving) but not the other three units. In terms of learning context, we found a positive relationship between the number of CS courses offered at school and student assessment performance for Unit 1.

The analysis results indicate the varying relationship between instructional strategies and student performance across units. Moreover, experience teaching ECS appears to be more important than prior experience teaching CS when it comes to student performance, particularly for Unit 2. The positive effect of having a well-established CS program at a school on student performance does not appear to last past Unit 1.

5. Discussion

Overall, the study did not reach strong conclusions that were consistent across the units. Some of this may be due to the reliance on teacher self-report, which were not externally validated. Often the results we found differed by unit. For example, while higher level of belief that ECS benefits all was related to better performance on Unit 2, this result was not found for the other units. While this may in part be due to the small sample size, it also may be in indicator that the factors that promote or impede success in teaching CS may differ depending on the content that is being taught.

One interesting result we found was that students of teachers who reported more experience teaching Computer Science courses performed significantly worse on the ECS unit assessments. This was not found to be the case for teachers who had more experience teaching ECS though. This may be because the focus of ECS is not the same as traditional CS courses, and to effectively teach ECS there are instructionally different strategies needed than those required for more traditional CS courses.

Related to this is the fact that students whose teachers reported higher inquiry and collaboration-based strategies performed significantly better on the assessments for two of the units. Higher reporting of collaboration-based strategies was related to higher performance on Unit 1, while higher inquiry-based strategies was related to higher performance on Unit 3.

Another finding that was expected is that teachers who had difficulty accessing technology tended to modify or skip lessons more than others, as they needed to make curricular adaptations to accommodate the issues with technology. Modifications of Units 1 and 3 was tied to lower performance of the students, while skipping of topics in Units 2 and 4 was tied to lower student performance. This indicates that care should be taken when deciding to modify or skip a lesson, as students may then not have the opportunity to achieve the learning goals of those lessons.

6. Conclusion

This study provides an overview of factors that can be considered when examining CS curriculum, and the development of measures for these factors. Overall, this study indicates that the factors for success in an introductory computer science course may not be the same across all CS concepts or CS classrooms. Further refinement of the factors that affect teaching quality and curriculum enactment may help tease out the relationship between teacher/classroom characteristics, teaching quality, curriculum enactment, and student success. In addition, future studies may examine other measures of success, such as future course-taking patterns.

ACKNOWLEDGMENTS

This work was conducted under NSF Grant-#1418149. We gratefully acknowledge all of the teachers and students who participated in the research.

REFERENCES

[1] Michal Armoni. 2011. Looking at Secondary Teacher Preparation Through the Lens of Computer Science. ACM Transactions on Computing Education 11, 4: 1–38. https://doi.org/10.1145/2048931.2048934

[2] Owen Astrachan and Amy Briggs. 2012. The CS Principles Project. ACM Inroads 3, 2: 38–42. https://doi.org/10.1145/2189835.2189849

[3] Andrea Arpaci-Dusseau, Owen Astrachan, Dwight Barnett, Matthew Bauer, Marilyn Carrell, Rebecca Dovi, Baker Franke, Christina Gardner, Jeff Gray, Jean Griffin, Richard Kick, Andy Kuemmel, Ralph Morelli, Deepa Muralidhar, Rebecca Brook Osborne, and Chinma Uche. 2013. Computer science principles: analysis of a proposed advanced placement course. In Proceeding of the 44th ACM technical symposium on Computer science education (SIGCSE), 251–256. https://doi.org/10.1145/2445196.2445273

[4] Marie Bienkowski, Nicole Shechtman, Julie Remold, and Jennifer Knudsen. 2014. Supporting STEM Teachers to Inspire through Everyday Innovation. Teacher Education and Practice 27: 356–375.

[5] Alec M. Bodzin and Karen M. Beerer. 2003. Promoting Inquiry-Based Science Instruction: The Validation of Science Teacher Inquiry Rubric. Journal of Elementary Science Education 15, 39: 1–11. Retrieved from https://doi.org/10.1007/BF03173842

[6] Jeanne Century and Amy Cassata. 2014. Conceptual foundations for measuring the implementation of educational innovations. In Treatment integrity: A foundation for evidence-based practice in applied psychology., Lisa M. Hagermoser Sanetti and Thomas R. Kratochwill (eds.). American Psychological Association, Washington, 81–108. Retrieved May 6, 2016 from http://content.apa.org/books/14275-006

[7] Jeanne Century, H. King, S. Rand, C. Heppner, Baker Franke, and Jill Westrick. 2013. Computer Science - Teacher Capacity Study - The Center for Elementary Mathematics and Science Education. Outlier. Retrieved September 1, 2018 from http://outlier.uchicago.edu/computerscience/OS4CS/teacher-capacity/

[8] Linda Darling-Hammond. 2000. Teacher quality and student achievement. Education policy analysis archives 8: 1. Retrieved April 1, 2015 from http://epaa.asu.edu/ojs/index.php/epaa/article/view/392

[9] Drew H. Gitomer and Courtney A. Bell. 2013. Evaluating teaching and teachers. In APA handbook of testing and assessment in psychology, Vol. 3: Testing and assessment in school psychology and education. American Psychological Association, Washington, DC, US, 415–444. https://doi.org/10.1037/14049-020

[10] Joanna Goode and Jane Margolis. 2011. Exploring Computer Science: A Case Study of School Reform. ACM Transactions on Computing Education 11, 2: 1–16. https://doi.org/10.1145/1993069.1993076

[11] Dan Leyzberg and Christopher Moretti. 2017. Teaching CS to CS Teachers: Addressing the Need for Advanced Content in K-12 Professional Development. In Proceedings of the 2017 ACM SIGCSE Technical Symposium on Computer Science Education (SIGCSE '17), 369–374. https://doi.org/10.1145/3017680.3017798

[12] Jane Margolis, Jean J. Ryoo, Cueponcaxochitl D. M. Sandoval, Clifford Lee, Joanna Goode, and Gail Chapman. 2012. Beyond Access: Broadening Participation in High School Computer Science. ACM Inroads 3, 4: 72–78. https://doi.org/10.1145/2381083.2381102

[13] Kata Mihaly, Daniel F. McCaffrey, Douglas O. Staiger, and J. R. Lockwood. 2013. A composite estimator of effective teaching. Seattle, WA: Bill & Melinda Gates Foundation. Retrieved May 9, 2015 from http://www.nbexcellence.org/cms_files/resources/Jan%202013%20%20A%20Composite%20Estimator%20of%20Effective%20Teaching%20Research%20Paper.pdf

[14] K-12 CS Framework Committee. 2016. K-12 Computer Science Framework. Retrieved April 11, 2017 from http://www.k12cs.org.

[15] Luis C. Moll, Cathy Amanti, Deborah Neff, and Norma Gonzalez. 1992. Funds of knowledge for teaching: Using a qualitative approach to connect homes and classrooms. *Theory Into Practice* 31, 2: 132–141. https://doi.org/10.1080/00405849209543534

[16] Robert P. Moses and Cobb, Charles E. 2001. Radical Equations: Civil Rights from Mississippi to the Algebra Project. Beacon Press, Boston, MA.

[17] C. L. O'Donnell. 2008. Defining, Conceptualizing, and Measuring Fidelity of Implementation and Its Relationship to Outcomes in K-12 Curriculum Intervention Research. Review of Educational Research 78, 1: 33–84. https://doi.org/10.3102/0034654307313793

[18] Outlier Research and Evaluation. n.d. Barriers and Supports to Teaching Introductory Computer Science (with Exploring Computer Science Materials). Retrieved September 1, 2018 from http://outlier.uchicago.edu/basics/

[19] William R. Penuel, Min Sun, Kenneth A. Frank, and H. Alix Gallagher. 2012. Using Social Network Analysis to Study How Collegial Interactions Can Augment Teacher Learning from External Professional Development. American Journal of Education 119, 1: 103–136. https://doi.org/10.1086/667756

[20] Janine T. Remillard and Daniel J. Heck. 2014. Conceptualizing the curriculum enactment process in mathematics education. ZDM 46, 5: 705–718. https://doi.org/10.1007/s11858-014-0600-4

[21] Pratim Sengupta, John S. Kinnebrew, Satabdi Basu, Gautam Biswas, and Douglas Clark. 2013. Integrating computational thinking with K-12 science education using agent-based computation: A theoretical framework. *Education and Information Technologies* 18, 2: 351–380. https://doi.org/10.1007/s10639-012-9240-x

[22] Eric Snow, Daisy Rutstein, Marie Bienkowski, and Yuning Xu. 2017. Principled Assessment of Student Learning in High School Computer Science. 209–216. https://doi.org/10.1145/3105726.3106186

[23] Carol Tate, Julie Remold, and Marie Bienkowski. 2018. Pursuing the Vision of CS for All: Views from the Front Lines. ACM Inroads 9, 3: 48–52.

Including Embedded Systems in CS: Why? When? and How?

Bill Siever (Moderator)
Washington University in St. Louis
St. Louis, Missouri
bsiever@gmail.com

Roger D. Chamberlain
Washington University in St. Louis
St. Louis, Missouri
roger@wustl.edu

Elliott Forbes
University of Wisconsin-La Crosse
La Crosse, WI
eforbes@uwlax.edu

Ingrid Russell
University of Hartford
West Hartford, CT
irussell@hartford.edu

ABSTRACT

Embedded systems pervade nearly every aspect of modern life. Moreover, the emergence of both mobile platforms and Internet of Things (IoT) is furthering their reach. Although embedded systems are one of the bodies of knowledge in the ACM/IEEE-CS *Computer Engineering* Curricula, they have only passing mention in the ACM/IEEE-CS *Computer Science* Curricula. Inclusion of embedded systems concepts in undergraduate computer science can facilitate many objectives: a) they are an example of Platform-Based Development, a prominent theme in the ACM 2013 CS Curricula, b) they are often a more suitable level of complexity for educational needs than other "real world" platforms (e.g., Arduinos may be used to introduce many AP CS Principles in a single course), c) they offer a novel form of engagement, which may enhance diversity, and d) emerging areas, like IoT, are increasing demand for professionals that understand the full span of systems, from low-level firmware, to middleware and cloud computing.

This panel represents three methods of including embedded systems concepts in undergraduate computer science: 1) use of embedded systems to improve engagement in a non-major computing course, 2) a required course covering core content for both computer science and computer engineering majors, and 3) a degree program offering a formal emphasis in embedded systems via a complementary set of courses. The panelists will share their motivations for including embedded systems concepts in their programs, their approaches to integrating the content into their curricula, the teaching methods they use, the challenges they faced, and challenges that remain.

CCS CONCEPTS

• **Social and professional topics → Computer science education**; **Computer engineering education**; **Computational science and engineering education**; *Professional topics*; *Computing education*; • **Hardware → Analysis and design of emerging devices and systems**; • **Software and its engineering →** *Software system structures*;

ACM ISBN 978-1-4503-5890-3/19/02.
https://doi.org/10.1145/3287324.3287327

KEYWORDS

Embedded Systems Education

ACM Reference Format:
Bill Siever (Moderator), Roger D. Chamberlain, Elliott Forbes, and Ingrid Russell. 2019. Including Embedded Systems in CS: Why? When? and How?. In *Proceedings of the 50th ACM Technical Symposium on Computer Science Education (SIGCSE '19), February 27-March 2, 2019, Minneapolis, MN, USA.* ACM, New York, NY, USA, 2 pages. https://doi.org/10.1145/3287324.3287327

1 SUMMARY

The goal of this panel is to share interest in and challenges of including embedded systems concepts in *undergraduate computer science.* The panelists were selected to represent three different approaches currently in practice. They also represent a diverse set of both objectives and institutions. The audience may include educators who are either already using or are considering an approach comparable to one of the panelists as well as those who haven't previously considered the benefits of embedded systems exposure. Significant potential outcomes of the panel include: a) sharing tips that help bootstrap inclusion of embedded systems concepts in other programs and b) cross-pollination of ideas between the approaches already in practice.

2 PANEL STRUCTURE

The discussion will:

(1) Start with a brief introduction
(2) Give each panel member 10-12 minutes to summarize their work, which will include:
   - a description of their institution, program, and students;
   - motivations for including embedded systems concepts;
   - the approach they use for content integration;
   - the pedagogical techniques they use; and
   - the challenges they've encountered (scaling, motivating students, costs, equipment, etc.)
(3) Open the floor to guided discussion, including comparison and contrast of the different approaches. The moderator will have a prepared list of questions if discussion lags.

3 INGRID RUSSELL

As part of the University of Hartford's efforts to integrate High Impact Practices into the undergraduate curriculum, the Computer Science Department developed a model for revitalizing an introductory computer science course for non-majors. The course provides a broad introduction to the use of computers as tools for creativity, problem solving, communications, and information organization. It is taken by many students in the College of Arts and Sciences to meet the technology component of the general education requirement and by students in other colleges to meet a requirement for their major. The overarching goal of our efforts was to enhance the learning experiences in the course by applying and relating fundamental computational thinking concepts of algorithmic thinking, data representation, and computational efficiency to real-world problems in the context of a highly visual embedded system, the Arduino Nano. The Arduino platform, which is cross-platform and easy-to-use for both non-science and non-engineering students, has great promise in teaching course concepts in both hardware and software within a visual context. The platform provides a rich opportunity to engage students by showing broad applications of computing in domains that are part of their daily life, thus introducing computing in a way that may broaden participation.

We have developed and tested adaptable curricular modules and associated hands-on laboratories that can be used in introductory courses in both computer science and engineering. Features of our materials include: a) emphasis on application of ideas through implementation, b) a practical approach to real-world applications, c) hands-on learning that fosters close faculty-student interaction, and d) engaging, team-based active learning. The approach has been effective. Students obtained a greater appreciation for technology and how different technologies work together. In addition to improving student learning, we expect this model to improve student retention rates and encourage broader participation in computer science and engineering.

The model was first implemented during the 2016–2017 academic year in one section of the course. During fall 2017 and spring 2018 semesters two other instructors implemented the model and curricula in their offerings of the course. Additional sections will follow in the successive semesters and we will continue to collect assessment data of the model's impact.

4 ROGER D. CHAMBERLAIN

At Washington University in St. Louis embedded systems principles are introduced in a first-year course that is required for both computer science and computer engineering majors. The focus of the course is computing in the physical world, recognizing that the majority of computing systems today don't reside on desktops or in server rooms, nor is their I/O limited to a keyboard, mouse, screen, and network connection. The course content, detailed in [1], is motivated by core concepts that are foundational to to both computer science and computer engineering. This includes information representation, timing (*when* something happens as a functional property), automata models (finite-state machines), physical I/O (both analog and digital), computer communications, and a brief introduction to computer architecture and assembly language.

Unlike many introductory embedded systems courses, which are upper-division offerings, this is intentionally designed to be a first-year course, accessible after only one semester of introductory computer science. The course is lecture-free, high enrollment, and meets twice a week in the instructional laboratories. One meeting is devoted to studio sessions, where students perform guided exercises through the material they are expected to master. The other session provides opportunities for both assistance on assignments and assessment purposes. This instructional approach is consistent with the department's decade-long investment in active learning [2].

5 ELLIOTT FORBES

Within the last 10-15 years the barriers to entry in embedded systems development have dramatically decreased. Development platforms of the past were often vendor-locked, required expensive hardware and software developer kits (SDKs), were difficult to use, and lacked a community that was accessible to newcomers. Now, however, the open-source hardware and software communities have rallied, largely solving these issues.

Recognizing this trend, the Computer Science Department of the University of Wisconsin-La Crosse gauged interest in embedded systems in spring of 2014 by offering a special topics course on the Internet of Things. This course was popular with students and prompted another offering. While these classes were successful, we found that the most compelling use for these systems was in their integration with sensors and actuators. Unfortunately students had very little experience with the electrical issues that arise when interfacing with a broad variety of systems. To solve this we introduced two more classes — the first is a class that covers DC analog circuit analysis and digital logic and the second explores microcontrollers, common ICs, communications protocols, and prototyping issues. These classes are now a prerequisite to the Internet of Things course. This three-course sequence is distinct enough from the typical computer science curriculum that students completing all three courses can add a special designation to their computer science degree indicating an emphasis in embedded systems.

REFERENCES

[1] Roger D. Chamberlain and Ron K. Cytron. 2017. *Computing in the Physical World* (pre-release ed.). http://www.ccrc.wustl.edu/~roger/cse132/cc_v0_06.pdf

[2] Ross Sowell, Yixin Chen, Jeremy Buhler, Sally A. Goldman, Cindy Grimm, and Kenneth J. Goldman. 2010. Experiences with active learning in CS3. *Journal of Computing Sciences in Colleges* 25, 5 (May 2010), 173–179.

Where Are We Now? Results from a National Study of Computer Science Teachers and Teaching

Eric R. Banilower
Horizon Research, Inc.
Chapel Hill NC USA
erb@horizon-research.com

Evelyn M. Gordon
Horizon Research, Inc.
Chapel Hill NC USA
egordon@horizon-research.com

ABSTRACT

The National Survey of Science and Mathematics Education has provided nationally representative data about the status of K–12 science and mathematics education periodically over the past 40 years. In 2018, the sixth iteration of the study, the study's scope was expanded to include a focus on K–12 computer science education and the study renamed The NSSME+. Data come from roughly 1,300 schools, 7,000 K–12 science and mathematics teachers (who were asked about their integration of computer science into their instruction), and 300 teachers of high school computer science. This session will engage participants with results related to computer science education in the U.S., including: how many, and which, students have access to computer science instruction; who teaches computer science and what pre-service preparation and in-service professional development they have; the nature of computer science instruction; and access to resources, including instructional materials, to support instruction.

CCS CONCEPTS

• **Social and professional topics~K-12 education**

KEYWORDS

K–12 Computer Science Education; Computer Science Teacher Preparation; Computer Science Teacher Professional Development

ACM Reference format:

Eric R. Banilower and Evelyn M. Gordon. 2018. Where are We Now? Results from a National Study of Computer Science Teachers and Teaching. In *Proceedings of The 50th ACM Technical Symposium on Computer Science Education, Minneapolis, MN, USA, February 27 - March 2, 2019 (SIGCSE'19). ACM, New York, NY, USA, 2 pages.* https://doi.org/10.1145/3287324.3287515

ACM ISBN 978-1-4503-5890-3/19/02.
https://doi.org/10.1145/3287324.3287515

1 Objective

National interest in providing computer science education at the K–12 level has grown steadily since ACM founded the Computer Science Teachers Association (CSTA) in 2004. This trend is evident in SIGCSE conference sessions focused on K–12 education, President Obama's Computer Science for All initiative, the growth of online instruction and advocacy sites such as CS for All and code.org, and the development of K–12 computer science standards by CSTA and an increasing number of states. However, there has been no nationally representative study of the status of computer science education at the K–12 level. The 2018 NSSME+ provides nationally representative results about K–12 computer science education, including who teaches it and what they are doing in their classrooms.

The 2018 NSSME+ administered surveys at approximately 1,300 schools, and included roughly 300 teachers of high school computer science and 7,000 teachers of K–12 science and mathematics throughout the U.S. The study consisted of both teacher- and school-level questionnaires, and the sample was designed to provide both national estimates and disaggregation of the data by various school and classroom factors. Results from the study include:

- The distribution of computer science classes and computer science teachers in the nation's schools, including the access of historically underrepresented students to these classes/teachers;
- The qualifications of computer science teachers;
- The instructional objectives and activities that characterize computer science instruction; and
- The integration of computer science concepts (including computational thinking) in mathematics and science instruction.

2 Outline

This session will share findings from the study and engage participants in considering the implications of the results for both the preparation and support of computer science teachers. The session will be divided into three main segments of approximately 25 minutes, each of which will include multiple strategies for participant engagement. The first segment will share findings related to the current computer science teaching force and how their preparation compares to recommendations described in CSTA's *Ensuring Exemplary Teaching in an Essential Discipline* [1] and the International Society for Technology in Education's *ISTE Standards for Computer Science Educators* [2]. Results show that although only about 1 in 4 high school computer science teachers nationwide have a degree in computer engineering, computer science, information science, or computer science education, almost half have completed coursework in at least 3 of the 4 content areas recommended by both CSTA and ISTE.

The teacher preparation recommendations will also inform the second and third segments, to consider related needs among the current teaching force. The second segment will focus on the amount and nature of professional development opportunities, including induction experiences, computer science teachers have access to and participate in. For example, over half of high school computer science teachers have completed more than 35 hours of professional development related to computer science teaching in the past three years, but nearly a fifth have not had any professional development in this time frame. The third segment will share data about the nature of computer science instruction, including the extent to which students are engaged in the types of computer science practices described in the *K–12 Computer Science Framework* [3]. Between 50 and 60 percent of high schools offer courses that include programming or require programming as a prerequisite, though 80 percent of schools provide access to these types of courses when online and offsite options are included. Only about a fifth offer AP computer science courses. Teachers reported that they have students work on programming activities using a computer at least weekly in over 95 percent of those courses, and in almost three-fourths of classes they have students comment their code to document purposes or features at least weekly. In contrast, in about a third of computer science classes teachers rarely or never have students systematically use test cases to verify program performance and/or identify problems, and they rarely or never have students write their reflections in about half of computer classes. Despite recent trends encouraging the incorporation of computer science into science and mathematics courses, a large majority of science and mathematics classes (71–89 percent, depending on grade level) never include coding as part of instruction.

In each segment, participants will first be asked to predict results, based on their experience and knowledge, and discuss their predictions in small groups before findings from the study are detailed. Participant questions and reactions will be encouraged throughout, particularly comparing their initial predictions to the empirical findings of the study. As part of each segment of the session, we will lead a discussion of the implications of the results for efforts to increase student access to high-quality computer science learning experiences. These conversations will include both small-group and whole-group discussions to provide opportunities for all participants to share their views and to hear the views of others.

3 Expectations

The intended audience for this session includes policy makers and practitioners who train, support, and provide instructional resources for computer science teachers.

As a result of this session, participants will gain a national perspective on the current state of the K–12 computer science teacher workforce and computer science teaching. Participants will also learn about areas of need for professional growth among new and veteran high school computer science teachers. Lastly, participants will share and develop new insights into how teachers of computer science can be effectively prepared in pre-service programs, supported with ongoing professional learning opportunities, and provided with the tools and resources to be successful in the classroom.

4 Suitability for a Special Session

Results from the study address multiple areas of interest to the SIGCSE community and could not be communicated effectively in a 25-minute paper session. In addition, we have designed the session to be more interactive than a typical paper or panel session to allow attendees to explore the implications of our findings for their own work. A special session organized specifically for these needs is an ideal alternative.

ACKNOWLEDGMENTS

This material is based upon work supported by the National Science Foundation under Grant No. DGE-1642413. Any opinions, findings, and conclusions or recommendations expressed in this material are those of the authors and do not necessarily reflect the views of the National Science Foundation. The presenters also wish to thank Daniel J. Heck, Kristen A. Malzahn, and P. Sean Smith for their contributions to the project.

REFERENCES

[1] B. Ericson, M. Armoni, J. Gal-Ezer, D. Seehorn, C. Stephenson, and F. Trees. 2008. *Ensuring exemplary teaching in an essential discipline: Addressing the crisis in computer science teacher certification.* New York, NY: Association for Computing Machinery and Computer Science Teachers Association. Retrived from https://www.csteachers.org/resource/resmgr/CertificationFinal.pdf.

[2] International Society for Technology in Education. 2011. *Standards for Computer Science Educators.* Retrieved from https://www.iste.org/standards.

[3] K–12 Computer Science Framework. 2016. Retrieved from http://www.k12cs.org.

The New NSF Requirement for Broadening Participation in Computing (BPC) Plans

Community Advice and Resources

Tracy Camp
Dept. of Computer Science
Colorado School of Mines
Golden, CO, USA
tcamp@mines.edu

Wendy DuBow
NCWIT
University of Colorado
Boulder, CO, USA
wendy.dubow@ncwit.org

Diane Levitt
Cornell Tech
2 West Loop Road
New York, NY, USA
diane.levitt@cornell.edu

Linda J. Sax
UCLA
3045 Moore Hall
Los Angeles, CA, USA
lsax@ucla.edu

Valerie Taylor
CMD-IT
2130 Harvey Mitchell Pkwy South
College Station, TX, USA
taylor@cmd-it.org

Colleen Lewis
(Moderator)
Harvey Mudd College
Claremont, CA, USA
lewis@cs.hmc.edu

ABSTRACT

The CISE directorate of the NSF is rolling out a requirement that all NSF grants include a Broadening Participation in Computing (BPC) plan (www.nsf.gov/cise/bpc/). This has the potential to drive important institutional change across CS departments in the U.S. This panel of BPC experts will offer their perspectives on meaningful BPC activities, talk about existing BPC programs, and share BPC-related resources that can help PIs and departments craft high-quality BPC plans. The panelists will offer contrasting perspectives on topics such as K-12 outreach, the allocation of department funds for BPC, faculty engagement, and first steps departments should take. Ultimately, NSF review panels made up of CISE community members will evaluate BPC plans, but we hope to spark productive conversations in the interest of fostering institutional change to achieve the social imperative of BPC.

KEYWORDS

Broadening Participation in Computing; inclusive teaching; culture change

ACM Reference format:

Tracy Camp, Wendy DuBow, Diane Levitt, Linda Sax, Valerie Taylor and Colleen Lewis. 2019. The New NSF Requirement for Broadening Participation in Computing (BPC) Plans: Community Advice and Resources. In *Proceedings of the 50th ACM Technical Symposium on Computer Science Education (SIGCSE'19). Feb. 27-Mar.2, 2019, Minneapolis, MN, USA.* ACM, New York, NY, 2 pages. https://doi.org/10.1145/3287324.3287332

SIGCSE '19, February 27-March 2, 2019, Minneapolis, MN, USA

ACM ISBN 978-1-4503-5890-3/19/02.
https://doi.org/10.1145/3287324.3287332

1 Summary

The On July 3, 2017, the Computer & Information Science & Engineering (CISE) directorate at the US National Science Foundation (NSF) released a Dear Colleague Letter (NSF 17-110; www.nsf.gov/pubs/2017/nsf17110/nsf17110.jsp) with a new set of initiatives for Broadening Participation in Computing (BPC). One component is that "all CISE PIs will be strongly encouraged to include meaningful BPC plans in the Broader Impacts section of submitted proposals, starting with deadlines in fall 2017."

"CISE recognizes that BPC will require an array of long-term, sustained efforts and that efforts to broaden participation must be innovative, varied, and welcoming of multiple pathways that eliminate or overcome barriers." (NSF 17-110). Each of our panelists wear multiple hats. We have panelists representing nonprofits focused on diversity in CS (NCWIT, CMD-IT, CRA-W, BRAID), academic institutions committed to inclusivity (e.g., Colorado School of Mines, Cornell Tech, UCLA), and researchers studying ongoing diversity efforts (Drs. DuBow and Sax). This breadth offers the expertise to provide nuanced advice around important topics that have no single answer, such as the following questions:

- How should you allocate funds between student affinity groups, conference travel, and staff support for BPC?
- How do you help faculty connect BPC activities to research in CS that does not otherwise relate to education or BPC?
- Should faculty who are resistant to BPC be encouraged to participate in fundamentally different ways?

Is K-12 outreach a distraction to creating within-institution culture change or an important dimension of BPC activity?

This panel addresses the topic of the NSF goal to help PIs "develop interest, skills, and activities in support of BPC at all levels." (NSF 17-110).

2 Panel Structure

5 minutes: The moderator, Colleen Lewis, will provide a brief introduction to the NSF initiative.
20 minutes: Each panelist will have three minutes to introduce themselves, their organization, and up to two resources for BPC.
35 minutes: Panelists will answer a set of questions based upon the interest of attendees.
15 minutes: Each panelist will have about two minutes to offer final thoughts and recommendations.

3 Panelists

3.1 Tracy Camp, Colorado School of Mines

Tracy Camp is a Full Professor and Head of the Department of Computer Science at Colorado School of Mines. Dr. Camp is a former co-chair of the Committee on the Status of Women in Computing Research (CRA-W), and continues to be involved today on the CRA-W Board and CRA-W Steering Committee. CRA-W has a variety of programs for BPC seeking to support women at every level of the research pipeline: undergraduate students, graduate students, faculty, and industry and government researchers. Dr. Camp is also a member of the Steering Committee for BPC-net, which is a new NSF-sponsored repository of BPC resources.

3.2 Wendy DuBow, NCWIT

Wendy DuBow is the director of evaluation and a senior research scientist at the National Center for Women & Information Technology (NCWIT). NCWIT exists to provide interested parties with research-backed techniques for increasing the meaningful participation of all girls and women in computing disciplines. We do through this sharing readable, professionally designed practical materials about how to recruit and retain underrepresented groups in computing. Because changing the status quo requires changing systems, not individuals, we encourage organizations to take a strategic, systemic approach to broadening participation in computing. DuBow will present NCWIT's strategic change model that enables faculty and administrators to identify which area(s) of change they will focus on and then supplies them with relevant practices (https://www.ncwit.org/recruit-and-retain-strategically). The six key focus areas for changing the environment for students are: recruiting, curriculum, pedagogy, supporting students, institutional policies, and evaluation.

3.3 Diane Levitt, Cornell Tech

Diane Levitt is the Senior Director of K-12 Education at Cornell Tech, the new graduate campus of Cornell University in New York City. She drives the campus engagement with the NYC computing education community, including the Dept. of Education's CS4All initiative, and works with individual schools to catalyze K-12 computer science, notably through the Teacher in Residence program which places CS master teachers as content coaches in public elementary and middle schools. Diane will present Cornell Tech's model for investing in K-12 computing education, wherein the campus acts as a hub for building the capacity of teachers to incorporate CS, involving faculty, graduate students and staff in these efforts. Levitt has been a panelist reviewing NSF BPC Plans. Some documentation of Cornell Tech's work can be found at:

- https://www.learntechlib.org/primary/p/181938/
- https://tech.cornell.edu/news/cornell-tech-program-prepares-k-12-teachers-to-teach-computer-science/
- https://tech.cornell.edu/news/transforming-computer-science-education-in-public-schools/

3.4 Linda J. Sax, UCLA

Linda J. Sax is Professor of Higher Education in the Graduate School of Education & Information Studies at UCLA. She is the Principal Investigator for the research component of the Building, Recruiting and Inclusion for Diversity (BRAID) initiative aimed at diversifying undergraduate computing. Dr. Sax will draw from interviews with computer science department chairs and surveys of computing students to discuss how BRAID institutions have engaged in BPC activities. She will also discuss the research methods used to study institutional adoption of BPC activities and their impact on students. Two key resources for this information are the BRAID website (https://braidresearch.gseis.ucla.edu/) and Dr. Sax's recently-published paper on the role of computer science department chairs in promoting gender and racial diversity (http://www.dl.begellhouse.com/journals/00551c876cc2f027,611065c054afe923,28d870d57ed75b8d.html).

3.5 Valerie Taylor, CMD-IT

Valerie Taylor is CEO and President of the Center for Minorities and People with Disabilities in IT (CMD-IT). CMD-IT offers a range of programs focused on professional development for students, faculty and professionals from the target groups. CMD-IT also has reports documenting the participation of minorities and people with disabilities in computing (http://www.cmd-it.org/resources/). These can be helpful resources for documenting patterns of underrepresentation. Additionally, these resources challenge the narrative that there are no minorities or people with disabilities in IT. CMD-IT is also the presenter of the Richard Tapia Celebration of Diversity in Computing Conferences (http://www.tapiaconference.org). Valerie Taylor is also the Director of the Mathematics and Computer Science Division at Argonne National Laboratory. Before joining Argonne in 2017, Dr. Taylor was on the faculty at Texas A&M. Taylor is a fellow of both IEEE and ACM. She has received numerous awards, including the Richard A. Tapia Achievement Award for Scientific Scholarship. Civic Science, and Diversifying Computing.

3.6 Colleen M. Lewis, CSTeachingTips.org

The moderator, Colleen Lewis, is the McGregor-Girand Associate Professor of computer science at Harvey Mudd College. Lewis curates CSTeachingTips.org, a NSF-sponsored project for disseminating effective computer science teaching practices. For example, http://csteachingtips.org/tips-for-department-inclusivity provides tips for creating an inclusive department culture, which could inform department BPC plans.

Shaping Curricular Guidelines for Associate-Degree Cybersecurity Programs

Cara Tang
Computer Information Systems
Portland Community College
Portland, OR, USA
cara.tang@pcc.edu

Cindy S. Tucker
Computer & Information Technologies
Bluegrass Community and Technical College
Lexington, KY USA
cindy.tucker@kctcs.edu

Christian Servin
Computer Science
El Paso Community College
El Paso, TX USA
cservin1@epcc.edu

Markus Geissler
Computer Information Science
Cosumnes River College
Sacramento, CA, USA
geisslm@crc.losrios.edu

Melissa Stange
Computer Science
Lord Fairfax Community College
Middletown, VA USA
mstange@lfcc.edu

ABSTRACT

As projections of the shortage of cybersecurity workers grow [4], the spotlight is on cybersecurity education. In December of 2017, the Joint Task Force on Cybersecurity Education published *Cybersecurity Curricula 2017: Curriculum Guidelines for Post-Secondary Degree Programs in Cybersecurity* [6] (CSEC2017), representing a new discipline in ACM's Computing Curricula Series [5]. Now the ACM CCECC (Committee for Computing Education in Community Colleges) is leading creation of a similar set of guidelines for two-year cybersecurity programs at the associate-degree level, called CSEC2Y.

This special session, led by the ACM CCECC, will engage participants in the curriculum development process for associate-degree programs in the increasingly important field of cybersecurity. Participants will have the opportunity to review the current CSEC2Y draft and related materials, to recommend changes, plan further revisions, and otherwise assist in crafting the curricular guidance.

CCS CONCEPTS

• **Social and professional topics → Professional topics → Computing education → Model curricula.**

KEYWORDS

Community College; Two-Year College; Cybersecurity Education; CSEC2017; CSEC2Y; Curriculum Guidelines

ACM ISBN 978-1-4503-5890-3/19/02.
https://doi.org/10.1145/3287324.3287516

ACM Reference format:

Cara Tang, Cindy Tucker, Christian Servin, Markus Geissler and Melissa Stange. 2019. Shaping Curricular Guidelines for Associate-Degree Cybersecurity Programs. In *Proceedings of ACM SIGCSE Technical Symposium (SIGCSE'19). ACM, New York, NY, USA, 2 pages.* https://doi.org/10.1145/3287324.3287516

1 Objective

As projections of the shortage of cybersecurity workers grow [4], the spotlight is on cybersecurity education. In December of 2017, the Joint Task Force on Cybersecurity Education published *Cybersecurity Curricula 2017: Curriculum Guidelines for Post-Secondary Degree Programs in Cybersecurity* [6] (CSEC2017), representing a new discipline in ACM's Computing Curricula Series [5]. This set of curriculum guidelines was endorsed by four professional computing societies: Association for Computing Machinery (ACM), IEEE Computer Society (IEEE-CS), Association for Information Systems Special Interest Group on Information Security and Privacy (AIS SIGSEC), and International Federation for Information Processing Technical Committee on Information Security Education (IFIP WG 11.8).

Now the ACM Committee for Computing Education in Community Colleges (CCECC) is leading creation of a similar set of guidelines for two-year cybersecurity programs at the associate-degree level. The CCECC has formed a task force to create cybersecurity curriculum guidance for two-year programs based on CSEC2017.

The CCECC serves and supports community and technical college educators in all aspects of computing education, with a focus on producing curriculum guidelines for associate-degree programs in ACM-recognized computing disciplines. The CCECC's most recent curricular volume is CSTransfer2017 (*Computer Science Curricular Guidance for Associate-Degree Transfer Programs with Infused Cybersecurity*) [2], published in June of 2017. Aligned with CS2013 [1] to facilitate transfer,

CSTransfer2017 offers over 200 learning outcomes across 17 knowledge areas that are appropriate for the first two years of a computer science program. In addition to the Cybersecurity knowledge area itself, cybersecurity has been infused throughout the guidelines, representing the importance of security in all aspects of computing. The learning outcomes focus on student achievement rather than knowledge, and each outcome has an associated assessment rubric. This curriculum structure follows in the style established with the ACM CCECC's *Information Technology Competency Model of Core Learning Outcomes and Assessment for Associate-Degree Curriculum* [3] published October 2014, for two-year career-oriented IT programs.

The current project focusing on curriculum guidelines for associate-degree cybersecurity programs, code named CSEC2Y, will maintain the focus on student achievement with measurable student learning outcomes. The scope includes both transfer and career-oriented associate-degree programs in cybersecurity. Based on CSEC2017, the content of the guidelines will be updated for currency and appropriateness at the two-year level. In addition to CSEC2017, other relevant sources will influence the guidelines, including the CAE-CD 2Y 2019 knowledge units (requirements of the NSA and DHS National Centers of Academic Excellence in Cyber Defense) [8] and the NICE cybersecurity workforce framework [7].

This special session will engage those interested in cybersecurity education at the undergraduate, lower division level in the development of these curricular guidelines. Participants will have the opportunity to review the current draft and related materials, to recommend changes, plan further revisions, and otherwise assist in crafting the curricular guidance. The session will serve an important role by engaging the broader community to provide input and dialog on opportunities, challenges, local needs, and successful models of cybersecurity computing curricula to shape the new guidelines.

2 Outline

The 75-minute session will be organized as follows:

2.1 Introduction (15 minutes)

Members of the ACM CCECC will describe the work of the committee, the current curricular project, and the goals for this special session. Presenters include Cara Tang (CCECC chair and CSEC2Y task group chair), Cindy Tucker (CCECC vice-chair), and Christian Servin (CCECC member).

2.2 Work on Knowledge Areas (45 minutes)

The current draft of the proposed associate-degree curricular framework will be presented. Participants will break into small groups, with each group to consider a subset of the knowledge areas with respect to CSEC2017 and other materials as appropriate. The small group discussion may include suitability of content for associate-degree programs, associated student learning outcomes, assessment metrics, and missing content. After a time, each small group will report out to the whole group and further discussion will take place.

2.3 Summary and Wrap-Up (15 minutes)

Changes to the curriculum framework that were proposed during the session will be summarized. The presenters will describe ways in which participants may continue to be involved in or stay connected to the curricular project.

3 Expectations

The intended audience for this session includes community college faculty, division chairs, and program coordinators, as well as educators from 4-year programs interested in 2-year curricula and articulation. The session will provide an overview of existing curricular guidelines for computing programs infused with cybersecurity, with the majority of time in the session spent working on and contributing to the creation of curricular guidance for associate-degree cybersecurity programs.

4 Suitability for a Special Session

The ACM CCECC's recent CSTransfer2017 curriculum guidelines were greatly influenced and improved by community input, including a special session at SIGCSE'16. As an emerging discipline in computing, cybersecurity is still being defined as a field and the CSEC2Y task group desires to engage the interested community to shape and improve these curricular guidelines. This session is designed to be highly interactive and would not be suitable as a paper or panel.

REFERENCES

[1] ACM and IEEE Computer Society. 2013. *Computer Science Curricula 2013.* ACM, New York, NY. DOI: http://dx.doi.org/10.1145/2534860.

[2] ACM Committee for Computing Education in Community Colleges. 2017. *Computer Science Curricular Guidance for Associate-Degree Transfer Programs with Infused Cybersecurity.* ACM, New York, NY. DOI: http://dx.doi.org/10.1145/3108241.

[3] ACM Committee for Computing Education in Community Colleges. 2014. *Information Technology Competency Model of Core Learning Outcomes and Assessment for Associate-Degree Curriculum.* ACM, New York, NY, USA. DOI: http://dx.doi.org/10.1145/2686614.

[4] $(ISC)^2$. 2017. Global Cybersecurity Workforce Shortage to Reach 1.8 Million as Threats Loom Larger and Stakes Rise Higher, https://www.isc2.org/News-and-Events/Press-Room/Posts/2017/06/07/2017-06-07-Workforce-Shortage

[5] Joint Task Force for Computing Curricula. 2005. *Computing Curricula 2005: The Overview Report.* ACM, New York, NY.

[6] Joint Task Force on Cybersecurity Education. 2017. *Cybersecurity Curricula 2017: Curriculum Guidelines for Post-Secondary Degree Programs in Cybersecurity.* ACM, New York, NY, USA. DOI: http://dx.doi.org/10.1145/3184594

[7] National Initiative for Cybersecurity Education (NICE). 2017. *NICE Cybersecurity Workforce Framework.* NIST Special Publication 800-181. DOI: https://doi.org/10.6028/NIST.SP.800-181.

[8] NSA and DHS, Centers of Academic Excellence in Cyber Defense (CAE-CD) 2019 Knowledge Units, https://www.iad.gov/NIETP/documents/Requirements/CAE-CD_2019_Knowledge_Units.pdf

SIGCSE Reads 2019: Discussion and Q & A

Rebecca Bates
Minnesota State University, Mankato
Mankato, MN
bates@mnsu.edu

Valerie Summet
Rollins College
Winter Park, FL
vsummet@rollins.edu

Nanette Veilleux
Simmons University
Boston, MA
veilleux@simmons.edu

Judy Goldsmith
University of Kentucky
Lexington, KY
goldsmit@cs.uky.edu

Naomi Kritzer
Saint Paul, MN
naomi.kritzer@gmail.com

ABSTRACT

This special session will allow discussion of how many common goals of CS educators (conveying core CS concepts, creating community for our students, discussing ethics, etc.) can be furthered through the use of literature in CS courses. We will present five goals which are common in CS education, and discuss how incorporating literature relates to them. We will present small case studies showing concrete examples of assignments and courses which have successfully utilized literature in common, core CS courses. We will showcase a Q & A with author Naomi Kritzer, winner of the 2016 Hugo Award for her short story "Cat Pictures Please".

CCS CONCEPTS

• **Social and professional topics → Computing education**; *Codes of ethics*;

KEYWORDS

Computing Education, Science Fiction, Building Community

ACM Reference Format:
Rebecca Bates, Valerie Summet, Nanette Veilleux, Judy Goldsmith, and Naomi Kritzer. 2019. SIGCSE Reads 2019: Discussion and Q & A. In *SIGCSE '19: 50th ACM Technical Symposium on Computer Science Education, February 27–March 2, 2019, Minneapolis, MN, USA.* ACM, New York, NY, USA, 2 pages. https://doi.org/10.1145/3287324.3287524

1 OBJECTIVE

We propose a special session to continue the SIGCSE multi-year, ongoing discussion on using literature to teach computer science centered around the 4 works selected by SIGCSE attendees in 2018: In honor of SIGCSE's 50th birthday, a novel and a short story from SIGCSE's early days: *Do Androids Dream of Electric Sheep* by Philip K. Dick and " I Sing the Body Electric!" by Ray Bradbury. Nonfiction work: *Algorithms of Oppression: How search engines reinforce racism* by Safiya Umoja Noble. A modern short story: "Cat Pictures Please" by Naomi Kritzer.[1]

By having a discussion of the common reading experience for the SIGCSE community and a concrete discussion of how works such as these can be incorporated into CS courses, we hope to support the development of a stronger sense of community and connection as well as engage members in discussions of topics of personal interest. We also hope to highlight how computer science education can be enhanced by using enjoyable books and stories to engage students in computer science learning.

The importance of creativity in computer science and the relationship between "traditional" creativity and technical creativity can be highlighted in a variety of courses through the use of literature. Our session will specifically focus on interdisciplinary creativity through a Q&A with Naomi Kritzer to highlight how she includes technical knowledge in her creative process.

Student reaction to classes that have used literature has been very positive, in part because students are able to connect something they (often) love to their future career. This has implications for retention and long-term persistence in the field. [3]

2 SESSION OUTLINE

The outline and timing of the session will be:

- Brief intro of SIGCSE Reads works (5 min.)
- Overview of 5 common goals and brief case studies (see section 5) (10 min.)
- Q&A with Naomi Kritzer (30 min.)
- Small group discussion (15 min.)
- Reporting out, including lists of new suggestions (14 min.)
- Request for survey participation (1 min.)

3 EXPECTATIONS

Audience: CS educators who are interested in incorporating more literature into their courses. While examples and discussion will center around the four specific works of this year's SIGCSE Reads, attendees will be given ample time to discuss other works and strategies.

Goals: Attendees will leave with examples of how to use literature in their courses to build community and discuss ethics and creativity, and information about contemporary Science Fiction trends.

Suitability: SIGCSE Reads publicizes all the common reads throughout the year, leading up to the conference. Everyone who chose

SIGCSE'19, February 27–March 2, 2019, Minneapolis, MN, USA

ACM ISBN 978-1-4503-5890-3/19/2.
https://doi.org/10.1145/3287324.3287524

[1] http://clarkesworldmagazine.com/kritzer_01_15/

to read the SIGCSE Reads book and story selections is equally equipped to participate in discussions and will wish to do so, making a panel format a poor fit for this special session.

4 DISCUSSION LEADERS

Four of the proposers of this session (Bates, Goldsmith, Summet, and Veilleux) have led a panel discussion and BOFs at many previous SIGCSE conferences. They are well versed in the use of fiction and popular non-fiction in their classes [1, 3]. Bates has taught "Artificial Intelligence & Science Fiction" for many years and incorporates fiction in many of her technical courses [2]. Goldsmith has taught "Science Fiction and Computer Ethics" and allows her AI students to use science fiction reviews as a gateway to AI research papers [4, 5]. Summet uses a series of non-fiction works and excerpts in a Senior Capstone course to encourage student reflection on the experience, purpose, and pitfalls of education and computer science. She has also used science fiction to foster discussion about society's perceptions of robotics and AI in her introductory courses. Veilleux uses science fiction, especially stories like "Cat Pictures Please", *Super Sad True Love Story* and *Hitchhiker's Guide to the Galaxy* to show the unintended consequences or results of ill-considered AI learning strategies in her Data Mining class.

5 CLASSROOM GOALS

Many professors perceive including non-textbook reading assignments as taking away from course material or as a distraction from the subject matter. This session is designed to highlight how relevant fiction and non-fiction works bring depth and nuanced understanding which students will not receive otherwise. Over the years, the organizers of SIGCSE Reads and this session have identified several goals of using science fiction in the classroom.

Building community

Including fiction and non-fiction work builds community – both in the classroom and as a larger body of computer scientists. Popular fiction, in particular, allows students to tap into a culture they may already be passionate about or intrigued by. However, this approach is a double-edged sword. An identity embraced by computer scientists can involve an attendant culture around Science Fiction. While this creates and strengthens communities (and therefore we serve our students by making them aware of this parallel culture), it can also exclude qualified professionals who are not immersed in, and possibly repulsed by, the sub-culture.

Connecting computing to students via the medium of literature

The most straight-forward use of science fiction in the classroom is as examples of scientific discovery without considering its impact. SIGCSE Reads anticipates lively discussion among participants on the challenges of introducing "futuristic" fictional worlds to students, when the fiction itself is so grounded in the social realities of the time the works were written. Participants should be interested in talking about how to effectively persuade students to explore the lessons of the hypothetical futures – evil overlords, dystopias, utopias, and sometimes simply odd side effects (e.g., "Cat Pictures Please"), while also acknowledging the sometimes pleasant and sometimes repulsive social and cultural realities of the past.

Non-fiction can directly explore the impact of technical progress, without fictional metaphors. Use of non-fiction can appeal to more literal-minded students, and also allow discussion of the historical contexts in which technical progress has been made.

Allowing for intentional discussion of problematic aspects of CS

Fifty years after SIGCSE began, we see meaningful efforts to confront implicit bias. Science fiction certainly has mirrored the historical bias in science, and can be illuminating, especially for those of us who grew up inoculated against seeing bias. At the same time, Science Fiction now includes a broader range of protagonists and situations, making it useful again as a community strengthening tool. We have come a long way from stories filled with remarks like Heinlein's "9 times out of 10 when a woman gets raped it's partly her own fault" in *Stranger in a Stranger Land.*

Broadening student perspectives

Over the 50 years of SIGCSE, writing about computer science topics in both fiction and non-fiction has come a long way. This expansion allows a modern curriculum to include works that more effectively reflect the interests and backgrounds of readers who come from a wider range of backgrounds. Care should be taken, when selecting works for a class, to select a variety of works – where variety is measured using many metrics.

Encouraging creativity, critical thinking and interdisciplinary interests

Reading fiction exposes students to imaginary situations, inspiring creativity, while reading non-fiction exposes students to developed arguments, modeling critical thinking. Furthermore, reading itself enhances writing skills. The student can then use these skills to better communicate in their professions, to branch into a science-adjacent fields as teachers or authors, or may simply participate in a lifelong, engaging hobby.

6 PROPOSED DISCUSSION QUESTIONS

(1) How have you used science fiction or other non-textbook works in your classes?
(2) What aspects of using these readings connect you to the larger, cultural community?
(3) How can some traditional science fiction favorites be used be used to discuss bias in science? Similarly, do current science fiction examples avoid these pitfalls?
(4) What are suggestions for texts for SIGCSE Reads 2020?

REFERENCES

[1] Rebecca Bates, , Judy Goldsmith, Rosalyn Berne, Valerie Summet, and Nanette Veilleux. 2012. Science Fiction in Computer Science Education. In *Proc. 2012 ACM SIGCSE Technical Symposium on Computer Science Education (SIGCSE '12).*
[2] Rebecca Bates. 2011. AI & SciFi: Teaching Writing, history, Technology, Literature, and Ethics. In *Proc. 2011 ASEE Annual Conference & Exposition.*
[3] Rebecca Bates, Valerie Summet, and Nanette Veilleux. 2017. SIGCSE Reads: Time for Book Discussion (Abstract Only). In *Proc. 2017 ACM SIGCSE Technical Symposium on Computer Science Education (SIGCSE '17).* 721–721.
[4] Emanuelle Burton, Judy Goldsmith, Sven Koenig, Benjamin Kuipers, Nicholas Mattei, and Toby Walsh. 2017. Ethical Considerations in Artificial Intelligence Courses. *AI magazine* 38, 2 (2017).
[5] Emanuelle Burton, Judy Goldsmith, and Nicholas Mattei. 2018. How to teach computer ethics through science fiction. *Commun. ACM* 61, 8 (2018), 54–64.

50 Years of CS1 at SIGCSE: A Review of the Evolution of Introductory Programming Education Research

Brett A. Becker
University College Dublin
Ireland
brett.becker@ucd.ie

Keith Quille
Institute of Technology Tallaght
Ireland
keith.quille@it-tallaght.ie

ABSTRACT

The SIGCSE Technical Symposium is celebrating its 50th year, and a constant theme throughout this history has been to better understand how novices learn to program. In this paper, we present a perspective on the evolution of introductory programming education research at the Symposium over these 50 years. We also situate the Symposium's impact in the context of the wider literature on introductory programming research. Applying a systematic approach to collecting papers presented at the Symposium that focus on novice programming / CS1, we categorized hundreds of papers according to their main focus, revealing important introductory programming topics and their trends from 1970 to 2018. Some of these topics have faded from prominence and are less relevant today while others, including many topics focused on students—such as making learning programming more appropriate from gender, diversity, accessibility and inclusion standpoints—have garnered significant attention more recently. We present discussions on these trends and in doing so, we provide a checkpoint for introductory programming research. This may provide insights for future research on how we teach novices and how they learn to program.

CCS CONCEPTS

• **Social and professional topics → Computer science education; CS1.**

KEYWORDS

CS1; CS 1; CS-1; programming; introductory programming; introduction to programming; novice programming; survey; review

ACM Reference Format:

Brett A. Becker and Keith Quille. 2019. 50 Years of CS1 at SIGCSE: A Review of the Evolution of Introductory Programming Education Research. In *Proceedings of the 50th ACM Technical Symposium on Computer Science Education (SIGCSE '19), February 27-March 2, 2019, Minneapolis, MN, USA.* ACM, New York, NY, USA, 7 pages. https://doi.org/10.1145/3287324.3287432

1 INTRODUCTION

The SIGCSE Technical Symposium (the Symposium) is celebrating its 50th year, and researching how novices learn to program has been a consistent theme throughout this history. We present a perspective on this research over these first five decades. We also situate the Symposium and its impact in the context of the wider literature on introductory programming research. From an initial selection of 777 papers presented at the Symposium, we categorized 481 CS1 papers and offer a discussion on their topics and trends, providing a checkpoint for introductory programming research going forward into the second half of the Symposium's first century. This may prove insightful for future research on how we teach novices and how they learn to program. Our research goals are:

- RG1 Identify the important topics in introductory programming education research, including their trends, over the first 50 years of the SIGCSE Technical Symposium
- RG2 Situate the introductory programming research presented at the SIGCSE Technical Symposium in the context of the wider literature

SIGCSE '19, February 27-March 2, 2019, Minneapolis, MN, USA

ACM ISBN 978-1-4503-5890-3/19/02...$15.00
https://doi.org/10.1145/3287324.3287432

2 RELATED WORK

Despite the large volume of work on introductory programming (commonly called 'CS1' [19]), there are relatively few surveys, reviews and meta-analyses with wide scope. Most relevant to the present work as it only considered papers presented at the Symposium, is a 2004 paper by Valentine [44], which focused on CS1 and CS2, including papers, workshops and panels. These were organized into a 'taxonomy' based on the paper approach (Marco Polo, Tools, Experimental, Nifty, Philosophy or John Henry), while our categorization is based on paper content/topic. A 2002 paper by Vasiga also provided data on CS1 and CS2 at SIGCSE, and stated: "To say there has been much discussion of CS1 and CS2 in SIGCSE circles is a gross understatement" [45, p. 28]. Table 1 shows the number of papers reported by these authors compared to the subsets of our papers that align with their dates. It is important to note that we only considered papers on CS1 (not CS2). We explain our method in Section 3.

Another effort relevant to our work is a 2018 ITiCSE Working group led by Luxton-Reilly & Simon which performed a large literature review of introductory programming research, citing over 700 references [29]. We discuss this further in Section 4.

	Valentine [44]	Vasiga [45]	this study
1984-1993	17	-	36
1994-2003	28	-	98
2000	-	18	8

Table 1: Number of papers reported at the Symposium on CS1 & CS2 [44, 45] and CS1 (this study). Note that these are subsets of our data as our study spans 1970-2018.

3 METHOD

We chose to analyze papers presented at the SIGCSE Technical Symposium focusing on introductory programming courses at the university level, commonly called CS1 [19]. We conducted a preliminary search of the ACM Digital Library (ACM DL) on January 21, 2018 and carried out a short feasibility study, mainly to refine the search parameters and method. On August 3, 2018 we conducted our final search, which was for papers including any of the following terms in the title, abstract, or keywords: CS1, "CS 1", "introductory programming", "introduction to programming", "novice programming", "novice programmers". This search returned 3,153 hits in the ACM DL Guide to Computing Literature, and 2,354 hits in the ACM DL Full-Text Collection. We then extracted all papers sponsored by SIGCSE (1,442 hits) and then filtered, leaving only papers presented at the SIGCSE Technical Symposium (777 hits). We then applied the exclusion criteria: (1) Papers less than three pages in length (eliminating 244), and (2) Papers not focusing on first-year university-level introductory programming (eliminating 52). This resulted in a final list of 481 papers. Our actual query was:

acmdlTitle: (CS1 "CS 1" "introductory programming" "introduction to programming" "novice programming" "novice programmers") OR recordAbstract: (CS1 "CS 1" "introductory programming" "introduction to programming" "novice programming" "novice programmers") OR keywords.author.keyword: (CS1 "CS 1" "introductory programming" "introduction to programming" "novice programming" "novice programmers")

3.1 Classification of papers

We acknowledge the inherent difficulty of reliably coding academic papers [41]. As this is not a systematic literature review, we allowed categories and subcategories to emerge as Author 1 processed all 481 papers. Our main goal was to categorize the papers fitting our criteria in a way that would accurately describe the landscape of CS1 research at the Symposium, and how it has changed in the last 50 years. For this reason we chose to categorize each paper into one category only (a many-to-one mapping). We discuss this and other threats to validity in Section 6. Once initial categories and subcategories were determined through Author 1 processing all 481 papers, Author 2 re-categorized a random sample of 10% placing 41 of 48 papers in the same categories, indicating 85% agreement. A third faculty member at the same institution as Author 1 repeated this re-categorization with a new random 10% sample and placed 40 of 48 papers in the same category as Author 1, indicating 83% agreement. After this, Authors 1 & 2 discussed the categories and made minor refinements resulting in eight top-level categories: (1) *First languages & paradigms*; (2) *CS1 design, structure & approach*; (3) *CS1 content*; (4) *Tools*; (5) *Collaborative approaches*; (6) *Teaching*; (7) *Learning & Assessment*; and (8) *Students*. In the interest of making this work useful for the community, details on these 481 papers including URLs, number of citations, and citations/year are included in a CSV file available at www.brettbecker.com/sigcse2019.

4 SITUATING THE SIGCSE TECHNICAL SYMPOSIUM IN THE WIDER LITERATURE

Before looking within the Symposium and the evolution of introductory programming education research over the last 50 years, we wanted to gain a picture of the Symposium within the broader literature. As mentioned in Section 2, Luxton-Reilly et al. conducted a 2018 review of introductory programming literature [29], using a similar but slightly broader search query and a much wider search space (not limited to the ACM Digital Library). This resulted in over 5,000 papers, reduced to 1,844 after applying exclusion criteria. We started with 1,442 papers which reduced to 481, approximately 26% of the 1,844 from the ITiCSE working group. This quick comparison reveals that the SIGCSE Technical Symposium represents not only a considerable space in the literature of introductory programming literature indexed by the ACM, but a healthy percentage of the introductory programming literature in general.

To gain a different perspective, we performed our search against: the ACM Digital Library Guide to Computing Literature; all papers published by ACM; and, all proceedings sponsored by SIGCSE. Table 2 shows our findings as a percentage of the hits from the Guide to Computing Literature. Like the comparison to the ITiCSE working group mentioned above, this shows that the SIGCSE Technical Symposium occupies a significant footprint in the wider literature; approximately 25% by this measure, almost the same as the 26% when compared to [29] in the above paragraph.

Search Space	hits	% total
ACM Digital Library Guide to Computing Literature	3,153	100%
Published by ACM	1,823	~58%
Conferences sponsored by SIGCSE	1,442	~46%
SIGCSE Technical Symposium	777	~25%

Table 2: Number of hits and percentage of total (ACM DL Guide to Computing Literature) for our search query.

5 THE EVOLUTION OF INTRODUCTORY PROGRAMMING EDUCATION RESEARCH

In this section we provide a view of the introductory programming research presented at the Symposium, followed by discussions on the evolution of each of the eight top-level categories we identified. We also discuss interesting subcategories.

Figure 1 shows a TreeMap of all 481 papers categorized into 8 top-level categories and 54 subcategories. Some top-level categories have a subcategory called 'General', reserved for papers that are broad in scope and represent the whole top-level category as opposed to a specific subcategory. Additionally, if we had a subcategory with less than five papers (other than a 'General' subcategory), we aggregated these into a single 'Other' subcategory. For instance, the top-level category *First languages & paradigms* has a subcategory called *Other* containing papers from any *First languages & paradigms* papers that were in subcategories with less than five papers. Thus, the only subcategories in Figure 1 that may have less than five papers are *General* and *Other* subcategories.

Figure 2 shows the evolution of each of the eight top-level categories over the last five decades. To compensate for the fact that the overall number of papers published in each decade has steadily increased, we normalized the number of papers per decade by dividing the number of papers per top-level category in each decade by the total number of papers in our dataset published in each given decade. This broadly shows the evolution of these eight top-level categories over the last 50 years. In the following subsections we discuss trends and a selection of notable developments/papers in each of these top-level categories, and some subcategories.

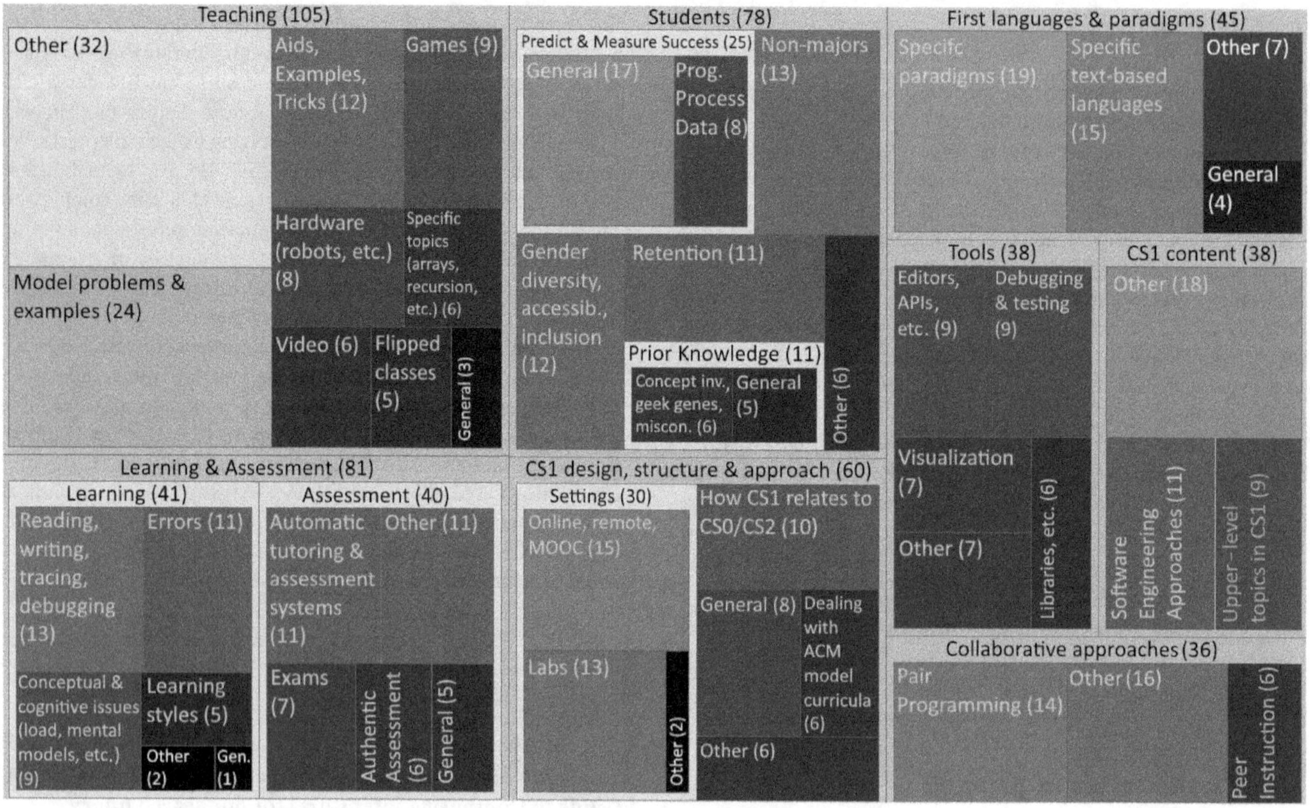

Figure 1: TreeMap of 481 papers in 8 categories and 54 subcategories. The area of each rectangle is proportional to the number of papers in each topic area. More details are discussed in Section 5.

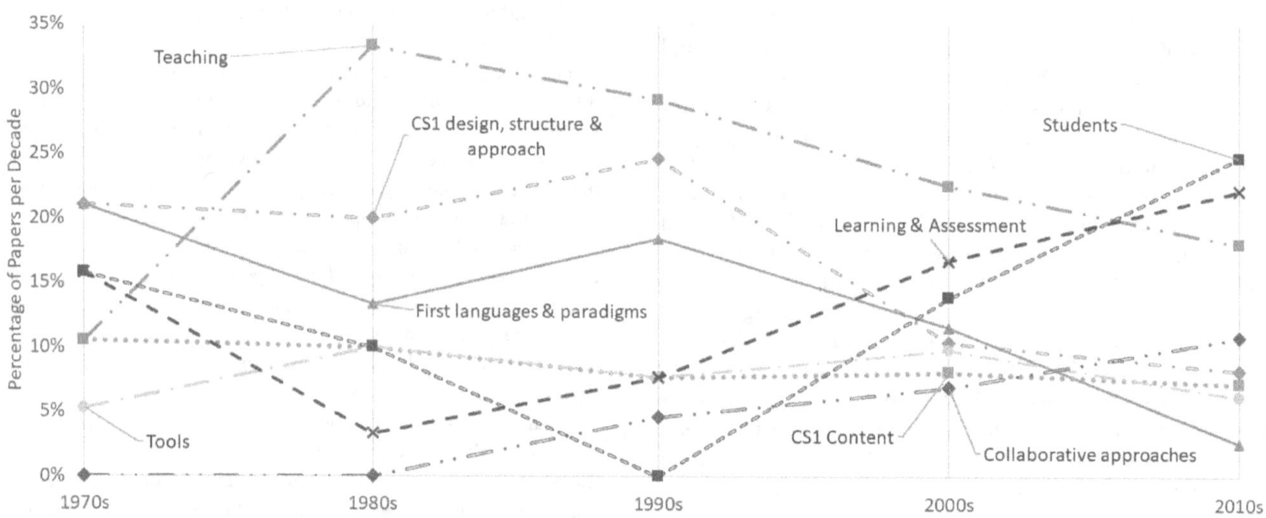

Figure 2: 50-year trends of the 8 top-level categories in introductory programming at the SIGCSE Technical Symposium. To compensate for the fact that the overall number of papers published in each decade has steadily increased, we normalized the number of papers per decade by dividing the number of papers per top-level category in each decade by the total number of papers in our dataset published in each given decade.

5.1 First Languages & Paradigms

	'70s	'80s	'90s	'00s	'10s
General languages & paradigms				2	2
Specific paradigms		1	7	10	1
Specific text-based languages		3	5	6	1
Other	4			2	1

Table 3: Number of papers in the First Languages & Paradigms category.

Table 3 shows the subcategories in this category and the corresponding number of papers published in each decade. As can be seen in Figure 2, interest in this area has slowly declined since the 1990s. Other than language/paradigm choice, one of the most discussed topics in this category has been objects first approaches [12]. At the 2018 Symposium, Simon et al. presented a survey of language choice in CS1 courses in Australasian and UK universities, revealing that the most popular teaching language is Java, followed by Python and C [39]. Interestingly, at the 2004 Symposium, Roberts called for educators to "take responsibility for breaking the cycle of rapid obsolescence [of teaching languages] by developing a stable and effective collection of Java-based teaching resources that will meet the needs of the computer science community" [37, p. 115]. Whether or not this call was met, and whether this was predictive of the prominence of Java reported by Simon et al. is beyond the scope of this paper, but it is interesting to note that the Roberts paper was published in 2004, near a peak in teaching language interest, and that in the current decade, interest has waned considerably, perhaps due to stability brought on by the popular use of Java and Python. Other factors that may have served to draw attention away from the language/paradigm debate recently include the 2004 adoption of Java for the APCS exam [37], which has remained unchanged since, and the evolution of ACM/IEEE model curricula—CC2001 categorized introductory languages by paradigm, while the CS2013 Fundamental Programming Concepts knowledge unit only identifies concepts common to all programming paradigms [23].

5.2 CS1 Design, Structure & Approach

	'70s	'80s	'90s	'00s	'10s
General design; structure; approach	3	1	2		2
How CS1 relates to CS0 or CS2				4	6
Dealing with ACM model curricula		1	3	2	
Physical Settings					
> Online, remote or MOOC delivery			2	8	5
> Labs		1	9	3	
> Other physical settings		1			1
Other	1	2		1	2

Table 4: Number of papers in the CS1 Design, Structure & Approach category.

Table 4 shows the subcategories in this category and the corresponding number of papers published in each decade. Papers in the *Other* category included those on learning outcomes, the impact of hardware decisions and cost-effective methods of teaching CS1. Interest in this category has also waned since the turn of the century, as shown in Figure 2.

It is noteworthy that interest in *Labs* peaked in the 1990s, and *Online, remote or MOOC delivery* peaked a decade or so later. The apparent fall-off in work on remote delivery mechanisms could be due to the advent of new conferences specifically addressing these topics, leading to a migration in where such research is presented. Papers *Dealing with ACM model curricula* peaked in the 1990s, while *How CS1 relates to CS0 and CS2* featured in ten papers, all appearing after 2002 (with four of these since 2016). Perhaps related to this, there has been relatively recent interest in completely rethinking the structure and approach of CS1 itself, as evidenced by a 2010 paper by Hertz titled "What do CS1 and CS2 Mean? Investigating Differences in the Early Courses" [19], and Harvard's 'reinventing' of CS1 resulting in their popular CS50 course, which was redesigned due to two problems that they hypothesized the course suffered from: poor perception and a dated design [31]. It is interesting to note that the idea of redesigning the CS1 course is not new; Cherniak delivered a paper at the 1976 Symposium on reconsidering the CS1 approach [10]. It is noteworthy that despite being presented over 40 years ago, this paper discussed high school programming syllabi. Other notable 'early mentions' were liberal arts colleges in 1980 [15] and delivering CS1 online in 1999 [9].

5.3 CS1 Content

	'70s	'80s	'90s	'00s	'10s
Upper-level topics in CS1				5	4
Software engineering approaches	1	1	4	3	2
Other	1	2	1	6	8

Table 5: Number of papers in the CS1 Content category.

Table 5 shows the subcategories in this category and the corresponding number of papers published in each decade. As seen in Figure 2, interest in this category has remained relatively flat, while the subcategories have varied individually. Topics in the *Other* subcategory include data science approaches, CS+X [5], and media computation [42], which have only appeared in the last two decades. Papers on *Software engineering approaches* [21] have been published in each of the five decades, while papers on *Upper-level topics in CS1* [16] have all appeared after 2000.

5.4 Tools

	'70s	'80s	'90s	'00s	'10s
Editors, APIs, etc.	1		2	2	4
Libraries, etc.			1	5	
Visualization			2	1	4
Debugging & testing		2		6	1
Other		1		3	3

Table 6: Number of papers in the Tools category.

Table 6 shows the subcategories in this category and the corresponding number of papers published in each decade. As seen in Figure 2, similar to *CS1 Content*, interest in this category has remained relatively flat over the decades. As noted in Section 5.1, most of the discussion on CS1 languages has converged on Java and Python, and this is somewhat reflected in the *Tools* category, where several tools for Python [14, 18] and Java [35] have been introduced.

Reis and Cartwright [35] also addressed the ongoing debate of pedagogical vs. 'industry relevant' tools, a theme also reflected in *First languages & paradigms*. Most of the papers on *Libraries* focus on GUI and graphics or games. It is noteworthy that several papers that focused on C or C++ tools were in the *Debugging & testing* and *Visualization* subcategories. It is also noteworthy that not all tools are for development. For instance, Kumar developed *Epplets* to help students solve Parsons Puzzles [26], and the Blackbox project [8] provides tools and a large programming dataset for researchers.

5.5 Collaborative Approaches

	'70s	'80s	'90s	'00s	'10s
Pair programming				5	9
Peer instruction				1	5
Other			3	6	7

Table 7: Number of papers in the Collaborative Approaches category.

Table 7 shows the subcategories in this category and the corresponding number of papers published in each decade. Papers in the *Other* subcategory included topics such as peer code review, studio-based instruction (which includes pedagogical code review) [22], POGIL [20], and group projects. As can be seen in Figure 2, interest in this area has risen dramatically since the turn of the century.

It is arguable that *Pair programming* [33] and *Peer instruction* [40] could be in the same subcategory but after an extensive look at the papers involved and searching the ACM Digital Library for these topics, we decided that they warrant separate subcategories. In fact, none of the six *Peer instruction* papers mentioned *pair programming*, and only one of the 14 *Pair programming* papers mentioned *peer instruction*, and the one that did, discussed the topics as separate approaches [1]. Beck et al. provided a discussion on cooperative learning vs. pair programming [3], and we found one paper categorized in *Other* which, in summarizing the importance of peer learning principles, suggested that 'peer instruction' is a more general term than 'pair programming', 'peer testing' or 'peer review' [17]. Regardless, collaborative approaches to teaching CS1 have steadily increased in popularity since 2000.

5.6 Teaching

	'70s	'80s	'90s	'00s	'10s
General teaching		1		1	1
Model problems & exercises		4	9	10	1
Specific topics (arrays, recursion, etc.)			1	2	3
Games				6	3
Hardware (robots, etc.)				8	
Aids, examples & tricks		2	3	4	3
Flipped approaches					5
Video				2	4
Other	2	3	6	6	15

Table 8: Number of papers in the Teaching category.

Table 8 shows the subcategories in this category and the corresponding number of papers published in each decade. Papers in the *Other* category included those on teaching assistants and mentors, feedback, plagiarism, and many more topics with less than 5 papers each. We chose these subcategories carefully - for instance, *Model problems & exercises* was not chosen as a subcategory of *Learning & Assessment* as by-and-large these are not used as assessment, but as teaching devices. Similarly, we saw *Games*, and *Hardware (robots, etc.)* as teaching devices. Despite *Teaching* being the category with the largest number of papers (105), Figure 2 shows that activity in this area peaked in the 1980s when these papers accounted for 33% of all papers that decade. Since then activity has steadily declined to 18% in this decade. It is worth noting that despite this, the category had the highest percentage of papers per decade in the 1980s, 1990s, and 2000s, and only this decade was surpassed by *Students* and *Learning & Assessment*. Several interesting trends are apparent in Table 8. *Games* first appeared in our data in 2006 [27], but is the third largest subcategory, behind *Model problems & exercises* [7], and *Aids, examples & tricks*. *Hardware (robots, etc.)* first appeared in our data in 2001, *Aids, examples & tricks* has been somewhat constant, and *Flipped approaches* [28] first appeared in 2013.

5.7 Learning & Assessment

	'70s	'80s	'90s	'00s	'10s
General learning					1
Conceptual or cognitive issues			2	4	3
Learning styles				1	4
Reading, writing, tracing & debugging	1	1		5	6
Errors				3	8
Other learning					2
General assessment				4	1
Automatic tutoring & assessment systems	1		1	3	6
Authentic assessment			2	3	1
Exams				2	5
Other assessment	1			4	6

Table 9: Number of papers in the Learning & Assessment category.

Table 9 shows the subcategories in this category and the corresponding number of papers published in each decade. As can be seen in Figure 2 and Table 9, this category has seen steady, sharp growth since the 1980s, moving from 3% to 22% of papers per decade (second only to *Students*). It is important to note however, that as our exclusion criteria eliminates papers less than three pages in length, we exclude tracks such as panels. Therefore our data does not accurately represent initiatives like "Nifty Assignments" which started as a panel at the Symposium in 1999 and is now a track of its own (nifty.stanford.edu). A number of subcategories have shown remarkable interest since the turn of the century, including *Reading, writing, tracing & debugging* [13], how students deal with *Errors* [4, 32], and *Learning styles*, including achievement goals and mastery learning [47], and *Conceptual or cognitive issues* which revealed papers on topics such as mental models [30].

5.8 Students

Table 10 shows the subcategories in this category and the corresponding number of papers published in each decade. Figure 2

	'70s	'80s	'90s	'00s	'10s
Non-majors	2			3	8
Retention		1		5	5
Gender, diversity, inclusion & accessibility				5	7
Prior knowledge				2	3
> Concept inventories, geek genes, misconceptions				1	5
Predicting & measuring success		2		5	10
> Programming process data				2	6
Other	1			1	4

Table 10: Number of papers in the Students category.

shows that this category went from 16% in the 1970s to 0% in the 1990s to 25% today (the most popular category). Several insights can be drawn from Table 10. It is interesting to note that *Non-majors* were considered as early as 1973 [38], yet interest has only recently gathered pace. *Gender, diversity, inclusion & accessibility* has only appeared since 2004, when Rich et al. proposed a CS1 course explicitly aimed at non-majors and women [36]. In 2004, Valentine noted that only half of Symposia between 1984 and 2004 had any 'appearances' on women in computer science. *Prior knowledge* including *Concept inventories* [43], *geek genes* (or the non-existence thereof) and *Misconceptions* [24] have also only appeared since 2000. In 2017, Kirkpatrick et al. introduced an alternative CS1 for students with prior programming knowledge [25]. *Predicting & measuring success* [6, 46] and research on *Programming process data* [2] have also only appeared since the turn of the century. It is interesting to note that concerns about large enrollments appeared as early as 1974 [11], while *Retention*, dating back as far as 1984, has shown significant interest more recently [34].

6 THREATS TO VALIDITY

We note several threats to validity, but do not believe that these significantly detract from achieving our goals set out in Section 1. Firstly, our search query may not be completely representative of the literature, but it is similar to a recent survey with a much wider scope [29], and as discussed in Section 4, we believe it is broadly representative of the wider literature. Also, if carried out by other researchers, the categories that emerged may have been different.

We acknowledged the "significant difficulty of reliably coding academic papers" [41, p. 223] and as this is not a systematic literature review, we allowed categories to emerge as we began classification. However as outlined in Section 3.1 our categorization proved to be acceptably reproducible. Next, in the interest of being succinct, we employed a many-to-one mapping of papers to categories (each paper has exactly one category, but a category may have more than one paper). Thus, we did not allow cross-categorization, which may have provided for a richer (but probably more complex) analysis and discussion. Additionally, our trends are coarsely based on decades. A finer resolution may have provided more subtle trends.

In excluding papers less than three pages in length, we excluded tracks such as panels, and therefore initiatives such as Nifty Assignments which provide valuable contributions. Finally, we remind the reader that we have specifically researched CS1 papers presented at the SIGCSE Technical Symposium only, and that that the trends observed may not necessarily be reflective of the broader trends of the computing education community.

7 CONCLUSION

We categorized 481 CS1 papers presented during the first 50 years of the SIGCSE Technical Symposium. We have endeavored to adopt best practice to categorize these papers in the interest of being fair and objective, and believe that the picture we present of the evolution of introductory programming research during the first 50 years of the Symposium is useful in terms of meeting the research goals set out in Section 1. Future work on a larger scale could address some of the threats identified in Section 6. Our analysis revealed several important trends and highlights the fact that CS1 research is not only focused on programming. We also situated the Symposium in the wider literature, revealing that it occupies a significant space in the CS1 literature.

This work provides a checkpoint for introductory programming research going forward into the second 50 years of the SIGCSE Technical Symposium and will hopefully provide insights for future research on how we teach novices and how they learn to program.

REFERENCES

[1] Onni Aarne, Petrus Peltola, Juho Leinonen, and Arto Hellas. 2018. A Study of Pair Programming Enjoyment and Attendance Using Study Motivation and Strategy Metrics. In *Proceedings of the 49th ACM Technical Symposium on Computer Science Education (SIGCSE '18)*. ACM, New York, NY, USA, 759–764. https://doi.org/10.1145/3159450.3159493

[2] Amjad Altadmri and Neil C.C. Brown. 2015. 37 Million Compilations: Investigating Novice Programming Mistakes in Large-Scale Student Data. In *Proceedings of the 46th ACM Technical Symposium on Computer Science Education (SIGCSE '15)*. ACM, New York, NY, USA, 522–527. https://doi.org/10.1145/2676723.2677258

[3] Leland L. Beck, Alexander W. Chizhik, and Amy C. McElroy. 2005. Cooperative Learning Techniques in CS1: Design and Experimental Evaluation. In *Proceedings of the 36th SIGCSE Technical Symposium on Computer Science Education (SIGCSE '05)*. ACM, New York, NY, USA, 470–474. https://doi.org/10.1145/1047344.1047495

[4] Brett A. Becker, Kyle Goslin, and Graham Glanville. 2018. The Effects of Enhanced Compiler Error Messages on a Syntax Error Debugging Test. In *Proceedings of the 49th ACM Technical Symposium on Computer Science Education (SIGCSE '18)*. ACM, New York, NY, USA, 640–645. https://doi.org/10.1145/3159450.3159461

[5] Tanya Berger-Wolf, Boris Igic, Cynthia Taylor, Robert Sloan, and Rachel Poretsky. 2018. A Biology-themed Introductory CS Course at a Large, Diverse Public University. In *Proceedings of the 49th ACM Technical Symposium on Computer Science Education (SIGCSE '18)*. ACM, New York, NY, USA, 233–238. https://doi.org/10.1145/3159450.3159538

[6] Susan Bergin and Ronan Reilly. 2005. Programming: Factors That Influence Success. In *Proceedings of the 36th SIGCSE Technical Symposium on Computer Science Education (SIGCSE '05)*. ACM, New York, NY, USA, 411–415. https://doi.org/10.1145/1047344.1047480

[7] Kevin Bierre, Phil Ventura, Andrew Phelps, and Christopher Egert. 2006. Motivating OOP by Blowing Things Up: An Exercise in Cooperation and Competition in an Introductory Java Programming Course. In *Proceedings of the 37th SIGCSE Technical Symposium on Computer Science Education (SIGCSE '06)*. ACM, New York, NY, USA, 354–358. https://doi.org/10.1145/1121341.1121452

[8] Neil Christopher Charles Brown, Michael Kölling, Davin McCall, and Ian Utting. 2014. Blackbox: A Large Scale Repository of Novice Programmers' Activity. In *Proceedings of the 45th ACM Technical Symposium on Computer Science Education (SIGCSE '14)*. ACM, New York, NY, USA, 223–228. https://doi.org/10.1145/2538862.2538924

[9] Jacobo Carrasquel. 1999. Teaching CS1 On-line: The Good, the Bad, and the Ugly. In *The Proceedings of the Thirtieth SIGCSE Technical Symposium on Computer Science Education (SIGCSE '99)*. ACM, New York, NY, USA, 212–216. https://doi.org/10.1145/299649.299758

[10] Bob Cherniak. 1976. Introductory Programming Reconsidered - a User-oriented Approach. In *Proceedings of the ACM SIGCSE-SIGCUE Technical Symposium on Computer Science and Education (SIGCSE '76)*. ACM, New York, NY, USA, 65–68. https://doi.org/10.1145/800107.803449

[11] Richard W. Conway. 1974. Introductory Instruction in Programming. In *Proceedings of the Fourth SIGCSE Technical Symposium on Computer Science Education (SIGCSE '74)*. ACM, New York, NY, USA, 6–10. https://doi.org/10.1145/800183.810430

[12] Stephen Cooper, Wanda Dann, and Randy Pausch. 2003. Teaching Objects-first in Introductory Computer Science. In *Proceedings of the 34th SIGCSE Technical Symposium on Computer Science Education (SIGCSE '03)*. ACM, New York, NY, USA, 191–195. https://doi.org/10.1145/611892.611966
[13] Stephen H. Edwards. 2004. Using Software Testing to Move Students from Trial-and-error to Reflection-in-action. In *Proceedings of the 35th SIGCSE Technical Symposium on Computer Science Education (SIGCSE '04)*. ACM, New York, NY, USA, 26–30. https://doi.org/10.1145/971300.971312
[14] Stephen H. Edwards, Daniel S. Tilden, and Anthony Allevato. 2014. Pythy: Improving the Introductory Python Programming Experience. In *Proceedings of the 45th ACM Technical Symposium on Computer Science Education (SIGCSE '14)*. ACM, New York, NY, USA, 641–646. https://doi.org/10.1145/2538862.2538977
[15] Robert J. Ellison. 1980. A Programming Sequence for the Liberal Arts College. In *Proceedings of the Eleventh SIGCSE Technical Symposium on Computer Science Education (SIGCSE '80)*. ACM, New York, NY, USA, 161–164. https://doi.org/10.1145/800140.804628
[16] Patrick Garrity, Timothy Yates, Richard Brown, and Elizabeth Shoop. 2011. WebMapReduce: An Accessible and Adaptable Tool for Teaching Map-reduce Computing. In *Proceedings of the 42Nd ACM Technical Symposium on Computer Science Education (SIGCSE '11)*. ACM, New York, NY, USA, 183–188. https://doi.org/10.1145/1953163.1953221
[17] Alessio Gaspar, Joni Torsella, Nora Honken, Sohum Sohoni, and Colin Arnold. 2016. Differences in the Learning Principles Dominating Student-Student vs. Student-Instructor Interactions While Working on Programming Tasks. In *Proceedings of the 47th ACM Technical Symposium on Computing Science Education (SIGCSE '16)*. ACM, New York, NY, USA, 255–260. https://doi.org/10.1145/2839509.2844627
[18] Philip J. Guo. 2013. Online Python Tutor: Embeddable Web-based Program Visualization for Cs Education. In *Proceeding of the 44th ACM Technical Symposium on Computer Science Education (SIGCSE '13)*. ACM, New York, NY, USA, 579–584. https://doi.org/10.1145/2445196.2445368
[19] Matthew Hertz. 2010. What Do "CS1" and "CS2" Mean?: Investigating Differences in the Early Courses. In *Proceedings of the 41st ACM Technical Symposium on Computer Science Education (SIGCSE '10)*. ACM, New York, NY, USA, 199–203. https://doi.org/10.1145/1734263.1734335
[20] Helen H. Hu and Tricia D. Shepherd. 2014. Teaching CS 1 with POGIL Activities and Roles. In *Proceedings of the 45th ACM Technical Symposium on Computer Science Education (SIGCSE '14)*. ACM, New York, NY, USA, 127–132. https://doi.org/10.1145/2538862.2538954
[21] Christopher Hundhausen, Anukrati Agrawal, Dana Fairbrother, and Michael Trevisan. 2009. Integrating Pedagogical Code Reviews into a CS 1 Course: An Empirical Study. In *Proceedings of the 40th ACM Technical Symposium on Computer Science Education (SIGCSE '09)*. ACM, New York, NY, USA, 291–295. https://doi.org/10.1145/1508865.1508972
[22] Christopher Hundhausen, Anukrati Agrawal, Dana Fairbrother, and Michael Trevisan. 2010. Does Studio-based Instruction Work in CS 1?: An Empirical Comparison with a Traditional Approach. In *Proceedings of the 41st ACM Technical Symposium on Computer Science Education (SIGCSE '10)*. ACM, New York, NY, USA, 500–504. https://doi.org/10.1145/1734263.1734432
[23] Association for Computing Machinery (ACM) Joint Task Force on Computing Curricula and IEEE Computer Society. 2013. *Computer Science Curricula 2013: Curriculum Guidelines for Undergraduate Degree Programs in Computer Science*. Technical Report. New York, NY, USA. 999133.
[24] Lisa C. Kaczmarczyk, Elizabeth R. Petrick, J. Philip East, and Geoffrey L. Herman. 2010. Identifying Student Misconceptions of Programming. In *Proceedings of the 41st ACM Technical Symposium on Computer Science Education (SIGCSE '10)*. ACM, New York, NY, USA, 107–111. https://doi.org/10.1145/1734263.1734299
[25] Michael S. Kirkpatrick and Chris Mayfield. 2017. Evaluating an Alternative CS1 for Students with Prior Programming Experience. In *Proceedings of the 2017 ACM SIGCSE Technical Symposium on Computer Science Education (SIGCSE '17)*. ACM, New York, NY, USA, 333–338. https://doi.org/10.1145/3017680.3017759
[26] Amruth N. Kumar. 2018. Epplets: A Tool for Solving Parsons Puzzles. In *Proceedings of the 49th ACM Technical Symposium on Computer Science Education (SIGCSE '18)*. ACM, New York, NY, USA, 527–532. https://doi.org/10.1145/3159450.3159576
[27] Scott Leutenegger and Jeffrey Edgington. 2007. A Games First Approach to Teaching Introductory Programming. In *Proceedings of the 38th SIGCSE Technical Symposium on Computer Science Education (SIGCSE '07)*. ACM, New York, NY, USA, 115–118. https://doi.org/10.1145/1227310.1227352
[28] Kate Lockwood and Rachel Esselstein. 2013. The Inverted Classroom and the CS Curriculum. In *Proceeding of the 44th ACM Technical Symposium on Computer Science Education (SIGCSE '13)*. ACM, New York, NY, USA, 113–118. https://doi.org/10.1145/2445196.2445236
[29] Andrew Luxton-Reilly, Simon, Ibrihim Albluwi, Brett A. Becker, Michail Giannakos, Amruth N. Kumar, Linda Ott, James Paterson, Michael James Scott, Judy Sheard, and Claudia Szabo. 2018. Introductory Programming: A Systematic Literature Review. In *Proceedings of the 2018 ITiCSE Conference on Working Group Reports (ITiCSE-WGR '18)*. ACM, New York, NY, USA. https://doi.org/10.1145/3293881.3295779 *in press.*
[30] Linxiao Ma, John Ferguson, Marc Roper, and Murray Wood. 2007. Investigating the Viability of Mental Models Held by Novice Programmers. In *Proceedings of the 38th SIGCSE Technical Symposium on Computer Science Education (SIGCSE '07)*. ACM, New York, NY, USA, 499–503. https://doi.org/10.1145/1227310.1227481
[31] David J. Malan. 2010. Reinventing CS50. In *Proceedings of the 41st ACM Technical Symposium on Computer Science Education (SIGCSE '10)*. ACM, New York, NY, USA, 152–156. https://doi.org/10.1145/1734263.1734316
[32] Guillaume Marceau, Kathi Fisler, and Shriram Krishnamurthi. 2011. Measuring the Effectiveness of Error Messages Designed for Novice Programmers. In *Proceedings of the 42Nd ACM Technical Symposium on Computer Science Education (SIGCSE '11)*. ACM, New York, NY, USA, 499–504. https://doi.org/10.1145/1953163.1953308
[33] Charlie McDowell, Linda Werner, Heather Bullock, and Julian Fernald. 2002. The Effects of Pair-programming on Performance in an Introductory Programming Course. In *Proceedings of the 33rd SIGCSE Technical Symposium on Computer Science Education (SIGCSE '02)*. ACM, New York, NY, USA, 38–42. https://doi.org/10.1145/563340.563353
[34] Leo Porter and Daniel Zingaro. 2014. Importance of Early Performance in CS1: Two Conflicting Assessment Stories. In *Proceedings of the 45th ACM Technical Symposium on Computer Science Education (SIGCSE '14)*. ACM, New York, NY, USA, 295–300. https://doi.org/10.1145/2538862.2538912
[35] Charles Reis and Robert Cartwright. 2004. Taming a Professional IDE for the Classroom. In *Proceedings of the 35th SIGCSE Technical Symposium on Computer Science Education (SIGCSE '04)*. ACM, New York, NY, USA, 156–160. https://doi.org/10.1145/971300.971357
[36] Lauren Rich, Heather Perry, and Mark Guzdial. 2004. A CS1 Course Designed to Address Interests of Women. In *Proceedings of the 35th SIGCSE Technical Symposium on Computer Science Education (SIGCSE '04)*. ACM, New York, NY, USA, 190–194. https://doi.org/10.1145/971300.971370
[37] Eric Roberts. 2004. The Dream of a Common Language: The Search for Simplicity and Stability in Computer Science Education. In *Proceedings of the 35th SIGCSE Technical Symposium on Computer Science Education (SIGCSE '04)*. ACM, New York, NY, USA, 115–119. https://doi.org/10.1145/971300.971343
[38] Gerard Salton. 1973. Introductory Programming at Cornell. In *Proceedings of the Third SIGCSE Technical Symposium on Computer Science Education (SIGCSE '73)*. ACM, New York, NY, USA, 18–20. https://doi.org/10.1145/800010.808068
[39] Simon, Raina Mason, Tom Crick, James H. Davenport, and Ellen Murphy. 2018. Language Choice in Introductory Programming Courses at Australasian and UK Universities. In *Proceedings of the 49th ACM Technical Symposium on Computer Science Education (SIGCSE '18)*. ACM, New York, NY, USA, 852–857. https://doi.org/10.1145/3159450.3159547
[40] Beth Simon, Michael Kohanfars, Jeff Lee, Karen Tamayo, and Quintin Cutts. 2010. Experience Report: Peer Instruction in Introductory Computing. In *Proceedings of the 41st ACM Technical Symposium on Computer Science Education (SIGCSE '10)*. ACM, New York, NY, USA, 341–345. https://doi.org/10.1145/1734263.1734381
[41] Andreas Stefik, Stefan Hanenberg, Mark McKenney, Anneliese Andrews, Srinivas Kalyan Yellanki, and Susanna Siebert. 2014. What is the Foundation of Evidence of Human Factors Decisions in Language Design? An Empirical Study on Programming Language Workshops. In *Proceedings of the 22Nd International Conference on Program Comprehension (ICPC 2014)*. ACM, New York, NY, USA, 223–231. https://doi.org/10.1145/2597008.2597154
[42] Allison Elliott Tew, Charles Fowler, and Mark Guzdial. 2005. Tracking an Innovation in Introductory CS Education from a Research University to a Two-year College. In *Proceedings of the 36th SIGCSE Technical Symposium on Computer Science Education (SIGCSE '05)*. ACM, New York, NY, USA, 416–420. https://doi.org/10.1145/1047344.1047481
[43] Allison Elliott Tew and Mark Guzdial. 2010. Developing a Validated Assessment of Fundamental CS1 Concepts. In *Proceedings of the 41st ACM Technical Symposium on Computer Science Education (SIGCSE '10)*. ACM, New York, NY, USA, 97–101. https://doi.org/10.1145/1734263.1734297
[44] David W. Valentine. 2004. CS Educational Research: A Meta-analysis of SIGCSE Technical Symposium Proceedings. In *Proceedings of the 35th SIGCSE Technical Symposium on Computer Science Education (SIGCSE '04)*. ACM, New York, NY, USA, 255–259. https://doi.org/10.1145/971300.971391
[45] Troy Vasiga. 2002. What Comes After CS 1 + 2: A Deep Breadth Before Specializing. In *Proceedings of the 33rd SIGCSE Technical Symposium on Computer Science Education (SIGCSE '02)*. ACM, New York, NY, USA, 28–32. https://doi.org/10.1145/563340.563350
[46] Christopher Watson, Frederick W.B. Li, and Jamie L. Godwin. 2014. No Tests Required: Comparing Traditional and Dynamic Predictors of Programming Success. In *Proceedings of the 45th ACM Technical Symposium on Computer Science Education (SIGCSE '14)*. ACM, New York, NY, USA, 469–474. https://doi.org/10.1145/2538862.2538930
[47] Daniel Zingaro, Michelle Craig, Leo Porter, Brett A. Becker, Yingjun Cao, Phill Conrad, Diana Cukierman, Arto Hellas, Dastyni Loksa, and Neena Thota. 2018. Achievement Goals in CS1: Replication and Extension. In *Proceedings of the 49th ACM Technical Symposium on Computer Science Education (SIGCSE '18)*. ACM, New York, NY, USA, 687–692. https://doi.org/10.1145/3159450.3159452

Camp or College?

Student Perspectives from College Computer Science Departments & Coding Boot Camps on Skills Learned

Quinn Burke
Digital Promise
San Mateo, CA, USA
qburke@digitalpromise.org

Cinamon Sunrise Bailey
College of Charleston
Charleston, SC, USA
cinamonsunrise@yahoo.com

ABSTRACT

The purpose of this paper is to investigate student perspectives of how college computer science (CS) programs compare to those of coding bootcamps. In particular, the research examines to what degree students report their respective programs instill the necessary interpersonal and intrapersonal skills (i.e., teamwork and resilience) necessary for workforce entry. Prior research from the authors suggests there is a perception among the software industry that college graduates often lack the necessary so-called "soft" skills for successful workforce entry; this research investigates to what degree students from each educational environment mirror this sensibility in the assessment of their own abilities, learning preferences, and educational experiences. Data is based on a series of fifty (50) one-on-one interviews with students, 22 of whom come from a coding bootcamp background and 28 who come from a four-year college. Alongside these interviews, students completed both pre-surveys (50 students) and post-surveys (19 students) on learning preferences and programmatic experience; 12 students also participated in follow-up interviews further articulating their learning experiences. Results indicate that despite significant differences in age and workforce experience, coding bootcamp students and undergraduates differ little in how they perceive themselves as learners. However, there were notable differences in reasons for application to respective programs as well as exposure to practical learning experiences through coursework. Discussion focuses on the degree to which the aforementioned "soft skills" are perceived as learned expertise versus personal attributes, and to what degree such perception may contribute to higher education's pedagogical and curricular approaches to CS instruction.

CCS CONCEPTS

User characteristics; collaborative and social computing; education

KEYWORDS

Coding bootcamp; experiential learning; soft skills; learning environment; learning preferences

SIGCSE '19, February 27-March 2, 2019, Minneapolis, MN, USA

ACM ISBN 978-1-4503-5890-3/19/02...$15.00
https://doi.org/10.1145/3287324.3287373

ACM Reference format:

Quinn Burke and Cinamon Sunrise Bailey. 2019. Camp or College? Student Perspectives from College Computer Science Departments and Coding Bootcamps on Skills Learned. In *Proceedings of ACM Special Interest Group on Computer Science Education (SIGCSE'19) Feb. 27-March 2, 2019, Minneapolis, MN, USA. ACM, New York, NY, USA, 6 pages.* https://doi.org/10.1145/1234567890

1 INTRODUCTION

The Bureau of Labor Statistics [20] projects the U.S. will have over one-million unfulfilled software engineering jobs by 2020, with Code.org [7] listing the current openings in the U.S. at over 600,000. While post-secondary computer science (CS) enrollments have steadily risen since 2006 [8], the software development industry indicates that college
graduates are lacking necessary skills for entry level positions [12,18,21]. What is particularly notable about this skills gap among recent graduates is that industry representatives perceive such a gap in fundamental, broad areas such as problem-solving, peer-to-peer collaboration, and graduates' wider capacity for team leadership. In 2018, LinkedIn [15]—a professional networking website with over 500 million members globally and the 34th most visited site online—conducted an internal investigation of the skills most commonly listed as integral to hiring. Software development skills were widely cited as a "must have" with 472,000 respondents citing these as integral to new hires. Nearly three times as many respondents (1.4 million total), however, indicated that more general communication and collaboration skills were essential of new hires, and pointed out that the demand for these wider "life" skills directly correlated with the increasingly "shorter shelf life" associated with particular technical skills [15].

Into this skills gap steps a new player. Over the past five years, so called "coding bootcamps" have emerged as a new post-secondary education option to help address unfulfilled software engineering jobs. Brief yet intense training programs, coding bootcamps are, on average, 10-12 weeks in duration, and emphasize teaching the programming skills that employers look for from new software developer hires (particularly front-end programming) while also enabling their graduates to grasp the most essential aspects of coding [9]. Such camps are attracting more mature students (Twenty-nine years-old, on average), with more work experience (six years, on average), which industry representatives report as being a unique value-added to their code camp hires [4,9]. Despite their prodigious growth over the past five years, coding bootcamps remain under-investigated in terms of the educational environments they foster; most information the U.S. public has about such camps is largely through popular press, with snippets on what they financially offer to unemployed and underemployed individuals and how the software development industry has likewise benefitted [11,16]. There is, in fact, little information about what their students actually think of the programs in terms of curricula and pedagogy. Nor is there much understanding as to how these programs compare to four-year CS degree programs or to what extent each training environment fosters the development of real world problem-solving and collaboration skills.

Funded by a National Science Foundation Core Research and Development Grant, our exploratory research intends to further examine the role of coding bootcamps in post-secondary STEM education. Over the initial stages of the research, we focused on the software industry's perspective of coding bootcamps and hiring managers' perceptions of the quality of bootcamp graduates in relation to those from four-year CS undergraduate programs. Our current focus is exploring student perspectives from both coding bootcamps and undergraduate CS programs in order to examine three research questions: *(1) Who are these programs attracting?* (2) *How do these students perceive their respective learning environments and their capacity to help them develop these requisite "soft" skill sets?* and (3) *What are the programmatic outcomes characteristic of each training ground?* Through student perspectives, this paper reports how each training ground promotes learning through collaboration and real-world experience. We also examine how these student perspectives contribute to the wider picture of career and adult education programs nationally.

2 BACKGROUND

A growing body of literature on post-secondary computing education [1,2,5,9] points to the very real need for post-secondary institutions to inculcate more than CS knowledge and coding skills among their graduates for successful entry into software development jobs. "Soft" skills, such as teamwork and clear communication, are likewise essential, and programs are increasingly revisiting where these skills can be explicitly addressed within their respective curricula. Striking a balance between "hard" and "soft" skills has long been a challenge for hiring managers from a range of industries [14-15], though software companies report to especially struggle with hiring able programmers who likewise have the requisite interpersonal and intrapersonal skills for meaningful collaboration as well as "transfer" capacity to bring their knowledge base to new and novel scenarios [8]. The skills that employers report valuing the most include networking, problem solving, leadership, adaptability, and collaboration [6,18], but Janush [13] reports that higher educational institutions do not necessarily provide graduates sufficient educational opportunities to foster these skills.

In 2018, initial research examined the software development industry's perspective of coding bootcamps and how they compared with traditional four-year CS programs [3-4]. Through a series of hour-long focus groups and interviews with hiring managers, "soft" skills, such as critical thinking, teamwork, and collaboration, were altogether twice as likely to come up than "hard" skills among participants [3]. However, this research also found that hiring managers nearly unanimously first sorted applicants based on whether they had obtained a four-year degree or not. The college degree, however, did not necessarily need to be in CS [3-4]. Despite this overwhelming trend of hiring college graduates, industry representatives noted that while a college degree was usually a requisite credential, they often preferred their boot camp hires based on the fact that these hires were usually older and had more experience with hands-on projects and team building [4], reinforcing prior findings [2-3] that the majority of code camp graduates who secured employment post-graduation also had college degrees.

3 METHODS

3.1 Participants

For this study, we recruited a total of fifty (50) students from four (4) different four-year college CS programs, as well as from a total of three coding boot camps. All programs were located in medium-sized (130K-150K population) southeastern U.S. cities. Table 1 offers a more detailed breakdown of participant geography, race/ethnicity, and gender.

TABLE 1: Participant/ institutional profile

Program	Participants/ Gender	Ethnicity/Race	Organization #/ Profile
Coding Boot Camp	**22** (9 females, 13 males)	**14** White/ Caucasian **3** Black/African American / African **2** Asian/ South Asian **1** Latinx **2** Unknown	**3** Bootcamps (2 mid-sized cities in GA and SC)
College / University	**28** (12 females, 16 males)	**16** White/ Caucasian **4** Black/African American / African **3** Asian/ South Asian **1** Latinx **1** Kurdish **3** Unknown	**4** Universities (2 mid-sized cities in SC)

Students were recruited through direct visits to bootcamp and college classrooms, as well as through flyers delivered to instructors. Some of the bootcamp students were recruited through "cold" email messages posted via the LinkedIn website.

3.2 Data Collection & Analysis

From April 2017 through February 2018, the researchers conducted fifty (50) one-on-one interviews with participating students. Questions focused on (1) admission processes (2) skills and knowledge obtained in each training ground, and (3) teaching methods and the learning environments characteristic of each training ground. Prior to the interviews, students were asked to complete a pre-survey focusing on how they perceived themselves as learners (*Were they open to new ideas/perspectives? Did they try multiple solutions when tackling a problem? Did they prefer to stick with a known solution as opposed to exploring other options?*). All focus groups and interviews were subsequently transcribed and qualitatively analyzed using NVivo software first, followed by Dedoose software, which supported the overall organization of the findings and the qualitative analysis of data.

Reliability was calculated based on three sample coding comparisons between two coders. Across these three, there was 100% agreement on the 4 primary codes, 94% agreement on the secondary codes, and 87% agreement on the tertiary codes. In order to establish 'descriptive validity', the open-ended interviews were transcribed verbatim, which lead to a more accurate reflection of what the participant had said; and the reporting of the data reflected the same accuracy in that it was coded into themes and portrayed the unfolding of the 'event' in an accurate manner [17]. 'Interpretive validity' was promoted through the reporting of direct answers and the establishment of intercoder reliability methods aimed at capturing data representing the participants' meaning of events as opposed to interpretations based on the researchers' perspectives [17].

In May 2018, a post-survey was sent out to all student participants. Questions focused on job status, workplace environment, and students' perceptions of workplace preparation. A smaller sample of the original participants responded (twelve code camp students and seven college/ university students). Twelve of these students also participated in a follow-up interview to further examine their survey responses.

4 RESULTS

The results reported here correspond to our three respective research questions around entering student profile, programmatic learning environment, and student outcomes.

4.1 Profile of entering students

Bootcamp students ranged in age from early 20s to mid 50s. Two students had a military background (though neither was funded through the GI bill). Four students had diversity scholarships or funding through the bootcamp. Nineteen bootcamp students (86.5%) decided to pursue this educational route in order to change careers, advance within their own company, or update their skill set to include computing and/ or software development; and six students (27%) indicated they chose bootcamp training because they wanted hands-on instruction and/or practical real-world experience. In terms of prior technological knowledge and/or experience prior to admission, twenty bootcamp students (91%) stated that they had some form of training or experience in database management, website development, back end and/ or front end programming, full stack development, software development, game creation, CS theory, and/or computer programming languages. Interestingly, six of these students (27%) indicated that they had some form of university or community college education in CS or website design; and ten students (45%) stated they were self-taught through free online courses via YouTube, free-Code-Camp, and Codecademy.

As Graph 1 indicates, 82% already had a bachelor's degree or higher (degrees included business, CS, education, engineering, finance, liberal arts, mass communications, music theory, and the sciences).

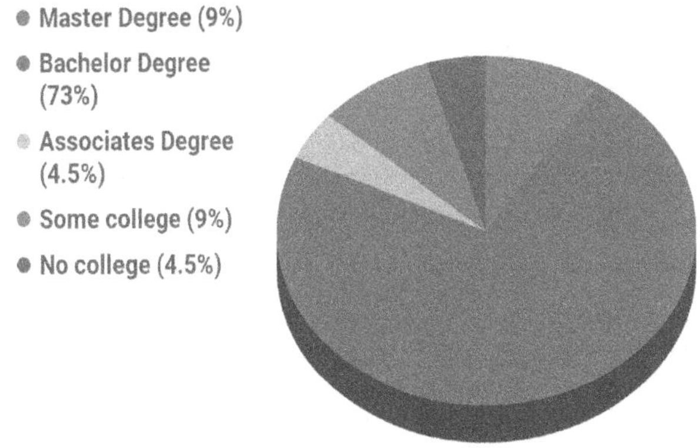

Graph 1: Post-Secondary Education of Boot Camp Students

Pre-surveys revealed that fifteen bootcamp students (68%) in this study believed that they are open to multiple perspectives when finding solutions and considered themselves multimodal learners, who are flexible about how they give and receive information. Thirteen students (59%) self-reported metacognition in that they monitor and are aware of their own learning techniques and processes. Interestingly, during their initial interviews, 68% described themselves as people who "like to learn", "enjoy building things from scratch", "like to problem-solve", and/or "want to challenge themselves".

The interviews with the **university students** (mean age approximately 22-years-old) revealed, perhaps unsurprisingly, that they had considerably less work experience prior to admission. The geographic origins of the students were broader and included GA, NC, MN, NJ, SC, and WA. Five of these participants were international students from Italy, the Philippines, Morocco, Ethiopia, and Canada, respectively. Fourteen of these participants (50%) entered as undecided without a CS major in mind. It is interesting to note that 100% of these undecided students stated that they were initially leaning towards degrees in math, science, and/or engineering. Of all undergraduates, only ten (36%) had prior work or internship experience.

Nineteen university students (68%) reported that they were exposed to CS related courses/assignments while in high school, had self-taught themselves via free computer programming online courses, and/or were taught about software and hardware development by tech adjacent family members and friends during high school. Seven of these participants (25%) chose this training ground due to financial aid or scholarships, and four students (14%) stated that they chose this route because of the importance industry places on having a bachelor's degree or higher.

Pre-surveys revealed that, like the bootcamp students, 68% of the university students in this study felt that they are open to multiple perspectives when finding solutions and considered themselves multimodal learners, who are flexible about how they give and receive information. 64% (as compared to 59% of bootcamp students) demonstrated metacognition in their survey responses in that they monitor and are aware of their own learning techniques and processes.

These results support Course Report's [9] national profile of bootcamp students being significantly older than four-year CS undergraduates, and with more work experience. This is, of course, not surprising; more notable is the fact that our findings suggest bootcamp applicants have more digital technological experience prior to programmatic entry, and such students were already highly-educated (82% of bootcamp applicants already had a bachelor's degree or higher). It also suggests that bootcamps, as opposed to graduate schools, are being utilized as an alternative continuing education resource for college graduates who wish to pivot towards a career in the software development field.

4.2 Student perceptions of learning environment

Interview responses showed that **bootcamp students** were notably focused on finding a job or obtaining a promotion immediately after (or even before) completion of their training. Many students' interviews reflected that they felt the coding camp was providing them with a foundation for learning computer programming languages, which would allow them to subsequently grasp other languages more fluidly. For example, a male student with a B.S. in neuro-behavioral biology and a B.A. in Economics, reported that bootcamps are able to help job candidates more immediately show potential employers that they "have the base, [they] have the foundation to analyze and to think about how to approach something." Some students noted their classmates included software development professionals, who came to the code camp in order to update their skill sets.

In regards to the learning environment, over 86% of bootcamp students reported that hands-on projects and peer collaboration were emphasized and were implemented immediately, and 77% mentioned that their boot camps work closely with industry with regards to collaboration on student projects and attending demo days to view student projects. Furthermore, several noted that the bootcamp environment was fast paced, encouraged innovation, and emphasized immediate feedback, mimicking their experiences in workplace environments, whether such employment was in software development or not.

Five code camp students (23%) found the coursework difficult, and three of these students had a CS foundation and/or technical training in the past. For example, one female student, who obtained a CS degree 20 years prior, stated that she "wish[ed] that they had a prep class, something a little bit more for beginners," and added that her instructor "doesn't realize he can't bring it down to [her] level like he should." This is interesting as it indicates that the CS foundations and technical skills, which were taught in her university 20 years ago, were not helpful for employment in today's software development industry. Several bootcamp students reported the fast-paced experience proved difficult due to work and family obligations. A male graduate (age range 41-50), who earned a B.S. in business and remained in the same finance job even after his bootcamp graduation, mentioned that he struggled with the coursework due to his "obligations and responsibilities outside of the camp...there wasn't enough time to process everything and then finish the homework."

Meanwhile, unlike the bootcamp students we interviewed, many of the **university students** did not have their career plans decided yet. Several, though, seemed optimistic about the job possibilities associated with CS. For instance, a 21-year-old male student, who started off in astrophysics prior to switching to CS, stated "anything I learn could be applied just about anywhere in computer science." Several students reported that their CS courses were providing them with a foundation of how to learn and/or problem solve.

Twenty-four college/university students (86%) agreed that they were required to take their introductory classes prior to working on more advanced projects in their junior and senior years, and only six students (21%) reported working on collaborative projects with industry (versus the 77% in bootcamps). Notably, four of these six students indicated they had sought out the internship on their own volition. Two university students were either enrolled in or in the process of enrolling in a coding bootcamp in order to get hands-on experience and foundational skills while they also attended their university classes.

According to interviews, a majority of the college students felt they had developed communication skills through group projects and collaboration with peers. Fourteen students (50%) indicated that their coursework outside of CS and/or campus organizations likewise helped them develop soft skills, such as teamwork, leadership, ability to communicate effectively, entrepreneurship, risk taking, critical thinking, and cultural awareness. The interviews revealed that there were mixed feelings amongst the students about whether or not the universities encouraged innovation and creativity. A male student, a CS and Math major, stated "I think some of it's particular to the professor. I've had some professors who in some of the classes really want it done the way that they've taught you to do it, and in other classes they're much more open to that innovation or that digging deeper to find something else."

Students from all four college programs reported receiving consistent feedback via grades, though some indicated more supplementary feedback would have been useful. For example, one male student stated "(Y)ou'll turn in some assignments and then you won't hear back for weeks about it, but [you] have to turn in your next assignment...I don't know how to improve, because I haven't gotten feedback yet." A former semi-professional hockey player, indicated that having different feedback from different professors may prove to be helpful toward future careers: "I think it gives you the flexibility and the dexterity you need depending on what kind of boss you have."

These results suggest that bootcamps provide more *immediate* emphasis on feedback, industry collaboration, job acquisition, and practical, hands-on experience than do four-year undergraduate programs. This is not to indicate that college CS programs are devoid of such content, but rather that their students reported it occurring later within their individual programs, usually during late junior and senior year of college. Bootcamp students reported on largely appreciating the fast-paced and immersive nature of their respective programs; however, what is less clear from their responses is the degree to which such structure and curricula inculcated their problem-solving and collaboration skills versus simply sharpened these as existing skills.

4.3 Programmatic Outcomes

A total of 12 **bootcamp students** from two different southeastern U.S. cities completed the follow up survey, and had graduated. Of these, seven had obtained a new job in the software industry (full-stack, web design, graphic design, software engineer, data entry, software quality analyst, and technical program manager); and two of these students received help from their instructor/ bootcamp in getting their jobs (both from the same camp). All worked within 20-40 miles from their training ground.

Of the students, who had not yet found new employment, two were still looking for a position; and three graduates reported being in the same position that they were in before code camp training and were hoping for a promotion and/or increased programming opportunities (network support manager, marketing, and UX design).

During their first and second interviews, several of the bootcamp students indicated that the ability to learn quickly was important in the workplace, and that they had to demonstrate this in their interviews. Six participants attributed their ability to get a job with their boot camp training and/or connections. For one bootcamp graduate, a male with a BS in Science and Psychology, having bootcamp training was both a positive and a negative attribute. For hiring, he stated, "Going from zero to 60 in three months I think was something I was able to tout as a skill." However, he was hired in a quality assurance position rather than in the engineering department he wanted "because they had had so many bad experiences that none of the managers, were actually willing to take on another boot camp grad." The student with only a high school education stated that "(h)aving only a highschool diploma and the coding school certificate doesn't really make [him] a very competitive worker, at least not on paper."

With regards to soft skills, first and second interviews revealed that thirteen of these participants indicated they had entered their bootcamp training with their soft skills already embedded through their college experience, work experience, and/or their own desire to continue learning and/or to problem-solve. For example, a female, with a master degree in music education, associated her soft skill development with her musical and teaching background, which had occurred years before entry into the camp. All thirteen of these students expressed that although they had come into their respective bootcamp programs with their soft skills intact, the bootcamp environment nonetheless emphasized the importance of such skills as particular levers they should use to their advantage as they prepared for software development careers. "[T]hey didn't necessarily train us in soft skills," explained one code camp graduate who likewise had a college degree. "They just provided the environment for us to learn those soft skills on our own in a non-corporate environment." On the other hand, five students (23%) indicated that the bootcamp setting very much helped them develop soft skills, such as collaboration, effective problem-solving, time management, determination, and accountability. For example, a female code camp graduate, who had already earned a master's degree, directly credits her job promotion and some of her soft skill development to her code camp experience. "(A)fter the class," she explained, "I feel more comfortable experimenting, trying, teaching myself." The sole international bootcamp student in our study seconded this sentiment, indicating that while he had such soft skills prior to admission, his bootcamp allowed him to learn "American soft skills" and more ably grasp U.S. customs, such as "being able to be friendly with your boss".

Within the post-survey, seven **university students** from two different southeastern U.S. cities responded. Of these students, two had graduated and acquired a job (data center infrastructure monitoring and software engineer). These jobs were located within 30-40 miles of their university. Two students were in internships with software development companies, while also attending classes; the remaining three were still solely focusing on coursework at the time of the survey.

In the second set of interviews, all three CS graduates indicated that they were able to learn "how to learn" in college. One stated that the university "gave [him] a very good framework even when presented with terms that [he] didn't have any experience with." Another added "I think that I have a very developed critical thinking ability from a university style education." An Italian international student, despite being pleased with his semester in a southeastern U.S university, indicated that "what was lacking in university was ... it was all very, let's say, 'theoretical'. We learned out of a textbook.... We don't really learn how to really directly implement it in the business setting."

These results indicate that bootcamp students more often perceive themselves as already personally and socially developed—perhaps unsurprising given their greater maturity and levels of experience. As noted earlier though, it is difficult to determine if these were innate skills or hard-earned through past work and prior educational pursuits. Students from both training grounds recognized that their programs were attempting to instill and/or reinforce soft skills, such as collaboration and problem-solving.

5. DISCUSSION

In *Soft Skills for Business Success,* Deloitte Access Economics [10] predicts that by 2030, company positions that are "soft skills intensive" can be expected to grow at more than double the rate of other types of positions. This trend is evident in the software industry's increased ownership of such skills development, with companies increasingly offering seminars and classes in-house to inculcate such soft skills among employees, especially for new hires [1,3-5,]. This is not however to imply that these same companies are happy about having to take ownership over such coursework [18], and many of these companies report of being all too aware that the majority of CS undergraduate programs are still not explicitly addressing the development of these crucial interpersonal and intrapersonal skills [6,15,18]. It is worthy to point out that 50% of the college and university students in this study indicated that they were developing soft skills like teamwork, collaboration, leadership, and problem solving through their respective CS programs and through their general education courses, electives, and campus organizations. But these undergraduates were not necessarily able to project why or how they would utilize these skills in the workplace. Meanwhile, 59% of bootcamp students emphasized that they had entered their respective programs already endowed with these soft skills based on prior educational and work experiences. These students provided specific examples of how they have demonstrated leadership, teamwork, and problem-solving within their career and why it was important that they utilized these particular skills in the workplace.

Still, it is altogether difficult to ascertain as to where and when the university and bootcamp students developed their reported soft skills, and whether such development occurred at stages far more nascent than post-secondary education. Here it is worthwhile to return to the existing literature [1, 5, 19], which suggests that post-secondary graduates' lack of such requisite interpersonal and intrapersonal skills often directly stems back to the wider (and persistent) conception among post-secondary college and university educators that these elements are not *learned skills* but rather personal *attributes* that individuals either have or do not have upon programmatic entry, and thus by extension, cannot be taught. This perception, to a degree, then can tacitly absolve said instructors and post-secondary programs from having to explicitly teach such content to their students. Bootcamp student perspectives meanwhile suggest that these programs are explicitly engaging in practices, which promote the soft skills that employers are seeking from new hires (i.e.

increased critical feedback to prepare students for giving and receiving feedback in the workplace, real world practice from week one in programs, and increased opportunities to be exposed to the industry). This perspective from code camp students is supported by our past research examining industry perspectives on such camps [3].

6 Limitations & Future Research

Of course, the conclusions presented here--though bolstered by a range of metrics and non-student perspectives--rely heavily on self-reporting from student participants. This and the modest sample size present significant limitations to this still exploratory research. Though there were fifty (50) student interviews coupled with surveys, this represents a relatively small number and was limited to the southeastern region of the U.S. Despite the limitations, the research presented here has significant educational implications for post-secondary computing education. By providing a learning environment that includes greater immersion into real world applications, increased industry collaborations, and more immediate critical feedback, colleges could contribute even more to closing the "soft skills gap" and more ably prepare students for entering and performing in the rapidly changing workplace characteristic of software development.

While the research here presents student perspectives and past research [3] presented industry perspectives, going forward, we will examine individual instructor perspectives from each learning environment: *How do they perceive these soft skills and to what degree do they teach (and think they can, in fact, teach) such skills to post-secondary students?*

In addition to examining instructors' perceptions, we will explore instructional practices with regards to how soft skills are incorporated into the curriculum, examining select syllabi and assignments across camp and college/ university classroom. Including further analysis of instructional perspectives will likewise act as an important supplement to the existing perspectives we have examined from industry reps and students.

ACKNOWLEDGMENTS

The writing of this paper was supported through a National Science Foundation (NSF) Core Research and Development Grant to the first author. The views expressed are solely those of the authors.

REFERENCES

[1] Ahmed, F., Capretz, L.F., Bouktif, S., & Campbell, P. 2013. Soft skills and software development: A reflection from software industry. *International Journal of Information Processing and Management, 4(3).* Doi:10.4156/ijipm.vol4.issue3.17

[2] Burke, Q., Bailey, C., Lyon, L.A., & Bowring, J. (2017, August 29). "Earning a college degree in order to go to camp?" Inside Higher Education. Available at https://www. insidehighered.com/views/2017/08/29/essay-how-coding-boot-camps-are-add-college-degree.

[3] Burke, Q., Bailey, C.. `Lyon, L., & Green, E. 2018. Understanding the software development industry's perspective on coding boot camps versus traditional 4-year Colleges. Proceedings from AERA '18. *The Dreams, Possibilities, and Necessities of Public Education, April 13–17, 2018 New York, NY, USA*

[4] Authors. 2018. Assessing industry's perspective of coding boot camps through the Lens of routine and adaptive expertise. Proceedings from SIGCSE '18*: The 49th ACM Technical Symposium on Computer Science Education, February 21 – 24, 2018, Baltimore, Maryland, USA*

[5] Capretz L.F. and Ahmed, F. 2010. Why do we need Personality diversity in software engineering. *ACM SIGSOFT Software Engineering Notes, 35(2).* doi: 10.1145/1734103.1734111.

[6] Casner-Lotto, J. & Barrington, L. 2006. *Are they really ready to work? Employers' perspectives on the basic knowledge and applied Skills of new entrants to the 21st Century U.S. workforce. Partnership for 21s Century Skills.* Washington, DC: Partnership for 21st Century Skills.

[7] Code.org. 2017. Computer science education stats. Retrieved from: https://code.org/promote

[8] Computing Research Association. 2017. Generation CS: Computer science undergraduate enrollments surge since 2006. Available at http://cra.org/data/Generation-CS/

[9] Course Report. 2017. Retrieved from: https://www.coursereport.com

[10] Deloitte Access Economics. 2017. Soft skills for business success. Retrieved from: https://www2.deloitte.com/

[11] Greenman, M. 2016. Intensive training helps coding newcomers land technology jobs. (September 2016). Available at: http://425business.com/intensive-training-helps-coders-land-technology-jobs/

[12] Indeed. 2017. What do employers really think about coding boot camps? Available at: http;//blog.indeed.com/2017/05/ 02/what-employers-really -think-about-coding-bootcamp/

[13] Janush, S. 2017. Bringing soft skills to the forefront: How higher ed (and continuing ed) must adapt

[14] Lapowsky, I. (2016, August 16). Can't afford a coding bootcamp? Available at https://www.wired.com/ 2016/08/white-house-rolls-student-loans-coding-camps/

[15] LinkedIn Learning. 2018. 2018 Workplace learning report: The rise and responsibility of talent development in the new labor market. Retrieved from: https://learning.linkedin.com/content/dam/me/learning/ en-us/pdfs/linkedin-learning-workplace-learning-report-2018.pdf

[16] Lohr, S. (2017). A new kind of tech job emphasizes skills, not a college degree. *The New York Times.* Available at https://www.newyorktimes.com/2017/06/28/technology/tech-Skills-college-degree, html?mcubz=2 Doi: http://dx.doi.org/10.18260/p.24716

[17] Maxwell, J. A., 1992, Understanding and validity in qualitative research. In A. M. Huberman & M. B. Miles (Eds.), *The Qualitative Researcher's Companion,* (pp. 37-64). Thousands Oaks, CA: Sage Publications.

[18] Mourshed, M., Farrell, D., & Barton, D. 2013. Education to employment. *National Partnership for Educational Access: Research Brief.* Available at https://npeac memberclicks.net /assets/education%20to%20employment.final.pdf

[19] Pritchard, J. 2013. The importance of soft skills in entry-level employment and post-secondary success: Perspectives from employers and community colleges. Available at http://www.seattlejobsinitiative.com/wp-content/uploads/SJI_SoftSkillsReport_vFINAL_1.17.13.pdf

[20] The U.S. Bureau of Labor Statistics. 2017. Available at https://www.bls.gov.

[21] Van Velsor, E.V. and Wright, J. 2012. Expanding the Leadership Equation Developing Next-Generation Leaders. *Center for Creative Leadership.* Available at https://ccl.org/wp-content/uploads/2015/04/Expanding LeadershipEquation.pdf

A Middle-School Code Camp Emphasizing Digital Humanities

Yesheng Chen, Zhen Chen, Shyamala Gumidyala, Annabella Koures, Seoyeon Lee, James Msekela, Halle Remash, Nolan Schoenle, Sarah Dahlby Albright, and Samuel A. Rebelsky
Grinnell College
{chenyesh,chenzhen,gumidyal,kouresan,leeseoyo,msekelaj,remashha,schoenle,dahlbysa,rebelsky}@grinnell.edu

ABSTRACT

Over the past decade, politicians, leaders, and pundits have called for computing and computer science education opportunities to be made available earlier and earlier. Such calls have led to the creation of a wide variety of offerings for students at middle-school and even elementary levels, including summer "code camps" targeted at middle-school students. Such camps often emphasize fun aspects of computing, such as games and robots. In contrast, research at the collegiate level suggests that meaningful applications of computing, such as computing for social good, are more successful at building and sustaining interest, particularly among students from groups traditionally underrepresented in computing.

In this project, we developed and offered a summer camp that draws upon ideas and approaches from the digital humanities (DH), which explore the use of algorithms and computation in support of broader humanistic inquiry. Because DH reveals different ways to apply algorithmic and computational thinking, DH has the potential to attract students who might not otherwise consider computing.

In this paper, we introduce central issues in the digital humanities, explain the rationale for the camp design, describe the camp curriculum, and reflect on successful and less successful aspects of the camp. Among other things, we consider how to introduce digital humanities topics to students who have not yet heard the term "humanities" and explore the utility of such topics for this age group. We also present preliminary data on the short-term effects of the camp on students' self-efficacy and interest in computing.

CCS CONCEPTS

• **Social and professional topics → Computing education**; **K-12 education**; Race and ethnicity; Gender.

KEYWORDS

Digital Humanities; Outreach (Middle School); Code camp; Racket; Natural language

ACM Reference Format:
Yesheng Chen, Zhen Chen, Shyamala Gumidyala, Annabella Koures, Seoyeon Lee, James Msekela, Halle Remash, Nolan Schoenle, Sarah Dahlby Albright, and Samuel A. Rebelsky. 2019. A Middle-School Code Camp Emphasizing Digital Humanities. In *Proceedings of the 50th ACM Technical Symposium on Computer Science Education (SIGCSE '19), February 27-March 2, 2019, Minneapolis, MN, USA.* ACM, New York, NY, USA, 7 pages. https://doi.org/10.1145/3287324.3287509

SIGCSE '19, February 27-March 2, 2019, Minneapolis, MN, USA

ACM ISBN 978-1-4503-5890-3/19/02...$15.00
https://doi.org/10.1145/3287324.3287509

1 INTRODUCTION

In spite of a host of efforts to diversify the field, computer science remains dominated by white and Asian males. A recent Taulbee survey suggests that only 17.9% of bachelor's degrees in computer science are awarded to students identified as female, 3.1% to students identified as Black or African-American, and 7.5% to students identified as Hispanic [19]. Many factors likely lead to this problem. Unfortunately, many parents and teachers still treat technical fields as a domain for boys and men. As Cheryan *et al.* [6] have demonstrated, one major factor is that perceptions of "who does computer science" lead many women and students of color to dismiss the field. But students are not just discouraged by issues of identity; Guzdial [11] suggests that there are also issues of interest; many students perceive computing as "irrelevant" and "asocial". These are complex issues to address; a single type or level of intervention is not enough. Because these biases start early, many educators are developing early interventions [7, 14].

Over the past few years, our research team has explored extracurricular approaches that target students in elementary and middle schools. In particular, we have considered novel approaches to summer "code camp" offerings that emphasize meaningful aspects of computing. Although such approaches have shown some success at the college level (e.g., [9, 10, 18]), they are rarely used at these earlier levels. For example, in a survey of 500 mainstream camps [8], we observed that most such camps focus on popular aspects of computing, like Minecraft, Lego robots, or App development.

While many of our camps have emphasized computing for social good, in this project we chose a different approach to computing, one that emphasizes the Digital Humanities (DH), a growing field that explores computing through a humanistic lens, not only exploring the human implications of computing, but also considering how computing can support broader approaches to humanistic inquiry. Because DH reveals different ways to apply algorithmic and computational thinking, DH-based approaches have the potential to attract students who might not otherwise consider computing. Of course, DH encompasses a wide variety of approaches, and it is not possible to employ them all; we focused primarily on problems related to language generation or analysis.

In section 2, we describe the local context of the camp, focusing on our community and the types of students who enrolled. In section 3, we provide additional detail about our approach to the digital humanities and describe the design and structure of the camp. In section 4, we describe the mechanisms we used to assess the efficacy of the curriculum and review data from camper surveys. Finally, in sections 5 and 6, we consider some implications of the data and suggest future steps.

2 LOCAL CONTEXT

"All politics is local", as they say. While there are broadly applicable approaches to computing outreach, local context is also important. The approaches appropriate to a community that has a strong tech industry are likely different than those to one in which tech is absent. Similarly, the interests of students in a high-SES[1] community may be different than those in a low-SES community, as will the ability of families to take advantage of enrichment activities. Hence, we begin with a consideration of our local context.

Our institution is situated in the middle of a small town (9,000 residents) in a midwestern farming state. Like many college towns, it includes people from a wide variety of backgrounds; the college attracts a broader and educated group of people, not just faculty and their families, but also others interested in the benefits of living near an institution of higher learning. We also have a large population of "working poor"; even though the unemployment rate in town is under 3%, the poverty rate in our county is over 30%.

While we knew that our camp would draw from the college community, our particular interest was students who, because of their background and the lack of a local tech industry, might not otherwise consider a career in computing or even attending college. We think that attracting such students is particularly important because computing careers are likely to be among the most lucrative available to them. We paid particular attention to ways to support such students, including a low initial camp fee with meals and snacks included, a "no questions asked" financial aid model, and free early-drop-off and late-pick-up options.

We drew students not only from our community, but also from surrounding communities. In addition, a few parents who regularly commute sixty miles or so to our town registered their children. Our target audience was middle-school students entering 5th through 8th grade. We had initially capped the camp at 32 students; however, experience from prior camps, which suggested that we'd have a bit of melt the first day,[2] led us to allow 38 students to enroll. Our estimates were close; we had approximately 34 students at each day of camp. Two students had previously attended our elementary-school camp, which emphasizes coding for tangible crafts [4]. Ten had participated in our middle-school camp on data science [5] in the prior year, five in our revised middle-school camp on data science [3] two weeks earlier, and five in both years.[3]

3 CAMP DESIGN

A core goal of the broader project is to explore alternative approaches to summer code camps. Spurred, in part, by a growing institutional emphasis on the Digital Humanities (DH), we decided to add a camp that drew upon DH to our repertoire.

3.1 Digital humanities

As in the case of many modern computational disciplines, such as data science, definitions of DH vary widely depending on the background and interests of those defining the field. Some focus on approaches to language, particularly of larger corpora of texts, to find patterns through statistical algorithms like topic modeling. Others emphasize the use of computers to visualize aspects of traditional humanistic data. Still others focus on ways in which computers permit new modes of interactive writing. Many also include humanistic approaches to computing. For example, authors of a recent text suggest that,

> *For us, digital humanities simply represents a community of scholars and teachers interested in using or studying technology. We use humanities techniques to study digital cultures, tools, and concepts, and we also use computational methods to explore the traditional objects of humanistic inquiry. [1]*

In choosing an approach for the camp, we drew upon an early DH offering at our institution that focused on literary studies [17]. Students in that class began the semester with an environmental scan of DH, identifying everything from markup languages for poetry to issues surrounding the dominance of America and Western Europe in DH work. Afterwards, the course focused on three primary approaches: writing, map-based analysis, and the use of coding as a tool to explore texts. That is, students first read and analyzed a variety of interactive online texts and used tools to build similar texts, from hypertexts in Twine[4] to Twitter 'bots using Tracery[5]. Next, students read a more traditional work of fiction and used tools like Google Maps to explore and explain the use of places in the text. Finally, students learned to use Python to write simple programs to look for patterns in texts and employed pre-written tools for more sophisticated analyses, such as topic modeling.

3.1.1 Why digital humanities? At first glance, DH may seem like an odd topic for a camp for middle-school students, few of whom likely know what the humanities are. However, by the time students reach college, we see a disproportionate number of women entering the humanities rather than the sciences. There is also a long-standing stereotype that girls are generally more drawn to language and literature than are boys. For example, in a recent Brookings report, Loveless [12] observes,

> *The most recent results from reading tests of the National Assessment of Educational Progress (NAEP) show girls outscoring boys at every grade level and age examined. Gender differences in reading are not confined to the United States.*

Loveless also describes effects on boys' interest in reading.

> *Cultural influences steer boys toward non-literary activities (sports, music) and define literacy as a feminine characteristic. This explanation believes cultural cues and strong role models could help close the gap by portraying reading as a masculine activity.*

While our primary hope was to use girls' likely interest in reading and literature to draw them to computing, observations like Loveless's suggest that DH could also help draw more boys to language and literature.

[1] socio-economic status

[2] One of the disadvantages of a low enrollment cost.

[3] We take the number of returners as a positive sign of the value students and parents place on the camp. However, returners complicated both the camp curriculum and the data analysis.

[4] http://twinery.org/

[5] https://github.com/galaxykate/tracery

Monday	Tuesday	Wednesday	Thursday	Friday
Camp Orientation Intro Algorithms I *Icebreakers*	Opening Slideshow Racket Review Pair Programming	Present: Web App ***Madlibs***	RegExp	SH Awards Ceremony Project Work Time
		Snack Break		
Intro Algorithms II Intro Racket I	Discuss Lang. & Code Intro Strings	Intro Conditionals Analysis w/Files & Lists I	***Analyze Web Pages I*** *Scavenger Hunt*	Project Work Time
		Lunch + Recess		
Intro Racket II *Intro Scavenger Hunt* Intro HTML & CSS	Language Generation Racket Web Server	Analysis w/Files & Lists II Present: Madlibs *Scavenger Hunt*	***Analyze Web Pages II*** Transform Web Pages *Scavenger Hunt*	Poster Prep Presentation Prep
		Snack Break		
Hypertext Stories Present: Stories	***Web App*** *Scavenger Hunt*	Project Intro Project Brainstorm	Project Work Time	Welcome Visitors Show and Tell

Table 1: Camp Curriculum. "Away from keyboard" activities appear in italic and mini-projects appear in bold italic.

3.2 Primary activities

Drawing our approach from the aforementioned literary theory course, we decided to focus primarily on the application of computer science to text, including text generation, text manipulation, and text analysis. That led to the creation of a series of core activities across the week of the camp. We chose to have students explore mechanisms for representing language, as illustrated by HTML; new ways of writing, including both hypertexts and the language generation sometimes associated with Twitter 'bots; and ways to create programs to analyze texts.

3.2.1 Building Web pages. We began with an activity in which students built and linked Web pages. This starting activity provides many benefits. Students are empowered as they realize that they can build pages that are available to "anyone" on the World-Wide Web. The use of cascading style sheets also makes it more fun, as they have broad freedom to style pages.[6] For students used to a block-based language,[7] HTML provides a relatively simple way to introduce issues of formal language and syntax.

3.2.2 Choose your own adventure. Web pages provide some benefit by themselves. However, as we had seen in the literary analysis course, having students build more sophisticated hypertexts offers an additional sense of agency. We phrased hypertexts as an opportunity to write short "choose your own adventure" stories. We provided students with an initial template and gave suggestions on possible directions. In addition to building interest and efficacy, these activities helped students understand issues of linking and naming. While some were frustrated by the need to get the target of a link "just right", most quickly learned that "computers are dumb; they can only do what you explicitly tell them to".

3.2.3 Language generation. Using Twitter 'bots as a motivating example, we guided through students through the design of programs that created language using simple generative grammars. We first introduced them to a simplified Haiku generator expressed as a series of rules in a programming language. For example,

- A Haiku is a capitalized five-syllable group of words, followed by a seven-syllable group of words, followed by a five-syllable group of words.
- A five-syllable group of words can be either (a) a two-syllable word followed by a three-syllable word; or (b) a two-syllable word followed by a one-syllable word, followed by a two-syllable word; or a one-syllable word followed by a three-syllable word, followed by a one syllable word.[8]
- A one-syllable word can be "fast" or "blue" or "code" or ....

After introducing the structure and showing some examples, We challenged them to add more words and more structure.

In the second language generation exercise, we worked with students to develop a framework for generating sentences using both simple subject plus intransitive verb and subject plus transitive verb plus object sentences. While few students knew this terminology, most were able to figure out the general structure.

Finally, we had students work in larger groups with a counselor to try to write procedures that generated longer stories. We knew that such procedures would be complicated, but with some pointers and gentle nudges, most groups were able to write self-referential procedures that generated stories.[9]

As one might expect, writing poetry and stories and then reading the results aloud produces a good deal of amusement. These initial forays into language generation also supported some appropriate learning outcomes. It helped students get accustomed to a new programming language; all that is necessary for the most straightforward forms of language generation are the ability to define new zero-parameter procedures and to use a few basic commands for appending strings or choosing between one of a few actions.[10] Looking at the forms of the different rules deepened students' understanding of the structure of language, which we expect to be useful for both artificial and natural languages.

[6]Although CSS was in our original plans for the camp, some constraints led us to leave them out of the original HTML lesson.

[7]Some students had seen a block-based language in the classroom. Others had encountered one in a previous camp.

[8]We realize that there are many other options. As we note to the students, this is intentionally a *simplified* grammar.

[9]E.g., a story is either a sentence or a sentence and a story.

[10]Although the latter procedure appears in few languages, it was relatively straightforward to write and provide to our students.

3.2.4 Madlibs. As a counterpart to the language generation activity, we also had students build Web-based "Madlibs" programs which prompt for a variety of types of words (e.g., an adjective, a color, a proper noun) and then put those into a template to construct a story. We provided students with a basic framework, both the form and the script that processes the form. They then added new inputs and revised the template.

Most students were familiar with Madlibs, which provided a level of comfort. As in the other exercises, students enjoyed having us read the generated stories aloud; knowing that we would do so proved motivational. The structure of the program provided an opportunity to deepen students' understanding of variables and to discuss some aspects of the architecture of the World Wide Web.

3.2.5 Language analysis. As the examples above suggest, most projects emphasized the creation of new computational language-based artifacts. We also considered it necessary to give the students experience with the use of computers as analytical tools. We chose two basic types of text files to analyze, a pre-screened set of Tweets from selected celebrities[11] and a few classic texts downloaded from Project Gutenberg. Some tasks helped students understand the need for a clear and common format for files and to learn how to scrape or download data, others asked them filter the lists of Tweets for particular words they chose or to recognize patterns of Tweets. We also provided resources for them to do more complex analyses of Web pages, such as to extract and count various tags or to search within particular sections. These kinds of exercises not only provided students with a broader understanding of the power of computers, it also gave us the opportunity to introduce a variety of other algorithmic concepts, such as conditionals.

3.2.6 Additional activities and topics. While the activities above provided the primary projects for the camp, we also introduced a variety of other ideas and tools in smaller lessons. For example, although we did not include a large text-manipulation project, we did include the basics of pattern matching and replacement using regular expressions and provided them with a framework in which they could apply those tools to transforming Web pages. These additional activities appear in Table 1.

3.3 Other camp design issues

3.3.1 Choosing a programming language. In our other camps, we begin with a block programming language, such as Scratch. However, a significant portion of this camp had either participated in a prior camp or had encountered block programming in school. Hence, we looked for languages that would feel less familiar to the students, but would still be age appropriate.

We settled on Racket, a language not regularly used in such camps. While a LISP descendant may not seem to be an appropriate language for middle school students, the Bootstrap project[12] [13, 15, 16] has shown that Racket can be quite successful for this age group. We saw many advantages to using Racket. It would be new to all students, which helped ensure that everyone felt like they were encountering something different. We also use Racket as the introductory language in our college curriculum; not only did that mean that the counselors were familiar with it, it also provided us with the opportunity to build self-efficacy by talking to students about the level of work they were doing. Racket also provides a wide range of available libraries, including a built-in Web server and libraries for Web processing.

3.3.2 Final projects. As in our other camp offerings, we concluded with an open-ended project of the form "*With your partner, do something interesting with what you've learned in camp and then present it to the class and to your parents.*" We introduced the project with a series of examples to help them envision a range of possibilities. We had them journal about topics and approaches they found interesting and then explore them further in small groups. Each student had the opportunity to "pitch" a project idea to the class. After the pitches, students ranked their top five projects. That evening, counselors used those rankings and their knowledge of student ability and personality to pair students into project groups. In addition to developing a project, each pair was also expected to make a poster that summarized the project and to give a short (2-3 minute) presentation to an audience of parents and friends and the end of the camp.

3.3.3 Structuring activities. Because our goal in the camp was primarily to build interest, we de-emphasized syntax and focused more on broader concepts. Rather than ask students to write programs from scratch, we often asked them to modify existing programs or to fill in gaps in partial programs. This approach allowed us to rapidly introduce a wide variety of topics.

The range of ages and backgrounds presented a challenge. Hence, we focused on a model in which each pair of students could work at the pace most appropriate for them. We minimized lecture and focused more on activities in which students could "go and try it yourself", doing a series of worksheets and program extensions. We also provided a wide variety of reference sheets and relied on a low camper-to-counselor ratio to ensure that help was readily available when students were stuck.

3.3.4 Organizing topics. While our camp emphasized computing, we knew that students also needed breaks and away-from-keyboard activities to maintain focus. Hence, in addition to providing lunch breaks and snack breaks, each day also included time for recess and a building or campus "scavenger hunt" activity.

Our experience from prior camps suggested that students were most amenable to learning new material in the morning and that focus tended to fade at the end of the day. By putting programming projects at the end of the day, we got students to focus more.

Table 1 provides an overview of the curriculum. As that overview suggests, we were not always able to maintain a consistent daily schedule. For example, the timing of scavenger hunts was constrained by the availability of locations on campus.

4 DATA AND ANALYSIS

As Decker, McGill, and Settle [7, 14] suggest, the effectiveness of these kinds of outreach activities should be measured primarily in terms of their long-term impacts. For example, how does the activity affect a student's likelihood to pursue other computing activities, particularly at the collegiate level?

[11] Beyonce was particularly popular.
[12] http://www.bootstrapworld.org/

1 *I look like a computer scientist.*
2 *Boys can do computing.*
3 *Girls can do computing.*
4 *I know a lot about computing.*
5 *I can become good at computing.*
6 *I know more than my friends about computers.*
7 *I like the challenge of computing.*
8 *Computer science is cool.*
9 *I feel comfortable using a computer.*
10 *I want to have a job in computing.*
11 *I want to learn more about computing.*
12 *Computer scientists are creative.*
13 *Solving problems is fun.*
14 *Computing involves people working together.*
15 *I like computing.*

Figure 1: Survey statements

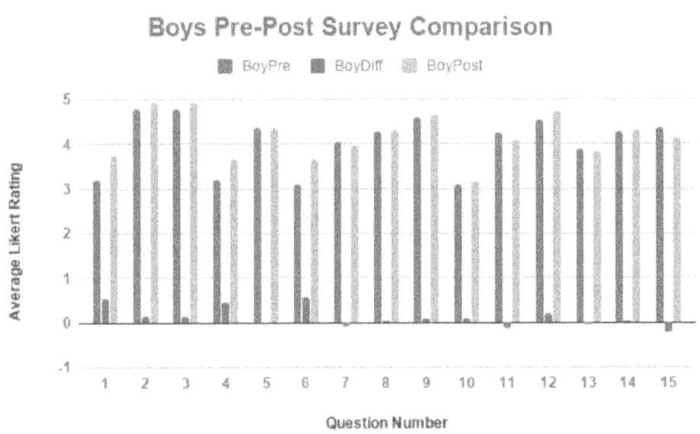

Figure 2: Survey data: Boys

Nonetheless, it seemed worthwhile to gather some data about the short-term effects of the camps. In order to measure the campers' change in self-efficacy and coding confidence quantitatively, we used pre-camp and post-camp survey instruments based on instruemnts from Georgia Computes! [2] that ask students to respond to various statements, such as "I look like a computer scientist" and "I like the challenge of computing" on a five-point Likert scale. Our questions appear in Fig. 1. Through these surveys, we hoped to be able to explore changes in student attitudes.

Figures 2 and 3 illustrate the changes among both boys ($n = 26$) and girls ($n = 8$). Informally, we saw an increase in student responses on all questions except questions 11 (*I want to learn more about computing*), 13 (*Solving problems is fun*), and 15 (*I like computing*). However, the decreases were not statistically significant at $\alpha \leq 0.1$, and the original rankings were relatively high (4.23, 3.88, and 4.35, respectively). Prior experience likely had some impact; given that many had attended a prior camp, it was unclear whether this new camp experience was likely to have an additional effect.

We ran a paired t-test using the pre-camp and post-camp surveys to explore changes in students' attitudes. In spite of camper prior experience , we found statistically significant growth on questions 1 (*I look like a computer scientist,* $p < 0.05$), 2 (*Boys can do computing,* $p < 0.1$), 4 (*I know a lot about computing,* $p < 0.05$), and 6 (*I know more than my friends about computers,* $p < 0.05$). We note that while there was a statistically significant increase in the question 2 responses and not in the question 3 responses, question 3 had a higher average score on the pre-surveys and the average post-survey score for the two questions was the same.

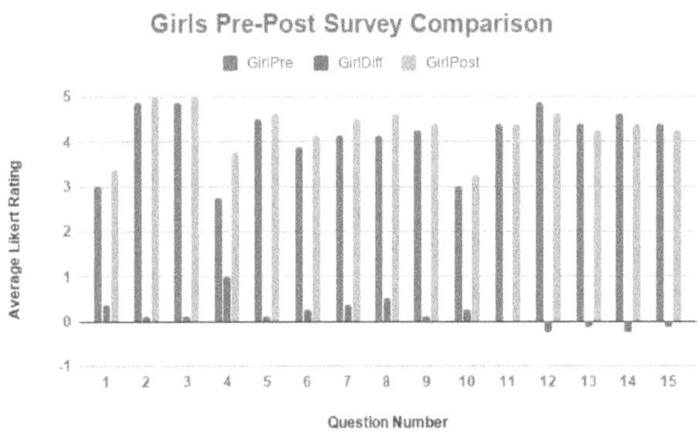

Figure 3: Survey data: Girls

5 DISCUSSION

Because we had a comparatively small number of campers (thirty-four), surprisingly few female participants (an issue we will discuss further), and a large number of repeat participants, we do not feel confident claiming that this curriculum has had a significant effect on the students. Nonetheless, it is worth exploring both the data and some informal observations we made during the camp.

We were surprised at the initial responses to questions 2 (*Boys can do computing*) and 3 (*Girls can do computing*). We did not expect either the high levels of agreement with those statements or the similarities of responses from boys and girls, particularly given that boys usually agree less about girls' ability to do computing. It may be that schools are doing a better job of encouraging students to think broadly. However, since these students come from a variety of school districts, it may be that returning students had already embraced this broader notion of who can do computing.

We also admit that we were both surprised and frustrated by the small number of female students enrolling in the camps. Our other camps on code crafts and on computing for social good tend to draw a nearly even mix of boys and girls. It may be that our hypothesis that the Digital Humanities would attract young women was incorrect. It may be that we failed to advertise the camp appropriately—while we thought a title of "Language and Code" would highlight the humanistic aspect, it may be that many potential students read it as "programming language". We will need to revisit this question if we are to offer the camp again.

5.1 Informal observations

We also observed some effects that we could not easily measure.

One returning student, who had been reluctant to work with others or to ask for help in a previous camp, thrived in this camp. He not only approached the project with enthusiasm, but showed great flair in his presentation.

Although our primary goal is to promote computing, we also expect that the camps can promote college. During one of the scavenger hunts, one of the campers said "I never thought about attending college. But this place is cool. Do you think I could get in?" We assured him that with hard work, he could.

A visiting K-12 teacher noted that they appreciated the ways that some of the exercises helped students think more deeply about language, particularly the Madlibs and language generation projects. It could be that this is a natural way to incorporate more computing in language courses not so much to teach computing, but to help students gain a deeper understanding of language.

5.2 Projects

We had hoped that students would evenly distribute among the various approaches to projects, drawing upon one or more of the methods from the mini projects: hypertext stories, language generation, Madlibs, text analysis, and Web page manipulation. However, the majority decided to write "choose your own adventure" hypertext stories.

There were, of course, exceptions. Two teams adapted the basic Madlibs model. Two teams worked with counselors to build more advanced projects that combined Madlibs with hypertext stories.[13] In one case, the initial Madlibs answers carried from page to page, so that characters and other words would reappear. In the other, students asked questions on each page and accumulated data for a final page. Two teams explored issues of language generation, creating more complex texts and, in one case, attempting to include rhyming in poems. A few teams avoided the "language and code" theme. One built a time-wasting click counter. A second started a role-playing-style fighting game with character stats. A third built a single page collection of useful links with affiliated images.[14]

In spite of these few detours, we consider the projects a success. Students worked hard on their projects, posters, and presentations. We also saw pride in their projects. Many parents and campers called and emailed after the camp asking for access to the projects.

5.3 Difficulties

That is not to say that the camp was a complete success. As we have already noted, we are frustrated to have attracted such a small proportion of female campers. It is also clear that we threw too much at the campers; by the time we got to the Web manipulation exercises on day four, many seemed lost. It appears that our approach of "focus more on concepts than underlying details" may not have been the best approach if we wanted students to branch beyond the examples we provided. While we have given the students a sense of power, particularly in their ability to create Web pages and hypertext stories that they can share on the Web, it may be that we have given them too little power to think computationally.

6 CONCLUSIONS AND FUTURE WORK

The underrepresentation of many groups in computing remains an issue of national concern, not only because computing has the potential to provide fulfilling and rewarding career opportunities, but also because the nation needs people from a wide variety of perspectives building the technologies that so frequently affect our daily lives. Although many approaches have started to make some difference, it is clear the computer science education and computing communities must continue to explore new ways to attract and support members of underrepresented groups. It's clear that no one method will work; we need a spectrum of approaches to support a range of people and perspectives.

In this paper, we have explored one particular approach, the use of language-based computing exercises associated with the Digital Humanities in a code camp for middle-school students. Our experience in this project was mixed. While students enjoyed the camp and we saw a few changes in attitude, the camp failed to attract a large number of students from our target groups. And we clearly packed too much material into a one-week camp.

Unfortunately, the size and character of the camper population made it difficult to show success or failure of the curriculum. Because we had so many returning students, we do not even know what the short-term effects on confidence or interest would have been on a cohort consisting of only students who had not attended a previous camp.

We may not offer this camp a second time. It is clear that if we do, we will need to make a variety of changes, cutting back on the number of activities and finding ways to better encourage a broader variety of projects. We will also need to find new ways to show the applicability of the topic.

Nonetheless, we do see a role for exercises drawn from DH as a tool in broadening participation in computing. As noted, the language generation and Madlibs exercises can help student learn not only about computing, but also about language. It may be that the projects are better used individually, in the context of other outreach activities, rather than combined into a single week-long experience. We also consider it worth exploring uses of DH at the college level as an avenue to broadening participation.

For those interested in adapting any of our work, the curriculum, slide decks, instructors guides, and worksheets are available online at https://codecamp.sites.grinnell.edu/languageandcode/.

ACKNOWLEDGMENTS

We are grateful to the Grinnell College Innovation Fund and the Grinnell College Student-Faculty Research Fund for providing the resources to offer this camp at low or no cost to our campers. The Mellon Foundation has supported the growth of Digital Humanities and Digital Liberal Arts at Grinnell through a joint "Digital Bridges" grant with the University of Iowa and, while it provided no direct funding to this project, that broader iniative influenced the direction of the project. Erik Simpson's *Lighting the Page* course was particularly influential. Our IRB provided useful feedback on the instrument and the project. Grinnell summer research students graciously worked with the campers on their research projects, providing advice on both posters and presentations. Junior counselors Gabby Dahlby Albright, Hans Larsson, and Daniel Rebelsky provided necessary support for this project; we know it's hard to support someone else's curriculum, and they did a great job. Finally, we appreciate the enthusiastic participation of our campers!

[13] While the students could modify existing programs, it was clear that they had not developed the mastery necessary to build more sophisticated programs. Counselors therefore provided additional support.

[14] Twenty years ago, they might have been as innovative as Yahoo.

REFERENCES

[1] Claire Battershill and Shawna Ross. 2017. *Using Digital Humanities in the Classroom: A Practical Introduction for Teachers, Lecturers, and Students.* Bloomsbury Academic, London and New York.

[2] Amy Bruckman, Maureen Biggers, Barbara Ericson, Tom McKlin, Jill Dimond, Betsy DiSalvo, Mike Hewner, Lijun Ni, and Sarita Yardi. 2009. "Georgia Computes!": Improving the Computing Education Pipeline. *SIGCSE Bull.* 41, 1 (March 2009), 86–90. https://doi.org/10.1145/1539024.1508899

[3] Caelin Bryant, Yesheng Chen, Zhen Chen, Jonathan Gilmour, Shyamala Gumidyala, Beatriz Herce-Hagiwara, Anh Thu Msekela, James Pham, Halle Remash, Marli Remash, , Nolan Schoenle, Jonah Zimmerman, Sarah Dahlby Albright, and Samuel A. Rebelsky. 2019. A Middle-School Code Camp Emphasizing Data Science for Social Good. In *Proceedings of the 50th ACM Technical Symposium on Computer Science Education (SIGCSE '19).* ACM, New York, NY, USA, 7. https://doi.org/10.1145/3159450.3162313

[4] Caelin Bryant, Jonathan Gilmour, Beatriz Herce-Hagiwara, Anh Thu Pham, Halle Remash, Marli Remash, Jonah Zimmerman, Sarah Dahlby Albright, and Samuel A. Rebelsky. 2018. The Craft of Code: Exposing Elementary Students to Computing Through Tangible Crafts (Poster). In *Proceedings of the 49th ACM Technical Symposium on Computer Science Education (SIGCSE '18).* ACM, New York, NY, USA, 1080–1080. https://doi.org/10.1145/3159450.3162321

[5] Caelin Bryant, Jonathan Gilmour, Beatriz Herce-Hagiwara, Anh Thu Pham, Halle Remash, Marli Remash, Jonah Zimmerman, Sarah Dahlby Albright, and Samuel A. Rebelsky. 2018. A Middle-School Code Camp Experience Emphasizing Data Science for Social Good (Poster). In *Proceedings of the 49th ACM Technical Symposium on Computer Science Education (SIGCSE '18).* ACM, New York, NY, USA, 1088–1088. https://doi.org/10.1145/3159450.3162313

[6] Sapna Cheryan and Victoria C. Plaut. 2010. Explaining Underrepresentation: A Theory of Precluded Interest. *Sex Roles* 63, 7 (01 Oct 2010), 475–488. https://doi.org/10.1007/s11199-010-9835-x

[7] Adrienne Decker, Monica M. McGill, and Amber Settle. 2016. Towards a Common Framework for Evaluating Computing Outreach Activities. In *Proceedings of the 47th ACM Technical Symposium on Computing Science Education (SIGCSE '16).* ACM, New York, NY, USA, 627–632. https://doi.org/10.1145/2839509.2844567

[8] Anita DeWitt, Julia Fay, Madeleine Goldman, Eleanor Nicolson, Linda Oyolu, Lukas Resch, Jovan Martinez Saldaña, Soulideth Sounalath, Tyler Williams, Kathryn Yetter, Elizabeth Zak, Narren Brown, and Samuel A. Rebelsky. 2017. What We Say vs. What They Do: A Comparison of Middle-School Coding Camps in the CS Education Literature and Mainstream Coding Camps (Abstract Only). In *Proceedings of the 2017 ACM SIGCSE Technical Symposium on Computer Science Education (SIGCSE '17).* ACM, New York, NY, USA, 707–707. https://doi.org/10.1145/3017680.3022434

[9] Michael Goldweber. 2018. Strategies for Adopting CSG-Ed In CS 1. In *Proceedings of the 3rd Conference for Research on Equity and Sustained Participation in Engineering, Computing, and Technology (RESPECT '18).*

[10] Michael Goldweber, John Barr, Tony Clear, Renzo Davoli, Samuel Mann, Elizabeth Patitsas, and Scott Portnoff. 2013. A Framework for Enhancing the Social Good in Computing Education: A Values Approach. *ACM Inroads* 4, 1 (March 2013), 58–79. https://doi.org/10.1145/2432596.2432616

[11] Mark Guzdial. 2009. Education: Teaching Computing to Everyone. *Commun. ACM* 52, 5 (May 2009), 31–33. https://doi.org/10.1145/1506409.1506420

[12] Tom Loveless. 2015. How Well Are Students Learning; With sections on the gender gap in reading, effects of the Common Core, and student engagement.

[13] Wendy S. McClanahan, Sarah K. Pepper, and Meridith Polin. 2016. "I program my own videogames": An Evaluation of Bootstrap. https://www.bootstrapworld.org/impact/EvalReportDec2015Medium.pdf

[14] Monica M. McGill, Adrienne Decker, and Amber Settle. 2015. Does Outreach Impact Choices of Major for Underrepresented Undergraduate Students?. In *Proceedings of the Eleventh Annual International Conference on International Computing Education Research (ICER '15).* ACM, New York, NY, USA, 71–80. https://doi.org/10.1145/2787622.2787711

[15] Emmanuel Schanzer, Kathi Fisler, and Shriram Krishnamurthi. 2013. Bootstrap: Going Beyond Programming in After-School Computer Science. In *SPLASH Education Symposium 2013.* ACM, New York, NY, USA, 7. http://cs.brown.edu/~sk/Publications/Papers/Published/sfk-bootstrap-after-school/

[16] Emmanuel Schanzer, Kathi Fisler, and Shriram Krishnamurthi. 2018. Assessing Bootstrap: Algebra Students on Scaffolded and Unscaffolded Word Problems. In *Proceedings of the 49th ACM Technical Symposium on Computer Science Education (SIGCSE '18).* ACM, New York, NY, USA, 8–13. https://doi.org/10.1145/3159450.3159498

[17] Erik Simpson. 2018. Sylabus for Lighting the Page: Digital Methods in Literary Studies. http://www.cs.grinnell.edu/~simpsone/Connections/Digital/Lighting/

[18] Ursula Wolz, Meredith Stone, Kim Pearson, Sarah Monisha Pulimood, and Mary Switzer. 2011. Computational Thinking and Expository Writing in the Middle School. *Trans. Comput. Educ.* 11, 2, Article 9 (July 2011), 22 pages. https://doi.org/10.1145/1993069.1993073

[19] Stuart Zweben and Betsy Bizot. 2017. 2016 Taulbee Survey. *Computing Research News* 29, 5 (5 2017), 3–51. https://cra.org/crn/wp-content/uploads/sites/7/2017/05/2016-Taulbee-Survey.pdf

A Middle-School Camp Emphasizing Data Science and Computing for Social Good

Caelin Bryant, Yesheng Chen, Zhen Chen, Jonathan Gilmour, Shyamala Gumidyala,
BeatrizHerce-Hagiwara, Annabella Koures, Seoyeon Lee, James Msekela, Anh Thu Pham,
Halle Remash, Marli Remash, Nolan Schoenle, Jonah Zimmerman, Sarah Dahlby Albright, and Samuel A Rebelsky
Grinnell College
{bryantca,chenyesh,chenzhen,gilmourj,gumidyal,hercehag,koursean,leeseoye,msekelaj,phamanht,remashha,
remashma,schoenle,zimmera2,dahlbysa,rebelsky}@grinnell.edu

ABSTRACT

The underrepresentation in computer science of women, domestic students of color, and students of lower socioeconomic status remains a national issue. Recent studies demonstrate two critical factors: Persistent stereotypes about "who does computer science" can preclude interest in the field for members of these groups; many also perceive computing as "irrelevant" and "asocial". While these issues must be addressed at multiple ages and levels, many suggest starting early, before students have developed stereotypes.

As a step in combating (mis-)perceptions of ability and relevance, we designed and conducted a spectrum of week-long summer "code camps" for regional middle-school students. These camps emphasize meaningful uses of computing, building self-efficacy, and broadening understanding of who does and can do computer science. In this paper, we focus on our "data science for social good" (ds4sg) camp, in which students explored computational approaches to data science through a lens of computing for social good, discovering how computing helps them not only better understand societal issues but also convince others to address problems.

We discuss the rationale for the curriculum and its content, including our uses of pair programming, personal projects, and a growth model that brings students from block-based programming to professional Jupyter data notebooks. We consider the short-term effects the camps have on students' self-efficacy and perceptions of computer science. We conclude with recommendations and guidelines for those intending to offer similar camps.

CCS CONCEPTS

• **Social and professional topics → Computing education**; **K-12 education**; Race and ethnicity; Gender.

KEYWORDS

Data Science; CSG-Ed; BBC micro:bits; Outreach (Middle School); Code Camp; Jupyter; ds4sg

ACM ISBN 978-1-4503-5890-3/19/02...$15.00
https://doi.org/10.1145/3287324.3287510

ACM Reference Format:
Caelin Bryant, Yesheng Chen, Zhen Chen, Jonathan Gilmour, Shyamala Gumidyala, Beatriz Herce-Hagiwara, Annabella Koures, Seoyeon Lee, James Msekela, Anh Thu Pham, Halle Remash, Marli Remash, Nolan Schoenle, Jonah Zimmerman, Sarah Dahlby Albright, and Samuel A Rebelsky. 2019. A Middle-School Camp Emphasizing Data Science and Computing for Social Good. In *Proceedings of the 50th ACM Technical Symposium on Computer Science Education (SIGCSE '19), February 27-March 2, 2019, Minneapolis, MN, USA.* ACM, New York, NY, USA, 7 pages. https://doi.org/10.1145/3287324.3287510

1 INTRODUCTION

For the past few decades, both computing in America and computer science in higher education have suffered from significant underrepresentation of women, domestic students of color, and students from lower socioeconomic backgrounds. A wide variety of projects have attempted to address these issues. In spite of these efforts only 17.9% of bachelor's degrees in computer science are awarded to students identified as female, 3.1% to students identified as Black or African-American, and 7.5% to students identified as Hispanic [20]. More work is needed.

Many issues are at play. Some identify a "pipeline problem", with members of these groups deciding early on that they do not belong in computer science [17]. Cheryan and Plaut [7] suggest that stereotypes about who "does computing" are one factor in this decision. Guzdial [18] suggests that student beliefs that computing may be "irrelevant" and "asocial" are also factors. To help address this problem, a variety of outreach activities have been developed that target students early in their careers [9, 19].

Over the past three years, our research team has explored the effect of summer code camps on student interest and self-efficacy. Rather than employing the more common approaches to computing the emphasize entertainment (e.g., robots, games, or Minecraft) [11], we emphasized meaningful uses of computing [6, 10], focusing primarily on issues of computing for social good [15]. We hypothesize that these more meaningful approaches will help build students' self-efficacy and interest, particularly among those from groups traditionally underrepresented in computing.

In this paper, we focus on a pair of middle-school camps offered in summer 2017 and 2018 in which campers explored computational techniques related to the emerging field of data science and applied their newly-developed skills to explore data sets relating to issues of social good. In section 2 of the paper, we describe the local context of the camp, particularly the characteristics of our community and the children who enrolled. In section 3, we describe the design and structure of the camp and provide additional detail about our approaches to data science and computing for social good. In section 4, we describe some changes we made in the second year. In section 5, we review data from camper surveys. In section 6, we conclude with a summary of the implications of the data and other observations from the camp.

2 LOCAL CONTEXT

Our institution is in a rural community (approximately 9,000 residents) in a comparatively white state—91.4% of the population identified as white in the latest census. Our community has a large population of working poor: While the poverty rate in our county is over 30%, the unemployment rate is under 3%. Surrounding communities have similar populations.

In designing the camp, we strove to address the particular concerns of our community. While we wanted to address the underrepresentation of girls and students of color, we also wanted to make sure that the camp was accessible to students of lower socioeconomic status. Building these students' self-efficacy seems particularly important as the opportunities presented by computing careers can make a huge difference in their lives. We used a variety of approaches to support these campers, including free tuition for those on free or reduced lunch programs[1], providing meals and snacks for every camper, subsidizing costs for all campers, and providing no-cost options for early drop-off and late pick-up.

Because there are few educational enrichment activities available to rural students, we drew students not only from our community, but also from neighboring communities. Some came from as far as sixty miles away, suggesting that there are far too few such opportunities for students in rural areas.

3 DESIGNING THE CAMP

Given the evidence of the value of computing for social good approaches [14, 15], our team's experience with such activities in a prior project [10], and the paucity of code camps that focus on computing for social good [11], we chose to make computing for social good a core theme of the camp. Adding a focus on data science incorporated a current and discipline-spanning approach to computing. The combination places our camp in a growing "data science for social good" (ds4sg) movement.[2] In the remainder of this section, we explore the themes and associated camp design issues.

3.1 Themes

3.1.1 Computing for social good. As Goldweber *et al.* [15] suggest, many women and students of color often avoid computing because they perceive that computing is incapable of making a difference in their primary areas of interest; such students often seek out careers which have the potential of positively impacting their communities. Hence, unlike students who enter computing because of a background in tinkering with computers or computational tasks, these students need to see that computing can have a positive impact on the world. To encourage a more diverse discipline, we developed the camp around the premise of "computing for social good" (CSG) [13], in which problems and context suggest ways in which computing can have a real impact. This approach promoted the social relevance of computer science while maintaining foundational programming concepts to give campers a broader and more informed perception of computer science as a whole.

The direct application of the CSG methodology to the camp provided much of its content. For example, Goldweber's "Reuniting Families" activity [12] helped us teach campers about developing algorithms in the context of societal disasters. We added a kinesthetic component to that activity so that campers not only designed algorithms for reuniting families, but also carried out each others' algorithms in a large public space. Our discussions about the current and future roles of technology encouraged campers to explore computing solutions to personal and societal issues. Similarly, case studies about weather patterns and car crashes favored an analytical approach to national events.

3.1.2 Data science. The field of data science is growing rapidly; however, its definition is tenuous, at best. As one of the statistics faculty noted when talking to us about possible ways to design a data science curriculum, "if you ask a dozen statisticians to define data science, you'll get at least a half-dozen different answers". Since we were focusing on the computational aspects of data science, we chose two primary ways of thinking about it: We taught campers that data science is a field in which you gain insight from existing data and that data science requires a series of replicable processes (e.g., cleaning and wrangling) carried out by algorithms that data scientists design and implement. We focused on how the components of algorithms (e.g., conditionals, loops, and subroutines) can be used to navigate a data set and how algorithms, along with visualization routines, help one develop a broader understanding of data and share that understanding with others. We also discussed issues of data cleaning, particularly algorithmic data cleaning (as opposed to manual data cleaning). In summary, we spent much of the week teaching campers practical data organization and manipulation skills so they could delve into data sets on their own.

Data science also supports many of our broader goals. We saw an opportunity further expand campers' perceptions of the capacity of computer science and computing to help people solve problems and to make a difference. Our focus on diversifying computing also ties to similar diversity goals in data science (e.g., [4]). Finally, choosing a "cutting edge" topic can show our rural students that they are able to engage with modern technologies.

3.1.3 Combining the themes: Data science for social good. At the time we were designing the first offering, we looked for a short and pithy title that covered the two core aspects of the camp. We settled on "Data science for social good". At the time, a new field with the same name was just beginning. As in the cases of both data science and computing for social good, it appears that there are a wide variety of meanings associated with these terms.

In choosing our own approach to computing and data science for social good, we identified a variety of approaches to help campers understand how the tools of data science can have an impact. For example, although much of our focus was on campers writing scripts

[1]Unfortunately, because many feel a stigma in our schools, many who would qualify for these programs choose not to enroll. The problem is most significant at the high-school level, but it is also in play at the middle-school level. To help address that stigma, we relied only on families' self-reports on the application form, and not on data from the school district.

[2]E.g., https://dssg.uchicago.edu/.

to explore and visualize data, we also exposed them to mechanisms for gathering environmental and other data. The latter approach helped them understand that they need not rely only on extant data sets, but could also create their own. Two sets of campers even designed attitudinal surveys as part of their broader projects.

More generally, it appears campers came to understand that the tools they were learning allowed them to identify or gather data relevant to a social or societal situation of interest and transform those data into a form in which they could make arguments relevant to that situation and to affect opinions. Focusing on computing for social good also helped us avoid some of the stigma that may be associated with data science, the sense that data science most frequently means "companies like Amazon and Facebook using their data to sell you something". Like all projects in computing for social good, our focus on ds4sg provided campers with the opportunity to think about issues that mattered to them.

The CSG-Ed community suggests that there are four levels of CSG activity [14],

- *Level 1*: The low hanging fruit: redefine an existing example/project with a CSG-Ed narrative.
- *Level 2*: Explicitly address a social good problem, though often in a simplified form.
- *Level 3*: A real world problem solved as an exercise.
- *Level 4*: A real world problem brought by stakeholders and with real world benefits rather than just an exercise

Our approach is somewhat tangential, although perhaps similar to level 2. While they are not "solving" a problem, they are explicitly addressing issues of social good, using a real data set to provide useful analysis.

3.2 Platforms and languages

We took particular care in selecting applicable programming languages and intuitive platforms. Other concerns included disparities in campers' prior programming experience and their broad age range. For reasons which will be introduced and elaborated in the following sections, we chose to base our camp in three main languages: A pair of block-based languages and Python.

3.2.1 BBC micro:bits—Hands-on activities with a block-based language. BBC micro:bits are cheap, pocket-sized programmable computers designed to act as an introductory interface for novice programmers. Each individual micro:bit has a five-by-five grid of LEDs forming a graphic interface, with two programmable buttons on either side for user input. The small size of the micro:bit might be deceiving due to its numerous additional features including a built-in radio, compass, and Bluetooth.[3]

We introduced the micro:bit Blocks Editor early in the week because it is an intuitive environment to introduce key programming concepts such as loops, conditionals, and variables.[4] The block-based language supported novice learners. It also gave students who had seen a prior block-based language a chance to explore a different language and extend their knowledge. The micro:bits served as a visual counterpart to indicate their progress, both successes and failures. As one of our primary goals of the camp was to increase the campers' confidence in the subject matter, it was important to give the campers a sense of accomplishment in a tangible and results-oriented way early on.

3.2.2 Jupyter Notebook—Programming like a data scientist. As we had hoped, the Data Science for Social Good Camp drew in campers who had not written much code before. It also appealed to campers who had learned block programming languages in schools and wanted to move on to a higher-level language. We also wanted to empower both sets of campers to think of themselves as real programmers. For these reasons, we looked to a platform that would permit campers to write realistic data science code without too much overhead. Python has long-standing success as a text-based introductory language [16] and is widely used in the data science community. We selected the cloud-based Jupyter Notebook environment[5] because it is moderately friendly for novice users, supports professional data scientists, and permitted campers to continue their work beyond the camp.[6]

Jupyter Notebook is a popular Web-based platform for exploring and analyzing data and is used by many professional data scientists. Like many modern computational systems for exploring data, it allows users to mix code, output, formatted text, and more into something much like a scientist's notebook, but an interactive one.

Each camp worksheet typically took the form of a Jupyter Notebook containing instructions, resources, and fill-in-the-blank partial code. These worksheets supplied campers with the means to practice concepts relating to data science, including a final analysis of their data. Campers incorporated data from a csv or Excel document, computed summary statistics, and created visualizations as prompted by worksheets. The partial code provided examples of syntax and common practice for code organization. These served as references for campers in later, more challenging exercises.

3.2.3 Bridging the gap—From blocks to text. To help campers adapt to a new programming environment, we designed the camp to help them bridge the gap between the Block Editor for micro:bits and Jupyter Notebooks, focusing less on syntactic differences and more on the consistency of algorithmic reasoning. We scheduled the transition early in the week so that campers would have more time to become comfortable with Python before beginning their final projects.

We first used the BlockPy[7] Web-based Python Block Editor to familiarize campers with Python [2]. BlockPy maintains the key infrastructure that we had covered with campers in the micro:bits, such as loops, variables, and conditionals, while introducing a split screen that displays Python code alongside the block programs. In introducing BlockPy, we had campers explore and compare the new interface to the old as they looked for pieces of code that would help them solve a multi-part word problem. This search allowed campers to reaffirm foundational computer science concepts and develop their deductive skills.

We implemented a review of BBC micro:bits in the middle of the week using the micro:bits Python Editor. During this activity,

[3]http://microbit.org/about/

[4]For reasons that we do not quite understand, the block language does not currently support subroutines.

[5]https://jupyter.org/documentation.html

[6]Many do not necessarily have access to their own computers. Those that receive computers from the local school district are not permitted install their own software. A cloud-based solution permits them to continue work in all situations.

[7]https://think.cs.vt.edu/blockpy/index/

Monday	Tuesday	Wednesday	Thursday	Friday
Camp Orientation Intro Algorithms *Icebreakers*	Simple Statistics Pair Programming I *Game Break* Python Syntax	Variables *Game Break* For-each loops	***Project Brainstorm*** *Scavenger Hunt*	***Project Work Time*** Visualization II *Game Break* ***Project Work Time***
		Lunch + Recess		
Intro micro:bits	Scavenger:bits Intro Jupyter	Lists Procedures	Data Frames II Visualization I ***Case Study*** ***Project Example***	Social Applications ***Work Time*** ***Presentation Prep***
		Snack Break		
Intro Conditionals Intro Data Science *Scavenger Hunt*	Intro Lists ***Intro Project***	*Scavenger Hunt* Dataframes I ***Project Prep***	***Project Work Time***	Welcome Visitors ***Presentations***

Table 1: Camp curriculum. "Away from keyboard" activities appear in italic and project activities appear in bold italic.

the campers were given documentation and example code so that they could code their micro:bits into compasses, radio communication devices, and more. Reexamining the capabilities of micro:bits gave campers an intermission from new material as well as the opportunity to get more hands-on experience with Python.

While three languages in one week may seem like a lot, we found the approach logical, campers progressed from a beginning block language that was straightforward but limited, through a more complex block language, and on to a professional tool. Because we tied ideas of each language to the next, and because pairs of language shared common characteristics, the transition seemed relatively smooth. In addition, our goal was not mastery, but exposure.

3.3 Final projects

Early on in designing curricula, we decided to end the week with a larger, more personally driven final project, which we titled "Final Findings" and introduced on the first day of camp. This project was intended to leave the campers with a tangible example of the skills they had acquired over the course of the camp and a way to connect to the material.

To enhance their sense of accomplishment, we concluded the camp with project presentations in which pairs of campers presented the data they chose to analyze, the significant data they discovered through calculations, and the visualizations that they programmed. After their hours of work on the data, campers readied their materials for presentation to others. We invited parents and community members[8] to those presentations, which were a highlight of the week. which We discuss the projects and presentations further below.

3.4 Organizing topics and days

In designing the camp, we considered both technical and more conceptual outcomes; in addition to teaching tools like loops and subroutines, we wanted campers to understand the power that comes with writing programs and to realize that they could write such programs. We had also identified a necessary set of skills for campers to complete the final projects in data science. As is the norm in designing such camps, we then considered the natural flow of ideas, reflecting on the transition from block-based languages to a text-based language and an appropriate spiral approach that helped campers revisit topics in different levels of depth.

While our primary focus was on computing topics, we knew from past experience that this age group would not learn well if they spent the day in front of the computer. Hence, the camp schedule incorporated frequent "away from computer" activities including short breaks to play active and engaging games. Snacks were offered during appropriate breaks before lunch.

Moving the activities away from the computer did not mean that we necessarily moved the campers away from thinking about core topics. For example, one the first day of camp we moved to an outdoor amphitheater to carry out the algorithms they had developed for reuniting families after a disaster. We also included CS Unplugged [3] activities to introduce Computer Science concepts in a fun and active environment. During afternoon breaks, we invited faculty and students in the Computer Science department to introduce campers to their research.

We also exposed campers to the broader view of ds4sg early and repeatedly. On many days, counselors presented a case study that integrated new concepts with social good data. For example, our second case study taught campers how to organize data about weather changes in a way that would allow them to analyze it in Python. Most of the last day was devoted to working on final projects, getting them ready to present to their friends and family.

Table 1 presents the curriculum for the second year of camp.

3.5 Extending the scavenger hunts

We have traditionally made scavenger hunts a key part of our camps. By exploring the science building, campers are exposed to a wide range of scientists and science, including both female scientists and scientists of color. When they explore the campus, they gain a sense of the resources associated with a typical college. One of our more successful scavenger hunts involves the campers taking "selfies" throughout the building. For example, *Take a picture of yourself with at least four women scientists, Take a picture of yourself with three pieces of safety equipment, Take a picture of yourself in a lab*

[8] An audience of roughly eighty people.

coat, and *Take a picture of yourself with the person this building is named for.*

For the second offering of the ds4sg camps, we enhanced two of the scavenger hunts with data problems. For one early scavenger hunt, which we termed Scavenger:bits, we tasked campers with recording data from throughout the science building. Students worked in teams to program the micro:bits to gather different kinds of data, raced off to gather the data, and then returned to record it. A second, campus-wide, scavenger hunt tasked the campers with using pre-programmed micro:bits to gather data at various locations across campus and then to process it when they returned.

The Scavenger:bits activity, which we offered on the second day of camp, exposed campers to the power of programming devices to gather data. It helped the campers transition into more serious programming efforts. It also helped the campers understand the power of crowd-sourcing and the potentials for inconsistent data. Since the campers entered the data in a common spreadsheet, they could see both the additional scope of data that are possible in crowdsourcing and also the variation that happens when different people gather what should be the same data.

4 LESSONS FROM YEAR ONE

The camp has evolved in many ways between the two years. The two data-enhanced scavenger activities described above are one such change. Another major change we made had to do with the data sets that campers used. In the 2017 camp, we asked campers to find their own data sets and convert them to CSV format. At the same time, we promised to finish any work they could not complete in a reasonable amount of time. In this endeavor, we were reminded of why many data science classes provide students with a limited menu of data sets: most groups of campers had difficulty locating data sets with appropriate and useful data, even armed with the searching and vetting tools we taught them. Most groups found this experience quite frustrating. Thus, counselors spent extra time finding data sets for some groups of campers as they had been unable to find suitable data themselves. Some groups also had to change their topics depending on the availability of the data that they intended to find. For example, a group interested in studying space debris ended up working with a data set on UFO sightings. Luckily, campers were gracious and willing to adapt to these changes and most tackled their new topics with vigor.

For the 2018 camp, we prepared a selected group of data sets for the campers to use, including data sets on animals (wildlife trade, threatened species), education, environment (carbon dioxide emission, earth surface temperature, food waste), equity & poverty (hate crimes, homelessness, multidimensional poverty, stop and frisk), politics, and broader society (public locations in our state, world happiness report, representation of LGBT people on broadcast television). The campers did not find these sets particularly limiting; most were able to tie their interests to one or more of the data sets. However, two groups decided to gather their own data (e.g., about their fellow campers' political leanings and opinions on particular data issues). The surveys also revealed to the class some of the risks of surveys; for example, since the surveys asked for age and sex, the campers could immediately identify which surveys belonged to the directors.[9] That provided an illustrative example of the responsibility of data scientists to consider the confidentiality of their subjects.

We also streamlined parts of the curriculum, limiting their exposure to micro:python, freeing time for deeper exposure to Jupyter.

In the first offering, we had assumed that campers would be excited by the micro:bits, and they were, enough so that many parents contacted us to find out how to get their own. However, the campers, by-and-large, told us that they were more excited by the work they did in Python and Jupyter Notebook. Although we can not pinpoint the precise reason, it seems that they felt like they were doing "real" programming when they were working in Jupyter because the environment they used matched that which working data scientists use. In contrast, our increased use of micro:bits for scavenger hunts in 2018 seems to have heightened student interest without diminishing their enthusiasm for Jupyter.

In the first offering, the rapid transition from block code to Python created syntactic confusion. Surprisingly, by spending less time on block code in 2018 and more on Python, we were able to better ease this transition. That is, rather than covering issues like loops and conditional deeply in the block language and then reintroducing them in Python, we covered only the basics in the block language and focused more strongly on them when we got to Python. Perhaps we should not have surprised about the difficulty campers had transitioning between languages. While there is an assumption that language transfer is natural, some studies have recently challenged that assumption (e.g., [1, 8]).

In the first offering, we gave campers relatively few guidelines for their presentations. Most used the features of Jupyter Notebook to develop presentations that mixed code, graphs, and text. Others hand-drew posters. And a few gave only oral presentations. During these presentations, the campers demonstrated knowledge and commitment to their topics, in addition to budding presentation skills. While there were some technical difficulties, such as a Jupyter notebook that would not load, the campers performed well and took setbacks in stride. However, some were clearly stressed by the openness of the choice, and too few showed off their programming skills; while a PowerPoint of charts can be compelling, it does not reveal the underlying work. Hence, for the 2018 camp, we asked campers to present from their Jupyter notebooks and provided tips for doing so. It was clear from audience reactions that the parents were surprised at the amount of code that the campers had written.

5 EXPLORING SHORT-TERM OUTCOMES

Thirty-eight (38) students enrolled in the camp in 2017[10] and twenty-five (25) students enrolled in 2018. Neither the length of the intervention nor the comparatively small n warranted a large-scale study.[11] Nonetheless, gathering some attitudinal data has shown value in the Georgia Computes! project [5] and we considered it equally useful to explore some short-term effects using a similar approach.

In order to measure the campers' short-term change in self-efficacy and coding confidence in a quantitative manner, we used

[9] Mr. Director, it appears you forgot to answer this question.

[10] That was a bit more than we planned for. But many campers showed up on the first day with a friend in tow.

[11] As Decker, McGill, and Settle suggest [9, 19], longitudinal studies are more appropriate to consider the long-term effects of such interventions.

1	*I look like a computer scientist.*
2	*Boys can do computing.*
3	*Girls can do computing.*
4	*I know a lot about computing.*
5	*I can become good at computing.*
6	*I know more than my friends about computers.*
7	*I like the challenge of computing.*
8	*Computer science is cool.*
9	*I feel comfortable using a computer.*
10	*I want to have a job in computing.*
11	*I want to learn more about computing.*
12	*Computer scientists are creative.*
13	*Solving problems is fun.*
14	*Computing is collaborative.*
14'	*Computing involves people working together.*
15	*I like computing.*

Figure 1: Survey statements

pre-camp and post-camp survey instruments based on upon the Georgia Computes! instruments [5] that ask students to respond to various statements, such as "I look like a computer scientist" and "I like the challenge of computing". For the 2017 camp, we used a seven-point Likert scale. Based on our experience from the 2017 camp, for the 2018 camp we revised the instrument to use a five-point Likert scale. The questions appear in Figure 1; Note that we changed question 14 in 2018 to provide more clarity for students.

In fourteen out of the fifteen questions on the 2017 survey, we saw an increase in the average response. Eight of those changes were statistically significant ($p < 0.05$). Notable positive changes (with t-test results far below the threshold of significance) occurred in the following questions: 1:*I look like a computer scientist*, which had a positive difference in average survey response of approximately .94 points, 4:*I know a lot about computing*, which had a positive difference of approximately 1.2 points, and 6:*I know more than my friends about computers*, with a positive difference of 1 point. It seems that campers, although somewhat apprehensive of their own potential at the start of the project, found themselves more sure of their abilities, not only in comparison with their peers outside of the project, but also as independent thinkers.

In the 2018 data, we also saw especially significant short-term growth ($p < 0.01$) in questions 1, 4, and 6. This year, we also saw similarly significant growth ($p < 0.01$) in question 14:*Computing involves people working together*[12] and 15:*I like computing*.

A few trends appeared when looking at the pre-camp and post-camp averages for female campers versus the averages for male campers in the 2017 data. In both pre-camp and post-camp surveys, female campers tended to have a larger increase in self-efficacy than the male campers. This intuition is supported in the case of questions 2:*Boys can do computing*, 3:*Girls can do computing*, 7:*I like the challenge of computing*, 9:*I feel comfortable using a computer*, 10:*I want to have a job in computing*, and 14:*Computing is collaborative*, where the change in the female campers' responses yielded significant results ($p < 0.05$) and the change in male campers' responses did not ($p > 0.05$). Only in question 5 did the male campers' difference in average response yield a significant change while the female campers' responses did not.

It seems that the curricula of this project had a more significant short-term effect on our female campers, which is in keeping with Goldweber *et al.*'s analysis [15]. The only negative difference in averages in the female campers' responses was with question 11:*I want to learn more about computing*, which, although discouraging to note, did not yield significant results when running a two-tail t-test (null hypothesis, $p < 0.01$).

These initial results suggest that, at least for the short term, we have and fulfilled our intent to make the concepts of computer science more accessible to youth who perhaps do not identify with the statement "I look like a computer scientist". The even more significant increase in confidence in our female campers is an especially encouraging outcome. Our results give us hope that the campers left inspired, and may collaborate with peers outside of the project to continue their education in computer science.

[12]It appears our choice of wording was important!

6 CONCLUSION

Although many middle-school outreach activities focus on students' perceived interests, such as video games or "exciting" technologies, our experiences suggest that computing for social good provides a platform for helping students grow in self-efficacy and interest.

As the assessment suggests, the camp was generally successful in making a positive short-term difference in students' sense of who can "do" computing and in their own self-efficacy and interest. While we were saddened to see that the female campers often began the camp with lower responses on most questions, we were encouraged to see their gains as higher than the male campers'.

The projects were central to the success of the camp and they provided some of the greatest benefits. As campers gained familiarity with data science tools, they became more comfortable with the idea of a final project on a subject of their choosing.

We have also found that while campers can be intimidated by a text-based programming language and a professional programming environment, they also feel empowered and gain additional self-efficacy in using such an environment. Our informal conversations with the campers suggest that the approach is worth investigating further. Resources from the camp, including curriculum, instructor guides, and presentations are available at https://codecamp.sites.grinnell.edu/dataforsocialgood/.

ACKNOWLEDGMENTS

We are grateful to the Grinnell Innovation Fund and the Grinnell Student-Faculty Research Fund for providing the resources to offer this camp at low or no cost to our campers. The Roy J. Carver Charitable Trust supported a broader Data Science initiative at Grinnell. Our IRB provided useful feedback on the instrument and the project. Our fellow students graciously spoke with the campers about their research projects. Professor Ursula Wolz provided us with advice about ways to approach teaching this age group and Professor Shonda Kuiper in statistics provided feedback on our approach to data science. Dr. Narren Brown supported the design of our instrument. Counselors Elise Brod, Gabby Dahlby Albright, David Kreis, Hans Larsson, and Jonathan B. Rebelsky provided necessary support for this project; we know it's hard to support someone else's curriculum, and they did a great job. Finally, we appreciate the enthusiastic participation of our campers!

REFERENCES

[1] Glenda Barlow-Jones and Jacqui Chetty. 2012. Bridging the Gap: the Role of Mediated Transfer for Computer Programming. , 5 pages.

[2] Austin Cory Bart and Dennis Kafura. 2017. BlockPy Interactive Demo: Dual Text/Block Python Programming Environment for Guided Practice and Data Science (Abstract Only). In *Proceedings of the 2017 ACM SIGCSE Technical Symposium on Computer Science Education (SIGCSE '17)*. ACM, New York, NY, USA, 639–640. https://doi.org/10.1145/3017680.3022383

[3] Tim Bell, Ian Witten, Michael Fellows, Robyn Adams, Jane McKenzie, Matt Powell, and Sam Jarman. 2015. *CS Unplugged: An Enrichment and Extension Programme for Primary-Aged Students*. csunplugged.org.

[4] Francine D. Berman and Philip E. Bourne. 2015. Let's Make Gender Diversity in Data Science a Priority Right from the Start. *PLOS Biology* 13, 7 (07 2015), 1–5. https://doi.org/10.1371/journal.pbio.1002206

[5] Amy Bruckman, Maureen Biggers, Barbara Ericson, Tom McKlin, Jill Dimond, Betsy DiSalvo, Mike Hewner, Lijun Ni, and Sarita Yardi. 2009. "Georgia Computes!": Improving the Computing Education Pipeline. *SIGCSE Bull.* 41, 1 (March 2009), 86–90. https://doi.org/10.1145/1539024.1508899

[6] Caelin Bryant, Jonathan Gilmour, Beatriz Herce-Hagiwara, Anh Thu Pham, Halle Remash, Marli Remash, Jonah Zimmerman, Sarah Dahlby Albright, and Samuel A. Rebelsky. 2018. A Middle-School Code Camp Experience Emphasizing Data Science for Social Good: (Abstract Only). In *Proceedings of the 49th ACM Technical Symposium on Computer Science Education (SIGCSE '18)*. ACM, New York, NY, USA, 1088–1088. https://doi.org/10.1145/3159450.3162313

[7] Sapna Cheryan and Victoria C. Plaut. 2010. Explaining Underrepresentation: A Theory of Precluded Interest. *Sex Roles* 63, 7 (01 Oct 2010), 475–488. https://doi.org/10.1007/s11199-010-9835-x

[8] Wanda Dann, Dennis Cosgrove, Don Slater, Dave Culyba, and Steve Cooper. 2012. Mediated Transfer: Alice 3 to Java. In *Proceedings of the 43rd ACM Technical Symposium on Computer Science Education (SIGCSE '12)*. ACM, New York, NY, USA, 141–146. https://doi.org/10.1145/2157136.2157180

[9] Adrienne Decker, Monica M. McGill, and Amber Settle. 2016. Towards a Common Framework for Evaluating Computing Outreach Activities. In *Proceedings of the 47th ACM Technical Symposium on Computing Science Education (SIGCSE '16)*. ACM, New York, NY, USA, 627–632. https://doi.org/10.1145/2839509.2844567

[10] Anita DeWitt, Julia Fay, Madeleine Goldman, Eleanor Nicolson, Linda Oyolu, Lukas Resch, Jovan Martinez Saldaña, Soulideth Sounalath, Tyler Williams, Kathryn Yetter, Elizabeth Zak, Narren Brown, and Samuel A. Rebelsky. 2017. Arts Coding for Social Good: A Pilot Project for Middle-School Outreach. In *Proceedings of the 2017 ACM SIGCSE Technical Symposium on Computer Science Education (SIGCSE '17)*. ACM, New York, NY, USA, 159–164. https://doi.org/10.1145/3017680.3017795

[11] Anita DeWitt, Julia Fay, Madeleine Goldman, Eleanor Nicolson, Linda Oyolu, Lukas Resch, Jovan Martinez Saldaña, Soulideth Sounalath, Tyler Williams, Kathryn Yetter, Elizabeth Zak, Narren Brown, and Samuel A. Rebelsky. 2017. What We Say vs. What They Do: A Comparison of Middle-School Coding Camps in the CS Education Literature and Mainstream Coding Camps (Abstract Only). In *Proceedings of the 2017 ACM SIGCSE Technical Symposium on Computer Science Education (SIGCSE '17)*. ACM, New York, NY, USA, 707–707. https://doi.org/10.1145/3017680.3022434

[12] Michael Goldweber. 2012. A Day One Computing for the Social Good Activity. *ACM Inroads* 3, 3 (Sept. 2012), 46–49. https://doi.org/10.1145/2339055.2339071

[13] Michael Goldweber. 2015. Computer Science Education for Social Good. *SIGCAS Comput. Soc.* 45, 2 (July 2015), 29–30. https://doi.org/10.1145/2809957.2809963

[14] Michael Goldweber. 2018. Strategies for Adopting CSG-Ed In CS 1. In *Proceedings of the 3rd Conference for Research on Equity and Sustained Participation in Engineering, Computing, and Technology (RESPECT '18)*.

[15] Michael Goldweber, John Barr, Tony Clear, Renzo Davoli, Samuel Mann, Elizabeth Patitsas, and Scott Portnoff. 2013. A Framework for Enhancing the Social Good in Computing Education: A Values Approach. *ACM Inroads* 4, 1 (March 2013), 58–79. https://doi.org/10.1145/2432596.2432616

[16] Philip Guo. 2014. Python is Now the Most Popular Introductory Teaching Language at Top U.S. Universities. *Commun. ACM BLOG* (2014).

[17] Denise Gürer and Tracy Camp. 2002. An ACM-W Literature Review on Women in Computing. *SIGCSE Bull.* 34, 2 (June 2002), 121–127. https://doi.org/10.1145/543812.543844

[18] Mark Guzdial. 2009. Education: Teaching Computing to Everyone. *Commun. ACM* 52, 5 (May 2009), 31–33. https://doi.org/10.1145/1506409.1506420

[19] Monica M. McGill, Adrienne Decker, and Amber Settle. 2015. Does Outreach Impact Choices of Major for Underrepresented Undergraduate Students?. In *Proceedings of the Eleventh Annual International Conference on International Computing Education Research (ICER '15)*. ACM, New York, NY, USA, 71–80. https://doi.org/10.1145/2787622.2787711

[20] Stuart Zweben and Betsy Bizot. 2017. 2016 Taulbee Survey. *Computing Research News* 29, 5 (5 2017).

Podcast Highlights: Targeted Educational Videos From Repurposed Lecture-capture Footage

Mia Minnes
UC San Diego
minnes@eng.ucsd.edu

Christine Alvarado
UC San Diego
cjalvarado@eng.ucsd.edu

Max Geislinger
UC San Diego
mgeislin@ucsd.edu

Joyce Fang
UC San Diego
jofang@ucsd.edu

ABSTRACT

Using instructional videos—either as supplemental content or in a flipped classroom—has become increasingly popular among students and instructors in higher education CS courses. However, producing or finding appropriate videos can be expensive and time-consuming. This experience report describes a novel, relatively low-cost approach to creating customized video resources that requires very little instructor time. This approach leverages widely available screen capture and podcasting technologies to produce a suite of 2-5 minute "podcast highlights" videos from full-length live lecture footage. Podcast highlights distill lecture concepts into short segments, and supplementary annotations help illustrate these concepts further. Podcast highlights can be created quickly by undergraduates with just a small amount of instructor supervision. We created podcast highlights videos for four undergraduate CS courses. In a pilot study with two of these classes, many students used the highlights videos regularly and praised their usefulness for both previewing and reviewing class concepts. This report presents the podcast highlights production process, student reaction to and use of podcast highlights videos, and best practices for creation and deployment of these customized educational videos.

CCS CONCEPTS

• **Social and professional topics** → **Computer science education**;

KEYWORDS

Pedagogical videos, CS education

ACM Reference Format:

Mia Minnes, Christine Alvarado, Max Geislinger, and Joyce Fang. 2019. Podcast Highlights: Targeted Educational Videos From Repurposed Lecture-capture Footage. In *Proceedings of the 50th ACM Technical Symposium on Computer Science Education (SIGCSE '19), February 27-March 2, 2019, Minneapolis, MN, USA.* ACM, New York, NY, USA, 7 pages. https://doi.org/10.1145/3287324.3287465

SIGCSE '19, February 27-March 2, 2019, Minneapolis, MN, USA

ACM ISBN 978-1-4503-5890-3/19/02...$15.00
https://doi.org/10.1145/3287324.3287465

1 INTRODUCTION

Over the last decade, videos have become pervasive in computer science (CS) education. From YouTube, to Khan Academy, to MOOC providers like EdX and Coursera, educational videos are clearly now a permanent part of the CS online education landscape. These generally available online videos resources can also be used to supplement in-person classes. However, especially in a field like computer science where there is a wide range of languages, examples, and even terminology, sourcing videos that match the specific content in a course is critical to students' learning, but can be challenging for instructors and students alike.

In part as a response to this challenge, many instructors turn to the production of videos more targeted to their specific course. One low-overhead example of such videos are lecture capture podcasts that allow students (and the public) to (re)watch class sessions soon after they are held. This lecture capture technology is supported at many large universities, and does not require any involvement from the instructor, other than teaching their class and perhaps wearing a microphone. Lecture capture videos are popular with students, alleviating the stress of note taking and providing a backup in case of missed classes [12, 13, 17, 19].

Some instructors, particularly those "flipping" their classrooms, produce custom, short, targeted videos. Students watch these videos (and usually complete a low-stakes assignment based on the videos) before class, and then work on interactive exercises in class. Such flipped classrooms have had promising results in CS learning [3]. A barrier to adopting this pedagogical approach, however, is the high cost of producing materials [11]. For example, at our institution, the studio production cost for a custom one-person educational video is about $30 per finished minute, and it takes about 2 weeks to film and edit a video [16]. Moreover, these figures do not include the cost of the instructor time required to plan and record the video, or to add additional annotations and edits that the studio team (who are not content experts) do not know to add.

In this experience report, we present an approach to leveraging lecture capture footage to create high-quality, customized, relatively low-cost videos appropriate for use in a flipped classroom or as supplementary resources for students. Instead of producing videos in a studio or even from scratch, we started with footage from full lecture-capture videos in four core CS classes. We edited and annotated this footage to produce a curated collection of "podcast highlights" videos for each course. The editing of full-length lectures to 2-5 minute highlights was done mostly by students, with light supervision by the instructor.

The podcast highlights from two of the four courses were offered as supplementary resources in two core CS classes in Fall 2017. Student feedback and analysis of usage patterns indicate that these podcast highlights were popular, with students watching the videos for many reasons including preparing for class and for exams.

While the videos themselves will be useful to us for many years, the contribution of this experience report is not the videos themselves. Rather, the two main contributions of this report are: (1) the podcast highlights approach to video production and (2) an understanding of student use-patterns and responses to these highlights videos. This experience report presents our production process, students' reactions to and use of podcast highlights videos, and best practices for production and deployment based on our experiences and data collected.

2 RELATED WORK

Studies on the use of lecture podcasts consistently find that students are happy to have these podcasts and that the availability of lecture videos has positive or neutral impacts on student learning. Many students (and instructors) report believing that lecture capture improves learning [12, 17]. Carle et al. compared two sections of an undergraduate course and found that students in the podcasting section were more engaged and did better [4]. Yet, other studies have found little to no difference in performance between students with access to podcasts and those without [1, 15, 17, 18].

The reality of whether lecture podcasts help students' performance is likely more nuanced, depending on the type of course and the ways in which students use the video resource. Danielson et al. found that podcasting was related to higher performance in courses that relied more heavily on lecture and were more science research focused, and that there was no significant relationship between podcasting and student performance for courses that relied less heavily on lecture and were more focused on science applications [6].

Giannakos et al. [10] and Brooks et al. [2] studied the qualitatively different use patterns in the ways students use lecture capture. Brooks et al. found that students who used lecture capture consistently throughout the term performed better than other patterns of use, including using lecture capture in a just-in-time fashion to study for exams. Heilensen's 2010 meta-study [13] on the learning outcomes of podcasting found that the most useful aspect of podcasting is to review portions of the lecture, and that students consider podcasts more reliable than their own notes. The 2015 meta-study by Witthaus and Robinson observed that students rarely use lecture capture videos to simply re-watch complete lectures, but instead "view specific sections of recordings to reinforce their understanding of concepts" [19]. In fact some studies have found that students who do re-watch complete lectures tend to perform worse [19]. This mismatch between the format of lecture capture and students' desired use is in part what motivates the work we present in this experience report.

In many of these studies, the availability of lecture capture videos did not seem to lower students' attendance in class [5, 14, 18]. However, there is recent evidence in the other direction: Edwards and Clinton found that the availability of lecture capture videos significantly reduced class attendance [9]. Dobkin et al. [8] demonstrates the value of class attendance, especially for students in the bottom half of the class. We conjecture that students are less likely to think of podcast highlights videos as class-replacements as compared to lecture capture footage. Replacing live footage with these video snippets may therefore mitigate concerns about dropping attendance rates while retaining the benefits of local, customized video resources for students.

Moreover, once podcast highlights videos are created, they can facilitate pedagogical practices such as flipping the classroom. Flipped classrooms have been shown to have positive learning outcomes both in CS [3] and in other disciplines [7, 11]. In a 2014 meta-study of research on flipped classrooms, Giannakos et al. highlights the recurring challenge of producing high-quality pre-class materials [11]. The relative ease of producing podcast highlights (as compared to creating videos from scratch) may help address this barrier to adoption of the flipped classroom pedagogy.

3 PODCAST HIGHLIGHTS CREATION

The core of the podcast highlights approach is the footage captured from regular in-person classes. At our institution, 125 classrooms are outfitted with lecture capture technology which records the content shown on the projector (slides, digital ink, live coding, etc.) as well as audio from a wireless microphone worn by the instructor. In the 2017-2018 academic year, over 17000 hours of footage were recorded, with viewership over 370000 hours [16].

We started with footage from courses two of the authors had taught in recent terms. This footage is archived on our campus servers and was readily available for download. The production of the podcast highlight videos was done by undergraduates who had previously taken the course, working under the lightweight supervision of the instructor of the course. The students used the class syllabus, class notes, and their own experiences to identify the most important and/or difficult topics in each course. They then matched these topics to explanations and examples presented in the full-length lecture podcast. Each explanation or example was extracted using video editing software (Camtasia). The students then enhanced the videos by adding call-outs, highlighting, simple post-production animations, and zooming. For example, in a code-tracing example, an animated marker directs viewers' attention to the current line being executed and a memory model displays variable values as they are updated.

The production process was piloted with a Basic Data Structures class (DS) and a Discrete Math (DM) class in summer 2017. A team of two students worked on video creation for each course, working on average ten hours per week for ten weeks. Both teams and the two instructors met weekly to review drafts of the videos, discuss editing best practices, and prioritize topics for video creation. Topics that are typically challenging for students received extra attention: for example, in the Discrete Math class six out of the 36 videos focus on induction; in the Data Structures class six out of the 51 videos discuss aspects of running time analysis. Table 1 summarizes the videos created for each class. This table includes videos created for two additional classes that were added to the project after initial deployment of the videos showed promising results. These additional classes were Introductory Programming (CS1) and Theory of Computation (Theory); video production is ongoing for the Theory class.

Table 1: Summary of podcast highlights videos created

	CS1	DS	DM	Theory
Number of videos	34	51	36	10 (so far)
Average duration	2:31	2:39	3:13	2:06
Total duration	1:25:18	1:54:25	1:43:12	0:21:00 (so far)

The time (and cost) to produce the podcast highlights videos was significantly less than it would have been to produce videos from scratch, particularly from the perspective of the instructor. In the pilot summer, the undergraduate person-time to produce 1 minute of finished video was about 110 minutes, while instructor person-time per minute of finished video was only about 5 minutes. This undergraduate time includes a significant startup cost. Once students became comfortable with the video editing software and process their speed increased considerably. Moreover, the students producing the videos received many educational benefits: they not only more deeply learned the course material but also learned how to present that material in an educationally beneficial way. Thus, depending on student preference and department budget, the work done by the student editors could be for pay and/or for credit.

4 PODCAST HIGHLIGHTS DEPLOYMENT

In Fall 2017, we deployed podcast highlights videos for Discrete Math and Data Structures as supplementary resources. Full-length lecture podcasts from the current quarter were also available to students in each course. Each course was taught by the instructor featured in the respective podcast highlights. Both courses are large lower-division courses required of CS-related majors. Our institution uses 10-week academic terms (plus a finals week).

Students in each course had two ways to access the podcast highlights videos: (1) students could access them via the same special-purpose campus video hosting website where they access the full-length lecture podcasts; (2) students could access the podcast highlights videos through each course's website. Each podcast highlights video was associated with a specific lecture or topic in the class and the link to the corresponding podcast highlight(s) was featured on the class website. In Data Structures, the videos were linked immediately next to all information about the week in the class calendar. In Discrete Math, the videos were categorized by week and displayed in a section of the homepage devoted to supplementary material and extra practice problems.

The podcast highlights were primarily used as an optional resource in both courses. Students in the Data Structures courses were assigned some podcast highlights videos as pre-class work in the second, third and fifth weeks of the course. No videos were assigned as required viewing in Discrete Math.

5 EVALUATION

We studied student use of and reaction to the podcast highlights videos in the two pilot courses. Following an IRB-approved protocol, we collected data in the form of (1) usage metrics of the online videos, (2) student performance in class assessments, and (3) opinion surveys of students about the perceived usefulness of the videos. The anonymized data were analyzed to explore the following questions:

- What were students' perceptions of podcast highlights videos?
- What were the usage patterns of podcast highlights videos (frequency, intensity, timing)?
- Was there correlation between these patterns and student performance in the class?

We include in our analysis only those students who received a grade in each course and did not opt out of the study. This group includes 326 students in the Data Structures class (3 opted out) and 250 students in the Discrete Math class (2 opted out). Of these students, 282 completed the end of course survey in Data Structures (86.5%) and 234 completed the survey in Discrete Math (93.6%).

Table 2: Self-reported use of video resources in two pilot classes: Data Structures (n = 282) and Discrete Math (n = 234)

	Never	Rarely	Occasionally	Frequently
Data Structures				
Podcast Highlights	7%	17%	37%	39%
Lecture Capture	7%	9%	34%	50%
Discrete Math				
Podcast Highlights	24%	22%	27%	27%
Lecture Capture	7%	13%	38%	42%

5.1 Student reactions to podcast highlights

Overall, students reacted positively to the podcast highlights videos, finding them useful for a variety of purposes. First, a significant number of students in both classes reported using them. Table 2 shows the self-reported use in each course of the podcast highlights and the full lecture capture videos. Podcast highlights were slightly less heavily used than full lecture podcasts in both courses and less heavily used in Discrete Math than in Data Structures. We discuss possible reasons for these differences in Subsection 6.3.

Students reported using podcast highlights videos for many reasons, which both overlapped with and complemented their reasons for watching the full lecture podcasts. Table 3 gives the percent of survey respondents who selected each of a set of possible reasons for using podcast highlights and full lecture podcasts; These possible reasons were given in the survey question, and students were invited to "select all that apply", so columns do not sum to 100. In addition to selecting from a list of possible reasons, students could write in a free-response reply. These free-responses included "had time", "[wanted to] Learn as much as possible" and other similar comments; these responses are aggregated in the last row of Table 3. While podcast highlights were often used for similar purposes as full lecture podcasts, they were not as popular for catching up on material from a missed class, likely because students were (rightfully) concerned about what else they had missed. In fact, podcast highlights videos were popular for preparing *before* material was covered in class. Full lecture capture videos could not be used for this purpose because they are recordings of the live class and thus only available after each class session.

Table 3: Percent of student survey respondents agreeing with specific reasons for using video resources in two pilot classes.

	DS Lecture (n = 265)	DS Highlights (n = 251)	DM Lecture (n = 214)	DM Highlights (n = 175)
To prepare before the material was covered in class	N/A	54.2	N/A	34.9
Because some of the material went too fast for me in class	42.1	31.5	52.8	46.9
Because I did not attend the corresponding class	64.4	22.7	50.5	25.1
To get information helpful to complete the homework	64.0	60.6	65.9	61.1
To study for the exam	59.8	51.4	61.68	57.7
Other	23.5	28.3	25.23	24.6

The survey also invited students to give open-ended feedback on the podcast highlights. The response rates for this question were lower, with 52 responses in the Data Structures class and 25 responses in the Discrete Math class. These responses reveal both enthusiasm for this resource, as well as some subtleties to using podcast highlights effectively.

In many cases (51% of DS comments and 16% of DM comments), student enthusiasm was short and vague, such as "Great" or "I like them." Other comments praised specific aspects of the podcast highlights. Six DS students commented positively on the short length of the videos, for example:

> I really like how the highlights condense important topics into short, digestible videos.

Three DS students and one DM student praised their utility in preparing for class. One DM student wrote:

> I think the podcast highlights are extremely beneficial in targeting which concepts to pay extra attention to.

Other students (two DM students and three DS students) praised the value of the highlights videos for reviewing class material. For example, a DS student wrote

> I liked how concise and information packed they were with a detailed example (typically), made it a lot easier to translate to the actual homework when writing one's own implementation and made it a lot easier to understand conceptually when preparing for exams.

Students also had some suggestions for how to improve the videos. A few students felt the videos were confusing or "too short." One student in each class observed that broken links to some of the podcast highlights videos discouraged them from fully utilizing the resource. A DM student suggested that captions be added to videos (which we plan to do). Another DM student asked for additional podcast highlights videos to be made, particularly on topics that are not covered as thoroughly in the class textbook. Finally, one DS student disliked that the highlights were separate from the full lecture podcasts and suggested that it would be more useful to simply have timestamps of "highlights" portions within the current term's full lecture podcasts. While this might be desirable, we note that it would be impractical to have a team of video editors create these time stamp annotations in real time during the current term.

It was also clear from student comments that the way podcast highlights were made available to students had a big impact on their perceived (and perhaps actual) utility, and that not all students fully recognized the podcast highlights as a resource. In 10% of DS and 44% of the DM comments, students conflated podcast highlights videos with full lecture capture podcasts. The details mentioned in these comments make it clear that students were describing the current quarter's full lecture capture footage rather than the highlights videos.

5.2 Podcast highlights usage patterns

To complement students' self-reported reactions, we analyzed when, how much, and by how many students the podcast highlights were actually used in the two courses of the pilot study.

We started by examining how many students watched each podcast highlight. In the DS class, each podcast highlights video was watched by between 48 and 210 distinct students (18% to 64% of the class), with a median of 98 students (30% of the class). In the DM class, the range was 8 to 130 students (3% to 52% of the class), with a median of 35 students (14% of the class). Across both classes we found four highlights videos that received zero views. In the DS class, the single highlights video with no views was not properly linked from the class website. In the DM class, one video was not properly linked while two others were on topics either not covered that quarter or covered fully by other highlights videos.

The topics of the five videos watched by the greatest number of students in each course are given in Table 4. Popular highlights topics in each class included topics that were challenging, and examples that would help students complete their assignments. In the DM class, the most popular podcast highlights video corresponded to a day when the professor was out of town and had another professor fill in during lecture.

Not surprisingly, videos that were explicitly assigned were watched by more students than those that were simply provided as a resource. For the DS course, the 11 videos watched by the most students were all assigned for pre-class viewing. Even though students had to complete short pre-class assignments based on the "required" videos, these videos were at best watched by 64% of the students. It is possible students watched these videos in a group (and hence their views were not logged), but this finding is also consistent with our anecdotal evidence from previous classes. For low-stakes pre-class assignments, some students either simply guess until they get (mostly) right answers or get the answers from others in the class.

In both classes we see that one of the most popular videos was early in the course, likely because students were trying out this new resource. Videos well into the middle of the course were popular in both classes. With the exception of the week 9 videos in DM, videos toward the end of the course were viewed by fewer students.

Table 4: Topics of the 5 most watched highlights videos in each course (both assigned and non-assigned in DS) including the number of unique students who viewed the video and the week the topic was covered.

Topic	# Stud.	Week
Data Structures (overall) (n = 326)		
Iterators, overview *(as.)*	210	2
Type parameters *(as.)*	191	1
Priority Queues, Intro *(as.)*	168	5
Priority Queues, Implementation *(as.)*	163	5
Java Wildcards *(as.)*	142	5
Data Structures (non-assigned) (n = 326)		
Big O	118	4
Big Theta	117	4
Calculating Big O from code	115	4
Big Omega	115	4
Hashtable running time	114	4
Discrete Math (n = 250)		
Contrapositive proof example	130	4
Greedy Alg. example	100	1
Relations on a set	76	9
Relations example	73	9
Direct proof example	56	4

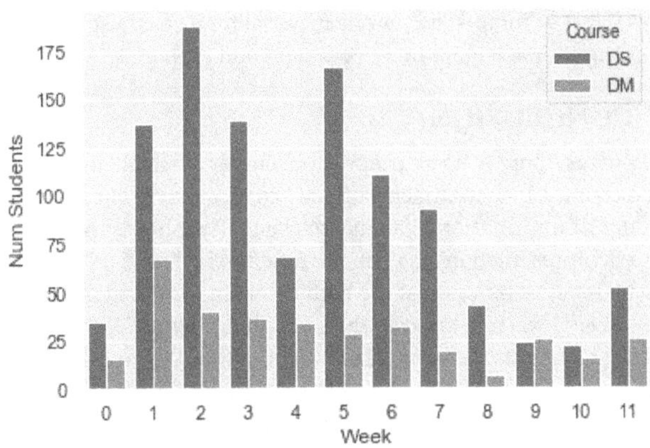

Figure 1: The number of unique students who watched any podcast video during each week of the course. Week 0 is a half-week at the start of term; week 11 is finals week.

This trend is likely related to the fact that the number of students who accessed any podcast highlights video (on any topic) during a particular week in the course dropped throughout the quarter, with a slight upturn during finals week, as shown in Figure 1.

The peaks in Figure 1 are lower than the numbers reported in Table 4, indicating that students watched the podcast highlights videos over a relatively spread out period, rather than immediately when the corresponding topic was covered in class. When we examined usage patterns for individual videos, we found that many views came several days or even weeks after the topic was covered.

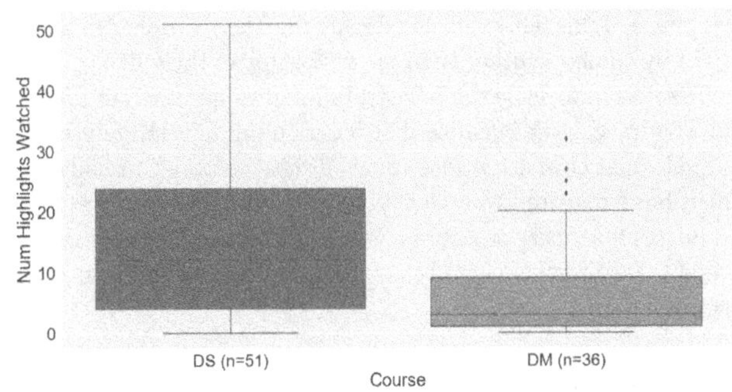

Figure 2: The distribution of the number of highlights videos viewed by students in each course.

This delay is likely due to students using the highlights videos to help with their homework or to review for the exams. Indeed, our finer-grained daily analysis of when students accessed podcast highlights (not shown here due to space limitations) revealed peaks before homework due dates and exam dates.

Figure 2 shows the distribution of the number of podcast highlights videos watched by each student in each course. In the DS course, students watched a median of 12 highlights videos (24% of the total available videos) while in the DM course they watched a median of 3 (8% of the total available videos). In both classes, the median is low but the distribution has a long tail with several outliers on the high end. Many students in each course watched most or all of the highlights videos.

5.3 Podcast highlights and class performance

We examined podcast highlights' use in comparison to class performance, and found no clear relationship between the number of podcast highlights viewed and a student's performance in the course. This was not a controlled study; podcast highlights were made available to all students, and all students were equally encouraged to use them. Future work might compare student performance when podcast highlights are assigned in different ways and examine the possible effects on subgroups of the class.

6 DISCUSSION

6.1 Benefits of podcast highlights

We found that highly customized videos featuring local instructors resonated with students. The advantage of the podcast highlights paradigm is that any school can adopt this strategy to answer the needs that are known best to those teaching there. For example, if the introductory programming courses are taught in a particular language and the data structures course switches to a new language, the podcast highlights videos would naturally address issues that come from switching programming languages.

Our students responded positively to having videos that featured their own instructors. For example, the DM podcast highlight that was watched by the most students was one covering material that had been taught by a substitute lecturer while the instructor was away. But creating separate collections of podcast highlights videos for each instructor who teaches a core course is impractical. In the next phase of this work, we will deploy the Theory videos in a class taught by someone other than the instructor in the video.

We selected to scale the podcast highlights approach to the CS1 and Theory classes because their curriculum is relatively stable. Foundational courses whose topics don't "go stale" quickly and which have matured to a steady state at an institution are great candidates for this approach: they will likely have the raw material available for the videos, and the videos will be useful for multiple terms to come.

6.2 Production best practices

Students who have recently taken the course are often attuned to which concepts were particularly challenging. An essential feature of this project was recruiting such students to do most of the heavy lifting in the video editing process. We found that the most effective student editors were not necessarily the A+ students; rather, they were students who were reflective about their own learning process and could articulate the common learning breakdowns in the course. One of the most common errors the novice editors made was to try to cram too much content in each video. A short sprint / review cycle where the instructors review rough drafts of videos helped diagnose such problems early and fix them by dividing out videos so each became short and focused.

As the team size grew and as the number of videos produced increased we found that a carefully described style guide helped the podcast highlights videos retain a cohesive look and message. A minimalist palette of text annotations, callout boxes, highlighting, and animations enriched the existing video content while effectively communicating to viewers how to interpret each piece of the video.

The most popular podcast highlights videos addressed more theoretical topics in the DS and DM classes: runtime analysis and proof strategies. For both of these, the students tended to watch videos that worked through examples. One reason for this trend may be that students have fewer opportunities for real-time feedback when working through theoretical concepts: there is no compiler or autograder they can run to certify their work is correct. Seeing detailed examples that relate closely to homework assignments may build student confidence in their own solutions.

The premise of the podcast highlights video initiative relies on the availability of lecture-capture footage. Many, but not all, universities have invested in technology to record this footage in real-time. Instructors without access to built in lecture-capture technology may effectively substitute their own recordings, such as screencasting, along with a voice recorder. Video editing software could then be used to overlay the audio over the video file.

6.3 Deployment best practices

As with most pedagogical resources, the ways in which podcast highlights are deployed appear to have a substantial effect on whether and how students use them. Based on our observations in the pilot classes, we propose the following as best practices:

- Teach students how you expect that they will use the podcast highlights videos. In particular, describe how these videos promote their learning differently from other class resources. Encourage students to watch podcast highlights videos to *preview* concepts before class, ideally incentivizing this behavior by assigning it for some form of class credit.
- Make the podcast highlights videos easy to find: promote them clearly on your website, preferably next to lecture slides, readings, and other frequently updated resources. Embed links in homework assignments when possible.
- Organize the podcast highlights videos for easy indexing. Make sure videos have appropriate and useful titles, and denote those videos that have complete solved examples.

6.4 Use of videos by students not in the class

Making podcast highlights videos publicly available contributes to our institution's general education outreach mission. It may also directly benefit students on our campus that are not currently enrolled in the classes for which videos are created. For example, many of our students transfer to our institution from community colleges after completing their lower division courses. They will need to take courses that rely on Data Structures and Discrete Math, for example, as prerequisites. By watching the podcast highlights videos, these students can efficiently review key concepts and acquaint themselves with local terminology and norms. Similarly, these videos can serve students who take breaks between successive courses in a sequence by acting as a refresher to improve readiness immediately before the post-requisite classes.

On the other end of the spectrum, the podcast highlights videos can be useful as a quick overview of a course *before* a student enrolls as well. Students, particularly those with less experience, often seek ways to get a "jump-start" on the material for a course so that they enter the course feeling more confident and prepared.

7 CONCLUSION

These days, there is no shortage of resources available to students in CS courses. In fact, students often become overwhelmed with the amount of information available to them. The podcast highlights approach presented in this paper can help distill this information into targeted resources that are both contextualized and focused, at a relatively low (time) cost to the course instructor. We found that podcast highlights videos were used for many of the same beneficial purposes as full lecture podcasts (e.g. studying for exams, helping with homework). On the other hand, they were not often used as a replacement for lecture, making it unlikely that the availability of podcast highlights alone would tempt students to skip class.

Podcast highlights were received positively by students, and we believe we have only begun to explore their potential as a supplementary, assigned, or targeted educational resource. Podcast highlights videos give an example where "less may be more" when it comes to aids for student learning, and may help students focus their attention and precious study time.

8 ACKNOWLEDGEMENTS

The podcast highlights initiative was supported by a UC San Diego Course Development and Instructional Improvement award. We also thank our undergraduate student teams who worked on video production: Hasan Al-Jamaly, Farhood Ensan, Julia Kapich, Nina Rothenhaus, Serena Shi, Alex Staninger, Anagha Subramanian, Yu Wu, and Jeffrey Yeung.

REFERENCES

[1] Grant Abt and Tim Barry. 2007. The Quantitative Effect of Students Using Podcasts in a First Year Undergraduate Exercise Physiology Module. *Bioscience Education* 10, 1 (2007), 1–9. https://doi.org/10.3108/beej.10.8 arXiv:https://doi.org/10.3108/beej.10.8

[2] Christopher Brooks, Graham Erickson, Jim Greer, and Carl Gutwin. 2014. Modelling and quantifying the behaviours of students in lecture capture environments. *Computers & Education* 75 (2014), 282 – 292. https://doi.org/10.1016/j.compedu.2014.03.002

[3] Jennifer Campbell, Diane Horton, Michelle Craig, and Paul Gries. 2014. Evaluating an Inverted CS1. In *Proceedings of the 45th ACM Technical Symposium on Computer Science Education (SIGCSE '14)*. ACM, New York, NY, USA, 307–312. https://doi.org/10.1145/2538862.2538943

[4] Adam C. Carle, David Jaffee, and Deborah Miller. 2009. Engaging college science students and changing academic achievement with technology: A quasi-experimental preliminary investigation. *Computers & Education* 52, 2 (2009), 376 – 380. https://doi.org/10.1016/j.compedu.2008.09.005

[5] Surendar Chandra. 2007. Lecture Video Capture for the Masses. In *Proceedings of the 12th Annual SIGCSE Conference on Innovation and Technology in Computer Science Education (ITiCSE '07)*. ACM, New York, NY, USA, 276–280. https://doi.org/10.1145/1268784.1268864

[6] Jared Danielson, Vanessa Preast, Holly Bender, and Lesya Hassall. 2014. Is the effectiveness of lecture capture related to teaching approach or content type? *Computers & Education* 72 (2014), 121 – 131. https://doi.org/10.1016/j.compedu.2013.10.016

[7] Louis Deslauriers, Ellen Schelew, and Carl Wieman. 2011. Improved Learning in a Large-Enrollment Physics Class. *Science* 332, 6031 (2011), 862–864. https://doi.org/10.1126/science.1201783 arXiv:http://science.sciencemag.org/content/332/6031/862.full.pdf

[8] Carlos Dobkin, Ricard Gil, and Justin Marion. 2010. Skipping class in college and exam performance: Evidence from a regression discontinuity classroom experiment. *Economics of Education Review* 29, 4 (2010), 566 – 575. https://doi.org/10.1016/j.econedurev.2009.09.004

[9] Martin R. Edwards and Michael E. Clinton. 2018. A study exploring the impact of lecture capture availability and lecture capture usage on student attendance and attainment. *Higher Education* (05 Jun 2018). https://doi.org/10.1007/s10734-018-0275-9

[10] Michail N. Giannakos, Letizia Jaccheri, and John Krogstie. 2015. Exploring the relationship between video lecture usage patterns and students' attitudes. *British Journal of Educational Technology* 47, 6 (2015), 1259–1275. https://doi.org/10.1111/bjet.12313

[11] Michail N. Giannakos, John Krogstie, and Nikos Chrisochoides. 2014. Reviewing the Flipped Classroom Research: Reflections for Computer Science Education. In *Proceedings of the Computer Science Education Research Conference (CSERC '14)*. ACM, New York, NY, USA, 23–29. https://doi.org/10.1145/2691352.2691354

[12] J. F. Groen, B. Quigley, and Y. Herry. 2016. Examining the Use of Reading Capture Technology: Implications for Teaching and Learning. *The Canadian Journal for the Scholarship of Teaching and Learning* 7, 1 (2016). https://doi.org/10.5206/cjsotl-rcacea.2016.1.8

[13] Simon B. Heilesen. 2010. What is the academic efficacy of podcasting? *Computers & Education* 55, 3 (2010), 1063 – 1068. https://doi.org/10.1016/j.compedu.2010.05.002

[14] David J. Malan. 2007. Podcasting Computer Science E-1. In *Proceedings of the 38th SIGCSE Technical Symposium on Computer Science Education (SIGCSE '07)*. ACM, New York, NY, USA, 389–393. https://doi.org/10.1145/1227310.1227446

[15] Blanche W. OâĂŹBannon, Jennifer K. Lubke, Jeffrey L. Beard, and Virginia G. Britt. 2011. Using podcasts to replace lecture: Effects on student achievement. *Computers & Education* 57, 3 (2011), 1885 – 1892. https://doi.org/10.1016/j.compedu.2011.04.001

[16] UC San Diego Educational Technology Services. 2018. personal communication (August 2018).

[17] Amber Settle, Lucia Dettori, and Mary Jo Davidson. 2011. Does Lecture Capture Make a Difference for Students in Traditional Classrooms. In *Proceedings of the 16th Annual Joint Conference on Innovation and Technology in Computer Science Education (ITiCSE '11)*. ACM, New York, NY, USA, 78–82. https://doi.org/10.1145/1999747.1999772

[18] Adrienne E. Williams, Nancy M. Aguilar-Roca, and Diane K. O'Dowd. 2016. Lecture capture podcasts: differential student use and performance in a large introductory course. *Educational Technology Research and Development* 64, 1 (01 Feb 2016), 1–12. https://doi.org/10.1007/s11423-015-9406-5

[19] G. Witthaus and C. Robinson. 2015. *Lecture capture literature review: A review of the literature from 2012 to 2015*. Technical Report. Centre for Academic Practice, Loughborough University. ttps://dspace.lboro.ac.uk/2134/25712

Student-Generated Videos for Promoting Better Attitudes towards Cryptography

Ana I. González-Tablas
Universidad Carlos III de Madrid
Leganés, Spain
aigonzal@inf.uc3m.es

Pablo Martín-González
Universidad Carlos III de Madrid
Leganés, Spain
pmgonzal@inf.uc3m.es

ABSTRACT

We present an active learning experience conducted on a Cryptography course within a Bachelor's Degree in Computer Science and Engineering with the goal of promoting better attitudes towards cryptography. Students were asked to create short videos that presented in an attractive way day-to-day topics or systems related with cryptography but not included in the course syllabus. Participation was optional although additional marks were assigned depending on a rubric-based assessment. Students, besides creating the videos, could participate also (or only) in evaluating some of the peer-created videos using the same rubric used by the teachers. Other active learning experiences consider student-generated videos but often topics are required to be within the course syllabus.

We describe the experience design and how we have used YouTube and Microsoft Class Notebook to seamlessly deploy the experience as an extra curricular activity, with minimum teachers overhead. To measure the effect of the experience on the students attitude, we have carried on a survey (pre-test and post-test), adapted from an already existing attitudes towards statistics scale, on two student groups (intervention and control). Results show that intervention group presents higher increments in attitudes in the three analysed dimensions (usefulness, likeness, and motivation) respect to the control group. We have also conducted a satisfaction survey on intervention group, that show that a mean of 80% of students evaluate as positive (agree or strongly agree) the experience. Final grades, however, do not present significant differences.

CCS CONCEPTS

• **Security and privacy → Cryptography**; • **Social and professional topics → Computational science and engineering education**.

KEYWORDS

Active learning; cryptography; student-generated videos; attitudes

ACM Reference Format:
Ana I. González-Tablas and Pablo Martín-González. 2019. Student-Generated Videos for Promoting Better Attitudes towards Cryptography. In *SIGCSE '19: 50th ACM Technical Symposium on Computer Science Education, February 27–March 2, 2019, Minneapolis, MN, USA.* ACM, New York, NY, USA, 7 pages. https://doi.org/10.1145/3287324.3287455

SIGCSE'19, February 27–March 2, 2019, Minneapolis, MN, USA

ACM ISBN 978-1-4503-5890-3/19/2...$15.00
https://doi.org/10.1145/3287324.3287455

1 INTRODUCTION

Cryptography is a topic considered in all ACM/IEEE Computer Science curriculum guidelines. It is often the first course students have related to cybersecurity, and an usual manner to learn fundamental cybersecurity concepts such as confidentiality, integrity and authentication. Computer Science students should learn these concepts not only because in most cases they will be relevant in their future professional practice but also as they underlie day-to-day digital life. In this work we present an experience we have conducted on the students of a Bachelor's Degree in Computer Science and Engineering in Spain. The Degree has several subjects related to cybersecurity, being cryptography the first one of them and the only one mandatory for the three offered specializations (inspired in the Computing, Computer Engineering and Information Technology curriculum guidelines).

Each of the teachers participating in this experience have been teaching the cryptography subject more than 10 years. In the last years, with the advent of cybersecurity field, we have informally noticed that students attitude towards cryptography is different depending on their career interests. Students interested in pursuing a cybersecurity career are initially highly motivated by the course, while students interested in information technology are curious but not significantly interested, and students interested in computer science specialization (mainly focused on artificial intelligence field) have no interest at all in most cases. Moreover, some cybersecurity oriented students lose interest in the course as they realize it is not going to help them hacking any system (at least not in the short-term). We perceive that, although knowing cryptography benefits all of them, not only because of their future professional practice but because of their future digital citizen activities, they are not fully aware of the relation of cryptography with their current and future life. And we think that this unawareness may hinder students developing a more positive attitude towards cryptography.

The main goal of the experience we have conducted is to promote better attitudes towards cryptography within the students, by highlighting its relation with day-to-day life and professional practice. As requirements for the experience design, we wanted to preserve the current curricular activities, so we decided to design the experience as an optional and extracurricular activity. Finally, we wanted to minimize teachers overhead caused by collaborating in the experience, so we decided to use supporting technology easy to deploy and ready-to-use.

Existing literature indicates that the general tendency seems to be that innovative teaching approaches do have positive effects on affective outcomes and/or achievements [4]. Moreover, more positive attitudes favour life-long learning [8]. Therefore, in order to achieve the stated goals, we decide to design and carry on an optional and innovative active learning activity that specifically targets promoting awareness of the relation of cryptography with day-to-day life and/or with computer engineering professional practice. The activity is two-fold, as it includes two separated sub-activities named as CREATE and EVALUATE. In the sub-activity CREATE, students are requested to form small groups and choose a topic that specifically promotes the awareness relation. Teachers accept and refocus, if necessary, topics to avoid overlapping and guarantee a minimum awareness promotion. Then, students have to design and produce a short video addressing the chosen topic. After students submit final videos at the end of the lecture period, links to the videos are published in a platform accessible to the participating students. In the sub-activity EVALUATE, students are requested to evaluate, individually, at least three of the peer-generated videos guided by a rubric. The activity therefore promotes active and quality learning, targeting the two highest levels in the cognitive dimension of the Bloom's revised taxonomy.

Main contributions of this work are (1) providing evidence of the positive effects of innovative learning activities on attitudes, and (2) describing in detail how the experience has been designed and implemented in order that other members of the community could replicate it, for cryptography courses or other courses in a similar situation.

2 RELATED WORK

Using multimedia material generated by teachers or subject-matter experts to teach and learn is not a new approach in the community, being commonly assumed to have positive effects, belief that is reinforced with the recent rise of flipped learning modalities. There is also a significant number of experiences in the literature that present positive results after making use of student-generated videos. For example, works in [3, 5] highlight the effects on student engagement. Other works focus on the effects of student-generated videos on learning outcomes. For example, work in [2] has as goal to measure whether students producing a video demonstrated a significant improvement in the understanding of complex concepts. However, although some works use student-generated videos that address open topics or projects closely related to the professional practice (see for example [7]), most of them request students to produce videos related to contents within the course syllabus.

The goal of our work is different as we want to promote a more positive attitude towards cryptography, by highlighting its relation with future student lives. Videos could somehow be seen as a the summary of a research project, but they are not just that, as the awareness promotion goal should underlie all of them.

3 COURSE BACKGROUND

The activity has been conducted in a mandatory cryptography course offered in the second trimester (teaching period of 14 weeks, 6 ECTS) of the second year of a Bachelor's Degree in Computer Science and Engineering in Spain. The teaching activities include lectures, exercise and problem resolution, and hands-on laboratories. Some of the assessment activities are conducted within the teaching period and give 60% of the course grade, obtaining the remaining 40% from the final exam held after the teaching period. The course covers most of the topics recommended in the ACM/IEEE Computer Science Curricula 2013 for cryptography [6].

4 METHODOLOGY

4.1 Experiment design

We design a quasi-experiment with an intervention and a control group, formed with students belonging to, respectively, three and four of the teaching groups linked to the cryptography course (with a maximum of 40 students each). Teaching groups are assigned to one or other experiment group such that size and the distribution of students' performance, based on previous courses results, are similar. Intervention group contains 108 students, from which 69 of them choose to participate in the experiment and collaborate in data collection. Control group contains 154 students, from which 114 of them choose to collaborate in data collection.

In order to measure the effects of the intervention on the students attitudes towards cryptography, we design a pre-test post-test experiment that uses as measurement instrument a reduced and adapted version of an existing five point Likert-type statistics attitude scale [1]. We choose this scale as it addresses in Spanish a specific math field (which we perceive to be in a similar situation as cryptography) and it is based on several well-known statistic attitude scales written in English. Table 1 shows the 12 items selected for our attitude towards cryptography questionnaire. We choose to only measure usefulness, likeness and motivation dimensions, discarding anxiety and self-confidence dimensions as they are less related to our goal. Following the original scale instructions, four scores can be obtained after using the questionnaire. Each item has a score equal to the points given to the item, needing those written in a negative way (I9-I12) some correction (inverse scale). A score for each dimension is computed by adding the scores of its item, and a Total Attitude Score (TAS) is computed by adding the scores of the three dimensions.

In order to measure the satisfaction of the students participating in the experience, we design a post-test only experiment that uses as measurement instrument a self-designed Likert-type survey with 14 questions addressing several issues (questions are listed in Figure 2): perception on achieved awareness and learning (Q1-Q6), enjoyment (Q7), experience design (Q8-Q9), future repetitions (Q10-Q11), and perceived effects on the course-related learning (Q12-Q14).

Finally, we have also compared student performance in intervention and control groups, although we did not expect significative differences after the intervention as we will discuss in Section 6.

4.2 Activity design

We design a two-fold activity targeting video creation (sub-activity CREATE) and video evaluation (sub-activity EVALUATE). Videos generated by students in the sub-activity CREATE are afterwards offered as candidate videos to be evaluated in the sub-activity EVALUATE. Students in the intervention group may choose to participate in zero, one or both sub-activities.

Next we describe the steps of the activity, along with their temporal planning within the weeks of the course (W1-W14) or after. Note that as it is a requirement not to disturb normal teaching

Table 1: Overview of the attitude towards cryptography questionnaire: Items for each dimension

Dimension	ID	Order	Item
Usefulness	I1	1	Cryptography is a very worthwhile and necessary subject
	I2	4	I would like to have a deeper knowledge of Cryptography
	I3	6	Knowing how to use Cryptography will increase my job opportunities
	I4	9	For the professional development of our career I consider that there are other more important subjects than Cryptography
Likeness	I5	2	Using Cryptography can be fun
	I6	7	I think Cryptography will be stimulating for me
	I7	10	I would like to have a job in which I had to use Cryptography
	I8	12	If I had the opportunity, I would enrol in more Cryptography courses besides the mandatory ones
Motivation	I9	3	Cryptography is too theoretical to be of practical use to the average professional
	I10	5	Cryptography can be useful for someone who is dedicated to research, but not for the average professional
	I11	8	I hope I will use just a little bit of Cryptography in my professional life
	I12	11	For the professional development of my career one of the most important subjects is Cryptography

activity, only the activity presentation step takes place within the teaching time, besides punctual and short communications to the students to motivate participation or remind some aspects.

(1) *Activity presentation* (W1) In the first session of the course, the activity is presented to the students in the intervention group, after describing the course.
(2) *Attitudes pre-test* (W1-W2) Students of the course are invited to answer the attitudes towards cryptography questionnaire.
(3) *Enrolment in the activity platform* (W3) A platform (virtual space) is set up specifically for the activity. All students willing to participate in the activity are invited to request enrolment in the platform.
(4) *Groups formation and topic selection (CREATE)* (W3-W7) Students participating in the sub-activity CREATE are requested to form small groups and register those groups in the platform. Students are encouraged to discuss possible topics among them and with the teachers. Once teachers accept a group's topic, it is published in the platform.
(5) *Video design (CREATE)* (W8-W13) Students are expected to search for information and resources related to the topic, experiment with video recording and edition technologies, and design the video. Students may request for help or guidance to teachers at any moment by writing an email or asking teachers before or after the class. Students may also use the platform to place information and drafts that want to share with teachers or the rest of the participants in the activity.
(6) *Video recording and edition (CREATE)* (W14) Students should record and submit their final videos by the end of this week. Teachers publish the links to these videos in the CREATE video catalogue, accessible through the platform.
(7) *Video evaluation (EVALUATE)* (W15) Students participating in the sub-activity EVALUATE have to select three videos from the CREATE video catalogue and fill an evaluation form based on a rubric for each of them, within the platform.
(8) *Attitudes post-test* (W16) Students of the course are invited to answer the attitudes towards cryptography questionnaire.
(9) *Satisfaction post-test* (W16) All students in the intervention group are invited to answer the satisfaction survey.

4.3 Using a rubric throughout the activity

Table 2 shows the rubric we have designed to evaluate student-generated videos. First criterion reflects the main goal of the activity, stating it clearly for all participants. Second criterion requires some relation with course syllabus; this way we expect students make a reasonable effort at generating and comprehending videos. Third and fourth criteria are straightforward, more when videos are going to be used in the sub-activity EVALUATE.

The rubric has been provided to the students at the beginning of the sub-activity CREATE, so students could better guide their efforts. This same rubric has been used by students participating in the sub-activity EVALUATE to evaluate peer-generated videos; in this case, students will also have to provide a justification of the given evaluation score for each criterion and a brief reflection on what they have learned, if they have enjoyed it and whether they would recommend other students to visualize it.

4.4 Technologies and ethical issues

We decided to use some virtual platform that allowed conducting most of the activity online but that did not require a large effort to deploy and set up. We choose to use Microsoft Class Notebook for several reasons. First of all, it basically provides a collaborative easy-to-use web-based edition and publication space and it requires zero deployment workload. Microsoft provides free accounts to teachers and students of educative institutions. Once a notebook is created, teachers may enrol students (mixing students from different teaching groups), and publish material in three sub-notebooks with different permissions: content library (all students can read), collaborative space (all students can read and write), and personal space (a private space for each students); teachers can read and write everywhere.

We conducted most of the activity through one of this notebooks with the exception of data collection (attitude questionnaire and satisfaction survey) and video storage. We collected data using the University's Moodle-based Learning Content Management system. Students were asked to publish their videos in YouTube and then share the link with teachers.

We structure the contents of the Class Notebook as follows:

- Content library: Here we include three sections. First one is devoted to the sub-activity CREATE and contains pages with a description of the steps together with the associated deadlines (hard or suggested), a list of topics provided as example, and the rubric. A second section is devoted to the sub-activity EVALUATE and contains the CREATE video catalogue and the template for evaluating videos. The third

Table 2: Rubric used to evaluate student-generated videos

Criterion	Excellent	Good	Fair	Needs improvement
Awareness promotion	Topic and contents explicit and clearly promote and highlight the relation	Topic and contents promote the relation but somehow contents could state the relation more clearly	Topic and contents slightly promote the relation; it is somehow difficult to grasp	Topic and contents poorly promote the relation; topic could promote it with difficulty, contents fail to do so
Relation with course syllabus	Relation exists and it is explicit and clearly stated	Relation exists but it could be stated more clearly	A small relation exists; it is somehow difficult to grasp	Either there is no relation, or topic and content exist within course syllabus
Correctness of technical content	Technical content is correct and enough to understand the topic	Technical content is correct but more could have been added for a better understanding	There is insufficient technical content or it is somehow incorrect	Either there is no technical content or it is clearly incorrect
Struture and clarity	Contents are well organized and ideas are clear and logically presented	Contents are well organized; most ideas are clear and logically presented	Contents are basically organized; only some ideas are clear and logically presented	Either contents are unstructured or ideas are not provided in a clear and logical manner

section is used to publish the additional grades earned by students as reward for participating in the activity.

- Collaborative space: Here we include two community sections for all participants and one section for each group participating in the sub-activity CREATE. First section is devoted to group formation (students can register a group and its members, or list groups or students seeking more members or a group, respectively). Second section lists useful references for the design, recording and edition of educative videos. Group sections are intended for being used as digital portfolios or as a communication means of drafts, ideas and references with teachers, within the sub-activity CREATE.
- Personal space: Students participating in the sub-activity EVALUATE copy the evaluation template in their personal space and fill it in here (teachers also have access).

To respect ethical issues, we stated very clear that participation was optional and that we were not asking students to appear in the videos if they did not want to. Data was anonymously collected with the Moodle-based system, so we cannot not link answers submitted by the same student to questionnaires/survey; we only know which students have not answered them. Regarding videos, to protect students privacy, we encouraged them to publish videos in a private way in YouTube. In this way, videos are not indexed by YouTube and are only accessible through the link.

4.5 Rewarding participation

We firmly believe that participating in the activity greatly benefits students in the medium and long-term. However, we are aware that they have very tight schedules and do not naturally commit to innovative activities that take their extracurricular time. Therefore, we offered additional marks for participating as follows:

- Sub-activity CREATE: All students forming a group could earn up till 1 additional mark, depending on how teachers evaluated their video using the rubric. These additional marks are added to their course grade.
- Sub-activity EVALUATE: Students could earn up till 1 mark, depending on how teachers evaluated their video evaluations. However, in this case, the obtained marks are not added but can substitute the smallest laboratory grade (also over 1 mark), in the case it benefits the student.
- Attitude questionnaire and satisfaction survey: We rewarded participation in pre-test and post-tests with 0.1 marks respectively. Therefore students could earn up till 0.2 additional marks that will be added to their course grade.

Two teachers were involved in the experiment. Marks were assigned by both of them for each video and each video evaluation. Marks assigned to students were computed as the mean among the two teachers marks, to minimize possible biases.

5 RESULTS

From the whole intervention group (N=108), 72 students (67%) enrolled in the platform, participating actively only 69 of them (64%). 64 students (59%) collaborated to create 18 videos and 42 students (39%) participated individually evaluating at least three peer-generated videos. Within the intervention group, 34% of the students participated both in the sub-activities CREATE and EVALUATE, 25% only in CREATE and 5% only in EVALUATE. Videos addressed topics such as crypto coins, ransomware, quantum and post-quantum cryptography, security of popular social messaging apps (such as Whatsapp), protection of video games, Person-in-the-Middle attack, WiFi pineapple and artificial intelligence applied to cryptography. In general, video quality (content, presentation) was high, being some videos highly creative and a few quite technical.

Figure 1 shows the results of data collected with the attitude towards cryptography questionnaire. Normalized Total Attitude Score (TAS) and scores for each attitude dimension are shown, for pre and post tests of control and intervention groups. Comparing pre and post tests results, it can be seen that students in both control and intervention groups enhance their attitude towards cryptography. However, although differences are not huge, students in the intervention group have increased their attitude towards cryptography more than students in the control group, specially when focusing in each dimension.

It is interesting to see that initially, control group presents a slightly better general attitude than the intervention group because of the differences in the likeness dimension. However, intervention group ends up with an increase of almost 5% in TAS because of the larger increment by 5% between pre and post tests in the first and second dimensions, and a positive bias in the third dimension towards larger scores.

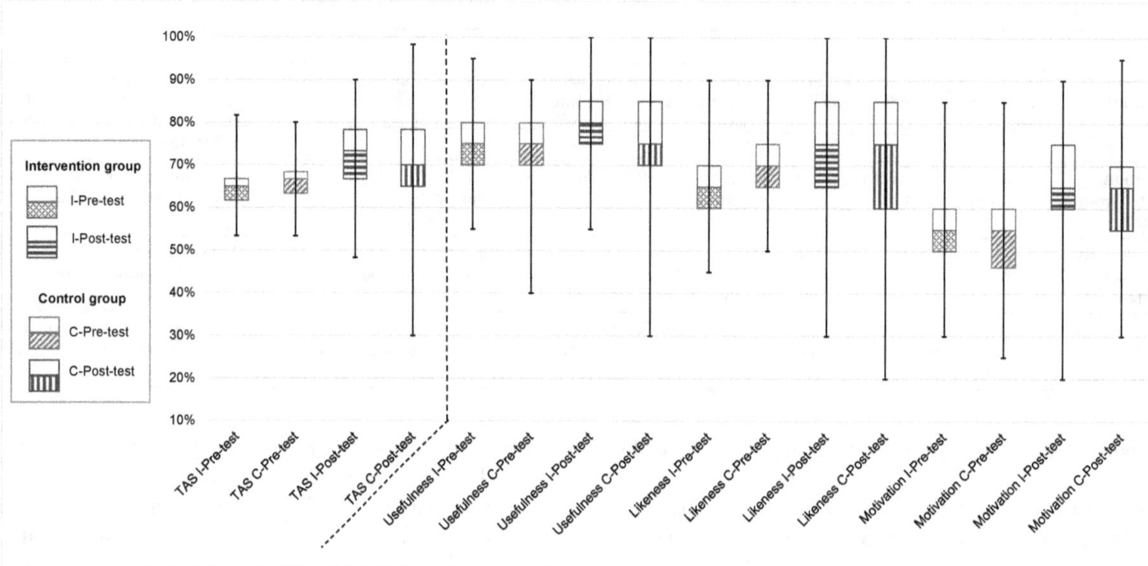

Figure 1: Results of the attitude towards cryptography questionnaire (N^I_{pre}=79, N^C_{pre}=94, N^I_{post}=79, N^C_{post}=114).

Figure 2 shows the results of data collected with the satisfaction survey. It can be seen that at least 80% of students answers with agree or strongly agree in 10 out of 14 questions. Very few students (at most three for each question) have answered with disagree or strongly disagree. We recall that data collection was anonymous and direction of answers were not linked to any reward. Therefore we assume that students are very satisfied with their participation.

Figure 3 analyses the distribution of the course grades for the different groups and sub-groups of the experiment, excluding marks earned by participating in the activity. It can be seen that no significant differences exist between course grades for intervention and control groups (p = .62 using the Wilcoxon Rank-Sum test). This was, somehow, an expected result, as the activity does not specifically target topics within course syllabus. It is also interesting to see that there is even no significant difference in course grades between students in the intervention group that have not participated in the activity or have only participated in the sub-activity CREATE. Some differences can be seen in course grades distribution in the students that have participated in the sub-activity EVALUATE, substantial in the case of only participating in EVALUATE and less obvious in the case of participating in both CREATE and EVALUATE.

Analysis of course grades against marks earned by participating in sub-activities CREATE and EVALUATE shows their unrelatedness. However, a majority of students have obtained more than fair marks in the sub-activities. Nonetheless, we highlight that some students that have participated in the activity earning good marks (greater than 0.7) have not passed the course.

Finally, both teachers involved in the experiment devoted approximately 6 work hours to evaluate videos (sub-activity CREATE) and another 6 to evaluate videos evaluations (sub-activity EVALUATE). Only one teacher devoted 2 additional hours to identify which students have participated in questionnaires and survey, and 3 additional ones to organize and include the additional marks in the course grade spreadsheet. Finally, both teachers had to dedicate an insignificant amount of time to enrol students in the platform, and some significant amount of time (7 hours each) to tutorship students in their topic search, their video design or just motivating students to participate in the activity. For both teachers, total workload amounts 43 work hours, excluding experiment design, instrument design and implementation, and design and edition of the rubric and pages in the Class Notebook created for the activity. Each teacher devoted then respectively 3 and 4 full working days.

6 DISCUSSION AND FUTURE WORK

Results obtained in the experience align with results of previous works [4]. That is, the experience has had a positive effect on student attitudes although not in a great extent. Taking into account student effort and teacher workload, we could question ourselves whether it is worth conducting such type of active learning experiences. We believe it is worth. We have perceived student enthusiasm because of participating on the activity (data collected through the satisfaction survey supports this perception). We believe that participating in the experience will have a long-term effect that cannot be measured just after conducting the experience.

Results show that usefulness dimension is the one that benefits more from the experience. After the experience, we think that it is probably more difficult to increase student likeness and motivation dimensions, as they are more subjective than usefulness. However, we also believe that knowing something better, as promoted by the activity, might help to increase likeness and motivation dimensions.

We have been surprised by the number of students that have not participated at all within both control and intervention group

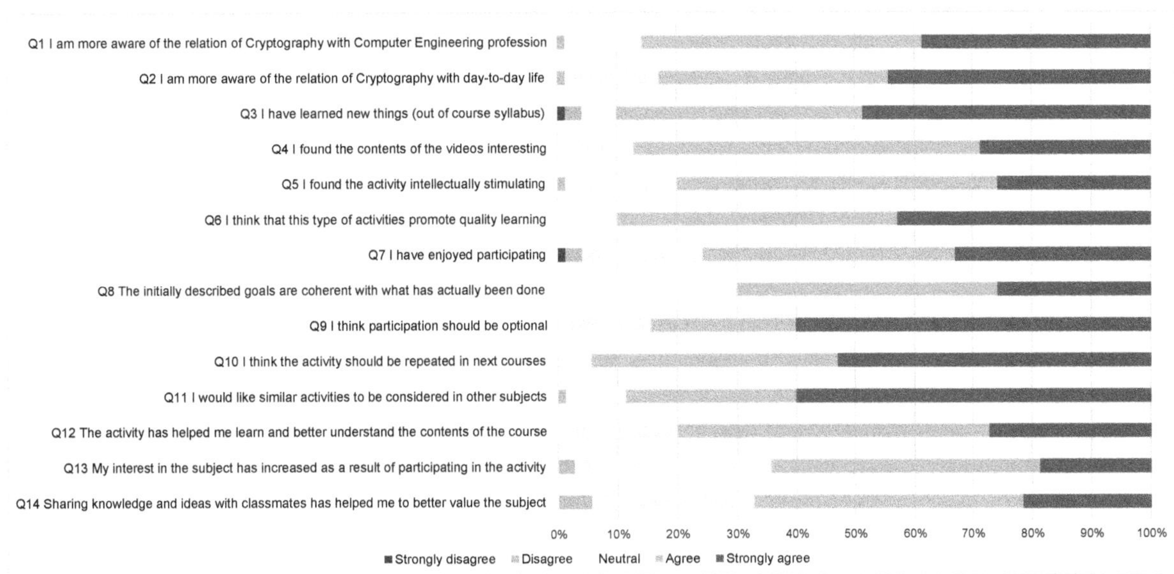

Figure 2: Results of the satisfaction questionnaire (N=67, students participating in the activity).

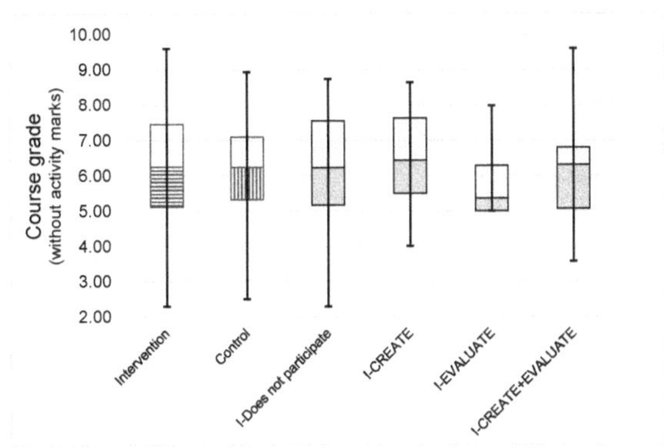

Figure 3: Course grades (not including marks earned with the activity in the intervention group).

(they have not answered the attitude questionnaires even answering them granted some marks). We think that some of these students might not have assisted to lectures (it is not mandatory) and this might have hindered their engagement.

This is the first time we have conducted the experience[1] and we have found some difficulties, being the most important one the temporal restriction. The activity targets topics that build on course syllabus, so, ideally, it should be conducted after the course. However, we are restricted to the course period, that includes teaching and final assessment weeks. Placing the activity at the end of the period means that students are requested an extra effort at their busiest weeks. This may also contribute to explaining the moderate participation in the activity (65%). However placing the activity earlier in the course will lose the benefit of building learning over previous knowledge. We do not find a solution to the temporal restriction and we think the best option to promote participation is to keep the effort required by the activity as moderate.

In general we think the experience has been very positive and plan to repeat it in next courses, refining aspects as the validation of the rubric or researching reasons for not participating in the activity. Implementing anonymous but linked questionnaires will allow us to better analyse data. However, we face an important challenge for extending the activity to all the groups of the course, as not all teachers are committed to assuming associated workload of an extracurricular activity. Finally, we think the activity design herein presented could be easily applied in other courses that are taught in the first years of computer science degrees, and have a high amount of abstract content (algorithms, models, maths...) relevant to students future professional practice, but that this relation is not clearly addressed within the course syllabus.

ACKNOWLEDGEMENTS

Authors want to thank suggestions provided by anonymous reviewers. This work is supported by the Comunidad de Madrid [S2013/ICE-3095 (CIBERDINE)]; by the Ministerio de Ciencia, Innovación y Universidades [TIN2016-79095-C2-2-R (SMOG)]; and by Universidad Carlos III de Madrid [15ª Convocatoria de Apoyo a Experiencias de Innovación Docente del curso 2017-2018].

[1]Several years ago we conducted a similar activity where students had to write a research report on some security-related topic. Teacher workload was significantly higher and it had the drawback that only teachers read those reports.

REFERENCES

[1] Elena Auzmendi Escribano. 1992. *Las actitudes hacia la matemática-estadística en las enseñanzas medias y universitaria: características y medición.* Ediciones Mensajero, Bilbao.

[2] Pablo Frank-Bolton and Rahul Simha. 2018. Docendo Discimus: Students Learn by Teaching Peers Through Video. In *Proceedings of the 49th ACM Technical Symposium on Computer Science Education.* ACM, 473–478.

[3] Juhani Pirhonen and Päivi Rasi. 2017. Student-generated instructional videos facilitate learning through positive emotions. *Journal of Biological Education* 51, 3 (2017), 215–227.

[4] Elwin R Savelsbergh, Gjalt T Prins, Charlotte Rietbergen, Sabine Fechner, Bram E Vaessen, Jael M Draijer, and Arthur Bakker. 2016. Effects of innovative science and mathematics teaching on student attitudes and achievement: A meta-analytic study. *Educational Research Review* 19 (2016), 158–172.

[5] Sandy Schuck and Matthew Kearney. 2006. Capturing learning through student-generated digital video. *Australian Educational Computing* 21, 1 (2006), 15–20.

[6] The Joint Task Force on Computing Curricula. 2013. *Computing Science Curricula 2013. Curriculum Guidelines for Undergraduate Degree Programs in Computer Science Final Report.* Technical Report. ACM/IEEE. https://doi.org/10.1145/2534860

[7] Kristie A Thomas and Liza Marks. 2014. Action!: Student-generated videos in social work education. *Journal of Technology in Human Services* 32, 4 (2014), 254–274.

[8] R Watanabe and B Mcgaw. 2003. Student learning: Attitudes, engagement and strategies. *Learning for tomorrow's world. First results from PISA* (2003), 109–158.

Story Programming: Explaining Computer Science Before Coding

Jennifer Parham-Mocello
Oregon State University, USA
parhammj@oregonstate.edu

Shannon Ernst
Oregon State University, USA
ernstsh@oregonstate.edu

Martin Erwig
Oregon State University, USA
erwig@oregonstate.edu

Lily Shellhammer
Oregon State University, USA
shellhal@oregonstate.edu

Emily Dominguez
Oregon State University, USA
domingue@oregonstate.edu

ABSTRACT

Story Programming is an approach for teaching complex computational and algorithmic thinking skills using simple stories anyone can relate to. One could learn these skills independent of a computer or with the use of a computer as a tool to interact with the computation in the tale. This research study examines the use of Story Programming before teaching coding in a computer science orientation course to determine if it is a viable alternative to the code-focused way of teaching the class in the past. We measure the viability of the Story Programming approach by evaluating student-success and learning outcomes, as well as student reactions to post-survey questions.

CCS CONCEPTS

• Social and professional topics ~ Computational thinking • Social and professional topics ~ Computer science education • Applied computing ~ Interactive learning environments

KEYWORDS

Story Telling; Computer Science Pedagogy; Introduction to Computer Science

ACM Reference format:

Jennifer Parham-Mocello, Shannon Ernst, Martin Erwig, Lily Shellhammer, and Emily Dominguez. 2019. Story Programming: Explaining Computer Science Before Coding. In Proc. of the 50th ACM Technical Symposium on Computer Science Education (SIGCSE '19), Feb. 27-March 2, 2019, Minneapolis, MN, USA. ACM, *NY, NY, USA, 7 pages.* https://doi.org/10.1145/3287324.3287397

1 INTRODUCTION

Many approaches to introducing computer science to students are predicated on programming, that is, they require an understanding of how to code an algorithm in a programming language. This approach is used in efforts such as *code.org* that promote coding and computer science to younger children, but the abstract nature of programming languages (block based or not) can pose a significant barrier to entry. A code-first approach can be effective when students have a good understanding of programming or are willing to acquire it. Since computer science is not synonymous with programming, there is no inherent necessity to tie the orientation to computer science to coding activities. Students who are not sure whether they want to study computer science but are curious about the subject should not be excluded because they are reluctant to the idea of having to become a programmer as a prerequisite to understanding computer science. The same applies to laypeople who want to get some basic understanding of a field of growing importance for society. Therefore, efforts to explain computer science without a computer, such as *csunplugged.org*, have gained popularity, especially among the K-12 community, and studies show that this approach broadens participation [3].

The researchers in this study believe that the state-of-the-art introductory computer science education at the university level could benefit from more creativity and computational thinking without the use of a computer. To reach a wide audience with a diverse background and set of expectations, we use an approach that uses well-known stories and everyday situations to explain computer science concepts before teaching coding [8]. Explaining computational concepts through popular stories has three complementary advantages.

First, identifying computing concepts in stories and everyday situations shows that computation is a universal phenomenon that does not only occur in machines. Pointing out the occurrence of computing in everyday situations emphasizes the relevance of computing and provides motivation for understanding basic concepts of computer science independent of the goal to become a programmer or computer scientist.

Second, the use of well-known stories can help with making the learning curve gentler, since students only need to understand the link between the story elements and the computing concepts. If they know the story, the objects and events are readily available as building blocks for computing metaphors. This is different in approaches that invent new stories to explain computing such as [2, 14] where students first have to absorb and understand the story and only then can process the links to computing concepts.

Third, stories can make people empathize more with the problems. Considering the problem of finding the shortest path from the couch to the fridge may be important, but it does not reach the level of importance of the path-finding problem that Hansel and Gretel face. Being emotionally engaged in a problem often means to care more about a problem, which helps to make the explanation provided by the story more memorable and effective. This aspect is probably stronger

* This work is partially supported by the National Science Foundation under the grant CCF-1717300.

SIGCSE '19, February 27-March 2, 2019, Minneapolis, MN, USA

ACM ISBN 978-1-4503-5890-3/19/02...$15.00
https://doi.org/10.1145/3287324.3287397

by using existing popular stories whose impact on the audience has already been demonstrated through their popularity.

In the remainder of this paper we report on a study that researches an approach called *Story Programming* as an alternative for teaching a computer science orientation course, CS 0. This approach is based on the book *Once Upon an Algorithm: How Stories Explain Computing* [7], and this research investigates whether this approach is a viable option for teaching a university-level computer science course. We define viable in terms of satisfying learning outcomes and positive student reactions to post-survey question.

2 BACKGROUND

The two most closely related areas to our approach are the so-called "unplugged" computational thinking approach and the other existing approaches to using stories for explaining computing concepts.

2.1 Unplugged Computational Thinking Activities

The most well-known approach to teaching computer science concepts without the use of a computer is the approach taken in *csunplugged.org* [4]. It is a collection of engaging activities that can illustrate computing concepts, but it does not use stories. Story Programming uses the idea of unplugged activities performed without a computer, but the actual activities in this project are different and relate to the stories in the book or stories students create.

Unplugged activities are primarily used in K-12 [1, 5, 11, 17, 18], but this research study employs the idea of teaching computational thinking without a computer at the university level. Most alternatives for teaching introductory computer science courses in institutions focus on changing the curriculum in their introductory computer science classes to improve success and retention [9, 16] and make topics covered more relevant and broader [15]. Some institutions have created interest-based classes allowing students to choose a class section based on what they like, such as game development, robotics, music, and mobile applications [9, 20], while others focus on adding computational thinking to their curricula with and without the use of a computer [10, 13, 16, 19]. These studies show that teaching computational thinking helps students think about different ways to attack problems, making them more effective problem solvers. This study uses a Story Programming approach to teach computational thinking skills using stories without a computer before teaching programming skills.

2.2 Story Programming Approaches

The use of stories to explain computing is not new. *Computational Fairy Tales* describes algorithms and data structures as part of a story about a princess on a quest to save her father's kingdom [14]. The target audience is middle school children, and the treatment of concepts is often quite brief. The selection of topics is ad hoc, and the book does not cover any language aspects. *Lauren Ipsum* [2] employs a similar approach. It tells a story about a girl who gets lost in a forest and wants to find her way back home. In her adventure, she has to solve several problems, which serve as a hook to introduce concepts of algorithms and math on a very high level. The target audience is also middle school children, and the story is like *Alice in Wonderland* with its playful and clever use of names. It contains an appendix that provides additional explanations of the concepts mentioned in the story, but it also does not cover any language aspects.

One study used *Computational Fairy Tales* to help the retention and academic performance of computer science majors, mostly aimed at students with little to no programming experience [16]. It found that "CS0 students without prior programming experience got significantly higher grades in CS1 than CS0 students who had programmed before"; the students were split on how useful the book was to their learning. This is different than the study presented in this paper, which determines if Story Programming is a viable alternative to the traditional programming-focused approach for teaching a computer science orientation class. Another study used physical simulations in class to explain concepts, which students said helped them to understand the computational concepts [13], arguing that computer science or programming concepts could be explained effectively using stories if the connection between concept and story is strong. One study claimed that using a story to learn a concept will be easily accessible because that is how many of us learn to begin with [12]. These claims align with the rationale for using Story Programming, but the study presented in this paper does not investigate these claims. One other study used "unplugged" activities and storytelling to introduce teachers to computational thinking, but it focused on teacher training and used contextual stories to relate different "unplugged" activities to specific computational skills for teachers as the storytelling approach [6].

3 RESEARCH METHOD

At Oregon State University, students in the College of Engineering are required to take an orientation course to fulfill a degree requirement, and Computer Science Orientation (CS 0) is offered once a year to fulfill that requirement for students interested in majoring in CS. This course is primarily taken by incoming first-year students who are declared Computer Science majors, but students with prior computer science experience or outside the major may take the course as well. In the past, Python was used as the coding language with students beginning to write small programs as early as week two in a ten-week term. The lectures are focused on teaching basic Python including variables, control flow (both conditional statements and looping), functions and lists with exposure to how to design solutions to computer science problems and the idea of testing. In-class exercises are completed in groups and used to stimulate learning in a computer-free environment.

We divided the Fall 2017 CS 0 course into three sections. One section remained taught in the traditional fashion with a focus on programming in Python. The other two sections were taught using a new approach supported by *Once Upon an Algorithm*. One Story Programming section was taught using Python in the second half of the class, and the other section used Haskell to investigate differences in language choice with the new approach. All sections were taught by the same instructor, and the students were placed in sections at random.

3.1 Course Structure

All three sections had about 100 students per lecture and utilized presentation slides to teach concepts, as well as live coding demonstrations through a terminal when programming was being taught. Every week students engaged in in-lecture, group exercises. While the traditional section primarily focused on programming concepts, these activities did not involve a computer. They often centered around writing pseudocode, designing a solution to a problem, or analyzing code. The Story Programming in-class exercises did not focus on pseudocode or code analysis until half way through the term, and most of their exercises focused on understanding the stories used in the book *Once Upon an Algorithm* from a computational perspective, coming up with new stories to explain computational concepts, and developing and tracing algorithms. Since these activities did not use a computer, they were referred to as computational thinking (CT) activities rather than coding activities.

The students in the Story Programming sections were required to read relevant chapters of the book before class with a weekly online quiz. Chapters were generally covered in a sequential fashion with some occasional skipping to group like concepts together. The traditional section did not have a textbook, but students were encouraged to use online documentation for Python to supplement their learning where needed. The use of the book in the Story Programming sections changed the emphasis placed on some of the concepts, allowing for greater breadth and depth of concepts. For example, the Story Programming sections covered the concept of data structures and decidability more deeply than the traditional section, which gave a cursory view of data structures only through lists and only mentioned the idea that not all problems are solvable.

Each section had one two-hour lab per week, but while the traditional section labs focused on programming activities beginning in week 1, the first 5 Story Programming labs focused on small group activities applying concepts to the real world. For example, one of the first activities examined path finding algorithms using the tale of Hansel and Gretel, and students were presented with three variants of the algorithm that they had to act out with pebbles. Another activity helped students learn about the runtime of different algorithms by having to count and transfer beans across the classroom using different methods. The programming activities in the last 5 labs mirrored in code the concepts that were covered in earlier labs, rather than relating to the new concepts.

Each section had weekly assignments. For the traditional section these focused on programming. The students were presented with a problem statement and were asked to implement a solution in Python by the end of the week. These programs often focused on interacting with a user. The Story Programming sections focused on describing algorithms and connecting concepts they were learning from the book to the real world. When the students in the Story Programming sections began programming, their programs were much smaller toy problems and did not involve user input. The problems given to the Story Programming sections were also slightly different depending on the programming language.

3.2 Research Questions

With clearly defined sections, a formal study on the differences in pedagogy can address the following broad research questions, which we will outline in more detail in section 4.

RQ1: Does the Story Programming approach satisfy the learning outcomes?

RQ2: How do students react to the Story Programming approach?

RQ3: How do students react toward the CT activities versus coding activities?

3.3 Data Collection

With IRB permission, course-level DWF rates and grade distribution information were collected from the registrar, and student-level post-survey data were collected from consenting participants. Conceptual questions about algorithms, representation, and abstraction on a post-survey addressed the first research question, and survey questions with a 4-point Likert scale addressed the other two research questions.

4 RESULTS AND DISCUSSION

The course-level student success results are out of 277 students, and the student-level post-survey results are out of 110 consenting participants (35 Story Python, 25 Story Haskell, and 50 Traditional). Since the data are not normally distributed and are based on a Likert scale, non-parametric statistical tests, such as Kendall's correlation tau, τ, and the Kruskal-Wallis hypothesis test are used to reject hypotheses with 95% confidence, α=.05.

RQ1: Does the Story Programming approach satisfy the learning outcomes?

A college-level learning outcome for this class is student success. Two measures of student success are DWF rates and the grade distribution of passing students. A course-level learning outcome in CS 0 is to gain an understanding of computer science, which is measured using a post-survey.

DWF Rates

The results in Table 1 do not show a significant difference in the DWF rates between the two Story Programming sections or between the Story Programming and traditional approaches.

Sections	Students and DWF rates	
	# Students	*DWF*
Story Python	105	8.6%
Story Haskell	65	9.2%
Traditional	107	6.5%

Table 1: Number of students and DWF in each section

This suggests that the Story Programming and traditional approaches have comparable student retention and performance, and the choice of language in the Story Programming approach does not affect this. As a side note, the average DWF rate across all sections is almost 11% lower than the previous year, when all students were in one section of 284. This suggests that class size has a bigger effect on retention and student success than the approach or language used in a computer science orientation class.

Grade Distribution

Statistical tests show no differences in grade distributions between the Story Programming populations using different languages or between the two different approaches. However, it is interesting to note that the

Story Programming sections differ the most (see Figure 1). The Haskell section has a lower percentage of As and a higher percentage of Bs.

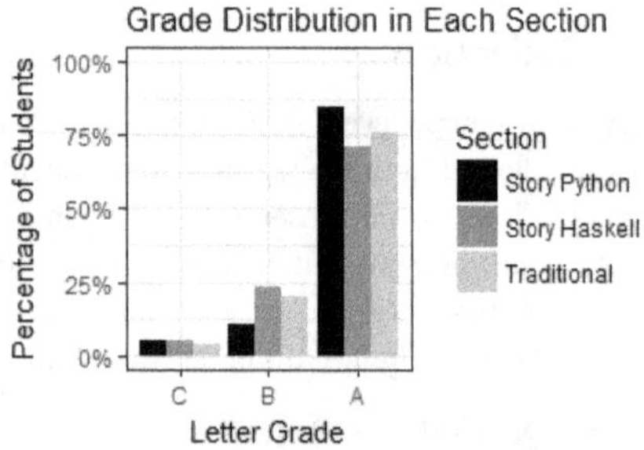

Figure 1: Grade Distribution among Story Programming approaches and the traditional programming approach.

Post-Survey Conceptual Questions

Out of the 110 consenting participants across all sections, there are no differences in the way students from the Story Programming sections or different approaches answer the conceptual post-survey questions (see Table 2). Interestingly, approximately half the students answer the algorithm and abstraction questions correctly, whereas most students answer the representation questions incorrectly.

Sections	Post-Survey Conceptual Questions		
	Algorithm (8)	*Representation (4)*	*Abstraction (4)*
Story Python	47.9%	42.1%	60.0%
Story Haskell	54.0%	35.0%	63.0%
Traditional	52.8%	36.5%	61.0%

Table 2: Percentage of students with Correct Answers to Post-Survey Conceptual Questions

RQ2: How do students react to the Story Programming approach?

Only students from the two Story Programming sections answer survey questions about the new approach and the use of the book. The following questions are answered by comparing these two sections,

Does the chosen language make a difference in how students feel about the Story Programming approach?

There is a significant difference in the student reactions toward the Story Programming approach based on the section (*pvalue=.003*). Figure 2 shows the distributions of student feelings about the approach in the two sections. The Story Programming section using Haskell tends to like the approach more than the section using Python. However, an average of 65% of the students in both sections really or somewhat like the Story Programming approach to teaching the orientation class with only 13% disliking the approach a great deal.

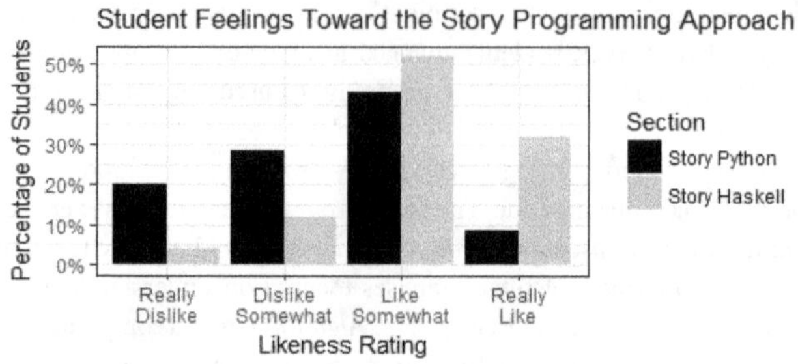

Figure 2: Distribution of students' feelings about the Story Programming approach in the different sections.

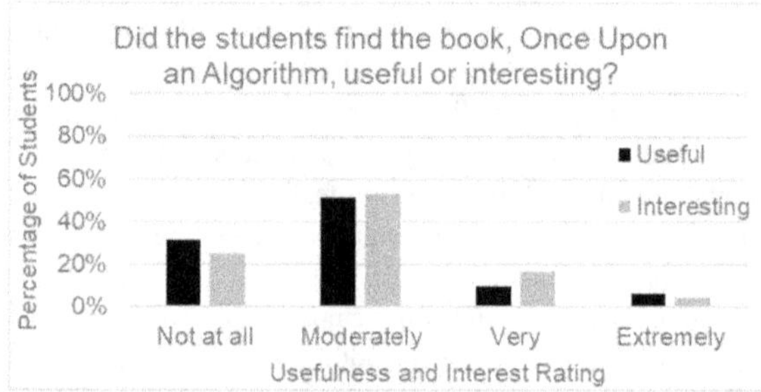

Figure 3: Percent of students who find the textbook useful to their learning or interesting.

Does the chosen language make a difference in the way students feel about the book used?

The two sections do not significantly differ in the responses regarding usefulness of and interest in the book, which means that students in both sections are consistent in the way they evaluate the book. This is observed in the strong positive, $\tau=0.70$, correlation between student ratings on how useful the book is to their learning and how interesting it is, and there is a moderately positive correlation between how they feel about the Story Programming approach and whether they find the book useful ($\tau=0.59$) or interesting ($\tau=0.52$). Only 25-32% from both sections do not at all find the book useful to their learning or interesting, but most only find the book moderately useful or interesting (see Figure 5).

Figure 4 shows the students' favorite chapters are 1 (about algorithms and computation), 4 (data structures), and 6 (sorting). Since each of these chapters use different stories, this means that students are not partial to one specific story. Moreover, no student seemed to like chapter 15 (about abstraction), which uses Harry Potter as the story. Interestingly, the two Story Programming sections did not differ significantly in the choice of favorite chapters, but they did differ significantly in their least favorite chapters (*pvalue=.02*). The least favorite chapters are more evenly distributed with no one disliking chapter 2 (runtime and resources). It is interesting to note that the students tend to like the first part of the book more, which is about algorithmic concepts, in contrast to the later chapters with more abstract content about language concepts.

Figure 4: Number of students who choose specific chapters in the textbook as their most and least favorite.

Does prior programming experience, gender, or class standing change the way students feel about the approach?

Figure 5 shows that many students enter CS 0 with prior programming experience, and there is not a significant difference between sections. Since approximately 60-70% of the students have prior programming experience, this is a variable worth considering.

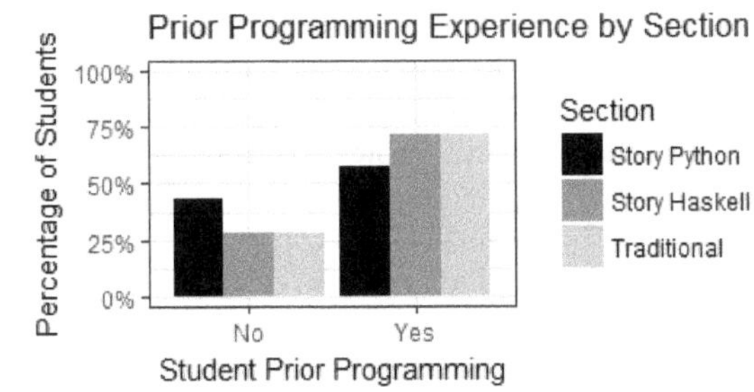

Figure 5: Prior programming experience across all three sections.

The data from the two Story Programming sections do not show a significant difference in the way students felt about the approach based on prior programming experience, and there is no strong correlation between prior programming experience and their feelings toward the Story Programming approach. However, it is interesting to note that there is a very low negative correlation, which means that there were a few more students with prior programming experience who have negative feelings toward the approach. There is also no difference in the usefulness and interest ratings of the book among those with and without prior programming experience.

There is no difference in gender or class standing distributions in the two Story Programming sections, and there is not a significant difference in class standing across all sections. However, Figure 6 shows a significant difference in gender across the Story Programming and traditional sections (*pvalue=.04*). The traditional section has more male students.

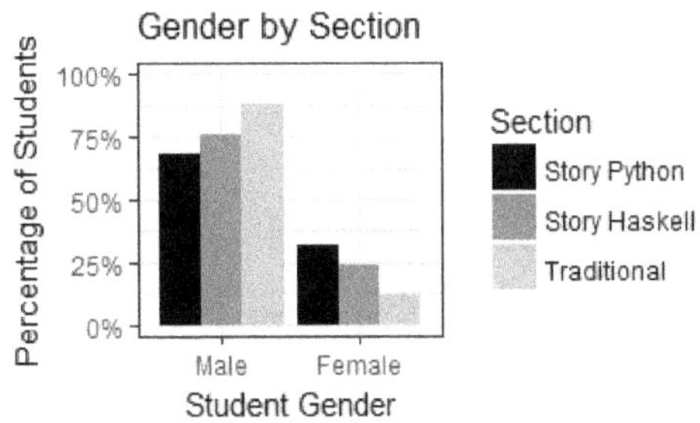

Figure 6: Gender demographics across all three sections.

Just as with prior programming experience, there is not a significant difference in the way students felt about the approach or textbook based on gender or class standing, and there is not a strong correlation between gender or class standing with how they felt about the approach or book.

RQ3: How do students react toward the CT activities versus coding activities?

There is a moderate to strong positive correlation, τ*=0.57-0.72*, between how students feel about the CT activities helping them learn, whether they feel the CT activities motivate them to learn more about computer science, and how engaging they rate the CT activities. There is a moderate correlation between how a student feels about the Story Programming approach with how they rate the CT activities. The students who like the approach are more likely to find the activities engaging (τ*=0.57*) or feel that they help them learn (τ*=0.49*). Likewise, the rating for the coding activities show similar correlations, τ*=0.58-0.72*, between how students feel about the coding activities helping them learn, whether they feel the coding activities motivate them to learn more about computer science, and how engaging they rate the coding activities.

Do the approaches lead to differences in the activities students consider helpful for learning, motivating, and engaging?

There is a significant difference in student reactions toward CT activities among the Story Programming sections, but there is not a significant difference in student reactions toward CT activities in the sections using different approaches. Students in the two Story Programming sections differ on whether they feel CT activities help them learn (*pvalue=.03*), motivate them to learn more about computer science (*pvalue=.01*), and engage them (*pvalue=.01*). Since the trends are the same for these students feelings toward CT activities, we include one figure showing the differences in motivation to learn more about CS among the various sections. Figure 7 shows that the students in the Haskell Story Programming section strongly agree more than those in the Python section, as well as disagreeing less.

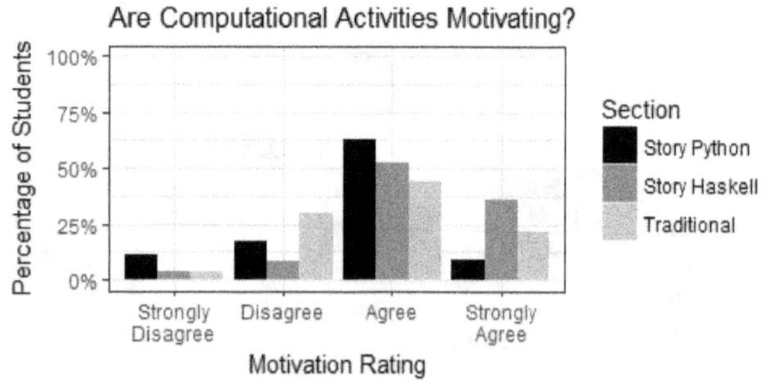

Figure 7: Distribution of agreement about whether computational thinking activities motivated students' learning.

There is not a significant difference in student reactions toward coding activities among Story Programming sections or across the different approaches. The Story Programming sections have about 10% more students who feel the coding activities help them learn, motivate them, and are engaging, but the traditional section has 24% more students who feel like the coding activities motivate them over the CT activities. This might be due to a heavier focus on writing code in the traditional approach, whereas the Story Programming approach focuses on CT using stories and non-coding activities for the first half of the term. Overall, the students in the traditional section disagree more about the helpfulness, motivation, and engagement of both kinds of activities, but the students in the Story Programming section with Python strongly disagree more than any other section.

Is there a correlation between the way students rate CT activities versus coding activities?

Most students who agree the CT activities are engaging also agree the coding activities are engaging, and this is the same for those who strongly agree. Even though there is not a strong linear relationship between most student ratings for CT activities and coding activities, there are other interesting patterns to observe. Across all sections, there are no students who strongly agree with the CT activities and then disagree or strongly disagree with the coding activities. Interestingly, the Haskell Story Programming section never disagrees or strongly disagrees to either activity. In all sections, if students disagree with CT activities, then they tend to agree with coding activities. However, if they disagree with the coding activities, then they continue to disagree with the CT activities.

None of the sections show a difference in the way students of different genders rate the CT or coding activities. Across all sections, there is a significant difference in the way students of different genders rate the engagement of coding activities (*pvalue=.01*), and female students tend to strongly agree with the engagement of these activities more than their male peers. However, students with different prior programming experiences in the Python Story Programming section differ in all their ratings of CT activities (*pvalues=.01-.05*), but ratings for the coding activities in this section do not differ based on prior programming. No other sections show differences in their ratings of CT or coding activities based on prior programming, and across all sections, there is a significant difference among students with prior programming experience and their ratings for the motivation and engagement of CT activities (*pvalues=.03 and .04*).

5 CONCLUSIONS

This study does not show any difference in student success or conceptual learning among either Story Programming sections or between the two approaches. However, it is interesting that the choice of Haskell provides a modest difference in the distribution of As and Bs. It appears that the approach or language choice across different sections of an orientation course does not impact DWF rates as much as having smaller sections does. This result supports making class sizes smaller and perhaps providing different choices for students when offering multiple sections of a course.

Student reactions to the Story Programming approach are mostly positive, and students' prior programming experience, gender, or class standing does not seem to impact the way students react to the new approach or the book. However, the choice of Haskell with the Story Programming approach seems to create more positive reactions than Python. In general, students find the book to be moderately useful or interesting. The students like the chapters in the beginning of the book the most, which suggests that students in an orientation course like concrete algorithmic concepts more than abstract computational concepts.

Interestingly, the two approaches show no significant difference in student reactions toward CT activities performed without the use of a computer and coding activities using a computer, but the language used with the Story Programming approach may affect reactions toward the CT activities. Students in the Haskell section strongly agree more than the Python section with the positive impact of the CT activities, but the reactions toward the coding activities in these sections do not differ. In all sections, students rank coding activities higher than CT activities, which suggests that students value coding more than the CT activities.

In summary, we conclude that Story Programming is a viable approach for teaching a CS orientation class with a mixture of students who do and do not have prior programming experience. The choice of language used with the Story Programming approach has some impact on student grades and reactions toward the approach and activities.

REFERENCES

[1] T. Bell, J. Alexander, I. Freeman, and M. Grimley. 2009. Computer Science Unplugged: school students doing real computing without computers. Journal of Applied Computing and Information Technology 13, 1.
[2] Carlos Bueno. 2014. Loren Ipsum. No Starch Press.
[3] Thomas J. Cortina. 2015. Reaching a broader population of students through "unplugged" activities. Commun. ACM 58, 3 (February 2015), 25-27. DOI: https://doi.org/10.1145/2723671
[4] CS Education Research Group. CS unplugged: Computer Science without a computer. http://www.csunplugged.org
[5] Paul Curzon. 2013. cs4fn and computational thinking unplugged. In Proceedings of the 8th Workshop in Primary and Secondary Computing Education (WiPSE '13). ACM, New York, NY, USA, 47-50. DOI: http://doi.acm.org/10.1145/2532748.2611263
[6] Paul Curzon, Peter W. McOwan, Nicola Plant, and Laura R. Meagher. 2014. Introducing teachers to computational thinking using unplugged storytelling. In Proceedings of the 9th Workshop in Primary and Secondary Computing Education (WiPSCE '14). ACM, New York, NY, USA, 89-92. DOI=http://dx.doi.org/10.1145/2670757.2670767.
[7] Martin Erwig. 2017. Once Upon an Algorithm: How Stories Explain Computing. MIT Press.

[8] Martin Erwig. 2017. The Real Ghost in the Machine. The World Today, 36-37 (Oct./Nov. 2017).

[9] Michael Haungs, Christopher Clark, John Clements, and David Janzen. 2012. Improving first-year success and retention through interest-based CS0 courses. In Proceedings of the 43rd ACM technical symposium on Computer Science Education (SIGCSE '12). ACM, New York, NY, USA, 589-594. DOI=http://dx.doi.org/10.1145/2157136.2157307

[10] Peter B. Henderson. 2011. Computing unplugged enrichment. ACM Inroads 2, 3 (August 2011), 24-25. DOI=http://dx.doi.org/10.1145/ 2003616.2003626

[11] Felienne Hermans and Efthimia Aivaloglou. 2017. To Scratch or not to Scratch?: A controlled experiment comparing plugged first and unplugged first programming lessons. In Proceedings of the 12th Workshop on Primary and Secondary Computing Education (WiPSCE '17), Erik Barendsen and Peter Hubwieser (Eds.). ACM, New York, NY, USA, 49-56. DOI: https://doi.org/10.1145/3137065.3137072

[12] William J. Joel. 2013. A story paradigm for computer science education. In Proceedings of the 18th ACM conference on Innovation and technology in computer science education (ITiCSE '13). ACM, New York, NY, USA, 362-362. DOI=http://dx.doi.org/10.1145/2462476.2466526

[13] Dennis Kafura and Deborah Tatar. 2011. Initial experience with a computational thinking course for computer science students. In Proceedings of the 42nd ACM technical symposium on Computer science education (SIGCSE '11). ACM, New York, NY, USA, 251-256. DOI=http://dx.doi.org/10.1145/1953163.1953242

[14] Jeremy Kubica. 2012. Computational Fairy Tales. CreateSpace Independent Publishing Platform

[15] David J. Malan. 2010. Reinventing CS50. In Proceedings of the 41st ACM technical symposium on Computer science education (SIGCSE '10). ACM, New York, NY, USA, 152-156. DOI: http://dx.doi.org/10.1145/ 1734263.1734316

[16] Cindy Marling and David Juedes. 2016. CS0 for Computer Science Majors at Ohio University. In Proceedings of the 47th ACM Technical Symposium on Computing Science Education (SIGCSE '16). ACM, New York, NY, USA, 138-143. DOI: https://doi.org/10.1145/2839509.2844624

[17] Brandon Rodriguez, Cyndi Rader, and Tracy Camp. 2016. Using Student Performance to Assess CS Unplugged Activities in a Classroom Environment. In Proceedings of the 2016 ACM Conference on Innovation and Technology in Computer Science Education (ITiCSE '16). ACM, New York, NY, USA, 95-100. DOI: https://doi.org/10.1145/2899415.2899465

[18] Renate Thies and Jan Vahrenhold. 2013. On plugging "unplugged" into CS classes. In Proceeding of the 44th ACM technical symposium on Computer science education (SIGCSE '13). ACM, New York, NY, USA, 365-370. DOI: http://dx.doi.org/10.1145/2445196.2445303

[19] Michele Van Dyne and Jeffrey Braun. 2014. Effectiveness of a computational thinking (CS0) course on student analytical skills. In Proceedings of the 45th ACM technical symposium on Computer science education (SIGCSE '14). ACM, New York, NY, USA, 133-138. DOI: http://dx.doi.org/10.1145/ 2538862.2538956

[20] Zoë J. Wood, John Clements, Zachary Peterson, David Janzen, Hugh Smith, Michael Haungs, Julie Workman, John Bellardo, and Bruce DeBruhl. 2018. Mixed Approaches to CS0: Exploring Topic and Pedagogy Variance after Six Years of CS0. In Proceedings of the 49th ACM Technical Symposium on Computer Science Education (SIGCSE '18). ACM, New York, NY, USA, 20-25. DOI: https://doi.org/10.1145/3159450.3159592.

OneUp: Engaging Students in a Gamified Data Structures Course

Darina Dicheva
Computer Science Dept.
Winston-Salem State University
Winston Salem, NC 27110, USA
dichevad@wssu.edu

Keith Irwin
Computer Science Dept.
Winston-Salem State University
Winston Salem, NC 27110, USA
irwinke@wssu.edu

Christo Dichev
Computer Science Dept.
Winston-Salem State University
Winston Salem, NC 27110, USA
dichevc@wssu.edu

ABSTRACT

Although many CS courses require extensive practice, a large number of students show low motivation for engaging in non-graded, self-directed learning activities. To address this problem, we developed OneUp - a highly configurable course gamification platform that enables instructors to tailor the gamification features to fit their preferences. This paper presents a case study of using OneUp to gamify a Data Structures course. The focus is on encouraging students' self-study and better engagement with out-of-class online practicing. We describe the utilized game elements - badges, leaderboard, virtual currency, and learning dashboards, and provide a descriptive analysis of their use. The results of our evaluation show that this gamification intervention has been well received by the students, resulting in significantly increased student engagement and out-of-class practicing and in a reduced failing rate.

CCS CONCEPTS

• **Applied Computing → Interactive Learning Environments**

KEYWORDS

Active learning, gamification, out-of-class study, Data Structures

ACM Reference format:

Darina Dicheva, Keith Irwin and Christo Dichev. 2019. OneUp: Engaging Students in a Gamified Data Structures Course. In *Proceedings of the 50th ACM Technical Symposium on Computer Science Education (SIGCSE'19), Feb. 27-Mar. 2, 2019, Minneapolis, MN, USA.* ACM, New York, NY, USA, 7 pages. https://doi.org/10.1145/3287324.3287480

1 INTRODUCTION

Student engagement and motivation in computing courses, especially at the lower level, is a commonly recognized problem [1]. Many of the courses are focused on skill development, where students are not merely memorizing concepts and principles, but applying them to solve everyday life problems. Central to the notion of skill-based learning is the notion of practice. For developing needed skills, learners need to spend significant time engaged in practicing problem solving and developing subject-related skills in a variety of hands-on scenarios

The majority of available educational tools for practicing are crafted to support skill development through self-study, which makes it hard to mandate and control their use. Self-study tools typically support recommended content/activities and as such, their use rarely counts towards the final grade, which results in a low usage [2]. Thus, although freely available, practicing problems that accompany self-assessment tools are rarely fully utilized. Our approach to ameliorating this problem is through increasing students' motivation by employing gamification. Gamification, the use of game design elements in non-game contexts [3], has attracted the interest of educators with its promises to foster motivation and behavioral changes in learning contexts, but there is a lack of appropriate tools to support instructors in gamifying their courses [4]. To bridge this gap we developed the OneUp Learning platform [5], which is aimed at facilitating the process of gamifying academic courses and enabling tailoring of the gamification features to meet the vision of the course instructor. To the best of our knowledge, it is the first highly configurable platform for gamifying courses. Our first evaluation of the OneUp platform was in a study to gamify a Data Structures course. In this study we aimed to address the following questions:

RQ1: Does gamification encourage out-of-class practice?

RQ2: Does gamification improve grades?

RQ3: What is students' perception of the usefulness of the gamification platform and their engagement with it?

The rest of the paper is organized as follows: Section 2 describes briefly the OneUp platform and Section 3 discusses the experiment for using it to gamify a Data Structures course. In Section 4 we present the results of the study and in Section 5 we introduce the related work. Section 6 concludes the paper.

2 THE ONEUP PLATFORM

The course gamification platform OneUp Learning (OneUp for short) supports the use of established game design principles and elements in the organization of academic courses. Being focused on skill development, it supports practicing, self-assessment, and testing particular skills. The system is described in [5], and here we only summarize its features. The main functionality of OneUp includes: (1) Support for instructors to incorporate game design principles and mechanics in the instructional methods they use in their course; (2) Support for creation and automatic checking of static and dynamic problems, and (3) Learning analytics and

SIGCSE '19, February 27-March 2, 2019, Minneapolis, MN, USA

ACM ISBN 978-1-4503-5890-3/19/02...$15.00
https://doi.org/10.1145/3287324.3287480

visualization to inform students and instructors of student performance and progress throughout the course.

2.1 ONEUP Gamification Features

OneUp can be viewed as a gamified Course Management System (CMS) that allows the instructor to enter assignments, practice exercises, and quizzes/tests and connect game elements to them by specifying appropriate rules. The gaming rules define under what conditions (based on activities, challenges, and skills) specific game elements will be applied. The following game elements are currently supported: points (skill points, challenge points, and activity points), avatars, badges, leaderboards, and virtual currency, along with immediate feedback and freedom to fail. The instructor selects the game elements at the time of creating and configuring the course in OneUp. A user-friendly graphical interface enables easy creating of badges and virtual currency rules. All elements of the framework - the targeted skills, learning content, activities, tests/quizzes, game design elements, and relations between them are configurable. Any game element can be turned on and off to fit the instructor's preferences. In addition, the instructor can enable the students to turn off some game features if found undesirable.

2.2 Practice Support

The OneUp adopted vocabulary reflects the game terminology: the learning objectives are skills, the tests and quizzes are challenges, and the questions included in them are problems. OneUp supports two types of automatically graded challenges: warm-up challenges (for student practice and self-assessment) and serious challenges (graded quizzes and tests). Instructors define the challenges and for each problem in a challenge, specify the challenge points earnable from that problem. The instructor could also specify skill points, which indicate how the problem contributes to increasing the level of student mastery of related course skills. Two types of problems are supported: static and dynamic. Static are problems for which the correct solution is given at the time of entering them in the system. These include multiple-choice questions, multiple answer questions, true/false questions, fill-in-the-blank questions, and matching questions. Dynamic problems are short computer programs, which use a random seed to generate a unique instance of a particular programming or calculating problem and then grade the correctness of the answer submitted for that problem.

2.3 Feedback and Learning Analytics

Feedback is provided to the students in a number of ways. At the problem level, the student gets feedback on their entered solution as specified by the instructor at the time of creation of the challenge. If the instructor specifies the course topical structure during the course configuration, the topics are used for grouping the displayed warm-up challenges. For each topic, the students see summarized information about their practicing performance on that topic – a row of colored squares indicating the score on each challenge: green ('You've got it!'), blue ('Getting there'), red ('Needs improvement'), and white ('Not attempted').

At the course level, students can see aggregated information about their performance in their personal learning analytics dashboard. This dashboard displays student experience points (XP), practice points (collected and possible), and course bucks they have earned so far. A central piece in the dashboard is the progress bar, which consists of four parts displayed in different colors: the course points earned so far (purple), the amount of course points that can be earned in the future (yellow), the amount of points already lost (red), and the learning predictor - the total amount of points that would be earned in this course if the student keeps the same level of performance in the course (black). The dashboard also shows the skill analytics and the student's results of taking serious challenges and warm-up challenges. Finally, it displays all badges earned by the learner. The instructors can see students' individual learning dashboards. In addition, they are presented with a grade book, visualizations of the class results on warm-up and serious challenges, and an instructor dashboard that summarizes students' engagement and outcomes: serious challenge points, activity points, number of warm-up challenges taken, earned virtual currency, and timestamp of the last action.

2.4 Social Comparison

OneUp supports social comparison in two ways. Firstly, for each of the performance indicators in the student individual learning dashboard there is an option for displaying the class average as well. Secondly, the course dashboard, which is shown on the main course website contains a leaderboard (XP ranking), skill ranking, and latest awarded badges to students from this course. The instructor can configure which of these to be shown and give the students the right to show/hide any of them on their own display.

3 CASE STUDY: GAMIFYING A DATA STRUCTURES COURSE

In this study we decided to use OneUp as both an online practice system and a gamified framework for maintaining information not only about student practicing but also about student overall course engagement and performance. We used OneUp in addition to the Blackboard CMS system. The instructor posted the course slides and assignments on Blackboard, however all grades were also entered in OneUp, so that students can benefit from the gamification intervention. Student usage of OneUp was voluntary. The goal of the study was to evaluate whether gamification would increase student motivation and course engagement, in particular, for out-of-class practicing, which is critically important for learning in STEM disciplines.

The preparation for gamifying the Data Structures course consisted of two parts: creating warm-up challenges for student practicing and configuring the course in the OneUp platform.

3.1 Challenges and Problems

We created 64 warm-up challenges with a total of 290 problems. The challenge distribution by topic is as follows: Java Classes (review) - 3, Recursion - 2, Bags - 14, Stacks - 14, Queues - 11, Lists - 12, and Trees - 5. Of the problems, 152 are multiple-choice,

9 multiple answers, 4 matching, 83 true/false questions, and 42 are dynamic problems. We created three types of dynamic problems:

1. Dynamic problems asking what would be the content of a particular data structure after applying a series of add/delete/ view operations on it. For those, we modeled the specific data structure and generated random sequences of statements.
2. Dynamic problems for traversing a tree.
3. Programming problems. These required supporting code for running the student program and a testing program.

3.2 Gamification Features

In the gamified Data Structures Course we used all gamification features supported by the OneUp platform. Accordingly, the students could create avatars, earn badges, earn virtual currency and spend it in the Course Shop, check their performance on their private learning dashboard and the class performance on the course dashboard. Moreover, they were enabled to select the gamification features they wanted to see and whether to have the class average for the performance matrixes displayed on their dashboard.

The rewards in the gamified course were in the form of badges and virtual currency (VC), which students could earn and spend based on rules specified by the instructor. We decided to use badges primarily to reward students for their performance and to use virtual currency mainly to reward their course engagement and efforts to learn, including practicing, attending classes, etc.

The instructor created the badges and VC rules in the OneUp instructor's interface. Table 1 shows some of the badge categories, and Table 2 - some earning and spending rules defined in OneUp.

Table 1: Sample Badge Categories Used in the Course

	*Game Changer* (Level 1, 2, 3): the difference of student's percent score of an assignment with the previous one is between 10% - 19% for Level 1, 20% - 29% for Level 2, and > 30% for Level 3
	*Highest Score for Assignment*
	*Perfect Score on Test*
	*Persistent Practice* (Level 1, 2, 3): completes 5 distinct warm-up challenges for Level 1, 20 for level 2, and 40 for Level 3.

Badges did not affect the course grade in any way but they served as a recognition with social effect [6], since they were displayed on the class leaderboard. Differently from the badges, the virtual currency could affect the course grades directly or indirectly, depending on the rules selected by the instructor. Examples of the former are buying some extra credit points for a specific homework or buying credit for one problem on a test. Examples for the latter are requesting a deadline extension or a resubmission of a homework. The idea here is to stimulate students to practice more for earning more 'course bucks' by incentivizing them with purchasable course related 'benefit'. This way the virtual currency offers a strategy for encouraging persistent practicing and an alternative method for rewarding student learning.

Table 2: Examples of Earning and Spending Rules

Earning Rules	
Condition	*VC*
First taking of a warmup challenge with a score > 80%	5
Taking a new warmup challenge with a score > 75%	1
Submitting an assignment 2 days before the due date	1
Attending 5 consecutive classes	1
Spending Rules	
Condition	*VC*
Buy 5 extra credit points for an assignment	10
Buy a 15-min extension of the time for a test	5
Get 1 different problem on a test	10
Buy another attempt (re-submission) for an assignment	10

3.3 Research Method

The CSC 2331 Data Structures course is offered each semester hence the enrollment is not high. Therefore, we conducted a quasi-experiment [7]: we used the fall 2017 class (16 students) as a control group and the spring 2018 class (11 students) as an experimental group. The same instructor taught both classes using the same instructional materials, teaching methodology, and student assessment. Both groups used the OneUp platform for out-of-class learning and practicing, but for the experimental group all gamification features were activated, while for the control group they were disabled. All students in both groups signed an Informed Consent Form to participate in the study.

To answer the research questions we used two complimentary methods. For the first two (R1 and R2), we used the OneUp system log to extract data for tracking student visits to the gamification-related pages, how many practice quizzes they have completed, etc. We also used student final course grades to evaluate the impact of gamifying the course on students' academic performance. To answer the third research question (R3), we conducted a survey with the experimental group at the end of the semester.

4 RESULTS

4.1 Platform Usage

The use of the OneUp gamification platform was not required for either the control group or the experimental group. For both groups the instructor created accounts for all students in the beginning of the semester and regularly reminded the students of the benefits of doing practice exercises in OneUp for their learning and course performance. However, our study revealed a significant difference in the OneUp usage for the experimental group compared to that of the control group. In this section, we first report statistics on the use of the OneUp gamification elements by the students in the experimental group, and then we compare the use of OneUp as a platform for practicing by the students of both the control and the experimental group.

4.1.1 Use of the gamification features of OneUp. As described in Section 3.2, the core features used in the gamified Data Structures course were avatars, badges, virtual currency, the course leaderboard, and the learning dashboard. The students were not required to use any of these features. Regarding the avatars, 27% of the students chose not to use a personal avatar. It is interesting that the "no avatar" group included students from both ends (high and low) of the OneUp usage spectrum. The distribution of the student accesses to the OneUp gamification-related pages is presented on Fig. 1, where LD stands for Learning Dashboard, VC-E – for VC Earning Transactions, VC-S for VC Spending Transactions, BI for Badges Info, and VC-I for VC Info.

As Fig. 1 shows, the page most frequently visited by the students is the Learning Dashboard, where they could see the aggregated information about their course performance. A possible reason is that the students could check their progress bar, which not only reflected their current course points but also gave a prediction about the total course points/course grade that the student would have at the end of the course if they kept the same performance. The next in popularity is the page reporting the student's virtual currency transactions. This was the place where students could track the status of a *purchase* made in the Course Shop and the corresponding message from the instructor. The Earning VC Transactions page gave information about how exactly the students earned their virtual currency. As expected, the least frequent visits were to the pages that gave information about what kind of badges one can get in this course and what are the rules for earning and spending virtual currency. It is possible that after a few visits the students retained that information.

4.1.2 Badges. During the semester, a total of 54 badges were awarded. Notably, all of the students received at least one badge, with 18% receiving more than 10 badges. As shown in Fig. 2 (where only categories with more than one badge are shown), the most badges have been awarded for Persistent Practice Level 1 (completed 5 distinct challenges) and Level 2 (completed 20 challenges). These are followed by Game Changer Level 1 and Level 3 (Level 1 is given when the difference between the percent score of a test or an assignment from the previous one is between 10% and 19%, and Level 3 when this difference is > 30%).

4.1.3 Virtual Currency. During the course, 595 VC earning transactions were recorded. Each VC earning transaction is a result of satisfying a VC earning rule as defined by the instructor. Fig. 3 shows the distribution of the VC earning transactions by category (VC rules). As it can be seen, students earned most of their VC for taking new warm-up challenges: with a score > 70% (147), with a score > 80% (135), and with a score > 90% (112). The remaining transactions include VC earned for turning correct labs in class, attending 5 consecutive classes, getting a grade greater than the class average on a homework, etc. Fig. 3 depicts the distribution of the students' earning transactions by category.

Students made 95 purchases in the Course Shop using their accumulated virtual currency. All but one student made purchases, with an average of 9.5 transactions per student. 18% of the students made more than 20 purchases. Fig. 4 depicts the distribution of the students' spending transactions by category. This distribution shows that students' favorite has been buying extra credit points for an assignment (they were allowed to buy max 5 points for an assignment with 150 possible points).

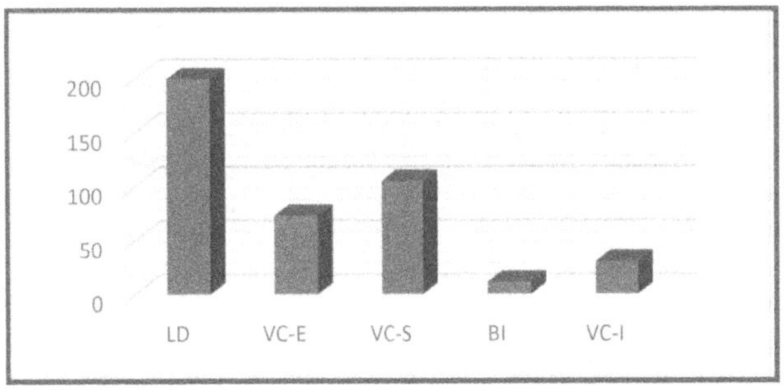

Figure 1: Access to gamification-related pages.

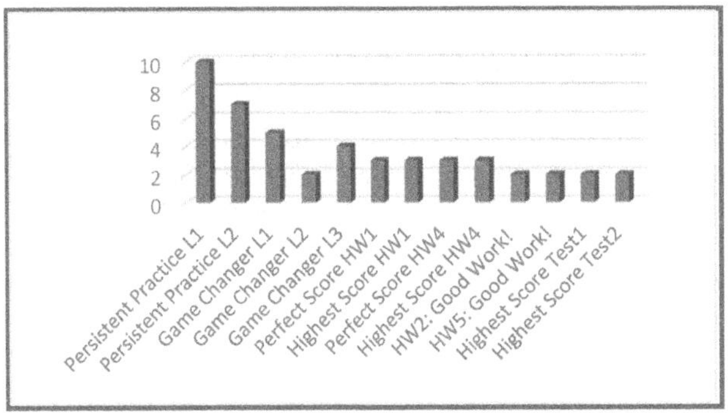

Figure 2: Earned badges by category.

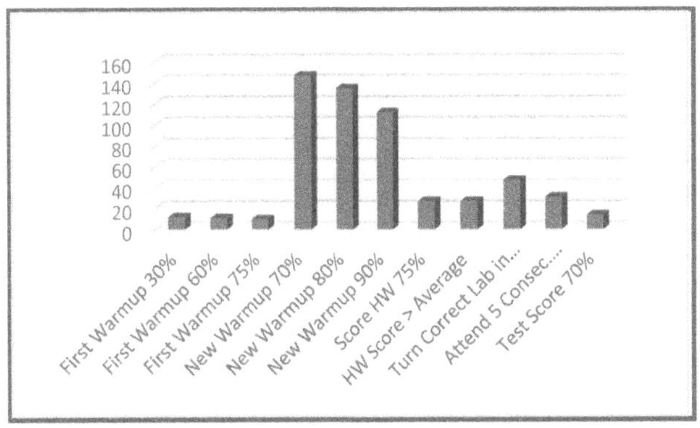

Figure 3: Student VC earned transactions by category.

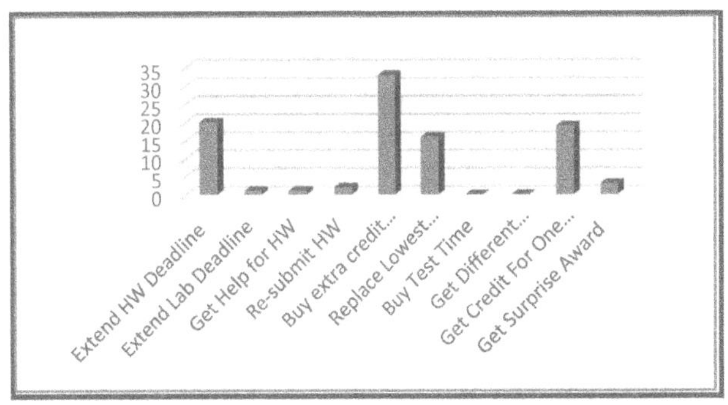

Figure 4: Student VC spent transactions by category.

This is followed by "Getting credit for 1 test question", "Extend the deadline of an assignment with 12 hours" and "Replace the lowest homework grade with the student average homework grade". Remarkably, no VC was spent for extending test time or getting a different problem on a test.

4.1.4 Taking Practice Tests. Adding gamification features resulted in a significant increase of the taken warmup challenges: the experimental group took 239 distinct warmup challenges with a total of 554 attempts, while the control group took only 45 distinct warmup challenges with a total of 73 attempts. Fig. 5 (a) shows the percent of students who have taken 1-10, 11-20, 21-30, or 31-50 challenges for both groups.

As evidenced in Fig.5 (a), most of the students in the control group (69%) have taken between 1 and 10 distinct challenges, with 25% - none, and only 6% between 11 and 20 challenges. No students have taken more than 20 distinct challenges. In contrast, all students in the experimental group have taken some challenges, with 46% of the students, between 21 and 30 challenges and 18% between 31 and 50 challenges. The difference in the number of warm-up attempts is even more pronounced (see Fig. 5 (b)): 25% of the students from the control group have not taken warm-ups and none of them have taken more than 20 warm-ups, while 37% of the experimental group students have taken between 51 and 60, 18% between 61 and 70, and 9% more than 70 warm-ups. The average number of warm-up challenge attempts for the control group was 4.5625, while the average number of challenges for the experimental group was 46.1667. The one-sided t test (t = -3.1574, p-value = 0.008895) shows that the difference is statistically significant. These results signal that after the gamification intervention, students' practicing has intensified significantly.

For the experimental group, we also looked at the distribution of warm-ups taken by date. This distribution shows clear picks around the dates of the three course exams. The results are consistent with previous findings reporting that the students take online practice exercises mainly before course milestones [10].

4.1.5 Performance. We use student final course grades to evaluate the impact of gamifying the course on students' learning and academic performance. We consider course failing rates as relevant and important measure of the impact. Fig. 6 depicts the distributions of the final course grades for both groups.

While we cannot claim statistical significance of these results, they reveal a drastic change of the numbers of Fs and a significant increase of the passing grade (C) for the experimental group. For comparison, the Fs and Ds for the previous two course offerings are as follows: F16 – 10% Ds and 10% Fs and for S17 – 15% Ds and 20% Fs. There is also a slight increase of the As and Bs.

The results in 4.1.4 and 4.1.5 positively confirm RQ1 and RQ2.

4.2 Student Feedback

At the end of the semester, we conducted a survey to gather further quantitative feedback about students' perception of usefulness of the system and engagement with it. We were particularly interested in understanding what motivated students to continue a practice session after taking one challenge. The survey used a 5-point Likert scale (1 = strongly disagree, 3 = neutral, 5 = strongly agree).

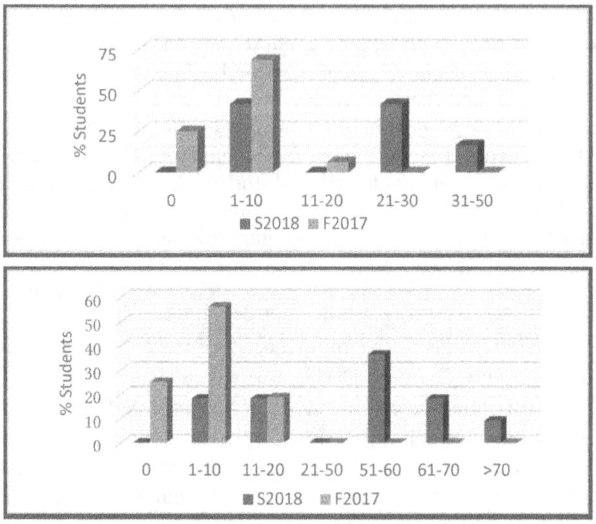

Figure 5: (a) Distinct warm-up challenges; (b) Attempts.

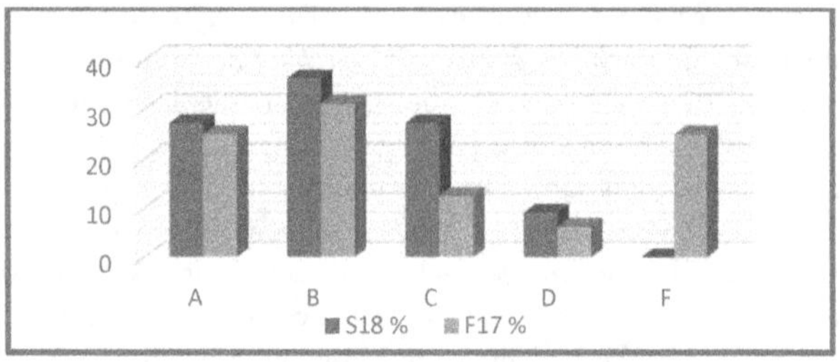

Figure 6: Final Course Grades.

Table 3 shows three sub-scales of the questionnaire: *Perception of usefulness* (Q1-Q3), *Motivation to keep using OneUp* (Q4-Q8), and *Level of engagement* while practicing (Q9-Q12). All students from the experimental group completed the survey. The results are presented in Fig. 7. The answers, indicate that the majority of students perceived OneUp as very useful, with a mean score of 4.33 for questions Q1 – Q3, with a particularly high score of 'Agree' and 'Strong Agree' (100%) on Q3 ('Using OneUp helped me to improve my grades'). The answers of the questions in the category 'Level of Engagement', characterized by a mean score of 3.90, with the highest score for Q9 (4.27) and lowest for Q10 (3.72) were also largely positive.

The overall result shows a good engagement of the students at the time of practicing, which, in turn, is an indication for an effective intervention. Of interest are student responses to questions about what motivates them to keep practicing once they have started. The desire to improve their grades (Q5) and to earn more virtual currency (Q7) are the leading factors for student persistency to practice (100% Agree and Strongly Agree for both). Enjoying the experience of using the system (Q8) elicited mixed but mostly positive responses. One possible interpretation of these results is that: (1) the motivation to use OneUp was mainly driven by the provided learning experience; (2) the enjoyment arose from the practicing experience with OneUp.

These data clearly indicates positive results for the indicators associated with RQ3.

Table 3: Survey Questions by Category

Q1. I felt more effective in self-learning when using OneUp.
Q2. Using OneUp made it easier for me to prepare for the tests.
Q3. Using OneUp helped me to improve my grades.
A desire to
Q4: improve my skills.
Q5. improve my grades
Q6. earn more badges
Q7. earn more virtual currency
Q8. enjoy the experience of using the system encouraged me to continue practice sessions in OneUp.
Q9. When taking a warm-up I put in effort to complete it.
Q10. I do not take the challenges in OneUp very seriously.
Q11. When taking a warm-up I do not pay much attention to my performance.
Q12. I intend to use OneUp if offered in future courses.

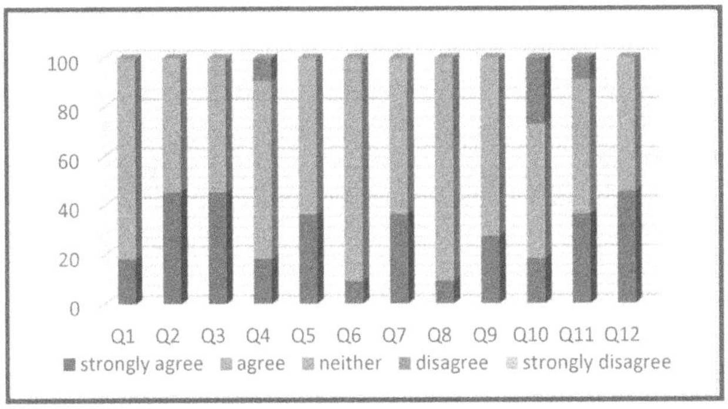

Figure 7: Answers to Survey Questions.

5 RELATED WORK

There have been several reports on using gamification in CS courses. In a "Data Structures and Algorithms" course, Haaranen and colleagues [8] used badges which students could earn by doing online exercises with certain restrictions, such as completing them a full week before deadline or getting them correct on the first try. The exercises contributed 20-30% to their course grade. The authors concluded that student behavior can be affected with badges but they did not have a significant effect on the course results because some students stopped doing the exercises once they had achieved their desired grade. In this context, the intervention was not aligned with students' goals. Latulipe et al. [9] used gamification to reward students for extra engagement in a flipped CS1 class with a focus on teamwork. The study has been constrained to using a leaderboard, stamps, and tokens and the evaluation showed positive ratings of the questions related to gamification. With the goal to increase attendance and engagement in the practical sessions for CS1 and CS2, Harrington et al. [10] used the TrAcademic system, a public leaderboard of points that could be awarded by TAs during the sessions for attendance, completion of problems, and assisting other students. The authors report that gamifying the practical sessions dramatically improved attendance and retention rates. Iosup and Epema [11] describe a Computer Organization gamified course, which uses points, levels, badges, leaderboards, and social engagement. Key features included enabling various paths of advancement and fostering social interaction inside and outside the classroom. Their evaluation found that gamification could help in many ways, from increasing passing rates and participation, to high student satisfaction. O'Donovan et al. [12] used a reward system based on Experience points, which students earned by completing quizzes, attending lectures, and participating in class exercises. They used Steam Points as an in-game currency: for every 200 XP, students get 1 SP. They can spend SP in the steam shop on quiz do-overs, puzzle hints, class rewards, and assignment extensions. The authors concluded that gamification improved student engagement and had a significant positive impact on student grades.

There are two main differences between our work and the previously reported works. The first one is that the authors of those reports have implemented gamification support for a specific course, which cannot be easily reused for another course. In contrast, we are using our course independent gamification platform, where any reconfiguration of the game features by the instructor is straightforward. The second difference is that all the reported works have gamified course activities, which were required, meaning that they were part of the course structure. In our experiment, we focus on student self-directed learning. In addition, we examine the use of virtual currency, one of the least explored gamification elements, which was favored by the students.

6 CONCLUSION

We have used the OneUp platform to gamify a Data Structures course and performed an experimental study of the use and effect of the gamification elements on student practicing, as well as the students' perception of the system. The results successfully confirmed our hypothesis that the addition of the OneUp gamification features to the online practicing platform would lead to increased self-study and practicing of the students. This, in turn, led to improved course performance.

The offered incentives were well received, with the majority of students expressing a preference for virtual currency compared to badges. Our interpretation of the high level of earning and spending of virtual currency is that this particular game design element was attracting students as a lever for improving their grades. The variety of badges earned shows that they also played a stimulating role, in particular, for strong students for which the grades were of less concern. The high frequency of visits to some gamification related pages suggests that the goal orientation and competition was driving those visits: students were curious to understand how they perform in relation to their goals and in relation to their classmates.

Overall, the results of the study indicate that the gamification intervention had a positive effect on students' learning experience.

ACKNOWLEDGMENTS

This material is based upon work funded by the NSF HBCU-UP TIP-1623236 Project and partially supported by the NSF DUE-1821189 Project.

REFERENCES

[1] P.R. Pintrich. 2003. A Motivational Science Perspective on the Role of Student Motivation in Learning and Teaching Contexts. *Journal of Educational Psychology*, 95(4), 667-686.

[2] T.D. Loboda, J. Guerra, R. Hosseini, and P. Brusilovsky. 2014. Mastery Grids: An Open Source Social Educational Progress Visualization. In: C. Rensing, S. de Freitas, T. Ley, P.J. Muñoz-Merino (Eds.) *Open Learning and Teaching in Educational Communities.* EC-TEL 2014. LNCS, Vol. 8719, Springer.

[3] S. Deterding, D. Dixon, R. Khaled, and L. Nacke. 2011. From game design elements to gamefulness: Defining "gamification". In *Proceedings of the 15th Int. MindTrek Conference*, Tampere, Finland, ACM, New York, NY, 9-15.

[4] D. Dicheva, C. Dichev, G. Agre, G., and G. Angelova. 2015. Gamification in Education: a Systematic Mapping Study. *Educational Technology & Society,* 18(3), 75-88.

[5] D. Dicheva, K. Irwin, and C. Dichev. 2018. OneUp: Supporting Practical and Experimental Gamification of Learning. *International Journal of Serious Games,* 5(3), 5 - 21.

[6] J. Hamari and J. Koivisto. 2013. Social Motivations to Use Gamification: An Empirical Study of Gamifying Exercise. *ECIS 2013 Completed Research.* 105.

[7] D. Campbell and J. Stanley. 1966. *Experimental and quasi-experimental designs for research.* Ravenio Books.

[8] L. Haaranen, P. Ihantola, L. Hakulinen, and A. Korhonen. 2014. How (not) to Introduce Badges to Online Exercises. In *Proceedings of the 45th ACM technical symposium on Computer science education* (SIGCSE'14), March 5-8, 2014, Atlanta, GA, ACM, New York, NY, 33-38.

[9] C. Latulipe, N.B. Long, and C.E. Seminario. 2015. Structuring Flipped Classes with Lightweight Teams and Gamification. In *Proceedings of the 46th ACM Technical Symposium on Computer Science Education* (SIGCSE'15), ACM, New York, NY, 392-397.

[10] B. Harrington and A. Chaudhry. 2017. TrAcademic: Improving Participation and Engagement in CS1/CS2 with Gamified Practicals. In *Proceedings of the 2017 ACM Conference on Innovation and Technology in Computer Science Education* (ITiCSE'17), July 3-5, 2017, Bologna, Italy, 347-352.

[11] A. Iosup, and D. Epema. 2014. An Experience Report on Using Gamification in Technical Higher Education. In *Proceedings of the 45th ACM technical symposium on Computer science education* (SIGCSE'14), March 3-8, 2014, Atlanta, GA, ACM, New York, NY, 27-32.

[12] S. O'Donovan, J. Gain, and P. Marais. 2013. A case study in the gamification of a university-level games development course. In Proceedings of the *South African Institute for Computer Scientists and Information Technologists Conference* (SAICSIT '13), East London, South Africa, 242-251.

Program Wars

A Card Game for Learning Programming and Cybersecurity Concepts

John Anvik
University of Lethbridge
john.anvik@uleth.ca

Vincent Cote
University of Lethbridge
vincent.cote@uleth.ca

Jace Riehl
University of Lethbridge
jace.riehl@uleth.ca

ABSTRACT

Although there are many computer science learning games with the goal of teaching programming, such games typically require the person to either learn an existing programming language or the game's own specialized language. This can be intimidating, confusing or frustrating for an individual when they cannot get their "program" to work correctly (e.g. syntax error, infinite loop). Additionally, such games commonly use a puzzle-solving approach that does not appeal to some demographics.

This paper presents a programming-language-independent approach to teaching fundamental programming and cybersecurity concepts using simple vocabulary. This approach also uses the familiar activity of playing cards against opponents to create a more dynamic and engaging learning experience. The approach is demonstrated by a web-based game called *Program Wars*. Results from a user study show that players are able to effectively connect game concepts to actual programming language structures; however, whether players' comprehension of computer programming is improved is unclear.

KEYWORDS

Programming language education; Cybersecurity education; web application; card game

ACM Reference Format:
John Anvik, Vincent Cote, and Jace Riehl. 2019. Program Wars: A Card Game for Learning Programming and Cybersecurity Concepts. In *Proceedings of the 50th ACM Technical Symposium on Computer Science Education (SIGCSE '19), February 27-March 2, 2019, Minneapolis, MN, USA.* ACM, New York, NY, USA, 7 pages. https://doi.org/10.1145/3287324.3287496

1 INTRODUCTION

Although there are many learning games and environments with the goal of teaching computer science concepts [4, 9, 13, 22] and software engineering [2, 7, 14, 17], those that focus on teaching programming typically fail in two respects.

First, most such games require the user to either learn an existing programming language (e.g. Javascript, Python, C) or their own specialized language (e.g. Scratch [21] or Alice [20]). For an individual not familiar with programming structures, it can be intimidating, confusing or frustrating when they cannot get their "program" to work correctly. For example, novices commonly create syntax errors when they do not understand the "programming language", or they create logical errors, such as an infinite loop. Bromwich et al. [5] observed that many educational programming languages and environments are often overly ambitious in what they teach.

Second, the gameplay generally falls into one of two different game styles: puzzle solving or sandbox. The premise of puzzle-solving style games tends to be a variation of getting a robot to navigate a maze, a problem domain that does not appeal to some demographics, such as females [18]. Sandbox games attempt to address this limitation by allowing the individual to create their own stories in an open-ended way, thereby connecting to an individual's interests. However, such flexibility requires the guidance of the individual by an outside influence, such as a teacher, to ensure the progression of learning [5].

Program Wars[1] is a web-based card game for teaching or reinforcing the fundamental concepts of programming and cybersecurity to those with limited or no programming experience. Being web-based, it is freely available for use by any institution wishing to adopt it.[2] In the game, players construct a computer program that meets or exceeds a goal number of statements. Players build their program using "instruction" cards and "repetition" cards. Some repetition cards allow the player to change the number of repetitions using "variable" cards. Players can also "group" instructions to protect portions of their program from being cyberattacked (i.e. "hacked").

Program Wars addresses both of the above limitations. First, Program Wars addresses the problem that "the bad usability of programming languages increases [the] difficulty [of learning programming]." [12]. It does this by using a programming-language-independent approach that focuses on the fundamental programming language concepts using a simple vocabulary (e.g. "instruction", "group", "repeat"). Second, Program Wars uses the familiar activity of playing cards, a game type that has been previously used for teaching such topics as algorithm analysis and design [8] and software engineering [1, 3, 19]. This game type has been found to have more general and long-term appeal [6, 11, 15, 16, 18] than solving a maze. In Program Wars the player faces one or more AI opponents for a dynamic and engaging learning experience.

Program Wars is similar in teaching scope to VISPROCON [5], which also focuses on only teaching the concepts of sequences, loops, and conditionals. Whereas VISPROCON uses the play model of navigating a robot through a maze, Program Wars uses the play model of a card game.

A pilot user study with non-computer science undergraduates was conducted to answer three research questions (see Section 3).

SIGCSE '19, February 27-March 2, 2019, Minneapolis, MN, USA

ACM ISBN 978-1-4503-5890-3/19/02...$15.00
https://doi.org/10.1145/3287324.3287496

[1] https://github.com/johnanvik/program-wars
[2] https://programming-wars.firebaseapp.com/

Participants completed a pre-game questionnaire, played several games of Program Wars, and completed a post-game questionnaire.

This paper proceeds as follows. First, a detailed description of Program Wars is presented. Next, a description of the pilot user study conducted to evaluate Program Wars is given followed by the results and a discussion of the study. Finally, improvements made to Program Wars subsequent to the pilot user study are described before concluding the paper.

2 PROGRAM WARS

This section presents a high-level view of the gameplay and a detailed description of the basic cards in Program Wars. Advanced cards are presented in Section 5.

2.1 Overview of Gameplay

At the start of Program Wars, the player chooses the target number of points (e.g. 35, 75, 105) and the number of opponents (1-3) against which they wish to play (the deck size is proportional to the number of players). Each player is dealt six cards and on each turn receives another card from the deck.

The gameplay of Program Wars is made up of a series of rounds in which each player has a turn. On a turn, a player can either play or discard a card from their hand. To win, a player needs to create a program that reaches a minimum number of points for the currently selected branch (see Section 2.2.1). The points are the total number of instructions that would be executed by the computer. Players use a variety of means to accumulate points, all the while fending off attacks from the other players. As the check for a winner happens at the end of each round, it is possible for more than one player to complete their program and win the game.

Figure 1 shows part of the way through a two-player game. Some of the elements shown in the figure are improvements made after the pilot user study (outlined by dotted red boxes and labelled "Version 2"; see Section 5 for details).

The top half of the screen (left to right) shows the current progress of the two players for each of their play area, the current player's hand, and the cyberattack and cybersecurity cards that are affecting the player.

The bottom half of the screen shows the current player's True and False play areas, with the False branch being the active play area for this round. In the True path, the player has one stack of cards totalling 15 instructions and another card stack totalling 18 instructions. Collectively, the True path contains 33 instructions. The False path contains two card stacks, each with one card, producing a total of 2 instructions for this path. However, due to the effect of a *Malware* card, the effective instruction total for the True path is reduced to 25 (see Section 5.1.1).

Three aids are provided to assist a player in learning the game. First, there is an 11-min video that shows a game being played. Second, players can access a page from the game that describes the rules of the game and all of the cards. Lastly, when a player clicks on a card, a description of the card is presented on the left side of the top area of the screen. Players can choose to disable this feature once they are familiar with the game.

2.2 Game Cards and Areas

The player builds their program using the basic building blocks of any program: instructions, groups of instructions, repetition, and branching. Also, the player can launch a cyberattack at an opponent, or prepare a defence against their opponents. This section describes each of the cards in the game and their relation to computer science concepts.

2.2.1 Branching. The programming concept of *branching* or *paths* is represented in the game by two playing areas, each representing the 'True' and 'False' path of the traditional *if-then* conditional statement. At the start of each round in the game, one of the two playing areas is randomly selected to be the 'active' branch and players build their program in that play area during their turn. [3]

2.2.2 Instructions. As in actual computer programs, instructions form the backbone of the player's created program. Each instruction card represents a fixed number of instructions (1, 2, or 3). These cards are the base of a card stack created in one of the two playing areas. As the player needs to play this type of card to start gaining points in the game, it is often the card played on their first turn.

Figure 1 shows examples of instruction cards. In the True play area, there is an example of an *Instruction-3* card, and in the False play area, there are two *Instruction-1* cards.

2.2.3 Repetition. Repeat cards allow the player to multiply the effect of an Instruction, Group, or another Repeat card. These cards represent the concept of a *loop*. There are three sizes of Repeat cards: 2, 3, and 4. By placing a Repeat card on another Repeat card, the player can form a nested loop. An example of Repeat cards forming a nested loop is shown in the True play area where a *Repeat-3* has been placed on a *Repeat-2*, which is on an *Instruction-3*, creating a card stack of 18 instructions.

In addition to the fixed-size Repeat cards, there is also a variable Repeat card (called *Repeat-X*). This card has no advantage by itself; it acts as a *Repeat-1* card. This card is used in conjunction with a Variable card. Figure 1 shows an example of its use, along with a Variable card, on the leftmost side of the True play area.

2.2.4 Variables. Variable cards represent the concept of a *variable*. Placing a Variable card on a *Repeat-X* increases its multiplicative power. The Variable cards have values of 3 through 6 inclusive. If the Variable card is on the top of the card stack (i.e. not buried by another Repeat card) it can be replaced by another Variable card on a player's turn.

Figure 1 shows an example where a *Variable-5* card is used (leftmost side of the True play area). If the player chooses, they could replace this card with the *Variable-3* or *Variable-4* card in their hand.

2.2.5 Groups. A Group card represents the concept of a *function*, *method*, or *procedure* in the game. A player can 'group' either a single instruction card or a stack of cards (i.e. a collection of Instruction, Repetition and Variable cards) that totals the value of the Group card. Group cards have fixed values of 2 through 6, inclusive. Group cards protect a portion of the player's program from a *Hack* cyberattack (see Section 2.2.6). The use of Group cards also

[3] We plan to explore the use of Variable cards and a conditional expression to more accurately represent this concept in a future version of the game.

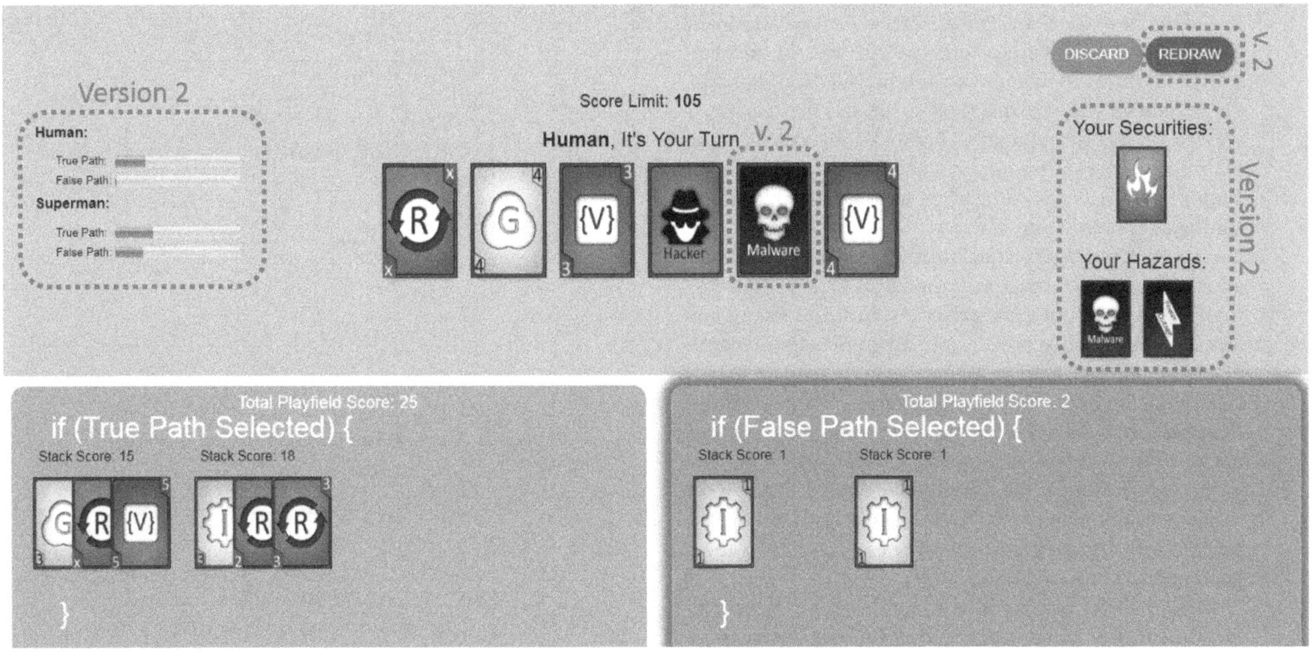

Figure 1: Partway through a game where the *False* path has been selected for the current round.

introduces players to the software engineering practice of source code refactoring [10].

For example, assume that in Figure 1, the False play area also contained an *Instruction-2* card. On their turn, the player could play the *Group-4* card from their hand to replace the two *Instruction-1* cards and the *Instruction-2* card, as the three card total is 4. We can see that a similar situation occurred previously on the True path, where a *Group-3* card is under a *Repeat-X* and *Variable-5*.

2.2.6 Cyberattack. As cybersecurity is an important aspect of modern day software development, Program Wars includes one cybersecurity concept in addition to programming language concepts. This card also makes the game interactive between the players.

The *Hack* card represents an attack by a malicious programmer. It allows a player to remove one stack of instructions from one of an opponent's play areas. Card stacks that contain a *Group* card are protected from being 'hacked'.

3 PILOT USER STUDY

This section presents a pilot user study that collected both quantitative and qualitative data regarding the playing of Program Wars. The objective of the study was to answer three research questions:

RQ1 Does playing Program Wars lead to players having a better understanding of a computer program?

RQ2 Is a player of Program Wars able to connect game concepts to elements in actual computer programs?

RQ3 What are the players' impressions of Program Wars?

The remainder of this section presents the methodology used to answer these research questions.

3.1 Methodology

To find answers to our research questions, we conducted a user study.[4] Participants in the study were asked to do the following:

(1) **Navigate to the URL for the study.** The study was conducted entirely in a web browser. The intent was to allow participants to participate in the study at their own choice of time and at their own pace without influence from the researchers. It was also believed that doing so would lead to more participation in the study.[5]
(2) **Complete a demographics questionnaire.** This questionnaire collected information about the participant's background including previous experience with programming concepts, software for teaching programming, and card games.
(3) **Complete a pre-game survey.** Participants were given five multiple choice questions to test their pre-existing skill at understanding a computer program. For each question, the participant examined a simple arithmetic program containing no input/output statements[6] and responded with what they thought was the computed value.
The programs were presented in one of four programming languages (C, Python, Pascal or Fortran), as a goal of Program Wars is to teach the fundamental concepts of programming independent of a specific programming language. The program for each question was the same with the programming language being randomly chosen. For example, assuming

[4] The practices and procedures for the user study were reviewed by a Human Subject Research Committee to ensure that standards for ethical treatment of participants, such as informed consent and privacy, were addressed.

[5] Althouigh participants may have received outside help from peers or online resources during the study, we believe this to be unlikely or to have a minimal effect given the questions asked in the questionnaires.

[6] This choice was made to limit the complexity of the programs and responses.

five different participants, for the first question Participant #1 was shown a C program, Participant #2 was shown a Fortran program, Participant #3 was shown a Pascal program, Participant #4 was shown a C program, and Participant #5 was shown a Fortran program. Figure 2 shows an example of one pre-game survey question using C.[7]

(4) **Play Program Wars.** Participants were asked to play three short games of Program Wars.

(5) **Complete a post-game questionnaire.** Participants were asked five multiple choice programming questions similar to those asked in the pre-game survey. Again, the programs presented were given in one of the four programming languages. The five questions in the post-game survey were paired with corresponding questions in the pre-game survey to require the same knowledge for understanding the program, but not necessarily presented using the same programming language. Figure 3 shows the corresponding post-game Python variant corresponding to the question given in Figure 2. Participants' post-game responses were compared with their pre-game responses to answer RQ1.

Participants were also given four multiple choice questions to assess if they could connect the Grouping, Instruction, Repetition and Variable cards used in Program Wars with elements of a computer program. Figure 4 shows an example of such a question. As with the programming questions, the connection questions were given using a randomly selected programming language from the four languages. The results of these questions were used to answer RQ2.

Finally, participants were asked for any qualitative feedback about Program Wars to answer RQ3.

Participants were expected to take 45 minutes to complete the study - 15 minutes for each of completing the pre-game questionnaire, playing three games, and completing the post-game questionnaire. In order to match pre- and post-game questionnaires, participants were asked to provide an email address in both questionnaires. This matching was done by only one of the authors to preserve privacy as much as possible. Once the matching between pre- and post-game questionnaires were completed, this personal identifying information was replaced by a unique study id. Qualtrics was used for presenting and collecting the questionnaire data.

3.2 Participants

The target population for Program Wars is those with little or no programming experience. For the study, participants were recruited from an undergraduate introductory course for non-computer science majors. The course provided a survey of computer science topics, including a one-week introduction to computer programming using Python and Scratch. It was believed that participants from this course would have a high probability of meeting the study criteria (although this was not guaranteed). The course had an enrollment of 80 students, of which over half (46 students) participated in the study.

[7]The corresponding Pascal, Python and Fortran programs have been omitted from the paper for reasons of space.

What is *value* after this program is run?

```
int value = 2;
for(int i=0; i<4; i++)
   // i % 2 means "i is even"
   if(i % 2 == 0)
      value = value * 2;
```

- 4
- 8
- 16
- An error.
- I don't know

Figure 2: A pre-game programming question (C).

What is *value* after this program is run?

```
value = 1;
for i in range (0, 12):
   # if i is divisible by 3
   if(i % 3 == 0)
      value = value * 2
```

- 4
- 8
- 16
- An error.
- I don't know

Figure 3: A post-game programming question (Python).

4 RESULTS

This section presents the results of our pilot study and discusses what we discovered in our evaluation.

4.1 Demographics

All forty-six participants were in the age range of 18-25 years, with 70% reporting as male and 30% as female. The participants were from a wide range of disciplines as shown in Table 1. Roughly half of the participants (56%) had previously used programming learning sites such as Scratch, Code.org, or Khan Academy. Figure 5 shows the participants' reported level of experience with counting card games (e.g. Poker or Bridge) and video games. Nearly all participants were familiar with such card games and play video games. As may be expected, participants played video games more frequently.

Table 1: Areas of study of the participants.

Arts	9	Humanities	1
Business / Management	9	Social Science	7
Education	4	Science	14
Health	1		

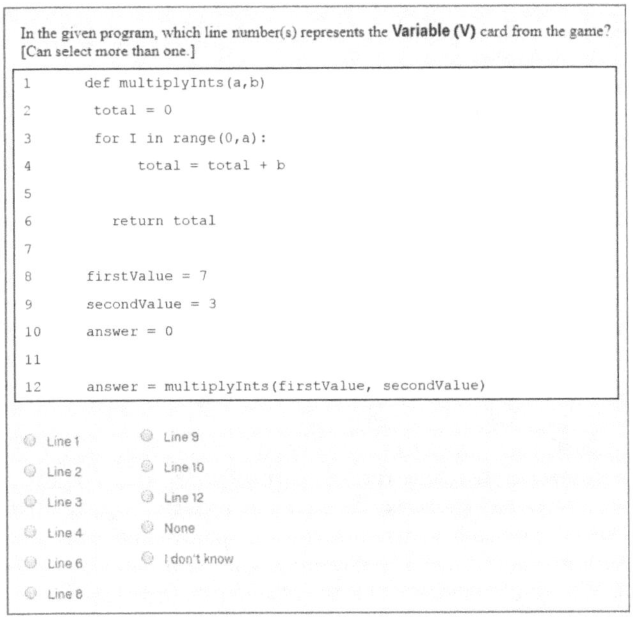

Figure 4: A post-game question connecting a game card to a programming concept (Python variant).

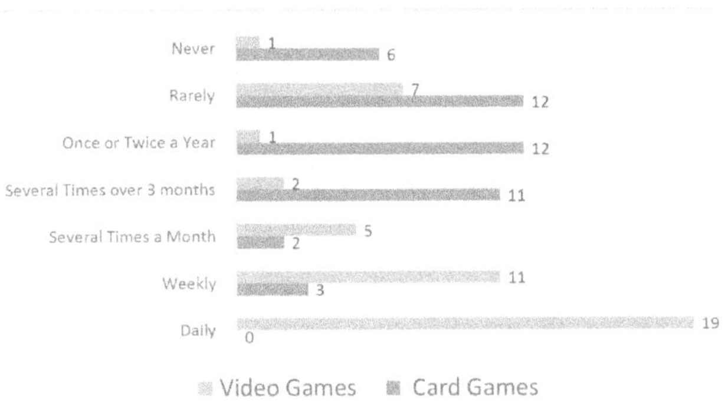

Figure 5: Participants' experience with card/video games.

4.2 Analysis

This section presents the results of the analysis regarding any improvements in the comprehension of programs written in a programming language (RQ1), how well the participants were able to connect the concepts in Program Wars to elements in an actual program (RQ2), and their impressions of the game (RQ3).

4.2.1 Comprehension of Computer Programs. Trends regarding participants' improvement in comprehension of a computer program were assessed by comparing whether or not a participant correctly answered similar questions before and after playing the game. If a participant was found to have answered more program comprehension questions correctly after playing the game, an improvement was considered to have occurred. If a participant was found to answer more questions incorrectly after playing the game, program comprehension was considered to have declined. The results show that, when using this approach to evaluate comprehension, 19 participants (56%) had a decline in program comprehension, with 7 (21%) showing improvement and 8 (24%) showing no change. Participants were found to have the most improvement regarding a question containing a simple calculation using variables.

We believe that two factors resulted in the observed decline in program comprehension:

Limited number of questions. The pre- and post-game questionnaires were set up so that the knowledge tested by a question was paired (i.e. Question #1 of the pre-game questionnaire tested similar knowledge as Question #1 of the post-game questionnaire). As study participants tend to favour answering fewer questions and to make the pairing manageable, only five questions were asked. Consequently, an incorrect answer in the post-game questionnaire has a significant impact on the results. We plan to have a wider variety and quantity of program comprehension questions in future studies.

Use of multiple programming languages To reinforce the program-language independent nature of Program Wars, the computer programs for each question were presented in one of four programming languages. However, it appears that this choice resulted in an unintended amount of confusion among the participants.

Although all programming comprehension questions presented "I don't know" as a response, it is possible that some participants just guessed at the answer.

Another threat to the study is the use of Python as one of the programming languages. Originally, the user study was to be conducted early in the semester, before students in the course were exposed to Python. However, due to unanticipated delays, the study was conducted later in the semester around the time when students were being introduced to Python and Scratch. It is unclear how much this timing affected the results of the study.

We plan to restrict the questions to using pseudocode in future studies to reduce this confusion and to remove the risk of participants having a knowledge of the programming language used in the questions.

Table 2: Participants who correctly connected card types to programming language elements in an actual program.

Card Type	Participants
Grouping	11 (31%)
Variable	24 (67%)
Instructions	19 (53%)
Repetition	17 (47%)

4.2.2 Connection to Programming Concepts. Table 2 presents the results regarding how well the participants were able to connect the card types in Program Wars to elements of a program expressed in a programming language. As shown by the table, participants most easily made a connection with the concept of a variable but had a harder time identifying the concept of grouping. Participants were also able to easily match *Instruction* and *Repetition* cards to elements in a program. It was found that 3 participants (8%) were able to correctly connect all card types, 10 participants (28%) were able to connect three card types, 10 participants (28%) were able to connect two card types, 9 participants (25%) were able to connect one card type, and 4 participants (11%) were not able to make any connection between card types and program elements. In other words, nearly two-thirds of participants were able to make a connection between two or more of the programming concepts represented in the game and elements of an actual program.

However, as the Variable card is only used with the Repetition card in the game, it is possible that some participants may not have understood that these two concepts are independent of each other. Also, as different programming languages use different constructs and syntax for representing these concepts, presenting programs in a more programming-language-neutral (e.g. pseudocode) may better assess the participant's improvement or decline in comprehension. We plan to address these two items in our next study.

4.2.3 Player Feedback. Twenty-two participants (61%) provided feedback on Program Wars. Twelve participants commented that once they understood the game's mechanics (either by watching the video, reading the rules or playing their first game), the game was fun, engaging and easy to play.

Three participants expressed frustration with the random number generator when either they were dealt a hand without instruction cards and it took several turns to make progress, or they completed their program on one path and the other path was repeatedly selected, leading to the AI winning instead. One participant expressed frustration at how often the AI hacked their program. Finally, responses from five participants indicated misunderstandings with how a game ends.

5 IMPROVEMENTS TO PROGRAM WARS

Following the user study, we made two significant improvements to Program Wars, as well as a number of improvements to the user interface (e.g. player's progress) and usability (e.g. redraw hand) (labelled as "Version 2" in Figure 1). This section provides details for these two improvements.

5.1 Cyberattacks and Cybersecurity

A participant of the study commented that "*...once I got the hang of the basics, there wasn't much room to improve.*", a sentiment echoed by two others. Therefore, we added two new cyberattack cards and corresponding counters for these cards to provide more complex player interactions and gameplay strategies.

5.1.1 Cyberattacks. The two new cyberattack cards are *Malware* and *Power Outage*.

The *Malware* card represents the concept of a computer virus, Trojan horse, worm, ransomware, spyware, scareware or adware. The intent of the *Malware* card is to slow down an opponent's computer, hence the card's effect is to reduce an opponent's instruction total by 25% (i.e. the player's program is only 75% effective).

The *Power Outage* card represents the occasion when electricity stops flowing to a computer, such as someone tripping on the power cord or hitting a power switch, or a tree branch knocking down a power line. The effect of the *Power Outage* card is to prevent a player from playing any further cards on their playing areas.

Figure 1 shows an example of both of these cards. Note that the player's True portion of their program has been reduced from 33 to 25 ($\lceil 33 * 0.75 \rceil$). The player's False portion is also affected, however as the number of instructions is small there is no practical effect ($\lceil 2 * 0.75 \rceil = 2$). The player is currently also under the effect of a *Power Outage* and can only play either the *Hack* or *Malware* card from their hand, or redraw their entire hand.

5.1.2 Cybersecurity. To counter the cyberattacks, two types of cybersecurity cards are provided: safeties and remedies. The safety cards are *Firewall*, *Generator*, and *AntiVirus*. The remedy cards are *Battery Backup* and *Overclock*.

Safety cards protect a player from specific cyberattacks for the remainder of the game. The *Firewall* card protects a player's program from *Hack* cards, the *Generator* card protects the player from *Power Outage* cards, and the *AntiVirus* card protects the player from *Malware* cards. There are only one of each of these cards in the deck no matter the size of the deck. Figure 1 shows the player with a *Firewall* safety card.

Remedy cards either prevent or counter one cyberattack, depending on whether the card is played before or after the player is attacked. The *Battery Backup* card counters a *Power Outage*, and *Overclock* counters a *Malware* attack. *Overclock* also 'speeds up' a player's program by 25% (i.e. the player's total number of instructions is 125% of the total of their cards). Once a remedy card is used to counter an attack, it and the cyberattack card are discarded.

5.1.3 Expanded Scoring. The winning condition for a game is reaching a target number of instructions on the currently selected True or False path. We expanded the scoring for the game to reward players for practising what may be considered good programming practices (e.g. the use of *Group* cards to promote the concept of "refactoring" [10]).

The scoring for the game now also considers the size of the player's program (i.e. the number of instructions in both play areas) and the use of 'good programming practices'. Players are rewarded for their use of modular programming (i.e. *Group* cards), repetition and variables. The player is also rewarded for completing their program, good cybersecurity practices (i.e. the use of Safety cards and having a malware-free system), and not overheating their system (i.e. no overclocking). These bonuses reinforce the need for a player to make strategic decisions during the game.

6 CONCLUSION

This paper presented the web-based card game, Program Wars. Program Wars uses simple vocabulary for teaching the fundamental programming language concepts in a programming-language-independent manner. A pilot user study conducted on Program Wars showed that connecting game concepts to actual programming language elements were possible for most participants. However, due to the choice of having multiple programming languages and other confounding factors, it was unclear if the participants' ability to understand a computer program was improved.

REFERENCES

[1] J. H. Andrews. 2013. Killer App: A Eurogame about software quality. In *2013 26th International Conference on Software Engineering Education and Training (CSEE T)*. 319–323. https://doi.org/10.1109/CSEET.2013.6595269

[2] Ufuk Aydan, Murat Yilmaz, Paul M. Clarke, and Rory V. O'Connor. 2017. Teaching ISO/IEC 12207 software lifecycle processes: A serious game approach. *Computer Standards & Interfaces* 54 (2017), 129 – 138. https://doi.org/10.1016/j.csi.2016.11.014 Standards in Software Process Improvement and Capability Determination.

[3] Alex Baker, Emily Oh Navarro, and André van der Hoek. 2005. An experimental card game for teaching software engineering processes. *Journal of Systems and Software* 75, 1 (2005), 3 – 16. https://doi.org/10.1016/j.jss.2004.02.033 Software Engineering Education and Training.

[4] Timothy Bell, Jason Alexander, Isaac Freeman, and Mick Grimley. 2009. Computer Science Unplugged: school students doing real computing without computers. 13 (01 2009).

[5] Kohl Bromwich, Masood Masoodian, and Bill Rogers. 2012. Crossing the Game Threshold: A System for Teaching Basic Programming Constructs. In *Proceedings of the 13th International Conference of the NZ Chapter of the ACM's Special Interest Group on Human-Computer Interaction (CHINZ '12)*. ACM, New York, NY, USA, 56–63. https://doi.org/10.1145/2379256.2379266

[6] Peter Drake and Kelvin Sung. 2011. Teaching Introductory Programming with Popular Board Games. In *Proceedings of the 42Nd ACM Technical Symposium on Computer Science Education (SIGCSE '11)*. ACM, New York, NY, USA, 619–624. https://doi.org/10.1145/1953163.1953338

[7] Anke Drappa and Jochen Ludewig. 2000. Simulation in Software Engineering Training. In *Proceedings of the 22Nd International Conference on Software Engineering (ICSE '00)*. ACM, New York, NY, USA, 199–208. https://doi.org/10.1145/337180.337203

[8] Joao F. Ferreira and Alexandra Mendes. 2014. The Magic of Algorithm Design and Analysis: Teaching Algorithmic Skills Using Magic Card Tricks. In *Proceedings of the 2014 Conference on Innovation & Technology in Computer Science Education (ITiCSE '14)*. ACM, New York, NY, USA, 75–80. https://doi.org/10.1145/2591708.2591745

[9] Charles Wesley Ford, Jr. and Steven Minsker. 2003. TREEZ - An Educational Data Structures Game. *J. Comput. Sci. Coll.* 18, 6 (June 2003), 180–185. http://dl.acm.org/citation.cfm?id=770818.770848

[10] Martin Fowler. 1999. *Refactoring: Improving the Design of Existing Code*. Addison-Wesley Longman Publishing Co., Inc., Boston, MA, USA.

[11] Bradley S. Greenberg, John Sherry, Kenneth Lachlan, Kristen Lucas, and Amanda Holmstrom. 2010. Orientations to Video Games Among Gender and Age Groups. *Simulation & Gaming* 41, 2 (2010), 238–259. https://doi.org/10.1177/1046878108319930 arXiv:https://doi.org/10.1177/1046878108319930

[12] Nicolas Guibert, Patrick Girard, and Laurent Guittet. 2004. Example-based Programming: A Pertinent Visual Approach for Learning to Program. In *Proceedings of the Working Conference on Advanced Visual Interfaces (AVI '04)*. ACM, New York, NY, USA, 358–361. https://doi.org/10.1145/989863.989924

[13] Lasse Hakulinen. 2011. Using Serious Games in Computer Science Education. In *Proceedings of the 11th Koli Calling International Conference on Computing Education Research (Koli Calling '11)*. ACM, New York, NY, USA, 83–88. https://doi.org/10.1145/2094131.2094147

[14] Apurva Jain and B. Boehm. 2006. SimVBSE: Developing a Game for Value-Based Software Engineering. In *19th Conference on Software Engineering Education Training (CSEET'06)*. 103–114. https://doi.org/10.1109/CSEET.2006.31

[15] Jennifer Jenson, Suzanne de Castell, and Stephanie Fisher. 2007. Girls Playing Games: Rethinking Stereotypes. In *Proceedings of the 2007 Conference on Future Play (Future Play '07)*. ACM, New York, NY, USA, 9–16. https://doi.org/10.1145/1328202.1328205

[16] Kristen Lucas and John L. Sherry. 2004. Sex Differences in Video Game Play:: A Communication-Based Explanation. *Communication Research* 31, 5 (2004), 499–523. https://doi.org/10.1177/0093650204267930 arXiv:https://doi.org/10.1177/0093650204267930

[17] E. O. Navarro and A. v. d. Hoek. 2005. Design and Evaluation of an Educational Software Process Simulation Environment and Associated Model. In *18th Conference on Software Engineering Education Training (CSEET'05)*. 25–32. https://doi.org/10.1109/CSEET.2005.16

[18] Mikki H. Phan, Jo R. Jardina, Sloane Hoyle, and Barbara S. Chaparro. 2012. Examining the Role of Gender in Video Game Usage, Preference, and Behavior. *Proceedings of the Human Factors and Ergonomics Society Annual Meeting* 56, 1 (2012), 1496–1500. https://doi.org/10.1177/1071181312561297 arXiv:https://doi.org/10.1177/1071181312561297

[19] Elizabeth Suescun Monsalve, A.X. Pereira, and Vera Werneck. 2017. Teaching software engineering through a collaborative game. (01 2017), 874–895.

[20] Carnegie Mellon University. 2018. Alice.org. Online. http://www.alice.org

[21] MIT University. 2018. Scratch Homepage. Online. https://scratch.mit.edu

[22] Atif Waraich. 2004. Using Narrative As a Motivating Device to Teach Binary Arithmetic and Logic Gates. In *Proceedings of the 9th Annual SIGCSE Conference on Innovation and Technology in Computer Science Education (ITiCSE '04)*. ACM, New York, NY, USA, 97–101. https://doi.org/10.1145/1007996.1008024

Analyzing Gamification Impact on a Mastery Learning Introductory Programming Course

Rafael G. de Pontes
UFCG
Campina Grande, Paraíba, Brazil
rafaelpontes@copin.ufcg.edu.br

Dalton D. S. Guerrero
UFCG
Campina Grande, Paraíba, Brazil
dalton@computacao.ufcg.edu.br

Jorge C. A. de Figueiredo
UFCG
Campina Grande, Paraíba, Brazil
abrantes@computacao.ufcg.edu.br

ABSTRACT

In recent years, the use of game elements in non-game contexts has been widely adopted in different contexts, one of which education. Concerned with investigating the effect of gamification on student engagement in the context of an undergraduate Introductory Programming course that applied that Mastery Learning approach, a gamified web application was developed and integrated to a pre-existing online platform used to conduct the syllabus. N = 60 students were randomly assigned to one of two groups: an experimental group with access to the gamified platform and a control group without access to it. The randomization guaranteed a similar number of students in relation to advancement in the course, in each group. The main features explored in the gamified approach were anonymous weekly leaderboards, many categories of badges and personal record-tracking. Each student profile was private. A first 90-minute experiment showed that the experimental group solved 37% more exercises than the control group, on average. From that point onward, student activity was monitored for a period of four weeks, until the end of the course. Though student-activity decreased over time as students completed the course, the experimental group increasingly solved more exercises per week compared to the control group (at least 46% more, on average). After the course was concluded, the experimental group answered a survey which showed that the badges were the feature that motivated them the most. This research's source code is available and may be easily replicated or incremented.

CCS CONCEPTS

• **Applied computing → Interactive learning environments**; **Computer-managed instruction**; *E-learning*;

KEYWORDS

Gamification, Badge, Leaderboard, Mastery Learning, Programming

ACM Reference Format:
Rafael G. de Pontes, Dalton D. S. Guerrero, and Jorge C. A. de Figueiredo. 2019. Analyzing Gamification Impact on a Mastery Learning Introductory Programming Course. In *Proceedings of the 50th ACM Technical Symposium on Computer Science Education (SIGCSE '19), February 27-March 2, 2019, Minneapolis, MN, USA.* ACM, New York, NY, USA, 7 pages. https://doi.org/10.1145/3287324.3287367

SIGCSE '19, February 27-March 2, 2019, Minneapolis, MN, USA

ACM ISBN 978-1-4503-5890-3/19/02...$15.00
https://doi.org/10.1145/3287324.3287367

1 INTRODUCTION

One of the objectives in programming courses is that students achieve mastery over the abstract theoretical concepts being taught. It is widely accepted that this kind of expertise starts with general problem solving skills and grows with deliberate and repeated practice[14][39][5][37]. This expertise is critical for students to hone their programming skills to become adept at it[38][26]. However, finding techniques to foster student engagement is not a trivial task. This is specially true in introductory programming (IP) courses when students who are new to the subject find difficulty in writing syntactically correct codes[17].

To that end, a possible complementary educational approach is with gamification, which was defined by Deterding et al as the use of game elements and mechanics in non-game contexts[11][12]. In education, gamification has become increasingly popular in researches aiming to improve engagement, behavioral change, as to promote learning and mastery of skills[27][9][13][24][26][4].

Based on some of the aforementioned studies on gamification in education, we hypothesized that:

Hypothesis H_1: In general, university students are interested in gamified experiences.

Hypothesis H_2: Gamifying a mastery learning introductory programming course leads to improved student engagement.

Therefore, we designed and developed a gamified web application that was integrated in a pre-existing online platform adopted in an undergraduate IP course that applied the mastery learning method, with the main objective of increasing student engagement. Here, we interpret student engagement as the number of completed programming assignments.

A survey was administered prior to the experiment to gather demographics information and student opinion on games and gamified experiences. It showed that the majority of students had some experience with games and a positive opinion towards gamification. During the experiment, students who were exposed to the gamified platform solved at least 46% more programming assignments per week, on average, in comparison with the equivalent control group. A post-experiment survey administered to the experimental group showed that they enjoyed the gamified experience.

2 BACKGROUND

This section presents relevant theoretical background that introduce important aspects of the IP context and gamification in education.

2.1 Introductory Programming Challenges

IP is an important and compulsory course in all Computer Science majors, in which the grasp of the essence of programming should be the main objective[8]. However, this may present itself as quite a challenge to novice students. Many struggle with the abstractions required to make software[1].

The truth is students' ability to grasp algorithmic thinking, associate it with elements found in a given programming language and finally be able to create software solutions for programming problems vary greatly among different people. In an attempt to mitigate this, some universities started adopting the mastery learning approach and observed positive effects even in subsequent programming courses[30]. The course in which this gamified experiment was held applied the mastery learning method.

2.2 Mastery Learning

Over the last decades, many educators have channeled their efforts into innovative instructional interventions, attempting to mitigate achievement gaps of diverse groups of students. Among the main educational approaches proposed and studied by researchers, mastery learning has long been in the spotlight [18] [19]. This methodology may be subdivided into two: Bloom's Learning for Mastery (LFM) [3] and Keller's Personalized System of Instruction (PSI) [25]. Though they differ in some aspects, both of them agree that the content of a given course be divided into short units and that students should take formative tests on each of these units. The main idea is that students should only move on to a subsequent unit upon mastering the current.

Kulik and Bangert-Drowns [28] conducted a meta-analysis of the effectiveness of the mastery learning methodology based on the findings of 108 controlled evaluations in various educational contexts. They revealed that weaker students may be the most positively affected in terms of attitude toward the course content, instruction and time on task.

More recently, McCane et al [30] studied the effect of this methodology in an introductory programming course. They revealed a moderate positive performance of students exposed to the mastery learning method in comparison with students from its traditional version. They have also presented results that indicated the mastery learning was more advantageous to lower performing students without harming higher performing students, which is desirable.

2.3 Gamification in Higher Education

A student once asked "Why can't we get achievements for being awesome?" [10]. Indeed, the structure of education in general has many similarities with those of games. There is a set of rules that must be followed in order to achieve a main goal. Therefore, the idea of actually adding game elements to the context of education is rather appealing. In fact, many studies in recent years have reported significant positive results for some of the tested motivational aspects [22] [9]. Some argue that gamification effect on engagement may vary due to factors such as user motivation or nature of the gamified system [23].

In their study, Decker *et al* [10] proposed a gamified solution whose core design principles included: being non-curricular and voluntary, game activities were external to main course website, varied achievement types and contexts, and it was accessible to casual players. Given their positive student feedback, we took some of these into consideration in our approach.

Khaleel *et al* proposed a framework for gamifying programming courses which suggested that the integration of game elements should aim at increasing student motivation and interest in learning programming. They listed game elements and associated them with programming requirements. According to them, badges and leaderboards may be used to increase student motivation. Furthermore, real-time results, dashboards, reports, percentage of competency, and profile information may be used to increase student interest in learning[26]. These concepts were all aggregated to our gamified online platform.

The badge, which is the main game element in our gamified platform, may be defined as optional sub-goals which are not a requisite for the completion of the main task at hand [31]. In their study with badge-based gamified platform, Haaranen et al [20] concluded that some students may have strongly negative emotions towards badges, therefore, they should be optional at some level. And, as much as they also made their badges private, students would talk about them with one another. They proposed that badges be public. Furthermore, they advised that making badges for achievements already happening in the course, like for grades, is not considered novelty and should be avoided. Most importantly, badges should be fun and creative. Finally, they suggested that badges do not hinder usability of the official learning platform used in the course. Taking all of this into consideration, we came up with a gamified solution that is rather modular and is independent of the main online platform used in our course. More details on the design of our platform may be seen on Section 4.3.

3 THE COURSE

The undergraduate course in which the subjects were enrolled was from the first term of a Computer Science major from a Brazilian Public University. Its syllabus was divided into 10 units (modules): units 1-3 introduced basic programs and fundamental concepts in programming, conditionals; units 4-6 ranged from definite/indefinite loops and functions; finally, units 7-10 introduced data structures such as arrays, lists, matrices, maps and some sort algorithms.

The course was self-paced, which means that each student individually advanced in the course at his/her own rhythm, following the aforementioned mastery learning approach. To manage this methodology, the professors developed an online platform, named TST[1], which gradually unlocked the units as students solved two assignments from his/her current unit in a weekly in-class mini-test. Besides, students would have to attend theoretical lessons specifically focused on his/her unit range. The course's full length was four months. The programming language taught was Python 2.7.

4 METHODOLOGY

Before introducing our methodology, we highlight that this study was approved by a Brazilian Institutional Review Board (IRB), namely, the Research Ethics Committee (REC) from the Alcides Carneiro University Hospital at UFCG (CAAE 70198817.3.0000.5182).

[1] Available at https://github.com/daltonserey/tst.git.

4.1 Initial Survey

In the second week of the course, a basic survey was administered to gather student opinion and experience regarding games and gamification in general (N = 79). The questions were:

(1) **Do you play?** Yes (86.1%). In the past, but not anymore (8.9%). No (5.1%).
(2) **What kind of games?** Digital games (93.7%). Board games (62%). Physical sports (38%). No experience with games (3.8%). Notice people could choose multiple options.
(3) **How often do you play?** A lot and every day (12.7%). Frequently (21.5%). Moderately (30.4%). Casually (31.6%). Never (3.8%).
(4) **How would you evaluate the impact of the insertion of game elements in educational contexts? (1: very negative, 5: very positive)** Average: 4.35.
(5) **Do you prefer traditional or gamified courses?** Gamified (93.7%). Traditional (6.3%).

4.2 Participants

The sample consisted of students from the aforementioned undergraduate IP course. Originally, at the time of the experiment, which was one month before the course was over, we had written experiment participation permission from 72 students. Based on the unit each student was the week before the initial experiment, a randomization script was developed to divide these students into two groups with similar number of students from each unit. The algorithm was the following: for each unit, starting from the first and following in ascending order, if the unit presented an even number of students, each group would receive the same amount of students. For the first occurrence of an odd number of students on a given unit, the extra one would be randomly assigned to one of the groups. In the following occurrences of odd number of students for a given unit, the group opposite to the one favored immediately before would receive the extra student.

Given the 72 aforementioned students, the proposed randomization algorithm allocated 36 students in each group. However, on the day of the first experiment, only 30 people in the experimental group actually used the gamified website. Hence, to keep balance, 6 students who were at the same unit as the non-participants from the experimental group were randomly discarded from the control group. Figure 1 shows the box-plots of distributions of units the $N = 60$ students were a week before the first intervention, per group. The colors indicate the gender of each student. Notice some students had already completed the course. Therefore, it was optional for them to solve assignments from the completed units.

Tables 1 and 2 show basic statistics concerning each group in relation to completed units status from the week before the pilot experiment, age and number of students in each group by gender.

Before performing further statistical analyses, two hypothesis tests were performed in order to check if the sample ($N = 60$) came from a normal distribution in relation to the number of completed units from a week before the first experiment. This was the chosen metric for measuring students' knowledge within the course and used for randomizing the control and experimental groups. First, a D'Agostino and Pearson's Omnibus test[7][6][32] returned $K^2 = 17.331$ and $p = 3.7 \times 10^{-4}$. Then, a Shapiro-Wilk

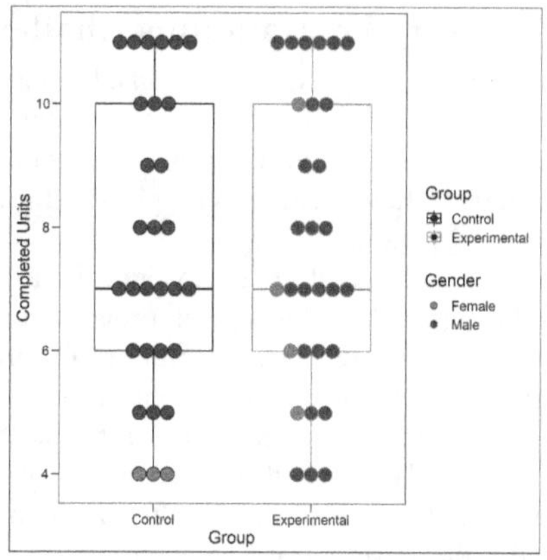

Figure 1: Box-plots with Completed Units per group.

Table 1: Mean (μ), median (Med), standard deviation (σ) for students' completed units a week before experiment.

Group	Completed Units		
	mu	Median	s
Control (N = 30)	7.7	7	2.36
Experimental (N = 30)	7.7	7	2.36

Table 2: Number of students per gender, Mean (μ), median (Med), standard deviation (σ) for ages.

Group	Count		Age		
	Male	Female	μ	Med	σ
Control (N = 30)	27	3	19.3	18	5.3
Experimental (N = 30)	26	4	19.4	19	2.3

test[35][33][34] yielded $W = 0.912$ and $p = 3.6 \times 10^{-4}$. The null hypothesis in both tests stated that the sample came from a normal distribution. Therefore, because both p-values were below $\alpha = 0.05$, the null hypothesis was rejected, and we cannot assume the sample is normally distributed.

Taking that and the sample data into consideration, a non parametric hypothesis test was chosen to check for the technical equivalence in groups: a two-sided Mann-Whitney rank test[29] comparing the number of completed units before the experiment. The null hypothesis stated that there was no difference in relation to the number of completed units between groups. This test returned $W = 450$ and $p = 0.994$. Therefore, we assumed that there was no significant difference between groups in relation to technical knowledge within the IP course.

4.3 The Gamified Platform

Taking some core design principles from previous studies (Sections 1 and 2) and the particularities of the IP course into consideration, the following main game mechanics were designed: a weekly leaderboard, badges, personal record-tracking. It was developed to be modular and can be easily integrated into any online platform with basic HTTP requests informing that a certain student completed a specific assignment at a given time. The administrator can register students by e-mail, preventing external users to access privileged information from students. The complete source-code, and some basic instructions for integration and usage are available[2].

One of the main design decisions was that each student's information would be private. This was meant to protect students from undesired exposure. Each user only had access to his/her achievements upon proper authentication within the system. More on this on Section 8.

Upon successful authentication, the user would see his profile picture, alongside name, e-mail and a navbar menu which showed him/her all the scrollable sections of the page.

The first information option on each student's profile was a table with the following data: number of consecutive days on which at least one assignment was solved, number of assignments completed on the current day, number of assignments completed in the current week (Monday through Sunday). Each of those values were sided with their respective corresponding personal records. These values were used to calculate some of the badges.

Secondly, the leaderboard was presented in the form of a graph. The vertical axis represented the number of completed assignments of all registered active users from the current week (Monday through Sunday). One thing to note, however is that there was no information on who each point in the curve. The only exception was the point that corresponded to the authenticated user, which was highlighted with a different size. Hence, each user would know where he/she was in comparison with the others, but the identity of the others would be secret. The percentage of top students amongst which the user was included was presented alongside the leaderboard graph. Since a weekly badge was awarded according to this percentage, a preview of the student's current competition badge status would be presented. All this info was updated in real time.

The badges were divided into five categories: daily, continuity, special, challenge, and competition. Further detail on each of these five categories bellow:

- **Daily:** they could be achieved once every day. There were 6 ranks for these. As the student did the amount[3] required for each rank, he would receive an extra badge for that rank.
- **Continuity:** these badges were designed as to promote the student to do exercises each day, continuously. If he/she spent two days in a row without doing exercises, the counters for achieving these badges would reset. Every 5-day streak would award a new rank of continuity badge. There were special badges for the 7 and 30-day streak as well.
- **Special:** these would be awarded for completing assignments on special occasions, such as early in the mornings, Friday nights, early in weekends, during the course laboratory classes etc. These also included some missables that could only be achieved during the 90-minute marathon in which the gamified platform was introduced.
- **Challenge:** these were awarded for students who solved some of the most difficult programming problems according to data from previous terms. Unique badges were personally designed for each of these problems and reflected their context.
- **Competition:** these were awarded once every week, according to the weekly leaderboard. There were 5 ranks: copper, silver, gold, platinum and diamond. To earn a badge for a given rank, the student would have to be within the percentage of students who did the most amount of assignments that week. The percentages were: [75-50%[, [50-35%[, [35-20%[, [20-5%[, 5%, respectively. For example, if a student were among the 5% of students who solved the most problems on the moment of the weekly leaderboard reset, he would be awarded with a Diamond Competitor Badge. This reset occurred on every Monday at 0:00 am.

[2]At https://github.com/rafaelpontes/achievement-profile.git.
[3]These varied from 1 through 25 problems a day.

4.4 Initial Experiment

The first 90-minute experiment was conducted during one of the laboratory lessons. Students who had been previously randomly assigned to be part of the experimental group were invited to go to a different laboratory. The rest of the students (control group) remained in the original laboratory. After all the students were accommodated and properly logged on a computer, 20 programming assignments were made available for everyone to try to solve. These problems were some of the most challenging ones from the course. The gamified platform was only introduced to the students in the experimental group. They were informed that there was a competition and, among the possible achievements, there were special badges that could only be unlocked within the 90 minutes that followed the start of the competition. Students from the control group were instructed to do as many exercises as they could, but did not know of the existence of nor had access to the gamified platform. After the competition was over, students from the experimental group received badges for their position on the leaderboard. They were also told that the gamified platform would remain online until the end of the course, and that they could follow up their achievements in real time or even be notified if they achieved any new badges. It is worth noting that this experiment took place when there was only one month left of the course. This decision was made because the platform was still in its alpha phase and tests were being done earlier in the course. When it was finally mature enough to be tested in production, it was released as explained above.

4.5 Final Survey

After the completion of the course, a survey was administered only to people who had used the gamified platform, but only 15 students answered it. Seven 5-point Likert-Scale questions were asked, whose results are on Table 5. The questions were the following:

(1) How easy was the usage of the website? (1: very hard, 5: very easy)
(2) How friendly was the website for you? (1: not friedly at all, 5: very friendly)
(3) What was the impact you feel the website had on your performance in the course? (1: very negative, 5: very positive)
(4) How much did the personal record-tracking help you want to surpass your own records? (1: very negatively, 5: helped a lot)

(5) How much did the weekly leaderboard help you wish to do more programming exercises? (1: very negatively, 5: helped a lot)
(6) How much did the badges help you wish to do more programming exercises? (1: very negatively, 5: helped a lot)
(7) How competitive do you consider yourself? (1: not competitive at all, 5: very competitive)

5 RESULTS

In order to verify impact on engagement over the course, the main metric was the number of completed assignments from both groups over five time frames: the initial 90-minute experiment and each of the four weeks that ranged from the beginning of this experiment until the end of the course. Each week was investigated independently. Table 3 presents basic statistics for each of those time frames.

Table 3: Mean (μ), median (*Med*) and standard deviation (σ) of completed assignments per time frame, per group.

	Control N = 30			Experimental N = 30		
Event	μ	**Med**	σ	μ	**Med**	σ
Experiment 1	4.67	4	2.02	6.40	6	3.10
Week 1	8.40	8.50	3.04	12.27	9.50	6.87
Week 2	4.23	2	5.43	6.63	6	7.49
Week 3	2.63	1	4.11	5.17	3	6.22
Week 4	0.43	0	1.68	1.33	0	3.12

Table 4 compares the percentage increases in the number of completed assignments between control and experimental group. Accounting weeks 1 through 4, the overall increase was +61.89%. These percentages were calculated according to Equation 1.

$$\frac{\mu_E - \mu_C}{\mu_C} \tag{1}$$

Where μ_C and μ_E correspond to the mean of completed assignments of the control and the experimental group, respectively, for each time frame.

To measure the significance of those statistics, one-sided Mann-Whitney U hypothesis tests were performed comparing the number of completed assignments for each of those time frames. The null hypothesis stated that the control group solved more programming assignments over each of the time frames. Table 4 shows the values of p and W for each of those tests.

Table 4: Percentages of increased number of completed assignments by the experimental group in comparison with the control group (%) and results for Mann-Whitney U one-sided tests (p and W), both per time frame. E1: Experiment 1. Wi, i = 1, 2, 3, 4 represent each i-th week time frame.

	E1	W1	W2	W3	W4
%	+37.04%	+46.07%	+56.74%	+96.58%	+209.30%
p	**0.01**	**0.01**	**0.04**	**0.02**	0.30
W	294.5	294.0	331.5	311.5	428.0

To visualize the number of completed assignments for each of the considered time frames, Figures 2 and 3 may be consulted. They present box-plots comparing this metric for both groups, by gender. Notice the right-hand side of Figure 2 is a version without gender highlight and whose notches indicate the medians.

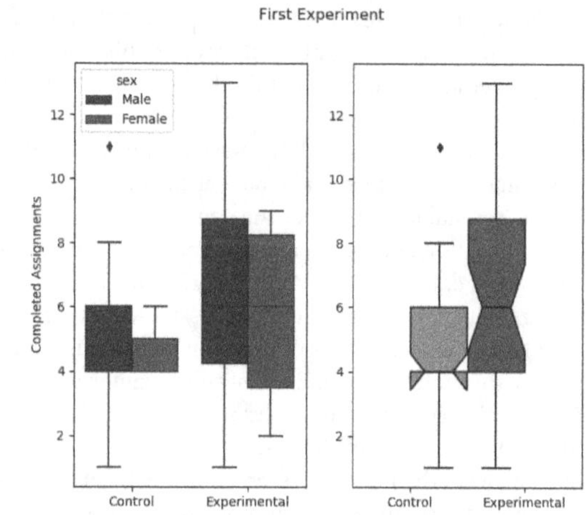

Figure 2: Box-plots with Completed Assignments on the first 90-minute experiment, per group, per gender.

The results for the final survey from Section 4.5 with people who used the gamified platform is available on Table 5. Questions may be seen on Section 4.5.

Table 5: Means (μ) for final survey with people who used the gamified platform, which only received 15 responses.

	Q1	Q2	Q3	Q4	Q5	Q6	Q7
μ	4.33	4.80	3.67	4.07	4.13	4.27	3.80

6 DISCUSSION

Starting from data obtained in the initial survey, we noticed the great majority (96.2%) had experience with at least one type of game and that most of them (93.7%) would be fond of the idea of participating in a gamified course. Furthermore, their answer for question 4 averaged 4.35. This supports our initial hypothesis (H_1).

Onto the overall experiment results, Table 3 indicates that the experimental group completed more assignments per time frame, on average, in comparison to the technically equivalent control group. Though Table 3 presents that the number of completed assignments per week decreased in both groups over time, Table 4 shows that the experimental group increased the ratio of completed assignments per week, taking the control group as a base reference. The overall decreasing number of assignments over time may be explained by the fact that, as students concluded the course, they no longer had to take tests, and completing new assignments or revisiting old ones would be less compelling.

One point to consider, however, is that the standard deviation in relation to completed assignments from the experimental group

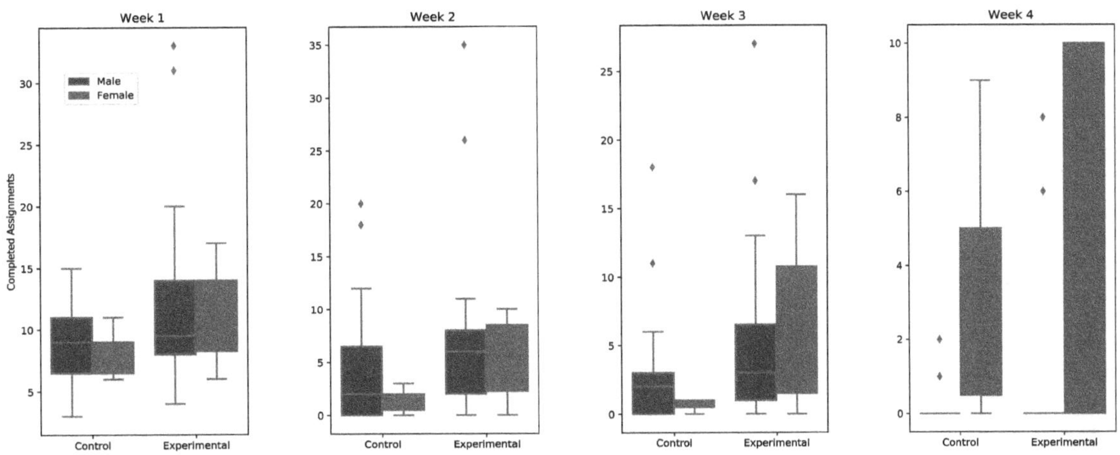

Figure 3: Box-plots with Completed Assignments per week, per group, per gender.

was higher than the control group's in all scenarios. This mathematically indicates the gamified platform had a more significant impact on some students than in others. More competitive and game-enthusiast students are more prone to being influenced by the game mechanics that aimed at stimulating problem-solving within the course. However, it is also possible that students were not limited by motivational factors.

In relation to the null hypothesis that states that the control group completed more programming assignments per week than the technically equivalent experimental group, the Mann-Whitney U tests whose results may be seen on Table 4 suggest that it was refuted for the 90-minute experiment and the period from week 1 through 3 (in bold), because the p-value was below $\alpha = 0.05$. Therefore, we assume that the alternative hypothesis (H_2) that states that people with access to a gamified platform complete more programming assignments than those who do not. Notice we are measuring engagement with the number of completed assignments. This directly correlates to other statistically significant increase on engagement in other gamified educational approaches [2] [36]. However, the test for week 4 resulted in $p = 0.3$, so we failed to refute the null hypothesis. We interpret that this was due to the fact that most of the students had already concluded the course by the last week, losing interest in doing more exercises from the given course to focus on other activities, regardless of the gamified platform.

Concerning the answers from the final survey, it is noticeable that the overall feedback was positive. Students enjoyed the gamified experience, in general, though they felt it did not have that great of an impact on the course as a whole (Question 3 averaged a 3.67 answer). This is possibly due to the fact that the gamified platform was only introduced into the last month of the course. We intend on replicating this longitudinal experiment with the introduction of the gamified platform earlier in the course.

7 THREATS TO VALIDITY

This research relied on the number of completed units for justifying the equality of groups. However, other cofactors could contribute to each student's engagement and level of expertise, such as previous experience with programming, age, personality, extra-class problems etc. Although the sample ($N = 60$) represented over 50% of the total number of students from the course, it is too bold an assumption to generalize these results for every undergraduate IP context, which may vary drastically. Another point to consider is that this intervention took place within the last month of the course, and several students had already concluded it by then. Different results would probably be obtained had it been introduced earlier in the course, as some researchers found gamification may not be long-term [15] [16] [21]. Finally, considering that the survey revealed that great majority of students from the sample were already predisposed to see gamification favorably, the results could have been different in case the students were not fond of gamification nor games in general.

8 FUTURE WORK

Given the prototype nature of the gamified platform, future experiments may include a richer gamification design, with the inclusion of progress bars, visualization of past leadearboards and statistics, the option for the student to make his/her the profile public to peers, integration with social networks, the option to engage in battle-like programming challenges with peers etc. Furthermore, new metrics could be taken into consideration in the analysis, such as student grades, age, prior programming experience and their relation to the gamified presence and engagement. Furthermore, we plan on integrating the gamified platform earlier in the course, as to present of a more detailed longitudinal analysis.

ACKNOWLEDGMENTS

The authors would like to thank the Software Practices Laboratory at UFCG and CAPES for the support. Additionally, we thank being partially sponsored by agreement 08200.315131/2016-10 between ePol/DPF and UFCG; and agreement SCON2018-00300 between e-CIS and UFCG.

REFERENCES

[1] Ana Paula Ambrósio, Fábio Moreira Costa, Leandro Almeida, Amanda Franco, and Joaquim Macedo. 2011. Identifying cognitive abilities to improve CS1 outcome. In *Frontiers in Education Conference (FIE), 2011*. IEEE, F3G–1.

[2] Paul E Anderson, Thomas Nash, and Renée McCauley. 2015. Facilitating programming success in data science courses through gamified scaffolding and learn2mine. In *Proceedings of the 2015 ACM Conference on Innovation and Technology in Computer Science Education*. ACM, 99–104.

[3] Benjamin S Bloom. 1968. Learning for Mastery. Instruction and Curriculum. Regional Education Laboratory for the Carolinas and Virginia, Topical Papers and Reprints, Number 1. *Evaluation comment* 1, 2 (1968), n2.

[4] Andharini Dwi Cahyani. 2016. Gamification approach to enhance students engagement in studying language course. In *MATEC Web of Conferences*, Vol. 58. EDP Sciences, 03006.

[5] Michelene TH Chi, Robert Glaser, and Marshall J Farr. 2014. *The nature of expertise*. Psychology Press.

[6] Ralph D'Agostino and Egon S Pearson. 1973. Tests for departure from normality. Empirical results for the distributions of b_2 and $\sqrt{b_1}$. *Biometrika* 60, 3 (1973), 613–622.

[7] Ralph B D'Agostino. 1971. An omnibus test of normality for moderate and large size samples. *Biometrika* 58, 2 (1971), 341–348.

[8] Kaiyu Dai, Yiming Zhao, and Ronghua Chen. 2010. Research and Practice on Constructing the Course of Programming Language. In *2010 10th IEEE International Conference on Computer and Information Technology (CIT 2010)*. IEEE, 2033–2038.

[9] Simone de Sousa Borges, Vinicius H. S. Durelli, Helena Macedo Reis, and Seiji Isotani. 2014. A Systematic Mapping on Gamification Applied to Education. In *Proceedings of the 29th Annual ACM Symposium on Applied Computing (SAC '14)*. ACM, New York, NY, USA, 216–222. https://doi.org/10.1145/2554850.2554956

[10] Adrienne Decker and Elizabeth Lane Lawley. 2013. Life's a game and the game of life: how making a game out of it can change student behavior. In *Proceeding of the 44th ACM technical symposium on Computer science education*. ACM, 233–238.

[11] Sebastian Deterding, Dan Dixon, Rilla Khaled, and Lennart Nacke. 2011. From Game Design Elements to Gamefulness: Defining "Gamification". In *Proceedings of the 15th International Academic MindTrek Conference: Envisioning Future Media Environments (MindTrek '11)*. ACM, New York, NY, USA, 9–15. https://doi.org/10.1145/2181037.2181040

[12] Sebastian Deterding, Miguel Sicart, Lennart Nacke, Kenton O'Hara, and Dan Dixon. 2011. Gamification. using game-design elements in non-gaming contexts. In *CHI'11 extended abstracts on human factors in computing systems*. ACM, 2425–2428.

[13] Darina Dicheva, Christo Dichev, Gennady Agre, and Galia Angelova. 2015. Gamification in education: A systematic mapping study. *Journal of Educational Technology & Society* 18, 3 (2015).

[14] K Anders Ericsson, Ralf T Krampe, and Clemens Tesch-Römer. 1993. The role of deliberate practice in the acquisition of expert performance. *Psychological review* 100, 3 (1993), 363.

[15] Rosta Farzan, Joan M DiMicco, David R Millen, Beth Brownholtz, Werner Geyer, and Casey Dugan. 2008. When the experiment is over: Deploying an incentive system to all the users. In *symposium on persuasive technology*.

[16] Rosta Farzan, Joan M DiMicco, David R Millen, Casey Dugan, Werner Geyer, and Elizabeth A Brownholtz. 2008. Results from deploying a participation incentive mechanism within the enterprise. In *Proceedings of the SIGCHI conference on Human factors in computing systems*. ACM, 563–572.

[17] Nobuo Funabiki, Yousuke Korenaga, Toru Nakanishi, and Kan Watanabe. 2013. An extension of fill-in-the-blank problem function in Java programming learning assistant system. In *Humanitarian Technology Conference (R10-HTC), 2013 IEEE Region 10*. IEEE, 85–90.

[18] Thomas R Guskey. 2007. Closing achievement gaps: revisiting Benjamin S. Bloom's "Learning for Mastery". *Journal of advanced academics* 19, 1 (2007), 8–31.

[19] Thomas R Guskey. 2010. Lessons of mastery learning. *Educational leadership* 68, 2 (2010), 52.

[20] Lassi Haaranen, Petri Ihantola, Lasse Hakulinen, and Ari Korhonen. 2014. How (not) to introduce badges to online exercises. In *Proceedings of the 45th ACM technical symposium on Computer science education*. ACM, 33–38.

[21] Juho Hamari. 2013. Transforming homo economicus into homo ludens: A field experiment on gamification in a utilitarian peer-to-peer trading service. *Electronic commerce research and applications* 12, 4 (2013), 236–245.

[22] Juho Hamari, Jonna Koivisto, and Harri Sarsa. 2014. Does gamification work?– a literature review of empirical studies on gamification. In *2014 47th Hawaii international conference on system sciences (HICSS)*. IEEE, 3025–3034.

[23] Juho Hamari and Janne Tuunanen. 2014. Player types: A meta-synthesis. (2014).

[24] Karl M. Kapp. 2012. *The Gamification of Learning and Instruction: Game-based Methods and Strategies for Training and Education*. Pfeiffer.

[25] Fred S Keller. 1968. "GOOD-BYE, TEACHER..." 1. *Journal of applied behavior analysis* 1, 1 (1968), 79–89.

[26] Firas Layth Khaleel, Noraidah Sahari Ashaari, Tengku Siti Meriam Tengku Wook, and Amirah Ismail. 2017. Gamification-based learning framework for a programming course. In *Electrical Engineering and Informatics (ICEEI), 2017 6th International Conference on*. IEEE, 1–6.

[27] Ana Carolina Tomé Klock, Aline Nunes Ogawa, Isabela Gasparini, and Marcelo Soares Pimenta. 2018. Does Gamification Matter?: A Systematic Mapping About the Evaluation of Gamification in Educational Environments. In *Proceedings of the 33rd Annual ACM Symposium on Applied Computing (SAC '18)*. ACM, New York, NY, USA, 2006–2012. https://doi.org/10.1145/3167132.3167347

[28] Chen-Lin C Kulik, James A Kulik, and Robert L Bangert-Drowns. 1990. Effectiveness of mastery learning programs: A meta-analysis. *Review of educational research* 60, 2 (1990), 265–299.

[29] Henry B Mann and Donald R Whitney. 1947. On a test of whether one of two random variables is stochastically larger than the other. *The annals of mathematical statistics* (1947), 50–60.

[30] Brendan McCane, Claudia Ott, Nick Meek, and Anthony Robins. 2017. Mastery Learning in Introductory Programming. In *Proceedings of the Nineteenth Australasian Computing Education Conference*. ACM, 1–10.

[31] Markus Montola, Timo Nummenmaa, Andrés Lucero, Marion Boberg, and Hannu Korhonen. 2009. Applying game achievement systems to enhance user experience in a photo sharing service. In *Proceedings of the 13th International MindTrek Conference: Everyday Life in the Ubiquitous Era*. ACM, 94–97.

[32] Derya Öztuna, Atilla Halil Elhan, and Ersöz Tüccar. 2006. Investigation of four different normality tests in terms of type 1 error rate and power under different distributions. *Turkish Journal of Medical Sciences* 36, 3 (2006), 171–176.

[33] Nornadiah Mohd Razali, Yap Bee Wah, et al. 2011. Power comparisons of shapiro-wilk, kolmogorov-smirnov, lilliefors and anderson-darling tests. *Journal of statistical modeling and analytics* 2, 1 (2011), 21–33.

[34] JP Royston. 1982. Algorithm AS 181: the W test for normality. *Journal of the Royal Statistical Society. Series C (Applied Statistics)* 31, 2 (1982), 176–180.

[35] Samuel Sanford Shapiro and Martin B Wilk. 1965. An analysis of variance test for normality (complete samples). *Biometrika* 52, 3/4 (1965), 591–611.

[36] Alexandru Topîrceanu. 2017. Gamified learning: A role-playing approach to increase student in-class motivation. *Procedia Computer Science* 112 (2017), 41–50.

[37] Jennifer Underdahl, Joycelyn Palacio-Cayetano, and Ron Stevens. 2001. Practice makes perfect. *Learn. Lead. Techn* 28 (2001), 26–31.

[38] Xianmin Wei. 2010. Research of practical course teaching of JAVA language. In *Educational and Information Technology (ICEIT), 2010 International Conference on*, Vol. 2. IEEE, V2–10.

[39] Leon E. Winslow. 1996. Programming Pedagogy – a Psychological Overview. *SIGCSE Bull.* 28, 3 (Sept. 1996), 17–22. https://doi.org/10.1145/234867.234872

Assessing Incremental Testing Practices and Their Impact on Project Outcomes

Ayaan M. Kazerouni, Clifford A. Shaffer, Stephen H. Edwards, and Francisco Servant
Virginia Tech
Blacksburg, VA
ayaan|shaffer|s.edwards|fservant@vt.edu

ABSTRACT

Software testing is an important aspect of the development process, one that has proven to be a challenge to formally introduce into the typical undergraduate CS curriculum. Unfortunately, existing assessment of testing in student software projects tends to focus on evaluation of metrics like code coverage *over the finished software product*, thus eliminating the possibility of giving students early feedback as they work on the project. Furthermore, assessing and teaching the process of writing and executing software tests is also important, as shown by the multiple variants proposed and disseminated by the software engineering community, *e.g.*, test-driven development (TDD) or incremental test-last (ITL). We present a family of novel metrics for assessment of testing practices *for increments of software development work*, thus allowing early feedback before the software project is finished. Our metrics measure the *balance* and *sequence* of effort spent writing software tests in a work increment. We performed an empirical study using our metrics to evaluate the test-writing practices of 157 advanced undergraduate students, and their relationships with project outcomes over multiple projects for a whole semester. We found that projects where more testing effort was spent per work session tended to be more semantically correct and have higher code coverage. The percentage of method-specific testing effort spent before production code did not contribute to semantic correctness, and had a negative relationship with code coverage. These novel metrics will enable educators to give students early, incremental feedback about their testing practices as they work on their software projects.

KEYWORDS

incremental development, process measurement, software repository mining

ACM Reference Format:

Ayaan M. Kazerouni, Clifford A. Shaffer, Stephen H. Edwards, and Francisco Servant. 2019. Assessing Incremental Testing Practices and Their Impact on Project Outcomes. In *Proceedings of the 50th ACM Technical Symposium on Computer Science Education (SIGCSE '19), February 27-March 2, 2019, Minneapolis, MN, USA.* ACM, New York, NY, USA, 7 pages. https://doi.org/10.1145/3287324.3287366

SIGCSE '19, Feb 27-Mar 2, 2019, Minneapolis, MN, USA

ACM ISBN 978-1-4503-5890-3/19/02...$15.00
https://doi.org/10.1145/3287324.3287366

1 INTRODUCTION

Software testing is an important aspect of software development, and one that is widely recognized to contribute to software quality [25, 32]. Unfortunately, teaching effective software testing often runs into many difficulties, *e.g.*, students in many US universities display a disinclination to practice regular software testing as they work toward project completion [13], and they often show poor testing ability [16, 37]. Furthermore, software testing is not a formal part of the typical CS undergraduate curriculum [25, 35].

In this paper, we focus on two major challenges for teaching software testing. First, existing approaches to assess student software testing can typically only be applied after students finish their project [15, 37]. As a consequence, by the time that these approaches provide students with feedback, they cannot really apply it to correct their practice for the same assignment. Examples of such measures include code coverage [15, 16, 37], bugs uncovered by running each student's test suite against every other student's implementation [17, 22], and coverage from mutation testing [1, 34]. In order to be able to provide students with early and continuous feedback, new approaches are necessary — to continuously assess the process that students follow *as they work on a software project.*

Second, there is a lack of strong understanding of *how specifically* software testing should be practiced [3, 28]. Existing studies measure the effects of testing methodologies [11, 19] by studying scenarios of complete adherence to a given well-known technique, *e.g.*, test-driven development (TDD) [4, 7], often with conflicting results [28, 31] [1]. However, the findings from these studies may not generalize to the context of students learning testing practices. The testing behaviors of students working on projects in uncontrolled environments (*e.g.*, at home) typically cannot be cleanly dichotomized into *fully test-first* or *fully test-last* styles of development. In our experience, since students are learning the practice, they typically follow various testing practices with varying rigor at different points in time.

To address these challenges, we propose a novel set of metrics that will enable educators to provide students with early, continuous feedback about their testing practices — as they are working on their software project. Our metrics quantitatively characterize how students write test code and production code *for work increments*, enabling the incremental assessment of their testing practices. These novel metrics measure the two testing behaviors that practitioners and software engineering researchers consider beneficial: the **balance of testing effort** (a common idea behind TDD and ITL [4, 7, 18, 19]), and the **sequence of testing effort** (the main idea behind test-first development [7]). In addition to

[1]Most industrial case studies lean toward an increase in program quality (external and internal), with a decrease in developer productivity

measuring work increments, our metrics are also *continuous* in nature: they measure the extent to which students followed beneficial practices within a work increment — instead of measuring *whether or not* they followed them. As a result, our metrics more faithfully represent (and thus allow us to study) the varying levels of student engagement with various testing practices at different times in the project life-cycle — without needing to classify their testing practices as any particular well-known technique (for neither work increments nor the whole project).

We performed an empirical study to learn the relationship between our metrics and the outcome of the software projects that students wrote. We analyzed the natural programming habits of 157 students working on complex projects with month-long life-cycles, with a median of 1.4K lines of code. We found that balancing the amount of test code and production code written during each work session (§3.2.1) — both project-wide and for specific pieces of the project — was related to better project outcomes. Additionally, we found that writing more test code *before* finalizing the relevant production code was not related to project correctness, and negatively related to test suite coverage. These findings show that our metrics can be used to incrementally provide students with feedback about their testing practices — as they work on their projects — to lead them to project success.

This paper provides the following contributions:

- A novel family of metrics to faithfully capture the extent to which students achieve balance and sequence of testing and production coding effort.
- An empirical study that measures the extent to which these metrics are related to successful project outcomes (correctness and test suite coverage)

2 PROPOSED METRICS OF TESTING EFFORT

In this section, we propose a new family of metrics to measure the balance and sequence of test and production code writing effort in a continuous fashion. Figure 1 shows an example sequence of developer activity, created from synthetic data. Each group of blocks represents a *work session*, and each individual block represents test code (shaded) or production code (solid) written for a given method. Figure 2 depicts the the metrics we describe in the following sections, in terms of the example activity sequence from Figure 1. Metrics are defined in terms of **the balance of testing effort** and the **sequence of testing effort**.

2.1 Balance of Testing Effort

We examine commits in the raw event stream in terms of *time* and *location*. Commits may be bucketed based on the *work session* in which they took place, or the *methods* they were related to.

Project-wide Overall Balance of Testing Effort (POB). This metric is depicted in the first row of Figure 2. It represents the test effort in the entire project regardless of the production methods being tested or the session in which test code was written. That is, notice how the visual dimensions for color (method), ordering, and block-group (sessions) have been eliminated for this metric.

"Effort" is captured as the number of line-level code-changes (additions, removals, or inline modifications) as captured by the `git diff` command (see §3.2). We define "**testing effort**" as the percentage of effort that was devoted to writing test code. By walking the code changes for a project, we compute the total size of all changes to test code T and the total size of all changes to production code P. Then we can calculate testing effort as a percentage of overall effort spent writing test code:

$$POB = \frac{T}{P+T} \tag{1}$$

Note that this is not equivalent to the percentage of source code that is test code. Additions, removals, and line-changes are included in this measure, as opposed to simple line counts at each snapshot. Therefore, this is a measure of *testing effort*, rather than a measure of *amount of test code.*

Method-specific Overall Balance of Testing Effort (MOB). This metric is depicted in the second row of Figure 2. In this metric, we determine testing effort while taking *location* into account, i.e., we measure the testing effort devoted to individual methods. We use the method-modification stream described in §3.2.2, and apply Equation (1) to each method in the project to compute the testing effort devoted to each method. Let this set of method-level test effort values be POB_m. Then we calculate the *MOB* metric as the median of the distribution of testing effort measured for all methods.

$$MOB = \widetilde{POB_m} \tag{2}$$

Project-wide per-Session Balance of Testing Effort (PSB). This metric is depicted in the third row of Figure 2. To determine testing effort while taking *time* into account, we compute *project-wide per-session balance* (PSB) of production code and test code. We grouped snapshots into work sessions as described in §3.2.1, and calculated the testing effort devoted to each work session using Equation (1).

Therefore, if POB_w is a set of values of testing effort devoted to each work session, this measure of testing effort over time (*PSB*) can be defined as the median testing effort across all work sessions:

$$PSB = \widetilde{POB_w} \tag{3}$$

Why use the median? Each project will *certainly* include some testing effort, because subjects were required to include test suites. Previous work has found that test code and production code do not co-evolve gracefully, whether written by students or by professionals [8, 9]. Using the mean testing effort, there would be no way to gauge whether this testing effort is put in gracefully over time. That is, a dearth of testing effort early on would be counteracted by an increase in testing effort at the end of the project, or vice versa.

Figure 3 shows the distribution of this metric across all projects. The distribution of medians indicates that a majority of students put in less than 20% testing effort in at least half of their work sessions. This could mean that subjects are not testing as much as they should. This would be in keeping with other work that finds that test code and production code do not co-evolve gracefully for students or for professionals [8, 9].

Method-specific per-Session Balance of Testing Effort (MSB). This metric is depicted in the fourth row of Figure 2. *MSB* determines testing effort while taking both *time* and *location* into account. That is, for the production code that is written in a given work session, we would like to know if the student tends to write *related* test code. We compute *method-specific balance over time* (*MSB*) of production

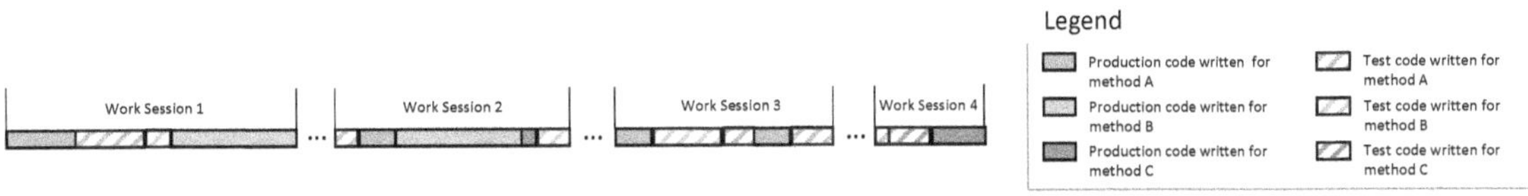

Figure 1: An example sequence of developer activity.

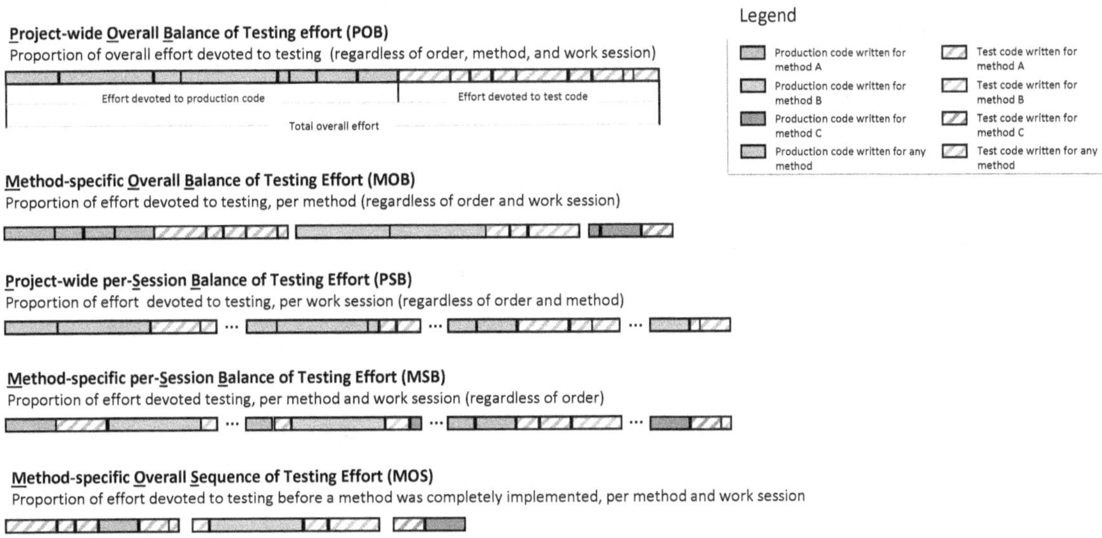

Figure 2: Measures to be derived from a programming activity event stream. Each row depicts a different method of aggregating the programming events from Figure 1.

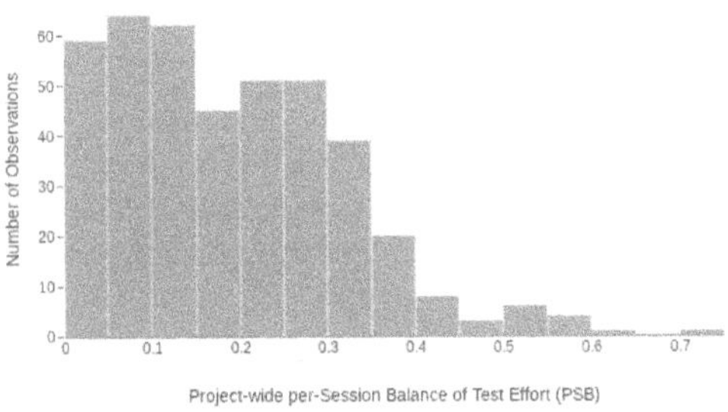

Figure 3: Distribution of median testing effort across work sessions

code and test code. To do this, we use *method-modification events* (§3.2.2) and divide them into *work sessions* based on their timestamps (§3.2.1).

Therefore, for all changes related to a given method that were made in a given work session, we may measure the testing effort using Equation (1). We are left with test effort values at two levels of grouping: **work session** and **method**. To compute *MSB*, we first find the project-wide per-session testing balance *for individual methods*, and call it PSB_m. Then we find the median per-session testing balance *across all methods*. Therefore, this metric can be represented as a "median of medians":

$$MSB = \widetilde{PSB_m} \tag{4}$$

2.2 Sequence of Testing Effort

We are interested in the balance of test code written *before* and *after* the relevant production code, and the relationship of that balance with project outcomes.

Only a small number of methods across the entire data set were invoked in a test before being declared themselves. This could be because test-first was not practiced at all, or because test-first developers declared incomplete stubs before writing tests, or because of some other reason. We can characterize this behavior by observing the central tendency of the size of changes to test code that take place before the relevant production code has been finalized.

Method-specific Overall Sequence of Testing Effort (MOS). This metric is depicted in the last row of Figure 2. We measure *sequence* as the percentage of test code that was written for a production method before the method was *finalized*[2].

Therefore, if m is a production method, then T_b is the total size of changes to test code before m was finalized, and T_a is the total size of changes to test code after m was finalized. Note than T_b and T_a only include changes to test methods that directly invoke m. Then we compute the percentage of test code for m that was

[2] A production method is 'finalized' when it is changed for the last time.

written before m was finalized as:

$$MOS_m = \frac{T_b}{T_b + T_a}$$

We compute the median MOS_m over all methods to get an overall measure for a student working on a project (MOS):

$$MOS = \widetilde{MOS_m} \quad (5)$$

3 RESEARCH METHOD

We performed an empirical study to understand the impact that **balance** and **sequence** of testing effort have on the quality of projects. We are driven by the following research questions:

RQ1: How do software product outcomes relate to the **balance** of effort devoted to writing test code and production code?

RQ2: How do software product outcomes relate to the **sequence** of effort devoted to writing test code and production code?

3.1 Study Setting

We studied software systems that were developed by Computer Science students enrolled in a third year Data Structures & Algorithms (DSA) course at a large R1 public university in the US in the Fall 2016 semester. Students in this course have taken several prerequisite programming courses, most of them in Java. Subjects became acquainted with the JUnit[3] testing framework in a previous course, and in the DSA course were taught material about project management and incrementally writing and testing code by one of the authors of this paper. We examine 157 students' programming habits as they work on four course projects over the course of the semester, for a total of 415 observations. Our design is unbalanced because not all students completed all 4 projects, typically because they withdrew from the course.

Subjects were given about four weeks for each project, and their solutions had a median size of 1.4K lines of source code, including tests. Each project asked the subjects to implement one or more data structures, along with its standard operations. Students were required to write JUnit tests for their code. In addition to correctness, students were graded on the percentage of conditions covered by their test-suites, providing strong incentive to eventually write test suites with near-total code coverage.

3.2 Data Collection

To operationalize the specific concepts that will soon be described, we collected and preprocessed the activities that our studied developers performed. We developed a custom Eclipse plugin to capture developer activity in the IDE [26, 29]. Our plugin creates a git repository and creates a new commit every time the developers click the "save" button in the IDE. Because the commits are maintained by our plugin and are not under the control of subjects, we avoid some "perils" of mining these snapshots [12]. That is, histories were not "re-written" using `git rebase` or `amend` commands. This rich data set captures the detail and nuance of test-writing behavior that is necessary to calculate the metrics to be described below. Repositories were mined using the open-source tool RepoDriller [2] [4].

[3]http://junit.org

[4]Now PyDriller [38]

3.2.1 Work sessions. Following Kazerouni et al. [27], we split the event stream for a subject working on a project into *work sessions*. Work sessions are sequences of activity, and are delimited by an hour or more of inactivity. In this context, 'activity' refers to automatically captured commits (driven by file save events), and they were grouped based on their timestamps.

3.2.2 Capturing Test-code and Production-code Modifications. To determine when changes affected test code vs. production code, and when test-code changes were related to production-code changes, we extracted developer activity on a per-method basis, and call these events *method-modification events*.

Using `git diff` output and an AST of the current snapshot, we determine which production methods and which tests for such production methods were modified in each commit. A test for a production method m is modified in a commit if the test directly invokes m. Therefore, we magnify the commit history into a series of method-specific events, meaning we expand commits into a series of method-specific `MODIFY_SELF` or `MODIFY_TEST_FOR_SELF` events.

3.2.3 Data Preprocessing. We filtered out some production methods from analysis. We excluded getters, setters, and printing methods. Exploratory analysis showed that 93% of projects in our dataset directly invoked at most 60% of all production methods in test code[5]. In other words, the distribution of testing effort across production methods is highly skewed. Both the mean and median values would be highly influenced by the skewed distribution, and would lead to a misleading 'score' for method-specific testing effort.

To account for this, we only examine the *top 60% most-tested* production methods in each project, where methods were ordered by the testing effort they were given. By examining only these most-tested methods, we are robust to the highly skewed distribution of testing effort across methods.

3.3 Data Analysis

Once we characterized the balance of writing test code and production code as a series of continuous independent variables, we used linear models to determine their effects on the following project outcomes:

- **Semantic Correctness (C)**: Measured as the percentage of tests passed from a suite of automated acceptance tests written by the course teaching staff.
- **Test Suite Coverage (T)**: Measured as the percentage of condition coverage achieved by the student's own test suite, measured using the JaCoCo[6] plugin. While subjects were required to submit test suites with nearly 100% code coverage, that might not happen until near the end of the development cycle.

We use linear mixed-effects ANCOVAs [6], with *students* and *projects* as crossed random effects. Experience suggests that no two students are the same, and this inherent variation might confound the model. Further, it is difficult to compare the programming process on different projects, even if they are assignments in the same

[5]Note that this is not the same as code coverage, which includes constructs that are invoked further down the call stack.

[6]https://www.eclemma.org/jacoco/

Table 1: Final ANCOVA Summary – Overall Testing Effort

	C		T	
Measure	Estimate	p	Estimate	p
POB	0.30	< 0.001*	0.23	< 0.001*
MOB	*NA*	0.12	*NA*	0.41
PSB	*NA*	0.83	*NA*	0.97
MSB	*NA*	0.97	0.08	0.01*
MOS	*NA*	0.74	-0.06	0.03*
	Residual Std. Err. = 0.23		Residual Std. Err. = 0.11	
	Marginal R^2 = 0.05		Marginal R^2 = 0.10	
	Conditional R^2 = 0.39		Conditional R^2 = 0.17	

course. Mixed-effects models allow us to control for the variation from these unaccounted-for effects.

We present *marginal* and *conditional* R^2 values [33] that describe the amount of variance in project outcomes explained by our models. Marginal R^2 values refer to the amount of variance in the outcome variable described by *fixed effects only* (in this case, our process measurements). Conditional R^2 values refer to the amount of variance in the outcome variable described by *the entire model* (in this case, the process measurements as well as individual students and assignments).

We fit the following linear mixed models for **semantic correctness** (C) and **test suite coverage** (T), using our metrics as fixed effects[7]:

$$C \sim POB + MOB + PSB + MSB + MOS + (1|student) + (1|project)$$
$$T \sim POB + MOB + PSB + MSB + MOS + (1|student) + (1|project)$$

The models are summarized in Table 1. Estimates suggest that project-wide overall balance (*POB*) of test code and production code is positively related with semantic correctness and test coverage. Additionally, test coverage has a positive relationship with method-specific per-session balance (and *MSB*) of test and production code, and a significant but weak negative relationship with the amount of testing effort put in before finalizing production code (*MOS*).

To gain a more fine-grained understanding of our measures and their effects, we fit another 'process-based' model for each outcome, only including the measures that took *time* into account:

$$C \sim PSB + MSB + MOS + (1|student) + (1|project)$$
$$T \sim PSB + MSB + MOS + (1|student) + (1|project)$$

The models are summarized in Table 2. Notice that *PSB* is significantly related to both outcomes under the process-based model, while it was not significant under the overall model in Table 1.

4 RESULTS

We now present our findings regarding **RQ1** and **RQ2**.

RQ1 – Balance: Both semantic correctness (C) and test coverage (T) showed positive relationships with project-wide per-session balance of test and production code (*PSB*). That is, project implementations tend to be more semantically correct, and their test-suites

[7]The notation $(1|factor)$ means that *factor* was used as a random effect.

Table 2: ANCOVA Summary – Process-Based Testing Effort

	C		T	
Measure	Estimate	p	Estimate	p
PSB	0.30	0.005*	0.12	0.008*
MSB	0.11	0.10	0.09	0.002*
MOS	-0.03	0.62	-0.06	0.02*

tend to have higher condition coverage, when students more often write test code when they sit down to work on the project.

Test coverage was also positively related to the balance of testing effort devoted to individual methods in each work session (*MSB*) That is, condition coverage tended to be higher when more testing effort was devoted to individual methods each time the project was worked on.

RQ2 – Sequence: Whether testing effort took place more predominantly before or after the relevant production code was finalized was irrelevant to semantic correctness. On the other hand, test coverage had a negative relationship with *MOS*, indicating that implementations tended to have higher condition coverage when a higher proportion of the testing effort devoted to a method was expended *after* the method was finalized.

5 DISCUSSION

Why is semantic correctness not associated with writing test code for relevant production code? Notice that method-specific per-session balance of test code and production code (*MSB*) was not significantly related to semantic correctness (Table 2). Does this mean that it does not matter *what* test code a developer writes, only that they write *some* test code? It would be surprising and counterintuitive to think so. However, it may be that, for this population, the variance in correctness explained by the specificity of test code written is subsumed by the variance explained by simply writing test code consistently.

Why is PSB significantly related to outcomes in the process-based model (Table 2), but not in the overall model (Table 1)? It may be that the variance explained by consistently writing software tests in each work session is subsumed by the variance in explained by maintaining an overall balance of testing effort.

How does one balance test code and production code over time, while also writing more test code after the relevant production methods have been finalized? The quantitative measure *MOS* measures the percentage of testing effort that tends to be put in before the relevant production method has been finalized, and is negatively related with the percentage of conditions covered by the test suite. These findings together suggest that while regular, balanced testing is important to test coverage, it is also important to put in testing effort after pieces of functionality have been completed.

What do the low marginal R^2 values suggest? The process measurements show significant relationships with semantic correctness and test suite coverage. Marginal (fixed effects only) R^2 values [33] for both models suggest that this effect size is small (5% for C and 10% for T). There are always likely to be numerous unexplained sources of variation when measuring human behavior. In other words, there could be any number of unaccounted factors that affect the quality of software produced by developers (particularly students). Those factors are not under study. The goal of this study was to determine the impact of balancing production and test coding effort on project quality, and the models are able to answer our research questions with statistical confidence.

It could also be that the assignments in this DSA course do not "hit the right switches", that is, success did not demand a high adherence to incremental testing. After all, they were not explicitly designed to do so. It would be interesting to conduct a similar study using semester-long projects from dedicated software engineering courses, more closely imitating real-world scenarios.

6 THREATS TO VALIDITY

Internal Validity. Since we do not have strictly defined experimental and control groups, we do not claim direct causality between process measurements and project outcomes. Our sample of student developers is sufficiently large and does not suffer from a selection bias [8]. Therefore, we do not believe that this is a serious threat to validity.

Subjects had mechanical experience with the JUnit testing framework from a previous course. Multiple class periods were devoted to teaching material about project management skills, including incremental software testing, before the first project was assigned. This fact might mitigate threats from differential experience.

External Validity. Findings based on this particular student population working on these assignments might not be generalizable to all junior level student programmers. Further, student behavior is often motivated by a number of unknown external factors (for example, deadlines and responsibilities from other courses). It is unclear if or how this might have affected our findings, other than to observe that this semester seemed typical of our long experience with the course.

Construct Validity. The largest threat to construct validity is related to the computation of the event stream described in §3.2.2. Specifically, we link test methods and production methods if a given test method directly invokes a given production method. However, it could be that the production method was not the 'focal point' [21] of the test method, and was only being invoked to set up the test case, or to gain access to the method that was actually being tested. This could have increased the number of `MODIFY_TEST_FOR_SELF` events for some production methods, affecting our process measurements.

However, if a production method is directly invoked in a test, it is reasonable to claim that the method is being tested, regardless of developer intent. Indeed, this is the basis for code coverage, which treats methods (or statements, branches, etc.) as "covered" as long as they are invoked "somewhere in the call stack".

7 RELATED WORK

In this section we review some related work on teaching, observing, and assessing software testing.

Teaching Testing. In the classroom, Desai [14] acknowledges the challenges associated with introducing testing into the curriculum, and notes that regular, reinforced learning of testing might be better than only an introduction to it at the start of the semester. Jones [25], Edwards [15, 16] and others [35, 36] have worked toward introducing testing into the curriculum. Unfortunately, most prior work in this area tends to focus on novice programmers working on small projects, where the benefits of testing are not readily apparent [5], and on 'after-the-fact' feedback. In this paper, we study advanced students working on larger, more complex projects, and we work toward a long-term goal of continuous feedback and self-correction on the testing process.

Observing Testing Behavior. The Test My Code (TMC) plugin [39] for NetBeans records events whenever the student saves, runs, or tests code using instructor-provided tests. Hosseini et al. [23] make use of this plugin in an attempt to reason about how students check their work as they program. In contrast, this work focuses on data about students' testing habits, i.e., how they go about writing and running their own software tests.

Assessing Testing. Beller et al. [8–10] developed WatchDog, a family of IDE plugins to capture and assess software testing. Using these data, they found that most professional and student developers do not practice testing actively and that solution code and test code do not co-evolve gracefully. WatchDog assesses how closely developers followed a given testing methodology. Our metrics allow feedback for how students balance and sequence testing effort regardless of whether they follow (or not) a specific methodology.

Industrial case studies measuring the effects of TDD [11, 30, 40] tend to focus on a single implementation of a large project. As a consequence, comparisons to other projects are difficult and these studies are rarely replicated. Other existing studies do controlled experiments, which tend to involve many implementations, but they focus on learning about a specific testing methodology which is used by the developers for the whole duration of the study [18–20, 24]. In this paper, we study a different setting, in which students may follow various testing methodologies with varying rigor at different times. In addition, we strengthen the external validity of our results by comparing implementations of the same project from over 100 students (for multiple projects).

8 CONCLUSION

In this paper, we presented a novel family of metrics to assess students' incremental testing practices. We also conducted an observational study examining the relationships of test-writing behaviors, as measured by these metrics, on project outcomes. Our findings support the conventional wisdom about continuously writing tests alongside production code, but we did not find evidence to support the notion that writing tests first leads to project success.

This work is a step toward enabling continuous feedback on students' programming process. Future work will include formulating and deploying feedback based on these assessments, helping instructors to better teach incremental development.

9 ACKNOWLEDGMENTS

This work is supported in part by the National Science Foundation under grant DUE-1245334. The authors would like to thank Jamie Davis for valuable feedback on drafts of the paper.

[8] The course we study is a required part of the CS undergraduate curriculum, and we included all consenting students (>96%) enrolled in the course as subjects.

REFERENCES

[1] Kalle Aaltonen, Petri Ihantola, and Otto Seppälä. 2010. Mutation Analysis vs. Code Coverage in Automated Assessment of Students' Testing Skills. In *Proceedings of the ACM International Conference Companion on Object Oriented Programming Systems Languages and Applications Companion (OOPSLA '10)*. ACM, New York, NY, USA, 153–160. https://doi.org/10.1145/1869542.1869567

[2] Maurìcio Finavaro Aniche. 2018. RepoDriller. https://github.com/ayaankazerouni/repodriller.

[3] Maurìcio Finavaro Aniche and Marco Aurélio Gerosa. 2010. Most common mistakes in test-driven development practice: Results from an online survey with developers. In *Software Testing, Verification, and Validation Workshops (ICSTW), 2010 Third International Conference on*. IEEE, 469–478. https://doi.org/10.1109/ICSTW.2010.16

[4] Dave Astels. 2003. *Test driven development: A practical guide*. Prentice Hall Professional Technical Reference.

[5] Elena García Barriocanal, Miguel-Ángel Sicilia Urbán, Ignacio Aedo Cuevas, and Paloma Díaz Pérez. 2002. An Experience in Integrating Automated Unit Testing Practices in an Introductory Programming Course. *SIGCSE Bull.* 34, 4 (Dec. 2002), 125–128. https://doi.org/10.1145/820127.820183

[6] Douglas Bates, Martin MÃd'chler, Ben Bolker, and Steve Walker. 2015. Fitting Linear Mixed-Effects Models Using lme4. *Journal of Statistical Software, Articles* 67, 1 (2015), 1–48. https://doi.org/10.18637/jss.v067.i01

[7] Kent Beck. 2003. *Test-driven development: by example*. Addison-Wesley Professional.

[8] Moritz Beller, Georgios Gousios, Annibale Panichella, and Andy Zaidman. 2015. When, How, and Why Developers (Do Not) Test in Their IDEs. In *Proceedings of the 2015 10th Joint Meeting on Foundations of Software Engineering (ESEC/FSE 2015)*. ACM, New York, NY, USA, 179–190. https://doi.org/10.1145/2786805.2786843

[9] Moritz Beller, Georgios Gousios, and Andy Zaidman. 2015. How (Much) Do Developers Test?. In *Proceedings of the 37th International Conference on Software Engineering - Volume 2 (ICSE '15)*. IEEE Press, Piscataway, NJ, USA, 559–562.

[10] Moritz Beller, Igor Levaja, Annibale Panichella, Georgios Gousios, and Andy Zaidman. 2016. How to Catch 'Em All: WatchDog, a Family of IDE Plug-ins to Assess Testing. In *Proceedings of the 3rd International Workshop on Software Engineering Research and Industrial Practice (SER&IP '16)*. ACM, New York, NY, USA, 53–56. https://doi.org/10.1145/2897022.2897027

[11] Thirumalesh Bhat and Nachiappan Nagappan. 2006. Evaluating the Efficacy of Test-driven Development: Industrial Case Studies. In *Proceedings of the 2006 ACM/IEEE International Symposium on Empirical Software Engineering (ISESE '06)*. ACM, New York, NY, USA, 356–363. https://doi.org/10.1145/1159733.1159787

[12] C. Bird, P. C. Rigby, E. T. Barr, D. J. Hamilton, D. M. German, and P. Devanbu. 2009. The promises and perils of mining git. In *2009 6th IEEE International Working Conference on Mining Software Repositories*. 1–10. https://doi.org/10.1109/MSR.2009.5069475

[13] Kevin Buffardi and Stephen H. Edwards. 2014. A Formative Study of Influences on Student Testing Behaviors. In *Proceedings of the 45th ACM Technical Symposium on Computer Science Education (SIGCSE '14)*. ACM, New York, NY, USA, 597–602. https://doi.org/10.1145/2538862.2538982

[14] Chetan Desai, David Janzen, and Kyle Savage. 2008. A Survey of Evidence for Test-driven Development in Academia. *SIGCSE Bull.* 40, 2 (June 2008), 97–101. https://doi.org/10.1145/1383602.1383644

[15] Stephen H. Edwards. 2003. Improving Student Performance by Evaluating How Well Students Test Their Own Programs. *J. Educ. Resour. Comput.* 3, 3, Article 1 (Sept. 2003). https://doi.org/10.1145/1029994.1029995

[16] Stephen H. Edwards and Manuel A. Perez-Quinones. 2008. Web-CAT: Automatically Grading Programming Assignments. In *Proceedings of the 13th Annual Conference on Innovation and Technology in Computer Science Education (ITiCSE '08)*. ACM, New York, NY, USA, 328–328. https://doi.org/10.1145/1384271.1384371

[17] Stephen H. Edwards, Zalia Shams, Michael Cogswell, and Robert C. Senkbeil. 2012. Running Students' Software Tests Against Each Others' Code: New Life for an Old "Gimmick". In *Proceedings of the 43rd ACM Technical Symposium on Computer Science Education (SIGCSE '12)*. ACM, New York, NY, USA, 221–226. https://doi.org/10.1145/2157136.2157202

[18] Hakan Erdogmus, Grigori Melnik, and Ron Jeffries. 2010. Test-Driven Development.

[19] D. Fucci, H. Erdogmus, B. Turhan, M. Oivo, and N. Juristo. 2017. A Dissection of the Test-Driven Development Process: Does It Really Matter to Test-First or to Test-Last? *IEEE Transactions on Software Engineering* 43, 7 (July 2017), 597–614. https://doi.org/10.1109/TSE.2016.2616877

[20] Davide Fucci, Giuseppe Scanniello, Simone Romano, Martin Shepperd, Boyce Sigweni, Fernando Uyaguari, Burak Turhan, Natalia Juristo, and Markku Oivo. 2016. An external replication on the effects of test-driven development using a multi-site blind analysis approach. In *Proceedings of the 10th ACM/IEEE International Symposium on Empirical Software Engineering and Measurement*. ACM, 3.

[21] M. Ghafari, C. Ghezzi, and K. Rubinov. 2015. Automatically identifying focal methods under test in unit test cases. In *2015 IEEE 15th International Working Conference on Source Code Analysis and Manipulation (SCAM)*. 61–70. https://doi.org/10.1109/SCAM.2015.7335402

[22] Michael H. Goldwasser. 2002. A Gimmick to Integrate Software Testing Throughout the Curriculum. In *Proceedings of the 33rd SIGCSE Technical Symposium on Computer Science Education (SIGCSE '02)*. ACM, New York, NY, USA, 271–275. https://doi.org/10.1145/563340.563446

[23] Roya Hosseini, Arto Vihavainen, and Peter Brusilovsky. 2014. Exploring problem solving paths in a Java programming course. (2014).

[24] Liang Huang and Mike Holcombe. 2009. Empirical investigation towards the effectiveness of Test First programming. *Information and Software Technology* 51, 1 (2009), 182–194.

[25] Edward L. Jones. 2000. Software Testing in the Computer Science Curriculum – a Holistic Approach. In *Proceedings of the Australasian Conference on Computing Education (ACSE '00)*. ACM, New York, NY, USA, 153–157. https://doi.org/10.1145/359369.359392

[26] Ayaan M. Kazerouni, Stephen H. Edwards, T. Simin Hall, and Clifford A. Shaffer. 2017. DevEventTracker: Tracking Development Events to Assess Incremental Development and Procrastination. In *Proceedings of the 2017 ACM Conference on Innovation and Technology in Computer Science Education (ITiCSE '17)*. ACM, New York, NY, USA, 104–109. https://doi.org/10.1145/3059009.3059050

[27] Ayaan M. Kazerouni, Stephen H. Edwards, and Clifford A. Shaffer. 2017. Quantifying Incremental Development Practices and Their Relationship to Procrastination. In *Proceedings of the 2017 ACM Conference on International Computing Education Research (ICER '17)*. ACM, New York, NY, USA, 191–199. https://doi.org/10.1145/3105726.3106180

[28] Sami Kollanus. 2010. Test-driven development-still a promising approach?. In *Quality of Information and Communications Technology (QUATIC), 2010 Seventh International Conference on the*. IEEE, 403–408. https://doi.org/10.1109/QUATIC.2010.73

[29] Joseph Abraham Luke. 2015. *Continuously Collecting Software Development Event Data As Students Program*. Master's thesis. Virginia Tech.

[30] E Michael Maximilien and Laurie Williams. 2003. Assessing test-driven development at IBM. In *Software Engineering, 2003. Proceedings. 25th International Conference on*. IEEE, 564–569.

[31] Hussan Munir, Misagh Moayyed, and Kai Petersen. 2014. Considering rigor and relevance when evaluating test driven development: A systematic review. *Information and Software Technology* 56, 4 (2014), 375 – 394. https://doi.org/10.1016/j.infsof.2014.01.002

[32] Glenford J Myers, Corey Sandler, and Tom Badgett. 2011. *The art of software testing*. John Wiley & Sons.

[33] Shinichi Nakagawa and Holger Schielzeth. [n. d.]. A general and simple method for obtaining R2 from generalized linear mixed-effects models. *Methods in Ecology and Evolution* 4, 2 ([n. d.]), 133–142. https://doi.org/10.1111/j.2041-210x.2012.00261.x

[34] Zalia Shams and Stephen H. Edwards. 2013. Toward Practical Mutation Analysis for Evaluating the Quality of Student-written Software Tests. In *Proceedings of the Ninth Annual International ACM Conference on International Computing Education Research (ICER '13)*. ACM, New York, NY, USA, 53–58. https://doi.org/10.1145/2493394.2493402

[35] Terry Shepard, Margaret Lamb, and Diane Kelly. 2001. More Testing Should Be Taught. *Commun. ACM* 44, 6 (June 2001), 103–108. https://doi.org/10.1145/376134.376180

[36] Jaime Spacco, David Hovemeyer, William Pugh, Fawzi Emad, Jeffrey K. Hollingsworth, and Nelson Padua-Perez. 2006. Experiences with Marmoset: Designing and Using an Advanced Submission and Testing System for Programming Courses. In *Proceedings of the 11th Annual SIGCSE Conference on Innovation and Technology in Computer Science Education (ITICSE '06)*. ACM, New York, NY, USA, 13–17. https://doi.org/10.1145/1140124.1140131

[37] Jaime Spacco and William Pugh. 2006. Helping Students Appreciate Test-driven Development (TDD). In *Companion to the 21st ACM SIGPLAN Symposium on Object-oriented Programming Systems, Languages, and Applications (OOPSLA '06)*. ACM, New York, NY, USA, 907–913. https://doi.org/10.1145/1176617.1176743

[38] Davide Spadini, Maurìcio Aniche, and Alberto Bacchelli. 2018. *PyDriller: Python Framework for Mining Software Repositories*. https://doi.org/10.1145/3236024.3264598

[39] Arto Vihavainen, Thomas Vikberg, Matti Luukkainen, and Martin Pärtel. 2013. Scaffolding Students' Learning Using Test My Code. In *Proceedings of the 18th ACM Conference on Innovation and Technology in Computer Science Education (ITiCSE '13)*. ACM, New York, NY, USA, 117–122. https://doi.org/10.1145/2462476.2462501

[40] Laurie Williams, E Michael Maximilien, and Mladen Vouk. 2003. Test-driven development as a defect-reduction practice. In *Software Reliability Engineering, 2003. ISSRE 2003. 14th International Symposium on*. IEEE, 34–45.

Pragmatic Software Testing Education

Maurício Aniche
Delft University of Technology
The Netherlands
m.f.aniche@tudelft.nl

Felienne Hermans
Delft University of Technology
The Netherlands
f.f.j.hermans@tudelft.nl

Arie van Deursen
Delft University of Technology
The Netherlands
arie.vandeursen@tudelft.nl

ABSTRACT

Software testing is an important topic in software engineering education, and yet highly challenging from an educational perspective: students are required to learn several testing techniques, to be able to distinguish the right technique to apply, to evaluate the quality of their test suites, and to write maintainable test code. In this paper, we describe how we have been adding a pragmatic perspective to our software testing course, and explore students' common mistakes, hard topics to learn, favourite learning activities, and challenges they face. To that aim, we analyze the feedback reports that our team of Teaching Assistants gave to the 230 students of our 2016-2017 software testing course at Delft University of Technology. We also survey 84 students and seven of our teaching assistants on their perceptions. Our results help educators not only to propose pragmatic software testing courses in their faculties, but also bring understanding on the challenges that software testing students face when taking software testing courses.

CCS CONCEPTS

• **Applied computing** → **Education**; • **Software and its engineering** → *Software verification and validation*;

KEYWORDS

software testing education, software engineering education, computer science education.

ACM Reference Format:
Maurício Aniche, Felienne Hermans, and Arie van Deursen. 2019. Pragmatic Software Testing Education. In *SIGCSE '19: 50th ACM Technical Symposium on Computer Science Education, February 27–March 2, 2019, Minneapolis, MN, USA*. ACM, New York, NY, USA, 7 pages. https://doi.org/10.1145/3287324.3287461

1 INTRODUCTION

Every software developer should be aware of the (high) impact that malfunctioning software can have in our society. We have seen huge losses in the financial market [30], and even researchers withdrawing their papers [33]; all of them caused by software bugs. Making sure software works is maybe the greatest responsibility of a software developer. Luckily, over the years, software testing moved away from being considered the activity that 'less skilled' software engineers do to one of the most important skills an engineer should have.

The act of inspecting large and complex code bases to find bugs is not a trivial task in the real world: engineers need to have a broad understanding of different practices that vary from simple manual exploratory testing, where a human tries to find bugs manually by interacting with the system, to advanced bleeding-edge testing techniques, such as automated testing and automated test generation, where engineers program machines to test their system.

Companies such as Facebook [12], Google [41], and Microsoft [35] take testing seriously and require their engineers to master such techniques. Surveys have shown that developers understand the importance of testing-related training [15] and yet many of them still lack formal testing education [6, 34].

Indeed, educating a student in the art of software testing is challenging, for both students and educators. From the educator's perspective, it is hard to keep a testing course up-to-date with the novelties of the field as well as to come up with exercises that are realistic [14]. Due to the importance of the topic, educators have been experimenting with the introduction of testing earlier in Computer Science programs [17, 19–21, 23, 27], introducing a test-first approach in CS courses [9, 10, 22], developing tools focused on software testing education [11, 38], and proposing more complete postgraduate courses focused on testing [39]. Educators also face the fact that some testing topics are not conceptually straightforward, not easy to demonstrate and generalize, and are not all available in a single textbook [40].

This paper has a twofold goal. First, to present how we have been teaching pragmatic software testing to the first year CS students at Delft University of Technology. Second, we explore students' common mistakes, hard topics to learn, favourite learning activities, and challenges they face when learning pragmatic software testing.

To this aim, we analyzed the 1,993 quotes from the feedback report that we, as teachers and teaching assistants, gave to each of the 230 students of the 2017 edition of the Software Quality and Testing course, which is taught at the first year of our Computer Science bachelor. In addition, we performed a survey with 84 students, which we augmented by also surveying seven of our TAs.

The main contributions of this paper are:

- A proposal for a pragmatic software testing course based on nine key principles that can be taught for computer science students, including building a test mindset and interaction with practitioners (Section 3).
- An empirical analysis of the students' most common mistakes (Section 6.1), their perceptions on the most difficult topics in software testing (Section 6.2), and the importance of different teaching activities (Section 6.3) when learning pragmatic software testing.

SIGCSE'19, February 27–March 2, 2019, Minneapolis, MN, USA

ACM ISBN 978-1-4503-5890-3/19/2...$15.00
https://doi.org/10.1145/3287324.3287461

2 RELATED WORK

Software Testing is an important part of any Software Engineering program [2, 8, 26, 42], and by itself poses *several other challenges* to educators. Unfortunately, the topic still does not receive its deserved attention in several CS programs. Wong [42] argues that many engineers are not well trained in software testing because most CS programs offer ST as an elective course. Clarke et al. [8] also points to the fact that due to the large number of topics to be covered in a Software Engineering program, little attention is given to Software Testing. Astigarraga et al. [2] show that most CS programs tend to emphasize development at the expense of testing as a formal engineering discipline. Lemos et al. [26] show that software testing education can improve code reliability in terms of correctness; however, authors also argue that university instructors tend to lack the same knowledge that would help students increase their programming skills toward more reliable code.

Educators have been suggesting different approaches on how to introduce testing in a CS curriculum: from students submitting their assignments together with test plans or sets [16, 17, 21], performing black-box testing in a software seeded with errors [21, 24, 31], students testing each others' programs [36], to suggesting students to use a test-first approach at the very beginning of the program [9, 10, 22, 27]. Many of these authors even suggest that tests should be incorporated to the Computer Science and Software Engineering curricula, not only as an elective discipline, but throughout the curriculum. More specifically, Jones [23] suggests that students need to see the practice of software testing as part of the educational experience and that each core course in the curriculum should impart one or more testing experiences.

In addition, educators have proposed tools that are solely focused on software testing education. Elbaum et al. [11] propose *BugHunt*. BugHunt is a tool that contains four different lessons on software testing (terminology, black box, white box, efficiency in testing). 79% of the students in their experiment agreed that BugHunt added significant value to the material presented in the lecture(s) on software testing, and 61% of the students agreed that BugHunt could replace the classes on testing. Spacco and Pugh propose *Marmoset* [38], a tool to help incentivize students to test their software. Marmoset's innovative element is that if a submission passes all of the public test cases, then students are given the opportunity to test their code against a test suite that is not publicly disclosed.

3 PRAGMATIC SOFTWARE TESTING EDUCATION

The *Software Testing and Quality Engineering* at Delft University of Technology is a course that covers several different aspects of software testing, ranging from topics in the ISTQB industry certification [5] to software testing automation, as well as the future of testing by means of selected research papers.

The course is currently a compulsory part of the 4th quarter of the first year in the Computer Science bachelor. The course corresponds to 5 ECTS (140 hours). Students have two lectures of 1.5 hours plus 4 hours of labwork a week. As a pre-requisite, students should have at least basic knowledge on Java programming language.

The teaching team is currently composed of two teachers and teaching assistants (TAs). The number of TAs vary as our university has a policy of 1 TA per 30 students. Teachers are responsible for the course design, lectures, creating and assessing multiple choice exams, and they have the overall responsibility of the course. TAs are responsible for helping students, grading all labwork deliverables, and for giving concrete and specific feedback on what students can improve.

Learning goals. At the end of the course, students (1) are able to create unit, integration, and system tests using current existing tools (*e.g.*, JUnit, Mockito) that successfully test complex software systems, (2) are able to derive test cases that deal with exceptional, corner, and bad weather cases by performing several different techniques (*i.e.*, boundary analysis, state-based testing, decision tables), (3) are able to measure and reflect on the effectiveness of the developed test suites by means of different test adequacy metrics (*e.g.*, line and branch code coverage, MC/DC), (4) are able to reflect on limitations of current testing techniques, when and when not to apply them in a given context, and to design testable software systems, (5) Participants are able to write maintainable test code by avoiding well-known test code smells (*e.g.*, Assertion Roulette, Slow or Obscure Tests).

Program. The course covers software quality attributes, maintainability and testability, manual and exploratory testing, automated testing, devops, test adequacy, model-based testing, state-based testing, decision tables, reviews and inspections, design-by-contract, embedded system testing, test-driven design, unit versus integration testing, mocks and stubs. More specifically:

- Week 1: Introduction to software testing, fault vs failure, principles of testing, (un)decidabilitily, introduction to JUnit, introduction to labwork.
- Week 2: Life cycle, validation vs verification, V-model, code reviews. Functional testing, partition testing, boundary testing, and domain testing.
- Week 3: Structural testing, adequacy criteria, code coverage. Unit vs integration vs system testing, mock objects, and test-driven development.
- Week 4: State-based testing, model-based testing, and decision tables.
- Week 5: Test code quality, test code smells. Design for testability. Design-by-contracts.
- Week 6: Security testing. Search-based software testing.
- Week 7: Guest lectures from industry.

Key elements. To achieve a pragmatic software testing course, we have devised and currently follow some key elements:

Theory applied in the lecture. We put our efforts into developing lectures where students can see theory being applied to practice. Our lectures often have the following structure: we present a (buggy) code implementation (initially on slides, and later in the IDE), we discuss where the bug is, we explore, at a conceptual level, a systematic approach to detect the bug, we apply the approach into a set of concrete examples. In other words, we do not only focus on explaining abstract ideas, but on concretely showing how to apply them on different real world problems, using real-world tools, like JUnit, Mockito, and Cucumber.

Real-world pragmatic discussions. Software testing is a challenging activity to be done in practice. This means that developers often make trade-offs in deciding what and how much to test. Engineering questions that arise when complex software systems are being tested, such as "how much should I test?", "how should I test a mobile application that communicates with a web server?", and "should I use mocks to test this application?" are often discussed in classroom so that students see how to extrapolate from our often small exercises to their future real lifes as developers.

Build a testing mindset. Software testing is not seen as an important task by many students. A software testing course should inspire students to think about testing whenever they implement any piece of code. In our testing course, we aim to achieve such a testing mindset by (1) showing how testing can be a creative activity, requiring strong developers, by means of several live coding sessions and rich pragmatic discussions, (2) demonstrating not only the usefulness of any testing technique we teach, but also how they are applied, as well as what trade-offs such techniques have in the real-world, (3) bringing guest lecturers who talk about the importance of software testing for their companies.

Software testing automation. The software engineering industry has long been advocating the automation of any software testing activity [12, 35, 41]. However, some software testing courses still focus on writing test case specifications solely as documents, and do not discuss how to automate them. In our course, to all the theoretical and systematic test design techniques we present, from functional testing to structural testing, from unit to system-level tests, students later write them in a form of an automated test. Mastering tools such as JUnit and Mockito, standard tools for test automation in Java, is a clear learning goal of our course. The importance of automation also strongly appears in our labwork, which we discuss next.

A hands-on labwork. We see the labwork as an important learning method. In our course, by means of a practical labwork assignment, students apply a selection of techniques to a 3k lines of code game written in Java, namely, JPacMan. The labwork contains a set of 50 exercises in which students are able to exercise all the techniques we teach. It is important to notice that students not only generate test cases on the paper, but also automate them. A great amount of their work is in actually producing automated JUnit test cases.

In the following, we present the main deliverables of our labwork. The complete assignment can be found in our online appendix [1].

- *Part 0 (Pre-requisites).* Clone the project from Github, configure the project in your IDE, write your first JUnit test, run coverage analysis.
- *Part 1.* Write a smoke test, functional black-box testing, boundary tests, reflect on test understandability and best practices.
- *Part 2.* White-box testing, mock objects, calculate code coverage and apply structural testing, use decision tables for complex scenarios, reflect on how to reduce test complexity and how to avoid flaky tests.
- *Part 3.* Apply state-based testing, test reusability, refactor and reflect on test smells.

Test code quality matters. Due to the importance of automated testing activities, software testers will deal with large test codebases. Empirical research has indeed shown that test code smells often happen in software systems, and that their presence has a strong negative impact on the maintainability of the affected classes [3]. We often reinforce the importance of refactoring test code and make sure they are free of smells. To any test code we write during live coding sessions, we make sure that they are as free of smells as possible. Test smell catalogues such as the ones proposed by Meszaros [32] are deeply discussed in a dedicated lecture.

Design systems for testability. Designing software in such a way that it eases testability is a common practice among practitioners [13, 18, 29]. This requires us to not only discuss software testing in our course, but software architecture and design principles of testable software systems, such as dependency inversion [28], observability and controllability, in an entire dedicated lecture for the topic. Questions like "Do I need to test this behavior via an unit or a system test?", "How can I test my mobile application?" are extensively discussed not only through the eyes of software testing, but also to the eyes of software design.

Mixture of pragmatic and theoretical books. The two books we use as textbooks in the course are the *"Foundations of software testing: ISTQB certification"* [5], which gives students a solid foundation about testing theory, and the *"Pragmatic Unit Testing in Java 8 with JUnit"* [25], which gives students concrete and practical examples on how to use testing tools, like JUnit. We believe both complement each other and both are important for students who will soon become a software tester.

Interaction with practitioners. We strongly encourage their interaction with practitioners throughout our course. Having guest lectures from industry practitioners helps us to show the pragmatic side of software testing. Guests focus their lectures on how they apply software testing at their companies, tools they use, their pros and cons, and on the mistakes and challenges they face. In the 2017 edition, we also experimented with Ask-Me-Anything (AMA) sessions, where we called experts from all over the world via Skype and students had 15 minutes to ask any software-testing related questions.

Grading. We currently use the following formula to grade our students: `0.25 * labwork + 0.75 * exam`. The labwork (as we explain below) is composed of 4 deliverables, each graded by our TAs in a range of [0..10]. We later average the grades of four deliverables, which compose the labwork component of the grade. At the end of the course, we propose a 40-question multiple choice exam. Students may take a resit 6 weeks later if they did not pass in the first time. We also offer an optional midterm exam for students who want to practice beforehand.

4 RESEARCH METHODOLOGY

The *goal* of this study is to provide a better understanding of the difficulties and challenges that students face when learning pragmatic software testing.

To that aim, we analyze the data from 230 students of the 2016-2017 edition of our software testing course. We propose three research questions:

RQ$_1$: What common mistakes do students make when learning software testing?

RQ_2: Which software testing topics do students find hardest to learn?

RQ_3: Which teaching methods do students find most helpful?

To answer our research questions, we collect and analyze data from three different sources: the feedback reports that TAs give to students throughout the course, a survey with students, and a survey with the TAs, both performed after the course. We characterize the participants in Section 5. In the following, we detail the three parts of our methodology.

Manual content analysis on the feedback. As we explain in Section 3, students work on and produce four deliverables during the course. After each deliverable, our team of TAs manually reads students' reports, source code, and tests, and with the help of a rubric, provides them with rich qualitative feedback.

This feedback usually contains several quotes that touch on a mix of different topics, such as mistakes they made in the exercises, tips on how to improve their existing work, issues on the written report, and even compliments for their good work. The language of such feedback reports is usually informal, as we do not give constraints to TAs on how the feedback should be.

We analyze the content of all feedback reports. To that aim, we first filter out any feedback that is not directly related to software testing (*e.g.*, comments on exercises that were not done, or compliments). We then follow an iterative process, derived from standard qualitative data analysis procedures [37]: (1) we assign a code for each quote in the feedback; the code summarizes the essence of the quote, (2) if a quote does not belong to any existing codes, we introduce a new code, (3) each quote has just a single code; if a quote tackles two different problems, we split the original quote into two quotes, (4) to assign the correct code to a quote, we used our knowledge of the testing course, labwork, and the existing rubrics. We assigned 40 different codes to a total of 1,993 quotes. As a next step, we started an iterative merging process to derive the final themes, by grouping similar codes into higher-level themes, *e.g.*, the theme "maintainability of test code" contains quotes from the "test quality", and "test duplication" codes. We ended up with eight themes that we present in the Results (Section 6).

Survey with students. With the goal of capturing their perceptions on learning software testing, we asked students to answer a questionnaire that contained both open and closed questions at the end of the course.

The survey contains a total of 18 questions, none of which are required. The two closed questions of the survey asked students about the difficulty of learning and putting into practice the concepts and techniques we taught, and about the importance of the different activities we used throughout the course. In these questions, students had to choose from a five point Likert-scale, ranging from strongly disagree to strongly agree (see Figures 2 and 3). The open questions were mostly focused on understanding the students' main challenges, difficulties, and suggestions of improvements for our testing course. We apply qualitative techniques to analyze the results of each open question individually, similarly to our analysis of the feedback reports. The full survey as well the full code book can be found in our online appendix [1].

We did not make answering the survey compulsory for the students. We received 84 complete answers out of the 230 students.

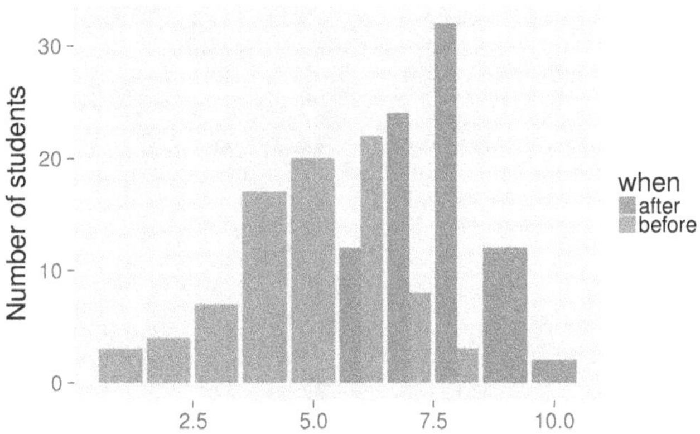

Figure 1: Histogram of the students' (X axis) perceptions in terms of their knowledge (Y axis) on software testing before and after the course. Scale: from 1 to 10.

Survey with Teaching Assistants. Our TAs support students throughout the course, by answering their questions, supporting their work during the lab, and by grading their assignments. As a consequence of such intense contact with students, TAs obtain a good perspective on the challenges of teaching software testing.

We also performed a similar survey with TAs, focusing on what they perceive as challenges for students. The survey contained the same two closed questions from the students' survey (challenges when applying software testing, and the importance of the different activities). In the open questions, we focused on asking about the common mistakes students do during the lab, as well as their perceptions on the challenges that students face.

We shared the survey internally at the end of our course. We also did not make answering the survey compulsory for TAs. At the end, we received 7 complete answers out of the 10 TAs.

5 CHARACTERIZATION OF THE PARTICIPANTS

Students. 66 students identify themselves as male, 8 as female, and 10 preferred not to answer. 89.3% of the students are between 18 to 24 years, five are between 25 and 34, and four are 17 or younger. Only three students were international students. In terms of Java knowledge, in a scale from 1 to 10, 9.5% of students consider their knowledge between 9 and 10, and 72% of them consider themselves between 7 and 8. Only 4 students consider themselves 5 or below.

Thanks to the introduction to JUnit that students receive during their very first course on programming, most of them already had some knowledge on software testing prior to our course. In fact, as we show in Figure 1, before the course starts, in a scale from 1 to 10, 39% of them consider themselves between 6 and 8, 44% between 4 and 5, and only 16% between 1 and 3. No student considered herself a 9 or 10. Students considered that their knowledge increased after the course. All of them considered their knowledge after the course as 6 or greater; 39% of them ranked themselves with a 8, and 14.6% with a 9. Two students ranked themselves with a 10.

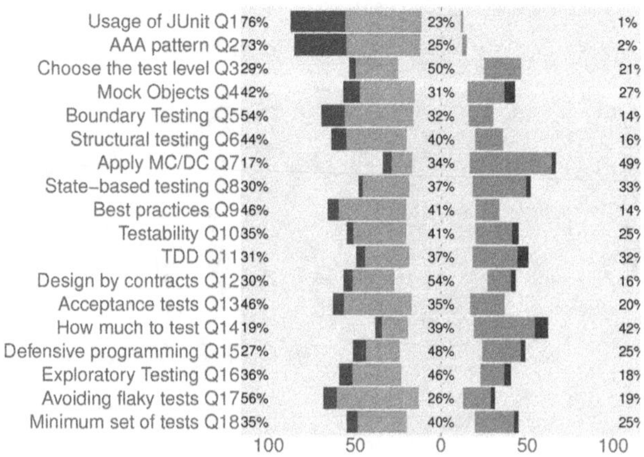

Figure 2: Students' perception on the difficulty of each testing topic. Scale: very easy, easy, neutral, hard, very hard. The full questionnaire can be found in our appendix [1].

Teaching Assistants. All TAs are between 18 and 24 years-old, one of them being female. They all ranked their Java knowledge between 8 and 10, and software testing knowledge between 7 and 8. Four of them are TAs for the first time in our software course; the other three TAs are performing this role for the third year in a row.

6 RESULTS

6.1 RQ_1: What common mistakes do students make when learning software testing?

We characterize the labwork feedback in eight different themes (ordered by their frequency): *test coverage, maintainability of test code, understanding testing concepts, boundary testing, state-based testing, assertions, mock objects,* and *tools.*

Test coverage (416 times, 20.87%). Students commonly either miss tests, *i.e.*, they do not provide all the expected tests for a given piece of code, or they write tests that are not totally correct, *e.g.*, the test does not actually test the piece of code, or the test exercises the wrong class. In addition, we also observed cases (14) where the student actually "overtested" (*i.e.*, wrote tests for more cases than required).

Maintainability of test code (407 times, 20.42%). Students often need advice on how to write maintainable test code. More specifically, test quality advices in general, such as better naming and excessive complexity (247), code duplication and lack of reusability (69), tests that could be split in two (31), better usage of test cleanup features, such as JUnit's Before and After (47).

Understanding testing concepts (306 times, 15.35%). Students provide incomplete answers or have difficulties when it comes to questions that involve testing concepts and ideas, such as what flaky tests are about, advantages and disadvantages of unit and system tests, and the importance of removing test smells.

Boundary testing (258 times, 12.95%). Students often miss all the tests required to cover a boundary (142). As we also ask them to first build a decision table and then derive the tests, we also see that they often miss elements in the table (50) and generate tables that are not fully correct (46).

State-based testing (247 times, 12.39%). When it comes to state-based testing, students often miss or create wrong states or events (56) and transitions (72), or develop non-clear or not legible state machines (68).

Assertions (158 times, 7.93%). Most feedback related to assertions focus on missing assertions, *i.e.*, the student forgot to assert one or more expected result, and on assertions that are wrong or should not exist in that test.

Mock Objects (117 times, 5.87%). Students required some feedback on how to use mock objects. More specifically, on how to properly verify interactions with mock objects (*i.e.*, Mockito's 'verify' method) and to explain when one should mock an object.

Tools (84 times, 4.21%). Students sometimes do not use the tools properly. More specifically to our course, students commonly use JUnit 4 features instead of JUnit 5, do not correctly use AssertJ's fluent API, and make wrong use of Cucumber features.

TAs perspective. Overall, the observations of TAs match with what we observed in the labwork analysis. In terms of testing best practices, TAs mentioned to help students in writing maintainable test code. According to one TA, students often write tests that contain unnecessary code and weird interactions with the class under test. In addition, according to one TA, students do not clearly see how to reuse test code. Another TA mentioned that a common question is on how to properly test exceptions. Finally, a TA also observed that students often write tests that actually do not exercise any production code (in this case, JUnit still shows a green bar, giving a false impression of success to the student).

6.2 RQ_2: Which software testing topics do students find hardest to learn?

In Figure 2, we show, based on the survey data, how students and TAs perceive the difficulty of each of the topics we teach.

Most students consider using the JUnit framework (Q1) as well as to think about the Act-Arrange-Assert pattern that composes any unit test (Q2) easy to learn. In fact, 76% and 73% of students consider it easy or very easy to learn JUnit and to use the AAA pattern, respectively. These perceptions are also shared by TAs, and matches with RQ_1 results, as the number of feedback related to bad tool usage is small (4.21%).

Interestingly, applying MC/DC (Modified Condition/Decision Coverage) [7] criteria to test complicated conditions (Q7) was considered hard or very hard by 49% of the students; this is the hardest topic among all of them. However, it seems that other coverage criteria are easier to learn, as only 16% of students considered structural testing hard (Q6).

Applying software testing in a pragmatic way, as expected, was considered hard for students. Deciding how much testing is enough (Q14) is also considered a hard topic by 42% of students (the second most hard topic). TAs agree and even perceive this topic harder than the students. This result also matches with our findings on RQ_1, where test coverage is the most prominent topic in feedback. In addition, writing the mininum set of tests that gives confidence (Q18) is considered hard for 25% of students and neutral for 40%. Choosing the right level of testing (*e.g.*, unit, integration, or system tests) is not considered easy to all of them; 29% consider it easy,

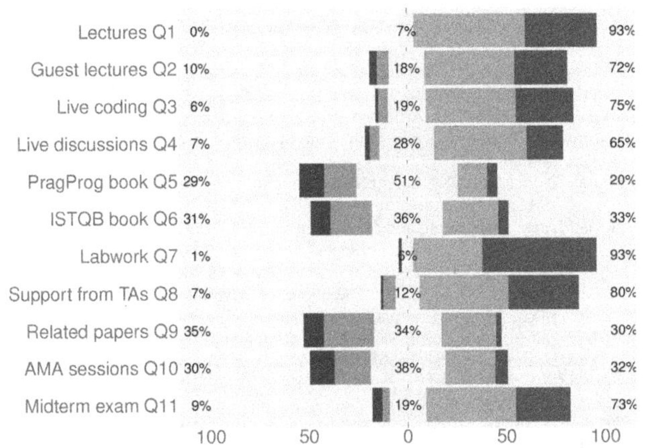

Figure 3: Importance of different activities in software testing learning. Scale=strongly disagree, disagree, neutral, agree, strongly agree. The full questionnaire can be found in our appendix [1].

50% of the students are neutral, and 21% perceive it as a hard topic (Q3). Not a single TA perceived this topic as easy. We believe these findings highlight even more the importance of discussing even more the pragmatic side of software testing.

When it comes to testing code best practices, students had a contradicting perceptions. The usage of mocks to simulate a dependency (Q4) and writing fast, reproducible, and non-flaky tests (Q17) were considered easy topics to be learned by 42% and 56% of students, respectively. TAs agree that students learn these topics with less difficulties. However, when it comes to following testing best practices (Q9), 46% of students perceive it as an easy topic, while 71% of TAs perceive it as a hard topic for students. The students' perceptions also contradicts the results of RQ_1, where we observe a large number of feedback focused on best practices in their assignments.

Finally, testability seems less challenging for students than for TAs. While students perceive optimizing code for testability (Q10) as just somewhat challenging (35% find it easy, 41% are neutral, and 25% find it hard), 67% of TAs belive that testability is a hard topic for students. As we conjecture that TAs have a better understanding of testability than the students, these findings suggest that the students are not sufficiently aware of the difficulty of testability.

6.3 RQ_3: Which teaching methods do students find most helpful?

In Figure 3, we show how students perceive the importance of each learning activity we have in our software testing course.

Students perceive activities that involve practitioners as highly important. More specifically, guest lectures from industry (Q2) were considered important by 72% of participants. The Ask-me-Anything sessions (Q10), on the other hand, was considered important by only 32% of participants; 38% are neutral, and 30% do not consider them important.

Moreover, different interactions during the lecture are also considered important for students. Teachers performing live code (Q3) and discussions and interactions during the lecture (Q4) are considered important by 75% and 65% of students, respectively. We conjecture that discussions and live coding are moments in which students have the opportunity to discuss the topics they consider hard, such as how much testing is enough, which test level to use, and test code best practices (as seen in RQ_1 and RQ_2).

On the other hand, the two books we use as textbooks in the course are not considered fundamental for students. More specifically, 31% of students find the ISTQB [5] not important and 36% are neutral (Q6), whereas 29% of them find the PragProg [25] not important and 51% are neutral (Q5). Reading related papers (Q9) is also considered not important for 35% of them.

6.4 Limitations of our study

The qualitative analysis of the open questions in the survey was manually conducted by the first author of this paper. The analysis, therefore, could be biased towards the views of the authors. To mitigate the threat, we make all the data available for inspection in our online appendix [1],

TAs were responsible for giving feedback to students throughout the study. Although we instruct all TAs on how to grade and what kind of feedback to give (they all follow the same rubrics), different TAs have different personalities. In practice, we observed that some TAs provided more feedback than other TAs. While we believe this could have little impact on the percentages of each theme in RQ_1, we do not expect any other theme to emerge,

In terms of generalizability, although we analyzed the behavior of 230 students, we do not claim that our results are complete and/or generalizable. Furthermore, most students were dutch (we only had 3 international students answering our survey), which may introduce cultural bias to our results. We urge researchers to perform replications of this study in different countries and universities.

7 CONCLUSIONS

Software testing is a vital discipline in any Software Engineering curriculum. However, the topic poses several challenges to educators and to students. In this paper, we proposed a pragmatic software testing curriculum and explored students' common mistakes, hard topics to learn, favourite learning activities, important learning outcomes, and challenges they face when studying software testing.

Researchers and educators agree that software testing education is fundamental not only to industry, but also to research. We hope this paper helps the community to improve even more the quality of their software testing courses. As Bertolino [4] states in her paper on the achievements, challenges, and dreams on software testing research: *"While it is research that can advance the state of the art, it is only by awareness and adoption of those results by the next-coming generation of testers that we can also advance the state of practice. Education must be continuing, to keep the pace with the advances in testing technology".*

ACKNOWLEDGMENTS

We thank all the students and teaching assistants that followed our course in the last years.

REFERENCES

[1] Maurício Aniche, Felienne Hermans, and Arie van Deursen. 2018. Pragmatic Software Testing Education: Appendix. (2018). https://doi.org/10.5281/zenodo.1459654.

[2] Tara Astigarraga, Eli M Dow, Christina Lara, Richard Prewitt, and Maria R Ward. 2010. The emerging role of software testing in curricula. In *Transforming Engineering Education: Creating Interdisciplinary Skills for Complex Global Environments, 2010 IEEE*. IEEE, 1–26.

[3] Gabriele Bavota, Abdallah Qusef, Rocco Oliveto, Andrea De Lucia, and Dave Binkley. 2015. Are test smells really harmful? An empirical study. *Empirical Software Engineering* 20, 4 (2015), 1052–1094.

[4] Antonia Bertolino. 2007. Software testing research: Achievements, challenges, dreams. In *2007 Future of Software Engineering*. IEEE Computer Society, 85–103.

[5] Rex Black, Erik Van Veenendaal, and Dorothy Graham. 2012. *Foundations of software testing: ISTQB certification*. Cengage Learning.

[6] FT Chan, TH Tse, WH Tang, and TY Chen. 2005. Software testing education and training in Hong Kong. In *Quality Software, 2005.(QSIC 2005). Fifth International Conference on*. IEEE, 313–316.

[7] John Joseph Chilenski and Steven P Miller. 1994. Applicability of modified condition/decision coverage to software testing. *Software Engineering Journal* 9, 5 (1994), 193–200.

[8] Peter J Clarke, Debra Davis, Tariq M King, Jairo Pava, and Edward L Jones. 2014. Integrating testing into software engineering courses supported by a collaborative learning environment. *ACM Transactions on Computing Education (TOCE)* 14, 3 (2014), 18.

[9] Stephen H Edwards. 2003. Rethinking computer science education from a test-first perspective. In *Companion of the 18th annual ACM SIGPLAN conference on Object-oriented programming, systems, languages, and applications*. ACM, 148–155.

[10] Stephen H Edwards. 2004. Using software testing to move students from trial-and-error to reflection-in-action. *ACM SIGCSE Bulletin* 36, 1 (2004), 26–30.

[11] Sebastian Elbaum, Suzette Person, Jon Dokulil, and Matt Jorde. 2007. Bug hunt: Making early software testing lessons engaging and affordable. In *Proceedings of the 29th international conference on Software Engineering*. IEEE Computer Society, 688–697.

[12] Facebook. [n. d.]. Building and Testing at Facebook. https://www.facebook.com/notes/facebook-engineering/building-and-testing-at-facebook/10151004157328920/. ([n. d.]). Last visited in October, 2017.

[13] Steve Freeman and Nat Pryce. 2009. *Growing object-oriented software, guided by tests*. Pearson Education.

[14] Vahid Garousi and Aditya Mathur. 2010. Current state of the software testing education in north american academia and some recommendations for the new educators. In *Software Engineering Education and Training (CSEE&T), 2010 23rd IEEE Conference on*. IEEE, 89–96.

[15] Vahid Garousi and Junji Zhi. 2013. A survey of software testing practices in Canada. *Journal of Systems and Software* 86, 5 (2013), 1354–1376.

[16] Judith L Gersting. 1994. A software engineering "frosting" on a traditional CS-1 course. In *ACM SIGCSE Bulletin*, Vol. 26. ACM, 233–237.

[17] Michael H Goldwasser. 2002. A gimmick to integrate software testing throughout the curriculum. In *ACM SIGCSE Bulletin*, Vol. 34. ACM, 271–275.

[18] Misko Hevery. 2008. Testability explorer: using byte-code analysis to engineer lasting social changes in an organization's software development process.. In *Companion to the 23rd ACM SIGPLAN conference on Object-oriented programming systems languages and applications*. ACM, 747–748.

[19] Thomas B Hilburn. 1996. Software engineering-from the beginning. In *Software Engineering Education, 1996. Proceedings., Ninth Conference on*. IEEE, 29–39.

[20] Thomas B Hilburn and Massood Townhidnejad. 2000. Software quality: a curriculum postscript?. In *ACM SIGCSE Bulletin*, Vol. 32. ACM, 167–171.

[21] Ursula Jackson, Bill Z Manaris, and Renée A McCauley. 1997. Strategies for effective integration of software engineering concepts and techniques into the undergraduate computer science curriculum. In *ACM SIGCSE Bulletin*, Vol. 29. ACM, 360–364.

[22] David Janzen and Hossein Saiedian. 2008. Test-driven learning in early programming courses. In *ACM SIGCSE Bulletin*, Vol. 40. ACM, 532–536.

[23] Edward L Jones. 2001. An experiential approach to incorporating software testing into the computer science curriculum. In *Frontiers in Education Conference, 2001. 31st Annual*, Vol. 2. IEEE, F3D–7.

[24] Edward L Jones. 2001. Integrating testing into the curriculum—arsenic in small doses. *ACM SIGCSE Bulletin* 33, 1 (2001), 337–341.

[25] Jeff Langr, Andy Hunt, and Dave Thomas. 2015. *Pragmatic unit testing in Java 8 with JUnit*. The Pragmatic Bookshelf.

[26] Otávio Augusto Lazzarini Lemos, Fábio Fagundes Silveira, Fabiano Cutigi Ferrari, and Alessandro Garcia. 2017. The impact of Software Testing education on code reliability: An empirical assessment. *Journal of Systems and Software* (2017).

[27] Will Marrero and Amber Settle. 2005. Testing first: emphasizing testing in early programming courses. In *ACM SIGCSE Bulletin*, Vol. 37. ACM, 4–8.

[28] Robert C Martin. 2002. *Agile software development: principles, patterns, and practices*. Prentice Hall.

[29] Robert C Martin. 2017. *Clean architecture: a craftsman's guide to software structure and design*. Prentice Hall Press.

[30] Scott Matteson. [n. d.]. Report: Software failure caused 1.7 trillion in financial losses in 2017. https://www.techrepublic.com/article/report-software-failure-caused-1-7-trillion-in-financial-losses-in-2017/. ([n. d.]).

[31] Renée McCauley and Ursula Jackson. 1999. Teaching software engineering early: experiences and results. *ACM SIGCSE Bulletin* 31, 2 (1999), 86–91.

[32] Gerard Meszaros. 2007. *xUnit test patterns: Refactoring test code*. Pearson Education.

[33] G. Miller. [n. d.]. A Scientist's Nightmare: Software Problem Leads to Five Retractions. http://science.sciencemag.org/content/314/5807/1856.full. ([n. d.]). Last visited in October, 2017.

[34] SP Ng, Tafline Murnane, Karl Reed, D Grant, and TY Chen. 2004. A preliminary survey on software testing practices in Australia. In *Software Engineering Conference, 2004. Proceedings. 2004 Australian*. IEEE, 116–125.

[35] Alan Page, Ken Johnston, and Bj Rollison. 2008. *How we test software at Microsoft*. Microsoft Press.

[36] James Robergé and Candice Suriano. 1994. Using laboratories to teach software engineering principles in the introductory computer science curriculum. In *ACM SIGCSE Bulletin*, Vol. 26. ACM, 106–110.

[37] Johnny Saldaña. 2015. *The coding manual for qualitative researchers*. Sage.

[38] Jaime Spacco and William Pugh. 2006. Helping students appreciate test-driven development (TDD). In *Companion to the 21st ACM SIGPLAN symposium on Object-oriented programming systems, languages, and applications*. ACM, 907–913.

[39] Muhammad Dhiauddin Mohamed Suffian, Suhaimi Ibrahim, and Mohamed Redzuan Abdullah. 2014. A proposal of postgraduate programme for software testing specialization. In *Software Engineering Conference (MySEC), 2014 8th Malaysian*. IEEE, 342–347.

[40] Joseph Timoney, Stephen Brown, and Deshi Ye. 2008. Experiences in software testing education: some observations from an international cooperation. In *Young Computer Scientists, 2008. ICYCS 2008. The 9th International Conference for*. IEEE, 2686–2691.

[41] James A Whittaker, Jason Arbon, and Jeff Carollo. 2012. *How Google tests software*. Addison-Wesley.

[42] Eric Wong. 2012. Improving the state of undergraduate software testing education. In *American Society for Engineering Education*. American Society for Engineering Education.

Software Testing in Introductory Programming Courses

A Systematic Mapping Study

Lilian Passos Scatalon
University of São Paulo (ICMC-USP)
São Carlos-SP, Brazil
lilian.scatalon@usp.br

Jeffrey C. Carver
University of Alabama
Tuscaloosa-AL, United States
carver@cs.ua.edu

Rogério Eduardo Garcia
São Paulo State University (FCT-Unesp)
Presidente Prudente-SP, Brazil
rogerio.garcia@unesp.br

Ellen Francine Barbosa
University of São Paulo (ICMC-USP)
São Carlos-SP, Brazil
francine@icmc.usp.br

ABSTRACT

Traditionally, students learn about software testing during intermediate or advanced computing courses. However, it is widely advocated that testing should be addressed beginning in introductory programming courses. In this context, testing practices can help students think more critically while working on programming assignments. At the same time, students can develop testing skills throughout the computing curriculum. Considering this scenario, we conducted a systematic mapping of the literature about software testing in introductory programming courses, resulting in 293 selected papers. We mapped the papers to categories with respect to their investigated topic (curriculum, teaching methods, programming assignments, programming process, tools, program/test quality, concept understanding, and students' perceptions and behaviors) and evaluation method (literature review, exploratory study, descriptive/persuasive study, survey, qualitative study, experimental and experience report). We also identified the benefits and drawbacks of this teaching approach, as pointed out in the selected papers. The goal is to provide an overview of research performed in the area, highlighting gaps that should be further investigated.

CCS CONCEPTS

• **Social and professional topics** → **Computing education**; *CS1*; • **Software and its engineering** → *Software testing and debugging*;

KEYWORDS

Software testing; introductory programming courses; systematic mapping

ACM Reference format:
Lilian Passos Scatalon, Jeffrey C. Carver, Rogério Eduardo Garcia, and Ellen Francine Barbosa. 2019. Software Testing in Introductory Programming Courses. In *Proceedings of Proceedings of the 50th ACM Technical Symposium on Computer Science Education, Minneapolis, MN, USA, February 27-March 2, 2019 (SIGCSE '19)*, 7 pages.
https://doi.org/10.1145/3287324.3287384

SIGCSE '19, February 27-March 2, 2019, Minneapolis, MN, USA

ACM ISBN 978-1-4503-5890-3/19/02...$15.00
https://doi.org/10.1145/3287324.3287384

1 INTRODUCTION

Because industrial software practitioners interact with testing, whether or not they hold a 'testing' job, they need to acquire testing skills [6]. Even so, we are graduating students from computing programs who have deficiencies in software testing skills [3, 12].

A way to deal with this issue is to address software testing earlier in the computing curriculum, beginning in introductory programming courses [4]. The idea is to provide students the opportunity to develop their testing skills incrementally throughout the curriculum [9]. Moreover, knowledge of testing can help students improve their programming skills [5, 8, 14].

However, the integration of software testing in this context is not straightforward, since there are many different ways to design the introductory programming sequence [10, 13]. The ACM/IEEE CS curricular guidelines point out some design aspects that vary in these courses, such as the institutional context (with different target audiences), the choice of programming paradigm and language, the platform (e.g. desktop/laptop, web, mobile devices), and the use of software development practices to support the programming activities (e.g. version control, refactoring, and design patterns) [1].

In this paper, our goal is to investigate the integration of testing into this diverse context and provide an overview of the research performed in the area. We conducted a systematic mapping of the literature [11], which resulted in 293 selected papers. We mapped the studies to categories of investigated topic and evaluation method.

Our results highlight elements that compose an integrated *teaching method* of programming and testing (course materials, programming assignments, programming process, supporting tools) and the *learning outcomes* that have been investigated in the area (program/test quality, concept understanding and students' perceptions and behaviors). We also discuss the benefits and drawbacks identified in the selected papers, aiming to help with trade-off decisions in curriculum/course design and with the conduction of further research in the area.

The remainder of this paper is organized as follows. Section 2 describes our research questions and the protocol we followed to conduct the systematic mapping. Section 3 presents the selected studies and provides answers to the proposed research questions. Section 4 discusses the obtained results and, finally, Section 5 presents conclusions, threats to validity and provides directions to future work.

2 RESEARCH METHOD

We followed the guidelines of Petersen et al. [11] to define the research protocol and to conduct the study. Briefly, we performed the following steps:

- definition of review scope (Section 2.1);
- search and selection of relevant papers (sections 2.2 and 2.3);
- definition of a classification scheme, composed by the categories for the mapping (Section 2.4), and
- data extraction from selected papers and mapping to the defined categories (Section 2.5).

2.1 Research Questions

To scope the study, we defined the following research questions:

RQ1: Which topics have researchers investigated about software testing in introductory programming courses?

RQ2: What are the benefits and drawbacks about the integration of software testing into introductory programming courses?

2.2 Search Strategy

We conducted the search for relevant papers in two steps: (i) an automatic search in databases, which provided a list of relevant papers and (ii) a backward snowballing from this preliminary list to identify additional relevant papers [15].

We performed the automatic search in five databases: ACM Digital Library[1], IEEEXplore[2], ScienceDirect[3], Scopus[4], Springer Link[5]. We selected these databases because they are among the most used ones by previous systematic reviews [16].

We constructed the search string following the approach by Zhang et al. [16]. We piloted a previous version of this protocol and formed a reference list composed of 158 papers. Since there was a high variability in the expressions authors use to refer to the teaching of programming and software testing in this context, we performed a frequency analysis of individual words from the titles, abstracts, and keywords of our reference list. We chose the most frequent ones that were able to retrieve all papers from the reference list and arranged them along three aspects: programming, testing and educational context.

The results of that process produced the following search string that we executed in the search engines:

(*programming* **OR** *program*) **AND**
(*testing* **OR** *test*) **AND**
(*student* **OR** *course* **OR** *learning* **OR** *teaching*)

[1]http://dl.acm.org
[2]http://ieeexplore.ieee.org
[3]http://sciencedirect.com
[4]http://scopus.com
[5]http://link.springer.com

2.3 Selection criteria

The included papers discuss or investigate software testing in the context of teaching programming fundamentals in higher education, according to the scope defined by the research questions.

Once we had all papers returned from the automatic search, we excluded duplicate papers and papers not written in English. Also, we excluded papers whose context was outside higher education or that only addressed advanced computing courses.

Finally, following a similar approach to Radermacher and Walia [12], we only selected papers since 2000, because papers published earlier than that would not represent current educational practices.

2.4 Classification Scheme

The classification scheme refers to the categories to which we mapped the selected papers. We defined categories for two facets: *investigated topic* and *evaluation method*.

The structure of **investigated topics** provides an overview of the area, helping to answer RQ2. We defined the categories by following the approach of keywording, as suggested by Petersen et al. [11]. Briefly, we looked for concepts that represented the contribution of each paper. Then, we combined these identified concepts in order to form the categories. The idea was to identify categories which would accommodate all selected studies.

For **evaluation method**, we adopted the categories used by Al-Zubidy et al. [2] in their review of Computer Science Education studies, since our mapping is within the scope of theirs. Namely, **literature review** (a review of existing studies in a given topic), **exploratory study** (involves observation and model building), **descriptive/persuasive study** (an overview of the current situation in a given topic), **survey** (subjects are surveyed about some intervention), **qualitative study** (involves the analysis of qualitative data), **experimental** (includes experiments, quasi-experiments and case studies), **experience report** (not a planned study, a report about the experience of applying an intervention) and **not applicable** (a proposal, but without an evaluation).

2.5 Data extraction

We extracted the following elements from each selected paper: year; publication venue (journal/conference); evaluation method; investigated topic; and benefits and drawbacks of software testing in introductory programming courses. One of the authors (Scatalon) did the reading and extraction of these elements for the selected papers.

3 RESULTS

Figure 1 shows the results of the search for relevant papers. The automatic search returned 9091 studies in total, from which we selected 229 relevant studies by applying the selection criteria. Next, we applied backward snowballing and obtained 64 additional relevant studies, arriving at a total of 293 selected papers.

As Table 1 shows, the selected papers appear in a wide variety of conferences and journals. We listed the more frequent ones. Most studies were published in venues about CS Education (SIGCSE,

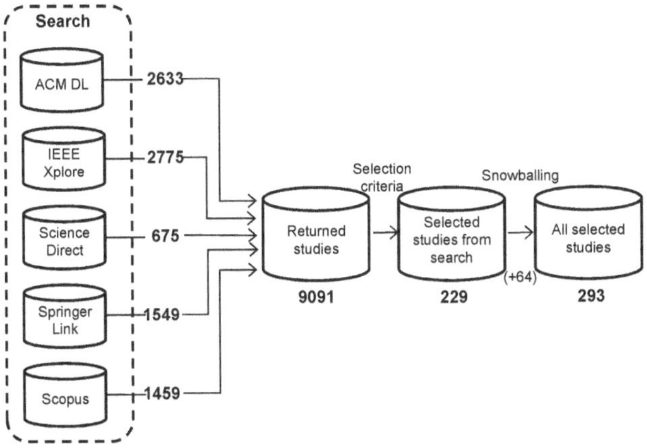

Figure 1: Results

ITiCSE, ACE, ICER, Koli Calling, SIGCSE Bulletin, Computer Science Education), followed by venues that address Software Engineering Education (ICSE and CSEE&T), education in computing-related curricula (FIE, Journal of Computing Sciences in Colleges, ACM TOCE), and, finally, venues with a more general focus in technology in education (L@S and Computers & Education).

The following subsections provide an analysis of the identified papers. Due to the large number of papers included in this mapping study, we are not able to include all references in the paper. A full list of papers along with the corresponding study number can be found at http://bit.ly/SIGCSE19-SM-Testing. This list of references is grouped based on the topics described in the next section.

Table 1: Distribution of publication venues

Venue Name	Venue Type	#
SIGCSE	conference	49
ITiCSE	conference	37
Journal of Computing Sciences in Colleges	journal	34
FIE	conference	23
OOPSLA/SPLASH	conference	13
ICSE	conference	10
CSEE&T	conference	9
ACE	conference	9
SIGCSE Bulletin	journal	9
ICER	conference	6
Koli Calling	conference	5
L@S	conference	4
Computer Science Education	journal	3
Software: Practice and Experience	journal	3
ACM JERIC/TOCE	journal	2
Computers & Education	journal	2
other		75
total		293

3.1 RQ1: Investigated topics

We identified nine *investigated topics* in the selected papers. Figure 2 shows the map of selected papers to the categories of topic and evaluation method. The topic **curriculum** includes papers about the integration of testing in the computing curriculum as a whole or in individual programming courses.

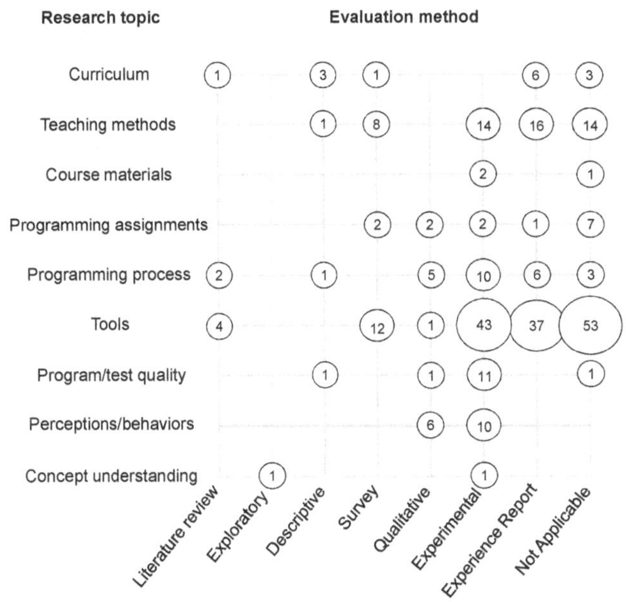

Figure 2: Map of research on software testing in introductory programming courses

Teaching methods include methods to teach programming with the integration of software testing. We identified general elements that compose a teaching method in this scenario. We also considered these elements as topics in our study: **course materials** (materials about testing for the context of introductory courses), **programming assignments** (guidelines to conduct programming assignments that include testing practices), **programming process** (programming processes for novices), and **tools** (supporting tools). When a selected paper addressed more than one of these elements, we mapped it to the topic *teaching methods*. Otherwise, it was mapped to the topic of the corresponding element.

The remaining topics concern the learning outcomes of the integration of testing in programming courses: **program/test quality** (assessment of students' submitted code), **perceptions/ behaviors** (students' attitudes towards software testing) and **concept understanding** (assessment of students' knowledge of programming and testing concepts). Next we provide an overview of the selected papers according to the investigated topics.

3.1.1 Curriculum. The papers mapped to the topic *curriculum* recommend testing concepts and practices should be distributed throughout the computing curriculum (S3, S5, S11, S12, S13). Moreover, the idea is to address testing earlier, beginning in introductory programming courses, by integrating testing practices into programming assignments (S1). Some papers address the design of a specific programming course with the integration of testing, such as S2, S4, S6 and S8.

3.1.2 Teaching methods. The papers mapped to this topic propose or investigate methods to teach programming with the integration of software testing, i.e. the different ways to teach these two subjects together in this context. Janzen and Saiedian (S35, S36) proposed *Test-Driven Learning* (TDL), which is a method to teach programming by introducing new concepts through unit tests. The authors provide several guidelines on how to apply it in the classroom. Edwards (S33, S17, S34) proposed the combination of TDD and the use of an automated assessment tool (Web-CAT) to leverage constant feedback as students submit their programs and test suites.

3.1.3 Course materials. There are only three selected papers investigating course materials about software testing that can be used in the context of introductory courses. Agarwal et al. (S68) and Barbosa et al. (S70) presented educational modules of software testing. They linked the materials according to the instructional sequence in which novice programmers should learn testing concepts. Desai et al. (S69) demonstrated how to adjust existing materials from a programming course to integrate software testing. They also report about their experience to apply the materials in the classroom.

3.1.4 Programming assignments. Papers about this topic discuss guidelines to design, conduct, and assess programming assignments that include testing practices. Some selected papers present descriptions of particular assignments (e.g. nifty assignments or programming projects) and include information about the appropriate context to apply them (S75, S78, S79, S80).

The design of assignments involving testing includes some additional important aspects to consider. First, there is the need to decide whether students should write test cases or work with instructor's tests (S77). Second, the problem specification should be clear enough so students are able to write tests (S74, S76).

Finally, testing is an inherent part of assessing students' programs, by providing a metric of correctness (S84). It can ease the grading process, especially when using an automated assessment tool. Tools can provide adequate results and feedback for formative assessment (such as homeworks and lab sessions) but might be less feasible for summative assessment (tests and exams), according to S72.

3.1.5 Programming process. Several proposals aim to teach students a systematic approach to develop programs, which can be seen as a lightweight version of a software development process. Given the scope of the systematic mapping, all processes addressed in the selected papers involve software testing, binding it somehow with programming.

The programming process can be easily overlooked in introductory courses, especially when students learn programming mostly by seeing examples of ready-made solutions. Instead, they should also learn how to stepwise create a solution for a given problem and to reflect about their own development process (S110).

Several studies investigate the use of **TDD** (*test-driven development*) by novice programmers (e.g. S92, S94, S96, S98, S99, S102, S103). There are other proposals of programming process, specifically designed for the educational context, which are also heavily influenced by TDD. Some examples are TBC (*Testing Before Coding*), POPT (*Problem-Oriented Programming and Testing*) and STREAM (Stubs, Tests, Representations, Evaluation, Attributes and Methods) from S87, S97 and S89, respectively.

Usually these processes address the testing activity from a high-level point of view, without giving details about how students should test their programs. In another perspective, two studies investigated the testing activity for novice programmers at a lower-level, focusing on test design and the use of testing criteria (S98 and S101).

3.1.6 Tools. The papers mapped to this topic present several kinds of tools, which automate different aspects of applying testing practices. We sort them into three groups:

- **Supporting mechanisms to write and execute test cases:**
  - **Testing frameworks/libraries:** besides the xUnit testing frameworks, there are testing libraries developed specifically to ease the learning curve for students (e.g. S201, S153, S226, S178).
  - **IDEs' testing facilities:** there are IDEs that offer mechanisms to help students test their programs, like BlueJ (S204).
- **Automated assessment systems:** automating the assessment process by means of software testing is fairly straightforward, since test cases are represented by code that can be executed along with submitted programs. In this sense, *automated assessment* permeates most tools used in this context. We sort them into the following categories:
  - **Submission and testing systems:** These systems usually are responsible for compiling the submitted program, executing tests and providing feedback to students. In some cases these tools also grades students' submitted code according to test results in a (semi-)automatic manner. In general, these systems are web-based (S254, S215, S138, S177) or plug-ins to other widely used systems such as IDEs (S208) or LMSs (S145).
  - **Online judges:** These tools present a catalog of problems to students, who should submit the corresponding programming solutions to be assessed by means of testing. Some of these systems are used in programming competitions (S133, S176).
  - **Games:** Some tools can be characterized as games, which aim to motivate students through fun and competition. They introduce software testing in different ways, such as implicit testing to solve programming "quests" (S223), or hints in the format of unit tests, which help students to guess a "secret implementation" in code duels (S142).
  - **Tutor systems:** Some tools combine course materials and interactive exercises or assignments, providing automatic orientation while students learn programming and testing. Usually this kind of tools is composed by materials (presented as slides or hypertext) and an automated assessment tool to test students' programs (S118, S121, S123, S167).

- **Automated assessment utilities**: Some papers focus on functionalities that compose or complement automated assessment systems. We provide an overview of these proposals, sorting them into the different aspects they address:
  - **Test automation:** There are several proposals that aim to make the execution of tests and students' programs as seamless as possible. One important aspect in this scenario is *interface conformance* between program and test suite (S258, S164, S241), seeking to assure that both are compiled together properly. Additionally, some precautions should be taken during execution, like running students' code in a sandbox to assure safety and having mechanisms to cope with infinite loops (S194, S174).
  - **Feedback:** Metrics of program and test quality can be used to suggest a grade and to provide feedback to students. Besides that, students need help with failed test cases and improving their test suites. Some tools provide this type of additional support to students, like mechanisms to detect inadequate memory management (S154) and the generation of execution traces (S131). Feedback can also help to influence students' testing behavior, with the adaptive release of hints as students achieve certain testing goals (S173, S179).

3.1.7 Program/test quality. Papers mapped to this topic address students' performance in programming assignments, assessed by means of their submitted code (program and/or tests). The program usually is assessed in terms of **correctness**, which in turn is calculated by the **success rate** of a given test suite. Besides correctness, there are also metrics that involve a static analysis of the source code structure, by analyzing modifications made by students between successive submissions (S270, S273).

When students are supposed to write tests in the assignments, the issue of assessing the quality of their test suites is raised. The most common metric is **code coverage**, which generates feedback that is easy for students to understand. However, code coverage can overestimate test quality, since it is possible to achieve 100% coverage even when a test suite is not thorough, e.g. when the tests do not check for missing features in the program. In this sense, other strategies like **mutation analysis** and **all-pairs testing** can provide more accurate metrics (S264, S266), though both are more computationally expensive.

3.1.8 Concept understanding. There are only two selected studies that address this topic (S277, S278). Both aim to investigate assessments of programming concepts, which include software testing concepts. Sanders et al. (S277) presented the Canterbury QuestionBank[6], a repository of 654 multiple choice questions about programming fundamentals, 3% of which about testing. Luxton-Reilly et al. (S278) present a comprehensive review of concepts that should be assessed in introductory programming courses. *Testing* appears under the category of programming process, along with other topics like debugging and design.

3.1.9 Students' perceptions and behaviors. Papers mapped to this topic investigate students' attitudes towards software testing. Students' perceptions indicate their opinions about the testing approaches, such as TDD acceptance (S280). Students' behaviors refer to what they actually do during programming assignments, in contrast with what they were instructed to do (S289, S291, S292, S293).

We can observe trends in student behavior when analyzing submissions of the whole class (S284, S282), such as "happy-path" testing in S286. There are also studies analyzing multiple subsequent submissions for a given assignment, i.e. "snapshots" of students' programs and test suites. Process adherence (e.g. whether students are adopting test-first or not) and mechanisms to influence students' behavior can be investigated using this strategy (S280, S287, S281).

3.2 RQ2: Benefits and Drawbacks

To answer RQ2, we identified benefits and drawbacks of integrating software testing into programming courses, as pointed out by the selected papers. We identified the following **benefits**:

- **Improvement in students' programming performance**: there are studies reporting improvements in students' performance, mainly in terms of program quality (S33, S101, S276, S272). There are also findings indicating improvements in the resulting program design (in S94, for TDD specifically). The papers argue the reason behind these improvements is that testing practices help developing students' comprehension and analysis skills (S34).
- **Feedback**: test results can provide students useful information about their programming and testing performance before the assignment deadline (S21, S34, S92, S119, S210). This issue of providing feedback to students is recurrent in the motivation for using automated assessment tools (S112 to S261). Automated feedback may decrease the amount of help students need from the instructor (S150). Moreover, since testing drives students to self-validate their work, it can help them make progress when they are stuck or recognize when they need help from the instructor (S62).
- **Objective assessment**: testing results provide an objective and consistent way to assign grades to the assignments (S192). This benefit of testing is also frequently discussed in the selected papers about supporting tools (S112 to S261). Besides helping in the grading process, the assessment through testing also helps students to better understand the correctness requirements of assignments (S62).
- **Better understanding of the programming process**: when software testing is introduced, students learn a simplified version of the development process (S89). Considering that they have to work on many programming assignments throughout the introductory sequence, students have an opportunity to learn the mechanics of the activities of programming and testing together (S104).

Conversely, we identified the following **drawbacks**:

- **Additional workload of course staff**: instructors and teaching assistants may have additional work to adjust course materials to include testing concepts, prepare reference test suites for assignments, and assess students' test suites (S33, S17, S62, S72).
- **Students' testing performance**: studies report the lack of proper testing by students. Students mostly check common

[6] web-cat.org/questionbank

program behavior, leaving out corner cases that would be crucial to reveal the presence of defects (S286). In order to be properly understood and applied, many testing ideas require previous knowledge and skill in programming, which students are also still acquiring in programming courses. In particular, the main difficulty may be related to students writing their own test cases (S38, S62).
- **Students' reluctance to conduct testing**: students may present a negative attitude towards software testing, even though they recognize the importance of the testing activity (S61). When the testing practice is voluntary, they may not develop test cases for their programs (S32).
- **Programming courses are already packed**: the integration of software testing brings the need to cover additional topics in courses that may be already full. In other words, it is the integration of additional content with the same amount of lecture hours (S123, S17, S34).

4 DISCUSSION

The map of papers in Figure 2 allows us to analyze the distribution of research in the area. In terms of investigated topics, over half of papers are about *tools*, 51.19% (150). Conversely, the topics *course materials* (1.02% – 3) and *concept understanding* (0.68% – 2) cover only a small amount of research performed in the area.

These less investigated topics can indicate areas in need of more research, which could be directed to minimize the identified drawbacks in Section 3.2. For example, if more course materials were available, it could help to minimize the additional workload of course staff. Also, these materials could help identify ways to integrate testing without disrupting programming courses. Similarly, more research in teaching novice's *programming process* and in fostering *concept understanding* (especially basic testing concepts) could help to improve students' testing performance and their reluctance to perform software testing.

As to evaluation methods, selected papers that present empirical studies (*survey, qualitative* and *experimental*) comprise 44.7% (131) of the studies. Conversely, papers classified as *not applicable* or *experience report* comprise 50.51% (148), slightly above half of selected papers. The problem with the latter kind of studies is the lack of empirical evidence. Papers in *not applicable* present only proposals with no evaluation. *Experience reports* are not planned studies, so the conclusions rely on the researcher's perceptions.

Still considering the distribution of research in the area, the investigation of TDD is noteworthy throughout the selected papers, because 27% (89) mention it. For the topic *curriculum*, Edwards (S1) argues that TDD should be used in all programming assignments of the computing curriculum, from the CS1 course. Adams (S2) advocates that it should start in the CS2 course instead. In *teaching methods*, Edwards (S33, S17, S34, S21) proposed and investigated the use of TDD combined with an automated assessment tool in the classroom. In *course materials*, Desai et al. (S69) showed how TDD can be integrated into existing course materials, considering the same amount of lecture hours and without reducing the coverage of programming topics. Marrero and Settle (S71) discussed *assignments* with TDD in the context of two different programming courses. Spacco and Pugh (S279), Janzen and Saiedian (S280), and Buffardi and Edwards (S281, S285) studied mechanisms to motivate students to apply TDD. Besides these papers that investigate TDD specifically, it is possible to see the TDD's influence on the definition of other proposals (e.g. S87, S97, S89).

5 CONCLUSIONS

In this paper we provide an overview of the research performed about the integration of software testing into introductory programming courses. We conducted a systematic mapping study, which resulted in 293 selected papers. We classified papers according to investigated topic and evaluation method. We also discussed benefits and drawbacks of the approach.

There is a wide variety of ways to integrate testing into introductory courses, as can be observed in the selected papers. We identified a structure of topics (Section 3.1) which outlines a *teaching method* of both subjects (course materials, programming assignments, programming process and tools) and the corresponding students' learning outcomes (program/test quality, perceptions/behaviors and concept understanding). These identified elements can be seen as variables involved in the integration of testing in programming courses.

Similarly, the identified benefits and drawbacks in Section 3.2 motivate further research, aiming to raise the benefits and minimize the drawbacks. Also, as discussed in Section 4, the distribution of research over the identified topics shows a high concentration of papers about supporting tools (above half of the selected papers). This may indicate researchers the need to consider other topics in the area as well.

In terms of evaluation method, our results show a high number of studies (slightly above half of the papers) that are either experience reports or proposals with no evaluation (classified as "not applicable"). This result means a significant amount of studies lack a planned evaluation. This practice is concerning, since there is the need to transition from this kind of study to generating theory through empirical studies, by generating and iterating on hypotheses in CS Education research [7].

This systematic mapping contains the following threats to validity. First, it is important to consider that the first author individually performed all the steps of this study, including the selection of papers, reading, definition of classification scheme, extracting data, and mapping of the studies. For validation, the other authors provided feedback on all steps. Second, piloting the protocol helped to minimize biases in this study results. Third, we limited the publication date of selected papers to after the year 2000. Again, we believe that papers before that would not represent current educational approaches, specially in a area such Computer Science.

As future work, we intend to investigate in detail the variables involved in the integration of testing into programming courses. More specifically, we intend to conduct a systematic review of a subgroup of the selected papers: the empirical studies (papers mapped to *survey, qualitative* and *experimental*). Our goal is to help in the designing and planning of future studies, which in turn can help to further investigate topics lacking of research.

ACKNOWLEDGMENTS

This work was supported by FAPESP (State of São Paulo Research Funding Agency) grants 2014/06656-8 and 2016/17575-4.

REFERENCES

[1] ACM/IEEE-CS. 2013. Computer Science Curricula 2013. (December 2013). Joint Task Force on Computing Curricula, available at www.acm.org/education/CS2013-final-report.pdf.

[2] Ahmed Al-Zubidy, Jeffrey C. Carver, Sarah Heckman, and Mark Sherriff. 2016. A (Updated) Review of Empiricism at the SIGCSE Technical Symposium. In *Proceedings of the 47th ACM Technical Symposium on Computing Science Education (SIGCSE'16)*. ACM, New York, NY, USA, 120–125. https://doi.org/10.1145/2839509.2844601

[3] J. C. Carver and N. A. Kraft. 2011. Evaluating the testing ability of senior-level computer science students. In *24th IEEE-CS Conference on Software Engineering Education and Training (CSEE&T)*. 169–178.

[4] Stephen H. Edwards. 2003. Rethinking Computer Science Education from a Test-first Perspective. In *Companion of the 18th Annual ACM SIGPLAN Conference on Object-oriented Programming, Systems, Languages, and Applications (OOPSLA '03)*. ACM, New York, NY, USA, 148–155. https://doi.org/10.1145/949344.949390

[5] Stephen H. Edwards. 2004. Using Software Testing to Move Students from Trial-and-error to Reflection-in-action. In *Proceedings of the 35th SIGCSE Technical Symposium on Computer Science Education (SIGCSE '04)*. ACM, New York, NY, USA, 26–30. https://doi.org/10.1145/971300.971312

[6] Vahid Garousi and Junji Zhi. 2013. A Survey of Software Testing Practices in Canada. *Journal of Systems and Software* 86, 5 (May 2013), 1354–1376.

[7] Mark Guzdial. 2013. Exploring Hypotheses About Media Computation. In *Proceedings of the Ninth Annual International ACM Conference on International Computing Education Research (ICER '13)*. ACM, New York, NY, USA, 19–26.

[8] David Janzen and Hossein Saiedian. 2008. Test-driven Learning in Early Programming Courses. In *Proceedings of the 39th SIGCSE Technical Symposium on Computer Science Education (SIGCSE '08)*. ACM, New York, NY, USA, 532–536. https://doi.org/10.1145/1352135.1352315

[9] Edward L. Jones. 2001. Integrating testing into the curriculum – arsenic in small doses. In *Proceedings of the Thirty-second SIGCSE Technical Symposium on Computer Science Education (SIGCSE '01)*. ACM, New York, NY, USA, 337–341.

[10] Arnold Pears, Stephen Seidman, Lauri Malmi, Linda Mannila, Elizabeth Adams, Jens Bennedsen, Marie Devlin, and James Paterson. 2007. A Survey of Literature on the Teaching of Introductory Programming. In *Working Group Reports on ITiCSE on Innovation and Technology in Computer Science Education (ITiCSE-WGR '07)*. ACM, New York, NY, USA, 204–223. https://doi.org/10.1145/1345443.1345441

[11] Kai Petersen, Robert Feldt, Shahid Mujtaba, and Michael Mattsson. 2008. Systematic Mapping Studies in Software Engineering. In *Proceedings of the 12th International Conference on Evaluation and Assessment in Software Engineering (EASE'08)*. British Computer Society, Swinton, UK, UK, 68–77.

[12] Alex Radermacher and Gursimran Walia. 2013. Gaps Between Industry Expectations and the Abilities of Graduates. In *Proceeding of the 44th ACM Technical Symposium on Computer Science Education (SIGCSE '13)*. ACM, New York, NY, USA, 525–530.

[13] Arto Vihavainen, Jonne Airaksinen, and Christopher Watson. 2014. A Systematic Review of Approaches for Teaching Introductory Programming and Their Influence on Success. In *Proceedings of the Tenth Annual Conference on International Computing Education Research (ICER '14)*. ACM, New York, NY, USA, 19–26.

[14] Jacqueline L. Whalley and Anne Philpott. 2011. A Unit Testing Approach to Building Novice Programmers' Skills and Confidence. In *Proceedings of the Thirteenth Australasian Computing Education Conference - Volume 114 (ACE '11)*. Australian Computer Society, Inc., Darlinghurst, Australia, Australia, 113–118. http://dl.acm.org/citation.cfm?id=2459936.2459950

[15] Claes Wohlin. 2014. Guidelines for Snowballing in Systematic Literature Studies and a Replication in Software Engineering. In *Proceedings of the 18th International Conference on Evaluation and Assessment in Software Engineering (EASE'14)*. ACM, New York, NY, USA, Article 38, 10 pages.

[16] He Zhang, Muhammad Ali Babar, and Paolo Tell. 2011. Identifying relevant studies in software engineering. *Information and Software Technology* 53, 6 (2011), 625 – 637. Special Section: Best papers from the APSEC.

The Zones of Proximal Flow Tutorial

Designing Computational Thinking Cliffhangers

Ashok Basawapatna
State University of New York, College at Old Westbury
Old Westbury, NY
basawapatnaa@oldwestbury.edu

Alexander Repenning
University of Applied Sciences and Arts Northwestern Switzerland
Windisch, Switzerland
alexander.repenning@fhnw.ch

Mark Savignano
Minnesota State University, Mankato
Mankato, Minnesota
mark.savignano@mnsu.edu

ABSTRACT

The creation of computer science tutorials is becoming critically important as hundreds of millions of students each year get their first CS experience through self-directed online activities. Creating a "cliffhanger" activity, with high engagement during and motivation to continue learning post activity, is a balancing act. If tutorials provide too much detailed information, users may be able to follow instructions but can feel overwhelmed or bored. On the other hand, tutorials that do not sufficiently explain crucial steps risk frustrating users who might drop out of the activity. Zones of Proximal Flow (ZPF) tutorials are simple to create and provide a navigation structure of differentiated instruction allowing users to choose appropriate detail based on their self-assessed state of flow, from bored to anxious. Using Retention of Flow analysis, two Hour of Code game design tutorials were analyzed: a sophisticated online tutorial for the creation of Frogger, and a simple ZPF tutorial for the creation of Pac-Man. One hope was that the simple ZPF Pac-Man tutorial would not do much worse than the sophisticated Frogger tutorial, but surprisingly the ZPF Pac-Man tutorial significantly outperformed the Frogger tutorial in terms of student retention. The Pac-Man tutorial also displayed a high student motivation to continue programming past the end of differentiated instruction.

CCS CONCEPTS

• **Applied computing → Interactive learning environments**; *Computer-assisted instruction*;

KEYWORDS

Zones of Proximal Flow, Flow, Zone of Proximal Development, Computational Thinking, Hour of Code, Tutorial, Cyberlearning, Retention of Flow, Retention, Exposure

ACM Reference Format:

Ashok Basawapatna, Alexander Repenning, and Mark Savignano. 2019. The Zones of Proximal Flow Tutorial: Designing Computational Thinking Cliffhangers. In *Proceedings of the 50th ACM Technical Symposium on Computer Science Education (SIGCSE '19), February 27-March 2, 2019, Minneapolis, MN, USA.* ACM, New York, NY, USA, 7 pages. https://doi.org/10.1145/3287324.3287361

SIGCSE '19, February 27-March 2, 2019, Minneapolis, MN, USA

ACM ISBN 978-1-4503-5890-3/19/02...$15.00
https://doi.org/10.1145/3287324.3287361

1 INTRODUCTION

The push to expose students to programming and computational thinking has led to many encouraging developments. One popular example is Computer Science Education Week (CS Ed Week) which includes the Hour of Code that challenges novice learners across the world to spend an hour programming [32]. Students, many with little to no prior computer science experience, choose from a group of scaffolded online activities offering a gentle-slope introduction to coding [19]. Over half a billion students have participated in the Hour of Code from 2013 to 2017 [9].

These massive participation numbers are only positive if Hour of Code activities keep students' interest throughout and motivate them to continue learning after activity completion. If a novice student has an apathetic or negative Hour of Code experience, that student might decide programming is hard and/or boring [12, 15]. If this experience is repeated with half a billion participants, the Hour of Code actually risks losing a generation of computer scientists. Thus, activity designers and evaluators need to give special care to create "cliffhangers" where students are engaged throughout and are motivated to continue programming after reaching the end of activity instruction [26].

To help facilitate a cliffhanger experience, activity designers must optimize how much information to provide participants at each activity instruction to maximize engagement. On one hand, giving participants too much information could overwhelm users, and previous studies into minimal manuals have shown users performing faster and better with less instruction [7, 21]. However, giving participants too little information can lead to incomplete tutorial steps [31] putting users in a state of anxiety or frustration as they request more information [20]. Morevoer, the online nature of Hour of Code activities means that anybody with an internet connection is a potential user, including international participation and varying age ranges. Therefore, few assumptions can be made about user skill level. How might a single activity go about creating a cliffhanger experience for the most amount of these diverse participants?

Differentiated instruction provides one possible solution. Differentiation is a form of user needs controlled scaffolding accomodating participants of differing skill level in an effort to engage all learners [16]. Differentiation has been successfully used to teach programming through formative progress monitoring and individualized instruction [14, 22]. How might one extend differentiated instruction to an Hour of Code context, optimally balancing online tutorial information for a variety of users? For the 2017 Hour of code, a tutorial was introduced that walked students through the creation of the classic arcade game Pac-Man. This tutorial was simple to create but featured differentiated instruction at each tutorial step based on a framework called the Zones of Proximal Flow [5]. The aim of this was to answer two specific research questions related to whether differentiated instruction could help create a cliffhanger activity.

- **RQ1 (Efficacy)**: Can a simple differentiated scaffolding tutorial match the efficacy of an optimized professional single path tutorial?
- **RQ2 (Perserverance)**: What effects does removing the differentiated scaffolding approach have on participant retention and willingness to continue?

The remainder of this paper will describe the development of this Pac-Man tutorial, including related work, and review the results of the tutorial in relation to the above research questions.

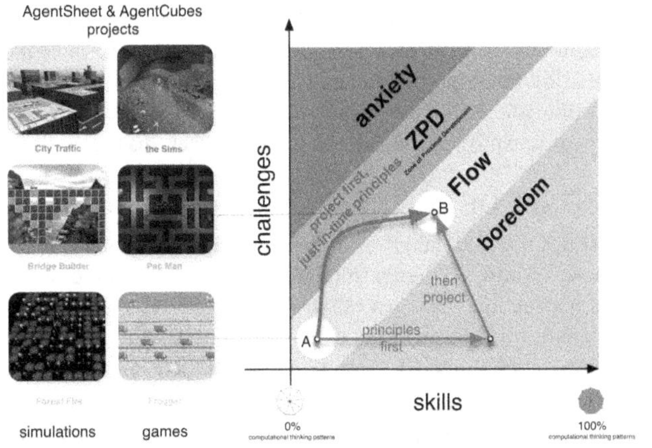

Figure 1: The Zones of Proximal Flow with Computational Thinking Skills on the x-axis and Challenges on the y-axis [5]

2 RELATED WORK

One strategy for motivating students in programming can be derived from previous theories on learner engagement and targeted instruction including the affective and cognitive experiences of the learner. Flow, as defined by Csikszentmihalyi, is a mental state of focused engagement that a person experiences when the current challenge matches the current skill [10, 11]. If the challenge exceeds skill, the person is put in a state of anxiety, and if the skill exceeds the challenge, the person is put into a state of boredom [10]. The Zone of Proximal Development, defined by Vygotsky, is the domain of challenges a learner can do given appropriate instruction [30]. The Zones of Proximal Flow (ZPF) is a conceptual framework that unifies Csikszentmihalyi's Flow [10] with Vygostky's Zones of Proximal Development (ZPD) [30]. The Zones of Proximal Flow framework argues that when a student is given a challenge that exceeds their skill, that students can be provided just in time scaffolding before reaching a state of anxiety, targeted to the their Zone of Proximal Development, guiding the learner back into a state of Flow [5].

Figure 1 depicts the Zones of Proximal Flow, in the context of the Scalable Game Design project, describing a scaffolding strategy employing a project-first approach to integrate game and simulation development units into middle school classrooms [5]. The y-axis of Figure 1 depicts the game and simulation design challenges present in the Scalable Game Design curricula [29]. The x-axis of Figure 1 depicts the computational thinking skills, entitled Computational Thinking Patterns (a list of which can be found in [1]), necessary to complete a given challenge [18]. At Point A in Figure 1, a student has recently completed creating the game Frogger and is now given another more sophisticated project to complete such as creating the game Pac-Man or creating a Bridge Building simulation (Point B in Figure 1). Since the student has not yet learned the necessary computational thinking skills to create this more advanced project, the challenge far exceeds the student skill level and the student starts to drift out of Flow into a state of anxiety. In the Zones of Proximal Flow model, before the student gets into an anxious state, the student is provided with scaffolding in the form of just-in-time principles aligned to the student's Zone of Proximal Development, guiding the student back into a state of Flow and allowing them to continue programming their project. These just-in-time principles can include embedded tutorial instruction [13], intelligent critiquing systems [2] and instructor intervention [4] among others.

How might one begin to evaluate the efficacy of Hour of Code activities to indicate how many participants are in Flow? Previous Hour of Code research has looked at student retention throughout a given activity to provide just-in-time information [23] and student engagement through qualitative measures [17]. The Retention of Flow is a method of evaluating these cyberlearning activities based on student retention [27, 33]. To better understand this notion, imagine 10,000 people, each one assembling an Ikea table on their own. At each step of the assembly process, some people in the population drop out of the activity, while others are retained and continue assembling their table. Points at which many more people than usual drop out might indicate a challenge step that far exceeds user skill given the current scaffolding (i.e. the Ikea instructions at that step). Similarly, the Retention of Flow uses participant retention, measured by a lines of code (also called program length) metric, which follows a negative exponential curve starting at 100%, at the beginning of the activity (0 lines of code), and declining as people drop out of the activity. The program length can then be matched to corresponding activity milestones in the retention plot to determine at which point of the activity students dropped out. Some assumptions behind the Retention of Flow are that, void of any external factors, the people retained at each step are the ones wherein the current challenge matches their skill, and it is the aim of any activity designer to create activity steps that have a high continuation probability yielding a higher retention.

Retention relates to Research Question 1 in that, assuming that an activity has a high educational value, a higher retention throughout the activity is ideal for the motivational purposes of the Hour of Code. Therefore, one can in-part use retention to compare two similar activities in terms of efficacy. Relating to Research Question 2, participant retention after activity instruction ends indicates a cliffhanger. To put this another way, devoid of the instructional scaffoding the student continues, implying a level of intrinsic motivation [6]. Instilling this intrinsic motivation in students should be the ultimate goal of any Hour of Code activity, and Retention of Flow begins to provide initial evidence of whether this has occurred.

3 ZONES OF PROXIMAL FLOW TUTORIALS

The Zones of Proximal Flow Tutorial attempts to extend the ZPF Framework into a cyberlearning activity [8] providing differentiated instruction. The idea of the ZPF tutorial is as follows; the participant works through the tutorial steps, and with each instruction encountered, self assesses their current state choosing from three possibilities:

(1) OK (Flow): The user understands the instruction and does not need any more guidance.
(2) How (ZPD): The user needs to learn a new concept before implementing the tutorial step.
(3) Show (Anxiety): The user still cannot, or does not have the time to, follow the instructions. A link to an example project is provided with the instruction implemented allowing the user to mimic or clone the implementation.

The 2017 Hour of Code featured an AgentCubes [28] game-design activity that guided students through the creation of the classic arcade game Pac-Man. The Pac-Man activity used the Zones of Proximal Flow tutorial strategy of differentiated instruction by giving the participant three choices at every activity step. Figure 2 depicts part of the Pac-Man Zones of Proximal Flow Tutorial that asks participants to create the Pac-Man characters. In Figure 2, the user initially encounters a slide describing What to do. In this case the user is asked to create the characters, also called agents, necessary for a simple Pac-Man game. These include Pac-Man, ghosts, a wall, and a background floor. If the user is able to follow that instruction, they can click the "OK" button and are taken to the next activity instruction. However, if the user does not understand that instruction, the user can click the "How" button, which will take the user to another slide with more detailed instructions. In the case depicted in Figure 2, the detailed instruction is in the form of a video that goes through adding an agent and drawing that agent. If this explanation makes sense, the user can implement the instruction and then click "OK" to be taken to the next activity instruction ("Program Pacman" in Figure 2). However, if the user still is having trouble understanding the instruction, the user can click "Show" to be taken to an example or "prebaked" project, for instance like a prebaked cake on a cooking show, with just the steps up to this point of the activity implemented. Once the project is opened, the user can play, explore, and mimic and/or clone the implementation allowing them to continue working.

The Pac-Man activity is 14 slides long and consists of two parts. Part one consists of a ZPF tutorial from slide one to slide ten, with the first slide describing how to use the tutorial. The first ten slides, corresponding to program lengths of 0 to 17, are dedicated to creating a simple Pac-Man game, including a keyboard controlled Pac-Man and ghosts that randomly move. ZPF instruction abruptly stops at slide ten. Part two, consisting of slides eleven to fourteen and corresponding to program lengths of 18 to 40, encourage participants to do extension activities adding extra functionality to their Pac-Man game including Pac-Man being consumed by ghosts, Pac-Man reorienting in the direction of movement, intelligent ghost movement based on collaborative diffusion [25], and pellets that Pac-Man can consume to win. However, from slides eleven to fourteen, no differentiated instruction is provided as to how to achieve this; the only support provided to students is a link to a sample prebaked project for each of these steps.

3.1 Pac-Man vs. Frogger

The Zones of Proximal Flow Pac-Man Tutorial is simple to create as compared to the other AgentCubes based Hour of Code tutorial offered since 2015: Frogger [13]. the Frogger tutorial features a video integrated directly into AgentCubes online allowing users to create the game as they watch step by step instructions. Furthermore, the video narration is multilingual, using professional voice over personnel, and is split up into chapters allowing students to navigate to a specific tutorial instruction on demand. The creation of the Frogger tutorial took a team of dedicated programmers, educational designers, and playtesters working together over the course of many months. In this sense, Frogger is an optimized single path tutorial aimed at providing instruction with the right amount of information to retain the widest audience. Previous research shows that the Frogger tutorial had a similar participant retention to the official Hour of Code Angry Birds activity [26].

The Pac-Man activity, on the other hand, was created by two people over the course of a two days in the form of a slideshow presentation. However, despite the low production value, the Pac-Man activity features a ZPF tutorial providing users with the agency to choose instruction appropriate to their skill level. Given this stark difference in production effort, can the simple Pac-Man Hour of Code tutorial, supporting students through the Zones of Proximal Flow via differentiated instruction, be nearly as effective as the professionally created Frogger tutorial in terms of student retention and motivation to continue post instruction?

4 METHODOLOGY

This research analyzed a collected sample of 1,468 Pac-Man games and 767 Frogger games submitted during the Hour of Code week. These games were initially identified as Pac-Man and Frogger through a script and manually checked to ensure they were indeed Pac-Man and Frogger. Answering the research questions necessitates one, determining how engaged students are during the activity and two, evaluating the probability of students to continue programming post activity scaffolding. By analyzing the retention of Pac-Man and Frogger at corresponding program lengths, we can begin to compare the retentions between the two activities during instruction and beyond. To answer Research Question 1, activity efficacy, we look at how the activity retention of Pac-Man compares to Frogger from program length 0 to 17 (Part 1 of the Pac-Man activity featuring the ZPF tutorial). To answer Research Question 2, we look at both the retention plot from program length 18 to 40, where the ZPF instruction ends and students are encouraged to program extension activities, as well as program lengths greater than 40, to determine to what extent, if any, students continue past the extension activities. It should be noted for purposes of comparison to previous research, the program length metric used in this

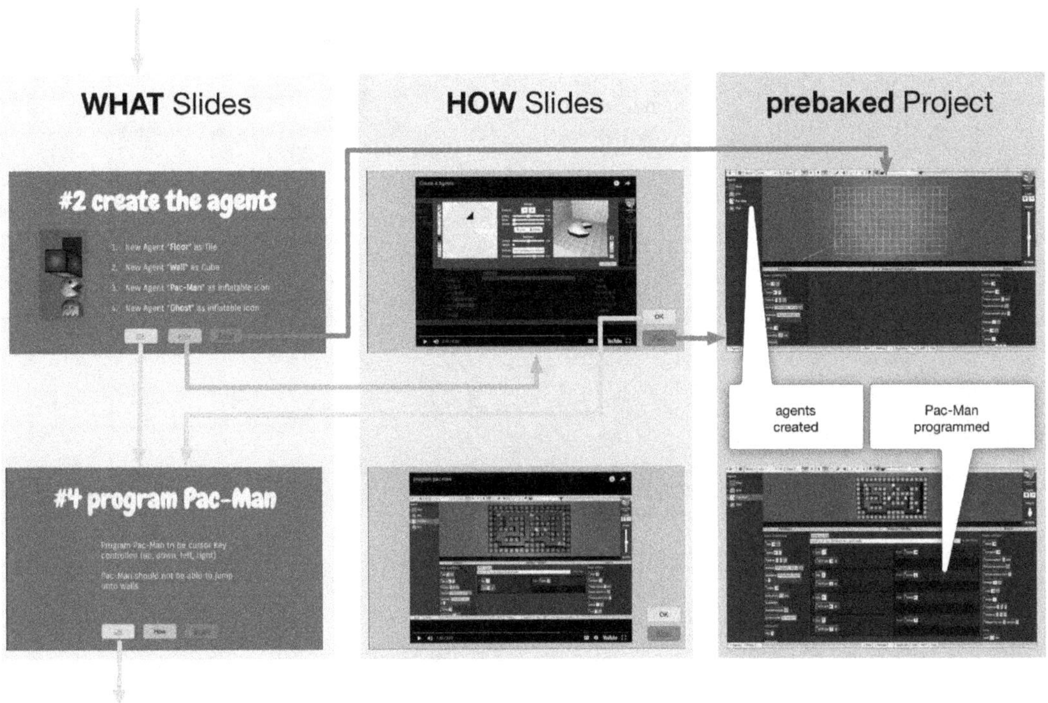

Figure 2: The ZPF Flow Chart depicting the green OK button leading to the next instruction slide, the orange button leading to a How slide that further explains the current tutorial step, and the red Show button leading to a "prebaked" project.

study is similar, but not identical, to [3]. A manual survey of the sample games was done to ensure the program lengths actually corresponded to activity milestones. Also of note, the collected sample of games does not include cloned projects unless they had significant programming time associated with them as not to bias the data.

5 RESULTS

Figure 3 plots the percent of Participants Retained vs Lines of Code. Pac-Man retention is plotted in red and Frogger in blue. The three shaded regions refer to the parts of the Pac-Man tutorial, with green being the ZPF Tutorial (program lengths 1 to 17), yellow being the extension activities (program lengths 18 to 40) and peach being everything past the end of the Pac-Man activity (program lengths greater than 40). The following results are organized according to the Research Questions.

RQ1: Efficacy. The part of Figure 3 shaded in green corresponds to the ZPF portion of the Pac-Man activity. Both Pac-Man and Frogger retentions start at 100% at the beginning of their respective activities, with the Pac-Man having a higher participant retention than the Frogger activity as program lengths increase. The difference in retention reaches a maximum at Program length 15 wherein the Pac-Man retention is almost 14% higher than the Frogger retention. At program length 17 the ZPF portion of the Pac-Man tutorial ends. A two sample z-test for proportions run at program length 17 found significantly more students in the Pac-Man activity retained through 17 lines of code (75%) than the Frogger activity (62%) with z=6.72, p=.05.

RQ2:Perserverance. The part of Figure 3 shaded in yellow, program length 18 to 40, refers to the Pac-Man extension activities described in Section 3. At this point of the activity the ZPF differentiated instruction part of the tutorial has competed. Figure 3 depicts a drop in retention of almost 10% between program length 17 and program length 18 with a continuation percentage of 87.9%. Around 57% of students who start the extension activities finish all of them (i.e. are retained to program length 40). A two sample z-test for proportions run at program length 40 showed significantly more students in the Pac-Man activity were retained through 40 Lines of code (38%) than the Frogger activity (27%) with z=5.16, p=.05. To put this another way, 38% of participants who start the Pac-Man Hour of Code activity end up programming past the ZPF instructional section and finish implementing all the extension activities.

An ANOVA analysis comparing the groups of Pac-Man and Frogger projects from Lines of Code 1 to 40 was completed using 105 random samples for each group (sample of size of 210) which it was estimated would achieve a power of 0.95 with a level of significance at 0.05. After running the analysis, the p-value was at .00017 which is lower than the level of significance of 0.05 suggesting that there is indeed a significant difference between the two groups throughout the duration of the Pac-Man activity spanning both the pre and post ZPF activity instruction.

At program length 40 to 41 there is a precipitous drop wherein the final slide of the Pac-Man activity is reached. About half the remaining students drop out at this point and half continue adding to their Pac-Man game. Frogger instruction continues to program length 58, and between program length 41 and 60, Frogger retains

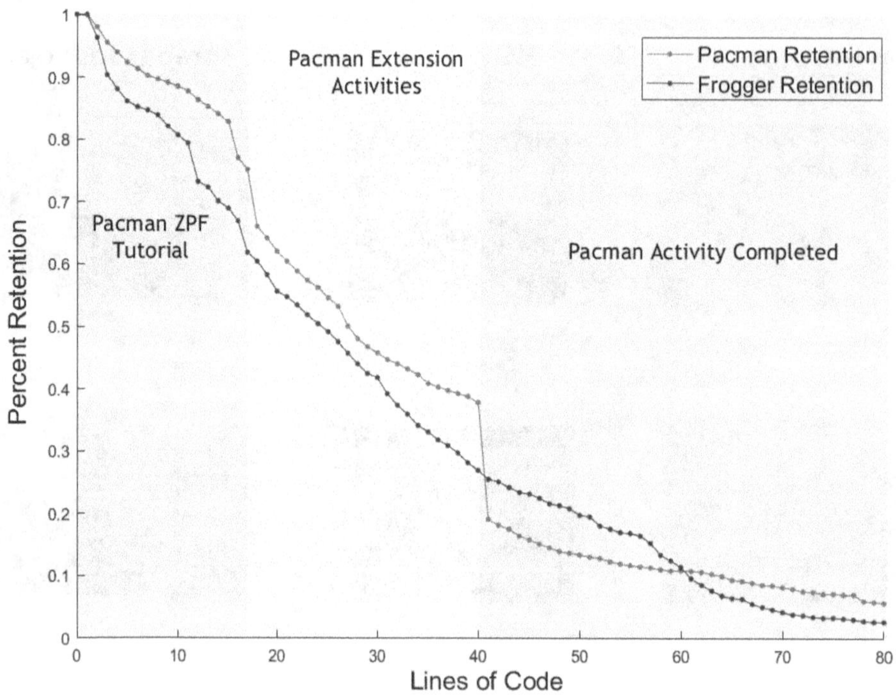

Figure 3: Pac-Man and Frogger Activity Retention. Shaded regions refer to parts of the Pac-Man Activity.

more students than Pacman. Overall 19% of students who start the Pac-Man tutorial continue programming past the end of the Pac-Man extension activities.

6 DISCUSSION

The above results begin to show the effectiveness of the Zones of Proximal Flow Tutorial both during the activity instruction (program length 1 to 17) and after activity instruction (from program length 18 to 40). The ANOVA analysis indicates a significant difference between participants doing the Pac-Man tutorial and the Frogger tutorial. This section will delve into these diferences by discussing the results corresponding to activity duration engagement (RQ1) and post-activity perseverance (RQ2). Finally the section will conclude with study shortcomings and implications.

6.1 Evidence of ZPF Tutorial Efficacy

The first research question attempts to answer how effective the ZPF tutorial is for participants. This spans program length 1 to 17 in the Pac-Man activity. Figure 3 depicts that during the activity, the Pac-Man Zones of Proximal Flow Tutorial consistently retained more participants than the Frogger tutorial. By the end of the ZPF tutorial portion of the Pac-Man activity, there is a significantly greater number of participants retained than in the Frogger activity. Furthermore, over three quarters of students who start the activity get through the ZPF portion of the tutorial. This begins to indicate the power of differentiated instruction and the Zones of Proximal Flow approach.

This result is surprising for a few reasons. The first is that major design effort was put into producing the Frogger activity, outlined in Section 3.1, and the Frogger activity itself is embedded in the programming environment. Given these advantages, one might expect that the Frogger activity would allow participants to more easily create their game. Previous research has posited the Retention of Flow conjecture which in part states that a tutorial step that is markedly more challenging than previous steps will exhibit a preciptious decline in retention [26]. The ZPF tutorial strategy attempts to avoid this by allowing users to choose the level of instruction that best support them based on their self-assessed current skill. In this manner, ZPF tutorials aim to keep students in the Flow by always providing them with the necessary on-demand scaffolding to ensure skill level in balance with the challenge. Given the significantly higher retention as compared to Frogger, the ZPF strategy seems to be successful.

6.2 Evidence of Perserverance Post ZPF Activity Instruction

At program length 18 the participant has created a basic Pac-Man game with a keyboard controlled Pac-Man and randomly moving ghosts. At this point, the ZPF tutorial strategy of differentiated instruction is abandoned and students are given extensions that they can add to their Pac-Man game. The only support for these extensions are a few example prebaked projects. There is a 10% drop in retention at this point, which could be due to this marked increase in challenge coupled with the end of creating a basic Pac-Man game.

However, well over one third of the students (38%) who start the Pac-Man activity end up programming past the instructional part of the tutorial and implementing all the Pac-Man extensions. This indicates that for these participants, Pac-Man is a cliffhanger as they program past activity instruction to add functionality to their game. At program length 40, the Frogger activity is still providing participants with step by step instructions, and at that point, the Pac-Man retention is still significantly higher than the Frogger retention. Therefore, student perserverance is such that the Pac-Man activity, devoid of any step by step instructions, still manages to retain a greater number of participants than the Frogger activity.

From Program length 40 to 41 there is another drop in Pac-Man retention (40% to 20% retention). This drop is to be expected as the Pac-Man extension activities end and students reach the end of the Pac-Man activity slides. This is the first point Pac-Man retention falls below Frogger retention, as the Frogger activity instruction does not end until program length 58. Still, half the participants who finished the extension activities continue to independently program past the end of the Pac-Man activity slides. Furthermore, one fifth of the total participants who start the Pac-Man activity end up programming past the end of the Pac-Man activity. At line 61, the Pac-Man activity retention once again overtakes the Frogger activity retention as people drop out once the Frogger activity is complete. At 64 lines of code, 20 lines past the final extension activity and at program lengths over three and a half times as long as the final ZPF instruction, 10% of participants are still retained in the Pac-Man activity.

6.3 Study Shortcomings and Implications

The results of this study begin to suggest that the ZPF tutorial approach with Pac-Man is an effective strategy. To come to this conclusion we compared the results of the ZPF tutorial to another Hour of Code AgentCubes tutorial: Frogger. However, it is hard to say whether the Frogger tutorial itself has a "normal" retention curve with so little Hour of Code retention data published. One interesting data point is that the Frogger tutorial has been improved over three years of the Hour of Code [2], and in past research showed similar retention to the official Hour of Code Angry Birds tutorial [26]. Though it would be nice to have more published Hour of Code retention data from a variety of activities, this provides a bit of outside validity to the comparison.

The ZPF tutorial approach might not be the only thing that engaged students during the activity. For example, one motivator could be that Pac-Man is a much more popular game than Frogger. In fact, more participants attempted the Pac-Man tutorial than Frogger indicating a greater initial interest. This motivation external to the activity could positively affect retention. However, one might not expect any external motivation to continue through the tutorial activity if the activity itself is not engaging.

The data shows that the ZPF tutorial had increased retention over corresponding places in the Frogger tutorial. A major difference between the ZPF tutorial and Frogger tutorial is the idea of differentiated instruction. However, one piece of instrumentation not included in the ZPF tutorial was the amount of users who clicked on each button. For example, in Figure 2, we do not know how many students clicked on the "OK", "How", and "Show" buttons. Therefore, it is hard to pinpoint which steps students might have found challenging and the tutorial paths they chose when they encountered these challenging steps. Click data, including per-user click data, would help pinpoint how users navigate the tutorial and give insight to which tutorial steps users find challenging and options they find useful. Furthermore, a post-activity a questionnaire could allow users to explain what they found helpful or unhelpful about the differentiated instruction approach, and a cognitive walk-through could show how clearly students perceived each potential choice at each tutorial step [24].

One additional artifact that occurs between program length 1 and 17 is a small drop of around 6% between program length 15 and 16. At program length 15 the participant has just completed programming Pac-Man to move with keyboard input. It is not clear why there would be a drop here, but it is interesting to note that an almost identical drop of 6% occurs in the Frogger retention plot, between program lengths 11 and 12, where again the participant has just completed programming the Frog to move. It could be that these are the first programming interactions users implement, and thus, some participants decide the activity is not for them at this point. Further research must be done to figure out exactly why this is the case.

This research begins to show the power of differentiation in self-directed learning, and adding differentiation might be an easy way to boost activity retention. Further research must be done to explore this, possibly by retrofitting the Frogger Hour of Code tutorial with differentiation to determine the retention effects. Finally, an emerging benefit of this research is that it provides an effective DIY strategy for teachers short on time looking to create Hour of Code activities.

7 CONCLUSION

This paper presents a new approach to Hour of Code style tutorials based off a simple differentiated instruction strategy guided by the Zones of Proximal Flow framework, and evaluated by analyzing activity retention. This evaluation shows that the Zones of Proximal Flow Tutorial has a significantly higher retention than a more professionally made Frogger tutorial, with students programming through the end of ZPF instruction and activity completion. To ensure the Hour of Code is effective in motivating the maximum numbers of students necessitates activities that keeps students in Flow. Zones of Proximal Flow Tutorials provide an avenue to better match instructional challenge to a diverse range of participant skill, hopefully yielding a cliffhanger first exposure computer science experience.

ACKNOWLEDGMENTS

Data used with permission from AgentSheets Inc. Inflatable Icon is patented under US Patent No. 7,630,580. This work is supported by the Hasler Foundation, the Swiss National Science Foundation under Grant CRAGP2_158545, and the National Science Foundation under Grant Numbers 0833612, 1345523, and 0848962. Any opinions, findings, and conclusions or recommendations expressed in this material are those of the authors and do not necessarily reflect the views of these organizations.

REFERENCES

[1] Ashok Basawapatna, Kyu Han Koh, Alexander Repenning, David C. Webb, and Krista Sekeres Marshall. 2011. Recognizing Computational Thinking Patterns. In *Proceedings of the 42Nd ACM Technical Symposium on Computer Science Education (SIGCSE '11)*. ACM, New York, NY, USA, 245–250. https://doi.org/10.1145/1953163.1953241

[2] Ashok Basawapatna and Alexander Repenning. 2017. Employing Retention of Flow to Improve Online Tutorials. In *Proceedings of the 2017 ACM SIGCSE Technical Symposium on Computer Science Education (SIGCSE '17)*. ACM, New York, NY, USA, 63–68. https://doi.org/10.1145/3017680.3017799

[3] Ashok Basawapatna, Alexander Repenning, Mark Savignano, Josiane Manera, Nora Escherle, and Lorenzo Repenning. 2018. Is Drawing Video Game Characters in an Hour of Code Activity a Waste of Time?. In *Proceedings of the 23rd Annual ACM Conference on Innovation and Technology in Computer Science Education (ITiCSE 2018)*. ACM, New York, NY, USA, 93–98. https://doi.org/10.1145/3197091.3197136

[4] Ashok Ram Basawapatna, Alexander Repenning, and Kyu Han Koh. 2015. Closing The Cyberlearning Loop: Enabling Teachers To Formatively Assess Student Programming Projects. In *Proceedings of the 46th ACM Technical Symposium on Computer Science Education (SIGCSE '15)*. ACM, New York, NY, USA, 12–17. https://doi.org/10.1145/2676723.2677269

[5] Ashok R. Basawapatna, Alexander Repenning, Kyu Han Koh, and Hilarie Nickerson. 2013. The Zones of Proximal Flow: Guiding Students Through a Space of Computational Thinking Skills and Challenges. In *Proceedings of the Ninth Annual International ACM Conference on International Computing Education Research (ICER '13)*. ACM, New York, NY, USA, 67–74. https://doi.org/10.1145/2493394.2493404

[6] Roland Benabou and Jean Tirole. 2003. Intrinsic and extrinsic motivation. *The review of economic studies* 70, 3 (2003), 489–520.

[7] John B. Black, John M. Carroll, and Stuart M. McGuigan. 1986. What Kind of Minimal Instruction Manual is the Most Effective. *SIGCHI Bull.* 18, 4 (May 1986), 159–162. https://doi.org/10.1145/1165387.275623

[8] Christine L Borgman. 2011. *Fostering learning in the networked world: The cyberlearning opportunity and challenge.* DIANE Publishing.

[9] Code.org 2018. Leaderboard for the Hour of Code. Retrieved August 28, 2018 from https://code.org/leaderboards

[10] Mihaly Csikszentmihalyi. 1997. *Finding flow: The psychology of engagement with everyday life.* Basic Books.

[11] Mihaly Csikszentmihalyi and Isabella Csikszentmihalyi. 1975. *Beyond boredom and anxiety.* Vol. 721. Jossey-Bass San Francisco.

[12] Jie Du, Hayden Wimmer, and Roy Rada. 2016. "Hour of Code": Can It Change Students' Attitudes toward Programming? *Journal of Information Technology Education: Innovations in Practice* 15 (2016), 52–73.

[13] Nora A Escherle, Silvia I Ramirez-Ramirez, Ashok R Basawapatna, Dorit Assaf, Alexander Repenning, Carmine Maiello, Yasko Ch Endo, and Juan A Nolazco-Flores. 2016. Piloting computer science education week in Mexico. In *Proceedings of the 47th ACM Technical Symposium on Computing Science Education.* ACM, 431–436.

[14] Nuno Gil Fonseca, Luís Macedo, and António José Mendes. 2018. Supporting Differentiated Instruction in Programming Courses Through Permanent Progress Monitoring. In *Proceedings of the 49th ACM Technical Symposium on Computer Science Education (SIGCSE '18)*. ACM, New York, NY, USA, 209–214. https://doi.org/10.1145/3159450.3159578

[15] Google CS Ed Research group et al. 2014. *Women who choose computer science–what really matters: The critical role of encouragement and exposure.* Technical Report. Technical report, Google. Retrieved from http://static.googleusercontent.com/media.

[16] Tracey Hall. 2002. Differentiated instruction. *Wakefield, MA: National Center on* (2002).

[17] CUNO Klopfenstein, Saverio Delpriori, BRENDAN DOMINIC Paolini, and Alessandro Bogliolo. 2018. X Marks the Bot: Online coding-based treasure hunt games for code literacy. *INTED PROCEEDINGS* (2018), 4867–4873.

[18] Kyu Han Koh, Hilarie Nickerson, Ashok Basawapatna, and Alexander Repenning. 2014. Early Validation of Computational Thinking Pattern Analysis. In *Proceedings of the 2014 Conference on Innovation & Technology in Computer Science Education (ITiCSE '14)*. ACM, New York, NY, USA, 213–218. https://doi.org/10.1145/2591708.2591724

[19] Deepak Kumar. 2014. Digital Playgrounds for Early Computing Education. *ACM Inroads* 5, 1 (March 2014), 20–21. https://doi.org/10.1145/2568195.2568200

[20] Benjamin Lafreniere, Tovi Grossman, and George Fitzmaurice. 2013. Community Enhanced Tutorials: Improving Tutorials with Multiple Demonstrations. In *Proceedings of the SIGCHI Conference on Human Factors in Computing Systems (CHI '13)*. ACM, New York, NY, USA, 1779–1788. https://doi.org/10.1145/2470654.2466235

[21] Adrianus W. Lazonder and Hans van der Meij. 1993. The minimal manual: is less really more? *International journal of man-machine studies* 39, 5 (1993), 729–752. https://doi.org/10.1006/imms.1993.1081

[22] Vinhthuy Phan and Eric Hicks. 2018. Code4Brownies: An Active Learning Solution for Teaching Programming and Problem Solving in the Classroom. In *Proceedings of the 23rd Annual ACM Conference on Innovation and Technology in Computer Science Education (ITiCSE 2018)*. ACM, New York, NY, USA, 153–158. https://doi.org/10.1145/3197091.3197128

[23] Chris Piech, Mehran Sahami, Jonathan Huang, and Leonidas Guibas. 2015. Autonomously Generating Hints by Inferring Problem Solving Policies. In *Proceedings of the Second (2015) ACM Conference on Learning Scale (LS '15)*. ACM, New York, NY, USA, 195–204. https://doi.org/10.1145/2724660.2724668

[24] Peter G. Polson, Clayton Lewis, John Rieman, and Cathleen Wharton. 1992. Cognitive walkthroughs: a method for theory-based evaluation of user interfaces. *International Journal of man-machine studies* 36, 5 (1992), 741–773.

[25] Alexander Repenning. 2006. Excuse me, I need better AI!: employing collaborative diffusion to make game AI child's play. In *Proceedings of the 2006 ACM SIGGRAPH symposium on Videogames.* ACM, 169–178.

[26] Alexander Repenning and Ashok Basawapatna. 2016. Drops and Kinks: Modeling the Retention of Flow for Hour of Code Style Tutorials. In *Proceedings of the 11th Workshop in Primary and Secondary Computing Education (WiPSCE '16)*. ACM, New York, NY, USA, 76–79. https://doi.org/10.1145/2978249.2978260

[27] Alexander Repenning, Ashok Basawapatna, Dorit Assaf, Carmine Maiello, and Nora Escherle. 2016. Retention of Flow: Evaluating a Computer Science Education Week Activity. In *Proceedings of the 47th ACM Technical Symposium on Computing Science Education (SIGCSE '16)*. ACM, New York, NY, USA, 633–638. https://doi.org/10.1145/2839509.2844597

[28] Alexander Repenning, David C Webb, Catharine Brand, Fred Gluck, Ryan Grover, Susan Miller, Hilarie Nickerson, and Muyang Song. 2014. Beyond minecraft: Facilitating computational thinking through modeling and programming in 3d. *IEEE Computer Graphics and Applications* 34, 3 (2014), 68–71.

[29] Alexander Repenning, David C. Webb, Kyu Han Koh, Hilarie Nickerson, Susan B. Miller, Catharine Brand, Ian Her Many Horses, Ashok Basawapatna, Fred Gluck, Ryan Grover, Kris Gutierrez, and Nadia Repenning. 2015. Scalable Game Design: A Strategy to Bring Systemic Computer Science Education to Schools Through Game Design and Simulation Creation. *Trans. Comput. Educ.* 15, 2, Article 11 (April 2015), 31 pages. https://doi.org/10.1145/2700517

[30] Lev Semenovich Vygotsky. 1980. *Mind in society: The development of higher psychological processes.* Harvard university press.

[31] Ron Wakkary, Markus Lorenz Schilling, Matthew A. Dalton, Sabrina Hauser, Audrey Desjardins, Xiao Zhang, and Henry W.J. Lin. 2015. Tutorial Authorship and Hybrid Designers: The Joy (and Frustration) of DIY Tutorials. In *Proceedings of the 33rd Annual ACM Conference on Human Factors in Computing Systems (CHI '15)*. ACM, New York, NY, USA, 609–618. https://doi.org/10.1145/2702123.2702550

[32] Cameron Wilson. 2015. Hour of Code—a Record Year for Computer Science. *ACM Inroads* 6, 1 (Feb. 2015), 22–22. https://doi.org/10.1145/2723168

[33] Yao Xiong, Hongli Li, Mindy L Kornhaber, Hoi K Suen, Barton Pursel, and Deborah D Goins. 2015. Examining the relations among student motivation, engagement, and retention in a MOOC: A structural equation modeling approach. *Global Education Review* 2, 3 (2015).

Infusing Computational Thinking across Disciplines: Reflections & Lessons Learned

Lori Pollock, Chrystalla Mouza, Kevin R. Guidry, Kathleen Pusecker
University of Delaware
Newark, DE 19716, USA
{pollock, cmouza, krguidry, klp}@udel.edu

ABSTRACT

In this work, we describe our effort to develop, pilot, and evaluate a model for infusing computational thinking into undergraduate curricula across a variety of disciplines using multiple methods that previously have been individually tried and tested, including: (1) multiple pathways of computational thinking, (2) faculty professional development, (3) undergraduate peer mentors, and (4) formative assessment. We present pilot instantiations of computational thinking integration in three different disciplines including sociology, mathematics and music. We also present our professional development approach, which is based on faculty support rather than a co-teaching model. Further, we discuss formative assessment during the pilot implementation, including data focusing on undergraduate students' understanding and dispositions towards computational thinking. Finally, we reflect on what worked, what did not work and why, and identify lessons learned. Our work is relevant to higher education institutions across the nation interested in preparing students who can utilize computational principles to address discipline-specific problems.

Keywords

Undergraduate CS education; computational thinking; CS principles

ACM Reference format:

YoLori Pollock, Chrystalla Mouza, Kevin R. Guidry, and Kathleen Pusecker. 2019. Infusing Computational Thinking Across Disciplines: Reflections & Lessons Learned. In *Proceedings of 50th ACM Technical Symposium on Computer Science Education (SIGCSE '19), February 27-Mar. 2, 2019, Minneapolis, MN, USA.* ACM, New York, NY, USA, 7 pages. https://doi.org/10.1145/3287324.3287469

1. INTRODUCTION

As a result of policy efforts seeking to improve science, technology, engineering and mathematics (STEM) learning as well as industry initiatives aimed at promoting a more technology-savvy workforce, the need to help all students acquire computational thinking (CT) skills has gained increased attention.

CT is a problem-solving methodology implemented with a computer that can be automated, transferred and applied across subjects [1]. Jeanette Wing [2] suggested that CT is a fundamental skill of analytical thinking for everyone, which influences all aspects of our lives, from protecting our personal privacy and understanding our legal rights to deciding how to efficiently find and analyze information. A report on CT by the National Research Council (NRC) [3] advanced a similar idea indicating that CT is a cognitive skill that the "average person is expected to possess" (p.13).

SIGCSE'19, February 27-March 2, 2019, Minneapolis, MN, USA.

ACM ISBN 978-1-4503-5890-3/19/02...$15.00.
DOI: http://dx.doi.org/10.1145/3287324.3287469

CT includes a broad range of mental concepts and tools from computer science that help students analyze and develop solutions to problems within their own disciplines, including: problem decomposition, abstraction, algorithms, data representation and analysis, and automation [1, 3]. For example, business students can use CT to collect, classify, and leverage social media data for marketing and sales (data representation and analysis). Exercise science and physical therapy students can use CT to collect, classify, and learn from fitness and health records data for customized health regimes for patients (data representation and analysis). Journalism students can use CT to decompose articles and identify patterns, determine missing information to design interviews and surveys, develop sound logical arguments in their stories, and produce videos (problem decomposition, abstraction, automation). Music students can use CT to create and manipulate music through various technologies using concepts from programming (problem decomposition, abstraction, data representation, automation). Engineering students can analyze traffic patterns and algorithms to control traffic lights (problem decompositions, algorithms, and data analysis). Finally, art students can use CT to transform biochemical data into geometric images with meaning and beauty (abstraction and algorithms).

Although the ability to think computationally is essential to productive disciplinary engagement, most university curricula are currently not designed to provide such knowledge to a broad student population [4]. Even when efforts are made to teach every student about computing as a general education requirement, the discussion of CT does not always reach out to the entire university community [3]. Through support from the National Science Foundation (NSF), institutions such as DePaul University [5], Union College [6], and Towson University [4] have pioneered ways of integrating CT into existing, discipline-specific undergraduate courses in the sciences, humanities, and social sciences by creating flavors of introductory computer science courses for broad audiences. Recognizing the need for these interventions to be contextual so that students appreciate and use CT in their own career paths, these institutions advanced frameworks and models for promoting the development of CT among a diverse body of undergraduate students. Previous work, however, did not provide recommendations for establishing such initiatives university-wide to reach all students within a variety of majors and disciplines. For instance, some efforts focused on honors students [4], others only on students in the humanities [5], and others only on students within STEM fields [7].

In this work, we present our effort to develop, pilot, and evaluate a model for infusing CT into undergraduate curricula across a variety of disciplines using multiple methods that have been previously tried and tested individually, including: (1) multiple pathways of CT, (2) faculty professional development (PD), (3) undergraduate peer mentors, and (4) formative assessment [4, 6, 8]. Locally, this work is motivated by the recent decision of our institution to add CT to its education objectives for all undergraduate students. Nationally, this project is motivated by the need to identify models and practices that help institutions across the nation infuse CT across undergraduate curricula in a variety of disciplines, to ensure that all students acquire computational competencies required to maintain the economic competitiveness of the U.S. in a 21st-century workforce [3].

2. MULTIPLE PATHWAYS TO CT

Creating multiple pathways to the development of CT knowledge and skills is not new. For example, Carroll University [9] replaced general education mathematics and computer science requirements with new courses focused specifically on CT for all Bachelor of Science students at the University (80% of the population). It also developed interdisciplinary programs in computational science and trained faculty to teach new courses as well as integrate CT throughout individual curricula. While this effort targeted developing distinct CT courses, other prior NSF-supported efforts focused explicitly on the integration of CT across a variety of disciplines. For instance, one effort addressed infusing CT in liberal arts and journalism by having students from diverse backgrounds work in groups to find technology solutions to real world problems [10]. Similarly, another effort brought together faculty leaders inside the CT community to collaborate with faculty and students from outside the CT community [6]. The goal was to attract non-traditional students to take introductory computer science courses as well as encourage faculty outside computer science to develop discipline-specific courses that built on the introductory computational course. DePaul University, collaborated with other Chicago area institutions to work to incorporate CT across liberal studies [5]. Finally, Towson University, developed an introductory course for freshmen called *Everyday CT* as well as offered a discipline-specific CT seminar [4].

Collectively, these efforts provided a set of curricular examples and syllabi that illustrate ways in which CT can be infused into a variety of disciplines. Most of these efforts, however, were primarily "bottom up" and did not lead to sustainable change. Our approach differs in that our institution has already mandated that CT be incorporated across undergraduate curricula across disciplines as a General Education objective for all students. Therefore, we are tasked with the objective of identifying implementation strategies that respond to this new mandate. In this work, we present *pilot instantiations* of CT integration in three different disciplines: sociology, mathematics, and music. We also present our faculty support model and discuss formative assessment during the pilot implementations. There are two unique elements in our approach compared to prior efforts. First, rather than developing new courses, our faculty integrated CT into existing courses in their discipline. Second, none of the faculty had a background in computer science. Rather, they were disciplinary experts with interests in identifying strategies for CT integration that were relevant to courses in their own field.

3. FACULTY PROFESSIONAL DEVELOPMENT

PD is key to facilitating ongoing course preparation and implementation particularly for faculty with minimal CT background. One-shot workshops, however, are rarely effective [11]. Rather, effective PD that leads to improved student outcomes is ongoing and is connected to content and specific teacher needs [11]. Earlier faculty PD models on CT consisted of short-term workshops [4] or co-teaching approaches where CS faculty were paired with faculty in a specific discipline to ensure accurate content instruction. While there are a number of benefits to co-teaching, it makes scaling up challenging.

Our PD model consists of participation in a multiday institute during the summer and bi-weekly meetings throughout the academic year with the faculty teaching the course(s) and a CT integration team. The team includes a faculty from computer science who brings CT-related expertise, a learning scientist, and professionals from our university's Center for Teaching & Assessment of Learning. The institute provides an introduction to CT and CT classroom activity ideas while the CT integration teams and undergraduate students with computer science background provide assistance and resources during the planning and implementation of the courses.

3.1. Summer Institute

Every year at the end of the spring semester, our university provides a Faculty Institute that focuses on teaching, learning, and assessment. To infuse CT across undergraduate curricula for all majors, the Center for Teaching & Assessment of Learning at our institution in concert with faculty in computer science and education established a CT-related PD track within the Summer Institute. This track focused specifically on helping faculty learn about CT, including approaches and strategies for integrating CT in their specific disciplines. The Summer Institute provided hands-on opportunities for faculty to learn more about CT and how to create classroom activities and assessments that promote CT-related skills among students. We began by introducing CT with a "CS Unplugged" activity - an activity that introduces a CT concept without technology. We then shared our draft rubric focusing on assessing artifacts that integrate CT with disciplinary content. The rubric, modeled after the Association American of Colleges and Universities VALUE rubrics, draws heavily on the literature on CT and has been vetted by CT experts (see Appendix A). Faculty participants used the rubric as a scaffold for developing CT related activities within their discipline. Faculty with whom we have worked to infuse CT into their courses also shared specific examples and activities from their courses. In addition to these sessions at the summer institute, we also piloted with one faculty an alternative PD model that consisted of a 3-day intensive workshop focused on course design rooted in backward design principles. Both of these models are adaptations of existing faculty support programs at our institution and models that are commonly used at many U.S. colleges and universities.

3.2. Year-Long Support

To ensure that participating faculty were supported in their efforts to integrate CT in their respective disciplines, we provided year-long support in bi-weekly meetings that included both time for collaborative discussions and sharing of practices as well as one-to-one consultation. As noted, the team meetings included the disciplinary expert professors, a learning scientist, a computer science professor, and two professionals from the Center for Teaching Assessment & Learning. Our discussion topics focused on identifying opportunities for CT integration into existing course modules, developing new modules that integrate CT in the specific discipline, providing feedback on module development, as well as developing instruments (e.g., surveys and rubrics) for assessing student CT knowledge and skills. We used the criteria in the draft rubric to guide many of our discussions and keep them focused on specific CT constructs that may be more fruitful in each discipline.

3.3. Undergraduate CT Fellows

Our work is uniquely characterized by the role of undergraduate peer mentors, called CT Fellows, who are responsible for ongoing faculty support. Specifically, CT-knowledgeable undergraduates not only assist participating faculty in the design and implementation of instructional activities that integrate CT with specific disciplinary content, but they also serve as peer mentors during the course. Our institution has a rich tradition of utilizing peer mentors in a variety of disciplines and contexts. This model is effective because the mentors are close enough to their peers to recognize confusion and perspectives that they themselves experienced while acquiring new knowledge. This "near peer" closeness helps mentors build rapport with students, encourage and provide emotional support, and set expectations with nondirective enabling [12].

To prepare CT Fellows, we draw on a model developed to prepare undergraduate students to assist K-12 teachers in teaching computing [13]. In this model, students interested in becoming Fellows participate in a university course called Field Experiences in Teaching Computing. The course, which is open to students who have completed at least one prior computer science course, is based on prior NSF-supported service-learning models and fulfills requirements for a computer science major, computer science minor, and discovery learning experience (a graduation requirement for undergraduate students at our institution). It has been offered continuously since spring 2013. Participants meet for 75-minutes on-campus once a week to identify and implement CT related teaching resources targeted toward specific disciplines, model classroom lessons that build on research-driven strategies, discuss teaching pedagogy, prepare and analyze lesson plans, and reflect on their experiences.

4. DESCRIPTION OF CT-INFUSED COURSES

In this section, we describe efforts to integrate CT across disciplines including sociology, mathematics, and music.

4.1. Sociology

In sociology, a faculty member infused CT into the *Introduction to Sociology* course for honors students in their freshman year. In this course, the instructor met with the CT Fellow and decided to focus primarily on the use of algorithms in relation to gender in children's products. Specifically, working in small groups, students researched and selected websites aimed at promoting and selling toys to children. Their task was to identify patterns such as slogans, colors, music, and activities associated with gender. Subsequently, their task was to develop algorithms, which is a key component of our rubric (see Appendix A), using terms such as AND, OR and NOT that helped a search engine identify gender on children's websites by specifying the salient patterns found in their analysis. Students were free to create an algorithm in a variety of formats (that did not include programming). For instance, some students provided lists of items while others wrote programs using pseudo-code.

Using the construct of algorithms in this context provided a means for gender socialization. Participants learned that websites selling toys to children could easily be analyzed using an algorithm and that these algorithms represent society's understanding of socially salient elements that help identify and recognize gender. In the process, students had an opportunity to recognize how rigid gender differences must be for an algorithm to identify gender. Thus, in this course, algorithms highlighted the process of socializing children into differences that are meaningful and how to identify and embody those differences. In essence, this assignment helped highlight the connections among CT and disciplinary content related to gender socialization.

4.2. Mathematics

In mathematics, CT was integrated into a course for non-majors titled *Contemporary Mathematics*. Specifically, the instructor consulted with the CT fellow and the PIs and integrated CT into an exercise related to data analysis which is a key component of CT and our rubric (see Appendix A). For example, the instructor asked students to identify a dataset from an online portal (https://www.statcrunch.com/). Subsequently, students were asked to identify a question that could be answered based on the dataset, analyze the data, display the findings using graphs, and write an interpretation of the findings.

Working in groups of 2-3, participants selected a variety of datasets from cereal (e.g., where cereal is stored in a supermarket, nutritional information, etc.) to social media to sports (e.g., NFL statistics) to music to presidential ratings. In the process, students learned about the data they were using and realized the value of using automation in the analysis as the data sets were too large to identify patterns manually. Further, students realized that meaningful representation of data was frequently dependent on the size of the dataset, which in turn influenced their choice of graphs and their interpretation of the findings.

4.3. Music

In music, a faculty member developed and taught a course called *Computational Thinking in Music*. This was the only instance where a new course was created as opposed to integrating CT into existing materials. This course was developed in collaboration with a music faculty who had previously integrated CT into a music appreciation course for non-majors. Although the course was successful, both faculty wanted to take a deeper dive into the connections among music and CT and thus established a pilot course focusing explicitly at the intersection of CT and music. Specifically, a key component of the course was the integration of programming in music and the use of online data (e.g., HookTheory.com) and Python code to explore music released by a popular artist and algorithmically write a portion of a song in the style of that artist.

The course was open to all students independent of prior background in music. As a result, there was variability in students' understanding of music from those with no background at all to amateur musicians. The first four weeks of the course were devoted to helping students fill in the gaps in terms of their understanding of music vocabulary and terminology. In Week 5, students downloaded pre-existing transcriptions of artists' music to form a corpus. Subsequently, they created harmonic progressions for a verse (chords and rhythms) based on a computer-based analysis of corpus data; this analysis was performed using Python programs developed by the CT Fellow assigned to support this course. Following the development of the progression, participants created melody for verse (pitches and rhythms) again using Python code. The basic string of pitches and layout for segmentations was suggested by computer analysis of their specific corpus that created a Markov model. Finally, participants repeated the harmonic progression and melody tasks for the chorus and revised as needed. To conclude the course, the instructor brought in a band of musicians who gave a live performance of students' work.

5. METHODS

In this paper, we report on formative evaluation of our approach to CT integration across the disciplines of sociology, mathematics, and music. Relatedly, we answer the question: *How does participation in a CT-infused discipline specific course influence undergraduate students' understanding and attitudes towards CT?*

Data were collected from all undergraduates enrolled in one of the pilot courses in sociology (N=22), mathematics (N=35), and music (N=10) through a tested pre-and-post course survey [14] that was slightly modified for our work. In addition to other questions, the survey included one open-ended question of interest to our work: *What do you think the term computational thinking means?* This question tested students' understanding of CT. The survey also used 20 Likert-type items (see Table 1) to assess student understanding and attitudes in four categories: *definition* (e.g., see items 1-4), *comfort* (see items 5-10), *interest* (see items 11-14), *career/future use* (see items 15-20). Likert-type responses were scored on a scale of 1- 4 where 1=*Strongly Disagree* and 4=*Strongly Agree.* Subsequently scores were entered into a spreadsheet and means were calculated. The pre and post open-ended survey response was analyzed qualitatively using the constant comparative method [15]. This approach helped identify common themes that cut across participants' responses.

6. RESULTS

Overall, results indicated positive improvements from the pre to the post administration of the survey in some categories but not others. Specifically, participants reported better understanding (items 1-4) and comfort (items 5-10) with CT. However, participants did not express greater interest in CT after their participation in the course (items 11-14). Further, there was some ambivalence regarding the importance and value of CT in participants' future careers, specifically within their discipline (items 15-20). The exception was item 20, where participants clearly indicated improvements in their understanding of tools that can be used in their discipline. It is important to note, however, that given the small sample size and the fact that not all students responded to each question we were not able to conduct a statistical analysis to test for the significance of the gain score from the pre to the post administration of the survey.

Table 1. Pre/Post Scores on Understanding and Attitudes Toward CT

	Sociology* (N=22)		Mathematics* (N=35)		Music* (N=10)	
	Pre	Post	Pre	Post	Pre	Post
1. CT focuses solely on understanding how computers work.	3.7	3.7	3.0	3.7	2.7	2.8
2. CT involves thinking logically to solve problems.	3.6	3.4	3.9	3.6	3.8	3.7
3. CT requires using computers to solve problems.	2.9	3.6	2.9	3.1	1.9	2.4
4. CT involves abstracting general principles and applying them to other situations.	3.3	3.4	3.5	3.5	3.6	3.9
5. It is possible to apply CT skills to solve problems in my major.	3.6	3.9	3.1	3.2	3.6	3.3
6. I am comfortable with CT concepts.	2.1	3.5	2.7	3.0	2.4	3.3
7. I can achieve good grades in courses that require CT.	3.1	3.7	3.2	3.1	2.8	3.4
8. I can learn to understand CT concepts.	3.7	3.6	3.6	3.5	3.4	3.8
9. I use CT skills in my daily life.	3.2	3.3	3.0	3.1	3.0	3.2
10. I can solve problems by using CT skills.	3.4	3.0	3.3	3.3	3.2	3.3
11. I think using CT skills is boring**.	1.7	1.7	2.4	2.2	2.1	2.1
12. The challenge of solving problems using CT appeals to me.	3.1	2.7	2.7	2.7	3.0	3.2
13. I am interested in using CT skills.	3.3	3.0	2.8	2.7	3.1	3.2
14. I will voluntarily take courses that use CT if I am given the opportunity.	3.2	3.2	2.3	2.4	3.0	3.1
15. Knowledge of CT skills will help me secure a better job.	3.4	3.7	3.1	3.1	3.6	3.4
16. My career goals require that I learn CT skills.	3.2	3.8	2.6	2.9	2.9	2.9
17. I expect that learning CT skills will help me to achieve my career goals.	3.4	3.4	2.8	2.9	3.3	3.3
18. I hope that my future career will require the use of CT skills.	2.9	3.0	2.6	2.5	2.8	3.2
19. Having background knowledge and understanding of CT skills is valuable in and of itself.	3.5	3.1	3.1	3.2	3.6	3.7
20. I know what CT tools are available to solve problems in my major.	2.2	3.1	2.7	2.9	2.6	3.3

* Not all participants responded to all items on the pre/post survey

** This item is a reverse statement and thus the lower score indicates disagreement that CT is boring.

Findings from the open-ended question also noted improvements in participants' understanding of CT related concepts before and after participation in a CT infused course. When asked to respond to the question *"What do you think the term CT means?"* initial responses focused primarily on the following:

- Logical thinking: *"Using logic and common sense when thinking", "Using logic and structured thinking to organize given information", "Using common sense and logic in daily activities."*
- Non-creative thinking: *"Thinking in a math-oriented kind of way, thinking in a strict way/not creatively."*

- Thinking like a computer: *"Thinking through tasks like an AI computer program to find the fastest and most efficient option".*

Further some participants simply noted that CT is about "using a computer", "computer knowledge" or "completing mathematical calculations". Only a small number of students recognized CT as a problem-solving methodology that can be implemented with a computer. One participant, for instance, explained: *"CT is defining a problem and trying to find a solution to it using a computer or machine".*

In contrast, post-survey data demonstrated an improved understanding of CT through more detailed and conveying responses. Most participants recognized CT as a problem-solving methodology, while others used specific CT concepts as they defined CT, including "decomposition" and "abstraction". One participant explained, *"CT is a thought process in which tasks are broken down into easier, more manageable steps. CT uses problem decomposition, algorithms, abstraction, and data."* Similarly, another student noted: *"CT involves considering a problem and breaking it down through decomposition in order to better carry out the task or solve the problem."* Further, participants recognized that CT is not a mechanistic approach to thinking but rather involves creativity and problem solving through multiple perspectives. One student explained, *"CT involves thinking abstractly and being able to decompose an issue at hand in order to see all possible solutions"* while another student noted that *"CT is being able to look at things or issues from multiple perspectives or lenses and come up with various solutions or answers".* Finally, more participants understood the relationship between CT and computers. One student explained, *"CT is being able to think or put ideas in terms that a computer could follow".* Overall, in the post-survey, a greater number of participants were able to articulate the relationship between CT, problem-solving, and computers.

7. DISCUSSION AND LESSONS LEARNED

In this section, we identify lessons learned from the pilot implementations in sociology, mathematics, and music.

- Faculty development is critical in learning about CT and honing an understanding of discipline-specific approaches to CT. Further, regular discussions between a CT integration team that includes both CT and disciplinary experts as well as experts on teaching and assessment are critical in developing course objectives and instructional activities that indeed provide a path to the design and implementation of CT into disciplinary courses without the need for co-teaching. The draft VALUE-style rubric that presents a succinct definition of CT with measurable criteria was tremendously helpful in not only facilitating discussions, but also in helping faculty modify their courses, creating assignments, and assessing students' work.
- Peer mentors in the form of CT knowledgeable undergraduates can support the faculty in a way that increases faculty confidence in the classroom as they enact CT activities. However, the role of CT Fellows varied among participants. For example, the music faculty required substantial technical support from a CT Fellow who wrote computer code and helped the faculty and students adapt and run that code on their computers. In sociology and mathematics, however, the CT Fellow served primarily as a brainstorming partner for the faculty members in developing and polishing course assignments that integrated CT with disciplinary content. As faculty gain confidence they are more likely to continue to build on their successes with additional CT-related activities and modules. The peer mentor for a given course may not require more than four hours a week including class time, thus the same CT Fellow may be able to support more than one faculty in a given year. This helps with scaling the model to support more faculty in CT integration each year. However, the logistics of coordinating, supervising, and supporting these students who also have many other responsibilities – their own coursework, enrollment in the CT fieldwork course, and attending some classes with their CT faculty member – can be formidable and cannot be underestimated. These challenges make it likely that we will make significant changes to this aspect of our support model as we continue infusing CT into additional courses at our institution.
- Students sometimes do not appreciate why they are learning CT within a disciplinary-specific course. This suggests that faculty need to begin the course and its advertising with strong motivation for integrating CT transparent learning objectives into the course, and reiterating the importance of those learning objectives throughout the course. This can be done by providing examples of how the CT-related activities are relevant to their discipline and the real world outside the classroom; in fact, situating CT within students' and faculty members' selected disciplines is why we have elected to infuse CT into many different courses instead of assigning this responsibility to computer science faculty or creating CT-specific courses co-taught by computer scientists.
- Formative assessment needs to account for the fact that artifacts created for assessment are different across disciplines. Thus, a common rubric for assessing CT knowledge and skills may need to be adapted when implemented on various kinds of student artifacts.

In conclusion, our findings indicate that a model for CT integration that applies multiple proven methods together holds promise for successfully meeting university goals of CT for all, without a co-teaching model or separate discipline-oriented computer science courses. In addition, the model provides service learning opportunities for CT knowledgeable undergraduates and creation of a network of faculty who can share their ideas, challenges, and experiences in integrating CT within their discipline. Our next challenge is scaling up the model to reach a greater number of faculty and students

Appendix 1. Draft Computational Thinking Rubric adapted from [1]. See also: http://www.udel.edu/005415

	Capstone	Milestones		Benchmark
	4	3	2	1
Decomposition *Breaks a problem into its constituent subproblems*	Creates a problem decomposition that breaks a complex problem into clearly described, well-defined, and distinct-but-related subproblems that are easier to solve than the original problem but when combined efficiently solves the original problem.	Creates a problem decomposition that breaks a complex problem into clearly described subproblems that are distinct-but-related but lack efficiency, although they solve the original problem.	Creates a problem decomposition that breaks a complex problem into subproblems that lack efficiency, fail to have sufficient descriptions, and overlap, although they solve the original problem.	Creates a problem decomposition that breaks a complex problem into subproblems that are inefficient, described poorly, overlap or closely related, and fail to completely solve the original problem.
Data *Analyze (or create) a data set that facilitates discovery of patterns and relationships*	Analyzes[1] a data set to ensure it is sufficiently comprehensive, efficiently organized, meaningfully labeled, and thoroughly described so that it can be analyzed to discover meaningful patterns and relationships.	Analyzes a data set to ensure it is sufficiently comprehensive, meaningfully labeled, and thoroughly described but fail to ensure that it is efficiently organized.	Analyzes a data set to ensure it is sufficiently comprehensive and meaningfully labeled but fail to ensure that it is thoroughly described and efficiently organized.	Analyzes a data set but fail to ensure that it is sufficiently comprehensive, efficiently organized, meaningfully labelled, and thoroughly described so patterns and relationships are obscured.
Algorithms *Creates a series of ordered steps to solve a problem or achieve a goal*	Creates an accurate, logical, efficient, and well-described sequence of steps or instructions to solve a problem or achieve a goal.	Creates accurate steps that are logical and well-described and solve a problem or achieve a goal but the steps are inefficient e.g., not in an optimal sequence, overlapping or duplicative.	Creates logical steps that solve a problem or achieve a goal but the steps are poorly described.	Creates a sequence of steps that do not solve a problem or achieve a goal. The steps lack efficiency, sufficient descriptions, and are not described or documented.
Abstraction *Reduces complexity to create a general representation of a process or group of objects so it is not only appropriate for the immediate purpose or goal but can also be used in different contexts*	Creates an accurate-but-simplified representation of a process or group of objects to solve the problem or meet the goal. Selects essential characteristics by filtering out unnecessary information. Can be used to solve other problems or goals.	Creates an accurate-but-simplified representation of a process or group of objects to solve the problem or meet the goal. Selects essential characteristics by filtering out unnecessary information. Cannot be used to solve other problems or goals.	Creates an accurate-but-simplified representation of a process or group of objects to solve the problem or meet the goal. Fails to select all essential characteristics by filtering out unnecessary information. Cannot be used to solve other problems or goals.	Creates an representation of a process or group of objects that is not accurate, not sufficiently simplified, or fails to solve the problem or meet the goal.

[1] Advanced courses or disciplines with a strong focus on CT may instead require students to create a data set instead of analyzing an existing one.

8. ACKNOWLEDGMENTS

This work is supported by a grant from the National Science Foundation (Award # 1611959). All opinions are the authors and do not necessarily represent those of the funding agency.

9. REFERENCES

[1] Barr, V., & Stephenson, C. 2011. Bringing computational thinking to K-12: What is involved and what is the role of the computer science education community? *ACM Inroads*, 2(1): 48-54.

[2] Wing, J. 2006. Computational thinking. *Communications of the ACM, 49*(3). 33-35.

[3] National Research Council. 2010. *Report of a Workshop on the Scope and Nature of Computational Thinking.* Washington, DC: National Academy of Sciences.

[4] Dierbach, C., Hochheiser, H., Collins, S., Jerome, G., Ariza, C., Kelleher, T., Kleinsasser, W., Dehlinger, J., & Kaza, S. 2011. A model for piloting pathways for computational thinking in a general education curriculum. In *Proceedings of the 42nd ACM Technical Symposium on Computer science education*, 257-262. doi: 10.1145/1953163.1953243.

[5] Perković, L., Settle, A., Hwang, S., & Jones, J. 2010. A framework for computational thinking across the curriculum. In *Proceedings of the 15th annual conference on Innovation and technology in computer science education*, 123-127. doi: 10.1145/1822090.1822126.

[6] Barr, V., Motahar, E., Liew, C. W., & Stewart-Gambling, H. 2009. Building a campus wide computation initiative: Panel discussion. *Journal of Computing Sciences in Colleges, 24*(3), 109-110.

[7] Alvarado, C., Dodds, Z., Kuenning, G., Hadas, R., & Shelton, C. 2010. *Modular CS1 from the inside out: Computational thinking for all STEM students.* CPATH PI Meeting, March 25-26, Arlington, VA.

[8] Pollock, L., Mouza, C., Atlas, J., & Harvey, T. 2015. Field experiences in teaching computer science: Course organization and reflections. *Proceedings of the 47th ACM technical symposium on Computer science education*, 374-379.

[9] Kuster, C., & Hu, C. 2012. CAPTH-1: Developing computational thinking skills across the Undergraduate curriculum. Retrieved from: http://grantome.com/grant/NSF/CNS-0939032.

[10] Pulimood, S. M., Pearson, K., & Bates, D. C. 2014. CABECT: collaborating across boundaries to engage undergraduates in computational thinking (Workshop - abstract only). In *Proceedings of the 45th ACM Technical Symposium on Computer Science Education*, Atlanta, Georgia, USA, March 05 – 08, 2014.

[11] Zepeda, S.J. 2011. Professional development: What works (2nd ed.). Larchmont, NY: Eye on Education, Inc.

[12] Harrington, K., O'Neill, P., & Bakhshi, S. 2008. *Making time and space for writing: Student writing mentors and the writing centre.* Presentation at Writing Development in Higher Education Conference, University of Strathclyde, Glasgow, Scotland.

[13] Pollock, L., Mouza, C., Atlas, J., & Harvey, T. 2015. Field experience in teaching computer science: Course organization and reflections. In *Proceedings of Special Interest Group in Computer Science Education*, March 4-7, Kansas City, MO.

[14] Yadav, A., Mayfield, C., Zhou, N., Hambrusch, S., & Korb, J. T. 2014. Computational thinking in elementary and secondary teacher education. *ACM Trans. Comput. Educ. 14*, 1, Article 5 (March 2014), 16 pages. DOI:http://dx.doi.org/10.1145/2576872

[15] Hatch, J. A.(2002. Doing qualitative research in education settings . New York, NY: Suny University Press.

Building Computational Creativity in an Online Course for Non-Majors

Markeya S. Peteranetz
Dept. of Computer Science and Engineering
University of Nebraska-Lincoln
256 Avery Hall, Lincoln, NE 68588-0115
markeya.dubbs@huskers.unl.edu

Leen-Kiat Soh
Dept. of Computer Science and Engineering
University of Nebraska-Lincoln
256 Avery Hall, Lincoln, NE 68588-0115
lksoh@cse.unl.edu

Elizabeth Ingraham
School of Art, Art History & Design
University of Nebraska-Lincoln
120 Richards Hall, Lincoln, NE 68588
eingraham2@unl.edu

ABSTRACT

In recent years, a growing number of universities have begun to offer specialized courses as a way to make computer science (CS) more accessible to students with little or no prior CS or programming experience, especially non-CS majors. One of the ways courses have been modified for these students is by supplementing the core problem solving and coding aspects of the curriculum with explicit instruction on computational thinking principles. These "computational thinking" courses are promising in that they ground computational thinking in discipline-specific contexts and emphasize application of computational principles. However, there is little empirical research evaluating the extent to which students learn computational thinking from these courses. The purpose of this study was to evaluate the impact of an online Computational Creativity course on students' computational thinking skills, creative competencies, and self-efficacy. Students in the Computational Creativity course were predominantly non-CS majors, and they completed four Computational Creativity Exercises (CCEs) that have previously been shown to improve learning and achievement. Results indicate that the Computational Creativity course was effective in increasing students' computational thinking knowledge and self-efficacy for applying computational thinking in their fields, but it did not have an impact on students' creative competencies. Additionally, students' reactions to the course and the CCEs were mostly positive. Thus, this study provides initial evidence that non-CS majors can learn computational thinking through the online Computational Creativity course.

CCS CONCEPTS

• Social and professional topics~Computational thinking • Applied computing~Collaborative learning • Applied computing~E-learning

ACM ISBN 978-1-4503-5890-3/19/02...$15.00.
https://doi.org/10.1145/3287324.3287346

KEYWORDS

Collaborative learning; Computational thinking; Computational creativity; Creativity; Non-majors

ACM Reference format:
Markeya S. Peteranetz, Leen-Kiat Soh, and Elizabeth Ingraham. 2019. Building computational creativity in an online course for non-majors. In *Proceedings of the 50th ACM Technical Symposium on Computing Science Education (SIGCSE '19). February 27-March 2, 2019, Minneapolis, MN, USA* ACM, New York, NY. https://doi.org/10.1145/3287324.3287346

1 Introduction

Online courses have come to be a common part of post-secondary education in the United States. Some degree programs are entirely online, and colleges are offering an increasing number of courses online. This trend is also present in computer science (CS) and computing education, and as a result there is interest in determining how effectively computational thinking skills can be taught through an online course. Though much has been written about the creation and implementation of online courses, especially Massive Open Online Courses (MOOCs), few studies have examined the *effectiveness* of teaching CS and computational thinking in an online format.

Early research on the effectiveness of teaching CS online yielded mixed results [1,2]. More recent research has shown students' test performance is comparable when CS classes are taught in-person or online [3]. Research in other disciplines [4–6] has also shown either equivalent performance across instructional formats or slightly better performance in online classes. When results show comparable outcomes in online and face-to-face courses, the conclusions about the effectiveness of online learning tend to differ based on whether the question of interest is, "can online instruction lead to better learning outcomes than face-to-face instruction?" or, "do the two methods yield equivalent outcomes?" In the former case, the idea is that online learning might be a solution to low achievement. In the latter case, the hope is that the administrative and monetary benefits of online instruction do not come at the expense of student learning. And, if the hope is that online instruction results in similar achievement, research showing no difference between the two methods, such as [3], gives reason to be optimistic about the wider adoption of online instruction.

The purpose of this study was to evaluate the impact of an online Computational Creativity course on students' computational thinking skills [7], creative competencies [8,9], and self-efficacy [10]. Students (who were predominantly *not* CS majors) enrolled in and completed a semester-long Computational Creativity course that was offered through the university's School of Art, Art History & Design.

The following sections review research related to teaching computational thinking and CS through online courses and teaching computational thinking and CS to non-CS majors, followed by a discussion of computational creativity and exercises that can be used to incorporate it into classrooms. Then, the design and results of the study investigating the impact of the Computational Creativity course are presented. Finally, the results of the study are discussed.

2 Related Research

2.1 Teaching Computer Science to Non-CS Majors

As the interdisciplinary potential of CS has come to be recognized more widely, colleges and universities have begun to offer CS courses specifically designed for students outside the CS major. For example, discipline-specific variations of CS were created through an "Applied Computer Science option" at Winona State University [11]. The applied option had separate tracks for students in bioinformatics, computer information systems, geographic information technology, and human computer interaction. Similarly, [12] outlined the design and evaluation of a CS1 course for science majors. The course took a "breadth-first" approach in order to familiarize students with as many topics as possible and taught the basics of programming in Python. Cortina [13] described a Principles of Computing course that was designed for non-technical non-CS majors. The course provided students an introduction to computing topics and the field of computer science separate from programming.

Soh et al. [14] went a step further and envisioned a suite of CS1 courses that integrated core CS curriculum with computational thinking rooted in a wide range of disciplines: engineering, the sciences, the arts, and humanities. In these courses, the same core CS1 content was taught, but the programming language, assignments, and lab activities were selected to be especially relevant for the different disciplines targeted by each class. This specialization and connection to different disciplines was intended to make the content more meaningful for students and also to make clearer the ways in which the knowledge and skills learned in the course could be applied to each discipline.

2.2 Computational Thinking Courses

The increased awareness of the interdisciplinary potential of CS and computational thinking has also led to attempts to reach non-CS majors through introductory computational thinking courses. For example, faculty at Purdue University developed a computational thinking course specifically for students majoring in a variety of science programs including physics, chemistry, and biology [15]. At Tuskegee University, an introductory bioinformatics course was designed specifically to foster biology students' computational thinking [16]. However, as recently as 2015, Czerkawski and Lyman [17] observed "There is not yet a coherent cross-institutional movement to incorporate [computational thinking] as a fundamental skill-set, outside of computer science and a few STEM disciplines." That is, although some institutions are taking steps to teach computational thinking to students outside of CS, non-CS computational thinking courses are still the exception rather than the rule.

One feature common to most computational thinking courses is a focus on grounding computational thinking principles and learning activities in a context that is familiar to most students. Often, making computational thinking familiar and accessible involves either eliminating or greatly reducing the presence of computer code in the curriculum. Czerkawski and Lyman [17] argued, "Engaging humanities and fine-arts majors in computational thinking projects requires field-appropriate introduction to [computational thinking] principles. ...focused on algorithms and principles of computational thinking without requiring any actual programming." Teaching computational thinking without code reduces the cognitive load [18] placed on students as they attempt to understand and apply computational thinking principles, and as a result, should make it easier for students without CS or coding experience to learning computational thinking.

Despite the reported instances of computational thinking courses being taught to non-CS majors (e.g., [15,16]), there is little available empirical research evaluating these courses. In one of the few cases where the course was evaluated, Chowdhury et al. [19] found that students had mostly positive experiences in the course and found the use of a collaborative cohort model to be beneficial. However, their evaluation focused on students' perceptions of and experiences with the course, it and did not include an analysis of students' learning of computational thinking. Thus, one goal of this study was to conduct a broad evaluation of the effectiveness of a computational thinking course for non-CS majors by examining students' learning and self-efficacy in addition to their perceptions of the course.

2.3 Computational Creativity

A novel way to teach computational thinking to non-CS majors (as well as CS students) is through computational creativity [20]. Computational creativity is the synergistic combination of computational thinking and creative thinking that can lead to more effective problem solving across disciplines and contexts. It takes the structure and versatility of computational thinking and infuses it with the flexibility and ingenuity of creative thinking. A computational creativity approach can be used to make computational thinking more accessible to students without CS or programming experience. In the computational creativity framework put forth by [20–23], the core components of computational thinking are abstraction, algorithm design, evaluation, generalization, pattern recognition, and problem decomposition [7], and creative thinking is rooted in Epstein's [8,9] creative competencies: *Broadening*, *Capturing*, *Challenging*, and *Surrounding*.

Computational creativity is reflected in the integration of CS and the fine arts in the *Performamatics* courses developed at the University of Massachusetts Lowell [24]. In these courses, computational thinking and creative thinking were combined as students used computers and coding as the medium through which they created art or music. For example, in the *Sound Thinking* course, students learned how computational concepts such as algorithms, loops, and modularization are part of digitally composing music and performed music using Scratch. By highlighting the intersection of computation and music, the *Sound Thinking* course offers an entry point into CS for students who might not otherwise be interested in learning about CS or computational thinking.

2.3.1 Computational Creativity Exercises. Computational Creativity Exercises (CCEs) have been created specifically as a vehicle for introducing computational creativity into courses both in and outside of CS. As discussed in [20,23], the principles underlying the design of the CCEs are (1) balancing of attributes between computational and creative thinking and (2) mapping between computational and creative concepts and skills as they manifest in different disciplines. A brief description of the CCEs is provided next, and the reader is referred to [20–22] for more detail.

Each exercise has four basic components: (1) Objectives, (2) Tasks, (3) CS Light Bulbs, and (4) Questions. Each exercise is presented and completed on an online collaborative wiki platform, which is available within most Learning Management Systems (LMS). For each CCE, the objectives include a set of creative objectives, computational objectives, and collaborative objectives. Creative objectives are based on Epstein's four competencies: capturing, challenging, broadening, and surrounding. Computational objectives include two aspects: CS concepts, such as sorting and logical conditionals, and computational thinking skills, such as problem decomposition and abstraction. The collaborative nature of the CCEs facilitates creative thinking by bringing together students from diverse backgrounds. These objectives help students contextualize the purpose of the exercises by showing how an exercise lacking any programming code is related to CS concepts and by also indicating how students can use relevant creative thinking skills to complete the exercises.

The Task component lists all the tasks the group must complete during the two weeks of the exercise. Tasks require collaboration among the students and some require individual contributions. The CS Light Bulbs are text boxes embedded within the exercise handout that explicitly connect the task activities and CS topics specific to each participating course. The Light Bulbs help students relate what they do for the exercise to real-world issues and practices that utilize computational thinking and CS concepts. The Questions component presents open-ended questions that require students to reflect on their solutions and analyze potential issues with their solutions, encouraging them to evaluate the results of their original tasks using computational thinking and imagine further improvements using creative thinking.

Prior research [22–23,25–26] has demonstrated the effectiveness of CCEs in improving undergraduate students' learning and achievement. Positive effects have been found for students in introductory [22-23,27] and upper-level [21,25] courses, for CS majors and non-CS majors [23], and for engineering students in introductory CS [26,27]. Although CCEs have been shown to improve computational thinking knowledge in CS courses, studies have not shown an impact on CS students' creative competencies [21,25]. Additionally, all studies of the CCEs impacts on learning and achievement have been conducted in CS courses, where the CCEs were used to supplement to standard CS and programming instruction. That is, the CCEs have been shown to increase computational thinking knowledge and skills *alongside* the standard CS curriculum. The effectiveness of CCEs in building computational thinking separate from CS curriculum, such as in a computational thinking course designed for non-CS majors, has yet to be investigated.

3 Research Questions and Hypotheses

In this study, we investigated the following research questions:

Research Question 1: Did students' computational thinking knowledge and skills increase after taking the Computational Creativity course?

Hypothesis 1: Students' computational thinking knowledge and skills would increase after taking the Computational Creativity course.

Research Question 2: Did students' creative competencies increase after taking the Computational Creativity course?

Hypothesis 2: Students' creative competencies would not be changed by the Computational Creativity course. As previous stated, prior research has found no impact of CCEs on creative competencies, and therefore, we did not expect the Computational Creativity course to have an impact on students' creative competencies.

Research Question 3: Did students' self-efficacy for applying computational thinking increase after taking the Computational Creativity course?

Hypothesis 3: Students' self-efficacy would increase after taking the Computational Creativity course.

Research Question 4: How did students feel about the Computational Creativity course?

Due to the exploratory nature of this research question, no hypotheses were specified.

4 Method

This section contains descriptions of the Computational Creativity course, the participants in the study, and the instruments used.

4.1 Course and Context

We developed the Computational Creativity course to make computational thinking and creativity accessible and applicable for a broad range of students. It was partially adapted from a previously developed course that was delivered in a traditional in-person lecture format. Both the in-person course and the online course were 3-credit hour courses, which is most common at this university. The course consisted of 6 modules. Each module centered on a set of ideas (e.g., "Module 4: Identifying creative blocks and applying creative blockbusters. Using your whole brain and managing time and stress."). They contained video-recorded lectures, discussion activities, and graded assignments. Four of the 6 modules contained a CCE, and the last 3 modules had assignments that were steps towards completing the final project. Students worked in groups for the CCEs, but all other activities were completed individually. The 4 CCEs used in this course were *Exploring, Thinking*

Inside the Box, *Storytelling*, and *Everyday Object*. An extended description of *Everyday Object* is provided by [23].

4.2 Participants

During the fall 2017 semester, 42 students were enrolled in the Computational Creativity course, and 37 students (15 male, 22 female; 13 freshman, 5 sophomore, 4 junior, 12 senior, 3 graduate/other) consented to participate and completed the beginning-of-semester survey. The middle-of-semester survey was completed by 25 students, and the end-of-semester survey was completed by 27 students. Surveys were completed voluntarily and accessed via a web link provided by the course instructor. Survey and responses were only accessed by the researchers.

4.3 Materials

Students completed a battery of instruments via web-based survey at the beginning, middle, and end of the semester. Instruments measured students' computational thinking skills, motivation, self-regulation tendencies, affective reactions to the course, and perceptions of the CCEs. Only the instruments that are used in the present study are described here.

4.3.1 Computational Thinking Test. An 18-item test of computational thinking knowledge and skills was administered at the beginning and end of the semester. Items pertained to abstraction, algorithm design, evaluation, generalization, pattern recognition, and problem decomposition, with each dimension being represented by three items. Test items were written by a member of the research team who has expertise in computational thinking. Item analysis was conducted on both sets of test items, and the removal of sub-optimal items resulted in a 16-item subset that was used for analysis. Participants' scores were the total number of correct responses out of 16 (coefficient alpha: pre-test = .72, post-test = .78).

4.3.2 Creative Competencies Scale. Creative competencies were measured with a researcher-developed instrument adapted from the Epstein Creative Competencies Inventory (ECCI) [29]. The scale consisted of 4 items, and the score used for analysis was the mean of the items (coefficient alpha: beginning = .65, end = .79).

4.3.3 Self-Efficacy Scale. Participants' self-efficacy was measured at all three time-points by asking them to rate their confidence in their ability to apply computational thinking in their field ("Your ability to use computational algorithms to solve problems in your field,") [30]. Ratings were done on a scale from 0 (Completely Unconfident) to 100 (Completely Confident). The self-efficacy score was the mean of the items (coefficient alpha: beginning = .92, middle = .96, end = .88).

4.3.4 Course and CCE Ratings. As part of the end-of-semester survey, participants were asked to provide ratings for various aspects of the course and the CCEs. Ratings pertained to perceived "effectiveness," "usefulness," and "interestingness" of various aspects. For the effectiveness rating items the response scale was 1 = not effective, 2 = neither effective nor ineffective, 3 = somewhat effective, 4 = effective, 5 = very effective, and for the usefulness and interestingness rating items the response scale was 1 = very unuseful/uninteresting, 2 = unuseful/uninteresting, 3 = somewhat unuseful/uninteresting, 4 = somewhat useful/interesting, 5 = useful/interesting, 6 = very useful/interesting.

5 Results

The results of the four research questions are presented next. Paired-samples t-tests were used to answer Questions 1 and 2. Repeated-measures analysis of variance (ANOVA) was used to answer Question 3. Descriptive statistics were used to answer Question 4.

5.1 Research Question 1: Did Students' Computational Thinking Knowledge and Skills Increase After Taking the Computational Creativity Course?

The comparison of pre-test and post-test performance was based on the scores of participants who completed both tests. A student who had one of the highest scores on the pre-test and one of the lowest scores on the post-test was determined to be an outlier and was therefore excluded from the analysis of computational thinking test scores. The removal of the outlier resulted in an analysis sample of 23 participants.

Change in Computational Thinking test scores from the beginning to the end of the semester was tested with a paired samples *t*-test. There was a significant increase in scores from the beginning to the end of the semester ($t(22) = 2.106$, $p = .047$, $D = 0.41$). This effect is medium according to the conventional interpretation of Cohen's D. Students' average score was 6.96 at the start of the semester and 8.30 at the end of the semester. This finding supports the hypothesis that test scores would increase for students who completed the Computational Creativity course. The positive effect suggests the online Computational Creativity course can be used to teach computational thinking knowledge and skills to non-CS students.

5.2 Research Question 2: Did Students' Creative Competencies Increase After Taking the Computational Creativity Course?

Change in students' creative competencies from the beginning to the end of the semester was tested with a paired samples *t*-test. There was not a significant change in creative competencies during the semester ($t(25) = -1.301$, $p = .205$, $D = 0.23$). Students' score on the creative competencies scale showed a slight, non-significant decrease from 3.29 at the start of the semester to 3.11 at the end of the semester. Thus, the hypothesis that students' creative competencies would not be impacted was supported.

5.3 Research Question 3: Did Students' Self-Efficacy for Applying Computational Thinking Increase After Taking the Computational Creativity Course?

Repeated-measures (ANOVA) was used to examine change in self-efficacy across all three time points at which data were collected during the semester. Only students who completed the self-efficacy scale at all three times were included in the analysis, resulting in an analysis sample of 20 participants. Students experienced a significant linear increase in self-efficacy during the semester (Wilks' $\Lambda = .408$, $F(2, 18) = 13.050$, $p < .001$, partial $eta^2 = .592$). This effect is large. On average, students' self-efficacy increased from 54.8 at the start of the semester, to 64.7 in the middle of the semester, to 72.9 at the end of the semester. This finding supports the hypothesis that students' self-efficacy would increase during the Computational Creativity course, and it suggests the online Computational Creativity course can be used to increase students' self-efficacy for applying computational thinking in their fields.

5.4 Research Question 4: How Did Students Feel About the Computational Creativity Course?

On the whole, students rated the course and the exercises positively. The following three tables provide descriptive statistics based on the ratings students gave to several aspects of the course and the exercises. Ratings pertain to perceived "usefulness," "interestingness," and "effectiveness." Means and standard deviations for all ratings are given in Tables 1-3.

As shown in Table 1, students generally found the CCEs to be useful and interesting. The Exploring exercise was rated as more useful than interesting, but the Storytelling exercise received considerably higher ratings for interestingness than usefulness. Thinking Inside the Box and Everyday Object were rated similarly in terms of usefulness and interestingness.

The means and standard deviations shown in Table 2 reveal that most students found the problem-solving tasks and analysis and reflection questions to be useful. The collaborative format and exercise Lightbulbs were rated as slightly less useful. Table 3 shows the effectiveness ratings of the CCEs as well as the Computational Creativity course as a whole. Students gave slightly higher ratings to the CCEs than the course, but all average ratings were above the "somewhat effective" threshold (i.e., > 3 out of 5).

6 Discussion and Conclusions

Overall, the findings of this study support the hypotheses: Students in the online Computational Creativity course improved their knowledge of computational thinking and experienced an increase in self-efficacy after taking the course. Prior research has shown that the CCEs improve students' computational thinking knowledge and skills when they are completed as part of a CS course, and these findings indicate they can also have a positive impact when implemented in courses that do not have the same elements of a traditional CS curriculum. The positive effects indicate that it is possible for students to learn computational knowledge and skills through an online course that is neither a programming course nor a CS course. This empirical evidence of the effectiveness of such an online course is reassuring as more and more college courses, in CS and other disciplines, are offered entirely online. The generally positive ratings of both the course and the CCEs is promising, especially considering this was the first time the course was offered entirely online.

Consistent with prior studies [21,25] the Computational Creativity course did not change students' creative competencies. Thus, it seems that instruction informed and supported by the computational creativity framework taps into students' existing creative competencies without necessarily growing them. It is yet to be determined whether the effects of the CCEs or the Computational Creativity course would change if more emphasis were placed on increasing creative competencies alongside learning and self-efficacy. Currently, the creative competencies are reflected in the Creative Objectives of each CCE, but Epstein's [8,9] creative competencies and the scale used to measure them have more to do with one's general habits and tendencies that increase the likelihood one will be creative than any potentially creative actions and ideas generated during individual learning activities like CCEs. For example, one component of *Capturing* is the practice of recording ideas, thoughts, or solutions in a notebook or journal. Students are required to Capture their ideas and work on the CCEs, but the CCEs and the Computational Creativity course do not explicitly encourage students to make this a more general habit, and it is the general habit of *Capturing* that is measured by our scale. Therefore, it is possible students use of *creativity* is changing as they complete CCEs, but not their *creative competencies*, as outlined by Epstein.

Table 1: Ratings of Exercise Usefulness and Interestingness

	Usefulness		**Interestingness**	
Exercises	Mean	SD	Mean	SD
Exploring	4.89	1.25	4.67	1.24
Thinking Inside the Box	4.33	1.44	4.41	1.53
Storytelling	4.48	1.19	4.89	1.09
Everyday Object	4.56	0.85	4.52	1.16

Note. Response scale was 1 = very unuseful (uninteresting), 2 = unuseful (uninteresting), 3 = somewhat unuseful (uninteresting), 4 = somewhat useful (interesting), 5 = useful (interesting), 6 = very useful (interesting). Statistics are based on responses from the 27 students who completed the post-survey.

Table 2: Ratings of CCE Components

How useful was...	**Mean**	**SD**
The collaborative group/teamwork format	4.07	1.52
Problem solving tasks	5.26	0.53
Analysis questions	4.96	0.76
Reflection questions	4.78	1.15
Lightbulbs	4.37	1.39

Note. Response scale was 1 = very unuseful, 2 = unuseful, 3 = somewhat unuseful, 4 = somewhat useful, 5 = useful, 6 = very useful. Statistics are based on responses from the 27 students who completed the post-survey.

The possibility of impacting students' creative competencies should be explored in future studies. It is possible that a curriculum that explicitly targets creative competencies could increase them and also change the impact the CCEs have on learning and self-efficacy. Future research should also compare online and face-to-face versions of computational thinking courses for non-CS majors. Though the study presented here indicates computational thinking skills can be learned through an online class, it does not address the question of whether online and face-to-face instruction yield different learning outcomes.

Table 3: Ratings of the Effectiveness of CCEs and the Computational Creativity Course

Question	Mean	SD
How effective do you think the computational creativity exercises in your course were in meeting their objectives?	4.00	0.86
How effective were the computational creativity exercises in preparing you to use computational thinking creatively in your field?	3.64	1.10
How effective were the computational creativity exercises in helping you understand and use computer science methods and tools in your field?	3.41	1.01
How effective were the computational creativity exercises in giving you ideas about how to think and problem solve more creatively in your field?	3.96	0.84
How effective was the "Computational Creativity" course in meeting its objectives?	3.78	1.39
How effective was the "Computational Creativity" course in preparing you to use computational thinking creatively in your field?	3.59	0.97
How effective was the "Computational Creativity" course in helping you understand and use computer science methods and tools in your field?	3.37	1.18
How effective was the "Computational Creativity" course in giving you ideas about how to think and problem solve more creatively in your field?	3.81	1.00

Note. Response scale was 1 = not effective, 2 = neither effective nor ineffective, 3 = somewhat effective, 4 = effective, 5 = very effective. Statistics are based on responses from the 27 students who completed the post-survey.

Additional research that uses stronger quasi-experimental designs is needed in order to determine how mastery of computational thinking skills through this course compares to that of other similar courses.And, it is important that future research examines the possibility of subgroup differences (e.g., men and women, first-year and advanced students) when teaching computational thinking online. If online computational thinking classes for non-majors, such as the Computational Creativity course, can effectively build students' computational thinking skills, they could be used to further the goal of introducing a wider range of students to computing and computational thinking.

ACKNOWLEDGMENTS

This work was partially supported by the National Science Foundation (Grants No. 0829647, 1431874, and 1122956).

REFERENCES

[1] Merry McDonald, Brian Dorn, and Gary McDonald. 2004. A statistical analysis of student performance in online computer science courses. In *Proceedings of the ACM Technical Symposium on Computer Science Education* (SIGCSE'04). Norfolk, VA, 71-74.

[2] Robert McCloud. 2004. Does an online course work in computer science?. *J. of Computing Sciences in Colleges*, 19, 5 (2004), 260-269.

[3] Joseph D. Dumas. 2016. Online vs. face-to-face student performance in an introduction to operating systems course. *J. of Computing Sciences in Colleges*, 32, 2 (2016), 185-191.

[4] Lynne N. Kennette and Bibia R. Redd. 2015. Instructor presence helps bridge the gap between online and on-campus learning. *College Quarterly*, 18, 4 (Fall 2015).

[5] Tuan Nguyen. 2015. The effectiveness of online learning: Beyond no significant difference and future horizons. *MERLOT J. of Online Learning and Teaching*, 11, 2 (Jun. 2015), 309-319.

[6] Tal Soffer and Rafi Nachmias. 2018. Effectiveness of learning in online academic courses compared with face-to-face courses in higher education. *J. of Computer Assisted Learning*, online first access (2018), 1-10. doi: 10.1111/jcal.12258

[7] Jenette Wing. 2006. Computational thinking. *Commun. of the ACM*, 49 (Mar. 2006), 33-35.

[8] Robert Epstein. 1996. *Cognition, creativity, and behavior: Selected essays.* Praeger, Westport, CT.

[9] Robert Epstein. 2005. Generativity theory and creativity. Theories of creativity. In *Theories of Creativity*, M.A. Runco and R.S. Albert (Eds.). Hampton Press, Cresskill, NJ.

[10] Albert Bandura. 1977. Self-efficacy: Toward a unifying theory of behavioral change. *Psychological Review*, 84, 2 (1977), 191-215.

[11] Mingrui Zhang, Eugene Lundak, Chi-Cheng Lin, Tim Gegg-Harrison, and Joan Francioni. 2007. Interdisciplinary application tracks in an undergraduate computer science curriculum. In *Proceedings of the ACM Technical Symposium on Computer Science Education* (SIGCSE'07). Covington, KY, 425-429.

[12] Zachary Dodds, Ran Libeskind-Hadas, Christine Alvarado, and Geogg Kuenning. 2008. Evaluating a breadth-first CS 1 for scientists. . In *Proceedings of the ACM Technical Symposium on Computer Science Education* (SIGCSE'08). Portland, OR, 266-270.

[13] Thomas J. Cortina. 2007. An introduction to computer science for non-majors using principles of computation. In *Proceedings of the ACM Technical Symposium on Computer Science Education* (SIGCSE'07). Covington, KY, 218–222.

[14] Leen-Kiat Soh, et al. 2009. Renaissance computing: An initiative for promoting student participation in computing. In *Proceedings of the ACM Technical Symposium on Computer Science Education* (SIGCSE'09). Chattanooga, TN, 59-63.

[15] Susanne Hambrusch, Cristoph Hoffmann, John T. Korb, Mark Haugan, and Antony L. Hosking. 2009. A multidisciplinary approach towards computational thinking for science majors. In *Proceedings of the ACM Technical Symposium on Computer Science Education* (SIGCSE'09). Chattanooga, TN, USA. 183-187.

[16] Hong Qin. 2009. Teaching computational thinking through bioinformatics to biology students. In *Proceedings of the ACM Technical Symposium on Computer Science Education* (SIGCSE'09). Chattanooga, TN, USA. 188-191.

[17] Betul Czerkawski and Eugene W. Lyman. 2015. Exploring issues about computational thinking in higher education. *TechTrends*, 59, 2 (Mar./Apr. 2015), 57-65.

[18] John Sweller. 1994. Cognitive load theory, learning difficulty, and instructional design. *Learning and Instruction*, 4, 4 (1994), 295-312.

[19] Bustra Chowdhury, Austin Cory Bart, and Dennis Kafura. 2018. Analysis of collaborative learning in a computational thinking class. In *Proceedings of the ACM Technical Symposium on Computer Science Education* (SIGCSE'18). Baltimore, MD, 143-148.

[20] Leen-Kiat Soh, Duane F. Shell, Elizabeth Ingraham, Stephen Ramsay, and Brian Moore. 2015. Learning through computational creativity. *Commun. ACM*, 58, 8 (Aug. 2015), 33–35.

[21] Duane F. Shell., Leen-Kiat Soh, Abraham E. Flanigan, Markeya S. Peteranetz, and Elizabeth Ingraham. 2017. Improving students' learning and achievement in CS classrooms through computational creativity exercises that integrate computational and creative thinking. In *Proceedings of the ACM Technical Symposium on Computer Science Education* (SIGCSE'17). Seattle, WA, 543-548.

[22] L. Dee Miller, Leen-Kiat Soh, Vlad Chiriacescu, Elizabeth Ingraham, Duane F. Shell, and Melissa Patternson Hazley. 2013. Improving learning of computational thinking using creative thinking exercises in cs-1 computer science courses. In *Proceedings of the 43th Annual Frontiers in Education Conference* (FIE'13). Oklahoma City, OK, 1426-1432.

[23] L. Dee Miller, Leen-Kiat Soh, and Duane F. Shell. 2014. Integrating computational and creative thinking to improve learning and performance in CS1. In *Proceedings of the ACM Technical Symposium on Computer Science Education* (SIGCSE'14). Atlanta, GA, 475-480.

[24] Alex Ruthmann, Jesse M. Heines, Gena R. Greher, Paul Laidler, and Charles

Saulters, II. 2010. Teaching computational thinking through musical live coding in Scratch. In *Proceedings of the ACM Technical Symposium on Computer Science Education* (SIGCSE'10). Milwaukee, WI, 351-355.

[25] Markeya S. Peteranetz, Shiyuan Wang, Duane F. Shell, Abraham E. Flanigan, and Leen-Kiat Soh. 2018. Examining the impact of computational creativity exercises on college computer science students' learning, achievement, self-efficacy, and creativity. In *Proceedings of the ACM Technical Symposium on Computer Science Education* (SIGCSE'18). Baltimore, MD, 155-160.

[26] Duane F. Shell, Melissa Patterson Hazley, Leen-Kiat Soh, L. Dee Miller, Vlad Chiriacescu, and Elizabeth Ingraham. 2014. Improving learning of computational thinking using computational creativity exercises in a college CS1 computer science course for engineers. In *Proceedings of the 44th Annual Frontiers in Education Conference* (FIE'13). Madrid, Spain, 3029-3035.

[27] Markeya S. Peteranetz, Abraham E., Flanigan, Duane F. Shell, and Leen-Kiat Soh. 2017. Computational creativity exercises: An avenue for promoting learning in computer science, *IEEE Transactions on Education*, 60, 4 (Oct. 2017), 305-313. DOI: 10.1109/TE.2017.2705152

[28] Markeya S. Peteranetz, Abraham E. Flanigan, Duane F. Shell, and Leen-Kiat Soh. 2018. Helping engineering students learn in introductory computer science (CS1) using computational creativity exercises (CCEs). *IEEE Transactions on Education*, advance online publication, (2018), 1-9. DOI: 10.1109/TE.2018.2804350

[29] Robert. Epstein, Steven M. Schmidt, and Regina Warfel. 2008. Measuring and training creative competencies: Validation of a new test. *Creativity Research J.*, 20, 7-12.

[30] Duane F. Shell, Leen-Kiat Soh, Abraham E. Flanigan, and Markeya S. Peteranetz., 2016. Students' initial course motivation and their achievement and retention in college CS1 courses. In *Proceedings of the ACM Technical Symposium on Computer Science Education* (SIGCSE'16). Memphis, TN, 639-644.

Facilitating Course Assessment with a Competitive Programming Platform

Daniel Coore
University of the West Indies
Kingston, Jamaica
daniel.coore@uwimona.edu.jm

Daniel Fokum
University of the West Indies
Kingston, Jamaica
daniel.fokum@uwimona.edu.jm

ABSTRACT

We present an initiative that introduced the use of a competitive programming platform as a mechanism for auto-grading assignments for an introductory course on algorithm design and analysis. The specific objective of the intervention was to increase the number of assessed programming exercises to an average of 1 per week. A traditionally large enrolment with only a few graduate assistants available meant that prior to the intervention, few assignments were given, and the duration that students waited for feedback was long. Fresh problems were developed for deployment on the platform, each one targeting the specific learning objectives of the week in which they were given. The assignments were given in the format of a contest, and students were permitted to submit multiple attempts without penalty. There was a public leaderboard that showed real-time standings, but a student's grades depended only on the number of test cases his submissions passed and not on its ranking on the leaderboard. Anecdotally, we observed an increased degree of engagement with the course content. However a statistical analysis shows that the impact of the intervention on student performance, relative to previous instances of the course, was mixed. We discuss these and other findings.

CCS CONCEPTS

• **Social and professional topics** → **Student assessment**; *Computational thinking*; *Computer science education*; *Adult education*; • **Theory of computation** → *Graph algorithms analysis*; *Data structures design and analysis*; Algorithm design techniques.

KEYWORDS

Competitive Programming, Managing Enrolment Growth

ACM Reference Format:
Daniel Coore and Daniel Fokum. 2019. Facilitating Course Assessment with a Competitive Programming Platform. In *Proceedings of the 50th ACM Technical Symposium on Computer Science Education (SIGCSE '19), February 27-March 2, 2019, Minneapolis, MN, USA.* ACM, New York, NY, USA, 7 pages. https://doi.org/10.1145/3287324.3287511

SIGCSE '19, February 27-March 2, 2019, Minneapolis, MN, USA

ACM ISBN 978-1-4503-5890-3/19/02...$15.00
https://doi.org/10.1145/3287324.3287511

1 INTRODUCTION

It is a common belief that student performance can be improved through regular assessments coupled with corrective feedback [4]. We subscribe to this belief; but in the face of growing undergraduate enrolments and static levels of graduate student assistance, achieving sufficient levels of student assessment with quick feedback can be difficult, especially in core classes for a computing major. We describe an intervention in a core computing class on algorithm analysis that uses a platform for competitive programming to deliver auto-assessed assignments. The initial motivation was to solve a challenge of available human resources, but the initiative also introduced an element of gamification to the course, which had interesting side effects. We discuss the impact of the intervention both in quantitative and qualitative terms.

COMP2211 (Analysis of Algorithms) is a core course in the Computer Science and Software Engineering majors, and introduces students to methods for analysing algorithm performance in general and to classic algorithms for common abstract problems (e.g. sorting, graph traversal, and path optimisation). The course is delivered through 3 lecture hours and 1 tutorial hour per week. The students have typically been at college for at least 1 year, and have completed a year of introductory courses on programming, exposing them to functional, procedural and object-oriented programming. They have also been exposed to rudimentary data structures, such as lists, trees, queues and stacks. Lectures are delivered primarily face to face, facilitated by an online virtual learning environment.

The course is assessed through a combination of written and/or programming assignments (30%), two online quizzes (10%), one midterm exam (10%) and a (written) final exam (50%). Enrolment in this course over the past 5 years has steadily increased from approximately 100 to nearly 150, but the allocation of two teaching assistants has not increased over that period.

Prior to the intervention, there were only two assignments totalling the 30% weight, and students were given 2 weeks to complete each. The number of assignments was primarily determined by the number that could be reasonably assessed and returned given the assistance available. The larger assignments (2 week duration) were given to compensate for the low number so that all of the topics of the course could be assessed by at least 1 item of coursework before students sat the comprehensive final exam.

The *Hacker Rank*™ platform [1] serves as an online judge for programming contests and provides facilities for members of its community to build custom problems and custom contests. A user with ordinary privileges may create a custom problem by supplying the text of the problem and a suite of tests (input and expected output pairs). The platform can accept solutions implemented in any of the supported programming languages (over 30 in all) and will automatically judge a submission to a problem by evaluating the submitted code on the associated test suite. In the context of a contest, it will assign points proportional to the weights assigned to the tests, and maintain a leaderboard for the problem, as well as for the overall contest. Contestants may submit solutions multiple times; potential penalties for incorrect submissions are configurable on the platform.

We used the *Hacker Rank™* platform to create a collection of contests, which served as graded assignments for the course, to be given out nearly[1] weekly. Each week's contest was populated with custom problems that tested knowledge of the topics taught in the preceding week's lectures. A student's grade for a problem was determined entirely by the subset of test cases passed, and not on his/her rank in the leaderboard. The other components of the course (quizzes, midterm and final) were unchanged, as were the nominal weights associated with each component. So, the essential difference was that the two (2) assignments of the previous incarnation, worth an average of 15% each, were now replaced with ten (10) assignments worth an average of 3% each. All other aspects of the course's assessment remained the same. Importantly though, since assignments were now being assessed through a contest platform, students had the opportunity to make multiple attempts. No penalties were given for repeated submissions to the same problem, so there was real potential for students to obtain a perfect score on each assignment. We expected this change to have had a positive impact on student engagement, and on overall performance in the course.

At the end of the course, we compared the students' performances on the final exam and the midterm exam with those of their counterparts in 2 previous cohorts. We restricted our comparison to only those years because there were other differences between earlier offerings of the course and that of 2017. A Welch t-test revealed that there was a statistically significant (at the 95% confidence level) improvement in the mean final exam score over the 2015 cohort, but the improvement over 2016 could only be asserted at the 90% confidence level. The relative improvement of performance in the midterm exams was also mixed, but this time the statistically significant improvement was over the 2016 cohort.

We also gathered evidence of student engagement from the statistics of attempts submitted to the platform. Qualitatively, we found that there were largely two categories of student responses to the problems posed in the assignments: those who were intimidated to the point of not submitting an attempt at any problem, and those who were spurred on to strive for perfection – sometimes going to efforts well beyond what they would normally be inclined to expend. We discuss the impact these observations may have had on the objective measures of individual performance, and how they might be mitigated in future attempts to use a competitive programming platform as a tool to assist assessment.

2 BACKGROUND

Eddy and Hogan [3] shows that increased course structure leads to better student performance. An example of a high-structure course is one where students have more than one reading quiz per week, students engage with the content for more than 40% of the class time, and students have more than one graded review assignment per week. A moderate structure course, which was what was used in [3] has an optional graded preparatory assignment per week, students engage with content in-class for 15–40% of the class time, and students have one optional graded review assignment per week. Such an intervention improved course performance for all students, but it worked especially well for black students [3].

There is a general belief in educational literature that indicates that more frequent testing raises performance [2]. For example, Kitchen et al. [7] indicated that students were better able to solve difficult items of experimental data interpretation in a cell biology course if they had been tested with multiple exams. As a result, Bailey et al. [2] studied the use of weekly formative exams and creative grading in an introductory biology course. This was also an instance of having improved course structure. Bailey et al. [2] found that using weekly formative exams and a creative grading scheme resulted in students who were more tenacious, and had improved performance on the final exam, particularly at higher levels of Bloom's taxonomy.

Gholami and Zhang [5] used weekly quizzes in a Computer Organization course and found that student performance in the quizzes was strongly correlated with final exam performance. One possible explanation of this correlation is that weekly quizzes develop good habits that lend themselves to better student performance. Gholami and Zhang [5] also noticed that students who performed poorly on the final exam tended to start the quizzes much closer to their due date. This latter finding from [5] is similar to what was found in [8].

Sheshadri *et al.* [9] studied log files from four online sources, viz., a learning management system (LMS), forum, version control, and homework sytem. They show that a student's class performance is associated with students' activity. As was found in [5, 8], students with good study habits tend to have better final grades [9].

With the leaderboard, and story-like problem definitions, our intervention has aspects of gamification, although peripheral to the primary purpose of the intervention. Ibáñez et al. [6] reviewed the use of gamification to teach aspects of the C programming language to undergraduate engineering students. They found that the gamified approach to C worked, because students continued working and learning programming topics, i.e., students were cognitively engaged, even after earning the maximum number of grade points [6]. Souza *et al.* [10] reported on the use of a leaderboard in a software engineering course. They reported that students used the leaderboard to compare themselves to others in the course, and changed their study habits when their performance lagged the class [10]. We expected to observe similar patterns of engagement, but we did not attempt to measure changes in study habits in this study. Rather, we confined ourselves to observations of assessment results in order to measure the impact of the intervention.

3 METHOD OF IMPLEMENTATION

A total of 10 contests were created for weekly distribution (in weeks not already containing one of the other types of coursework assessment). Each contest was associated with a set of topics from the week(s) of lecture falling between it and its immediate predecessor (typically a span of one week). Questions were then designed to

[1] No assignments were given out in the same week as another coursework component

populate each contest. Each question would target one or more of the topics identified. Question difficulty and overall contest difficulty were moderated by assigning point value to questions based on the time a student would be expected to spend on the question. Each week's contest contained a total of 50 points (except for an occasional bonus question) comprised of 2 to 3 questions, each of which was valued at between 10 and 30 points.

Below is a summary of the approximate interpretation of the relative difficulty of a question, based on its value in points.

10 points Very Easy: the problem is directly related to a lecture topic, and requires little else to implement its solution

15 points Easy: the problem has one main idea related to a lecture topic, but may require some additional ideas that have either been learned in a prerequisite course or relatively early in this course.

20 points Par: The solution to the problem requires use of multiple topics from recent lecture(s), or one in an indirect way, or may require a fair amount of code to fully implement.

25 points Harder: The problem is like a "Par" question, but somehow is slightly more difficult: either through more code required, a less direct connection to lecture material, or relies on multiple recent topics from the course

30 points Hard: The problem requires more code than typically is required, and probably requires a number of ideas previously taught to be well understood in order for the solution to be successfully implemented.

The qualitative associations with the point values above were suggestive and not enforced in any rigorous way. Often we would use a comparative reference to a problem in a previous week with a given point value to determine what might be appropriate for a given problem in the current week. This was done as a kind of independent determination of the relative difficulty of a problem to try to ensure that the 50 points associated with each week's contest, amounted to an equal amount of time that we believed students would need to complete each week's assignment. Students were not told of the qualitative interpretations of the point values of each problem. They did know the actual point values though.

The *Hacker Rank™* platform permits multiple submissions to the same problem. The penalty for incorrect submissions is configurable. We opted not to penalize multiple submissions, so that students could use the assignments in a formative way. It was our intention that the opportunity to repeatedly submit a solution and tweak it until it worked would encourage students to engage with the content more than if they had a single opportunity to submit (as would have been the case in the previous instances of the course).

Points were awarded to solutions purely on the basis of the total weight of the test cases that were passed. Although the *Hacker Rank™* platform permits full customization of the weights of each test case, we opted to keep each test case at the same point value, and modulate the degree of success through the design of the test case suite. Since this was an algorithms course, the difficulty of a test case was often measured by the size of the input. Like any other online judge, the *Hacker Rank™* platform gives each submission a limited time to execute on each test case. So test cases can be designed to distinguish between solutions of different time complexities. Test cases were typically divided into 4 bands based on input-size:

Small: Often, even a brute force solution could pass these tests. These were present to indicate correctness of the algorithm. Students were told that if they got these right, then it implied that they probably at least understood the problem to be solved.

Moderate 1: These aimed to rule out brute force solutions that did not even attempt to make any optimizations (if any were readily available). Clever or efficient implementations of sub-optimal algorithms (ones that used an algorithm of higher computational complexity than the one intended) could perhaps still pass these test cases.

Moderate 2: These were aimed at ruling out a solution that implemented an algorithm that was sub-optimal by at least a factor of n (where n is the input size). For example, if the expected solution would be a $\Theta(n)$ time algorithm, these test cases would rule out a $\Theta(n^2)$ time algorithm, but a $\Theta(n \log n)$ time algorithm might pass, depending on the size of the hidden constant in the Θ notation.

Large: These were aimed at ruling out any solutions with slower running times than the intended algorithm. They would often be sized at the very upper limits of the constraints for the inputs.

A typical problem would have a test suite containing 15 test cases, which were typically divided across the 4 size bands in the ratio 5:4:3:3, with each test case being valued the same. This approach allowed students who understood the problem sufficiently well to at least muster a brute force solution to score some points, while trying to proportionately reward them for their additional effort at applying the concepts taught in lectures.

Of course, some problems had more than one solution with the same time complexity, all of which would pass these test cases. In these cases, we would examine the alternative solutions that we could imagine, and determine whether each merited full marks in the spirit of the question. If each alternative solution was based on knowledge from the course (or perhaps even a more advanced course) we would leave the problem as it was. On the other hand, if the problem could be solved equally efficiently using only knowledge from a prerequisite course, we would modify the problem (or replace it altogether).

For example, a problem that we may have anticipated solving in $\Theta(n \log n)$ time, using a binary heap, but which turned out to be solvable in the same asymptotic running time using a clever combination of an efficient sort and only native vectors (Python lists) or arrays would probably have been left intact, even if the targeted topic was binary heaps. On the other hand, if the sorted vector implementation was the "most natural" approach (e.g. if the data input to the problem was static) then the problem would have been modified.

A part of our testing process for the quality of a question was to adjust the test suites to ensure that a solution that violated the spirit of the problem would not earn too many points. For example, a problem that intended for a limited number of binary searches to be performed would be tested with a brute force solution that used unrestricted exhaustive searches to ensure that such a solution did not get more than a particular threshold score. That threshold varied with the relative point of the semester where the contest fell; the earlier in the semester, the higher the tolerance for brute force solutions, and therefore the higher the threshold was set.

The first week (called *Week 0*) was used as an orientation exercise to ensure that students performed the necessary steps to obtain a user ID on the *Hacker Rank™* platform and learned how to submit code to the platform for judging. The problems for *Week 0* were related to topics that would have been taught in prerequisite courses. So, in some ways, it also set expectations for the level of programming skill anticipated in the student.

4 RESULTS

The course had 146 students at the last offering, with 74.7% of these being male. The average age of the students was 21. In addition, approximately 70% of the students were taking the course for the very first time.

We hypothesized that the objective measures of student performance would improve, so we chose to compare performances on written exams (both the final and the midterm) between the cohort with the intervention, and each of the previous cohorts dating back to 2015. In each of the 3 years reported on, the course structure and content was identical, apart from the intervention, and it was delivered by the same lecturer. All elements of the course's assessment have remained the same throughout the 3 years reported, apart from the number and weight of the assignments as defined by the intervention.

Question 1 of the final exam is a compulsory question which tests for the ability to analyse the running time of a code fragment, as well as to use tools such as the Master Theorem to solve recurrence relations. We chose to assess it along with the overall final and midterm grades, because it represented a more focused assessment component whose results could be reliably interpreted, in the event that either of the other two measurements proved to be inconclusive.

4.1 Statistics

On each of the final exam and the midterm exam, the maximum score achievable was 50 marks. The maximum achievable marks on Question 1 of the final was 20. The mean aggregate score for the final of the 2017 cohort was 24.7 and the standard deviation was 11.4. The Shapiro-Wilk test indicated that the distribution of the aggregate scores was normal.

An unpaired Welch two sample t-test (no assumption of equal variance) was performed on each pair of cohorts being compared for each of the mentioned assessed components. The null hypothesis in each case was that the difference between the mean score for the 2017 cohort and that of the other year's was zero. So the p-value reflects the significance level at which we can say that the mean performance was actually different (i.e., if it is less than 0.05, we may say that we are 95% confident that the means do differ, and in the same direction as the sign of the t parameter). Table 1 presents a summary of the tests.

Table 1 shows that the results of our intervention are inconclusive when considered in terms of the overall final grade or midterm grade. For example, it is statistically significant at the 0.05 level that the mean final grade in 2017 was larger than that of 2015, but we cannot say the same when comparing 2017 to 2016 (the significance

Table 1: Results of two-sided Welch t-tests comparing performances in 2017 with those of 2016 and 2015.

	2017	2016	2015
Mean Final Exam	24.693	22.636	20.876
d.o.f.		240.33	231.06
t		1.6575	3.2381
p-value		0.09872	0.00138
Mean Q1 of Final	12.062	9.556	6.767
d.o.f.		243.95	232.35
t		4.4205	9.7026
p-value		1.483×10^{-5}	$< 2.2 \times 10^{-16}$
Mean Midterm	21.454	18.206	20.885
d.o.f.		298.01	243.17
t		2.6851	0.42579
p-value		0.007657	0.6706

is only at the 0.10 level). The results are reversed when we examine the midterm grade: the 2017 grades are better than the 2016 grades, but not than the 2015 grades. Interestingly, we can conclude that the intervention appears to have had a definite impact on the performance on Question 1 of the final. When the results of 2017 were compared with each of 2016 and 2015, the difference in 2017 was better than in each year, and these results were statistically significant even at levels below 0.0001. This result, although narrow, is qualitatively useful since Question 1 always covers the basic elements of algorithm analysis, including: simplifying orders of growth, solving recurrence relations, and analysing the asymptotic running time of a given code fragment using a rigorous methodology.

4.2 Student Engagement

Feedback from students on the intervention was collected in an informal way, sometimes briefly at the start of the first lecture of the week, but most often in a free session after a lecture or a tutorial. The students offering feedback were prompted to respond to open-ended questions about the level of difficulty of the assignments, their apparent relevance to lectures, and their contribution to the students' learning. The collection of students responding would be ad hoc, according to who happened to be present at the time of the solicitation.

We observed from the anecdotal student feedback that some were struggling with the frequent demands of critical thinking exercises that were now being assessed (such exercises had always been present in tutorial assignments, but those are not assessed). Some admitted having weaknesses with programming competence that were now being exposed by the problems. Interestingly, some students welcomed this because they claimed it helped them to focus on topics they recognised that they did not know well enough. Unfortunately, we were also told of some students who had been discouraged to the point of surrender. On the other hand, some students reported that the exercises were refreshing, and made them feel empowered by an improvement in their problem solving competence.

Our examination of the statistics of interaction with the *Hacker Rank™* platform reflect the generality of some of these anecdotal reports. The platform provides statistics on the total number of

Table 2: Student engagement as measured by attempts at each assignment.

Week	HackerRank Logins	HackerRank Submissions	Student Submissions	Adjusted Logins	Adjusted %
0	124	98	91	117	78%
1	157	135	131	153	86%
2	156	136	131	151	87%
3	148	115	108	141	77%
4	140	60	59	139	42%
5	133	81	78	130	60%
6	142	114	110	138	80%
7	130	67	62	125	50%
8	141	88	80	133	60%
9	121	51	48	118	41%

logins and submissions; however, it is also publicly accessible to anyone with the link to the contest. We observed that a few students who were not in the course were actually regularly attempting the problems. To capture data on student engagement from these statistics, we adjusted the *Hacker Rank™* data by observing the actual number of scores reported by students each week. (Due to the public nature of the platform the students were asked to report their scores through the course's virtual learning environment to ensure that only the scores of students registered for the course were recognised by the assessment process.) Table 2 shows all the data captured about logins and submissions. It reflects the adjusted measures of, for each week's assignment: the number of students logging in (accessing the questions), the number submitting a solution at least once, and the corresponding percentage of logins who submitted.

We consider this percentage to be a measure of the degree to which students made an attempt at each week's assignment. Most weeks it was over 60%. The low attempt rate of week 4 was a reflection of the difficulty of that week's assignment, and should be considered an outlier. Students complained in that week of the difficulty of one of the problems in particular.

The relatively high numbers of logins, but low percentage of submissions towards the end of the course is an interesting data point. It is an indication that many students were at least reading the problems, but they were either unwilling or unable to even produce a rudimentary (e.g. brute force) solution to them. We regard this as a kind of conditional engagement, where it appears that students would be willing to attempt the problems only if they found them tractable (whether at first glance, or after some effort). The causes for the observations certainly warrant further investigation – whether they are related to time management, competence, or motivation (or some combination of the three) should inform any intervention to try to improve the submission rate.

The *Hacker Rank™* statistics also provided access to each attempt made by each student to each problem. We tallied up the total number of attempts, distinguishing between attempts that were made before the deadline, and those after. The fine-grained data could potentially be examined deeper than we have done, but doing so would have required better analytic tools, than we had at our disposal, for extracting summary information from the web pages containing that data. Nevertheless, examining the effort put in by students after the deadline provided us with a measure of their cognitive engagement, since there was no direct reward from the assessment process for doing that. Table 3 presents the total number of submissions made for each assignment, and the average number per student per problem.

Table 3: Student engagement as measured by submissions made to all problems in each week's assignment.

Week	Submissions before deadline	Submissions after deadline	Total	Avg. per student per problem
0	837	27	864	4.41
1	2823	50	2873	7.09
2	1754	44	1798	3.31
3	1956	44	2000	5.80
4	686	16	702	5.85
5	797	64	861	3.54
6	1900	57	1957	8.58
7	717	27	744	5.55
8	953	76	1029	5.85
9	452	4	456	4.47

All students were aware that their grade would be determined purely by the number of points reflected on the leaderboard for a particular assignment. Furthermore, they were aware that once the contest closed, it would stop updating the leaderboard. Therefore, it is reasonable to interpret all submissions after the deadline (especially those many minutes, hours or days after) as attempts made in the interest of learning.

The average number of submissions per person per problem is also an indicator of deliberate effort that was probably leading to learning. An assignment with a high average implies that students were repeatedly attempting to obtain a perfect score, and therefore believed that it was within their ability to do so. A finer measure of the data would be required to extract better information, because in some instances, a low average was obtained because one question was perceived to be very difficult, and it consequently had very few attempts.

4.3 Effects of Gamification

The *Hacker Rank™* platform maintains a leaderboard for the overall contest, as well as for each question. Rank on the leaderboard is determined by an entrant's score (in points) and in the case of ties, by time of completion. For the purposes of their grade, a student's rank on the leaderboard had no role to play. Yet, we see from Table 4 that for many of the assignments, an attempt to solve at least one problem was made within 1 hour of release of the assignment. Assignments were released on Sunday night at midnight, and the first lecture for the week was on Monday at 11am. Since there was no assessment credit given for rank, and the release time of the assignment was not a time when students would typically

Table 4: Student engagement as measured by time in minutes for first submission after the release of each assignment at midnight on Sunday.

Week	Earliest Submission (mins)
0	844
1	1041
2	17
3	297
4	1
5	44
6	45
7	487
8	2118
9	78
Mean	497.2

begin an assignment due the following week, we interpret this degree of eagerness as a form of engagement that was fueled by the gamification aspect of the use of the platform.

The data in Table 4 illustrates the effect of gamification on student behaviour. We believe that gamification had at least two observable effects on student behaviour arising from the use of the *Hacker Rank™* platform:

- Students started the assignments sooner, a few even immediately upon release.
- Students used others' performances as motivation or demotivation, depending on how they viewed their own abilities relative to those would typically be at the top of the leaderboard.

Informal discussions with students also made it clear that they paid attention to which students were at the top of the leaderboard. Interestingly, we observed two types of reactions to who was at the top of the leaderboard. Students who viewed themselves as contenders strived harder to make it to the top, and students who did not would become demotivated if they noticed that the usual top scorers had not yet done a problem.

4.4 Correlation between Assignments and Final Exam

Figure 1 shows, from the relatively narrow confidence interval, that there was good correlation between students' performances on the assignments and their performances on the final exam. We speculate that the mixed overall results of the t-tests is a consequence of separate populations of the class being affected in opposite directions by the weekly programming assignments.

5 DISCUSSION AND CONCLUSION

Given the large increase in frequency and number of assignments, we predicted that the objective measures of student individual performance would improve over that of previous cohorts. Therefore, we were somewhat surprised to discover that the improvement of the final exam over the 2016 cohort could not be established at the 0.05 significance level. Nevertheless, we noted that our predictions

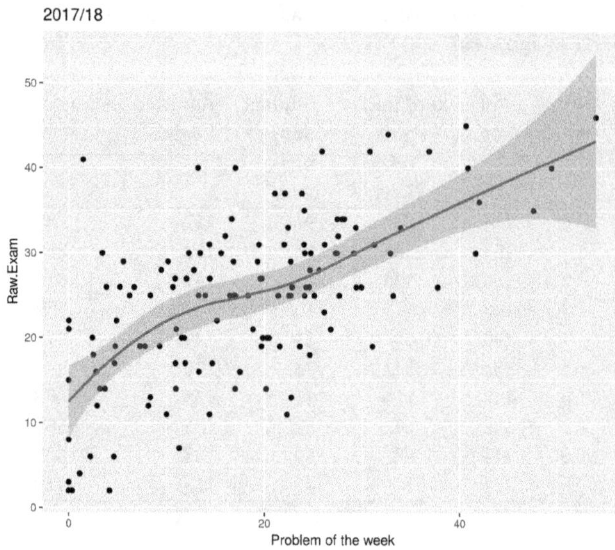

Figure 1: Scatterplot of raw exam scores versus weighted problem of the week scores

were fulfilled relative to the 2015 cohort, and that at least on the compulsory Question 1 of the final (which tended to focus on the fundamentals of the course) the performance of the 2017 cohort was an improvement over the previous two years.

Anecdotally many students described how having to pass all of the test cases on the *Hacker Rank™* platform made them better appreciate how running times and computational complexity were related to each other. Perhaps this is the explanation for the improved performance on Question 1 of the final. A more formal mechanism for collecting feedback should be developed in order to probe the interventions that could help students who are unable (or unwilling) to submit a solution, when faced with a challenging question, as revealed by the data in Table 2. Such an investigation would probably require a closer look at the negative effects of gamification on students who have low self-confidence.

The intervention is worth repeating because the degree of engagement as measured by times to start the assignment, and the number of attempts per question was high. Anecdotally, some students reported feeling more competent and better equipped to address novel problems. Admittedly these were the better students, and perhaps the mixed results on overall scores of either the midterm or the final is a reflection that the intervention did not have a uniform effect on all the different types of learners in the class. A further study would be required to try to discern the degree of benefit to each type of learner of such an intervention. Furthermore, we expect that data over more years would help to clarify the mixed results that we observed.

REFERENCES

[1] 2018. HackerRank. (2018). https://www.hackerrank.com/

[2] E. G. Bailey, J. Jensen, J. Nelson, H. K. Wiberg, and J. D. Bell. 2017. Weekly Formative Exams and Creative Grading Enhance Student Learning in an Introductory Biology Course. *CBE–Life Sciences Education* 16, 1 (2017), ar2. DOI: http://dx.doi.org/10.1187/cbe.16-02-0104

[3] S. L. Eddy and K. A. Hogan. 2014. Getting Under the Hood: How and for Whom Does Increasing Course Structure Work? *CBE–Life Sciences Education* 13, 3 (2014), 453–468. DOI: http://dx.doi.org/10.1187/cbe.14-03-0050

[4] S. Freeman, D. Haak, and M. P. Wenderoth. 2011. Increased Course Structure Improves Performance in Introductory Biology. *CBE–Life Sciences Education* 10, 2 (2011), 175–186. DOI: http://dx.doi.org/10.1187/cbe.10-08-0105

[5] A. Gholami and L. Y. Zhang. 2018. Student Behaviour in Unsupervised Online Quizzes: A Closer Look. In *Proceedings of the 23rd Western Canadian Conference on Computing Education (WCCCE '18)*. ACM, New York, NY, USA, 8:1–8:6. DOI: http://dx.doi.org/10.1145/3209635.3209650

[6] M. B. Ibanez, A. Di-Serio, and C. Delgado-Kloos. 2014. Gamification for engaging computer science students in learning activities: A case study. *IEEE Transactions on Learning Technologies* 7, 3 (7 2014), 291–301. DOI: http://dx.doi.org/10.1109/TLT.2014.2329293

[7] E. Kitchen, J. D. Bell, S. Reeve, R. R. Sudweeks, and W. S. Bradshaw. 2003. Teaching Cell Biology in the Large-Enrollment Classroom: Methods to Promote Analytical Thinking and Assessment of Their Effectiveness. *Cell Biology Education* 2, 3 (2003), 180–194. DOI: http://dx.doi.org/10.1187/cbe.02-11-0055

[8] A. M. Metz. 2008. The effect of access time on online quiz performance in large biology lecture courses. *Biochemistry and Molecular Biology Education* 36, 3 (5 2008), 196–202. DOI: http://dx.doi.org/10.1002/bmb.20184

[9] A. Sheshadri, N. Gitinabard, C. F. Lynch, T. Barnes, and S. Heckman. 2018. Predicting Student Performance Based on Online Study Habits: A Study of Blended Courses. In *Proc. 11th International Conference on Educational Data Mining*, K. E. Boyer and M. Yudelson (Eds.). Buffalo, NY, 411–417. http://educationaldatamining.org/files/conferences/EDM2018/papers/EDM2018_paper_147.pdf

[10] M. R. A. Souza, K. F. Constantino, L. F. Veado, and E. M. L. Figueiredo. 2017. Gamification in Software Engineering Education: An Empirical Study. In *IEEE 30th Conference on Software Engineering Education and Training (CSEE&T)*. IEEE, 276–284. DOI: http://dx.doi.org/10.1109/CSEET.2017.51

Development of a Lean Computational Thinking Abilities Assessment for Middle Grades Students

Eric Wiebe†
North Carolina State University
Raleigh, NC USA
wiebe@ncsu.edu

Jennifer London
London & Assoc.
Raleigh, NC USA
londonje@gmail.com

Osman Aksit
Dhahran Ahliyya Schools
Dammam, Saudi Arabia
osmanaksit@gmail.com

Bradford W. Mott
North Carolina State University
Raleigh, NC USA
bwmott@ncsu.edu

Kristy Elizabeth Boyer
University of Florida
Gainesville, FL USA
keboyer@ufl.edu

James C. Lester
North Carolina State University
Raleigh, NC USA
lester@ncsu.edu

ABSTRACT

The recognition of middle grades as a critical juncture in CS education has led to the widespread development of CS curricula and integration efforts. The goal of many of these interventions is to develop a set of underlying abilities that has been termed computational thinking (CT). This goal presents a key challenge for assessing student learning: we must identify assessment items associated with an emergent understanding of key cognitive abilities underlying CT that avoid specialized knowledge of specific programming languages. In this work we explore the psychometric properties of assessment items appropriate for use with middle grades (US grades 6-8; ages 11-13) students. We also investigate whether these items measure a single ability dimension. Finally, we strive to recommend a "lean" set of items that can be completed in a single 50-minute class period and have high face validity. The paper makes the following contributions: 1) adds to the literature related to the emerging construct of CT, and its relationship to the existing CTt and Bebras instruments, and 2) offers a research-based CT assessment instrument for use by both researchers and educators in the field.

CCS CONCEPTS

• Social and professional topics → Computational thinking; Student assessment; K- 12 education

KEYWORDS

computational thinking, IRT, psychometrics, K-12 computer science education, middle grades, assessment

SIGCSE '19, February 27-March 2, 2019, Minneapolis, MN, USA

ACM ISBN 978-1-4503-5890-3/19/02...$15.00
https://doi.org/10.1145/3287324.3287390

ACM Reference format:
E. Wiebe, J. London, O. Aksit, B. W. Mott, K. E. Boyer and J. C. Lester. 2019. Development of a Lean Computational Thinking Abilities Assessment for Middle Grades Students. In *Proceedings of the 50th ACM Technical Symposium on Computer Science Education (SIGCSE'19), Feb. 27-Mar. 2, 2019, Minneapolis, MN, USA.* ACM, New York, NY, USA, 6 pages. https://doi.org/10.1145/3287324.3287390

1 INTRODUCTION

The recognition of middle grades as a critical juncture in CS education has, expectedly, led to the development of curricula and other interventions in both formal and informal educational settings [1-4]. An equal effort has gone into elective classes in areas such as robotics (e.g., [5]), maker-based activities (e.g., [6]), in addition to block-based programming (e.g., [7]). It follows that work has gone into developing assessments for the targeted knowledge and practices that these curricula and interventions address [8].

Part of the assessment challenge is that the goal of such interventions has, over the past ten years, shifted away from only a specific goal of teaching CS concepts and programming abilities, to developing a set of underlying abilities that has been termed computational thinking (CT) [9, 10]. The emergence of CT as a conceptual framework guiding curricular development and assessment [11, 12] has happened in parallel with a move to think more broadly as to which types of educational contexts might be appropriate for students to engage in CT-based activities. In particular, this has included a strong move to integrate CT activities into established STEM courses at the middle grades and high school level [2, 13-15]. Such approaches appropriately demand a strategy that assumes that CT ability is being developed across multiple formal and informal academic contexts [5]. Similarly, assessments that measure both what students bring to a particular intervention and how that intervention impacts their knowledge and abilities, to be effective, would need to be decontextualized to some degree from the particular application or academic subject area.

The growth of interest in integrated CT interventions points to a need to develop CT assessments that can work in such diverse instructional contexts [16-18]. However, most assessments developed for either CS or CT at the middle grades level are still based on CS frameworks around the construction or analysis of coding artifacts [4, 8, 19, 20]. These assessments use a range of text-based, block-based, and pseudo-code, but still use coding artifacts based on CS concepts as the paradigm for analysis [21, 22]. It raises questions as to whether such instruments would be appropriate as a pre-test for students who have never had experience with developing code or for interventions where coding is not the basis of the CT curricular intervention [23]. For example, many interventions utilize unplugged activities that may be independent of specific code-based representational schemes and syntaxes [3, 9, 24]. In addition, many assessments are not only written with programming artifacts as the task, but also represent CS-centric conceptual frameworks, rather than CT frameworks [19]. In summary, an assessment—particularly a pre-assessment—should reflect core CT abilities being developed in the intervention but be free from specialized representational notations (e.g., programming languages) or knowledge that a student would not have been exposed to outside the intervention. Put another way, you may want to distinguish abilities related to underlying CT constructs apart from specialized knowledge of programming ability, and a code-centric assessment would not allow you to do this. Additional associated problems from a code-centric assessment might include both floor effects of pre-assessment scores and/or frustration on the part of students faced with what amounts to a foreign language.

The goal of the work presented in this paper is pragmatic. Leveraging both theoretical and empirical work done to date, we have set out to identify assessments associated with a current emergent understanding of key cognitive abilities underlying CT. These assessments should avoid the abovementioned concerns related to specialized knowledge related to programming languages or other allied CS knowledge. In doing this work, we will explore the psychometric properties of items appropriate for use with middle grades (U.S. grades 6-8; ages 11-13) students. We will also investigate whether these items represent a single dimension of ability. Finally, we will strive to recommend a set of items that has a relatively short administration (i.e., can be completed in a single 50-minute class period) and have high face validity for both teachers and students.

2 RELATED WORK

An important line of work to develop a CT assessment independent both of specific programming languages and curricular contexts has been led by Román-González and colleagues [25-27]. They chose to take a psychometric approach rooted in the CHC model of intelligence [28, 29]. Román-González [26] and a small number of other researchers (e.g., [30]) have conjectured a relationship between CT constructs such as abstraction, pattern generalization, algorithmic thinking, and conditional logic, and the CHC constructs of fluid intelligence, visual processing, and working memory. The design of their items were informed both by prior assessments developed around CS-centric programming tasks [31, 32], as well as other efforts developing programming-independent assessments [33, 34].

Using a 28-item version of his computational thinking assessment (CTt) [26] on a sample of 1,251 Spanish students, boys and girls from 24 different schools enrolled from 5th to 10th grade, Román-González established reliability as internal consistency with a Cronbach's Alpha = 0.793. Criterion validity was explored first by looking at correlations between the CTt and the PMA battery of cognitive tests, and then through a multiple linear regression through the CTt score. The CTt moderately correlated with the PMA spatial (r = 0.44) and reasoning ability (r = 0.44), and weakly correlated with verbal reasoning (r = 0.27). In addition, it was strongly correlated with the RP30 problem-solving test (r = 0.67) which is considered a proxy for fluid intelligence. The regression with these same subscales was also significant ($p < 0.01$), with spatial and reasoning ability as significant predictors. However, 73% of the CTt scores' variance was left unexplained. Román-González, Pérez-González, & Jiménez-Fernández [26] observed a near-normal distribution (M=16.38, .058 skewness, and -.446 kurtosis) among 1,251 Spanish students from 5th-10th grade. Items spanned a wide array of difficulty with later questions being hardest. The average success rate along the 28 items was p = 0.59 (medium difficulty); ranging from p = 0.16 (item 23; very high difficulty) to p = 0.96 (item 1; very low difficulty). In summary, the CTt was shown to have an appropriate distribution of item difficulty for middle grades students. In addition, the CTt seems to measure abilities related to fluid intelligence and spatial ability, however a majority of the differences in student performance ability on the assessment was not explained by these particular cognitive abilities.

The authors conclude that the CTt provides a decontextualized assessment that compliments assessments designed to be more context-specific. It is interesting to note that many of the CTt items have block-based programming-like elements in them, raising concerns that this assessment would suffer from floor effects with students not familiar with block-based programming concepts. However, a recent study using the CTt did not find this effect with a population of students of whom a high proportion self-reported little or no prior programming experience [35]. Further work by Román-González and colleagues continued to explore the complimentary utility of CTt with other either programming-centric or more general assessments. In a convergent validity study, they found a high correlation between the CTt and Dr. Scratch [36] (r = 0.44) and with the CTt and a selected set of Bebras [33, 34] items (r = 0.52). They conclude that the correlational results point to a partial but not complete overlap between the three assessments, reflecting the designers' differing measurement goals. Thus the conclusion was that CTt and Bebras are measuring somewhat different abilities.

Bebras, it should be said, started not as an assessment, but as an international competition with the stated goal of raising awareness and interest in informatics (i.e., computing/computer science) education and career paths [33, 34]. It was designed to promote informatics learning in school by solving short, conceptually-based tasks that make up the heart of the competition. Since its beginnings in Lithuania in 2004, it has grown to the point that more than 1.3 million individuals across Europe and elsewhere participated in the competition during Bebras week in November 2015 [34]. Like the CTt, Bebras was designed to not depend on prior knowledge of programming/coding [37], but instead has puzzle-like problem-solving tasks readily accessible to students with no programming background. Though Bebras' roots are not as an assessment instrument (CS or otherwise), researchers have noted the ability to map its items to problem-solving constructs that underlie CS/CT, such as algorithmic thinking and working with structures and patterns [38]. For that reason, Bebras has increasingly been utilized in research and applications related to CT assessment [39].

As part of this interest in utilizing Bebras tasks as part of CT assessments, IRT-based analyses have been conducted on Italian [40], Slovenian [41], and German [42] versions of the Bebras competition task set. In perhaps the largest-scale analysis of Bebras data, performance data on Bebras tasks from 115,400 students in grades 3-12 in seven countries were analyzed by Izu and colleagues [43]. They specifically looked at gender differences, where none was found in either participation or performance except at older grade ranges where there was higher male participation. They concurred with other studies that identified an apparent discrepancy between the tasks' estimated and perceived difficulty, finding that the Bebras versions had more "harder than expected" than "easier than expected" items. This has been noted as perhaps the result of the task set being designed as a competition and not an assessment [44]. As noted by the researchers conducting IRT analyses on Bebras tasks, this approach is particularly appropriate for assessing the difficulty of items if they are to be used as an assessment.

In summary, CTt and Bebras have emerged as two instruments with a mounting base of evidence linking them to core constructs underlying current conceptualizations of CT. Both instruments have set out to create items that are appropriate for middle grades students who have no prior experience with block-based or other programming languages. However, they originate from goals somewhat different from each other; while CTt was designed from the start as an assessment of CT, Bebras started as a task set for a competition and only more recently has been researched as an assessment tool. Another important distinction is that though the developers of the CTt and a small set of additional research has shown the instrument appropriate for use with students with no programming background, items such as the one shown in Figure 1 use what is, in effect, block-based programming code. In contrast, Bebras items use common, everyday visual metaphors in their puzzle-like items. It is worth reiterating that the CTt took inspiration from Bebras and has been shown to be correlated at a complementary rather than wholly overlapping level [25].

3 DATA AND METHODS

3.1 Test Items

The initial version of our assessment consisted of 43 items, which was the combination of 28 items from the CTt (Figure 1) and 15 items from the Bebras challenge (Figure 2). All 28 multiple-choice items of the CTt were included without making any modifications. Fifteen items were selected out of 18 items from the UK Bebras 2016 task set that were targeted for students of age 10 to 12 years old (referred as Juniors age group). Eleven of the 15 Bebras items were single-select multiple-choice, one item was multi-select multiple-choice, one item was drag and drop ranking-order type, one item required matching and lastly one item required students to enter a number. One of the Bebras items (Robot Exit) was modified to make it a multiple-choice question as it originally required an interactive drag and drop of instructional blocks guiding the robot. Both CTt and Bebras items were given to 15 middle school students before the main data collection to make sure that the questions are appropriate for this age group.

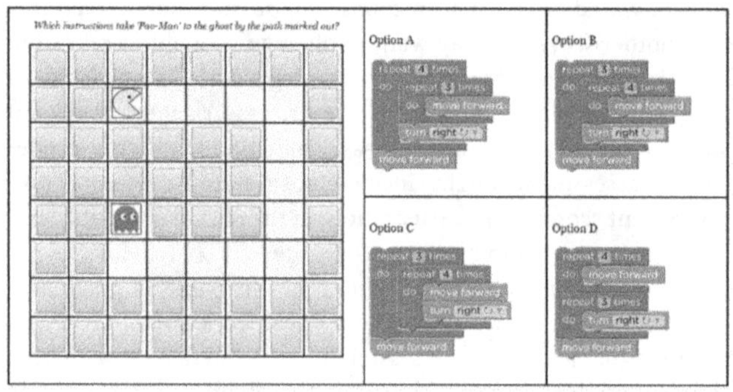

Figure 1: A sample item from CTt

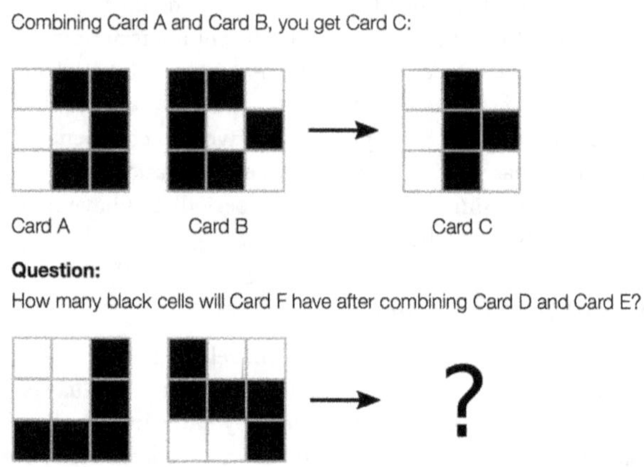

Figure 2: A sample item from the Bebras Challenge

3.2 Data Sources

A Non-Equivalent Anchor Test (NEAT) design was used to maximize the data collected from our sample as it was infeasible to administer the 43-item assessment due to time constraints in the classroom. A NEAT design is one in which multiple versions of an exam are given; in this study there were 10 separate versions. All versions share a subset of anchor items (i.e., common items) and also contain a number of unique items. Anchor items are used to equate student scores on different versions of the assessment. The first set of 5 versions each contained 26 items, as that was the estimated number that could be completed in the allotted time (~45 min). The 26 items consisted of 17 items from the CTt (14 anchor, 3 unique) and 9 items from the Bebras challenge (7 anchor, 2 unique). The selection of anchor items from the CTt was based on the computational concepts (e.g., "basic directions and sequences", "simple functions") that each item addresses in the test. The CTt aims to assess seven computational concepts in total and each concept was addressed by four questions (Roman-Gonzalez et al., 2017, p. 681). We selected two questions addressing each concept as anchor questions, so each version of the assessment included 14 questions from the CTt that addressed all seven computational concepts defined by Roman-Gonzalez et al. [25]. The rest of the CTt items were then distributed across the 5 versions as items unique to each version. The selection of anchor items from the Bebras challenge was based on the difficulty level of the items (A = easy, B = moderate, C = difficult) set by the creators of the tasks. We selected three items from A level, two from B, and two from C as anchor items. Then, we distributed the rest of the items as unique items across the five versions in a way that each version included at least one C level item and one A/B level item. The second set of 5 shortened versions each contained 16 items, which consisted of 10 items from the CTt (7 anchor, 3 unique) and 6 items from the Bebras challenge (4 anchor, 2 unique), and did not include some items that were eliminated based on preliminary results. Since the items unique to each version had the highest amount of missing data, we decided to keep the unique items in the shortened versions and drop some of the anchor items in a way that it does not change our rationale for selecting those items. While the NEAT design is popular and efficient for deploying more items, it does result in a great deal of data that is missing by design.

We then used concurrent equating to put all items from all test versions onto the same scale, allowing all of our administrations of smaller numbers of tests to be considered together and with equal contribution to the model. When the sample size reached 160, a preliminary Rasch analysis was conducted for the purpose of identifying items which were not performing well or as expected; 3 items were eliminated based on negative point-biserial correlation or very low variance. The remaining rounds of data collection were then conducted with the most problematic items removed. In addition, a subset of 21 students took the assessment twice in order to inform additional discussion of test-retest reliability. In total, 309 students completed the assessment.

3.3 Results

3.3.1 Preliminary Item Fit Analysis. To help select the best items to include in a final assessment, a form of Item Response Theory (IRT), Rasch analysis, was used to both look at the performance of individual items tested and the relationship of student responses on individual items with other items [45]. Rasch measures a sample of respondents' (i.e., students) performance on each question as a function of a latent trait θ. A model of each item, an Item Characteristic Curve (ICC), maps the probability (y-axis) that an individual would answer correctly against the individual's proficiency (θ, x-axis). One parameter for an item's ICC is its difficulty (β), where a higher β would indicate that a student would need to have a higher θ in order to have the same probability of answering it correctly. The discrimination parameter (α) indicates how effectively an item can discriminate between high and low-ability students. A high α would create a steeper sloped ICC, whereby small changes in θ would mean relatively larger shifts in probability of correct response. The approach here is to use these parameter characteristics, at the individual item level and collectively (i.e., across all items), to select a set of items with a range of difficulty and high discrimination, and which all behave statistically in a homogeneous fashion (e.g., have similar amounts of response variability).

With a goal of reducing the length of the test to the best performing items, our general approach was to use Rasch analysis [45] to investigate bad fit first for causes such as data entry errors or miskeys, and then eliminate items that still showed poor fit to the IRT model. We followed the recommendations of Linacre [46], for the order and priority of assessing items based on these statistics. Items with negative point-biserial correlations with either overall score or θ were removed first, next were violations of outfit and infit, then finally for mean-square and standardized mean square fit. Items that were very high or very low difficulty tended to be eliminated as they tended not to differentiate high and low ability participants well; this had the effect of trimming the correct response probability distribution somewhat. However, the resulting distribution was in line with the person ability distribution. In total, 17 items were eliminated via these methods.

Finally, as noted above, we re-administered the test to a small subset of 21 students that had taken the test during the prior semester. We found that one Bebras item, Bebras_Q2, showed a great deal more improvement than all other items. At time 1, 10% of participants answered correctly but at time 2, 43% answered correctly. Other than this item, items were reliable between administrations, with a tendency towards slight improvement at time 2. Because it was impossible to determine if there was an event that influenced a collective response to Bebras_Q2 or if the pattern was due to exposure effect, we decided to eliminate Bebras_Q2.

In summary, we eliminated 18 total items based on these criteria, and the final IRT model was refit to the data. Using the above-described techniques the remaining items, by process of elimination, demonstrated stable patterns of response across students and were of a range of difficulty that was both appropriate for middle grades students, but would still allow discrimination between levels of ability.

3.3.2 Analysis of Dimensionality. With the goal of evaluating whether the remaining items were measuring a single dimension of ability, a Rasch analysis was conducted with a final sample size of 308, after one student was eliminated for having all missing data after item reduction. Item parameters were estimated using the marginal maximum likelihood (MML) with an expectation-maximization (EM) algorithm using XCalibre software (Version 4.2; Assessment Systems, 2014). Items that were omitted by individuals were calculated as being incorrect. After the IRT model was fit to the data, maximum likelihood estimation (MLE) was used to calibrate the items.

We first tested whether the 1-parameter Rasch model was greatly violating the assumption of a reasonably stable item discrimination (alpha parameter) by examining item plots and by comparing model fit to a 2 parameter (2PL) model ([47], pg. 141). The item plots showed that the discrimination, indicated by the slope of the traces, was stable for almost all items. Furthermore, a comparison of AIC and BIC statistics (see Table 1) indicate that there is no meaningful difference between the 1PL (Rasch) and 2PL models, therefore the 1PL model is suitable for these data.

Based on our use of a NEAT design, we chose to compare model fit for a unidimensional vs. a two-dimensional model that was comprised of CTt items in one dimension and Bebras items in the other. The mirt package in R [48] was used for this task using item parameters from the XCalibre program output as starting values. The same estimation techniques were used (MML-EM) to calculate IRT model fit statistics for each confirmatory model (see Table 1) and the results showed a non-meaningful improvement of about 1%, indicating the more parsimonious 1PL, 1 factor model is preferable [47].

In summary, each instance of analysis, the unidimensional Rasch model was roughly equivalent or superior [48]. Under the new model, there were no violations of item fit statistics, and a person ability-item difficulty map indicated that there was good coverage of person ability levels by the assessment.

Model	-2LL	Relative Change	AIC	BIC
1PL,1 Factor	4626.892	Reference	4628.893	4632.623
2PL,1 Factor	4799.596	0.005	4651.596	4744.848
1PL,2 Factor	4699.452	-0.016	4703.453	4710.913

Table 1: Comparison of 1PL (Rasch) and 2PL Models

4 CONCLUSIONS AND FUTURE WORK

One of the main purposes of this study was to reduce a longer, preliminary hybrid Román-González – Bebras CT assessment into a short and well-performing assessment that could be administered in a reasonable time period. The conjecture by Román-González that CTt and Bebras items could be used together in a complimentary fashion seems to have been borne out based on our IRT-guided process of item reduction. Our final recommended set of 25 items contain both CTt (n=19) and Bebras (n=6) items.

This CT assessment instrument is designed to be used as a pre-assessment for students who may not have had any previous experience programming. While there might have been concerns that some of the CTt items may have used block-based programming representations requiring prior programming experience, prior literature [35] and this analysis seems to indicate otherwise. There is reason to be conservative in this conclusion until further research is conducted.

The instructional implication of a short, easily administered CT pre-assessment is the ability for both teachers and researchers to gauge the initial ability of students to engage in tasks (programming or otherwise) that require the current, generally recognized CT skill set. When used as a pre and post-assessment instrument it has the potential to provide insight as to the efficacy of the intervention or instruction to develop CT ability. The CTt has demonstrated sensitivity to relatively short interventions [35], but more research is needed to explore how this new 25-item instrument responds.

Another motivation for continued validation work on this set of 25 items is the NEAT data collection design. Though necessary and appropriate for the logistical constraints of this data collection, it resulted in some sparsity of responses. A new round of data collection with just the final 25 items, randomly administered across participants will help alleviate data sparsity and address any ordering effects. While the results of this study suggest that the hybrid assessment is unidimensional, further research focusing on the shortened exam alone would allow for a deeper look into dimensionality. Finally, while some of the prior research has pointed to the strong conceptual and theoretical relationship of the CTt and Bebras instruments to current CT frameworks, more work will be needed to continue to explore the criterion validity of this new instrument against the CHC model of intelligence, programming ability, and other related measures of CT.

ACKNOWLEDGMENTS

This work is supported in part by the National Science Foundation through Grants CNS-1138497 and DRL-1640141. Any opinions, findings, conclusions, or recommendations expressed in this report are those of the participants, and do not necessarily represent the official views, opinions, or policy of the National Science Foundation.

REFERENCES

[1] Goode, J. and Chapman, G. *Exploring Computer Science.* University of Oregon, Eugene, OR, 2016.

[2] Lee, I., Martin, F. and Apone, K. Integrating computational thinking across the K-8 curriculum. *ACM Inroads*, 5, 4 (2014), 64-71.

[3] Mannila, L., Dagiene, V., Demo, B., Grgurina, N., Mirolo, C., Rolandsson, L. and Settle, A. 2014. Computational Thinking in K-9 Education. In *Proceedings of the Proceedings of the Working Group Reports of the 2014 on Innovation and Technology in Computer Science Education Conference.* ACM, 1-29.

[4] Zur-Bargury, I., Parv, B. and Lanzberg, D. 2013. A nationwide exam as a tool for improving a new curriculum. In *Proceedings of the Proceedings of the 18th ACM conference on Innovation and technology in computer science education.* ACM, 267-272.

[5] Witherspoon, E. B., Higashi, R. M., Schunn, C. D., Baehr, E. C. and Shoop, R. Developing Computational Thinking through a Virtual Robotics Programming Curriculum. *ACM Trans. Comput. Educ.*, 18, 1 (2017), 1-20.

[6] Martin, L. The promise of the Maker Movement for education. *Journal of Pre-College Engineering Education Research (J-PEER)*, 5, 1 (2015), 4.

[7] Rodger, S. H., Hayes, J., Lezin, G., Qin, H., Nelson, D., Tucker, R., Lopez, M., Cooper, S., Dann, W. and Slater, D. 2009. Engaging middle school teachers and students with alice in a diverse set of subjects. In *Proceedings of the Proceedings of the 40th ACM technical symposium on Computer science education (SIGCSE)*. ACM, 271-275.

[8] Bienkowski, M., Snow, E., Rutstein, D. W. and Grover, S. *Assessment design patterns for computational thinking practices in secondary computer science: A first look.* SRI International, Menlo Park, CA, 2015.

[9] Grover, S. and Pea, R. Computational Thinking in K–12: A Review of the State of the Field. *Educational Researcher*, 42, 1 (2013), 38-43.

[10] Wing, J. M. Computational Thinking. *Communications of the ACM*, 49, 3 (2006), 33-35.

[11] K12CS *K–12 Computer Science Framework*. 2016.

[12] NRC, N. R. C. *A Framework for K-12 Science Education: Practices, Crosscutting Concepts, and Core Ideas.* The National Academies, Washington, DC, 2011.

[13] Buffum, P. S., Martinez-Arocho, A. G., Frankosky, M. H., Rodriguez, F. J., Wiebe, E. N. and Boyer, K. E. 2014. CS principles goes to middle school: learning how to teach Big Data. *Proceedings of the 45th ACM technical symposium on computer science education (SIGCSE '14)*. ACM, 151-156.

[14] Jona, K., Wilensky, U., Trouille, L., Horn, M., Orton, K., Weintrop, D. and Beheshti, E. 2014. Embedding computational thinking in science, technology, engineering, and math (CT-STEM). *Future Directions in Computer Science Education Summit Meeting*.

[15] Weintrop, D., Beheshti, E., Horn, M., Orton, K., Jona, K., Trouille, L. and Wilensky, U. Defining computational thinking for mathematics and science classrooms. *Journal of Science Education and Technology*, 25, 1 (2016), 127-147.

[16] Grover, S. 2017. Assessing Algorithmic and Computational Thinking in K-12: Lessons from a Middle School Classroom. In *Emerging Research, Practice, and Policy on Computational Thinking. Educational Communications and Technology: Issues and Innovations.* Springer, 269-288.

[17] Grover, S., Cooper, S. and Pea, R. 2014. Assessing computational learning in K-12. In *Proceedings of the 2014 conference on Innovation & technology in computer science education (ITTICSE '14)*. ACM, 57-62.

[18] Shute, V. J., Sun, C. and Asbell-Clarke, J. Demystifying computational thinking. *Educational Research Review*, 22 (2017), 142-158.

[19] Brennan, K. and Resnick, M. 2012. New frameworks for studying and assessing the development of computational thinking. In *Proceedings of the 2012 annual meeting of the American Educational Research Association*. AERA.

[20] Denner, J., Werner, L. and Ortiz, E. Computer games created by middle school girls: Can they be used to measure understanding of computer science concepts? *Computers & Education*, 58, 1 (1// 2012), 240-249.

[21] Tew, A. E. and Guzdial, M. 2011. The FCS1: a language independent assessment of CS1 knowledge. In *Proceedings of the Proceedings of the 42nd ACM technical symposium on Computer science education*. ACM, 111-116.

[22] Weintrop, D. and Wilensky, U. 2015. Using Commutative Assessments to Compare Conceptual Understanding in Blocks-based and Text-based Programs. In *International Computing Education Research Conference (ICER '15)*. ACM, 101-110.

[23] Taylor, C., Zingaro, D., Porter, L., Webb, K. C., Lee, C. B. and Clancy, M. Computer science concept inventories: past and future. *Computer Science Education*, 24, 4 (2014), 253-276.

[24] Curzon, P., McOwan, P. W., Plant, N. and Meagher, L. R. 2014. Introducing teachers to computational thinking using unplugged storytelling. In *Proceedings of the 9th Workshop in Primary and Secondary Computing Education*. ACM, 89-92.

[25] Román-González, M., Moreno-León, J. and Robles, G. 2017. Complementary tools for computational thinking assessment. In *Proceedings of international conference on computational thinking education (CTE 2017)*. The Education University of Hong Kong, 154-159.

[26] Román-González, M., Pérez-González, J.-C. and Jiménez-Fernández, C. Which cognitive abilities underlie computational thinking? Criterion validity of the Computational Thinking Test. *Computers in Human Behavior* 72 (2016), 678-691.

[27] Román-González, M., Pérez-González, J.-C., Moreno-León, J. and Robles, G. Extending the nomological network of computational thinking with non-cognitive factors. *Computers in Human Behavior*, 80 (2018), 441-459.

[28] Alfonso, V. C., Flanagan, D. P. and Radwan, S. *The impact of the Cattell-Horn-Carroll theory on test development and interpretation of cognitive and academic abilities*. Guilford Publications, City, 2005.

[29] McGrew, K. S. CHC theory and the human cognitive abilities project: Standing on the shoulders of the giants of psychometric intelligence research. *Intelligence*, 37, 1 (2009), 1-10.

[30] Ambrósio, A. P., Xavier, C. and Georges, F. 2014. Digital ink for cognitive assessment of computational thinking. In *Proceedings of the 2014 IEEE Frontiers in Education Conference (FIE)*. IEEE, 1-7.

[31] Basawapatna, A. R., Koh, K. H. and Repenning, A. 2010. *Using scalable game design to teach computer science from middle school to graduate school.* In *Proceedings of the fifteenth annual conference on Innovation and technology in computer science education*. ACM, 224-228.

[32] Werner, L., Denner, J. and Campe, S. 2012. *The Fairy Performance Assessment: Measuring Computational Thinking in Middle School.* In *Proceeding of the 44th ACM technical symposium on computer science education (SIGCSE '12)*. ACM, 421-426.

[33] Dagienė, V. and Futschek, G. 2008. Bebras international contest on informatics and computer literacy: Criteria for good tasks. In *International Conference on Informatics in Secondary Schools-Evolution and Perspectives*. Springer, 19-30.

[34] Dagienė, V. and Sentance, S. 2016. It's Computational Thinking! Bebras Tasks in the Curriculum. In *International Conference on Informatics in Schools: Situation, Evolution, and Perspectives*. Springer, 28-39.

[35] Aksit, O. *Enhancing Science Learning through Computational Thinking and Modeling in Middle School Classrooms: A Mixed Methods Study.* Dissertation, North Carolina State University, Raleigh, NC, 2018.

[36] Moreno-León, J. and Robles, G. 2015. Dr. Scratch: A web tool to automatically evaluate Scratch projects. In *Proceedings of the workshop in primary and secondary computing education (WiPSCE '15)*. ACM, 132-133.

[37] Blokhuis, D., Millican, P., Roffey, C., Schrijvers, E. and Sentance, S. *UK Bebras Computational Thinking Challenge 2016.* University of Oxford, Oxford, UK, 2015.

[38] Barendsen, E., Mannila, L., Demo, B., Nata, Grgurina, A., Izu, C., Mirolo, C., Sentance, S., Settle, A., Gabriel, S. 2015. Concepts in K-9 Computer Science Education. In *Proceedings of the 2015 ITiCSE on Working Group Reports*. ACM, 85-116.

[39] Dagienė, V., Stupurien, G. and Vinikien, L. 2016. Promoting Inclusive Informatics Education Through the Bebras Challenge to All K-12 Students. In *Proceedings of the Proceedings of the 17th International Conference on Computer Systems and Technologies 2016*. ACM, 407-414.

[40] Bellettini, C., Lonati, V., Malchiodi, D., Monga, M., Morpurgo, A. and Torelli, M. 2015. How Challenging are Bebras Tasks?: An IRT Analysis Based on the Performance of Italian Students. In *Proceedings of the 2015 ACM Conference on Innovation and Technology in Computer Science Education*. ACM, 27-32.

[41] Gujberova, M. and Kalas, I. 2013. Designing productive gradations of tasks in primary programming education. In *Proceedings of the 8th Workshop in Primary and Secondary Computing Education*. ACM, 108-117.

[42] Hubwieser, P. and Muhling, A. 2014. Playing PISA with Bebras. In *Proceedings of the 9th Workshop in Primary and Secondary Computing Education*. ACM, 128-129.

[43] Izu, C., Mirolo, C., Settle, A., Mannila, L. and Stupuriene, G. Exploring Bebras Tasks Content and Performance: A Multinational Study. *Informatics in Education*, 16, 1 (2017), 39-59.

[44] Dagienė, V., Mannila, L., Poranen, T., Rolandsson, L. and Derhjelm, S. 2014. Students' performance on programming-related tasks in an informatics contest in Finland, Sweden and Lithuania. In *Proceedings of the 2014 conference on Innovation; technology in computer science education*. ACM, 153-158.

[45] Fischer, G. H. and Molenaar, I. W. *Rasch models: Foundations, recent developments, and applications*. Springer Science, 2012.

[46] Linacre, J. M. *Winsteps®*. Winsteps.com, 2018.

[47] de Ayala, R. J. *The Theory and Practice of Item Response Theory.* Guilford Press, New York, 2009.

[48] Chalmers, R. P. mirt: A multidimensional item response theory package for the R environment. *Journal of Statistical Software*, 48, 6 (2012), 1-29.

On the Fairness of Multiple-Variant Multiple-Choice Examinations

Paul Denny
The University of Auckland
Auckland, New Zealand
paul@cs.auckland.ac.nz

Sathiamoorthy Manoharan
The University of Auckland
Auckland, New Zealand
s.manoharan@auckland.ac.nz

Ulrich Speidel
The University of Auckland
Auckland, New Zealand
ulrich@cs.auckland.ac.nz

Giovanni Russello
The University of Auckland
Auckland, New Zealand
g.russello@auckland.ac.nz

Angela Chang
The University of Auckland
Auckland, New Zealand
a.chang@auckland.ac.nz

ABSTRACT

Academic dishonesty is a widely acknowledged problem in tertiary education, and a range of safeguards and tools exist to both deter and detect cheating. During tests and examinations students are often monitored closely by invigilators, however incidents of misconduct still occur. Multiple-choice questions (MCQs) are particularly susceptible in this regard due to the simplicity with which answers can be communicated. Nonetheless, they are commonly used in large classes due to their convenience. In this work we investigate multiple-variant MCQs, where answer options are randomly selected from predefined sets. This format is less prone to student cheating and overcomes several weaknesses of similar methods. We evaluate this approach in two large computer science courses through student questionnaires and simple item analysis. We find that multiple-variant MCQ exams are perceived as an effective way to reduce cheating behavior, however not all question variants are equally difficult. This introduces concerns around fairness and we discuss approaches to mitigate these issues in the future.

CCS CONCEPTS

• **Social and professional topics → Computing education.**

KEYWORDS

examinations, plagiarism, MCQs, multiple-variant MCQs

ACM Reference Format:
Paul Denny, Sathiamoorthy Manoharan, Ulrich Speidel, Giovanni Russello, and Angela Chang. 2019. On the Fairness of Multiple-Variant Multiple-Choice Examinations. In *Proceedings of the 50th ACM Technical Symposium on Computer Science Education (SIGCSE '19), February 27-March 2, 2019, Minneapolis, MN, USA.* ACM, New York, NY, USA, 7 pages. https://doi.org/10.1145/3287324.3287357

SIGCSE '19, February 27-March 2, 2019, Minneapolis, MN, USA

ACM ISBN 978-1-4503-5890-3/19/02...$15.00
https://doi.org/10.1145/3287324.3287357

1 INTRODUCTION

Multiple-choice questions (MCQs) allow instructors to grade quickly and easily, and are therefore widely used in tests and examinations across many disciplines. As research instruments, MCQs permit the automated analysis of responses from a large number of students, which can reveal insights into student understanding and misconceptions [6]. MCQs that are well designed can measure a broad range of competencies [5], however they are difficult to create. A large body of literature exists outlining best practice and guidelines for creating effective MCQs, including the importance of plausible distractors and concise, unambiguous question stems [22]. In computer science courses, especially in large CS1 classes, MCQs remain a popular form of assessment [20]. In 2013, an ITiCSE working group generated a repository of MCQs targeting CS1 and CS2 topics which now serves as a free resource for educators [23].

There are two primary drawbacks to using MCQs in computer science tests and exams. The first problem relates to limitations of the question format with respect to assessment. MCQs are not well suited for assessing certain skills, such as the ability to write complete programs, however they are suitable for targeting some concepts. In first-year computer science courses, MCQs are frequently used to assess code comprehension and numerous studies of novice programmers involve this format [11]. Moreover, most programming instructors believe that MCQs provide adequate assessment of low level programming concepts [26].

The second problem with using MCQs in high-stakes tests and exams is a more practical one and relates to conducting the assessment in a fair manner. Cheating in multiple-choice examinations – whether deliberate collusion between peers or copying from unaware classmates – is unfair to honest students and difficult to detect [7, 31]. The limited choice of answer options and the simplicity of the answer format make cheating easier. Preventing all forms of collusion or cheating, particularly in very large classes where examinations are conducted in vast rooms or halls, is a difficult challenge. One approach is to increase the number of invigilators available to oversee an exam, and although this is perceived as an effective strategy by faculty it is not always practical [30]. Another approach is to personalize the questions for each student, making it more difficult for students to collude during the exam.

We see personalization as a way of reducing incidents of cheating in large classes [14]: personalization is achieved by generating *multiple-variant* MCQs, in which the answer options for a question

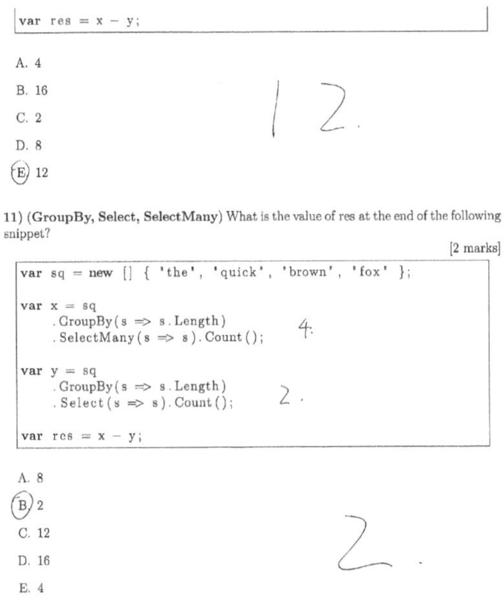

Figure 1: One strategy for colluding with others nearby, regardless of the order in which the five answer options are presented

are drawn at random from a pool of options defined by the instructor. In this paper we explore the *fairness* of this approach in terms of the difficulty of the generated questions and as perceived by students sitting exams composed of multiple-variant MCQs. Our research questions are as follows:

(1) When questions are generated by random selection of the answer options, are some variants of a question significantly more difficult than others?
(2) How do students perceive the fairness of exams that are personalized in this way?

2 BACKGROUND

Almost all academic institutions have a code of academic honesty for students [16], yet it is estimated that nearly 70% of students admit to some form of cheating [2]. Reported rates are even higher in computing courses [25]. A variety of reasons are given for this behaviour, including lack of ability, laziness and being unaware of the risks and consequences of being caught [28].

Cheating is prevalent not only in take-home assessments but also, to a lesser extent, in examinations [12, 13, 15, 30, 33]. Cheating on tests and exams is viewed, by faculty and students alike, as a particularly serious act [8, 17]. The results of independent surveys conducted by Sims [29] and by Sheard and Dick [24], in which scenarios of academic dishonesty were ranked by students, revealed that items related to exam misconduct were deemed the most serious. Using a similar methodology, Pincus and Schmelkin examined faculty perceptions of academic dishonesty and, other than deliberately sabotaging another student's work or forging University documents, acts of cheating in tests and exams were considered the most severe [21].

Exam invigilators find themselves having to deal with a mixture of cheating mechanisms and strategies. Classical cheat sheets are being replaced by modern bluetooth-enabled communication devices that enable communications with outside of the exam centre [1, 27]. Popular e-commerce site eBay, for example, has a dedicated "cheat exam" permalink[1] that offers a range of cheating devices. Recent reviews on some of these devices indicate that they are being used as advertised, although the set up is not always straightforward. For example, a tiny hidden earpiece claiming to be the "best way of hiding your cheating notes" was reviewed positively by one purchaser who also suggested: "you need to get that positioning right and test it out each time you want to use it before walking into [the] exam hall with it".

Despite the growing sophistication of methods for cheating in exams, direct communication between students in the exam room is still the most simple and common technique. Paper-based exams may eventually be replaced by digital exams, where students use a device or computer to submit answers to questions, and this mode may permit a wider variety of question types and technical safeguards to make cheating more difficult [4, 9, 18, 32]. In addition, a number of promising systems for invigilating online programming exams are now emerging, along with strategies for countering cheating behaviour such as preventing communication between students while allowing access to read-only web resources [10]. Nevertheless, with very large student cohorts posing significant resource requirements, the simplicity of paper-based MCQ exams means they are likely to remain popular for some time yet.

3 COUNTERING CHEATING

A common approach to counter cheating in paper-based MCQ exams involves the production of the question booklets. It is standard practice for multiple *versions* of the booklets to be produced, where each version has the answer options for the questions shuffled in a random order. For practical reasons, usually only a small number of distinct versions (often four) of the examination booklets are produced. Therefore, students are usually seated such that they are not adjacent to other students with an identical version of the exam.

Most incidents of cheating that we have observed in our own local four-version MCQ examinations involve low-tech strategies where students attempt to communicate with, or copy from, other students sitting nearby. One particular technique we have seen involves students writing answer keys for MCQs in large letters on their examination booklets so that they are visible to those sitting around them. As the correct answer to a question is the same across all versions, the students write keywords or phrases that identify the answer rather than the letter of the option, as illustrated in the picture of a question booklet shown in Figure 1.

Premeditated communication between students can be countered by randomly assigning students their seat locations. While this is quite effective, it greatly increases the time needed for students to be seated. This can be an important factor if the room is only available for a limited time, for example when tests are conducted "in-class" according to the standard lecture schedule. Anecdotally, in a rare case where a random seating allocation was announced at the

[1] https://www.ebay.com/bhp/cheat-exam

beginning of a test at our own institution, we noticed small groups of students very reluctant to be separated. On another occasion, invigilators physically obstructing the last few rows of an exam room (with a good view of rows below) had to deal with several students highly determined to seat themselves in these rows.

Where time pressure or class size prevents specialized seating plans, another approach to tackling collusion is personalization of the exam questions. There are several different strategies for generating personalized questions. One is to develop a large pool of unique questions from which each student receives a random selection of questions that are of equal difficulty and target the same topics as other students. This approach enables the instructor to carefully tailor each question, for example to ensure that distractors target common misconceptions, however the effort required to generate a large bank of similar questions is significant. A more automated approach is to use parametrized questions, where an instructor prepares a smaller set of questions that contain parameters which are instantiated randomly for each student [3]. This has proven effective for low-stakes self-assessment exercises, however generating parametrized distractors that target subtle misconceptions can be challenging.

The approach to personalization that we evaluate in this work is conceptually very simple [14]. It requires less effort than generating many distinct questions, yet still allows an instructor to carefully design answer options. For a given question stem, the instructor creates a pool of multiple *true* answers (all of which are correct solutions to the question) and a separate pool of multiple *false* answers (which are all incorrect). We then automatically select the appropriate number of true and false answers randomly for each variant of the question (e.g., for single-response MCQs we select one true answer and an appropriate number of false answers). With a sufficient number of options in each answer pool, many different question variants are possible thus making it difficult for students to collude.

3.1 Generating question variants

We now present an example of the process that we use for generating question variants. Consider the following code tracing question (using the C language) that might appear in a typical CS1 course.

Consider the following code that processes an array of integers (note that the values in the array are not displayed below):

```
int values[5] = { ..... };
int x = 0;
for (int i = 0; i < 5; i++) {
   if (i < 2) {
      x = x + values[i];
   } else if (i > 2) {
      x = x - values[i];
   }
}
printf("x = %d", x);
```

Which array initialization would lead to the output `x = 0`?

There are many possible ways that the array, *values*, could be initialized that would not be valid solutions to this question. Five such invalid initializations are: {1,2,3,4,5}, {-2,-1,0,1,2}, {2,1,0,-1,-2}, {5,4,3,2,1} and {5,0,4,0,4}. There are also many possible *correct* solutions (where the sum of the first two values in the array is equal to the sum of the last two values) such as: {0,1,1,0,1}, {1,9,1,5,5}, {2,1,4,3,0}, {2,3,5,1,4} and {1,-2,3,4,-5}. A question variant is then generated by random selection from these two pools of correct and incorrect answer options.

3.1.1 *Single-response MCQs.*
Single-response MCQs are the most common format used in practice. To generate a single-response MCQ, one correct option and $p-1$ incorrect options are selected at random from the respective banks, where p is the total number of answer options desired. The number of possible variants for a single-response MCQ is $N_t\binom{N_f}{p-1}$ where N_t and N_f are the number of true and false answers in the respective banks.

3.1.2 *Multiple-response MCQs.*
A less common form of MCQ is the multiple-response multiple-choice question [19]. These questions may have multiple correct answers, and when answering such a question students are required to select all correct options, reducing the probability of students correctly answering a question by guessing. To generate a multiple-response MCQ, m_t true answers and m_f false answers are selected at random from the respective banks, such that $m_t + m_f$ is equal to p. The number of possible variants for a multiple-response MCQ is $\sum_{i=0}^{p}\binom{N_t}{i}\binom{N_f}{p-i}$.

In addition, for any given question variant, the options can be presented in $p!$ ways due to random shuffling of the answer options.

4 METHODOLOGY

In this work we explore the actual and perceived fairness of generating personalized exam questions the following way: we examine the actual fairness by comparing the measured difficulty of the question variants generated for a given question stem; we examine the perceived fairness by asking students to provide feedback on this style of personalization and, specifically, we ask them to comment on any negative aspects.

Our evaluation involves two courses, both second-year computer science courses, taught at the University of Auckland in 2018. The first course (Course A) is an introduction to data communications and the second course (Course B) is an intermediate course on object-oriented software development. In total, personalized questions were generated for three mid-semester tests (one for Course A and two for Course B). Each of the three tests consisted of 22 single-response MCQs. After the mid-semester test for Course A, students in that course were invited to complete a questionnaire containing the following two questions:

- *"In your view, what were the negative aspects, if any, of the personalized test?"*
- *"If there is any feedback you would like to provide to improve personalized tests, please provide this feedback here".*

Similarly for Course B, after the first mid-semester test students were invited to complete a short survey. In this case, students were asked to respond to the following two questions on a standard 5-point Likert scale:

- *Personalized tests help to reduce the level of cheating*
- *Personalized tests ensure everyone needs to work equally hard to achieve good scores*

Our analysis of question difficulty involves a subset of the test questions. We focus on questions for which there are a small number of correct and incorrect options in the answer pools, and therefore a relatively small number of unique variants. In such cases, each variant will be answered by a relatively large number of students. This allows us to compare the difficulty of the variants, computed as the proportion of students that answer each variant correctly, with good statistical power. For example, Question 12 on the second test for Course B was generated from a pool of 2 correct options and 4 incorrect options. As each question presents a total of 5 options, only two different variants of this question are possible and roughly half of the nearly 300 students that sat the test would have answered each variant. On the other hand, some questions have a large number of unique variants. Question 8 on the same test had 420 unique variants, as it had 6 correct options and 8 incorrect options in the answer pool. In this case, many students would have had a unique variant on their version of the test and no variants would have been answered by more than a few students.

We analyze all questions, across the three tests, for which there are 2 or 3 correct options and fewer than 6 incorrect options in the answer pools (for a maximum of 15 variants of any one question). In terms of presenting our results, we categorize question variants based on the correct answer only. That is, for each possible correct answer of a question variant, we report the proportion of students who selected this answer.

Students provided open responses to the questionnaire for Course A, and we categorized these responses into high level themes. For each of the two questions, we report the number of responses that commented on the fairness of using personalized questions, and we include a sample of typical responses. The questionnaire for Course B consisted of Likert scale questions, and we tabulate the responses to these questions. For both courses, responding to the questionnaires was optional (ungraded) and responses were anonymous.

5 RESULTS

A total of 298 students sat the test for Course A (Test A), and 294 and 284 students sat the two tests for Course B (Test B1 and Test B2) respectively.

5.1 Fairness of questions

Table 1 shows the proportion of students who correctly answered each question variant (V_i) for the subset of questions we analyzed across the three tests. Question numbers shown in the table correspond to the questions as they appeared on the tests. We compare the difficulty of the question variants using chi-squared tests based on a classification of whether students answered each variant correctly. More than half of the questions we analyzed had variants of similar difficulty, however some questions had variants that were significantly easier than others, putting the students who received those variants at an advantage. The most striking example of this is Test B1.Q14, where the hardest variant saw 28 out of 107 students answer correctly (26.2%), compared with 56 out of 80 students who had the easiest variant of this question (70.0%).

Examining some of the problematic questions in more detail uncovers problems with their design. For example, the stem for

Table 1: Comparison of student performance on each question variant

n	Question	V_0	V_1	V_2	χ^2 (p)
299	Test A.Q07	66.4%	70.5%	-	0.526
	Test A.Q08	49.3%	45.5%	-	0.584
294	Test B1.Q14	49.5%	26.2%	70.0%	**0.000**
	Test B1.Q19	24.0%	27.7%	-	0.555
	Test B1.Q24	34.0%	51.0%	-	**0.005**
284	Test B2.Q06	56.2%	66.1%	79.1%	**0.006**
	Test B2.Q07	35.2%	44.4%	42.9%	0.399
	Test B2.Q12	56.1%	72.4%	-	**0.006**
	Test B2.Q13	37.2%	38.2%	-	0.949
	Test B2.Q26	55.9%	46.9%	51.2%	0.447

Test B1.Q14 showed a code fragment which initialized an ArrayList of points:

```
ArrayList<Point> points = new ArrayList<Point>();
points.add(new Point(10, 20));
points.add(new Point(30, 40));
points.add(new Point(50, 60));
```

Students were required to identify the code fragment that would correctly print the elements of the ArrayList. The pool of answer options contained three correct alternatives (denoted as V_0, V_1 and V_2 in Table 1) and five incorrect alternatives (which targeted errors such as directly indexing the ArrayList and using an incorrect type when extracting an element). The correct answer option for variant V_1 was selected by only 26.2% of students. This correct option was simply `System.out.println(points);`, and this was the only option (out of all correct and incorrect alternatives) in which a *for* loop was not explicitly used. The fact that this alternative was a trivial solution, and was unusual compared to the other options in which an explicit loop was used, may have contributed to the low success rate for this variant of the question.

Question Test B2.Q12 showed students a superclass definition (Base), and asked them to identify the correct constructor definition for a subclass (Derived). The question read as follows:

Consider the superclass (Base). Its subclass (Derived) implements a boolean instance variable p. Which of the following is NOT a correct implementation for the constructor of Derived?

```
class Base {
   protected int x;
   protected double y;
   public Base() { }
   public Base(int x, double y) {
      this.x = x;
      this.y = y;
   }
   public Base(double y) {
      x=-1;
      this.y = y;
   }
}
```

and students were then shown a series of possible definitions for the subclass constructor. The correct option (which is *not* a valid constructor definition) that was shown to students who received variant V_1 of this question was as follows:

```
public Derived(boolean p, int x, double y) {
   super(p, x, y);
}
```

and this was selected by 92 out of 127 (72.4%) students. Across all of the correct and incorrect options available for generating this question, this was the only option where three parameters were passed to the constructor. As with question Test B1.Q14, this unique feature of this option may explain why variant V_1 was significantly easier for students.

5.2 Student perceptions

The first question asked of students in Course A was *"In your view, what were the negative aspects, if any, of the personalized test?"*. There were 47 responses to this question, and more than half (25 responses) directly commented on the potential lack of fairness of the multi-variant approach due to the random nature of the questions. Examples of these comments are below:

- *Some people got easier questions, while others got harder*
- *Some people got some subjectively more difficult questions*
- *Not really equal, some student may get questions easy to solve*
- *Test score is highly dependent on the random generation of the test*

Two student responses noted that if the content was understood well, differences in question difficulty may not be unfair:

- *Some people may get hard versions which does take up more time to do. However, if you knew the topic reaaaaaaly well, it wouldnt affect too much*
- *Sure some people mentioned getting weird numbers for which they had to calculate but I feel like thats just life and if you learn't the concepts properly you wouldn't have any problem answer questions with different values*

Interestingly, several responses indicated that students like to compare their answers with one another after the test, and the personalization makes this more difficult:

- *it would take more time to check answers with others after the test*
- *harder to compare answers afterwards with friends*
- *Everyone just became even more curious of what each other's questions were*
- *Hard to compare with peers - they may have not had that question*

There were 18 responses to the second question, *"If there is any feedback you would like to provide to improve personalized tests, please provide this feedback here"*. In this case, only 4 students commented that changes should be made to improve the fairness of the tests.

One student suggested a different approach (modifying the order of the questions) to counter cheating:

- *perhaps the order of questions could be randomized to reduce cheating, rather than completely randomize the tests*

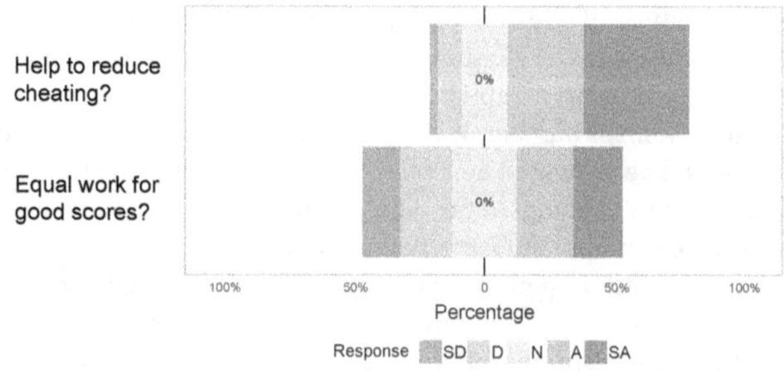

Figure 2: Student responses to the questions *"Personalized tests help to reduce the level of cheating"* and *"Personalized tests ensure everyone needs to work equally hard to achieve good scores"*

Several students indicated that they liked the personalized approach and would not recommend changes:

- *No, I like the personalized tests*
- *Fine at the moment – no feedback*

Finally, one student recommended using personalization only for certain types of questions, and using a more traditional approach of shuffling common options for other questions:

- *I think that randomization can be good for mathematical questions, because the numbers that you get don't affect your ability to do the problem, but with some of the "which of these statements are true" style questions it is harder to be sure that they are all equally difficult, so maybe just randomize the order of answers and combinations of options rather than which questions you get*

A total of 234 students responded to the survey for Course B. Figure 2 summarizes responses to the two Likert scale questions. Students appear to agree, quite strongly, that personalized questions reduce the level of cheating in tests and exams. More than 40% of responses strongly agreed with this statement. However, students are more neutral about the fairness of the approach. In response to the question of whether everyone needs to work equally hard to achieve good scores, the most common response (25%) to this question was "Neutral". In summary, personalizing exam questions is considered by students to be effective at reducing cheating behavior, but there remains uncertainty about the fairness of the approach.

6 DISCUSSION

Personalized exams are an effective way to reduce the opportunity for students to cheat, however our questionnaire indicated that many students are concerned about the fairness of this form of assessment. Moreover, despite our test questions undergoing several rounds of internal review, there is clear evidence that some question variants were significantly easier than others. This highlights the difficulty of defining questions using our approach, where answer options are selected at random from pools of correct and incorrect alternatives, such that in all cases the generated questions are of similar difficulty. Of course, student cheating on exams introduces a different kind of unfairness, however we cannot say whether the measures we have taken to eliminate this results in an assessment that is more or less fair overall.

Certain types of questions may be better suited to the kind of personalization we have described. Questions which involve mathematical calculations or mechanical steps may be more suitable, for example code tracing questions (such as the one shown in Section 3.1) where several sets of inputs can be defined such that the presence or absence of a particular pattern determines the output produced. In fact, one of the students we surveyed suggested restricting personalization to questions of this type.

A different approach for generating personalized questions is to construct parametric questions that can lead to many concrete question instances. For example, consider the following question on pre- and post-increment operators.

Study the following code fragment:

```
int z = x++ + --y;
System.out.printf("x=%d, y=%d, z=%d", x, y, z);
```

What gets printed if `x` *and* `y` *had been initialized to 4 and 11 respectively?*

This question could be parameterized by supplying different initialization values for x and y. Assuming the initial values of x and y are n and m respectively, the correct final values for x, y and z are $(n + 1, m - 1, n + m - 1)$. A student who mistook the order in which the pre- and post-operator expressions are evaluated would end up with the incorrect answer $(n + 1, m - 1, n + m + 1)$; a student who might have thought both pre- and post- operator expressions are evaluated in the same way would come up with the incorrect answer $(n + 1, m - 1, n + m)$. These give rise to three possible final values for z. Finally, considering the possibility that a student might think the increment and/or decrement operators do not modify the object, this misconception gives rise to three additional incorrect answer options: $(n, m, n + m)$, $(n, m, n + m - 1)$, $(n, m, n + m + 1)$. This type of parametrization works well for numerical questions, but is less flexible when customizing non-numerical answer options.

A limitation of the MCQ format can also lead to unfairness. If we have only 5 answer options available, as is typical for many multiple-choice questions, only 4 of the previously highlighted 5 false answer options will be used. It is therefore possible that the answer option that captures a particular student's misunderstanding might not feature in the student's list of answer options. This limitation may lead to the student getting an unfair advantage since they can see that their initial answer is wrong. This, in fact, is an artifact of the constraint around the number of answer options permitted, and is equally applicable to standard MCQ examinations (i.e., examinations without personalized content).

In the questions we analyzed, most of the unfairness stemmed from poor design of the questions and/or answer options. A careful look at some of the selected questions from Table 1 can attest to this. The most problematic questions appeared to be the result of answer options which have an obviously unique or unusual feature. A more critical review of the questions before the examination is conducted (and upon reflection afterwards) may help to reduce such unfairness in the future.

7 LIMITATIONS AND FUTURE WORK

Our current analysis has two main limitations. Firstly, we only examined a small subset of the test questions so that we could compare question variants with large numbers of student responses. While this meant that many test questions were not examined, we were able to identify questions where the difficulty varied significantly between variants. Secondly, we only measured the difficulty of the question variants with respect to the correct answer options. This limited the number of variants that we needed to compare, however the choice of incorrect answer options can also have an impact on the difficulty of a question. A trivial example is when a student gets a set of incorrect answer options that can easily be eliminated from consideration, compared to another student who receives more effective distractors which may be harder, and take more time, to rule out.

Another limitation of this work is that we only consider single-response MCQs. The approach that we have described for generating question variants can be applied equally well to construct multiple-response MCQs by selecting an appropriate number of correct and incorrect options for a given question.

8 FUTURE WORK

As class sizes grow, the use of MCQs in tests and examinations will continue to be an attractive option for academics. Approaches to counter valid concerns around collusion and copying during exams, such as question personalization, are worth exploring.

Our future work will focus on improving the quality of the questions that we can generate with this approach. This will involve analysing student responses to questions to remove problematic options from the pools, as well as designing new options. We also plan to evaluate multiple-response MCQs which can be generated automatically once sufficiently large option pools are available.

9 CONCLUSION

Many large courses use multiple-choice examinations for ease of grading, however this question format is susceptible to cheating which is a widely acknowledged problem in higher education. To address this, we describe an approach for generating personalized questions which is based on random selection of alternatives from pools of correct and incorrect answer options. This approach to personalization is simpler than creating large banks of unique questions, yet allows the instructor the ability to carefully tailor question distractors. We evaluate the use of this approach to generate tests in two large computer science courses in the light of fairness. Students strongly believe that the approach reduces cheating behavior, however they are concerned about its fairness. These concerns are supported by our analysis of question difficulty which shows that some questions are significantly easier than others. Future work will look to address these problems, and evaluate other kinds of personalized questions.

10 ACKNOWLEDGEMENTS

This project was approved by the University of Auckland Human Participants Ethics Committee, Reference Number 017990.

REFERENCES

[1] Shashank Bengali. 2014. India's renowned education system has a flip side: Ingrained cheating. *Los Angeles Times* (16 April 2014).

[2] M.A. Broeckelman-Post. 2008. Faculty and Student Classroom Influences on Academic Dishonesty. *IEEE Transactions on Education* 51, 2 (May 2008), 206–211. https://doi.org/10.1109/TE.2007.910428

[3] Peter Brusilovsky and Sergey Sosnovsky. 2005. Individualized Exercises for Self-assessment of Programming Knowledge: An Evaluation of QuizPACK. *J. Educ. Resour. Comput.* 5, 3, Article 6 (Sept. 2005). https://doi.org/10.1145/1163405.1163411

[4] Kameswari Chebrolu, Bhaskaran Raman, Vinay Chandra Dommeti, Akshay Veer Boddu, Kurien Zacharia, Arun Babu, and Prateek Chandan. 2017. SAFE: Smart Authenticated Fast Exams for Student Evaluation in Classrooms. In *Proceedings of the 2017 ACM SIGCSE Technical Symposium on Computer Science Education (SIGCSE '17)*. ACM, New York, NY, USA, 117–122. https://doi.org/10.1145/3017680.3017754

[5] Steven Downing and Thomas Haladyna. 2006. *Handbook of Test Development.* 792 pages.

[6] Robert J. Dufresne, William J. Leonard, and William J. Gerace. 2002. Making sense of students' answers to multiple-choice questions. *The Physics Teacher* 40 (2002), 174–180.

[7] Robert B. Frary. 1993. Statistical Detection of Multiple-Choice Answer Copying: Review and Commentary. *Applied Measurement in Education* 6, 2 (1993), 153–165. https://doi.org/10.1207/s15324818ame0602_4

[8] Melody Graham. 1994. Cheating at Small Colleges: An Examination of Student and Faculty Attitudes and Behaviors. 35, 4 (1994), 255–260.

[9] Arto Hellas, Juho Leinonen, and Petri Ihantola. 2017. Plagiarism in Take-home Exams: Help-seeking, Collaboration, and Systematic Cheating. In *Proceedings of the 2017 ACM Conference on Innovation and Technology in Computer Science Education (ITiCSE '17)*. ACM, New York, NY, USA, 238–243. https://doi.org/10.1145/3059009.3059065

[10] An Ju, Ben Mehne, Andrew Halle, and Armando Fox. 2018. In-class Coding-based Summative Assessments: Tools, Challenges, and Experience. In *Proceedings of the 23rd Annual ACM Conference on Innovation and Technology in Computer Science Education (ITiCSE 2018)*. ACM, New York, NY, USA, 75–80. https://doi.org/10.1145/3197091.3197094

[11] Raymond Lister, Elizabeth S. Adams, Sue Fitzgerald, William Fone, John Hamer, Morten Lindholm, Robert McCartney, Jan Erik Moström, Kate Sanders, Otto Seppälä, Beth Simon, and Lynda Thomas. 2004. A Multi-national Study of Reading and Tracing Skills in Novice Programmers. *SIGCSE Bull.* 36, 4 (June 2004), 119–150. https://doi.org/10.1145/1041624.1041673

[12] Sathiamoorthy Manoharan. 2017. Personalized Assessment as a Means to Mitigate Plagiarism. *IEEE Transactions on Education* 60, 2 (May 2017), 112–119. https://doi.org/10.1109/TE.2016.2604210

[13] Sathiamoorthy Manoharan. 2017. Towards Mitigating Cheating in Multiple-Choice Examinations. In *Proceedings of the 2017 TERNZ Conferece.*

[14] Sathiamoorthy Manoharan. 2019. Cheat-Resistant Multiple-Choice Examinations using Personalization. *Computers & Education* (2019), to appear. https://doi.org/10.1016/j.compedu.2018.11.007

[15] Helen Marsden, Marie Carroll, and James T Neill. 2005. Who cheats at university? A self-report study of dishonest academic behaviours in a sample of Australian university students. *Australian Journal of Psychology* 57, 1 (2005), 1–10. https://doi.org/10.1080/00049530412331283426

[16] Donald L. McCabe and Linda Klebe Trevino. 1993. Academic Dishonesty: Honor Codes and Other Contextual Influences. *The Journal of Higher Education* 64, 5 (1993), 522–538.

[17] Elizabeth M. Nuss. 1984. Academic Integrity: Comparing Faculty and Student Attitudes. *Improving College and University Teaching* 32, 3 (1984), 140–144.

[18] Julia Opgen-Rhein, Bastian Küppers, and Ulrik Schroeder. 2018. An Application to Discover Cheating in Digital Exams. In *Proceedings of the 18th Koli Calling International Conference on Computing Education Research (Koli Calling '18)*. ACM, New York, NY, USA, Article 20, 5 pages. https://doi.org/10.1145/3279720.3279740

[19] Andrew Petersen, Michelle Craig, and Paul Denny. 2016. Employing Multiple-Answer Multiple Choice Questions. In *Proceedings of the 2016 ACM Conference on Innovation and Technology in Computer Science Education (ITiCSE '16)*. ACM, New York, NY, USA, 252–253.

[20] Andrew Petersen, Michelle Craig, and Daniel Zingaro. 2011. Reviewing CS1 Exam Question Content. In *Proceedings of the 42Nd ACM Technical Symposium on Computer Science Education (SIGCSE '11)*. ACM, New York, NY, USA, 631–636. https://doi.org/10.1145/1953163.1953340

[21] Holly Pincus and Liora Schmelkin. 2003. Faculty Perceptions of Academic Dishonesty: A Multidimensional Scaling Analysis. *The Journal of Higher Education* 74, 2 (2003), 196–209.

[22] Michael Rodriguez and Anthony Albano. 2017. *The College Instructor's Guide to Writing Test Items.* Routledge, New York. 172 pages.

[23] Kate Sanders, Marzieh Ahmadzadeh, Tony Clear, Stephen H. Edwards, Mikey Goldweber, Chris Johnson, Raymond Lister, Robert McCartney, Elizabeth Patitsas, and Jaime Spacco. 2013. The Canterbury QuestionBank: Building a Repository of Multiple-choice CS1 and CS2 Questions. In *Proceedings of the ITiCSE Working Group Reports Conference on Innovation and Technology in Computer Science Education-working Group Reports (ITiCSE -WGR '13)*. ACM, New York, NY, USA, 33–52. https://doi.org/10.1145/2543882.2543885

[24] Judy Sheard and Martin Dick. 2011. Computing Student Practices of Cheating and Plagiarism: A Decade of Change. In *Proceedings of the 16th Annual Joint Conference on Innovation and Technology in Computer Science Education (ITiCSE '11)*. ACM, New York, NY, USA, 233–237. https://doi.org/10.1145/1999747.1999813

[25] Judy Sheard, Selby Markham, and Martin Dick. 2003. Investigating Differences in Cheating Behaviours of IT Undergraduate and Graduate Students: The maturity and motivation factors. *Higher Education Research & Development* 22, 1 (2003), 91–108.

[26] Shuhaida Shuhidan, Margaret Hamilton, and Daryl D'Souza. 2010. Instructor perspectives of multiple-choice questions in summative assessment for novice programmers. *Computer Science Education* 20 (2010), 229–259.

[27] David Sim. 2017. Students use hidden wireless devices to cheat in exams. *International Business Times* (7 June 2017).

[28] Simon and Judy Sheard. 2015. In Their Own Words: Students and Academics Write About Academic Integrity. In *Proceedings of the 15th Koli Calling Conference on Computing Education Research (Koli Calling '15)*. ACM, New York, NY, USA, 97–106. https://doi.org/10.1145/2828959.2828977

[29] Randi L. Sims. 1995. The severity of academic dishonesty: A comparison of faculty and student views. *Psychology in the Schools* 32, 3 (1995), 233–238.

[30] Sami W. Tabsh, Akmal S. Abdelfatah, and Hany A. El Kadi. 2017. Engineering students and faculty perceptions of academic dishonesty. *Quality Assurance in Education* 25, 4 (2017), 378–393.

[31] Wim J. van der Linden and Leonardo Sotaridona. 2004. A Statistical Test for Detecting Answer Copying on Multiple-Choice Tests. *Journal of Educational Measurement* 41, 4 (2004), 361–377.

[32] Craig Zilles, Robert Deloatch, Jacob Bailey, Bhuwan Khattar, Wade Fagen, Cinda Heeren, David Mussulman, and Matthew West. 2015. Computerized testing: A vision and initial experiences. In *Proceedings of the American Society for Engineering Education 122nd Annual Conference and Exposition (ASEE 2015)*.

[33] Justin Zobel. 2004. "Uni Cheats Racket": A Case Study in Plagiarism Investigation. In *Proceedings of the 6th Australasian Conference on Computing Education*, Vol. 30. 357–365.

Teaching Explicit Programming Strategies to Adolescents

Andrew J. Ko
University of Washington
Information School
Seattle, WA, USA
ajko@uw.edu

Thomas D. LaToza
Department of Computer Science,
George Mason University
Fairfax, VA, USA
tlatoza@gmu.edu

Stephen Hull
Department of Computer Science,
George Mason University
Fairfax, VA, USA
shull4@gmu.edu

Ellen A. Ko
Juanita High School
Kirkland, WA, USA
s-eko@lwsd.org

William Kwok
University of Washington
Information School
Seattle, WA, USA
wkwok16@uw.edu

Jane Quichocho
University of Washington
Information School
Seattle, WA, USA
janeq97@uw.edu

Harshitha Akkaraju
University of Washington
Information School
Seattle, WA, USA
akkarah@uw.edu

Rishin Pandit
Thomas Jefferson High School for
Science & Technology
Alexandria, VA, USA
rishin.pandit@gmail.com

ABSTRACT

One way to teach programming problem solving is to teach explicit, step-by-step strategies. While prior work has shown these to be effective in controlled settings, there has been little work investigating their efficacy in classrooms. We conducted a 5-week case study with 17 students aged 15-18, investigating students' sentiments toward two strategies for debugging and code reuse, students' use of scaffolding to execute these strategies, and associations between students' strategy use and their success at independently writing programs in class. We found that while students reported the strategies to be valuable, many had trouble regulating their choice of strategies, defaulting to ineffective trial and error, even when they knew systematic strategies would be more effective. Students that embraced the debugging strategy completed more features in a game development project, but this association was mediated by other factors, such as reliance on help, strategy self-efficacy, and mastery of the programming language used in the class. These results suggest that teaching of strategies may require more explicit instruction on strategy selection and self-regulation.

ACM Reference Format:
Andrew J. Ko, Thomas D. LaToza, Stephen Hull, Ellen A. Ko, William Kwok, Jane Quichocho, Harshitha Akkaraju, and Rishin Pandit. 2019. Teaching Explicit Programming Strategies to Adolescents. In *Proceedings of the 50th ACM Technical Symposium on Computer Science Education (SIGCSE '19), February 27-March 2, 2019, Minneapolis, MN, USA.* ACM, New York, NY, USA, 7 pages. https://doi.org/10.1145/3287324.3287371

SIGCSE '19, February 27-March 2, 2019, Minneapolis, MN, USA

ACM ISBN 978-1-4503-5890-3/19/02....$15.00.
https://doi.org/10.1145/3287324.3287371

1 INTRODUCTION

Programming is hard to learn [21]. It requires the mastery of programming language semantics [18], common patterns of computation [15], ever-changing APIs and tools [13], and several software engineering skills, such as testing, debugging, and program design [12]. Learners also need strong self-regulation skills, both to regulate their learning [7], but also to regulate their programming process [16, 17]. The range of skills required in programming may be one reason why teaching programming is so difficult [11, 21].

One approach to improving learning is to teach *strategic* skills [19]. For example, one strategic skillset is self-regulation, helping students to reflect on and change their strategies when they find them to be ineffective. Studies show that learners' self-regulated learning skills tend to be shallow, but when strong, are associated with learning success [10, 16, 20]. Others have investigated the self-regulated learning strategies that higher education CS students find effective [7], including explicitly assessing task difficulty. One study developed adolescents' self-regulation skills by prompting learners to reflect on their strategies; this increased students' independence, sustained their growth mindset, and increased their productivity [17], mirroring findings in science education (e.g., [1]).

While self-regulation appears to be key in helping learners select strategies, a related approach has been to teach explicit, step-by-step strategies for solving specific problems. For example, a strategy for debugging might involve prompting students to first find strong evidence of the cause of a failure, and only then edit their program to repair the defect. Experiments on explicit strategies for program design [8, 22], program tracing [23], code reviews [5], and spreadsheet modification [3] have all showed promising short term gains in adult problem solving. Our recent work has further shown that explicit strategies supported by a tool for managing the execution of strategy steps [14] cause experienced developers to have greater task success and more confidence in their progress [14].

While this prior work establishes that self-regulation skills may be important and that explicit strategies for specific programming tasks can help in controlled settings with adults, there is little prior work investigating the teaching of explicit programming strategies in classrooms. Moreover, even less work has considered teaching strategies to adolescents, who may have distinct challenges from students in higher education, due to their still-developing executive functioning [2]. These gaps in prior work leave open several important questions about the efficacy of strategies in classrooms:

- RQ1: *What barriers do students face trying to use explicit programming strategies in their problem solving?* For example, from an adoption perspective, do students welcome the guidance that explicit strategies can offer, or do they view them too structured and time-consuming?
- RQ2: *To what extent is scaffolding necessary to support the execution explicit strategies?* Can strategy support eventually be removed or is it augmentation that remains valuable even after having learned a strategy?
- RQ3: *To what extent is using explicit strategies associated with more success at programming problem solving?* And to what extent do other factors such as prior knowledge and self-efficacy mediate this success?

To answer these questions, we conducted a classroom study of explicit programming strategies, teaching a 5-week summer course to a group of 17 adolescents. We taught students the game design subset of Code.org's CS Discoveries curriculum and two explicit programming strategies for debugging and code reuse. In the rest of this paper, we detail the course, the strategies, our answers to the questions above, and their implications.

2 METHOD

Our approach to teaching explicit strategies was to offer deliberate practice [6], including direct instruction on two strategies, concrete contextual guidance on using the strategies, and feedback on their use throughout the duration of our. In the rest of this section, we detail the classroom context of this strategy practice, the strategies we taught, and the data we gathered.

2.1 Setting and Participants

We focused on students aged 14-18 in U.S. high schools who were novice to programming. To reach diverse students, we partnered with a university's Upward Bound (UB) program. UB is a U.S. federally-funded college preparation program that helps students who are low-income and/or have no parent or guardian with a bachelor's degree access higher education. The program we worked with served four public high schools and reached about 180 students per year. The program was free; students received lunch money to attend and a stipend upon completion.

UB's summer session last 5-weeks. We offered a "Game Design" elective. The UB staff solicited students' elective preferences and then randomly assigned students to their 1st and 2nd choices. After enrollment stabilized, we had 17 students. The group was mostly low-income racial minority students with little to no programming experience. Students were aged 14-17 years old. Of the 17 students, 9 identified as boys and 8 as girls. All but one student identified as Asian, African American, Hispanic, and Middle Eastern. About 65% of students reported speaking a language other than English fluently, as well as 71% speaking a non-English language at home. The languages reported included English (15), Vietnamese (3), Bengali (2), Somali (2), Cham (2), Mien (1), Russian (1), Nepali (1), and Amharic (1). Students' parents' education mostly ranged between completing some high school to some college.

Students had little to no prior experience with programming: 12 reported never having written a program, but 9 reported having used at least one programming language, including HTML (4), Minecraft (3), Excel (3), Scratch (2). Three students mentioned professional languages such as Java (2), Python (2), and JavaScript (1). To assess prior programming knowledge, we gave students a pre-test which measured their knowledge of basic programming principles such as variables, conditionals, loops, and Game Lab APIs, all in JavaScript. Out of 10 points on the pre-test, the median was 3. One outlier student correctly answered 8 questions.

2.2 Course design

Our course spanned 18 contact hours across 18 days. Class was in a computer lab that seated 25. The 1st author taught the class with the help of four teaching assistants (three undergrads and one high school student). The class followed Code.org's game design curriculum, which used Game Lab, a simple web-based IDE with both a block-based and text-based editor for authoring 2D interactive games with JavaScript. The Code.org curriculum spans more than 30 hours of instruction, so we excluded some lessons. The first 3 weeks of the course covered the subset of JavaScript used in Game Lab and key Game Lab APIs on sprites, animations, and collision detection. Each class began with a brief 5-10 minutes of direct instruction on the lesson for the day, followed by a 45 minute period of self-guided Code.org instruction.

After 3 weeks of instruction, we administered a midterm, then began a 2-week period of game development in which students worked alone or in pairs to design and implement a simple game of their own design across ten class periods. To receive full credit, students' projects needed to: 1) have a background, 2) have a sprite controlled by the player, 3) have a sprite that moves automatically, 4) draw at least one shape, 5) have an animated sprite, and 6) have at least one sprite that responded to collisions. We offered students extra credit for features they wrote down and implemented beyond the basic requirements, incentivizing independent work.

2.3 Explicit strategies

We taught two explicit strategies during the class. To represent strategies, we used a format called Roboto [14], and a tool that helps students execute each step of a Roboto strategy while tracking their progress. Figures 1 and 2 show the text of the strategies and Figure 3 shows the strategy tracker.

The *debug* strategy, shown in Figure 1, was a generic approach to localizing a defect by brainstorming possible causes and investigating each one systematically. If this approach failed, the strategy prompted students to ask the teacher for ideas on possible causes. We taught the strategy just after the lesson that introduced conditionals. To teach the strategy, we discussed the metaphor of fixing a car engine. We asked students if they would use a strategy of unscrewing something without first understanding how the engine worked; most agreed that would be a bad strategy. We then discussed how debugging programs was they same, requiring one to

```
# If you need help finding the problem, ask for help.
Find what your program is doing that you do not want it to do
# Write the line number inside of the program
# and separate with commas.
SET 'possibleCauses' to any lines of the program that
    might be responsible for causing that incorrect 'behavior'
FOR EACH 'cause' IN 'possibleCauses'
    Navigate to 'cause'
    # Ask for help if you need guidance on how.
    Look at the code to verify if it causes the incorrect behavior
    IF 'cause' is the cause of the problem
        # If you need help finding the problem, ask for help.
        Find a way to stop 'cause' from happening
        # Ask for help if you need guidance on how.
        Change the program to stop the incorrect behavior
        # Ask for help if you need guidance on how.
        Mark the task as finished
        RETURN nothing
IF you did not find the cause
    Ask for help finding other possible causes
    Restart the strategy
RETURN nothing
```

Figure 1: The debug strategy.

```
# Describe the behavior as specifically as possible.
SET 'behavior' TO the behavior youd like 'program' to exhibit
IF I know how to implement 'behavior'
    Write code for the 'behavior'
    Run 'program' to test if it exhibits 'behavior' as you expect
    Mark this task as finished
    RETURN nothing
# Use a search query that contains the language you are using and
# describes 'behavior'
Using a search engine such as Google search for relevant examples
UNTIL you have looked at ALL relevant examples
    IF 'result' example seems to be related to your goal
        Click on the link and read the text
        IF the example seems like it might help
            Copy and paste the code into your code editor and ask a
                teacher for help if you don't understand it
            # Change any values to match your needs
            Adapt the code to your needs deleting any lines that you
                are confident are not necessary
            Test your program to ensure the behavior works
            IF the program does not work
                Use the debug strategy to find out why
                RETURN nothing
IF you have not yet found a example
    Ask your teacher for guidance
```

Figure 2: The reuse strategy.

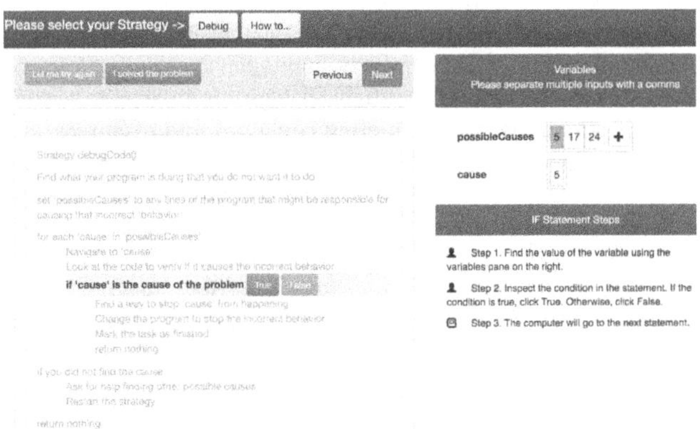

Figure 3: The strategy tracker, showing a conditional step of the debug strategy. The tracker acts as a scratchpad for relevant information and enforces the steps of the strategy.

first understand how the program works and only then edit it. We walked through an example of using the strategy. Then, for the next week, when students asked for help debugging, we prompted them to use the debugging strategy, modeling each step for them, and showing how the strategy could structure their process.

Just before students began developing their own games, we taught the *reuse* strategy shown in Figure 2. The goal of this strategy was to guide program design, helping students to identify the behavior they wanted to implement, then utilize resources such as the web, documentation, and instructors to identify an example to adapt to their game. (To students, we called this the "how to" strategy, but we will call it the *reuse* strategy in this paper). To teach this strategy, we provided direct instruction about how to use it, walked the class through an example, and then modeled its use during one-on-one help requests by showing students how to execute each step of it.

When students had questions in class, we solicited information about their strategy use as follows: 1) we asked "What is your goal right now?", 2) then asked "What strategy are you using to achieve the goal?", and 3) then provided help. While this disincentivized independent use of strategies, it was an opportunity to provide individualized instruction on the strategies, as well as gather data about strategy use. Additionally, not providing help would have subverted the learning goals of the class, which took priority over the research goals. Because of this, we did not expect all students to have a strategy or be using a strategy that we taught. When a student did report using a strategy, it was evident, because they either referred explicitly to a strategy we had taught or struggled to articulate a strategy, instead describing actions they had taken.

One confounding factor in the study was that students needed to feel safe asking for help, otherwise they would not see the strategies modeled, or learn effectively. To mitigate this, we focused on developing trust and rapport with the students, sharing personal details about our experiences with games, game development, programming, and college. All instructors learned students' names and worked with them one-on-one.

2.4 Data collection

To measure barriers to using strategies (RQ1), we gathered three forms of data. The first was during the help requests described above, in which we gathered students' reactions to being taught the strategy (e.g., reluctance, eager opening of the tracker), what help we provided, the outcome of providing the help, and students' reaction to the help we provided. A second source was a daily survey at the end of each class involving programming in which we asked "If you used the debugging strategy, did it help you find the problem?" The third source were two one-on-one interviews in which we asked each student, "What do you like about the strategies?", "What do you not like about the strategies?", and "What strategy do you prefer to use?" We performed these interviews just before the midterm and on the last day of class.

Measuring strategy use (RQ2) was challenging because strategies occur in the mind and are not directly observable. Therefore, we triangulated three sources of data. The first was the use of the Roboto strategy tracker tool. We used usage logging to determine whether students had stepped through any part of a strategy on each day of instruction. The second source was help requests during class; we gathered data about whether students were using the strategy we taught, which we defined to students as "using the strategy tracker or reading the strategy to guide your work." The third source was self-report via an end of class survey asking students whether they used one of the strategies to solve a problem on that day, with or without the tracker. We collated all three data sources for each student, combining them into a single binary variable of whether the strategies had been used.

To measure the relationship between strategy use and productivity (RQ3), we measured productivity by analyzing students' final games for a set of game features (described later). To control for knowledge of JavaScript, we used the midterm scores assessing knowledge of variables, conditionals, Boolean logic, and Game Lab APIs. To measure strategy self-efficacy, our daily debrief survey asked students to express their agreement with the statements "I can follow the debugging strategy that [the instructor] taught to find and fix defects in my programs." and "I can follow the 'how to' strategy to find and adapt examples for my programs." on a 5-point scale of strongly disagree to agree. We asked this each day for each strategy that had been taught on that day or prior.

3 RESULTS

To contextualize our results, we begin by describing the classroom environment. Most students were engaged, but some were tired and slept, some occasionally used their smartphones, and some were distracted by sitting next to friends. The instructor and assistants wandered the lab, proactively offering help, responding to questions, and ensuring students were on task. Since most students spoke English as a second language, students moved at very different paces and the instructors and TAs regularly needed to give further explanation of the Code.org content. As suggested by prior work [11], the purely content-driven instruction in Code.org's curriculum was insufficient to produce robust knowledge of JavaScript's semantics, which led to many defects in students' programs.

3.1 RQ1: Barriers to using strategies

To answer RQ1, we performed several qualitative analyses. We followed Hammer and Berland's views on qualitative coding, not treating the results of our category generation as data itself, but as an organization of claims about data [9].

3.1.1 Strategy Interviews. The first analysis we performed was of the responses to our two interviews about the strategies, one prior to the midterm concerning the debugging strategy, and the second at the end of the course covering both strategies[1]. One author began by identifying categories of sentiments that students expressed about the strategies. This author then discussed the substance of the categories with the rest of the authors and resolved disagreements. The quotes we include paraphrase students' verbatim responses.

The first round of interviews about the debug strategy revealed that 46.7% of students preferred to guess the cause of defects and edit the program to verify their guess, 26.7% preferred asking for help, and 13.3% preferred reading and analyzing their code. Only 13.3% preferred the debug strategy. Out of the 13 distinct sentiments students expressed, only three were positive. Students claimed that they liked the step-by-step nature of the debugging strategy, feeling it helped them stay on track, one calling it a "formula for when you get stuck." Many students reported liking the debug strategy because it gave them an alternative to their ineffective editing strategy. One student said that it "forces us to actually look at our code instead of adding random stuff."

Although many students said that the debug strategy made it easier to solve their problems, the majority of their sentiments about it were negative. These included not being able to use the strategy independently, being unsure where to start, having difficulty identifying possible causes of defects, finding the strategy too time consuming, finding the strategy tracker interface confusing, disliking the tracker's design (having to log in, the website "looking boring"), and finding the strategy as too general and repetitive.

In the second round of interviews, conducted after 2 weeks of open-ended game development, 13.3% students preferred the debug strategy over guessing and editing (33.3%), asking for help (33.3%), and analyzing their code (20.0%). A chi-squared analysis on the frequency of the preferred strategies in the middle and end of the class showed no significant change in strategy preference (χ^2=0.64, p=.89). Students expressed many of the same sentiments about the debug strategy as before, but none of the students reported disliking the interface, being annoyed by having to log in, feeling unsure where to start, or feeling that the strategy was too general. Two new sentiments also emerged: students reported that the steps of the strategies were harder to remember without the tool, and that they disliked strategies rarely gave them solutions right away.

In responses about the reuse strategy, 60% of students claimed not having used it. Students preferred strategies including looking for resources without the tool (26.7%), asking for help (33.3%), and guessing implementation details (20.0%). Only 20.0% preferred the reuse strategy. Students reported liking that the reuse strategy helped them find solutions and that it prompted them to search for resources, whether online or from peers. They disliked, however, that it did not help them find solutions right away and found it harder to remember the steps without the tool. They also reported feeling like the reuse strategy was "pretty much cheating" because it used resources online, that they struggled to interpret the code they found online, that they often could not find resources, and that their lack of prior knowledge hindered their use of it: "kind of hard to know, because some of the things you're trying to learn you don't know yet."

3.1.2 Reactions to Strategy Modeling. To further understand barriers to using strategies, we analyzed notes about the 239 help requests for students' reactions to the help we provided when modeling strategy use. We conducted an inductive, qualitative coding of these notes, which involved generating and refining a set of categories from students' reactions, then classifying and resolving inconsistencies. Table 1 shows the range of reactions.

Students exhibited both positive and negative reactions toward the strategies. Positive reactions were characterized by compliance with, expressions of belief in, or an indication of learning as a result of the strategy. Negative reactions included impatience with the time strategy use required, frustration when the intended goal was not met, or inclination to revert back to guessing and editing.

[1]Our analysis omitted data from 2 students who missed one of the interviews.

Table 1: Categories of student reactions to strategy modeling

Category	Definition	Example notes about student reaction	Frequency
Reaction Not Recorded	Reaction to the help given was not recorded		53
Reaction Irrelevant to Strategy	Reaction was not regarding strategy usage		17
Indifference	No positive or negative feelings toward the strategy	"No reaction to mentioning the debug strategy"	15
Positive Sentiments			
Confidence in Strategy	Indication of a belief in the effectiveness of strategy use	"Seemed satisfied following the strategy and that it helped"	30
Compliance	Willing or enthusiastic use of the strategy	"Willingly participated in using the strategy tool"	19
Internalization	Ability to use strategy without the tool	"Was using the strategy in her head, but not online"	5
Negative Sentiments			
Reluctance	Indications of mild unwillingness to use the strategy	"Smiled and reluctantly agreed to using the strategy tool"	27
Dissatisfaction	Expressions negative emotions in response to the strategy	"He said 'I don't think [the strategy] is useful.'"	12
Resistance	Decision to revert to personal strategy	"Didn't use the strategy because he thought it wasn't helping"	16
Strategy Understanding			
Indicated Learning	Better understanding of the subject from strategy use	"He navigated to the causes and noticed missing parameters"	94
Indicated Difficulty	Confusion or missteps in the process of strategy use	"Didn't know possible causes"	38

These reactions reveal perceived barriers such as reluctance, dissatisfaction, and resistance. External factors, such as the strategy tracker's interface or strategy presentation, might have influenced sentiments, introducing other barriers.

Help request reactions also revealed expressions of struggle. These included difficulty completing the step of the debug strategy that required students to identify possible causes of failures and the step of the reuse strategy that required translating solutions into code. Conversely, students reported that they gained an ability to achieve a goal and indicated a greater understanding of the subject on which they received help by using a strategy.

3.1.3 Sentiments about Strategy Utility. We analyzed students' daily sentiments about the utility of the strategies based on the daily debrief surveys. We present these sentiments as percentages of the total student sentiments at the end of the course, added throughout each day the students were surveyed.

According to students' self-reported data over the whole class, 73% of students said they either agreed or strongly agreed to being able to understand the debug strategy, while 51% of students either agreed or strongly agreed to being able to understand the reuse strategy. Only 53% of the students said that the debug strategy was either helpful or somewhat helpful, while 46% of students said that the reuse strategy was either helpful or somewhat helpful. Only 1% of student responses claimed that both strategies were unhelpful and they were unable to follow said strategy. A large portion of the student responses claimed they never used a strategy: throughout the class, only 54% of students claimed they used the debug strategy, while 47% claimed they used the reuse strategy, at the end of the day. Fishers exact tests showed a significant association between students who reported using the each strategy and students who reported it helpful (both p<.00001).

3.2 RQ2: Scaffolding or tool?

To investigate whether the strategy tracker was scaffolding that eventually could be removed or a tool of consistent utility, we analyzed the use of the strategies over time and how they were used. Figure 4 and 5 show the debug and reuse strategy use over time respectively, including four measures. The first (blue) was the total number of students using the strategies, as indicated by a help request (yellow) in which someone was independently using the strategy, log data (green) showing the students using the strategy tracker, or self-reported use of the strategies (orange) in the daily surveys. These figures show that while use of the strategy tracker rapidly declined over several days, use of the strategies without the tracker continued throughout the course.

Figure 4: Debug strategy use

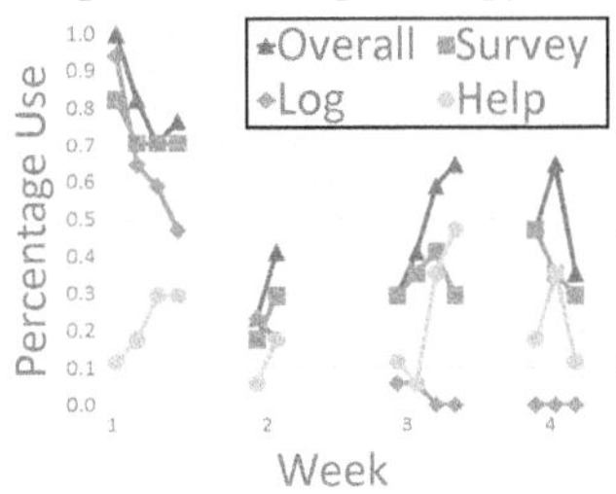

Figure 5: Reuse strategy use

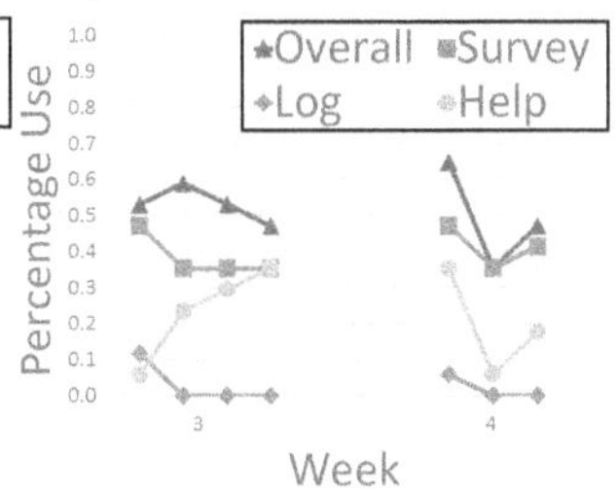

3.3 RQ3: Is strategy use related to productivity?

Our last question concerned the relationship between strategy use and problem solving success. We defined productivity as successful implementation of game features. To identify these features, the teaching team analyzed all 13 final games as a group, generating a comprehensive list of game functionality. The final list of features and their respective frequencies included: keyboard input (13), collisions (13), score tracking (11), enemies (8), sound effects (8), scrolling background (6), lives (4), obstacles (2), gravity (3), animated sprites (8), falling objects (8), collectibles (7), levels (6), dynamic background music (4), title screen (6), game over screen (8), multiplayer (4), bouncing (3), instructions (1), mouse input (1), and restart functionality (1). Students' feature counts ranged from 7 to 12 with a median of 9.

To answer RQ3, we sought to model the relationship between strategy use and this productivity metric. We measured strategy use as the total number of days a student used a strategy via any of our three measures of strategy use and number of features implemented. We first checked for correlations between between game feature count and strategy use for each strategy. We found that using the debug strategy was significantly correlated with productivity (R^2 = 0.2627, $p < 0.05$), but using the reuse strategy was not (R^2 = 0.1414, $p > 0.05$).

Table 2: Ordinal logistic regressions

	Odds Ratio	SE β	Wald	Pr > χ^2
Debug Self Efficacy	0.70	0.75	0.23	0.63
Team	2.15	0.99	0.61	0.44
Debug Usage	1.56	0.36	1.54	0.22
Midterm Score	1.05	0.25	0.04	0.85
Help Request Count	0.98	0.07	0.08	0.77
Reuse Self Efficacy	0.55	0.68	0.76	0.38
Team	1.82	0.99	0.36	0.55
Reuse Usage	1.15	0.26	0.30	0.58
Midterm Score	1.01	0.26	0.00	0.96
Help Request Count	1.03	0.05	0.37	0.54

To account for other factors that may have mediated productivity, we next created ordinal logistic regressions for each strategy including more possible factors that influence the number of implemented features. The other factors we included were 1) prior knowledge of the Game Lab API based on midterm score, as brittle knowledge of the API would have limited productivity; 2) the most frequent response to the self-efficacy question for the strategy on the daily surveys after the midterm, as self-efficacy should have mediated successful use of the strategies; 3) whether or not they were on a team, as teams may have been more productive; and 4) the number of times they requested help from an assistant, as help seeking was likely to play a significant role in successfully building game features. Table 2 shows the resulting regressions. Neither model significantly explained the variation in productivity, suggesting that additional factors, or interactions between factors, were responsible for the number of game features students implemented.

4 DISCUSSION

Our case study revealed several trends. First, with respect to barriers (RQ1), all of our data sources suggest that while the adolescents in our class could see the merits of the strategies in the abstract, many did not see enough value to use them. Most chose to engage in rapid cycles of editing and testing, without deeply understanding their code, rather than the more systematic strategies we taught that required reasoning about program behavior. Student sentiments suggest that this was partly because of a perception that strategies slowed them down, but also because many of the skills the strategy required were something students' did not feel confident performing without help, such as identifying possible causes of defects or finding and reasoning about relevant code online. Our results on scaffolding (RQ2) suggest that having a tool that aided strategy execution may have scaffolded strategy learning over time, but that students who used the strategies appeared to do so by internalizing the them, rather than use the tracker. Our results on productivity (RQ3) suggest that while there was an association between using the debug strategy and how many game features students implemented, the relationship was not a direct one: there were likely many interacting factors that we did not model that determine whether students' were able to use explicit strategies to effectively guide their problem solving.

There are several possible interpretations of these results. One is that while explicit strategies may be more effective in principle, unless students believe they can perform them independently, they will be reluctant to use them, even when they have directly observed their benefits. A related interpretation is that providing effective, explicit strategies may only be effective for learners that have strong self-regulation skills, as prior work shows that learners with weaker regulation skills are often unaware of the need for better strategies [7, 10, 17, 20]. Another interpretation is an "attention economic" one [4]: in a classroom environment with substantial teaching support, asking for help is a more efficient strategy than trying to independently use a programming strategy a student has just learned; after all, both strategies had numerous failure modes that encouraged students to ask for help if they got stuck. Another interpretation is that the strategies were simply too sophisticated to learn while also learning basic programming concepts. Perhaps simpler strategies, scaffolded by instructor guidance, would be more likely to be adopted and more likely to impact behavior, even if they are less effective. For example, future work could explore a debugging strategy that simply prompts students to "find and understand the cause before editing," or a reuse strategy that prompts students to "ask an expert for an example and then work with them to adapt it to your needs." This level of strategic detail might be more appropriate for rank novices, and the level of complexity of problems they tend to face. Finally, perhaps most adolescents, who are known to have not yet fully developed executive functioning [2], do not yet have the self-regulation skills yet to delay gratification in a way that explicit programming strategies require.

Our study's limitations complicate these interpretations. Students might have been more positive in the interviews and surveys because of participant response bias. Our class was students' last of the day, and so many of their self-regulation skills may have been exhausted by a long day of math, writing, college prep, and other electives. The students we studied are also not representative of all adolescents learning to code.

Despite these limitations, our results have important implications for future research and teaching. First, our data suggest that there appear to be many interacting factors that influence adoption and use of explicit strategies in classrooms, such as students' willingness to delay gratification, the availability of help, the strength of their self-regulation skills, self-efficacy with the specific strategies taught, the likelihood of students' encountering problems that benefit from strategy use, and the alignment between the specific strategies taught and students' prior knowledge. This suggests that studying strategies in strictly controlled settings that omit these factors is not likely to be fruitful. Second, despite having a tool that carefully taught the strategies, an instructor that patiently explained the strategies, and an entire team of teaching assistants model the use of strategies with individual students, most students did not adopt the strategies. If we are to succeed in teaching adolescents programming strategies we know to be effective, future work must invent more effective, scalable ways to teach strategies. We hope our results are a solid foundation for this work.

ACKNOWLEDGMENTS

We thank our study participants for their time, the Upward Bound team for their support, and Dastyni Loksa for his feedback on the study design. This work was supported in part by the National Science Foundation under grants CCF-1703734 and CCF-1703304.

REFERENCES

[1] Roger Azevedo and Jennifer G Cromley. 2004. Does training on self-regulated learning facilitate students' learning with hypermedia? *Journal of Educational Psychology* 96, 3 (2004), 523.

[2] Roy F. Baumeister and Kathleen D. Vohs. 2003. Self-regulation and the executive function of the self. *Handbook of self and identity* 1 (2003), 197–217.

[3] Suresh K. Bhavnani, Frederick A. Peck, and Frederick Reif. 2008. Strategy-Based Instruction: Lessons Learned in Teaching the Effective and Efficient Use of Computer Applications. *ACM Transactions on Computer-Human Interaction* 15, 1, Article 2 (May 2008), 43 pages. https://doi.org/10.1145/1352782.1352784

[4] Alan F. Blackwell. 2002. First steps in programming: A rationale for attention investment models. In *IEEE Symposium on Visual Languages and Human-Centric Computing*. 2.

[5] Ryan Chmiel and Michael C. Loui. 2004. Debugging: From Novice to Expert. In *ACM SIGCSE Technical Symposium on Computer Science Education*. 17–21. https://doi.org/10.1145/971300.971310

[6] K Anders Ericsson, Ralf T Krampe, and Clemens Tesch-Römer. 1993. The role of deliberate practice in the acquisition of expert performance. *Psychological review* 100, 3 (1993), 363.

[7] Katrina Falkner, Rebecca Vivian, and Nickolas JG Falkner. 2014. Identifying computer science self-regulated learning strategies. In *Proceedings of the 2014 conference on Innovation & technology in computer science education*. ACM, New York, NY, 291–296.

[8] Matthias Felleisen, Robert Bruce Findler, Matthew Flatt, and Shriram Krishnamurthi. 2018. *How to design programs: an introduction to programming and computing*. MIT Press, Cambridge, MA.

[9] David Hammer and Leema K Berland. 2014. Confusing claims for data: A critique of common practices for presenting qualitative research on learning. *Journal of the Learning Sciences* 23, 1 (2014), 37–46.

[10] Matthias Hauswirth and Andrea Adamoli. 2017. Metacognitive calibration when learning to program. In *Proceedings of the 17th Koli Calling Conference on Computing Education Research*. 50–59.

[11] Ada S Kim and Andrew J Ko. 2017. A pedagogical analysis of online coding tutorials. In *ACM SIGCSE Technical Symposium on Computer Science Education*. 321–326.

[12] Andrew J Ko, Robin Abraham, Laura Beckwith, Alan Blackwell, Margaret Burnett, Martin Erwig, Chris Scaffidi, Joseph Lawrance, Henry Lieberman, Brad Myers, et al. 2011. The state of the art in end-user software engineering. *Comput. Surveys* 43, 3 (2011), 21.

[13] Andrew J Ko, Brad A Myers, and Htet Htet Aung. 2004. Six learning barriers in end-user programming systems. In *IEEE Symposium on Visual Languages and Human-Centric Computing*. 199–206.

[14] Thomas D LaToza, Maryam Arab, Dastyni Loksa, and Andrew J. Ko. 2018. Explicit Programming Strategies. *In review* (2018).

[15] Raymond Lister, Elizabeth S. Adams, Sue Fitzgerald, William Fone, John Hamer, Morten Lindholm, Robert McCartney, Jan Erik Moström, Kate Sanders, Otto Seppälä, Beth Simon, and Lynda Thomas. 2004. A Multi-national Study of Reading and Tracing Skills in Novice Programmers. *SIGCSE Bulletin* 36, 4 (June 2004), 119–150. https://doi.org/10.1145/1041624.1041673

[16] Dastyni Loksa and Andrew J Ko. 2016. The role of self-regulation in programming problem solving process and success. In *ACM International Computing Education Research Conference*. 83–91.

[17] Dastyni Loksa, Andrew J Ko, Will Jernigan, Alannah Oleson, Christopher J Mendez, and Margaret M Burnett. 2016. Programming, problem solving, and self-awareness: effects of explicit guidance. In *ACM SIGCHI Conference on Human Factors in Computing Systems*. 1449–1461.

[18] Greg L Nelson, Benjamin Xie, and Andrew J Ko. 2017. Comprehension First: Evaluating a Novel Pedagogy and Tutoring System for Program Tracing in CS1. In *ACM International Computing Education Research Conference*. 2–11.

[19] Devon H. O'Dell. 2017. The Debugging Mindset. *ACM Queue* 15, 1, Article 50 (Feb. 2017), 20 pages. https://doi.org/10.1145/3055301.3068754

[20] James Prather, Raymond Pettit, Kayla McMurry, Alani Peters, John Homer, and Maxine Cohen. 2018. Metacognitive Difficulties Faced by Novice Programmers in Automated Assessment Tools. In *Proceedings of the 2018 ACM Conference on International Computing Education Research*. 41–50.

[21] Yizhou Qian and James Lehman. 2017. Students' Misconceptions and Other Difficulties in Introductory Programming: A Literature Review. *ACM Transactions on Computing Education* 18, 1, Article 1 (Oct. 2017), 24 pages. https://doi.org/10.1145/3077618

[22] Emmanuel Schanzer, Kathi Fisler, and Shriram Krishnamurthi. 2018. Assessing Bootstrap: Algebra Students on Scaffolded and Unscaffolded Word Problems. In *ACM Technical Symposium on Computer Science Education*. 8–13.

[23] Benjamin Xie, Greg L. Nelson, and Andrew J. Ko. 2018. An Explicit Strategy to Scaffold Novice Program Tracing. In *ACM Technical Symposium on Computer Science Education*. 344–349. https://doi.org/10.1145/3159450.3159527

Teachers' Experiences of using PRIMM to Teach Programming in School

Sue Sentance*
King's College London
sue@raspberrypi.org

Jane Waite
Queen Mary University of London
j.l.waite@qmul.ac.uk

Maria Kallia
King's College London
maria.kallia@kcl.ac.uk

ABSTRACT

PRIMM is an approach to teaching programming at K-12 that facilitates the structure of lessons in a purposeful way. PRIMM stands for Predict-Run-Investigate-Modify-Make, and draws on recent research in programming education. In particular the PRIMM approach recognises that starting with existing code and being able to explain what it does gives novice programmers the confidence to write their own programs. Using the PRIMM approach, teachers can devise scaffolded and targeted tasks for students which helps engender understanding, particularly for those who may have previously struggled to understand programming concepts. In this techniques paper, we consider what PRIMM is, and the experiences that teachers have had of using the structure in the classroom. PRIMM materials have been trialled in schools in a study involving around 500 students aged 11-14. From interviews with nine participating teachers we have found that teachers particularly value the collaborative approach taken in PRIMM, the structure given to lessons, and the way that resources can be differentiated. We propose that PRIMM is an approach that could be adopted in all phases of programming education as well as in teacher training.

CCS CONCEPTS

• **Social and professional topics → K-12 education; Computer science education;**

KEYWORDS

K-12 education, programming education, K-12 teachers

ACM Reference Format:
Sue Sentance, Jane Waite, and Maria Kallia. 2019. Teachers' Experiences of using PRIMM to Teach Programming in School. In *Proceedings of the 50th ACM Technical Symposium on Computer Science Education (SIGCSE '19), February 27-March 2, 2019, Minneapolis, MN, USA.* ACM, New York, NY, USA, 7 pages. https://doi.org/10.1145/3287324.3287477

1 INTRODUCTION

The reformation of school computing in England has been a welcome development given that it is essential that we prepare all young people with the digital skills they need to fully participate in society. The introduction of new computer science concepts and skills into the curriculum, particularly in the area of computer programming, has been challenging for students and teachers, firstly because models for pedagogy are either not fully formed or shared with teachers, and secondly, because computer programming can be difficult to learn [24]. It is thus recognised that more research needs to be conducted with a focus on appropriate pedagogy [31].

Computing teachers benefit from access to proven teaching strategies and pedagogies relating to programming. Much research has been carried out in this area, mostly in higher education settings, but only recently in schools, and this has not been widely translated into usable structures for teachers. Consequently, computing teachers are being called to deliver a challenging subject with insufficient knowledge of effective teaching strategies and on how to develop and enhance vital competencies to accomplish this task. To address these issues, we have developed and are evaluating a new pedagogical model for teaching and learning programming (PRIMM) [26]. PRIMM can be used to structure lessons and sequences of lessons with the following activities:

- **Predict** what code will do
- **Run** the code to test predictions
- **Investigate** the structure of code
- **Modify** the code to add functionality
- **Make** a new program using the same/modified structures.

PRIMM stands for **Predict**, **Run**, **Investigate**, **Modify** and **Make**. Using PRIMM, classroom activities can be designed which involve predicting the output of code, code comprehension and gradually making new programs. It is a method of teaching programming that counters the known problem of novices trying to write programs before they are able to read them [15]. It incorporates activities that scaffold learning for students and provides a structure for lessons.

In this techniques paper, we describe the rationale for this approach, exemplify it, and describe teachers' experiences. In a study of the PRIMM methodology we interviewed nine experienced K-12 Computing teachers about their teaching of programming to students aged 11-14 using PRIMM. From our analysis we identified that teachers particularly value predicting what code does, the potential for differentiation to a wide range of abilities, and the structure provided by PRIMM.

2 TEACHING PROGRAMMING: INSTRUCTIONAL APPROACHES

Much research associated with the teaching of programming has focused on pedagogy and instructional approaches to teaching. From the 1980s we see an emphasis on learners constructing knowledge as they explore [22]; applying ideas from Papert's constructionism

*The first author now works at the Raspberry Pi Foundation

SIGCSE '19, February 27-March 2, 2019, Minneapolis, MN, USA

ACM ISBN 978-1-4503-5890-3/19/02...$15.00
https://doi.org/10.1145/3287324.3287477

we see instructional approaches based around open-ended activities, through which students can develop a personal understanding of newly introduced concepts or devices.

More recent research has highlighted the need for guided instruction to ensure that learners circumnavigate a carefully constructed progression to develop a complete mental model [8, 9, 17, 20, 25]. Grover et al. suggest that to foster deep learning a combination of guided discovery and instruction rather than pure discovery and 'tinkering' would be more successful[9]. This sentiment is echoed by a number of studies with emerging evidence that some of the more difficult concepts such as initialisation, variables and loops need to be explicitly taught [11, 12, 20]. Other studies raise the need for learners' cognitive load to be managed by more closely controlling learning opportunities and learning experiences [1, 32, 33]. This research has implications for pedagogy in school, suggesting that targeted teaching is needed for difficult concepts within a controlled progression of learning experiences [35].

Research in the teaching of programming has also included a focus on the levels of abstraction involved in understanding how to write programs. Cutts et al. reviewed university students use of vocabulary when solving multiple choice questions [6] and suggested a teaching model of student understanding of programs called the Abstraction Transition Taxonomy (ATT) which included three levels of language in programming: English, CS Speak and Code. The recommendation from this research was to support learners to be able to transition across all levels. Another framework, the Levels of Abstraction (LOA) framework, has been developed for introductory programming courses [2, 23, 28]. Four levels are described: *execution*; *program*; *algorithm* and *problem* [2]. The focus of the LOA framework is on learners knowing what level they are working at and being able to transition between the levels.

Another focus has been on reading and tracing code. Work by Lister and colleagues over many years has highlighted the importance of reading code and being able to trace what it does before writing new code[15, 16]. Comparing tracing skills to code writing, they demonstrated that novices require a 50% tracing code accuracy before they can independently write code with confidence [16, 34]. Learning to program is sequential and cumulative, and tracing requires students to draw on accumulated knowledge to conceive a big picture. Work by Teague and Lister in this area suggests that novice learners should be focused on very small tasks with single elements [30]. Another study concluded that as well as inferring meaning from code from its structure, the first step should be to make inferences about the execution of the program [5].

Studies related to code comprehension have also highlighted the importance of reading code to address misconceptions of algorithm efficiency [7] and the use of worked examples to understand how variables change over time [29]. Gujberova and Kalas recommended a sequence of carefully graded learning activities for primary students to improve programming and computational thinking, including activities where learners read and interpreted each line of code, as well as a stage for reading the entire program and predicting the outcome [10]. Another approach is subgoal modelling, where meaningful labels are added to worked examples to visually group steps into subgoals - thereby highlighting the structure of code. Two higher education studies [18, 21] used this strategy with exemplar text, worked examples and problems. Both reports concluded that those students given subgoals performed significantly better than those who had no subgoals or who added their own subgoals.

Another approach used in the teaching of programming is Use-modify-create (UMC). UMC is a teaching framework for supporting progression in learning to program [14]. Learners move along a continuum from where they first *use* programs made by someone else to finally *create* their own programs. Between these points they *modify* work made by someone else so that the modified material becomes 'theirs'.

3 THE PRIMM APPROACH

The PRIMM approach builds on some of the research cited above. In particular it draws primarily on three areas of research:

- **Tracing and read-before-you-write**[15, 16]. PRIMM draws on tracing and reading code as an important principle for teaching programming [15]. The *predict* phase of PRIMM encourages students to practice reading code and working out what it will do when executed.
- **Use-Modify-Create** [14]. PRIMM is influenced by the work on Use-Modify-Create (UMC) [14]. PRIMM's *predict, run* and *investigate* phases map to the *use* stage. *Modify* is the same across both frameworks. PRIMM's *make* phase is equivalent to *create*. PRIMM has partly built on UMC to gradually transfer ownership of the program to the student. It supports the student's confidence as they are not burdened by the prospect of failure until they understand how the program works.
- **Levels of Abstraction** [6, 23]. Thirdly, PRIMM draws on work relating to abstraction [6, 23], in that the different activities focus on different levels of abstraction. The *Predict* and *Run* phases focuses very much on the execution of code, whereas the *Investigate* stage is about the program, or Cutts et al's *Code* level. When students reach the *Make* stage they have developed skills to focus on the 'problem' that needs to be solved.

4 A PRIMM LESSON

In this section, we briefly describe a PRIMM lesson or sequence of lessons, and the materials that exemplify this. The intention is that teachers can develop their own PRIMM-like materials at an appropriate level for their students.

4.1 Predict and Run

At the beginning of a PRIMM lesson, students are given a short program on the board, or on paper, to look at in pairs. The task is for them to write down the output of the program. Our examples use Python; two examples are shown in Figures 1 and 2.

The teacher discusses the students' answers with the class, and students then download code and run to check their prediction. It is important that they do not copy the code as this is a completely different process. Access to a shared area where starter programs are stored is important, and multiple **predict** activities can be used.

4.2 Investigate

In this phase of the lesson or sequence of lessons, students are asked code comprehension questions about the same program or snippet

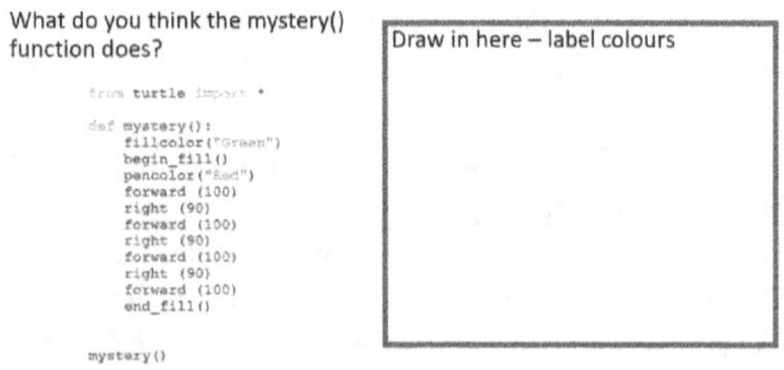

Figure 1: A predict activity from one of the first lessons

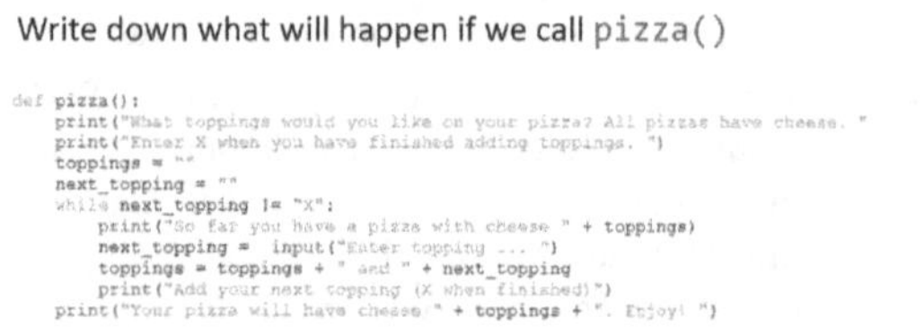

Figure 2: A predict activity from a more advanced lesson

Figure 3: Sample question in the investigate phase

of code. These questions pick out certain aspects of the program to develop understanding. Developing good questions in this section requires a good understanding of programming and student misconceptions, and the Block Model [25] can help to structure questions. For example, students may be asked a question about the execution of the whole program, which requires an understanding of the underlying algorithm and program execution. In the pizza example shown in Figure 2, the student may be asked what happens if the user does not add any toppings. In addition questions can be asked which enable the students to discuss individual snippets of codes, such as that shown in Figure 3. Discussion of the question should ideally take place in pairs or groups to enable students to develop the vocabulary they need to talk about the program [6].

4.3 Modify and Make

In this phase of the lesson the learners are able to build on the existing program to modify and create new programs. Carefully structured activities allow progression from simple changes to more substantial functional changes to the program. Having an existing program in place gives the student confidence and something to build on. Sometimes the *modify* task is to remove obvious glitches with the program. For example, following the Pizza example in Figure 2, a *modify* task may to be to improve the program so that the output does not end with *"and"*. Subsequently, in the *make* phase, the students will be asked to create a new program from a problem description, drawing on what they have learned about loops and string manipulation from the previous program [6].

5 THE STUDY

As part of our research into the effectiveness of PRIMM, we applied design-based research methodology [4] to evaluate and test the materials implementing the PRIMM approach. The goal of design-based research (DBR) is to *"use the close study of learning as it unfolds within a naturalistic context that contains theoretically inspired innovations, usually that have passed through multiple iterations, to then develop new theories, artifacts, and practices that can be generalized to other schools and classrooms."* [p.151][3]. DBR takes materials that have been developed through a particular theoretical perspective and implements them in a naturalistic setting, iterating with the results of the materials in context. The PRIMM materials are on their third iteration: firstly in a small study in a CPD setting [26], secondly used in a pilot study with six teachers (Section 5.1), and the third iteration developed for the main study (Section 5.2). We used DBR to consider both the structure of PRIMM as a teaching aid and the actual materials produced to exemplify PRIMM.

5.1 The pilot study

We designed and implemented a short pilot study to evaluate the effectiveness of PRIMM and understand it better. The pilot study involved 6 teachers and approximately 80 students over 4-7 lessons, followed by individual interviews with the teachers to consider their views of PRIMM and the materials. Interviews were recorded, transcribed, coded and analysed. Teachers were enthusiastic about the PRIMM structure; our analysis of the interviews enabled us to further develop the materials and to devise appropriate research instruments for the subsequent main study. For the pilot we developed PRIMM-style worksheets for teachers to use with the intention of teachers developing them further and becoming co-creators of PRIMM materials. We concluded that we needed to provide more comprehensive materials and that teachers had limited confidence and time to develop their own resources in the PRIMM style.

5.2 The main study

For the main study we built on the pilot study in refining both the study materials and the analysis process. 14 teachers were recruited, of whom 13 completed the trial and taught just less than 500 students using PRIMM for a period of three to four months at the beginning of 2018. As a separate part of the study we used a quasi-experimental approach to investigate the impact of PRIMM on students' performance [27], with an experimental group of 493 students performing significantly better ($p<.05$) than a comparison group of 180 students in a post-test. In this paper, we focus on the qualitative analysis, and the teachers' experiences of PRIMM.

5.3 Participants

Teachers were recruited to the study via a number of channels, being selected on the basis of having students undertaking an appropriate programming module within the timeframe of our study. Teachers attended a one-day training session on the PRIMM approach and materials, which included the rationale behind DBR; teachers were invited to adapt, edit and upload edited materials as they wished during the study. Teachers completed evaluations of the PRIMM lessons that they taught, and interviews were arranged at the end of the trial with PRIMM materials. All ethical procedures were adhered to. Information about the teachers is shown in Table 1.

Table 1: Summary of teacher and lesson characteristics

ID	Teacher gender	Grade	Class gender in study	No. classes	No. topics covered	No. lessons \topic
A	Female	8th	Girls	2	10	1
B	Male	8th	Boys	3	7	2
C	Male	7th	Mixed	2	8	2
D	Female	6th	Mixed	1	5	2-3
E	Male	8th	Mixed	2	10	2-3
F	Female	7&8th	Mixed	4	4	2
G	Male	7th	Girls	3	7	1
H	Male	7th	Mixed	6	7-9	1-2
I	Male	8th	Girls	2	8	1

5.4 Data collection: interviews

Semi-structured interviews were designed and conducted. After the pilot study (see Section 5.1) we reviewed the interview questions for their contribution and usefulness and adapted them for the follow up study interview. In the pilot study teachers were asked questions on general information about sessions with PRIMM and questions on PRIMM experiences. The general questions were retained as they were useful to verify subject material covered; the experience questions were expanded and grouped over three sections, resulting in four sections of questions for the main study:

- Section A General information about PRIMM sessions
- Section B Impact of PRIMM on students' programming skills
- Section C Impact of PRIMM on teachers' confidence
- Section D Use of PRIMM resources and the future

In total nine interviews were held with teachers from the 13 participating schools: these 9 were representative of the sample of 13 (see Table 1). All interviews and focus groups were completed in the spring of 2018.

5.5 Data analysis

All interviews were conducted online, audio recorded and transcribed. A thematic qualitative data analysis (QDA) approach was used to analyse the transcribed interviews and outcomes of tasks based on the methodology detailed by [13]. NVivo was used to support the process of coding text segments. Two of the authors worked on the coding of the interviews.

In the pilot study we had first generated high level categories deductively from the research questions [13]. We had also created sub-categories at this stage, based on knowledge of the field [19]. However, in the main study we started by coding inductively from the interviews [19]. The rationale for this decision was to investigate whether there were any significant differences in the emergent themes. The overall objective at this point was to create main themes which would lead to a structure for reporting which would not be pre-determined by any initial constraints.

Table 2: Summary of codes

Overarching theme	% segments coded to this theme
A Practical details of implementation	9%
B Skills needed to program	4%
C. Stages of PRIMM	18%
D. Impact and use of PRIMM	23%
E. Differentiation and assessment	24%
F. Adaptation and future use	12%
G. Teachers' feelings and emotions	11%

One author coded two of the interviews adding and amending categories and sub-categories inductively. After this first pass of coding, we reviewed and revised the resultant categories to confirm they matched the data coded. Two interviews provided approximately 1/5th of the overall transcripts in line with recommendations from [13] of 10 to 20% for the first pass. Following this, all interviews were coded. Emergent patterns were recognized and new codes created to hierarchically group codes. This process was repeated across the categories creating, merging and splitting codes inductively [13, 19]. Once the more elaborate category system had been created, we checked that all data adhered to the new coding structure and recoded as necessary [13]. A second researcher then coded three of the nine interviews (33% of the text) a second time, with a Cohen's Kappa reliability score of 0.75, which is considered as good agreement between researchers.

6 RESULTS: TEACHERS' EXPERIENCES

Through an iterative coding process seven key themes emerged from the data, as shown in Table 2, which shows the themes and the % of coded segments for each theme. In total there were 1603 coded segments. Within the 6 themes, categories were divided and further sub-divided to capture teachers' contributions. In total there were 87 separate sub-categories of themes. The 20 most commonly occurring of these 101 sub-categories is shown in Table 3.

From the 20 most common sub-categories and from our own theming exercise, we can see that teachers were commenting largely on the structure and use of PRIMM, differentiation for different groups of students, and also their own response to teaching in this way as teachers.

6.1 The structure and use of PRIMM

Teachers commented on a range of aspects of PRIMM that supported their teaching. Several teachers liked the way the lessons were divided up into different activities and maintained interest of students of different abilities:

> *"...it's chunking it up ... and each lesson having a new challenge that builds on the previous one so it keeps the interest of the ones that have raced ahead in the previous lesson."* (Teacher A)

One teacher commented that the **predict and run** part of the lesson promoted student engagement:

Table 3: Most common sub-categories

No	Sub-category	No. segments
1	Use and adaptation of PRIMM	147
2	Use for lower ability children	91
3	Predict aspect of PRIMM	78
4	Teacher emotions	70
5	Progress made by pupils	63
6	Modify aspect of PRIMM	59
7	Investigate aspect of PRIMM	58
8	Use for higher ability children	50
9	PRIMM being fun	46
10	Future use of PRIMM	42
11	Make aspect of PRIMM	35
12	Routine nature of PRIMM	34
13	Differentiation by group	32
14	Assessment	32
15	Run aspect of PRIMM	31
16	Repeating or interwoven concepts	30
17	Differentation by task	30
18	Flow of control and tracing	27
19	Differentiation by teacher guidance	25
20	Pupil/pupil communication	23

> *"I think the Predict bit drew them into the lesson from the start and then they were focused and that's what made them want to get involved."* (Teacher I)

Generally, asking students to predict what code would do without writing any was a new strategy for teachers. Teacher C commented that he felt it set much higher expectations of his students. Several other teachers referred to the collaborative nature of PRIMM:

> *"I think the starter activity, where they actually have a clear activity, that was very good because it got them to work with each other, help them help each other, really. And then, moving on, [we had] the code to be given to the students to actually work with."* (Teacher H)

Teachers also commented on the independence and thinking skills generated by predicting what the code would do:

> *"With the starters, quite often I used a whiteboard where they actually had to write down what they thought the program was going to do, what values they thought the program was going to create. Because they were having to work out and write down what the program was doing, they were having to actually think about for themselves, rather than me telling them what the program was doing."* (Teacher C)

Teachers could see the value of asking questions to demonstrate code comprehension, although the **investigate** part of the process was felt to be a difficult part of the lesson for some students. In part this was caused by the pitch of the materials (written by the research team) being too high, and including some challenging questions. However alongside these concerns teachers acknowledged that they helped students gain an understanding of what was going on in the program:

> *" They were spotting how things happened or the significance of particular bits of the code and realising that essentially that the task was easier than they might previously have thought."* (Teacher I)

Teacher I linked enjoyment of the **modify** stage and independence as he said:

> *"The less able ones [students] enjoyed it (modify) because they got what they were doing when they were at that stage. They were more sure of themselves than they have been in previous Python lessons where they've relied on my telling them. This was them doing it themselves ... the difference was tangible."* (Teacher I)

Eight of the nine teachers mentioned how clear the PRIMM process was, how easy it was to follow the PRIMM structure or the routine repeatable nature of PRIMM:

> *"By the third lesson they were familiar with the structure and they were happy to go with it. They knew what was coming next, if you like, without necessarily knowing what the content was going to be, they knew what was coming up next."* (Teacher I)

Some of the content provided in the PRIMM materials was felt to be too advanced for students at some schools, and teachers felt they were pushing students through it. For example, Teacher D pointed out that he felt pressurized to get learners to complete work:

> *"In one sense, it was very well structured because it meant that the high-performance students never run out of work. In none of the lessons did I have students who completed every single thing. But it also meant that I was sort of pushing on a lot."* (Teacher D)

The PRIMM **modify** stage was linked to learner confidence:

> *"...previously, when they're writing their own programs, we have so much trouble with syntax errors and half the lesson is just them sorting out syntax. So actually being able to modify it, they can think a little bit more about what their code is doing rather than whether they've got a colon in the right place or whatever. And then I think, moving on, once they get to making their own, they've got that little bit more confidence that they've got a starting point to move on from"* (Teacher A)

Teachers reported valuing and making time for the *make* aspect, despite being short of time:

> *"One of the reasons I didn't get through ten activities is that the geography quiz was a really interesting make project for them, yet most of them barely started their first question within the time available in one hour across that lesson. I actually sacrificed the next lesson ... it was a nice lesson to have as an extension without introducing new concepts. We actually gave up another hour to making and peer reviewing the geography quiz"* (Teacher A)

6.2 Accessibility to a range of learners

One of the motivations behind PRIMM was that mandatory computing needs to be accessible to students with a wide range of abilities, and those who may not have any innate interest in the subject. For example, Teacher D mentioned that if students were not interested at all in programming, they could get into the content of the lesson much more quickly *"because they didn't have to go through the process of typing it out themselves"*.

Three of the teachers described how they adapted some of the resources in the **investigate** stage, for example making missing word activities. Some teachers described how their lower-ability learners did not get on to the final **make** activities but that they had still achieved some of the learning outcomes:

> *"I found that the resources for each lesson had enough stretch for those that got it straight away and wanted to go ahead, but also there was enough so that those that didn't get it. They could carry on modifying, not necessarily getting onto the make part... and they didn't have that sense of frustration that they weren't doing anything."* (Teacher D)

Teacher D also saw starting with an existing program an advantageous way to make progress:

> *"It's like a writer, isn't it? You write an essay. If you start with a blank bit of paper, that scares some people. I think the same can be true of a blank IDLE screen. So I think having a structure to hinge what they're doing on and not starting blank and the idea of tinkering is actually a good one."* (Teacher D)

Many of the lower-ability students lack confidence in programming but teachers felt that the PRIMM structure enabled students to gradually build up confidence through the repetitive nature of the exercises, and be more comfortable about making mistakes:

> *"At first, they weren't confident by themselves to predict, and so I'd ask them to talk in pairs, for example, as I think they were scared of getting it wrong ... But as we went on and it became a routine that we did it, and I had to build up the fact that they probably will fail as resilience ... as a normal way of working. Once they got to that point, they realised if they got it wrong, it didn't actually matter, because it actually gave us more to talk about and about why they thought it was wrong, and mistakes were completely acceptable and a normal part of computer science."* (Teacher D)

6.3 Teachers' personal experience

Teachers talked a lot about how they experienced teaching with PRIMM personally. Several teachers discussed gaining more confidence or insight into their own teaching methods.

> *"I felt that the structure, it's something that I could hand over to someone that wasn't such a confident coder and they could go with it as well. "* (Teacher A)

Other teachers mentioned that using PRIMM made them more confident in their own students ability to learn new concepts:

> *"I think that's one of the things that I'd take away from PRIMM. It's something that had changed my practice and it made me I suppose more confident in kids' ability to grasp functions or user-defined functions and procedures. I'd say that was one of the few things in which I'd changed in terms of confidence."* (Teacher B)

Another teacher explained how they had more idea of students' progress during the lesson, which made them more effective:

> *"I found I could get round the room much more quickly, and I was seeing everyone's screen or I was being shown things. Things were being explained to me, instead of me asking for explanations from them."* (Teacher I)

One of the most confident and experienced teachers in the study, who found keeping to the PRIMM structure through the whole trial quite constraining, talked about the PRIMM approach as something he would use amongst other approaches, and repeated several times that he thought of PRIMM as a 'philosophy' rather than a 'methodology'. From this we infer that the structure was restrictive to him, but that the inherent ideas implicit were useful:

> *"I think the structure of PRIMM every lesson is a bit constraining. But I think as a philosophy, it's great. And I hope that the post-test against the control group shows that PRIMM is successful because it seems to make sense. It seems to me that, as a philosophy, it would be great. As a methodology, it's quite constricting."* (Teacher B)

Teachers also talked about adapting the resources for future use, which implies a confidence to develop their teaching further. Finally, teachers had comments on improvements to the materials, or how they might adapt the approach for their particular students. Overall teachers were positive: *"It really does work! "* (Teacher I)

6.4 Summary

Our study to date indicates that teachers value the structure provided by PRIMM. Many comments related to the *Predict* phase particularly. This aligns with the work around the importance of reading and tracing code [15, 30, 34] as well as the importance of understanding transition between different levels of a program [2, 6, 23, 28]. Teachers like the idea of students modifying existing code, supported by the UMC approach [14], although in some cases the materials were too weighty for the teachers to reach those sections in the time available. In terms of the materials we developed to exemplify PRIMM, our research indicates that while the *structure* of the lessons suited the lower ability students in the class, the quantity of *content* in the materials meant teachers could not complete all the activities planned. This does not necessarily reflect on the PRIMM structure but indicates that both the structure and content of PRIMM lessons are equally important.

Some teachers in our study were very willing to adapt materials and create new ones for students, for topics that we had not yet covered, in particular. Other teachers were less confident to do this and felt constrained by being in a research study. We reflected that, although we had built up good relationships with teachers in the study, in future studies we would ensure that materials were co-constructed and owned more definitively by teachers.

7 CONCLUSION

In this paper we have described the structure of the PRIMM approach and the materials we developed to exemplify it. Through interviews with teachers we have gained an understanding of the extent to which PRIMM is useful in school.

From teacher feedback, we can conclude that teachers find the approach useful and indicate that it helps students to gain a better understanding of programming, as well as structuring productive lessons. We have shown that teachers particularly value the collaborative approach taken in PRIMM, and the structure given to the lessons. Teachers also could see the potential for differentiation to a wide range of abilities, and the focus on subject-specific vocabulary that PRIMM engenders.

Although there has been much research around programming pedagogy, with a range of strategies suggested, our experience to date suggests that this approach offers teachers a clear and easy-to-follow structure for lessons that other approaches have not provided. For this reason, in our future work we plan to revisit the methodology used to ensure that teachers feel able to engage more with the materials design and take an enhanced participatory role in the research. We are collecting PRIMM-style resources that teachers have developed to use in their classrooms to use as exemplars for a wider body of teachers. We anticipate that this approach may be of use to other researchers of school-based computing education.

REFERENCES

[1] Giora Alexandron, Michal Armoni, Michal Gordon, and David Harel. 2014. Scenario-based Programming: Reducing the Cognitive Load, Fostering Abstract Thinking. In *Companion Proceedings of the 36th International Conference on Software Engineering (ICSE Companion 2014)*. ACM, New York, NY, USA, 311–320. https://doi.org/10.1145/2591062.2591167 00023.

[2] Michal Armoni. 2013. On Teaching Abstraction in Computer Science to Novices. *Journal of Computers in Mathematics and Science Teaching* 32, 3 (2013), 265–284.

[3] Sasha Barab. 2014. Design-based research: A methodological toolkit for engineering change. In *The Cambridge Handbook of the Learning Sciences, Second Edition*. Cambridge University Press.

[4] Sasha Barab and Kurt Squire. 2004. Design-based research: Putting a stake in the ground. *The journal of the learning sciences* 13, 1 (2004), 1–14.

[5] Teresa Busjahn and Carsten Schulte. 2013. The Use of Code Reading in Teaching Programming. In *Proceedings of the 13th Koli Calling International Conference on Computing Education Research (Koli Calling '13)*. ACM, New York, NY, USA, 3–11.

[6] Quintin Cutts, Sarah Esper, Marlena Fecho, Stephen R. Foster, and Beth Simon. 2012. The Abstraction Transition Taxonomy: Developing Desired Learning Outcomes Through the Lens of Situated Cognition. In *Proceedings of the Ninth Annual International Conference on International Computing Education Research (ICER '12)*. ACM, New York, NY, USA, 63–70.

[7] Judith Gal-Ezer and Ela Zur. 2004. The efficiency of algorithmsâĂŤmisconceptions. *Computers & Education* 42, 3 (April 2004), 215–226. https://doi.org/10.1016/j.compedu.2003.07.004

[8] Varvara Garneli, Michail N. Giannakos, and Konstantinos Chorianopoulos. 2015. Computing education in K-12 schools: A review of the literature. In *Global Engineering Education Conference (EDUCON), 2015 IEEE*. IEEE, 543–551. 00017.

[9] Shuchi Grover, Roy Pea, and Stephen Cooper. 2015. Designing for deeper learning in a blended computer science course for middle school students. *Computer Science Education* 25, 2 (April 2015), 199–237. https://doi.org/10.1080/08993408.2015.1033142

[10] Monika Gujberova and Ivan Kalas. 2013. Designing Productive Gradations of Tasks in Primary Programming Education. In *Proceedings of the 8th Workshop in Primary and Secondary Computing Education (WiPSE '13)*. ACM, New York, NY, USA, 108–117. https://doi.org/10.1145/2532748.2532750 00012.

[11] Peter Hubwieser, Michal Armoni, Michail N. Giannakos, and Roland T. Mittermeir. 2014. Perspectives and Visions of Computer Science Education in Primary and Secondary (K-12) Schools. *Trans. Comput. Educ.* 14, 2 (June 2014), 7:1–7:9. 00041.

[12] Paul A. Kirschner, John Sweller, and Richard E. Clark. 2006. Why Minimal Guidance During Instruction Does Not Work: An Analysis of the Failure of Constructivist, Discovery, Problem-Based, Experiential, and Inquiry-Based Teaching. *Educational Psychologist* 41, 2 (June 2006), 75–86. https://doi.org/10.1207/s15326985ep4102_1 05793.

[13] Udo Kuckartz. 2014. *Qualitative text analysis: A guide to methods, practice and using software.* Sage.

[14] Irene Lee, Fred Martin, Jill Denner, Bob Coulter, Walter Allan, Jeri Erickson, Joyce Malyn-Smith, and Linda Werner. 2011. Computational thinking for youth in practice. *ACM Inroads* 2, 1 (2011), 32.

[15] Raymond Lister, Elizabeth S Adams, Sue Fitzgerald, William Fone, John Hamer, Morten Lindholm, Robert McCartney, Jan Erik Moström, Kate Sanders, Otto Seppälä, et al. 2004. A multi-national study of reading and tracing skills in novice programmers. In *ACM SIGCSE Bulletin*, Vol. 36. ACM, 119–150.

[16] Raymond Lister, Colin Fidge, and Donna Teague. 2009. Further Evidence of a Relationship Between Explaining, Tracing and Writing Skills in Introductory Programming. In *Proceedings of the 14th Annual ACM SIGCSE Conference on Innovation and Technology in Computer Science Education (ITiCSE '09)*. ACM, New York, NY, USA, 161–165.

[17] Sze Yee Lye and Joyce Hwee Ling Koh. 2014. Review on teaching and learning of computational thinking through programming: What is next for K-12? *Computers in Human Behavior* 41 (2014), 51–61. 00303.

[18] Lauren E. Margulieux and Richard Catrambone. 2016. Improving problem solving with subgoal labels in expository text and worked examples. *Learning and Instruction* 42 (2016), 58–71. 00015.

[19] P Mayring. 2000. Forum: Qualitative Social Research Sozialforschung, 2. History of Content Analysis. In *Forum: Qualitative Social Research. Sozialforschung*, Vol. 1.

[20] Orni Meerbaum-Salant, Michal Armoni, and Mordechai (Moti) Ben-Ari. 2013. Learning computer science concepts with Scratch. *Computer Science Education* 23, 3 (Sept. 2013), 239–264. https://doi.org/10.1080/08993408.2013.832022

[21] Briana B. Morrison, Lauren E. Margulieux, Barbara Ericson, and Mark Guzdial. 2016. Subgoals Help Students Solve Parsons Problems. In *Proceedings of the 47th ACM Technical Symposium on Computing Science Education (SIGCSE '16)*. ACM, New York, NY, USA, 42–47. https://doi.org/10.1145/2839509.2844617 00025.

[22] Seymour Papert. 1980. *Mindstorms: children, computers and powerful ideas.* Vol. Harvester studies in cognitive science. Harvester, Brighton.

[23] Jacob Perrenet, Jan Friso Groote, and Eric Kaasenbrood. 2005. Exploring students' understanding of the concept of algorithm: levels of abstraction. *ACM SIGCSE Bulletin* 37, 3 (2005), 64–68.

[24] Anthony Robins, Janet Rountree, and Nathan Rountree. 2003. Learning and Teaching Programming: A Review and Discussion. *Computer Science Education* 13, 2 (2003), 137–172.

[25] Carsten Schulte. 2008. Block Model: An Educational Model of Program Comprehension As a Tool for a Scholarly Approach to Teaching. In *Proceedings of the Fourth International Workshop on Computing Education Research (ICER '08)*. ACM, New York, NY, USA, 149–160.

[26] Sue Sentance and Jane Waite. 2017. PRIMM: Exploring pedagogical approaches for teaching text-based programming in school. In *Proceedings of the 12th Workshop in Primary and Secondary Computing Education*. ACM. https://doi.org/10.475/123_4

[27] Sue Sentance, Jane Waite, and Maria Kallia. [n. d.]. Teaching computer programming with PRIMM: a sociocultural perspective. Paper in review. ([n. d.]).

[28] David Statter and Michal Armoni. 2016. Teaching Abstract Thinking in Introduction to Computer Science for 7th Graders. In *Proceedings of the 11th Workshop in Primary and Secondary Computing Education (WiPSCE '16)*. ACM, New York, NY, USA, 80–83. https://doi.org/10.1145/2978249.2978261 00010.

[29] Leigh Ann Sudol-DeLyser, Mark Stehlik, and Sharon Carver. 2012. Code comprehension problems as learning events. In *Proceedings of the 17th ACM annual conference on Innovation and technology in computer science education*. ACM, 81–86. http://dl.acm.org/citation.cfm?id=2325319

[30] Donna Teague and Raymond Lister. 2014. Programming: Reading, Writing and Reversing. In *Proceedings of the 2014 Conference on Innovation and Technology in Computer Science Education (ITiCSE '14)*. ACM, New York, NY, USA, 285–290.

[31] The Royal Society. 2017. After the Reboot: Computing Education in UK Schools. Policy Report.

[32] Chia-Yin Tsai, Ya-Fei Yang, and Chih-Kai Chang. 2015. Cognitive Load Comparison of Traditional and Distributed Pair Programming on Visual Programming Language. In *Educational Innovation through Technology (EITT), 2015 International Conference of*. IEEE, 143–146. 00001.

[33] Jeroen J. G. van MerriÃńnboer and John Sweller. 2005. Cognitive Load Theory and Complex Learning: Recent Developments and Future Directions. *Educational Psychology Review* 17, 2 (June 2005), 147–177. https://doi.org/10.1007/s10648-005-3951-0 00000.

[34] Anne Venables, Grace Tan, and Raymond Lister. 2009. A Closer Look at Tracing, Explaining and Code Writing Skills in the Novice Programmer. In *Proceedings of the Fifth International Workshop on Computing Education Research Workshop (ICER '09)*. ACM, New York, NY, USA, 117–128.

[35] Jane Waite. 2017. Pedagogy in teaching Computer Science in schools: A Literature Review. https://royalsociety.org/ /media/policy/projects/computing-education/literature-review-pedagogy-in-teaching.pdf The Royal Society.

Survey Results on Why CS Faculty Adopt New Teaching Practices

Christopher Lynnly Hovey
University of Colorado Boulder
Boulder, CO USA
hoveyc@colorado.edu

Lecia Barker
University of Colorado Boulder
Boulder, CO USA
barkerl@colorado.edu

Vaughan Nagy
University of Colorado Boulder
Boulder, CO USA
vaughan.nagy@colorado.edu

ABSTRACT

In a previous paper, we explored results from the first stage of a two-part research project designed to uncover what influences computer science (CS) faculty to adopt new teaching practices. In the first phase, we conducted interviews, classroom observations, and focus groups with faculty to better understand the organizational, individual, and social factors that influence faculty adoption. Here we discuss findings from the second phase of the project, which uses survey data from 821 CS faculty at 595 institutions in the U.S. to investigate the prevalence of themes uncovered during the qualitative phase. Results show that faculty who tried an innovation were motivated primarily by concerns for students' learning and course experience, including their engagement and participation. Also important were the "fit" with existing practices and tools, and the logistics of implementing an innovation. Factors that reduced faculty willingness to try an innovation include a lack of time, logistical issues, and satisfaction with their current teaching practices. Faculty learned about the innovations they later adopted through presentations and workshops at conferences and at their home institutions, and through conversations with respected colleagues who teach in similar contexts. Implications for encouraging more widespread usage of teaching techniques that improve diversity and student learning are discussed.

KEYWORDS

faculty adoption of teaching innovations; propagating student-centered teaching; interactive learning dissemination; lecturing; pedagogy

ACM Reference format:

Christopher Lynnly Hovey, Lecia Barker, and Vaughan Nagy. 2019. Survey Results on Why CS Faculty Adopt New Teaching Practices. In *Proceedings of the 50th ACM Technical Symposium on Computer Science Education (SIGCSE '19), February 27-March 2, 2019, Minneapolis, MN, USA, 7 pages.* https://doi.org/10.1145/3287324.3287420

ACM ISBN 978-1-4503-5890-3/19/02···$15.00
https://doi.org/10.1145/3287324.3287420

1 INTRODUCTION

Many computer science (CS) departments in the U.S. are experiencing a "surge" in the number of students declaring the major [5]. However, it is unclear whether or not the standard repertoire of teaching practices that are used in CS classrooms will be able to address incoming students' expectations for more interactive, dynamic instruction [4]. Innovative, evidence-based teaching stragies for CS education like Peer Instruction [17], media computation [10,19], and using meaningful, socially relevant examples and content [3] are effective ways of attracting more diverse students, of improving students' performance, engagement, and intention to continue in the major, and of addressing growing enrollments. However, recent research indicates that most CS faculty describe their teaching as encompassing both instructor- and student-centered practices [8,9]. Findings associated with the research we present here [13] indicate that when asked about the frequency of using various teaching practices in a specific course, most CS faculty reported presenting content by lecturing more frequently than using any of the seven student-centered instructional techniques provided in the survey. These results collectively suggest that there is a need to increase the use of evidence-based teaching practices among CS faculty in higher education. Addressing this need requires knowing more about why faculty change the way they teach, to better inform the design of intentional propagation strategies [18].

To that end, this paper reports on the second of a two-phase research project intended to increase our understanding of what influences CS faculty to try out new teaching practices. In the first phase of the project, we interviewed and conducted classroom observations with 66 CS faculty, the results of which were presented in [2] and summarized below. The analysis of our qualitative data provided us preliminary insights and rich description about faculty adoption in CS higher education, but those results do not allow us to generalize beyond those participants. In the present paper, we investigate how our qualitative findings relate to the rest of the field of CS higher education, using survey data from 821 CS faculty teaching in an estimated 595 universities, colleges, and community colleges in the United States.

2 A SUMMARY OF QUALITATIVE RESULTS

In [2], and to a lesser degree in [1], we described the results of a qualitative study in which we conducted theory-driven, semi-structured interviews and observations with 66 faculty who teach CS introductory courses. Participants were selected using parameters intended to maximize the diversity of opinions and experiences, including institutional and personal criteria. Faculty, ranging from adjunct instructors to department chairs, were asked to describe their teaching and occupational contexts; their experiences with using student- and instructor-centered teaching practices; their beliefs about teaching, research, learning, and the nature of academia; and their interactions with and attitudes towards their students, peers, department administration, and the community of CS educators. Recordings were transcribed and then analyzed using both emergent and theory-based coding. More information about the research methods used in this phase is available in [1] and [2].

The remainder of this section describes principle findings from phase 1 of our project, with additional anecdotes from the qualitative data. Where applicable, we also cite studies from CS and other STEM fields as they support or contradict our findings. A more encompassing review of propagation and adoption research in CS and STEM higher education is available in [18].

2.1 Why Faculty Try New Teaching Practices

Mirroring theory and empirical findings in physics education research [12], and Ni, Guzdial, and colleagues' work in CS [7,14,15], we found that faculty typically try a new teaching practice or technique because they intentionally seek out solutions to a problem they have identified. The most common problems that motivated CS faculty to try new teaching practices were sub-par student learning (usually expressed as low student performance), insufficient pre-college or pre-course preparation, and low perceived student engagement (e.g., students looking bored or inattentive)—results also found in other CS studies [7,14,15]. Faculty often described responding to explicit or implicit student feedback (see [1] for more detail), especially regarding whether or not to continue using a practice; in some cases, faculty also gained awareness from students through direct and indirect suggestions via overhearing conversations, end-of-term reviews, etc. Some faculty mentioned being motivated to try a new practice because they believed that instructor-centered teaching might deter underrepresented students (women and minorities) from pursuing CS degrees, a motivation also discussed in [15].

Some faculty described hearing about a new teaching strategy or tool that they felt sounded interesting, without necessarily having a problem to address. The practice was typically described as being superior to whatever was already in use, by virtue of the advantages that it offered or simply because it offered a deviation from the status quo. In some cases, faculty were asked to try the practice by a colleague or a developer.

Some faculty reported substantial challenges, or were disincentivized to seek out or try new teaching techniques. Some junior faculty reported that they were less willing to try new teaching because they felt that experiementing with teaching could be detrimental to their tenure case, especially if the new practice would not be well-received by students. One interviewee described having difficulty in her tenuring case because she had received high performance evaluations in both research and teaching; she was treated incredulously by at least one member of her tenuring committee who did not believe someone could be good at both aspects of the job. Other faculty reported not trying or discontinuing certain practices on the pretext that it might not "go over well" with their students.

Faculty discussed other reasons for abstaining from trying a practice. Weighing the amount of time needed to learn about, prepare, and implement an innovation against the time needed for other teaching work was a common consideration among respondents. This finding is echoed in [14], which found that prep time was among the most common concerns for CS faculty (and among physics faculty [11]). Our respondents reported a willingness to put in time to investigate and try a new practice as part of the regular teaching workload, but they needed to feel secure that it would benefit students. Faculty described unfamiliarity with innovative teaching as being a barrier, contrasting their personal experiences as students that often only included passively sitting through "straight lecture" and doing independent study. Conversely, one respondent discussed trying an innovative teaching strategy that they had experienced as a student because it had excited them about computing.

Some faculty described how their department's culture, insitutional policies or context, and physical resources influenced adoption and continued use. For example, classroom layouts and available equipment often preemptively stopped faculty from trying practices they had considered. Stadium-style seating often prompted lecture-style presentations simply because the space was not conducive to interaction. In other cases, the room provided a necessary, but not sufficient, boon to the instructor's willingness to try an innovation. For example, one respondent reported that collaborative work was aided because lecture and lab were colocated in the same room.

Faculty also frequently discussed a tension between trying new teaching and "covering material"; in other words, they felt innovative teaching might increase students' depth of learning, but it would slow down the pace of the course and reduce the instructor's ability to relay a breadth of knowledge (e.g., more topics). This tension was particularly in evidence when faculty taught courses that were part of a sequence or set curriculum; faculty were afraid of frustrating or disappointing their peers if students were not adequately prepared for the next course(s) in the sequence. In rare cases, what was seen as inflexible department committee or administrative control over curriculum also influenced faculty not to try certain pedagogical techniques.

2.2 How Faculty Hear about Practices

Faculty reported several different communication channels through which they were exposed to an innovative practice. Most commonly, faculty found out about an innovation from informal conversations with peers, or from conference presentations at CAHSI, SIGCSE, FIE, or the NCWIT Summit. Personal discussions between colleagues about teaching or classroom issues often spurred adoption. For others, teaching new classes caused them to ask colleagues for syllabi and teaching materials; these resources required innovative teaching methods that would then be "tried out" on an experiemental basis along with the curriculum. Recommendations were typically persuasive if they came from peers with personal connections, including former mentors or graduate students, or from respected strangers with strong personal or institutional reputations (for teaching or research). Similarities in institutional, teaching, or research contexts—what Everett Rogers would describe as "homophily" or sameness [16]—were also persuasive elements for conference presenters. Evidence from empirical studies was not typically a consideration, and in at least one case, a faculty member dismissed evaluative studies as being inherently biased.

Faculty also mentioned learning about innovations through funded initiatives, either through grant opportunities from organizations like the National Science Foundation or through their campus's center for teaching and learning. Funding also factored heavily into faculty routinely using the innovation.

Qualitative results provide a rich description of how faculty learn of innovations and why they adopt them. Phase 2 of our project involved constructing and disseminating a survey to investigate how prevalent these, and other theory-based concerns, are among CS faculty. Below we describe our methods and results, followed by a discussion of how insights might contribute to increasing adoption of teaching practices.

3 METHODS

3.1 Survey Construction and Design

The survey was constructed using themes that emerged from transcripts of the interviews, observations, and focus groups from the first phase of the project. Survey items were crafted using the word choices and thematic considerations that faculty volunteered in interviews. This was done in an effort to reduce respondents' cognitive load and survey fatigue, and improve response validity and reliability [6,20]. The survey asked faculty to provide the name and enrollment of a course they had taught recently, preferably one that students take early in the curriculum, and the frequency of using certain practices. Faculty were then asked whether or not they had ever tried using a teaching practice in that course that they had not used before, and if so, what was it. Responses to this question were then used to route "yes" participants, and the name of their innovation, to various banks of questions about how they found out about the innovation, what motivated them to try it, what outcomes occurred when they tried it, whether they still used it, and why. Faculty who said that they had not tried something new were branched past these questions. Faculty were also asked to select an innovation that they had not tried from set list, and then were asked a battery of follow up questions regarding reasons for non-use (lack of info, various hypothesized inhibitors, etc.). The survey was piloted among 10 CS faculty of various ranks at a large, public university. Their feedback was incorporated into a final survey, which was disseminated online.

3.2 Sample Development

To develop the sample, we used the U.S. Department of Education's Integrated Postsecondary Education Database System (IPEDS) [21] to generate a list of institutions per institutional type that awarded bachelor's or associate degrees in 2014 and 2015 in "computer science" (Classification of Instructional Program (CIP) code 11.07) or in "computer and information sciences and support services" (CIP 11). We then used department websites to acquire email contact information for between 1 and 4 faculty from each institution. Emphasis was given to identifying faculty who teach lower division introductory courses. In total, links to the incentive/survey were sent to 4,088 faculty from 1,310 institutions.

3.3 Data Collection and Respondent Profile

3.3.1. Data Collection. To administer the survey, potential respondents were sent personalized invitations (e.g., Dear Professor <LastName>) with a link to a survey landing page offering an incentive. Faculty could voluntarily provide a contact email to receive a $20 Amazon.com gift card. Methodology studies have shown that using pre-survey incentives and personal salutations are more likely to entice respondents who otherwise would have abstained from the survey, which increases the sample size [6]. This data set was stored separately from the actual survey, so there was no way to match email addresses with survey responses. Respondents also had the option of skipping the incentive and proceeding to the survey. The "submit" button for the incentive screen forwarded participants to one of eight survey "collector groups," which retained their institutional type without storing any personal information.

3.3.2. Sample Size. Responses were collected from the beginning of May until the end of July 2017. In total, 849 faculty accessed the link to the incentive landing page; 751 claimed the incentive, and 821 faculty continued to and completed at least the first page of the survey, resulting in a response rate of 20%. Confidentiality settings prevent us from knowing the exact number, but a conservative estimate calculated from incentive-to-survey transfers by institutional type suggests that at least 595 institutions are represented in the data.

3.3.3. Respondent Profile. Table 1 shows the distribution of respondents by institutional type, which intentionally approximates the proportions of institutions for each type found in IPEDS to strengthen the representativeness of the data. The timing and frequency of reminders for participation were sent to specific groups based on the evolving distribution of the sample.

How long faculty had been teaching was normally distributed across three intervals: "up to 5 years" (25%), "between 6 and 20 years" (49%), and "more than 20 years" (26%). Faculty were well distributed across ranks: adjuncts and instructor (20%), assistant professor (25%), associate professor (25%), and full professor (27%)—with an additional 3% reporting being either a chair or dean, or having no rank system. Rank strongly correlated with tenure status categories: non-tenure track (21%), tenure-track (25%), and tenured (55%). Women comprised 22% of the sample, and an additional 8% of the sample described their

Table 1: Respondents by Institutional Types

Institutional Type	N	Percent
Two-Year Associate-Granting	164	20.0%
Research Intensive/Extensive	133	16.2%
Historically Black College/University	26	3.2%
Hispanic Serving Institution	101	12.3%
Tribal College	5	0.6%
Small (enrollment = 1-4,999)	209	25.5%
Medium (enrollment = 5,000-9,999)	47	5.7%
Large (enrollment = 10,000+)	136	16.6%
Total	**821**	**100%**

gender identity as "not listed," "prefer not to respond," or opted to leave the question blank. Of the 646 respondents who provided their race/ethnicity via an open-ended question, 81% were White, 12% were Asian, and 8% were Black, Hispanic, Native/Indian, or other. We were unable to find data on the demographic features of the full population of CS faculty with which we could compare our sample.

4 RESULTS

In total, 72.4% (n=584) of faculty responded that they had tried a new teaching practice. These respondents were then asked questions about how they learned of the practice and what influenced them to try it. Values displayed in the following tables reflect the percentage (%) and number (N) of respondents who selected each response option. "Don't know/not applicable," auto-skipped, and non-response answers are excluded. Items are ordered by descending levels of overall agreement.

4.1 Why Faculty Try New Teaching

4.1.1. Reasons for Trying. Faculty were asked two banks of questions regarding their considerations and motivations for trying a new practice. Results are displayed in Table 2. Four of the top five considerations center on intended positive outcomes for students regarding the course, i.e., their understanding, engagement, performance, and participation. "Fit" with existing practices and tools was also important to a majority of faculty. The next three items represent logistical considerations, including the knowledge and time required to try the innovation. Concerns over how much time it would take to try, and potential interference with covering material, were less important than interviews led us to expect, although over 50% of respondents agreed to each item. Less than half of respondents felt their decision was motivated or influenced by an interest in students' social skills development, covering more material, saving time, or satisfying a request to try it from either students or colleagues. One-fourth of respondents received help from a learning center.

4.1.2. Reasons for Not Trying (Yet). Respondents were also asked to select an innovative teaching practice that they "had heard of but had not (yet) tried" from a set list. They were then asked to report their level of agreement or disagreement with statements about why they had not tried it. Specific responses and percentage frequencies are reported in Table 3. Results indicate that not having time to try the practice is the strongest and most common inhibiter of faculty adoption. Satisfaction with current teaching practices was also very common. Not having access to the necessary resources, and not being familiar with the practice—essentially logistical concerns—were also somewhat common reasons why faculty abstained from using a practice.

Less than half of the sample expressed concerns about how students would respond to using the innovation (akin to "fit" with how students learn), or that the practice might interfere with covering material. Given their importance for adoption (see Table 1), these two considerations appear to be "heat" factors for motivating adoption, but their absences are not necessarily "chilling" factors for adoption, metaphorically speaking.

Similar proportions of faculty, about 15% to 20%, had issues with classroom physical setups or with class enrollments. Tenure considerations, as well as direct discouragement from peers or departmental regulations were very uncommon, receiving less than 10% agreement each.

Table 2: Motivations and Considerations for Adoption

Motivation* or Consideration		Strg Dis.	Dis.	Agr.	Strg Agr.
I wanted to improve my students' understanding of course content*	%	0%	1%	28%	70%
	N	1	7	159	392
I wanted to increase my students' engagement or interest*	%	0%	2%	31%	66%
	N	2	13	173	372
I wanted to improve my students' performance in the class*	%	0%	4%	34%	62%
	N	1	20	189	348
I believed it would be a better "fit" with how my students learn	%	0%	5%	51%	43%
	N	1	29	275	232
I wanted to increase my students' participation in class*	%	1%	6%	27%	65%
	N	7	36	150	363
I felt I had enough resources (e.g., funding, hardware, etc.) to try it	%	2%	8%	52%	38%
	N	9	42	274	198
I had clear expectations for what I thought it would do	%	1%	12%	60%	27%
	N	3	67	334	151
I understood the necessary logistics (time, resources, etc.) before trying it	%	1%	18%	53%	28%
	N	7	100	292	154
I wanted to better prepare students for their careers*	%	11%	11%	39%	40%
	N	56	58	206	213
It was recommended by someone I trust	%	12%	13%	45%	30%
	N	50	55	190	128
I wanted to be more inclusive of underrepresented students*	%	19%	22%	37%	22%
	N	91	106	176	103
I thought I would be able to use it in all of the courses I teach	%	10%	33%	37%	21%
	N	53	179	201	113
I was concerned that it would take a lot of time to implement	%	11%	41%	37%	12%
	N	59	223	202	65
I was concerned that I would not be able to cover as much material	%	19%	42%	31%	8%
	N	101	229	171	43
I wanted students to improve their social skills*	%	30%	31%	28%	11%
	N	146	152	137	55
I wanted to cover more material*	%	30%	44%	17%	9%
	N	159	236	91	48
I received help from my institution's center for teaching	%	42%	32%	16%	9%
	N	201	153	78	43
I wanted to save time*	%	39%	40%	13%	7%
	N	211	213	72	39
A colleague asked me to try it *	%	46%	39%	10%	4%
	N	221	187	49	20
My students suggested that I try it*	%	59%	33%	6%	2%
	N	301	166	30	10
My department required me to try it*	%	71%	27%	1%	2%
	N	360	136	6	8

Notes: Strg Dis. = Strongly Disagree; Dis. = Disagree; Agr. = Agree; Strg Agr. = Strongly Agree, and N = Number of respondents. Items are listed in descending order by percentage of total agreement (i.e., Agree + Strongly Agree).
Items without asterisks were prompted in the survey as, "Please reflect on your thoughts about the teaching practice '<piped text>' when you were *first deciding* if you would try it. To what extent do you agree or disagree with the following considerations?" Asterisks indicate the survey prompt asked, "To what extent do you agree or disagree that the following considerations *motivated* your decision to try the teaching practice '<piped text>'?"

Table 3: Reasons for Not (Yet) Trying an Innovation

Reason for Not (Yet) Having Tried an Innovation		Strg Dis.	Dis.	Agr.	Strg Agr.
I have not had enough time to try it	%	5%	17%	46%	32%
	N	29	103	275	190
I am satisfied with how I teach now	%	2%	27%	54%	16%
	N	15	172	341	103
I have not had access to the resources needed to try it	%	7%	35%	38%	20%
	N	41	196	217	113
I am not familiar with the logistics/resources needed	%	11%	35%	38%	16%
	N	71	224	243	100
It might not work for the type of students I teach	%	13%	43%	36%	8%
	N	70	226	190	43
There is not enough evidence that it works	%	9%	50%	33%	8%
	N	41	221	145	33
My students might not like it	%	10%	51%	33%	6%
	N	47	250	161	31
It might negatively impact my ability to cover material	%	13%	48%	30%	9%
	N	72	262	162	50
My classroom's physical setup prevents me from trying it	%	20%	59%	16%	5%
	N	109	316	86	27
My class enrollment is too large to use it in my class(es)	%	24%	58%	12%	6%
	N	132	311	64	33
My class enrollment is too small to use it in my class(es)	%	27%	59%	12%	3%
	N	141	307	62	14
It might interfere with getting tenure or promotion	%	50%	41%	6%	3%
	N	269	219	33	17
A colleague or peer has discouraged me from trying it	%	41%	53%	5%	2%
	N	228	293	28	9
It would not be possible to try it because of how my department sets curriculum	%	45%	49%	5%	1%
	N	249	274	29	7

Notes: Strg Dis. = Strongly Disagree; Dis. = Disagree; Agr. = Agree; Strg Agr. = Strongly Agree, and N = Number of respondents. Items are listed in descending order by percentage of total agreement (i.e., Agree + Strongly Agree).
Survey prompt: "To what extent do you agree or disagree that the following influenced you to *not* try '<piped text>'?"

4.2 How Faculty Learn About Innovations

Faculty were asked to describe both the source of information and the context in which they learned about their innovations. Response options included people and settings derived from interviews, as well as open-ended options where faculty could describe each in their own words. Because of the interdependence and complexity of sources and contexts, we realized that these two survey items would need to be manually cross tabulated into a single variable. The results of this reorganization are presented in Table 4, listed in descending order of prevalence. Because we were not able to ask follow-up questions or seek clarification about the awareness situation, these results should be interpreted as preliminary indications.

Table 4: Awareness Situations

Institutional Type	N	Percent
Conversation with another faculty member	161	38.5%
Presentation/workshop at a conference	90	21.5%
Presentation/workshop at my institution	74	17.7%
Research, media, or publication	68	16.3%
From a student (grad or undergrad)	9	2.2%
Experience while being a student	7	1.7%
Sales pitch	5	1.2%
Email from center for teaching and learning	4	1.0%
TOTAL	**418**	**100%**

The two most common situations in which faculty learned of an innovation they later adopted were through conference presentations and workshops (either at conferences or the home institution), and through informal conversations with colleagues. Collectively, these made up approximately three-fourths of all awareness situations. Somewhat in contrast to our qualitative data, approximately one-tenth of situations involved personally directed research, popular media like prominent CS educators' blog posts, and academic publications. This finding suggested that the degree to which formal evidence diffuses among CS faculty may hinge on endorsement and active promotion of mavens—highly visible, well-respected, notable persons with strong reputations in the CS education community.

Students explicitly asking faculty to change how they teach was not common. Nine respondents described hearing the recommendation from either a graduate or undergraduate student, corroborating evidence from Table 2 in which only eight respondents agreed to some level that student recommendations had been a consideration in their decision to adopt. We caution that this result does not negate the importance students have in encouraging or discouraging continued usage [1,2]. Similarly, personal experience as a student, being approached by a sales representative, and emails from centers for teaching and learning were relatively uncommon avenues through which faculty discovered new teaching practices.

In the qualitative data, we found that reputation and contextual similarities were important mediators in the persuasiveness of people who encouraged adoption. Therefore, respondents who reported that the awareness source was another faculty member (or who responded "other" and reported that the person was working in higher education) were asked a bank of questions related to personal and institutional reputations, and contextual similarities of the person from whom they learned about their new teaching practice. Response options and results, ranked in order of total agreement, are reported in Table 5.

The teaching reputation of the individual, and of her or his institution, were highly ranked by almost all respondents. Institutional similarity and teaching the same type of students (i.e., institutional homophily) also received a high level of overall agreement. Conversely, research and industry reputations received much less agreement. Therefore, we can conclude that the persuasiveness of a champion or propagator is strongly associated with teaching reputation, of both the individual *and* the institution in which they work.

5 DISCUSSION AND IMPLICATIONS

Many of the hypotheses generated by the qualitative phase of our project were supported in the quantitative phase. Faculty adoption is often strongly motivated by concerns for student learning and students' experience of a course, including their engagement and participation. As hypothesized by Rogers [16], a practice must "fit" with (or be compatible with) existing practices, although we found only limited evidence that concerns about "fit" were related to *not* trying an innovation. We also found strong evidence that the logistics of implementing an innovation, meaning the requisite knowledge, time, and

Table 5: Source Reputation and Similarities

Source Reputation and Similarities		Strg Dis.	Dis.	Agr.	Strg Agr.
This person has a strong teaching reputation	%	0%	2%	42%	55%
	N	1	7	134	177
This person's institution has a strong teaching reputation	%	2%	6%	48%	43%
	N	7	19	144	128
This person works at an institution similar to mine	%	4%	11%	28%	57%
	N	14	35	88	182
This person teaches students that are similar to mine	%	6%	10%	44%	40%
	N	18	33	140	129
This person has a strong research reputation	%	10%	22%	42%	27%
	N	24	54	106	67
This person teaches course topics that are similar to mine	%	11%	21%	36%	31%
	N	38	70	120	103
This person's institution has a strong research reputation	%	10%	28%	37%	25%
	N	26	76	100	66
This person has a strong industry reputation	%	25%	30%	32%	13%
	N	50	61	64	27
This person does research in my research area	%	38%	32%	19%	11%
	N	98	84	50	29

Notes: Strg Dis. = Strongly Disagree; Dis. = Disagree; Agr. = Agree; Strg Agr. = Strongly Agree, and N = Number of respondents. Items are listed in descending order by percentage of total agreement (i.e., Agree + Strongly Agree).
Survey prompt: "You said you first heard about the teaching practice from'<piped text>.' To what extent do you agree or disagree with the following statements about this person?"

resources, also factored into faculty's trial of an innovation, and conversely, the absence of these inhibited trying a new practice.

The most prevalent awareness situation involved learning from colleagues through conversations and through conference presentations; a strong personal or institutional reputation for teaching plays a factor in eliciting new users to try an innovation.

There were a few surprises regarding the relationship between the qualitative and quantitative results. Tenure considerations were not as prevalent as expected. We found no statistical differences among faculty of different tenure statuses. Also, in the qualitative phase, we found evidence that some faculty disregard empirical studies. Survey results suggest that faculty do in fact seek out highly reputed blogs, popular media, and academic publications for teaching strategies on their own.

Although holding workshops and actively supporting faculty in learning new approaches to teaching are likely to result in long-term use, the resources for getting the word out and funding such efforts are minimal. Thus, we hope to continue this work by mining the findings for improving communication and messaging to increase the likelihood that faculty will find out about, experiment with, and routinely use effective teaching practices. As is suggested by the percent of faculty who discovered a practice in a research publication or similar medium (16%), raising awareness of the innovation requires more than publishing results, regardless of how important evaluations are to the integrity of evidence-based practices. Many CS faculty members do not access the CS teaching literature. Personal accounts shared at conferences and through personal conversations in departments may be more persuasive than research reports. Finding "mavens" who communicate across boundaries may be a useful approach. An important way to disseminate new teaching strategies is to have faculty from a variety of contexts and environments that have successfully implemented the innovation share their experiences with their colleagues. Faculty are more likely to adopt an innovation, even if they have reservations, when the idea is promoted by someone they hold in esteem, or whom they believe is similar to them and has similar circumstances. Developers and advocates might circumvent biases by demonstrating understanding of faculty concerns and shared values, and by communicating these to faculty. They may also identify the sources most trusted by particular target audiences. Conference presenters and advocates should elucidate the "how-to" of the innovation and include honest experiences about what motivated the innovation, what worked well, how much time it took, what was challenging, and what can be improved.

Developers and advocates should seek to understand the constraints and circumstances of specific adoption audiences, especially time, funding, tenure and promotion policies, curricular sequencing and rigidity, physical space, student and departmental culture, and personal concerns. In particular, grants and other funding opportunities can allow faculty the release time, infrastructure, and curriculum vitae boost that may encourage them to innovate their teaching. By understanding these tensions, developers and advocates may be more successful at diffusing better education practices throughout CS higher education to promote retention and learning.

6 LIMITATIONS

As in all research, there are several limitations to this study. Despite incorporating best practices into our research methods, it is possible that our respondents are not reflective of all CS faculty. Invitations emailed to faculty described the study as, "a 15-minute survey on how faculty find out about, try out, and decide to routinely use teaching practices in their [CS] classes." This would likely deter faculty who are disinterested in teaching. And while the survey was disseminated over several months in the summer in order to decrease the risk of competing responsibilities, some educators may not have checked their email during the recess or had time to fill out the survey. Respondents may have interpreted question prompts or response options in ways that differed from our intent, as they did for our questions about the awareness situation. Nonetheless, this study hopefully gives developers and propagators useful information about why faculty change the way they teach, which can be leveraged in developing propagation plans to encourage more widespread use of effective teaching strategies.

ACKNOWLEDGEMENTS

Thank you to the survey respondents who participated in this study, especially those that identified a scripting error that helped us fix the survey. Thank you to our colleagues Erin Arneson, Brittany Kos, Shauna Montoya, and Hannah Weber, whose help with the survey design, data wrangling, and analysis were instrumental. Thanks to Margaret Luebs, Sandra Hovey, and our SIGCSE reviewers for providing excellent substantive feedback and proof editing suggestions. Finally, thank you to the National Science Foundation for funding this study under award DUE#1123332.

REFERENCES

[1] Lecia Barker and Jane Gruning. 2014. The Student Prompt: Student Feedback and Change in Teaching Practices in Postsecondary Computer Science. In *Proceedings of the 44th Annual Frontiers in Education Conference*, 1–8. DOI:https://doi.org/10.1109/FIE.2014.7044464

[2] Lecia Barker, Christopher Lynnly Hovey, and Jane Gruning. 2015. What Influences CS Faculty to Adopt Teaching Practices? In *Proceedings of the 46th ACM Technical Symposium on Computer Science Education* (SIGCSE '15), 604–609. DOI:https://doi.org/10.1145/2676723.2677282

[3] Lecia Barker, Christopher Lynnly Hovey, and Leisa D. Thompson. 2014. Results of a large-scale, multi-institutional study of undergraduate retention in computing. In *Proceedings of the 44th Annual Frontiers in Education Conference* (FIE '14), 1693–1700. DOI:https://doi.org/10.1109/FIE.2014.7044267

[4] David Buckingham. 2007. *Beyond Technology: Children's Learning in the Age of Digital Culture.* Polity, Cambridge, MA.

[5] Computing Research Association. 2017. *Generation CS: Computer Science Undergraduate Enrollments Surge Since 2006.* Retrieved March 20, 2017 from http://cra.org/data/generation-cs/

[6] Don A. Dillman, Jolene D. Smyth, and Leah Melani Christian. 2014. *Internet, phone, mail, and mixed-mode surveys: the tailored design method* (Fourth edition ed.). Wiley, Hoboken, New Jersey.

[7] Davide Fossati and Mark Guzdial. 2011. The Use of Evidence in the Change Making Process of Computer Science Educators. In *Proceedings of the 42Nd ACM Technical Symposium on Computer Science Education* (SIGCSE '11), 685–690. DOI:https://doi.org/10.1145/1953163.1953352

[8] Scott Grissom, Sue Fitzgerald, Renée McCauley, and Laurie Murphy. 2017. Exposed! CS Faculty Caught Lecturing in Public: A Survey of Instructional Practices. In *Proceedings of the 2017 ACM SIGCSE Technical Symposium on Computer Science Education* (SIGCSE '17), 261–266. DOI:https://doi.org/10.1145/3017680.3017702

[9] Scott Grissom, Renée Mccauley, and Laurie Murphy. 2017. How Student Centered is the Computer Science Classroom? A Survey of College Faculty. *ACM Trans Comput Educ* 18, 1 (November 2017), 5:1–5:27. DOI:https://doi.org/10.1145/3143200

[10] Mark Guzdial and Allison Elliott Tew. 2006. Imagineering Inauthentic Legitimate Peripheral Participation: An Instructional Design Approach for Motivating Computing Education. In *Proceedings of the Second International Workshop on Computing Education Research* (ICER '06), 51–58. DOI:https://doi.org/10.1145/1151588.1151597

[11] Charles Henderson and Melissa H. Dancy. 2007. Barriers to the use of research-based instructional strategies: The influence of both individual and situational characteristics. *Phys. Rev. Spec. Top. - Phys. Educ. Res.* 3, 2 (September 2007), 020102. DOI:https://doi.org/10.1103/PhysRevSTPER.3.020102

[12] Charles Henderson and Melissa H. Dancy. 2008. Physics faculty and educational researchers: Divergent expectations as barriers to the diffusion of innovations. *Am. J. Phys.* 76, 1 (January 2008), 79–91. DOI:https://doi.org/10.1119/1.2800352

[13] Christopher Lynnly Hovey, Lecia Barker, and Margaret Luebs. forthcoming. Frequency of Instructor- and Student-Centered Teaching Practices in Introductory CS Courses. In *Proceedings of the 50th ACM Technical Symposium on Computer Science Education* (SIGCSE '19). DOI:https://doi.org/10.1145/3287324.3287363

[14] Lijun Ni. 2009. What Makes CS Teachers Change?: Factors Influencing CS Teachers' Adoption of Curriculum Innovations. In *Proceedings of the 40th ACM Technical Symposium on Computer Science Education* (SIGCSE '09), 544–548. DOI:https://doi.org/10.1145/1508865.1509051

[15] Lijun Ni, Tom McKlin, and Mark Guzdial. 2010. How Do Computing Faculty Adopt Curriculum Innovations?: The Story from Instructors. In *Proceedings of the 41st ACM Technical Symposium on Computer Science Education* (SIGCSE '10), 544–548. DOI:https://doi.org/10.1145/1734263.1734444

[16] Everett M Rogers. 2003. *Diffusion of innovations.* Free Press, New York.

[17] Beth Simon, Sarah Esper, Leo Porter, and Quintin Cutts. 2013. Student Experience in a Student-centered Peer Instruction Classroom. In *Proceedings of the Ninth Annual International ACM Conference on International Computing Education Research* (ICER '13), 129–136. DOI:https://doi.org/10.1145/2493394.2493407

[18] Cynthia Taylor, Jaime Spacco, David P. Bunde, Zack Butler, Heather Bort, Christopher Lynnly Hovey, Francesco Maiorana, and Thomas Zeume. forthcoming. Propagating the Adoption of CS Educational Innovations. In *Proceedings of the 23rd Annual ACM Conference on Innovation and Technology in Computer Science Education* (ITiCSE Companion '18). DOI:https://doi.org/10.1145/3293881.3295785

[19] Allison Elliott Tew, Charles Fowler, and Mark Guzdial. 2005. Tracking an Innovation in Introductory CS Education from a Research University to a Two-year College. In *Proceedings of the 36th SIGCSE Technical Symposium on Computer Science Education* (SIGCSE '05), 416–420. DOI:https://doi.org/10.1145/1047344.1047481

[20] Roger Tourangeau. 2000. *The psychology of survey response.* Cambridge University Press, Cambridge; New York.

[21] U.S. Department of Education. 2016. Integrated Postsecondary Education Data System. Retrieved from https://nces.ed.gov/ipeds/

Broadening Participation in Computing

Putting Our Work in Context

Jennifer M. Blaney
(moderator)
Utah State University
jennifer.blaney@usu.edu

Linda J. Sax
University of California, Los Angeles
lsax@ucla.edu

David Feldon
Utah State University
david.feldon@usu.edu

Ann Gates
University of Texas at El Paso
agates@utep.edu

ABSTRACT

Broadening the participation of women in computing has increasingly become a focus of computing education research over the past several years. To be sure, the field of computing has unique challenges that merit close examination. At the same time, social scientists have built large bodies of literature related to gender equity across disciplines that span several decades, much of it critical to how we understand (in)equity in computing. This panel will provide perspectives from scholars with expertise in a variety of disciplines, including computer science, higher education, and educational psychology. Panelists will share relevant research from their home disciplines and initiate a discussion on the future of computing education research.

1 Summary

While many STEM fields have made significant progress toward parity, computing lags behind other fields, with women making up only 18% of bachelor's degree recipients across computing majors [9]. Given these persistent inequities, broadening participation in computing has become a central focus of computing education research. For example, at the 2018 SIGCSE Symposium, scholars presented on computing bootcamps, pair programming activities, bridge programs, and other efforts to recruit women students. While these types of studies on the unique nature of gender dynamics and recruitment efforts in computing are certainly needed, it is also imperative that the computing education community utilize existing resources from the large bodies of literature on gender equity across disciplines. This panel will draw on literature from STEM disciplines and the social sciences to frame how we explore equity within the SIGCSE community.

1.1 Comparing to Other STEM Disciplines

Within the computing education community, some have argued that computing educators should look to other STEM disciplines (e.g., biology) for guidance on how to diversify [2]. Indeed, there is much that the field of computing can learn from fields like biology, where women now represent approximately half of bachelor's degree recipients [9]. However, despite the strides that have been made in the biological sciences, educational research has documented key ways that inequities persist. For example, while women represent approximately half of medical school students, women and men remain largely segregated by specialty, with women being more likely to pursue medical specialties that are associated with lower average salaries [7], leading to gender stratification among medical school graduates. Other recent research has documented gender inequities in introductory biology class participation [3], doctoral student lab experiences, and publication rates among biology students [4]. Together, these examples reveal that representation is only one facet of gender equity, and that increasing the representation of women in STEM fields will not necessarily increase gender equity in these domains. In this panel session, we will discuss this further, focusing on how the biological sciences may provide important guidance for how the computing field can recruit more women to computing while also addressing persistent gender inequities *within* education environments.

1.2 Looking to Existing Social Science Research

In our efforts to identify strategies that advance gender equity in computing environments, it is imperative that we begin by carefully considering the wealth of existing research relevant to this topic. Fortunately, there are fields we can look to for guidance in how to direct our efforts. For example, researchers in education and psychology have been exploring the climate for women in STEM for decades [6]. This scholarship largely concludes that addressing structural inequities in the *environment*, such as a chilly climate for women, is imperative so that we are able to not only recruit more women to STEM disciplines, but also retain and provide women with equitable learning environments [1; 6]. Applying this to the computing context, we can expect that if we focus all of our efforts on recruiting women to computing, we may reveal strategies to increase women's representation in the field. However, we will likely be left with significant gender stratification, as seen in the biological sciences. Such stratification is already visible in computing, evidenced by recent research revealing that women with computing degrees are disproportionately tracked out of technical roles and into administrative positions within tech companies [5]. In this panel, we will discuss ways to pull from existing literature in the social sciences to direct our research efforts, focusing on structural inequities.

1.3 Seeking Methodological Rigor

Finally, as we expand upon existing research in the social sciences to examine gender equity in computing, we can look to social science literature for guidance in how to utilize rigorous methodological approaches. A lack of methodological rigor in both quantitative and qualitative inquiry has been a longstanding concern in the computing education community [8] and can both threaten the legitimacy of the field and lead to false assumptions about presumed best practices in computing

SIGCSE '19, February 27-March 2, 2019, Minneapolis, MN, USA

ACM ISBN 978-1-4503-5890-3/19/02.
https://doi.org/10.1145/3287324.3287330

education. Because of the interdisciplinary nature of computing education research, rigorous methods require a fluency in literature from social science and computing disciplines. By bringing together experts from these various disciplines, this panel will initiate a discussion of different disciplinary perspectives on methodological rigor.

2 Panel Structure

The moderator will introduce the panel topic and provide a very brief discussion of the literature. Each panelist will have 10 minutes to present their perspective on what they would like to see in future research on broadening participation in computing. The moderator will facilitate a small group discussion to give all participants an opportunity to discuss the concepts raised by the panelists and share expertise from their home disciplines. Participants will then have the opportunity to share ideas from their small groups and ask questions of the panelists.

3 Panelists

3.1 Jennifer M. Blaney

Dr. Jennifer M. Blaney is a postdoctoral scholar in Instructional Technology and Learning Sciences at Utah State University. She earned her Ph.D. in higher education with a graduate concentration in gender studies from the University of California, Los Angeles, where she also worked as the Senior Data Manager for BRAID Research. Dr. Blaney's research is interdisciplinary and explores gender equity and college student development in STEM fields, focusing on undergraduates in computing programs. Dr. Blaney has collaborated with scholars in gender studies, computer science, social psychology, and other disciplines, and her work builds on the robust literature from feminist and critical researchers who have developed methods of inquiry for exploring gender (in)equity (e.g., feminist standpoint theory). Most recently, Dr. Blaney has conducted research on how gender shapes the way undergraduates develop their conceptions of leadership in computing.

3.2 Linda J. Sax

Dr. Linda J. Sax is a Professor of Higher Education in the Graduate School of Education & Information Studies at UCLA. Dr. Sax's research focuses on gender differences in college student development, with an emphasis on women in STEM fields. She is currently the Principal Investigator for the research component of the BRAID initiative aimed at diversifying the computer science major. Her research has been funded by the National Science Foundation, the U.S. Department of Education, the Alfred P. Sloan Foundation, the Computing Research Association, AnitaB.org, and the Women's College Coalition, among others. Dr. Sax previously served as national director (from 1997 to 2005) of the Cooperative Institutional Research Program (CIRP) at the Higher Education Research Institute (HERI), the nation's largest and longest-running multi-institutional study of college students. Dr. Sax is the author of more than 100 publications, including The Gender Gap in College: Maximizing the Developmental Potential of Women and Men (Jossey-Bass, 2008), and is the recipient of the 2005 Scholar-in-Residence Award from the American Association of University Women and the 1999 Early Career Award from the Association for the Study of Higher Education.

3.3 David Feldon

Dr. David Feldon is a Professor of Instructional Technology and Learning Sciences at Utah State University. His research examines two lines of inquiry that are distinct but mutually supportive. The first characterizes the cognitive components of expertise as they contribute to effective and innovative problem solving (e.g., computational thinking) as well as how they affect the quality of instruction that experts can provide. The second examines the development of research skills within STEM disciplines as a function of instruction and other educational support mechanisms. He also conducts some research into technology-facilitated instructional approaches and the research methods for examining them. Dr. Feldon earned his Ph.D. in educational psychology and his M.S. in instructional technology from the University of Southern California, completed his postdoctoral fellowship at UCLA, and earned his tenure at the University of Virginia prior to joining the Utah State University faculty. He has published extensively on issues of instruction and assessment in various STEM disciplines, including an analysis of students' development of programming skills using recursion published in the *Journal of Learning Sciences.* His expertise in measurement, evaluation, and instruction will bring a unique perspective to this panel discussion.

3.4 Ann Gates

Dr. Ann Quiroz Gates is an AT&T Distinguished Professor and Chair of the Computer Science Department at the University of Texas at El Paso, and the past Associate Vice President of Research and Sponsored Projects. Dr. Gates directs the NSF-funded Cyber-ShARE Center of Excellence, serves on the NSF CISE AC Subcommittee on Education and Broadening Participation, and leads the NSF-funded Computing Alliance for Hispanic-Serving Institutions. She received the 2015 Great Minds in STEM's Education award, the CRA's 2015 A. Nico Habermann Award, the 2010 Anita Borg Institute Social Impact Award, and the 2009 Richard A. Tapia Achievement Award for Scientific Scholarship, Civic Science, and Diversifying Computing. She was named to Hispanic Business magazine's 100 Influential Hispanics in 2006 for her work on the Affinity Research Group model that focuses on development of undergraduate students involved in research.

4 REFERENCES

[1] Blickenstaff, J. C. (2005). Women in science careers: Leaky pipeline or gender filter? *Gender and Education, 17*(4), 369-386.

[2] Cohoon, J. M. (2002). Women in CS and biology. *ACM SIGCSE Bulletin, 34*(1), 82-86.

[3] Eddy, S. L., Brownell, S. E., & Wenderoth, M. P. (2014). Gender gaps in achievement and participation in multiple introductory biology classrooms. *Life Sciences Education, 13,* 478-492.

[4] Feldon, D. F., Peugh, J., Maher, M. A., Roksa, J., & Tofel-Grehl, C. (2017). Time-to-credit gender inequities of first-year PhD students in the biological sciences. *Life Sciences Education, 15*(1).

[5] Hewlett, S., Luce, C., Servon, L., Sherbin, L., Shiller, P., Sosnovich, E., & Sumberg, K. (2008). The Athena Factor: Reversing the Brain Drain in Science, Engineering, and Technology. *Harvard Business Review: Research Report.*

[6] Kanny, M. A., Sax, L. J., & Riggers-Piehl, T. A. (2014). Investigating forty years of STEM research: How explanations for the gender gap have evolved over time. *Journal of Women and Minorities in Science and Engineering, 20*(2), 127-148.

[7] Jagsi, R., Griffith, K. A., DeCastro, R. A., & Ubel, P. (2014). Sex, role models, and specialty choices among graduates of US medical schools in 2006–2008. *Journal of the American College of Surgeons, 218*(3), 345-352.

[8] Lishinski, A., Good, J., Sands, P., & Yadav, A. (2016). Methodological rigor and theoretical foundations of CS education research. In *Proceedings of the 2016 ACM Conference on International Computing Education Research.*

[9] National Center for Education Statistics. (2017). Digest of Education Statistics: Bachelor's Degrees Conferred by Postsecondary Institutions, by Race/Ethnicity and Sex of Student: Selected Years, 1976–77 through 2015–2016.

Special Session: AI for K-12 Guidelines Initiative

David Touretzky
AI for K-12 Working Group Chair
Carnegie Mellon University
Pittsburgh, PA
dst@cs.cmu.edu

Fred Martin
CSTA Board of Directors Chair
UMass Lowell
Lowell, MA
fred_martin@uml.edu

Deborah Seehorn
CS4NC/NC ECEP
CSTA Curriculum Committee Chair
Cary, NC
deborah.seehorn@outlook.com

Cynthia Breazeal
Director Personal Robots Group
MIT Media Laboratory
Cambridge, MA
cynthiab@media.mit.edu

Tess Posner
CEO
AI4ALL
Oakland, CA
tess@ai-4-all.org

ABSTRACT

In May 2018, the Association for the Advancement of Artificial Intelligence (AAAI) and the Computer Science Teachers Association (CSTA) formed a joint working group to develop national guidelines for teaching K-12 students about artificial intelligence [1]. Inspired by CSTA's national standards for K-12 computing education [2], the *AI for K-12* guidelines (ai4k12.org) will define what students in each grade band should know about artificial intelligence, machine learning, and robotics. The working group is also creating an online resource directory where teachers can find AI-related videos, demo software, and activity descriptions they can incorporate into their lesson plans. The goal of this session is to raise the SIGCSE community's awareness of the initiative, its deliverables, and outcomes, and to foster a community-wide conversation about AI education in K-12. This initiative parallels other recent initiatives in K-12 AI education and community-wide initiatives and discussions around CS For All and CS in K-12. This Special Session is aimed toward K-12 CS educators, researchers, and curriculum and tool designers.

Categories and Subject Descriptors

Social and professional topics → Professional topics → Computing education → K-12 education

Keywords

Artificial Intelligence; AI Education; K-12 CS Education; Instructional Resources; Guidelines; Standards

ACM ISBN 978-1-4503-5890-3/19/02.
https://doi.org/10.1145/3287324.3287525

1. OVERVIEW

The SIGCSE and CSTA communities have been central in the national expansion of CS Education in K-12 for all students across the country. This work has been undergirded by Code.org and the development and implementation of the College Board's AP Computer Science Principles courses and exam, the CS K-12 Framework [3], the CSTA 2017 Standards for K-12 Computing education [2], along with countless other research projects, tools, and professional and curriculum development efforts from within this community. At the same time as investments in CS for K-12 have been increasing, advances in AI have spawned development of intelligent personal assistants (e.g., Alexa and Siri), autonomous robots, self-driving cars, and machine learning algorithms that beat Go world champions [4-7].

However, despite increased media attention and the growing presence of AI technologies in our everyday lives, little guidance is available for American K-12 educators who would like to explain AI to their students. There are only two sentences about AI in the 2017 CSTA K-12 Computing Standards, both in the 11-12 grade band [2]. There is nothing for children in earlier grade bands. Moreover, teachers do not have easy access to appropriate resources for teaching AI to audiences outside of university courses.

In response to these needs, the Association for the Advancement of Artificial Intelligence (AAAI) and the Computer Science Teachers Association (CSTA) formed a joint working group in May 2018 to develop national guidelines for teaching students about artificial intelligence [1]. Inspired by CSTA's national standards for K-12 computing education [2], the "AI for K-12" guidelines will define what students should know about AI, and also what they should be able to do. Other organizations including AI4ALL (ai-4-all.org) and the International Society for Technology in Education (ISTE) have also recognized these needs and are beginning to address them [8, 9].

The guidelines unpack AI's "Big Ideas" along five thematic strands, and are organized by four grade bands: K-2, 3-5, 6-8, and 9-12. The working group is also creating an online resource directory where teachers can find AI-related videos, demo software, and activity descriptions they can incorporate into their lesson plans. The working group's web site is http://ai4k12.org. The goal of this special session is to raise the SIGCSE community's awareness of the initiative and foster a community-wide conversation about AI education in K-12.

Specific Objectives of the proposed session will be to:

1. Review the AI for K-12 initiative's goals and introduce the working group.
2. Describe the process for developing the guidelines.
3. Discuss draft guidelines and current challenges in developing them and needed input.
4. Share resources from the curated AI for K-12 Resource Directory and opportunities for development.

2. OUTLINE

- **Introduction (5 mins)** – David Touretzky - The AI for K-12 Working Group Chair will introduce the initiative's goals, steering committee, working group participants, and project timeline
- **The Need for AI in K-12 (20 mins)** Cynthia Breazeal (Personal Robots Group – MIT Media Lab) and Tess Posner (AI For ALL CEO/President).
- **Big Ideas in AI (10 mins)** - Fred Martin - Introduce the Big Ideas in AI: what every K-12 student should know and be able to do
- **Guideline Development Process & Draft Guidelines (10 mins)** - Deborah Seehorn - describe the process for guideline development, draft guidelines, and input needed
- **Overview Resource Directory (10 mins)** - David Touretzky - an interactive demonstration of the directory, tools, and other resources.
- **Feedback & Discussion (15 mins)** – Attendees will have an opportunity to ask questions about the AI Big Ideas, the guidelines, and the resources.

3. EXPECTATIONS

This special session is directed toward K-12 CS educators, researchers, and curriculum and tool designers. The AI for K-12 Steering committee plans to use this session to disseminate resources, get feedback from the SIGCSE community on the five "Big Ideas" in AI, draft guidelines, and resource repository, and increase the SIGCSE Community's involvement in the initiative. We will provide attendees with paper-based drafts of the guidelines, the link to the resource directory, and a walk-through of the resources. We plan to gain feedback in two ways: (1) an interactive question and answer feedback segment at the end of the session and (2) an online feedback survey. Attendees will be provided with a link to complete the survey and an invitation to join the AI for K-12 interest group.

We hope the special session will:

- Increase enrollment in our AI4K12 Interest Group mailing list (ai4k12-list@aaai.org) so that people can receive updates on the project and provide feedback on future drafts.
- Inspire attendees to try out the tools and activities in the resource library at home.
- Motivate attendees to integrate AI activities and modules into their K-12 courses or research projects.
- Inspire tool designers to think about how they can design tools to fill in the gaps in our resource directory.

4. SUITABILITY

AI for K-12 is a national initiative focused on providing guidance about what K-12 students should know about AI. The initiative is a collaboration between two international organizations and brings together people and ideas from across communities. The goal of this session is to raise the SIGCSE community's awareness of the project, its deliverables, and outcomes, and to foster a community-wide conversation about AI education in K-12. This project parallels similar community-wide initiatives and discussions around CS For All and CS in K-12.

5. REFERENCES

[1] Association for the Advancement of Artificial Intelligence (AAAI). (2018, May 15). AAAI Launches "AI for K-12" Initiative in Collaboration with the Computer Science Teachers Association (CSTA) and AI4All [Press release]. Retrieved from https://aaai.org/Pressroom/Releases/release-18-0515.php

[2] Computer Science Teachers Association (2017). CSTA K-12 Computer Science Standards, Revised 2017. Retrieved from http://www.csteachers.org/standards

[3] K-12 Computer Science Framework Steering Committee. 2016. K-12 Computer Science Framework. Technical Report. ACM, New York, NY, USA. Retrieved from https://k12cs.org/

[4] Molnar, M. (2018, July 10). K-12 Artificial Intelligence Market Set to Explode in U.S. and Worldwide by 2024. EDWeek: Market Brief, Retrieved from https://marketbrief.edweek.org/marketplace-k-12/k-12-artificial-intelligence-market-set-explode-u-s-worldwide-2024/

[5] Fuller, C. (2018, April 16). 6 Ways AI Is Revolutionizing Daily Life. AT&T, Retrieved from https://www.attsavings.com/resources/internet/ai-is-revolutionizing-daily-life/

[6] Simonite, T. (2017, December 21).As Artificial Intelligence Advances, Here Are Five Tough Projects For 2018. WIRED:, Retrieved from https://www.wired.com/story/as-artificial-intelligence-advances-here-are-five-projects-for-2018/

[7] Newman, J. (2018, January 4). Eight Trends That Will Define The Digital Assistant Wars In 2018. FastCompany. Retrieved from https://www.fastcompany.com/40512062/eight-trends-that-will-define-the-digital-assistant-wars-in-2018

[8] International Society for Technology in Education (ISTE). (2018, June 25). Bold New Program Helps Teachers and Students Explore the Power of AI [Press release]. Retrieved from https://www.iste.org/explore/articleDetail?articleid=2229&category=Press-Releases&article=Bold+New+Program+Helps+Teachers+and+Students+Explore+the+Power+of+AI

[9] Baloch, H., Crompton, H., Gerl, M., Harrison, S., Law, D., McGirt, F., Ramos, Y., South, J. (June 25, 2018). Artificial Intelligence Goes to School [Text, Audio]. Retrieved from https://conference.iste.org/2018/program/search/detail_session.php?id=110888525

The Reality of Inclusion: The Role of Relationships, Identity, and Academic Culture in Inclusive and Equitable Practices for Broadening Participation in Computing Education

Jamie Payton (Moderator)
Computer & Information Sciences
Temple University
Philadelphia, PA USA
payton@temple.edu

Jamika D. Burge[†]
STEM+CS Research
Thurgood Marshall College Fund
Washington, DC USA
jamika.burge@gmail.com

Jill Denner
Science Department
Education, Training, Research
Scotts Valley, CA USA
jill.denner@etr.org

ABSTRACT

During the 2018 *RESPECT* Conference, a group of us facilitated a conversation about inclusion in computing. The discussion focused on critical issues of equity and inclusion and how to engage people from all groups in learning key concepts in computing. For this SIGCSE panel, we propose to continue the conversation through a broader conversation around the terms "broadening participation" and the roles of relationships, identity (cultural and personal), and academic, political, and professional perspectives when supporting equity and inclusion in computing education. This panel seeks to disrupt the conversation about computer science education, and participants to this session will leave having had a safe space in which to discuss issues of identify, race, and privilege that are critical to spaces like SIGCSE.

CCS CONCEPTS

• Computing Education • Computer Science Education

KEYWORDS

Equity and Inclusion, Intersectionality, Computer Science Education, Broadening Participation, CS for All, Social Justice

1. SUMMARY

The CS for All movement is in full swing and, importantly, challenges notions of who should participate (and succeed) in technical ecosystems. Equally important is the reality that many are still being left out of this movement, amplifying, in stark ways, the largely white, male presence that continues to dominate our schools and workplaces [1]. Despite the benefits of increased financial returns and innovative technical solutions informed by a diversity of perspectives [2, 3], true tech inclusion is still elusive. Based on our 2018 session and collective experience of attending SIGCSE for many years, we have identified the following needs:

- SIGCSE members have good intentions about inclusion, but need spaces where they can ask questions and learn from others.
- Theoretical constructs like intersectionality are coming into mainstream conversations, but people need models of how to apply them in research methods, and in presentations.
- Many are ready to embrace a justice-centered approach to equity in computer science education, but are not sure how to navigate that within their institutions.

This session brings back the original *RESPECT* panelists and will raise these issues thoughtfully to push the boundaries of broadening participation by modeling how to have these conversations in our classrooms and research teams.

2. PANEL STRUCTURE

The moderator will give context for the panel topic (5 mins), followed by brief introductions for panelists. As panelists are introduced, each will give a 5-10-minute framing of their perspectives relative to the topic. After all (four) panelists have joined, the moderator will facilitate a Q&A offering 2-3 questions to the panel (15-20 minutes). The questions will be designed to generate strategies and address struggles related to incorporating inclusive approaches to our work, research, and teaching. Examples include: "What is the role of theory in keeping an inclusive research agenda?", "Which research methods help you maintain a focus on equity and inclusion?", and "Are there online groups or in-person meetings that people with an interest in this topic should participate in?". The floor will then be opened for discussion and questions from the audience (25-30 minutes). The moderator will collect and read anonymous questions and comments in order to include the voices that are not usually heard during conference sessions. We have learned, from prior experience, that audiences are eager to engage on topics raised by this panel, often requiring more time than is allotted. This panel is designed to be led by the contributions of the expert panelists, not dominated by it. Thus, there will be sufficient time for audience participation.

[†]Corresponding author

SIGCSE '19, February 27-March 2, 2019, Minneapolis, MN, USA

ACM ISBN 978-1-4503-5890-3/19/02.
https://doi.org/10.1145/3287324.3287337

3. JAMIE PAYTON

Jamie Payton is an Associate Professor and the Chair of the Computer & Information Sciences Department at Temple University. Her research interests include pervasive computing systems for smart health and well-being, broadening participation in computing, and evidence-based approaches to improving computer science education. She is the Director of the STARS Computing Corps, an NSF-funded national alliance of over 50 colleges and universities with the mission to broaden participation in computing; STARS has engaged over 2,600 college students in service learning projects with regional K12 schools, industry, and community partners to inform, engage, and prepare over 140,000 future students for entry and success in college computing programs. She is also the PI of the Research Experiences for Undergraduates (REU) Site program on Pervasive Computing for Smart Health, Safety, and Well-being, which provides intensive summer research opportunities to a diverse group of talented undergraduate students. Jamie moderated this discussion at *RESPECT 2018*, and will do so again for this panel.

4. JAMIKA D. BURGE

Jamika D. Burge is a Senior Research Scientist at the Thurgood Marshall College Fund (TMCF), where she serves as co-PI for the NSF-funded Building Student Retention through Individuated Guided coHort Training in CS (BRIGHT-CS) project, which is developing a CS ecosystem for girls of color in the New York City and Northern Virginia metro areas, and she is co-PI for Girls ROCK Tech!, which, in partnership with Black Girls ROCK!, is developing a leadership curriculum that combines computational thinking with a powerful cultural and gender empowerment model for middle and high school girls. Jamika also leads *Communities of Practice* for ONE Design at Capital One. In this role, she supports designers through research empowerment, career growth, and skills development. She is an authority on intersectionality research which led her to co-found blackcomputeHER.org, an organization dedicated to supporting computational & design thinking and workforce development for black women and girls. On this panel, she will discuss intersectionality, identity, and the narrative used to describe people who are traditionally excluded from computing and tech.

5. JILL DENNER

Jill Denner is a Senior Research Scientist at Education, Training, Research (ETR), a non-profit organization in California. Her research focuses on broadening participation in computing from K-12 to community college. This work is done in partnership with schools, community-based organizations, and colleges. She has been the PI on 20 federal grants focused on understanding how to create learning environments that leverage the cultural strengths and agency of youth and families. In this panel, she will discuss the role of equity and power in research-practice partnerships that cross ethnic and socioeconomic lines, how sociocultural and critical race theories have increased the relevance of her research, and her experience as a white middle class woman doing research on/with Latinx communities.

6. CELINE LATULIPE

Celine Latulipe is a Professor of Human-Computer Interaction and Computer Science Education in the College of Computing and Informatics at UNC Charlotte. Celine has performed extensive research into reformulating and reengineering the college learning experience to make large core computing courses social, collaborative, engaging and empowering for women, African-American and Hispanic students. She is known for pioneering the lightweight teams approach to learning, with teams that are both diverse but also include pairs of under-represented students, and for promoting gender-paired programming in CS1 labs to enact early empowerment in the degree. Celine is the PI on a recently awarded NSF grant that will require all incoming (freshman and transfer) computing majors at UNC Charlotte over the next two years to engage in participatory Exclusion Response Workshops. These workshops make use of Augusto Boal's Theatre of the Oppressed methodology as a mechanism for rehearsing social change. She will bring her expertise in creating social change, gender dynamics, and intersectional analysis to bear on this panel.

7. YOLANDA A. RANKIN

Yolanda is currently an Assistant Professor in the College of Communication & Information at Florida State University. Her research interests include identifying best practices and pedagogical strategies for Computer Science (CS) education K-16, utilizing videogames to promote Second Language Acquisition (SLA), and engaging members of underserved populations in participatory design of information-based technologies. Yolanda has accumulated more than twelve years of industry experience working as a software engineer & project manager engineer at Lucent Technologies Bell Labs and as a Research Staff Member at IBM Research Lab in San Jose, CA. As such, she is acutely aware of the underrepresentation of African American women in industry and is currently investigating African American women's pathways into the field of computing. Yolanda's most recent book, Moving Students of Color from Consumers to Producers of Technology, represents a collation of effective strategies for broadening the participation of underrepresented groups in CS. Yolanda believes in engaging members of underrepresented populations as co-designers of equitable learning environments that embrace diverse populations, and she will present this perspective on this panel.

8. REFERENCES

[1] B. Myers, *Women and Minorities in Tech, by the numbers*, https://www.wired.com/story/computer-science-graduates-diversity/.

[2] S. A. Hewlett, M. Marshall, & L. Sherbin. (2013). How diversity can drive innovation. *Harvard Business Review*, 91(12), 30-30.

[3] A. D. Rayome, *5 eye-opening statistics about minorities in tech*, https://www.techrepublic.com/article/5-eye-opening-statistics-about-minorities-in-tech/

ACM Task Force on Data Science Education

Draft Report and Opportunity for Feedback

Andrea Danyluk*
Williams College
Williamstown, Massachusetts, USA
andrea@cs.williams.edu

Paul Leidig
Grand Valley State University
Allendale, Michigan, USA
leidig@gvsu.edu

Lillian Cassel
Villanova University
Villanova, Pennsylvania, USA
lillian.cassel@villanova.edu

Christian Servin
El Paso Community College
El Paso, Texas, USA
cservin1@epcc.edu

ABSTRACT

The ACM Data Science Task Force was established by the ACM Education Council and tasked with articulating the role of computing discipline-specific contributions to this emerging field. This special session seeks to introduce the work of the ACM Data Science Task Force as well as to engage the SIGCSE community in this effort. Members of the task force will introduce key components of a draft report, including a summary of data science curricular efforts to date, results of ACM academic and industry surveys on data science, as well as the initial articulation of computing competencies for undergraduate programs in data science. This session should be of interest to all SIGCSE attendees, but especially faculty developing college-level curricula in Data Science.

CCS CONCEPTS

• **Social and professional topics → Computing education**; • **Applied computing → Education**.

KEYWORDS

Data Science; Curriculum.

ACM Reference Format:

Andrea Danyluk, Paul Leidig, Lillian Cassel, and Christian Servin. 2019. ACM Task Force on Data Science Education: Draft Report and Opportunity for Feedback. In *Proceedings of the 50th ACM Technical Symposium on Computer Science Education (SIGCSE '19), February 27–March 2, 2019, Minneapolis, MN, USA.* ACM, New York, NY, USA, 2 pages. https://doi.org/10.1145/3287324.3287522

1 OBJECTIVE

A particular challenge of developing data science curricula is that the field is inherently interdisciplinary. An important requirement is the balance of computing, statistics, and domain knowledge. At the August 2017 ACM Education Council meeting, a task force was initiated to add to the broad, interdisciplinary conversation on data science, with an articulation of the role of computing discipline-specific contributions to this emerging field. Specifically, the task force is seeking to define what the computing/computational contributions are to this new field, in order to provide guidance for computer science or similar departments offering data science programs of study at the undergraduate level. A draft report is available as of late 2018 – early 2019. The goal of this special session is to provide an overview of the project and draft report, and – more importantly – to actively engage the SIGCSE community in discussions that will help to inform the final published volume. Holding this special session at SIGCSE is an important step in the outreach that the Task Force plans to do over the next year.

Important work has already been done in the data science curriculum space. For example, in October 2015, the National Science Foundation (NSF) sponsored a workshop with representatives of many perspectives on data science. Some attendees represented established programs; others represented societies with an interest in data science. The final report [2] describes the discussions and reflects the diversity of opinions. The EDISON Data Science Project was launched in 2015 with the purpose of "accelerating the creation of the Data Science profession."[4] The EDISON consortium, comprised of partners from across Europe, recently made available Release 2 of their Data Science Competence Framework.[3]. The Park City Math Institute brought together an interdisciplinary faculty group to devise curriculum guidelines for undergraduate programs in data science.[6] And recently, the National Academies of Sciences, Engineering, and Medicine released an extensive report on Data Sciences for Undergraduates.[5].

The goal of the ACM Data Science Task Force is not to duplicate these important efforts but to further articulate the contributions of the computing discipline to data science, as well as to provide additional detail on computing discipline-specific competencies. The task force and associated advisory committee are global committees, with representatives from four continents, as well as from academia and industry.

2 OUTLINE

This special session is organized by four members of the ACM Data Science Task Force. The session is modeled on panels and special sessions organized to gather input on previous ACM curricular volumes, such as CS2013.[1]. While we hope that attendees will have

*Also at Northeastern University, Boston, MA.

SIGCSE '19, February 27–March 2, 2019, Minneapolis, MN, USA

ACM ISBN 978-1-4503-5890-3/19/02.
https://doi.org/10.1145/3287324.3287522

read the draft report, we will not expect this, and will introduce the report contents to provide context for the following discussion. We will reserve more than half of the session for questions, discussion, and feedback. Our plan is to do this in a "whole group" setting, so that participants can hear each others' questions and comments and respond to them. Our intent is for this to be an exchange of ideas that will inform subsequent drafts of the curricular recommendations. Our outline for the session is as follows:

- Introduction (5 minutes) – an introduction to the goals and purpose of the ACM Data Science Task Force.
- Current landscape in data science curriculum development (5 minutes) – an articulation of the work already done, particularly in the undergraduate curriculum space.
- Outcomes of academic and industry surveys (10 minutes) – In spring/summer 2018, the task force fielded parallel surveys to gather input on computing discipline-specific contributions to data science, including their relative importance to companies that hire in this area. We will present some of our findings.
- Computing knowledge areas for data science (10 minutes) – Following the framework of ACM curricular volumes – e.g., [1] – the task force is organizing its report around knowledge areas, such as Data privacy, security, integrity; Data management, storage, retrieval; Systems considerations for data mining "in the large" – big data, distributed systems, parallel computing, and high-performance computing; Machine learning; and others. We will itemize the knowledge areas and provide some examples of competencies.
- Timeline and process (5 minutes) – Before opening the session for discussion, we will articulate our timeline, next steps, and opportunities for involvement.
- Open discussion (40 minutes) – Time for questions and feedback.

3 EXPECTATIONS

This session should be of interest to all SIGCSE attendees, but especially faculty developing college-level curricula in Data Science. Our expectations are that attendees will learn about this new ACM curricular project and will be able to contribute to forthcoming iterations of the work, either in person at the session or by following up with the task force.

REFERENCES

[1] ACM/IEEE-CS Joint Task Force on Computing Curricula. 2013. *Computer Science Curricula 2013.* Technical Report. ACM Press and IEEE Computer Society Press. https://doi.org/10.1145/2534860

[2] Boots Cassel and Heikki Topi. 2015. *Strengthening Data Science Education Through Collaboration.* Technical Report. http://www.computingportal.org/sites/default/files/Data%20Science%20Education%20Workshop%20Report%201.0_0.pdf

[3] EDISON. [n. d.]. The EDISON Data Science Competence Framework. http://edison-project.eu/edison/edison-data-science-framework-edsf. Accessed: 2018-08-30.

[4] A. Manieri, S. Brewer, R. Riestra, Y. Demchenko, M. Hemmje, T. Wiktorski, T. Ferrari, and J. Frey. 2015. Data Science Professional Uncovered: How the EDISON Project will Contribute to a Widely Accepted Profile for Data Scientists. In *2015 IEEE 7th International Conference on Cloud Computing Technology and Science (CloudCom).* 588–593. https://doi.org/10.1109/CloudCom.2015.57

[5] National Academies of Sciences, Engineering, and Medicine. 2018. *Data Science for Undergraduates: Opportunities and Options.* The National Academies Press, Washington, DC. https://doi.org/10.17226/25104

[6] Richard De Veaux, Mahesh Agarwal, Maia Averett, Benjamin Baumer, Andrew Bray, Thomas Bressoud, Lance Bryant, Lei Cheng, Amanda Francis, Robert Gould, Albert Kim, Matt Kretchmar, Qin Lu, Ann Moskol, Deborah Nolan, Roberto Pelayo, Sean Raleigh, Ricky Sethi, Mutiara Sondjaja, Neelesh Tiruviluamala, Paul Uhlig, Talitha Washington, Curtis Wesley, David White, and Ping Ye. 2017. Curriculum Guidelines for Undergraduate Programs in Data Science. *Annual Review of Statistics and Its Application* 4 (Mar 2017), 15–30.

CS Principles Higher Education Pathways

Crystal Furman (moderator)
College Board
Duluth, Georgia
cfurman@collegeboard.org

Owen Astrachan
Duke University
Durham, North Carolina
ola@duke.edu

Daniel D. Garcia
UC Berkeley
Berkeley, California
ddgarcia@berkeley.edu

David Musicant
Carleton College
Northfield, Minnesota
dmusicant@carleton.edu

Jennifer Rosato
College of St. Scholastica
Duluth, Minnesota
jrosato@css.edu

ABSTRACT

With approximately 37,000 students entering college with an AP CSP credit, students, parents, and teachers are wondering how that AP credit "counts" in college. In this panel, we will share perspectives from the College Board and higher education institutions of pathways from CS Principles to CS majors. While over 500 institutions have indicated they have credit and placement policies for CSP, they may vary quite a bit [1]. (Credit gives students units of credit on their college record while placement means the AP credit can meet a particular course requirement.) For example, some institutions offer credit only, while others allow the course to count as part of a general education program, as a major elective, or even require CSP in the major. Panelists will share institutional context and reasoning behind their policies.

CCS CONCEPTS

• **Social and professional topics → Computing education**;

KEYWORDS

Advanced Placement, CS Principles, K-12 Education

ACM Reference Format:

Crystal Furman (moderator), Owen Astrachan, Daniel D. Garcia, David Musicant, and Jennifer Rosato. 2019. CS Principles Higher Education Pathways. In *Proceedings of the 50th ACM Technical Symposium on Computer Science Education (SIGCSE '19), February 27-March 2, 2019, Minneapolis, MN, USA.* ACM, New York, NY, USA, 2 pages. https://doi.org/10.1145/3287324.3287438

1 SUMMARY

The CS Principles course was designed to be a breadth-first introduction to CS, with a goal of broadening participation. Creating it as an Advanced Placement course was one way to ensure widespread adoption in high schools, however, the course must also be considered rigorous enough for colleges. The College Board ensures AP courses align to comparable college level courses through syllabus studies, surveys of high education, and focus groups. Once the course and exam are developed and the exam administered for the first time, a standard setting panel of higher education and high school faculty assists in determining the level of student performance required to earn each score (2, 3, 4, and 5) [2].

Session participants will be provided with achievement level descriptors that illustrate the anticipated performance level of students who score 3, 4, or 5 as well as examples of questions from recently developed practice exams and exemplars of student work which demonstrate the equivalent college-level performance required of students. Panelists will share credit and placement policies from a variety of institutions (public and private, liberal arts and research-focused), including how those policies align with program goals to broaden participation. Audience members will have a better understanding of the breadth of credit and placement options and considerations for adopting credit and placement policies for AP CSP at their own institution.

2 PANEL STRUCTURE

After a brief introduction of the AP CSP course and exam, each panelist will be given 8 minutes to present their respective positions on higher education credit and placement policies for AP CSP at their institutions. Following the presentations, the moderator will facilitate the audience discussion. We anticipate questions regarding how AP CSP fits into CS pathways, creation of credit and placement policies, and how AP CSP aligns to comparable courses in higher education.

3 OWEN ASTRACHAN

Duke University is a highly-selective undergraduate institution with 6400 undergraduate students in schools of Arts and Science, Engineering, Environment, and Public Policy. For purposes of AP credit there are two schools: Arts and Science+others and Engineering. Computer Science is in the school of Arts and Science and gives credit for Compsci 92: Information and the Internet, for a score of 5 on the AP CSP exam. This course fulfills a quantitative reasoning requirement, but students must take two such courses at Duke, so effectively the course is for credit only (this policy applies to all AP courses). We have offered two versions of this course since 2008, changing to a course modeled as a CS Principles course in 2013. We have used ideas from CSP in broadening participation in our introductory course for majors so that its composition reflects that of the student body (50% male/female). Because we are expanding

ACM ISBN 978-1-4503-5890-3/19/02.
https://doi.org/10.1145/3287324.3287438

our introductory course for majors to be an interdisciplinary programming course there is less demand for our Compsci 92 course than there has been in the past.

Owen Astrachan is a Professor of the Practice of Computer Science course, designed Compsci 92 at Duke, and was the Principal Investigator on the NSF/College Board grant that created the AP CS Principles course.

4 DANIEL D. GARCIA

The University of California (all campuses) grants elective units[1] for AP CSP: 8 units in the quarter system, or 5âĚŞ units for semesters. At UC Berkeley, credit varies by the overseeing college. The College of Engineering allows a score of 3 or above to count for our equivalent non-majors course, *CS10: The Beauty and Joy of Computing (BJC)*, whereas the the College of Letters and Science allows a score of 3 or above to count for the Quantitative Reasoning requirement.

UC Berkeley, similar to most big public schools, has a general service CS0 and a CS1 for students interested in a CS major. The CS0 class is not required by any major, and it serves dual purposes. It stands alone as a single course for students wishing to learn computational thinking, how to program, and to think about the social implications of computing. It also serves students who intend to major in computing but need a little practice, support and a less-steep learning curve than CS1. Many of the students who take the course for the first reason find themselves fascinated by the subject and follow it up with CS1, and many end up choosing a CS minor or major. It is wonderful to draw students in from the entire campus for our CS0 course BJC; our gender diversity is among the highest in the country-in the spring of 2018 we had 65% female enrollment! We owe a fair bit to the appeal of the curriculum and pedagogy that come from AP CSP: team projects of the students' own choice, global impact and data big ideas, and collaboration and communication practices.

In February of 2017 (just before the first AP CSP exam), the UC Office of the President reached out to undergraduate admissions, and eventually to EECS to see if they should give credit for the course. We offered a resounding yes, which was followed by full support from our department chair and the undergraduate study committee. Critical to this all was the strong support in the department for our CS0 course, which had been a pilot for AP CSP, and which has been serving to add much-needed diversity to CS1.

Dan Garcia is a Teaching Professor at UC Berkeley, was a member of the AP CSP development committee, and was the co-creator of the Beauty and Joy of Computing course.

5 DAVID MUSICANT

Carleton College is a top-ranked liberal arts school located in Northfield, MN, with 2000 students. We offer a CS1 class that over half of the students at Carleton take, and a score of 4 or 5 on the AP CS A exam grants incoming students credit for it. We don't currently offer a course that resembles AP CSP. We do offer an occasional course aimed at the CS0 audience titled "Life in the Age of Networks," that serves much of the same purpose, but the content is very different. We did have a course called "Explorations in Computer Science" that was fairly similar to AP CSP, but that course is no longer offered.

We've struggled with how to handle AP CSP with regards to credit at Carleton. We believe that the AP CSP curriculum is wonderful, and serves as a great introduction to CS and are thrilled to see that it is getting the uptake in schools that it is. We're also very much encouraged by the broadening participation from high schools. We do have some concerns about whether success on the AP CSP exam indicates achievement at a level that would correspond to our expectations of college level work. We originally decided not to grant credit for AP CSP, based on an early draft of some sample exam questions that we thought weren't challenging enough. After an entire prototype exam was released, with some uncertainty, we chose to grant credit for a score of 5 on the exam. Since we don't offer a course that matches it, this means that the student is merely granted a course's worth of credits that can contribute to the total number of credits needed to graduate. We continue to be concerned about the scoring guidelines for the Explore performance task, which seem to be focused on the structure of the student's submission rather than on correct content.

Dave Musicant is a Professor of Computer Science at Carleton, teaches CS1 and more advanced courses at Carleton College, and also teaches workshops for high school teachers regarding the AP CS A exam.

6 JENNIFER ROSATO

The College of St. Scholastica is located in Duluth, MN, with 4500 students (1700 traditional and 1000 online or extended undergraduates). For the Computer Information Systems major, a CS0 course has been required for over 20 years. In the past, the course has included programming, databases, and spreadsheets, however, it has now been replaced by the Mobile CSP course. It also fulfills a general education math requirement, is a required course for Health Informatics majors and CS Education minors. About half of the students take the course online, serving both traditional and adult learners. A majority of students are first generation and come from communities unlikely to offer high school CS. The CSP course serves as an introduction to the major areas of study in CS and its social implications, in alignment with School of Business & TechnologyâĂŹs focus on ethics. For St. Scholastica, the CS0 course provides an engaging first course for the majority of students who have little background in CS and a recruitment pathway to the CS major.

Jennifer Rosato is the Director of the National Center for Computer Science Education, leads the Mobile CSP project, and is a member of the AP CSP development committee.

REFERENCES

[1] College Board. [n. d.]. AP Computer Science Principles Higher Education Credit and Placement. Retrieved August 30, 2018 from https://apcentral.collegeboard.org/courses/ap-computer-science-principles/higher-education-credit-and-placement?course=ap-computer-science-principles
[2] College Board. [n. d.]. Score Setting and Scoring. Retrieved August 30, 2018 from https://apcentral.collegeboard.org/about-ap/how-ap-develops-courses-and-exams/score-setting-and-scoring

[1]Elective units "can be applied to UC graduation requirements for specific subjects and/or for general education/breadth requirements, as determined by each campus"

Negotiating Varied Research Goals in Computing Education Research

Mark Guzdial
Electrical Engineering & CS Dept.
University of Michigan
Ann Arbor, MI, USA
mjguz@umich.edu

Colleen M. Lewis
Computer Science Dept.
Harvey Mudd College
Claremont, CA, USA
lewis@cs.hmc.edu

Lauren Margulieux
Dept. of Learning Sciences
Georgia State University
Atlanta, GA, USA
lmargulieux@gsu.edu

Greg L. Nelson
Computer Science & Engineering Dept.
University of Washington, Seattle
Seattle, WA, USA
glnelson@uw.edu

Leo Porter
Computer Science and Engineering Dept.
University of California, San Diego
La Jolla, CA, USA
leporter@eng.ucsd.edu

ABSTRACT

As we celebrate the 50th SIGCSE Symposium, this panel explores how computing education researchers chart a course individually and as a community to build our research practices and collective knowledge of computing education. This navigation involves developing our research goals, which tools we use to work towards those goals, and which academic communities outside of computing education we seek to learn from and contribute to. However, these processes of navigation are rarely discussed as a community. Paper and grant submissions and reviews provide an imperfect way for our community to communicate our varied values and priorities. This panel brings together experts in computing education research who differ in their research goals, tools, and external communities. We can expect a lively discussion amongst the panelist and we hope to spark important discussions within the computing education research community!

KEYWORDS

Research goals, research practices and methods, interdisciplinary

1 PANEL STRUCTURE

In honor of the 50th SIGCSE Symposium, this panel considers the various fields that contribute to computing education research (CER) and how researchers integrate diverse goals, tools, and products in their research. This panel brings together experts in CER who differ in their academic training, professional goals, and memberships in external communities.

SIGCSE '19, February 27-March 2, 2019, Minneapolis, MN, USA

ACM ISBN 978-1-4503-5890-3/19/02.
https://doi.org/10.1145/3287324.3287329

15 minutes: The panelists will provide background about the goals, tools, and products that define their research.
20 minutes: The panelists will discuss strengths, weaknesses and limitations of their approach, and collaborations that they have with researchers who take different approaches.
30 minutes: The panel will invite attendees to contribute questions of individual panelists or for the panelists to discuss.
10 minutes: The panel will close with brief comments regarding how they would like CER to evolve over the next 10 to 30 years.

2 GOALS, TOOLS, AND PRODUCTS

CER, like other discipline-based educational research, brings together people with different goals:

- practitioners (i.e., educators and curriculum and tool developers) who primarily want to optimize learning,
- discipline-based education researchers who primarily want to understand and improve learning within computing, and
- general education researchers who primarily want to understand how people learn in general.

Each group values the goals of the other groups. In addition, researchers can belong to multiple groups or collaborate across groups, but they must negotiate their priorities to determine the research tools that they should use.

- action research is a rapid method to implement and evaluate design decisions and improve learning environments but it does not normally include many scientific controls, making it difficult to explain why changes occur or generalize findings.
- design-based research (DBR) tests designs of learning environments, tools, or interventions that are based on theory. In the early stages of DBR, the focus is on improving design with a specific context, and in the later stages, the focus shifts to building generalizable theory.
- highly-controlled experiments examine factors that affect learning independently from other contextual factors to

isolate the effects of variables in the learning environment and build general learning theory.

The tools that are used throughout a project can greatly impact the products of the work and how external communities engage it.

- action research generally produces directly applicable solutions, such as tools and instructional materials for a specific context (i.e., course, topic, or school) and can provide insight for education researchers,
- early stage DBR generally produces domain-specific theory and design of learning environments, tools, and interventions of interest to discipline-based ed researchers and can guide practice and development or application of learning theory,
- late stage DBR and highly-controlled experiments produce global theories or interventions that generalize across topics and domains and guide practice and future research.

Each of these research goals, tools, and connections to external communities provide valuable contributions to CER. We will explore the benefits and challenges of different approaches. We will also explore how to contribute to and communicate in research projects that include multiple approaches.

3 POSITION STATEMENTS

3.1 Mark Guzdial, University of Michigan

Position: I am a computer scientist who did a PhD in CS and Education. I was trained as a learning scientist who worked in computing. I recognize that I need to collaborate with educational psychologists and other learning scientists who know research methods and theories that I don't. I can provide them with insights into computing, a field with growing importance for all learners.
Expertise and background: Mark Guzdial is a professor in CS & Engineering and Engineering Education Research. His focus is on making computing available to a wide audience, particularly non-CS majors, end-user programmers, and high school teachers. He tends to publish in ACM SIGCSE venues, but he sometimes publishes in the education and learning sciences communities.

3.2 Colleen Lewis, Harvey Mudd College

Position: I will focus on my experience as a practitioner and my work documenting and disseminating knowledge about teaching CS (i.e., pedagogical content knowledge or PCK) through CSTeachingTips.org. As an educator, general and domain-specific theory inform my actions, but may never provide the granularity to guide every decision. While examples of CS PCK are often dismissed as anecdotes, these anecdotes can match the granularity of my decisions and help me notice and respond to important aspects of my students' learning.
Expertise and background: Colleen Lewis is the McGregor-Girand Associate Professor of CS. Trained as a learning scientist and teaching CS, her scholarship is spread across these boundaries and builds upon research in social psychology and higher ed.

2.3 Lauren Margulieux, Georgia State Univ.

Position: As a learning scientist, my primary research goals are to build general theory for how people develop cognitive skills and develop interventions to improve learning outcomes. I often work with discipline-based education researchers to conduct research in authentic learning environments. This approach allows my research to make both applied contributions within a domain and theoretical contributions to the learning sciences. I have found that satisfying the needs of both general and domain-specific research goals takes extra design and development time but leads to high quality and well-devised research and products.
Expertise and background: Lauren Margulieux is an assistant professor in the Department of Learning Sciences. Her training is in cognitive psychology, instructional design, and learning technologies. She conducts research on problem solving in STEM. In addition to ACM SIGCSE, she is a member of the International Society of the Learning Sciences and American Educational Research Association.

2.4 Greg Nelson, University of Washington

Position: As a pragmatic design-focused researcher, I prioritize finding more effective designs for learning computing. I have written about tensions between pursuing design and explanatory research goals. I create and evaluate learning tools, including discontinuous designs like learning to read a programming language first instead of learning reading and writing at the same time. I also develop domain-specific theories of what computing knowledge is and assessments for them, such as program tracing.
Expertise and Background: Greg Nelson is a senior CS PhD student under Andy Ko, trained in HCI, computing education, and statistics. His research focuses on assessment and instructional design for computing education, including tutorial systems and other learning environments beyond in-person classrooms.

2.5 Leo Porter, UC San Diego

Position: I am a computer scientist whose PhD is in computer architecture. Having moved into CS education in 2011, I bring the focus on benchmarking, standards, and empirical research from architecture to my research in CS education. On the panel, I will focus on my work evaluating the effectiveness of Peer Instruction in CS and in ongoing work predicting which students are at-risk and which factors lead to them being at-risk. I have found that empirical research based on data from measurable outcomes and from qualitative studies with students both helps us better understand the impact of known phenomena while discovering new lines of inquiry.
Expertise and background: Leo Porter is an Associate Teaching Professor. He teaches a wide variety of classes across the curriculum including courses on introductory programming, upper division data structures and architecture, and graduate courses on architecture and CEd research. His research focuses on evaluating pedagogical practices, developing instruments to measure student learning, and predicting and understanding at-risk students.

Computing Education as a Foundation for 21st Century Literacy

Mark Guzdial
University of Michigan, Computer Science & Engineering
Ann Arbor, Michigan
mjguz@umich.edu

ABSTRACT

Teaching programming as a way to express ideas, communicate with others, and understand our world is one of the oldest goals for computing education. The inventor of the term "computer science" saw it as the third leg of STEM literacy. In this talk, I lay out the history of the idea of universal computational literacy, some of what it will take to get there, and how our field will be different when we do.

CCS CONCEPTS

• Social and professional topics → Computing education; • Applied computing → Interactive learning environments.

KEYWORDS

computational literacy, CS for All, computational thinking, history

ACM Reference Format:
Mark Guzdial. 2019. Computing Education as a Foundation for 21st Century Literacy. In *Proceedings of the 50th ACM Technical Symposium on Computer Science Education (SIGCSE '19), February 27-March 2, 2019, Minneapolis, MN, USA.* ACM, New York, NY, USA, Article 4, 2 pages. https://doi.org/10.1145/3287324.3290953

1 OUR MISSION: "AT ALL EDUCATION LEVELS"

The mission of the ACM Special Interest Group on Computer Science Education[1] is to serve as a global forum for educators about the learning and teaching of "computing" (not just *computer science*) "at all levels." SIGCSE has a bold and noble mission. One of the earliest goals of computer science was to provide computing to teachers and students at all levels.

Alan Perlis, the first ACM Turing Award laureate, argued in 1961 that all university students take a course in "computers," and that they should all learn programming [9]. He argued that programming gave students a new way to see the world and solve problems – within their own discipline. He said, "Given then the appropriate computer, the capability of developing programming systems, the proper freshman course[2], and possibly a good follow-up program, the computer will achieve its ultimate role as handmaiden to scholarly university activities."

[1]https://sigcse.org/sigcse/about/profile
[2]Even Perlis saw the challenge of computing education as mostly about CS1.

SIGCSE '19, February 27-March 2, 2019, Minneapolis, MN, USA

ACM ISBN 978-1-4503-5890-3/19/02.
https://doi.org/10.1145/3287324.3290953

Like Perlis, Seymour Papert was interested in the computer as a support for learning activities, especially for children. He made the claim "that children can learn to program and learning to program can affect the way that they learn everything else" [8]. His point is not to teach computer science for its own sake, or as vocational training, but as a support for learning in any discipline.

The earliest reason for teaching students about computers was to support learning in science, engineering, and mathematics (what we now call *STEM*). George Forsythe invented the term *computer science* in an article in the *Journal of Engineering Education* [4]. For Forsyth, computers were the third leg of literacy for STEM students. He wrote in 1968 [5], "The most valuable acquisitions in a scientific or technical education are the general-purpose mental tools which remain serviceable for a lifetime. I rate natural language and mathematics as the most important of these tools, and computer science as a third."

Alan Kay [7] and Andrea diSessa [2] used the term "literacy" to describe this use of computation as a medium, like reading and writing. Kay wrote, "Computer literacy is a contact with the activity deep enough to make the computational equivalent of reading and writing fluent and enjoyable." We can study reading and writing for their own sake, but for most of us, reading and writing is what enables us to express ideas, to communicate with others, and to understand our world. Literacy supports and affects how we learn.

When I read SIGCSE's mission, I hear the mandate of Forsythe, Perlis, and everyone who has wanted computation to play a role in learning "at all levels." This is our organization's mission, to serve educators who bring computing to all students.

2 WHEN COMPUTING IS LIKE MATHEMATICS AND SCIENCE

Computing education will look entirely different when we teach students at all levels to use computing as a literacy, like reading, writing, and mathematics. We are currently struggling with the overwhelming weight of rapidly rising enrollments [1], but we need to prepare for much greater numbers if we are to meet this mandate. We need to plan for dramatic growth.

Here is one way to think about the scale of that growth. The SIGCSE Technical Symposium draws about 1300 attendees. ACM SIGCSE's International Computing Education Research Conference (ICER) has about 150 attendees. The K-12 CS teachers conference (CSTA) had about 750 attendees last year. Let's consider the difference in scale when we are reaching students "at all education levels." Mathematics and science today is taught to all students, and there are conferences dedicated to supporting those teachers. Here in the US, the National Council of Teachers of Mathematics had 1,000 attendees at their research conference, and 9,000 at their annual meeting. The National Science Teachers Association has 9–12,000 attendees annually at their national conference. Computing education may not ever look exactly like science or mathematics, but the scale to reach *everyone* is likely comparable.

Computing education will need decades to reach this scale. We are a young discipline, at 50 years old. In contrast, the American Society of Engineering Education (ASEE) just celebrated their 125th year. The National Council of Teachers of Mathematics was started in 1920, so it soon will be 100 years old. At SIGCSE's 100th anniversary, we may still be talking about achieving Forsythe's vision of computing as a literacy alongside text and mathematics.

3 CHANGING COMPUTING EDUCATION

Meeting the needs of students "at all education levels" is going to require changes in what we teach and how we teach. My thinking about the core principles of computing education has been shaped by an award-winning paper at ICER 2017 [10]. Katie Rich and her co-authors defined learning trajectories for K-12 computer science concepts, but their work is not limited to elementary and secondary school students. Their goal was to identify the most fundamental ideas needed to learn programming. Some of those ideas are:

- Precision and completeness are important when writing instructions in advance.
- Different sets of instructions can produce the same outcome.
- Programs are made by assembling instructions from a limited set.
- Some tasks involve repeating actions.
- Programs use conditions to end loops.

For most of us, these are so automatic that we may not even explicitly teach them. However, students (at all levels) do not know these ideas and need to be taught them. Even subsets of these fundamental ideas are important and powerful.

Computing education means different things to different audiences [6]. Millions of children use the programming language Scratch, but most use only a small part of Scratch's capabilities. For example, a great many Scratch projects use no repetition at all, or never use conditionals to end loops [3]. Computing is so powerful that you can say something useful and interesting without even including everything on Katie Rich's list. Literacy does not require mastery or even use of all the concepts of programming. Fluency is the goal, and scholarly interests can be served with only a small piece of computing.

This last summer, I visited the London Science Museum and saw the device in Figure 1, an printing telegraph machine from 1860. It is an anachronism today, not just because it's a telegraph machine. The developers of this device recognized the powerful idea of generating the Morse code for a letter with a keystroke. But the only keyboard they had at hand was a piano keyboard. Printing telegraph machines date from 1840, but the QWERTY keyboard was only patented in 1868. For almost 30 years, if you wanted a keyboard, a piano keyboard was the only option.

Computing education is only 50 years old. We may be in the period before our QWERTY keyboards are invented. Some of what we are inventing may not last long. It may become an anachronism. We have to consider that what we see as computing education may be a great idea with a piano keyboard attached. Things will change.

Figure 1: An 1860 Hughes' Printing Telegraph Machine.

4 A CALL TO ACTION

We need to make more computing educators, of all kinds, at all educational levels. Some of these teachers will be in science, mathematics, or other non-CS disciplines. Some of them will not know enough to pass our current CS1's. That's okay. Expressive power does not require everything we currently teach in our CS1.

We have to find our allies. I draw on research and practice from physics education research, educational psychology, and learning sciences. Creating a literacy for the 21st century is a large multi-disciplinary endeavor.

We need to invent, to mutate, to evolve. We should not just replicate our existing computing education tools, curricula, and classes. We have to make new kinds of computing education to meet the goals of computing literacy at all educational levels. Be on the lookout for the QWERTY keyboards, which may seem awkward at first (and may even be sub-optimal), but will allow us to expand our reach and to grow our field to meet the needs of all students and teachers.

REFERENCES

[1] Tracy Camp, W Richards Adrion, Betsy Bizot, Susan Davidson, Mary Hall, Susanne Hambrusch, Ellen Walker, and Stuart Zweben. 2017. Generation CS: the growth of computer science. *ACM Inroads* 8, 2 (2017), 44–50.
[2] Andrea diSessa. 2001. *Changing Minds.* MIT Press.
[3] Deborah A. Fields, Yasmin B. Kafai, and Michael T. Giang. 2017. Youth Computational Participation in the Wild: Understanding Experience and Equity in Participating and Programming in the Online Scratch Community. *ACM Trans. Comput. Educ.* 17, 3, Article 15 (Aug. 2017), 22 pages. https://doi.org/10.1145/3123815
[4] George Forsythe. 1961. Engineering students must learn both computing and mathematics. *Journal of Engineering Education* 52 (1961), 177–188.
[5] George Forsythe. 1968. What to do till the computer scientist comes. *Amer. Math. Monthly* 75 (1968), 454–462.
[6] Mark Guzdial. 2018. What We Care About Now, What We'll Care About in the Future. *ACM Inroads* 9, 4 (Nov. 2018), 63–64. https://doi.org/10.1145/3276304
[7] Alan Kay. 1984. Computer Software. *Scientific American* 251, 3 (1984), 52–59.
[8] Seymour Papert. 2000. What's the big idea? Toward a pedagogy of idea power. *IBM systems journal* 39, 3.4 (2000), 720–729.
[9] Alan J. Perlis. 1962. The Computer in the University. In *Computers and the World of the Future*, Martin Greenberger (Ed.). MIT Press.
[10] Kathryn M. Rich, Carla Strickland, T. Andrew Binkowski, Cheryl Moran, and Diana Franklin. 2017. K-8 Learning Trajectories Derived from Research Literature: Sequence, Repetition, Conditionals. In *Proceedings of the 2017 ACM Conference on International Computing Education Research (ICER '17)*. ACM, New York, NY, USA, 182–190. https://doi.org/10.1145/3105726.3106166

Understanding Learning Curves and Trajectories in CSS Layout

Meen Chul Kim
Drexel University
Philadelphia, PA, USA
meenchul.kim@drexel.edu

Thomas H. Park
Codepip
Philadelphia, PA, USA
thomas@codepip.com

Ruixue Liu
Worcester Polytechnic Institute
Worcester, MA, USA
rliu2@wpi.edu

Andrea Forte
Drexel University
Philadelphia, PA, USA
aforte@drexel.edu

ABSTRACT

Web development is a learning context with the potential to support rich computational thinking. Large-scale analysis of compilation and runtime errors have been used in introductory programming courses and similar approaches can be used to understand learning in web development environments. We investigated activity logs of a novel web coding game to uncover learning trajectories and what people struggle with when learning flexible box (flexbox), a collection of new CSS layout features. We designed a game called Flexbox Froggy, in which learners solve challenges by writing a few lines of CSS code, moving from simple levels that require knowledge of one flexbox property, to complex levels combining multiple properties. We investigate learning curves based on the changes in syntactic and semantic errors learners make as they complete the game. Our findings show that people performed better encountering a single new property than combined with properties they had already practiced. Clusters of learners at different levels did not demonstrate expected error rates based on learning curve theory. Also unexpectedly, advanced groups that mastered syntax had higher semantic error rates than the beginner group, especially when attempting new properties or complex use cases. We conclude with implications for designing and developing introductory web programming games and other instructional materials.

KEYWORDS

Clustering, CSS layout, Educational game, Learning analytics, Learning curve analysis, Web development

ACM Reference Format:
Meen Chul Kim, Thomas H. Park, Ruixue Liu, and Andrea Forte. 2019. Understanding Learning Curves and Trajectories in CSS Layout. In *SIGCSE '19: 50th ACM Technical Symposium on Computer Science Education, February 27–March 2, 2019, Minneapolis, MN, USA.* ACM, New York, NY, USA, 7 pages. https://doi.org/10.1145/3287324.3287387

ACM ISBN 978-1-4503-5890-3/19/2...$15.00
https://doi.org/10.1145/3287324.3287387

1 INTRODUCTION

As learning analytics and educational data mining techniques improve and expand, analyzing code-writing data at scale has become an increasingly productive way to investigate how people learn programming and what they struggle with. Studies in this space have used quantitative methods to explore mastery in introductory computer programming [4, 29, 33], common errors and misconceptions such as compiler errors [2, 13], and learning behavior in virtual learning environments such as MOOCs [11, 21], online communities [1, 7, 10, 34], and games [14, 16].

Web development is one context in which people practice rich and multi-layered computation. For many, web development is a first experience in creative computation [8, 30]. Because of its potential bridging role between early programming exposure and later mastery [27], web development is a fruitful area of inquiry for computing education research, but it's difficult to measure learning in the often informal, idiosyncratic contexts where people attempt to solve web development problems. Learning analytics, though not without limitations, is an interesting approach because we can develop creative proxies for measuring learning in contexts where collecting data on learning outcomes is challenging or not possible.

This work presents our preliminary investigation of web programming data at scale. We designed an online game to create playful, motivating experiences with concrete learning goals [20, 22]. Flexbox Froggy (https://flexboxfroggy.com) supports people in learning Flexible Box (flexbox), a collection of CSS features that makes it easier to design web pages with responsive layouts. In this game, people write a few lines of CSS code to guide frogs to lily pads of matching colors, while gradually exposed to core properties of flexbox such as aligning content and items. We explored the changes in learner errors through completion of the game. Learning curve analysis was employed to model the trajectories of such learning where the likelihood of error-making is expected to decrease over the course of engagement. Clustering was also applied to understand aggregate patterns of learning. Our investigation was guided by the following research questions:

(1) How can we measure learning based on users' successes and failures at different game levels?
(2) How can knowledge components and learning curves be modeled in this context?
(3) What patterns of behavior emerge as people progress to increasingly difficult levels?

2 RELATED WORK

This paper builds on three areas of computing education: 1) web development, 2) educational games, and 3) learning analytics. Literature on web development as a context for computational learning examines formative experiences and misconceptions. Early work examined the established practices and conceptions of web developers [8, 30] and uncovered computational features that novice and non-programmers frequently struggle with such as hyperlinks [9, 28] and nesting [23, 24]. Visual layout was found to be difficult for both beginning and experienced programmers [23, 27, 30]. WYSIWYG interfaces are reported to construct unproductive mental models which could block a later sense of mastery [26].

Educational games research explores how to provide authentic, playful experiences for learning computation. Some research stresses creating gaming environments with explicit instructional goals [16, 18]. Others focus on providing game-like environments where people learn through exploration, tinkering, and creation of personally meaningful projects [6, 19, 32]. These platforms are often designed for informal learning opportunities. Environments that provide open-ended, unstructured environments require learners to sustain high levels of motivation while they master the basic but often challenging coding skills necessary to create interesting projects. In our game design efforts, we aim to provide an enjoyable gaming experience with clear goals [15, 19] to foster motivation and understanding and, in turn, elicit prolonged engagement in learning computational features.

The third literature we leverage is the growing body of learning analytics and educational data mining research focused on understanding computing education through large scale analysis of trace data. Such studies have investigated compilation and runtime errors [2, 13], coding patterns [12, 29, 35] of novice programmers [3, 4, 33] and structured computational learning in various environments [11, 17, 21]. Others have explored learning computation in online communities given manipulative toolkits [1, 7, 10, 34]. In order to uncover significant trajectories of learning, these studies employed a variety of quantitative techniques such as learning curve analysis, error quotient, and machine learning. In this work, we aim to identify quantitative analytics that can be applied to large-scale code-writing data generated by learners.

3 METHOD

3.1 Design of Flexbox Froggy

Flexbox Froggy is designed to challenge learners to solve simple puzzles by writing CSS code. We were inspired by computer literacy games such as Gidget, CSS Diner, and Erase All Kittens where people learn about various computational features while solving problems. We chose flexbox because it is a new module and therefore relevant for both beginners and experienced web developers, additionally, both novice and expert programmers struggle with web layouts [23, 27, 30].

In Flexbox Froggy, users learn flexbox's eight core properties, namely, **justify-content**, **align-times**, **flex-direction**, **order**, **align-self**, **flex-wrap**, **flex-flow**, and **align-content** through 24 levels. Most levels have one or two solutions. The game marks solutions correct based on the position of the frogs. We designed levels to provide a smooth learning curve, flat in the beginning so as not to intimidate learners, and then gradually ramp up the challenge. The last level is treated as the final "boss level" and combines nearly all the CSS properties learners have encountered, providing a tougher challenge and hopefully a sense of accomplishment when solved. The first level introduces justify-content, one of most basic properties and its values. Next, learners are exposed to the same property again in another straightforward use case, which leads to a more complex use case. Learners then explore the next property and its use cases, with subsequent levels eventually combining multiple properties.

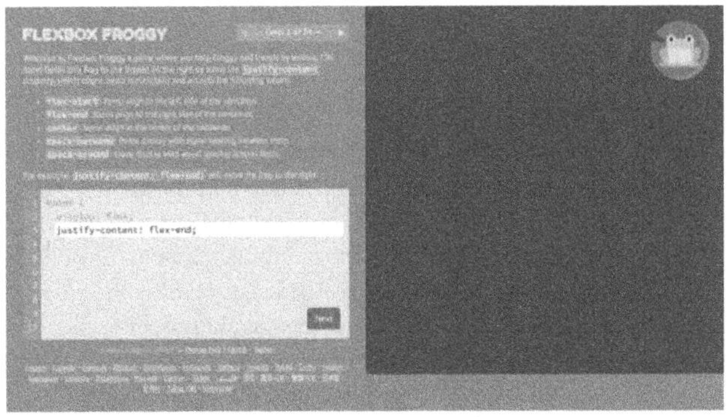

Figure 1: Game Interface with Code Submission

Figure 1 shows the game's interface, which mainly consists of two panes: 1) left pane for in-game reference and code completion and 2) right pane for instant assessment of code-writing. The left pane features a reference guide, instructions and explanations of each stage, property, and value. Reference material is also available in context as tooltips. The code editor provides a partial structure to be completed by users who submit a CSS code snippet by clicking "next." Learners can proceed to next levels only if the current level is solved. Completed levels can be revisited using navigation at the upper-right. The right pane updates as the users edit code to provide within-tool scaffolding in the form of immediate feedback to aid with debugging [18, 25]. If a submitted answer is correct, the frog appears on the lily-pad. If not, the entire screen trembles.

3.2 Data Collection and Processing

Flexbox Froggy is playable in a browser and requires no registration. We did not directly recruit players. Upon release of the game, it was registered to Hour of Code on Code.org. Hacker News and some subreddits featured it, and it is still shared on a regularly on Twitter. We collected anonymous data related to completion of game tasks, input of correct and incorrect answers, and completed levels. To distinguish unique learners, we assigned a random alphanumeric token to each learner based on browser information and epoch time of first access. We collected 4,865,200 submitted answers by 9,980 unique learners. Then, subpopulation who completed all levels was selected, which reduced the submissions to 2,293,681. We considered the level complete once a user submitted a correct answer and discarded subsequent submissions for the same level. Thus, the data was reduced to 2,152,670 answers submitted by 5,520 unique users. We evaluated keystroke-level feedback about

Table 1: Game Levels and Knowledge Components

Level	Properties	Knowledge Components
1	justify-content	horizontal alignment
2	justify-content	horizontal alignment
3	justify-content	horizontal alignment
4	justify-content	horizontal alignment
5	align-items	vertical alignment
6	justify-content align-items	horizontal alignment vertical alignment
7	justify-content align-items	horizontal alignment vertical alignment
8	flex-direction	horizontal direction
9	flex-direction	vertical direction
10	justify-content flex-direction	horizontal alignment horizontal direction
11	justify-content flex-direction	horizontal alignment vertical direction
12	justify-content flex-direction	horizontal alignment vertical direction
13	justify-content align-items flex-direction	horizontal alignment vertical alignment horizontal direction
14	order	horizontal order
15	order	horizontal order
16	align-self	vertical order
17	order align-self	horizontal order vertical order
18	flex-wrap	horizontal wrapping
19	flex-direction flex-wrap	vertical direction horizontal wrapping
20	flex-flow	vertical direction horizontal wrapping
21	align-content	horizontal alignment
22	align-content	horizontal alignment
23	flex-direction align-content	vertical direction horizontal alignment
24	justify-content flex-direction flex-wrap align-content	horizontal alignment vertical direction horizontal wrapping horizontal alignment

syntactic and semantic errors through the W3C CSS Validation Service (http://www.css-validator.org); an answer is tagged as having a syntactic error if its result is incorrect and validity returns false. If it is incorrect while validity is true, the answer was regarded as having a semantic error. Based on this validation, the data set ended up having 48 feature dimensions, according to the number of syntactic and semantic errors per level. To build better fitting learning curve and clustering models, we used the interquartile range to remove outlying learners based on the total number of code submissions, which yielded a final data set of 1,775,039 answers submitted by 5,282 unique users.

3.3 Learning Curve Analysis and Clustering

Learning curve analysis is an approach that models learners' performance over time. Based on the power law of practice underlying this approach, the probability that a learner will make an error is expected to decrease as they repeatedly practice a target knowledge component (KC) [5]. In intelligent tutoring where learning curve analysis is often used to estimate student performance, problems are easily broken down into multiple smallest units of action [31]. However, it is less clear what is a meaningful unit of action in our data. Before applying learning curve analysis to our data, therefore, we need to define knowledge components. Table 1 describes the properties expected to be learned at each game level. As described, we designed the game to have learners practice different properties in multiple levels. Failing a given level does not necessarily mean that every knowledge component represented in the code is incorrect, only a subset may be incorrect. Therefore, each level was tagged with one or more knowledge components intended to practice. Just as submissions can be measured for correctness, each of the knowledge components can also be analyzed for changes in correctness over time.

Clustering is an unsupervised machine learning technique that uncovers latent structure in data without ground truth or a priori idea of what should be found. In learning analytics, clustering is used to identify groups of learners that share characteristics. As discussed in Related Work, a range of clustering algorithms such as hierarchical clustering, *k*-means clustering, and EM algorithm have been applied to code-writing data. To investigate collective trajectories of learning, we employ the *k*-means++ algorithm implemented in scikit-learn, a widely used Python machine learning library. We decided to use *k*-means++ over regular *k*-means as the latter is more sensitive to initial cluster centroid seeds. An individual learner's syntactic and semantic errors at each level were considered as feature dimensions. Then, we investigated the existence of different learning trajectories and characteristics per group.

4 RESULTS

4.1 Patterns between Syntax and Semantics

Figure 2 illustrates patterns of syntactic and semantic errors per level. The upper figure shows a stacked mean error rate chart, the lower one depicts a ratio column chart between two types of errors. Syntactic errors take up the largest fraction of incorrect submissions. As expected, learners struggled most with the final "boss" level. Unexpectedly, mean error rates in total do not decrease as the users move on to more advanced levels. Moreover, the ratios of semantic errors tend to increase and jag even though learners have had more opportunities to practice the properties of the flexbox module. These patterns violate our expectations of learning curve analysis described in the methodology section. Instead of a smooth curve, we found that learners struggled more than expected as they encountered familiar properties in new configurations.

4.2 Finding Homogeneous Trajectories

Any variant of *k*-means algorithms requires a manual selection of the number of clusters. To find an optimal *k*, we examined the changes in within-cluster sum of squared error by increasing *k*

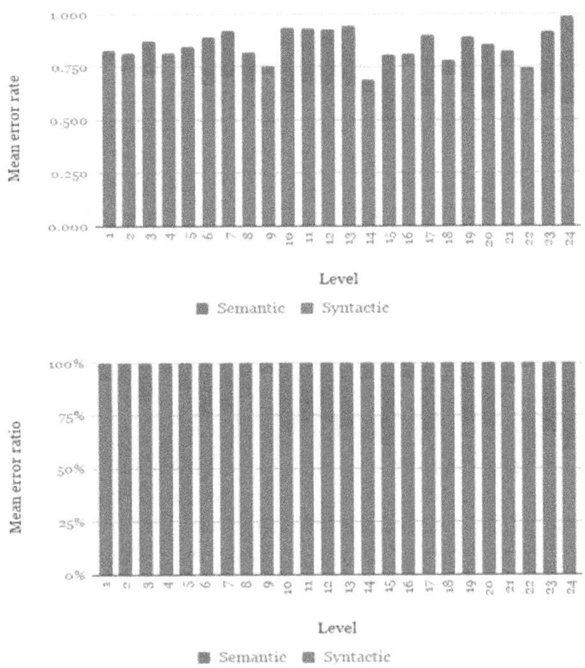

Figure 2: Syntactic and Semantic Errors. Stacked Rate Chart (Upper) and 100% Stacked Ratio Chart (Lower)

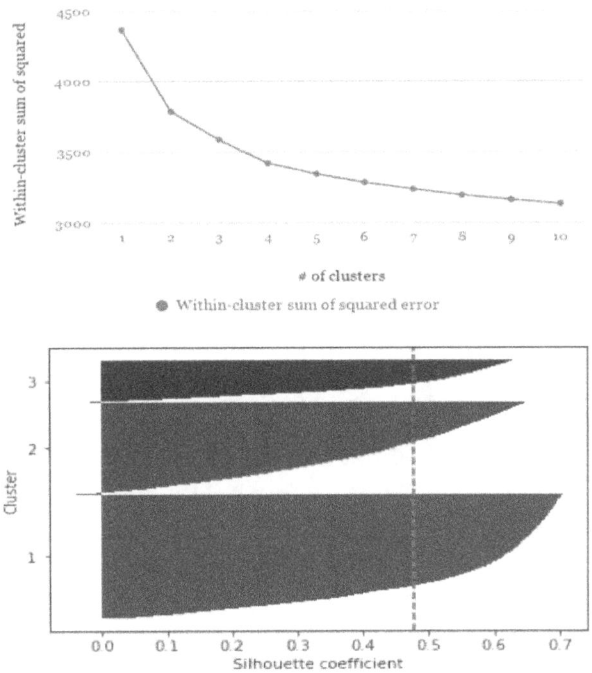

Figure 3: Changes in Within-cluster Sum of Squared Error (Upper) and Silhouette Coefficient at 3 as k (Lower)

ranging from 1. As shown in Figure 3 upper, increasing the number of clusters beyond 3 minimally affects the error values. To validate the consistency within clusters of data given 3 and 4 as candidate ks, we investigated the silhouette coefficient, using the Euclidean distance (See Figure 3 lower). Given the silhouette ranges between -1 and 1, the learner groups showed a clearer homogeneity when 3 is chosen as the number of clusters. Based on these observations, 3 was chosen as the number of clusters. In order to build a final model, k-means++ was run 500 times on the 48 feature dimensions of 5,282 users and the model with the least within-cluster sum of squared error was used.

First, we wanted to see learning trajectories and curves for the whole data set. As described, trajectories were expected to start with a high error intercept, curve downwards, and then plateau near a zero-error rate as users acquire the mastery. Figure 4 top displays the trajectories of learners considering the average rate of all types of errors per level. Based on error trends, we labeled learners in three groups: Gr1 (n=1,892), Gr2 (n=1,546), and Gr3 (n=1,844). Learning curves corresponding to each cluster are also rendered. As illustrated in the figure, three groups of learners show similar patterns of rising-falling-rising learning curves which do not match the general expectations above. They start with an increasing curve over the first seven levels. Even after repeated opportunities to practice the same KC groups, the number of errors tends to increase. One interpretation is that flexbox is a new concept to both the novice programmer and the experienced developer; however, it is surprising that better performing learner groups, *i.e.* Gr2 and Gr3, would not exhibit transfer from experience with other, similar CSS properties. After declining for levels 8 and 9, the errors spike between the 10th and 13th levels. This indicates the learners were most challenged when multiple KCs were combined despite prior exposure to the properties and values. Afterwards, the errors decline and increase again. While Gr1's low error rate persists when practicing a new property (order) at the 14th level, Gr2 and Gr3 error rates spike. Overall, all the groups share indistinct patterns with little arithmetic difference and almost no persistent learning curves.

The rest of the subfigures depict learning trajectories and curves by error types. Syntactic errors show good learning curves that decrease and plateau over time (See Figure 4 middle). In these learning curves, the error rates start between 70% and 80%, high enough to indicate that around three out of four learners struggle with the KC at the first attempt. Although Gr2 and Gr3 have spikes in error rates when moving from level 14 to 15 (See Figure 4 top), their syntactic error rates decreased (See Figure 4 middle). Instead, semantic error rates spike (See Figure 4 bottom). While trajectories with syntactic errors show good learning curves, the learning trajectories and curves derived from semantic errors add richer interpretations to the findings: even though learners get familiar with syntactic operations such as declaring relevant properties and assigning syntactically acceptable values, they still struggle with assigning proper values.

4.3 Learning Curves and Clusters by KCs

Although our findings do not match what we expected based on learning curve theory, this does not necessarily invalidate these

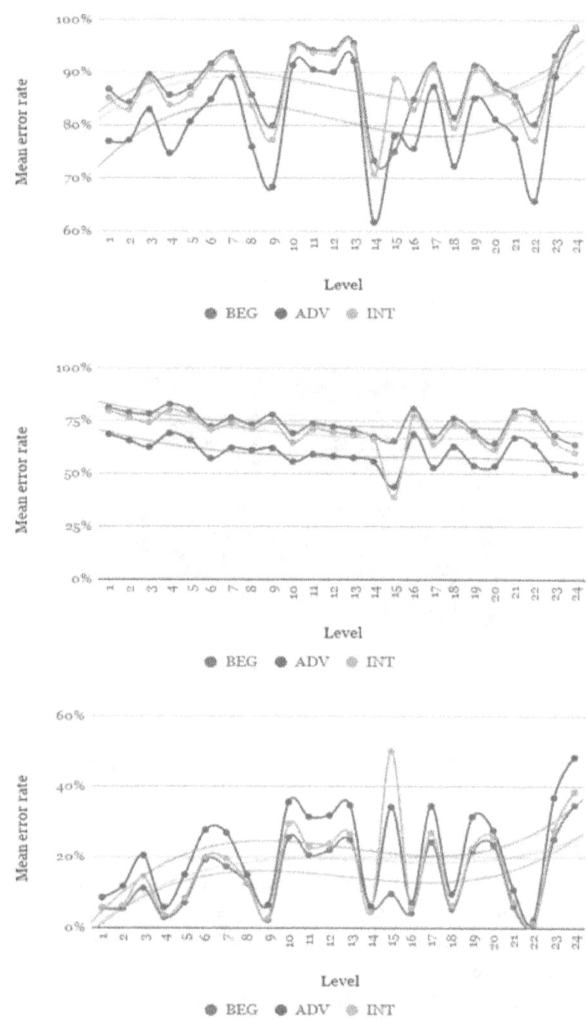

Figure 4: Learning Curves for All Levels: All (Top), Syntactic (Middle), and Semantic (Bottom) Errors

models. Instead, we suggest that investigating learning patterns and trajectories in a game that relies on accumulative knowledge components requires interpreting the game as a more complex learning experience with additional dimensions. Toward that end, we categorized levels in two KC groups based on similarity of visual operations, namely 15 levels that involve **alignment** and 10 that involve **direction**.

Figure 5 shows learning curves for the 15 levels in the alignment KC group, sequentially ordered. The uppermost figure shows rising-falling learning curves including all types of errors for each learner group; notably there are almost no clear learning trajectories that suggest mastery. All learner groups show similar patterns rising at the end. Learning curves by error type are depicted in the middle (syntactic errors) and bottom (semantic errors) for the alignment KC group. In these cases, all of the groups show good learning curves for syntax that slope downwards over time (See Figure 5 middle). It is notable that although syntactic errors decrease, semantic error rates increase as the learners encounter more complex use cases; additionally, Gr1 struggle more with syntax while Gr2 and Gr3 make more semantic errors (See Figure 5 bottom).

Figure 6 illustrates learning curves for the 10 levels in the direction KC group. Again, combining error types shows jagged learning curves for all types of learners, indicating no clear learning trajectory (See Figure 6 top). The middle and bottom figures depict learning curves by error types, demonstrating again that all the groups show good learning curves in mastering syntax (See Figure 6 middle). Semantic error rates keep jaggedly increasing despite opportunities to practice, with Gr3 exhibiting the most errors (See Figure 6 bottom).

5 SUMMARY AND DISCUSSION

In this paper we explored the quantitative generation of KC models, learning curves, and learner clusters with the code-writing data submitted to a web development game. We investigated the efficacy of models generated using all errors versus two discrete error types (syntax and semantic) and explored knowledge component groups as an additional strategy for understanding learning curves. We identified three distinct user groups that we labeled Gr1, Gr2 and Gr3. Models inclusive of both types of errors showed learning curves that tended to rise-fall-rise, indicating no clear learning trajectory. While the different learner groups had similar learning patterns, the learner groups who performed better over the entire course of levels, namely Gr2 and Gr3, struggled more with the semantic operations, especially in levels with new properties or more complex use cases. Overall, all groups of users were generally found to have good learning curves in syntactic manipulation as they were exposed to more opportunities to practice the properties. Contrary to learning curve theory, however, the general learning curves did not show the expected reduction in error rate. This led us to examine patterns by the KC groups, *i.e.* alignment and direction. The results showed Gr1 performed better when challenged with complex combinations of KCs and all learner groups showed clear learning trajectories in practicing syntax.

Our efforts to employ learning curve analysis and clustering in analyzing web programming data can be used to consider the design of instructional materials and games that introduce learners to syntactic and semantic knowledge components. Although learners demonstrated increased proficiency with syntax while learning new knowledge components, our findings suggest that when introducing combinations of components, learning trajectories become less easily identified.

Based on these experiences, we identified several opportunities to refine our instruments as well as data collection. The fact that the learners semantically struggled with complex use cases in spite of multiple exposure to the same KC groups might be a sign that the skill required to use a single layout operation is different from the skill of combining multiple components, and that the two should be separated into different KCs (and taught as separate concepts as well). In addition, to stabilize learning curves, a prep session or lengthier level design as well as greater quantity and variety in the use cases may be required. Finally, we could experiment with features like code mirror and syntax highlighting.

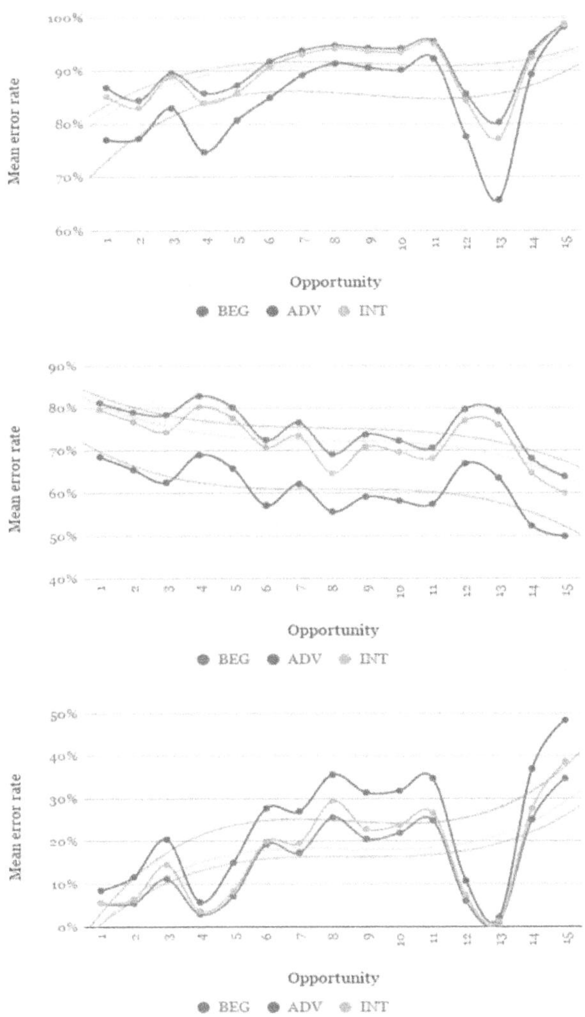

Figure 5: Learning Curves for Alignment: All (Top), Syntactic (Middle), and Semantic (Bottom) Errors

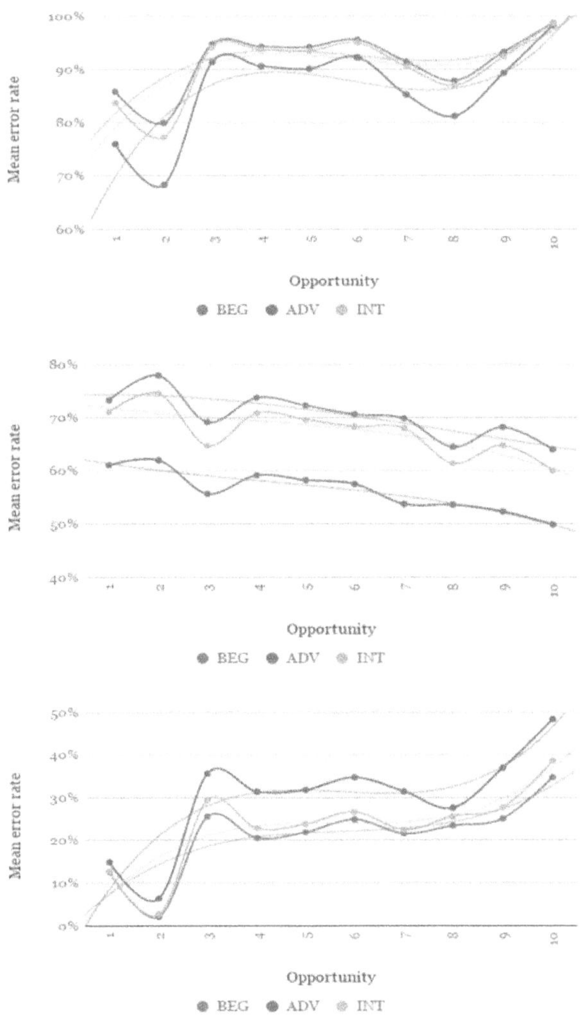

Figure 6: Learning Curves for Direction: All (Top), Syntactic (Middle), and Semantic (Bottom) Errors

Limitations of this work include the absence of observational or other data to aid in our interpretations and the restricted context of Flexbox Froggy as a learning environment. In future work, we plan to expand our work in the context of another introductory web programming game. We also seek a clear explanation for extreme outlier data. In continuation of this work, we aim to compare complete and incomplete sequences of learner actions with keystroke-level learning behavior modeling to further understand learner-generated web coding data as a resource for learning analytics.

ACKNOWLEDGMENTS

This work is supported by the NSF under Grant No.: 1339344.

REFERENCES

[1] Efthimia Aivaloglou and Felienne Hermans. 2016. How Kids Code and How We Know: An Exploratory Study on the Scratch Repository. ACM Press, 53–61. https://doi.org/10.1145/2960310.2960325

[2] Brett A. Becker. 2016. A New Metric to Quantify Repeated Compiler Errors for Novice Programmers. ACM Press, 296–301. https://doi.org/10.1145/2899415.2899463

[3] Matthew Berland, Taylor Martin, Tom Benton, Carmen Petrick Smith, and Don Davis. 2013. Using Learning Analytics to Understand the Learning Pathways of Novice Programmers. 22, 4 (2013), 564–599. https://doi.org/10.1080/10508406.2013.836655

[4] Adam S. Carter, Christopher D. Hundhausen, and Olusola Adesope. 2015. The Normalized Programming State Model: Predicting Student Performance in Computing Courses Based on Programming Behavior. ACM Press, 141–150. https://doi.org/10.1145/2787622.2787710

[5] Hao Cen, Kenneth R. Koedinger, and Brian Junker. 2006. Learning factors analysis – a general method for cognitive model evaluation and improvement. (2006), 164–175.

[6] Stephen Cooper, Wanda Dann, and Randy Pausch. 2000. Alice: a 3-D tool for introductory programming concepts. 15, 5 (2000), 107–116.

[7] Sayamindu Dasgupta, William Hale, Andrés Monroy-Hernández, and Benjamin Mako Hill. 2016. Remixing as a pathway to computational thinking. (2016), 1438–1449.

[8] Brian Dorn and Mark Guzdial. 2010. Discovering computing: perspectives of web designers. ACM Press, 23. https://doi.org/10.1145/1839594.1839600

[9] Alain Désilets, Sébastien Paquet, and Norman G. Vinson. 2005. Are wikis usable? ACM Press, 3–15. https://doi.org/10.1145/1104973.1104974

[10] Deborah A. Fields, Yasmin B. Kafai, and Michael T. Giang. 2017. Youth Computational Participation in the Wild: Understanding Experience and Equity in Participating and Programming in the Online Scratch Community. 17, 3 (2017), 1–22. https://doi.org/10.1145/3123815

[11] Elena L. Glassman and Robert C. Miller. 2016. Leveraging learners for teaching programming and hardware design at scale. (2016), 37–40.

[12] Elena L. Glassman, Rishabh Singh, and Robert C. Miller. 2014. Feature engineering for clustering student solutions. ACM Press, 171–172. https://doi.org/10.1145/2556325.2567865

[13] Andrew Head, Elena Glassman, Gustavo Soares, Ryo Suzuki, Lucas Figueredo, Loris D'Antoni, and Björn Hartmann. 2017. Writing Reusable Code Feedback at Scale with Mixed-Initiative Program Synthesis. ACM Press, 89–98. https://doi.org/10.1145/3051457.3051467

[14] William Jernigan, Amber Horvath, Michael Lee, Margaret Burnett, Taylor Cuilty, Sandeep Kuttal, Anicia Peters, Irwin Kwan, Faezeh Bahmani, Andrew Ko, Christopher J. Mendez, and Alannah Oleson. 2017. General principles for a Generalized Idea Garden Image 1. 39 (2017), 51–65. https://doi.org/10.1016/j.jvlc.2017.04.005

[15] Yasmin B. Kafai. 2006. Playing and Making Games for Learning: Instructionist and Constructionist Perspectives for Game Studies. 1, 1 (2006), 36–40. https://doi.org/10.1177/1555412005281767

[16] Michael J. Lee, Faezeh Bahmani, Irwin Kwan, Jilian LaFerte, Polina Charters, Amber Horvath, Fanny Luor, Jill Cao, Catherine Law, Michael Beswetherick, Sheridan Long, Margaret Burnett, and Andrew J. Ko. 2014. Principles of a debugging-first puzzle game for computing education. IEEE, 57–64. https://doi.org/10.1109/VLHCC.2014.6883023

[17] Michael J. Lee and Andrew J. Ko. 2015. Comparing the Effectiveness of Online Learning Approaches on CS1 Learning Outcomes. ACM Press, 237–246. https://doi.org/10.1145/2787622.2787709

[18] Michael J. Lee, Andrew J. Ko, and Irwin Kwan. 2013. In-game assessments increase novice programmers' engagement and level completion speed. (2013), 153–160.

[19] John Maloney, Mitchel Resnick, Natalie Rusk, Brian Silverman, and Evelyn Eastmond. 2010. The Scratch Programming Language and Environment. 10, 4 (2010), 1–15. https://doi.org/10.1145/1868358.1868363

[20] M. J. Mayo. 2009. Video Games: A Route to Large-Scale STEM Education? 323, 5910 (2009), 79–82. https://doi.org/10.1126/science.1166900

[21] N. Myller, J. Suhonen, and E. Sutinen. 2002. Using data mining for improving web-based course design, Vol. 1. IEEE Comput. Soc, 959–963. https://doi.org/10.1109/CIE.2002.1186125

[22] Harold F. O'Neil, Richard Wainess, and Eva L. Baker. 2005. Classification of learning outcomes: evidence from the computer games literature. 16, 4 (2005), 455–474. https://doi.org/10.1080/09585170500384529

[23] Thomas H. Park, Brian Dorn, and Andrea Forte. 2015. An analysis of HTML and CSS syntax errors in a web development course. 15, 1 (2015), 4:1–4:21.

[24] Thomas H. Park, Meen Chul Kim, Sukrit Chhabra, Brian Lee, and Andrea Forte. 2016. Reading Hierarchies in Code: Assessment of a Basic Computational Skill. ACM Press, 302–307. https://doi.org/10.1145/2899415.2899435

[25] Thomas H. Park, Ankur Saxena, Swathi Jagannath, Susan Wiedenbeck, and Andrea Forte. 2013. openHTML: Designing a transitional web editor for novices. (2013), 1863–1868.

[26] Thomas H. Park and Susan Wiedenbeck. 2010. First Steps in Coding by Informal Web Developers. IEEE, 79–82. https://doi.org/10.1109/VLHCC.2010.20

[27] Thomas H. Park and Susan Wiedenbeck. 2011. Learning web development: Challenges at an earlier stage of computing education. (2011), 125–132.

[28] Ljubomir Perković, Amber Settle, Sungsoon Hwang, and Joshua Jones. 2010. A framework for computational thinking across the curriculum. ACM Press, 123. https://doi.org/10.1145/1822090.1822126

[29] Kelly Rivers, Erik Harpstead, and Kenneth R. Koedinger. 2016. Learning curve analysis for programming: Which concepts do students struggle with? (2016), 143–151.

[30] Mary B. Rosson, Julie Ballin, and Heather Nash. 2004. Everyday programming: Challenges and opportunities for informal web development. (2004), 123–130.

[31] Kurt VanLehn, Kenneth R. Koedinger, Alida Skogsholm, Adaeze Nwaigwe, Robert G. M. Hausmann, Anders Weinstein, and Benjamin Billings. 2007. What's in a step? Toward general, abstract representations of tutoring system log data. (2007), 455–459.

[32] Karen Villaverde and Daniel Jaramillo. 2010. Game design and development course taught with Alice. 26, 2 (2010), 22–29.

[33] Christopher Watson, Frederick W.B. Li, and Jamie L. Godwin. 2013. Predicting Performance in an Introductory Programming Course by Logging and Analyzing Student Programming Behavior. IEEE, 319–323. https://doi.org/10.1109/ICALT.2013.99

[34] Seungwon Yang, Carlotta Domeniconi, Matt Revelle, Mack Sweeney, Ben U. Gelman, Chris Beckley, and Aditya Johri. 2015. Uncovering trajectories of informal learning in large online communities of creators. (2015), 131–140.

[35] Hezheng Yin, Joseph Moghadam, and Armando Fox. 2015. Clustering Student Programming Assignments to Multiply Instructor Leverage. ACM Press, 367–372. https://doi.org/10.1145/2724660.2728695

Captioning Online Course Videos: An Investigation into Knowledge Retention and Student Perception

Michael Whitney
Computer Science and Quantitative Methods
Winthrop University
Rock Hill, SC
whitneym@winthrop.edu

Bryan Dallas
Rehabilitation Counseling
Northern Illinois University
DeKalb, Il
bdallas@niu.edu

ABSTRACT

The expansion of computer science programs into the digital world has significantly increased the use of videos as an instructional medium. In an effort to improve student performance in a video driven learning environment, this paper explores the impact of captions on learning performance. Previous work has focused on the benefits of captions for persons with disabilities, those learning English as a second language, and reading instruction for children. This work expands on the caption knowledge base by investigating (1) if the inclusion of captions significantly improves knowledge retention amongst all students in an online computer science course, and (2) if students perceive videos with captions as beneficial to learning. Our results show a statistically significant performance improvement after watching videos with captions vs. videos without captions. Students reported using captions as a learning resource as they helped reinforce video material, maintain focus, and enhance comprehension.

CCS CONCEPTS

• Social and professional topics → Computing education;

KEYWORDS

Computing education, captions, subtitles, online instruction

ACM Reference format:

Michael Whitney and Bryan Dallas. 2019. Captioning Online Course Videos: An Investigation into Knowledge Retention and Student Perception. In *SIGCSE '19: The 50th ACM Technical Symposium on Computer Science Education, Feb. 27-Mar. 2, 2019, Minneapolis, MN, USA.* ACM, NY, NY, USA, 7 pages. https://doi.org/10.1145/3287324.3287347

ACM ISBN 978-1-4503-5890-3/19/02...$15.00
https://doi.org/10.1145/3287324.3287347

1 Introduction

The continued expansion of education into the digital world has opened up an immense opportunity to utilize videos as a means for education. Massive Open Online Courses (MOOCs) such as Udemy, Coursera, and Udacity enroll millions of students [3] who use video lectures and tutorials as a primary method of instruction [34]. Other approaches that incorporate instructional videos include local online and hybrid courses which combine face-to-face with online instruction. In addition, flipped classes commonly have students watching lecture videos outside of class and then applying concepts during in-class activities.

A challenge for all the aforementioned approaches is the engagement of the student with the video content. Some approaches that have helped to overcome this challenge include embedding questions in videos, integrating video critiques, and providing integrated collaborative opportunities [5, 9, 13, 26]. Other approaches include modeling student engagement using interaction measures (e.g., video summarization) and video production (e.g., length, talking heads, enthusiasm, etc.) [6, 25].

In this paper, we discuss a means to further overcome the challenge of video engagement using captions. While typically viewed as an accommodation for persons with disabilities, based on our review of the literature, the utilization of captions as a learning resource for students without disabilities has experienced minimal research. To this end, our goal was to examine if the inclusion of captions on course videos further engaged students without disabilities in the learning process and, consequently, increased knowledge retention.

2 Background

The terms open captions, closed captions, and subtitles are often used synonymously as they all provide a text alternative for a video's dialog. Both open and closed captions complement the dialog with the addition of pertinent sound elements (i.e., phone ringing, horn blowing, etc.) found in the video. In addition, open captions are always on and closed captions can be turned on or off. Collectively, this group of terms can be referred to as captions which we use throughout this paper for the purpose of clarity.

Historically, the use of captions has been influenced by legislation, a universal design approach, or both. Federal legislation like the Americans with Disabilities Act [1] and the Rehabilitation Act [21,

22] (i.e., Sections 504 and 508) require postsecondary educational videos to include captions to ensure persons with disabilities have equal access to information provided in videos. Ideally, all institutional videos should be captioned so they are available at the time of need but realistically, many institutions wait for a caption request by a student with a disability prior to taking action.

Some faculty and institutions incorporate a universal design approach when creating videos. Such an approach attempts to design "products and environments to be usable by all people, to the greatest extent possible, without the need for adaptation or specialized design" [12, p. 1]. Based on this approach, the provision of captions ensures access to video-related information when audio is not possible (e.g., restaurant, gym, disability) or has been diminished (e.g., crowded auditorium). It also might be a useful learning tool.

2.1 Related Work

Decades of educational research on captions has mostly focused on individuals with disabilities or individuals learning a new language. Researchers have found captions to effectively help individuals who are deaf or hard of hearing [33], individuals learning a new language [28, 29, 30], and children learning to read [11]. It is less clear however as to the benefits of captions amongst a general audience of learners. To this end, researchers have begun to investigate the educational impact of captions on the general population. Findings suggest that reading captions seems to be an automatic activity [32] and that captions help students without disabilities maintain focus, retain information, compensate for poor audio quality, better understand new terms and unfamiliar words, and aid in note-taking [4, 15]. In contrast, others have reported no significant difference in subsequent assessment results after viewing educational videos [23]. It is also important to note that no studies have found that captions are a detriment to learning video-based information.

2.2 Theoretical Influences

Paivio's Dual Coding Theory [17, 18] is based on the concept that redundant information increases comprehension. The theory sets forth that "cognition consists of two separate but interconnected mental subsystems [channels], a verbal system and a nonverbal system" [24, p. 463]. The verbal deals directly with language and nonverbal is related to nonlinguistic stimuli. Information for these two channels is coded differently and exist as separate sensorial representations which can be retrieved independently or collectively for subsequent use. An example is the naming of an object such as using the word "chair" and also showing a picture of an actual chair. Both representations are stored separately but work in parallel. To this end, the utilization of these two channels provide a means to better facilitate knowledge storage and retrieval. In other words, complementing information with another source of redundant information affords individuals the opportunity to better understand said information. Multiple researchers have found the provision of such redundant information (e.g., captions) to be beneficial to learning [10, 14, 32].

However, the addition of captions requires the visual channel to process two different sets of information - the captions and the scene. According to the Cognitive Load Theory, an extensive increase on information complexity or amount to be processed can have a negative effect on information processing [27]. Some have indicated that the addition of captions do increase the cognitive load [2, 16] which can be detrimental to learning. In contrast, other researchers have found that the visual attention distribution between subtitles and other sources of information do not have any significant impact on performance [7, 20, 31]. In addition, Kruger, Este, & Matthew [8], were able to find that the inclusion of same language captions reduced cognitive load for students studying English as a second language.

3 Captioning Process

In the recent past, the process to caption a video was a costly / labor intensive process where an individual would transcribe the video, timecode the transcription, and then create a new video by combining the original video with the transcription. Thanks to speech-to-text engines that are built into many video services, the time and cost to produce captioned videos has been greatly reduced. Services such as Microsoft Stream and YouTube offer a free captioning service while Vimeo requires videos to be captioned with a third-party tool prior to uploading it to Vimeo. Free online tools include Amara.org, DotSub.com, and Subtitle Horse. The process for captioning is very similar in all aforementioned tools and services. Of the free services, many utilize YouTube due to the accuracy of speech recognition and the ease of distributing the videos.

In 2009, YouTube [35] introduced their auto-caps to make videos accessible everywhere and to everyone. While accuracy is high, there exists a need to edit the captions to ensure the created transcript appropriately represents the content [19]. The following are the steps needed to upload, edit, and publish a video.

1. Create account / upload video
2. Navigate to Video Manager
3. Next to the video, click the drop-down menu next to the Edit button and select Subtitles/CC.
4. Choose language
5. Wait for video to be processed
6. In the "Published" section, click the language button (e.g., English) to review and edit as necessary
7. Click save changes when complete

The time needed to edit a transcription is directly related to the approach taken to correct errors. If the speed of the video is set to 2x, and the transcript accuracy is high, then the errors can be corrected in less than the overall time of the video.

4 User Study Methodology

In this study, we are motivated by the identification of an online teaching practice that enhances student learning through the use of captions. The research questions we address are how the inclusion of captions impact student performance and student perception of learning with captions.

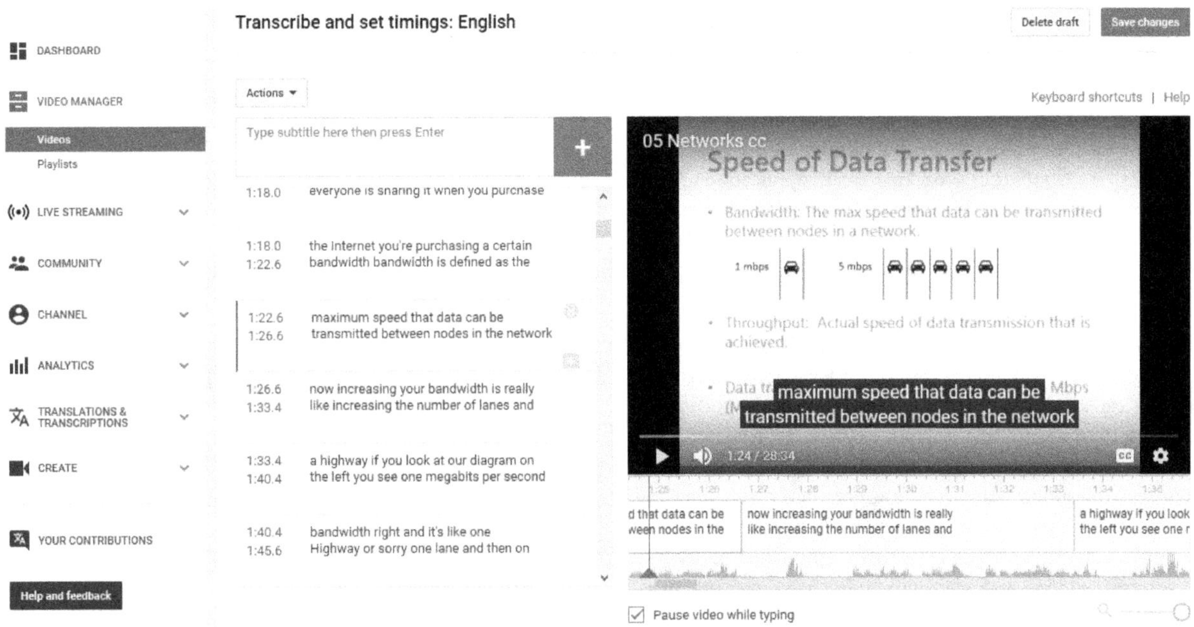

Figure 1: Editing transcription in YouTube

We propose that the addition of captions on course videos can promote further engagement with course content which results in increased learning performance. In addition, students will perceive captioned videos as a benefit to the learning process. To this end, this study examines the following research questions:

- RQ1: Does the inclusion of captions significantly improve knowledge retention?
- RQ2: Do students perceive videos with captions as beneficial to learning?

Our rationale behind the first research question is that the extra sensory exposure to lecture materials (i.e., captions) will enhance learning. Previous studies have found mixed results warranting further study. Importantly, the first research question examines exposure to and availability of captions rather than a read along requirement. To this end, students can read what they perceive as more difficult content and just listen to more understandable content.

We based the second research question on our belief that captions are perceived as a useful learning tool as opposed to an accommodation requirement. More so, it is a common notion that many believe captions only benefit persons who are deaf or hard of hearing. Due to technology advancements and multimedia caption availability, we believe this notion is outdated. Recent studies have found that learners without disabilities are generally supportive of the use of captions in a learning environment.

4.1 Study Setup

Student participants were recruited from an online CSCI 101 course taught by one instructor during the spring semester of 2018 at a small south-eastern public university. During the course, students were required to watch weekly videos and then take online quizzes related to those videos during the same week. In total, 25 students agreed to participate.

We used a mixed method design, manipulating exposure to videos with captions over a six-week period. We used surveys to collect student perceptions. Objective measures for learning are based on quiz performance. In addition, 13 of the 25 students participated in a focus group at the end of the study. Details of our design, measures, and student participants are to follow.

4.2 Implementation Procedure

All students were randomly placed into one of two groups. Both groups were required to watch six videos and take corresponding quizzes on a weekly basis for six weeks. Each group would alternate between a video with captions and a video without captions in a counterbalanced fashion. A new video and quiz set became available each week. At the end of the week, quizzes were closed for submission. Access to the videos with or without captions and corresponding quizzes was controlled through Blackboard settings. Students had unlimited access to videos and could watch them as many times as needed.

4.2.1 Videos. We utilized YouTube captioning services to create captions for six lecture videos. The captions for each video was reviewed and corrected as needed by the instructor. Each video with captions also had a non-captioned counterpart to ensure captions were not available for non-captioned portions of the study. Conversely, captioned videos provided captions by default. The videos were hosted by YouTube and embedded into Blackboard for a seamless student learning experience. Each video ranged from 20-30 minutes.

4.2.2 Quizzes. Each video had a corresponding quiz that consisted of 10-15 multiple choice questions. Time limits on quizzes ranged from 30-45 minutes depending on the amount of questions. No disability accommodation requests were made (e.g., extra time) for quizzes. Researchers chose Lockdown Browser to ensure a controlled and fair test taking environment. Lockdown Browser controls the online testing environment by restricting access to other computer programs and applications (e.g., browsers, text editor, etc.). In addition, Lockdown Browser records a video of the students to ensure they are alone and did not have any external resources such as a textbook or notes available to them.

4.2.3 Data Collection: Scores, Survey, and Focus Group. To evaluate RQ1, our measures of learning effects include student performance on six quizzes. Additionally, students reported the percent of captions read while watching videos. To evaluate RQ2, surveys were administered at the end of each captioned related quiz. Survey questions addressed caption use and personal impressions of captions. The survey included both Likert scale and open-ended questions. In addition, a focus group met to discuss interaction with videos and learning preferences and practices. Data gathered included researcher notes and written responses to discussed topics.

5 Analysis and Results

In total, there were 25 participants: 10 male and 15 female. A subgroup of 13 participants attended the focus group session: 4 male and 9 female. We performed analysis on the data collected during the study using a combination of descriptive statistics, qualitative data, and pairwise t-tests. We started with statistical analysis on the distributions of captioned quiz scores and quiz scores without captions. We then employed a matched sample t-test to determine if watching videos with captions significantly improve the overall quiz performance. Lastly, we used descriptive statistics to represent student perceptions on learning with captions. We chose the alpha value of 0.05 to determine the significance of our results.

5.1 Student Performance

In Figure 2 and Figure 3, we present the two datasets. The first dataset (Figure 2) consists of student quiz scores for all videos without captions. Here the distribution is skewed left which implies that most students performed in an expected range for given quiz questions. The second dataset (Figure 3) consists of student scores for all videos with captions. This distribution's short tail indicates better performance when captions were available. In addition, 76% of students obtained a passing grade for the non-captioned quizzes while 100% passed the captioned quizzes. As all students were exposed to both conditions, it is evident that the addition of captions does have a positive effect on scores and passing rates.

In Figure 4, we present the mean scores for the student participants. The two datasets consist of average scores for videos with and without captions.

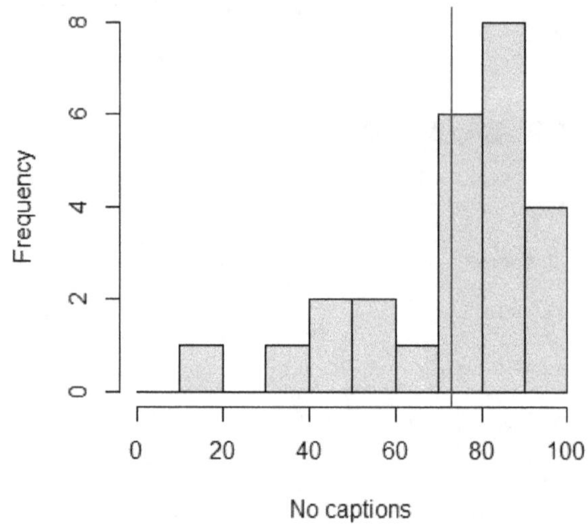

Figure 2: Histogram no captions quiz scores

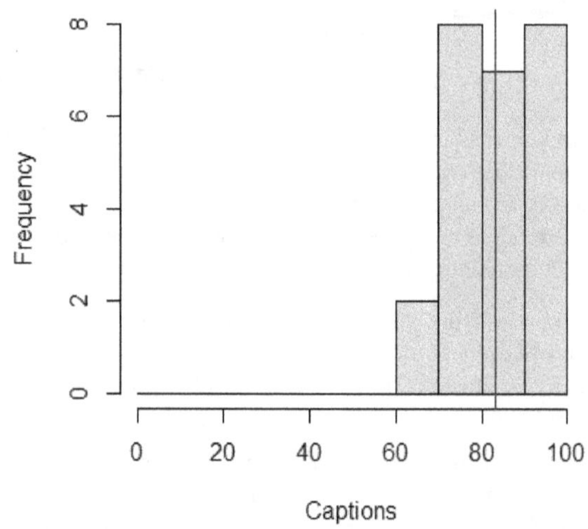

Figure 3: Histogram of captions quiz scores

In every instance, the average quiz score was higher when captions were available. In addition, students reported reading an average of 57% - 81% of the available captions (Table 1). To this end, it is evident that students are taking the opportunity to further engage with materials which, ultimately, produce positive results.

Table 1: Grade Results, Percent of Captions Read, Perception of Caption Helpfulness 1-5

	No Captions	Captions	% Read	Captions Help SD, D, N, A, SA
Quiz 1	73.75%	80.00%	50.00-74.00	4.00
Quiz 2	70.00%	72.50%	66.67-91.33	4.17
Quiz 3	79.48%	93.33%	53.71-78.00	4.00
Quiz 4	80.55%	85.42%	55.55-80.00	4.14
Quiz 5	71.21%	80.00%	50.17-74.33	4.00
Quiz 6	81.00%	87.50%	61.11-85.67	4.13
Total	73.07%	83.24%	52.92-81.35	4.07

5.2 Research Question 1

Does the inclusion of captions significantly improve knowledge retention?

Our first research question examines knowledge retention based on the inclusion of captions. Our testing of RQ1 relies on scores based on videos with and without captions. The matched sample t-test revealed a significant difference between performance without captions (M=73.07, SD=20.24) and with captions (M=83.24, SD=10.14); t(24)=2.62, p=.014. These results suggest that captions have a positive effect on knowledge retention. More specifically, our results suggest that the provision of captions has a significant positive effect on knowledge retention.

5.3 Research Question 2

Do students perceive videos with captions as beneficial to learning?

Our testing of RQ2 is dependent on responses to survey questions and focus group contributions. Survey results show that a majority of students perceive the inclusion of captions as beneficial to learning. More so, 84% of the students responded positively (rating of 4 out of 5) to feeling that captions had helped in learning and understanding the material (mean of 4.07). Individual survey comments supporting the use of captions include:

- I like that captions help reinforce the video material.
- I like captions, they help me focus on the material.
- It helps me understand more when I read the words.
- I like the captions because it helps me understand what the speaker is saying. I am a visual learner, so seeing it helps me comprehend more.
- I think that the video captions are very useful and it is better for me to see and read it.
- I like the use of captions, it helps me understand what the professor is saying.
- It helps to match the words with the sounds and follow along more clearly.

On the other hand, some students provided comments about why they might not appreciate the use of captions:

- The captions didn't affect me one way or another.
- Some of the captions got in my way on the video.
- They were getting in the way of me taking notes on my MacBook but if I wasn't taking notes or had the video full screen, I'm sure they wouldn't have been in the way.
- I liked the videos, I just find that I learn better with no captions.

During the focus group, students explained that captions were a helpful learning resource. While they did not read 100% of the available captions, they tended to read when they perceived the content to be more difficult. Additionally, a common theme was the use of captions to help stay focused. More so, students reported that reading captions helped control for mind wandering due to internal or external distractions.

The group also discussed whether the captions were distracting from the visual materials on the screen. The group felt that the combination of captions and visual information did not cause an overload. More so, they felt it was easy to balance between captions and scene. In the case where they did not understand something in the video, they would back up the video and watch the section again. While none reported the duality of captions and scenes as the cause, there was an indication that on consecutive views they would place more focus on captions or scene depending on what they felt better support their learning needs.

During the focus group, 7/13 reported that they would continue using captions as a learning tool. This was an interesting find as all students indicated that they read the available captions to some degree and most felt the captions had helped in learning and understanding the material. When asked why, students reported that captions were easy to use during the study but that they did not think they would actively search them out if they were not on by default.

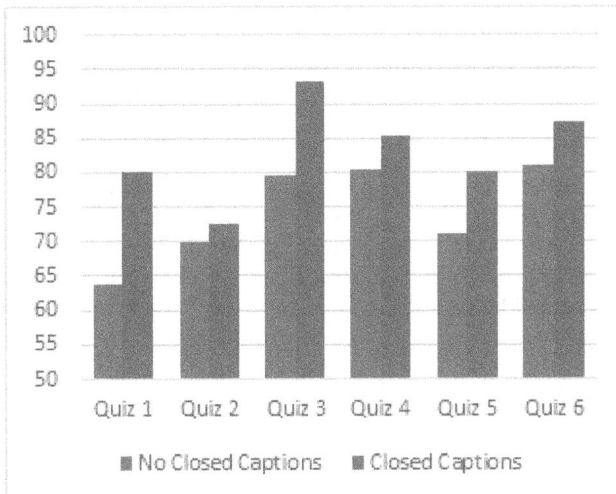

Figure 4: Mean scores for each assessment broken out by the availability of captions

6 Discussion

Our primary objective for this study was to understand the effect of captioned videos in a computing course. Drawing from theory, we created an effective learning environment where students engage in learning through captioned videos. Our findings provide strong support for the use of captions in course videos. In addition, the results afford us the opportunity to contribute to the current knowledge base in a few key areas.

Based on the results in Figure 4, students performed better whenever captions were available. So much so, that their average quiz score was 10% higher with captions (Table 1) which we found to be statistically significant. While the students did not read 100% of the captions, they utilized the captions to keep focus and provide further clarification when needed. In addition, the passing rates (Figure 2 & 3) are much better when captions are available than when they are not available (100% vs 76%). Based on these findings, our answer for RQ1 is yes, the inclusion of captions can significantly improve knowledge retention.

According to survey responses and focus group discussions, most of the participants (84%) perceive captions as beneficial to learning (Table 1). In addition, participants reported that captions allow them to further engage with the learning process and by doing so, better learn the materials. In response to RQ2, our findings indicate that students do perceive captions as beneficial to learning.

Our interpretation of these results are that (1) students engage with captions for various learning needs (e.g., clarification, focus, reinforcement, etc.) and this engagement has a strong positive influence on student learning, and (2) students appreciate when captions are provided as they perceive them as a resource that helps them learn. We were pleased to discover that many of the focus group participants will continue using captions as a learning resource. For the few that reported discontinued use, we suspect some would continue use if they had been informed of the increase in learning performance as discovered in the study.

Our findings also inform Dual Coding Theory and Cognitive Load Theory. As predicted by the Dual Coding Theory, we found that processing information through multiple channels facilitated better performance. As explored in the focus group, we found that the addition of captions did not cause a cognitive overload as described in the Cognitive Load Theory. Participants reported the ability to switch between captions and visual content in a controllable manner. This reported ability to switch was also experienced by participants when they watch the same material multiple times.

Although more research is needed, our findings suggest a need for instructors at the postsecondary level to "turn on" captions when showing videos in a classroom or online learning environments. The current study contributes to a growing body of research indicating captions' positive effects on learning in an educational setting. Students are also very open to using captions when learning new information. Instructors are encouraged to seek out educational videos that have captions readily embedded for use in their course. When needed, instructors should request institutional assistance in embedding captions in videos that have not yet been captioned. Finally, as a professional development exercise, instructors should learn how to create and embed their own captions when possible.

Based on the results of the current study, further research on the educational benefits of captions is warranted. Researchers can focus on a wide variety of educational subjects, settings (e.g., online, on-campus), and grade levels. It is recommended that future research include a more detailed study of how often students actually use captions when exposed to the technology. This could be done through measuring students' eye gaze when viewing educational videos.

7 Limitations

The findings of our study should be interpreted with consideration to its limitations. The study was conducted at one university by one instructor in one undergraduate computer science course. While such sampling is common, it limits generalizability of the findings. To this end, caution should be used when generalizing the implications of this study. In addition, students did have the ability to turn off captions for the duration of the available videos. While none reported doing so, it is possible that some may have turned off captions without reporting that they had done so. Finally, Lockdown browser was utilized to control the testing environment, but it is possible that topics were shared amongst students. By doing so, averages could have been inflated in our datasets.

8 Conclusion

In conclusion, our findings have important implications for computer science programs as the information gained indicates positive effects of captions. Computer science faculty can draw from this information to design better learning mediums for students. In doing so, all students will have the opportunity to benefit from an engaging and supportive learning process.

In the future, we are interested in investigating the benefits that captions have on long-term memory. In addition, we intend to examine the benefits of captions in more complex courses found in the computer science curriculum. Lastly, we also intend to explore the influence that captions have on the cognitive load in complex computing courses.

ACKNOWLEDGMENTS

We thank all faculty, students, and participants for their time.

REFERENCES

[1] Americans with Disabilities Act. 1990. 42 U.S.C. § 12101 et seq. Retrieved from https://www.ada.gov/2010_regs.htm

[2] Roland Brunken, Jan L. Plass, and Detlev Leutner. 2003. Direct Measurement of Cognitive Load in Multimedia Learning. Educational Psychologist 38, 1: 53–61. https://doi.org/10.1207/S15326985EP3801_7

[3] Class Central. 2018. A Product at Every Price: A Review of MOOC Stats and Trends in 2017 – Class Central. Class Central's MOOC Report. Retrieved August 4, 2018 from https://www.class-central.com/report/moocs-stats-and-trends-2017/

[4] Bryan K. Dallas, Amanda K. McCarthy, and Greg Long. 2016. Examining the Educational Benefits of and Attitudes toward Closed Captioning among Undergraduate Students. Journal of the Scholarship of Teaching and Learning 16, 2: 50–65.

[5] Jacob Enfield. 2013. Looking at the Impact of the Flipped Classroom Model of Instruction on Undergraduate Multimedia Students at CSUN. TechTrends 57, 6: 14–27. https://doi.org/10.1007/s11528-013-0698-1

[6] Philip J. Guo, Juho Kim, and Rob Rubin. 2014. How Video Production Affects Student Engagement: An Empirical Study of MOOC Videos. In Proceedings of the First ACM Conference on Learning @ Scale Conference (L@S '14), 41–50. https://doi.org/10.1145/2556325.2566239

[7] Jan-Louis Kruger, Esté Hefer, and Gordon Matthew. 2013. Measuring the Impact of Subtitles on Cognitive Load: Eye Tracking and Dynamic Audiovisual Texts. In Proceedings of the 2013 Conference on Eye Tracking South Africa (ETSA '13), 62–66. https://doi.org/10.1145/2509315.2509331

[8] Jan-Louis Kruger, Esté Hefer, and Gordon Matthew. 2014. Attention distribution and cognitive load in a subtitled academic lecture: L1 vs. L2. Journal of Eye Movement Research 7, 5. https://doi.org/10.16910/jemr.7.5.4

[9] Lisa L. Lacher, Albert Jiang, Yu Zhang, and Mark C. Lewis. 2018. Including Coding Questions in Video Quizzes for a Flipped CS1. In Proceedings of the 49th ACM Technical Symposium on Computer Science Education (SIGCSE '18), 574–579. https://doi.org/10.1145/3159450.3159504

[10] Juha Lång. 2016. Subtitles vs. narration: The acquisition of information from visual-verbal and audio-verbal channels when watching a television documentary. In Eyetracking and Applied Linguistics, Silvia Hansen-Schirra and Sambor Grucza (eds.). Language Science Press, 59–81.

[11] Deborah L. Linebarger. 2001. Learning To Read from Television: The Effects of Using Captions and Narration. Journal of Educational Psychology 93, 2: 288–98.

[12] Ron Mace. The Center for Universal Design - About UD. Retrieved August 6, 2018 from https://projects.ncsu.edu/design/cud/about_ud/about_ud.htm

[13] Mary Lou Maher, Celine Latulipe, Heather Lipford, and Audrey Rorrer. 2015. Flipped Classroom Strategies for CS Education. In Proceedings of the 46th ACM Technical Symposium on Computer Science Education (SIGCSE '15), 218–223. https://doi.org/10.1145/2676723.2677252

[14] Richard E. Mayer and Roxana Moreno. 1998. A split-attention effect in multimedia learning: Evidence for dual processing systems in working memory. Journal of Educational Psychology 90, 2: 312–320.

[15] Karla Kmetz Morris, Casey Frechette, Lyman Dukes, Nicole Stowell, Nicole Emert Topping, and David Brodosi. 2016. Closed Captioning Matters: Examining the Value of Closed Captions for "All" Students. Journal of Postsecondary Education and Disability 29, 3: 231–238.

[16] Fred G. W. C. Paas and Jeroen J. G. Van Merriënboer. 1993. The Efficiency of Instructional Conditions: An Approach to Combine Mental Effort and Performance Measures. Human Factors 35, 4: 737–743. https://doi.org/10.1177/001872089303500412

[17] Allan Paivio. 1990. Mental Representations: A Dual Coding Approach. Oxford University Press.

[18] Allan Paivio. 2007. Mind and Its Evolution: A Dual Coding Theory Approach. Mahwah, NJ: Lawrence Erlabaum Associates.

[19] Becky Parton. 2016. Video Captions for Online Courses: Do YouTube's Auto-generated Captions Meet Deaf Students' Needs? Journal of Open, Flexible, and Distance Learning 20, 1: 8–18.

[20] Elisa Perego, Fabio Del Missier, Marco Porta, and Mauro Mosconi. 2010. The Cognitive Effectiveness of Subtitle Processing. Media Psychology 13, 3: 243–272. https://doi.org/10.1080/15213269.2010.502873

[21] Rehabilitation Act, Section 504. 1973. 29 U.S.C. § 701. Retrieved from from https://www.dol.gov/oasam/regs/statutes/sec504.htm

[22] Rehabilitation Act, Section 508. 1973. 29 U.S.C § 794 (d). Retrieved from https://www.section508.gov/manage/laws-and-policies

[23] Richard M. Ruggiero. 1986. Impact of Television Captioning on Hearing Audiences. In Proceedings of the Annual Meeting of the California Educational Research Association, 15.

[24] Mark Sadoski, Allan Paivio, and Ernest T. Goetz. 1991. Commentary: A Critique of Schema Theory in Reading and a Dual Coding Alternative. Reading Research Quarterly 26, 4: 463–484. https://doi.org/10.2307/747898

[25] Klaus Schoeffmann, Marco A. Hudelist, and Jochen Huber. 2015. Video Interaction Tools: A Survey of Recent Work. ACM Comput. Surv. 48, 1: 14:1–14:34. https://doi.org/10.1145/2808796

[26] Vikash Singh, Sarah Abdellahi, Mary Lou Maher, and Celine Latulipe. 2016. The Video Collaboratory as a Learning Environment. undefined. Retrieved August 4, 2018 from /paper/The-Video-Collaboratory-as-a-Learning-Environment-Singh-Abdellahi/18aa68c53a75f6ca0ace1555a80a3b7c909b42a7

[27] John Sweller. 1988. Cognitive Load During Problem Solving: Effects on Learning. Cognitive Science 12, 2: 257–285. https://doi.org/10.1207/s15516709cog1202_4

[28] Gregory Taylor. 2005. Perceived Processing Strategies of Students Watching Captioned Video. Foreign Language Annals 38, 3: 422–427. https://doi.org/10.1111/j.1944-9720.2005.tb02228.x

[29] Robert Vanderplank. 1988. The value of teletext sub-titles in language learning. ELT Journal 42, 4: 272–281. https://doi.org/10.1093/elt/42.4.272

[30] Paula Winke, Susan Gass, and Tetyana Sydorenko. 2010. The Effects of Captioning Videos Used for Foreign Language Listening Activities. Language Learning & Technology 14, 1: 65–86.

[31] Géry d'Ydewalle and Wim De Bruycker. 2007. Eye Movements of Children and Adults While Reading Television Subtitles. European Psychologist 12, 3: 196–205. https://doi.org/10.1027/1016-9040.12.3.196

[32] Géry d'Ydewalle, Johan Van Rensbergen, and Joris Pollet. 1987. Reading a message when the same message is available auditorily in another language: The case of subtitling. In Eye Movements from Physiology to Cognition, J. K. O'regan and A. Levy-schoen (eds.). Elsevier, Amsterdam, 313–321. https://doi.org/10.1016/B978-0-444-70113-8.50047-3

[33] Joong-O Yoon and Heaeun Choi. 2011. The effects of captions on deaf students' contents comprehension, cognitive load and motivation in online learning. American Annals of the Deaf 156, 3: 283–289.

[34] A. M. F Yousef, U. Schroeder, M Wosnitza, and H Jakobs. 2014. A Review of the State-of-the-Art. Proceedings of CSEDU: 9–20.

[35] YouTube. Innovation in accessibility. Official YouTube Blog. Retrieved August 6, 2018 from https://youtube.googleblog.com/2009/11/innovation-in-accessibility.html

Facing Backwards While Stumbling Forwards: The Future of Teaching Web Development

Randy Connolly
Dept. Mathematics & Computing
Mount Royal University
Calgary, AB, Canada
rconnolly@mtroyal.ca

ABSTRACT

Web development continues to grow as an essential skill and knowledge area for employed computer science graduates. Yet within the ACM CS2013 curriculum recommendation and within computing education research in general, web development has been shrinking or even disappearing all together. This paper uses an informal systematic literature review methodology to answer three research questions: what approaches are being advocated in existing web development education research, what are current trends in industry practice, and how should web development be taught in light of these current trends. Results showed a significant mismatch between the type of web development typically taught in higher education settings in comparison to web development in industry practice. Consequences for the pedagogy of web development courses, computer science curriculum in general, and for computing education research are also discussed

CCS CONCEPTS

• **Social and professional topics → Professional topics → Computing education**; Model curricula;

KEYWORDS

Web Development; CS Education; Cloud Computing

ACM Reference format:

Randy Connolly. 2019. Facing Backwards While Stumbling Forwards: The Future of Teaching Web Development. In *Proceedings The 49th ACM Technical Symposium on Computer Science Education*, Minneapolis, MN, USA, Feb. 27–Mar. 2, 2019 (SIGCSE '19), 6 pages. ***https://doi.org/10.1145/3287324.3287433***

1 INTRODUCTION

In Canto XX of Dante's ***Inferno***, the narrator and his guide through the underworld come across a slow procession of chanting sufferers whose heads are reversed on their necks, so "their faces looked down on their backs; / they had to move ahead by moving backward, for they never saw what was ahead of them" [10]. In the ***Inferno***, the punishments are always meant to be poetically appropriate for the specific sin being punished, so Dante the Pilgrim in the book is not surprised to learn that those he sees are the soothsayers, those who claimed to see forward into the future, and are punished in the afterlife by never seeing what's just ahead of them. While some might be pleased to think that all those Silicon Valley prognosticators of inflated expectations have a special room awaiting them, making predictions of future technological trends is something most computing curriculum designers and planners have to do on a semi-regular basis. Perhaps no computing curriculum area contains more peril of misjudged divination than within the web development area.

The pace of change within web technology is well known and the difficulty in crafting curricula in such a rapidly changing context has been a constant complaint in the published literature on the teaching of web development [2, 17, 22, 24, 26]. These difficulties have perhaps resulted in the key problem with many courses in this area, namely their content becomes out-of-date too quickly. This problem is reflected in the titles of two papers documenting these flaws: "Partying Like It's 1999" [8] and "Awakening Rip Van Winkle" [9]. The latter paper argued that "there has been a certain dormancy to the way that the web is being taught in the computer science curriculum." This paper is going to take another stab at providing advice for what curricula in the area of web development should look like moving forward. Unlike Dante's soothsayers, I will not exactly be predicting the future, but instead will look sideways at the present and backwards to the recent past of web development and use that as a guide for what teaching web development today and in the near future should look like.

As an author of the principal textbook in this area, used at well over a hundred universities and colleges worldwide, I certainly have a vested interest in this topic, which might explain my advocacy for its place in computing education. But as any examination of industry requirements of computing graduates will make clear, from an employment perspective at least, there is an argument for web development's place within the computer science curriculum. A 2017 analysis of ITS intern postings (which arguably are an excellent measure of employer expectations of graduate competencies in computing) found that the Web Systems and Technologies area was by far the most frequently requested technological competency, larger than the combined values for the second and third most frequently requested competencies [27]. Similar recent studies of job advertisements

SIGCSE '19, February 27-March 2, 2019, Minneapolis, MN, USA

ACM ISBN 978-1-4503-5890-3/19/02...$15.00
https://doi.org/10.1145/3287324.3287433

for the emerging "hot" field of Data Analyst / Data Scientist found that web development skills were an essential requirement of most job listings in this area [16, 28].

Given the strong and on-going industry demand for graduates knowledgeable in web topics, it might be surprising to learn that web development has in fact been disappearing from computer science curricula in North America. As the introduction to the special issue on Web Development in ***ACM Transactions on Computing Education*** noted, "you can see web development everywhere except in the curricula of the various computing programs" [31]. For instance, in the ACM CS2013 curricula guidelines [1], web development has shrunk to being just one of several sub-areas within the elective-only Platform- Based Knowledge area. Of the 84 course exemplars at the end of CS2013, not a single one contains any topics from the Web Platforms sub-area. This absence does not go unnoticed outside academia. An engineer for Stack Overflow writing recently in the ***Communications of the ACM*** [25] "spoke to a roomful of third-year CS majors and was shocked to learn that most did not know HTML" or any other web technology.

Other ACM computing discipline curricula, however, such as IT and SE, advocate for some required commitment to aspects of web development as a required knowledge area. In Europe and the UK, many institutions offer specialized degrees dedicated to web development [4]. This paper is ultimately going to argue that web development as it is practiced today is a worthy topic for more than minimal coverage within computer science. To this end, this paper will endeavor to articulate the nature of contemporary web development, which hopefully will be of value to those teaching or revising courses containing web development content.

2 RESEARCH METHODOLOGY

While this paper is much less rigorous than a formal systematic literature review or systematic mapping study, it is inspired by such approaches [21]. Such studies are widely used in software engineering to both summarize current research and practice and help transfer results to both educators and practitioners (e.g., [20] and [33]). These studies revolve around a specific set of research questions which are then addressed via a content analysis of a large set of academic and professional studies.

For this study, the research questions were as follows:

- **RQ1**. What approaches are being advocated within web development education research?
- **RQ2**. What are the current trends in industry practice?
- **RQ3**. How should web development be taught in light of the findings from RQ2?

A total of 125 mainly peer-reviewed papers published between 2000 and 2018 were analyzed for all three of these questions.[1] For RQ1, 80 papers were examined; of those, only 18 were from the past four years, evidence of a slow-down of education research in this area attested to in [31]. A categorization content analysis was performed on a subset of these 80 papers in order to extract common, reoccurring themes and ideas. It should be noted that only the author performed this categorization step. This is a substantial limitation of this study; a proper systematic literature review should have at least two judges for the content analysis so that reliability analysis can be performed.

This author has previously published an earlier study on RQ1 [9], and will not duplicate the findings here, and in this paper will focus instead on aspects of RQ1 in relationship to RQ2 and RQ3. For RQ2, the papers were limited to those between 2013 and 2018. This paper's answers to RQ3 are a bit more opinionated and leans on my own interpretation of the answers to RQ2 in light of my experience as a practitioner and as a textbook author.

3 RESULTS

3.1 Current Approaches to Teaching Web Development

While always an uncommon topic within computing education research, there does appear to be declining interest in the teaching of this material [31] with most research falling between 2000 and 2007. More recent research tends to appear in less known regional computing education conferences or in the ***Journal of Computing Sciences in Colleges***, perhaps reflecting the continuing importance of web development as a topic area within the more vocationally-oriented two-year programs.

One of the key difficulties with teaching web development is that it has a large amount of potential topics, more than can possibly be covered in a single course. As a result, educators need to make difficult decisions about what to cover and what to ignore. As a result, most published accounts indicate that their courses begin with HTML and CSS, and then move on to backend programming using something like PHP, ASP.NET, or Ruby on Rails, alongside some form of relational database access. Other courses include JavaScript on the client, and more recently, on the server as well.

Several studies argued (for instance [34]) that web development can act as an important conceptual link between the early stages of a student's computing education, their day-today "normal" use of computers, and the broader range of Computer Science / Computational concepts. Muibi, Dorn, and Park [32] in a somewhat analogous manner argued that web development courses need to balance, following Shafer and Resnick [37], four types of pedagogical authenticity: personal authenticity to the students' interests, real-world authenticity, authenticity to the specific computing discipline, and assessment authenticity (that is, assessments that reflect what is covered). What makes web development courses especially difficult, they argued, is that these four authenticities can be in direct conflict with one another within a web development course. In particular, they found students with a design preference disliked the coding, while students with a coding preference disliked design aspects. But as an inherently interdisciplinary field, a web development course

[1] A complete list of research papers examined in this study along with a more fulsome description of the methodology used in the content analysis can be found at https://www.randyconnolly.com/papers/sigcse2019.

that aspires to some form of real-world authenticity will need to blend instructional content that will likely not align with all students' interests (nor indeed with the instructor's as well) [11].

3.2 Changes in Industry Practice

Earlier, it was mentioned that the number of computer education papers about the teaching of web development has declined significantly over the past half decade. One potential explanation for this is the changing nature of real-world web development practice.

In, say, 2008, web development meant learning HTML, and depending on the design orientation of the developer, either a little or a lot of CSS. Application logic was implemented using back-end/server-side coding using PHP, ASP.NET, JSP, or some other related technology. From a software design perspective, a more advanced developer might use an MVC architecture in PHP or make use of the Front Controller pattern in JSP or ASP.NET, but this was relatively uncommon. JavaScript was used sparingly in most sites, though the spread of so-called AJAX (Asynchronous JavaScript and XML) support in all browsers demonstrated that the future of the web was going to make heavier use of JavaScript. The architecture of the web at that point of time was also relatively straightforward. It consisted of a handful of protocols (HTTP, TCP/IP, DNS, and URLs), routers and load balancers, and servers often combined with web farms with vertical differentiation around tasks (e.g., data servers, application servers, media servers). The use of formal development processes or methodologies was relatively rare; developers typically FTP'd software changes to testing servers and then production servers and hoped/prayed that not too much would break each time code changes were uploaded.

By 2013, JavaScript had indeed become an essential part of almost all real world-web sites. Back-end systems had become thinner with less application logic and often acted as providers of JSON data using REST web services (now called web APIs). Node.js, a JavaScript-based server environment, was gaining popularity as the ideal speedy scripting environment for these "thin" back-ends. This data may have been queried from a relational database, or it may have been pulled from one of several different no-SQL databases such as MongoDB or Cassandra. Architectures were getting much more complicated as more and more logic moved from the server to the client. Variations of MVC such as MVVM and MVP tried to address the implementation complexity of the hybrid nature of these new web applications. But perhaps the largest two changes just developing at this time were the emergence of DevOps and cloud computing.

DevOps, a development methodology that combined software development with implementation operations, used collaborative agile approaches to software development and made use of version control software (such as git) in conjunction with automated build, deployment and testing tools [20]. As Christensen as noted [7], from an educational perspective, DevOps is challenging because it emphasizes hybrid skills that cross over the boundaries between the typical courses in university computer science programs. Furthermore, operations skills are typically not an area of expertise of most university computing teachers. As well, to do DevOps in a manner that reflects at least some real-world complexity "requires highly complex execution architectures consisting of 5-10-20 servers which pose a challenge on setting up the execution context for exercises and even more so on how to evaluate the systems developed and submitted by our students" [7].

Virtualization environments in general and cloud platforms such as Amazon Web Services (AWS), Google Cloud Platform, and Microsoft Azure was the other innovation that was just beginning to transform the practice of web development in 2013. Instead of deploying to physical testing servers then production servers, servers were becoming almost entirely virtualized, living on dynamically-allocated virtual servers provided by one of these large cloud platforms.

By 2018, many of the trends visible in 2013 had become the working reality of most web sites (indeed, as single-page applications have become more common, the term "web site" should be replaced now with the more accurate term "web application"). The JavaScript-centric nature of contemporary web development has resulted in a virtual avalanche of JavaScript frameworks. Many large enterprise development teams embraced Google's Angular, while the front-end focused React framework by FaceBook has become widely adopted by both large and small development teams. New JavaScript APIs have opened up the hardware context of the browser and allows developer access to vibration, orientation, battery status, ambient lighting, geolocation, etc. Local storage APIs within the browser in conjunction with parallel processing in the browser via the service worker API now allows developers to create Progressive Web Apps (i.e., web applications that work with or without internet connectivity). Together, these enhancements to the web environment have displaced many of the main benefits of proprietary native apps, making web technology not just ***a*** platform (as it is in CS2013), but likely ***the*** platform for software development now and into the future.

DevOps and Cloud environments have also changed since 2013. A complex DevOps workflow is now common using command-line tools for module building, transpiling, version control, continuous integration, and automated testing. The Cloud in 2018 has become much more than just an environment for provisioning virtualized server instances. Many services previously implemented by a development team, such as databases, file storage, search, and authentication, are often outsourced to third-party services and consumed via an API directly in JavaScript [38].

New software application architectures have emerged that take advantage of these changes in the cloud-based web development context. **Microservices** is a cloud-native architectural pattern than replaces monolithic applications with smaller, loosely-coupled, independently-deployable services managed by smaller teams using the technology stack and languages best suited to the task and the team [14, 33]; this approach takes advantage of a new, light-weight virtualization mechanism known as containers that make use of new DevOps tools such as Docker and Kubernetes. **Serverless computing** has continued this movement towards smaller and smaller units of execution [3,5]. In it, server and application management is hidden from the developers, who instead create small, stateless functions (typically written in JavaScript, Java, or Python using a platform such as AWS Lambda) that are executed within a cloudbased function container; such function containers are launched when the function is invoked and put to sleep after execution is complete. **Edge or Fog Computing** is another new trend in cloud-based web development [6, 13, 38], which redistributes computer processing out to the edge of the network, closer to the devices of the end-user. This architecture pattern is especially helpful for the Internet-of-Things, in which the size and scope of sensor data is such that centralized topologies cannot economically handle the processing load.

All this change and technological churn can be hard to visualize and assimilate even for veteran web developers, much less for an educator whose expertise may not be in this area. To this end, Fig. 1 illustrates the degree to which contemporary web development exists within a complex infrastructure and process flow architecture, one typically required even for relatively small operations (in this case, uploading and processing an image file). This example illustrates the serverless computing approach and could also be understood as a single larger microservice, or a series of smaller ones connected via message queuing.

Looking at this diagram, one might see that the term "web development" itself is a bit behind-the-times. Some authors are now using the much broader terms "cloud native application development" or simply "cloud development" to capture not only the virtualization technologies integral to the modern web, but also that web development now involves a lot more than the explicit web technologies of HTML, CSS, HTTP, and JavaScript [23, 38].

3.3 How should web development be taught now?

The educational problem with the complexity of today's web picture is nicely summed up by Guo and Koufako [18]: it "involves a large variety of technologies, such as networks, distributed systems, databases, security, and data analytics ... [and] it is a challenge to educators when it comes to developing a course [that covers this content]."

Table 1 provides a historic overview of the key knowledge areas potentially needed by full-stack (that is, front-end, backend, and DevOps) developers across the three time frames covered in Section 3.2.

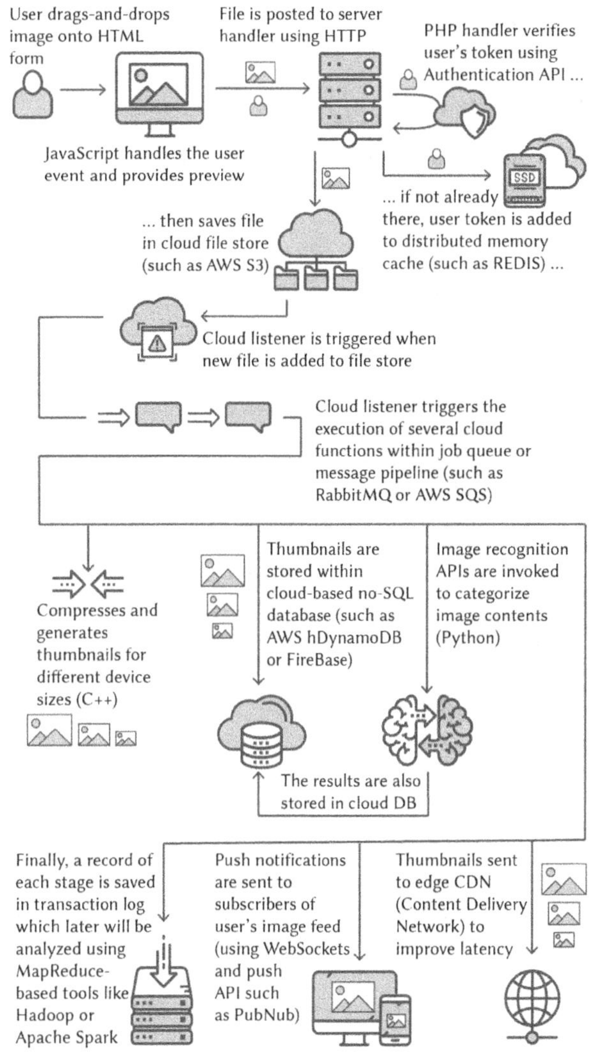

Figure 1: Uploading and processing an image file in 2018.
Artistic Images: Figure 1 © Randy Connolly
Image Credits: Randy Connolly

The obvious problem here is that it is not at all possible to cover all this content (or even a majority of it) within a single course. This is, no doubt, the reason why in Europe and the UK there are dozens and dozens of dedicated undergraduate computing programs dedicated just to web development [4]. In the North American context, where web development, if covered at all, is typically shoehorned into a single course within a CS, SE, or IT program, it is usually not possible to cover an adequate amount of web development topics. For this reason, self-learning has become one of the principle ways of learning web development in North America, a trend noticed by [12], [25], and [29]. Today coding bootcamps, hackathons, and numerous private online course offerings have emerged as a way of filling this very large gap in the education of computing students.

Table 1: Web Development Concepts/Technologies/Knowledge Areas

2008
HTML, CSS, Protocols (HTTP, DNS, IP), Architecture (Client/Server), JavaScript (basics), Server Configuration (Linux + Apache), Server-Side Scripting (PHP/ASP.NET/JSP/Ruby), SQL + Database API, Security Basics
2013
All the above plus: JavaScript (lots and lots), Asynchronous Coding Patterns, Web API Consumption+Creation, CSS Preprocessors, Responsive CSS Design + Implementation, Package Managers + Build Tools + Task Runners, Automated Testing Frameworks, NoSQL databases, Process Monitoring + Analytics, Cloud Management (IaaS), Web Design Patterns (esp. MVC)
2018
All the above plus: JavaScript Frameworks, Authentication Frameworks, Caching/Name-Value Stores, Message Brokers, Continuous Integration/Deployment, Container and Infrastructure Provisioning, Cloud Native Architectures, WebSockets + Push APIs, Functional/Reactive Programming, Server-Side Renderers, Parallel Coding Patterns

Unfortunately, there is no easy answer to the question in the heading of this section. In a previous paper [9], I have argued that dedicating several courses to this content is a good start to answering this question. Another approach to answering this problem is to integrate current web practices throughout the curriculum. For instance, we could use DevOps tools and approaches across multiple courses, or replace console outputs with web page outputs, or by forcing students to work more often with legacy, web-based code bases, as advocated by [15] and [25]. Another promising approach advocated by [4] and [30] is to focus on the key concepts underlying these technologies and then selecting subsets of them that best exemplify these concepts.

4 DISCUSSION AND CONCLUSION

As forcefully indicted by [25], students in CS are often "not learning best practices in the classroom" and are more likely to learn "through extracurricular involvement in open-source projects than from their university professors ... This is a disgrace that should make every CS department bow their heads in shame." The results of this study provides some evidence in support of this accusation. Why then has this disjunction between computing in the world outside university and computing in academic CS programs occurred?

One of the key teaching problems in any computing program is that concepts, techniques, and technologies are taught within subdisciplinary course silos (e.g., databases, networks, programming), but in practice, they are parts of larger heterogeneous environments. Adams [2] and Grove [17] back in 2007 noted that both undergraduate and graduate students "struggle to put the pieces together" from these silos and rarely understand how they work together. This, by and large, is still the case. Web development for many years has potentially provided curriculum developers with a valuable opportunity: namely, to help students put these pieces together and to experience the kind of integration issues that are at the heart of most computing projects outside of academia, all within a rich technology stack that is in extremely high demand by employers. This is arguably even more the case today. Web development can and should be much more than just one of several elective platforms (as it is in CS 2013) that students optionally can learn. It should instead be a required part of the curriculum whose job it is to teach the key integrative aspects of computing.

One potential argument for why CS2013 reduced the amount of web development coverage in comparison to the CS2001 and CS2008 versions is that CS is about teaching foundational computational concepts that prepare students for a changing future, and not about teaching particular technology skills. While there is certainly some truth to this claim, it can also be a too-convenient excuse against the need to face and adapt to a changing computing world. There is no necessity other than familiarity for using, for instance, Java and console output, to teach traditional CS courses such as data structures, algorithms, and the introduction to programming. As argued by [25], simply making use of contemporary web technologies instead to teach CS topics would go a long way to rectifying the imbalance between how CS is taught and how it is practiced outside the university.

Furthermore, the argument that CS is not involved in the teaching of flavor-of-the-day skills but in the teaching of computational concepts that have been used in the past, the present, and no doubt the future, is a bit disingenuous. This distinction between concepts and skills is not at all clear-cut. For instance, the ACM Computing Curricula 2020 project recognizes the importance of skills in its competency model. In it, competency = knowledge + skill + disposition, where skill "refers to capabilities that develop and become refined over time through practice and perseverance, usually manifested through 'hands-on' activity" [19]. Recent research, as well, on Threshold Concepts in computer science [4, 30, 35, 36], has moved away from just trying to discover and articulate concepts and instead is interested in discovering, threshold skills. That is, it is just as important for computing students to know ***how*** as to know ***what***. Playing music, learning programming, creating good software designs, and implementing complex web architectures are all examples of threshold skills: tricky procedural knowledge that is best learned through practice and which in turn help students learn essential computing concepts.

CS programs have long recognized this pedagogical truth by integrating practical hands-on labs and assignments into the typical CS course. As CS curriculum planners, we can decide which specific technologies to use in our classrooms as the means of better understanding CS concepts. One way to expose our students to more contemporary development techniques is to simply decide to make significantly greater use of web platforms in the teaching of traditional CS topics.

Hopefully, as the ACM CS curricula is revised early in the next decade, web development will be reintegrated into its recommendations (or, at the very least, not completely ignored). Until that time, it is hoped that web development also returns as an active area for computer education researchers. Now, more than ever, educators need guidance in how to best teach the complexities of 2018 web development, much less what it will look like in 2023. Experience reports on unique web teaching configurations are always valuable, but as noted by [31], "what would be especially useful moving forward are additional evidence-based articulations of the conceptual core of web development ... [and] evidence-based research into the nature of student learning within web development." But for interest in the educational study of the teaching of web development to be reignited, effort must continually be made to reassert the need for including the teaching of web development topics and tools within CS.

REFERENCES

[1] ACM/IEEE. 2013. Computer Science Curricular 2013: Curriculum Guidelines for Undergraduate Degree Programs. https://www.acm.org/education/curricula-recommendations.

[2] D. R. Adams. 2007. Integration early: A new approach to teaching web application development. ***J. Comput. Sci. Colleges*** 23(1), 97–104.

[3] G. Adzic and R. Chatley. 2017. Serverless computing: economic and architectural impact. In ***Proceedings of the 2017 11th Joint Meeting on Foundations of Software Engineering (ESEC/FSE 2017)***. ACM, New York, NY, USA, 884-889. DOI: https://doi.org/10.1145/3106237.3117767

[4] P. Alston, D. Walsh, and G. Westhead. 2015. Uncovering "Threshold Concepts" in Web Development: An Instructor Perspective. ***Trans. Comput. Educ.*** 15(1), 18 pages. DOI: http://dx.doi.org/10.1145/2700513

[5] I. Baldini, P. Castro, K. Chang, P. Cheng, S. Fink, V. Ishakian, et al. 2017. Serverless computing: Current trends and open problems. In ***Research Advances in Cloud Computing***. Springer, Singapore, 1-20.

[6] R. Buyya, S. N. Srirama, G. Casale, R. Calheiros, Y. Simmhan, B. Varghese, et al. 2017. ***A Manifesto for Future Generation Cloud Computing: Research Directions for the Next Decade***. arXiv preprint arXiv:1711.09123

[7] H. B. Christensen. 2016. Teaching DevOps and Cloud Computing using a Cognitive Apprenticeship and Story-Telling Approach. In ***Proceedings of the 2016 ACM Conference on Innovation and Technology in Computer Science Education (ITiCSE '16)***. ACM, New York, NY, USA, 174-179. DOI: https://doi.org/10.1145/2899415.2899426

[8] R. Connolly. 2009. No longer partying like it's 1999: designing a modern web stream using the it2008 curriculum guidelines. In ***Proceedings of the 10th ACM conference on information technology education (SIGITE '09)***. ACM, New York, NY, USA, 74-79. DOI: http://dx.doi.org/10.1145/1631728.1631752

[9] R. Connolly. 2011. Awakening Rip Van Winkle: modernizing the computer science web curriculum. In ***Proceedings of the 16th annual joint conference on Innovation and technology in computer science education (ITiCSE '11)***. ACM, New York, NY, USA, 18-22. DOI: https://doi.org/10.1145/1999747.1999756

[10] Dante. 2002. ***The Divine Comedy. Volume 1: Inferno***. Trans. M. Musa. Penguin. New York.

[11] B. Dorn and M. Guzdial. 2010. Discovering computing: perspectives of web designers. In ***Proceedings of the sixth international workshop on Computing education research (ICER '10)***. ACM, New York, NY, USA, 23-30. DOI: http://dx.doi.org/10.1145/1839594.1839600.

[12] B. Dorn and M. Guzdial. 2010. Learning on the job: characterizing the programming knowledge and learning strategies of web designers. In ***Proceedings of the SIGCHI Conference on Human Factors in Computing Systems (CHI '10)***. ACM, New York, NY, USA, 703-712. DOI: https://doi.org/10.1145/1753326.1753430.

[13] M. Díaz, C. Martín, and B. Rubio. 2016. State-of-the-art, challenges, and open issues in the integration of Internet of things and cloud computing. ***Journal of Network and Computer Applications***, 67, 99-117.

[14] N. Dragoni, S. Giallorenzo, A. L. Lafuente, M. Mazzara, F. Montesi, R. Mustafin, & L. Safina. 2017. Microservices: yesterday, today, and tomorrow. In ***Present and Ulterior Software Engineering***. Springer, Cham., 195-216.

[15] A. Fox and D. Patterson. 2012. Crossing the software education chasm. ***Commun. ACM*** 55, 5 (May 2012), 44-49. DOI: https://doi.org/10.1145/2160718.2160732

[16] A. Gardiner, C. Aasheim, P. Rutner, and S. Williams. 2018. Skill requirements in big data: A content analysis of job advertisements. ***Journal of Computer Information Systems***, 58(4), 374-384.

[17] R. F. Grove. 2007. Trends in teaching web-based development: A survey of pedagogy in web development courses. In ***Proceedings of the 3rd International Conference on Web Information Systems and Technologies***.

[18] D. Guo and A. Koufakou. 2018. A Comprehensive and Hands-on Undergraduate Course on Cloud Computing. In ***Proceedings of the ASEE Southeastern Section Conference***.

[19] J. Impagliazzo and A. N. Pears. 2018. The CC2020 project— computing curricula guidelines for the 2020s. In ***Global Engineering Education Conference (EDUCON)***, 2021-2024.

[20] R. Jabbari, N. bin Ali, K. Petersen, and B. Tanveer. 2016. What is DevOps?: A Systematic Mapping Study on Definitions and Practices. In ***Proceedings of the Scientific Workshop Proceedings of XP2016 (XP '16 Workshops)***. ACM, New York, NY, USA, 11 pages. DOI: https://doi.org/10.1145/2962695.2962707

[21] B. Kitchenham and S. Charters, 2007. Guidelines for Performing Systematic Literature Reviews in Software Engineering. ***Technical Report EBSE 2007-001***. Keele University and Durham University Joint Report.

[22] F. Klassner. 2000. Can Web development courses avoid obsolescence?. In ***Proceedings of the 5th annual conference on Innovation and technology in computer science education (ITiCSE '00)***. ACM, New York, NY, USA, 77-80. DOI: http://dx.doi.org/10.1145/343048.343083

[23] N. Kratzke and P. C. Quint. 2017. Understanding cloud native applications after 10 years of cloud computing-a systematic mapping study. ***Journal of Systems and Software***, 126, 1-16.

[24] A. H. Lee. 2003. A manageable web software architecture: Searching for simplicity. ***ACM SIGCSE Bull.*** 35 (1), 229–233.

[25] T. A. Limoncelli. 2017. Four ways to make CS and IT more immersive. ***Commun. ACM*** 60, 10 (September 2017), 50-52. DOI: https://doi.org/10.1145/3106633

[26] Y. Liu and G. Phelps. 2011. Challenges and professional tools used when teaching web programming. ***J. Comput. Sci. Colleges*** 26(5), 116–121.

[27] M. A. Mardis, J. Ma, F. R. Jones, C. R. Ambavarapu, H. M. Kelleher, L. I. Spears, and C. R. McClure. 2018. Assessing alignment between information technology educational opportunities, professional requirements, and industry demands. ***Education and Information Technologies***, 23(4), 1547-1584.

[28] A. D. Mauro, M. Greco, M. Grimaldi, and P. Ritala. 2018. Human resources for Big Data professions: A systematic classification of job roles and required skill sets. ***Information Processing & Management***, 54(5), 807-817.

[29] R. McCartney, J. Boustedt, A. Eckerdal, K. Sanders, L. Thomas, and C. Zander. 2016. Why Computing Students Learn on Their Own: Motivation for Self-Directed Learning of Computing. ***Trans. Comput. Educ.*** 16(1), 18 pages. DOI: http://dx.doi.org/10.1145/2747008

[30] M. Mick and S. E. Conners. 2018. Peering Through the Portal: An Investigation into Threshold Concepts in Web Development. ***International Journal of the Academic Business World***, 9.

[31] C. S. Miller and R. Connolly. 2015. Introduction to the Special Issue on Web Development. ***Trans. Comput. Educ.*** 15(1), 5 pages. DOI: http://dx.doi.org/10.1145/2724759

[32] H. Muibi, B. Dorn, and T. Park. 2015. Teacher Perspectives on Web Design Instruction. In ***Proceedings of the 2015 ACM Conference on Innovation and Technology in Computer Science Education (ITiCSE '15)***. ACM, New York, NY, USA, 231-236. DOI: http://dx.doi.org/10.1145/2729094.2742606

[33] C. Pahl, and P. Jamshidi. 2016. Microservices: A Systematic Mapping Study. In ***CLOSER*** 1, 137-146.

[34] T. H. Park and S. Wiedenbeck. 2011. Learning web development: challenges at an earlier stage of computing education. In ***Proceedings of the seventh international workshop on Computing education research (ICER '11)***. ACM, New York, NY, USA, 125-132. DOI: http://dx.doi.org/10.1145/2016911.2016937

[35] K. Sanders, J. Boustedt, A. Eckerdal, R. McCartney, J. E. Mostrom, L. Thomas, and C. Zander. 2012. Threshold concepts and threshold skills in computing. In ***Proceedings of the eighth international workshop on Computing education research (ICER '12)***, 23-30.

[36] K. Sanders and R. McCartney. 2016. Threshold concepts in computing: past, present, and future. In ***Proceedings of the 16th Koli Calling International Conference on Computing Education Research (Koli Calling '16)***. ACM, New York, NY, USA, 91-100. DOI: https://doi.org/10.1145/2999541.2999546.

[37] D. W. Shaffer and M. Resnick. 1999. "Thick" Authenticity: New Media and Authentic Learning. ***Journal of interactive learning research***, 10(2), 195-216.

[38] B. Varghese and R. Buyya. 2018. Next generation cloud computing: New trends and research directions. ***Future Generation Computer Systems***, 79, 849-861.

The Error Behind The Message: Finding the Cause of Error Messages in Python

Tobias Kohn
University of Cambridge
Cambridge, UK
tk534@cam.ac.uk

ABSTRACT

The interaction between a novice programmer, and the compiler plays a crucial role in the learning process of the novice programmer. Of particular importance is the compiler's feedback on errors in the program code. Accordingly, compiler error messages are an important and active field of research. Yet, a language that has largely been left out of this discussion so far is Python.

We have collected Python programs from high school students taking introductory courses. For each collected erroneous program, we sought to classify the effective error, and assess if the student was able to fix the error. Our study is a precursor to providing improved error messages in Python, and assess their effectiveness. As such, we are eventually interested in finding ways to automatically determine the effective error, so as to base the displayed message on.

From our data, we found that a considerable part of students' errors can be attributed to minor mistakes, which can easily be identified and corrected. However, beyond such minor mistakes, a proper error diagnosis might have to be based on a goal/plan analysis of the entire program. Likewise, proper assessment of whether an error has been fixed frequently requires more context than is provided by the program alone.

ACM Reference Format:

Tobias Kohn. 2019. The Error Behind The Message: Finding the Cause of Error Messages in Python. In *Proceedings of the 50th ACM Technical Symposium on Computer Science Education (SIGCSE '19), February 27-March 2, 2019, Minneapolis, MN, USA.* ACM, New York, NY, USA, 7 pages. https://doi.org/10.1145/3287324.3287381

1 INTRODUCTION

Making mistakes and correcting them is an important aspect of learning. A central piece of this process is good feedback to the learner, which then leads to the correction and effective learning process. In programming, students' mistakes manifest themselves as syntax errors or bugs in the program. While syntax errors prohibit a successful compilation and execution of the program, bugs become visible through the program's output. Unfortunately, the feedback given by compilers on syntax errors is often inadequate and provides little assistance for the student to correct the program.

SIGCSE '19, February 27-March 2, 2019, Minneapolis, MN, USA

ACM ISBN 978-1-4503-5890-3/19/02...$15.00
https://doi.org/10.1145/3287324.3287381

In order to improve the automated feedback produced by compilers, we need to study how good the displayed message matches the actual, underlying error in the program code, as well as if the message then enables the student to successfully correct the error. That is, good and helpful feedback relates both to the student's error, as well as the correction.

We are undertaking endeavours to develop helpful error messages for Python. To that end, we have written a parser that detects and identifies over one hundred different syntax errors [11]. In order to assess the quality of the error messages, we want to develop a metric that measures how well the messages fit the underlying errors and if the messages enable students to correct their code.

As a first step towards a metric, we have collected and analysed about 4000 Python programs with errors from high school students. Based on the data, we sought to distinguish between trivial errors, such as misspellings or inadvertent slips, and errors that might indicate some misconception or problem. Inadvertent slips are to be expected quite frequently even in programs of professionals.

Measuring the effects of error messages on the students is far from trivial, and there is no single, accepted metric. We thus tried to find patterns in the data, which might lead to a reliable automated assessment.

2 RESEARCH QUESTIONS

We have collected 4091 instances of error messages, each with the student's program that led to the error message, as well as the subsequent program the student tried to run. Analysing the data, we address the following questions:

- **(RQ1)** How often are errors due to minor, superficial mistakes, which should be easily fixed when pointed out?
- **(RQ2)** Do the displayed error messages correspond to the actual underlying errors?
- **(RQ3)** Is there any evidence that the error messages have an effect on the students at all?
- **(RQ4)** Can we derive a metric for measuring automatically if a student has fixed a certain error?

RQ1: What is the number of minor mistakes? The study of compiler error messages in education is to some extend based on the premise that the syntax errors are due to misconceptions of the students. While misconceptions are an important source of errors, some syntax errors are simply due to "typing mistakes" or "inadvertent slips" [19].

We assume that students do not profit from long, explanatory error messages in the case of minor mistakes. Rather, the error messages should be kept as short as possible, and act as brief reminder. Moreover, minor mistakes are not related to misconceptions of students. Hence, the amount of minor mistakes leading to a certain error message being displayed should be taken into account when enhancing error messages.

The classification of an error as a minor mistake depends on the student and the exact situation. For our study, we decided to count as a minor mistake what could be fixed with a simple edit, such as, e. g., inserting a character.

RQ2: Do the error messages report the actual underlying errors? As pointed out by i. a., Dy and Rodrigo [8], or McCall and Kölling [13], there is a difference between the true error in the student's source code and the compiler error message (CEM) displayed. The improvement of error detection is aimed at closing the gap between the underlying error, and the CEM. We are therefore interested in assessing if the data shows limitations to how close true errors and their messages can get.

RQ3: Do error messages have an effect on students? During classroom sessions, we observed that some students would not read the displayed error message, but rather focus on the code at the highlighted position in their source code. This seemed particularly true for longer, explanatory messages. If the hypothesis that a significant part of errors is easy to fix when pointed out holds, then the error messages might be irrelevant for this class of errors. On the other hand, for more complex errors, the error messages might not provide enough information for the students to fix the error at all. It is therefore not obvious that the error messages itself play a non-trivial role.

If the error message does play a role, then the collected data should contain samples, where the students' response correlates with the error message, even when alternative modifications to the source code would make more sense.

RQ4: Can we decide if an error has been fixed? When proposing new enhanced error messages, we need to assess if the messages help the students fix the problem pointed out by the message. One possibility is to check if the student's subsequent compilation attempt succeeds, or if and where the student has modified the source code. For our study, we were interested if a student's editing of the source code and the disappearance of an error are a reliable metric.

3 RELATED WORK

It has been noted early on that compilers often produce inadequate error messages of poor quality [5]. Numerous projects have therefore been put forward to address the problem, and enhance or improve the error messages presented to the novice programmers, e. g., [3, 9, 18], often with limited success [4, 6, 14]. More recent research has started to investigate if the displayed error messages actually correspond to the underlying error [8, 13], or if students read and react to error messages [2, 12, 16].

Most research agrees in that a small set of syntax errors in novices' programs make up for the bulk of all errors encountered. This has been established for Java by, e. g. Jackson et al. [10], Denny et al. [7], and Altadmri and Brown [1], and for Python by Pritchard [17]. It thus makes sense to concentrate research on these most frequent compiler error messages (CEMs) to assess if enhancing or improving CEMs has an effect on the students.

Students have difficulties understanding CEMs and relating them to their code. One approach to address this issue is to *enhance* CEMs with additional information about what kind of error could be the cause of the CEM, or how it might be fixed, thus providing the novice with the knowledge an expert might have.

However, evaluating the effectiveness of enhanced CEMs proves to be difficult, and studies have found mixed results. Denny et al. [6] studied the number of compilations attempts (submissions), and whether the enhanced CEMs led to a reduction in submissions with errors, but found no effect. Becker [3] found that enhanced CEMs do have a positive effect on the number of erroneous submissions, however, a later study [4] could not confirm these results. Nienaltowski et al. [14] also studied the effect of enhanced CEMs, but found that longer messages with additional information did neither improve the number of correct answers, nor the response time of students in their questionnaire. Odekirk and Zachary [15] concluded from their study with C programmers that those who received enhanced feedback needed less help from the teaching assistants. Finally, Marceau et al. [12] note that "there is no single metric for the 'effectiveness' of an error message". They propose a metric based on whether the students make a reasonable edit. Their metric requires the judgement from an experienced instructor.

Since enhancing error messages has resulted in little success so far, Barik et al. [2] and Prather et al. [16] have investigated if students actually read the error messages. Using eye tracking, Barik et al. found that, indeed, students spend considerable time on reading CEMs and conclude that reading and understanding error messages is about as hard as reading program code. Prather et al. also found that students read the error messages, but also note that some students were so unfamiliar with the materials that the CEMs were of little help to them.

The need to add typical causes for error messages already hints at the obvious difference between the actual underlying error, and the displayed error message. Dy and Rodrigo [8] investigated "non-literal" error messages: messages that do not match the actual error. They note that inaccurate CEMs are a source of problems for novice programmers. Furthermore, there are errors in novices' programs, whose nature remains ambiguous even to expert programmers. McCall and Kölling [13] clearly distinguish between the *programmer's misconception*, the concrete *error* in the program, and the *diagnostic message* displayed by the compiler. They point out that the compiler error message often depends on the compiler's internal structure, and that there is no simple correspondence between the underlying error, and the displayed message. Depending on the context, the same misconception or error can lead to different CEMs being displayed. On the other hand, different errors can also lead to the same CEM.

Traver [19] presents an extensive study of the problem of compiler error messages. Among other things, Traver remarks that the most frequent errors do not necessarily represent the most difficult errors to fix. Furthermore, errors are not only due to lack of knowledge, or misconceptions, but also due to inadvertent slips. Traver also states that the quality of compiler error messages matters, as adequate messages can help the programmer to not simply make random edits to address the error. Additionally, helpful error messages can reduce the workload of instructors explaining the same messages over and over to students.

4 METHOD

Collection of Data. We made our Python editor publicly available[1]. The editor/parser came with the option to send error reports and anonymised copies of the programs back to us. This option was not enabled by default, but was on an opt-in basis. Each student could decide at any time whether to take part in our study or not.

Upon start up, the editor would generate a large random sequence as unique identifier, and send all reports together with this identifier. This allowed us to track a student's progress during a session. Typically, a session would last for an hour at school, but if the editor was restarted, it would generate a new identifier.

Swiss high schools with participating students teach their programming courses between grades 9 and 12, with the majority taking place in 10th grade. The courses serve as a first introduction to programming, but typically 5 % to 10 % of students in these classes have some prior programming experience.

The introductory classes followed a common curriculum, which is based on turtle graphics. Students are introduced to functions, simple loops, parameters, variables, conditional execution, and lists.

Size of Data. All error reports were collected during one year. During this period, we have collected a total of 5440 user sessions, each containing several subsequent Python programs along with all errors reported to the student. The number of programs within a session, as well as the number of reported errors varied greatly. We extracted 6981 raw error messages from the recordings, but only 4091 were directly relevant for our study (see below).

In order to get an estimate of the number of participating students, we looked at the number of recorded sessions each week. On average, we recorded 121 weekly sessions, with a median of 120, and a standard deviation of $\sigma = 76.34$. The highest number was 298 sessions during one week. When looking at the distribution of weekly sessions, holiday weeks can easily be recognised: the number of submissions dropped then to an average of 26.6 with a median of 31. Counting only the non-holiday weeks, the overall average is 152 with $\sigma = 60.28$, and a median of 130. Based on these numbers, and given weekly classes at school, we estimate the number of participating students in the order of 100 to perhaps 150 students.

Selection of Data. Not all recorded error messages were directly usable for our study. Accordingly, we had to remove some of the collected submissions from our data set, leaving 4091 of the total of 6981 error reports for further analysis.

Our editor only recorded the main programs, but not additional files or modules. Thus, if the error was located inside an imported module, we were unable to inspect the erroneous code.

[1]The IDE is freely available under http://jython.tobiaskohn.ch

Program 1 We classified the extra space in the += operator as a minor misspelling.

```
x = 0
sum = 0
while x < 100:
    x += 1
    sum+ = x
```

```
x = 0
sum = 0
while x < 100:
    x+= 1
    sum = x
```

Runtime errors were mostly filtered out. While we retained *name errors* and *type errors*, we discarded other runtime errors such as "file not found" or "division by zero". We only kept errors that directly stemmed from syntactic or semantic issues with the code.

5 RESULTS: THE NATURE OF ERRORS

5.1 Minor Mistakes

Among the 4091 error instances, we classified 1233 instances as minor, superficial mistakes or misspellings, hence about 30 % of all instances. Most of these misspellings produced name error messages, as well as various messages indicating not properly closed tokens and statements (see Table 1). That students were able to directly fix 95 % of these error instances supports the idea of minor mistakes, which pose little problems to the students.

Displayed error message (CEM)	[ALL]	[FIX]
Name Error	570	544
Missing ')'	144	132
Missing Comma	109	102
Missing ':'	94	94
Inconsistent Indentation	64	60
Unterminated String	50	48
Total	1233	1174

Table 1: Of the 1233 instances of minor mistakes, 46 % **led to a name error being displayed. Students where then able to directly fix it in over** 95 %.

An error instance classified as minor if the underlying error could be corrected by a simple edit, i. e. swapping two characters, replacing a character by a different one, or inserting or deleting a character. However, the code around the minor mistake needed to be correct otherwise. For instance, a missing colon at the end of a line would only count as a minor mistake if the body beneath was properly indented. The juxtaposition of two statements as in Program 13 was not counted as a minor mistake, even though it can be corrected by a single edit. However, such an instance has a high probability to come from a misconception. When in doubt, we chose to rather not classify a particular instance as minor.

Program 2 The displayed error "NameError: name S is not defined." is caused by a simple mismatch of upper-/lower case. The student "fixed" the CEM by filling in a value for the parameter (which we classified as a "rewrite").

```
def hexagon(s):
    for i in range(6):
        forward(S)
        right(60)

hexagon(100)
```

```
def hexagon(s):
    for i in range(6):
        forward(100)
        right(60)

hexagon(100)
```

Nonetheless, Program 1 and Program 2 both show instances where the students modified the program to avoid further error messages, but did not fix the actual underlying error. Given the rather trivial nature of the errors, it is unclear as of why the students seemed unable to fix it.

Program 3 Python finds that the name s cannot be resolved (raising a "NameError" at runtime), whereas the actual error is due to incorrect indentation of the **for**.

```
def square(s, color):
    pencolor(color)
for i in range(4):
        forward(s)
        right(90)
```

```
def square(s, color):
    pencolor(color)
    for i in range(4):
        forward(s)
        right(90)
```

Program 4 Two examples where the student typed a comma instead of a dot. These errors were reported as "NameError", and "TypeError: wrong number of arguments", respectively.

```
for i in range(100):
    x = randint(0, 10)
    numbers,append(x)
```

```
def circle(r, clr):
    ...
circle(0,5, "red")
```

Program 5 The error message "else without if" might be confusing, because there is, in fact, even more than one **if**. The true error is the wrong indentation of the **else**.

```
    if key in [LEFT, RIGHT]:
        if key == LEFT:
            heading(-90)
        elif key == RIGHT:
            heading(90)
else:
    forward(10)
```

Program 6 Python reports a "name p not found" error in the second line. But the obvious intention of this statement is not to define *n*, but rather *p* as the square root of *n*.

```
n = input("Enter␣a␣number:")
n = p * p
if p % 1 == 0:
    print "This␣is␣a␣square␣number"
```

In addition to the minor mistakes, we found another 35 instances of random artefacts, and remarks. Examples of artefacts include line numbers at the start of each line, or small notes and remarks, which have the character of comments. Most of these notes simply read "Exercise 4.2" or similar.

5.2 Actual and Displayed Errors

Python only has a limited set of error categories. In our context, *SyntaxError*, *IndentationError*, *NameError*, and *TypeError* are relevant. On first sight, this small set suggests that each error can easily be assigned to the correct category. However, as the examples in Program 3, Program 4, and Program 5 show, even in this limited range of error categories, the reported error might not be the actual error.

For instance, of the 1462 name errors in the data set, 47 were due to incorrect indentation or scoping. In another 30 instances, the student used the name of a parameter in a function call instead of providing an argument value. We also found 120 cases where the name error was due to missing string delimiters, as in, e. g., `pencolor(red)`.

In the case of "else without if", 11 of the 13 instances were due to wrong indentation. As Python allows loops to have an else clause, the compiler might often not be able to detect a misplaced else (consider Program 5 with a **while** at the top).

Errors as in Program 4 are difficult to identify. Python is dynamically typed, which is to say that functions do not specify the type of their arguments. Moreover, it is often not even possible to clearly determine the correct number of arguments, or even know the function's signature in advance. In fact, the turtle module in Python defines all its functions dynamically, which means that virtually no information is available at compile time. In a case like `pencolor(dark red)`, it is therefore difficult for the parser to determine that there are string delimiters missing. There could, for instance, also be a comma missing between "dark" and "red".

Another case where the error cannot be automatically identified is shown in Program 8. Possibilities include that the last line should be indented, that the body of the if-statement is missing entirely, or even that the if-statement should not be part of the function "onClick".

In seven instances, the students had flipped the assignment, and wrote `3 = x` instead of `x = 3`. The underlying error of putting the target of an assignment on the right instead of on the left becomes much more difficult to recognise in cases like `x = y`. Misconceptions can even lead to examples such as shown in Program 6, where two errors ("assignment to right" and "assignment to expression") are combined, and thereby lead to valid, albeit wrong, syntax.

Program 7 In this instance of "NameError: name s is not defined.", the student simply removed the offending variable. The entire structure of this program hints at a basic misconception concerning the scope of variables, or the effect of the return statement.

```
def average(a, b):
    s = (a+b)/2
    return s
average(2,6)
print s
```

```
def average(a, b):
    s = (a+b)/2
    return s
average(2,6)
print
```

6 RESULTS: STUDENTS' REACTIONS

6.1 Statistics

Table 2 provides an overview of the most frequent error messages encountered in the collected data. For each instance in our collection, we looked at the students' reaction to the CEM, and applied a metric similar to the one found in Marceau et al. [12]. In contrast to Marceau et al., we were more concerned with *how* the students fixed the CEM, rather than their reaction in general, leading to different categories. [FIX] means that the student has directly fixed the proximate error in a meaningful way (although other errors might persist). [DEL] means that the student deleted the entire problematic passage (deleting, e. g., an entire function). [RWR] stands for rewrites. As discussed below, these are edits where the student has somehow addressed the CEM by rewriting the code, but not actually fixed the error itself. If a student just deleted individual tokens, but left the overall structure, we counted it as a rewrite rather than a deletion. Finally, there were other kinds of edits not captured by these three categories.

Error Category	Total	[FIX]	[RWR]	[DEL]
Name Error: Cannot Find Name	1462	1252	59	97
Wrong/Inconsistent Indentation	608	485	16	82
Type Error	349	287	17	18
Missing Comma or Operator	249	197	3	22
Missing/Mismatched Brackets	240	223	12	2
Total	4091	3428	176	345

Table 2: The most common error categories with students' reactions.

A case as seen in Program 13 was classified as [FIX], because the resulting program worked as expected, even though putting a comma is not necessarily a "good" edit.

6.2 Rewrites

Falling Back on Familiar Techniques. Using new programming techniques can be a challenge to students. The data contains examples, where students have tried to use a probably new programming construct, but failed because of some (syntactic) detail. In these examples the students then fall back to using familiar techniques instead of fixing the syntax error (Program 10, Program 9).

From the perspective of the compiler, it seems that the students successfully addressed the error and fixed the problem. If we want to evaluate if the error message has been helpful, however, the picture changes. Even though the program behaves correctly, the student was clearly unable to really fix the error at hand.

Fixing the Wrong Thing. Fixing a CEM does not necessarily mean that the underlying problem is solved at all. In some cases, the result compiles (and executes) without error, but does not behave as intended. It is possible to discern two basic student behaviours here. In some instances, the students merely removed the offending part (Program 7). In other instances, the students applied some change to fix the CEM, but thereby introduced logical bugs (Program 8).

Program 8 Instead of fixing the error according to the message "there is a body or indentation missing", the student un-indented the if-statement. The program will run without further problems, because *dotsize* is a global variable. Nevertheless, the if-statement never really takes effect.

```
dotsize = 10
def onClick(x, y):
    global dotsize
    dot(dotsize)
    dotsize += 5
    if dotsize > 30:
    dotsize = 10
```

```
dotsize = 10
def onClick(x, y):
    global dotsize
    dot(dotsize)
    dotsize += 5
if dotsize > 30:
    dotsize = 10
```

Program 9 After the message "there is a body or indentation missing", the student unrolled the loop, altogether.

```
for i in range(4):
draw_figure(100)
```

```
draw_figure(100)
draw_figure(100)
draw_figure(100)
draw_figure(100)
```

Program 10 After the message "to call a function, you must add parentheses", the student directly inlined the function's body instead of adding the necessary parentheses.

```
def square500(red):
    for i in range(4):
        forward(500)
        right(90)

forward(20)
square500
```

```
def square500(red):
    ...

forward(20)
for i in range(4):
    forward(500)
    right(90)
```

Program 11 Even though the error message "there is an else without an if" is technically correct, it does not capture the actual problem of the unindented break statement. The student obviously fixed the displayed syntax error, but did not address the true issue here.

```
t = 2
while t < x:
    r = x % t
    if r == 0:
        print "not␣prime"
    break
    else
        t += 1
```

```
t = 2
while t < x:
    r = x % t
    if r == 0:
        print "not␣prime"
    break
    if r != 0:
        t += 1
```

6.3 The Case of "Missing Comma"

A particular case did not receive the necessary attention during the construction of the parser. When, during the parsing process, an expression is immediately followed by another expression, our parser displays the message that there is a comma missing. We did not, however, anticipate that such a case would occur rather frequently and that putting a comma would be wrong most of the time (see Program 12).

Of the 214 instances that the parser classified as "comma missing", putting a comma would have been correct only in 86 instances (40 %). This means that the students got wrong advice in the remaining 128 instances. In 23 of these instances, the students did put a comma, even though this was not correct, and in 9 additional cases, the students put a comma to separate statements (Program 13). In other words, 32 instances in our data set show that the students read the error message and followed its implied course of action.

6.4 Misconceptions

Program 13 shows an example from our collection, where a student reacted to the "missing comma" message by inserting a comma. Python uses the semicolon to separate statements on the same line. In this case, however, the comma works, too, as it forms a tuple of the values returned by the two function calls.

Later on, several programs contained longer tuples of turtle commands, such as, e. g., `fd(80),rt(120),fd(80),...`. However, once programs include more than simple function calls, the chaining as tuples breaks down, as shown by the two error instances in Program 14. In these instances, the comma has become part of the expression and can no longer be used to separate statements.

The samples where a comma is used to chain statements are rather isolated instances in our data set. This example, however, indicates that error messages can, indeed, help students to learn,

Program 12 Examples of where the parser displayed a "missing comma" error message. Only in the first case is the message correct.

```
[(20, 25) (60, 25)]            pen color("red")
forward 100                    input()"your␣name:"
```

Program 13 After the error message "missing comma", the student added, indeed, a comma, arriving from the statement on the left to the tuple on the right. In Python, the tuple is legal code, and will execute as intended.

```
forward(100)right(100)         forward(100),right(100)
```

Program 14 Two instances, where using the comma as separator between statements does not work as intended.

```
print "...", i+=1              x = 0, y = 0
```

and form conceptual theories about the programming language, and its syntax and semantics. When enhancing error messages, care must be taken so as not to build or foster new misconceptions.

7 DISCUSSION

RQ1: What is the number of minor mistakes? With 30 %, minor mistakes make up a significant part of all the errors collected in our study. Almost half of these minor mistakes manifest themselves as name errors. The errors of a missing closing parenthesis, however, are more serious: there are several cases where standard Python keeps parsing the file, and then reports a completely unrelated error at a later location. Improved error detection can go a long way in helping students in such a case.

RQ2: Do the error messages report the actual underlying errors? Reporting the actual errors in the program code is not only hard in the case of failed compiling attempts. Even syntax errors might just alter a program's logic, and still satisfy the syntactic rules. Moreover, different possible errors can lead to patterns indistinguishable to the compiler, as has also been found in [13].

Not all errors lead necessarily to syntax errors and, moreover, a proper identification of errors requires deeper analysis of a program than is usually performed by a compiler. Hence, the compiler might be the wrong tool to identify and report errors in the first place. Finally, some errors remain ambiguous even to humans, without knowledge of the programmer's goals and plans. This finding is in accordance with [8].

Furthermore, notes and artefacts, such as "`exercise 4`", are for a machine virtually impossible to distinguish from actual code. Even more so as the same program might contain such an artefact, and a function named "exercise4".

On the other hand, even when the compiler error message does not reflect the actual error (as, e. g., in Programs 3 to 5), the message might still give enough information about the problem to be helpful. After all, students were able to fix the errors in over 80 % of the collected instances.

RQ3: Do error messages have an effect on students? Our parser issued incorrect error messages in 128 instances. In 25 % of these cases, the students followed the parser's implicit suggestion. Even though the sample size is very small, this indicates that at least some students rely on the CEM displayed to them. Other possible effects such as reducing the time needed to fix a program, or reducing the number of attempts needed to write a correct program were not considered in this study.

RQ4: Can we decide if an error has been fixed? Apart from the difficulty of reliably diagnosing the error in the underlying program, automatically classifying a student's response proves to be extremely difficult. In various instances, the students addressed the CEM rather than the underlying error. Among the strategies employed by students to cope with the error, we found that some students would just remove any problematic parts, or rewrite them in a simpler way, probably more familiar to them. Conversely, in the case of irrelevant artefacts and notes in the source file, deleting the offending part is, indeed, the right course of action. Checking subsequent compilation attempts for the reported CEMs, or the nature of edits seems therefore an unreliable metric.

Deciding if a particular error has been fixed depends highly on additional circumstances. Additional information such as the goal a program is supposed to achieve might be indispensable.

8 THREATS TO VALIDITY

The manual assessment of program code runs the danger of a strong bias or subjective component. Various examples of students' code illustrate the difficulty of properly assessing the exact type of error, the student's true intention, or even the student's response to the CEM. Furthermore, Python only provides rather crude categories for CEMs, making comparisons difficult.

Probably the largest problem is a proper definition of when an error should be considered a minor, superficial mistake as in RQ1. We decided to be as conservative as possible, only counting instances that clearly satisfy a hard rule and do not show a strong likelihood of an actual misconception.

9 CONCLUSION

Helpful compiler error messages (CEM) should help the programmer correct syntax errors in the program code. Assessing the quality of CEMs involves two independent metrics: the representation of the actual error in the code by the message and the information given to the programmer. In particular, a good metric should measure if the student is able to fix the actual error, instead of just reacting to the CEM.

We have analysed about 4000 error instances of Python programs from high school students and found that a considerable part of the errors are due to minor mistakes, such as misspellings. The nature of other errors or the students' responses, however, cannot always be reliably determined, even by humans, without knowing the goals and plans behind the program. Moreover, the compiler is not even able to detect all syntax errors or correctly classify them.

The reason why enhancing CEMs so often appears to be ineffective might thus be due to many errors being easy to fix even without further help, while other errors are not actually captured by the CEM at all. Moreover, if students try to fix the CEM rather than the error itself, the recurrence of CEMs, say, might not be a good indicator for a student's progress.

REFERENCES

[1] A. Altadmri and N. C. Brown. 37 million compilations: Investigating novice programming mistakes in large-scale student data. In *Proceedings of the 46th ACM Technical Symposium on Computer Science Education*, SIGCSE '15, pages 522–527, New York, NY, USA, 2015. ACM.

[2] T. Barik, J. Smith, K. Lubick, E. Holmes, J. Feng, E. Murphy-Hill, and C. Parnin. Do developers read compiler error messages? In *Proceedings of the 39th International Conference on Software Engineering*, ICSE '17, pages 575–585, Piscataway, NJ, USA, 2017. IEEE Press.

[3] B. A. Becker. An effective approach to enhancing compiler error messages. In *Proceedings of the 47th ACM Technical Symposium on Computing Science Education*, SIGCSE '16, pages 126–131, New York, NY, USA, 2016. ACM.

[4] B. A. Becker, K. Goslin, and G. Glanville. The effects of enhanced compiler error messages on a syntax error debugging test. In *Proceedings of the 49th ACM Technical Symposium on Computer Science Education*, SIGCSE '18, pages 640–645, New York, NY, USA, 2018. ACM.

[5] P. J. Brown. Error messages: The neglected area of the man/machine interface. *Commun. ACM*, 26(4):246–249, Apr. 1983.

[6] P. Denny, A. Luxton-Reilly, and D. Carpenter. Enhancing syntax error messages appears ineffectual. In *Proceedings of the 2014 Conference on Innovation & Technology in Computer Science Education*, ITiCSE '14, pages 273–278, New York, NY, USA, 2014. ACM.

[7] P. Denny, A. Luxton-Reilly, and E. Tempero. All syntax errors are not equal. In *Proceedings of the 17th ACM Annual Conference on Innovation and Technology in Computer Science Education*, ITiCSE '12, pages 75–80, New York, NY, USA, 2012. ACM.

[8] T. Dy and M. M. Rodrigo. A detector for non-literal java errors. In *Proceedings of the 10th Koli Calling International Conference on Computing Education Research*, Koli Calling '10, pages 118–122, New York, NY, USA, 2010. ACM.

[9] M. Hristova, A. Misra, M. Rutter, and R. Mercuri. Identifying and correcting java programming errors for introductory computer science students. *SIGCSE Bull.*, 35(1):153–156, Jan. 2003.

[10] J. Jackson, M. Cobb, and C. Carver. Identifying top java errors for novice programmers. In *Proceedings Frontiers in Education 35th Annual Conference*, pages T4C–T4C, Oct 2005.

[11] T. Kohn. *Teaching Python Programming to Novices: Addressing Misconceptions and Creating a Development Environment.* PhD thesis, ETH Zurich, 2017.

[12] G. Marceau, K. Fisler, and S. Krishnamurthi. Measuring the effectiveness of error messages designed for novice programmers. In *Proceedings of the 42Nd ACM Technical Symposium on Computer Science Education*, SIGCSE '11, pages 499–504, New York, NY, USA, 2011. ACM.

[13] D. McCall and M. Kölling. Meaningful categorisation of novice programmer errors. In *2014 IEEE Frontiers in Education Conference (FIE) Proceedings*, pages 1–8, Oct 2014.

[14] M.-H. Nienaltowski, M. Pedroni, and B. Meyer. Compiler error messages: What can help novices? In *Proceedings of the 39th SIGCSE Technical Symposium on Computer Science Education*, SIGCSE '08, pages 168–172, New York, NY, USA, 2008. ACM.

[15] E. Odekirk-Hash and J. L. Zachary. Automated feedback on programs means students need less help from teachers. In *Proceedings of the Thirty-second SIGCSE Technical Symposium on Computer Science Education*, SIGCSE '01, pages 55–59, New York, NY, USA, 2001. ACM.

[16] J. Prather, R. Pettit, K. H. McMurry, A. Peters, J. Homer, N. Simone, and M. Cohen. On novices' interaction with compiler error messages: A human factors approach. In *Proceedings of the 2017 ACM Conference on International Computing Education Research*, ICER '17, pages 74–82, New York, NY, USA, 2017. ACM.

[17] D. Pritchard. Frequency distribution of error messages. In *Proceedings of the 6th Workshop on Evaluation and Usability of Programming Languages and Tools*, PLATEAU 2015, pages 1–8, New York, NY, USA, 2015. ACM.

[18] T. Schorsch. Cap: An automated self-assessment tool to check pascal programs for syntax, logic and style errors. In *Proceedings of the Twenty-sixth SIGCSE Technical Symposium on Computer Science Education*, SIGCSE '95, pages 168–172, New York, NY, USA, 1995. ACM.

[19] V. J. Traver. On compiler error messages: what they say and what they mean. *Advances in Human-Computer Interaction*, 2010, 2010.

First Things First: Providing Metacognitive Scaffolding for Interpreting Problem Prompts

James Prather
Abilene Christian University
Abilene, Texas, USA
jrp09a@acu.edu

Raymond Pettit
Abilene Christian University
Abilene, Texas, USA
rsp05b@acu.edu

Brett A. Becker
University College Dublin
Dublin, Ireland
brett.becker@ucd.ie

Paul Denny
The University of Auckland
Auckland, New Zealand
paul@cs.auckland.ac.nz

Dastyni Loksa
University of Washington
Seattle, Washington, USA
dloksa@uw.edu

Alani Peters
Abilene Christian University
Abilene, Texas, USA
alp13d@acu.edu

Zachary Albrecht
Abilene Christian University
Abilene, Texas, USA
zca16a@acu.edu

Krista Masci
Abilene Christian University
Abilene, Texas, USA
klc10b@acu.edu

ABSTRACT

When solving programming problems, novices are often not aware of where they are in the problem-solving process. For instance, students who misinterpret the problem prompt will most likely not form a valid conceptual model of the task and fail to make progress towards a working solution. Avoiding such errors, and recovering from them once they occur, requires metacognitive skills that enable students to reflect on their problem-solving processes. For these reasons, developing metacognitive awareness is crucially important for novice students. Previous research has shown that explicitly teaching key steps of programming problem-solving, and having students reflect on where they are in the problem-solving process, can help students complete future programming assignments. Such metacognitive awareness training can be done through personal tutoring, but can be difficult to implement without a high ratio of instructors to students. We explore a more scalable approach, making use of an automated assessment tool, and conduct a controlled experiment to see whether scaffolding the problem-solving process would increase metacognitive awareness and improve student performance. We collected all code submissions by students in both control and experimental groups, as well as data from direct observation using a think-aloud protocol. We found that students who received the intervention showed a higher degree of understanding of the problem prompt and were more likely to complete the programming task successfully.

SIGCSE '19, February 27-March 2, 2019, Minneapolis, MN, USA

ACM ISBN 978-1-4503-5890-3/19/02...$15.00
https://doi.org/10.1145/3287324.3287374

CCS CONCEPTS

• **Social and professional topics → CS1**; • **Human-centered computing → User studies**;

KEYWORDS

CS1, automated assessment tools, metacognitive awareness

ACM Reference Format:
James Prather, Raymond Pettit, Brett A. Becker, Paul Denny, Dastyni Loksa, Alani Peters, Zachary Albrecht, and Krista Masci. 2019. First Things First: Providing Metacognitive Scaffolding for Interpreting Problem Prompts. In *Proceedings of the 50th ACM Technical Symposium on Computer Science Education (SIGCSE '19), February 27-March 2, 2019, Minneapolis, MN, USA.* ACM, New York, NY, USA, 7 pages. https://doi.org/10.1145/3287324.3287374

1 INTRODUCTION

Solving a programming problem requires careful navigation through multiple learning steps [25]. With only one mistake, the novice programmer could find themselves lost in the weeds without any idea as to why they are lost or stuck [36]. This is because novice programmers usually lack metacognitive awareness [14, 24, 28, 38] – the ability to think about and reflect on their problem-solving process – and cannot articulate it to a peer or instructor. The lack of this crucial skill in novice programmers could help to explain the tremendously high failure rate in computer science [4, 47], especially since the highest-performing novices tend to display some aspects of metacognitive awareness or other self-regulated learning strategies [10].

There are two general approaches to solving this problem: explicit instruction in the classroom [24, 25] or implicit training through careful design of the automated assessment tool or intelligent tutoring system used in the course, through which students complete their homework [36]. Loksa et al. [25] investigated metacognitive awareness in novice programmers using an explicit strategy by making students aware of and coaching them through six problem-solving stages: (1) *reinterpret the prompt*, (2) *search for analogous problems,* (3) *search for solutions,* (4) *evaluate a potential solution* , (5) *implement a solution,* (6) *evaluate implemented solution.* Before receiving help, students had to identify to an instructor where they were in these six stages, therefore reflecting on their programming process and practicing metacognitive awareness. Prather et al. [36] took this framework and applied it to the design of an automated assessment tool (AAT) to understand where the tool currently failed to implicitly support novice metacognition. They found five points at which the design of the AAT adversely impacted novice metacognitive awareness and called for future work to investigate each one. Three of the difficulties they highlighted applied to the first learning stage, *reinterpret the prompt.* Their analysis revealed the importance for students to correctly interpret the problem statement from the outset. They highlighted several difficulties that resulted if an incorrect conceptual model was formed early in the problem-solving process, such as a reluctance to reconsider a misconstrued conceptual model. They hypothesize that an explicit prompt from an AAT, checking that students understand a problem initially, may be particularly useful in this regard.

Prior work has suggested that focusing on the problem prompt can provide enough scaffolding to help novices build metacognitive awareness [17]. In this paper, we investigate whether asking novice programmers to solve a randomly generated test case immediately after reading the problem prompt can help them overcome metacognitive difficulties encountered at that learning stage and, therefore, should be incorporated into the design of AATs for better implicit metacognitive training.

We investigate the following research question:

- **RQ:** Can solving a randomly generated test case immediately after reading a problem prompt help novice programmers overcome metacognitive difficulties encountered in the early stages of problem-solving?

We report on a think-aloud study with CS1 students completing a timed programming exercise in order to determine if the intervention produces a noticeable impact on metacognitive awareness in an experimental group, over those in a control group.

2 RELATED WORK

2.1 Automated Assessment Tools

As this study centers around the use of automated assessment tools (AATs) and their design, it is important to first briefly consider AATs, their history, and how they have been designed (or not) to support metacognitive awareness. There is a long history of development, testing, and improvement of AATs [1, 12, 20, 21, 26, 34]. However, these AATs are not generally designed to improve the user's metacognitive awareness [36]. The only discussion in the literature about AATs that could be related to one of the stages from Loksa's framework [25] addresses stage 5, *implement a solution,* which centers on enhancing compiler error message feedback. Compiler error messages have long been documented to be a great source of confusion and frustration to students [9, 29, 32, 46]. How novices encounter error messages has been linked to success through Jadud's EQ [22] and enhanced compiler error messages (ECEMs) have shown potential in reducing EQ and to have positive effects on similar error metrics [5, 8]. This indicates that the addition of ECEMs can help students to better understand the errors in their solution and therefore reduce the overall amount of errors encountered. Accordingly, several researchers have attempted to add ECEMs into their AATs [3, 16, 41, 48]. A few researchers have reported empirical results on the efficacy of ECEMs, though the efficacy of this approach is an ongoing debate [6, 7, 11, 35, 37]. Likewise, a few researchers have attempted to take a human-factors approach to the design of ECEMs, highlighting the importance of human-centered design in AATs [18, 29, 30, 37, 46].

2.2 Metacognition in Novice Programmers

Introductory programming courses often focus solely on syntax and data structures, but there is a growing consensus among computer science education researchers that there should be more emphasis on assisting the novice in building a mental scaffold around which they can correctly place knowledge and in doing so, develop metacognitive awareness [10, 14, 19, 25, 28, 38, 43]. Metacognitive awareness is, simply put, knowing about knowing. Applied to programming, it is not just knowledge of the problem and how to solve it, but knowledge of where one is in the problem-solving process and self-reflection on that state [31].

A few studies, such as Falkner et al. [15] and Hauswirth & Adamoli [19] report on experiments designed to measure novice programmers' metacognitive awareness, self-reflection, or self-awareness of learning strategies. The most comprehensive study to date on promoting metacognitive awareness in novice programmers is by Loksa et al. [25]. As discussed in Section 1, they identified six distinct problem-solving stages that learners iteratively progress through. They reported on an intervention at a code camp where the control group was taught how to code and the experimental group was additionally trained in these six problem-solving stages and the use of an IDE with an Idea Garden. They reported that students with this training were significantly more productive, required less help, and displayed a positive shift in growth mindset. This indicates that modified pedagogical approaches and programming environments warrant development. Some successful modifications, however, are difficult to scale or hard to implement for online learning technologies, such as massively open online courses, which Loksa et al. acknowledged as a limitation of their work.

Prather et al. [36] recently reported on an intervention designed to explore the metacognitive difficulties faced by novices when using AATs, using the work of Loksa et al. as a theoretical framework. They conducted a think-aloud study with novice programmers solving a programming problem while using Athene, an AAT with a long history of empirical work [33, 35–37, 45]. The five metacognitive difficulties they report are shown in Table 1. The first three of these identified difficulties involve forming an appropriate conceptual model of the problem. They found that the students who successfully solved the problem were consistently more likely to correctly interpret the problem statement before beginning to write code. Moreover, the most common error made by those students unable to complete the programming problem was failure to build a correct conceptual model of the problem. Prather et al. argue that the single greatest weakness of modern AATs is that they merely present a problem to be solved, assuming that students will eventually conceptualize the problem correctly and allowing the

Table 1: Observed difficulties to metacognitive awareness by novices using AATs from [36].

Metacognitive Difficulty	Explanation
Forming	Forming the wrong conceptual model about the right problem
Dislodging	Dislodging an incorrect conceptual model of the problem may not be solved by re-reading the prompt
Assumption	Forming the correct conceptual model for the wrong problem
Location	Moving too quickly through one or more stages incorrectly leading to a false sense of accomplishment and poor conception of location in the problem-solving process
Achievement	Unwillingness to abandon a wrong solution due to a false sense of being nearly done

submission of code without any assurances as to how the problem has been interpreted by the student.

3 METHODOLOGY

In this paper we investigate whether providing an explicit metacognitive prompt - one that requires solving a test case immediately after reading the problem prompt in an AAT - will assist novice programmers in overcoming the metacognitive difficulties identified by Prather et al. [36]. We presented the programming problems in our automated assessment tool, Athene, and the test cases were crafted in the Canvas LMS.

3.1 Think-Aloud Study

During the sixth week of CS1 at Abilene Christian University, one researcher, who was not the professor of record, appeared in both sections of the course to solicit student participation, discuss the study, and administer IRB requirements. Students were asked to participate in exchange for three perfect daily quiz scores, which they would receive regardless of how well they performed in the study. Not participating was guaranteed to not have any negative consequences on their grades. A total of 36 out of 41 students chose to participate. Because there were two sections of the course, the first section was chosen as the control group (n=17) and the second section as the experimental group (n=21). Students in both control and experimental groups signed up for a time slot to meet one of the researchers in the lab for an hour-long one-on-one session where the student was observed completing a programming assignment using the think-aloud protocol [39]. The session consisted of a five-minute warm-up exercise to help the student become familiar with the task of talking aloud as suggested by [44] and [49], a 35-minute programming task where the student was given a problem in Athene and asked to solve it in the allotted time, and a 20-minute detailed feedback session where each student was given personalized advice based on the observations of the researcher. This hour-long one-on-one format is based on the methodology of Prather et al. [36]. The programming language students used was C++.

The general format of the think-aloud study follows the usability testing guidelines found in Rubin and Chisnell [39], including pre- and post-testing checklists and scripts. At the beginning of each think-aloud session, the evaluator read from a script outlining the reason for the session, the goal of the session, and what was expected of the student. The warm-up exercise was to write a program that would output "Hello, world." This particular task was chosen to reduce cognitive load introduced by the programming task during the warm-up. After completing the warm-up exercise, students were asked to complete the programming task within a time limit of 35 minutes. The task was this: given n integers, compute whether there were more positive or negative integer numbers provided as input. For this problem, students would need to understand the following concepts: console input, console output, conditionals, and loops. This problem is identical to the one used by Prather et al. [36]. The course was structured in such a way that the problem correlated with course topics at the time and therefore should have been familiar but moderately challenging. While each student worked to solve the problem, a researcher took extensive notes on what the student did and said. Interactions during the programming task between the researcher and student were kept to a minimum, as per Ericsson and Simon [13]. After reading the problem prompt, the control group was allowed to immediately begin coding, while the experimental group was immediately directed to solve a test case quiz inside of Canvas simply asking students to calculate the output of the program described in the prompt given a random set of input. Once the students in the experimental group had passed the test case quiz, they were allowed to begin writing code. This meant that the experimental group had slightly less time to complete the task than the control. We discuss and reject this as a potential threat to validity in Section 3.3.

Prior work has shown that participants trained in metacognitive strategies exhibit a positive shift in growth mindset [25]. We also explored this, by investigating whether participants had a shift towards a growth mindset from pre- to post-testing scores. In both groups, before reading the problem prompt and after solving the problem or time had expired, students were asked to answer how they felt about three growth mindset statements, which we took from Scott and Ghinea [42]. One statement endorsed a fixed mindset (Q1. "I do not think I can really change my aptitude for programming") and two statements endorsed the growth mindset (Q2. "I do not have a fixed level of programming aptitude and hard work can change it"; and Q3. "I believe I am able to achieve a high level of programming aptitude, with enough practice"). Participants were asked to rate how much they agreed with the three statements on a five-point Likert scale.

3.2 Qualitative Coding Process

Participant observation allowed us to record the participants' actions, apparent thought and problem-solving process, and external reactions to error messages and other feedback. Participant-specific data were separately recorded, tagged, and then moved into ATLAS.ti, a qualitative software analysis package. We used a collaborative coding process for the initial stage of coding the qualitative observation session notes [40]. The codebook was developed collaboratively among multiple researchers. Two researchers then independently coded 10% of the data (without knowing how the other had coded the data). A third researcher used Cohen's Kappa [2] to measure agreement between coders and found an interrater reliability rate of 67.2%, which is classified as "substantial agreement" [27]. With this initial step complete and having verified the accuracy of the double-blind coding process, a second step was taken where the two coders worked through their disagreements about which codes were used, refining the codebook [27]. Following this, the lead researcher proceeded to code the rest of the data. When the first stage was completed, we used ATLAS.ti to identify major themes within the data. These themes, grounded on the data, are explored in Section 4.2.

3.3 Threats to Validity

Four threats to the validity of this study are: 1. the potential for increased cognitive load during the think-aloud sessions; 2. the fact that the two groups were naturally split into two course sections; 3. the fact that the experimental group had slightly less time than the control group to complete the main task; and 4. students in the experimental group may have taken cues from the tasks researchers asked them to do. We address these in order here

Participants in the think-aloud study were in a one-on-one setting, were asked to think-aloud, and did not have access to any of their previously written assignments. It is possible that all of these factors increased student cognitive load in the think-aloud study. We attempted to offset this 'think-aloud factor' by adding in the warm-up exercise as suggested by Teague et al. [44] and Whalley and Kasto [49]. Furthermore, students who did not complete the warm-up exercise were given a correctly working warm-up exercise to help ensure that students were starting from a common place. In terms of writing code for the programming task, we asked all students to use Notepad, which is a plain text editor. This was to ensure that all students used the same environment, and to prevent students with knowledge of more advanced programming tools from utilizing their features for an advantage.

As the control and experimental groups were determined by the two sections of the course, we conducted a post-test analysis on midterm test scores to compare the similarity of students in each group. The mean score of students in the control group was 0.73 (SD = 0.19) and the mean score of students in the experimental group was 0.81 (SD = 0.15). An independent samples t-test (unequal variances, two-tail) showed that the difference in these scores is not statistically significant ($t(29) = 1.43$, $p = 0.16$), allowing us to conclude that that there is no significant difference in ability between the groups.

As discussed in Section 3, by design, the control group was allowed to immediately begin coding, while the experimental group was immediately directed to solve a quiz inside of Canvas consisting of a randomly generated test case. Once the students in the experimental group had passed the test case quiz, they were allowed to begin writing code. This meant that the experimental group had slightly less time to complete the task than the control. We do not believe this is a serious threat to validity for two reasons. First, no participant in the experimental group spent more than a minute on the test case quiz. Second, we believe that by requiring students to reflect on the prompt, we merely formalized a necessary step that students should have been taking anyway, and is an essential part of the study design.

Finally, the students in the experimental group may have taken their involvement in the experiment somewhat more seriously than those in the control. Students in the experimental group were asked to solve the test case before coding and so may have spent more time reading the prompt to pass the quiz and more carefully thinking about the solution where they would have otherwise not done so. This is an artifact of our methodology and one we hope to address in future work.

4 RESULTS

The quantitative data collected from the experiment consisted of answers to the growth mindset statements, completion times for both control and experimental groups, number of code submission attempts, and the number of attempts on the test case quiz by each student in the experimental group. We first present this quantitative data, followed by insights from the qualitative coding process discussed above.

4.1 Quantitative Results

Table 2 shows the completion rate, mean time and mean number of submissions for the experimental and control groups. "Submissions" refers to a compilation and run against test cases. Participants in the control group completed the programming task at a rate of 52.94% and those that completed it took 23.82 minutes on average with an average of 7.59 code submission attempts. In contrast, participants in the experimental group completed the programming task at a rate of 76.19% and those that completed it took 22.62 minutes on average with an average of 4.48 code submission attempts. From these basic results, it appears that the intervention helped more participants complete the programming task compared to those that did not receive the intervention - the experimental group had a higher completion rate, faster time, and fewer attempts required to complete. However, several of the other data points were inconclusive as we discuss below.

Table 2: Programming task performance of control and experimental groups

	Control	Experimental
Correct completion rate	52.94%	76.19%
Mean time (minutes)	23.82	22.62
Mean code submissions	7.59	4.48

Participants answered the growth mindset questions on a five-point Likert scale and we mapped their answers into a delta change value from before and after the programming task. This revealed a change of +0.308 on average in the control group and +0.000 on average in the experimental group. This seems to indicate that the intervention did not have a positive impact on participants' growth mindset. This could be explained by the fact that the experimental group displayed a higher level of growth mindset overall from the beginning. Another possible explanation for the increase in growth mindset in the control group (vs none in the experimental), is that perhaps working a problem and completing it in 35 minutes increased participants' confidence in their own abilities. Finally, recent research has begun to question whether the mindset of a student impacts performance, with one recent study (published after we conducted this experiment) concluding that it did not [23].

Finally, only one participant in the experimental group needed to submit the test case quiz more than once. In that one case, the student arrived at the correct answer on the second attempt, but did not complete the programming task. The four other participants in the experimental group that did not complete the programming task all correctly answered the test case quiz on the first attempt. Therefore, this data alone explains very little as there was no correlation between the number of test case attempts and programming task completion.

4.2 Qualitative Results

We tagged data in 1,116 places in the observation notes and post-session interviews, using Loksa et al. [25] and Prather et al. [36] as our theoretical frameworks. As we tagged and coded the data, trends began to naturally emerge from the data, which are explored below.

4.2.1 Experimental Group. Participants in the experimental group who submitted a correct code solution tended to display and verbalize higher metacognitive skills and behaviors. For instance, when asked to describe how he/she normally goes about solving a problem in Athene, participant 27 (P27) described themselves as walking through five of the six stages of problem-solving. Furthermore, all participants in the experimental group, except for one, verbalized a correct understanding of the purpose of the intervention when asked directly about it. P31, who completed the problem in 9 minutes, said that the intervention "help[ed] you understand the problem beforehand, make sure you understand the logic behind it." Most participants verbalized something similar. However, P31 also added that it, "helped me understand that when you dont enter anything it would be equal," which is an edge case not explicitly described in the instructions. P43, who completed the problem in 15 minutes, voiced their appreciation for the intervention, saying, "I usually freak out reading the prompt, but doing a test case helped me breathe and know that I know how to do it." P29, who completed the problem in 20 minutes, described how solving a test case immediately after reading the prompt, "made me realize that I didn't read the problem very well because I needed to go back and read it again before I answered the quiz." However, requiring students to solve a test case before coding did not entirely eliminate students from struggling with the *Assumption* metacognitive difficulty (see Table 1). P21, who completed the problem in 30 minutes, correctly solved the test case on their first attempt, and then went on to attempt to solve a similar problem students in CS1 had already seen, "More Even or Odd", where the program must determine if there are more even or odd numbers provided as input. After the eighth submission, P21 re-read the prompt, but continued to attempt to solve the wrong problem, struggling with both the *Location* and *Achievement* metacognitive difficulties. Only after 11 submissions did P21 re-read the prompt a third time and realize their mistake. In the post-session interview, P21 said that the intervention was, "Probably to evaluate the psychology of walking into something and thinking you may not be able to do it... but it helps you know that you can do it", which was not at all the intended purpose.

Participants in the experimental group who did not submit a correct code solution tended toward two behaviors: those that understood the intervention and those that did not. A few participants in this group were able to understand the prompt but were unable to implement a solution, usually becoming stuck on syntax or edge test cases. For instance, P33's code was extremely close to a correct solution, but they did not understand the purpose of the intervention, saying, "it wants to see if I can read a program." Others, however, suffered from various metacognitive difficulties. P39 faced the *Assumption* difficulty, thinking that he/she was solving the problem about even and odds, but discovered this error upon re-reading the prompt after 12 minutes. Other participants suffered from the *Forming* difficulty, such as P42 who struggled to understand the problem, even after correctly solving a test-case, and re-read the instructions five times, each time saying things like, "okay, I'm stupid...that was stupid...dang that changes everything," and, "Oh. Okay. I see now. Well that just makes all that work pointless." P36 also suffered from the *Forming* difficulty, but did not re-read the problem after initially correctly solving a test case. In the post-session interview, he/she said they did not know why they were required to solve a test case before beginning to code. The only participant to incorrectly solve the first test case was P34, who solved it on the second attempt. He/she also struggled with the *Forming* difficulty as he/she repeatedly attempted to count the number of times there were an equal amount of positive or negative numbers before the input had ended. In the post-session interview, he/she said that solving the test case, "tests our problem skills instead of the computer's to see if we can spot the differences first...it made me count how I was formatting the text 'cause my compiler does it for me." It is clear that P34 did not understand the intervention.

4.2.2 Control Group. The control group, who were not asked to solve a test case before they could begin writing code, naturally separated itself during the qualitative tagging and coding process into two distinct groups: those that reconsidered the prompt at least once and those that did not. Ten out of 17 participants did not once re-read the problem prompt, but only one out of that ten, P07, faced any kind of metacognitive difficulty. Even though four of the ten did not arrive at a correct solution, only P07 failed due to an incorrect conceptual model of the problem (a manifestation of the *Forming* difficulty), while the others all struggled with syntax. The other seven participants in the control group who re-read the prompt more than once were often inclined to go back multiple times looking for clues when they became stuck, with one re-reading only once, four re-reading three times, and one re-reading five times. P18, who re-read the problem prompt five times, faced the *Forming* difficulty, and despite so much time spent re-reading the prompt, also faced the *Dislodging* difficulty as re-reading did not appear to change his/her incorrect conceptual model.

However, metacognitive difficulties involving the participants' conceptual models of the problems were not the only ones encountered. For instance, P17, who re-read the prompt three times, submitted an incorrect solution 13 times (none of which included a loop). This was despite the fact that he/she verbalized their confusion as to Athene not recognizing their loop. None of the error messages that he/she encountered in Athene helped him/her to realize that they had failed to correctly adapt and implement a solution, representing a *Location* difficulty. The others in this group all re-read the problem prompt displaying multiple metacognitive behaviors, including forming a correct conceptual model, but faced syntax issues, some of which were overcome.

5 DISCUSSION

The unexpected results from this study lead to some interesting implications and a call for further research. First, those in the experimental group were much more successful at solving the problem than the control group. The qualitative results suggest that, for those in the experimental group, understanding why the intervention took place seems to correlate with success. Most participants verbalized that the intervention helped them think through the problem, including P31 and P29 who said that it helped them understand the problem or address a wrong idea very early in the problem-solving process.

Second, contrary to our expectations, two participants in the experimental group still thought they were solving a different problem ("More Even or Odd", which they remembered from another part of the course) than they actually were. This behavior was also noted by Prather et al. [36] and was the motivating example for designing this particular intervention. We expected this intervention would prevent students from forming the wrong conceptual model because students were explicitly made to choose what the output should be for a given set of input, which included the words "More Positive," "More Negative," or "Equal". Even more perplexing is that there were no negative numbers used in the input of the intervention test case quiz, so even if they thought they were solving the "More Even or Odd" problem, there was no case where answering *Equal* would have made sense if a participant was trying to solve that problem with the input provided. However, we cannot know how many students would have confused the present problem for another, but were prevented from doing so due to the intervention. Based on the overwhelmingly positive qualitative feedback from the experimental group indicating how much the intervention helped them, it is possible that it helped a few escape this issue. One possible explanation for the described phenomenon is that it is an artifact of the intervention using randomly generated test cases and that some sets of input could be interpreted as from the "More Even or Odd" problem. Therefore, one outstanding question is: *How do randomly generated test cases impact studies like this?* Perhaps if students had to solve two or three test cases that were carefully crafted to expose different gaps in their conceptual models, then it might prevent the *Assumption* difficulty, and perhaps help mitigate against the *Forming* difficulty as well. Overall, there was no clear distinction between the groups in terms of qualitative results, with the experimental group showing difficulty with at least four of the five difficulties (*Assumption, Location, Achievement,* and *Forming*), and the control group demonstrating at least three (*Location, Forming,* and *Dislodging*).

Third, we expected that re-reading the problem prompt would be associated with a higher likelihood of solving the problem for those in the control group, but from our results, that is clearly not the case. In fact, it seems like exactly the opposite. One possible explanation for this effect is that the students who already possess some metacognitive abilities only need to read the prompt once before successfully reinterpreting the prompt and creating an accurate conceptual model. This suggests that re-reading the prompt could be an indicator of metacognitive difficulties. This leads us to another outstanding question: *Is there a correlation between number of times a student re-reads a problem prompt and the number and severity of metacognitive difficulties faced?* Understanding this relationship would provide a better look into how and why students lacking metacognitive abilities are struggling to create correct abstractions and conceptual models of the problems they are asked to solve and could provide a fruitful avenue for future automated assessment tool modification.

6 CONCLUSION

In this paper, we presented a think-aloud study of CS1 students in order to determine if specific modifications to an automated assessment tool would improve metacognitive awareness in novice programmers.

Our quantitative data showed promising results, particularly with a higher completion rate, faster completion time, and fewer attempts required to complete for the experimental group. However, data on the pre- and post-test questions, and results on the test case quiz completion were not conclusive. Nonetheless, qualitative data showed that participants in the experimental group who submitted a correct code solution tended to display and verbalize higher metacognitive skills and behaviors, especially regarding correct conceptual models of the problem.

Other indicators showed mixed results, with some participants demonstrating signs of good metacognitive awareness, but others obviously struggling with several of the metacognitive difficulties that novices face when using automated assessment tools identified by [36] (Table 1). There was no clear distinction between the groups, with the experimental group showing difficulty with at least four of the five difficulties (*Assumption, Location, Achievement,* and *Forming*), and the control group demonstrating at least three (*Location, Forming,* and *Dislodging*).

The primary contribution of this work is two-fold. First, our results indicate that this line of research, although not conclusive, warrants future work. Second, we have identified two specific questions for future work: 1. *How do randomly generated test cases impact studies like this?* and 2. *Is there a correlation between the number of times a student re-reads a problem prompt and the number and severity of metacognitive difficulties faced?*

Our future work includes replicating this work at a larger scale, with higher numbers of participants from multiple diverse institutions. We feel this is required as the results from this study are promising but not conclusive. In addition we aim to work towards answering the two questions set out above.

REFERENCES

[1] Kirsti M Ala-Mutka. 2005. A survey of automated assessment approaches for programming assignments. *Computer science education* 15, 2 (2005), 83–102.

[2] Mousumi Banerjee, Michelle Capozzoli, Laura McSweeney, and Debajyoti Sinha. 1999. Beyond kappa: A review of interrater agreement measures. *Canadian journal of statistics* 27, 1 (1999), 3–23.

[3] Titus Barik, Jim Witschey, Brittany Johnson, and Emerson Murphy-Hill. 2014. Compiler error notifications revisited: an interaction-first approach for helping developers more effectively comprehend and resolve error notifications. In *Companion Proceedings of the 36th International Conference on Software Engineering.* ACM, 536–539.

[4] Theresa Beaubouef and John Mason. 2005. Why the high attrition rate for computer science students: some thoughts and observations. *ACM SIGCSE Bulletin* 37, 2 (2005), 103–106.

[5] Brett A Becker. 2016. A new metric to quantify repeated compiler errors for novice programmers. In *Proceedings of the 2016 ACM Conference on Innovation and Technology in Computer Science Education.* ACM, 296–301.

[6] Brett A Becker, Graham Glanville, Ricardo Iwashima, Claire McDonnell, Kyle Goslin, and Catherine Mooney. 2016. Effective compiler error message enhancement for novice programming students. *Computer Science Education* 26, 2-3 (2016), 148–175.

[7] Brett A Becker, Kyle Goslin, and Graham Glanville. 2018. The Effects of Enhanced Compiler Error Messages on a Syntax Error Debugging Test. In *Proceedings of the 2018 ACM Conference on Innovation and Technology in Computer Science Education.* ACM, 640–645.

[8] Brett A Becker and Catherine Mooney. 2016. Categorizing compiler error messages with principal component analysis. In *12th China-Europe Int'l Symposium on Software Engineering Education (CEISEE 2016), Shenyang, China.* 28–29.

[9] Brett A. Becker, Cormac Murray, Tianyi Tao, Changheng Song, Robert McCartney, and Kate Sanders. 2018. Fix the First, Ignore the Rest: Dealing with Multiple Compiler Error Messages. In *Proceedings of the 49th ACM Technical Symposium on Computer Science Education.* 634–639.

[10] Susan Bergin, Ronan Reilly, and Desmond Traynor. 2005. Examining the role of self-regulated learning on introductory programming performance. In *Proceedings of the first international workshop on Computing education research.* ACM, 81–86.

[11] Paul Denny, Andrew Luxton-Reilly, and Dave Carpenter. 2014. Enhancing syntax error messages appears ineffectual. In *Proceedings of the 2014 conference on Innovation & technology in computer science education.* ACM, 273–278.

[12] Christopher Douce, David Livingstone, and James Orwell. 2005. Automatic test-based assessment of programming: A review. *Journal on Educational Resources in Computing (JERIC)* 5, 3 (2005), 4.

[13] Karl Anders Ericsson and Herbert Alexander Simon. 1993. *Protocol analysis.* MIT press Cambridge, MA.

[14] Anneli Eteläpelto. 1993. Metacognition and the expertise of computer program comprehension. *Scandinavian Journal of Educational Research* 37, 3 (1993), 243–254.

[15] Katrina Falkner, Rebecca Vivian, and Nickolas JG Falkner. 2014. Identifying computer science self-regulated learning strategies. In *Proceedings of the 2014 conference on Innovation & technology in computer science education.* ACM, 291–296.

[16] Thomas Flowers, Curtis A Carver, and James Jackson. 2004. Empowering students and building confidence in novice programmers through Gauntlet. In *Frontiers in Education, 2004. FIE 2004. 34th Annual.* IEEE, T3H–10.

[17] Xun Ge and Susan M Land. 2003. Scaffolding studentsâĂŹ problem-solving processes in an ill-structured task using question prompts and peer interactions. *Educational Technology Research and Development* 51, 1 (2003), 21–38.

[18] Björn Hartmann, Daniel MacDougall, Joel Brandt, and Scott R Klemmer. 2010. What would other programmers do: suggesting solutions to error messages. In *Proceedings of the SIGCHI Conference on Human Factors in Computing Systems.* ACM, 1019–1028.

[19] Matthias Hauswirth and Andrea Adamoli. 2017. Metacognitive calibration when learning to program. In *Proceedings of the 17th Koli Calling Conference on Computing Education Research.* ACM, 50–59.

[20] Jack Hollingsworth. 1960. Automatic graders for programming classes. *Commun. ACM* 3, 10 (1960), 528–529.

[21] Petri Ihantola, Tuukka Ahoniemi, Ville Karavirta, and Otto Seppälä. 2010. Review of recent systems for automatic assessment of programming assignments. In *Proceedings of the 10th Koli Calling International Conference on Computing Education Research.* ACM, 86–93.

[22] Matthew C Jadud. 2006. *An exploration of novice compilation behaviour in BlueJ.* Ph.D. Dissertation. University of Kent.

[23] Antti-Juhani Kaijanaho and Ville Tirronen. 2018. Fixed versus Growth Mindset Does not Seem to Matter Much: A Prospective Observational Study in Two Late Bachelor level Computer Science Courses. In *Proceedings of the 2018 ACM Conference on International Computing Education Research.* ACM, 11–20.

[24] Dastyni Loksa and Andrew J Ko. 2016. The role of self-regulation in programming problem solving process and success. In *Proceedings of the 2016 ACM Conference on International Computing Education Research.* ACM, 83–91.

[25] Dastyni Loksa, Andrew J Ko, Will Jernigan, Alannah Oleson, Christopher J Mendez, and Margaret M Burnett. 2016. Programming, Problem Solving, and Self-Awareness: Effects of Explicit Guidance. In *Proceedings of the 2016 CHI Conference on Human Factors in Computing Systems.* ACM, 1449–1461.

[26] Andrew Luxton-Reilly, Simon, Ibrihim Albluwi, Brett A. Becker, Michail Giannakos, Amruth N. Kumar, Linda Ott, James Paterson, Michael James Scott, Judy Sheard, and Claudia Szabo. 2018. Introductory Programming: A Systematic Literature Review. In *Proceedings of the 2018 ITiCSE Conference on Working Group Reports (ITiCSE-WGR '18).* ACM, New York, NY, USA. *in press.*

[27] Kathleen M MacQueen, Eleanor McLellan, Kelly Kay, and Bobby Milstein. 1998. Codebook development for team-based qualitative analysis. *CAM Journal* 10, 2 (1998), 31–36.

[28] Murali Mani and Quamrul Mazumder. 2013. Incorporating metacognition into learning. In *Proceeding of the 44th ACM technical symposium on Computer science education.* ACM, 53–58.

[29] Guillaume Marceau, Kathi Fisler, and Shriram Krishnamurthi. 2011. Measuring the effectiveness of error messages designed for novice programmers. In *Proceedings of the 42nd ACM technical symposium on Computer science education.* ACM, 499–504.

[30] Guillaume Marceau, Kathi Fisler, and Shriram Krishnamurthi. 2011. Mind your language: on novices' interactions with error messages. In *Proceedings of the 10th SIGPLAN symposium on New ideas, new paradigms, and reflections on programming and software.* ACM, 3–18.

[31] Janet Metcalfe and Arthur P Shimamura. 1994. *Metacognition: Knowing about knowing.* MIT press.

[32] Laurie Murphy, Gary Lewandowski, Renée McCauley, Beth Simon, Lynda Thomas, and Carol Zander. 2008. Debugging: the good, the bad, and the quirky–a qualitative analysis of novices' strategies. In *ACM SIGCSE Bulletin*, Vol. 40. ACM.

[33] Raymond Pettit, John Homer, Roger Gee, Susan Mengel, and Adam Starbuck. 2015. An empirical study of iterative improvement in programming assignments. In *Proceedings of the 46th ACM Technical Symposium on Computer Science Education.* ACM, 410–415.

[34] Raymond Pettit and James Prather. 2017. Automated Assessment Tools: Too Many Cooks, Not Enough Collaboration. *J. Comput. Sci. Coll.* 32, 4 (April 2017), 113–121. http://dl.acm.org/citation.cfm?id=3055338.3079060

[35] Raymond S Pettit, John Homer, and Roger Gee. 2017. Do Enhanced Compiler Error Messages Help Students?: Results Inconclusive. In *Proceedings of the 2017 ACM SIGCSE Technical Symposium on Computer Science Education.* ACM, 465–470.

[36] James Prather, Raymond Pettit, Kayla Holcomb McMurry, Alani Peters, John Homer, and Maxine Cohen. 2018. Metacognitive Difficulties Faced by Novice Programmers in Automated Assessment Tools. In *Proceedings of the 2018 ACM Conference on International Computing Education Research.* ACM, 74–82.

[37] James Prather, Raymond Pettit, Kayla Holcomb McMurry, Alani Peters, John Homer, Nevan Simone, and Maxine Cohen. 2017. On Novices' Interaction with Compiler Error Messages: A Human Factors Approach. In *Proceedings of the 2017 ACM Conference on International Computing Education Research.* ACM, 74–82.

[38] Ido Roll, Natasha G Holmes, James Day, and Doug Bonn. 2012. Evaluating metacognitive scaffolding in guided invention activities. *Instructional science* 40, 4 (2012), 691–710.

[39] Jeffrey Rubin and Dana Chisnell. 2008. *Handbook of usability testing: how to plan, design and conduct effective tests* (2 ed.). John Wiley & Sons.

[40] Johnny Saldaña. 2015. *The coding manual for qualitative researchers.* Sage.

[41] Tom Schorsch. 1995. CAP: an automated self-assessment tool to check Pascal programs for syntax, logic and style errors. In *ACM SIGCSE Bulletin*, Vol. 27. ACM, 168–172.

[42] Michael J Scott and Gheorghita Ghinea. 2014. On the domain-specificity of mindsets: The relationship between aptitude beliefs and programming practice. *IEEE Transactions on Education* 57, 3 (2014), 169–174.

[43] Teresa M Shaft. 1995. Helping programmers understand computer programs: the use of metacognition. *ACM SIGMIS Database* 26, 4 (1995), 25–46.

[44] Donna Teague, Malcolm Corney, Alireza Ahadi, and Raymond Lister. 2013. A qualitative think aloud study of the early neo-piagetian stages of reasoning in novice programmers. In *Proceedings of the Fifteenth Australasian Computing Education Conference-Volume 136.* Australian Computer Society, Inc., 87–95.

[45] Dwayne Towell and Brent Reeves. 2009. From Walls to Steps: Using online automatic homework checking tools to improve learning in introductory programming courses. (2009).

[46] V Javier Traver. 2010. On compiler error messages: what they say and what they mean. *Advances in Human-Computer Interaction* 2010 (2010).

[47] Christopher Watson and Frederick WB Li. 2014. Failure rates in introductory programming revisited. In *Proceedings of the 2014 conference on Innovation & technology in computer science education.* ACM, 39–44.

[48] Christopher Watson, Frederick WB Li, and Jamie L Godwin. 2012. Bluefix: Using crowd-sourced feedback to support programming students in error diagnosis and repair. In *International Conference on Web-Based Learning.* Springer, 228–239.

[49] Jacqueline Whalley and Nadia Kasto. 2014. A qualitative think-aloud study of novice programmers' code writing strategies. In *Proceedings of the 2014 conference on Innovation & technology in computer science education.* ACM, 279–284.

The Error Landscape: Characterizing the Mistakes of Novice Programmers

Rebecca Smith
Rice University
Houston, Texas
rjs@rice.edu

Scott Rixner
Rice University
Houston, Texas
rixner@rice.edu

ABSTRACT

The software development process often follows a circuitous path, littered with mistakes and backtracks. This is particularly true for novice programmers, who typically navigate through a variety of errors en route to their final solution. This paper presents a quantitative analysis of a large dataset of Python programs written by novice students. The analysis paints a multifaceted picture of the errors that students encounter, providing insight into the distribution, duration, and evolution of these errors. Ultimately, this paper aims to incite further conversation on the mistakes made by novice programmers, and to inform the decisions instructors make as they help students overcome these mistakes.

KEYWORDS

Education; Runtime errors; Syntax errors; Novice programmers

ACM Reference Format:

Rebecca Smith and Scott Rixner. 2019. The Error Landscape:, Characterizing the Mistakes of Novice Programmers. In *Proceedings of the 50th ACM Technical Symposium on Computer Science Education (SIGCSE '19), February 27-March 2, 2019, Minneapolis, MN, USA.* ACM, New York, NY, USA, 7 pages. https://doi.org/10.1145/3287324.3287394

1 INTRODUCTION

Novice programmers make lots of mistakes along the way to writing correct programs. They may grapple with certain errors early in the development process, dwell on others over multiple consecutive versions of code, or even revert to prior errors. Instructors likely have opinions about the errors made by novices, informed by experience and anecdotal evidence. Quantitative studies that identify patterns in the way that novice programmers experience errors can help instructors evaluate the veracity of those opinions so they can validate or adjust their teaching methods.

A wealth of past work has explored the question of which errors arise most frequently [1–6, 8–19, 21, 23]. However, such work has typically studied Java programs, with a primary focus on syntactical errors that can be detected by the compiler [1–6, 13, 14, 18, 21, 23]. There have been very few studies that examine other types of errors, and even fewer that investigate other languages, such as Python. Because Python has become a popular language in introductory programming courses [20], characterizing the errors made by novice Python programmers can provide valuable insight into the development process of modern introductory students. Moreover, interpreted languages such as Python exhibit a rich variety of runtime errors; yet, such runtime errors have received substantially less scrutiny than compile-time errors [7, 12, 19].

Furthermore, past work has largely focused on quantifying the frequency distribution of errors. However, other facets of the error landscape, including the duration and evolution of errors, merit further exploration in order to provide a more extensive characterization of novice mistakes. Although several Java studies have expanded their scope to investigate factors such as duration — in time [2, 4, 9–11, 14] or number of compilations [8, 15] —, reoccurrence frequency [11, 14], and correlations between error frequency and student success [1, 3, 6, 10], similar data does not exist for Python. Additionally, none of these past studies have focused on the progression of errors.

This paper presents a quantitative analysis of the distribution, duration, and evolution of the errors made by novice Python programmers. This extends and augments the prior work in three key ways. First, it focuses on one of the common programming languages that novice programmers often encounter early. Second, it presents a holistic study of syntax, runtime, and logical errors in combination, for a more comprehensive profile of the error landscape. Finally, it addresses temporal and relational questions such as which errors students tend to encounter earlier in the development process and which pairs of errors students frequently transition between as they work towards their final solution. Some of the specific research questions that this paper addresses include:

- How common is each type of error?
- How often does a program exhibit varied errors across tests?
- How far into the development process does each type of error typically occur?
- For how many versions are students typically stuck?
- How often does each type of error typically re-occur?
- Between which errors do students most often transition?
- How often do students backtrack?
- How often does each type of error persist in the final version?

While this paper focuses on the above questions, the data presented could also be used to explore other aspects of the error landscape.

2 METHODOLOGY

This paper characterizes a large corpus of student implementations of eight programming problems. These eight functions were drawn from four different programming assignments (modules) across

SIGCSE '19, February 27-March 2, 2019, Minneapolis, MN, USA

ACM ISBN 978-1-4503-5890-3/19/02...$15.00
https://doi.org/10.1145/3287324.3287394

Table 1: Functions Under Test

Func. Index	Function: Module Name	Function: Function Name	Num Test Cases	Num Impls	Num Hashes	Min Hash Length	Avg. Hash Length	Max Hash Length
1	DNA Alignment	`build_scoring_matrix`	2	4450	1473	1	3.02	135
2	Graph Theory	`compute_in_degrees`	4	18002	6975	1	2.58	68
3	Graph Theory	`in_degree_distribution`	5	20055	7165	1	2.80	49
4	Graph Theory	`make_complete_graph`	3	15447	6309	1	2.45	55
5	Yahtzee	`expected_value`	12	49322	11381	1	4.33	115
6	Yahtzee	`gen_all_holds`	6	49137	10742	1	4.56	346
7	Yahtzee	`score`	9	33990	10728	1	3.17	162
8	2048 Game	`merge`	31	146508	41009	1	3.57	176

Table 2: Test Results

Func. Index	Version Data: Impls Freq.	Incorrect, incl. Err. Freq.	Incorrect, incl. Err. Pct.	Erroneous Freq.	Erroneous Pct.	RT Erroneous Freq.	RT Erroneous Pct.	Mixed Errors Freq.	Mixed Errors Pct.	Transition Data: Regressions Freq.	Regressions Pct.	Error Swaps Freq.	Error Swaps Pct.
1	4450	2813	(63.21%)	1246	(28.00%)	944	(21.21%)	17	(0.38%)	130	(2.92%)	0	(0%)
2	18002	7759	(43.10%)	4505	(25.02%)	3508	(19.49%)	235	(1.31%)	1019	(5.66%)	75	(0.42%)
3	20055	11220	(55.95%)	6341	(31.32%)	5347	(26.66%)	550	(2.74%)	1486	(7.41%)	102	(0.51%)
4	15447	6737	(43.61%)	3071	(19.88%)	2002	(12.96%)	28	(0.18%)	646	(4.18%)	49	(0.32%)
5	49322	32877	(66.66%)	15762	(31.96%)	14217	(28.82%)	1012	(2.05%)	2738	(5.55%)	479	(0.97%)
6	49137	35148	(71.53%)	14647	(29.81%)	12358	(25.35%)	538	(1.09%)	4236	(8.62%)	136	(0.28%)
7	33990	17240	(50.72%)	8423	(24.78%)	7565	(22.26%)	223	(0.66%)	1615	(4.75%)	429	(1.26%)
8	146508	82521	(56.33%)	40603	(27.71%)	32095	(21.91%)	1739	(1.19%)	12974	(8.86%)	4330	(2.96%)
Total	336906	196315		94598		78136		4342		24844		4236	

three massive open online courses (MOOCs) comprising a Coursera specialization on introductory Python programming. Student implementations were aggregated across multiple iterations of the courses.

Students developed their code in CodeSkulptor, a browser-based IDE [24]. In CodeSkulptor, students can save their progress using a button in the GUI or Ctrl+S. The initial save generates a unique file in cloud storage named in the form `<hash>_<version>`. The `<version>` is initialized to 0 and incremented on each subsequent save; the `<hash>` remains the same across saves. Thus, each hash approximates a single student's end-to-end development process.

Table 1 shows, for each function, the total number of implementations, the number of unique hashes to which these implementations belonged, and the min, average, and max hash "lengths" (number of versions). It assigns each function an index, which will be used in subsequent tables for brevity. In total, the corpus contained over 330,000 implementations from over 95,000 development chains.

The exhaustive approach to data collection helped preserve external validity by avoiding potential threats such as selection bias. However, because files are anonymous, the precise demographics of the students responsible for developing these programs is unknown. In general, the students enrolled in the three MOOCs represented a very heterogeneous population, hailing from 180 countries and ranging in age from 16 to 94, with an average age of 39. That this study represents such a diverse set of learners is arguably a strength; that said, it is a potential threat to internal validity if these results were applied to a more traditional population of college students, which would likely exhibit different demographics.

Implementations were evaluated using auto-generated test suites that have been shown to provide better coverage than carefully hand-crafted tests [22]. Table 1 indicates the number of tests used for each function. Note that this has a multiplicative effect on the dataset: within a single version, different tests may yield different errors, so the frequencies and percents in Section 3 are relative to the number of implementations multiplied by the number of tests.

3 RESULTS & ANALYSIS

Table 2 gives an overview of the test results. The sub-columns under "Version Data" classify implementations into five overlapping categories, each of which is a subset of the previous category. First, the set of all implementations ("Impls"). Second, incorrect implementations, *i.e.* those that failed at least one test due to an error or incorrect result ("Incorrect, incl. Err.)". Third, programs with either compile-time or runtime errors ("Erroneous"). Fourth, those which contained runtime errors ("RT Erroneous"). Last, implementations which exhibited multiple different runtime errors simultaneously – *i.e.*, different errors on different tests ("Mixed Errors").

The sub-columns under "Transition Data" count patterns within pairs of consecutive versions belonging to the same hash. First, the number of regressions: transitions to a higher number of failed tests than in the previous version. Second, the number of error swaps: transitions where the student fixed at least one test, but simultaneously broke at least one other test that previously passed. Error swaps were infrequent and correlated with test suite size

Table 3: Reasons for Failure

		Individual Function Distributions (Impls)								Aggregate Distribution			
										Normalized			Unnorm.
		1	2	3	4	5	6	7	8	Avg. (Impls)	Stdev (Impls)	Avg. (Hashes)	Avg. (Impls)
Runtime Errors	AssertionError	0%	0.05%	0.03%	0.20%	0.06%	0%	0.01%	0.02%	0.05%	0.07%	0.09%	0.03%
	AttributeError	3.18%	1.72%	1.90%	2.13%	1.85%	2.22%	1.83%	0.56%	1.92%	0.72%	2.57%	1.09%
	EOFError	0%	0%	0%	0%	0%	0%	0%	0.00%	0.00%	0.00%	0.00%	0.00%
	Exception	0%	0%	0%	0.04%	0.00%	0%	0.01%	0%	0.01%	0.01%	0.01%	0.00%
	ImportError	2.87%	3.78%	2.68%	4.50%	1.09%	1.41%	2.10%	2.54%	2.62%	1.14%	2.65%	2.06%
	IndexError	0.26%	2.46%	1.28%	0.27%	5.65%	1.79%	15.62%	8.62%	4.49%	5.34%	6.62%	7.21%
	KeyError	2.75%	15.19%	8.51%	0.64%	2.25%	0.27%	6.03%	0.01%	4.46%	5.26%	5.31%	1.18%
	MemoryError	0%	0%	0.00%	0%	0%	0%	0%	0%	0.00%	0.00%	0.00%	0.00%
	NameError	7.60%	10.03%	10.22%	10.41%	11.17%	8.04%	11.72%	10.94%	10.02%	1.46%	10.37%	10.89%
	OverflowError	0%	0%	0%	0%	0.01%	0.00%	0.02%	0%	0.00%	0.01%	0.01%	0.00%
	RuntimeError	0.07%	0.16%	0.77%	0.12%	0.10%	9.09%	0.01%	0.12%	1.31%	3.16%	1.47%	0.39%
	StopIteration	0%	0%	0%	0%	0%	0%	0%	0.00%	0.00%	0.00%	0.00%	0.00%
	TypeError	14.03%	7.98%	9.84%	9.13%	11.97%	9.31%	4.91%	4.16%	8.92%	3.30%	9.54%	7.06%
	UnboundLocalError	0.42%	1.22%	0.80%	0.83%	1.60%	1.04%	1.05%	1.63%	1.07%	0.41%	1.96%	1.57%
	ValueError	0.15%	0.30%	2.48%	0.12%	1.44%	0.55%	0.48%	0.51%	0.75%	0.81%	1.54%	0.86%
	ZeroDivisionError	0%	0.06%	0.48%	0.07%	0.99%	0.01%	0%	0.01%	0.20%	0.36%	0.64%	0.34%
	All Runtime Errors	31.33%	42.94%	39.00%	28.45%	38.18%	33.75%	43.78%	29.11%	35.82%	6.02%	42.79%	32.69%
Other	SyntaxError	11.09%	16.46%	11.49%	21.01%	6.13%	7.57%	6.32%	14.62%	11.94%	5.28%	9.43%	11.57%
	Incorrect Result	57.58%	40.45%	49.25%	49.26%	54.15%	51.42%	49.33%	50.91%	50.29%	4.92%	46.07%	51.81%
	Timeout	0%	0.15%	0.25%	1.28%	1.55%	7.26%	0.56%	5.37%	2.05%	2.73%	1.17%	3.93%

($r = 0.97$). Regressions occurred anywhere from 2.92–8.86% of the time, and were more common for functions that had a larger test suite and/or a larger total percentage of incorrect implementations.

3.1 Error Frequency Distribution

Table 3 presents a detailed breakdown of why each implementation failed on each test. As seen in Tables 1 and 2, the number of total implementations varied widely across functions. Since results are on a per-test basis, variance in the test set sizes compounded any disparities in the raw tallies. Thus, for ease of comparison, results are reported as a percentage of the product of the total number of implementations and the number of tests. Note that 0% indicates a true zero result, whereas 0.00% indicates a round to zero.

The aggregate results on the right-hand side of the table include four values. First, the "normalized" average percentage of files in which a given type of error occurred, which give equal weight to each function. Second, the corresponding standard deviation between the per-function values. Next, the average percentage of *hashes* that contained at least one incidence of a given error. In general, the per-hash occurrence rates were slightly higher than the corresponding per-implementation rates. However, per-hash occurrence rates of SyntaxErrors and timeouts were lower than the per-file rates, indicating that these errors were more heavily concentrated in a smaller number of students' development chains. The final column is the "unnormalized" average, computed from the raw frequencies. The normalized average is arguably a more accurate representation, as it represents each function's failure profile equally. The unnormalized average is skewed heavily towards functions that have a larger number of implementations and/or test cases. Thus, all ensuing discussions will focus on the normalized average, and refer to it simply as the "average" for brevity.

Figure 1: Runtime Error Duration (Any Error)

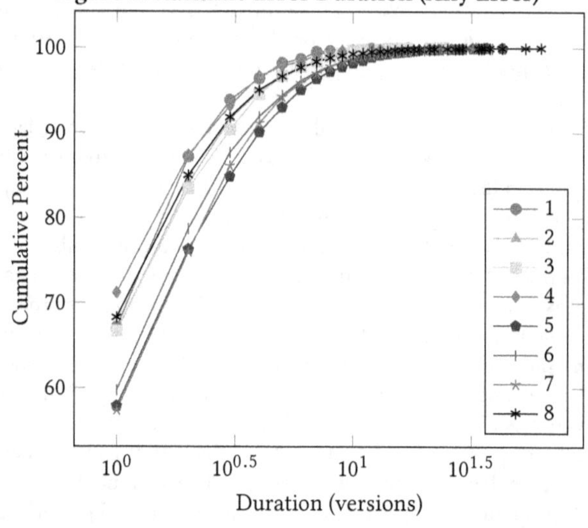

Individual runtime errors are at the top of the table, followed by the total percentage of failure attributable to any kind of runtime error. Other possible reasons for failure include SyntaxErrors, timeouts (typically due to infinite loops), or incorrect results.

Across the board, the most common reason for failure was an incorrect result, with an average rate of occurrence of 50.29%. Taken

Table 4: Runtime Error Duration (Same Error)

	Duration (Consecutive Versions)				
	Min	Max	Normalized		Unnorm.
			Avg.	Stdev	Avg.
AssertionError	1	6	1.59	0.41	1.94
AttributeError	1	24	1.44	0.17	1.43
EOFError	1	1	1	0	1
Exception	1	2	1.58	0.5	1.44
ImportError	1	63	1.50	0.25	1.56
IndexError	1	44	1.92	0.31	1.81
KeyError	1	21	1.85	0.43	2.12
MemoryError	1	1	1	0	1
NameError	1	43	1.55	0.17	1.58
OverflowError	1	5	1.43	0.37	1.57
RuntimeError	1	46	1.57	0.45	2.10
StopIteration	1	1	1	0	1
TypeError	1	43	1.59	0.13	1.66
UnboundLocalError	1	32	1.34	0.08	1.30
ValueError	1	14	1.66	0.48	1.79
ZeroDivisionError	1	43	1.92	0.77	1.86
Any Runtime Error	1	63	1.86	0.24	1.85

collectively, runtime errors were the next most common reason for failure (35.82%), with the biggest contributors being NameErrors (10.02%), and TypeErrors (8.92%). However, no individual type of runtime error occurred as often as SyntaxErrors, which on average accounted for 11.94% of failures. SyntaxErrors also exhibited the second-greatest standard deviation, with occurrence rates ranging from 6.13%–21.01%. In fact, in half of the functions, at least one type of runtime error — NameError, TypeError, or both — occurred more frequently than SyntaxErrors.

Certain types of runtime errors also exhibited high standard deviations, including IndexErrors (5.34%) and KeyErrors (5.26%). IndexErrors naturally spiked in functions that made heavy use of Python lists, such as functions 7 and 8, while KeyErrors cropped up in functions that frequently accessed Python dictionaries, like functions 2 and 3. Other types of errors appeared with striking consistency. For example, the rate of occurrence of NameErrors was nearly always close to 10%. Clearly, students often encountered NameErrors regardless of the problem they were solving.

3.2 Error Duration

Error duration is also an interesting avenue of exploration. When a student encounters an error, for how many consecutive versions are they typically stuck? Figure 1 displays the per-function cumulative distributions of the number of consecutive versions for which the student was stuck on *any* runtime error. For the sake of space, the error-specific results are summarized by the statistics in Table 4, rather than including individual plots for each type of error.

These results indicate that most students remained stuck on a runtime error for just one version at a time. Figure 1 reveals this to be true for any error 57.38–71.20% of the time, depending on the function in question, with an average of 64.36%. The plot then exhibits a pattern of exponential decay; runtime errors lingered for two, three, four, or five consecutive versions an average of 17.90%,

Figure 2: Regression Frequency

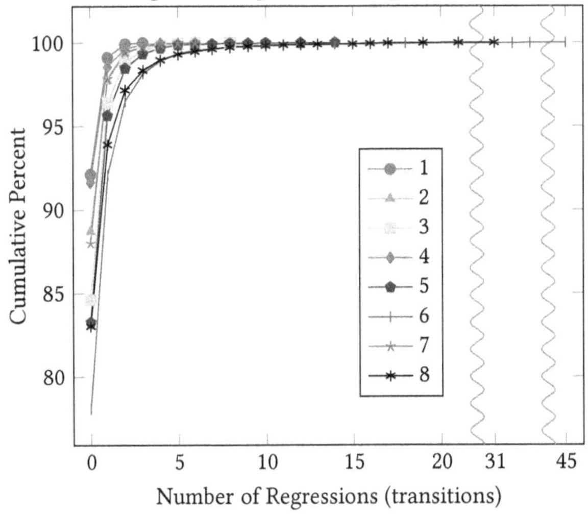

7.69%, 3.87%, and 2.16% of the time, respectively. However, the curve has a long tail, with several instances of students remaining stuck for a much longer duration — up to a max length of 93. This same pattern held true for the durations of specific error types, with the values shifted slightly higher. For example, the average probability of an individual runtime error being resolved within a single version ranged from 63.52–74.42% of the time.

Examining each type of error independently, as in Table 4, reveals that certain errors — those with low average durations — tended to be resolved more quickly than others. The low average durations of UnboundLocalErrors, AttributeErrors, ImportErrors, and NameErrors reflect the fact that they were resolved within one version an average of 83.2%, 76.5%, 75.6%, and 75.2% of the time, respectively. Others, such as RuntimeErrors, KeyErrors, ValueErrors, and IndexErrors proved more difficult for students to track down. For these, resolution was reached within one version on average only 52.0%, 56.1%, 63.8%, and 64.3% of the time, respectively.

3.3 Error Evolution

Another facet of interest is the evolution of errors during development. The development process is not linear; students may re-encounter the same types of errors multiple times, or even introduce new errors that cause previously-passed tests to fail. Table 5 and Figure 2 look at re-occurrence and regression, respectively. The sub-columns under "Re-Occurrence Frequency" in Table 5 average the error re-occurrence frequency across the eight functions, where the re-occurrence frequency is defined as the number of distinct times that an error appears. Multiple consecutive versions with the same error count as a single appearance; only non-consecutive instances are deemed distinct. In general, this table shows that students typically do not re-encounter the same type of error on many separate occasions during the development process; however, they are most likely to re-encounter TypeErrors and NameErrors.

Figure 2 plots the number of regressions per hash as a cumulative distribution, where regression is defined as moving from a state of m failed tests to a state of $n > m$ failed tests. Much like duration,

Table 5: Error Occurrence: Frequency and Position

		Re-Occurrence Frequency			Average Point of Occurrence			% Occurrence as Final State		
		Normalized		Unnorm.	Normalized		Unnorm.	Normalized		Unnorm.
		Average	Stdev	Average	Average	Stdev	Average	Average	Stdev	Average
Runtime Errors	`AssertionError`	1.15	0.25	1.22	10.65%	14.12%	20.00%	0.02%	0.03%	0.00%
	`AttributeError`	1.13	0.08	1.15	28.43%	5.40%	28.93%	0.36%	0.41%	0.11%
	`EOFError`	1	0	1	0%	0%	0%	0.00%	0%	0.00%
	`Exception`	1	0	1	8.58%	17.16%	11.44%	0%	0%	0%
	`ImportError`	1.11	0.07	1.15	15.58%	5.94%	18.13%	1.14%	0.88%	0.72%
	`IndexError`	1.12	0.10	1.25	24.37%	7.66%	29.11%	0.85%	0.93%	1.47%
	`KeyError`	1.10	0.06	1.09	23.43%	7.20%	20.57%	0.90%	0.84%	0.21%
	`MemoryError`	1	0	1	0%	0%	0%	0.00%	0%	0.00%
	`NameError`	1.16	0.08	1.18	24.44%	3.16%	24.78%	2.25%	0.81%	2.47%
	`OverflowError`	1	0	1	40.11%	23.13%	31.01%	0.00%	0.00%	0.00%
	`RuntimeError`	1.12	0.09	1.18	31.90%	15.56%	30.14%	0.34%	0.91%	0.12%
	`StopIteration`	1	0	1	18.44%	0%	18.44%	0.00%	0%	0.00%
	`TypeError`	1.17	0.13	1.20	21.17%	5.56%	26.91%	1.76%	0.96%	1.00%
	`UnboundLocalError`	1.11	0.06	1.09	32.73%	4.76%	31.31%	0.16%	0.10%	0.25%
	`ValueError`	1.15	0.10	1.15	23.34%	9.66%	30.01%	0.19%	0.24%	0.12%
	`ZeroDivisionError`	1.07	0.07	1.12	21.26%	13.45%	28.72%	0.07%	0.11%	0.03%
Other	`SyntaxError`	1.27	0.11	1.38	22.36%	4.96%	25.92%	0%	0%	0%
	Incorrect Result	1.24	0.11	1.34	18.78%	3.89%	21.37%	12.24%	4.61%	10.48%
	Timeout	1.21	0.10	1.23	32.29%	6.24%	31.54%	0.76%	1.35%	0.97%

the regression distribution is heavily skewed towards small values and roughly exhibits a pattern of exponential decay. Because of this, there are breaks in the x-axis in Figure 2 to allow for plotting outliers on the high end of the spectrum without unduly crowding the low end. For every function, over 78% of hashes exhibited no regressions, and over 92% had one or fewer regressions.

Further, Table 5 explores the question of how far into the development process certain errors tended to occur, as well as the likelihood of a given type of error remaining unresolved in the final version. The sub-columns under "Average Point of Occurrence" quantify the average relative point of occurrence of each error type. This heuristic was collected by taking the sequence of states for each hash for each test, filtering out correct results, collapsing consecutive instances of the same state into a single instance, and then defining the relative point of occurrence of the ith element in the sequence of length n as i/n. Relative, rather than absolute, point of occurrence was used to normalize across hashes of varying lengths.

As an example, the value of 0% for `EOFError` indicates that it only appeared as the first error encountered, and once resolved was never seen again. On the other hand, certain errors tended to arise later in students' progressions, such as `OverflowErrors` (40.11%).

Additionally, the sub-columns under "% Occurrence as Final State" count the number of times each type of error appeared in the final version of a student's code. This data indicates that logical errors (incorrect results) were by far the most likely to remain, accounting for 12.24% of final states. In contrast, not a single final version contained a `SyntaxError`. Runtime errors were also unlikely to linger, though certain types such as `NameErrors` (2.25%) and `TypeErrors` (1.76%) persisted with slightly higher frequency.

Finally, Tables 6 and 7 examine how errors changed between versions. These tables represent first-order Markov chains with state transitions between subsequent versions on the same hash. In each table, the leftmost column defines pre-transition states, the topmost row defines post-transition states, and the value within a given (row, column) is the probability of transitioning from that row's state to that column's state. Error types with an overall frequency $\leq 0.01\%$ (as in Table 3) were omitted for the sake of space.

Table 6 adopts a fine-grained focus on inter-error transitions, eliding transitions into error-free terminating states (*i.e.*, incorrect result or correct result). It also collapses consecutive versions that contained the same error, eliminating self-loops, as denoted by asterisks along the diagonal. Instead, it examines only those transitions that ended in a different error or timeout state. Amongst these, it computes the probability of each specific inter-error transition.

These results are influenced by overall incidence rates, with common errors such as `SyntaxErrors` and `NameErrors` being probable destinations for all. Still, certain transitions occurred with notably high frequency. For instance, timeouts and incorrect results transitioned to `SyntaxErrors` especially often: 42.94% and 31.10% of the time, respectively. Others, like `ZeroDivisionErrors` (6.71%) and `RuntimeErrors` (10.10%), were less likely to make this transition.

`KeyErrors` were consistently a common destination, but accounted for a particularly high percentage of transitions from `IndexErrors` (14.07%), `TypeErrors` (14.00%), and `NameErrors` (13.68%). `ValueErrors` were a less common destination, but transition rates to `ValueErrors` from `ZeroDivisionErrors` (11.47%) and `IndexErrors` (4.84%) were notably high — more than double the transition rates from the next-highest initial states.

Table 7 bins the possible destinations into several coarse-grained categories: the same state ("No Change"), any *different* error state ("New Error"), timeout, incorrect result, and correct result. Across the board, the most common "transition" was remaining in the same

Table 6: Markov Chain: Fine-Grained

Initial State	Next State: Assert.	Attr.	Import	Index	Key	Name	Runtime	Type	Unbound	Value	ZDiv.	Syntax	Timeout
Assert.	*	0.00%	0.00%	0.99%	0.00%	0.00%	0.00%	67.07%	0.00%	0.00%	0.00%	22.57%	9.37%
Attr.	0.00%	*	1.55%	5.86%	6.54%	20.43%	3.00%	37.48%	2.25%	1.37%	0.23%	17.74%	3.54%
Import	0.00%	4.43%	*	8.51%	12.60%	29.13%	1.98%	28.12%	0.20%	0.84%	0.44%	11.42%	2.33%
Index	0.00%	5.60%	1.59%	*	14.07%	21.25%	1.94%	18.73%	2.99%	4.84%	0.26%	23.73%	5.00%
Key	0.00%	5.59%	1.11%	6.02%	*	25.16%	2.98%	16.22%	2.86%	1.18%	0.49%	24.38%	14.01%
Name	0.09%	7.76%	2.74%	8.90%	13.68%	*	2.65%	26.99%	4.21%	1.77%	0.51%	25.86%	4.83%
Runtime	0.00%	13.32%	2.44%	2.39%	5.86%	16.44%	*	35.20%	2.84%	1.97%	0.00%	10.10%	9.43%
Type	0.10%	9.48%	1.68%	13.43%	14.00%	22.84%	2.78%	*	2.93%	1.47%	0.71%	26.04%	4.53%
Unbound	0.00%	5.93%	0.35%	6.21%	8.32%	27.24%	1.69%	18.96%	*	1.92%	0.43%	24.73%	4.22%
Value	0.00%	4.36%	0.37%	6.97%	6.17%	18.49%	1.44%	20.41%	7.62%	*	2.76%	22.95%	8.46%
ZDiv.	0.00%	0.00%	0.00%	5.09%	4.26%	13.50%	0.00%	29.84%	0.61%	11.47%	*	6.71%	28.52%
Syntax	0.03%	7.17%	2.67%	9.58%	10.05%	30.85%	1.97%	26.33%	3.76%	1.69%	0.36%	*	5.53%
Timeout	0.03%	6.45%	0.32%	10.96%	3.62%	12.99%	1.90%	14.32%	3.03%	2.28%	1.16%	42.94%	*
Incorrect	0.01%	5.00%	2.02%	6.58%	5.97%	19.72%	2.22%	18.31%	3.62%	1.34%	0.39%	31.10%	3.72%

Table 7: Markov Chain: Coarse-Grained

Initial State	Next State: No Change	New Error	Timeout	Incorrect Result	Correct Result
Assert.	43.39%	4.49%	1.15%	26.19%	24.78%
Attr.	33.35%	19.46%	0.85%	23.39%	22.94%
Import	46.00%	6.29%	0.23%	10.68%	36.80%
Index	53.22%	9.21%	0.64%	18.17%	18.76%
Key	51.45%	10.71%	2.61%	14.06%	21.17%
Name	40.91%	13.64%	0.73%	17.30%	27.42%
Runtime	33.81%	9.82%	0.85%	24.32%	31.20%
Type	42.69%	12.73%	0.67%	20.65%	23.26%
Unbound	28.03%	20.74%	0.94%	22.88%	27.42%
Value	41.02%	12.43%	1.13%	26.37%	19.04%
ZDiv.	49.19%	11.88%	7.16%	10.65%	21.11%
Syntax	35.73%	18.21%	1.04%	22.91%	22.11%
Timeout	46.64%	13.52%	*	18.62%	21.22%
Incorrect	57.98%	13.65%	0.59%	*	27.78%
Correct	89.07%	6.97%	0.25%	3.71%	*

state. Unsurprisingly, of all initial states, a correct result was least likely to change – though 10.93% of the time students did break previously-working code. Incorrect results were also quite likely to remain the same; it seems that students took longer to fix logical errors than Python errors. Table 7 also reveals which states were most likely to transition directly to a correct result. The clear leader in this category was the `ImportError`, transitioning to correct 36.80% of the time. In contrast, `IndexErrors` and `ValueErrors` had transition probabilities of 18.76% and 19.04%, respectively, indicating that they were less likely to precede a working solution.

4 CONCLUSION

This paper has characterized the errors that occurred in more than 330,000 Python implementations of eight functions by novice programmers, which were drawn from over 95,000 unique chains of development. The discussion in Section 3 highlighted some of the most notable results, providing insight into the frequency, duration, and evolution of errors. Certain clear patterns emerged, pointing to areas that merit additional attention by instructors and researchers alike. Future studies should aim to tease out the underlying reasons behind these patterns to better inform the decisions instructors make as they help students overcome these mistakes.

As an example, `TypeErrors` were not only one of most frequently-occurring runtime errors, but were also the most likely to re-occur and one of the most likely to linger in the final version. While further investigation might offer insights into the specific misconceptions students hold, these preliminary results already motivate additional attention to ensuring that students have a solid understanding of type theory, even (and perhaps especially) when using a dynamically-typed language like Python. Other types of errors cropped up less frequently, but persisted longer when they did appear, such as `IndexErrors` and `KeyErrors`. For such errors, instructors would do well to educate students not only on how to avoid them, but on effective debugging practices. `SyntaxErrors` were common, yet disproportionately concentrated in a smaller subset of the hashes; to remedy this imbalance, instructors may need to identify those students that struggle with syntax and provide targeted instruction.

These are just three examples of the pedagogical implications of the results presented in this paper. Moreover, while this paper highlighted many of the most striking results pertaining to the eight research questions stated in the introduction, the raw numbers presented in this paper could offer answers to countless other questions regarding students' development practices. Ultimately, this paper aims to serve as a jumping-off point for further investigation into the patterns of mistakes that novice programmers make, and to shape the pedagogical approaches used by instructors.

ACKNOWLEDGEMENTS

This work is supported in part by NSF Award CNS-1619124.

REFERENCES

[1] Alireza Ahadi, Vahid Behbood, Arto Vihavainen, Julia Prior, and Raymond Lister. 2016. Students' Syntax Mistakes in Writing Seven Different Types of SQL Queries and its Applications to Predicting Students' Success. In *Proceedings of the 47th Technical Symposium on Computer Science Education (SIGCSE '16)*. Memphis, TN.

[2] Alireza Ahadi, Raymond Lister, Shahil Lal, and Arto Hellas. 2018. Learning Programming, Syntax Errors and Institution-Specific Factors. In *Proceedings of the 20th Australasian Computing Education Conference (ACE '18)*. Brisbane, Queensland, Australia.

[3] Marzieh Ahmadzadeh, Dave Elliman, and Colin Higgins. 2005. An Analysis of Patterns of Debugging Among Novice Computer Science Students. In *Proceedings of the 10th International Conference on Innovation and Technology in Computer Science Education (ITiCSE '05)*. Caparica, Portugal.

[4] Amjad Altadmri and Neil C. C. Brown. 2015. 37 Million Compilations: Investigating Novice Programming Mistakes in Large-Scale Student Data. In *Proceedings of the 46th Technical Symposium on Computer Science Education (SIGCSE '15)*. Kansas City, MO.

[5] Brett A. Becker and Catherine Mooney. 2016. Categorizing Compiler Error Messages with Principal Component Analysis. In *Proceedings of the 12th China-Europe International Symposium on Software Engineering Education (CEISEE '16)*. Shenyang, China.

[6] Jeff Bulmer, Angie Pinchbeck, and Bowen Hui. 2018. Visualizing Code Patterns in Novice Programmers. In *Proceedings of the 23rd Western Canadian Conference on Computing Education (WCCCE '18)*. Victoria, BC, Canada.

[7] Yuliya Cherenkova, Daniel Zingaro, and Andrew Petersen. 2014. Identifying Challenging CS1 Concepts in a Large Problem Dataset. In *Proceedings of the 45th Technical Symposium on Computer Science Education (SIGCSE '14)*. Atlanta, GA.

[8] Paul Denny, Andrew Luxton-Reilly, and Dave Carpenter. 2014. Enhancing Syntax Error Messages Appears Ineffectual. In *Proceedings of the 19th International Conference on Innovation and Technology in Computer Science Education (ITiCSE '14)*. Uppsala, Sweden.

[9] Paul Denny, Andrew Luxton-Reilly, and Ewan Tempero. 2012. All Syntax Errors Are Not Equal. In *Proceedings of the 17th International Conference on Innovation and Technology in Computer Science Education (ITiCSE '12)*. Haifa, Israel.

[10] Stephen H. Edwards, Nischel Kandru, and Mukund B. M. Rajagopal. 2017. Investigating Static Analysis Errors in Student Java Programs. In *Proceedings of the 13th International Computing Education Conference (ICER '17)*. Tacoma, WA.

[11] Andrew Ettles, Andrew Luxton-Reilly, and Paul Denny. 2018. Common Logic Errors Made by Novice Programmers. In *Proceedings of the 20th Australasian Computing Education Conference (ACE '18)*. Brisbane, Queensland, Australia.

[12] Juha Helminen, Petri Ihantola, and Ville Karavirta. 2013. Recording and Analyzing In-Browser Programming Sessions. In *Proceedings of the 13th Koli Calling International Conference on Computing Education Research (Koli Calling '13)*. Koli, Finalnd.

[13] James Jackson, Michael Cobb, and Curtis Carter. 2005. Identifying Top Java Errors for Novice Programmers. In *Proceedings of the 35th Frontiers in Education Conference (FIE '05)*. Indianapolis, IN.

[14] Matthew C. Jadud. 2005. A First Look at Novice Compilation Behavior Using BlueJ. *Computer Science Education* 15, 1 (March 2005).

[15] Sarah K. Kummerfeld and Judy Kay. 2003. The Neglected Battlefields of Syntax Errors. In *Proceedings of the 5th Australasian Computing Education Conference (ACE '03)*. Adelaide, Australia.

[16] Einari Kurvinen, Niko Hellgren, Erkki Kaila, Mikko-Jussi Laakso, and Tapio Salakoski. 2016. Programming Misconceptions in an Introductory Level Programming Course Exam. In *Proceedings of the 21st International Conference on Innovation and Technology in Computer Science Education (ITiCSE '16)*. Arequipa, Peru.

[17] Davin McCall and Michael Kolling. 2014. Meaningful Categorisation of Novice Programmer Errors. In *Proceedings of the 44th Frontiers in Education Conference (FIE '14)*. Madrid, Spain.

[18] Ioana Tuugalei Chan Mow. 2012. Analyses of Student Programming Errors in Java Programming Courses. *Journal of Emerging Trends in Computing and Information Sciences* 3, 5 (May 2012).

[19] David Pritchard. 2015. Frequency Distribution of Error Messages. In *Proceedings of the 6th Workshop on Evaluation and Usability of Programming Languages and Tools (PLATEAU '15)*. Pittsburgh, PA.

[20] Esther Shein. 2015. Python for Beginners. *Commun. ACM* 58, 3 (Feb. 2015), 19–21. https://doi.org/10.1145/2716560

[21] Emily S. Tabano, Maria Mercedes T. Rodrigo, and Matthew C. Jadud. 2011. Predicting At-Risk Novice Java Programmers Through the Analysis of Online Protocols. In *Proceedings of the 7th International Computing Education Conference (ICER '11)*. Providence, RI.

[22] Terry Tang, Rebecca Smith, Scott Rixner, and Joe Warren. 2016. Data-Driven Test Case Generation for Automated Programming Assessment. In *Proceedings of the 21st International Conference on Innovation and Technology in Computer Science Education (ITiCSE '16)*. Arequipa, Peru.

[23] Arto Vihavainen, Juha Helminen, and Petri Ihantola. 2014. How Novices Tackle Their First Lines of Code in an IDE: Analysis of Programming Session Traces. In *Proceedings of the 14th Koli Calling International Conference on Computing Education Research (Koli Calling '14)*. Koli, Finland.

[24] Joe Warren, Scott Rixner, John Greiner, and Stephen Wong. 2014. Facilitating Human Interaction in an Online Programming Course. In *Proceedings of the 45th Technical Symposium on Computer Science Education (SIGCSE '14)*. Atlanta, GA.

How Many Abilities Can We Measure in Computational Thinking? A Study on Bebras Challenge

Ana Liz Souto O. Araujo
Federal University of Campina Grande
Federal University of Paraíba
Paraíba, Brazil
analiz@dcx.ufpb.br

Wilkerson L. Andrade
Federal University of Campina Grande
Paraíba, Brazil
wilkerson@computacao.ufcg.edu.br

Dalton D. Serey Guerrero
Federal University of Campina Grande
Paraíba, Brazil
dalton@computacao.ufcg.edu.br

Monilly Ramos Araujo Melo
Federal University of Campina Grande
Paraíba, Brazil
monillyramos@gmail.com

ABSTRACT

While several approaches have been proposed to assess computational thinking (CT) abilities, it is still unclear how many and which these abilities are. Despite the undisputed importance of assessment, the fact is that there is not enough evidence on which abilities are merely theoretical and which can be empirically observed in the context of CT. This paper is part of a larger investigation in which we try to answer a simple question: can CT abilities be quantitatively defined and measured? In this particular study, we try to answer a simple question: How many CT abilities can be empirically observed using factor analysis? We approach this question, using a dataset containing answers of 1564 students from Lithuania in the Bebras Challenge from 2015. Firstly, we used confirmatory factor analysis to verify a theory that claims that five CT abilities are assessed by the contest. Our analysis shows the theory is not statistically supported. Secondly, we used principal component analysis as an exploratory analysis to try to derive an appropriate number of factors from the data. Surprisingly, the analysis suggests there are only two main recognizable factors. Finally, we briefly discuss these factors and hypothesize that the first is called *evaluation ability*, which would include abstraction, generalization, and decomposition, while factor 2 is *algorithmic thinking and logical reasoning*.

CCS CONCEPTS

• **Social and professional topics** → **Computational thinking**;
• **Applied computing** → *Education*;

KEYWORDS

Computational Thinking; Bebras Challenge; Assessment

SIGCSE '19, February 27-March 2, 2019, Minneapolis, MN, USA

ACM ISBN 978-1-4503-5890-3/19/02...$15.00
https://doi.org/10.1145/3287324.3287405

ACM Reference Format:
Ana Liz Souto O. Araujo, Wilkerson L. Andrade, Dalton D. Serey Guerrero, and Monilly Ramos Araujo Melo. 2019. How Many Abilities Can We Measure in Computational Thinking? A Study on Bebras Challenge. In *Proceedings of the 50th ACM Technical Symposium on Computer Science Education (SIGCSE '19), February 27-March 2, 2019, Minneapolis, MN, USA.* ACM, New York, NY, USA, 7 pages. https://doi.org/10.1145/3287324.3287405

1 INTRODUCTION

In the recent history of Computer and Education, Computational Thinking has been pointed out as a key element because it promotes understanding of how to bring the core of computational processes to solve problems [2]. Computational Thinking (CT) is a term referring to the concepts, skills, and ideas of Computer Science applied in problem solving in an interdisciplinary way. Jeannette Wing initially defined that "CT involves solving problems, design systems, and understanding human behavior, by drawing on the concepts fundamental to computer science" [23]. Since her seminal article, CT has been gaining attention from teachers as well as from researchers.

Several countries have organized working groups to disseminate how to promote CT and the involved skills. The Computational Thinking Task Force[1] is an American group created by Computer Science Teachers Association (CSTA) that defines CT as a problem solving process involving skills and attitudes that help in the process. Nine abilities are pointed out as the core CT concepts and capabilities [2]: data collection, data analysis, data representation, problem decomposition, abstraction, algorithms and procedures, automation, parallelization, and simulation. In the same direction, the CompuThink study[2] is an European group funded by the Joint Research Centre of the European Commission that describes CT as a thinking process involving the formulation of a problem that can be solved by computational solution [4]. In this process, six abilities can be involved: abstraction, algorithmic thinking, automation, decomposition, debugging, and generalization. In addition, Computing at school[3] is the United Kingdom group that provides guidance to teachers and researchers involved in Computing Education. They have proposed that CT is a thinking process associating

[1] https://www.csteachers.org/page/CompThinking
[2] https://ec.europa.eu/jrc/en/computational-thinking
[3] http://community.computingatschool.org.uk/resources/2324/single

logical reasoning to solve problems. For this purpose, five abilities can be explored: abstraction, decomposition, algorithmic thinking, evaluation, and generalization [7, 21].

Defining how many and which are the core CT abilities depends on the theoretical support chosen by each researcher. This occurs because there is not a general agreement on which are the concept and skills involved in CT. Therefore, each study should present the theoretical definition of CT and the stimulated skills.

Although researchers diverge from concept and skills of CT, students of more than 50 countries have participated in the Bebras Challenge[4]. It is the most popular CT contest whose goals is to promote and stimulate CT skills and Computer Science among students [9]. The Bebras Challenge is composed by tasks that are elaborated to be solved without previous knowledge of Computer Science, but some computer concepts are involved. All Bebras tasks are related to CT, involving one or more of these abilities: abstraction, algorithm thinking, decomposition, evaluation, and generalization [10].

Despite the literature has pointed out the above-mentioned abilities as theoretically related to CT, the fact is that there is not enough evidence on which abilities are merely theoretical and which can be empirically observed. Few studies, for instance, have properly analyzed CT abilities as latent factors [16]. In fact, we do not know how many skills can be associated with the essential CT abilities.

This paper is part of a larger investigation in which we try to answer a simple question: can CT abilities be quantitatively defined and measured? In this particular study, we try to answer an even simpler question: how many CT abilities can be empirically observed and measured using factor analysis? We approach this question, using a dataset containing answers of 1564 students from Lithuania in the Bebras Challenge from 2015. Firstly, we used confirmatory factor analysis to verify a theory that claims that five CT abilities are assessed by the contest. Our analysis shows the theory is not statistically supported. Secondly, we used principal component analysis as an exploratory technique in order to try to derive an appropriate number of factors from the data.

This paper has been divided into eight sections. We start in Section 2 with a background on CT abilities. In Section 3, we explain how Bebras Challenge works. In Section 4, we detail the adopted methodology. In Section 5 and 6, we present and discuss the results, respectively. In Section 7, we compare related works with our study. Finally, in Section 8, we draw the concluding remarks.

2 COMPUTATIONAL THINKING ABILITIES

CT has been historically associated with Jeannette Wing and her influential article "Computational Thinking" published in 2006 [23]. She introduced the relation on solving problems with fundamental concepts of Computer Science as abstraction, decomposition, thinking recursively, and heuristic reasoning. More than that, she argued that CT is not only programming, it involves human behavior as a way that humans can think to solve problems.

Over the years, the definition of CT has been discussed as well as the associated skills [12, 13, 22, 24]. CSTA and ISTE (International Society for Technology in Education) put forth an operational definition of CT which say that CT is a problem solving process associated with some following characteristics, but not limited to them [1]: (i) Defining problems into one we know how to solve by using a computer or another tool; (ii) Analyzing and organizing data logically; (iii) Using abstraction to represent data; (iv) Organizing the solution as an algorithm to automate solutions; (v) Producing the better solution using resources efficiently and effectively; and (vi) Generalizing and using the problem solving process to several similar problems.

Beyond the operational definition, Selby and Woollard identified the most frequently skills and terms used in the CT literature [21]. Their study pointed out that although CT has a broad definition, it is a cognitive process which encompasses abstraction, algorithmic thinking, decomposition, evaluation, and generalization. Besides, it is the set of abilities most cited among the studies. The Computer Education of the United Kingdom and other countries around the world have been exploring those five abilities in teaching practices [7, 10, 16]. In the following, those abilities are presented in more details.

Abstraction can be understood as a way of paying attention to the essential information to solve a problem. In this process of looking at the problem, we need to choose the core details and ignore those that are not useful to accomplish the task [7]. A map for tourists, which represents the main tourist attractions, is an example of abstraction. The map highlights the localization of museums, gardens, parks, and at the same time ignore other buildings that can not be interesting for tourists.

Abstraction is also about choosing a representation of a situation [10] to reduce the complexity of a problem [7]. Because of this utility, abstraction pointed out as the core element of CT [24] and one of the most assessed abilities in literature [12].

Algorithmic thinking is associated with planning a solution by following steps [23]. It involves developing sequences and rules in order to reach the final goal [7]. Understanding, creating, and executing are the expected actions when we are exploring the ability to think in an algorithmic way [10]. For example, learning the steps for doing multiplication or division is an illustration of a basic algorithm that all students should learn at school. This example makes clear that algorithms are not only used by computer scientists but also it is widely applied in other fields [21].

Algorithmic thinking is also related to abstraction regarding a way to represent one solution. Wing argued that "an algorithm is an abstraction of a step-by-step procedure for taking input and producing some desired output" [24] p.3718. In fact, algorithmic thinking is one ordinary ability associated with CT and also one of the most assessed CT ability, as abstraction [12].

Decomposition is the ability to break problems down into small and manageable parts to solve them [7]. It is also applied to massive problems or complex tasks [21]. For example, making arrangements for a party can be decomposed into distinct activities such as reserving a location, inviting guests, buying beverages, ordering foods, and so on. Each one of these activities may be broken down into smaller activities and be integrated later in the process. Through decomposition of the original task, a large and complex task can be better managed.

Evaluation is the ability to find the best solution to a problem considering the resources. This process may include a set of questions suggested by Csizmadia *et. al.* [7] page 7: "Are the properties

[4]bebras.org

of the solution correct? Are they fast enough? Do they use resources economically? Are they easy for people to use? Do they promote an appropriate experience?". Those questions assist us to find a solution that suits our purpose [10].

Generalization is the ability to recognize patterns on how to solve specific problems and apply the solution to similar problems [21]. In other words, we can associate a previous solution to a new problem. Particularity, generalization involves identifying similarities and connections among activities. For example, if we have to organize a wedding, we can start from a list of activities created when we organized a party because we recognize the similarities between those two events. Generalization also includes induction, e.g., using one general solution to accomplish the activity [10].

3 BEBRAS CHALLENGE

Bebras is an international educational community that organizes an annual CT contest [9, 10]. The main goal of the group is to stimulate pupils' interest to the Computer Science. Students from more than 50 countries participated in the annual contest. The contest addresses primary and secondary education separating students in five groups: Mini (grades 3-4, ages 8-10), Benjamin (grades 5-6, ages 10- 12), Cadet (grades 7-8, ages 12-14), Junior (grades 9-10, ages 14-16), and Senior (grades 11-12, ages 16-18). The name and the number of groups can change depending on the country.

The main activity of the Bebras Challenge is the contest [10, 11]. The annual contest is composed of a set of questions, called tasks. The number of tasks and time to solve them can change among countries, but usually are between 15-21 tasks to be solved in 45-55 minutes. The task is designed to be solvable without previous knowledge from Computer Science or programming. Nevertheless, each task is related to one computational concept and one or more CT skills. Multiple-choice and dynamic questions, including interactive components and open-ended questions, are the primary types of tasks.

The development of Bebras' tasks is a process involving some steps every year [11]. Firstly, national organizers formulate tasks and submit them to Bebras International Task Workshop. In this step, all tasks are written in English. Secondly, during the workshop, experts from Bebras community review and improve the submitted tasks. In this case, a database is used to store all these reviewed tasks. Thirdly, national organizers select tasks from the database according to each grade. Then, the selected tasks are translated into the national language. Finally, national organizers prepare the final version of the tasks.

Throughout the history of Bebras Challenge, the organizers have classified the tasks into several categorization schemes. However, Dagiene *et al.* have proposed a new two-dimensional categorization system, including computational concepts and CT skills explored in each task [10]. The computational concepts are called informatics domain. It is divided into five areas, such as: *(i)* Algorithms and programming; *(ii)* Data, data structures, and representations; *(iii)* Computer processes and hardware; *(iv)* Communication and networking; and, *(v)* Interactions, systems, and society [10]. Besides the informatics domain, the categorization of CT skill adopted is that proposed by Computing At School [7, 10, 21]. The five CT skills are abstraction, algorithmic thinking, decomposition, evaluation, and generalization. Therefore, a task is associated with one informatics domain and one to three CT skills [10].

4 METHODOLOGY

In this study, we try to figure out how many CT abilities can be empirically observed in the context of CT questions. We approach this objective considering the CT abilities as latent variables (constructs) in the tasks of the Bebras Challenge. The Bebras Challenge was chosen because the tasks are designed to be answered by exploring CT abilities requiring no prior knowledge [10]. As a statistical resource, we used the Confirmatory Factor Analysis (CFA) and Principal Component Analysis (PCA). These two techniques are mathematical procedures that enable us to observe factors as a latent variable considering the intercorrelated variables [6, 14]. More specifically, the tasks are the variables that can be intercorrelated, considering they may represent the constructs.

We used a dataset containing answers of 1564 students from Lithuania in the Bebras Challenge from 2015 (grades 11 and 12). Initially, the dataset contained answers of 3304 students, but we removed students with no answer (NA) from our analysis. This decision was taken to avoid bias because, with NA, we could not control whether the student did not know the answer or did not respond due to unforeseen circumstances, for example, he/she did not feel motivated to participate to the contest. All things considered, our analysis encompassed eighteen tasks available at [8].

The factor analysis was conducted according to the procedure presented by Hair *et al.* [14]. Firstly, we used CFA to verify a theory that claims that the contest assesses five CT abilities. The theoretical model used in this study, i.e., the association between the tasks and an ability, was based on [10] and [3]. Unfortunately, our analysis showed that the theory was not statistically supported. Because of that, we moved on trying to search for how many factors could be found. Then, we employed PCA[5], as an exploratory analysis, trying to derive an appropriate number of factors from the data.

All statistical analysis was performed using the R language [17]. For CFA, we used *lavaan* library and *cfa( )* function [20]. As a measure of the goodness of fit, we used TLI (Tucker-Lewis Index), CFI (Comparative Fit Index), and RMSEA (Root Mean Square Error of Approximation) [6]. We conducted the PCA using *psych* library and *principal( )* function with *oblimin* rotation [18]. Indeed, we used Bartlett test, KMO (Kaiser-Meyer-Olkin), and MSA (Measure of Sampling Adequacy) as measures of the goodness of fit [14]. The eigenvalues were the chosen approach to estimate the number of factors in PCA. In this case, we used *scree( )* function.

5 RESULTS

In this Section, we present the results of the factor analysis. Firstly, we detail the data screening. Secondly, we show the CFA results of the theoretical model of five abilities on Bebras Challenge. Finally, we present the results of the exploratory analysis with PCA.

[5]According to Hair *et al.* [14], Principal Component Analysis and Common Factor Analysis are both factor analysis techniques. The main difference is that, in Common Factor Analysis, the extracted factors are based only on the common variance, while in Principal Component Analysis, the factors are based on the total variance.

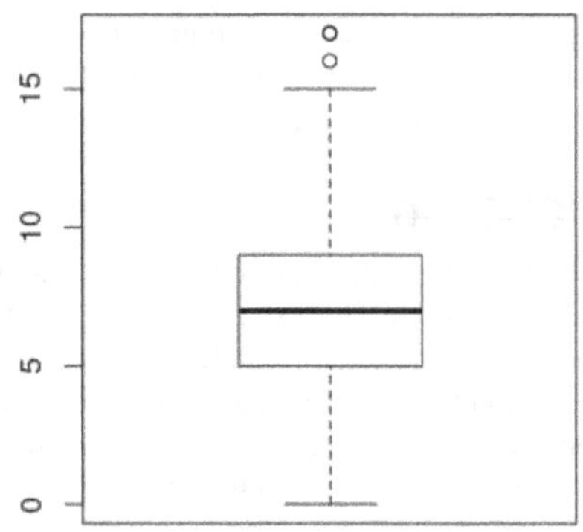

Figure 1: Boxplot of grades 11-12.

5.1 Data screening

In the first place, as the data came from different classes, we analyzed if the answers of students of grade 11 and 12 came from the same population. This procedure is needed to ensure the students' answers in these two groups can be analyzed in the same dataset (together). For this purpose, we used the Pearson's chi-squared test. The result of the test indicated we could accept that there is no difference between the grades. From now on, we consider the students' answers of grades 11 and 12 in the same dataset.

Figure 1 shows the boxplot of grades 11-12. The dataset has eighteen tasks (questions) containing answers of 1564 students (ages 16-18). Apart from some outliers, the mean of score was 6.98, and the standard deviation was 2.88.

5.2 Confirmatory Factor Analysis

In CFA, we used a previous classification that showed the relation between the tasks and the abilities to design the theoretical model tested in this study [3, 10]. In some cases, we need to choose one ability that was the most significant to solve the task, considering the proposed solution by Bebras' organizers. The ability and the tasks in our theoretical model were related as follows: **(i) Abstract** ability was associated with "Stack computer", "Mobiles", "Building a chip", and "Raid arrays" tasks; **(ii) Algorithmic thinking** was associated with "You won't find it", "Decorating chocolate", "Bowl factory", and "Busy beaver" tasks; **(iii) Decomposition** was associated with "Pirates" and "Beaver the alchemist" tasks; **(iv) Evaluation** was associated with "Birds", "Popularity", "email scam", "Beaver tutorials", and "Turn the cards" tasks; and finally, **(v) Generalization** was associated with "Word chains", "Drawing stars", and "Fireworks" tasks.

In Table 1, we describe the factor loadings and standard error (SE) of CFA. Based on the factor loading (less than 0.256), we have no statistical support to accept the model, despite it had a good indicator of goodness of fit, with a TLI of 0.99, CFI of 0.99, and RMSEA of 0.004. Considering the standardized coefficient ranging from 0.056 to 0.256 and two negative coefficients -0.007 and -0.098, the indicators did not show significant factor loadings.

Nevertheless, we blamed our theoretical model as it did not show good statistical results. Then, we redesigned different theoretical models, considering a variety of combinations between tasks and abilities. Despite all efforts, none of the theoretical models seemed

Table 1: Confirmatory Factor Analysis

Latent Factor	Tasks	Factor loadings	SE
Abstraction	Stack computer	0.256	0.017
	Mobiles	0.183	0.016
	Building a chip II	0.019	0.004
	Raid arrays	0.078	0.014
Algorithmic Thinking	You won't find it	0.209	0.016
	Decorating chocolate	0.139	0.014
	Bowl factory	0.141	0.014
	Busy beaver	0.062	0.013
Decomposition	Pirates	-0.007	0.026
	Beaver the alchemist	-0.098	0.318
Evaluation	Birds	0.036	0.013
	Popularity	0.117	0.014
	email scam	0.153	0.018
	Beaver tutorial	0.119	0.016
	Turn the cards	0.056	0.01
Generalization	Word chains	0.189	0.016
	Drawing starts	0.151	0.016
	Fireworks	0.133	0.015

to fit. Then, we may conclude that this dataset did not fit the model of five factors as it was proposed.

5.3 Principal Component Analysis

As the theoretical model of five factors was not confirmed by CFA, we further investigated on how many factors could be derived from the dataset. We initiated the exploratory analysis with PCA, calculating the goodness of fit to figure out whether we could continue with the factor analysis. All values were suitable for applying factor analysis [14]: (i) the Bartlett test indicated that there was a significant relation among the variables ($p - values < 2.2^{e-16}$), (ii) the KMO was 0.82, and (iii) all tasks presented MSA higher than 0.50.

The process of extraction of the final pattern matrix are described below. The eigenvalues point out four factors to be extracted (considering eigenvalues > 1), but this did not arise from the data. When four factors were considered, only one task was loaded onto third and fourth factors, respectively. So, the analysis was reduced to two factors. Then, we calculated the pattern matrix with *oblimin* rotation. The PCA was initiated with 18 tasks. In the first iteration, "Mobiles" task had cross-loading and was removed. In the second iteration, "Building a chip II", "Birds", and "Raid Arrays" tasks presented loading < 0.30 and were discarded (we considered 0.30 as a sufficient factor loading [14]). The "Pirates" task was removed because it presented MSA < 0.50. In the third iteration, the "Turn the cards" task presented cross-loading and was removed. After this time, all factor loading were > 0.30 in only one factor, KMO > 0.76, and MSA > 0.50 (we considered the values of KMO > 0.60 and MSA > 0.50 are acceptable [14, 15]).

In Table 2, we show the result of pattern matrix with two factors with *oblimin* rotation. Considering factor loading > 0.30, we can notice "Popularity", "Word chains", "Drawing stars", "Beaver the Alchemist", "You won't find it", "email scan", "Beaver tutorials",

Table 2: Pattern Matrix with 2 Factors (*oblimin* rotation)

Tasks	Factor 1	Factor 2	Commonalities
You won't find it	**0.62**	0.01	0.39
Word chains	**0.61**	-0.15	0.37
Beaver the alchemist	**0.52**	0.24	0.36
email scam	**0.50**	-0.11	0.25
Popularity	**0.42**	0.00	0.18
Drawing stars	**0.42**	0.03	0.18
Beaver tutorials	**0.36**	0.06	0.14
Fireworks	**0.32**	0.22	0.17
Busy beaver	-0.14	**0.69**	0.46
Decorating chocolate	0.15	**0.58**	0.38
Turn the cards	0.05	**0.42**	0.19
Bowl factory	0.26	**0.37**	0.23
Loadings	2.00	1.29	
Proportion Variation	0.17	0.11	
Cumulative Variation	0.17	0.27	

and "Fireworks" tasks have loading on factor 1. On the other hand, "Bowl factory", "Decoration chocolate", "Busy Beaver", and "Turn the card" tasks have loading on factor 2.

Based on our analysis, two factors can be derived from PCA. In an attempt to aptly name each factor, we investigated if some of the five abilities of the theoretical model are suitable in one of these factors. Analyzing tasks which have loading on factor 1, we tried to observe which is the most used ability to solve the set of tasks. We found that evaluation was needed to answer all tasks, but also could apply abstraction, generalization, and decomposition in another way. We noted that factor 2 could be algorithmic thinking and logical reasoning because three tasks described steps to follow and one task was related to logic reasoning implication. Therefore, we hypothesize that the first should be called *evaluation ability*, which includes abstraction, generalization and decomposition, while factor 2 should be *algorithmic thinking and logical reasoning*.

6 DISCUSSION

In this section, we discuss the result of factor analysis and also examine some Bebras' characteristics that may impact on the study.

6.1 Factor Analysis

CFA did not confirm the theoretical assumption of five abilities on Bebras Challenge. This result can be explained by reasoning that tasks are associated with more than one ability, instead of a single one per task [10]. CFA is a statistical process that demonstrates how a set of observed variables are related to the underlying latent factor(s), considering that each variable was loaded into only one factor [14]. If the last condition is violated, the statistical results cannot support the allegation [6]. Consequently, the theoretical model of five abilities cannot be statistically supported by CFA as proposed in Section 5.2.

In fact, the result with PCA suggests there are only two main distinguishing factors. We begin the analysis of factors by hypothesizing that factor 1 could be seen as mainly the *evaluation ability*, including abstraction, generalization as well as decomposition, and factor 2 could be seen as *algorithmic thinking and logical reasoning*. In a primary analysis, we observed that **evaluation** was the most common ability because all tasks, in some way, involved the need to find the best solution and fitness for purpose. **Abstraction** was also used considering that tasks need to choose a representation of a system and spot key elements in the problem. **Generalization** was applied when patterns were identified. At lastly, **decomposition** could be a strategic solution when the tasks were breaking down into small tasks. Regarding factor 2, **algorithmic thinking** and **logical reasoning** are closely related because algorithms can be translated into standard logical form and vice versa. Moreover, logical reasoning is part of the description of the concept of algorithms and programming ability in Bebras Challenge [10]. Then, *algorithmic thinking and logical reasoning* could represent factor 2.

However, the proposal mentioned earlier to name the two factors is not the only way to interpret it. Factor 2 was more natural to interpret because the content of the tasks was clearly executing an algorithm and using logical reasoning. On the other hand, factor 1 diverged from how many abilities could be used to solve those tasks and how strong the abilities can be associated. For example, abstraction can be related to generalization, as Barr and Stephenson declared on page 52 "abstraction - simplifying from the concrete to the general as solutions are developed" [2]. Nevertheless, all these allegations are still theoretical. Furthermore, other aspects of PCA can justify the difficulty in interpreting factors, for example, values of commonalities and proportion of variation.

The commonalities can justify the difficulty in naming the emergent factors because they show how much of a question's variability can be explained by the set of factors extracted. Thereby, higher commonalities are better because the variability can better explain the set of factors extracted. Whether commonalities are low (values between 0.0 and 0.4), then a variable may attempt to load on any factor. In Table 2, all commonalities are lower than 0.4, except for "Busy beaver" task. This value means it is possible that some task is loaded onto another factor. For example, "Fireworks" task has the lower commonalities, plus, the factor loading is 0.32 on factor 1 and 0.22 on factor 2. As we used 0.30 as a sufficient factor loading [14], then, we considered that "Fireworks" is loading on factor 1.

The lower proportion of variation may also influence the difficulty in naming the emerged factor because it can indicate that the tasks are different in some aspect from each other. The proportion of variation shows how good a factor solution explains what the tasks represent together. The higher the loading factor, the higher it is explained by the proportion of variance. In Table 2, the cumulative proportion of variance is 28%. This result means that only 28% of the variance can be explained by the factor solution presented in Section 5. The other 72% can be due to several aspects and error variance.

6.2 Characteristics of Bebras Challenge

Some characteristics of Bebras Challenge may have influenced the factor analysis. We examine the computation contents of the tasks, the number of the abilities involved in each task, and the tasks development process.

Several computation contents in the same test may have contributed to the low commonalities and loadings. When the stakeholders of each country are selecting the tasks to the contest, they must cover as many computation domains as possible, i.e., they must select different computation contents [10]. Remember that commonalities are a measure of variability, a varied range of computation contents may high the difference among tasks, and consequently, make it tricky to identify the construct that explains the results.

Because tasks may explore more than one ability simultaneously, these multiple possible classifications may influence the theory of five abilities not be confirmed by CFA. During the task development process, the organizers are free to involve one or more ability to solve the task. Moreover, the student can answer the task in a different way to the way that the task was designed. Consequently, another ability may be used beyond the expected one. In fact, the new categorization system proposed by Dagiene *et al.* recognized that more than one CT ability might be associated with each task [10]. Whether the task can be solved using more than one ability, it is expected that we can not measure the skills separately.

The development of Bebras tasks may have biased the variability of skills. Some abilities may have more numbers of tasks at the expense of others. For example, one or two abilities can be the favorite among all abilities. Consequently, more tasks about few abilities were available on the database. When the national organizer selects the tasks, it may have the probability of choosing more tasks about the same ability.

Another aspect is a specific informatics domain may be more related to one ability than other. For example, the tasks under the informatics domain "Algorithms and programming" addresses sorting (bubble sort, quick sort, etc.), IF conditions, and program execution. These contents are closely related to the algorithmic thinking ability, but not limited to it. As a consequence, if it has many tasks under "Algorithms and programming" domain, the greater is the probability of algorithmic thinking ability is involved.

7 RELATED WORK

CT skills have been investigated in several approaches toward figuring out which cognitive abilities we can asses. Román-González *et al.* related CT skills measured by the Computational Thinking Test (CTt) with other cognitive abilities using standardized psychological tests [19]. The CTt addresses computational concepts, such as basic directions and sequences, loops, repeat and conditional statements. They found that CT skills have moderate correlations with spatial ability, reasoning ability, and problem-solving ability. Likewise, Boom *et al.* have been examined the relationship of CT to intelligence [5]. They used Bebras tasks as an assessment of CT and an intelligence test to measure general problem-solving skills. The result indicated a large and significant correlation between these two instruments. The approach used in our investigation is similar to that used by Palts *el. al.* [16], but we performed some differences. Palts *el. al.* executed a factor analysis in order to test which CT abilities from the Bebras Challenge were well distinguishable. They used answers from Lithuania at grades 5-6 (ages 10-12) as the dataset. Indeed, they not only did not support the theory of five abilities but also found two main factors using exploratory factor analysis. In our study, we conducted a PCA under a different set of tasks (for grades 11-12). Our results showed the same number of factors, even analyzing another group of questions. However, we hypothesized divergent skills. Different from previous study, we detailed the reasons that may influence the results. We considered both the methodology of factor analysis and the characteristic of the Bebras Challenge. This discussion may assist the development of future questions in the context of measuring CT abilities as well as the Bebras community.

8 CONCLUDING REMARKS

The present research aimed to figure out how many CT abilities can be empirically observed using factor analysis. We approached the problem using Bebras tasks as a measure of CT. Firstly, we tried to confirm a theoretical model of five abilities measured in the Bebras Challenge, but the theory was not statistically supported. Then, we attempted to discover an appropriate number of factors from the data. Unexpectedly, the analysis suggested there are only two main recognizable factors. On top of these investigations, we theorize and propose that the first factor could be called *evaluation ability*, encompassing abstraction, generalization, and decomposition, while the second could be *algorithmic thinking and logical reasoning*.

One of the more significant findings that emerged from this study was that although CFA did not confirm the theory of the five abilities, they are present in the tasks in some way. This result may mean that the skills cannot be found disconnectedly in these tasks. The Bebras Challenge organizers have recognized that more than one ability can be related to each task. Besides, the student can solve it in a way that is different from the one expected by the task designer. Consequently, distinct abilities may be used beyond the expected one. These central aspects can be related to the fact that CFA did not confirm the theory of five abilities in Bebras Challenge.

A second significant finding was that two main factors emerged from the Bebras Challenge, even analyzing a different group of tasks. We observed that one of these factors might encompass four abilities while the second seems related to the other two abilities. However, identifying those two factors depends on how tasks can be solved using more than one ability as well as the conceptual definition of the abilities themselves. These are the two main aspects that can influence the proper naming of factors.

All involved aspects of factor analysis do not affect the importance of Bebras Challenge as a contest to promote CT skills around the world. The present study explored how tasks can be used to measure CT abilities, i.e., beyond the original goal of the contest. The overall findings point out that more empirical investigation should be performed toward uncovering which are the cognitive abilities that have been involved in CT.

9 ACKNOWLEDGEMENT

We thank Professor Dr. Valentina Dagiene (Vilnius University) for sharing the dataset of Lithuania Bebras Challenge.

REFERENCES

[1] Computer Science Teachers Association et al. 2018. Operational definition of computational thinking. http://www.iste.org/docs/ct-documents/computational-thinking-operational-definition-flyer.pdf.

[2] Valerie Barr and Chris Stephenson. 2011. Bringing computational thinking to K-12: what is Involved and what is the role of the computer science education community? *Acm Inroads* 2, 1 (2011), 48–54.

[3] Daphne Blokhuis, Peter Millican, Chris Roffey, Eljakim Schrijvers, and Sue Sentance. 2015. UK Bebras Computational Thinking Challenge. http://www.bebras.uk/uploads/2/1/8/6/21861082/ukbebras2015-answers_1.pdf

[4] Stefania Bocconi, Augusto Chioccariello, Giuliana Dettori, Anusca Ferrari, Katja Engelhardt, et al. 2016. *Developing Computational Thinking in Compulsory Education-Implications for policy and practice.* Technical Report. Joint Research Centre (Seville site).

[5] Kay-Dennis Boom, Matt Bower, Amaël Arguel, Jens Siemon, and Antonia Scholkmann. 2018. Relationship between computational thinking and a measure of intelligence as a general problem-solving ability. In *Proceedings of the 23rd Annual ACM Conference on Innovation and Technology in Computer Science Education.* ACM, 206–211.

[6] Timothy A Brown. 2014. *Confirmatory factor analysis for applied research.* Guilford Publications.

[7] A Csizmadia, P Curzon, M Dorling, S Humphreys, T Ng, C Selby, and J Woollard. 2015. Computational thinking: A guide for teachers. *Google Scholar* (2015). http://community.computingatschool.org.uk/files/8550/original.pdf

[8] Valentina Dagienė, Simona Feiferytė, Eglė Jasutė, Alvida Lozdienė, Bronius Skupas, Elena Sutkutė, and Gabrielė Stupurienė. 2015. Informatika: Bebras 2015. http://bebras.lt/wp-content/uploads/2015/09/Uzdaviniu-2015-m.-knygele.pdf

[9] Valentina Dagienė and Gerald Futschek. 2008. Bebras international contest on informatics and computer literacy: Criteria for good tasks. In *International Conference on Informatics in Secondary Schools-Evolution and Perspectives.* Springer, 19–30.

[10] Valentina Dagienė, Sue Sentance, and Gabrielė Stupurienė. 2017. Developing a two-dimensional categorization system for educational tasks in informatics. *Informatica* 28, 1 (2017), 23–44.

[11] Valentina Dagienė, Gabrielė Stupurienė, and Lina Vinikienė. 2017. Implementation of Dynamic Tasks on Informatics and Computational Thinking. *Baltic Journal of Modern Computing* 5, 3 (2017), 306.

[12] Ana Liz Souto O de Araujo, Wilkerson L Andrade, and Dalton D Serey Guerrero. 2016. A systematic mapping study on assessing computational thinking abilities. In *Frontiers in education conference (FIE), 2016 IEEE.* IEEE, 1–9.

[13] Shuchi Grover and Roy Pea. 2013. Computational thinking in K–12: A review of the state of the field. *Educational Researcher* 42, 1 (2013), 38–43.

[14] Joseph F Hair, William C Black, Barry J Babin, Rolph E Anderson, Ronald L Tatham, et al. 1998. *Multivariate data analysis.* Vol. 5. Prentice hall Upper Saddle River, NJ.

[15] Julie Pallant. 2013. *SPSS survival manual.* McGraw-Hill Education (UK).

[16] T. Palts, M. Pedaste, V. Vene, and L. VinikienĂŮ. 2017. Tasks for Assessing Skills of Computational Thinking. In *ICERI2017 Proceedings (10th annual International Conference of Education, Research and Innovation).* IATED, 2750–2759. https://doi.org/10.21125/iceri.2017.0784

[17] R Core Team. 2016. *R: A Language and Environment for Statistical Computing.* R Foundation for Statistical Computing, Vienna, Austria. https://www.R-project.org/

[18] William Revelle. 2017. *psych: Procedures for Psychological, Psychometric, and Personality Research.* Northwestern University, Evanston, Illinois. https://CRAN.R-project.org/package=psych R package version 1.7.8.

[19] Marcos Román-González, Juan-Carlos Pérez-González, and Carmen Jiménez-Fernández. 2017. Which cognitive abilities underlie computational thinking? Criterion validity of the Computational Thinking Test. *Computers in Human Behavior* 72 (2017), 678–691.

[20] Yves Rosseel. 2012. lavaan: An R Package for Structural Equation Modeling. *Journal of Statistical Software* 48, 2 (2012), 1–36. http://www.jstatsoft.org/v48/i02/

[21] Cynthia Selby and John Woollard. 2013. Computational thinking: the developing definition. (2013). https://eprints.soton.ac.uk/356481/

[22] Joke Voogt, Petra Fisser, Jon Good, Punya Mishra, and Aman Yadav. 2015. Computational thinking in compulsory education: Towards an agenda for research and practice. *Education and Information Technologies* 20, 4 (2015), 715–728.

[23] Jeannette M Wing. 2006. Computational thinking. *Commun. ACM* 49, 3 (2006), 33–35.

[24] Jeannette M Wing. 2008. Computational thinking and thinking about computing. *Philosophical transactions of the royal society of London A: mathematical, physical and engineering sciences* 366, 1881 (2008), 3717–3725.

(Re)Validating Cognitive Introductory Computing Instruments

Ryan Bockmon
University of Nebraska - Lincoln
Lincoln, Nebraska
ryan.bockmon@huskers.unl.edu

Stephen Cooper
University of Nebraska - Lincoln
Lincoln, Nebraska
scooper22@unl.edu

Jonathan Gratch
Texas Woman's University
Denton, Texas
jgratch@twu.edu.

Mohsen Dorodchi
University of North Carolina at Charlotte
Charlotte, North Carolina
mdorodch@uncc.edu

ABSTRACT

Cognitive tests have been long used as a measure of student knowledge, ability, and as a predictor for success in engineering and computer science. However, these tests are not without their own problems relating to priming, difficulty (resulting in test fatigue) and time on exam. This paper discusses efforts to modify Parker et al.'s Second CS1 aptitude test (SCS1) [13] to reduce the time spent on the exam, provide greater customization to match concepts taught across three universities, and reduce redundancy of test questions all while maintaining the instrument's reliability. This instrument was modified for use on an ongoing grant investigating whether spatial abilities impact the success of students in introductory CS courses. The instrument developed in this paper is a revised shortened version of Second Computer Science 1 (SCS1) aptitude test, designated as SCS1R.

CCS CONCEPTS

• **Social and Professional topics → Student assessment**;

KEYWORDS

Assessment; CS1; Validity; Replication

ACM Reference Format:
Ryan Bockmon, Stephen Cooper, Jonathan Gratch, and Mohsen Dorodchi. 2019. (Re)Validating Cognitive Introductory Computing Instruments. In *Proceedings of the 50th ACM Technical Symposium on Computer Science Education (SIGCSE '19), February 27-March 2, 2019, Minneapolis, MN, USA.* ACM, New York, NY, USA, 6 pages. https://doi.org/10.1145/3287324.3287372

1 INTRODUCTION

Computer science instructional intervention projects center on determining the impact that they have on student learning. To accurately measure the level of success of an intervention, researchers must have and use valid and reliable instruments. However, the field of computing has few valid and reliable assessments for pedagogical or research purposes [2].

Our goal was to identify valid and reliable instruments to collect baseline data used for our research grant investigating whether improving first year computing students' spatial skills impacts their success in computer science, as well as looking into how other factors might play a role in student success in first year computing classes. To meet these needs, the project required a valid instrument to test students' computing ability, a valid instrument to measure affective interests, and a valid instrument to test students' spatial skills. Many of the instruments available for use did not completely fit project needs.

During the summer of 2014 Cooper et al. ran a two-week summer coding workshop where they taught both a control and a treatment group of rising twelfth grade students [8]. The treatment group received a 45-minute spatial skills training session each morning in place of a review of the previous day's material. Four instruments were used to collect data. The first instrument collected data on demographics. The second instrument gathered information about students' confidence towards learning computing as well as gender roles concerning computing. The third and fourth instruments were the AP Computer Science exam [6] to test students' programming abilities and the Revised Purdue Spatial Visualization Test: Rotations (PSVT:R) to assess student spatial visual acuity [20]. At the end of the workshop, the researchers concluded that the treatment group had a greater gain between pre-test and post-test scores on the computer science instrument as well as having higher confidence with respect to their perceived programming experience.

In planning to replicate and expand on Cooper's study we ran into a few issues. One of which was the use of the AP Computer Science exam. While Cooper study was ran on a small group of students our project is being conducted across three universities, where each participating university teaches CS1 using different programming languages while the AP Computer Science exam is written for Java. This paper discuses the efforts of finding and revalidating a CS1 aptitude test for our study. While the validity of the other three instruments are of interest to us as well they fall outside the scope of this paper.

1.1 CS Aptitude Tests

Aptitude tests are a systemic means of testing a learner's abilities to perform specific tasks and react to different situations. Generally, the exam has a standardized method of administration and

SIGCSE '19, February 27-March 2, 2019, Minneapolis, MN, USA

ACM ISBN 978-1-4503-5890-3/19/02...$15.00
https://doi.org/10.1145/3287324.3287372

scoring, with results quantified and compared to other test takers. For CS, these competencies can include concepts such as logical or numerical reasoning, pattern recognition, or program simulations. As they represent a standardized exam, they can be used to measure a CS student's overall aptitude toward success in the field. However, variations within required competencies and curriculum valued or accepted at a specific location may differ resulting in incongruous matches between taught content and exam content.

Our spatial skills project is being conducted at three universities. Each participating university teaches CS1 using different programming languages, so the project required a single content instrument that could be used at our three schools. There are a few attempts to create and validate content instruments.

The most well-known CS content instrument is the AP Computer Science exam [6]. However, the AP CS asks questions in Java, which does not work for our study, given that two of our schools teach CS1 in other languages.

Tew's Foundational CS1 Assessment instrument (FCS1) [18] attempted to create a CS assessment test independent of any single programming language. FCS1 tests student ability using pseudo code written in the style of imperative languages. The validation process was conducted through a multi-step process that included an expert review panel, large-scale comparison between the FCS1 and language-dependent isomorphic tests [17, 18]. The study was conducted with 952 participants across two different universities with three different programming languages being taught: Java, Matlab, and Python. Because there was no other test validated beforehand they used the final exam scores of each participant and tested for correlations. Results showed that Java having the highest correlations with a Pearson's $r = .511$, $p < 0.001$. Python originally had the lowest correlation, but after splitting into two subgroups results showed that the CS-python focused section had a Pearson's $r = .679$, $p < 0.001$ and Media-Python had a Pearson's $r = .262$, $p < 0.001$. It was concluded that the FSC1 is a valid instrument [18]. This instrument met our multi-language needs. Unfortunately this instrument was unavailable for use.

The Second CS1 (SCS1) exam [13], a successor of the FCS1, was created in 2016. The study was conducted by testing a group of students (n = 183) on both the SCS1 and the FCS1 exams. The results found that there was a strong positive correlation between student scores on both the SCS1 and the FCS1 with a Pearson's correlation = 0.566, $p < 0.001$. Running a quantitative analysis using a 3 parameter Item Response Theory (IRT), the researchers indicated that both the FCS1 and the SCS1 were quite difficult. Testing reliability showed that both the FCS1 and the SCS1 failed to reach a Cronbach's alpha of a 0.65 [9] with their FCS1 having a Cronbach's alpha of a 0.53 and the SCS1 with a Cronbach's alpha of a 0.59 [13]. Like the FCS1, the SCS1 is multi-language (and was validated in Java, Python, and Matlab). The problem with using this exam as written was the length of time it takes students to complete.

The Computer Programming Aptitude Test was created by the University of Kent and designed to be free of any knowledge of programming languages. It consists of 26 questions composed of numerical problem solving, logical reasoning, attention to detail, pattern recognition and the ability to follow complex procedures [1]. To date, there has been no attempt to fully validate this test. A study has indicated that there is a correlation between scores on Computer Programming Aptitude Test and final grades [11]. The lack of formal validation and the requirement of an instrument that consisted of programming questions resulted in this instrument not being selected.

Despite concerns over the instrument's length, we decided to use the SCS1 and modify the instrument by taking a subset of the original SCS1 questions. The modification to the original SCS1 required us to establish the reliability for the new version of the test.

2 METHODS

Our data was collected in a pre-post format in introductory computing classes during the fall semester of 2017 across three universities: the University of North Carolina at Charlotte, Texas Woman's University, and the University of Nebraska - Lincoln. The instrument was available for students to take during the first 3 weeks of class as a pre-test and offered during the final 3 weeks as a post-test. 635 students took our modified SCS1R.

As part of the study, students were administered four different surveys: SCS1R to measure student computer science content knowledge, an attitudes instrument to examine the students' current attitudes and perceptions on CS, the Revised Purdue Spatial Visualization Test: Rotations (RPSVT:R) to assess student spatial visual acuity, and a demographics survey to collect information on students' background. To help reduce test fatigue we aimed to keep the time to complete all four surveys under 45 minutes. All participation was voluntary, with incentives used to encourage students to participate. All incentives were approved by each institution's IRB process and varied between institutions, consisting of either time slotted during labs, $10 gift cards, and/or extra credit.

2.1 SCS1R Design

The original SCS1 consists of 27 pseudo code questions, covering the typical CS1 topic coverage. Faculty taking the test required over an hour to complete. Students pre-flighting the test required 2 to 3 hours to complete it. The researchers wanted the test duration to be no more than 20-30 minutes to complete given that the spatial skills test would take up to 20 minutes and the demographics survey combined with the attitudes test would take about 10 minutes to finish. To keep the test length to a maximum of 20 minutes we selected 9 questions, retaining one item for each major topic covered at each of the first year computing course at the participating universities. These topics include; *if* statements, logic operations, variable declaration, arrays, return values, code completion, code tracing, and *for* and *while* loops. When multiple questions covered a given topic, we selected the one question we judged to be the best fit for our study. In the end we retained questions 1, 3, 8, 9, 11, 22, 25, 26, and 27 from the original SCS1, now labeled as Q1 - Q9. Question 1 covered basic *for* loop logic. Question 3 covered infinite *while* loops. Question 8 covered more advanced *for* loops having embedded loops. Question 9 covered more advanced *while* loops with the *mod* operator and basic boolean logic. Question 11 covered function calls and boolean logic. Question 22 covered arrays and array adding and subtracting. Question 25 covered converting math equations to code. Question 26 covered advanced boolean logic, and question 27 covered function calls and variable declaration. The interested reader should contact the instrument authors [13] for access to the questions.

3 ANALYSIS

A Rasch Model (Item Response Theory (IRT)) was used to test reliability and validity of the SCS1R. We used Ganz Rasch, a free software program, to apply IRT [3]. Running IRT on the SCS1R we were able to calculate the difficulty level of each question, plotted each question's item characteristic curve (ICC), and tested the fit of each item. There also exist 1-par, 2-par and 3-par IRT Models. The recommend sample size to run a 1-par is N = 150 for a 10 item test and N = 750 for a 2-par and 3-par IRT [15]. Due to the sample size (N = 635) and limited access to software, the Rasch model was decided to be the best fit. The researchers intend to switch over to a 2-par or 3-par as the sample population increases.

Calculations of Cronbach's α was used to test reliability of the SCS1R. An acceptable minimum value of .70 is considered acceptable for both Cronbach's α and ordinal α in educational research [12].

We used a t-test to compare students SCS1R scores to their final letter grades. Where the final letter grades was split into two groups. A t-test was used to determine if there was a significant difference of SCS1R scores between the two groups. While a chi-square and an ANOVA tests for significance differences of scores between multiple groups, a t-test is the best fit for comparing two groups [16].

3.1 Item Response Theory

Item response theory attempts to model the relationship between an examinee's ability, Θ, and the probability, P, of the examinee correctly responding to any particular test question, i [5]. The Rasch Model is defined below. β is the difficulty of a given question, i, and θ the ability of an examinee.

$$P_i(\Theta) = \frac{e^{(\Theta-\beta_i)}}{1+e^{(\Theta-\beta_i)}} \tag{1}$$

Abilities are calculated based on how well an examinee does on the overall test (equation 2). Equation 2 does not work for examinees who score a 100% or 0%. While you might want the examinee to get a 100% on the test, that does not assist in developing an understanding of their abilities and points to other typical explanations such as a low difficulty level of the exam. The same is true for examinees who score 0. The specific details, while beyond the scope of this paper, can be found in Baker and Kim [5].

$$\Theta_j = ln\frac{\%Correct}{1-\%Correct} \tag{2}$$

Difficulties are calculated based on how many examinees answer a question correctly. Equation 3 displays a rough estimate on the calculation of a question's difficulty. We used conditional maximum likelihood (CML) estimation. Further details are available in [4, 5]. Similarly to equation 2, equation 3 does not work for questions that have 100% correct responses or 0% correct responses. In a similar way as not wanting an examinee to get a score of 100 or 0, having a question that examinees get right 100% or 0% of the time will not benefit the research when trying to accurately measure examinees' abilities.

$$\beta_j = ln\frac{1-\%CorrectResponses}{\%CorrectResponses} \tag{3}$$

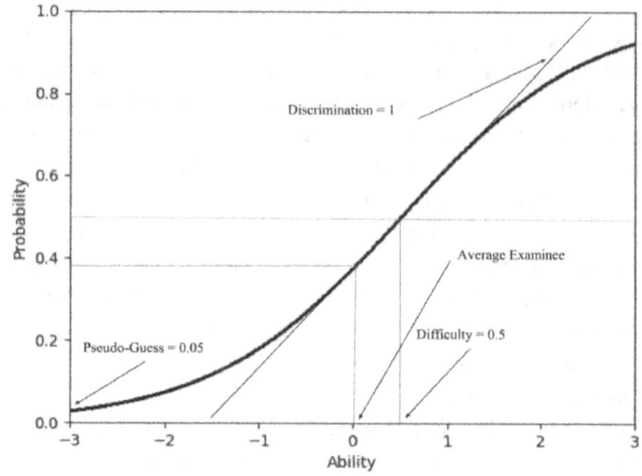

Figure 1: An example ICC

Both abilities and difficulties range from -3 to 3. An ability of -3 means the lowest ability, 0 is average, and 3 is the highest ability. As for difficulties -3 means the easiest difficulty, 0 is average, and 3 is the hardest. Using equation 1 and the difficulty of a test question, we can calculate the probability over the spectrum of all abilities ranging from -3 to 3 giving us an Item Characteristic Curve (ICC) of the question (equation 4).

$$P_i(\Theta) = \frac{e^{(\Theta_j-\beta_i)}}{1+e^{(\Theta_j-\beta_i)}} \tag{4}$$

The ICC represents the probability of an examinee obtaining the correct response to a question. The X axis ranges across examinees' ability. The Y axis is the probability an examinee of ability(x) getting a correct response to the question, ranging from 0 to 1 where 1 means that the chance of an examinee with ability(x) getting the correct response to the given test question is 100% [7, 10]. Figure 1 shows a sample ICC of a slightly difficult question $\beta(0.5)$, where an average examinee ($\Theta = 0$) has a 40% chance of getting the answer correct.

Plotting every test question's ICC gives the distribution of test items and how difficult a test is. A good test would have a large distribution across all items. "In developing any test, our aim would be to put enough stepping-stones along the path to represent all the stepping-points useful for our testing purposes, between little development and much development" [7]. Another way to look at it is, while testing the physical strength of a group of people you will not start them off by lifting 200lbs and increasing from there. Though some people might be able to lift that at first it does not give a good representation of how weak someone might be. Someone who can lift 190lbs will be considered just as weak as someone who can lift 10lbs. The same logic applies for not having a high enough difficulty.

Another aspect when creating a valid test is looking at the fit of each question. If a question is difficult, was that difficulty because it was designed to be challenging, or was there a misunderstanding in comprehension? Calculating the likelihood ratio (LR, equation 5) [5] can help. LR is calculated by splitting up the sample into two

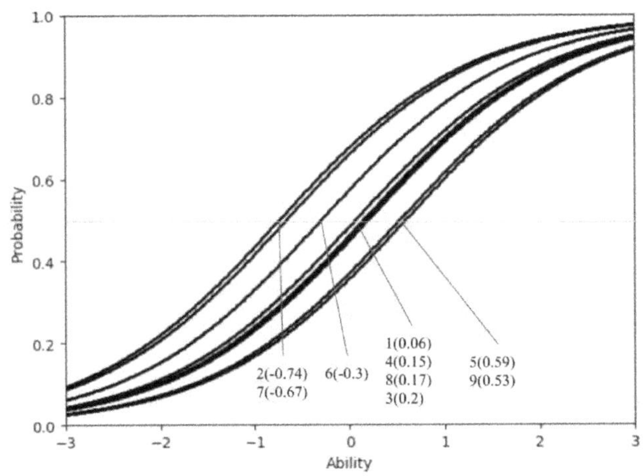

Figure 2: SCS1R ICC's

subgroups by the median score, where $\hat{\beta}_i$ consists of all students who scored below the median score and $\hat{\beta_{i_g}}$ consists of all students who scored above the median score. $l(\hat{\beta}_i)$ is the likelihood function under the overall approach. $l_g(\hat{\beta_{i_g}})$ is the likelihood function under the restricted approach. In other words, theoretically, the high ability students should have more correct responses across all test questions than low ability students. If low ability students are getting close to the same number of correct responses as high ability students to a certain question, there might be something wrong with the question. More detail can be found in [5].

$$LR = \frac{l(\hat{\beta}_i)}{\sum_{g=1}^{n-1} l_g(\hat{\beta_{i_g}})} \tag{5}$$

The Likelihood Test Statistic or z-value (Equation 6) provides a measurement as to the extent to which higher ability students perform better on a question than lower ability students. A significant z value indicates the item difficulty parameters differ across the raw score groups and that the Rasch model does not hold for that question [5]. Desirable values are routinely accepted to be those where $|z| \leq 2$ [7].

$$z = -2log(LR) = 2\sum_{g=1}^{n-1} logl_g(\hat{\beta_{i_g}}) - 2log(l(\hat{\beta}_i)) \tag{6}$$

As mentioned before, there is also a 1-par, 2-par and 3-par IRT. A 1-par IRT is commonly referred to as the Rasch model because it has the same number of parameters, but there are two significant differences. One difference is that difficulties of items in a 1-par IRT are centered around the average abilities of all examines while the difficulties of items in a Rasch model are centered around the average difficulty or all items. A second difference is that the discrimination parameter(α) of a Rasch model is set at a constant of 1 while a 1-par IRT can be set to a different constant. A 2-par IRT allows α to vary among test items. A 3-par adds in c, a lower asymptote or guessing parameter (equation 7). Changing α causes the slope of the ICC to either steepen or flatten out based on whether the question has high discrimination or not. A higher discrimination leads to a steeper slope. Changing c will cause the y asymptote to move up or down based on how easily a question can be guessed correctly [7, 10, 14].

Table 1: SCS1R Difficulties (N = 635)

Question	n+	% correct	CML
Q1	195	30.7	0.063
Q2	304	47.9	-0.740
Q3	179	28.2	0.199
Q4	185	29.1	0.148
Q5	138	21.7	0.589
Q6	241	38.0	-0.296
Q7	293	46.1	-0.665
Q8	182	28.7	0.173
Q9	144	22.7	0.528

$$P_i(\Theta) = 1 - c(\frac{e^{\alpha(\Theta_j - \beta_i)}}{1 + e^{\alpha(\Theta_j - \beta_i)}}) \tag{7}$$

4 RESULTS

4.1 IRT

4.1.1 Difficulties. Table 1 shows each item and its difficulty parameter (CML) after running a Rasch Model. n+ indicates the number of students that answered the question correctly. Arranging the questions from easiest to hardest we get Q2 being the least difficult of -0.740 followed by Q7, Q6, Q1, Q8, Q3, Q9 and Q5 being the most difficult of 0.589.

All questions had less than 50% of students correctly answering the questions, labeling all questions as hard. Parker et al. [13] note that a moderate question is one where between 50% and 85% of participants answer the question correctly, while an easy question is answered correctly by more that 85% of the respondents.

4.1.2 ICC. With the difficulties calculated we are able to plot the ICC of every question. Figure 2 shows the ICC for each question. Our results indicate that there is little variation between the 9 questions. Grouping questions based on their difficulties, 4 main groups emerge. Questions 2 and 7 mark the lower end, then question 6, then questions 1, 4, 8 and 3 and questions 9 and 5 being the last and most difficult. Even though the range of difficulty is small we can still categorize students into 5 main categories; 0 questions correct, 1-2 questions correct, 3 questions correct, 4-7 questions correct, and 8+ questions correct.

4.1.3 Fit. Table 2 shows the results of running a likelihood ratio test. After splitting the population into the 2 subgroups, where the first group (indicated as low abilities in Table 2) is all students who scored below the median score of 4 and the second group (indicated as high abilities in Table 2) is those students who scored a 4 or above. An ideal test should have a significant difference between the two groups and the percentage of students who answered the question correctly for each question. Question 7 is the best fit having a z-value of 0.659. We see that 32.7% of low ability students answered

Table 2: SCS1R Frequencies and Estimates

Question	Total			Low Abilities			High Abilities			|z- value|
	n+	% correct	CML	n+	% correct	CML	n+	% correct	CML	
Q1	195	30.7	0.063	69	15.9	0.260	126	62.7	-0.190	2.229
Q2	304	47.9	-0.740	145	33.4	-0.654	159	79.1	-0.973	1.566
Q3	179	28.2	0.199	77	17.7	0.135	102	50.7	0.289	0.786
Q4	185	29.1	0.148	72	16.6	0.212	113	56.2	0.072	0.702
Q5	138	21.7	0.589	46	10.6	0.708	92	45.8	0.488	1.022
Q6	241	38.0	-0.296	114	26.3	-0.337	127	63.2	-0.210	0.666
Q7	293	46.1	-0.665	142	32.7	-0.625	151	75.1	-0.755	0.659
Q8	182	28.7	0.173	66	15.2	0.310	116	57.7	0.013	1.477
Q9	144	22.7	0.528	87	20.0	-0.008	57	28.4	1.266	6.197

that question correctly, while 75.1% of high ability students answered that question correctly. Question 9 had the worst $|z|$-value at a 6.197. We see little difference between the two groups: 20.0% of the low ability students and only 28.4% of the high ability students answering the question correctly. Since question 9's $|z|$-value is so much greater than 2 it should be either edited or removed.

4.2 Reliability

For reliability, we calculated a Cronbach's alpha of a 0.499, indicating that at least 49.9% of the total score variance was due to true score variance in this sample. With further analysis, we determined that question 9 had a negative impact on the total reliability. After removing question 9, we calculated a Cronbach's alpha of a 0.57, still below our .70 minimum cut off [12]. We note that the low Cronbach's alpha is in line with the original SCS1 reliability of 0.59 as reported by [13], suggesting a practical level of reliability in keeping with the original unmodified exam.

4.3 Comparison

We used a t-test to compare students' SCS1R scores and their final letter grades. Because we didn't plan on collecting final letter grades until later in the collection process, the total number of final letter grades that were collected was 148. Final letter grades were split up into two groups. Group 1 consisted of students received a B+ or higher(n = 102) and group 2 consisted of students who receiving a B or below(n = 46). We wanted to split students up between a B and above and a B- and below. We were unable to do so because group 2 sample size wouldn't be large enough.

Running a t-test showed that there was a significant difference of scores between students who received a B+ or above (Mean = 3.4, Median = 3, SD = 1.7) and students who received a B and below (Mean = 2.7, Median = 3, SD = 1.3) at a p-value < 0.04 which is below the minimum cut off of a 0.05 [19]. Figure 3 Shows the the box plot of both groups. While the median of both groups are the same there was a significant difference between the two means (statistic=2.1, p-value=0.039). Stating that students who received a final letter grade of a B+ or higher scored higher on the SCS1R than those who received a final letter grade of a B or below.

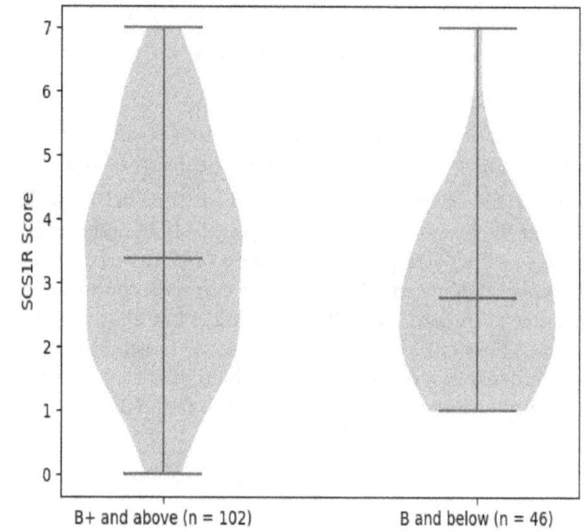

Figure 3: Violin Plot of Final letter grades and SCS1R scores (n = 148)

5 DISCUSSION

Conducting this study provided us a better understanding of the reliability of the instruments selected for use and enabled us to catch mistakes early in the data collection process for our overall study of spatial skills. Overall the SCS1R was found to be quite difficult for students, confirming the results obtained by Parker et al. [13]. Resulting data analysis suggests that this test should be further revised for difficulty and re-validated, a notion also suggested by the original authors. In our findings, beyond the difficulty level, question 9 specifically should be revised for better clarity or removed. In the case of question 1, which also fell (slightly) outside the recommended $|z|$-value, we determined that the item was necessary and beneficial to the study, while its removal caused the reliability of the SCS1R results to drop.

We where unable to reach significance while running a linear regression across all final letter grades and SCS1R scores. We chose to split students letter grades into two groups to show that the instrument is still able to differentiate between student of higher ability (course grades B+ and above) and students with lower abilities (as signified by those students earning a grade in CS1 of B and bellow). There were a few factors that play a role in why we couldn't reach significance of the chi-squared (linear regression). The biggest one is that the SCS1R is difficult. Students who received a B or below obtained scores that were not demonstrably different from guessing. There was also a strong bias when looking at final letter grades where the majority of students who participated received a grade in the A range. Another factor is that grading is not consistent across each university and their CS1 courses. Different professors have different grading scales and foci (e.g. emphasizing projects versus exams).

6 CONCLUSION

After taking a subset of the original SCS1 we were able to reduce time and redundancy, and alleviate student apprehension in taking a long and hard exam. Our Cronbach's alpha of 0.57 was close to the original Cronbach's alpha of 0.59 as reported by [13]. We also note that there was a clear correlation between student performance on the SCS1R and their performance in the CS1 course. This helped to convince us that the SCS1R exam is a reasonable predictor of student comprehension of CS1 content across the three universities data was collected.

ACKNOWLEDGEMENT

This material is based upon work partially supported by the National Science Foundation under Grant Numbers 1711780, 1711830, and 1712331. Any opinions, findings, and conclusions or recommendations expressed in this material are those of the author(s) and do not necessarily reflect the views of the National Science Foundation.

REFERENCES

[1] [n. d.]. Computer programming aptitude test. https://www.kent.ac.uk/careers/tests/computer-test.htm. ([n. d.]). Accessed: April 1, 2018.
[2] [n. d.]. CS education evaluation tools. https://csedresearch.org/tools/. ([n. d.]). Accessed: April 1, 2018.
[3] R. Alexandrowicz. 2012. "Ganz Rasch": A free software for categorical data analysis. *Social Science Computer Review* 30, 3 (2012), 369–379.
[4] E. Andersen. 1973. A goodness of fit test for the Rasch model. *Psychometrika* 38, 1 (1973), 123–140.
[5] F. Baker and S. Kim. 2004. *Item Response Theory: Parameter estimation techniques* (2nd. ed.). CRC Press.
[6] College Board. 2010. *2009 ap computer science a released exam.* The College Board, New York.
[7] T. Bond and C. Fox. 2001. *Applying The Rasch Model: Fundamental measurement in the human sciences.* Laurence Erlbaum Associates.
[8] S. Cooper, K. Wang, I. Maya, and S. Sorby. 2015. Spatial skill training in introductory computing. *ICER '15* (2015), 13–20.
[9] A. Field. 2009. *Discovering statistics using SPSS.* Sage publications.
[10] D. Harris. 1989. Comparison of 1-, 2- and 3-Parameter IRT Models. *Educational Measurement: Issues and Practice* 8, 1 (1989), 35–41.
[11] L. Lacher, A. Jiang, Y. Zhang, and M. Lewis. 2017. Aptitude and previous experience in cs1 classes. *Int'l Conf. Frontiers in Education: CS and CE* 17 (2017), 87–91.
[12] C. Lance, M. Butts, and L. Michels. 2006. The sources of four commonly reported cutoff criteria: What did they really say? *Organizational Research Methods* 9, 2 (2006), 202–220.
[13] M. Parker, M. Guzdial, and S. Engleman. 2016. Replication, validation, and use of a language independent cs1 knowledge assessment. *ICER '16* (2016), 93–101.
[14] Ayala R.J. de. 2009. *The theory and practice of item response theory.* The Guilford Press.
[15] A. Sahin and A. Duygu. 2016. The effects of test length and sample size on item parameters in item response theory. *Educational Sciences: Theory Practice* 17, 1 (2016), 321–335.
[16] Student. 1908. The Probable Error of a Mean. *Biometrika* 6, 1 (1908), 1–25.
[17] A. Tew, B. Dorn, and O. Schneider. 2012. Toward a validated computing attitudes survey. *ICER '12* (2012), 135–142.
[18] A. Tew and M. Guzdial. 2011. The FCS1: A language independent assessment of cs1 knowledge. *SIGCSE '11* (2011), 111–116.
[19] R. Wasserstein and N. Lazar. 2016. The ASA's Statement on p-Values. *The American Statistician* 70, 2 (2016), 129–133. https://doi.org/10.1080/00031305.2016.1154108
[20] S. Y. Yoon. 2011. Revised Purdue Spatial Visualization Test: Visualization of rotations (Revised PSVT:R) [Psychometric Instrument]. (2011).

A Topical Review of Evaluation Instruments for Computing Education

Adrienne Decker
Department of Engineering Education
University at Buffalo
Buffalo, NY, USA
adrienne@buffalo.edu

Monica M. McGill
Computer Science Department
Knox College
Galesburg, IL, USA
mmmcgill@knox.edu

ABSTRACT

As computing education research continues to grow and mature as a field, it becomes more important to focus on the quality and rigor of our research studies. One important aspect of any research study is its formal evaluation. Using standardized and validated instruments relevant to computer science education to perform evaluations can increase the quality of the study and the value of its results. However, researchers often create their own instruments rather than using existing ones, perhaps due to their lack of knowledge of the value of using an existing instrument or due to the challenge of finding such instruments. Through a review of relevant computing education literature, this paper presents a listing of 47 evaluation instruments specifically designed for measuring programs or constructs related to computing that can influence student achievement and learning. Analysis of purpose, target audience, reliability, and validity of the instruments is also presented. The paper ends with a call for the community to begin to make more regular use of validated instruments in their studies when possible and to develop and validate additional instruments in areas where few exist.

CCS CONCEPTS

• Social and professional topics~Computing education programs • Social and professional topics~Computer science education • Social and professional topics~Student assessment

KEYWORDS

Evaluation instruments, validation, assessment

ACM Reference format:
Adrienne Decker and Monica M. McGill. 2019. A Topical Review of Evaluation Instruments for Computing Education In *Proceedings of 50th ACM Technical Symposium on Computer Science Education (SIGCSE '19), February 27-March 2, 2019, Minneapolis, MN, USA.ACM, New York, NY, USA, 7 pages.* https://doi.org/10.1145/3287324.3287393

SIGCSE '19, February 27-March 2, 2019, Minneapolis, MN, USA

ACM ISBN 978-1-4503-5890-3/19/02.
https://doi.org/10.1145/3287324.3287393

1 INTRODUCTION

Since the publication of Computer Science Education Research in 2004 [9], there has been a handbook for conducting research in computing education and an increased scrutiny of the methods used in such studies. Many have argued that as a community we need to a better job of both designing and reporting on the research done in this space [1, 13, 19, 21].

One key aspect of doing a better job at our research is in measurement and evaluation. Recent studies that looked at data across multiple other studies have noted that there is a lack of both standardization in variables that are measured and how they are measured [5, 6, 10, 16].

It is critically important to adopt validated measures so that the variables that are measured are being done reliably. Using standardized instruments will also help us as a community to be able to better compare results. However, in order to achieve this goal, researchers need to be aware of what instruments are available to them and choose to use them when appropriate for their research. One problem that faces researchers is the lack of ability to easily find such instruments, which often results in individual studies developing instruments for their own use that are not able to be validated.

Therefore, this study was undertaken to provide a taxonomy of existing research-based evaluation instruments that are available in publications and publicly-accessible websites and databases. For the collection and analysis, our overarching research question is: *What evaluation and assessment instruments are available in accessible computing education venues and online databases?*

It is our hope that by providing such a list, researchers will use these instruments in their studies. In addition, researchers and evaluators can potentially re-validate these instruments as well as creating new instruments in areas where there are few. The long-term goal of this research is to promote the creation and usage of standardized measures within the computer science education community for commonly measured constructs across a wide-range of learners.

2 METHODOLOGY

To determine the set of evaluation instruments that have been designed for computing education and recently used in research studies, we began a systematic search of the computing education literature and other related databases. To do so, we:

- Examined 297 articles in the https://csedresearch.org database (2012-2016), noting any instruments used within studies as well as articles related to instrument validation, [15]
- Examined the table of contents for the proceedings of the ACM ICER conference, the ACM journal Transactions on Computing Education, and Taylor and Francis' Computer Science Education in the years 2012-2016 to determine if additional instrument validation studies were published that were not covered by the database above (as it is specialized to research in pre-college computing activities),
- Searched several online databases for instruments, including American Evaluation Association [2], STELAR [7] The Pear Institute [18], Institute for the Integration of Technology into Teaching and Learning [11], MSPNet [4], Engineering is Elementary [3], and
- Used search engines to perform searches based on relevant keywords (e.g., computer science, inventory, survey, instrument, evaluation, interest, self-efficacy, etc.).

After creating the initial list, we solicited the CS education community for additional instruments using the SIGCSE-Members listserv and computing education social media sites. At the end, we had a total of 47 evaluation instruments.

Demographics for each instrument were initially coded by a student assistant, with instructions and training from the research team, followed by verification by an independent coder (one of the researchers on the project).

The following data was collected for each instrument:

- Title of instrument
- Authors
- Year of publication
- Brief description of instrument
- Cost to use instrument
- Number of questions
- Type of questions
- Time required to complete instrument (or time limit)
- Target demographic
- Constructs assessed
- Reliability evidence presented
- Validity evidence presented
- URL to relevant article explaining instrument
- URL of instrument

3 RESULTS

Table 3 presents a list of these instruments and gives an indication of what type of construct it measures (cognitive, noncognitive, or program assessment). References for each instrument are given in Appendix A.

3.1 Cost and Availability

The cost to use the instrument and its availability seem to be intrinsically linked in our field. Of the 47 instruments studied, 39 (83%) were available, usually in the article that first used the instrument in a research study or a separate article that focused on the validation of the instrument. Many of those articles are not open access, but would be available through university libraries. Once a researcher had access to the article, the instrument does not have a cost to use it.

Of those instruments that were not available from the aforementioned articles, four were obtained from the authors who agreed to allow them to be housed in https://csedresearch.org database for free usage by anyone interested. Due to its nature, SCS1 [A-31] is available to anyone who requests access and is free to use, but is not publicly available to protect those using it for research purposes. That is, if the questions on the instrument become available to anyone, then it its efficacy to show knowledge of programming concepts is diminished.

In the end, 44 (94%) of the instruments are available to other researchers and do not require the researcher to pay a fee to administer. We attempted to reach out to the authors of the remaining instruments, and if the instrument is provided at some point in the future, it can be accessed in the https://csedresearch.org database.

3.2 Constructs Assessed

We divided the constructs assessed by the instruments into two main categories, cognitive and noncognitive constructs. For the purposes of this analysis, we considered cognitive constructs to be content or domain knowledge of computing or computer science, and noncognitive constructs are everything else.

There were 13 instruments (28%) that measured cognitive constructs. Of these, the types of knowledge measured were: computational thinking (6), CS1 concepts (3), CS2 concepts (1), digital logic (1), algorithmic analysis (1), and research skills (1).

There were 31 instruments (66%) that measured noncognitive constructs which included constructs such as self-efficacy, anxiety, confidence, enjoyment, sense of belonging, intent to persist, and perceptions.

There were four instruments that were categorized as measuring both cognitive and noncognitive constructs.

During analysis, it became clear that there was actually a third category of construct that was coded separately from cognitive and noncognitive. That third category is program evaluation. Program evaluation instruments seek to measure the effectiveness of a specific program and have items that address the issues pertinent to determining problems with delivery or execution of the program/intervention as well as ways to improve. Eight of the 47 instruments (17%) were categorized as having some or all of their items concerned with program evaluation.

3.3 Number of Items

The number of items on an instrument can generally give an idea of how long it would take to administer such an instrument. The amount of time needed to complete the survey or interview for the instruments ranges from 5 minutes to 1 hour. Table 1 shows the breakdown of number of items on the instruments.

The largest segment of the instruments (40%) had between 11 and 30 items. It is important to note that the instruments with over 50 items generally have subscales of smaller numbers of items that can be administered independently of each other. One of the instruments [A-42] is an observational protocol and item count does not make sense in that context. Project Quantum [A-8] is a contribution-driven question bank for creating evaluations and currently has over 8000 contributed questions, but is specifically designed so that a user only gives questions with topics of interest to their assessment needs.

Table 1: Number of items in studied instruments

Number of items	Number of instruments (%)
1 – 10	11 (23%)
11 – 30	19 (40%)
31 – 50	6 (13%)
> 50	9 (19%)

3.4 Item Type

In analyzing the collected demographic data, we noticed three main categories of item types, Likert-type prompts, multiple choice, and open-ended questions. Several of the instruments (29%) combined these three types of items and few had item types that did not fit into these categories. Table 2 shows the breakdown of types of items for the instruments studied.

The largest segment of the instruments (38%) had only Likert-type prompts. Including those with the instruments that combine Likert-type prompts with other types of items that percentage raises to 64%. Of the seven remaining instruments not covered by the table two were interview protocols; one was an observation protocol; two asked for answers on a 100-point scale; one had Likert-type prompts and semantic differential items; one had questions that asked the participant to choose the level of use of technology that best describes their level; and one was an autograding/machine grading assessment.

Table 2: Types of items in studied instruments

Type	No. of instruments (%)
Likert-type items only	18 (38%)
Multiple choice items only	6 (13%)
Open-ended items only	2 (4%)
Likert and Multiple Choice	6 (13%)
Likert and Open Ended	2 (4%)
Multiple Choice and Open Ended	2 (4%)
All three types	4 (9%)

3.5 Target Demographic

Figure 1 shows the breakdown of the target demographics for the instruments. The grade levels indicated are based on the United States system. For purposes of the reporting, an instrument can be included for more than one demographic category (e.g., it targets all K-12 students). The target of undergraduates has the largest percentage of instruments (26%), but if you consider instruments targeting K-12 (and remove duplicated counting), there are actually 20 instruments (43%) that target that demographic. Pre-service and in-service teachers are targets of 15% of the instruments.

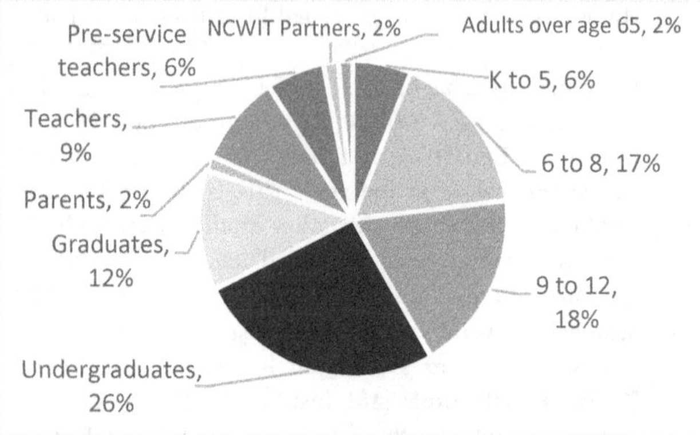

Figure 1: Target Demographics of Instruments Studied

3.6 Reliability

Reliability of an instrument is a statement about its consistency in measurement. Ideally, an instrument will provide the same results or score for the same answers each time it is given. Reliability information was found for 28 (60%) of the instruments. The most common form of reliability information was Cronbach's alpha or some other measure of internal consistency. There were two instruments that showed evidence of test-retest reliability within the data set.

3.7 Validity

Validity of an instrument helps us determine if we are measuring what we think we are measuring. Reliability is a necessary, but not sufficient condition to establish an instrument's validity. Reliability and/or validity have been checked for the specified particular demographic in a particular setting. Using a validated, reliable instrument does not necessarily mean that the instrument will be reliable and/or valid in different settings. It can provide, however, a greater measure of confidence than an instrument that has not been validated or determined to be reliable.

Validity can come in many forms and we see primarily two forms reported in the data. Of the 47 instruments studied, 24 (51%) provide some evidence for their validity. It was common in the data to see expert opinion give evidence of face validity and several instruments reported on construct validity evidence through various measures.

4 DISCUSSION

The instruments found are able to be used for free, with the exception of a few that require access to the publication in which they are included. This is a limitation for some, but often not those in the research community that have access to the most common journals and conference proceedings through college and university libraries. One positive step that could be taken for the instruments is to make the instrument freely accessible by making it available outside the article which describes it. That way, those interested in using it do not need access to the article to get the items from the instrument.

A majority of the instruments had under 30 items, which means that they should be relatively quick to administer. Couple that with the fact that the most common type of item was Likert scale and we have a collection of instruments that are not onerous on a participant's time. As pointed out, even those with a large number of items have subscales that allow the researcher to give a smaller number of items that best suit their needs. Multiple choice is also another popular option for these instruments. Aside from time to administer, another advantage of these item types is their ability to be scored quickly and consistently.

The instruments tend to strongly favor measuring noncognitive constructs (ie., those that are not domain or content knowledge). However, it was observed, although not studied rigorously for this analysis, that several of the constructs appeared across many of the instruments. Further analysis is needed to uncover duplication of constructs being measured or gaps where the instruments fail to cover factors that have been shown to impact student achievement and learning [8, 12, 14]. The beginnings of this gap analysis is available in [17].

It is very promising to see such a large number of these instruments providing either reliability (60%) or validity evidence (51%). There are actually 20 instruments (43%) that provide both. Assessment and evaluation specialists will tell you that there are many types of both reliability and validity and that more is always better [20]. While we did not specifically analyze what type of validity evidence was presented for this study, content or face validity was very commonly cited as the only validity evidence. While that is a start, for sure, more is needed. Further, many of the instruments rely on self-report, which can be a threat to construct validity. Self-report threat can occur because the participant wants to make themselves "look better" to the researcher/research project [20].

4.1 Limitations

There are a number of limitations of this study. First, the search space for instruments, while quite large in some aspects, is still limited. It is possible that there instruments in the literature outside our date range for the searched databases that exist, particularly newer instruments that were not revealed through our searches or calls to the community for input. Future work to expand the collection of instruments and to add to this taxonomy is already planned and will include additional years, venues, and targeted searches.

Further, we are often limited in the evidence presented about a particular instrument to one paper or website entry. It is quite possible that other papers exist that were not found during this search that would provide additional information about the instrument. One of our next steps is to contact the authors to verify the data we curated for each instrument and to provide us with additional evidence or links that describe the evidence about the instruments. This will be time-consuming work, but will provide greater assurance that the publicly available collection of instruments and their summaries is accurate and useful for the community.

4.2 Future Work

The next steps for this taxonomy are to make it more accessible to those in the community. To that end, each one of the instruments identified here and the data extracted from each is presented in searchable form at https://csedresearch.org.

As identified previously, we believe more instruments are available than what we were able to identify for this taxonomy at this time. New instruments will be added to the website as soon as we are made aware of them. The website will provide a way for instrument authors to contribute information about an instrument not listed and to provide additions and corrections to entries already there.

Additionally, we continue work with a group of evaluators who are also collecting a large set of evaluation instruments for both STEM and computing education. We will continue to share our collection of instruments with them in order to promote their usage far and wide.

5 CONCLUSION

We take this work as a starting point for the community. Not only do measures of many constructs and programs already exist, many of them have already been shown to be reliable and/or validated. We encourage those conducting research in computing education and wanting to measure specific constructs to first look to see if there is an instrument already available that measures those constructs.

There is also a need to validate existing instruments that have not yet been validated as well as validate instruments in different contexts. Doing so will help improve the results of the initial research as well as providing a validated measure of the construct for others.

We recognize that the instruments available may not measure exactly what is needed for a particular research study. However, adaptation of an existing instrument is favorable to creating a brand new instrument, especially if constructs are similar. When faced with the challenge of an instrument not being available, we as a community should also look outside our own literature to see if other educational/learning sciences literature provides a starting point. If not, that truly represents a need in the community to create and/or adapt a measure for use in future research.

ACKNOWLEDGMENTS

This material is based upon work supported by the U.S. National Science Foundation under Grant Nos. 1625335 and 1757402.

Table 3: List of Evaluation Instruments

Program Evaluation	Cog-nitive	Noncog-nitive	Evaluation Instrument Title	Appendix Citation
	X		Algorithm Analysis Concept Inventory	[A-11]
		X	BASICS Study Student Implementation Questionnaire	[A-32]
		X	BASICS Study Teacher Implementation Questionnaire	[A-33]
X			BASICS Study Teacher Interview Guide	[A-34]
X	X	X	CISE REU A La Carte Student Survey	[A-37]
		X	Cognitive Load Component Survey	[A-21]
	X		Commutative Assessment	[A-40]
	X		Computational Thinking Pattern Analysis (CTPA)	[A-17]
	X	X	Computational Thinking Survey	[A-44]
	X		Computational Thinking Test	[A-36]
		X	Computer Anxiety Scale	[A-43]
		X	Computer Attitude Questionnaire (CAQ 5.14)	[A-15]
		X	Computer Attitude Questionnaire (CAQ 5.22)	[A-15]
		X	Computer Attitude Scale	[A-19]
		X	Computer Programming Self-Efficacy Scale	[A-31]
		X	Computer Science Attitude and Identity Survey (CSAIS)	[A-38]
		X	Computer Science Attitude Survey (Hoegh and Moskal)	[A-14]
		X	Computer Science Attitude Survey (Weibe et al)	[A-42]
		X	Computer Science Interest Survey	[A-2]
		X	Computing Attitudes Survey	[A-10]
	X		Digital Logic Concept Inventory (DLCI) (Form A)	[A-13]
		X	Draw-a-Computer-Scientist Test	[A-12]
		X	Effectiveness of Technology Outreach Survey	[A-20]
X			Evaluation of Faculty Participation in POSSE	[A-7]
	X	X	Evaluation of Student Participation in HFOSS	[A-7]
	X		Fairy Assessment	[A-41]
		X	Microcomputer Beliefs Inventory for Middle School Students	[A-35]
X			NCWIT Computing Major Pace and Workload Experience	[A-22]
		X	NCWIT Incoming Student Survey	[A-23]
X			NCWIT Overall Computing Major Satisfaction: Student Survey	[A-24]
X			NCWIT Pair Programming Student Final Assessment	[A-25]
		X	NCWIT Parent Survey	[A-26]
X			NCWIT Program Partner Survey	[A-27]
		X	New Computer Game Attitude Scale	[A-18]
	X		Project Quantum	[A-8]
	X		Project TREES Survey	[A-3]
		X	Robotics Activities Attitudes Scale	[A-9]
	X		SCS1	[A-30]
		X	Self-Efficacy for Computational Thinking (SECT)	[A-1]
		X	Stages of Adoption of Technology (SA)	[A-4]
	X	X	Student Centered Observation Protocol for computer-science Education (SCOPE)	[A-39]
		X	Student Computing Interest: Post Survey for Outreach programs	[A-28]
X			Student Outreach Experience: Interview Protocol for Students	[A-29]
		X	Teacher Attitudes toward Computers (TAC)	[A-5]
		X	Teachers' Attitudes Toward Information Technology (TAT)	[A-16]
		X	Teachers' Self-Efficacy in Computational Thinking (TSECT)	[A-1]
		X	Technology in Education Competency Survey (TECS)	[A-6]

APPENDIX A. INSTRUMENT REFERENCES

Please see https://csedresearch.org/evaluation-instruments/ for more information about instruments.

[A-1] Nathan Bean, Joshua Weese, Russell Feldhausen, and R Scott Bell. 2015. Starting from scratch: Developing a pre-service teacher training program in computational thinking. In Frontiers in Education Conference (FIE), 2015 IEEE. IEEE, 1–8.

[A-2] Janet Seeley Blouin. 2011. High school seniors' computer self-efficacy and interest in computer science careers. Ph.D. Dissertation. University of Georgia.

[A-3] Guanhua Chen, Ji Shen, Lauren Barth-Cohen, Shiyan Jiang, Xiaoting Huang, and Moataz Eltoukhy. 2017. Assessing elementary studentsâĂŹ computational thinking in everyday reasoning and robotics programming. Computers & Education 109 (2017), 162–175.

[A-4] Rhonda Christensen. 1997. Effect of technology integration education on the attitudes of teachers and their students. Unpublished doctoral dissertation, University of North Texas. Available: https://digital.library.unt.edu/ark:/67531/metadc277676/?q=christensen.

[A-5] Rhonda Christensen and Gerald Knezek. 1996. Constructing the Teachers' Attitudes Toward Computers (TAC) Questionnaire. (1996).

[A-6] Rhonda Christensen and Gerald Knezek. 2001. The Technology in Education Competency Survey (TECS): A self-appraisal instrument for NCATE standards. In Society for Information Technology & Teacher Education International Conference. Association for the Advancement of Computing in Education (AACE), 2288–2289.

[A-7] HFOSS Community. Foss2Serve. Evaluation Instruments. Retrived from: http://foss2serve.org/index.php/Evaluation_Instruments

[A-8] Computing at School. Project Quantum: tests worth teaching to. Retrieved from: https: //community.computingatschool.org.uk/resources/4382/single

[A-9] Jennifer Cross, Emily Hamner, Lauren Zito, Illah Nourbakhshh, and Debra Bernstein. 2016. Development of an assessment for measuring middle school student attitudes towards robotics activities. In Frontiers in Education Conference (FIE), 2016 IEEE. IEEE, 1–8.

[A-10] Brian Dorn and Allison Elliott Tew. 2015. Empirical validation and application of the computing attitudes surve. Computer Science Education, 25, 1, 1-36,

[A-11] Mohammed F Farghally, Kyu Han Koh, Jeremy V Ernst, and Clifford A Shaffer. 2017. Towards a concept inventory for algorithm analysis topics. In Proceedings of the 2017 ACM SIGCSE. ACM, 207–212.

[A-12] Alexandria K Hansen, Hilary A Dwyer, Ashley Iveland, Mia Talesfore, Lacy Wright, Danielle B Harlow, and Diana Franklin. 2017. Assessing children's understanding of the work of computer scientists: the draw-a-computer-scientist test. In Proceedings of the 2017 ACM SIGCSE. ACM, 279–284.

[A-13] Geoffrey L Herman, Michael C Loui, and Craig Zilles. 2010. Creating the digital logic concept inventory. In Proceedings of the 41st ACM technical symposium on Computer science education. ACM, 102–106.

[A-14] Andrew Hoegh and Barbara M Moskal. 2009. Examining science and engineering students' attitudes toward computer science. In Frontiers in Education Conference, 2009. FIE'09. 39th IEEE. IEEE, 1–6.

[A-15] Gerald Knezek and Rhonda Christensen. 1996. Validating the Computer Attitude Questionnaire (CAQ). (1996).

[A-16] Gerald Knezek and Rhonda Christensen. 1998. Internal consistency reliability for the teachers' attitudes toward information technology (TAT) questionnaire. In Proceedings of the society for information technology in teacher education annual Conference. 831–836.

[A-17] Kyu Han Koh, Hilarie Nickerson, Ashok Basawapatna, and Alexander Repenning. 2014. Early Validation of Computational Thinking Pattern Analysis. In Proceedings of ITiCSE '14. ACM, New York, NY, USA, 213–218. https://doi.org/10.1145/2591708.2591724

[A-18] Eric Zhi-Feng Liu, Chun-Yi Lee, and Jen-Huang Chen. 2013. Developing a New Computer Game Attitude Scale for Taiwanese Early Adolescents. Journal of Educational Technology & Society 16, 1 (2013).

[A-19] Brenda H Loyd and Clarice Gressard. 1984. Reliability and factorial validity of computer attitude scales. Educational and Psychological measurement 44, 2 (1984), 501–505.

[A-20] Monica M McGill, Adrienne Decker, and Amber Settle. 2016. Undergraduate students' perceptions of the impact of pre-college computing activities on choices of major. ACM Transactions on Computing Education (TOCE) 16, 4 (2016), 15.

[A-21] Briana B Morrison, Brian Dorn, and Mark Guzdial. 2014. Measuring cognitive load in introductory CS: adaptation of an instrument. In Proceedings of the tenth annual conference on International computing education research. ACM, 131–138.

[A-22] National Center for Women & Information Technology. NCWIT Computing Major Pace and Workload: Student Survey. Retrieved from https://www.ncwit.org/file/computing-major-pace-and-workload-student-survey

[A-23] National Center for Women & Information Technology. NCWIT Incoming Student Survey. Retrieved from https://www.ncwit.org/file/incoming-student-survey

[A-24] National Center for Women & Information Technology. NCWIT Overall Computing Major Satisfaction: Student Survey. Retrieved from https://www.ncwit.org/file/incoming-student-survey

[A-25] National Center for Women & Information Technology. NCWIT Pair Programming Student Final Assessment. Retrieved from https://www.ncwit.org/file/pair-programming-student-final-assessment

[A-26] National Center for Women & Information Technology. NCWIT Parent Survey. Retrieved from https://www.ncwit.org/file/parent-survey

[A-27] National Center for Women & Information Technology. NCWIT Program Partner Survey. Retrieved from https://www.ncwit.org/file/program-partner-survey

[A-28] National Center for Women & Information Technology. NCWIT Student Computing Interest: Post Survey for Outreach Programs. Retrieved from https://www.ncwit.org/file/student-computing-interest-post-survey-outreach-programs

[A-29] National Center for Women & Information Technology. NCWIT Student Outreach Experience Interview Protocol for Students. Retrieved from https://www.ncwit.org/file/student-outreach-experience-interview-protocol-students

[A-30] Miranda C Parker, Mark Guzdial, and Shelly Engleman. 2016. Replication, validation, and use of a language independent CS1 knowledge assessment. In Proceedings of the 2016 ACM conference on international computing education research. ACM, 93–101.

[A-31] Vennila Ramalingam and Susan Wiedenbeck. 1998. Development and validation of scores on a computer programming self-efficacy scale and group analyses of novice programmer self-efficacy. Journal of Educational Computing Research 19, 4 (1998), 367–381.

[A-32] Outlier Research & Evaluation. 2017. BASICS Study ECS Student Implementation and Contextual Factor Questionnaire Measures [Measurement scales]. Technical Report. Outlier Research & Evaluation at UChicago STEM Education | University of Chicago; Chicago, IL. https://s3.amazonaws.com/cemse/basics/files/findings/BASICS_SQ_Measures_FINAL.pdf

[A-33] Outlier Research & Evaluation. 2017. BASICS Study ECS Teacher Implementation and Contextual Factor Questionnaire Measures [Measurement scales]. Technical Report. Outlier Research & Evaluation at UChicago STEM Education | University of Chicago; Chicago, IL. https://s3.amazonaws.com/cemse/basics/files/findings/BASICS_TQ_Measures_FINAL.pdf

[A-34] Outlier Research & Evaluation. 2017. BASICS Study ECS Teacher Interview Guide [Measurement scales]. Technical Report. Outlier Research & Evaluation at UChicago STEM Education | University of Chicago; Chicago, IL. https://s3.amazonaws.com/cemse/basics/files/findings/BASICS_TI_Guide_FINAL.pdf

[A-35] Iris M Riggs and Larry G Enochs. 1993. A microcomputer beliefs inventory for middle school students: Scale development and validation. Journal of Research on Computing in Education 25, 3 (1993), 383–390.

[A-36] Marcos Román-González, Juan-Carlos Pérez-González, Jesús Moreno-León, and Gregorio Robles. 2018. Can computational talent be detected? Predictive validity of the Computational Thinking Test. International Journal of Child-Computer Interaction (2018).

[A-37] Audrey S Rorrer. 2016. An evaluation capacity building toolkit for principal investigators of undergraduate research experiences: A demonstration of transforming theory into practice. Evaluation and program planning 55 (2016), 103–111.

[A-38] Alicia N Washington, Shaefny Grays, and Sudhipta Dasmohapatra. 2016. The Computer Science Attitude and Identity Survey (CSAIS): A Novel Tool for Measuring the Impact of Ethnic Identity in Underrepresented Computer Science Students. In Proceedings of the ASEE's 123rd Annual Conference & Exposition 2016.

[A-39] DC Webb, SB Miller, H Nickerson, R Grover, and K Gutiérrez. 2014. Student Centered Observation Protocol for computer-science Education (SCOPE). University of Colorado at Boulder (2014).

[A-40] David Weintrop. 2015. Comparing Text-based, Blocks-based, and Hybrid Blocks/Text Programming Tools. In Proceedings of the Eleventh Annual International Conference on International Computing Education Research (ICER '15). ACM, New York, NY, USA, 283–284. https://doi.org/10.1145/2787622.2787752

[A-41] Linda Werner, Jill Denner, Shannon Campe, and Damon Chizuru Kawamoto. 2012. The fairy performance assessment: measuring computational thinking in middle school. In Proceedings of the 43rd ACM technical symposium on Computer Science Education. ACM, 215–220.

[A-42] Eric Wiebe, Laurie Williams, Kai Yang, and Carol Miller. 2003. Computer science attitude survey. computer science 14, 25 (2003), 0–86.

[A-43] Katherine V Wild, Nora C Mattek, Shoshana A Maxwell, Hiroko H Dodge, Holly B Jimison, and Jeffrey A Kaye. 2012. Computer-related self-efficacy and anxiety in older adults with and without mild cognitive impairment. Alzheimer's & Dementia 8, 6 (2012), 544–552.

[A-44] Aman Yadav, Ninger Zhou, Chris Mayfield, Susanne Hambrusch, and John T Korb. 2011. Introducing computational thinking in education courses. In Proceedings of the 42nd ACM technical symposium on Computer science education. ACM, 465–470.

REFERENCES

[1] Ahmed Al-Zubidy, Jeffrey C. Carver, Sarah Heckman, and Mark Sherriff. 2016. A (Updated) Review of Empiricism at the SIGCSE Technical Symposium. In Proceedings of the 47th ACM Technical Symposium on Computing Science Education (SIGCSE '16). ACM, New York, NY, USA, 120-125. DOI: https://doi.org/10.1145/2839509.2844601

[2] American Evaluation Association. N.d. American Evaluation Association. Retrieved from: http://www.eval.org/

[3] Boston Museum of Science. Research Instruments. Retrieved from: https://www.eie.org/engineering-elementary/research/research-instruments

[4] Center for School Reform at TERC. MSPNet Resource List. Retrieved from: http://hub.mspnet.org/index.cfm/msp_tools

[5] Adrienne Decker, Monica M. McGill, and Amber Settle. 2016. Towards a Common Framework for Evaluating Computing Outreach Activities. In Proceedings of the 47th ACM Technical Symposium on Computing Science Education (SIGCSE '16). ACM, New York, NY, USA, 627-632. DOI: https://doi.org/10.1145/2839509.2844567

[6] Adrienne Decker and Monica M. McGill. 2017. Pre-College Computing Outreach Research: Towards Improving the Practice. In Proceedings of the 2017 ACM SIGCSE Technical Symposium on Computer Science Education (SIGCSE '17). ACM, New York, NY, USA, 153-158. DOI: https://doi.org/10.1145/3017680.3017744

[7] Education Development Center, Inc. STELAR – STEM Learning and Research Center. Retrieved from: http://stelar.edc.org/resources

[8] Camille A Farrington, Melissa Roderick, Elaine Allensworth, Jenny Nagaoka, Tasha Seneca Keyes, David W Johnson, and Nicole O Beechum. 2012. Teaching Adolescents to Become Learners: The Role of Noncognitive Factors in Shaping School Performance–A Critical Literature Review. ERIC

[9] S. Fincher and M. Petre, eds., Computer Science Education Research, Taylor & Francis, The Netherlands, Lisse, 2004.

[10] Petri Ihantola, Arto Vihavainen, Alireza Ahadi, Matthew Butler, Jürgen Börstler, Stephen H. Edwards, Essi Isohanni, Ari Korhonen, Andrew Petersen, Kelly Rivers, Miguel Ángel Rubio, Judy Sheard, Bronius Skupas, Jaime Spacco, Claudia Szabo, and Daniel Toll. 2015. Educational Data Mining and Learning Analytics in Programming: Literature Review and Case Studies. In Proceedings of the 2015 ITiCSE on Working Group Reports (ITICSE-WGR '15). ACM, New York, NY, USA, 41-63. DOI: https://doi.org/10.1145/2858796.2858798

[11] Institute for the Integration of Technology into Teaching and Learning. UNT Institute for the Integration of Technology. Retrieved from: https://iittl.unt.edu/content/instruments

[12] Jihyun Lee and Valerie J Shute. 2010. Personal and social-contextual factors in K–12 academic performance: An integrative perspective on student learning. Educational Psychologist 45, 3 (2010), 185–202.

[13] Alex Lishinski, Jon Good, Phil Sands, and Aman Yadav. 2016. Methodological Rigor and Theoretical Foundations of CS Education Research. In Proceedings of the 2016 ACM Conference on International Computing Education Research (ICER '16). ACM, New York, NY, USA, 161-169. DOI: https://doi.org/10.1145/2960310.2960328

[14] Robert J Marzano. 2003. What works in schools: Translating research into action. ASCD.

[15] Monica McGill and Adrienne Decker. (2017). Computer Science Education Repository. Available online: https://csedresearch.org.

[16] Monica M. McGill, Adrienne Decker, and Zachary Abbott. 2018. Improving Research and Experience Reports of Pre-College Computing Activities: A Gap Analysis. In Proceedings of the 49th ACM Technical Symposium on Computer Science Education (SIGCSE '18). ACM, New York, NY, USA, 964-969. DOI: https://doi.org/10.1145/3159450.3159481

[17] Monica M. McGill, Adrienne Decker, Tom McKlin, and Kathy Haynie. 2019._A Gap Analysis of Noncognitive Constructs in Evaluation Instruments_Designed for Computing Education. In Proceedings of the 50th ACM Technical Symposium on Computer Science Education (SIGCSE '19), ACM, New York, NY, USA. 7 pages. DOI: https://doi.org/10.1145/3287324.3287362

[18] Pear Institute. PEAR (Program in Education, Afterschool and Resiliency). Retrieved from: http://www.pearweb.org/atis/tools/jump

[19] J. Randolph, G. Julnes, E. Sutinen, S. Lehman, "A Methodological Review of Computer Science Education Resarch," Journal of Information Technology Education, vol. 7, 2008, pp. 135-162

[20] Trochim, W. M. 2006. The Research Methods Knowledge Base, 2nd Edition. Retrieved from http://www.socialresearchmethods.net/kb/.

[21] D. W. Valentine, "CS Education Research: A Meta-Analysis of SIGCSE Technical Symposium Proceedings," Proc. of the 35th SIGCSE Technical Symposium on Computer Science Education, Norfolk, VA, USA, March 3-7, 2004, pp. 255-259.

Automating Systems Course Unit and Integration Testing

Experience Report

Dee A. B. Weikle
James Madison University
Harrisonburg, VA
weikleda@jmu.edu

Michael O. Lam
James Madison University
Harrisonburg, VA
lam2mo@jmu.edu

Michael S. Kirkpatrick
James Madison University
Harrisonburg, VA
kirkpams@jmu.edu

ABSTRACT

Introducing software testing has taken on a greater importance in undergraduate computer science curricula in the last several years, with many departments using JUnit or other testing frameworks in the programming sequence and software engineering courses. We have developed an automated framework for unit and integration testing and grading for our intermediate-level systems course projects. Our system–designed to test C programs–combines the Check unit testing framework, custom Bash scripts for integration testing, and the Valgrind Memcheck memory leak detection tool. Although our courses use Linux, the framework is platform-independent and has been tested on a variety of other platforms.

We have used this framework for seven semesters with four different instructors as part of the computer science program at a primarily undergraduate university with an emphasis on liberal arts. We distribute both public and private tests so that students get immediate feedback on their progress without knowing the actual contents of every test. We have observed that knowing their code is not completely working motivates more students to figure out what they don't understand before the project deadline. It also gives students examples of different levels of tests to use to debug their code, encourages them to develop a deeper understanding of the project specification, and reduces student anxiety about grades.

ACM Reference Format:

Dee A. B. Weikle, Michael O. Lam, and Michael S. Kirkpatrick. 2019. Automating Systems Course Unit and Integration Testing: Experience Report. In *Proceedings of the 50th ACM Technical Symposium on Computer Science Education (SIGCSE '19), February 27-March 2, 2019, Minneapolis, MN, USA.* ACM, New York, NY, USA, 6 pages. https://doi.org/10.1145/3287324.3287502

1 INTRODUCTION

Software testing has become a fundamental skill for computer science graduates entering the industry. Many employers expect their new hires to be familiar with methodologies that integrate testing and software development, such as test-driven development. Given this increased emphasis from industry, many computer science programs have explored ways to reinforce these concepts in courses beyond software engineering.

SIGCSE '19, February 27-March 2, 2019, Minneapolis, MN, USA

ACM ISBN 978-1-4503-5890-3/19/02...$15.00
https://doi.org/10.1145/3287324.3287502

One common approach to increase students' exposure to testing practices is to bring unit testing into other domains, such as courses on human-computer interaction [3]. JUnit provides a standard industry framework for courses that use Java [12]; additionally, the rich features of JUnit facilitate using it for integration testing. In other areas, instructors have created their own languages and tools to bring unit testing to courses with C++ [2] or assembly language [7] projects. To support our intermediate-level systems courses, we have built a similar tool to facilitate automated testing in C.

Our system is designed to provide support for more than just unit testing. Specifically, our system provides an integrated framework for several automated testing components, including unit testing, integration testing, and dynamic analysis for memory leaks. Our system relies on common freely available tools, including the Check unit testing framework, the `diff` utility, and Valgrind's Memcheck memory leak detector. The framework uses Bash scripts to automate much of the processing. While our courses use Linux, the framework is platform-independent and has been tested on macOS and Cygwin for Windows.

Our design goals for this work go beyond just technical concerns, as well. In our experiences, many students struggle with systems courses for a variety of reasons. For most students, these courses are their first introductions to the C language and its related tools; consequently, they have no prior experience with explicit memory management. Most have minimal exposure to navigating the Linux command line. Furthermore, as our earlier courses are Java-based and assume no prior knowledge, many students are reluctant to move away from lightweight Java IDEs, such as Dr. Java or jGRASP.

By the end of the first semester in the systems sequence, our goal is for students to be able to develop command-line systems programs in C. Given the students' background, achieving this goal requires a significant amount of instructor support, both in the form of content scaffolding and motivational guidance. To facilitate both of these goals, our system provides students with all tests that will be used for evaluating their work. This includes a combination of public tests (to provide initial guidance) and private tests (precompiled and stripped of debugging symbols). Keeping the source code for the latter private is important, as many of these tests include code that would leak details about how to implement certain features.

A key feature of our approach is the structure of the test cases and their relationship to student grades. We adopt a specifications grading approach [10], in which subcomponents have a given specification that is evaluated in a pass/fail manner. The project requirements indicate which components are required to earn at least a grade of C, which for at least a B, and which are required for an A.

The advantage of this transparency is that it empowers students to monitor their progress independently.

This specifications grading approach has both cognitive and affective benefits for students. From the cognitive perspective, the grading structure provides scaffolding for students to learn how to break the project down into steps. They cannot earn a C or higher if *any* of the C tests fail, even if they pass several A or B tests; consequently, the grading structure guides them from simpler to more complex tasks. From the affective perspective, the tests serve as proximal subgoals [1] that reinforce motivation. Passing one test or group of tests increases the student's expectancy that they can pass the next, which is only slightly more complicated. And as the C tests are intentionally easy to pass with only modest effort, students quickly get the feedback–as they are working–that they are in no danger of failing.

Through course evaluations and informal discussions, we have observed anecdotal feedback that suggests students view the framework as helpful. Students have indicated that seeing the immediate feedback of their current grade status provided reassurance that kept them focused on making gradual progress. They have also identified the projects as being helpful preparation for exams by creating a platform to apply theoretical concepts.

We have used this framework for seven consecutive semesters with four different instructors leading the classes. Our department maintains a primary focus on undergraduate education within the context of a Master's university with a liberal arts emphasis. The majority of our students enter as computer science majors with little or no prior exposure to programming. Since adopting this testing framework in our systems curriculum, we have observed qualitatively improved student submissions and reduced student anxiety in these courses. In this experience report, we will describe some of the guiding principles of our approach, outline the major components of the system, and discuss lessons learned and tips for instructors who may want to use the system in their own courses.

2 BACKGROUND AND MOTIVATION

The automated testing tool that we present here is part of a larger departmental effort to redesign our systems curriculum [6]. Specifically, our aim has been to adopt a learner-centered philosophy that supports and encourages student autonomy within the constraints of a discipline with a rapidly growing and evolving body of knowledge. As part of this curriculum redesign, we have created a two-semester intermediate-level sequence that provides a foundation of the core knowledge for advanced systems work. Beyond normal cognitive learning outcomes, this two-semester sequence also emphasizes metacognitive objectives, with the aim that students leave these courses with the ability to use tools that are appropriate to the systems domain for later courses.

The first semester of this sequence focuses on the structure and execution of sequential software. These C-based projects revolve around binary executables structured in a simplified version of ELF (called Mini-ELF) and targeting the Y86 architecture [4]. Figure 1 shows a short description of each project, along with the specific learning goal for this phase.

The primary goal of this tool is to automate the delivery of feedback, which is an essential component of learning [9]. However, the quality and learning benefit of the feedback depends on several characteristics relating to how it is structured and given [13]. For instance, good feedback is goal-referenced and actionable, allowing the student to monitor their learning progress. In addition, good feedback is timely and user-friendly. Satisfying all of these properties is particularly challenging within the constraints of systems work that often relies on command-line tools. As such, one design goal of our system is to integrate the output from multiple tools into a single summary report that informs students regarding the tests their code passes, whether there are non-obvious concerns (such as memory leaks), and how their work will be measured for grading purposes. Since the students have immediate access to all of the tests, they get this feedback immediately *even though some tests are kept private to prevent leaking implementation hints.*

In addition to the intuitive goals of automating grading and feedback, our goals for this system are inspired by other work relating to motivation and persistence. Specifically, grades are a form of extrinsic motivation that reduces students' ability for self-regulation and control; as grades are perceived as either a reward or punishment, the net effect on students' intrinsic motivation is negative and detrimental to learning [11]. To counter this effect, we strove to structure our tests as an incremental approach based on the notion of proximal subgoals [1]. That is, with both unit and integration tests progressing through a series of closely related stages from simple to complex, successfully passing one test supports the students' expectation of passing the next.

3 TESTING FRAMEWORK

The testing framework is publicly available at *https://github.com/JMU-CS/c-test-framework*. The framework is designed for C99 on Linux, intended to be used in an academic course. It uses the Check[8] framework for unit testing, some custom Bash scripts for integration testing, and the Memcheck memory leak tool based on Valgrind[5]. We have attempted to clean up and generalize the code in this repository, but you may still find references to our course in these files. When downloaded a project directory would contain all the source files given to the student for the project. Some of these files will be "boiler-plate" templates that students will fill in with their solution. Included in this directory, is another directory called tests that contains the framework that we describe below.

This framework consists of unit tests for each function executed (in public.c and private.c), along with integration tests (in integrations.sh) that test overall output differences from running the student solution against a reference solution using diff on a given set of inputs. These tests form a testsuite that is then broken down into tests that are required for a particular grade. The sections below describe the unit tests, integration tests, the distribution and grading in more detail.

3.1 Unit Tests

Figure 2 shows sample code for creating a unit test according to the Check framework. The example here is setting up a test for a C-language function the students are asked to write for p0 that returns the sum of the absolute value of two numbers. This is a public test (i.e. one for which students can see the source code) and only tests the most straightforward case for this problem, adding two positive

Project	Description	Goal
p0-intro	Introductory set of C functions ranging from the absolute value add shown in this paper to more complex file manipulation problems	Master basic C programming
p1-check	Read in a Mini-ELF header and display it	Write standard Linux command-line programs and reinforce the idea that information is bits plus context
p2-load	Load Mini-ELF file into memory array	Reinforce the relationship between a compiled executable and the standard Linux/C memory model
p3-disas	Decode and disassemble machine code instructions	Reinforce assembly code concepts and the standard components of executable files
p4-interp	Simulate execution of machine code instructions	Reinforce assembly code and CPU architecture concepts, focusing on the execution of machine code instructions

Figure 1: Five programming projects used in our introduction to systems course

```
START_TEST (C_addabs)
{
    ck_assert_int_eq (add_abs(2,3), 5);
}
END_TEST
```

Figure 2: Example test case using the Check framework

```
START_TEST (A_sortarray)
{
    const size_t N = 4;
    int nums[] = { 5, 2, 11, 8 };
    int ref[]  = { 2, 5, 8, 11 };
    sort_array(nums, N);
    for (int i=0; i<N; i++) {
        ck_assert_int_eq (nums[i], ref[i]);
    }
}
END_TEST
```

Figure 3: More complex example test case using the Check framework

numbers. The name of the test starts with "C" indicating this test must be passed for the student to get a C grade. The test case including negative numbers in one or more of the two operands is a private test, also required for a C grade. Note that all of the tests have somewhat descriptive names so even failure of the private tests provides some feedback to students about what is wrong with their code. As an example, the name of the private test just referred to is C_addabs_negative_ints. Figure 3 shows a more complex test case.

3.2 Integration Tests

Integration tests are intended to test whole-program behavior and are written using input/output file pairs. Tests are specified in a configuration file, which contains one line for each integration test. The line specifies the name of the test (the output file must match this) as well as the command line intended to evoke the corresponding output.

```
int addabs (int num1, int num2)
{
    // BEGIN_SOLUTION
    return abs(num1) + abs(num2);
    // END_SOLUTION
    // BOILERPLATE: return 0;
}
```

Figure 4: Reference solution

```
int add_abs (int num1, int num2)
{
    return 0;
}
```

Figure 5: Distribution (boilerplate) version

The actual testing is handled by a Bash script that runs the program once per test with the specified command line and uses the diff utility to compare the actual output to the expected output. The script is designed to be generic enough to handle any project.

Because memory management is such an important part of coding in a low-level language, the script also runs each test in Valgrind/Memcheck to check for memory leaks.

3.3 Distributions

Scripts are provided for building project distributions to give to students. These scripts remove solution code and package up the project into a tarball. For convenient testing, it also saves a snapshot of both the distribution files and the full solution.

To mark solution code for removal, the instructor should surround it with BEGIN_SOLUTION and END_SOLUTION one-line comments. If the removal of the code would result in invalid code (e.g., no return value), a BOILERPLATE tag can provide alternative code for the distribution. Figure 4 shows one example of a reference function that has been marked prior to distribution, and Figure 5 shows how the same function appears in the generated file.

3.4 Grading

We also provide a sample grading script. To use this script, the instructor must collect student submissions using a specific file structure as described in the framework documentation. The instructor must also provide a configuration file with the relevant filename and path information for the reference solution, submission folders, and results.

When the grading script is run, it copies all of the student submissions into sub-folders in a temporary folder. It also copies the test files from the reference solution to prevent students from gaming the system by modifying the test files. It then builds and runs all tests on all submissions. The results are printed to standard output in a summary format, with overview test results for each student as well as information about compiler warnings, memory leaks, or insecure functions (e.g., `gets`). Figure 6 shows sample output from this script.

All unit and integration tests are labeled with a grade level. The lowest grade tests are the easiest to write code to solve and are the least dependent on other functionality. Also, to pass the lowest level tests does not require passing any of the upper level tests. The higher grade tests may be dependent on the lower grade tests and to get a higher grade, a student must also pass all of the lower grade tests. For example, to get a C the student's code must have passed all of the F, D and C tests that are given. This structure gives an overall road map to students of how to work on the project - starting with the lowest grade functionality and moving upward. As they pass each level of tests, this success gives them both confidence and a new incremental goal to pass the next level.

3.5 Student Use

Students primarily interact with the framework through provided Makefiles. They build their project using the default `make` command, or they can run the test suite using `make test`. Figure 7 shows sample output for an incomplete submission; the unit test output is provided by the Check library and the integration test output is from our script. Figure 8 shows sample output for a complete submission.

We encourage students to run the integration tests themselves outside of the test framework. The command line and input file(s) for all integration tests are listed in a configuration file so there is enough transparency for students to reproduce the tests. This enables them to iterate faster once they have identified tests that they are failing, and it enables them to run the test in an interactive debugger.

3.6 Docker Support

The framework has been designed to be platform-independent and has been tested on a variety of Linux platforms as well as macOS High Sierra and Windows 10 (using Cygwin). In addition, we provide Docker files so that the framework can be used on non-supported platforms. The resulting Docker containers can be used to build the project distributions, run the test suite, or start the program in an interactive debugging session using the GNU debugger, regardless of the host platform.

4 DISCUSSION

Below is a list of benefits we have experienced from using this automated framework with a brief discussion of each.

- **Having a built-in test suite forces students to read the project specification more carefully.** Many skim the description and don't spend time reading and thinking about it. Being confronted with failure when they expect success reinforces that they are working with a machine not a human ("machine as other"), and even tiny differences or misunderstanding can cause catastrophic failure. Details matter.
- **Having unit tests for the students to use increased their motivation, and subsequently their learning.** Students come with questions *before* the assignment is due as they are motivated to understand what is going wrong in order to improve their grade. In addition, the smaller unit tests allow them to focus on a specific goal and ask questions targeting that goal.
- **Scaffolded (grade-specific) tests give students specific, smaller goals and a road map through a large project.** Though not always apparent to students, the thoughtful labeling of the tests so that they are encouraged to work on the D tests first, then the C tests, etc. gives them a subtle road map on how to approach the large project. This support is then available for students who needed it without requiring individual graded milestones. It is a good middle-ground between short-term deadlines and a long-term project without interim support.
- **Providing some built-in unit and integration tests scaffolds students into creating their own tests.** Students seem to have very little idea of how to create test cases of their own (and particularly integration tests) when they arrive in this third semester course. Although some of this may just be unfamiliarity with the C language, providing example tests gives them a starting point and encourages them to create their own.
- **Having unit and integration tests encourages students to understand the difference.** Passing unit tests and then failing integration tests seems to highlight the importance of communicating the interface between pieces of software clearly as well.
- **The distribution of a testing framework facilitates exploration and learning beyond what we consider "necessary" to pass the class.** While some students will run `make test` and treat it like a magic oracle for the entire semester, other students dig in deeper to learn how it works, and a few will even tinker and experiment with it. When a test fails on a later project, the explorers and tinkerers have a greater understanding of how to begin debugging. This ends up performing as differentiated instruction based on interest and ability. Students can learn at the pace and depth that is appropriate for them.
- **Our test-based baseline grading scheme reduces student uncertainty about their grade.** This reduction in uncertainty reduces anxiety for most students and gives them an indicator of where they are in addition to how much time they will likely need to complete the project. It also allows

```
studentid1  C D D  25%: Checks: 20, Failures: 15, Errors: 0   Integration failures: 14   No memory leak found.
studentid2      X  (no submission)
studentid3  D D D  25%: Checks: 20, Failures: 14, Errors: 1   Integration failures: 14   No memory leak found.
studentid4  F D F  20%: Checks: 20, Failures: 16, Errors: 0   Integration failures: 14   No memory leak found.
studentid5  A A A  100%: Checks: 20, Failures: 0, Errors: 0   Integration failures: 0    No memory leak found.
```

Figure 6: Example grading script output

```
========================================
             UNIT TESTS
15%: Checks: 20, Failures: 17, Errors: 0
D_addabs:0: Assertion 'add_abs(2,3) == 5' failed [...]
C_addptr:0: Assertion 'ans == 5' failed [...]
C_factorial:0: Assertion 'factorial(1) == 1' failed [...]
C_isprime:0: Assertion '!is_prime(4)' failed
[...]
========================================
          INTEGRATION TESTS
D_hello        FAIL (see outputs/D_hello.diff for details)
C_goodbye      FAIL (see outputs/C_goodbye.diff for details)
[...]
No memory leak found.
========================================
```

Figure 7: Excerpt from test run for incomplete submission (some output omitted for brevity)

```
========================================
             UNIT TESTS
100%: Checks: 20, Failures: 0, Errors: 0
========================================
          INTEGRATION TESTS
D_hello                        pass
C_goodbye                      pass
[...]
No memory leak found.
========================================
```

Figure 8: Excerpt from test run for complete submission

the instructor to give quick feedback the day before something is due to prevent surprise zeros because of incorrect submissions.

- **Having some tests public and some private with more detailed error messages, enables more detailed feedback to students.** The detailed error messages let students and faculty know where student code is failing. Faculty can then spend more time on code inspection of individual submissions for style and approach if desired.

We have also observed some potential obstacles to learning introduced by our framework:

- **The framework initially confuses students because they don't understand the output, so they often have trouble getting started.** To address this, we accompany the framework with an extensive description of the framework and spend a lot of time in office hours working with any students who have difficulty understanding it. We also provide an online discussion forum for students to ask questions, and in our experience some of these questions are answered before we even see them by peers who learned the framework more quickly. Ultimately, we feel that mastering a non-trivial testing framework is an important experience in systems programming.
- **The framework reduces incentive for students to write their own tests even as it also scaffolds them into it better.** We feel a framework like this could be more appropriate at lower-level class work (our course is a second-year systems introduction course) before we really expect students to be able to rigorously test their own code. Future work could include adding hidden tests that are used for grading but aren't distributed to students in order to encourage more self-testing.

5 CONCLUSIONS AND FUTURE WORK

The most exciting conclusion from using this framework is the increased motivation and engagement by the students to dig deep and finish the projects. Anecdotal feedback from students is that they would not have worked so hard and gotten the details right if they had not known they did not yet have the grade they wanted. Additional anecdotal feedback is that by the end of the course the relationship of the project to the theoretical course content clicks and they are able to firmly grasp the theoretical concepts while studying for the final exam. The specification of specific tests for attaining each grade level, allows the introduction of a subtle road map to finish the project while avoiding the "hand-holding" of very short term graded milestones in earlier courses. In addition, these grade level tests introduce a mastery-model of sorts, encouraging students with short-term achievable goals and giving them confidence as they attempt more and more difficult pieces. As a result, we see more students perform better in later classes in the curriculum because they have mastered the basic material. This has reinforced the benefit of the learner-centered redesign of the curriculum.

In future work, we will investigate adding static analysis such as that provided by lint to the testing framework. This would expand the immediate feedback available to students and support them in writing cleaner and safer code. We will also experiment with expanding the projects to include optional parts that could differ in rotations over semesters. In addition, changing the output and formatting of the tests to provide more encouragement and direction to students is an option. An example might be, "Congratulations on passing test X, you should consider working on test Y." Trade-offs on autonomy vs. direction would need to be considered here, but in some cases this encouragement could be helpful.

REFERENCES

[1] Albert Bandura and Dale H. Schunk. 1981. Cultivating Competence, Self-Efficacy, and Intrinsic Interest Through Proximal Self-Motivation. *Journal of Personality and Social Psychology* 41, 3 (September 1981), 586–598.

[2] Don Blaheta. 2015. Unci: A C++-based Unit-testing Framework for Intro Students. In *Proceedings of the 46th ACM Technical Symposium on Computer Science Education (SIGCSE '15)*. ACM, New York, NY, USA, 475–480. https://doi.org/10.1145/2676723.2677228

[3] Christopher Brown, Robert Pastel, Marika Seigel, Charles Wallace, and Linda Ott. 2014. Adding Unit Test Experience to a Usability Centered Project Course. In *Proceedings of the 45th ACM Technical Symposium on Computer Science Education (SIGCSE '14)*. ACM, New York, NY, USA, 259–264. https://doi.org/10.1145/2538862.2538964

[4] Randal E. Bryant and David R. O'Hallaron. 2015. *Computer Systems: A Programmer's Perspective (3rd Edition)*. Boston.

[5] Julian Seward et al. 2017. Valgrind. http://valgrind.org/

[6] Michael S. Kirkpatrick, Mohamed Aboutabl, David Bernstein, and Sharon Simmons. 2015. Backward Design: An Integrated Approach to a Systems Curriculum. In *Proceedings of the 46th ACM Technical Symposium on Computer Science Education (SIGCSE '15)*. ACM, New York, NY, USA, 30–35. https://doi.org/10.1145/2676723.2677264

[7] Zachary Kurmas. 2017. MIPSUnit: A Unit Testing Framework for MIPS Assembly. In *Proceedings of the 2017 ACM SIGCSE Technical Symposium on Computer Science Education (SIGCSE '17)*. ACM, New York, NY, USA, 351–355. https://doi.org/10.1145/3017680.3017747

[8] Arien Malec, Branden Archer, Chris Pickett, Fredrik Hugosson, and Robert Lemmen. 2014. Check: Unit Testing Framework for C. https://libcheck.github.io/check/

[9] National Research Council. 2000. *How People Learn: Brain, Mind, Experience, and School: Expanded Edition*. The National Academy Press, Washington, DC. https://doi.org/10.17226/9853 Edited by John D. Bransford, Ann L. Brown, and Rodney R. Cocking.

[10] Linda B. Nilson. 2014. *Specifications Grading: Restoring Rigor, Motivating Students, and Saving Faculty Time*. Stylus Publishing, Sterling, VA.

[11] Richard M. Ryan and Edward L. Deci. 2000. Self-Determination Theory and the Facilitation of Intrinsic Motivation, Social Development, and Well-Being. *American Psychologist* 55, 1 (2000), 68–78.

[12] Michael Wick, Daniel Stevenson, and Paul Wagner. 2005. Using Testing and JUnit Across the Curriculum. In *Proceedings of the 36th SIGCSE Technical Symposium on Computer Science Education (SIGCSE '05)*. ACM, New York, NY, USA, 236–240. https://doi.org/10.1145/1047344.1047427

[13] Grant Wiggins. 2012. Seven Keys to Effective Feedback. *Educational Leadership* 70, 1 (2012), 10–16. Feedback for Learning.

Gamifying a Software Testing Course with Code Defenders

Gordon Fraser, Alessio Gambi, Marvin Kreis
University of Passau
Passau, Germany
{gordon.fraser,alessio.gambi}@uni-passau.de
kreis03@gw.uni-passau.de

José Miguel Rojas
University of Leicester
Leicester, United Kingdom
j.rojas@leicester.ac.uk

ABSTRACT

Software testing is an essential skill for software developers, but it is challenging to get students engaged in this activity. The Code Defenders game addresses this problem by letting students compete over code under test by either introducing faults ("attacking") or by writing tests to reveal these faults ("defending"). In this paper, we describe how we integrated Code Defenders as a semester-long activity of an undergraduate and graduate level university course on software testing. We complemented the regular course sessions with weekly Code Defenders sessions, addressing challenges such as selecting suitable code to test, managing games, and assessing performance. Our experience and our data show that the integration of Code Defenders was well-received by students and led them to practice testing thoroughly. Positive learning effects are evident as student performance improved steadily throughout the semester.

CCS CONCEPTS

• **Social and professional topics → Software engineering education**; • **Software and its engineering → Software testing and debugging**;

KEYWORDS

Software testing education, mutation analysis, testing game, software engineering education, unit testing

ACM Reference Format:
Gordon Fraser, Alessio Gambi, Marvin Kreis and José Miguel Rojas. 2019. Gamifying a Software Testing Course with Code Defenders. In *Proceedings of the 50th ACM Technical Symposium on Computer Science Education (SIGCSE '19), February 27-March 2, 2019, Minneapolis, MN, USA*. ACM, New York, NY, USA, 7 pages. https://doi.org/10.1145/3287324.3287471

1 INTRODUCTION

Software testing – the activity of systematically executing a program with the aim of finding faults – is an essential skill for software developers, but it is one they are often not well-prepared for. The 2017 Software Fail Watch report [18] describes $1.7 trillion in lost revenue due to software problems, some of which could have been avoided with a more thorough approach to testing. This problem is rooted in education, where testing unfortunately is a relatively neglected component of the computer science curriculum [3], and even when it is taught, then engaging students is challenging. Common testing theory is heavy on management aspects and lighter on actual hands-on testing experience. As a result, students perceive testing as boring and repetitive, and do not acquire the practice and experience that software testing requires.

Gamification is recently heralded as a means to improve testing, both in education [1, 5] and practice [4, 7, 15]. In the wake of this trend, the Code Defenders game [16] aims to engage students with software testing in a competitive and entertaining way. Students compete over program code under test by either introducing software defects that evade the existing test suite ("attacking"), or by improving the test suite to fend off these attacks ("defending"). There is evidence that the game is engaging and players write better tests than outside the game [17], and there is anecdotal evidence of individual Code Defenders sessions being used to spice up university courses. However, to really provide learning effects, we argue that Code Defenders should be integrated more tightly as a semester-long activity of software engineering and testing courses.

In this paper, we describe our integration of Code Defenders into a course on software testing taught at undergraduate and graduate level. Such an integration causes numerous challenges: There are *organisational* challenges, such as managing games with fluctuations in student attendance; *technical* challenges, such as scaling up the game to handle large classes and coping with students trying to find ways to cheat or break the system; and *pedagogical* challenges, such as ensuring fairness and grading student participation. We describe how we overcame these challenges, and use the data collected from the first instance of the course, taken by 123 students who played a total of 197 team-based games, to provide detailed insights into the behaviour of the students, their engagement, and their satisfaction. The data from our experience provides the following insights:

RQ1: How do students engage with the game? Students actively participate and practice their testing skills. On average, students wrote 120.54 tests (with a maximum of 350), and inserted 158.66 artificial faults (maximum of 515).

RQ2: Does student performance improve over time? Students improved their testing performance throughout the course. We observed a moderate correlation of 0.51 between the number of sessions played and the quality of the tests written.

RQ3: Does student engagement correlate with exam grades? We observed a moderate correlation of -0.58 between the number of tests written in the game and exam marks, suggesting that better students are more active players.

RQ4: Do students appreciate using Code Defenders in class? In a survey students commented very favourably about their experience, and agreed that the integration is useful and fun.

ACM ISBN 978-1-4503-5890-3/19/02...$15.00
https://doi.org/10.1145/3287324.3287471

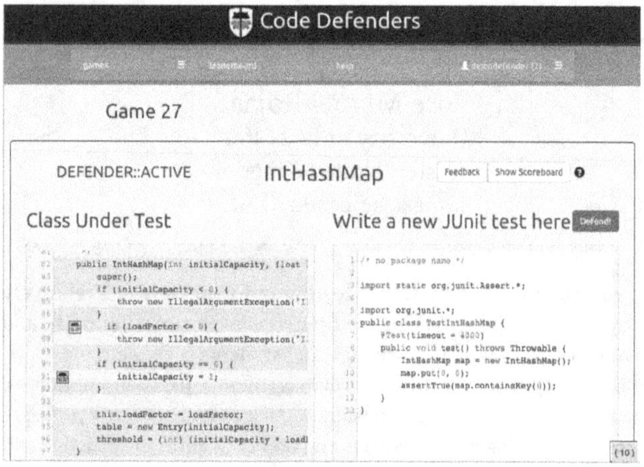

Figure 1: The Code Defenders game in action.

2 THE CODE DEFENDERS GAME

Two challenging activities in software testing are (1) assessing how well a program is tested by a given test suite, and (2) improving the test suite by creating additional tests. Code Defenders [16] is a game intended to engage students in these activities in the context of a Java object-oriented class under test and its test suite: *Attackers* aim to introduce artificial bugs into the class under test that reveal weaknesses in the test suite, while *defenders* aim to improve the test suite by adding tests. Since this process resembles the software testing technique of mutation analysis [2], the artificial bugs are called *mutants*. If a test which passes on the original program fails on a mutant, then that mutant is detected and the defender scores points, whereas the attacker scores points if the mutant is not detected. The number of points a mutant is worth depends on the number of tests it "survives", which further encourages players to create as subtle as possible mutants, and as strong as possible tests.

Attackers can create mutants that are syntactically different but semantically equivalent to the original program. In mutation analysis, this is known as the *equivalent mutant* problem [10], and equivalent mutants cannot be detected by tests by definition. Equivalent mutants may be used by attackers by accident, or intentionally as part of their strategy. If defenders cannot succeed in detecting a mutant and suspect it might be equivalent, then they can flag the mutant and trigger an *equivalence duel*. The attacker who created the mutant has to resolve this equivalence duel either by providing a test that detects the mutant – hence proving non-equivalence – or by accepting that the mutant is indeed equivalent – thus revealing their bluff and losing all points earned for the mutant.

Code Defenders is implemented as a web-based game (screenshot shown in Figure 1), and can be played in teams or pairs. Players get to see the source code of the Java class under test, with colour highlighting to indicate the coverage of the defenders' test suite, and with bug-shaped icons labelling the locations and status of the attackers' mutants. Attackers can create mutants by editing the source code of the Java class, and defenders have a code editor to write tests using JUnit [11], which is the de-facto standard test automation framework for the Java programming language. Besides the information displayed with the class under test (code, coverage, and mutant locations), defenders get to see all tests that have been submitted in the game, while attackers see all mutants. There is also a scoreboard that breaks down the game's current score for each team and player and summarises the status of the mutants.

Whenever humans play games, it is natural that they will try to cheat and bend the rules to their own advantage. Code Defenders uses rules, heuristics, and restrictions to avoid unfair mutants and tests. For example, it does not allow addition of new `if`-conditions into the code, because that would make it easy to create mutants that cannot reasonably be detected by a test without knowledge of the change (e.g., by comparing a variable against an arbitrary numeric value that a tester would hardly guess). Similarly, the restrictions prevent tricks with logical operators, bitshift operators, casts, and include some further specialised restrictions. There are fewer restrictions on defender actions; to ensure that players produce tests like they would in practice (e.g., [13]), the number of JUnit assertions per test is limited, with a default value of two.

By default, Code Defenders counts unresolved equivalence duels as lost for the attacker after a game ends. To prevent that players exploit this (e.g., by waiting until seconds before the end of the game to mark mutants as equivalent), "grace periods" can be used to gradually reduce the possible game actions towards the end of the game. If the game duration is too small to include grace periods (as in our case), Code Defenders can also be configured to ignore unresolved equivalence duels, but *force* attackers to handle equivalence duels before being allowed to submit new mutants.

3 CODE DEFENDERS IN THE CLASSROOM

3.1 Course Organisation

The context of our Code Defenders integration is a regular software testing course, organised around the standardised International Software Testing Qualification Board (ISTQB) foundation level tester curriculum [8], plus additional material on more advanced testing techniques. Thus, it consists of regular theoretical lectures, and weekly exercise sessions with exercise sheets featuring examples related to the theory, and introducing the technologies implementing the theoretical concepts, including JUnit. We extended this standard course design with weekly two-academic-hour practical sessions throughout the whole semester [6]. These practical sessions featured the use of Code Defenders in the computer lab.

Each practical session revolved around one dedicated Java class under test, on which students competed in teams. In the first session each student took the role of attacker and defender once each; in all successive sessions students participated only in one game, alternating between attacker and defender roles weekly. We bootstrapped each session with a couple of minutes of explanations of the class under test, and also provided some examples of how to write tests to speed up the code understanding phase.

A difficult challenge for the instructor is the selection of appropriate Java classes under test. If a class is too complex, it makes it more challenging for defenders to create good tests, thus allowing the attackers to safely mutate untested code, rather than having to think about how to evade the existing tests and reason about the effectiveness and fault finding potential of the existing tests. On the other hand, if a class is too simple, then the defenders can quickly produce a test suite that covers all testable behaviour, leaving the attackers frustrated and with little room to make changes that are

Table 1: Java classes used in the 12 Code Defenders sessions.

ID	Class	Project	LOC	Methods	Fields
1	Lift	Custom	53	12	5
2	Complex	Math4J	103	24	3
3	Rational	Dittrich Java Intro	114	17	3
4	Option	Apache Commons CLI	260	41	13
5	XmlElement	Inspirento	221	33	6
6	SparseIntArray	Android	161	22	5
7	IntHashMap	Apache Commons Lang	148	14	5
8	ByteVector	Objectweb ASM	154	12	3
9	CharRange	Apache Commons Lang	87	17	5
10	CaseInsensitiveString	Squirrel SQL	177	10	8
11	Document	Apache Lucene	113	15	6
12	Options	Apache Commons CLI	139	16	5

not immediately found. Additionally, the complexity of the chosen classes under test gradually needs to increase over the course of the semester, to keep students appropriately challenged as they improve their testing skills. While there are some standard code metrics that can support the selection (e.g., lines of code), ultimately judging the difficulty of testing a class is down to experience. There are also technical considerations, for example since Code Defenders offers no support for players to explore dependency classes.

Table 1 summarises the classes we used in the 12 sessions. We created the `Lift` class specifically to introduce Code Defenders. For successive sessions we selected real classes from open-source projects to increase motivation. To avoid that students find the original project online and use its tests, we removed context information, e.g., package name. For the two sessions following the introduction session we used classes implementing mathematical concepts familiar to students (`Rational` and `Complex`), thus allowing interesting gameplay to emerge more quickly. For the remaining sessions we selected pairs of classes that are somewhat similar in nature, so that each student would play as attacker and defender on similarly complex classes. Data structures are particularly well-suited since they usually have no dependencies, and students are familiar with the general concept. We also included more specialised classes to increase the level of difficulty and challenge the students. In the last two sessions we used classes that had simple dependencies, but replaced the dependencies with a skeleton interface, such that players were forced to use Java mocking frameworks in their tests.

Although students closely followed their game scores in the overall leaderboard, the score is not suitable as a means for assessment since it depends on many factors beyond the abilities of an individual student (e.g., the abilities and actions of the other players in the game or the use of unfair techniques in the game). We made the Code Defenders sessions count for 10% of the overall course grade, and graded students based on their level of participation. Students were expected to participate in at least 10 out of 12 sessions, and would be awarded one point for each active game participation (capped at 10 points). For each Java class we determined thresholds for the number of tests and mutants that represented "active" participation; to determine the number of suitable tests/mutants we cross-checked all tests and mutants on *all* games for the same class to remove any bias caused by the specific game context. A test is counted if it compiles, passes on the original version of the Java class, and detects at least one mutant; a mutant is counted if it is non-equivalent (i.e., detected by at least one test).

3.2 Game Management

There are several challenges when managing regular sessions with Code Defenders. First, it is desirable that only students physically present in the lab participate in the games. Second, fluctuations in student attendance make it difficult to set up games prior to the actual practical sessions. This was made even more difficult by restrictions in our lab size (40 computers only), which required us to run three smaller successive sessions each week (in which some students worked on their own laptops). We therefore started each session by taking attendance, and then creating a set of games only for the students present in that session. We extended Code Defenders with an administrative interface that supports this process.

Once the students present in a lab session are known, games need to be balanced for a number of factors: First, each student should alternate weekly between attacker and defender roles. Second, there is substantial variation in the skills of students, which may negatively affect games. For example, if a particularly strong defender plays a game where the other players are not so skilled, then that defender would dominate the testing tasks. This might frustrate the other defenders who get fewer chances to reveal mutants, and would make it difficult for attackers to score points. To avoid this issue, we ranked students by their game scores achieved in previous games before creating games, such that students with similar scores (and thus hopefully similar abilities) were teamed up.

We aimed for games with 3 attackers vs. 3 defenders since we observed good game dynamics with these team sizes in the past (for smaller teams it takes longer for mutants and tests to properly interact; for larger teams there tend to be players who cannot, or decide not to, keep up with their teammates). However, we allowed for some variation to accommodate for variations in attendance; in particular, we often made teams of weaker students larger to balance out games. We also used latecomers to equilibrate unbalanced games, e.g., by supporting the losing side with an additional player. Our administrative interface allows monitoring of running games, so that we could react to obvious problems. For example, sometimes defending teams would take long before creating the first test, in which case we located the students in the lab and tried to help. Although we aimed to use the full academic two hours (2 × 45 minutes) for the game, we would usually end games slightly earlier. Once a game is finished, students get to see all tests and mutants, allowing them to reflect, which often led to interesting and active debates among groups of students. Effectively, this means that games lasted on average around 70 minutes.

4 EVALUATION

To evaluate whether Code Defenders can be integrated into a testing course in a way that is beneficial and engaging for students, we investigate the following research questions:

RQ1: How do students engage with the game?
RQ2: Does student performance improve over time?
RQ3: Does student engagement correlate with exam grades?
RQ4: Do students appreciate using Code Defenders in class?

4.1 Experimental Setup

We collected data while running the course at the University of Passau in the winter semester 2017/2018. We deployed our own

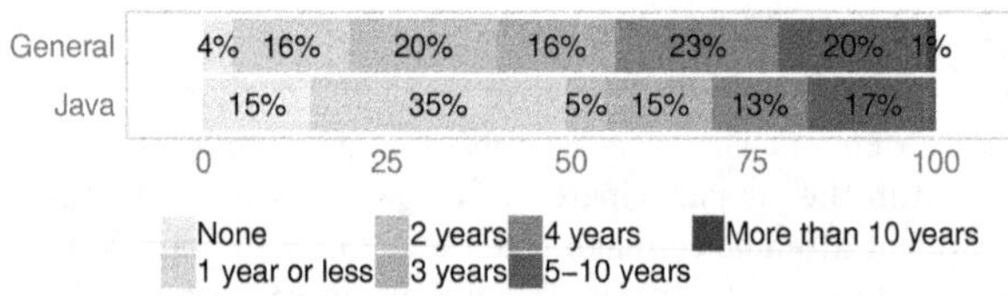

Figure 2: Students' programming experience.

Table 2: Game statistics.

Class	Games	Wins			Averages per Game			
		Att.	Def.	Draw	Players	Tests	Mutants	Duels
1	41	29	12	2	4.02	8.15	25.09	1.26
2	19	15	4	0	6.05	19.53	80.37	5.89
3	15	13	2	0	6.67	42.73	113.00	16.93
4	17	14	2	1	6.47	45.71	84.47	9.24
5	17	10	7	0	6.41	39.41	101.47	6.59
6	14	13	1	0	7.14	45.71	96.50	11.93
7	15	13	2	0	6.47	54.20	86.47	18.13
8	13	12	1	0	6.31	52.62	118.46	12.92
9	13	6	7	0	6.62	64.85	64.23	11.77
10	14	12	2	0	6.21	39.21	100.21	14.57
11	12	9	3	0	6.75	40.83	56.50	10.67
12	7	3	4	0	6.43	30.86	88.14	7.43

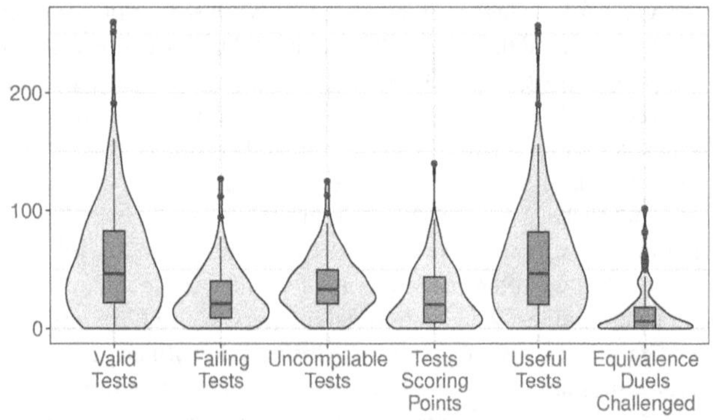

Figure 3: Statistics of defender actions per player; boxplots show quartiles, violinplots show distribution density.

installation of Code Defenders rather than using the public version, since (1) a large number of students would quickly hit the limits of the public server, (2) we wanted to avoid interactions between students and external remote players, and (3) we wanted to prevent students from creating their own games instead of focussing on the tasks set by us. The course was available to undergraduate and graduate students. In total, it was taken by 123 students (34 female, 89 male), of which 52 were undergraduate students and 71 were at graduate level. The average semester for undergraduate (bachelor) students was 5.77, and for graduate (master) students 1.83, which means that most students were in the final year of their degree. Figure 2 shows the programming experience of the students: 80% of the students declared to have more than two years of general programming experience, while almost half had only recently started using Java (1 year or less) or had not used Java before at all. Consequently, in the initial sessions we had to provide general programming support to some of the students. It is desirable for players to have reasonable Java experience so they can focus on the game.

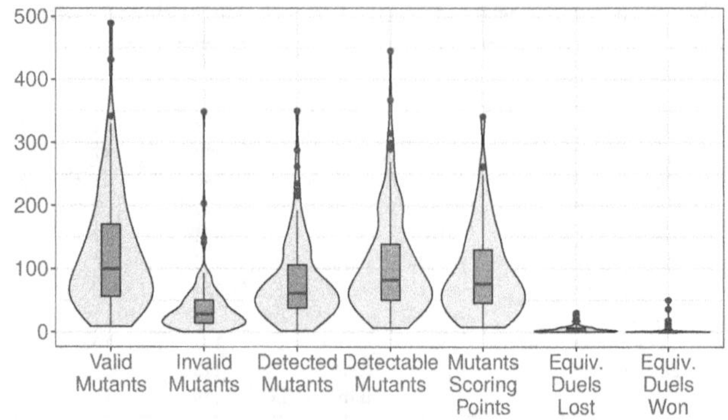

Figure 4: Statistics of attacker actions per player; boxplots show quartiles, violinplots show distribution density.

In total, the students played 197 games on the 12 classes, as summarised in Table 2. On the first class, each student played two warm-up games to experience both player roles, resulting in a higher number of games. Because points for active participation were capped at 10, the last class resulted in fewer participants and games. More games were won by attackers; we conjecture that this is because we did not deduct points for unresolved equivalence duels after games ended, as Code Defenders would normally do when using grace periods. On average, games were played with teams of three players each (i.e., 3 vs. 3 games).

4.2 RQ1: Student activities

We assess engagement by analysing the students' actions throughout the course. On average, each student participated in 8.66/12 sessions, and submitted 120.54 tests and 158.66 mutants over all games (average of 19.11 tests and 35.92 mutants per game per student). These numbers varied across games (see Table 2), with a maximum of 91 tests submitted by a student playing as defender in a single game, and a maximum of 157 mutants submitted by a student playing as attacker in a single game. In total, 18 students did not attend any of the last 6 (out of 12) game sessions, which suggests they abandoned the (optional) course prematurely.

Figure 3 provides more details on the actions performed by students playing as defenders. Although the majority of submitted tests were valid (i.e., compile and pass on the original class under test), a large number of them either had compilation errors or resulted in a failure when run on the original class under test (i.e., had incorrect test oracles). We conjecture that a common strategy to support the understanding of the code is to run a test and observe the behaviour based on the resulting test failure. On average, 37% of all valid tests scored at least one point, i.e., detected a previously undetected mutant. However, on average 98% of the valid tests have the potential to detect a mutant, and are counted as useful during grading. Finally, as expected the number of equivalence duels challenged is much lower than the number of tests submitted per game, although it increased over time as students gained experience.

Figure 4 summarises the actions performed by students when playing as attackers. In contrast to test submissions, the number of erroneous mutant submissions (compilation errors, violations of the constraints on mutations, or duplicate submission of already existing mutants) is much lower than the number of successful

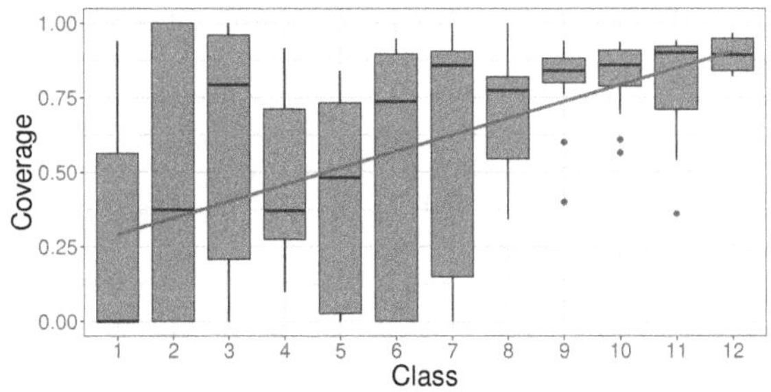

Figure 5: Code coverage achieved throughout the semester.

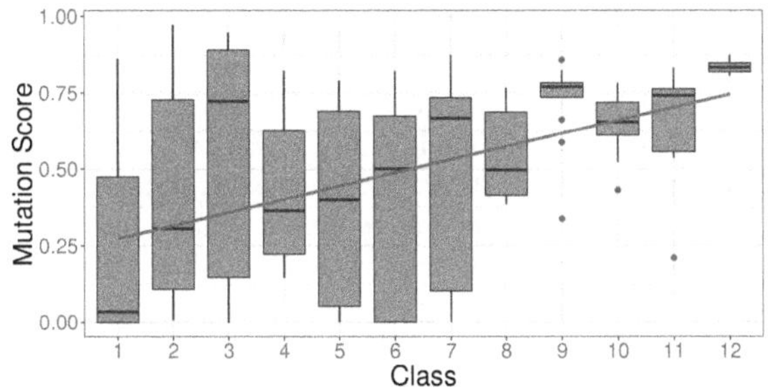

Figure 6: Mutation scores (measured with the Major mutation tool [12]) achieved throughout the semester.

submissions. This is not surprising since a mutant is valid if it follows basic syntactic rules. On average, 64% of the valid mutants were detected by the defenders' tests. By executing all tests from all games on the mutants we can estimate how many could have been detected; on average, 85% of the valid mutants could have been detected, showing that there is ample potential for defenders to further improve; this suggests that defenders might have needed more time, a better way of communication to organising the defense, or that teams of defenders could be made larger. A mutant is only useful if it "survives" at least one test (i.e., is covered but not detected) and thus scores at least one point. On average, 75% of the valid mutants scored at least one point, while the remaining valid mutants either were not covered by any tests, or were accepted as equivalent; the plot suggests that only a small ratio of the mutants were accepted as equivalent. More equivalence duels were lost than won, indicating that attackers either accepted more equivalences or struggled to produce mutant-detecting tests themselves.

Overall our average results indicate that most students engaged well both when playing as attackers and as defenders.

4.3 RQ2: Improvement throughout semester

To determine whether student performance improved throughout the course, we look at the quality of the test suites and mutants resulting from each game. In contrast to RQ1, for this we need an objective measurement of quality that is not dependent on player actions. For tests, the standard metrics are *code coverage* and *mutation score*. Code coverage measures how much of the source code has been executed by a given test suite. Complementary to this, the mutation score measures how good the test suite is at detecting a systematically produced set of mutants. We expect that students playing Code Defenders over time will gain more experience and produce test suites that cover more code and detect more mutants.

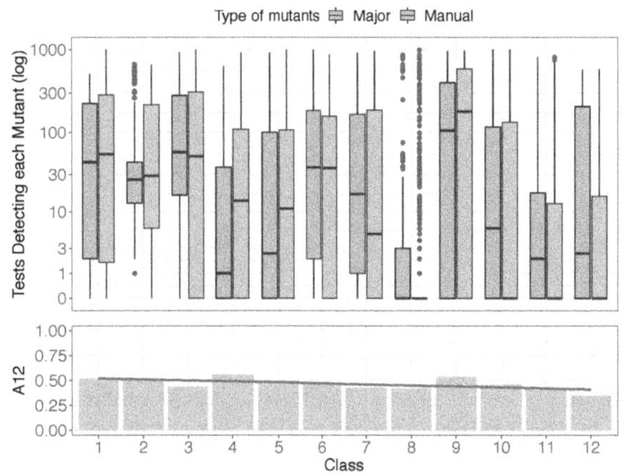

Figure 7: Mutant detection rate throughout the semester.

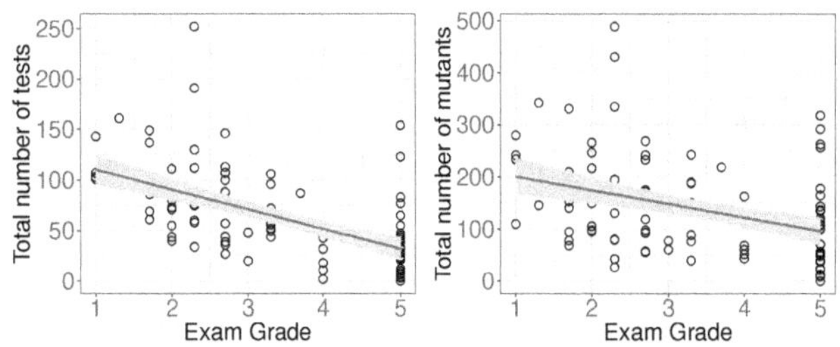

(a) Test submissions vs. exam grades. (b) Mutant submissions vs. exam grades.

Figure 8: Correlation of exam scores with player actions.

We used JaCoCo [9] to measure branch coverage per game, i.e., on the test suite consisting of all the tests for a game. Figure 5 shows the overall branch coverage achieved per game. Even though the classes under test gradually became more complex and challenging, a clear increase in the coverage throughout the semester is visible, suggesting an improvement in students' testing skills (Pearson's correlation between session number and coverage is 0.51, p-value < 0.001). We measured the mutation scores on the same test suites using the Major mutation tool [12]. Figure 6 confirms the trend already observed in the coverage data (correlation between session number and mutation score is 0.47, p-value < 0.001).

For mutants, determining whether there is an improvement is more challenging, since there is no standard metric of mutant quality. In general, we expect that (detectable) mutants are better if they are more *subtle*, i.e., if there are fewer tests that detect them. However, the tests written as part of the game are influenced by the mutants, which may skew such a measurement. Therefore, we follow the procedure used by Rojas et al. [17] to estimate mutant quality: For each Java class, we use the Randoop [14] test generator to produce 1,000 random tests. Then, we execute each mutant against each random test and count how many tests detect the mutant – the fewer, the harder to detect the mutant is. Since the performance of Randoop may vary across different classes, we use Major [12] to automatically produce a set of baseline mutants on which we also measure the hardness with the 1,000 random tests. This enables us to estimate student advancement in terms of the relative performance of the mutants compared to Major mutants.

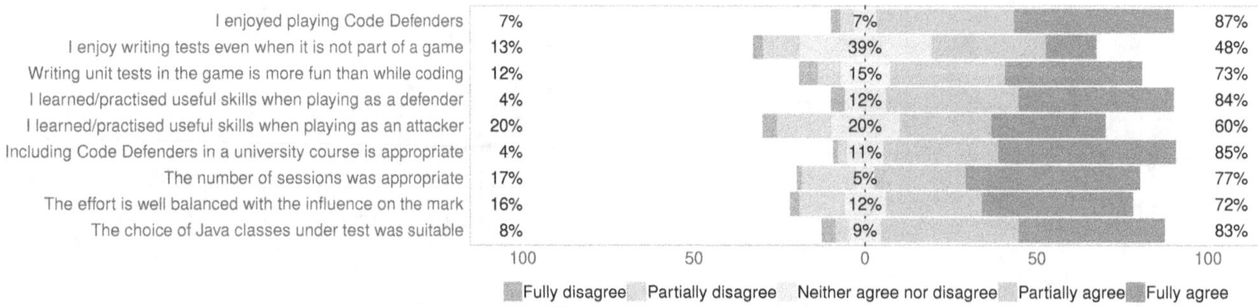

Figure 9: Exit survey responses.

Figure 7 shows the number of tests that detect each of the mutants for the two categories: manual (student-written) and Major mutants. While initially students produced mutants that were detected by more tests, the median mutant quality slowly improved, and from week six onwards the student-written mutants are *better* than the ones produced by Major. One exception is the ninth session (class `CharRange`), where the student-written mutants appear to be substantially worse. A closer look reveals that, in this class, changes to certain statements in the constructor lead to state changes that are detected by almost any test, and students happened to mutate these statements quite thoroughly, leading to more easy-to-detect mutants than the Major tool. Figure 7 statistically compares the mutant quality of the two types of mutants using the $\hat{A}_{12}$ Vargha-Delaney effect size measurement; a value of < 0.5 in this case means that the student-written mutants are better. The Pearson correlation between the number of the session and the $\hat{A}_{12}$ effect size is -0.6 (p-value = 0.04), showing that although effect sizes are small, there is a statistically significant improvement throughout the semester.

4.4 RQ3: Game activity vs. exam grades

In order to establish whether there is a relation between player engagement and final exam mark, we calculate the Pearson correlation between test/mutant submissions and the overall grade achieved on the end-of-term written exam. Exam grades are given on a scale of 1–5 (with intermediate steps of .3 and .7), with 1 being the best mark, and 5 being a fail. Figure 8(a) and Figure 8(b) show the correlation between the number of defender actions and mutant submissions, respectively, and the resulting final term exam grade (the exam was taken by 97 students). For both player roles there is a moderate correlation of -0.58 and -0.38, respectively (both p-values < 0.001), confirming that better students are more active players. The correlation is higher for test submissions, which is likely because it is easier to submit a mutant even without fully understanding the code and the tests. While we cannot conclude from this whether the game *influences* the exam marks without further experimentation, the relation of in-game performance and exam performance suggests that including Code Defenders gameplay in the grading is indeed appropriate, which is a prerequisite for making the game a mandatory part of a testing course.

4.5 RQ4: Student satisfaction

After the last Code Defenders session, we ran an anonymous survey among the students, in which we asked them to reflect on their experience and satisfaction with the Code Defenders integration. We announced the survey in-class and via email, and allowed students to voluntarily complete it in their own time. In total, 75 students responded to the survey. Figure 9 summarises the main questions (we omit feedback on how to improve the Code Defenders game itself as it falls out of the scope of this paper), which are overwhelmingly positive: Only two students did not like the integration, and three partially disliked it; the free-text responses suggest that the main points of criticism are limitations of the code editor, performance issues, and a desire to integrate more diverse testing concepts from the lectures into the game sessions, rather than just unit testing.

Although students tend to claim they do like to write tests even outside the game, they confirm it is more fun to do so as part of the game. A vast majority of students felt that they learned useful skills while playing as defender, and while they still agree that they learn useful skills when playing as attacker, there is less agreement compared to the defender role. This is in line with our observations of students submitting mutants with less consideration compared to tests. Students felt that using a game in a university course is appropriate; while the majority of students felt the number of sessions was appropriate, 17% of them disagreed on this. The explanations in the free-text responses reveal that a few students thought the tasks became a bit repetitive, and they would have liked to see more challenging classes over time. Even though the game sessions required no preparation time for the students, 16% of them thought that being awarded 10% of the overall course mark for the game sessions was not appropriately balanced (according to free-text responses it should contribute more), although the majority was satisfied with this marking decision. Finally, on balance the students were satisfied with the choice of classes under test and even suggested more challenging classes could have been used.

5 CONCLUSIONS

Overall, students engaged actively and enjoyed playing Code Defenders as part of our gamified testing course, while at the same time improving their testing skills. This positive outcome encourages us to continue using Code Defenders in the future, and we hope this experience report will inspire and assist other educators to integrate Code Defenders as an educational resource as part of their own software testing courses. Code Defenders is open-source and available on GitHub: https://github.com/CodeDefenders. A public installation is also available to play online at http://code-defenders.org.

ACKNOWLEDGEMENTS

This research has been supported by the Erasmus+ project IMPRESS 2017-1-NL01-KA203-035259 and DFG grant FR 2955/2-1.

REFERENCES

[1] Jonathan Bell, Swapneel Sheth, and Gail Kaiser. 2011. Secret ninja testing with HALO software engineering. In *Int. Workshop on Social Software Engineering (SSE)*. ACM, 43–47.

[2] Timothy Alan Budd. 1980. *Mutation Analysis of Program Test Data*. Ph.D. Dissertation. Yale University, New Haven, CT, USA.

[3] David Carrington. 1997. Teaching software testing. In *Australasian Conference on Computer Science Education (ACSE)*. ACM, ACM, 59–64.

[4] Tommaso Dal Sasso, Andrea Mocci, Michele Lanza, and Ebrisa Mastrodicasa. 2017. How to gamify software engineering. In *IEEE Int. Conference on Software Analysis, Evolution and Reengineering (SANER)*. IEEE, 261–271.

[5] Sebastian Elbaum, Suzette Person, Jon Dokulil, and Matt Jorde. 2007. Bug Hunt: Making early software testing lessons engaging and affordable. In *ACM/IEEE Int. Conference on Software Engineering (ICSE)*. 688–697.

[6] Gordon Fraser, Alessio Gambi, and José Miguel Rojas. 2018. A Preliminary Report on Gamifying a Software Testing Course with the Code Defenders Testing Game. In *European Conference of Software Engineering Education (ECSEE)*. ACM, 50–54.

[7] Félix García, Oscar Pedreira, Mario Piattini, Ana Cerdeira-Pena, and Miguel Penabad. 2017. A framework for gamification in software engineering. *Journal of Systems and Software* 132 (2017), 21–40.

[8] Int. Software Testing Qualification Board (ISTQB). 2011. Certified Tester Foundation Level Syllabus. https://www.istqb.org/downloads/send/2-foundation-level-documents/3-foundation-level-syllabus-2011.html4.

[9] JaCoCo. 2018. JaCoCo Java Code Coverage Library. https://www.eclemma.org/jacoco/. [Online; accessed October 27, 2018].

[10] Yue Jia and Mark Harman. 2011. An Analysis and Survey of the Development of Mutation Testing. *IEEE Transactions of Software Engineering* 37, 5 (2011), 649–678.

[11] JUnit. 2018. JUnit. https://junit.org/junit4/. [Online; accessed October 27, 2018].

[12] René Just. 2014. The Major mutation framework: Efficient and scalable mutation analysis for Java. In *ACM Int. Symposium on Software Testing and Analysis (ISSTA)*. 433–436.

[13] Gerard Meszaros. 2007. *xUnit test patterns: Refactoring test code*. Pearson Education.

[14] Carlos Pacheco, Shuvendu K Lahiri, Michael D Ernst, and Thomas Ball. 2007. Feedback-directed random test generation. In *ACM/IEEE Int. Conference on Software Engineering (ICSE)*. IEEE Computer Society, 75–84.

[15] Reza Meimandi Parizi. 2016. On the gamification of human-centric traceability tasks in software testing and coding. In *IEEE Int. Conference on Software Engineering Research, Management and Applications (SERA)*. IEEE, 193–200.

[16] José Miguel Rojas and Gordon Fraser. 2016. Code Defenders: A Mutation Testing Game. In *Int. Workshop on Mutation Analysis*. IEEE, 162–167.

[17] José Miguel Rojas, Thomas D White, Benjamin S Clegg, and Gordon Fraser. 2017. Code Defenders: Crowdsourcing effective tests and subtle mutants with a mutation testing game. In *ACM/IEEE Int. Conference on Software Engineering (ICSE)*. IEEE Press, 677–688.

[18] Tricentis. 2017. Software Fail Watch: 5th Edition. https://www.tricentis.com/software-fail-watch/. [Online; accessed October 27, 2018].

Measuring Unit Test Accuracy

Kevin Buffardi
California State University, Chico
Chico, California
kbuffardi@csuchico.edu

Pedro Valdivia
California State University, Chico
Chico, California
pvaldivia1@mail.csuchico.edu

Destiny Rogers
California State University, Chico
Chico, California
drogers14@mail.csuchico.edu

ABSTRACT

Unit testing is widely adopted in software development to automate verification of individual functions. Likewise, computer science curricula are increasing their emphasis on teaching unit testing skills. However, coverage and other measurements of test quality have limitations and may even encourage poor practices when used as an assessment and/or feedback mechanism for students. In this paper, we introduce test accuracy as a measurement that compares how well unit tests perform at distinguishing acceptable from unacceptable function implementations. To study measurements of test quality, we evaluated an assignment where students (n=103) developed a class along with accompanying tests for each of its functions.

Our quantitative analysis compares test accuracy with coverage and bug identification measurements by examining each of their relationships with a lack of bugs in the students' implementations. Of the three measurements, accuracy had the strongest positive correlation (ρ=.648, p<.001) with a lack of bugs in the entire program. When examining the subset of tests for a particular function-under-test, both accuracy and coverage were significant predictors of a lack of bugs within the corresponding function's implementation.

CCS CONCEPTS

• **Social and professional topics** → **Software engineering education**; • **Software and its engineering** → **Software testing and debugging**; • **Hardware** → *Coverage metrics*;

KEYWORDS

unit test, software testing, verification, function under test

ACM Reference Format:
Kevin Buffardi, Pedro Valdivia, and Destiny Rogers. 2019. Measuring Unit Test Accuracy. In *Proceedings of the 50th ACM Technical Symposium on Computer Science Education (SIGCSE '19), February 27-March 2, 2019, Minneapolis, MN, USA.* ACM, New York, NY, USA, Article 4, 7 pages. https://doi.org/10.1145/3287324.3287351

1 INTRODUCTION

In software engineering, typically about half of a project's costs are spent on testing [16]. Recent trends place an emphasis on incremental development with a particular prevalence of unit testing. Unlike system testing that verifies a software program in its entirety, unit tests are meant to verify individual functions. Incremental approaches to unit testing like Test-Driven Development (TDD) [3] take advantage of unit tests to build confidence in code and to help localize bugs when tests fail [17].

Despite its prominence and widespread adoption in industry, unit testing still does not get much attention in many computer science academic programs. However, the most recent curriculum recommended by the Association for Computing Machinery (ACM) identifies a need for increasing emphasis on testing within both "Software Development Fundamentals" and "Software Engineering" core knowledge areas. In addition, the curriculum specifically suggests including unit testing as early as introductory programming courses [2]. By incorporating more testing in computing education, students may learn to improve their debugging strategies and further their metacognitive problem-solving skills [8].

In recent years, educational tools [5][12][19] and pedagogical approaches [11][14] to teaching software testing have emerged. However, there is not a consistent de facto standard for how students' unit tests should be evaluated for their quality. While coverage is commonly used to measure thoroughness of testing, it does not reflect the true purpose of unit tests: distinguishing acceptable from unacceptable implementations.

Some preliminary studies have explored variations of evaluating students' tests by running them against a corpus of implementations that are known to contain bugs [1][5][12][14][19]. This approach shows promise to approximate how well tests identify bugs [9]. However, concentrating solely on failing bugs discounts the role of tests to also positively verify acceptable solutions. One might predict that tests' effectiveness at failing buggy code is inherently combined with an ability to pass good solutions. To the contrary a previous study revealed that it is common for students to struggle with either task independently. Moreover, deficiencies in accomplishing either goal is associated with producing similar number of bugs in the students' own implementations [7].

Likewise, approaches that involve running all of a student's tests at once against an entire program strays from the purpose of unit tests verifying individual functions. Consequently, this paper introduces test accuracy as a technique for measuring how well students' unit tests distinguish between both acceptable and unacceptable implementations. We compare accuracy to traditional bug identification and coverage metrics in a study of three semesters of a programming assignment that required unit tests and implementations for an object oriented class. In the study, we investigated the relationships between each metric and the number of bugs in the students' class (as a whole) as well as those within specific functions.

SIGCSE '19, February 27-March 2, 2019, Minneapolis, MN, USA

ACM ISBN 978-1-4503-5890-3/19/02...$15.00
https://doi.org/10.1145/3287324.3287351

2 BACKGROUND

Unit testing has grown in popularity along with an increasing prevalence of xUnit frameworks for modern programming languages [17]. These unit testing frameworks follow a common structure as a test class is dedicated to a corresponding object oriented class. A test class contains multiple unit tests. Each unit test is intended to invoke a particular function within the class and then assert the expected outcome for that particular test case. The aggregate of all test cases is referred to as a test suite, and when they are run, each unit test either passes (when the expected outcome is met) or fails (when its execution produces a fault or other unexpected outcomes). A test suite also provides automated regression tests. Ideally, all tests passing should impart confidence that the software behaves correctly, while a failing unit test should help developers identify the origin of a bug because it focuses on verifying a specific function [4].

Along with the prevalence of xUnit frameworks, tools to determine code coverage of test suites are also common. Coverage measures what segments of code execute within an implementation when tests run. While there are variations–such as condition/decision coverage that checks whether each part of a boolean condition has been evaluated as both true and false–a lack of qualifiers usually refers to statement coverage. Statement coverage (sometimes imprecisely called "line coverage") identifies which statements have been executed and can be reported as a percentage of total statements in the implementation.

However, coverage does not evaluate the actual outcomes of unit tests. Instead, it only indicates what code has (and has not) been tested at all. A statement that has been run and produced the expected outcome under one scenario does not guarantee that it will always behave correctly under all other cases. Nevertheless, once a statement has be executed by at least one test, it has been "covered" and therefore, coverage is a fairly superficial evaluation of unit tests.

Alternatively, mutation testing involves automatically generating variations of an implementation to create a corpus of artificial bugs (mutants) and check whether the unit tests can fail those bugs. Aaltonen, et al. recognized the convenience of mutation testing but also the potential that mutants may not accurately resemble naturally occurring bugs and therefore recommended assessing students' tests using a combination of mutation testing and coverage [1]. However, an experiment found that neither mutation testing nor coverage were as strongly correlated with identifying bugs as running students' tests against a corpus of implementations with naturally occurring bugs [9].

Goldwasser initially introduced all-pairs testing as a technique for introducing testing into programming assignments. With this approach, each student submits an implementation along with corresponding tests. Each students' tests are then evaluated by how well they fail other students' implementations that have been deemed imperfect by failing one or more of the instructor's reference tests. In an initial investigation of the technique, students whose implementations passed all the reference tests also submitted tests that exposed 87% of their peers' flawed programs. Meanwhile, students with incorrect solutions only exposed 63% of the imperfect programs [14]. Edwards, et al. reconciled the original all-pairs approach with support of a modern xUnit framework as well as integration with an online autograder [11]. In an evaluation of the updated all-pairs approach, students often achieved high coverage but the researchers also observed that most students' tests were ineffective at detecting hidden bugs [10].

Similarly, eLearning tools for practicing how to test have focused on whether or not students' tests can fail a corpus of buggy solutions [12][19]. Unlike coverage, evaluating students' tests against known bugs assesses the test outcomes. Unit testing best practices include giving proper attention to writing both "happy and sad tests" [4] to affirm that both common and unusual cases behave correctly. Failing incorrect behavior is a primary goal for testing. On the other hand, tests are inaccurate if they either pass buggy code or if they fail code that actually behaves correctly.

When tests report inaccurate conclusions, they represent similar Type I and Type II errors that are observed in hypothesis testing or medical diagnostic tests [18]. Inaccurately passing code that contains bugs may lead to poor software quality. In the least, this outcome results in additional cost when the bug is discovered later and has to be localized and patched; in the meantime it may also propagate other bugs. On the other hand, inaccurately failing code that behaves correctly is also potentially costly. Doing so requires re-evaluating both the implementation and the test, which takes time and increases cost. Even worse, if the implementation is blamed for the failure, the tests inaccurately document the expected behavior, which then results in changing it to misbehave.

We previously studied assignments where students wrote implementations and corresponding tests to investigate whether students exhibited both types of testing errors [7]. We found that students' tests commonly exhibited either type of error. Although it is possible to reject good solutions and accept bad solutions for the same function, we did not find any students who produced high rates of both errors for the same function.

However, we found that students made both types of errors independently and that individuals commonly produced different types of errors (or lack thereof) when testing different functions. More notably, we found that tests with high rates of failing good solutions was associated with just as many bugs as those with high rates of passing bad solutions when examining the student's corresponding implementation. Accordingly, this paper introduces a technique for assessing students' tests for their combined performance at bug identification and positive verification.

3 METHOD

To evaluate unit tests for their *accuracy*, we propose running them against a corpus of acceptable and unacceptable solutions and measuring the rate at which the tests distinguish between them. Accordingly, accuracy is measured by the sum of acceptable solutions passed and unacceptable solutions failed, divided by the total number of solutions in both corpora. Accuracy is contrasted with the traditional *bug identification rate*, which is calculated as only the percentage of unacceptable solutions failed by the tests.

Since accuracy accounts for both bug identification and positive verification, we predicted that test accuracy is a more effective measurement of testing than bug identification alone. In theory, accuracy's inclusion of both Type I and Type II error measurements is inherently more precise than the traditional bug identification assessment. However, it does not necessarily follow that measuring accuracy adds any more meaningful evaluation in practice.

Improved test quality should also improve a student's ability to verify their implementation and decrease the number of bugs it contains. Consequently, we compared both measurements of test quality by how strongly they are associated with a lack of bugs in students' corresponding solutions. For due diligence, we also compared these measurements to coverage, the other leading metric for test quality. We hypothesized that: **(H1) test accuracy is positively associated with implementations containing a lack of bugs**; and **(H2) accuracy is more strongly associated with a lack of bugs than both bug identification rate and coverage.**

3.1 Data Collection

Across three semesters of Software Engineering courses (n=103), students attempted a testing assignment. The courses included three offerings of an upper-division undergraduate class (n=95) and one offering of a graduate class (n=8), that are required for a Bachelors and Masters in Computer Science, respectively. Prerequisites for both courses prepared students with multiple object-oriented programming courses, none of which teach unit testing. The software engineering courses incorporate project-based experiential learning, complemented by lessons on the software development lifecycle and contemporary tools as well as approximately three weeks (6 lecture hours) spent on software design and another 6 hours spent on software testing. The testing module included lessons with demonstrations and assignments on: unit tests (using GoogleTest, an open source xUnit framework for C++ [15], Test-Driven Development [3], and coverage (using gcov, a coverage tool packaged with the GNU GCC compiler [13]).

The assignment used for this study was a take-home summative assessment of students' unit testing at the end of the courses' testing module. The assignment required students to implement a C++ class that included three public functions (with provided signatures including return values and parameters) in addition to a constructor and a private function (with void return and no parameters). Plain word documentation described the desired behavior of the class as a whole as well as each individual function. In addition to implementing the class, students were instructed to write accompanying unit tests that were sufficient for accurately verifying the class.

3.2 All-Function-Pairs Evaluation

The instructor wrote a comprehensive test suite to verify students' implementations and identify acceptable and unacceptable solutions. While we followed a model similar to all-pairs testing, the previous implementations classified entire programs as either entirely good (not failing any reference tests) or bad (failing at least one reference test). However, that approach tends to yield very few–if any–entirely correct programs [11]. Likewise, doing so only provides an evaluation of an entire test suite rather than assessing whether unit tests accurately verify individual functions.

Instead, we performed all-function-pairs analysis, which determines students' unit test outcomes for each public function in the class. We used a python script that performed prompt static analysis on each unit test to identify its function-under-test. Most non-trivial functions require multiple unit tests to verify its behavior in multiple different cases. A function that contains a bug should fail at least one unit test, but not all unit tests for that function-under-test (FUT) should necessarily fail because they describe different cases.

Therefore, we categorized each unit test within a student's test suite by its FUT: which function it is meant to verify. Each public function within the class should have a subset of the test suite with a corresponding FUT. Common procedure of a unit test involves setting the state for a test case, calling its FUT, and comparing the FUT's behavior to the expected outcome with an assertion statement. Accordingly, the static analysis identified each unit test's FUT by which of the class' functions is called in the assertion. If the assertion does not directly call any of the class' functions, the last of the function calls before the assertion is selected instead.

Sometimes, mostly for readability reasons, the FUT's return value is stored in a variable and then the variable is used in the assertion. There may be other approaches to identifying a FUT, such as dynamically analyzing the call stack when the unit test is run. However, static analysis is less costly and reliable by our observations. On rare occasion, static analysis found unit tests with no function calls (such as sanity checks that just verify that the test suite is setup correctly so that it can compile and run). Those tests are just disregarded because they did not test the class implementation in any way.

In the same static analysis, we identified the FUT subsets of the instructor's reference tests. GoogleTest runs an entire test suite by default, but a specific unit test can also be specified to run in isolation–a common feature in xUnit test runners. Accordingly, we ran each FUT subset from the reference tests against each student's implementation to classify whether that student's implementation of each function was acceptable (by passing its subset) or unacceptable (by failing one or more unit tests). Subsequently, we ran each FUT subset from each student's test suite against every other student's implementation.

In some cases, a student did not have any unit tests for a particular FUT; such a null subset passes every implementation as defined by the absence of any failures. If the student's FUT subset outcome matched the reference's outcome for the corresponding FUT implementation, it was considered the proper test outcome. Passing a function implementation that the reference tests also passed was recorded as a *positive verification* while matching a failure to the reference tests' failure was recorded as *bug identification*. FUT outcomes that differed from the reference tests are recorded as *false verification* and *false bug identification*.

This process of evaluating of each function implementation individually increases the likelihood of yielding a sizeable corpus of acceptable implementations. Given a challenging programming assignment, few students will pass *all* reference tests for the *entire program*. However, many more students will pass all the reference tests for any given function. This all-function-pairs testing method is illustrated and discussed in detail in our previous work [7]. While previous studies involved manually inspecting each unit test to identify its FUT, this study offers a more efficient and scalable solution by completely automating all-function-pairs evaluation.

3.3 Analysis

In addition to evaluating the test and implementation outcomes, we also used gcov [13] to evaluate students' coverage on each of their own function implementations (and program as a whole). However, unlike test and implementation outcomes, coverage scores for the program are not strictly the sum of each function. As is common in object-oriented programming, the class used in the assignment had some functional code that was not directly accessible via the public interface and therefore it was not a FUT, but it could be covered (indirectly, if any of the public functions invoked the private statements).

Overall, student programs averaged passing 80% of the reference tests (sd=.25). Similarly, accuracy (M=.78, sd=.13), bug identification rate (M=.71, sd=.24), and coverage (M=.86, sd=.25) scores were fairly good but with moderate variance between students. We performed a Shapiro-Wilk test on each metric and found that none of them were normally distributed (p<.001).

We evaluated the hypothesis **(H1) test accuracy is positively associated with implementations containing a lack of bugs** by performing Spearman's rho correlation (for non-parametric data) between students' program implementation scores and their corresponding test quality metrics. To conservatively correct for increased likelihood of yielding significant results when multiple correlations are performed, we adjusted the critical value (α=.0167) using the Bonferroni method.

For a more direct comparison between accuracy, bug identification rate, and coverage, we also modeled a multiple linear regression to explain the program implementation score response variable. We evaluated the hypothesis that **(H2) accuracy is more strongly associated with a lack of bugs than both bug identification rate and coverage**. Comparing the correlations of each test metric provides the strength of each metric's association with a corresponding lack of bugs in the student's implementation. The correlations consider each metric independently. However, the regression formula's coefficients also indicate how well each predicts the implementation score when modeled all together. To support H1 and H2, accuracy must have a significant (less than α) correlation with a higher positive coefficient than either bug identification rate or coverage. Likewise, accuracy should have a significant and larger coefficient in the regression model, indicating stronger predictive value.

In addition, we explored if accuracy maintained an association with a lack of bugs when evaluated for individual functions-under-test (FUT). To do so, we calculated correlations for each of the three FUT with their corresponding implementations by the same student. A good measurement of test quality should have consistent correlations across each function. Finally, we considered that functions with different degrees of difficulty may skew overall program evaluations so we performed mixed model regression. The mixed model coefficients should indicate each metric's prediction of the function implementation score, while accounting for differences between functions.

4 RESULTS

Spearman's rho indicated a significant (p<.001), strong positive correlation (ρ=.648) between accuracy and the implementation score for a program. Implementation score was also moderately correlated with bug identification rate (ρ=.355, p<.0167) and with coverage (ρ=.514, p<.001). These correlations are illustrated in **Figures 1-3** in independent scatterplots for each of the three metrics.

Next, we calculated a multiple linear regression model for predicting students' program implementation scores based on accuracy,

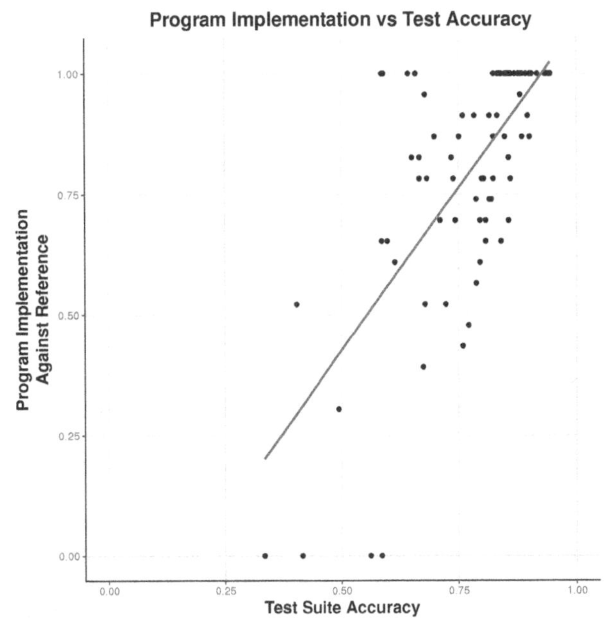

Figure 1: Correlation between program accuracy and implementation score

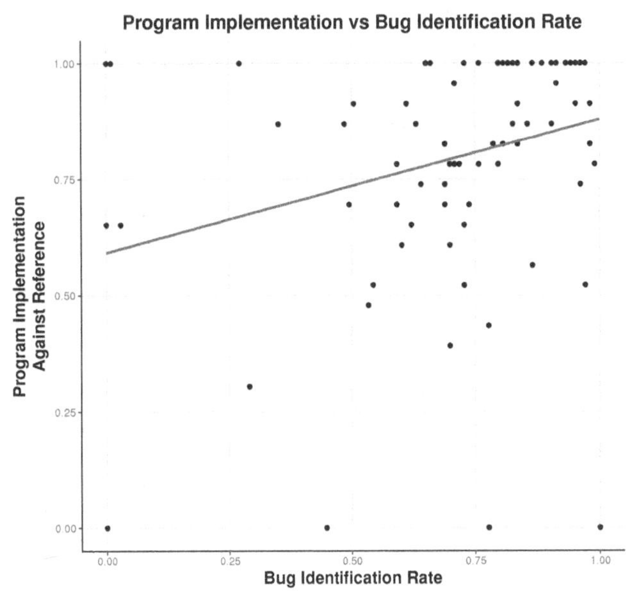

Figure 2: Correlation between program bug identification rate and implementation score

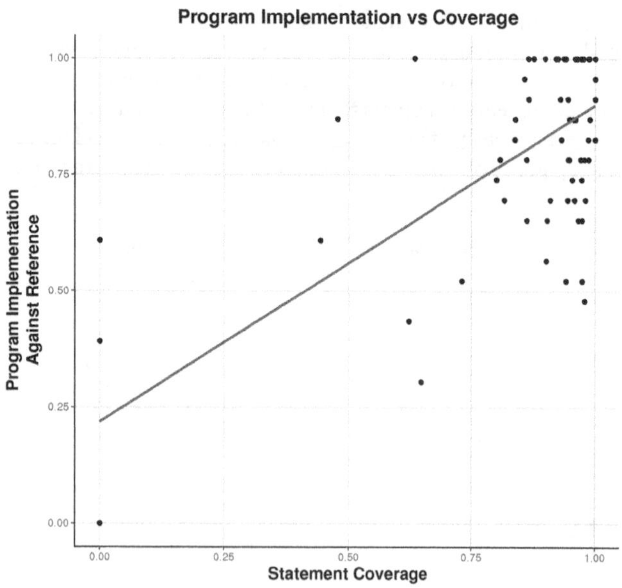

Figure 3: Correlation between program coverage and implementation score

bug identification rate, and coverage. We found that bug identification rate (B=-0.07, Std. Error=0.08) was not significant (p=.409) while both accuracy (B=0.83, Std. Error=0.18) and coverage (B=0.49, Std. Error=0.08) had significant coefficients (p<.001). We recalculated the model while excluding the non-significant bug identification rate factor and found a significant regression equation (E(2,77)=66.03, p<.001, R^2=.632). Students' predicted implementation scores were equal to: -0.20 + .749*accuracy + .489*coverage. Implementations scores increased by approximately 75 percentage points for achieving perfect (1.0) accuracy and about 49 percentage points for achieving full (1.0) coverage. Both accuracy and coverage were significant predictors of implementation scores (p<.001).

The correlation results support the hypotheses that **(H1) test accuracy is positively associated with implementations containing a lack of bugs** and that **(H2) accuracy is more strongly associated with a lack of bugs than both bug identification rate and coverage**. Accuracy had a moderately strong positive correlation and was also greater than that of either bug identification rate or coverage metrics. Beyond evaluating the metrics independently, the multiple linear regression strengthened support for both hypotheses by indicating that accuracy was a strong predictor of implementation scores even when bug identification rate and coverage were included in the same model. While coverage was also a significant predictor, accuracy had a greater coefficient, indicating stronger prediction of a lack of bugs in the corresponding implementation. These analyses reflect a comparison between accuracy and the two leading assessment metrics for students' test quality: coverage and bug identification rate against a corpus of buggy solutions using the all-pairs method [14].

However, we also explored accuracy's validity and relationship with individual function implementations using the all-function-pairs method [7]. The assignment used in this study required three public methods that modify and inspect the state of a board game (of the instructor's creation). The accuracy for each FUT, *dropPiece* (M=.83, sd=.18), *pieceAt* (M=.78, sd=.17), and *gameState* (M=.72, .17) was moderately high. We also observed a similar performance in implementations of those functions, where difficulty increased and scores decreased from *dropPiece* (M=.87, sd=.27) to *pieceAt* (M=.83, sd=.28) and finally to the most challenging function, *gamestate* (M=.74, sd=.30).

We posited that a good test metric should be relatively consistent at evaluating tests regardless of FUT so we evaluated the correlations between the accuracy and implementation scores for each FUT. We found that accuracy and implementation were significantly correlated for *dropPiece* (ρ=.503, p<.001), *pieceAt* (ρ=.510, p<.001), and *gameState* (ρ=.523, p<.001). Each correlation was moderately positive and relatively consistent, although it appears possible that the more difficult the function is, the relationship may grow slightly stronger. These correlations are illustrated in a scatterplot in **Figure 4**, with coded plots and regression lines for each FUT.

For a frame of reference, we also calculated the correlations between each FUT implementation and their respective bug identification rates and coverage. Students demonstrated a fairly consistent bug identification rate for *dropPiece* (M=.73, sd=.34), *pieceAt* (M=.73, sd=.29), and *gameState* (M=.70, sd=.30). *DropPiece* (ρ=.398, p<.001) and *pieceAt* (ρ=.315, p<.0167) had moderate, positive correlations with FUT implementation scores. However, there was no correlation between bug identification for *gameState* (ρ=.001, p=.99) and its implementation.

Meanwhile, students achieved relatively high coverage for *dropPiece* (M=.87, sd=.28), *pieceAt* (M=.89, .27), and *gameState* (M=.85, sd=.28). FUT implementation had a moderate, positive correlation with coverage for *dropPiece* (ρ=.414, p<.001), *pieceAt* (ρ=.445,

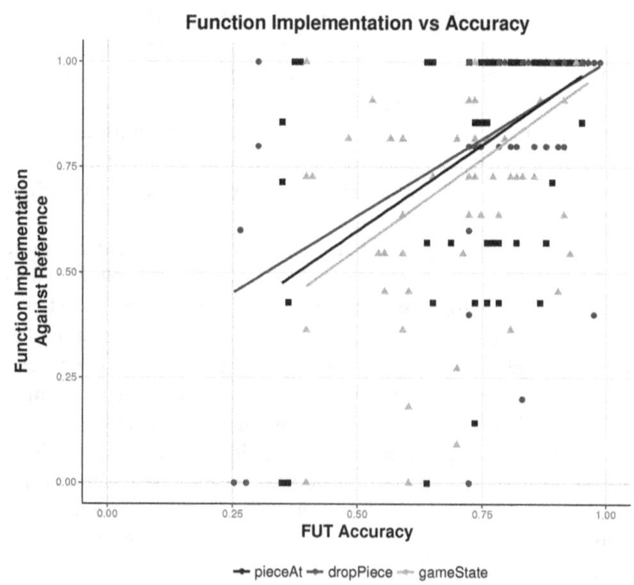

Figure 4: Correlations between accuracy and implementation on each of three functions-under-test

p<.001), and *gameState* (ρ=.527, p<.001). The magnitude of the correlations varied to a degree, but similarly to accuracy, the relationship appears to strengthen with more difficult functions.

When considered independently, accuracy and coverage were both relatively consistent. However, bug identification rate was not significantly correlated with implementation scores for each FUT. As found in analysis of entire programs, accuracy also demonstrated the strongest association with a lack of bugs within individual FUT implementations.

We also evaluated each metric as a predictor of FUT implementation scores while controlling for within-FUT comparisons to account for differences in difficulty. A repeated measures mixed model found that students' predicted FUT implementation scores were equal to: -0.06 + .575*coverage + .406*accuracy + .077*bug finding rate. Again, accuracy and coverage were the strongest predictors. However, in this case, coverage uniquely had a higher coefficient than accuracy. This discrepancy may be somewhat explained by the inclusion of bug finding rate in the model, which confounds as a similar (but weaker) measurement of categorizing test outcomes.

5 DISCUSSION

By its definition, accuracy should be expected to be an improved metric for evaluating quality of unit tests over bug identification rate using the all-pairs method. In our empirical analysis of the metrics applied to evaluating a real programming assignment, we found that accuracy is a much stronger assessment of unit test quality in practice as well.

However, we were somewhat surprised to find that coverage was also a significant predictor of a lack of bugs in students' corresponding implementations. Analyses of both the program as a whole as well as each of the individual functions suggest a fairly consistent association between accuracy and implementation scores. Nevertheless, these outcomes should also be interpreted within the limits of the study's design.

The study was limited to one assignment in Software Engineering classes so in future work we plan to extend our evaluation to include more programming and testing assignments across other courses. The subjects performed the assignment after about three weeks of exposure to unit testing so the observed phenomena may differ after gaining further experience. Each of these factors should be considered potential threats to the validity of the study.

Our integration of the all-function-pairs technique helped the study gain insight into how well students test individual functions. This provides more nuanced evaluation of unit testing metrics as they apply to individual functions-under-test (FUT) by advancing the traditional all-pairs method [14]. Calculation of both bug identification rate and accuracy can be automated but are not well suited for real-time feedback because large corpora are considerably more costly to analyze than simple metrics like coverage. Nevertheless, accuracy also evaluates unit tests for their purpose: distinguishing between acceptable and unacceptable implementations.

On the other hand, coverage is less costly to compute. However, when it is used as the only measurement for evaluating students' tests, students may develop poor habits. Previous studies have found that when coverage is used for feedback and assessment (via an autograder), students tend to only write "happy path tests" [10] since their goal of testing orients toward achieving high coverage, rather than toward identifying bugs and verifying each function [6].

6 CONCLUSIONS

This paper introduces the accuracy metric for assessing students' unit tests on programming assignments. In a study of unit test quality, we evaluated three semesters of students' tests (n=103) on a software engineering assignment. We found that accuracy had a strong, positive correlation with the lack of bugs in the students' corresponding implementations. A regression model found that *accuracy* was a stronger predictor than both *coverage* and *bug identification rates* for explaining program implementation scores. The study used a novel approach to also evaluate unit tests' performance at verifying individual functions-under-test (FUT). Both *accuracy* and *coverage* had moderate predictive power for a lack of bugs in corresponding FUT implementations. However, *accuracy* demonstrates fewer risks than *coverage* as an assessment metric due to its indication of how well students' test outcomes correspond with instructors' reference tests.

REFERENCES

[1] Kalle Aaltonen, Petri Ihantola, and Otto Seppälä. 2010. Mutation analysis vs. code coverage in automated assessment of students' testing skills. In *In Proceedings of the ACM international conference companion on Object oriented programming systems languages and applications companion (OOPSLA '10)*. ACM, New York, NY, USA, 153–160. https://doi.org/10.1145/1869542.1869567

[2] ACM. 2013. Computer Science 2013: Curriculum Guidelines for Undergraduate Programs in Computer Science. http://www.acm.org/education/curricula-recommendations

[3] Kent Beck. 2003. *Test-driven development by Example*. Addison Wesley.

[4] David Bowes, Tracy Hall, Jean Petrić, Thomas Shippey, and Burak Turhan. 2017. How good are my tests?. In *In Proceedings of the 8th Workshop on Emerging Trends in Software Metrics (WETSoM '17)*. IEEE Press, Piscataway, NJ, USA, 9–14. https://doi.org/10.1109/WETSoM.2017..2

[5] Michael K. Bradshaw. 2015. Ante Up: A Framework to Strengthen Student-Based Testing of Assignments. In *In Proceedings of the 46th ACM Technical Symposium on Computer Science Education (SIGCSE '15)*. ACM, New York, NY, USA, 488–493. http://dx.doi.org/10.1145/2676723.2677247

[6] Kevin Buffardi and Stephen H. Edwards. 2015. Reconsidering Automated Feedback: A Test-Driven Approach. In *In Proceedings of the 46th ACM Technical Symposium on Computer Science Education (SIGCSE '15)*. ACM, New York, NY, USA, 416–420. http://dx.doi.org/10.1145/2676723.2677313

[7] Kevin Buffardi and Pedro Valdivia. 2018. Bug Hide-and-Seek: An Educational Game for Investigating Verification Accuracy in Software Tests. In *In Proceedings of the 2018 IEEE Frontiers in Education Conference (FIE '18)*. IEEE Press, San Jose, CA, USA.

[8] Stephen H. Edwards. 2004. Using software testing to move students from trial-and-error to reflection-in-action. 36, 1 (2004), 26–30. http://dx.doi.org/10.1145/1028174.971312

[9] Stephen H. Edwards and Zalia Shams. 2014. Comparing test quality measures for assessing student-written tests. In *In Companion Proceedings of the 36th International Conference on Software Engineering (ICSE Companion 2014)*. ACM, New York, NY, USA, 354–363. http://dx.doi.org/10.1145/2591062.2591164

[10] Stephen H. Edwards and Zalia Shams. 2014. Do student programmers all tend to write the same software tests?. In *In Proceedings of the 2014 conference on Innovation & technology in computer science education (ITiCSE '14)*. ACM, New York, NY, USA, 171–176. http://dx.doi.org/10.1145/2591708.2591757

[11] Stephen H. Edwards, Zalia Shams, Michael Cogswell, and Robert C. Senkbeil. 2012. Running students' software tests against each others' code: new life for an old "gimmick". In *In Proceedings of the 43rd ACM technical symposium on Computer Science Education (SIGCSE '12)*. ACM, New York, NY, USA, 221–226. http://dx.doi.org/10.1145/2157136.2157202

[12] Sebastian Elbaum, Suzette Person, Jon Dokulil, and Matt Jorde. 2007. Bug Hunt: Making Early Software Testing Lessons Engaging and Affordable. In *In Proceedings of the 29th international conference on Software Engineering (ICSE '07)*. IEEE Computer Society, Washington, DC, USA, 688–697. http://dx.doi.org/10.1109/ICSE.2007.23

[13] GNU. [n. d.]. Gcov-a test coverage program. https://gcc.gnu.org/onlinedocs/gcc/Gcov.html
[14] M. H. Goldwasser. 2002. A gimmick to integrate software testing throughout the curriculum. In *In Proceedings of the 33rd ACM Technical Symposium on Computer Science Education (SIGCSE '02)*. ACM.
[15] Google. [n. d.]. GoogleTest. https://github.com/google/
[16] Rafaqut Kazmi, Dayang N. A. Jawawi, Radziah Mohamad, and Imran Ghani. 2017. Effective Regression Test Case Selection: A Systematic Literature Review. 50, 2 (2017), 32. https://doi.org/10.1145/3057269
[17] Gerard G. Meszaros. 2010. XUnit test patterns and smells: improving the ROI of test code. In *In Proceedings of the ACM international conference companion on Object oriented programming systems languages and applications companion (OOPSLA '10)*. ACM, New York, NY, USA, 299–300. https://doi.org/10.1145/1869542.1869622
[18] Jerzy Neyman and Egon S. Pearson. 1967. *On the Use and Interpretation of Certain Test Criteria for Purposes of Statistical Inference, Part I.* Cambridge University Press.
[19] Rebecca Smith, Terry Tang, Joe Warren, and Scott Rixner. 2017. An Automated System for Interactively Learning Software Testing. In *In Proceedings of the 2017 ACM Conference on Innovation and Technology in Computer Science Education (ITiCSE '17)*. ACM, New York, NY, USA, 98–103. https://doi.org/10.1145/3059009.3059022

An Analysis of Using Many Small Programs in CS1

Joe Michael Allen[1], Frank Vahid[1,2], Alex Edgcomb[1,2], Kelly Downey[1], and Kris Miller[1]
[1]Computer Science and Engineering, University of California, Riverside
[2]zyBooks, Los Gatos, California
jalle010@ucr.edu, vahid@cs.ucr.edu, alex.edgcomb@zybooks.com, kelly@cs.ucr.edu, kmiller@cs.ucr.edu

ABSTRACT

Modern program auto-graders enable new CS1 approaches. Instructors can easily create new assignments, with students receiving immediate score feedback and resubmitting assignments. With such auto-graders, one approach assigns many small programs (MSPs) each week instead of one large program (OLP). Earlier research showed MSPs in CS1 yielded happier students and better grades. Our university and other schools have switched to MSPs in CS1. This paper addresses common questions about MSPs. We analyzed submissions for a 76-student section of our MSP CS1 course. Given 7 MSPs per week each worth 10 points, students needed 50 points for full credit. Students averaged 17 minutes per MSP and 120 minutes per week. Given 7 days, students on average started 2.2 days ahead of the due date, with 37% starting at least 3 days ahead. 40% of students exceeded the required 50 points per week (no extra credit was given). 50% of students "pivoted" -- switching to another program before completing the previous one. 54% used MSPs to study for exams. Students used MSPs in ways beneficial to their learning and stress reduction: spending sufficient time, completing more than necessary, preparing for exams, and pivoting to avoid getting stuck. A common concern is that MSP CS1 students will do poorly in a CS2 using OLPs. We analyzed 5 quarters of CS2 and found MSP students do fine (in fact slightly better). These results encourage use and refinement of MSPs in CS1 and other courses.

CCS CONCEPTS

• Human-centered computing~Empirical studies in HCI • Social and professional topics~CS1 • Social and professional topics~Student assessment • Applied computing~Interactive learning environments • Applied computing~E-learning

KEYWORDS

CS1; MSPs; Auto-grader; Programming; Time spent; Days before due; Threshold; Pivot; Exam preparation; CS2

SIGCSE '19, February 27-March 2, 2019, Minneapolis, MN, USA

ACM 978-1-4503-5890-3/19/02...$15.00
https://doi.org/10.1145/3287324.3287466

ACM Reference format:

Joe M. Allen, Frank Vahid, Alex Edgcomb, Kelly Downey, and Kris Miller. 2018. An Analysis of Using Many Small Programs in CS1. *In SIGCSE '19: 50th ACM Technical Symposium on Computer Science Education, Feb 27–Mar 2, 2019, Minneapolis, MN, USA.* ACM, NY, NY, USA, 7 pages. DOI: https://doi.org/10.1145/3287324.3287466

1 Introduction

Student success in CS1 classes is critical to keeping students in the computer science (CS) major, training students in other majors who need some programming, and attracting students to CS. High-stress, poor performance, and negative evaluations in college-level introductory programming classes (CS1) are well known [2, 4, 6]. As such, improving CS1 teaching attracts much research attention, such as peer instruction [7, 8, 9, 10, 11, 14], media focus [3, 7, 10], student self-selection of projects [12], and pair programming [5, 7, 10, 13].

One improvement approach makes use of modern program auto-graders like zyBooks [18], Mimir [16], CodeLab [17], or Cody Coursework [15], to give students immediate feedback, thus allowing for resubmission and improved grades (while conserving limited instructor grading time). Modern commercial auto-graders make assignment creation easier than in the past, causing a dramatic increase in their use in CS1 and other courses; for example, since zyBooks' auto-grader was released in 2016, over 200 courses (mostly CS1) have started using an auto-grader that did not before. With the ease of creating and grading programming assignments, more instructors are creating and assigning many small programs (MSPs) per week rather than the more common one large program (OLP) per week. Our 2018 paper [1] summarized a study showing that MSPs led to happier less-stressed students, without hurting student performance -- and in fact leading to improved code-writing scores on exams, likely due to students having more practice on focused concepts.

This paper's purpose is to answer various common questions about MSPs. This research presents data and analysis on our experience using MSPs in CS1 at our university.

Section 2 describes our methodology, describing our CS1 course and detailing our data collection techniques. Section 3 addresses the question "How much time do students spend working on MSPs?" Section 4 addresses the question "How many days before the due date do students start MSPs?" Section 5 addresses the question "What percent of MSPs do students complete each day?" Section 6 addresses the question "Will students complete more MSPs than required?" Section 7 addresses the question "Do students take advantage of switching among MSPs when stuck (pivot)?" Section 8 addresses the question "Do students use MSPs to study for exams?" Section 9 addresses the question "Do students who learn using MSPs in CS1 do poorly in a CS2 using OLPs?" Section 10 concludes.

2 Methodology

2.1 Course

The study was conducted at our U.S. public research university, whose CS department typically ranks in the top 60 by U.S. News and World Report. The university operates on the quarter system. Each academic year is divided into three "regular" 10-week quarters (fall, winter, spring) and one compressed 5-week summer session. Throughout the academic year, the CS1 course serves around 300-500 students each quarter. The course is required for all computing majors and for various engineering, science, and math majors, such that about half the students are computing majors and half are non-computing majors. The course topics include basic input/output, assignments, branches, loops, functions, and vectors. The weekly structure of the course includes three hours of instructor-led lecture, two hours of TA-led labs, interactive online readings, and auto-graded homework assignments. The course teaches C++ as the programming language. The course has a midterm during week six and a final after week 10. Each exam's points come half from multiple choice questions and half from free-response coding questions. The course uses active learning and peer learning in lectures.

2.2 Data collection

We analyzed data from a Spring 2017 76-student section of our CS1 course that used MSPs. Our CS1 used an online textbook published by zyBooks for all class readings, activities, and programming assignments. At the quarter's end, we collected all student submissions and explores for programming assignments from zyBooks and combined them into one spreadsheet. A submission is defined as when the student "turns in" their assignment for grading. An explore is defined as when a student runs their code through the zyBooks compiler for testing without grading (development was done in the built-in zyBooks coding windows; students were not introduced to an external development environment). Each student submission has metadata about the assignment title, a userID (anonymized and generated from zyBooks), the submission score, the max score possible for the submission, and a timestamp. An explore has the same metadata as a submission but without a score and a max score. For this study, we collected data from the 76 students for 61 MSPs. In total, we collected 16,106 submissions and 48,186 explores for a total of 64,292.

3 How much time do students spend working on MSPs?

We generally expect students to spend about 3 hours per week working on their programming assignments. Our past surveys and analyses showed students on average spending about 2 hours, the average pulled down by students who submit few or no programs (of course some students spend more than 3 hours as well). We designed the MSPs to take about the same total time per week as the traditional OLP approach. A key question is how much time do students actually spend working on MSPs.

To calculate the total time students spent on MSPs, we used each timestamp for an explore or submit, calculated the difference between each timestamp, and summed the differences. We excluded a difference that exceeded 10 minutes, assuming the student took a break. Note that our calculations are thus an underestimate, as some breaks may have actually involved the student working or researching, and we also cannot capture time spent understanding and working on the program before the first explore or submit.

Figure 1 summarizes the average time spent by students on MSPs per week, as calculated above. The x-axis is the week number and the y-axis is the time spent in minutes. On average, students spent 17 minutes per MSP, and 120 minutes per week, excluding week 1 (which had easy introductory programs) and week 9 (which had fewer programs to complete). The two most challenging weeks were week 4 covering loops, and week 8 covering vectors. The dips in weeks 6 and 7 are due to several MSPs having students rewrite earlier MSPs, but using user-defined functions.

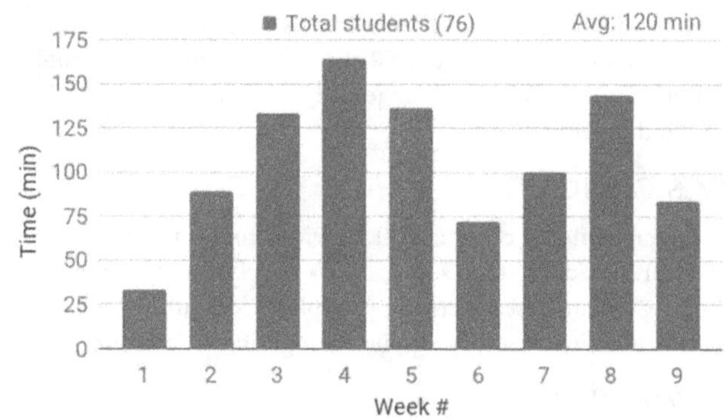

Figure 1: Average time spent by students each week on MSPs. Students with 0 submissions or 0 time spent were excluded from calculations.

We compared our analyses with a survey during lecture of week 8 that had 21 questions, one of which being "*The average hours per week spent on all zyLab programming assignments that week was?*" with response options 1-2, 2-3, 3-4, ..., 10+. Figure 2 summarizes student responses. 67 students responded. A weighted average yields about 5 hours per week, which is higher than our calculated time of 2 hours a week. This higher value may be due to various factors including: our calculations being an underestimate as mentioned earlier, students may overestimate or overreport time spent, weaker students may skip lecture and not be included in the survey, the survey's options may bias students towards selecting higher values, and the weighted sum may unintentionally round up.

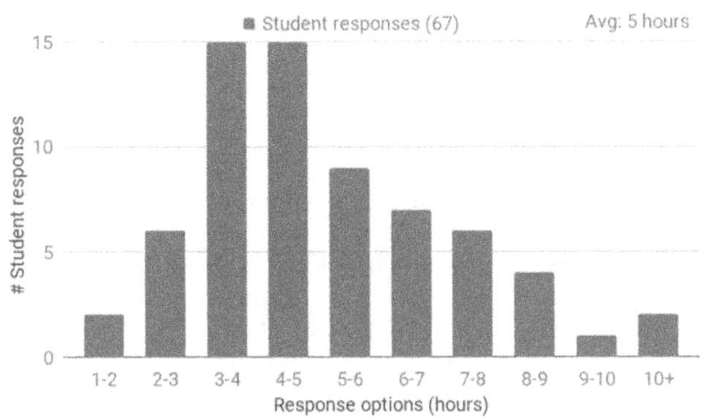

Figure 2: CS1 Spring 2017 survey responses (67 students) for "The average hours per week spent on all zyLab programming assignments that week was?" A weighted sum yields an average of 5 hours per week.

Figure 3 shows the time spent per MSP, using a box-and-whisker plot. The x-axis is the MSP (61 total) and the y-axis is the time spent in minutes. Dashed lines separate MSPs by week. The y-axis is capped at one hour (60 minutes). Students who did not attempt the given MSP are excluded from the calculations.

4 How many days before the due date do students start MSPs?

We released each week's MSPs on Tuesday, all due the following Tuesday at 9:00 pm. That week's readings and lectures (Tuesday and Thursday, 80 minutes each) taught the concepts covered by that week's MSPs. That week's 2-hour lab (Thursday) also taught those concepts, with about 30 minutes at the end for students to work on the MSPs and ask questions. A key question is how many days before the due date do students start working on MSPs.

Figure 4 summarizes the average number of days students began working on MSPs before the due date. The average was computed by finding students' first submission for all MSPs, computing the days between the first submission and the MSP due date, calculating the percent of students that started T-7, T-6, ..., T-0 days before the due date, and then averaging across all MSPs. The x-axis is the number of days prior to the due date. Using "NASA countdown-like" terminology, we use "T-2" to mean two days before the due date (or Sunday). The y-axis is the average percent of students that fall under each category. Week 1 is excluded from these calculations since week 1 MSPs were very easy.

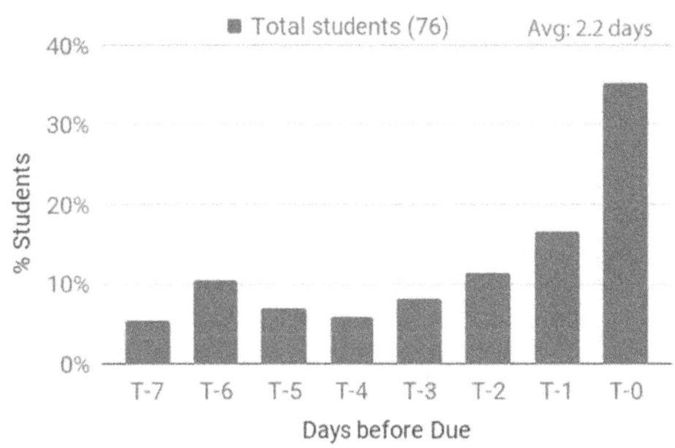

Figure 4: Percent of students who began MSPs each week T-X days prior to the due date - Spring 2017.

To our pleasure, 37% of students (28) started 3 days ahead or more. To our displeasure, 63% of students started only 2 days ahead or less, with 35% of students (27) starting on the due date. Students on average began 2.2 days ahead of the due date.

Figure 5 shows start times for the other two CS1 sections that quarter, which used OLPs. Those students began on average 2.1 days ahead of the due date. Only 28% (48) started 3 days ahead or more, and 25% (43) started on the due date. Note that the due dates were different between the sections, but this comparison still gives valuable insight.

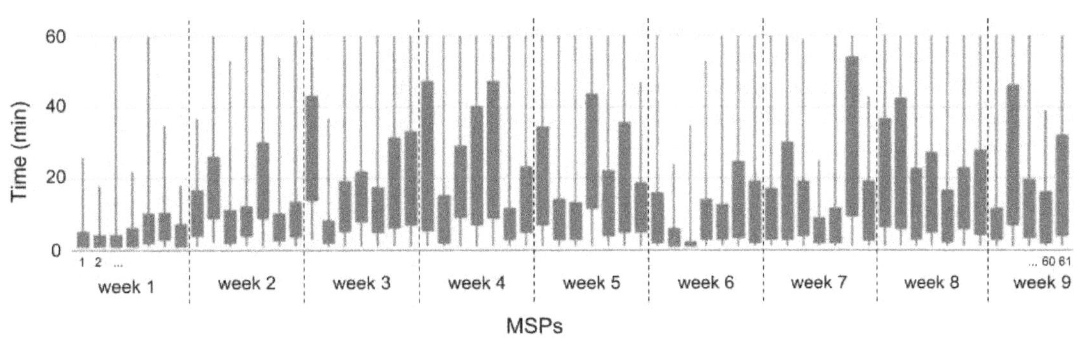

Figure 3: Box-and-whisker plot of student time spent for each MSP. On average, students spent 17 minutes per MSP excluding weeks 1 and 9.

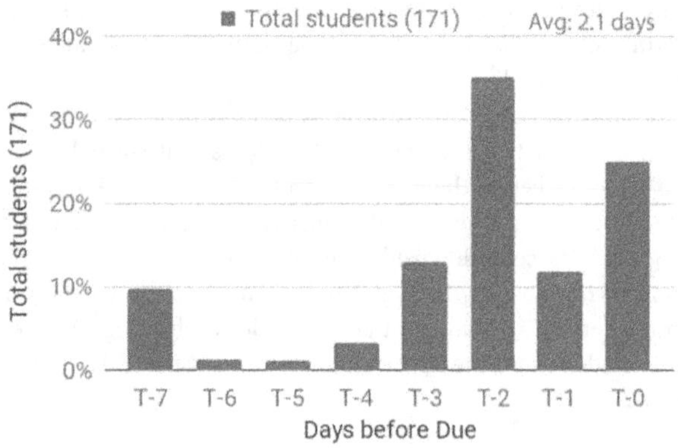

Figure 5: Percent of students who began OLPs each week T-X days prior to the due date - Spring 2017.

We had hoped that MSPs' less-intimidating nature would have led to earlier starts by most students. MSPs had a mild impact on students starting earlier, but many students still started on or near the due date. We believe starting earlier is good practice, and thus decided to try to encourage earlier starts. MSPs made such encouragement easy. In our Fall 2018 course, we simply included the following policy in our syllabus: "To discourage procrastination, you will be required to complete at least 20 points out of the 50 points each week by Sunday at 10 pm", which is 2 days prior to the Tuesday, 10 pm deadline. That small change led to substantial modification in student behavior, with start dates shifting from 2.5 (weeks 2 – 5) to 5.3 days before the due date. At the time of this publication, that Fall 2018 course covered up to week 5, and also excludes week 1 like the earlier data. Future work is needed to see if this improvement also helps to reduce student stress and improve grade performance.

5 What percent of MSPs do students complete each day?

The previous section showed when students started, defined as achieving at least 1 point on the MSP (out of 10 points). Here, we analyze total completion percent per day. A key question is what percentage of MSPs do students complete each day.

Figure 6 summarizes the completion rate of MSPs per day. The x-axis is the number of days prior to the due date and the y-axis is the completion percentage. The top bar is the percent completed on that day and the bottom bar is the cumulative completion prior to that day. Recall that only 50 of 70 points (71%) were required for full credit.

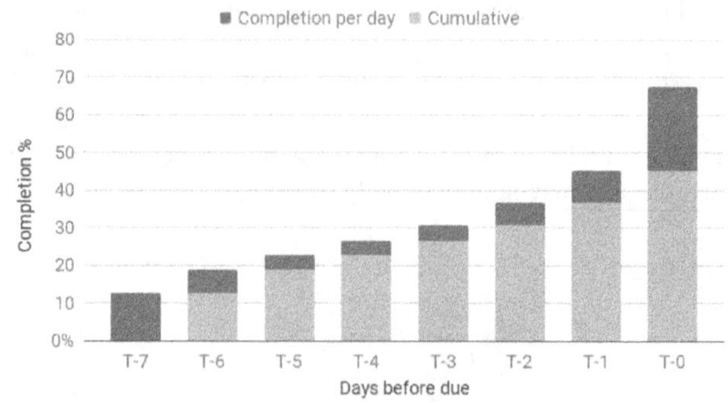

Figure 6: MSP completion T-X days prior to the due date. The top bar is the percent completed on that day, and the bottom bar is the percent completed prior to that day.

Figure 6 shows a gradual increase in the completion rate throughout the week. The completion rate increases 5-10% each day except for the last day (T-0) which has about a 20% increase. Because students need only complete 50 of 70 points, some MSPs have 0% completion, pulling down the averages shown.

6 Will students complete more MSPs than required?

Each week, students were assigned 7 MSPs (10 points each) and were only required to complete 50 points of 70 to score 100% on programming assignments for the week. No extra credit was given for exceeding 50 points. We refer to the 50-point cutoff as the full-credit threshold. A key question is whether students would willingly complete more MSPs than required, which would suggest that they find MSPs useful and/or enjoyable.

Figure 7 shows the percent of students that scored equal to or above the full-credit threshold each week. The bottom bar is the students that completed above the threshold and the top bar is the students that completed equal to the threshold. In weeks 1, 2, 3, and 6, a higher percentage of students scored above the threshold than equal to the threshold. Across the quarter, an average of 40% of students scored above the threshold.

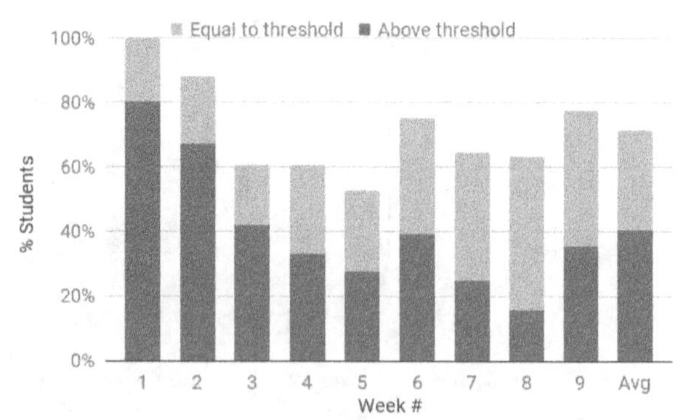

Figure 7: Percent of students who completed equal to or above the full-credit threshold each week.

Figure 8 provides a more detailed analysis via a bubble chart. The x-axis is the week number and the y-axis is the total points scored per week. The bubble size represents the number of students that scored that number of points. For example, the largest bubble in week 1 is labeled 53 because 53 students scored 70 points on MSPs for that week. Note that students who scored 0 points for the week are not included because those students likely dropped the class or decided not to submit labs for the week. The dashed line represents the full-credit threshold for each week. Note that week 9's threshold is lower since only five MSPs were given to students. On average, students who scored more than the full-credit threshold scored an additional 13 points. As each MSP is worth 10 points, this translates to completing an additional 1.3 MSPs each week.

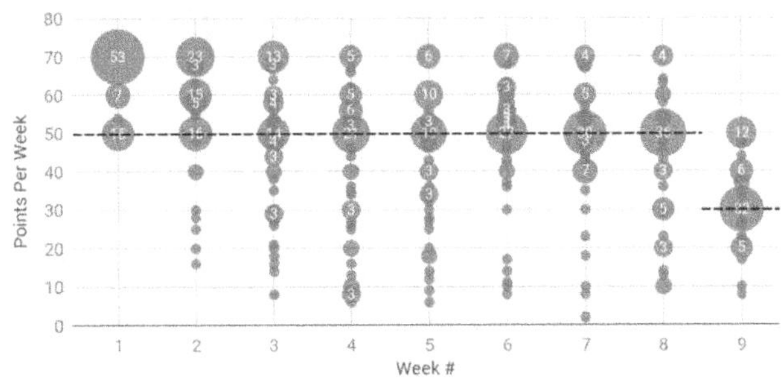

Figure 8: Points students scored each week. Students who scored 0 points for the week are excluded. Dashed line indicates max points for the week.

We were pleased to find that so many students were able to meet the full-credit threshold and that a substantial number were willing to do more than the minimum required work.

7 Do students take advantage of switching among MSPs when stuck (pivot)?

Pivoting is when a student partially completes an MSP (e.g., scores 6 of 10 points) and then decides to work on a different MSP. Typically, with traditional OLPs, students only have the option to work on the program until completion. If stuck, a student has few or no options. With MSPs, the students can pivot to another MSP. A key question is do students take advantage of the opportunity to pivot, and if so how often.

A submission is defined as a pivot if all following rules are met:

1. The current submission is not the student's first submission for the week
2. The current submission is for a different MSP than the previous submission
3. The current submission is for an MSP that has not been completed
4. The previous submission has not been completed
5. The current submission and previous submission are for MSPs assigned in the same week

Figure 9 shows the percent of students who pivoted at least once in a given week. The x-axis is the week number and the y-axis is the percent of students that pivoted that week.

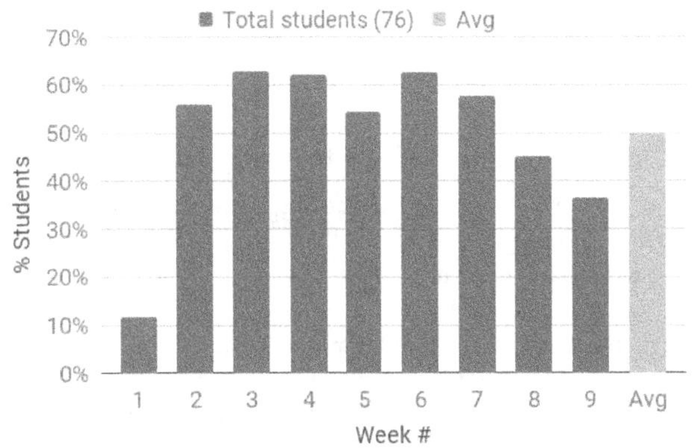

Figure 9: Percentage of students who pivoted at least once in a given week. An average of 50% of students pivoted at least once each week.

We found that students pivot on average 1.3 times each week. The highest number of pivots was one student who pivoted 12 times in week 4. Week 1 had few pivots due to the programs being easy. With more challenging programs beginning in week 2, students made much use of pivots. Students who pivoted at least once a week pivoted on average 2.5 times.

For insight, we highlight three actual pivoting scenarios.

7.1 Pivot at 0% - Week 8 (vectors)

A student attempted MSP 5 three times but received 0 points on all submissions. Instead of continuing MSP 5, the student switched to MSP 7 and scored 10 points. The student did not return to complete MSP 5. The student scored 50 points on MSPs for the week, meeting the 50-point full-credit threshold.

7.2 Single pivot - Week 3 (branches)

A student worked on MSP 4 and scored 8 points. The student switched to MSP 6 and scored 10 points. The student did not return to complete MSP 4. The student scored 48 points on MSPs for the week, nearly meeting the 50-point full-credit threshold.

7.3 Multiple pivots (3 or more) - Week 4 (loops)

A student worked on MSP 4 and scored 2 points. The student switched to MSP 5 and scored 10 points. The student returned to MSP 4 and improved their score from 2 points to 8. The student moved to MSP 7 and scored 9 points. The student then worked on MSP 6 and scored 10 points. Finally, the student returned to MSP 4 and improved their score from 8 points to 10. The student scored 69 points on MSPs for the week, exceeding the 50-point full-credit threshold and nearly hitting the 70-point max.

Students seem to take advantage of the pivot benefit that MSPs offer, especially when a threshold is used. 94% of students (71 students) pivoted at least once throughout the 10-week quarter. As a result, we hope to do future work to investigate whether students who pivot score higher than those who do not, whether there any detriments to pivoting, and whether students who pivot return and solve the MSP they switched away from.

8 Do students use MSPs to study for exams?

Given that MSPs are short, concise, and focus on a single concept, a key question is whether students voluntarily redo MSPs to prepare for exams.

Given the dates for the midterm and final exams, we defined criteria to determine if a student used an MSP for exam practice. We said that a student used an MSP for exam practice if the student had, for that MSP, a submission or explore timestamp that was after the MSP's due date and within one week prior to the exam. The midterm occurred during week six of the quarter and the final occurred at the end of the quarter.

Table 1 shows the results of how many students used MSPs for practice and how many unique MSPs were used to study. 54% of students (41) used MSPs to study for either the midterm or final. 98% of all MSPs (60) were used by at least one student to study for an exam.

Table 1: Student use of MSPs for exam preparation.

Total number of students	76
Total number of MSPs	61
% of students that used MSPs to study for the midterm	38%
% of students that used MSPs to study for the final	37%
% of students that used MSPs to study for either exam	54%
% of MSPs that were used to study for the midterm	97%
% of MSPs that were used to study for the final	90%
% of MSPs that were used to study for either exam	98%

We are pleased to see many students using MSPs to study for exams. For comparison, we looked at the other two sections of CS1 from Spring 2017, which used OLPs. Only 10% of students (17) used OLPs to study for exams.

9 Do students who learn using MSPs in CS1 do poorly in a CS2 using OLPs?

A common concern regarding MSPs in CS1 is the impact MSPs will have on students when they reach CS2 using OLPs. A key question is how do students taught via MSPs in CS1 fare in CS2, compared to students taught via OLPs in CS1.

We gathered data from our CS2 course from Winter 2017 through Spring 2018 (5 quarters). We determined which students took CS1 using MSPs and which took CS1 using OLPs. To be conservative, we excluded students who did not take CS1 at our university. We found 241 students that took MSPs and 312 students that took OLPs. In total, 553 students who took CS2 at our university were considered in our analysis.

Figure 10 shows CS2 performance results. The x-axis shows the class work categories we analyzed (participation activities, labs, programming assignments, midterm exams, final exam, and total grade in the class) and the y-axis is student grade performance. OLP students are the light bars on the left and MSP students are the dark bars on the right.

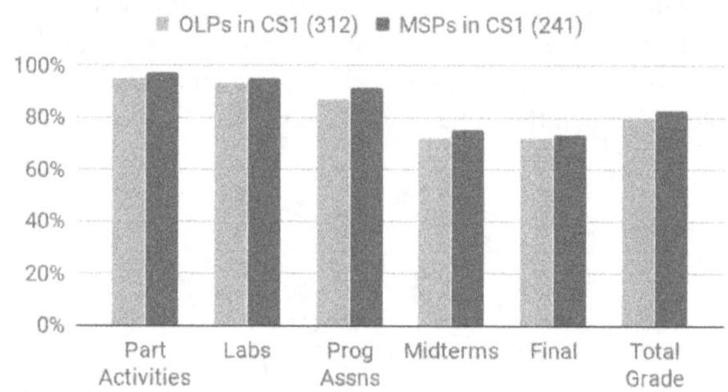

Figure 10: CS2 performance for MSP CS1 students vs. OLP CS1 students. MSP CS1 students do no worse, and in fact do slightly better.

Figure 10 shows that students who took CS1 with MSPs perform similarly, and in fact slightly better, than the students who took CS1 with OLPs. Note that the purpose of this analysis is not to claim MSPs in CS1 lead to better performance in CS2. Instead, the analysis shows that MSPs are not harming students in CS2. We hope to do further research to better understand the effects that using MSPs in CS1 has on students in CS2.

10 Conclusion

Modern easy-to-use auto-graders enable new teaching approaches in CS1 courses, like using MSPs instead of OLPs for weekly programming assignments. Our previous research showed that using MSPs in CS1 yielded happier students and better grades in the course. This paper analyzed how students use MSPs. We conclude that students are making good use of MSPs to aid in their learning process: Students spend sufficient time working on MSPs each week, begin working on MSPs earlier than for OLPs, complete more MSPs than necessary with a full-credit threshold, take advantage of pivoting between MSPs, and use MSPs to study for exams. We also see that MSP CS1 students do just as well, even slightly better, than OLP CS1 students in an OLP CS2. Our department now uses MSPs in all CS1 sections, and we are aware of dozens of other schools that have switched to MSPs as well.

ACKNOWLEDGEMENTS

This work was supported by the U.S. Dept. of Education (GAANN fellowship) and by Google.

REFERENCES

[1] Joe Michael Allen, Frank Vahid, Kelly Downey, and Alex Edgcomb. 2018. Weekly Programs in a CS1 Class: Experiences with Auto-graded Many-small Programs (MSP). In Proceedings of 2018 ASEE Annual Conference & Exposition. DOI: https://peer.asee.org/31231

[2] Theresa Beaubouef and John Mason. 2005. Why the high attrition rate for computer science students: some thoughts and observations. SIGCSE Bull. 37, 2 (June 2005), 103-106. DOI: http://dx.doi.org/10.1145/1083431.1083474

[3] Mark Guzdial. 2003. A media computation course for non-majors. In Proceedings of the 8th annual conference on Innovation and technology in computer science education (ITiCSE '03), David Finkel (Ed.). ACM, New York, NY, USA, 104-108.DOI: http://dx.doi.org/10.1145/961511.961542

[4] Päivi Kinnunen and Lauri Malmi. 2006. Why students drop out CS1 course?. In Proceedings of the second international workshop on Computing education research (ICER '06). ACM, New York, NY, USA, 97-108. DOI: http://dx.doi.org/10.1145/1151588.1151604

[5] Nachiappan Nagappan, Laurie Williams, Miriam Ferzli, Eric Wiebe, Kai Yang, Carol Miller, and Suzanne Balik. 2003. Improving the CS1 experience with pair programming. In Proceedings of the 34th SIGCSE technical symposium on Computer science education (SIGCSE '03). ACM, New York, NY, USA, 359-362. DOI:http://dx.doi.org/10.1145/611892.612006

[6] Andrew Petersen, Michelle Craig, Jennifer Campbell, and Anya Tafliovich. 2016. Revisiting why students drop CS1. In Proceedings of the 16th Koli Calling International Conference on Computing Education Research (Koli Calling '16). ACM, New York, NY, USA, 71-80. DOI: https://doi.org/10.1145/2999541.2999552

[7] Leo Porter and Beth Simon. 2013. Retaining nearly one-third more majors with a trio of instructional best practices in CS1. In Proceeding of the 44th ACM technical symposium on Computer science education (SIGCSE '13). ACM, New York, NY, USA, 165-170. DOI: http://dx.doi.org/10.1145/2445196.2445248

[8] Leo Porter, Cynthia Bailey Lee, and Beth Simon. 2013. Halving fail rates using peer instruction: a study of four computer science courses. In Proceeding of the 44th ACM technical symposium on Computer science education (SIGCSE '13). ACM, New York, NY, USA, 177-182. DOI: http://dx.doi.org/10.1145/2445196.2445250

[9] Leo Porter, Cynthia Bailey Lee, Beth Simon, and Daniel Zingaro. 2011. Peer instruction: do students really learn from peer discussion in computing?. In Proceedings of the seventh international workshop on Computing education research (ICER '11). ACM, New York, NY, USA, 45-52. DOI: http://dx.doi.org/10.1145/2016911.2016923

[10] Leo Porter, Mark Guzdial, Charlie McDowell, and Beth Simon. 2013. Success in introductory programming: what works?. Commun. ACM 56, 8 (August 2013), 34-36. DOI: https://doi.org/10.1145/2492007.2492020

[11] Beth Simon, Michael Kohanfars, Jeff Lee, Karen Tamayo, and Quintin Cutts. 2010. Experience report: peer instruction in introductory computing. In Proceedings of the 41st ACM technical symposium on Computer science education (SIGCSE '10). ACM, New York, NY, USA, 341-345. DOI: http://dx.doi.org/10.1145/1734263.173438

[12] Jeffrey A. Stone and Elinor M. Madigan. 2008. The impact of providing project choices in CS1. SIGCSE Bull. 40, 2 (June 2008), 65-68. DOI: https://doi.org/10.1145/1383602.1383637

[13] Laurie Williams, Kai Yang, Eric Wiebe, Miriam Ferzli, and Carol Miller. 2002. Pair Programming in an Introductory Computer Science. OOPSLA Educator's Symposium, Seattle, WA.

[14] Daniel Zingaro. 2014. Peer instruction contributes to self-efficacy in CS1. In Proceedings of the 45th ACM technical symposium on Computer science education (SIGCSE '14). ACM, New York, NY, USA, 373-378. DOI: http://dx.doi.org/10.1145/2538862.2538878

[15] Cody Coursework. https://coursework.mathworks.com/. Accessed: August, 2018.

[16] Mimir. https://www.mimirhq.com/. Accessed: August, 2018.

[17] Turing's Craft: CodeLab. https://www.turingscraft.com/. Accessed: August, 2018.

[18] zyBooks. https://www.zybooks.com/catalog/zylabs-programming/. Accessed: August, 2018.

Reducing Instructor Workload in an Introductory Robotics Course via Computational Design

Devon J. Merrill
UC San Diego
devon@ucsd.edu

Steven Swanson
UC San Diego
swanson@ucsd.edu

ABSTRACT

Physical computing and building robots has important benefits for novice engineers and computer scientists. However, lab time and hardware debugging comes with a high cost of instructor time and effort. To reduce this workload, we implemented a computational design tool that simplifies printed circuit board (PCB) design and manufacture, assembly, and programming. We pilot tested our computational design tool in a one-unit introductory physical computing course for 196 CS1 students. The students designed, assembled, and programmed a custom robot with minimal instructor assistance. The robots are Arduino-based and each included a student designed PCB. The students assembled the robots from off-the-shelf electronic components according to automatically generated assembly instructions. Students programmed their robots using simple APIs that were automatically generated and customized for each unique robot. A minimum of two quarters after the completion of the course, grade point average (GPA) for the students who completed the course, was found to be 0.15 higher than a comparison group of similar student ($n = 498, p < 0.05$). We present a detailed description of our computational design tool and course curriculum, identify challenges encountered by the students and instructional staff, make recommendations to increase student achievement, and address the scalability of the course.

ACM Reference Format:
Devon J. Merrill and Steven Swanson. 2019. Reducing Instructor Workload in an Introductory Robotics Course via Computational Design. In *Proceedings of the 50th ACM Technical Symposium on Computer Science Education (SIGCSE '19), February 27-March 2, 2019, Minneapolis, MN, USA.* ACM, New York, NY, USA, 7 pages. https://doi.org/10.1145/3287324.3287506

1 INTRODUCTION

A diverse range of computing devices are becoming deeply embedded in almost all aspects of our day-to-day lives. The increasing importance of computing and its growing economic impact are driving enormous growth in undergraduate demand for computing courses. These two trends lead to challenges in providing large numbers of students with experiences that straddle the boundary between software and the real world. Furthermore, growing enrollments often lead to large undergraduate classes that can be impersonal and make it difficult to have effective small-group interactions.

SIGCSE '19, February 27-March 2, 2019, Minneapolis, MN, USA

ACM ISBN 978-1-4503-5890-3/19/02.
https://doi.org/10.1145/3287324.3287506

We have developed Robot Parade, a lightweight lab course for freshmen computer science students taken concurrently with CS1, usually during their first quarter at college. We built the course to show students that they can conceive, build, and program a complete computing device of their own design. Robot Parade aims to provide a low-stress, enjoyable venue for students to practice what they learn in CS1 while interacting with other students in a smaller, more intimate setting than the large lecture format of our CS1 course can offer. Students complete nearly all the coursework in class during weekly two-hour labs, held nine times during the quarter.

Using robots in introductory programming courses can improve attitudes toward computers in general [4], and this approach has been developed as a direct application of Piaget's constructionism learning theory (e.g., by Rosenblat and Choset [5]). However, teaching these courses can be resource- and time-intensive. Rosenblat's course, for instance, relied on a low student-to-instructor ratio and pairing experienced senior students with less advanced students. These problems are especially acute for courses targeted at less-experienced students.

We developed Robot Parade to make a hands-on programming and building experience accessible to students during their first term studying computer science in college. A key motivation for targeting students early is to reduce attrition among underrepresented groups of CS and CE majors.

The course centers around a single project: students design, build, and program a simple wheeled robot that can sense and react to the environment. The project includes creating and assembling a custom printed circuit board (PCB).

Enabling first-term students who are learning to program and have little (or no) experience with electronics to complete the project has required us to carefully craft the course's content and schedule and develop a robot design tool that is accessible to our students.

During the first half of the course, students complete several robot programming labs using pre-built robots that include all the elements they will eventually use in their own designs. Each lab focuses on a different aspect of sensing or control (such as driving, controlling lights and a speaker, using a distance sensor). These labs help students learn the basics of Arduino-style microcontroller programming, and grapple with the vagaries of using code to gather data from sensors and control physical devices. They also encounter the rudiments of C++ (we teach CS1 in Java), gain experience assembling electronics (i.e., soldering and wiring), and learn their way around the "Makerspace" where we teach the class and some of the tools (e.g., 3D printers) it provides.

Figure 1: Several student designed robots.

Next, they design a robot to carry out a task of their choosing. "Tasks" include things like "look and act like a duck," "be polite to other robots," or "drive around and pop wheelies."

The key component of the robot is a printed circuit board (PCB) that will host its electronics and serve as its body. Designing PCBs is a complex task that usually requires experience with electronics and the steep learning curve of conventional PCB design tools.

To make PCB design tractable for our students, we have built a web-based, what-you-see-is-what-you-get (WYSIWYG) robot design tool called *The Robot Factory*. The Robot Factory lets students design a working robot in a single class period with very little training. Behind the scenes, The Robot Factory uses computational design to algorithmically generate a PCB that implements the circuitry for their design.

We have their PCBs manufactured, and the students solder them together by following customized assembly instructions for their robot that The Robot Factory generates. Students program the robots with the Arduino IDE using a customized library that The Robot Factory generates to match their particular robot design.

We have taught Robot Parade in five academic quarters over the last three years. Space is limited primarily by instructor "bandwidth," so we select students by lottery from those that submit a simple application. We typically run two sections of 20-30 students working in pairs. We have been working steadily to increase the number of students that may enroll the course by streamlining our curriculum and refining our robot design tool.

We recruit students who concurrently take a CS1 course alongside our robot course. The majority of the participants do not initially have basic programming skills such as knowledge of variables, functions, and control structures.

The following sections describe The Robot Factory and its interface (Section 2), detail the course content (Section 3), provide a pilot evaluation of the course's impact on student academic success (Section 4), and discuss plans for future improvements to the course (Section 5). Section 6 draws conclusions from our work.

2 THE ROBOT FACTORY

We want students to have the experience of building a real, working robot without requiring them to scale the steep learning curves that hardware design tools usually require. To make the task tractable and allow the students to focus on the *design* of the robot rather than the details of its implementation, we developed a computational design tool called The Robot Factory that makes designing a robot easy and automates much of the implementation.

The Robot Factory caters to students that have no electronics design or programming experience, and it minimizes the amount of instructor assistance and prompting required for success. To achieve both of these goals at once, we built it to be simple to use, provide real-time feedback about potential design problems, and use a familiar "drag-and-drop" paradigm for design. As a result, students can create a valid robot design after just a short two-minute introductory demonstration.

The Robot Factory also generates an easy-to-use high-level application programming interface (API) for each robot. The API uses concepts familiar to students taking CS1 so programming the robots is relatively easy as well.

Below, we describe the tool's interface and give an overview of how it works internally. It is available for anyone to use (http://robots.gadgetron.build/).

2.1 User Experience

The Robot Factory provides a web-based, drag-and-drop GUI that students use to design the shape of their robot and the components it will comprise. When it opens, it presents students with a minimal robot design on a green polygon that represents the PCB. The minimal design includes a ProTrinket [3] Arduino board and four AA-size batteries.

Students add *functional components* to the PCB from a library. They can choose from motorized wheels, buttons, single LEDs, LED arrays, IR distance sensors, actuated claws, bump switches, and a few other items.

The Robot Factory automatically adds *utility components* that the robot must include to work properly and synthesizes the PCB circuits to connect all the components together. Utility components include resistors and capacitors, motor drivers, and protection diodes. Large utility components that will significantly affect the appearance of the robot (e.g., the batteries and large capacitors) are visible in the user interface so students can choose where to place them. The tool automatically places small utility components (e.g., resistors).

After students are satisfied with their design they press the "build" button. This button sends the robot specification to synthesis servers running in the cloud.

Placement errors. The locations of the components are subject to several constraints that the student designs must satisfy (the wheels must be off the board, parts cannot overlap, etc.). Typical PCB design tools provide a separate design rule check (DRC) command to check some of these constraints, but the output can be confusing, the tools tend to generate many redundant errors, and it can take several iterations to resolve all the problems. Furthermore, some errors can safely be ignored, but knowing which ones are spurious requires expert knowledge.

The Robot Factory makes it easy to design correct robots with real-time feedback about placement restrictions. Difference colors indicate each of the three types of constraint (must be on the board,

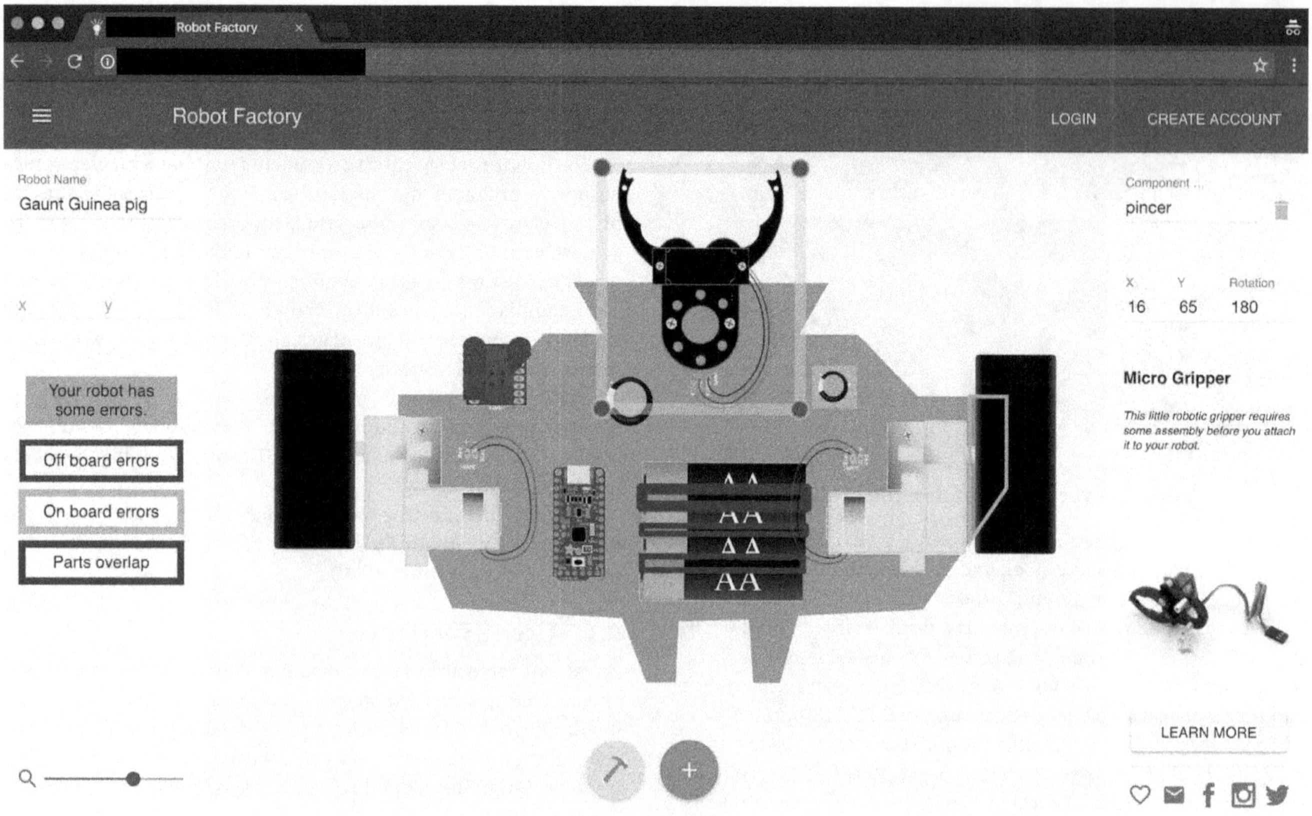

Figure 2: The computational design tool GUI.
An in-progress robot design showing several types of placement errors.

must be off the board, and no overlap). When a constraint is violated, the area of the component that violates the constraint is highlighted with a pulsing, outline. The first time each type of error is detected, a pop-up window explains the error and how to resolve it.

If an error exists, a prominent indicator in the GUI informs the user "Your robot has errors." If no component has a placement error, the indicator becomes green and reads, "Your robot looks great!" Students can only submit error-free designs.

To ensure students learn to deal with errors quickly, we place the components of the initial design so they overlap. Students typically respond by resolving this placement error as their first interaction with the tool. This seems to facilitate student willingness to experiment with component placement and resolve errors on their own.

Board shape. Letting students express their creativity is an important part of the class, but our initial implementation of the tool restricted students to rectangular boards, limiting the range of designs. Since then, we have added support for more complex shapes.

When we first introduced the ability to create complex robot shapes, we noticed that almost every student-created robot still had a rectangular board. We believed that this is because the starting board shape was rectangular. In the latest iteration of the tool, we randomized the vertices of the starting polygon. This has led to a much larger diversity of student designs. For instance, one team designed their board in the shape of the letters "LA" and then programmed the robot to dance to music from the movie "LA LA Land."

2.2 Back-end

The Robot Factory must be as automatic as possible to support scaling the number of student that we can support in a single class. In the vast majority of cases, translating a student's design into the hardware and software required to implement it must not require any direct intervention from the course staff. Furthermore, it must, to the extent possible, guide the students through the process of assembling and programming their robot.

The Robot Factory synthesizes a complete manufacturing specification from the students' designs. This includes PCB computer aided manufacturing (CAM) files, C++ API files, assembly instructions, and bill of materials. The complete process takes between one and five minutes, with the majority of that time spent on auto-placement and routing for the circuit board.

Synthesizing a complete manufacturing specification from an incomplete graphical specification is a multi-step process. We discuss each of them below.

Component-level synthesis. Component-level synthesis makes the necessary electrical connections between the functional components in the design and adds utility components that are not visible in the tool's interface. For example, students add motorized wheels to their design and choose where to put them, but the motors require more current than the microcontroller can provide. In response, The Robot Factory automatically adds and connects a motor driver board and a large capacitor. The motor driver board requires several GPIO connections to the microcontroller, logic level power, and motor power, so The Robot Factory connects (and adds if not already present) batteries and the microcontroller.

Some robot designs are not synthesizable. For example, if the student adds 20 LEDs, but the microcontroller only has 10 GPIO pins available, not all of the LEDs can be connected. Our tool reports this error to the student. It lists of all components that use GPIO pins and suggests removing some of them.

We provide guidelines to the students so these errors occur infrequently, but the details of these connection constraints are complex. For example, many of the Arduino's pins are multi-function and some functions require access to limited microcontroller resources such as timers. We encode these constraints in a generalized, abstract interface specification for each component. Using heuristic search, The Robot Factory is able to perform component-level synthesis on student robot designs in less than 30 seconds.

Auto-placement. Components must be placed on the PCB without violating their placement constraints. The Robot Factory real-time feedback ensures that the students have already correctly placed the functional components and the utility components that are visible. The Robot Factory adds additional utility components and must find places for them on the PCB. A general solution to the placement problem is not feasible (it is at least NP-complete), but our robot designs are not space-constrained, so a simple "first fit" is appropriate and usually completes in under 15 seconds. If auto-placement cannot find a valid placement, The Robot Factory returns an error and asks the student to make more open space in their design. The auto-placer has never failed in practice.

Electrical auto-routing. The routing process translates the logical connections created during component-level synthesis into metal traces on the PCB.

PCB routing can be very challenging. As with placement, however, the relative simplicity of The Robot Factory designs lets us successfully automate the process. The Robot Factory uses Autodesk Eagle's autorouter.

If a design fails to route, synthesis aborts and the student is prompted to try an alternate placement of their components. Out of the more than 100 designs students have created with our tool, fewer than five have failed to automatically route.

Source code generation. Students in the course are concurrently taking a first programming course, taught in Java. The robots we generate are Arduino-based, so they must program in (a simple subset of) C++. Java and C++ are similar enough that students are capable of creating simple programs for their robots. We typically spend about 15 minutes discussing the differences between Java and C++, and students do not usually struggle with the transition.

The Arduino API presents a larger obstacle. Arduino provides a low-level pin-oriented API that can read and write digital and analog values to and from pins on the microcontroller. The link between these low-level operations and higher-level robot behaviors is not always simple. For instance, driving forward requires manipulating several pins at once.

To streamline the process of programming their robots, The Robot Factory provides a "starter" program built specifically for each robot. The program runs "out of the box" on their robot and tests the operation of each component. It flashes any LEDs, drives forward, etc. The starter files also instantiate a C++ object for each functional component in the design with a name that corresponds to the name of the component the student specified in GUI. These objects support simple, intuitive methods such as LED.turnOn(), LED.turnOff(), wheels.forward(), and wheels.turnLeft().

These starter programs are very effective in reducing instructor workload in class. When used without modification they quickly identify malfunctioning components. This speeds up troubleshooting tremendously because students can accurately report and demonstrate issues.

Also, if a robot is not working when loaded with student code, students tend to blame the robot's hardware. By reloading the starter code, they can retest the hardware quickly. If the test code works, they know it is a problem with their code and they usually attempt to fix it themselves.

Assembly Instructions. Since each robot is different, the process of assembling them varies. To help students assemble their robots, The Robot Factory provides customized assembly instructions as a web page that includes an illustrated parts list, shows them where each part goes, and provide instructions for assembly. The instructions also include videos illustrating basic soldering techniques.

2.3 Design management

Student teams create an account in our tool that includes a team name, password, recovery email address, and association with a class section.

When a student's design is finished, the design is saved and becomes visible to instructors. When the students are satisfied with the design, an instructor confirms the design and it is ready to be manufactured. When all the designs are ready, The Robot Factory generates a combined bill of materials and makes the PCB design files easily available for ordering.

3 COURSE CONTENT

Robot Parade has two phases. In the first, students program robots similar to those they will eventually build. They also learn what is feasible with the components that The Robot Factory provides. In the second phase, they use this knowledge to guide the design of their own robots and then assemble and program them.

We teach the class in a makerspace. Students use 3D printers and other tools to create decorations for their robots and soldering equipment for assembly. We encourage students to use other equipment or bring in materials for decoration. The only out-of-class homework assignment in the course is to 3D something by the end of the fourth week. This helps engage them with the tools in the makerspace.

3.1 Grading

Robot Parade is meant to be a low-stress, fun opportunity for students to practice programming and broaden their horizons within computer science. The grading structure reflects this goal. The course is "Pass/Fail" and does not affect student GPA. We record attendance and the completion of the lab assignments. We use these records to identify students who may need additional coaching and encouragement, not for assigning grades.

3.2 Introductory Labs

The course begins with two introductory labs in which the students program two pre-designed robots to complete a variety of tasks. The labs are spread across three to four class meetings (a total of 6-8 hours). Groups work at their own pace with some encouragement from the course staff to stay on schedule.

The first lab involves driving the robot around on paper and using a marker to trace the path the robot has taken. This directly connects to a "turtle graphics" assignments they are working on in their concurrent CS1 course and that is common as an introduction to both procedural and object-oriented programming [2]. Students are eager to engage in the familiar task and quickly connect with the platform.

Drawing with a robot and drawing with a virtual "turtle" provide vivid lessons about the differences between programming the digital and physical worlds. For example, turning the robot precisely is hard while turning a turtle precisely is trivial.

The major tasks assigned in the first lab are to "draw your favorite shape" using the robot and marker, and to program the robot to "sing and dance" using LEDs and a small speaker on the robot.

Both of these assignments are freeform and credit is given for any attempt. However, if there is time left in class, we encourage them to do more. Although the students know that they will receive the same mark for any attempt, they become invested in the free-form assignments and often create elaborate programs.

The second lab involves interacting with the environment using a distance sensor and a motorized gripper. Students program the robot to maintain a constant distance from a moving object, "explore the room without getting stuck," and locate, grasp, and move a 3D-printed object. Students are told that they must use a state machine programming pattern to complete the final task, and we preface the lab with a brief lecture about the state machines and how they apply to robots.

We have taken steps to reduce the dependence of students on course staff during labs. The most helpful of these has been to put together a troubleshooting list. This list contains seven solutions to common problems that students have. These problems are:

(1) Plugging the programmer in the wrong orientation
(2) Not plugging the USB cable in (properly or at all)
(3) Selecting the incorrect serial port
(4) Selecting the incorrect Arduino board type
(5) Selecting the incorrect programmer type
(6) Using the wrong version of the Arduino IDE
(7) Having a dead battery

We have found that if the student's trouble is not on this list, then the problem generally cannot be solved quickly in class and the student should move to another workstation or switch to a different robot.

By using this list we have been able to focus the majority of in-class instructor effort on coaching program design and encouragement. However, the students need frequent reminders to check the list if they have trouble.

3.3 Robot Design

We weave the concept of creating a robot into the class from the beginning, culminating in "design day" when students design robots with The Robot Factory.

During the introductory labs, we encourage students to come up with a concrete, specific concept for their robot. This leads to the more interesting designs. Some examples of successful concepts include Polite Bot (which would drive around a tip a 3D printed top hat at other robots), Duck Bot (which acted like a duck), Smash Bot (which would wave around a big pair of 3D-printed fists. See Figure 1, top-right), R2-D2 bot (which looked like R2-D2 from Star Wars), etc. Concepts like "it's going to drive around and grab things" lead to less interesting designs and less student engagement.

The bulk of the design process takes most teams 60-90 minutes, but many teams spend the full two-hour class period tweaking their design. By the end of the class period, all the student designs are ready to be manufactured.

3.4 Robot Assembly Logistics

The next step is manufacturing the PCBs and assembling the robots. We order the boards from Advanced Circuits [1], quick-turn PCB manufacturer that will make boards for students for $33/board. The boards take at least seven days to arrive, so there is effectively a 2-week delay between design and assembly. The students spend the intervening class period working on 3D-printed decorations for their robots.

We have engineered the robots so that the most expensive components (the distance sensor, servo motors, drive motors, microcontroller, and LED arrays) are reusable. They all have "headers" that plug into sockets that students solder to the board. The components that are soldered to the board (resistors, capacitors, diodes, and so on) are disposable. Altogether, it costs about $50 to build each robot.

3.5 Robot Assembly in Class

Assembling the robots requires basic soldering as well as screwing and hot-gluing some components together. Most students have never assembled PCB or soldered before.

Assembly proceeds in several stages. These steps typically consume between one and two class periods.

Lecture We give a very brief lecture about the assembly process (described below) and explain the notion of polarized components (that is, components with a symmetrical arrangement of pins that must be inserted in the correct orientation) and how to tell if they have them assembled correctly.

Part collection Before class, the course staff sets out trays with all the components the students will need. The trays are arranged in the same order that the parts appear on illustrated parts lists for their robots and are labeled with the same pictures. Students take a small plastic bin, form a line, and move down the row of bins collecting their parts.

Dry fitting Students "dry fit" the components to their PCBs by using tape and inserting and bending the wire leads to hold them in place. A member of the course staff checks that everything is correct.

Solder lesson An instructor gives a quick soldering lesson to between one and three groups at a time. It covers how soldering works, what a good solder joint looks like, and a demonstration of how to solder each kind of connection they will need to make on their board.

Soldering! Students solder all the components to their PCB.

Solder check and final assembly Course staff checks each soldering job. If it looks good, the students trim the leads on the components. Then, they plug in the microcontroller and other reusable parts. They have a robot!

Testing The last step is to run the test program that The Robot Factory provides. If something does not work, the course staff helps them resolve the issue.

3.6 Robot Programming

The rest of class time in the course (1-2 weeks) is allocated to programming, decorating, and fine-tuning the software for the robots. We coach the students to use a state machine pattern to enable responsive interactivity. Because students have spent several weeks in the beginning of the course programming similar robots, they are generally able to program their own robot without assistance.

We notice an over-reliance on delay statements for program coordination (similar to other observations of early programmers [7]). We are continuing to develop strategies to help students be successful in creating real-time interactive programs in an embedded environment.

4 EVALUATION

We have taught the course in five academic quarters, Fall 2015, Spring 2016, Fall 2016, Winter 2017, and Fall 2017 and performed a preliminary analysis of how taking the class impacts student success over time. Between Fall 2015 and Fall 2017, 498 students applied to take the course. We admitted students from the applicant pool using a random lottery.

Our analysis shows that completing Robot Parade resulted in a statistically significant increase in overall GPA (Welch's t-test $p=0.0011$). The mean, cumulative GPA of students who completed the course, as of Summer 2018, is 3.43 (196 students, standard deviation 0.45 points, 4.0 scale). The mean GPA of the comparison group of students who applied to take the course, as of Summer 2018, is 3.29 (302 students, sd=0.56). The difference between the means is 0.148 points.

This pilot analysis indicates that completion of Robot Parade resulted in improved academic performance, and we are encouraged to continue developing the course. A full analysis, including the effect on major retention and with regards to gender is in progress.

Anecdotally, students enjoy designing, building, and programming (and decorating) their robots a great deal. Students attribute unique personalities to their robots, and to other students robots. Many students create elaborate stories about their robots' motivations and behaviors. We have observed that these student storytelling behaviors seem to be absent or strongly attenuated in similar first-year seminar robotics classes where all students are given identical robots. Students "owning" the robot that they designed and built themselves seems to be very engaging and motivating, echoing the findings of previous work [6]. Students often express a desire to keep and to continue working on their robot after the course is completed.

Also, because of the PCBs that forms the core of the robots, students feel that their robots are "real" electronics, as opposed to bread-boarded electronics or toolkits such as Lego Mindstorm. The concept of students designing and building "real" embedded devices seems to be empowering and motivating to the students.

5 FUTURE IMPROVEMENTS

Although the Robot Parade class and The Robot Factory design tool have met their original technical goals, we will continue to evolve the course with two further ambitions in mind.

The first is to continue increasing class size. To date, we have increased the scale of the class from 5 robots per class to 15 robots per class without adding course staff. We have plans to scale the course to 60 students (30 robots) per section in the next iteration (Fall 2018). Scaling the initial labs to that size should be easy, but we expect that efficiently assembling that many robots will become challenging.

One option would be to use solder-free assembly. To achieve this we could build (or buy) a standardized robot board and have students attach it to a laser-cut frame that would correspond to the robot shape they designed with The Robot Factory. They would connect electrical components with "hookup" wire. The resulting robots would be cheaper and easier to assemble, and it would open up more time in the course for programming, but we are worried they would be less engaging and exciting for the students.

Our second ambition is to integrate the course more deeply into our CS curriculum. Currently, the course is optional and loosely coupled to the introductory CS courses. Coupling it more tightly or expanding it to be an alternative format for introductory computing, perhaps in conjunction with our robotics program, would be very exciting.

6 CONCLUSION

The Robot Factory makes it possible for Robot Parade to give students hands-on experience building working robots early in their computer science careers. Of equal practical importance, The Robot Factory makes it easier for student to guide themselves through key parts of the design process, facilitates debugging, and eases the burden on course staff of organizing and ordering robot components.

The feedback from students and the growing demand for the course shows that there is a great appetite for this kind of class among CS students. Our preliminary data suggest it may have a positive impact on their long-term success. We plan to continue refining the class and exploring how to increase the benefits to students.

REFERENCES

[1] Advanced circuits. www.4pcb.com/.

[2] Michael E. Caspersen and Henrik Baerbak Christensen. Here, there and every-where - on the recurring use of turtle graphics in cs1. *Proceedings of the Australasian conference on Computing education - ACSE 00*, 2000.

[3] Adafruit Industries. Pro trinket 5v 16mhz. https://www.adafruit.com/product/2000.

[4] Seong-Won Kim and Youngjun Lee. The effect of robot programming education on attitudes towards robots. *Indian Journal of Science and Technology*, 9(24), 2016.

[5] M. Rosenblatt and H. Choset. Designing and implementing hands-on robotics labs. *IEEE Intelligent Systems*, 15(6):32–39, 2000.

[6] Yuan Sun and S. Shyam Sundar. Psychological importance of human agency how self-assembly affects user experience of robots. *2016 11th ACM/IEEE International Conference on Human-Robot Interaction (HRI)*, 2016.

[7] David Weintrop, Alexandria K. Hansen, Danielle B. Harlow, and Diana Franklin. Starting from scratch: Outcomes of early computer science learning experiences and implications for what comes next. In *Proceedings of the 2018 ACM Conference on International Computing Education Research*, ICER '18, pages 142–150, New York, NY, USA, 2018. ACM.

Frequency of Instructor- and Student-Centered Teaching Practices in Introductory CS Courses

Christopher Lynnly Hovey
University of Colorado Boulder
Boulder, CO USA
hoveyc@colorado.edu

Lecia Barker
University of Colorado Boulder
Boulder, CO USA
barkerl@colorado.edu

Margaret Luebs
University of Colorado Boulder
Boulder, CO USA
margaret.luebs@colorado.edu

ABSTRACT

Despite growing promotion of student-centered teaching, few studies have assessed how widely these practices have diffused throughout computer science (CS) higher education. Studies on teaching practices often treat instructor- and student-centered learning as being dichotomous. Recent research indicates that this reductionist model misinterprets what actually goes on in CS classrooms. For example, a recent study found that most CS faculty categorized their teaching practices as equally student-centered and instructor-centered. We contribute to this scholarship by reporting the results of a survey disseminated to 821 CS educators in 595 universities, colleges, and community colleges in the U.S. Participants were asked to report how frequently they employed several instructor- or student-centered teaching practices and tools during the most recent semester that they taught a specific course. Results indicate that when asked to reflect on specific behaviors within a certain timeframe, faculty reported using instructor-centered teaching practices, especially delivering content via lecture, more than student-centered practices. However, most faculty also reported using at least one student-centered technique, albeit less frequently, throughout the semester. This study found few differences across certain situational and demographic variables (e.g., institution type, tenure status, etc.). Faculty justify their teaching choices with concern for negative evaluations, desire for student learning, large enrollments, heavy teaching loads, and retaining underrepresented students.

CCS CONCEPTS

• **Social and professional topics ~ Computing education**

KEYWORDS

undergraduate computing education; lecturing; instructional techniques and strategies; student-centered teaching; evidence-based practices; faculty adoption; signature pedagogies

ACM ISBN 978-1-4503-5890-3/19/02...$15.00
https://doi.org/10.1145/3287324.3287363

ACM Reference format:

Christopher Lynnly Hovey, Lecia Barker, and Margaret Luebs. 2019. Frequency of Instructor- and Student-Centered Teaching Practices in Introductory CS Courses. In *Proceedings of the 50th ACM Technical Symposium on Computer Science Education (SIGCSE '19), February 27-March 2, 2019, Minneapolis, MN, USA.* 7 pages. https://doi.org/10.1145/3287324.3287363

1 INTRODUCTION

Despite the attention that funding agencies, educational specialists, social scientists, and computer science (CS) faculty have given to developing and propagating active, student-centered teaching practices, few studies have assessed how well these practices have diffused throughout CS higher education. Student-centered practices are promoted for good reason. A recent meta-analysis of 225 empirical studies provides strong evidence that active learning approaches improve students' performance [11]. Student-centered teaching practices early in the curriculum have also been shown to positively impact undergraduates' decisions to declare and remain in a major [6, 23]. Studies in other STEM fields suggest that instructor-centered teaching is still the most predominant approach [8, 15], but these studies often dichotomize instructor- and student-centered learning, describing faculty's instructional proclivities as falling squarely into only one category.

Recent research in CS education suggests that this dichotomous model may misinterpret what actually goes on in CS classrooms. Grissom, et al. [12] used the Postsecondary Instructional Practices Survey (PIPS) [28] to gauge the teaching practices of 365 CS faculty from 45 U.S. and one Canadian institution. The PIPS asks faculty to rate teaching practices on two independent scales of instructor- and student-centered instructional practices. Practices are rated based on the degree to which the respondent believes they are "descriptive of their teaching." The PIPS was piloted at four institutions to develop the instructor-centered and student-centered scales used by [12]. According to the pilot [28], the 15-item student-centered scale had high reliability (α=.877), and the 9-item instructor-centered scale had lower reliability (α=.677). In Grissom et al.'s use of PIPS among CS faculty, CS faculty were equally likely to describe their teaching practices as student-centered *and* instructor-centered. However, the survey did not report on the use frequency of instructor- and student-centered practices, so it is not clear what specific practices were most commonly selected.

We contribute to this growing body of scholarship by reporting the results of a survey taken by 821 post-secondary CS educators in 595 diverse institutions. The survey was grounded in interviews and classroom observations with CS faculty in every region and institution type in the U.S. Participants were asked to think about a specific course they had recently taught, and then report how frequently they had employed several teaching practices and tools. Our results indicate that when primed to think about concrete teaching practices in the context of a specific course, faculty reported using instructor-centered teaching practices—especially delivering content via lecture—more frequently than student-centered practices. However, consistent with [12], most faculty reported using both instructor- and student-centered practices, rarely just one or the other.

In the next section, we briefly review scholarship on student- and instructor-centered teaching practices, followed by a description of our research methods and sample profile. Then, we present results, including differences in the selection of certain teaching practices by different groups of faculty by institutional type, tenure status, and gender. We then describe respondents' unsolicited justifications for their teaching choices. We conclude by summarizing and discussing the findings.

2 STUDENT- AND INSTRUCTOR-CENTERED TEACHING

Student-centered teaching practices are curricular, pedagogical, or administrative techniques intended to increase interactivity among students and their peers, instructors, and the material in a way that privileges students' experiences, identities, intellectual growth, and personal development [18]. In CS, these practices include a broad range of instructional techniques such as pair programming and flipping the classroom, and teaching strategies such as emphasizing collaborative teamwork in or out of class.

Instructor-centered practices emphasize one-way information delivery from the educator, as the locus of knowledge, to a more or less passive audience of students, who act as receptacles of information. Knowledge is often communicated to students as a set of established formulas that they must accumulate and master, which are assessed against a preset standard [4, 13, 14]. Some scholars (e.g., [18]) have even argued that the goal of instructor-centered techniques is to produce homogenized, interchangeable workers for the industrialized workforce.

In our current era of post-industrial globalism [7, 22], it is clear that the education system must evolve to produce a diverse workforce of innovative, creative workers who can address the complex and dynamic needs of the (post)modern economy [20, 21]. Student-centered teaching practices have been shown to produce the following benefits:

Benefits for Student Performance. A recent, often-cited meta-analysis of 225 empirical studies across STEM fields provides strong evidence that active learning approaches improve students' performance [11]. A study focused specifically on CS classes also found that student-centered approaches greatly improved student performance [24].

Benefits for Student Engagement. Student-centered teaching practices have been shown to greatly increase student engagement in college science classes [25].

Benefits for Student Retention. The use of student-centered teaching practices, especially early in the curriculum, can positively impact undergraduates' decisions to declare a major and remain in that major [6, 23].

Benefits for Diversity. A large-scale study compared mathematics courses that used student- and instructor-centered teaching. Women's confidence and interest increased in the student-centered courses but declined in the instructor-centered courses [19].

3 METHODS

The analysis presented here is part of the second phase of a multi-method study examining what influences faculty to try new teaching practices. The first phase consisted of interviews and focus groups, which informed the construction and dissemination of a survey in the second phase. Topical selections and findings from the survey reflect the qualitative data. A more extensive investigation into the results regarding faculty adoption are explored in [16].

3.1 Survey Development

In [2] and [3], we reported the results of the qualitative phase of the two part study, which used interviews, focus groups, and classroom observations with 66 U.S. CS faculty members at 36 postsecondary institutions. Purposive sampling was used to maximize the range of experiences of faculty, seeking diversity in research or teaching focus, tenure status, institutional focus, student body characteristics, highest degree offered, public/private funding, minority/majority serving status, and geographic location. We conducted one hour, semi-structured interviews, or focus groups, with participants and observed the classroom teaching of most (n=55) to enhance our interpretation of the interviews. Data were transcribed and reviewed extensively by members of the research team to allow for emergent coding of the data, and we used keyword searches and targeted, thematic coding for hypothesis testing. Findings were then used, in conjunction with relevant theory and literature, to inform topics, content, and specific word choices in the survey.

3.2 Survey Design

The survey was designed and disseminated in accordance with best practices outlined in the *tailored design method* [9, 10] and other social science surveying methodology scholarship [1, 27]. To increase the accuracy of respondents' memories, the first survey item asked faculty to think of "a CS course you have taught in the past few years, preferably a course undergraduates take early in the major/minor," and write the course name or number in a text box. To further elicit grounded memories, the second survey item asked faculty to provide that course's enrollment. Asking people to reflect on their behavior over a set timeframe within a specific context is more likely to result in an accurate representation of behaviors than asking about "typical" behavior or general inclinations [10, 27]. The contents of the first text box (the course name or number) were then piped into the next set of survey items, to increase the likelihood that respondents were continuing to think of one specific course as they responded to questions. Survey items then asked faculty to report the frequency with which they had used practices and tools in that specific class, using a 5-point ordinal scale: "never," "one class session," "some class sessions," "most class sessions," and "every class session." A "don't know" option was provided.

In the last two sections of the survey, we also asked questions about respondents' organizational and occupational contexts, as well as personal demographics. Rather than asking respondents what type of institution they worked in, we stored responses to the survey invitation, which were sent out based on institutional type (explained in the next section) since faculty often work at multiple institutions. Incentive and survey data was stored in separate databases to protect confidentiality.

The survey went through several cycles of revision to incorporate feedback from CS faculty and doctoral students. A near-final version of the survey was piloted with additional faculty and Ph.D. students teaching introductory CS courses. The final survey was disseminated in the summer of 2017.

3.3 Sampling and Respondent Profile

The sample was developed from all U.S. postsecondary computer science departments that awarded at least one associate or bachelor's degree in 2015. We downloaded data from the National Center for Education Statistics Integrated Postsecondary Educational Data System (IPEDS [17]), selecting all U.S. public and not-for-profit private institutions that had awarded CS degrees in "computer science" or "computer and information sciences." We created separate download files for institutional categories (listed in Table 1). Because some institutions fit multiple categories, we assigned schools to only one group to avoid confusion. Then we searched online to identify one to four faculty members for each department who were shown as the instructor of record for a lower-division course. Email addresses were stored in separate "collector" files, enabling us to send targeted invites per category based on the evolving distribution of participants. The result was a sample stratified by institution types in the U.S.

We sent email invitations to 4,088 faculty, offering a $20 Amazon gift card as a pre-incentive.[1] We followed up with reminders until the number of respondents was proportional to the number of institutions listed per category. For some categories, e.g., Historically Black Colleges and Universities (HBCUs), we continued to search for and invite more faculty until we had adequate representation.

The survey was completely anonymous. Although we collected email addresses to send gift cards and logged invitation acceptances to prevent double-sampling, the survey required respondents to click through the incentive request form to access the anonymized survey. Data from each form were stored in completely separate databases. Limited by funds and our promise of gift cards, we closed the survey when we reached 751 incentive claims. However, many faculty members chose not to request the gift card, resulting in 821 complete surveys. The overall response rate of individuals for this study is 20 percent.

When the incentive request form redirected to the actual survey, the collector name (i.e., institutional category) was retained, allowing us to do analysis by institution type. Although the exact number is unknown, based on opened invitations and incentive hits, we estimate that the data represents about 595 institutions. The number of participants for each institutional type is shown in Table 1. The proportions of respondents by institutional type are within 4 percent on average of those listed in IPEDS data for CS degree-granting institutions [17]. Underrepresented categories in the sample, two-year degree and Hispanic-Serving institutions, have sufficiently large sample sizes to be able to report significance levels for inferential statistics.

Table 1: Final Sample Respondents by Institutional Type

Institution Type	Number
Two-year, Associate Degree Only Granting Institutions	164
Research Intensive/Extensive	133
Historically Black Colleges and Universities	26
Hispanic-Serving Institutions	101
Tribal Colleges	5
Small Colleges (Enrollments<5,000 Students)	209
Medium Colleges and Universities	47
Large Universities (Enrollments>10,000)	136
Total	**821**

4 RESULTS

4.1 Frequency of Using Teaching Practices

We asked faculty to report how often they used several teaching practices and tools the last time they had taught a specific course. These teaching practices are based on the content of interviews, as discussed in section 3.1. **Error! Reference source not found.** displays the results, which are ordered from "most used" to "least used." "Don't know/not applicable" responses are not shown in the table, but were used to help assess the relative use of each practice.[2]

Consistent with most studies of teaching in STEM, the most commonly selected and most frequently used practices were instructor-centered. "Presented content by lecturing" was by far the most commonly and frequently used practice: over 75 percent of respondents reported having lectured in most or all class sessions. Using whiteboards and chalkboards was also very common, perhaps reflecting that faculty work out problems in real time, express algorithms visually, etc. This could reflect student-centered teaching, if students use them, but in classroom observations mentioned in section 3.1, we found board work often consisted of faculty transmitting information to passive students—hence, we classified it as instructor-centered. Using slides, a clearer manifestation of instructor-centered practcices, were used in most or all class sessions by half of the sample and used in some class sessions by another 22 percent. Taken together, the frequencies of these three practices indicate that instructor-centered teaching practices are more widely and frequently used in CS higher education than the student-centered practices included in our study.

[1] Pre-incentives have been shown in survey research studies to outperform post-incentives. Invitation links took respondents to a page where they could request the incentive. Once they requested it, they were asked to follow another link to the survey itself. Information about who requested the incentives was stored in a completely separate database from the final survey results and we had no way of identifying respondents in the substantive survey.

[2] "'Most used' to 'least used'" was assessed by a scale based on the sum of weighted rankings for each practice, ranked and weighted according to how many faculty selected each response option and what practical interpretation each response option represented (e.g., "every class session" was weighted by 4x while "never" was weighted by -1x).

Table 2: Reported Frequencies of Using Teaching Practices

Teaching Practice		Every class session	Most class sessions	Some class sessions	One class session	Never
Presented content	%	39%	38%	20%	1%	2%
by lecturing*	N	310	307	159	9	19
Used whiteboards	%	34%	32%	25%	2%	6%
or chalkboards*	N	274	257	201	18	50
Used slide	%	26%	24%	22%	6%	22%
presentations*	N	208	192	179	48	174
Used examples intended to	%	19%	36%	39%	2%	3%
connect to students' interests	N	148	288	315	13	25
Led in-class	%	12%	26%	42%	5%	14%
discussions	N	99	206	335	40	113
Used recording of your own lectures	%	10%	5%	13%	3%	68%
for student use outside of class*	N	82	38	105	28	546
Used online	%	9%	10%	24%	3%	53%
discussions	N	74	79	192	25	421
Collected student	%	8%	13%	33%	4%	42%
input in real time	N	67	106	260	31	332
Flipped or inverted	%	6%	8%	25%	7%	49%
the class	N	47	66	198	58	395
Required students to use Agile or pair	%	4%	7%	23%	5%	58%
programming	N	29	60	182	44	466
Used process-oriented guided	%	1%	4%	10%	3%	64%
inquiry learning (POGIL)	N	8	30	77	21	513

Note: * Indicates an instructor-centered teaching practice; all others are identified as student-centered teaching practices.

However, similar to [12], results suggest that faculty often used a combination of instructor-centered and student-centered practices. Only three respondents reported using only instructor-centered practices and only five faculty relied solely on student-centered practices. Instead, faculty typically reported using two or all three of the instructor-centered practices *in conjunction with* three or more student-centered practices.

Among the eight student-centered instructional techniques shown in the table, employing "examples intended to connect to students' lives and interests" was the most frequently used practice, with 55 percent of faculty using it in most or every class session. Nonetheless, 3 percent of respondents reported never using this practice, 2 percent used it only once, and 39 percent reported making content meaningful only in some class sessions. In other words, almost half the faculty (45 percent) do not use this technique regularly.

In-class discussions were also commonly used, clustering around "some" or "most class sessions." Other student-centered practices, however, were used less frequently. More than half of respondents reported never using online discussions. And despite the notoriety of certain practices in conferences and workshops, faculty rarely (or infrequently) used prescriptive student-centered instructional techniques, such as flipping the classroom, requiring students to learn through the Agile method or pair programming, using process-oriented guided inquiry learning (POGIL), and recording lectures as videos for later student use.

4.2 Differences Across Variables

In order to understand under what conditions faculty use certain practices, we conducted statistical analyses to find out whether there are differences in the usage of each practice by institutional type, tenure status, career duration, teaching load, gender, and race. Tests consisted of analyses of variance (ANOVAs), with appropriate post hoc tests depending on whether or not variances were equal between groups; Mann-Whitney U tests, which are essentially t-tests for non-parametric data; Spearman's rho correlations, which are essentially Pearson's correlations for non-parametric data; and chi-squared tests. Because institution types can overlap, comparisons are only made between groups based on size, degree conferral, and populations served.

Overall, we found that usage of practices varies slightly by some variables, but effect sizes are very small. In the subsections below we briefly describe some of the more interesting results.

4.2.1. Differences by Institutional Types. Regarding the use of instructor-centered practices, we observed a few statistically significant differences between institutional types. However, the magnitude and effect sizes of these differences are slight.

Faculty at large institutions used both lecturing and slides slightly more frequently than faculty at small institutions (lecturing mean difference [Δ]=.45 on the five-point ordinal scale, P<.001; slides Δ=.67, p<.001). Both effect sizes are small (η^2=.05 and .04, respectively), accounting for five percent or less of the variance. This difference may be a byproduct of the classes' enrollment sizes, which were larger by about 80 students on average for faculty at large institutions (p=.001). Given the high level of overall use of lecturing and slides across all faculty, this difference amounts to using it extremely often versus very often, in practical terms.

Regarding the use of student-centered practices, faculty from two-year institutions used most of the student-centered practices slightly more frequently than other faculty, though those differences and their effect sizes are small. Both in-class and online discussions, relevant examples, and POGIL mean differences are between .44 and .22, with effect sizes accounting for less than 4 percent of the variance ($\eta^2 \leq .04$). However, two-year faculty used Agile/pair programming less than four-year colleagues on average (Δ=-.25, p=.035, $\eta^2 \leq .01$). Perhaps differences in department structure or culture could be at play, though further study would be necessary.

Faculty at minority-serving institutions had a higher average frequency than those at majority-serving institutions for using online discussions (Δ=.35, p=.005, $\eta^2 \leq .01$) and POGIL (Δ=.28, p=.004, $\eta^2 \leq .01$), but again, these differences are slight in magnitude and effect size.

4.2.2. Differences by Tenure Status. We asked respondents to report whether they were non-tenure track, tenure track[3], or tenured. Overall, very few differences were observed. Regarding instructor-centered practices, tenured faculty used slide

[3] By "tenure-track," we mean faculty who are in positions leading to tenured positions, but are not yet tenured.

presentations slightly less often than both tenure track (Δ=-.61, p<.001) and non-tenure track faculty (Δ=-.65, p<.001). The effect size was very small (η^2=.04). Speculatively, this relationship may relate to what level of course faculty teach (e.g., intro versus upper-division). The variability in how faculty reported the name or title of their courses in the survey question prevents us from exploring this hypothesis with our data, but no differences were observed in class sizes.

Regarding student-centered practices, tenured faculty used examples intended to connect to students' lives and interests less frequently than tenure-track faculty by .22 on the five-point ordinal scale (p=.043) and faculty without a tenuring system by .51 (p<.001). The overall effect size was small (η^2=.03).

4.2.3. Differences by Gender. Of the four identified instructor-centered practices, only lecturing differed statistically between men and women, with men having higher frequencies of using lectures to deliver content than women (Δ=.25, p=.001, η^2=.01). This difference was slight, amounting to one-quarter of an interval point; gender accounted for only one percent of the variance in lecturing.

Out of the seven student-centered practices, women used three with greater regularity than men: POGIL, flipping or inverting the class, and conducting online discussions. Of the three, flipped classrooms had the highest mean difference (at slightly over half an ordinal point), but even for this practice, gender only explained three percent of the variance in usage. POGIL and online discussions each had a mean difference less than .25 and an effect size of .01.

4.3 Faculty Explanations for Teaching Choices

The final survey question was optional, stating, "We value your thoughts and opinions. If you have any additional comments or questions, or if you have comments about this survey, please write them here." Although we did not explicitly ask for explanations, many respondents gave accounts for their teaching choices.

Some faculty expressed concerns about students' negative judgments. For example, "I worry that making the students think and participate in class is harder for them than sitting and listening and they might not enjoy them as much, and give me lower evaluation scores, even if they are learning more effectively." This concern for course evaluations is consistent with some of our interview findings. Another respondent was also concerned with students' reactions, writing, "My college is pushing the flipped classroom approach far more than I think it should. Most of my students have expressed displeasure with this approach." Perhaps a more cavalier attitude is shown in this comment, "My school gives merit pay and a large percentage of it is based on student evaluations. I am currently receiving high student evaluations so there is very little personal reward for trying innovative teaching techniques."

Others expressed concern about student learning. Concerned that students would not learn without the lecture, a respondent wrote, "Our students simply will not read anything technical unless it is a requirement for completing an assignment or know there will be a quiz the next class period." Another expressed concern with making sure the required material was covered, writing, "There are just times where I would like to ensure material is covered."

Others use instructor-centered approaches because of large enrollments or heavy teaching loads. For example, "There are many innovating and effective ways to teach a class with up to 50 students. The challenge is how to effectively teach a class of 150 and 300 students" and, "Time is the biggest problem when you are teaching 20+ hours a semester."

Other faculty provided justification for using student-centered approaches, sometimes based on educational research literature, like this instructor: "Research has shown that when students are interacting and discussing a subject area they tend to learn better than in the traditional lecture setting." Others simply feel that they are less effective at engendering student learning using instructor-centered approaches. One respondent wrote, "I have taught in lecture halls and hate doing so, as I feel like I'm wasting everyone's time. I only teach in computer labs now, in groups of 40 students at a time, and intersperse lab and lecture." Some faculty have adopted student-centered practices in an attempt to retain certain types of students: "I wanted to improve retention of students in CS courses beyond intro, especially underrepresented groups and personalities that can be turned off by arrogant, socially-awkward, domineering students, of which there are often many in CS classes."

5 DISCUSSION

5.1 Summary of Findings and Differences

This study combines with [12] to build a clearer understanding of the frequency with which CS faculty use instructor- and student-centered teaching practices. Using a survey technique designed to spur respondents' recall of teaching in a recent lower-division course, we focused on specific teaching practices rather than more abstract, self-categorization of practice. Thanks to the funding for this study, we were able to more deliberately reach more institutional types.

Our findings confirm that CS faculty in the U.S. rely heavily on instructor-centered teaching approaches, especially lecturing and using slides. However, while more CS faculty tended to use instructor-centered teaching practices, and used them more frequently, they also tried out student-centered practices, at least on (what appears to be) and experimental basis.

Though we found few, and slight, differences among faculty types, some of them are of interest. For example, the observation that faculty at schools with small overall enrollments use lecture and slides less frequently than do faculty from other institutional types suggests that schools with a teaching mission may be slightly more successful at fostering student-centered teaching. Considering huge enrollment increases in the past several years in CS, we speculate that instructor-centered practices are rising.

Two-year school faculty reported a student-centered focus in a variety of teaching practices. Two-year schools have not been heavily studied in terms of typical teaching practices. This study shines some light on this issue. Faculty in two-year schools have special challenges, as students come in with very different levels of preparation and goals. For example, some students may not have qualified for a four-year institution, some simply want to sample courses and not seek degrees, and others are specifically focused on certifications for jobs. In addition, a large percentage of minority students and those who are first in family to attend college begin at two-year schools, potentially bringing diversity to the CS field—if they can be induced to stay.

Faculty at minority-serving institutions were more likely to use just two student-centered practices: online discussions, and, surprisingly, POGIL. However, since very few faculty overall used POGIL, this difference is likely not indicative of much except that POGIL has perhaps been marketed to MSIs more rigorously.

Junior faculty on the tenure track more frequently used examples intended to be personally meaningful to students than did tenured faculty, possibly related to the age of faculty or recency of their own student experience. Non-tenure track and not-yet-tenured faculty also used slides more often than tenured faculty, perhaps reflecting some flavor of "born digital" for a younger generation. In [12], it was reported that women were more likely to use student-centered practices and less likely to use instructor-centered practices than men. Our results suggest that the relationship is more complex, as we found only a very weak association between women and student-centered practices.

Faculty account for their teaching approaches in a number of ways. Faculty justifying the use of instructor-centered approaches wrote open-ended comments about negative judgments by students and student course evaluations, making sure students learned the material, large enrollments, and heavy teaching loads. Faculty justified using student-centered approaches based on research evidence, feelings of effectiveness, and to retain underrepresented students.

5.2 Limitations of the Study

In addition to unavoidable self-selection and response biases risks inherent to the sampling and survey design methods, there is a risk that respondents might interpret terms such as "lecturing" or "flipping the classroom" differently. Although we tried to describe each teaching practice clearly in the survey, misinterpretation by respondents or misclassification by us in terms of instructor- or student-centered are still possible. This is why we focused on less ambiguous practices (lecture and slides). In addition, some faculty may think they are using a particular practice but are only implementing part of it, possibly in a way that jeopardizes the effectiveness of the innovation [5]. Implementation fidelity is a particular issue for prescriptive innovations like POGIL and pair programming.

A potential solution for future studies would be to survey both students and faculty using descriptive language rather than formal titles. Connecting faculty perceptions about their teaching with student perceptions may help establish validity and better gauge the fidelity of implementation.

A major limitation of this study is that the bank of practices and tools used in the survey is far from comprehensive. A large number of student-centered practices have been developed over the last few decades. Many CS faculty use student- and instructor-centered approaches that we did not list in our survey; our selection process of using examples that emerged in interviews or that were notable examples we felt were common in the field may have led us to omit other, potentially more common practices. Other studies should expand this inventory, and preferably, establish longitudinal patterns of usage.

6 CONCLUSION

Despite the demonstrated and perceived value of student-centered teaching approaches, it is unlikely that lecture and slides will die off in CS in the near future. Our results show that while most faculty lecture frequently, they also combine instructor-centered practices with student-centered practices in ways that make sense to them, such as leading in-class discussions and using examples that "connect to students' lives and interests." There is room for using more student-centered approaches, but currently most faculty are not *only* lecturing, and that is a good thing.

Faculty teach under a variety of conditions, including in situations where student evaluations are used to make nontrivial judgments about promotion, salary, and tenure. In such a case, it is understandable that faculty may stick to a safe path using practices that they perceive as what students expect [2]. The huge increases in CS enrollment as well as the limitations of the physical spaces where faculty teach are also likely to affect the practices faculty choose in classes. Those wishing to encourage better propagation of student-centered teaching in CS higher education should leverage the practices—and their motivations—that faculty actually use, in ways that accommodate the constraints faculty face.

The SIGCSE community may want to consider approaches to increasing the use of student-centered practices beyond the community itself. That is, faculty who attend SIGCSE are probably more likely to hear about and talk about innovations in their teaching than their peers who have never attended SIGCSE, but instead use their travel funds for technical SIGS.

We close with a provocation to the SIGCSE community. Shulman [26] argues that disciplines have signature pedagogies, which are particular teaching approaches that are useful for showing and demonstrating concepts; assumptions about the best ways of teaching concepts; and a tacit moral dimension that describes what is valued by a profession. Instead of seeking to do away with what is apparently a signature pedagogy in CS (and therefore, heavily entrenched in CS education), perhaps educational development specialists should provide instruction on improving the content of lectures and the form with which they are delivered. Instead of advocating for taking the instructor off the stage, we can teach instructors to perform better on the stage—improving the form with which they present ideas, using whiteboards more effectively and interactively. Showing practical applications of computing and connecting with students' interests and real world concerns using analogies and metaphor can make content meaningful, engage students, and improve learning. Sages who refuse to give up the stage might be persuaded to at least begin to share it, which could be a good gateway to student-centered teaching.

ACKNOWLEDGMENTS

Thank you to our survey respondents, research assistants, and reviewers who improved this study at every turn. Thank you to the National Science Foundation for funding this study under award DUE #1123332.

REFERENCES

[1] Babbie, E.R. 1990. *Survey research methods.* Wadsworth Publishing Co.

[2] Barker, L. and Gruning, J. 2014. The Student Prompt: Student Feedback and Change in Teaching Practices in Postsecondary Computer Science. *Proceedings of the 44th Annual Frontiers in Education Conference* (Madrid, Spain, Oct. 2014), 1–8.

[3] Barker, L., Hovey, C.L. and Gruning, J. 2015. What Influences CS Faculty to Adopt Teaching Practices? *Proceedings of the 46th ACM Technical Symposium on Computer Science Education* (Kansas City, Missouri, March 4-7, 2015, 2015), 604–609.

[4] Bell, T., Cockburn, A., Mckenzie, B. and Vargo, J. 2001. Flexible Delivery Damaging to Learning? Lessons from the Canterbury Digital Lectures Project. (2001).

[5] Borrego, M., Cutler, S., Prince, M., Henderson, C. and Froyd, J.E. 2013. Fidelity of Implementation of Research-Based Instructional Strategies (RBIS) in Engineering Science Courses. *Journal of Engineering Education.* 102, 3 (Jul. 2013), 394–425. DOI:https://doi.org/10.1002/jee.20020.

[6] Braxton, J.M., Doyle, W.R., Hartley, H.V., Hirschy, A.S., Jones, W.A. and McLendon, M.K. 2013. *Rethinking college student retention.* Jossey-Bass.

[7] Castells, M. 2009. *The Rise of the Network Society: The Information Age: Economy, Society, and Culture Volume I.* Wiley-Blackwell.

[8] Dancy, M. and Henderson, C. 2010. Pedagogical practices and instructional change of physics faculty. *American Journal of Physics.* 78, 10 (Oct. 2010), 1056–1063. DOI:https://doi.org/10.1119/1.3446763.

[9] Dillman, D.A. 2007. *Mail and Internet Surveys: The Tailored Design Method.* Wiley.

[10] Dillman, D.A., Smyth, J.D. and Christian, L.M. 2014. *Internet, phone, mail, and mixed-mode surveys: the tailored design method.* Wiley.

[11] Freeman, S., Eddy, S.L., McDonough, M., Smith, M.K., Okoroafor, N., Jordt, H. and Wenderoth, M.P. 2014. Active learning increases student performance in science, engineering, and mathematics. *Proceedings of the National Academy of Sciences.* 111, 23 (Jun. 2014), 8410–8415. DOI:https://doi.org/10.1073/pnas.1319030111.

[12] Grissom, S., Fitzgerald, S., McCauley, R. and Murphy, L. 2017. Exposed! CS Faculty Caught Lecturing in Public: A Survey of Instructional Practices. *Proceedings of the 2017 ACM SIGCSE Technical Symposium on Computer Science Education* (New York, NY, USA, 2017), 261–266.

[13] Hake, R. 1998. Interactive-engagement versus traditional methods: A six thousand student survey of mechanics test data for introductory physics students. *American Journal of Physics.* 66, 1 (1998), 64–73.

[14] Henderson, C. and Dancy, M.H. 2007. Barriers to the use of research-based instructional strategies: The influence of both individual and situational characteristics. *Physical Review Special Topics - Physics Education Research.* 3, 2 (Sep. 2007), 020102. DOI:https://doi.org/10.1103/PhysRevSTPER.3.020102.

[15] Henderson, C. and Dancy, M.H. 2009. Impact of physics education research on the teaching of introductory quantitative physics in the United States. *Physical Review Special Topics - Physics Education Research.* 5, 2 (Dec. 2009), 020107. DOI:https://doi.org/10.1103/PhysRevSTPER.5.020107.

[16] Hovey, C.L., Barker, L. and Nagy, V. forthcoming. Survey Results on Why CS Faculty Adopt New Teaching Practices. *Proceedings of the 50th ACM Technical Symposium on Computer Science Education* (Minneapolis, Minnesota, forthcoming).

[17] Integrated Postsecondary Education Data System: 2016. *http://nces.ed.gov/ipeds/.*

[18] Kaput, K. 2018. *Evidence for Student-Centered Learning.* Technical Report #ED581111. Education Evolving.

[19] Laursen, S.L., Hassi, M.-L., Kogan, M. and Weston, T.J. 2014. Benefits for Women and Men of Inquiry-Based Learning in College Mathematics: A Multi-Institution Study. *Journal for Research in Mathematics Education.* 45, 4 (2014), 406–418. DOI:https://doi.org/10.5951/jresematheduc.45.4.0406.

[20] National Academy of Engineering 2004. *The Engineer of 2020: Visions of Engineering in the New Century.* National Academies Press.

[21] National Academy of Sciences (US), National Academy of Engineering (US), and Institute of Medicine (US) Committee on Underrepresented Groups and the Expansion of the Science and Engineering Workforce Pipeline 2011. *Expanding Underrepresented Minority Participation: America's Science and Technology Talent at the Crossroads.* National Academies Press.

[22] Obi-Okogbuo, J. 2015. Science, Technology, and Globalization: A Re-Appraisal in the Philosophy of Science and Technology. *European Scientific Journal.* 11, 14 (May 2015).

[23] Pascarella, E.T. and Terenzini, P.T. 2005. *How college affects students. Volume 2: A third decade of research.* Jossey-Bass.

[24] Porter, L., Guzdial, M., McDowell, C. and Simon, B. 2013. Success in Introductory Programming: What Works? *Communications of the ACM.* 56, 8 (Aug. 2013), 34–36. DOI:https://doi.org/10.1145/2492007.2492020.

[25] Russell, J., VanHorne, S., Ward, A.S., Bettis, E.A., Sipola, M., Colombo, M. and Rocheford, M.K. 2016. Large Lecture Transformation: Adopting Evidence-Based Practices to Increase Student Engagement and Performance in an Introductory Science Course. *Journal of Geoscience Education; Bellingham.* 64, 1 (Feb. 2016), 37–51. DOI:https://doi.org/10.5408/15-084.1.

[26] Shulman, L.S. 2005. Signature pedagogies in the professions. *Daedalus.* 134, 3 (Jun. 2005), 52–59. DOI:https://doi.org/10.1162/0011526054622015.

[27] Tourangeau, R. 2000. *The psychology of survey response.* Cambridge University Press.

[28] Walter, E.M., Henderson, C.R., Beach, A.L. and Williams, C.T. 2016. Introducing the Postsecondary Instructional Practices Survey (PIPS): A Concise, Interdisciplinary, and Easy-to-Score Survey. *CBE-Life Sciences Education.* 15, 4 (Dec. 2016), ar53. DOI:https://doi.org/10.1187/cbe.15-09-0193.

Harnessing the Wisdom of the Classes

Classsourcing and Machine Learning for Assessment Instrument Generation

Sam Saarinen
Brown University
Providence, Rhode Island, USA

Shriram Krishnamurthi
Brown University
Providence, Rhode Island, USA

Kathi Fisler
Brown University
Providence, Rhode Island, USA

Preston Tunnell Wilson
Brown University
Providence, Rhode Island, USA

ABSTRACT

Generating questions to engage and measure students is often challenging and time-consuming. Furthermore, these questions do not always transfer well between student populations due to differences in background, course emphasis, or ambiguity in the questions or answers. We introduce a contributing student pedagogy activity facilitated by machine learning that can generate questions with associated answer-reasoning sets. We call this process Adaptive Tool-Driven Conception Generation. A tool implementing this process has been deployed, and it explicitly optimizes the process for questions that divide student opinion. In a study involving arrays in Java, this novel process: generates questions similar to expert-designed questions, produces novel questions that identify potential student misconceptions, and provides statistical estimates of the prevalence of misconceptions . This process allows the generation of quiz and discussion questions with less expert effort, facilitates a subprocess in the creation of concept inventories, and also raises the possibility of running reproduction studies relatively cheaply.

CCS CONCEPTS

• **Social and professional topics** → **Student assessment**; • **Computing methodologies** → Machine learning;

KEYWORDS

Contributing Student Pedagogy, Instrument Development, Learning Analytics

ACM Reference Format:
Sam Saarinen, Shriram Krishnamurthi, Kathi Fisler, and Preston Tunnell Wilson. 2019. Harnessing the Wisdom of the Classes: Classsourcing and Machine Learning for Assessment Instrument Generation. In *Proceedings of the 50th ACM Technical Symposium on Computer Science Education (SIGCSE '19), February 27-March 2, 2019, Minneapolis, MN, USA.* ACM, New York, NY, USA, 7 pages. https://doi.org/10.1145/3287324.3287504

ACM ISBN 978-1-4503-5890-3/19/02...$15.00
https://doi.org/10.1145/3287324.3287504

1 INTRODUCTION

Student conceptions and learning benefit from a diversity of assessment instruments. In an ideal world, educators would have access to a concept inventory (CI) for each topic they cover. A CI [8] is a *validated, robust,* and *interpretable* instrument that pinpoints student conceptions. It can examine the knowledge of students coming into a course [7], measure their change across the course [7], and help identify misunderstandings on the spot, e.g., in conjunction with clickers [13]. Therefore, there is value to having a large number of CIs across the whole spectrum of computer science topics.

Unfortunately, generating a CI or similar instrument is painstaking. Furthermore, a CI for a certain topic may not be very useful in a particular instructor's setting due to differences of covered material, prior preparation, choice of programming language, and numerous other factors. Finally, the number of actual CIs in computer science is fairly small [9] [14] and are relatively concentrated in introductory computing, failing to cover large parts of the field. Thus, CIs appear to be difficult-to-attain holy grails.

Absent such a rigorous instrument, an instructor might have to make do with a quiz of their design, which lacks any of the properties listed above. Due to the expert blind spot [11] the quiz may fail to cover some topics. It may also miss many mistakes that students have, may not necessarily clearly line up mistakes with misconceptions, and so on.

In this paper we attempt to find a happy middle between these extremes. We define the process of *Adaptive Tool-Driven Conception Generation* (ATCG), which uses a pair of techniques in conjunction:

crowdsourcing to obtain a large number of contributors with diverse views, but using students in a class; and,

machine learning to efficiently infer which contributions are most robust.

It is instructive to compare the ATCG process with a traditional CI process. Both are shown in Figure 1, with CI on the left and ATCG on the right. The CI steps are clearly much more heavy-weight, resulting in valuable instruments generated at great human (especially expert) expense. The ATCG steps are cheap and benefit from automation. They do not offer the same guarantees, but can be applied in many settings easily.

This naturally raises the question, what is the quality of the results from ATCG? We present a first set of results in this direction. First, we describe a tool, Quizius, that implements ATCG (section 3). We have used Quizius in three settings, two of which have nothing remotely resembling a computing CI: higher-order functional programming (which is used in many contexts, and even supported by the Snap! block programming language), and quantifier use in an upper-level course on mathematical logic in computer science. Due to space limitations we will focus on the third: generating an instrument for arrays in a Java CS2 course. We pick this because we can compare the result against an existing CI [9]. Perhaps somewhat surprisingly, the ATCG output fares quite positively (section 4), showing that this process has potential and is worth studying further.

Due to space requirements, we cannot include the full details here. A repository containing relevant documents is available at http://cs.brown.edu/research/plt/dl/quizius-2019/. Additionally, the Web-hosted Quizius tool is available (with a demo) at www.quizi.us, which other instructors are welcome to use to generate instruments for their courses.

2 RELATED WORK

Concept Inventories in Computer Science. Taylor et al. [14] provide a survey of the concept inventory efforts in computer science. They acknowledge that these are expensive to run due to the strong validation demands. In this paper we focus specifically on the instrument of Kaczmarczyk et al. (2010), based on extensive student interviews on topics validated by experts as important and difficult for beginning programming students, resulting in 16 questions, with most referencing snippets of Java code. We focus on the array portion of it, which is represented as four questions in Figure 3 (reproduced here with permission).

Contributing Student Pedagogy. ATCG can be viewed as a form of Contributing Student Pedagogy (CSP) [6]. This literature suggests that writing questions and answering other students' questions has a positive effect on course outcomes. ATCG has most of the attributes of a CSP, though simply generating an instrument provides only limited opportunity to "value the contribution of others", which for now has to be done through other channels. (ATCG also shares elements with *action research* [2], including a focus on action and reflection, and students as the main driver of scope.)

Quizius shares much with the CSP system PeerWise [3], but:

- When answering questions in our system, all answers are free-response so that the student answers will be unbiased.
- Rather than using student ratings of problem difficulty and usefulness, we empirically measure the informativeness of each question by using machine learning to examine the diversity of answers and optimize answer collection.
- After Quizius has run, an expert curates the most informative contributed questions for the purpose of creating an instrument, whereas no such engagement is necessary with PeerWise, where the activity is the goal in itself.

Bandit Processes and Machine Learning. To construct a quality instrument, we need robust questions. But measuring robustness accurately requires collecting responses from many students for that question. Additionally, out of consideration both for the students and the quality of data, we would like to not waste students' time on questions that are not likely to be interesting. One approach is to continually estimate the likelihood that a question is interesting, and prioritize data collection for questions that are already suspected to produce interesting responses. But we should not prematurely rule out a question because the first few responses were all the same (suggesting the question is uninteresting).

The problem of choosing an action (*a question*) out of many, where taking the action produces some reward (*we might get an interesting response*) and also gives us more information about the action (*we have a better estimate of how interesting the question is*), is a well-studied reinforcement learning problem called the Multi-Armed Bandit. Efficient solutions have been derived that are guaranteed to converge to selecting the best action as more data are acquired ([1], for example), which we use in Quizius.

3 THE QUIZIUS TOOL

To facilitate ATCG, we created the Web-based Quizius tool (Figures 4 and 5). It allows students to join classes, participate in quiz activities, write questions, answer questions with rationales, and review question and answer distributions after the quiz ends. Quizius also allows instructors to contribute their own questions, to review the distribution of student responses, and to automatically grade students based on participation and late-day use.

In addition to streamlining the data collection process, the tool implements the critical machine learning step to filter out informative questions from the large pool, spending as few student answers as possible on questions that are not very informative. Quizius models picking questions for students to answer as a multi-armed bandit problem. We define the reward (the objective we are seeking to maximize) for the bandit problem as the likelihood that the next response duplicates a non-majority answer. We believe this is a good proxy for questions that elicit diverse student mental models (section 4.5). Note that the objective of the ATCG method is to identify misconceptions for the purpose of evaluating pedagogical efficacy or tailoring instruction, not to place students on a scale of ability, as in item response theory [10]. This necessitates a different measure of question reliability than is typically used for so-called high-stakes assessments.

Ordinarily, upper-confidence-bound algorithms (what we are using to solve the multi-armed bandit problem) converge to selecting the single best option. Since we are trying to find not the best question but rather a small set of questions, we select from among the top $\sqrt{n}$ questions, where n is the number of students who have used the system so far.

One difficulty is that students may write the same answer in different formats (e.g., "1000" versus "1,000"). We found it annoying to manually cluster these. Therefore, after students answer a question, they are shown previous representative answers and asked whether theirs is the same as any of these. In effect, we ask the students to cluster their answers themselves. This is easy for them, and in practice catches most duplicates. Of course, on seeing the previous answers, students may change their response (e.g., if they feel they were mistaken). Thus, Quizius also lets them explicitly mark that they are changing their answer. This switch provides a very useful signal about student understanding that we have not yet exploited.

When the student process is done, the expert is given: a collection of questions; for each question, a collection of answers; for each answer, a collection of rationales for that answer. The expert then

(1) experts set the scope of the assessment (using a Delphi Process to choose important and difficult topics)
(2) students articulate mental models and experts identify misconceptions (through interviews to find interpretations for student responses)
(3) experts develop questions (to distinguish mental models)
(4) experts validate the assessment (using statistical and qualitative analysis across several trial administrations to iterate towards robust and validated questions)

Figure 1: A traditional process for creating new CIs. Steps are taken from [5] and are based on recent practice in several disciplines [4].

(1) experts write a prompt setting the scope for contributions
(2) students contribute questions
(3) students contribute answers and rationales (by answering other students' questions and providing a brief justification)
(4) a machine learning algorithm prioritizes responses to informative questions (in order to find robust questions)
(5) experts select questions for relevance (thus validating the questions)
(6) experts identify misconceptions (by reviewing student rationales for each answer and interpreting the responses)

Figure 2: The novel ATCG process.

selects the questions that appear most interesting to assemble into an instrument. Examining the rationales gives insight into the mental models responsible for the student responses. In practice, we find that most answers arise for the same reason, but a careful reading finds a few other "outlier" reasons. If ATCG is being used to help build a CI, such questions would have to be modified so that different (mis)conceptions do not result in the same answer.

The ATCG protocol has a bootstrapping problem: What questions do the first students answer? Quizius permits multiple options: let them simply finish early, or use pre-populated questions. The latter may be various sources: instructor-provided, from an existing CI, or even from previous iterations of using Quizius (e.g., if the process is re-run across years—which is what we did in our study in section 4).

4 A COMPARATIVE STUDY

We now compare an ATCG-generated instrument for CS2 Java arrays (the *generated* instrument), against Kaczmarczyk et al.'s CI (the *expert* instrument). G1-G6 in Figure 6 show the student-generated questions. At a high level, we find:

- The generated instrument contains most of the same topics and distractors as the expert instrument.
- The generated instrument misses some of the content of the expert instrument; we conjecture why this is so.
- The generated instrument contains array use topics—and distractors for them, along with explanations of misconceptions—*not* included in the expert instrument.

While performing this comparison, we also identify possible points of confusion in the expert instrument.

4.1 The Study Population and Iteration

We generated this instrument from two iterations of a CS2 class at a mid-size competitive private research US university. Although the course covered algorithms and data structures typical of CS2, it was also a first course using Java and a first course with object-orientation (the students had previously studied functional programming). Each time, the study was run midway through the course, after students had completed a lab assignment on each of objects and arrays. Just over 120 students participated in each iteration of the study, and we note (based on results from an entry survey) that less than half of these students had high school programming experience in Java.

The study was structured as an online homework assignment, and students were given a week to complete it. The first time the study was run, students were required to write one question (consisting of a short program in Java whose printed output demonstrated something they considered interesting about arrays; Figure 4 shows an example prompt), then to answer 15 questions written by other students in free-response style (to predict the printed output of the written programs without running them). They were also asked to answer the 4 array-related questions from the expert instrument. Figure 3 shows their counts for each answer in brackets; note that many answers were chosen by no students.

In the second iteration, we seeded the system with contributions from the previous year. We note that we observed qualitatively similar distributions of mental models between the two years. To reduce student effort, we made question submission optional (23 out of 128 students submitted one voluntarily anyway). Because of improvements to the question allocation algorithm and a tighter semester schedule, we only asked them to answer 10 questions. Section 4.6 gives more results on engagement and student time. *All* questions and responses in Figure 6 are student-generated; the responses are all from the second iteration of the study.

4.2 Similar Questions – Indexing and Length

To begin, we note that both the generated and the expert questions contain questions involving indexing (is Java 1-indexed or 0-indexed) and array length (E1 and E2 in Figure 3 (expert instrument) and G1, G2, G4, and G7 in Figure 6 (generated instrument)). We discuss 1-indexed misconceptions quantitatively in Section 4.6.

4.3 Missing Questions – Memory and Type

Although there is a diversity of questions in the generated instrument, we note that there are no questions about memory allocation or type of an array object similar to E3 and E4 (Figure 3). We conjecture that this was precluded by the prompt used in this study, which required students to write a short Java program whose output would be printed. We consider it likely that most CS2 students do not have access to the reflection capabilities necessary to phrase such questions as Java programs. Perhaps if given a different prompt, students might write questions regarding type or memory allocation, but it is also possible that a less-structured activity would be harder for students. Thus, an open-ended CI interview offers possibilities that a closed, computer-based process may make more difficult.

E1. What should the values of x and y be, in order to fill all elements of the following array with values of -1? [Distractors are based on thinking that arrays start at index 1 and/or a for loop stepping through an array will need to go until < the array's length - 1]

```
int[] myArray = new int[10];
int i;
int x;
int y;
for (i = x; i < y; i++) {
    myArray[i] = -1;
}
```

(a) x = 1, y = the length of myArray [1x]
(b) **x = 0, y = the length of myArray** [109x]
(c) x = 1, y = the length of myArray - 1 [0x]
(d) x = 0, y = the length of myArray - 1 [22x]

E2. How many elements are in myArray? [Distractors are based on thinking that an array's length is off by 1 or equal to the number of letters in the array's name]

(a) 7 [0x]
(b) 9 [1x]
(c) **10** [124x]
(d) 11 [0x]

E3. Which of the following answers most accurately describes the parts of the declaration of myArray? [Distractors are based on thinking the type of an array is just an array or a general object and/or declaring the length of an array instead sets the first element or all elements in the array to the value of the length] [remove answer e for non-Java languages]

```
int[] myArray = new int[5];
```

(a) **type is an integer array, length is 5** [124x]
(b) type is an array, each element has a value of 5 [0x]
(c) type is an integer array, each element has a value of 5 [0x]
(d) type is an integer array, the value of the first element is 5 [0x]
(e) type is an object array, the constructor is passed a value of 5 [2x]

E4. Which of the following answers most accurately describes the memory allocation of myArray in E3? [Distractors are based on thinking memory is not allocated for the elements in the array or only the 1st element or plus an extra element]

```
int[] myArray = new int[5];
```

(a) memory is allocated for 6 spaces [7x]
(b) **memory is allocated for 5 spaces** [120x]
(c) no memory is allocated [0x]
(d) memory is only allocated for the first element [0x]

Figure 3: Four questions from the expert instrument. Out of the 16 total questions, these related somehow to arrays. Questions, answers, and interpretations (mental models) are from Kaczmarczyk and collaborators (private correspondence, extending [9]). Answers are followed by the number of *our* respondents who selected that answer. Note that not all respondents answered all questions.

4.4 Novel Questions – Assignment, Aliasing, and Equality

Finally, we note that there are a number of concepts tested by the generated instrument that are not present in the expert instrument. For example, G1 (Figure 6) involves nested arrays, G3 tests aliasing after assignment of one array to another, G4 involves mutation of an array passed to a method, and G5 and G6 test array equality. These are all concepts that are not addressed by the expert instrument. The authors of this paper were surprised at some of the things students thought to write questions about, and we conjecture that student-authored questions may help to get beyond expert blind spots. In particular, G2 (which reveals a mutation and aliasing misconception–this is discussed in Section 4.6) is not a question that occurred to us.

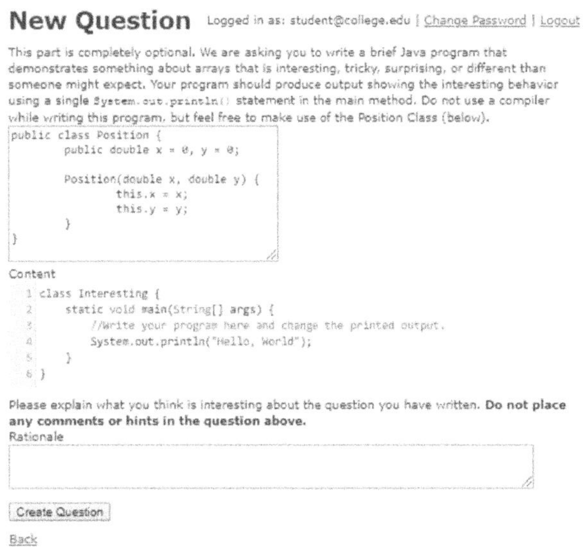

Figure 4: The Question Writing Interface for students.

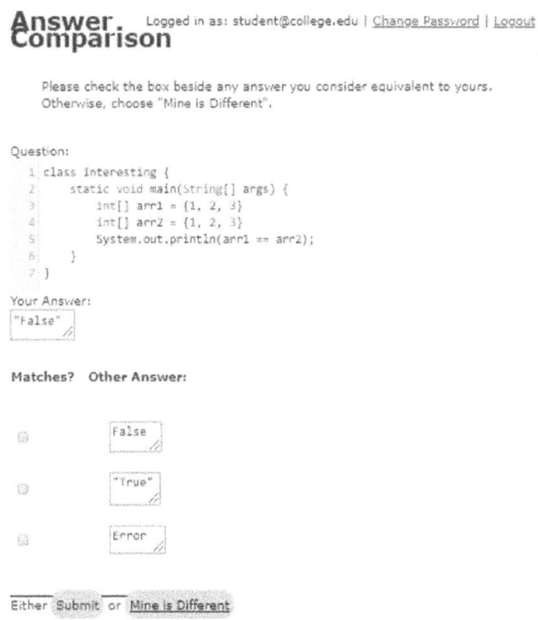

Figure 5: The Answer Grouping Interface for students. After giving a free response answer and a brief rationale, students are taken to this screen where they either combine their answer with an existing group, or indicate that their answer is different from the others.

4.5 Novel Mental Models

This study allowed us to identify new mental models related to multiple indexing, equality comparison, and initialization of arrays. Additionally, by analyzing over a hundred student responses to expert instrument question E4 (Figure 3), we identified a new mental model relative to those previously identified: one student believed that 6 spaces were allocated for a `new int [5]`, because they were aware that Java caches the length of an array as an integer, and

The provided Position class could be used freely:

```
public class Position {
    public double x = 0, y = 0;
    Position(double x, double y) {
        this.x = x;
        this.y = y;
    }
}
```

G1.

```
public class Interesting {
    public static void main(String[] args) {
        int[][][][][] arr = {{{{{1, 2}, {3, 4}}, {{5, 6}, {7, 8}}},
                             {{{9, 10}, {11, 12}}, {{13, 14}, {15, 16}}}},
                            {{{{17, 18}, {19, 20}}, {{21, 22}, {23, 24}}},
                             {{{25, 26}, {27, 28}}, {{29, 30}, {31, 32}}}}};
        System.out.println(arr[1][1][1][1][1]);
    }
}
```

(a) 32 [24x]
(b) 1 [9x]
(c) 16 [4x]
(d) {3,4} {11,12}, {19,20}, {27, 28} [2x]
(e) {{{{1, 2}, {3, 4}}, {{5, 6}, {7, 8}}}
{{{{1, 2}, {3, 4}}, {{5, 6}, {7, 8}}}
{{{{1, 2}, {3, 4}}, {{5, 6}, {7, 8}}}
{{{{1, 2}, {3, 4}}, {{5, 6}, {7, 8}}}
{{{{1, 2}, {3, 4}}, {{5, 6}, {7, 8}}}
[1x]
(f) illegible answer in console [3x]
(g) other [10x, including 30, 28, 12, 14, and 31]

G2.

```
public class Interesting {
    public static void main(String[] args) {
        int x = 3;
        int[] test = {x,1,1,1};
        x = 1;
        System.out.println(test[0]);
    }
}
```

(a) 3 [42x]
(b) 1 [8x]

G3.

```
public class Interesting {
    public static String posString(Position p) {
        return "(" + p.x + ", " + p.y + ")";
    }
    public static void main(String[] args) {
        Position[] whatIsJava = new Position[5];
        Position[] otherArray = whatIsJava;
        otherArray[4] = new Position(5.5, 2.2);
        System.out.println(posString(whatIsJava[4]));
    }
}
```

(a) (5.5, 2.2) [23x]
(b) null [14x]
(c) error [10x]
(d) (0, 0) [7x]
(e) other [2x]

G4.

```
public class Interesting {
    public static void reverse(int[] input) {
        int lastPlace = input.length - 1;
        int middlePlace = input.length / 2;
        for (int x = 0; x <= middlePlace; x++) {
            int temp = input[x];
            input[x] = input[lastPlace - x];
            input[lastPlace - x] = temp;
        }
    }
    public static void main(String[] args) {
        int[] arr = { 2, 16, 8, 42, 89 };
        reverse(arr);
        System.out.println(arr);
    }
}
```

(a) [89, 42, 8, 16, 2] [24x]
(b) Some memory address [19x]
(c) {89, 42, 8, 16, 2} [7x]
(d) other [4x]

G5.

```
public class Interesting {
    public static void main(String[] args) {
        int[] first = {1, 2, 3, 4};
        int[] second = {1, 2, 3, 4};
        System.out.println(first==second);
    }
}
```

(a) false [31x]
(b) true [11x]
(c) error [10x]

G6.

```
public class ArraysExample {
  public static void main(String[] args) {

    Position[] array1 = new Position[2];
    Position[] array2 = new Position[2];

    Position posn1 = new Position(2.5, 3.5);
    Position posn2 = new Position(2.5, 3.5);

    array1[0] = posn1;
    array1[1] = posn2;

    array2[0] = posn2;
    array2[1] = posn1;

    System.out.println(array1.equals(array2));
  }
}
```

(a) False [39x]
(b) true [10x]
(c) Error [2x]
(d) other [3x]

G7. [Note that Quizius ranked this question as having low information (limited diversity in answers). We include it here for comparison with answers to G1.]

```
public class Interesting {
    public static void main(String[] args) {
      try {
        Integer[] intArray = new Integer[] {1, 2, 3, 4, 5};
        System.out.println(intArray[5]);
          // print out the 5th element of the array
        } catch (ArrayIndexOutOfBoundsException e) {
      System.out.println("intArray does not contain an element at index 5");
        }
    }
}
```

(a) "intArray does not contain an element at index 5" [53x]
(b) Error [2x]

Figure 6: A selection from the most informative questions generated using ATCG. Each question is a program, whose output students were asked to predict. Each answer is followed by the number of respondents who agreed with it. Some answers are combined as "other" for brevity.

reasoned that that was allocated in addition to the 5 spaces for the 5 elements of the array. Although it is a rare mental model in our population, this suggests a refinement to that question. This mental model may have been lost in the much smaller sample size for which it is feasible to conduct extensive interviews.

4.6 Quantitative Analysis

Space precludes a detailed analysis of the questions in the two instruments, and student responses to them (and the mental models they reveal). However, we enumerate some salient points:

- The expert instrument (Figure 3) is able to detect up to 12 misconceptions (either or both of 2 for E1, 3 for E2, 4 for E3, and 3 for E4) related to arrays. Our population exhibited a ceiling effect on the expert instrument, however, as only 5 of those misconceptions appeared in our population, and the majority of students got all the CI questions correct. (Figure 3 contains detailed incidence counts.) The generated instrument (considering only programs 1-6, as presented in Figure 6) detected 13 misconceptions in our student population.
- The top-ranking generated questions are ones that produce a spread of student responses. Although this spread is not always due to a difference in mental models (G4 in Figure 6), other questions capture misconceptions in a nuanced way. In particular, on G1 on the generated instrument, 9 out of the 53 students exhibited a 1-indexing misconception (answer b). Interestingly, this 1-indexing misconception did not occur on a student-generated question involving a 1-dimensional array (G7), and on E1 from the expert instrument (Figure 3), only one student chose an answer consistent with a 1-indexing misconception. This is likely an instance of the well-known phenomenon of fragile student knowledge [12].
- For our student population, the generated questions detected misconceptions more frequently than the CI questions. There are many possible reasons for this, which we do not have space to discuss further. We do find interesting mental models in answers that claim a program is erroneous. We speculate this may not happen as frequently if students believe the programs were written by an expert.
- We measured the amount of time each student spent on the question authoring page and on the answer writing page, which is a reasonable proxy for student time, although some large outliers (one answer took 8.8 hours) suggest that students may have left the page open while doing other things. The median time to write a question was just over 11 minutes, and the median time to answer a question was 1 minute and 17 seconds. Furthermore, just over 30% of our students voluntarily answered more questions than required to complete the homework assignment—some by a significant margin, which suggests some of them may even have found this process educational or fun.

  Across all students, about 90 hours of student time were used in total. About 8 expert hours over the course of a week were used to design and refine the protocols for the study, and about 15 expert hours over the course of two weeks were spent on selecting the relevant questions and interpreting student rationales. In total wall clock time, the second iteration of this study took 4 weeks to run end-to-end, which is substantially faster than any CI-creation process.

5 DISCUSSION

It is not clear whether it is better to ask students to write questions before, during, or after answering the questions of other students. Having them write questions before answering any occasionally results in questions that are nearly isomorphic, although the written questions are unbiased by the work of other students. Having them write questions during or after allows students to benefit from the examples they have seen, and deliberately write different questions, but it may artificially constrain their responses based on what they have seen; more studies will need to be done to evaluate the relative strength of these effects quantitatively.

We found that some students submitted questions unrelated to arrays in Java, although they did produce a broad spread of answers. (In particular, a question about object equality comparison left even the authors searching carefully through the Java language specification to understand the correct answer.) Although the tool could be altered to allow students to flag off-topic questions, the instructor may wish to keep those questions that reveal a spread of mental models, even if they are off-topic.

Though we did not encounter instances of abusive use, it is also important for users to be able to flag offensive content (as they can in Quizius). Malicious users might write an abusive answer that others would have to read; more subtly, they might submit a program whose output is offensive, which everyone else would then be forced to type. Working in a graded course, rather than on the open Internet, probably helped us avoid such incidents.

6 CONCLUSION

This paper presents ATCG as an intriguing mid-point, and potential sweet spot, between the heavy-weight CI process and entirely instructor-generated evaluation instruments. Augmenting instructor work with that of students can reveal a rich set of models, working around expert blind-spots. In a comparative study, we find that *purely* student-generated questions and answers, with relatively little effort (and with some of the auxiliary benefits of CSP), can compare very favorably to ones generated with considerable effort by a team of experts. Our tool, Quizius, helps run the ATCG process, presenting a Web interface and embodying a machine learning algorithm. We have already begun to apply ATCG in two other computing contexts, and we feel this process should be applied to all of computer science (indeed, Quizius is not even computing-specific), especially in areas where it may take a very long time and considerable expense to cover with a CI.

ACKNOWLEDGMENTS

We are grateful to Lisa Kaczmarczyk for contributing questions from an expert instrument. We thank Leo Porter and Daniel Zingaro, as well as Mike Clancy and Cynthia Taylor, for their elucidating conversations on Concept Inventories and for pointing us to action research. This work was partially supported by the National Science Foundation.

REFERENCES

[1] Peter Auer, Nicolo Cesa-Bianchi, Yoav Freund, and Robert E Schapire. 2002. The nonstochastic multiarmed bandit problem. *SIAM journal on computing* (2002).

[2] Mary Brydon-Miller, Davydd Greenwood, and Patricia Maguire. 2003. Why action research? *Action Research* (2003).

[3] Paul Denny, John Hamer, Andrew Luxton-Reilly, and Helen Purchase. 2008. PeerWise: students sharing their multiple choice questions. In *ICER*. ACM.

[4] DL Evans, Gary L Gray, Stephen Krause, Jay Martin, Clark Midkiff, Branislav M Notaros, Michael Pavelich, David Rancour, Teri Reed-Rhoads, Paul Steif, et al. 2003. Progress on concept inventory assessment tools. In *Frontiers in Education*. IEEE.

[5] Ken Goldman, Paul Gross, Cinda Heeren, Geoffrey Herman, Lisa Kaczmarczyk, Michael C Loui, and Craig Zilles. 2008. Identifying important and difficult concepts in introductory computing courses using a delphi process. *ACM SIGCSE Bulletin* (2008).

[6] John Hamer, Quintin Cutts, Jana Jackova, Andrew Luxton-Reilly, Robert McCartney, Helen Purchase, Charles Riedesel, Mara Saeli, Kate Sanders, and Judithe Sheard. 2008. Contributing Student Pedagogy. *SIGCSE Bull.* (2008).

[7] Charles Henderson. 2002. Common concerns about the force concept inventory. *The Physics Teacher* (2002).

[8] David Hestenes, Malcolm Wells, Gregg Swackhamer, et al. 1992. Force concept inventory. *The Physics Teacher* (1992).

[9] Lisa C Kaczmarczyk, Elizabeth R Petrick, J Philip East, and Geoffrey L Herman. 2010. Identifying student misconceptions of programming. In *SIGCSE*. ACM.

[10] Frederic M Lord. 2012. *Applications of item response theory to practical testing problems*. Routledge.

[11] Mitchell J Nathan, Kenneth R Koedinger, Martha W Alibali, et al. 2001. Expert blind spot: When content knowledge eclipses pedagogical content knowledge. *ICCS*.

[12] DN Perkins and Fay Martin. 1986. Fragile knowledge and neglected strategies in novice programmers. In *Empirical Studies of Programmers*.

[13] Beth Simon, Michael Kohanfars, Jeff Lee, Karen Tamayo, and Quintin Cutts. 2010. Experience report: peer instruction in introductory computing. In *SIGCSE*. ACM.

[14] C. Taylor, D. Zingaro, L. Porter, K.C. Webb, C.B. Lee, and M. Clancy. 2014. Computer science concept inventories: past and future. *Computer Science Education* (2014).

An Assessment of Oral Exams in Introductory CS

Peter Ohmann
College of Saint Benedict / Saint John's University, USA
pohmann001@csbsju.edu

ABSTRACT

Assessment of student knowledge is a crucial and challenging part of course design. Especially in computer science courses in the United States, written examinations are very common. While written exams offer a number of advantages in convenience and familiarity, they are also inflexible and prone to question misinterpretation. In contrast to written tests, oral exams offer the prospect of an interactive conversation where students can express their knowledge in a variety of ways while asking clarifying questions.

In this paper, we present and assess our implementation of oral exams in an introductory computer science course. We describe the motivation for and resulting features of our design, including a simplified rubric style for equitable, on-the-fly grading. We also perform an assessment relative to more traditional written exams. We find the time commitment for instructors to be manageable and comparable to traditional exams. Through post-semester surveys, students self-report spending slightly more time studying for oral exams, but rate the difficulty as similar to written exams. Both qualitative and quantitative student feedback indicates that oral exams can be effective and well-received.

CCS CONCEPTS

• **Social and professional topics** → **Computer science education**; **CS1**; **Student assessment**; Computational thinking;

KEYWORDS

Oral exam, written exam, student survey

ACM Reference Format:

Peter Ohmann. 2019. An Assessment of Oral Exams in Introductory CS. In *SIGCSE '19: 50th ACM Technical Symposium on Computer Science Education, February 27–March 2, 2019, Minneapolis, MN, USA.* ACM, New York, NY, USA, 7 pages. https://doi.org/10.1145/3287324.3287489

1 INTRODUCTION

This work was undertaken while the author was a faculty member at Xavier University in Cincinnati, OH, USA. All discussion of curriculum and course design refer to the Computer Science program and course offerings of Xavier University during the 2017–2018 academic year.

Individual assessment of student knowledge is a crucial component of any course design. Rigorous in-class examinations (exams) are typically a core method. While exams vary immensely across universities and cultures, two common types of exams are well-known: the written exam and the oral exam.

In a written exam, students are given questions on paper and work alone to write answers to the questions. Usually, written exams have a fixed time limit. When a student has finished with the exam (or at the end of the time limit), they turn in the written copy for later grading by the instructor or course grader. Written exams typically involve little to no direct interaction between the student and instructor, aside from short clarification questions.

Oral exams are, instead, intended to foster unscripted discussion between the evaluator and student. An individual student (or, sometimes, a group of students) meets face-to-face with the evaluator at their own unique time, separate from the rest of the class. The student(s) are then asked a smaller set of questions, which they answer orally, perhaps with the occasional use of paper or whiteboard. Oral exams are typically graded during or immediately after the exam ("on-the-fly" in some fashion).

This paper describes our experience in implementing oral exams as the final examination for an introductory computer science course in a university setting. Through oral exams, we hoped to better assess the depth of student knowledge on exam topics (without question wording or guessing getting in the way). Ideally, we also hoped to reduce stress associated with writing under time pressure. We describe our design for the exam, our goals, and how we attempted to minimize some commonly-cited negative aspects of oral exams. We also include sample questions that we used in our exam implementation, and describe our use of pre-scripted prompts to ensure consistency across students' exams. These samples also help to demonstrate our simplified "check-box" rubric format, which is designed to reduce unintended bias during examination. We found this rubric format to be easy to use and efficient for on-the-fly grading; it may be useful to others hoping to implement oral exams into an introductory computer science course.

We also perform a preliminary evaluation of our design by comparing student reactions and our own perceptions to those when students took a traditional written exam in the same course. While our sample sizes are insufficient for an extensive experiment at this stage, we nevertheless glean encouraging indicators from a post-semester student survey. Students find the oral exams to be approximately as difficult as written exams, but report spending about 50% more time studying for oral exams. Student comments indicate that some students found the oral exam unique and forgiving, and some felt more relaxed (somewhat contrary to prior research on oral exam anxiety). From an instructor standpoint, we found the exam organization, scheduling, and grading to be as manageable as a traditional written exam, though we raise some concerns with scalability to large class sizes. We also saw positive signs in student performance on the exam. Overall, both instructor and student reactions to the oral exam format were positive and encouraging.

SIGCSE'19, February 27–March 2, 2019, Minneapolis, MN, USA

ACM ISBN 978-1-4503-5890-3/19/02...$15.00
https://doi.org/10.1145/3287324.3287489

1.1 Paper Organization and Contributions

Our primary contributions are as follows:

- We describe an instantiation of final oral exams into an introductory CS course.
- We provide sample questions and formatting/grading rubric styles to allow others to implement similar exams.
- We present preliminary qualitative and quantitative student and instructor feedback on the effectiveness of the oral exams. We especially focus on comparisons in student and instructor reactions to oral versus standard written exams.

This paper is organized as follows. Section 2 provides background on written versus oral exams in computer science, and discusses related work. Section 3 discusses our implementation of oral examinations into an introductory computer science course, our design goals, and includes sample questions from the exam. In section 4, we discuss preliminary comparisons of student and instructor feedback for the oral and written exam styles. Section 5 concludes.

2 BACKGROUND AND RELATED WORK

Prior work suggests that oral exams have both advantages and disadvantages (when compared with written exams). On the positive side, Asklund and Bendix [1] and Gharibyan [5] note that oral exams allow the instructor to more directly assess student levels of understanding, and provide prompt feedback on student performance. Further, Roecker [13] finds that oral exams can lead to improved student performance, allow freedom in students' problem-solving approaches, and can even expose flaws in course instruction. However, on the negative side, oral exams can be very time-consuming for larger class sizes [13], and give rise to concerns about reliability and fairness (since each student will, inevitably, have a slightly different exam) [6, 12].

Oral exams have historically been common outside of the United States (especially in the German education system [11]). However, written exams are by far the more popular style of exam in computer science courses within the United States. In fact, oral exams are uncommon in most disciplines at US universities [6, 10], outside of foreign languages [3, 7]. In computer science, oral exams are extremely rare outside of evaluating Ph.D. candidates [14]. Further, studies and reflections on their effectiveness are limited in the literature. Oral exams have been studied in other STEM areas, including physics [15], biology [8], and mathematics [9]. Prior work in computer science, however, is limited to older reports [4] and those offering general recommendations for implementation of oral exams (rather than comparisons between oral and written exams in the same course) [2, 5]. For example, Gharibyan [5] assesses the pros and cons of oral versus written exams, and offers advice on how to administer an oral exam for a theoretical computer science course. Gharibyan also describes written exam disadvantages, including the drastic effects of time pressure, the lack of flexibility (e.g., question wording becomes all-important), and the possibility of cascading minor errors. Other related work by Asklund and Bendix [1, 2] describes a design for group oral evaluations in a software configuration management course.

In the following sections, we extend this prior work in two key ways. First, we present an oral exam design used in introductory (rather than upper-division) computer science courses. Second, we present preliminary data comparing our implementation to a parallel offering of the same course with traditional written exams.

3 APPROACH

The first course in the Xavier University computer science sequence is a broad introduction to the field (traditionally called a CS0 course). For the course offerings/sections referenced in this paper, approximately 50% of topics are directly taught via programming in Python (traditionally associated with a CS1 course), 25% of topics involve no programming whatsoever, and the remaining 25% (related to algorithmic complexity) use programming in a smaller support role. Thus, throughout this paper, we use the term "CS 0/1 course."

Most prior offerings of this course have given a final, cumulative, written exam. In this section, we detail our design for a new final, cumulative, *oral* exam.

3.1 Exam Format and Goals

Both the paper and oral exams that we evaluate in this paper primarily cover four high-level topics from the semester:

- Sorting Algorithms; implementation is not expected
- Data Representation; specifically, binary and hexadecimal representations for positive and negative integers
- Algorithms and Complexity; specifically, analyzing complexity for an algorithm that the student designs
- Abstraction; specifically, its purpose and relevance to various course topics

Of course, the types of questions differ greatly between the two styles of exam. In designing the oral exam, we targeted the following core goals.

Flexibility Students should be given as much freedom as possible in demonstrating their knowledge of each topic. Of course, this freedom must be balanced with ensuring that all students receive substantively the same examination.

Consistency The exam should be a similar experience for each student. This is a major challenge for an exam based on free-form conversation.

Equity The exam should be equally accessible to students of various backgrounds. This is a continual challenge in any exam design, whether oral or written.

Overall, the exam proceeds like a *conversation*, wherein the instructor prompts for a particular topic, allows the student to demonstrate knowledge, and asks questions along the way. Students are graded on their ability to say or cover specific aspects of the topic; for example, a student might be expected to recognize that computers represent numbers in *binary* (and note that this is an alternative to *decimal*). Students earn points by satisfying the expected prompts, which the examiner has listed as check-boxes. In general, we did not expect a student to satisfy all check-boxes in order to earn full points; we thus had more boxes than the maximum possible exam score. This is especially important for open-ended questions, where the student is not expected to mechanically list every detail of an entire topic area. For example, in the binary number example, the examiner might have a check-box for "Mention binary numbers" and another for "Mention alternative to decimal."

Of course, not all students will naturally be driven to the expected sub-topics, and students may not always know how to proceed with

We covered "complexity" these past few weeks. What can you tell me about complexity?
☐ How long an algorithm will take
☐ It is based on input size
☐ Operations are counted (rather than time)

(a) Free topic discussion

How might we represent a decimal number as a binary number?
☐ Correct description given
(Could you give me an example?)
☐ Example partially correct
☐ Example completely correct
(Can we represent negative numbers too?)
☐ Basics of how negatives can be represented
☐ Some specific representation (sign-magnitude, 2s complement)
(Can you give me an example of how to represent a negative number?)
☐ Example partially correct
☐ Example completely correct

(b) Discussion of an example

What is "functional" abstraction?
☐ Understanding of abstraction, generally
☐ Definitional / Understanding of functional abstraction
(No answer: Functional abstraction is giving a name to a series of operations)
Why is functional abstraction useful?
☐ Use of name, abstraction of implementation details
(How about in Python? How about outside of coding?)
☐ Example from Python
☐ Example outside Python

(c) Discussion on the purpose of a topic

Figure 1: Sample Oral Exam Questions and Rubric

a question. The examiner needs some way to help orient the student, or give a subtle "hint." In our design, the exam rubric contains pre-scripted prompts. This helps ensure consistency for each student, i.e., that no particular student receives more extensive guidance. One could consider entirely restricting examiners to the prescribed prompts; in our case, we allowed ourselves, as instructors, some flexibility to stray from prompts when the conversation involved question clarity (rather than hints).

3.2 Question Design

Next, we shift our attention to the types of questions that appear on our exam. Loosely, we used three high-level types of questions. Each of the question parts in figure 1 demonstrates a question type, and is a (sometimes simplified) version of an actual question from our CS0/1 exam. Of course, our actual exam consisted of more and longer questions.

The first type of question initiates a free-form conversation about an important course topic. These questions are of the general form "tell me about X." An example is shown in figure 1a. Note that the student is expected to hit three important aspects of complexity learned in class: that it relates to how long an algorithm will take to run (we cover only time complexity), that it is an equation over input size, and that we count operations rather than seconds. Pre-scripted prompts would be given in parentheses (), so no hints are given here. There are, of course, follow-ups to this initial discussion (including having the student analyze a complete algorithm), but it is clear that this specific question part is worth up to 3 points.

The second type of question is of the general form "please give me an example of X." Figure 1b shows an example. Here, the initial question simply asks *how* to represent decimal numbers in a computer; however, the instructor has numerous prompts to use, all directed at getting the student up to the board, working examples.

The final type of question targets the core of many breadth-based introductory courses: the "why" questions. These questions are of the general form "explain why X is good/better/useful." Figure 1c shows an example. Here, we see a case where a pre-scripted instructor prompt gives the answer to a previous question (in this case: the definition of functional abstraction) so that the student is able to continue, even if they were unable to give a satisfactory answer to the initial question.

3.3 Running the Exam

Our goal was for oral exams to last approximately 20 minutes for an average student. To allow for struggling students, each student

Exam Type	Total Students	Respondents	Course Grade Difficulty Scaled: −5 to +5	Relative Exam Difficulty Scaled: −3 to +3	Study Hours
Written	24	5	−1.00	−0.40	4.00
Oral	53	17	−1.00	−0.44	6.13

Table 1: Survey Result Data

scheduled a 30-minute slot to take the exam; we cut off the discussion at that time. To help students manage time, we estimated maximum times for each topic (varying from 7–10 minutes) and warned students if they neared this threshold. We also provided the four exam topics (listed in section 3.1) at the start of the exam, and allowed students to reorder them (though no one did so). Students with special accommodations (e.g., due to documented disabilities) received extra time (e.g., 1.5× or 2×) just as on written exams.

Scheduling oral exams can be a challenge. In our case, students were given a random 2-hour time window in which their registration survey for final exam times "opened" (much like class registration at many universities). Slots included morning, daytime, and evening times, to accommodate students with varying commitments (e.g., work, family, class, etc.), based on the instructor's availability during the week of final exams.

As instructors, we need to determine when a student has satisfied a check-box in the rubric. This can be challenging when students give multiple, contradictory responses. Whenever we encountered this situation, we explicitly pointed it out to students, and forced them to take a stand. This is also slightly complicated by scripted prompts, which might help a muddled response get back on track. We planned for this inevitability: check-boxes that appear *before* the prompt in the rubric are generally "lost" once the hint is given. Figure 1c is a perfect example of this: once the student is given the definition of functional abstraction, they can no longer earn points for the initial "What is functional abstraction?" question.

Because of the "on-the-fly" check-box grading, we were able to give students a reasonable estimate for their grade immediately following the exam. We first asked students what grade *they* thought they earned, and then quickly counted check-boxes to determine their actual estimated grade. (The grade was an estimate to leave flexibility for scaling, though we did not need to do so.)

4 FEEDBACK AND RESULTS

We performed a preliminary evaluation of our oral exam design from section 3. To do so, we investigated two offerings of our CS0/1 course, taught in the Fall 2017 and Spring 2018 semesters. Both offerings were taught by the same instructor (the author of this paper), and covered the same material in the same order. In Fall, the final exam was given as an oral exam; in Spring, the final exam was written. The Fall semester had two sections totaling 53 students; the Spring semester had one section of 24 students.

Our assessment is in three parts. We begin by examining results from a survey sent to students following the completion of both semesters. First, section 4.1 investigates quantitative measures from the survey, focusing on perceptions of exam difficulty. Second, section 4.2 analyzes free-form survey comments, with an emphasis on student reactions to oral exams (from the Fall semester). Lastly, section 4.3 provides our own reflections, and a break-down of instructor time for the two styles of exam.

The results in this section are not statistically significant, due to the small sample size and low survey response rate (noted in section 4.1). Nevertheless, we find the results encouraging, and glean positive indicators from student comments and our reflections.

4.1 Survey

To begin, we examined quantitative data from student surveys. Some of this data is summarized in table 1. Here we see the total number of students who took each type of exam, and the number of students who responded to our post-semester survey. Clearly, response rates were low (e.g., 21% for Spring 2018 students who took the written exam); as noted above, the results cannot be considered statistically significant. We instead view them as preliminary indicators worthy of further study.

The next column, "Course Grade Difficulty," asked students to rate the difficulty of obtaining their desired course grade (compared with other courses). Specifically, we asked:

> "On a scale from −5 to +5, how difficult was earning the grade you desired (or needed) in this class?"

Negative numbers indicated that our CS0/1 course was easier than other courses, while positive numbers indicated that it was harder. The absolute numbers here are of lesser importance. Our key observation is that final exam style (which is the final thing that students will remember about a course) did not impact student perception of overall course difficulty for our small sample of students.

The column labeled "Relative Exam Difficulty" asked students to rate the difficulty of all exams (not just the final) relative to homework assignments. Specifically, we asked:

> "How relatively difficult were the homeworks and exams?"

Negative numbers indicated that homework was harder, while positive numbers indicated that exams were harder. Note that both groups completed the same set of homeworks (differing only in their final exam style). Once again, we see similar responses regardless of exam style.

We also asked students to rate the difficulty of their final exam relative to the difficulty of prior exams; students could respond that the exam was "Easier than the first two exams, " "Harder than the first two exams," or "About the same." Note that mid-semester exams were written (not oral) in both semesters. Figure 2 shows the results, given as the percentage of respondents who selected each option. The vast majority of students indicated that their final exam was either easier or about the same difficulty as the prior exams, with oral exams being marked as "easier" slightly more often. Of course, with our small sample size, these results may not be entirely representative of all students. Nevertheless, we consider this result encouraging, especially when coupled with the data on

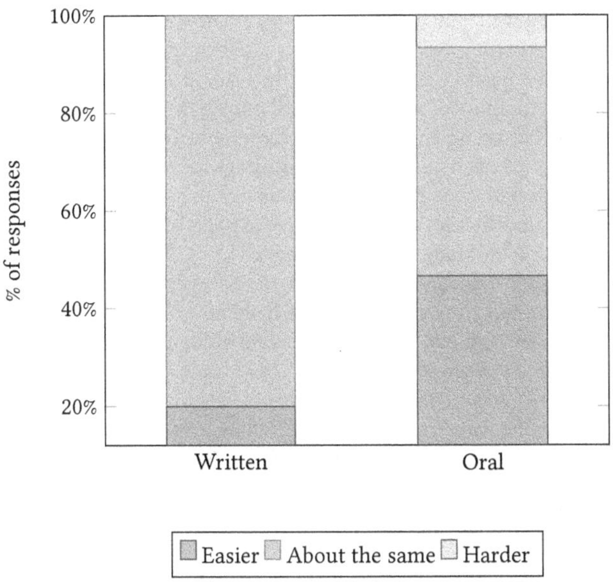

Figure 2: Relative difficulty of final vs. mid-semester exams

course difficulty and exams relative to homework. Our goal was not to make oral exams easier or harder than their written counterparts; rather, we hoped oral exams might spur deeper engagement with (and evaluation of) course material.

Finally, returning to the last column of table 1, we asked students to estimate the total number of hours they studied for the final exam (column "Study Hours"). Students who had an oral exam self-reported studying over 50% more than those who took another written exam. We again take this as a positive indicator. One feasible explanation is that students felt that they required a deeper understanding in order to have a *conversation* about a course topic.

4.2 Student Feedback

To better understand student reactions to oral versus written exams, we also asked students to provide free-form comments with their survey. Some common themes emerged. Students found the oral exam unique, and enjoyed the conversational style.

> "It was unlike any final I have ever taken before [...] I think that it really showed if you learned the material or not."

> "I liked the oral exam [...] it allows students to talk out their thinking process which I believe to be helpful."

> "I liked how exams were done as reflections of the examples we did in class."

> "It kind of made me feel like I was the teacher, which was pretty fun!"

The fact that the instructor could prompt students, who were given the freedom to explain and talk through answers, was also positive.

> "I liked the not having to write. Also being able to personally explain answers."

> "I liked that [the instructor] helped you come to an answer if you were close. When he dropped key words it helped me remember the topic better and give a better answer."

Surprisingly, and contrary to some prior research [7, 8], two students explicitly noted feeling more comfortable and/or experiencing less anxiety in the oral exam setting.

> "I liked the oral exam more so than the paper exam because I felt more relaxed and was having a conversation that highlighted what I had learned from the class rather than an extremely rigid exam where I tend to second guess myself."

> "It was more forgiving. I could take my time. I also enjoyed the immediate feedback."

Of course, not all comments were positive. In contrast to the above quotes, one student explicitly noted:

> "I did not like the oral exam as it made me nervous"

Written exam comments were less insightful, likely because the format was so familiar to students. This comfort, though, should not be dismissed: it can be both an advantage (in reducing anxiety) and a disadvantage (students who are simply "good test takers").

> "I liked that the exam was very similarly laid out to previous exams so we were comfortable with it."

> "The exams were well presented & straightforward."

4.3 Instructor Impacts

As instructors, we noted both positive and negative aspects to our oral exam design. In preparing the exam, we found that we could focus on question content, and spent much less time worrying about question wording, since we could always clarify during the exam. Instead, we shifted our focus to the rubric, which (per section 3) had to be written ahead of time. This was a major challenge, though we suspect that our skill would improve with further practice, and as questions are re-used and refined.

We were also pleasantly surprised by some students who had fared poorly on prior written exams. We suspect that encouraging students to use examples to explain their answers was a major benefit. Multiple times during the exam, we witnessed a student struggle initially with a question, but, through giving a free-form example, recover from an earlier misstep. These are situations where, on a written exam, the student may have been unable to make progress.

Our class size (53 students) was large by oral exam standards, and we were initially concerned about our ability to schedule all students within our final exam week. However, scheduling all students in limited time slots was not an issue, despite the large number of students and single instructor. In one case, we had to make special arrangements with a student who had a late registration slot; the student was able to swap exam times with a classmate.

We also tracked instructor time commitment for the Fall and Spring semesters; figure 3 shows the results. The plot shows time broken down into pre-exam preparation, exam delivery (proctoring for the written exam, or individual meetings for the oral exam), and post-exam grading (for oral exams, this essentially consisted of verifying and entering grades). While we did track work time, the times shown are approximate: most preparation and grading time overlapped with other unrelated duties.

For direct comparison, we scaled the oral exam delivery time so as to match the (smaller) number of students who took the written exam. This was feasible because each student was given a standard, fixed amount of time (30 minutes) for the oral exam. Naturally, since

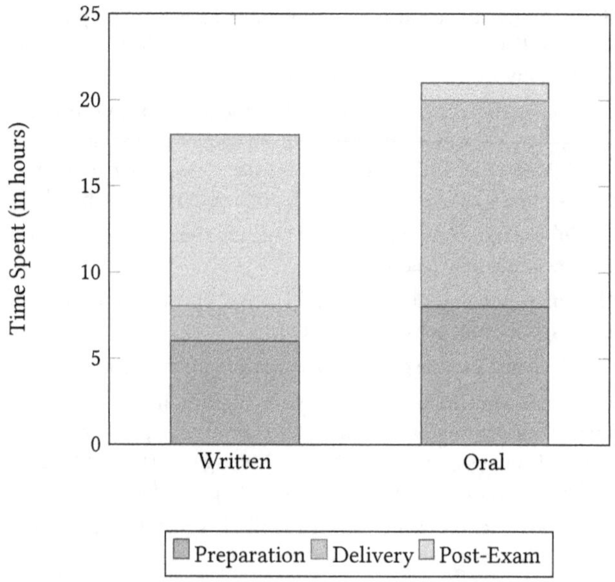

Figure 3: Instructor time spent on the exam (scaled to a 24 student class size)

we have only one semester of data for each exam type, we cannot compare their scalability. (For example, while adding one student to the oral exam adds exactly 30 minutes, it would be reasonable to assume that one additional written exam student would add significantly less post-exam grading time.) In all cases, we excluded additional time given to students with disabilities.

For our class sizes, our results are largely consistent with Roecker [13], who notes that overall time commitment for oral exams does not significantly exceed that of paper exams, but the time instead shifts from post-exam grading to time spent directly examining students. Overall, the oral exam required about 21 hours, while the written exam required 18. Preparation time was a significant factor, requiring 8 hours over the 6 required for the written exam. As noted previously, designing the check-box rubric was the primary time contributor prior to exam delivery.

4.4 Discussion and Practical Implications

Overall, we were pleased with our implementation of oral exams. Student and instructor reactions were positive, and we genuinely felt that students demonstrated a deeper level of engagement with the material.

We felt confident in our assessment of students' knowledge. As previously noted, we were able to directly interact with students to avoid question wording issues, and provide scripted hints so that students were not blocked from fully demonstrating the depth of their understanding. Rubric scores seemed to correspond with our perception of a student's performance during the exam. The only major exception was that the difference between B and C students often felt artificial (though this is often true of written exams as well). We attribute this, partially, to the rigidity of the check-box rubric; some method of adding more flexibility for the instructor would be welcome. Balancing this with our stated goals of equity and consistency, however, poses an interesting challenge.

On the positive side, our check-box rubric allowed the instructor to remain focused on discussion during the exam. It also gave a clear-cut argument for grade assignments; though, in our case, no students challenged the grading afterward. Ensuring equity in rubric design is an ever-present difficulty. Involving more instructors in rubric design may help to decrease bias (though this struggle is certainly not unique to oral exams).

Another challenge involves students discovering exam questions prior to their time slot. While we have no evidence that this occurred, we also had no way to prevent students from discussing the exam between sessions. In fact, our exams were given over the course of 5 days, so we consider this to be a major risk. In smaller courses, the danger could be mitigated by scheduling all exams in sequence, but this was not feasible for us (with 53 students).

Instructor time commitment, though not wholly unreasonable, was significant. For comparisons in section 4.3, we calculated as if both sections had 24 students. In actuality, the oral exam group of 54 students required 27 hours of dedicated examination time (one student was allowed double time). This was a burden for a single instructor, who, fortunately, had few other commitments during finals week. Regularly scaling to class sizes larger than 20 or 30 students appears challenging. With sufficiently-detailed rubrics, and well-scripted prompts, using multiple instructors (or TAs) may be an option.

5 CONCLUSION

Through our design, implementation, and evaluation, we find positive signs of effectiveness for oral exams in an introductory computer science course. Both qualitative and quantitative student reactions were largely positive. Students enjoyed the unique conversational style, and indicated that the oral exam was of comparable difficulty to a written exam, though they spent more time preparing. While instructor time commitments did increase slightly, we found ourselves better able to assess student knowledge at exam time.

Perhaps most importantly, though, our experiences and findings support the need for more research into oral exams in undergraduate computer science curricula. Scaling to larger class sizes while continuing to keep instructor time commitments reasonable and maintain consistency across students are open challenges. Further rigorous assessment of student reactions, student performance and grade impacts, and instructor attitudes would also be valuable, and would help pave the way for ever-improving assessment in an ever-changing discipline.

ACKNOWLEDGMENTS

The author would like to thank Dr. Kathleen Timmerman and Dr. Michael Goldweber for their advice and assistance with this paper and oral exam designs. He would also like to thank the members of the Xavier University *Center for Teaching Excellence* for their support. As previously noted, this work was undertaken while the author was a faculty member at Xavier University. Opinions, findings, conclusions, or recommendations expressed herein do not necessarily reflect the views of Xavier University or the author's present affiliated university.

REFERENCES

[1] Ulf Asklund and Lars Bendix. 2003. Oral vs. written evaluation of students. *LTHs 1: Pedagogisk inspirationskonferens, Lund, Sweden* (2003).

[2] Ulf Asklund and Lars Bendix. 2003. A Software Configuration Management Course. In *Software Configuration Management, ICSE Workshops SCM 2001 and SCM 2003 Toronto, Canada, May 14-15, 2001 and Portland, OR, USA, May 9-10, 2003. Selected Papers (Lecture Notes in Computer Science)*, Bernhard Westfechtel and André van der Hoek (Eds.), Vol. 2649. Springer, 245–258. https://doi.org/10.1007/3-540-39195-9_18

[3] Barbara Gross Davis. 2009. *Tools for teaching.* John Wiley & Sons.

[4] Ian Gent, Bill Johnston, and Patrick Prosser. 1999. Thinking on your feet in undergraduate computer science: A constructivist approach to developing and assessing critical thinking. *Teaching in Higher Education* 4, 4 (1999), 511–522.

[5] Hasmik Gharibyan. 2005. Assessing students' knowledge: oral exams vs. written tests. In *Proceedings of the 10th Annual SIGCSE Conference on Innovation and Technology in Computer Science Education, ITiCSE 2005, Caparica, Portugal, June 27-29, 2005*, José C. Cunha, William M. Fleischman, Viera K. Proulx, and João Lourenço (Eds.). ACM, 143–147. https://doi.org/10.1145/1067445.1067487

[6] M Hairer. approx 2007. Oral examinations/presentations. *Mathematics Research Centre, University of Warwick, UK* (approx 2007). http://homepages.warwick.ac.uk/~masbm/PCAPP/Projects/Oral_exams.pdf

[7] Elaine Hewitt and Jean Stephenson. 2012. Foreign language anxiety and oral exam performance: A replication of Phillips's MLJ study. *The Modern Language Journal* 96, 2 (2012), 170–189.

[8] Mark Huxham, Fiona Campbell, and Jenny Westwood. 2012. Oral versus written assessments: a test of student performance and attitudes. *Assessment & Evaluation in Higher Education* 37, 1 (2012), 125–136.

[9] Paola Iannone and A Simpson. 2012. Oral assessment in mathematics: implementation and outcomes. *Teaching Mathematics and Its Applications: International Journal of the IMA* 31, 4 (2012), 179–190.

[10] Gordon Joughin. 2010. *A short guide to oral assessment.* Leeds Met Press in association with University of Wollongong.

[11] Barbara M Kehm. 2001. Oral examinations at German universities. *Assessment in Education: Principles, Policy & Practice* 8, 1 (2001), 25–31.

[12] Muhammed Ashraf Memon, Gordon Rowland Joughin, and Breda Memon. 2010. Oral assessment and postgraduate medical examinations: establishing conditions for validity, reliability and fairness. *Advances in health sciences education* 15, 2 (2010), 277–289.

[13] Lee Roecker. 2007. Using oral examination as a technique to assess student understanding and teaching effectiveness. *Journal of Chemical Education* 84, 10 (2007), 1663.

[14] Kathryn E. Sanders and Robert McCartney. 2003. Program assessment tools in computer science: a report from the trenches. In *Proceedings of the 34th SIGCSE Technical Symposium on Computer Science Education, 2003, Reno, Nevada, USA, February 19-23, 2003*, Scott Grissom, Deborah Knox, Daniel T. Joyce, and Wanda Dann (Eds.). ACM, 31–35. https://doi.org/10.1145/611892.611926

[15] Yitong Zhao. 2018. Impact of Oral Exams on a Thermodynamics Course Performance. In *ASEE Zone IV Conference.* ASEE Conferences, Boulder, Colorado. https://peer.asee.org/29617.

On the Effect of Question Ordering on Performance and Confidence in Computer Science Examinations

Brian Harrington
Dept. of Computer and Mathematical Sciences
University of Toronto Scarborough
brian.harrington@utsc.utoronto.ca

Jingyiran Li
Dept. of Computer and Mathematical Sciences
University of Toronto Scarborough
jingyiran.li@mail.utoronto.ca

Mohamed Moustafa
Dept. of Computer and Mathematical Sciences
University of Toronto Scarborough
mohammad.moustafa@mail.utoronto.ca

Marzieh Ahmadzadeh
Dept. of Computer and Mathematical Sciences
University of Toronto Scarborough
marzieh.ahmadzadeh@utoronto.ca

Nick Cheng
Dept. of Computer and Mathematical Sciences
University of Toronto Scarborough
nick@utsc.utoronto.ca

ABSTRACT

Most computer science examinations tend to start with the easiest questions and progress towards the more difficult material. Whether this is because of the highly scaffolded nature of the course, an attempt to 'ease students in', or simply by convention, is unclear. However, there is a great deal of data from the psychology literature to suggest that human perception of the difficulty or discomfort of a task is disproportionately affected by the last part of the task completed. Therefore, is it possible that by structuring our exams in an easy-to-hard fashion, we are causing students to perceive the test as more difficult than it actually is? Could changing the question order allow us to change students' perception of their own achievement? What effect could this have on actual performance? This paper attempts to answer these questions by randomly assigning students to write exams ordered either easy-to-hard (referred as 'Easy-Difficult') or hard-to-easy ('Difficult-Easy), then ask them to predict their marks on per-question basis. We find that the question ordering has a small but not statistically significant effect on the performance, and virtually no effect on predicted marks when treating the entire class as one unstratified sample. However, the effect was significant for certain subgroups created via stratification. In particular, swapping the order of the questions may have hurt the performance of international students, but significantly raised both the performance and confidence of female students.

CCS CONCEPTS

• **Social and professional topics → Computing education; Computer science education; CS1;**

SIGCSE '19, February 27-March 2, 2019, Minneapolis, MN, USA

ACM ISBN 978-1-4503-5890-3/19/02...$15.00
https://doi.org/10.1145/3287324.3287398

KEYWORDS

CS1, examination, question ordering, confidence, gender, international students

ACM Reference Format:
Brian Harrington, Jingyiran Li, Mohamed Moustafa, Marzieh Ahmadzadeh, and Nick Cheng. 2019. On the Effect of Question Ordering on Performance and Confidence in Computer Science Examinations. In *Proceedings of the 50th ACM Technical Symposium on Computer Science Education (SIGCSE '19), February 27-March 2, 2019, Minneapolis, MN, USA.* ACM, New York, NY, USA, 7 pages. https://doi.org/10.1145/3287324.3287398

1 INTRODUCTION

When creating final examinations for courses, the natural tendency is to either include questions in the order in which they were covered in class, or to start with the easiest questions and work towards the most difficult ones. Quite often these two orderings are the same. However, there is much research in the psychology and education literature that shows us that human perception of the difficulty or unpleasantness of a task follows the 'peak-end' rule rule[8]. This rule says that a subject's perception is generally estimated as the mean between the most extreme and last remembered experiences in a task. Translating this idea to examinations implies that students perceptions of the difficulty of a test will be largely influenced by the most difficult question and the last question attempted. If the exam is ordered easy-to-hard, assuming students attempt the questions in order, then the hardest questions will likely be doubly weighted. If the order is reversed, encouraging students to start with the hardest problems and end with the easiest, then the weighting should be shared between the hardest and easiest questions, thus giving the student an overall reduced perception of the difficulty of the test.

In this paper, we first replicate and then extend our previous work which uses students estimation of their own marks on an introductory computer science final examination as a proxy for confidence and difficulty[6]. We support the initial study's hypotheses that there is a strong correlation between predictive ability and exam performance, and that student perception is linked more strongly to previous mark history than to actual exam performance.

We fail to replicate the study's finding that male students overestimate marks more than females, however we then extend the study to look at domestic and international students and find that the male overestimation trend is present in domestic students, but not international.

After replicating the initial study, we move on to evaluating the performance and grade estimation of students by question ordering. Our initial finding is that, when taking the class as a whole, there is no evidence of any impact of re-ordering the question. However, when analyzing sub-groups, we find that reversing the traditional ordering of easy-hard may have a negative impact on the performance of international students. Most interestingly, we find that the non-traditional hard-easy ordering has a statistically significant impact on female students, slightly improving their performance, but greatly improving their confidence.

2 BACKGROUND

The effect of question ordering on multiple choice tests has been long studied for both general knowledge[17] and topic specific questions [14]. While results show that the ordering of the questions from the easiest to most difficult results in more optimistic prediction of performance by participant regardless of where in a test participants are asked to estimate their performance, it affects participants' judgment of test fairness [5] and the difficulty rating of the questions [18].

Balch [1] reported that students perform better if questions are given in the same order as the material covered in lectures or presented in textbook as opposed to when the questions are ordered randomly. This result was later contradicted by Neely et al., [12] who ran three experiments with sequential and random order multiple choice question and found no significant differences in terms of performance. They did however find that randomizing the questions increased students' anxiety.

Gender differences in student populations has also been a topic of interest for many research activities ranging from performance evaluation and leadership ability [7, 9] to their attitude towards technology [10, 13]. A few studies have researched the gap between students' predictive and actual performance with regards to their gender[15]. The general findings have been that while there was no significant difference between female and male students' performance in Introduction to Computer Science courses, female students regularly predict their marks significantly lower than male students [6] These results supports the claim that female students underestimate their performance in computer science courses[3]. The reasons behind this low self-efficacy of female students have been discussed in numerous studies. Stereotype threats [4, 16] and lack of female role models [11] are regularly cited as causes.

One part of this study attempts to replicate earlier work[6] where students were asked to predict their own marks after completing the final examination of an introductory computer science course. They found that exam performance was strongly correlated with predictive ability, students with prior programming experience tended to over-predict their marks, and that while there was no difference in mark between male and female students, male students over-predicted significantly more than females.

3 METHODOLOGY

CSCA08: Introduction to Computer Science I is an introductory computer science (CS1) course at The University of Toronto Scarborough focusing on computer science fundamentals for first year students intending to major or specialize in Computer Science. The final exam for the course is a three hour pen and paper exam worth 40% of the final grade, and is cumulative across the entire semester. A total of 243 students completed the course, 62 females and 154 males (the other 27 choosing not to specify). 104 students were domestic, 116 were international, with an additional 23 not permitting access to their status information.

Following the methodology of [6], a bonus question was added to the final exam with the following question:

> Predict your mark on each question of this examination. If your estimate is within 10% of your actual grade, you get this bonus mark.

As with the prior study, marks were awarded to all students who completed the question with sensible results regardless of how close they were to their final marks.

After the non-bonus questions had been prepared by the teaching team[1], the questions were presented to a group of experienced instructors in random order. The instructor were then asked to rank the questions in order of difficulty, as perceived by a CS1 student. The opinions were unanimous with the initial suspicions of the teaching team, and thus a fully ordered ranking of question difficulty was established.

Two exams were prepared, version A (hereafter called easy-difficult) ordered the questions from easiest to most difficult, and version B (hereafter called difficult-easy) ordered the questions from most difficult to easiest. The same questions were used on both tests, and in both tests the bonus questions remained at the end. The only other distinction on the tests was a small **A** or **B** in the corner of the cover page, which, to the best of our knowledge, went entirely unnoticed by the students in the course. Exams were distributed randomly so that each student had an equal chance of receiving either type of exam.

Student gender was determined by the student's choice of honorific, as self declared in the university administration system ('Mr.' or 'M.' for males, 'Mrs.', 'Miss.', 'Ms', 'Mme', or 'Mlle' for female. An additional option of 'Mx.' was offered, but not chosen by any students in this study), students could also choose not to declare an honorific.

Domestic or international status was determined by the student's current tuition status, whether they were paying domestic or international fees for the course.

We did not have access to a student prior programming experience survey, so we were unable to replicate that part of the initial study or compare the effects of question ordering by prior experience.

All data was collected and interpreted post-hoc, and anonymized by members of the study group who had no ability to set or alter student grades. To determine the effect of the test ordering, we performed factorial ANOVA for each of the following: actual grade,

[1]In the interest of full disclosure, two of the members of the teaching team are co-authors on this paper, however they had no role in the marking of the examinations or the statistical calculations of the data

predicted grade, and over-prediction of grade. The ANOVA assumptions hold based on results from *qqnorm* plots, residual plots, Cook's Distance plots, and leverage plots. By Bartlett's test for homogeneity of variance[2], the model has constancy of variance holding under each factor ($p = 0.4835$).

4 RESULTS

In this section we will first explain how we replicated an existing study and then expanded upon it. We will then provide the results for our question ordering study.

4.1 Replication

In the first phase of the study, we attempted to replicate our earlier findings[6] with a new cohort of students. The results will be presented here in brief. For further discussion and analysis, the authors refer the reader to the original paper.

The correlational results were found to hold with similar results. Actual and predicted mark showed a strong correlation (Spearman $\rho = 0.702, p < 0.001$). As did mark with both prediction error and prediction error magnitude ($\rho = -0.292, p < 0.001$ and $\rho = -0.293, p < 0.001$).

As in the initial study, we found that exam under-performers over-predicted their marks more than their counterparts, and the results were strongly statistically significant (over-performer mean = 9.575, under-performer mean = 14.848, t-test $p = 0.0017$).

With respect to gender, we also found no significant difference between the actual grades of male and female students (male mean = 68.301 female mean = 64.486, t-test $p = 0.1379$), but unlike the previous study, we did not find a statistically significant difference in the predictions of male and female students (male mean = 80.308, female mean = 76.955, t-test $p = 0.2112$). While male students did predict slightly higher averages, they also performed slightly better, so that the over-prediction was essentially the same for both groups (male mean = 12.006, female mean = 12.470). However, this may be due to the confounding nature of question ordering and gender which will be further explored in Section 4.3.3.

4.1.1 Extension of Replicated Study. One additional piece of information we included in the study was domestic vs international student status which was not considered in the initial study. We found that in this case, there was no statistically significant difference in either the actual or predicted marks of domestic or international students. It can be discerned from Figure 1 that the predicted and the actual grade of international students in both genders have almost identical means, in particular, the average actual grade for male and female international students are 79.54298 and 79.60192, respectively (t test $p = 0.808$). The average predicted mark for male and female international students are 66.74737 and 65.99038, respectively (t test $p = 0.9864$). Furthermore, the overprediction of grades appeared very similar for both genders. On the contrary, the difference in the average of predicted and actual grade for the domestic students in both genders appeared visibly different from Figure 1. In addition, male domestic students seemed to overpredict their grade compared to the domestic female students.

While we were unable to replicate the effects found in the initial study with respect to gender confidence, separating the data by both gender and student status shows some interesting effects. As seen in Figure 1, the difference in confidence (as estimated by over-prediction of marks) can be clearly seen in domestic students, but was almost non-existent in international students. The average overprediction for male international students is 12.49386, for female international students is 13.05769 (t test $p = 0.824$). While the mean of overprediction for male domestic students is 13.1, and for female domestic students is 10.3825 (t test $p = 0.5926$).

However, none of the differences are statistically significant based on the results reported by a two-sample t-test despite of the obvious differences of the values. Such a result can be attributed to the presence of interaction effects which rendering the t-test an insufficiently robust hypothesis testing procedure.

4.2 Question Ordering

The primary concern of the study was the impact of question ordering on exam performance. To that end, we found that while students did perform slightly better in the easy-difficult ordering group with an average grade of 68.26620 versus an average of 66.21687 for the difficult-easy ordering, the result were not significantly different (t test $p = 0.4192$). Furthermore, we found that the average predicted grades of the two groups were nearly identical with a mean of 79.77817 for easy-difficult ordering group versus a mean of 78.90301 for difficult-easy ordering group. However, the difference is statistically insignificant with a $p = 0.7174$. This runs counter to our initial assumptions, and the generally accepted 'peak-end' rule, which would expect students ending with the easier questions to have perceived the exam as being easier, and thus predict higher marks on average, however as can be seen in Figure 2, the question ordering did not seem to have a large impact in either direction. This may be attributed to the confounding nature of question ordering and gender which demonstrated that the effect of these factors seem to cancel out. The ANOVA results suggested that the interaction effect between gender and question ordering in all students' predicted grade as well as their overprediction of the grade is indeed statistically significant with a p-value of p=0.0135 and p = 0.00415, respectively. If the significance of the interaction effect between gender and question ordering is not neglected, then it must be concluded that the main effect of the corresponding factors, namely, gender and question ordering, on the overprediction of grade is also statistically significant. Furthermore, the interaction variable of gender and question ordering is a potential effect modifier which differentially modifies/influences the observed main effects of these factors on the outcome response variable (whether it is actual grade, predicted grade, or the overprediction of grade) depending on the combinations of factorial levels as seen in Section 4.3.3.

4.3 Sub-Group Effects

Our initial analysis indicates that question ordering has little to no effect on students. However, this is taking the student population as a homogeneous group. Indeed, the main effect of question ordering on students' actual grade is statistically insignificant with the p-value of p=0.342 for the F-test. Unsurprisingly, its F-test has a p-value of 0.342 suggesting statistical insignificance of the main effect of question ordering does not affect students' prediction when considered as a whole without considering sub-groups. Therefore,

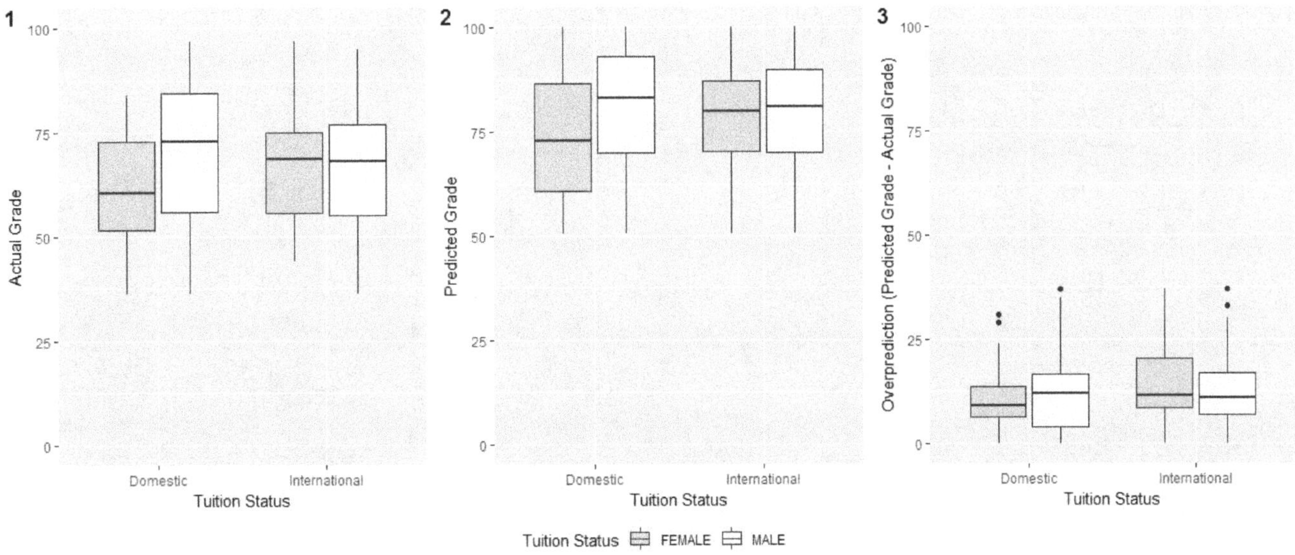

Figure 1: Exam Mark by Tuition Status and Gender

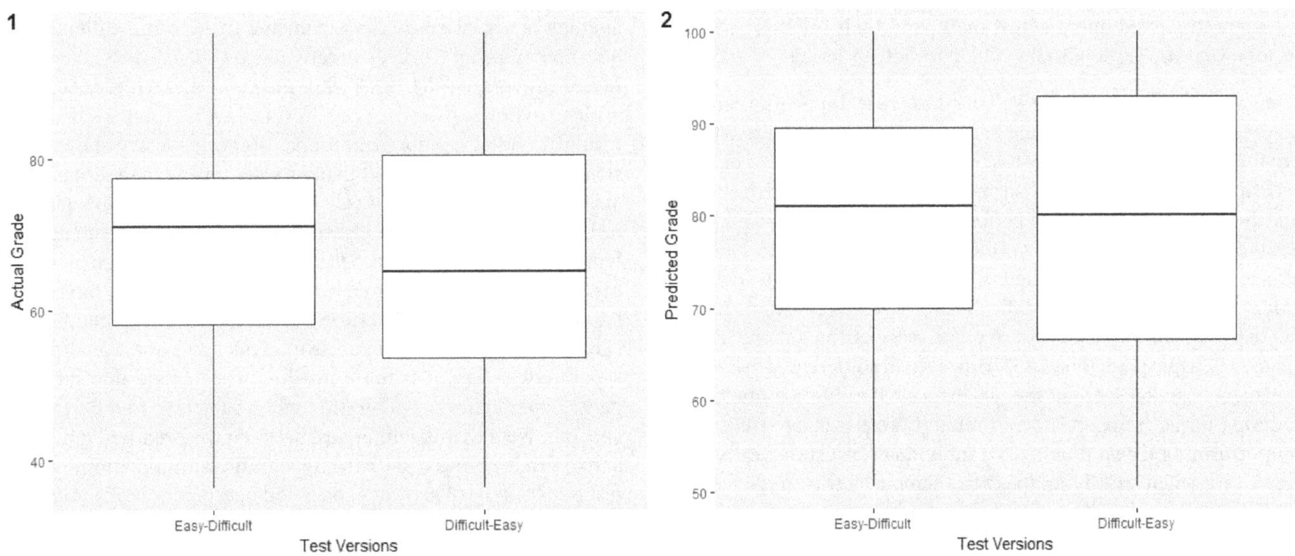

Figure 2: Exam Mark by Question Ordering

we further analyzed the data to determine whether the effect was equally benign in all sub-groups.

4.3.1 Domestic vs International Students. When the data is organized by student status (domestic vs international students) as in Figure 3, we can see that for the traditional easy-difficult ordering, the domestic and international students perform almost identically, but the international students predict slightly higher marks with an average prediction of 80.96047 while the domestic students attained an average of 77.9625. When the question order is reversed, it has very little impact on the domestic students performance, but does appear to boost their confidence slightly with an average prediction of 79.68953 , while it appears to have a negative impact on both the performance and predicted grades for international students who possessed an actual grade of 64.63375 and a predicted grade of 78.0575 on average.

The data in Figure 3 suggest that question ordering appear to affect international students more heavily in comparison to the domestic students. However, we found that in this case, there was no statistically significant difference in the actual marks (F-test p value p=0.493), predicted marks (F-test p value p = 0.6258), and their difference (F-test p-value p = 0.44949) of domestic or international students based on the ANOVA model of regressing each of the

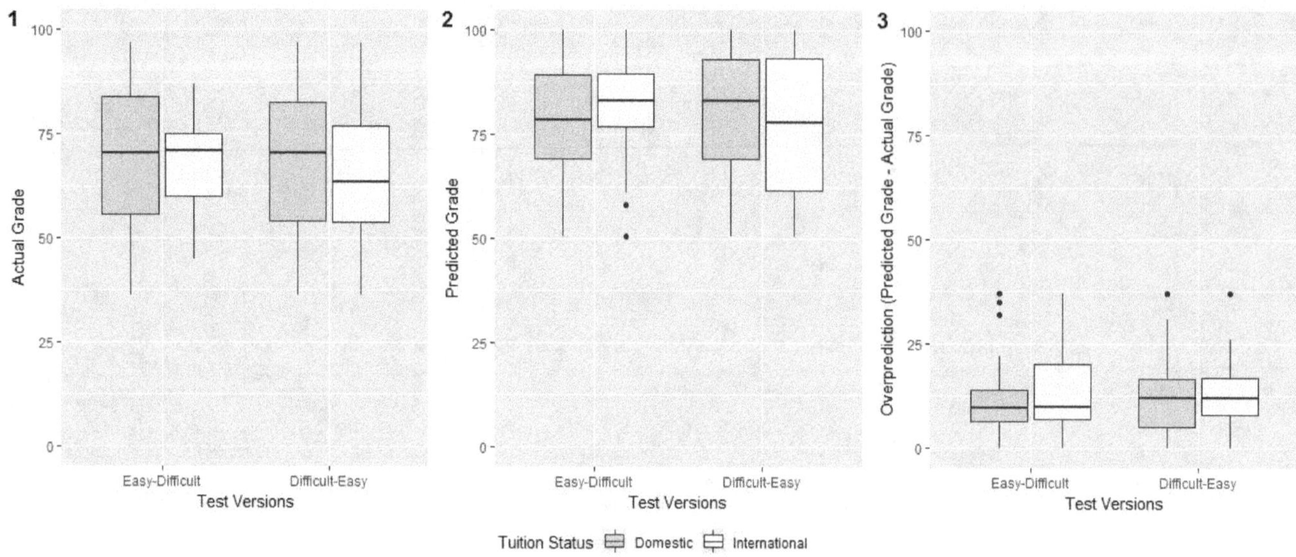

Figure 3: Exam Mark by Question Ordering and Tuition Status

values of predicted mark, actual mark, and their difference on 3 factors: Gender, Tuition Status, and Question Ordering.

4.3.2 Exam Performance Relative to Expectations. As seen in Figure 4, the question ordering had little effect on students when grouped by their performance relative to expectations. It can be discerned that students who have generally performed better throughout the semester continue to perform well on the final exam. Students who underperformed on the final exam seemed to be less affected by the question ordering considering the mean for the students who took the easy-difficult exam obtain a score of 55.410 while predicting 71.73 and the average score of the difficult-easy exam is 54 while predicting 70.52. However, the differences between the average actual score of the two exams with different question ordering for both the underperforming (t test $p = 0.5555$) and the outperforming (t test $p = 0.1831$) individuals are statistically insignificant when stratifying the entire sample by this single factor of performance. Similarly, the difference between the predicted grade of both question ordering groups does not show statistical significance with a t-test $p = 0.7489$ for the underperforming group and $p = 0.1636$ for the overperforming group. This result could be attributed to multicollinearity of the predictors (term test marks) of the regression model that is used to stratify students into outperforming and underperforming groups. Multicollinearity could render the regression model unstable in terms of their prediction power and accuracy. Furthermore, bias can be enlarged and obscure the inferences solely basing on t-tests.

4.3.3 Gender. When the data is organized by gender, the effects of question ordering become quite stark. While the effects on the population overall are negligible, this appears to be because of offsetting opposite impacts on male and female students. While male students appear to have performed better in the more traditional easy-difficult exam setup, reversing the order seems to have all but eliminated the difference in performance the difference of the average of actual grade for female and male in the difficult-easy question ordering has been greatly narrowed. Female students obtained an average of 64.79762 while male students achieved 66.69758 with an average difference of 1.9 on the actual exam grade. Interestingly, while the more traditional ordering clearly showed the strong male over-prediction that we were unable to replicate when analyzing the tests without considering the order, the difficult-easy ordering produced almost identical predicted marks for males and females, and in fact produced the opposite effect, with females over-predicting more than their male counterparts. Since the interaction variable of gender and question ordering is an effect modifier, we cannot interpret the main effects of gender and question ordering separately, rather, it is more justified to conclude that different genders perform very differently when subjected to different test versions. Note that the difference between the predicted grade and actual grade shows a statistically significant interaction term (F-test p-value p = 0.00659) of gender and question ordering, the large difference of grade over-prediction under different test versions for both genders can be attributed to the confounding effects of gender with question ordering and potentially tuition status.

5 CONCLUSIONS

In this paper, we set out to replicate an existing study on confidence and self prediction in CS1 students. We were able to reproduce all of the findings in the areas replicated, aside from the relative over-prediction of marks by male students. However, we then extended this study by subdividing the groups by status (domestic vs international). While this division did not have an impact on its own, the data shows that the gender confidence gap previously found does not hold equally across domestic and international students. However, a larger sample size is required to establish statistical significance.

This study is based on a single examination with a single cohort of students, though it does replicate (most of) the results of our

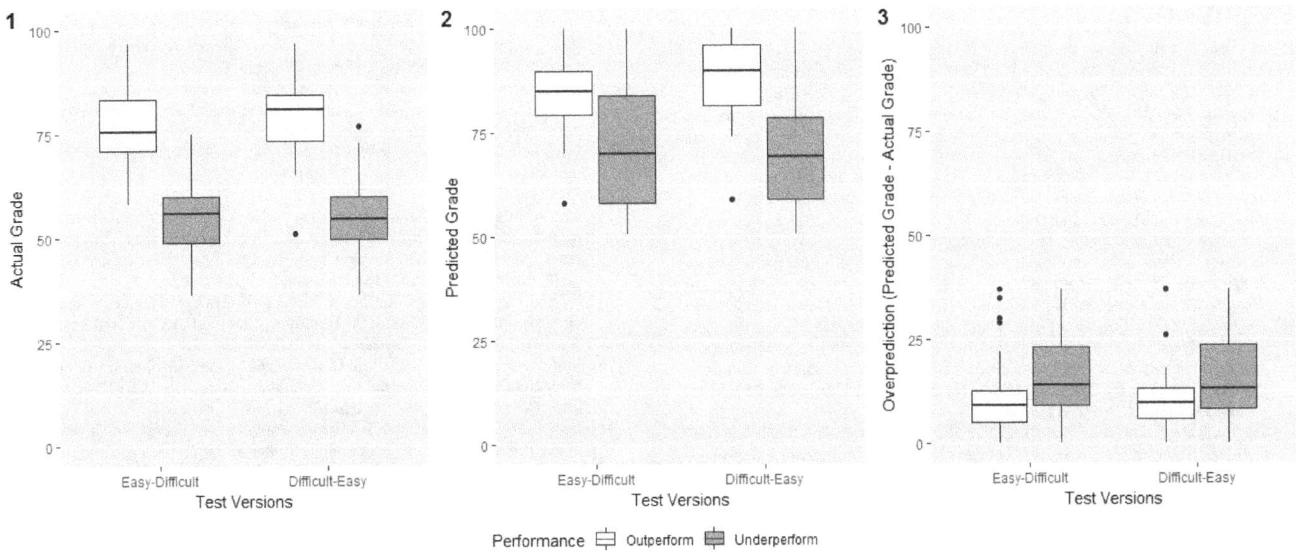

Figure 4: Exam Mark by Question Ordering and Term Test Performance

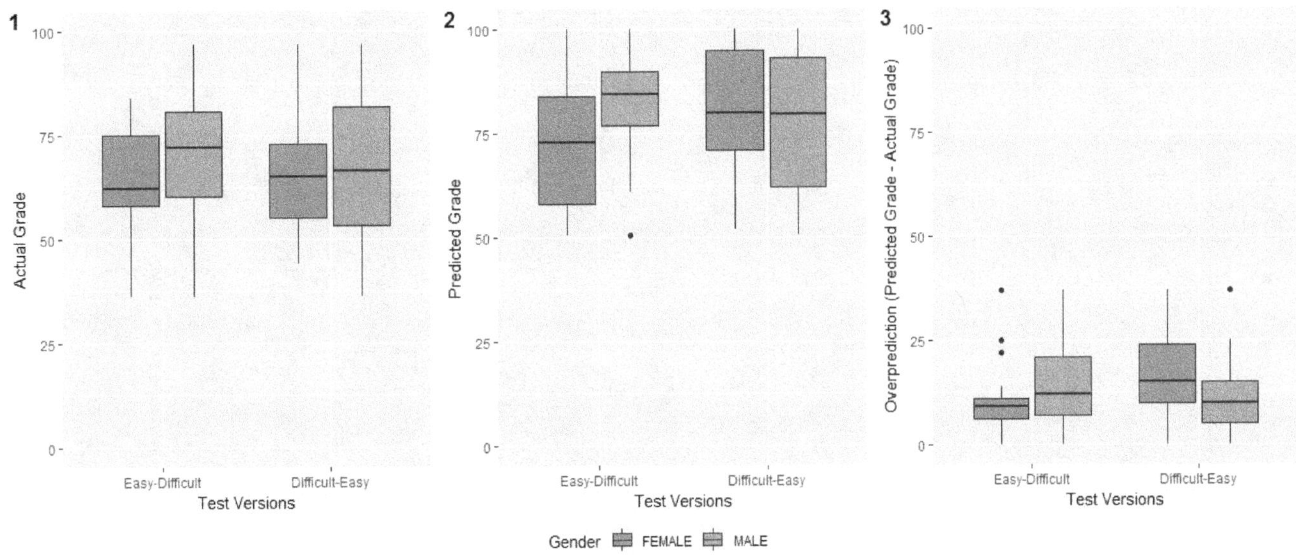

Figure 5: Exam Mark by Question Ordering and Gender

earlier studies. The questions were not specifically designed for the purposes of this study, so it is possible that floor and ceiling effects may have contributed to the results or lack thereof. The data is not conclusive enough to recommend a specific question ordering for all students, nor indeed to say conclusively that there is a global impact of question ordering. The results do show that question ordering can have significant effects on certain sub-groups, but further work and replication will be needed to determine the magnitude and direction of these effects across populations and to begin to provide actionable guidance on question ordering for examinations.

Our initial assumption that we would see an impact of the peak-end rule when re-ordering exam questions proved to be false for the student population as a whole. However, this was because the effect was only present in females, and actually reversed in males. Further work is needed to explain why re-ordering would have an opposite impact on males and females. However it is clear from this initial study that the simple assumption that exams should be structured with the easiest questions first and the hardest questions last needs to be challenged, especially as this ordering seems to have a negative impact on both the performance and confidence of female students.

REFERENCES

[1] William R. Balch. 1989. Item Order Affects Performance on Multiple-Choice Exams. *Teaching of Psychology* 16, 2 (1989), 75–77. https://doi.org/10.1207/s15328023top1602_9 arXiv:https://doi.org/10.1207/s15328023top1602$_9$

[2] Maurice S Bartlett. 1954. A note on the multiplying factors for various χ 2 approximations. *Journal of the Royal Statistical Society. Series B (Methodological)* (1954), 296–298.

[3] Tor Busch. 1995. Gender differences in self-efficacy and attitudes toward computers. *Journal of educational computing research* 12, 2 (1995), 147–158.

[4] Joel Cooper. 2006. The digital divide: The special case of gender. *Journal of Computer Assisted Learning* 22, 5 (2006), 320–334.

[5] Michael L. Dean. 1973. The Impact of Exam Question Order Effects on Student Evaluations. *The Journal of Psychology* 85, 2 (1973), 245–248. https://doi.org/10.1080/00223980.1973.9915653 arXiv:https://doi.org/10.1080/00223980.1973.9915653

[6] Brian Harrington, Shichong Peng, Xiaomeng Jin, and Minhaz Khan. 2018. Gender, Confidence, and Mark Prediction in CS Examinations. In *Proceedings of the 23rd Annual ACM Conference on Innovation and Technology in Computer Science Education (ITiCSE 2018)*. ACM, New York, NY, USA, 230–235. https://doi.org/10.1145/3197091.3197116

[7] Nagore Iriberri and Pedro Rey-Biel. 2017. Stereotypes are only a threat when beliefs are reinforced: On the sensitivity of gender differences in performance under competition to information provision. *Journal of Economic Behavior Organization* 135 (2017), 99 – 111. https://doi.org/10.1016/j.jebo.2017.01.012

[8] Daniel Kahneman and Richard H Thaler. 2006. Anomalies: Utility maximization and experienced utility. *Journal of Economic Perspectives* 20, 1 (2006), 221–234.

[9] Harsh K. Luthar. [n. d.]. Gender differences in evaluation of performance and leadership ability: Autocratic vs. democratic managers. *Sex Roles* 35, 5 ([n. d.]), 337–361. https://doi.org/10.1007/BF01664773

[10] Anahita Mahzari and Marzieh Ahmadzadeh. 2013. Finding Gender Preferences in E-Commerce Website Design by an Experimental Approach. *International Journal of Applied Information Systems* 5, 2 (2013).

[11] David M Marx and Jasmin S Roman. 2002. Female role models: Protecting womenâĂŹs math test performance. *Personality and Social Psychology Bulletin* 28, 9 (2002), 1183–1193.

[12] Darlene L Neely, Frederick J Springston, and Stephen JH McCann. 1994. Does item order affect performance on multiple-choice exams? *Teaching of Psychology* 21, 1 (1994), 44–45.

[13] Antonio Padilla-MelÃĺndez, Ana Rosa del Aguila-Obra, and Aurora Garrido-Moreno. 2013. Perceived playfulness, gender differences and technology acceptance model in a blended learning scenario. *Computers Education* 63 (2013), 306 – 317. https://doi.org/10.1016/j.compedu.2012.12.014

[14] II Pettijohn, F Terry, and Matthew F Sacco. 2007. Multiple-Choice Exam Question Order Influences on Student Performance, Completion Time, and Perceptions. *Journal of Instructional Psychology* 34, 3 (2007).

[15] Monika Sieverding and Sabine C. Koch. 2009. (Self-)Evaluation of computer competence: How gender matters. *Computers Education* 52, 3 (2009), 696 – 701. https://doi.org/10.1016/j.compedu.2008.11.016

[16] Jessi L Smith and Camille S Johnson. 2006. A stereotype boost or choking under pressure? Positive gender stereotypes and men who are low in domain identification. *Basic and Applied Social Psychology* 28, 1 (2006), 51–63.

[17] Yana Weinstein and Henry L. Roediger. 2010. Retrospective bias in test performance: Providing easy items at the beginning of a test makes students believe they did better on it. *Memory & Cognition* 38, 3 (01 Apr 2010), 366–376. https://doi.org/10.3758/MC.38.3.366

[18] Yana Weinstein and Henry L. Roediger. 2012. The effect of question order on evaluations of test performance: how does the bias evolve? *Memory & Cognition* 40, 5 (01 Jul 2012), 727–735. https://doi.org/10.3758/s13421-012-0187-3

Author Index

www.ingramcontent.com/pod-product-compliance
Lightning Source LLC
LaVergne TN
LVHW080110011026
849160LV00013B/1066
9781450367417